German Liberalism
and the Dissolution of the
Weimar Party System,
1918–1933

German Liberalism and the Dissolution of the Weimar Party System, 1918–1933.

Larry Eugene Jones

The University of North Carolina Press
Chapel Hill and London

Publication of this work was made possible in part through a grant from the Division of Research Programs of the National Endowment for the Humanities, an independent federal agency whose mission is to award grants to support education, scholarship, media programming, libraries, and museums, in order to bring the results of cultural activities to a broad, general public.

The paper in this book meets the guidelines for permanence and durability of the Committee on Production Guidelines for Book Longevity of the Council on Library Resources.

92 91 90 89 88   5 4 3 2 1

Library of Congress Cataloging-in-Publication Data

Jones, Larry Eugene.
German liberalism and the dissolution of the Weimar party system,
1918–1933 / by Larry Eugene Jones.
p. cm.
Bibliography: p.
Includes index.
ISBN 0-8078-1764-3 (alk. paper)
1. Deutsche Volkspartei (1918–1933)—History. 2. Deutsche
Demokratische Partei—History. 3. Germany—Politics and
government—1918–1933. 4. Liberalism—Germany—History—20th
century. I. Title.
JN3970.D38J66 1988   87-34904
943.085—dc19   CIP

Portions of this work appeared earlier in somewhat different form in "Crisis and Realignment: Agrarian Splinter Parties in the Late Weimar Republic, 1928–33," in *Peasants and Lords in Modern Germany: Recent Studies in Agricultural History*, ed. Robert G. Moeller, pp. 198–232 (London: Allen and Unwin, 1986); " 'The Dying Middle': Weimar Germany and the Fragmentation of Bourgeois Politics," *Central European History* 5 (1972): 23–54 (© 1972 Emory University); "Inflation, Revaluation, and the Crisis of Middle-Class Politics, 1923–28: A Study in the Dissolution of the German Party System," *Central European History* 12 (1979): 143–68 (©1979 Emory University); and "Gustav Stresemann and the Crisis of German Liberalism," *European Studies Review* 4 (1974): 141–63 (© Sage Publications Ltd.) and are reproduced here by permission of the publishers.

To my parents

Contents

Preface

THE FAILURE OF GERMAN liberalism and the collapse of the Weimar Republic are questions of enduring historical interest, inseparably linked to what Willson Coates and Hayden White have called the "ordeal of liberal humanism." Not only has the German experience between 1918 and 1933 given rise to persistent doubts about the viability of democratic institutions during periods of acute social and economic stress, but more importantly it has done much to challenge the liberal faith in the essential rationality of man. Given the profound implications that the fate of Weimar democracy and the rise of Nazism hold for the western liberal tradition and its faith in progress through reason and law, it is essential that we as products, if not adherents, of that tradition develop a fuller understanding of the specific processes, both long-term and short-term, that led to the collapse of the German liberal movement and to the destruction of the political order with which it was so closely associated.

Almost all historians are in essential agreement that one of the principal reasons for the failure of the Weimar Republic was the fragmentation of the German party system and the inability of those parties upon whose support the fate of the republic ultimately depended to produce a viable consensus for the conduct of national policy. At the crux of this problem lay the irreversible decline of the German liberal parties and the progressive disaffection of Germany's liberal electorate from the system of government in whose founding their leaders had played such a prominent role. The reasons for the collapse of the German liberal movement from 1918 to 1933, however, are extremely complex and defy reduction to some sort of simple formula or common denominator. One should be particularly careful about simply dismissing the failure of Weimar liberalism as a consequence of German liberalism's historic failures in the nineteenth century or the result of what some scholars have identified as the essentially illiberal character of Germany's political culture. On the contrary, there is considerable evidence to suggest that the founding of the Weimar Republic marked both the culmination of a liberal revival underway since the turn of the century and the beginning of a bold new era in the history of the German liberal movement. This does not, of course, mean that the fate of Weimar liberalism was not affected—and in some instances profoundly—by long-range factors such as the historic schism between the two wings of the German liberal movement or the heterogeneity of liberalism's social base. Still, it should serve as a valuable corrective to those who all too frequently have argued that Weimar liberalism—and with it the Weimar Republic—was doomed to failure by the weight of historical tradition.

The following study represents the culmination of more than twenty years of research and writing on the history of the German party system during the Weimar Republic. It originated at the University of Wisconsin in the late 1960s as a dissertation on the efforts to create a united liberal party from 1924 to 1930 and was subsequently expanded to cover the entire Weimar period. Research for the dissertation was made possible by a Fulbright Fellowship at the University of Bonn from 1966 to 1968. A later fellowship from the Alexander von Humboldt-Stiftung made it possible for me to spend two years (1975–77) at the Ruhr-Universität in Bochum. It was then that the present project began to take shape and that much of the primary research was completed. Smaller grants from the Deutscher Akademischer Austauschdienst, the American Philosophical Society, and the Canisius College Faculty Fellowship Program enabled me to return to Germany for short research trips in the summers of 1979, 1980, and 1983. I was also extremely fortunate to be affiliated from 1978 to 1983 with an international project on "Inflation und Wiederaufbau in Deutschland und Europa 1914–1924" financed through a generous grant from the Volkswagen-Stiftung and coordinated by a four-man consortium consisting of Gerald Feldman, Carl-Ludwig Holtfrerich, Gerhard A. Ritter, and Peter-Christian Witt. Lastly, a grant from the American Council of Learned Societies for the 1983–84 academic year and a faculty fellowship from Canisius College for the summer of 1985 made it possible for me to complete the writing of the manuscript. Subventions from the National Endowment for the Humanities and Canisius College helped defray the costs of publication.

The completion of this work would not have been possible without the cooperation and assistance of a large number of archives, libraries, and research institutes on both sides of the Atlantic. I am particularly indebted to the staff of the Bundesarchiv in Koblenz for the continuous help and support they have provided ever since my first visit in the winter of 1966–67 and would like to single out my good friend Hans-Dieter Kreikamp not only for his tireless labors on my behalf but also for his hospitality and generosity. I would also like to take this opportunity to thank the Politisches Archiv des Auswärtigen Amts in Bonn, the Archiv für Christlich-Demokratische Politik at the Konrad Adenauer-Stiftung in Sankt-Augustin, the Geheimes Staatsarchiv Preußischer Kulturbesitz in Berlin-Dahlem, the Hauptstaatsarchiv in Stuttgart, the Bayerisches Hauptstaatsarchiv in Munich, the Nordrhein-Westfälisches Hauptstaatsarchiv in Düsseldorf, the Staatsarchiv Hamburg, the Generallandesarchiv Baden in Karlsruhe, the Landesarchiv Schleswig-Holstein in Schleswig, the city archives in Brunswick, Cologne, Mönchen-Gladbach, and

Munich, and the Yale University archives in New Haven, Connecticut, for their cooperation. I have also drawn heavily upon the holdings of the Preußische Staatsbibliothek in West Berlin, the Bayerische Staatsbibliothek in Munich, the Institut für Weltwirtschaft an der Universität Kiel, the Weltkriegs-bücherei at the Württembergische Landesbibliothek in Stuttgart, the Institut für Zeitgeschichte in Munich, the university libraries at Bochum, Bonn, and Cologne, the Hoover Institution on War, Revolution, and Peace at Stanford University, and the University of Michigan Library in Ann Arbor. My only regret is that I was unable to use the holdings of the Zentrales Staatsarchiv der Deutschen Demokratischen Republik in Potsdam, although it is uncertain how much that would have altered the story I have to tell here.

In addition to these records in the public domain, I have also been fortunate in gaining access to a number of important holdings still in private possession. Industrial archives, as historians well know, constitute a particularly valuable source of information on the political history of the Weimar Republic. I remain deeply grateful to Bodo Herzog for having granted me access to the holdings of the Historisches Archiv der Gutehoffnungshütte in Oberhausen at a time when my youth and inexperience might have made other industrial archivists shudder at the thought of doing so. His example, however, was quickly followed by Sigfrid von Weiher and Lothar Schoen of the Siemens-Museum in Munich, Peter Göb of the Werksarchiv Farbenfabrik Bayer AG in Leverkusen, and Renate Köhne-Lindenlaub of the Historisches Archiv der Friedrich Krupp GmbH in Essen. I am also grateful to a number of private individuals who allowed me to inspect papers and records in their possession. The generosity of Friedrich Hiller Freiherr von Gaertringen in granting scholars access to the Westarp Papers is legendary, and his cooperation during the early stages of my work proved indispensable. I would also like to express my gratitude to Paul Bausch, Ferdinand Friedensburg, Frau Konrad Frühwald, Wolfgang Hardt-wig, Felix Hirsch, Hans Albert Kluthe, Wilhelm Kohlhaas, Ada Rambeau, and Kurt Weinhold for having permitted me to use materials in their posses-sion. Otto Bornemann, Ernst Lemmer, Wilhelm Ridder, Wilhelm Simp-fendörfer, Werner Stephan, G. R. Treviranus, and Josef Winschuh were kind enough to grant me private interviews.

No work—and particularly not one that has taken as long in preparation as this—is ever the product of a single scholar. Scholarship is, after all, a collective enterprise and presupposes a community of scholars willing to share their knowledge, experience, and conclusions with each other. The publication of this work, therefore, affords me an excellent opportunity to pay special tribute to five scholars who have exercised a decisive influence upon my development as an historian and to whom I remain deeply indebted. Charles Sidman, now at the University of Florida at Gainesville, originally stimulated my interest in German history and suffered through my fledgling efforts as a master's candidate at the University of Kansas to become one of my most enthusiastic supporters. Theodore S. Hamerow, who first witnessed the inception of this project as a doctoral dissertation at the University of Wisconsin, has followed its progress with a discerning, if not impatient, eye and has remained one of my truest professional friends. Hans Mommsen, whom I had the good fortune to meet in the spring of 1973, served as my mentor for the two years I was at the Ruhr-Universität in Bochum and has done more than anyone else to inspire me with the confidence necessary to undertake a project as challenging as this. Likewise, Gerald Feldman of the University of California at Berkeley was instrumental in helping me appreciate the significance of my work, has been a constant source of moral as well as material support, and read an early version of the manuscript for the University of North Carolina Press. My work has benefited immensely from his criticism and insight. Thomas Childers of the University of Pennsylvania, whose work on Weimar voting behavior and the emergence of the Nazi electorate complements my own interest in the collapse of the Weimar party system, took an early interest in this project and also read an early version of the manuscript for the University of North Carolina Press. Not only has Tom been particularly generous in his encouragement ever since the beginning of this project, but he has enriched it with his criticism and insight into the Byzantine complexities of Weimar party politics.

A special debt of thanks is also due Georg Iggers of the State University of New York at Buffalo and Konrad Jarausch of the University of North Carolina at Chapel Hill for their constant support and encouragement. Modris Eksteins, Dieter Gessner, Peter Hayes, Martin Schumacher, Henry A. Turner, Jr., and Bernd Weisbrod were all kind enough to share with me the results of their own research and helped me gain access to collections that might otherwise have remained closed. I have also profited, though not necessarily in a way easily recognizable to my colleagues, from the exchange of ideas and information with David Abraham, William Allen, Attila Chanady, Geoff Eley, Bruce Frye, Andreas Kunz, and Robert Moeller. By no means is this list exhaustive, and I would like to offer a brief word of apology to anyone whose help I have failed to recognize. I would, however, be extremely remiss in my expressions of gratitude if I did not also mention a trio of department chairmen at Canisius College—Walter Sharrow, David Costello, Edwin Neville—who were extraordinarily forthcoming in helping me see this project to a conclusion. In retrospect, I feel fortunate to have taught at a place like Canisius, where I was not under pressure to publish and where a project like this could develop and mature at its own pace. I am also deeply indebted to Lewis Bateman and Ron Maner of the University of North Carolina Press for the skillful and conscientious job they did in helping me bring this project to fruition. At the same time,

I would like to express my gratitude to all of my students at Canisius who have helped me at one point or another in the preparation of the manuscript. Of these, three—Gretchen Hollmer, Peter Kirchgraber, and Tom Maulucci— warrant a special vote of thanks. And last, but not least, no words can ever adequately express the debt of gratitude I owe to Nancy, without whose support, encouragement, and dedication this work might not ever have seen the light of day.

Abbreviations

The following abbreviations for parties and other organizations are used in the text.

ADGB Allgemeiner Deutscher Gewerkschaftsbund/General German Trade-Union Federation

ADV Alldeutscher Verband/Pan-German League

BBB Bayerischer Bauernbund/Bavarian Peasants' League

BdL Bund der Landwirte/Agrarian League

BVP Bayerische Volkspartei/Bavarian People's Party

CNBLP Christlich-Nationale Bauern- und Landvolkpartei/Christian-National Peasants and Farmers' Party

CSVD Christlich-sozialer Volksdienst/Christian-Social People's Service

CV Centralverein deutscher Staatsbürger jüdischen Glaubens/Central Association of German Citizens of the Jewish Faith

DBB Deutscher Bauernbund/German Peasants' League

DBP Deutsche Bauernpartei/German Peasants' Party

DBS Deutsche Bauernschaft/German Peasantry

DDGB Deutsch-demokratischer Gewerkschaftsbund/German Democratic Trade-Union Federation

DDP Deutsche Demokratische Partei/German Democratic Party

DFP Deutsche Fortschrittspartei/German Progressive Party

DGB Deutscher Gewerkschaftsbund/German Trade-Union Federation

DHP Deutsch-Hannoversche Partei/German-Hanoverian Party

DHV Deutschnationaler Handlungsgehilfen-Verband/German National Union of Commercial Employees

DKP Deutschkonservative Partei/German Conservative Party

DNV Deutscher Nationalverein/German National Association

DNVP Deutschnationale Volkspartei/German National People's Party

DStP Deutsche Staatspartei/German State Party

DVFP Deutschvölkische Freiheitspartei/German Racist Freedom Party

DVP Deutsche Volkspartei/German People's Party

FNG Freiheitlich-nationaler Gewerkschaftsring deutscher Arbeiter-, Angestellten- und Beamtenverbände/Free National Ring of German Worker, Employee, and Civil Servant Unions

FVP Fortschrittliche Volkspartei/Progressive People's Party

GdA	Gewerkschaftsbund der Angestellten/Federation of Employee Unions
Gedag	Gesamtverband deutscher Angestelltengewerkschaften/United Federation of German Employee Unions
GCG	Gesamtverband der christlichen Gewerkschaften Deutschlands/United Federation of Christian Trade Unions of Germany
HB	Hansa-Bund für Gewerbe, Handel und Industrie/Hansa-Bund for Commerce, Trade, and Industry
KVP	Konservative Volkspartei/Conservative People's Party
LV	Liberale Vereinigung/Liberal Association
MSPD	Mehrheits-Sozialdemokratische Partei Deutschlands/Majority Social Democratic Party of Germany
NLP	Nationalliberale Partei/National Liberal Party
NLV	Nationalliberale Vereinigung/National Liberal Association
NRK	Nationaler Reichsklub/National Reich Club
NSDAP	Nationalsozialistische Deutsche Arbeiterpartei/National Socialist German Workers' Party
RDI	Reichsverband der deutschen Industrie/National Federation of German Industry
RjV	Reichsgemeinschaft junger Volksparteiler/Reich Association of Young Populists
RLB	Reichs-Landbund/National Rural League
RPD	Republikanische Partei Deutschlands/Republican Party of Germany
SPD	Sozialdemokratische Partei Deutschlands/Social Democratic Party of Germany
TLB	Thüringer Landbund/Thuringian Rural League
VKV	Volkskonservative Vereinigung/People's Conservative Association
VNR	Volksnationale Reichsvereinigung/People's National Reich Association
VRP	Reichspartei für Volksrecht und Aufwertung/People's Justice Party
WBWB	Württembergischer Bauern- und Weingärtnerbund/Württemberg Peasants' and Wine Growers' League
WP	Wirtschaftspartei or Reichspartei des deutschen Mittelstandes/Business Party

German Liberalism and the Dissolution of the Weimar Party System, 1918–1933

INTRODUCTION

The Liberal Legacy of Imperial Germany

MUCH OF THE TRADITIONAL literature on nineteenth- and twentieth-century German history has attributed the failure of the Weimar Republic and the rise of National Socialism to certain deformities in Germany's social, economic, and political development.[1] This argument, which received its classical formulations in the writings of Karl Marx, Max Weber, and Thorstein Veblen, maintained that the central feature of Germany's historical development since the end of the Napoleonic Wars was her failure to achieve a social and political revolution comparable to those experienced by England and then France during the seventeenth and eighteenth centuries. This, in turn, meant that the rapid economic modernization that Germany experienced in the second half of the nineteenth century took place within the framework of a social system that was still essentially feudal, thereby producing an anomaly which Ralf Dahrendorf has conveniently labeled the "feudal-industrial society."[2] Elevated to the status of what one distinguished historian of nineteenth-century German liberalism has called the "new orthodoxy,"[3] the emphasis upon the discrepancy between Germany's economic modernization and her political retardation has served as the conceptual paradigm for an entire school of recent German historians, the principal representatives of which are Hans-Ulrich Wehler, Jürgen Kocka, and Hans-Jürgen Puhle. The implications of this approach for an understanding of Weimar liberalism are, however, both profound and misleading. For not only does the preoccupation with the failure of Germany's bourgeois revolution belittle the actual accomplishments of the German liberal movement in the second half of the nineteenth century, it also seeks to explain the collapse of the Weimar Republic and the establishment of the Nazi dictatorship as the inescapable consequence of long-range historical processes that had been set in motion well before the republic itself had come into existence. The practical consequence of this has been to absolve the historian of any responsibility for explaining the weakness of Weimar liberalism and the collapse of the Weimar Republic in terms of the specific crises, both economic and political, that gripped Germany between 1918 and 1933.[4]

Recently, however, the "new orthodoxy" of Wehler, Kocka, and Puhle has come under increasingly heavy criticism from a brace of British historians, David Blackbourn and Geoff Eley, who have challenged many of its essential assumptions. Specifically, Blackbourn and Eley have argued that the notion of

Germany's abortive bourgeois revolution rests upon assumptions about the nature of the revolutionary experience in England and France that students of those countries' political traditions have become increasingly reluctant to accept. At the same time, they have also stressed the extent to which the German bourgeoisie was able to achieve many of its most important objectives with the creation of the Second Empire, albeit not in the heroic fashion of those who had failed at the barricades in 1848 and 1849.[5] As Blackbourn has persuasively argued in an essay entitled "The Discreet Charm of the Bourgeoisie," the 1860s and 1870s witnessed a silent bourgeois revolution from above during which the German bourgeoisie was able to realize many of its most cherished goals in the social and economic sphere. Not only the definitive triumph of the capitalist mode of production but also the establishment of equality before the law, the creation of a rich and variegated associational life, and the rise of a public sector based upon the principle of equal accessibility all bore subtle testimony to the way in which the German bourgeoisie had begun to remold society in accordance with its own interests, values, and aspirations. That these accomplishments were not accompanied by similar success in the political sphere should not, argues Blackbourn, be allowed to obscure the very real gains that the German bourgeoisie recorded in the social and economic.[6]

In challenging the "new orthodoxy" of Wehler and his associates, the "new revisionism" of Blackbourn and Eley has raised questions of profound significance for the history of German liberalism in the twentieth century. For while Blackbourn and Eley do not deny the role of continuity in modern German history, they are extremely critical of the "teleological blandness" that preoccupation with the notion of Germany's abortive bourgeois revolution and her subsequent deviation from the path that England and France took to the promised land of political modernity has produced in the historiography of the Second Empire and the Weimar Republic. Seeking to restore a sense of contingency to the study of German history between 1880 and 1933, Blackbourn and Eley have sharply criticized the tendency of Wehler and his followers to dismiss the collapse of the Weimar Republic and the rise of Nazism as the inescapable consequence of the general course of historical development that Germany had followed since the middle of the nineteenth century.[7] By ascribing, as Kocka has done, causal primacy to the persistence of "pre-industrial"—in other words, antimodern and antiliberal—traditions within influential sectors of German society, the disciples of the "new orthodoxy" have obscured an understanding of National Socialism in terms of the specific social, economic, and political crises that produced it.[8]

This criticism is particularly well taken with respect to the emphasis that not only Dahrendorf but an entire legion of German historians has placed upon the supposedly illiberal character of German social and intellectual life. Originally a term used to describe certain features of Germany's political culture in the nineteenth century, "illiberalism" has assumed almost causal primacy at the hands of Dahrendorf and his followers. As Dahrendorf himself writes: "Because the new illiberalism of the National Socialists fell on the soil of an illiberal, namely an authoritarian rather than a liberal tradition, it succeeded in seizing the power in Germany that it failed to achieve in more liberal countries."[9] But while use of the term by Dahrendorf, Fritz Stern, and others is helpful in illuminating a particular aspect of the German political tradition, it fails to carry the interpretational burden assigned to it for several crucial reasons. In the first place, the concept of illiberalism remains necessarily vague, referring at some times to a particular cast of mind and at others to institutionalized patterns of social and political behavior. At the same time, the concept has been transferred from the late nineteenth century, where it is useful in describing the general reaction against liberalism that took place in Germany after 1880, to a later temporal context in which its validity is far less apparent. Not only has this resulted in a skewed view of German history that selectively highlights particular aspects of the country's political tradition at the expense of others, but it overlooks contrary evidence that might suggest that German society was actually more liberal than it appears through the prism of illiberalism.[10]

The purpose of the following study is to take a fresh look at the history of German liberalism during the Weimar Republic, unhampered by the tyranny of historical hindsight, by placing the successes and failures of Weimar liberals against the background of the specific problems with which they were forced to deal. It aims to supplement the excellent monographs that Lothar Albertin, Jürgen Hess, and a host of others have produced on specific aspects of the history of Weimar liberalism[11] with a comprehensive history of the German liberal movement from the founding of the Weimar Republic in 1918 until its eventual destruction in 1933. Its principal focus will be the two liberal parties—the German Democratic Party (Deutsche Demokratische Partei or DDP) and the German People's Party (Deutsche Volkspartei or DVP)—to whose success or failure the fate of Germany's short-lived experiment in democracy was so closely tied. The central assumption upon which this study rests is that the collapse of the Second Empire and the founding of the Weimar Republic marked the beginning of a bold new era in the history of the German liberal movement and that the checkered fate of Weimar liberalism is therefore best understood not by reciting the all too familiar litany of failure that inscribed the history of German liberalism in the nineteenth century but by examining the specific factors that did so much to rob liberalism of its vitality and promise between 1918 and 1933. In this respect, it seeks to relate the specific crises experienced by the German liberal parties in the Weimar Republic first to the more general crisis and dissolution of the Weimar party system and second to the general course of German social and economic development in the first third of the twentieth century.[12]

The history of Weimar liberalism was marked by several distinct phases.

The first years of the Weimar Republic were marked by a bitter fratricidal conflict between the two liberal parties, as each tried to justify its existence at the expense of the other. Throughout this period it was the DDP's inability to pursue a consistent course of action with respect to the two questions that dominated the republic's political agenda—economic reconstruction and the Versailles peace settlement—that provided the DVP with the opening it needed to transform middle-class dissatisfaction with the DDP's performance as a member of the Weimar Coalition into a stunning victory at the polls in the 1920 Reichstag elections. Although the two liberal parties had begun to draw closer together by the middle of 1922, the benefits of such a rapprochement were all but nullified by the onset of the hyperinflation in 1922 and 1923. Not only did the runaway inflation of the early 1920s leave both the finances and organizations of the two liberal parties in a complete shambles; more important, it traumatized those social strata upon which the German liberal movement had traditionally depended for the bulk of its popular and electoral support. Moreover, the authoritarian manner in which the mark was stabilized at the end of 1923 and the beginning of 1924 severely compromised the legitimacy of the two liberal parties at the same time that the government's stabilization program inflicted further economic hardship upon those elements that constituted the social backbone of the German liberal movement. This, in turn, marked the beginning of an ever deepening legitimacy crisis, the most tangible manifestations of which were the continued decline of the two liberal parties, the emergence of middle-class splinter parties that addressed themselves to specific sectors of Germany's middle-class electorate, the increasingly prominent role of organized economic interests in the legislative process, and widespread appeals for a reform and reorganization of the German party system. These appeals, which reached a crescendo following the defeat of the two liberal parties in the 1928 Reichstag elections, drew much of their impetus from the idealism of the younger generation and were accompanied by a vigorous effort on the part of Germany's liberal leadership to unite the German bourgeoisie into a truly comprehensive liberal party. If the existence of such a party might have helped stem the rise of National Socialism, the failure of these efforts only dramatized the ineffectiveness of Germany's liberal leadership, undermined established patterns of voter identification within Germany's middle-class electorate, and facilitated Nazi penetration into the ranks of Germany's more moderate bourgeois parties. With the outbreak of the world economic crisis at the beginning of the 1930s and the turn to government by decree under the mantle of Reich President Paul von Hindenburg, the fate of the German liberal parties—as well as that of the Weimar Republic—was effectively sealed. In the final analysis, only the NSDAP was able to overcome the social and economic cleavages that had become so deeply entrenched within the German middle class and thus to satisfy the deep-seated psychological longing for bourgeois solidarity to which both the increasing fragmentation of the German party system and the deepening economic crisis had given rise.[13]

While historians should be careful to avoid the "fallacy of misplaced concreteness" that has characterized so much of the traditional literature on nineteenth- and twentieth-century German history, it would be no less imprudent to disregard the role of continuity altogether. The student of modern German history needs to strike a delicate balance between the concepts of continuity and contingency in his explanation of what happened to Germany between 1870 and 1933, a balance combining an appreciation of the role that longrange historical forces have played in modern German history with careful attention to the specific social, economic, and political conditions under which those forces became manifest. Of the long-range historical forces that helped shape the fate of German liberalism in the Weimar Republic, none was more important than the social and political fragmentation of those elements from which the German liberal movement traditionally recruited the bulk of its popular support. Although German liberalism derived its intellectual inspiration from the philosophical revolution that took place in Germany at the beginning of the nineteenth century and that was associated with the names of men like Immanuel Kant, Johann Gottlieb von Fichte, and G. W. F. Hegel,[14] it is not as an intellectual but as a social movement that German liberalism is to be understood.[15] Not only was the development of German liberalism during the course of the nineteenth century closely tied to the social and political emancipation of the German bourgeoisie,[16] but the extremely rapid and uneven pace of industrialization that Germany experienced from the founding of the Second Empire to the outbreak of World War I threatened German liberalism with the disintegration of the social milieu out of which it had originally emerged.[17] By the outbreak of World War I the German *Mittelstand* no longer represented a homogeneous social unit but consisted of at least five separate subgroups: the small business sector, the liberal professions, civil servants, white-collar employees, and the peasantry, or rural middle class. With little in common save their intermediary position between the extremes of big business and organized labor, these elements did not constitute a *Stand* or corporate estate in any sense of the word. On the contrary, their material interests were often so discordant that it is more appropriate to speak of them as the German middle strata than as a class, with all that implies in terms of social, economic, and ideological cohesiveness.[18]

The social and economic fragmentation of Germany's middle-class interest structure was paralleled by the political fragmentation of the German liberal movement. Almost from the moment of its inception, German liberalism was fraught with internal divisions over its relationship to the state, the economy, and the *Volk*.[19] Above all else, the fact that the struggle for political emancipation was to become closely, if not inseparably, linked with the quest for national unification produced a curious synthesis of liberalism and nationalism that tended to obscure the more illiberal impulses at work within the German national movement. The tension between these two concepts of emancipation did not become fully apparent until the Prussian constitutional conflict of 1862–66, when Bismarck succeeded in driving a permanent political wedge into the ranks of his liberal opponents. At the heart of Bismarck's success lay his ability to mobilize the strong national feeling that had played such a prominent role in the early history of the German liberal movement against those liberal parliamentarians who were unwilling to pay for national unification by sanctioning Bismarck's repeated violations of the Prussian Constitution. The resulting split in the vote on the Indemnity Bill that Bismarck presented to the Landtag in the fall of 1866 was destined to become a permanent feature of Germany's political landscape when, over the course of the next nine months, Bismarck's supporters in the German Progressive Party (Deutsche Fortschrittspartei or DFP) seceded from that party to found a new organization of their own entitled the National Liberal Party (Nationalliberale Partei or NLP).[20]

The years from 1866 to 1879 marked the zenith of liberal influence in the Second Empire and witnessed a series of major legislative accomplishments that not even the sweeping realignment of political forces initiated by Bismarck at the end of the 1870s could erase.[21] Still, Bismarck's break with the National Liberals in 1878–79 marked the end of the liberal ascendancy in Prusso-German affairs and ushered in a period of liberal decline that was to continue until the end of the century. This decline was accompanied by the further fragmentation of Germany's liberal forces and a series of liberal reversals at the polls. Between 1871 and 1890 the liberal portion of the national popular vote fell from 46.6 percent to 34.9 percent. By 1912 this figure had fallen to 26.5 percent, thereby consigning the German liberal movement to the status of a permanent minority in the political culture of Wilhelmine Germany. The fact, however, that the number of votes received by the various liberal parties from 1890 to 1912 remained relatively constant suggests that the decline of the German liberal movement should be seen in relative rather than absolute terms and that the German liberal parties had effectively exhausted their electoral potential at a time when their principal rivals on the German political scene—namely the German Center Party (Deutsche Zentrumspartei), the Social Democrats (Sozialdemokratische Partei Deutschlands or SPD), and the German Conservative Party (Deutschkonservative Partei or DKP)—had just begun to mobilize theirs.[22] At the heart of this problem lay the archaic form of party organization that existed in liberal circles before the outbreak of World War I. In terms of their underlying organizational structure, all of the German liberal parties, including the NLP, were essentially *Honoratiorenpar-*

teien, or loose associations of politically like-minded dignitaries that functioned only at the time of elections but otherwise maintained a shadow existence without benefit of a permanent national organization, membership dues, or even a comprehensive party program.[23]

Although the National Liberals launched a vigorous effort to modernize their party organization following their defeat in the 1890 Reichstag elections, it was only with the emergence of special interest organizations in the last decades of the twentieth century that the structure of the German party system began to change. The founding of the Central Association of German Industrialists (Centralverband deutscher Industrieller) in 1876 marked the appearance of a new type of economic interest organization that sought to influence the legislative process by bringing pressure to bear not only upon the governmental bureaucracy but upon the political parties themselves. The emergence of such organizations reached a climax in the 1890s with the creation of the Agrarian League (Bund der Landwirte or BdL), the League of Industrialists (Bund der Industriellen), and a host of middle-class interest organizations such as the German National Union of Commercial Employees (Deutschnationaler Handlungsgehilfen-Verband or DHV), the German Middle-Class Association (Deutsche Mittelstandsvereinigung), the Bavarian Peasants' League (Bayerischer Bauernbund or BBB), and the Association of Christian Peasant Unions (Vereinigung der christlichen Bauernvereine).[24] Not only did these developments underscore the increasing fragmentation of Germany's middle-class interest structure, but the situation in which these elements found themselves was further complicated by the rapid rise of the industrial working class in the period following Bismarck's dismissal from office. What resulted was a curious dialectic in which the impulse to unite in the face of increased working-class pressure was subverted by the disintegrative impact of economic modernization on the structure of Germany's middle-class interests.[25]

Just as the German liberal movement had split some thirty years before over the terms of national unification, it was destined to split once again in the face of what one renowned German historian has called the *Gretchenfrage* of German liberalism, that is, its attitude toward Social Democracy.[26] The National Liberals hoped to contain the threat that the rise of Social Democracy posed to the existing social order by establishing closer ties with other bourgeois parties. Johannes Miquel's campaign in 1897 for the consolidation of all "state-supporting bourgeois forces" was essentially an attempt to resurrect the old agrarian-industrial cartel which, after having dominated German politics since the middle of the 1870s, had collapsed in the wake of Caprivi's tariff policy.[27] Miquel's initiative paralleled a similar effort by Navy Secretary Alfred von Tirpitz to unite the German nation behind a program of naval construction aimed at securing German supremacy on the seas. Whereas the integrative component of Miquel's initiative lay in its antisocialism, in Tirpitz's case it was imperialism colored by the promise of expanded economic activity that served as the ideological axis around which the German nation, including the more nationalistic elements of the German working class, were to unite.[28] To Germany's left liberals, however, appeals such as these represented little more than ill-disguised attempts to promote the vested interests of the propertied bourgeoisie at the expense of the industrial working class. For them the task lay not in suppressing the working class as the National Liberals had proposed but in building a bridge between the bourgeoisie and industrial proletariat so that they might cooperate in those areas where their goals were compatible.

The principal architect of this strategy was Friedrich Naumann, who in 1899, as chairman of the short-lived National Social Union (Nationalsozialer Verein), intoned what was to become the rallying cry of Germany's moderate Left by calling for the creation of a united political front "from Bebel to Bassermann."[29] A former Christian-social, who under the influence of the famous German sociologist Max Weber had moved from a Christian to a more nationalistic brand of socialism, Naumann was emphatic that the optimum development of German national power presupposed the full integration of the German working class into the social and political fabric of the nation. His ultimate objective, outlined in his classic work, *Demokratie und Kaisertum* (1900), was to reconcile the forces of German nationalism with the German working class in a process that simultaneously involved the democratization of the German Empire and the nationalization of the Social Democrats.[30] Following the demise of the National Social Union in 1903, Naumann and most of his followers went over to the Radical Association (Freisinnige Vereinigung), where they joined forces with Theodor Barth in a determined campaign to bring about a regeneration of German liberalism. At the heart of their campaign lay an impassioned appeal for the consolidation of the various liberal groups that stood to the left of the National Liberals into a united liberal party. Only through the creation of such a party, argued Naumann and Barth, would it be possible for the German bourgeoisie to survive the two-front war it was currently waging against political reaction and Social Democracy.[31] Not only should such a party possess a mass political organization similar to that of the Social Democrats, but it should also identify itself as unequivocally as possible with the social and economic interests of the German bourgeoisie. "In the broadest sense of the word," wrote Naumann in 1904, "the entire future of liberalism depends upon the free and open recognition of its class character. For only a liberalism that is class conscious has the strength to hold its own in the universal class struggle that exists today."[32]

Naumann's appeal for the creation of a united liberal party inspired by a new vision of Germany's national mission and prepared to cooperate with the Social Democrats in the democratization of German political life had an electric effect upon an entire generation of German liberals and initiated a dramatic revival of German liberalism that was to continue for the better part of the next two decades. The effects of Naumann's appeal could be seen almost immediately in Hamburg, where in 1906 thirteen deputies in the Hamburg city council seceded from their respective delegations to reconstitute themselves as the United Liberals (Vereinigte Liberalen) in protest against the way in which a recent change in the local electoral law had discriminated against the lower classes.[33] In a similar vein, representatives from the various factions of the Bavarian liberal movement came together the following year to form the National Association for Liberal Germany (Nationalverein für das liberale Deutschland) in an attempt to lay the foundation for the eventual creation of a united liberal party.[34] The most important indication of Naumann's influence, however, could be seen in the progress that leaders of Germany's left-wing liberal parties began to make toward a resolution of their differences. In the spring of 1906 the first tangible step in the direction of a united liberal party was taken with the adoption of a common political platform by the Radical Association and a regional liberal party from southwest Germany known as the German People's Party (Deutsche Volkspartei). The following November the Radical People's Party (Freisinnige Volkspartei) lent its name to the cause of liberal unity by joining the other two left-wing parties in a joint party congress in Frankfurt. Yet in spite of the widespread support for the idea of a united liberal party that existed among influential sectors of Germany's liberal elite, the refusal of Eugen Richter's followers in the Radical People's Party—Richter himself had died in 1906—to compromise their laissez-faire social and economic policies continued to stand in the way of an accommodation with the more social-minded liberals around Naumann and Barth. It was only when Naumann began to retreat from many of his earlier positions on social and economic reform that the last obstacles to a merger of the three left-wing liberal parties were removed. In the summer of 1909 a special four-man committee was created to negotiate the outlines of an agreement that was ratified by the German People's Party in February 1910 and by the two radical parties at a joint convention in Berlin on 5 March. On the following day the three left-wing liberal parties formally dissolved their separate organizations and merged to found the Progressive People's Party (Fortschrittliche Volkspartei or FVP).[35]

All of this—and particularly the founding of the Progressive People's Party —pointed to the reemergence of a viable liberal infrastructure among the more progressive sectors of the German bourgeoisie and bore dramatic testimony to the renewed vitality that the German liberal movement began to show in the first decades of the twentieth century. Still, Naumann did not look upon the merger of the three left-wing liberal parties as an end in itself but as the prelude to their eventual fusion with the progressive elements on the left wing of the

NLP.[36] In this respect Naumann could only have been heartened by developments within the NLP itself. At the turn of the century the leaders of the NLP
had created the Reich Association of National Liberal Youth (Reichsverband
der nationalliberalen Jugend) in an attempt to enhance their party's image with
the younger generation. Regarding themselves as the "pioneers of liberal
unity," the Young Liberals had dedicated themselves to the regeneration of the
NLP so that it might serve as the crystallization point around which the "great
liberal party of the future" could form.[37] Although the Young Liberals were
repeatedly frustrated in their efforts to reform the NLP by the intransigence of
the heavy industrial interests that sat on the party's right wing,[38] the crusade
for a united liberal party received new impetus from the founding of the
Hansa-Bund for Commerce, Trade, and Industry (Hansa-Bund für Gewerbe,
Handel und Industrie or HB) and the German Peasants' League (Deutscher
Bauernbund or DBB) in the summer of 1909. Closely tied to Germany's
commercial and financial elites, the Hansa-Bund combined its demands for a
more equitable system of taxation and tariffs with an impassioned appeal for
greater political involvement on the part of Germany's liberal bourgeoisie. In
this respect the Hansa-Bund's ultimate objective was to consolidate the artisanry, small business sector, and newly emergent white-collar class into a
united political force capable of challenging the hegemony that the reactionary
social forces currently represented by the Agrarian League had exercised over
German political life for nearly half a century.[39] In a similar vein, the German
Peasants' League had been founded by liberal farm leaders with close ties to
the NLP in an attempt to organize peasant opposition to the tariff policies of
the Agrarian League and the conservative grain-producing interests that controlled it.[40]

Like the creation of the Progressive People's Party, the agitation of the
Young Liberals for a reform of the NLP and the formation of the Hansa-Bund
and German Peasants' League reflected the renewed vitality that surged
through the German liberal movement in the last years of the Second Empire.
Still, the forces with which Wilhelmine liberalism had to contend remained
formidable, and it is by no means certain that the leaders of the German liberal
movement would have been able to accomplish their objectives had not the
outbreak of World War I intervened to bring about the demise of the Second
Empire. Moreover, the divisions that had historically plagued the German
liberal movement still possessed considerable potential for frustrating the
process of liberal renewal. At no point was this more apparent than in the
Reichstag elections of January 1912. For although the Hansa-Bund, the Young
Liberal League, and a host of other liberal organizations prevailed upon the
two liberal parties to set aside their differences for the sake of a common
crusade against the forces of political reaction in the first trip to the polls on 12
January, the will to cooperate all but evaporated in the wake of the Social

Democratic landslide that characterized the outcome of the elections. The Progressives, for example, were so impressed by the SPD's performance in the preliminary elections that they proceeded to conclude an agreement to support each other's candidates in face-to-face contests with conservative opponents, while the National Liberals were so frightened by the spectre of Social Democracy that they concluded a similar agreement with the parties of the German Right.[41]

The two parties paid for their folly with one of the most puzzling defeats in the annals of German liberalism. For although the Progressives polled 260,000 more votes than the three left-wing liberal parties had received in 1907, they elected six fewer deputies, while the NLP saw its number of parliamentary seats reduced by nine in spite of the fact that it had improved upon its performance in the 1907 elections by more than 26,000 votes.[42] For the leaders of the German liberal movement the results of the 1912 Reichstag elections were both frustrating and ambiguous. At no point in the history of the Second Empire had the German liberal parties received more votes than in 1912. And yet their share of the popular vote had fallen to 26.5 percent and their combined parliamentary strength to 87 deputies. Moreover, the outcome of the elections had all but paralyzed the movement for liberal unity at a time when the need for some sort of accommodation between the two liberal parties seemed stronger than ever. Not only were the two liberal parties profoundly estranged from each other as a result of the conflicting strategies they had pursued in the runoff elections on 19 January 1912, but the fact that the Social Democrats had received more than a third of all votes cast sent shock waves through the National Liberal organization that had the advocates of liberal unity—and particularly the Young Liberals—running for cover. For the next six years the NLP was caught in the grip of a bitter internal crisis that both neutralized the crusade for a reform of the existing political order and foreshadowed the party's eventual demise in the fall of 1918. Meanwhile, Naumann and his associates were left with no alternative but to bide their time and wait for a more auspicious moment to resume their efforts on behalf of a united liberal party capable of cooperating with the Social Democrats in the creation of a viable parliamentary democracy.[43]

By no means, however, were the forces of liberal regeneration dead. To be sure, the last years of the Second Empire were characterized by a political stalemate that neither the champions nor the opponents of reform were able to turn to their advantage.[44] Moreover, the German Right had begun to show new signs of life, recovering from the devastating defeat it had suffered in the 1912 Reichstag elections by adopting techniques of political agitation and mobilization that were actually more in tune with the exigencies of mass politics than those of the two liberal parties.[45] Still, in many essential respects the German liberal movement—and this is particularly true of the more progressive elements on its left wing—was more vibrant than at any time since Bismarck's break with the National Liberals in 1878–79. Above all else, the forces around Naumann and the Progressive People's Party were in the process of breaking out of the political isolation in which Germany's left-wing liberal parties had found themselves ever since the founding of the Second Empire. Though the forces arrayed against it remained formidable, Naumann's appeal for the creation of a grand bloc "from Bebel to Bassermann" contained the seeds of an alliance that would eventually secure passage of the peace resolution in the summer of 1917, assume the reins of power with Prince Max von Baden's appointment as chancellor in the fall of 1918, and found the Weimar Republic a half-year later. While it is not at all certain—and indeed the preponderance of evidence seems to suggest otherwise—that these forces would have triumphed on their own had not the war intervened to hasten the collapse of the Second Empire, the fact nevertheless remains that the potential for democratic reform was greater on the eve of World War I than at any time since the emergence of the German liberal movement in the first half of the nineteenth century. Far from being an aberration in Germany's historical development, the founding of the Weimar Republic represented the culmination of a democratic and liberal revival that had been underway since the beginning of the twentieth century.

PART ONE

A New Beginning
1918–1920

CHAPTER ONE

Revolution and Realignment

THE END OF WORLD WAR I and the collapse of the Second Empire marked the beginning of a critical new era in the history of the German liberal movement. To Progressives and National Liberals alike, the outbreak of the November Revolution and the abdication of the Kaiser threatened to sweep away much of what they had managed to achieve over the course of the previous half-century. Not only was the monarchy a symbol of power and stability to which all but a few of their number felt a certain emotional attachment, but the spectre of Bolshevism injected a note of increasing urgency into the more generalized uncertainty with which the leaders of the German liberal establishment greeted their country's military defeat. Their uneasiness was compounded by the fact that the war had also done much to radicalize the social strata from which the two liberal parties had traditionally recruited the bulk of their electoral support.[1] Yet for all of the apprehension that Germany's liberal leadership may have felt about the fate of liberal institutions and values in the postwar period, the collapse of the Second Empire also created a moment of unprecedented opportunity for those liberals who hoped to put an end to the schism that had developed within their ranks during the course of the previous century. At no point after the constitutional conflict of the mid-1860s were conditions for the creation of a united liberal party more favorable than in the fall and winter of 1918–19.

From the elections of 1912 until the final days of World War I, the movement for liberal unity had made little, if any, progress. The defeat of the Young Liberals within the NLP had virtually paralyzed Progressive efforts to found a united liberal party, and with the outbreak of the war and the proclamation of the *Burgfriede* by Kaiser Wilhelm II in his speech from the throne on 4 August 1914, all domestic political issues, including that of liberal unity, had receded into the background. It was not until the spring and summer of 1917, when the *Burgfriede* collapsed in the altercation over electoral reform and war aims, that the two liberal parties began to emerge from the political limbo in which the outbreak of the war had placed them. Still, the divisions that had separated the two liberal parties before the war persisted with undiminished intensity. Whereas the Progressives had long endorsed the introduction of direct and equal suffrage in Prussia as the first step toward a genuine democratization of the Second Empire,[2] the leaders of the NLP's right wing feared that abolition of the three-class franchise would mean the end of bourgeois supremacy in Germany and consistently blocked the overtures of those on the party's left wing who advocated a reform of the Prussian electoral law as a way of rewarding the German working class for its loyalty during the war.[3] No less disturbing was the split that had developed between the Progressives and the National Liberals on the question of German war aims. For while the Progressives joined the Center and the Majority Socialists (Mehrheits-Sozialdemokratische Partei Deutschlands or MSPD) in sponsoring the Peace Resolution of 19 July 1917, the National Liberals continued to insist upon territorial annexations as a *conditio sine qua non* for the conclusion of hostilities and refused to support the resolution on the grounds that it might be interpreted as a sign of German weakness.[4]

With the collapse of the Ludendorff offensive in the summer of 1918 and the subsequent installation of Prince Max von Baden as chancellor in early October, the cleavages that had existed within the German liberal movement seemed suddenly superfluous. The appointment of Prince Max represented a major triumph for the Progressives, and his political program fulfilled virtually every objective for which they, along with the Center and Majority Socialists, had been working since the July crisis of 1917.[5] While the National Liberals were admittedly less enthusiastic than the Progressives about the changes that Prince Max had instituted in Germany's political system, whatever reservations they may have had about his constitutional experiment became academic in the wake of the revolution that spread throughout Germany from the port city of Kiel in the first week of November. The immediate effect of the outbreak of the revolution was to renew interest on the part of Germany's liberal leadership in the establishment of closer ties between the two liberal parties. Representatives from the Progressive and National Liberal delegations to the Reichstag had already met in early November to discuss the conclusion of an alliance for the national elections that they expected to take place following the conclusion of hostilities. These discussions were resumed immediately after the abdication of the Kaiser and resulted in a general consensus that the deteriorating domestic situation made a merger of the two liberal parties imperative. Acting on their own initiative, the negotiators proceeded to constitute themselves as a provisional executive committee for the purpose of exploring the possibility of such a merger and drafted a joint political program as the basis upon which the founding of a united liberal party was to take place.[6]

Prompted in large measure by the fear of social revolution, the rapprochement between the two liberal parties in the stormy days of November 1918 represented a first, tentative step toward the creation of a united liberal party. But before these developments could reach a conclusion, they were undercut by the emergence of a third and more radical group under the leadership of newspaper editor Theodor Wolff and university professor Alfred Weber. On 10 November a number of prominent personalities from all walks of German life had met in the home of Berlin industrialist Theodor Vogelstein to discuss the founding of an entirely new political party as an alternative to the "broken" and "morally bankrupt" parties that still claimed to represent Germany's liberal bourgeoisie. Later that afternoon a delegation from the Vogelstein group met with Wolff, who agreed to place his influential *Berliner Tageblatt* at the disposal of the new party. On the following morning Wolff received a visit from Weber, an impulsive young intellectual whose enthusiasm for the idea of a new party was sustained by a mixture of democratic idealism and apocalyptic fervor. Neither Wolff nor Weber harbored much sympathy for the idea of a united liberal party as envisaged by the Progressives and National Liberals. On the contrary, both men regarded the existing liberal parties as hopelessly compromised by their uncritical support of the German war effort and sought the creation of an entirely new party that would, at least in the eyes of the Francophile Wolff, serve as a German counterpart to the Radical Socialists in France.[7]

Having assured themselves of Wolff's cooperation, Vogelstein and his associates set out to secure the support of prominent Progressives such as Georg Gothein and Otto Fischbeck. The situation in which the Progressives found themselves was particularly desperate in light of the radicalizing effect that the war had had upon their party's middle-class electorate. Though deeply suspicious of the political naivete of Wolff and his entourage, Gothein and Fischbeck were fearful that the creation of a new bourgeois party to the left of the FVP would result in their own party's annihilation at the polls and therefore saw no alternative to an accommodation with the Wolff-Vogelstein faction.[8] On 13 November Gothein wrote to twenty-one members of the FVP Reichstag delegation and urged them to attach their signatures to an appeal for the founding of a comprehensive democratic party that Wolff and his associates were in the process of drafting.[9] Gothein's initiative, however, met with a cool response in traditional liberal strongholds such as Baden, Württemberg, and Bavaria, where the local leadership of the two liberal parties had already begun negotiations between themselves in the absence of any sort of clear signal from their superiors in Berlin.[10] Consequently, when the appeal appeared in Wolff's *Berliner Tageblatt* on 16 November, it carried the signatures of only two Progressive deputies in addition to those of Gothein and Fischbeck.[11]

The immediate effect of Wolff's appeal for a new democratic party uncompromised by the sins of the past was to sabotage the negotiations that the leaders of the Progressive and National Liberal parties had been conducting on behalf of an alliance for the upcoming national elections. This turn of events was particularly distressing to Gustav Stresemann, the thirty-nine-year-old chairman of the NLP Reichstag delegation and the driving force within the party ever since Bassermann's death a few years earlier. At the urging of the Young Liberals and the leaders of the NLP's left wing,[12] Stresemann had met with representatives from the FVP on 15 and 16 November in hopes of arranging an alliance for the national elections that were expected to take place in the first month or so after the end of the war. To be sure, Stresemann had deep personal reservations about an accommodation with the Progressives, but in light of the NLP's organizational collapse throughout much of the country, he saw no alternative to an alliance with the FVP and was even prepared to go along with a merger of the two parties after the elections had taken place.[13] With the emergence of the group around Wolff and Weber, however, Stresemann's own role in the movement for liberal unity became increasingly problematic, particularly in view of the deep-seated antipathy that he and the *Berliner Tageblatt* faction harbored toward each other.[14] Moreover, the industrial interests that had traditionally formed the nucleus of the NLP's right wing were adamantly opposed to any accommodation with the Progressives or any other political group that might hamper the effectiveness of their party's campaign against the Social Democrats.[15] But as local party leaders from one part of the country after another began to deluge Stresemann with reports of the NLP's organizational demise and pleas for an alliance with other liberal groups, Stresemann had no choice but to set aside his personal hostility to the *Tageblatt* faction and join the Progressives in their search for an accord with the Wolff-Weber group.[16]

The meeting between Stresemann, the Progressives, and the leaders of the Wolff-Weber group on the afternoon of 18 November marked a critical turning point in the efforts to create a united liberal party. While Stresemann went to the meeting hoping that a separate accommodation with the Progressives might still be possible, he was fully prepared to retire from active political life rather than stand in the way of a united liberal party.[17] The meeting, however, took an entirely unexpected turn when Weber, speaking on behalf of the faction from the *Berliner Tageblatt*, announced that he and his colleagues had officially constituted themselves as a new political party earlier that morning and that a merger with the two liberal parties was possible only under conditions that guaranteed the dominance of the group he represented. Specifically, Weber stipulated that anyone who had compromised himself by annexationist activities during the war was to be barred from a position in the leadership of the party and demanded that the new party's executive committee be constituted in such a way that the group from the *Berliner Tageblatt* receive as many seats as the two liberal parties combined.[18] Not only Stresemann but the Progressives as well were outraged at the way in which Weber and his supporters had tried to usurp leadership of the movement for liberal unity and left the meeting deeply depressed over its outcome.[19] But at a meeting of National Liberal and Progressive party leaders on the following day, the Progressives showed great reluctance to break off negotiations with the Wolff-Weber faction and announced that they would continue to seek a modus vivendi with the founders of the new party. Consequently, when the founding of the new party—the German Democratic Party—was officially announced on 20 November, the Progressives responded two days later with a public appeal calling upon their supporters throughout the country to place themselves at the service of the new party.[20]

Whereas the Progressives felt that they had no choice but to go along with with Wolff and his associates, the outcome of the meeting on 18 November had only confirmed Stresemann in his conviction that an agreement with the group around the *Berliner Tageblatt* was impossible. Immediately after the fateful meeting on 18 November, Stresemann cabled his supporters throughout the country in a desperate attempt to prevent them from going over to the Democratic Party and to keep what still remained of the old National Liberal organization intact.[21] At the same time, he and two other members of the NLP central executive committee, Robert Friedberg and Paul Vogel, issued a public appeal calling upon those who had remained true to the principles of the National Liberal Party to throw their support to the new German People's Party that he and the leaders of the NLP were in the process of founding.[22] Stresemann's hopes of rallying the National Liberal faithful to the cause of the DVP, however, had already suffered a serious setback with the defection of Baron Hartmann von Richthofen and Johannes Junck, both members of the NLP Reichstag delegation, earlier in the negotiations.[23] Stresemann's situation was further complicated by the virtual collapse of the National Liberal organization in Bavaria, Württemberg, and other parts of the country. In Württemberg, for example, local party leaders from both the FVP and NLP had already gone over to the DDP in an attempt to force the national leadership of their respective parties to resolve their differences on behalf of a united liberal party,[24] while in the Rhineland all but a handful of the NLP's local leaders had come out in support of the Democrats.[25]

Stresemann's decision to found the German People's Party ran strongly counter to the express wishes of many of his closest associates. This was particularly true of the Young Liberals, who at a meeting with Stresemann, Otto Hugo, and other party leaders on 23 November pressed their case for a united liberal party.[26] At the same time, both Stresemann and the founders of the DDP found themselves under increasingly heavy pressure from influential middle-class interest organizations to resume negotiations between their respective parties. On 28 November over 120 representatives from more than twenty special-interest organizations such as the Hansa-Bund, the German National Union of Commercial Employees, and the German Middle-Class Association met in Berlin to petition the leaders of the DDP and DVP for a resumption of efforts on behalf of a united liberal party, stipulating in particular that Stresemann as well as a sizable number from their own ranks should be accepted into the leadership of the new party.[27] Although Stresemann himself refused to become involved in further negotiations with the likes of Wolff and Weber, he could hardly ignore what amounted to a virtual ground swell of popular sentiment in favor of a merger between the DDP and DVP, with the result that he reluctantly agreed to meet with delegates from the newly founded DDP.

The decisive meeting took place on the afternoon of 2 December. The People's Party was represented by Friedberg and Eugen Leidig, both high-ranking members of the National Liberal delegation to the Prussian Landtag. The Democrats, on the other hand, were represented by Otto Fischbeck, a former Progressive parliamentarian who was strongly critical of the *Berliner Tageblatt* faction, and Hjalmar Schacht, a prominent Young Liberal who had been actively involved in the series of events leading to the founding of the DDP. While the founders of the DDP were resolutely opposed to any agreement that might make it possible for Stresemann to secure a position of influence within the new party,[28] Stresemann was prepared to go along with an accommodation with the Democrats, provided that his colleagues from the NLP received the measure of influence over the policies of the new party to which he thought they were entitled.[29] With this in mind, Stresemann provided Friedberg and Leidig with a set of specific instructions outlining the conditions under which a merger with the DDP would be acceptable to himself and the National Liberal leadership. But at the decisive meeting on 2 December Friedberg completely ignored the instructions he had received from Stresemann and proceeded, over Leidig's vigorous protests, to accept a merger with the DDP on terms that included the co-optation of himself and two other representatives from the DVP into the DDP executive committee. At the conclusion of the meeting Friedberg issued a statement that confirmed the unification of the two liberal parties and called for the creation of a "united front of the liberal and democratic bourgeoisie on the basis of the Democratic Party."[30]

When Stresemann returned to Berlin on the following day, he immediately denounced Friedberg's action as a complete capitulation to the Democrats and tried desperately to counter the effect that it had had upon the National Liberal organization throughout the country.[31] In one part of the country after another Friedberg's declaration of support for the DDP had destroyed what still remained of National Liberal resistance to the founding of a united liberal party. The entire National Liberal organization had already defected to the DDP in southern and southwestern Germany, and similar signs of the party's organizational collapse could be seen in Saxony, Silesia, and West Prussia.[32] At the same time, the leaders of the Young Liberal movement had come out in public support of the DDP in hopes that this might force Stresemann into joining the party.[33] But Stresemann, deeply embittered by what he regarded as Friedberg's betrayal of the National Liberal cause, remained unshaken in his determination to rally what still remained of the NLP organization to the support of the German People's Party. In this respect, Stresemann scored a critical victory when on 6 December the party organization in Hanover voted to repudiate Friedberg's merger with the DDP and called for an emergency session of the NLP central executive committee to determine the fate of the party.[34] The meeting took place in Berlin on 15 December in the midst of a fierce winter snowstorm that prevented more than two-thirds of the committee members from attending. Hopeful that his might work in their favor, those National Liberals who favored a merger with the DDP refused to consider a postponement of the meeting so that party members from outside of Berlin could attend. The subsequent debate centered around two resolutions, one introduced by former NLP Reichstag deputy August Weber that called for the dissolution of the National Liberal organization and its absorption into the DDP, and the other by Paul Vogel and his associates that proposed that the party organization be kept intact and placed at the service of the German People's Party. In the decisive vote Vogel's resolution on behalf of the DVP passed by a 33–28 margin, thus clearing the way for the official founding of the DVP at a demonstration later that afternoon in Berlin's fashionable Hotel Savoy.[35] "And with that fateful decision," wrote the DDP's Otto Nuschke a decade later, "the historic moment for the creation of a united liberal-democratic party had passed."[36]

In the polemics that followed the founding of the German People's Party, the Democrats tried to saddle Stresemann with the blame for the failure to achieve liberal unity in November and December 1918 and for the perpetuation of the historic schism within the ranks of the German liberal movement.[37] In point of fact, however, ultimate responsibility for the failure of efforts to create a united liberal party in the days following the collapse of the Second Empire rested not so much with Stresemann as with the Democrats around Wolff, Weber, and the *Berliner Tageblatt*. For Stresemann, as a careful reading of the historical record will reveal, was fully prepared not only to enter into a far-reaching alliance with the Progressives before the founding of the DDP ever took place but also to retire from active political life so as not to stand in the way of an accommodation with the Democrats. Two developments, however, prevented Stresemann from following through on this resolve. In the first place, the emergence of the Democrats in the second week of November and their appeal for the creation of a new political party unencumbered by the sins of the past effectively sabotaged whatever progress Stresemann and the Progressives had been making toward a resolution of their differences and left the latter with no alternative but to reach an accord with the Wolff-Weber faction. Secondly, the faction from the *Berliner Tageblatt* was adamantly opposed to any involvement on the part of Stresemann in the leadership of the new party—a point that Weber made manifestly clear with his attack against *Anne-xationspolitiker* at the meeting on 18 November—and consequently refused to grant even the minimal concessions that might have made it possible for him to join the DDP. Even then, Stresemann was still willing to step aside for the sake of a united liberal party until Friedberg's capitulation to the Democrats in the first week of December.

In the campaign for the elections to the National Assembly on 19 January 1919, the founders of the German Democratic Party sought above all else to prevent the working-class parties on Germany's socialist Left from capturing an absolute majority. In its official campaign appeal the DDP called for the reconstruction of the German fatherland on the basis of the republican form of government and pledged itself to the defense of private property and the free enterprise system.[38] While clearly dissociating themselves from socialist de- mands for a reorganization of the German economy, the Democrats were careful not to offend the more moderate elements within the German working class and rejected a DVP proposal for the creation of a united bourgeois front for fear that this might force the Majority and Independent Socialists closer together.[39] In this respect, the Democrats portrayed themselves as a bridge between the bourgeoisie and proletariat and repeatedly stressed that only the creation of a powerful bourgeois bloc willing to cooperate with the Majority Socialists on the basis of parity could prevent the state from falling under the domination of Germany's revolutionary Left.[40] By drawing a critical distinc- tion between the political and socioeconomic goals of the November Revolu- tion, the Democrats were able to present themselves both as the allies and the adversaries of German Social Democracy.

From a purely tactical point of view, the DDP's principal objective in the elections to the National Assembly was to extend its appeal beyond those social and political groups that had supported the old Progressive People's Party in the Reichstag elections of January 1912. At that time the Progressives had scored a major victory at the polls only to be denied the full fruits of their victory by the peculiarities of the German electoral law. Now, under a system of proportional representation, the Democrats hoped to improve upon that performance with one of the most highly sophisticated and well-organized campaigns Germany had ever witnessed. In adapting their campaign to the exigencies of mass politics, the Democrats consciously imitated techniques of political agitation and mobilization that had been in use in the United States for some time. In the two months between the party's founding and the elections to the National Assembly, the Democrats saturated the German public with nearly 20 million pieces of campaign literature, approximately a fourth of which were directly targeted at the newly enfranchised woman voter. At the same time, the Democrats also relied upon films, loudspeakers, and illustrated placards as supplemental means of carrying their message to the people. All of this represented a radical departure from the way in which the German liberal parties had traditionally conducted their campaigns and constituted part of a concerted attempt by the Democrats to transform the DDP into a mass political party fundamentally different from the liberal *Honoratorienparteien* of the 19th century.[41]

In their efforts to expand their party's electoral base beyond those groups that had supported the Progressives in 1912, the Democrats focused their immediate attention upon former Young Liberals and members of the now-defunct NLP. On 15 December forty-one former National Liberals published an appeal characterizing the DDP as a merger of all those committed to the liberal concept of freedom and calling upon their colleagues to support it as the only alternative to a socialist dictatorship.[42] Several days later, the executive committee of the Young Liberal League (Jungliberaler Reichsverband) issued a similar appeal in which the founders of the DVP were held responsible for the failure of liberal unity in the fall and early winter of 1918.[43] In a similar vein, the Democrats were able to achieve a major breakthrough into the ranks of the National Liberal electorate in the countryside. Here the principal figure was Karl Böhme, a National Liberal Reichstag deputy who had helped found the German Peasants' League in 1909 as a liberal counterweight to the protectionist policies of Germany's conservative rural elite. Following the collapse of the Second Empire, Böhme and the leaders of the German Peasants' League were quick to realign themselves with the DDP on the assumption that it represented the best bulwark against the twin dangers of social revolution and feudal reaction. More specifically, Böhme hoped that the DDP would take the lead in initiating a program of rural resettlement that would put an end to the social and political hegemony of the landed aristocracy and encourage those who had left the farm since the beginning of the century to return to the countryside.[44] Gratified by Böhme's declaration of support, the DDP reciprocated by publishing an agrarian program that underwrote the DBB's most important objectives and placed 250,000 marks at his organization's disposal for use in the campaign.[45]

The German Peasants' League was not the only middle-class interest organization to rally to the DDP's support in the aftermath of the November Revolution. In urban areas throughout the country, the DDP proved remarkably successful in attracting the support of organizations representing the so-called "new middle class" of civil servants and white-collar employees. In December 1918 the various civil servant organizations that had been founded during the war merged to form the German Civil Servants' Association (Deutscher Beamtenbund) under the chairmanship of Ernst Remmers. A member of the Democratic Party, Remmers was quickly co-opted into the DDP executive committee, where he served as a liaison to the civil servant movement and was

nominated as a candidate for election to the National Assembly.[46] In much the
same way, the Democrats also sought to establish a foothold within the German white-collar movement through the cooperation of Gustav Schneider. As
it had among civil servants, the war had also done much to stimulate a move
toward unionization on the part of white-collar employees. As chairman of the
Leipzig-based Federation of German Clerks (Verband deutscher Handlungsgehilfen), Schneider had spearheaded wartime efforts to consolidate the various
nonsocialist employee organizations throughout the country into a national
federation of white-collar unions. Like Remmers, Schneider was quick to
affiliate himself with the DDP after its founding in the fall of 1918 and
received a prominent place on the Democratic ticket for the National
Assembly.[47]

   The DDP's image as a socially progressive party accounted in large measure
for the support that it received from the new middle class in the campaign for
the elections to the National Assembly. Such an image held little appeal,
however, for the artisanry and small business sector, whose interest in the DDP
stemmed more from the need to contain the tide of social and political radicalism that had been unleashed by the November Revolution than from the party's
progressive social policies.[48] The ambivalence the more traditional elements
of the German middle class felt toward the DDP was compounded by the
overtures that the party made in the direction of the German working class.
Here the principal impulse came from a group of former Progressives who,
inspired by Friedrich Naumann's vision of a social monarchy, had long sought
to overcome the historic cleavage between liberalism and the German working
class under the auspices of the Hirsch-Duncker trade-union movement. By
1919 the movement's nominal leader was Gustav Hartmann, chairman of the
Federation of German Labor Associations (Verband der deutschen Gewerkver-
eine) and one of the DDP's co-founders. At the height of the November
Revolution, Hartmann had joined forces with Adam Stegerwald, a prominent
Christian labor leader, in founding the German Democratic Trade-Union Federation (Deutsch-demokratischer Gewerkschaftsbund or DDGB) as a basis for
consolidating the nonsocialist elements of the German working class—liberal
as well as Christian.[49] Anxious to secure an organizational foothold within the
German labor movement, the Democrats nominated Hartmann and several
other activists from the Hirsch-Duncker trade-union movement to safe candidacies for the National Assembly.[50]

   In their efforts to forge a broad-based alliance of middle-class and working-
class interests, the Democrats were helped in no small measure by the massive
financial support they received from the German industrial establishment. The
leaders of the German business community felt threatened by the outbreak of
the November Revolution and were anxious to check the tide of social and
political radicalism that was sweeping the country. It was with this in mind that

a group of Berlin businessmen under the leadership of Carl Friedrich von Siemens and Ernst von Borsig decided in December 1918 to found the Curatorium for the Reconstruction of German Economic Life (Kuratorium für den Wiederaufbau des deutschen Wirtschaftslebens) for the purpose of coordinating the collection and allocation of industrial funds for use in the elections to the National Assembly. The Curatorium's immediate objective was to prevent the socialist parties from gaining a majority in the National Assembly.[51] To accomplish this goal, the Curatorium collected more than 3 million marks for use by the three nonconfessional bourgeois parties in the election campaign. The founders of the Curatorium were particularly interested in the DDP because, of all the nonsocialist parties, it seemed to offer the best prospect of developing into a comprehensive bourgeois *Sammelpartei* capable of holding the working-class parties in check. On 31 December the Curatorium met with a four-man delegation from the DDP executive committee and, after receiving minimal assurances about the party's future political course, agreed to contribute 1 million marks to its campaign coffers.[52] The DVP and conservative German National People's Party (Deutschnationale Volkspartei or DNVP), by comparison, had to be satisfied with 500,000 marks apiece.[53]

The electoral coalition that the Democrats put together in the winter of 1918–19 embraced virtually every sector of the German middle strata as well as a sizable contingent from the Hirsch-Duncker trade-union movement. Only the artisanry and small business sector seemed inadequately represented on the Democratic ticket for the National Assembly. In an attempt to exploit the latent cleavages within the DDP's electoral base, Stresemann structured his party's campaign around three antitheses whose chief value lay in their conceptual and rhetorical simplicity: bourgeois-social, national-international, and liberal-democratic. The first of these tried to take advantage of the DDP's failure to draw a sharp line between itself and the Social Democrats. For while the leaders of the DDP rejected the designation "bourgeois" and continued to portray themselves as a bridge between the bourgeoisie and the industrial working class, Stresemann attacked the Democrats for their flirtations with Social Democracy and insisted that the DVP was the only genuine party of bourgeois concentration. With the second of these antitheses Stresemann was trying not only to capitalize upon the DDP's refusal to dissociate itself from the party of international socialism but also to exploit the prominence of a faction within the DDP that had espoused pacifist views during the war and had castigated him for his defense of the German war effort. In contrast to the internationalist, cosmopolitan character of the DDP, Stresemann portrayed the DVP as a "national" party whose mission was to nurture a sense of national consciousness on the part of the German people. The last antithesis, that of liberalism to democracy, was rooted in a similar antagonism toward the DDP and came to assume more and more importance as the two liberal parties tried to legitimize the failure of liberal unity in ideological terms. Equating the democratic doctrine of popular sovereignty with de Tocqueville's "tyranny of the majority," Stresemann and the founders of the DVP insisted that there was a fundamental and ultimately irreconcilable difference between liberalism and democracy. Specifically, Stresemann argued that democracy threatened to obliterate the uniqueness of the individual by submerging him in an amorphous and undifferentiated mass, while liberalism sought to emancipate the individual from anything that might interfere with the free development of his personality.[54]

At the heart of Stresemann's liberalism lay a deep and abiding commitment to the values of political and economic individualism. Stresemann was particularly concerned about the social impact of the changes that had taken place in the structure of the German economy during the war. Speaking in Stuttgart in November 1917, Stresemann had deplored the effect that the large-scale concentration of economic power during the war had had upon the German middle strata and called for the social and economic rehabilitation of those strata as the first order of business once hostilities ceased.[55] Stresemann returned to this theme in a speech at the Osnabrück city hall on 19 December 1918 when he denounced socialization schemes—bourgeois as well as socialist—as "Nietzsche translated into economics" and as the "path from capitalism to super-capitalism."[56] Throughout the campaign for the National Assembly the DVP continued to champion the cause of the independent middle class and demanded the immediate suspension of wartime economic controls as the first step toward its economic rehabilitation. By the same token, the founders of the DVP hoped to attract the support of the independent peasantry by advocating a program of rural resettlement designed to reverse the century-long pattern of emigration from the country to the city.[57] Yet at the same time that Stresemann sought to mobilize the peasantry and independent middle class in support of the DVP, he also made an unprecedented bid for the support of the Protestant wing of the Christian labor movement. Following the collapse of Stegerwald's efforts to found an interconfessional Christian workers' party in early December 1918,[58] Stresemann succeeded in winning the cooperation of a small yet influential group of Christian labor leaders headed by Hans Bechly from the German National Union of Commercial Employees, Friedrich Baltrusch and Georg Streiter from the United Federation of Christian Trade Unions (Gesamtverband der christlichen Gewerkschaften Deutschlands or GCG), and Wilhelm Gutsche from the newly founded German Trainmen's Union (Gewerkschaft deutscher Eisenbahner). While the more conservative Protestant labor leaders proceeded to affiliate themselves with the right-wing German National People's Party, the cooperation of Bechly, Gutsche, and their associates provided Stresemann and the DVP with what promised to be the beginning of a solid organizational foothold within the Christian labor movement.[59]

In terms of its underlying conception, the DVP constituted a "people's party" every bit as heterogeneous as the DDP. But the DVP's efforts to generate mass political support were severely handicapped by a variety of factors, not the least of which was the lack of adequate funding. For although the DVP had received 500,000 marks from the Curatorium for the Reconstruction of German Economic Life, the Ruhr industrial interests upon which the National Liberals had relied for financial support in the prewar period were extremely slow in coming to the DVP's help in the campaign for the National Assembly.[60] The Commission for the Collection, Administration, and Allocation of the Industrial Campaign Fund (Kommission zur Sammlung, Verwaltung und Verwendung des Industriellen Wahlfonds) that had traditionally channeled industrial funds to the NLP and more conservative bourgeois parties had been virtually paralyzed by the outbreak of the November Revolution and was in no position to support the DVP in the manner to which its predecessor had been accustomed. Consequently, the DVP lacked the financial resources to repair the damage that Friedberg's announcement of a merger between the DDP and DVP had done to the National Liberal organization throughout the country. In Bavaria, Baden, Württemberg, Silesia, West Prussia, and parts of Saxony the NLP district organizations had gone over to the DVP virtually intact, while in other parts of the country the party organization had either ceased to exist or had been immobilized by the confusion in Berlin. Only in Hesse, the Palatinate, and Lower Saxony did the National Liberal organization show any signs of life in the aftermath of Friedberg's announcement, with the result that the DVP was unable to present a full slate of candidates in much of the country.[61]

The outcome of the elections to the National Assembly only confirmed the tremendous advantage that the DDP had enjoyed going into the campaign. With more than 5.6 million votes—or 18.5 percent of the popular vote—the DDP improved upon the performance of the prewar Progressive People's Party in the 1912 Reichstag elections by more than 5 percentage points, while the DVP, on the other hand, saw its share of the popular vote fall from the 14 percent that the National Liberals had received in 1912 to a mere 4.4 percent seven years later. Although official election statistics make it impossible to determine the precise social character of the Democratic electorate, comparison with the results of the 1912 elections reveals that the DDP had managed to score a decisive breakthrough into National Liberal strongholds in the central and southwestern parts of the country. This was particularly true of Baden, Württemberg, Bavaria, Thuringia, and parts of Saxony, where the entire National Liberal organization had gone over to the DDP. Only in the Ruhr and Lower Saxony did the Democrats fail to make significant inroads into the National Liberal electorate, although even there they managed to score modest gains in comparison with the FVP's performance seven years earlier. About the only places where the DDP failed to match the percentage of the popular vote received by the Progressives in 1912 were large urban centers like Berlin and Hamburg, where potential Democratic voters had defected not only to the DVP and DNVP but to the Social Democrats as well. On the whole, however, such losses were minimal and did little to detract from the overall strength of the DDP's performance in the elections to the National Assembly.[62]

The outcome of the elections was nonetheless significant for the German People's Party, if for no other reason than the fact that it confirmed the party's survival under extremely adverse circumstances. Not only had the DVP been banished from traditional National Liberal strongholds in southwestern and central Germany, but the defection of the Young Liberals had cost the DVP the support of many of the NLP's more active, younger members. Still, in spite of the fact that the DVP was unable to field a slate of candidates in eleven of Germany's thirty-six electoral districts and had to rely upon alliances with either the DDP or DNVP in four others, the party had managed to poll 1.35 million votes and elect twenty-two deputies to the National Assembly. This meant that in those parts of the country where the DVP still possessed something in the way of a local organization it performed extremely well, sometimes receiving as much as 10 to 15 percent of the popular vote. Party leaders were particularly encouraged by the DVP's performance in the Palatinate, Hesse-Nassau, and the three north German districts of Posen, Oldenburg, and Pomerania, while in Berlin the DVP succeeded in electing a deputy in a city where the NLP had not even run a candidate in 1912. Even though the DVP was a mere shadow of what the NLP had been before the war, the party's performance in the elections to the National Assembly indicated that it was far from dead.[63]

In many respects, the collapse of the Second Empire and the founding of the Weimar Republic had done little to change the fundamental structure of the German party system as it had developed during the course of the nineteenth century. Although the November Revolution had witnessed the founding of three new bourgeois parties in the German Democratic Party, the German People's Party, and the German National People's Party, the constellation of political forces that emerged from the revolution bore a strong resemblance to that which had existed before the war. The element of continuity could be seen not only in the failure to create a united liberal party but also in the survival of the German Center Party with its national organization and ideological identity essentially intact.[64] Within the German liberal movement, however, the November Revolution had produced a fundamental realignment of political forces that belied the appearance of continuity. For although the efforts to found a united liberal party had once again ended in failure, the DDP was far more than a mere continuation of the prewar Progressive People's Party. Not only did the DDP embrace elements that stood to the left and the right of the old

FVP, but the party had succeeded in breaking out of the mold of a classical liberal *Honoratiorenpartei* by giving itself a strong popular base that none of the prewar liberal parties had ever possessed. Just as the collapse of the Second Empire marked the beginning of a bold new era in the history of the German people, so did the founding of the German Democratic Party represent the beginning of a new era in the history of the German liberal movement.[65] Whether or not this new beginning could thrive under the myriad of problems that beset the German people in the aftermath of the war remained to be seen.

CHAPTER TWO

The Burden of Responsibility

THE DDP'S VICTORY IN THE elections to the National Assembly did not represent an aberration in Germany's historical development but rather the culmination of the general revival of German liberalism that had begun with Naumann's arrival on the political scene at the end of the previous century. The emergence of the Hansa-Bund and the German Peasants' League, the founding of the Progressive People's Party and its strong performance in the 1912 Reichstag elections, and the prominent role that left liberals had played in national politics from the Peace Resolution in the summer of 1917 to Prince Max's "revolution from above" in the fall of 1918 all represented different facets of the general revival of political liberalism that reached its culmination in the founding of the German Democratic Party and its victory at the polls in January 1919.[1] Yet while the collapse of the Second Empire marked the beginning of a dramatic new era in the history of the German liberal movement, it was by no means certain whether or not German liberalism could overcome its own historical legacy. The fate of political liberalism in the Weimar Republic depended upon the successful resolution of a series of critical questions that had persistently plagued its development since the middle of the previous century. Could, for example, the German liberal movement ever overcome the traditional German antipathy toward political parties as institutions representing only parts of the whole but never the whole itself? Or, by the same token, would German liberalism ever succeed in overcoming the increasing fragmentation of Germany's middle-class interest structure to create a truly comprehensive liberal party? Would the leaders of the German liberal movement be able to replace the increasingly obsolete *Honoratioren-parteien* that had developed during the nineteenth century with a more modern organizational structure? Would German liberals ever overcome the historic antipathy of the German bourgeoisie toward the industrial working class? And last, but by no means least, would the intensity of German national feeling, particularly within the German middle strata, serve as an obstacle to the development of a viable liberal movement in a nation scarred by military defeat?

The fate of Germany's new republican order depended upon the extent to which the parties of the so-called democratic middle—specifically the Democratic Party, the Center, and the Majority Socialists—would be able to integrate the German middle strata and the more moderate elements from the German working class into an effective and durable political force. While efforts to construct a viable republican consensus were severely handicapped by the deep-seated animosity that influential sectors of the German bourgeoisie continued to harbor for the industrial working class, the stabilization of the new republican order was further complicated by the fact that the party system that the Weimar Republic had inherited from the Second Empire was archaic and ill suited to meet the needs of a modern parliamentary democracy. The democratization of German political life in general and the introduction of proportional representation in particular had increased the influence that organized economic interests were able to exercise in the internal affairs of the various bourgeois parties. Whereas before the war special interest organizations such as the Agrarian League and the Central Association of German Industrialists had characteristically bypassed both parliament and its constituent political parties in favor of direct contact with the ministerial bureaucracy, after 1918 political parties became the principal vehicle through which special economic interests could influence the legislative process.[2] At the same time, the introduction of proportional representation had greatly enhanced the importance of special interest organizations such as the German National Union of Commercial Employees or the newly formed German Civil Servants' Association—not to mention the Christian, Hirsch-Duncker, or socialist trade-union movements—that possessed a mass membership base.[3] The net effect of these changes was to severely complicate the task of political integration within the various nonsocialist parties that had emerged from the collapse of the Second Empire and to intensify the disintegrative potential of social and economic conflict.

As the German Democratic Party emerged from the elections to the National Assembly in January 1919, it remained to be seen whether or not it could translate its impressive performance at the polls into a coherent and effective program of political action. The internal cohesiveness of the DDP, however, was threatened not only by the horizontal tensions that existed between the diverse and potentially antagonistic social and economic groups that constituted the party's material base but also by the lack of a genuine ideological consensus among the leaders of the party. The Democratic Party represented the fusion of at least four or five different strains of German liberalism. By far the most prominent group within the DDP, particularly during the first months of its existence, was the so-called democratic faction around Theodor Wolff and Alfred Weber. Cosmopolitan, urbane, and inwardly alienated from much that had passed for Germany's national greatness, this group differed both in its ambivalence toward nationalism and in the intensity of its commitment to the welfare of the German worker from the Progressives, many of whom had been schooled in Friedrich Naumann's eclectic, if not grandiose, synthesis of liberalism, nationalism, and socialism.[4] Aside from Naumann himself, the principal representatives of the National Social tradition within the DDP were Gertrud Bäumer, a well-known feminist with close ties to the prewar German youth movement,[5] and Anton Erkelenz, a dedicated trade-union leader from the Rhineland who had been active in liberal politics ever since the turn of the century.[6] Other prominent Progressives within the DDP were Otto Fischbeck and Georg Gothein, both political pragmatists with close ties to middle-class business interests, while the South German Democrats, who of all the various liberal factions retained the strongest identification with the ideals and aspirations of 1848, were represented by Friedrich von Payer and Conrad Hauß-mann.[7] The fifth major group within the DDP consisted of former National Liberals like Hartmann von Richthofen and Robert Friedberg who had gone over to the Democratic Party in November and early December 1918. This group, which also included Young Liberal activists such as Hjalmar Schacht, Hermann Fischer, and Curt Köhler, possessed close ties to the German business community and along with Fischbeck and Gothein came to form the nucleus of the party's right wing.[8]

From the very outset, there was a profound difference—to extend an analogy from Max Weber's argument in *Politik als Beruf* on the irreconcilability of an "ethics of intention" with an "ethics of responsibility"—between the doctrinaire moralism of the group around Wolff and Weber and the political pragmatism of those like Fischbeck, Gothein, and Haußmann to whom politics was the art of the possible and not that of the impossible dream. Indeed, as Sigmund Neumann has suggested in his classic study of the German party system during the Weimar Republic, the entire history of the DDP could be seen as a case study of Weber's thesis.[9] Responsibility for leadership of the party originally rested in the hands of a provisional three-man executive committee consisting of Weber from the *Berliner Tageblatt* group, Fischbeck from the Progressives, and Richthofen from the left wing of the NLP.[10] The Progressives, however, regarded the political dilettantism of the faction around Wolff and Weber as a serious liability, and in early December Fischbeck and his associates launched a concerted campaign to drive them from control of the party.[11] Weber helped expedite matters himself with an inept and ill-considered attack against Hugo Stinnes and other Ruhr industrialists for having supposedly supported French plans to establish a separate Rhenish state in the western part of Germany.[12] When Weber's allegations proved totally unfounded, he was forced to resign from the leadership of the Democratic Party, thus providing the Progressives with their first victory in their efforts to undercut the influence of the *Berliner Tageblatt* faction.[13]

With Weber's resignation from the party leadership in December 1918 and the elections to the National Assembly a month later, the Progressives were able to solidify their control over the party organization and emerged as the dominant faction within the Democratic delegation at Weimar. By the middle of April Wolff had become so distressed by his loss of influence within the party that he announced his resignation from the DDP executive committee, citing the autonomy of the party's Weimar delegation as the reason for his decision.[14] The Progressives sealed their triumph several months later when Naumann was elected to the party chairmanship at the DDP's first national party congress in Berlin.[15] A statesman of charismatic vision, Naumann was without question the most dynamic figure in the German liberal movement since the turn of the century, and his election, in spite of his notorious disdain for the more mundane aspects of political leadership, promised to propel the DDP toward fulfillment of the ideals that had inspired its founding. But within six weeks of his election, Naumann was dead, the victim of a stroke suffered during a convalescence on the Baltic. Naumann's untimely death deprived the DDP of its most magnetic leader and created a void into which none of his associates was prepared to step. His successor, elected provisionally at a meeting of the DDP party council in September 1919[16] and then confirmed in office by the DDP party congress in December,[17] was Carl Petersen, a former Progressive from Hamburg who enjoyed the support of virtually every faction within the party. But Petersen, his obvious talents as a mediator notwithstanding, lacked the vision, the passion, and the ability to inspire that had set Naumann so far apart from his contemporaries.[18]

That the lack of effective and unified leadership constituted one of the major problems confronting the founders of the DDP became manifestly clear following the convocation of the National Assembly in early February 1919. As far as the Democrats were concerned, the immediate task was to contain the socialistic impulse that had been unleashed by the November Revolution while at the same time making certain that the conditions for the establishment of a viable democratic order had been secured. Convinced that this could best be accomplished by cooperating with the more moderate elements of the socialist movement, the Democrats joined the Majority Socialists and the Center in a coalition government headed by the MSPD's Philipp Scheidemann.[19] While the Democrats recognized the necessity of such a coalition in order to secure the foundations of the new democratic order, they were nevertheless extremely apprehensive about their party's relatively weak position in the government. Cabinet posts had been distributed among the Majority Socialists, the Center, and the DDP according to the formula 7:3:3, with the Foreign Ministry going to Count Ulrich von Brockdorff-Rantzau, a politically unaffiliated diplomat with close, though unofficial, ties to the DDP. Not only did this arrangement make it mathematically impossible for the two bourgeois parties to override the policy decisions of their working-class ally, but the fact that the selection of ministers was left in the hands of the parties themselves made it impossible for the Democrats to block the appointment of someone like the Center's Matthias

Erzberger whom they regarded as an unwanted liability.[20] Equally distressing from the Democratic point of view were the various schemes for a reorganization of the economy that emerged from the ranks of the working-class parties. In a major programmatic speech on 13 February, Naumann admitted that the creation of a socialist order was a moral obligation but clearly dissociated himself and the DDP from the various proposals for the socialization of the means of production.[21] In an equally important speech two days later, the DDP's Eugen Schiffer, whom the Democrats had delegated as the minister of finance in the Scheidemann government, categorically ruled out any economic experiments in view of the chaotic state of German finances and publicly committed himself to the restoration of the free enterprise system at the earliest possible opportunity.[22]

The Democrats hoped to offset their numerical inferiority in the Scheidemann government by controlling key cabinet posts such as the ministries of Finance, Treasury, and Interior. But their party's overall effectiveness as a member of the governmental coalition was severely handicapped by the lack of a clear conception of what it hoped to accomplish in the area of social and economic reform. At a meeting of the Democratic delegation on 1 March labor leader Anton Erkelenz encountered sharp criticism from the party's right wing when he suggested that the moment for at least limited economic experimentation had arrived. Particularly outspoken in his criticism of Erkelenz's proposal was Württemburg's Conrad Haußmann, who insisted that the goal of Democratic policy should be to wrest leadership of the national government from the Social Democrats and pursue a more independent, pro-middle-class line.[23] The cleavages within the Democratic delegation to the National Assembly became even more pronounced when a few days later the Socialist minister of labor, Rudolf Wissell, introduced legislation establishing the general guidelines for the socialization of the German economy and for the regulation of the coal industry in particular.[24] Not only were the leaders of the DDP irritated by the fact that neither they nor the Democratic ministers in the Scheidemann government had been consulted before the introduction of Wissell's legislation, but the proposal overstepped the terms of the "action program" to which the three government parties had agreed when the Weimar Coalition had first been formed.[25] Originally the Democrats hoped that it might be possible to amend the more odious aspects of Wissell's bill, but they were unable to reach agreement within their own ranks and rejected a compromise proposal from Erkelenz that would have committed the DDP to a program of socialization for those sectors of the economy that were deemed essential to the welfare of the nation as a whole.[26] Still, the Democrats could not afford to vote against Wissell's bill for fear that this would result in the collapse of the Scheidemann government and put an end to their work on the new constitution.[27] As a result, the Democrats were left with no choice but to support the government's socialization legislation when it came before the National Assembly for a final vote on 13 March. Only the fact that the bill was of little immediate consequence made it possible for the Democrats to set aside their reservations—as fundamental as they may have been—and support it in the interest of governmental solidarity.[28]

The failure of the DDP's Weimar delegation to take a clear and unequivocal stand against the socialization schemes of the Majority Socialists created serious problems for the Democratic leadership and seriously jeopardized the party's middle-class support.[29] The situation within the party assumed an even more ominous tone when on 10 April Schiffer, a former National Liberal and an outspoken exponent of the free enterprise system, announced his resignation as minister of finance in what could only have been interpreted as a protest against the social and economic policies of the Scheidemann government.[30] While Schiffer's action clearly reflected the frustration that the DDP leaders felt over their party's weakness as a member of the Weimar Coalition, the Democrats were not prepared to go so far as to withdraw from the government and end their cooperation with the Center and Majority Socialists. Not only would this have torpedoed the German peace delegation at Versailles, but there was no suitable alternative to a government based on the Weimar Coalition.[31] On 11 April Friedrich von Payer, chairman of the DDP's Weimar delegation, publicly reaffirmed his party's commitment to the Weimar Coalition in a speech before the National Assembly. Essentially a catalog of the Democrats' accomplishments as a member of the national government, Payer's speech was designed not merely to dispel doubts regarding the DDP's loyalty to the governmental coalition but also to remind the party's rank and file of the positive contribution which the DDP had made to the stabilization of the political situation in postwar Germany.[32]

Payer's defense of the DDP's political record as a member of the Weimar Coalition did little to defuse the potentially explosive situation that had developed within the Democratic party organization. At a meeting of the DDP executive committee on 12–13 April the party's Weimar delegation came under a sharp attack from right-wing Democrats for its failure to dissociate itself from the government's socialization proposals. Here the principal critics were Bruno Marwitz, an erstwhile Young Liberal who had played a decisive role in the founding of the DDP, and Otto Keinath, another former National Liberal who had risen to prominence as a lawyer for the Central Association of German Wholesalers (Zentralverband des deutschen Grosshandels). Marwitz drew special attention to the increasing disaffection of the party's middle-class electorate and warned that continued equivocation on matters such as socialization would doom the DDP's effort to establish itself as a party of bourgeois concentration. But these arguments fell on deaf ears as the DDP executive committee proceeded to adopt a resolution that ignored the demands of those who were either overly sympathetic or overly hostile to the idea of socialization.[33] This, in turn, did little either to reassure those on the party's right wing who had become wary of the party's collaboration with the Majority Socialists or to heal the rift that had developed within the party's electoral base.

The controversy over socialization revealed a fundamental ambiguity in the DDP's self-image. For although the DDP had been founded in an attempt to provide Germany's liberal bourgeoisie with the strong, broad-based political organization it needed in order to sustain its vital interests within the framework of the new republican order, the party also conceived of itself as a bridge between the bourgeoisie and the more moderate elements of the German working class. As a result, the Democrats had been obliged to make concessions in the field of social and economic policy, as in the case of the socialization debates in the spring of 1919, that threatened to alienate much of their party's middle-class support. The DDP's failure to press for a suspension of wartime economic controls and an end to governmental interference in the economic sector was widely perceived, particularly by those on the party's right wing, as a sign of its increasing dependence upon the Social Democrats and as a serious obstacle to Germany's economic recovery.[34] Unable to formulate an economic policy that satisfied both its middle-class and working-class constituencies, the DDP floundered between the Scylla of governmental crisis and the Charybdis of middle-class disenchantment.

The controversy over the DDP's social and economic policies was soon to be eclipsed by an even more divisive conflict, this time over acceptance or rejection of the Allied peace proposal. The Democrats had hoped for a peace settlement based upon the principles of Woodrow Wilson's "Fourteen Points," but their hopes were dashed with the publication of Allied peace terms on 7 May 1919. The terms of the proposed peace settlement provoked a wave of national indignation that swept the entire country and engulfed the leaders of the Democratic Party. On 12 May the DDP's Conrad Haußmann and Ludwig Quidde joined representatives from the government and every parliamentary delegation from the Independent Socialists to the German Nationalists in a demonstration of national solidarity against the Allied peace terms. While Haußmann denounced the Versailles peace proposal as a death sentence for countless thousands of innocent Germans and as a repudiation of the very principles upon which a lasting peace had to be based, the venerable Quidde, whose agitation for a negotiated peace during the last years of the war had earned him the wrath of the German High Command, protested that the Allied peace terms were totally incompatible with the ideals to which he as president of the German Peace Society (Deutsche Friedensgesellschaft) had devoted his life.[35] Meeting in Berlin six days later, the DDP executive committee unanimously endorsed the position that Haußmann and Quidde had taken on 12 May and passed a resolution expressing the hope that the terms of the Allied peace proposal could be revised in accordance with the principles of international justice so that a lasting peace might be possible.[36] At the same time, the three Democratic ministers—Gothein, Hugo Preuß, and Bernhard Dernburg, who had replaced Schiffer as head of the Finance Ministry—worked diligently behind the scenes to prevent the Scheidemann government from capitulating to Allied pressure.[37]

Throughout the late spring and early summer of 1919, the Democrats sought to establish themselves as the focal point of national resistance to Allied peace terms.[38] But as it became increasingly clear by the second week of June that there was little the German government, the German Reichstag, or the German delegation at Versailles could do to moderate the terms of the Allied peace proposal and that rejection of the proposal would almost certainly mean the occupation and perhaps dismemberment of the German Empire, the so-called *Ablehnungsfront* that had crystallized on 12 May began to fall apart. For their part, the Democrats were particularly concerned about the weakness of the Scheidemann government and feared that the increasing vacillation of the Majority Socialist and Centrist members of the cabinet foreshadowed a shift of sentiment in favor of accepting the peace terms.[39] These fears proved fully vindicated, for on the morning of 18 June—two days after an Allied ultimatum demanding unconditional compliance with the conditions dictated on 7 May— the German government split eight to six in favor of acceptance, with the three Democratic ministers joining Scheidemann and Brockdorff-Rantzau in the minority. Later that evening, the Majority Socialist delegation to the National Assembly repudiated Scheidemann's leadership of the government and voted to accept the Allied peace terms by almost a two-to-one margin. On the following day the Center delegation followed their example and at Erzberger's persistent urging voted in favor of acceptance by an overwhelming four-to-one margin.[40]

These developments set the scene for a critical test of principle within the Democratic Party. For although both the Center and Majority Socialists recognized the futility of further resistance to Allied pressure, the national leadership of the DDP remained intractible in its opposition to the Allied peace terms and was fully prepared to break ranks with its coalition partners for the sake of Germany's national honor. At a stormy meeting of the DDP's Weimar delegation on 19 June, Walther Schücking, a renowned pacifist and a member of the German delegation at Versailles, denounced the proposed peace treaty as a mockery of the principles of international justice upon which any lasting peace must be based and called upon his colleagues to reject it not only in order to defend Germany's national honor but to demonstrate to all the world the true meaning of pacifism and national self-determination.[41] Coming from a member of the party's small yet vociferous pacifist faction, Schücking's remarks made a profound impression upon the rest of the delegation and received warm support from representatives of the DDP's right wing such as Haußmann and Gothein.[42] But while the delegation may have been unanimous in its condemnation of the Allied peace terms, a small minority under the leadership of Friedrich von Payer, chairman of the Democratic delegation to the National Assembly, was no longer willing to ignore the possible consequences of rejecting the Allied demands. Convinced that Germany was militarily incapable of defending herself against the threat of Allied occupation, Payer warned his colleagues that rejection of the Allied peace proposal might very well mean the French annexation of the Rhineland, the establishment of a permanent French presence in the Ruhr, and the dissolution of the German Empire into a collection of independent states. In view of what might result from rejection of Allied peace terms, there was, Payer argued, no responsible alternative to voting for its acceptance, albeit under vigorous protest.[43] But Payer's remarks, motivated in large part by fears of what might happen to his native state of Württemberg if the Allies' peace proposal were rejected, had little effect upon the delegation as a whole. Supported only by Erkelenz and a handful of labor leaders who feared that rejection of the Allied peace proposal might force their party out of the government and put an end to its work in the field of social and economic reform, Payer and his supporters were outvoted by a decisive 55–8 margin.[44] The advocates of rejection had prevailed.

In the meantime, the position of the Scheidemann government had become untenable, and at three o'clock in the morning of 20 June it announced its resignation. The lead in forming a new government was immediately seized by Erzberger, who succeeded in persuading Germany's acting chief executive, Friedrich Ebert, to appoint Social Democrat Gustav Bauer as head of a minority government whose first item of business would be to accept Allied peace terms.[45] While the official installation of the Bauer government did not take place until the early afternoon of 21 June, any hopes that the DDP might support it received a sharp blow when on the morning of 20 June the Democratic delegation to the National Assembly adopted a resolution sponsored by Haußmann that explicitly ruled out Democratic participation in any government willing to accept the Allied peace terms. The Democrats hardened their position later that afternoon with the adoption of a second resolution stipulating that any member of the delegation who joined the government without its express approval would be subject to immediate expulsion.[46] Not only did the passage of this resolution torpedo whatever hopes Ebert or Erzberger might have had of enticing one or two prominent Democrats into the Bauer government, but it represented a clear triumph for those like Haußmann and Schiffer who were determined to prevent Erzberger and his supporters from finding a parliamentary majority for acceptance of the Allied peace terms.[47]

An overwhelming majority of the Democratic delegation to the National Assembly remained irreconcilably opposed to efforts by Erzberger and the

Majority Socialists to organize a government that would be willing to accept the Allied peace proposal. Yet in spite of the strong support this group was able to marshal in the delegation caucuses on 19 and 20 June, there still remained a cadre of approximately ten to sixteen deputies who strongly opposed the position taken by the delegation majority. When the delegation met again on the morning of 21 June to reaffirm its decision against joining the government that was to be presented to the Reichstag later in the day,[48] the dissidents within the Democratic delegation to the National Assembly met separately to determine whether they should submit to the will of the majority or secede from the delegation and join the Center and Majority Socialists in forming a new government. As drastic as the latter of these two alternatives must have seemed, such a step had been under consideration for some time by Erkelenz and the more determined advocates of acceptance, and they had even gone so far as to draw up a list of candidates for possible ministerial positions in the Bauer cabinet. But the idea of a secession from the DDP's Weimar delegation received little encouragement from the venerable Payer, who, in spite of his disagreement with the Democratic leadership over acceptance or rejection of the Allied peace terms, remained deeply committed to the party. Without Payer's support Erkelenz was obliged to abandon plans for a secession from the DDP's Weimar delegation and decided to make his peace with the party leadership.[49] On the following morning Erkelenz informed the delegation that he, Schneider, and two other proponents of acceptance were prepared to join the majority in voting for the rejection of the Allied peace proposal.[50]

Although a secession from the Democratic delegation to the National Assembly had been averted, the party remained deeply divided over acceptance or rejection of the peace terms. In the plenary debate on the afternoon of 22 June Schiffer, who had succeeded Payer as chairman of the Democratic delegation to the National Assembly, defended the position of the delegation majority with a blistering attack against the Center and Majority Socialists for having betrayed the spirit of national solidarity that had surfaced so visibly in the demonstration of 12 May against the Allied peace terms. Contending that the consequences of rejecting the Allied peace proposal could not possibly be worse than those that would result from its acceptance, Schiffer indicated that the leadership of his party had decided not only to oppose acceptance of Allied peace terms but also to abstain in the vote of confidence on the Bauer government.[51] When the question of acceptance or rejection of the Allied peace terms came before the National Assembly for a final vote later that afternoon, only seven members of the Democratic delegation—Payer, Richthofen, Schneider, Karl Hermann-Reutlingen, Christian Meismer, Wilhelm Vershofen, and Georg Zöpfel—joined the government parties in voting for acceptance of the Allied peace terms. As a result, the Allied peace terms were formally accepted by a 237–138 margin with five deputies abstaining and fifty-two others—

almost all of whom were members of the Democratic delegation—failing to
cast a vote. In a subsequent vote of confidence on the Bauer government the
number of abstentions rose to sixty-nine as those Democrats who had either
voted for acceptance of the Allied peace proposal or had refrained from voting
altogether joined their colleagues in withholding support from the government
that Erzberger had organized for the explicit purpose of signing the Allied
peace terms. In this instance Democratic solidarity was tarnished only by the
fact that five members of the delegation, including the pacifist Quidde, voted
against the Bauer government in a further demonstration of their implacable
opposition to the peace terms that had been imposed upon their country at the
point of a bayonet.[52]

The Bauer government had made its willingness to accept Allied peace
terms contingent upon concessions on the "War Guilt Clause" and other points
that the Germans regarded as matters of national honor. With the arrival at nine
o'clock that evening of an Allied communiqué stipulating that no further
concessions or extensions of the deadline would be considered, the position of
the Bauer government became increasingly desperate as support within both
the Center and the Majority Socialists for the acceptance of the Allied peace
terms began to evaporate. This turn of events created a sense of virtual panic
within the Democratic delegation. Meeting on the morning of 23 June under
what one of its leading spokesmen portrayed as the spectre of social revolution
and Bolshevism, the delegation proceeded to reaffirm its opposition to acceptance of the Allied peace proposal, though by a narrower margin than before.[53]
As it became increasingly clear during the course of the early afternoon that a
parliamentary majority for acceptance of the Allied peace terms no longer
existed and that neither the parties of the Right nor those of the Left were
willing to assume the reins of power, the leaders of the DDP searched desperately for a way out of the impasse that was paralyzing Germany's political
leadership. It was against the background of these developments that Rudolf
Heinze, chairman of the DVP delegation to the National Assembly, proposed
at a meeting of party leaders only hours before the expiration of the Allied
deadline that the government accept the peace proposal on the basis of the
authorization it had received the day before in return for an official declaration
from the parties opposed to signing the Allied peace proposal that the patriotic
motives of those who supported acceptance were beyond reproach. Although
the German Nationalists balked at going along with the DDP and DVP in
issuing such a declaration before the National Assembly, Heinze's initiative
broke the deadlock that had developed in the government's relations with the
National Assembly and helped clear the way for a final vote confirming its
authority to accept the Allied peace terms.[54] Assured of parliamentary support, the Bauer government then proceeded to notify Allied authorities at
Versailles of its intention to sign the treaty.

The significance of the DDP's struggle against acceptance of the Allied peace proposal was essentially twofold. In the first place, the intensity with which the Democrats fought acceptance of the proposed peace settlement can only be fully understood as part of a concerted effort by Haußmann and the Democratic leadership to wrest the conduct of German foreign policy from the hands of Erzberger and the Majority Socialists. Embittered over the manner in which Erzberger and his associates had sabotaged the sense of national solidarity that had surfaced in the protest demonstration of 12 May, the Democrats sought not only to introduce a more stridently nationalistic tone into the conduct of German foreign policy but more importantly to establish themselves as the nucleus around which all of those who opposed acceptance of the Allied peace proposal could unite. But the failure of the DDP's Weimar delegation to present a united front against acceptance of the Allied peace proposal completely undercut the party's efforts to produce a general reorientation in the conduct of German foreign policy and left the party exposed to attacks from those on the German Right who publicly decried the lack of unity on the part of the Democratic leadership. Secondly, the crisis over acceptance or rejection of the Allied peace proposal provided those Democrats like Schiffer who had become increasingly critical of cooperation with the Majority Socialists ever since the socialization debates earlier that spring with the leverage they needed to force the DDP out of the government, thereby undermining government assaults against the free enterprise system. As far as this faction was concerned, domestic considerations weighed every bit as heavily as the crisis over the conduct of German foreign policy, and its leaders were fully prepared to use the latter as a means of bringing about the collapse of the Weimar Coalition.

Although Schiffer and his supporters may have rejoiced at the demise of the Weimar Coalition, neither they nor the leaders of the Democratic delegation to the National Assembly could look upon the outcome of their bid for a greater voice in the conduct of German foreign policy with much satisfaction. Not only were Erzberger and the pro-peace elements within the Majority Socialists in clear control of German foreign policy, but the crisis over the Allied peace proposal had produced severe divisions within the ranks of both the Democratic party leadership and the DDP's national organization. The split in the party's Weimar delegation on the vote over acceptance of the Allied peace terms had produced widespread disaffection within the Democratic electorate throughout the country. This was compounded by the fact that a severe rift had developed between the party organization as a whole and state organizations in southwestern Germany, where the threat of foreign occupation had made acceptance of the Allied peace terms somewhat more palatable.[55] By the same token, the crisis over the conduct of German foreign policy had done much to intensify intraparty divisions over questions of social and economic policy.

The white-collar and working-class elements on the DDP's left wing had supported acceptance of the Allied peace terms partly out of concern that failure to do so would result in the collapse of the Weimar Coalition and seriously jeopardize the progress that had already been made in the field of social and economic reform. While these elements consequently urged the DDP's reentry into the government at the earliest possible opportunity, they were joined by the business interests on the party's right wing, which throughout the recent crisis had conspired to bring about the collapse of the Weimar Coalition. Now that the DDP was no longer in power, the DDP's business wing was alarmed at its lack of influence over the social and economic policies of the Bauer-Erzberger government and was anxious to reenter the government as a way of preventing further damage to the free enterprise system.[56]

It was against the background of this situation that the Democratic party leadership decided to hold a special party congress in Berlin during the second week of July. The Berlin congress opened as the debates on the Weimar Constitution were drawing to a close, and the party leaders could point with pride to the role that they and their colleagues had played in shaping the new constitutional order.[57] But the real purpose of the congress, as party leader Heinrich Gerland explained in a lengthy article written for one of the DDP's leading journals, was to restore party unity and provide a clear sense of the direction in which the party was moving. Writing with the tacit approval of the party's national leadership, Gerland suggested that the overriding goals of Democratic policy should be the peaceful revision of the Versailles Treaty, the pursuit of social reform within the framework of the existing economic system, and the consolidation of Germany's new democratic order.[58] Efforts to restore party unity along the lines suggested by Gerland, however, all but collapsed on the first day of the congress, when a heated exchange erupted between Naumann and Richthofen, one of the seven Democratic deputies who had voted for acceptance of the Allied peace terms, over the patriotic motives of those who had supported the government in the critical vote on 23 June.[59] No less ominous for the prospect of unity—particularly in light of the acrimony that had accompanied the passage of the government's socialization legislation earlier that spring—were the sharp differences of opinion that surfaced during the debate on a resolution that Erkelenz and the leaders of the DDP's social-liberal wing had introduced in support of a comprehensive new labor law designed to democratize labor-management relations throughout Germany.[60] While reluctant to go so far as to oppose the resolution outright, both Hermann Fischer from the Hansa-Bund and Otto Keinath from the Central Association of German Wholesalers warned the party against a one-sided social policy that sacrificed the interests of the German business community to those of organized labor.[61]

The Berlin congress failed to resolve many of the issues that threatened the

DDP's internal solidarity. Although the Democrats could take justifiable pride in the role that Preuss, Haußmann, and other party leaders had played in the adoption of the Weimar Constitution, the DDP remained deeply fragmented along sociological and ideological lines. As the dispute over socialization and the vote on the Versailles Peace Treaty clearly revealed, party unity was at best ephemeral and difficult to maintain. The immediate effect of this situation was to severely frustrate the DDP's political legitimation among those who had originally supported it as the best, if not last, bulwark against Bolshevism. From this pespective, therefore, the DDP was not so much a victim as a cause of the dramatic shift of sentiment that took place in Germany during the course of 1919. Whereas the year had begun amid hopes that the pain of military defeat might find meaning in the birth of a new and more equitable political order, the Versailles Treaty only mocked those who had championed the cause of political reason by producing a wave of national hysteria against the system of government in whose creation the DDP had played such a prominent role. Crippled by the legacy of Versailles, the German Democratic Party saw its greatest accomplishment, the Weimar Constitution, transformed into a symbol of Germany's national disgrace.

CHAPTER THREE

The Luxury of Opposition

THE DEMOCRATS' SUCCESS in the elections to the National Assembly stemmed from the curious mixture of euphoria and apprehension with which the German middle strata had greeted the fall of the Second Empire. By the middle of 1919, however, it had become increasingly clear that the leaders of the DDP had failed to translate the mandate they had received at the polls into a positive program of political action. At the heart of this failure lay the DDP's inability to pursue a consistent course of action with respect to the two questions that dominated Germany's political landscape in the immediate postwar period: the future of the free enterprise system and the peace treaty that Germany had just concluded with the Allies. Just as the DDP's equivocation on the question of socialization had severely compromised its credibility as an advocate of middle-class economic interests, so its failure to present a united front against acceptance of the Versailles Peace Treaty had left it vulnerable to charges from the Right of softness on the so-called national question. The combined effect of these developments was to produce a strong move away from the DDP on the part of its more nationalistic middle-class supporters.

The principal beneficiary of the growing middle-class disenchantment with the DDP's performance as a member of the Weimar Coalition was the German People's Party under the leadership of Gustav Stresemann. Of the various political parties that had emerged from the ruins of the Second Empire, none was more closely identified with a single individual than was the DVP with Stresemann. Stresemann's liberalism represented a synthesis of three basic principles.[1] The first of these was a deep and abiding commitment to the values of economic and political individualism. The son of a Berlin beer distributor whose business had been ruined by the competition of a large commercial brewery, Stresemann always retained a strong attachment to the economic values of the independent middle class into which he had been born. It was no accident, therefore, that Stresemann began his professional career as a lobbyist for light industrial interests in Saxony, where within two years of his appointment he had managed to create a statewide lobby that enabled Saxon light industry to defend its interests against those of heavy industry on both the state and national levels.[2] Yet while Stresemann was deeply committed to protecting the small private entrepreneur against the social and economic forces that threatened him with economic extinction, his commitment to the values of economic individualism was complemented by a social awareness that derived much of its inspiration from the teachings of Friedrich Naumann. As a student at the University of Leipzig in the late 1890s, Stresemann had come into contact with a group of professors associated with Naumann's ill-fated National Social Union, and in 1901 he had even attended its national convention as a member of the Dresden delegation. Stresemann remained deeply impressed by Naumann's argument that the optimum development of German national power presupposed the full integration of the German working class into the social and political fabric of the nation, and years later he eulogized Naumann as one who had provided German liberalism with the social dimension that had made it possible for his generation to embrace the liberal cause.[3] The third element of Stresemann's liberalism was a profound faith in the burgeoning power of the German nation. Not only did Stresemann regard the acquisition of colonies as a necessary precondition for Germany's continued economic development, but, as a firm believer in the "primacy of foreign policy," he continued to insist that the effective development of national power always take precedence over the demands of special economic interests.[4]

Following the demise of the National Social Union in 1903, Stresemann cast his lot with the National Liberal Party. With the support and encouragement of NLP party chairman Ernst Bassermann, Stresemann was elected to the Reichstag in 1907 and to the NLP central executive committee in 1916. From the outset, Stresemann received his strongest support within the party from the leaders of its left wing, and he actively encouraged them and their colleagues from the Young Liberal movement in their efforts to reform the party.[5] Upon Bassermann's death in 1917, Stresemann was elected to the chairmanship of the NLP Reichstag delegation, where he promptly incurred the wrath of his party's right wing by calling for a reform of the Prussian electoral law and the introduction of effective parliamentary government more than a year and a half before these goals were realized with Prince Max's "revolution from above" in October 1918.[6] Yet for all of the support that Stresemann had lent to the cause of domestic political reform before and after the outbreak of the war, he was also an outspoken German nationalist who unabashedly endorsed the most extravagant war aims of the German Right.[7] Stresemann's wartime record as one of Germany's most outspoken annexationists accounted for much of the vehemence with which Theodor Wolff and his associates had tried to block his entry into the DDP in the fall and early winter of 1918. For his own part, Stresemann found the spirit that animated Wolff and his supporters diametrically opposed to the national and liberal values that lay at the heart of his own political philosophy, and he was fully prepared to leave active political life if the faction from the *Berliner Tageblatt* had succeeded in dictating the terms upon which the creation of a united liberal party was to take place.[8]

Following the collapse of efforts to found a united liberal party in the fall and early winter of 1918, Stresemann proceeded to rally what still remained of the old National Liberal organization behind the newly founded DVP. But Stresemann's efforts to found a new liberal party to the right of the DDP received little support from his former associates on the NLP's left wing, most of whom had gone over to the Democrats despite their reservations about the predominant position that Wolff and the *Berliner Tageblatt* faction held within it. Stripped of what had once been the NLP's left wing, the DVP possessed a political profile that was decidedly more conservative than that of its predecessor. The most serious liability under which the DVP had to labor in the elections to the National Assembly, however, was the virtual collapse of the old NLP organization in former National Liberal strongholds such as Baden, Württemberg, West Prussia, and parts of Saxony. Had it not been for the strong support that Stresemann received from leaders of the NLP organization in Brunswick, Hanover, and parts of Westphalia, the DVP would almost certainly have gone down to an annihilating defeat in the elections to the National Assembly. As it was, the DVP emerged from the elections with more than 1.3 million votes and twenty-two seats in the National Assembly in what was both a tribute to Stresemann's effectiveness as a political campaigner and a testimonial to the strength of antidemocratic sentiment within influential sectors of the German bourgeoisie.[9]

In contrast to the Democratic delegation to the National Assembly, the twenty-two DVP deputies constituted a far more homogeneous and cohesive political group. In spite of the fact that only three of its members had served in the old imperial Reichstag, the DVP's Weimar delegation was in Stresemann's own estimation qualitatively better than the National Liberal delegation that had sat in the Reichstag before and during the war. Aside from Stresemann, the delegation's most prominent members were Rudolf Heinze, a former Reichstag deputy from Saxony who was elected to the chairmanship of the DVP's delegation at Weimar, and Jakob Riesser, the founder and first president of the Hansa-Bund. Both had previous parliamentary experience, and together with Stresemann they formed the delegation's executive committee and were responsible, particularly during the first months of 1919, for the party's day-to-day operations.[10] By no means, however, was the DVP delegation as socially heterogeneous as that which represented the DDP. For although the DVP took great pains to portray itself as a "people's party" whose social composition was supposed to reflect that of the nation as a whole, representatives from the artisanry, lower civil service, and white-collar class were noticeably absent from the delegation. And while the Christian trade-union movement was represented in the person of August Winnefeld from the Union of Christian Mine Workers (Gewerkverein christlicher Bergarbeiter), his presence did little to alter the fact that the delegation was dominated by higher civil servants, party functionaries, professional politicians, and industrial representatives. If the DVP conceived of itself as a people's party whose social structure corresponded to that of the nation as a whole, this was hardly reflected in the composition of its delegation to the National Assembly.[11]

At Weimar the DVP emerged as a resolute and outspoken opponent of the new democratic order to which the November Revolution had given birth. Even before the convocation of the National Assembly Stresemann had made little effort to conceal his strong monarchist sympathies, and on 28 January— scarcely a week after the elections to the National Assembly had taken place— he openly associated the DVP with the monarchist cause by joining two other members of his party in sending a congratulatory birthday telegram to the exiled Kaiser in Doorn.[12] Stresemann's display of sentiment, however, provoked such a storm of protest from various quarters within the party that he was obliged to moderate his position on monarchism for the sake of party unity. Speaking at a DVP rally in Weimar's Philharmonic Hall on 22 February, Stresemann conceded that the struggle over Germany's form of government had been decided in favor of the republic and that the DVP, in spite of its attachment to the old imperial order, could ill afford to adopt a posture of uncompromising opposition to the new republican order that had emerged to take its place.[13] Over the course of the next several months, Stresemann's position on monarchism underwent further modification, partly in recognition of the fact that the Weimar Constitution embodied many of the goals for which he and the left wing of the old NLP had been working ever since the turn of the century[14] and partly in response to a resolution by the Austrian National Assembly in favor of *Anschluß* with Germany. In his keynote address at the DVP's first national congress in the middle of April, therefore, Stresemann not only reaffirmed his allegiance to the symbols and traditions of the old imperial order but emphatically ruled out the DVP's participation in a monarchist countermovement on the grounds that this could only lead to civil war and make union with Austria impossible.[15] Hoping to capitalize upon mounting middle-class disillusionment with the DDP, Stresemann was clearly searching for a compromise formula that would allow republicans as well as monarchists to support his party. Consequently, the official party program that the DVP adopted at its second national congress in Leipzig in October 1919 contained a provision reaffirming its commitment to monarchism as the form of government that best corresponded to the character and traditions of the German people but sanctioning collaboration with the existing system of government for the sake of Germany's political and economic recovery.[16]

In spite of Stresemann's qualified acceptance of the Weimar Republic, the leaders of the DVP remained deeply suspicious of the new republican order, and in the decisive vote on 19 July 1919 they joined the Nationalists and Independent Socialists in voting against the Weimar Constitution.[17] In justify-

ing their stand, the leaders of the DVP found fault not only with the outspoken
republican character of the new constitution, but also with what Heinze,
chairman of the DVP delegation to the National Assembly, denounced as its
"radical parliamentarism." By this Heinze meant the fact that the new constitution had completely subordinated the functions of government to the will of
the parliamentary majority, a situation that in his eyes made governmental
stability and effective political leadership impossible. Equally distressing from
the DVP's point of view, according to Heinze, was the fact that the new
constitution had also left the federalism of the old Bismarckian Empire virtually intact, thereby perpetuating the particularism that had consistently frustrated Germany's development as a unified national state.[18] Yet while the
leaders of the DVP rejected the Weimar Constitution as a product of the
"ultrademocratic forces" that had triumphed with the November Revolution,
their criticism was directed not so much against the constitution itself—for
here, in fact, they found much to be commended—as against the Democrats
for having failed to check the radical excesses of their Social Democratic
allies. No party, exclaimed Stresemann in a blanket indictment of the DDP at
the DVP's Leipzig congress in October 1919, had ever failed so miserably in
its responsibility to promote the interests and ideals of the German bourgeoisie
as the Democratic Party.[19]

For Stresemann, the historic mission of the German People's Party was to
serve as a receptacle or *Sammelbecken* for those who had supported the DDP
in the elections to the National Assembly only to become disillusioned with its
performance as a member of the Weimar Coalition.[20] In this respect Stresemann and the leaders of the DVP assailed the Democrats both for the shortcomings of the Weimar Constitution and for their failure to present a united
front in the struggle against acceptance of the Versailles Treaty.[21] At the same
time, the DVP tried to capitalize upon middle-class uncertainty over the DDP's
social and economic policies by openly championing the cause of the artisanry
and independent middle class at Weimar. The specific proposals that the DVP
outlined at Weimar not only sought the suspension of wartime economic
controls but also contained provisions for the establishment of state-supported
credit facilities, parity for the artisan in the allocation of raw materials, and the
elimination of whatever competitive advantage municipal and cooperative
retail associations might enjoy over the small, independent shopkeeper.[22] In a
parallel move, the DVP also tried to recapture the support that the NLP had
enjoyed among the farmers of central and north central Germany. Before the
war this group had generally supported the National Liberals, but after the
November Revolution it had followed Böhme and the leadership of the German Peasants' League into the ranks of the DDP. In their efforts to regain the
support of the independent peasantry, the leaders of the DVP placed highest
priority upon the return to prewar production levels and demanded that war-

time economic controls be immediately lifted in order to achieve this goal. Similarly, the party called for a comprehensive land reform and a program of rural resettlement as means of realizing the old National Liberal slogan "Free Peasants on Their Own Soil."[23]

While Stresemann and the leaders of the DVP devoted much of their energy in the immediate postwar period to winning the support of the more traditional elements of the German middle class, they also sought to extend their party's influence into the ranks of what contemporary social theorists had come to label the "new middle class." Stresemann was distressed by the fact that neither the German Civil Servants' Association nor the organized white-collar movement were represented in the DVP's delegation to the National Assembly. His ties to the latter dated back to the last decade before the outbreak of the war, when his sponsorship of a comprehensive social insurance program for salaried employees had won him the respect and friendship of Hans Bechly, the future chairman of the German National Union of Commercial Employees.[24] Bechly joined the DVP in December 1918 after efforts to found a united liberal party had collapsed, and although the DHV pursued a policy of bipartisan neutrality with respect to all of Germany's nonsocialist parties, both he and Otto Thiel, his closest associate in the DHV's national leadership, actively supported Stresemann in his efforts to establish more permanent ties between the DVP and DHV.[25] In the meantime, the DVP had begun to establish a similar relationship with the German Civil Servants' Association through the offices of Albrecht Morath, a postal union official who, along with Thiel, was co-opted into the DVP managing committee in May 1919.[26] At the same time, the DVP tried to strengthen its position within the German Civil Servants' Association by coming out in strong support of its demands for a professional civil service free from partisan political influence and for a reform of Germany's civil service salary structure that would redress the loss in real income suffered by civil servants since the outbreak of the war.[27]

The DVP's solicitation of white-collar and civil servant support promised to provide it with a broader and more diversified social base than the prewar National Liberal Party had ever possessed. In large measure, however, the success of these efforts depended upon the extent to which the leaders of the DVP could overcome the organizational problems that had plagued their party's performance in the elections to the National Assembly. The collapse or defection of the NLP organization in one National Liberal stronghold after another had prevented the DVP from fielding its own slate of candidates in no less than eleven of Germany's thirty-six electoral districts, while in four others it had been obliged to conclude an alliance with either the DDP or DNVP.[28] Throughout the spring and summer of 1919 no task consumed the energies of Stresemann and his associates more fully than that of building a strong national organization capable of providing a new political home for those former

National Liberals who had gone over to DDP for want of a better alternative. It
was with this in mind, for example, that a group of former National Liberals
under the leadership of Paul Gustav Reinhardt founded a local chapter of the
DVP in Leipzig in late May 1919.[29] Over the course of the next several
months this scenario was repeated in one part of the country after another,
though not always with the desired results. The DVP's position remained
particularly precarious in southwestern Germany, where it never succeeded in
recapturing the ground that the NLP had held before the war. In Baden, where
in December 1918 the state NLP organization had gone over to the DDP
virtually intact, the DVP had managed to establish the beginning of a new state
organization in Mannheim, Heidelberg, and several other important cities.[30]
But the DVP's efforts to secure a decisive breakthrough into the ranks of the
local DDP were hampered by its constant equivocation on the question of
monarchism and by its unclear relationship to the DNVP.[31] The situation was
scarcely better in Württemberg, where the founding of a state DVP organization in the fall of 1919 received strong support from those National Liberals
who had gravitated to the political Right but not from those who had gone over
to the DDP.[32]

By the time of the Leipzig party congress in October 1919, the People's
Party had succeeded in establishing, in spite of indifferent results in areas like
Baden and Württemberg, the beginnings of a national party organization in all
but four of Germany's electoral districts. At the same time, party leaders had
also begun the creation of an elaborate horizontal structure designed to integrate specific vocational groups such as farmers, civil servants, and the independent middle class more firmly into the party organization.[33] Still, claims in
the fall of 1919 that the DVP embraced more than 500,000 registered members
seem to have been grossly inflated, with the actual number only slightly more
than half that figure.[34] For all intents and purposes—and despite protestations
to the contrary—the DVP remained, to a much greater extent than the Democratic Party, frozen in the mold of a traditional nineteenth-century *Honoratiorenpartei* whose members could be effectively mobilized at the time of
general elections but were otherwise excluded from a meaningful role in party
affairs. Moreover, the People's Party was much less centralized in terms of its
basic organizational structure than was the DDP. For although responsibility
for the party's parliamentary leadership lay almost exclusively in the hands of
the party chairman and a ten-man party executive committee, the various DVP
district organizations throughout the country were essentially autonomous
from the party headquarters in Berlin.[35] In the final analysis, the DVP retained
many of the structural defects of the old National Liberal Party and demonstrated only a limited capacity for adapting to the changes that had taken place
in Germany's political system as a result of the November Revolution.

One of the most serious defects of the DVP party organization lay in its method of raising funds to cover its operating expenses. To be sure, the leaders of the DVP were fully aware of the need for a more rational method of financing their party's operations than that employed by the old National Liberal Party.[36] But whereas the Democrats sought to make their party independent of outside financial support through the regular collection of dues from their party's rank-and-file membership, Stresemann showed little scruple about soliciting and accepting financial contributions from German big business. In January 1919, for example, the DVP had received 500,000 marks from the Curatorium for the Reconstruction of German Economic Life for use in the elections to the National Assembly.[37] But the costs of rebuilding the party's national organization constituted a heavy drain on the DVP's resources, and in the spring of 1919 Stresemann was obliged to turn to the business community for additional financial support.[38] On March 10 Stresemann wrote to Wilhelm von Siemens, the brother of Carl Friedrich von Siemens and a founding member of the Curatorium for the Reconstruction of German Economic Life, in an attempt to raise 100,000 marks for use in expanding the DVP's national organization.[39] Stresemann also approached Johannes Flathmann, secretary general of the Commission for the Collection, Administration, and Allocation of the Industrial Campaign Fund, in hopes that the heavy industrial interests behind it might come to his party's assistance. But whereas Siemens and the directors of the Curatorium declined to provide Stresemann with the funds he requested,[40] Flathmann agreed to make 150,000 marks available for the DVP's use—though not on an annual basis over the next three years, as Stresemann had hoped—on the condition that the final disposition of this fund be subject to approval by Albert Vögler, general director of the German-Luxemburg Mining and Foundry Concern (Deutsch-Luxemburgische Bergwerks- und Hütten A.G.) and a close associate of Ruhr coal magnate Hugo Stinnes.[41] Although Stresemann was still bitter over the way in which the leaders of the Ruhr industrial establishment had conspired to exclude him from a position of influence in the leadership of the newly founded National Federation of German Industry (Reichsverband der deutschen Industrie or RDI),[42] his party's finances left him with no alternative but to accept Flathmann's stipulation so that he might proceed with the task of rebuilding the DVP's national organization.[43]

In spite of generous support from Flathmann and the leaders of German heavy industry, the DVP continued to experience severe financial difficulties as a result of the expenses involved in rebuilding its national organization. In May 1919 the party allocated more than 100,000 marks—or approximately a third of the funds at its disposal—to the neediest of its district organizations in order to cover outstanding election debts and underwrite the cost of new organizational development.[44] Although the DVP hoped to raise the bulk of these funds from the party rank and file, its district organizations were so

negligent in collecting and transferring membership dues to the party headquarters in Berlin that by the end of the summer Stresemann and his associates
had no alternative but to turn once again to the German business community
for the financial assistance they so desperately needed. While the DVP's
request for supplemental financial support again met with a negative response
from Siemens and the leaders of the Curatorium for the Reconstruction of
German Economic Life,[45] the group around Flathmann recognized the DVP's
importance as an alternative to the Democratic Party and arranged to raise an
additional 100,000 marks for its use through a second round of solicitations
among the members of the Commission for the Industrial Campaign Fund.[46]

By no means did the financial assistance that the DVP received from
Flathmann and his associates come without a heavy political price. The leaders
of the Ruhr industrial establishment were intent upon transforming the DVP
into an instrument of their own political will and sought to use its increasing
dependence upon their financial contributions as a way of entrenching themselves within the party's national organization. In October 1919 Vögler and
those party leaders with close ties to Ruhr heavy industry succeeded in coales-
cing the six DVP district organizations from the Rhineland and Westphalia into
a regional *Arbeitsgemeinschaft*, which for all intents and purposes stood under
their direct political control. By creating such a body within the DVP's national organization, the leaders of Ruhr heavy industry sought to provide
themselves with sufficient leverage to influence not only the policies of the
DVP's delegation to the National Assembly but also the selection of candidates for the new national elections that were scheduled to take place as soon
as the National Assembly had completed its work.[47] The founding of the
DVP's Rhenish-Westphalian *Arbeitsgemeinschaft* coincided with Flathmann's
own efforts to tie further contributions from the Commission for the Industrial
Campaign Fund to the nomination of Hugo Stinnes, Kurt Sorge, and other
prominent industrialists to secure candidacies for the upcoming national elections.[48] From the very outset, these developments posed a serious threat both
to the DVP's political integrity and to its image as a socially heterogeneous
people's party.

An immediate consequence of the increasingly active role that German
industry had begun to play in the DVP's internal affairs was renewed pressure
for a merger with the right-wing German National People's Party. To be sure,
little seemed to separate the two parties during the first months of their
existence. Not only did they both appeal to the same social strata and rely upon
nationalism as the integrative component of their respective ideologies, but
both were profoundly alienated from the changes that had taken place in the
structure of Germany's political life as a result of the November Revolution.
Moreover, the fact that the DVP and DNVP were the only bourgeois parties to
oppose both the signing of the Versailles Peace Treaty and the ratification of

the Weimar Constitution lent further credence to the thesis that the German Right would be better served by one rather than two parties of national opposition.[49] But Stresemann, fearful that the agitation for a merger with the DNVP might frighten away those Democrats who had become disillusioned with their own party's performance as a member of the Weimar Coalition,[50] tried to dispel speculation about such a merger by reaffirming the DVP's independence vis-à-vis both the Democrats and the German Nationalists as unequivocally as possible.[51] Although sentiment for a merger with the DNVP was particularly strong among the industrial leaders on the DVP's right wing, the overwhelming majority of the party's leaders remained resolutely opposed to any accommodation with the DNVP that might compromise their own freedom of action and demanded the establishment of a sharper line of demarcation with respect to the Nationalists.[52] By no means insensitive to pressure of this sort, Stresemann responded at the DVP's Leipzig congress in October 1919 by drawing a fundamental distinction between the "constructive opposition" of the DVP and the DNVP's blanket rejection of everything associated with the new republican order. At the same time Stresemann dismissed rumors of a merger with the DNVP as altogether premature since, in his opinion, the latter was not so much a homogeneous political group as an unwieldy conglomeration of increasingly antagonistic factions that seemed on the verge of going their separate ways. How could a merger between the DVP and DNVP possibly take place, Stresemann asked, when it was not yet certain if the DNVP would survive as a viable political force?[53]

The Leipzig party congress in October 1919 represented the final act in a process of political legitimation that established the German People's Party as a permanent feature of Weimar's political landscape. Though its pedigree was tarnished by the circumstances that had surrounded its birth, the DVP had succeeded in creating a political home for itself between the parties to its immediate right and left. In sharp contrast to the uncertainty and discord that had prevailed at the DVP's first party congress in Jena six months earlier, the affair in Leipzig presented the picture of a party united in purpose and confident of the role it was to play in Germany's political future. The highpoint of the congress was the proclamation of a new party program entitled "Grundsätze der Deutschen Volkspartei." The program was a masterpiece of political compromise, reconciling the divergent views within the party on one major issue after another. Nowhere was the spirit of compromise more evident than on the question of monarchism, where the party tempered its attachment to the symbols and traditions of the old monarchial order by tacitly recognizing the need to work within the republican government for the sake of national recovery.[54] At the same time, the party tempered its rejection of socialization and its defense of the free enterprise system with an appeal for a thorough overhaul of the existing system of labor-management relations under the auspices of the

Central Association of Industrial and Commercial Employer and Employee Associations (Zentralarbeitsgemeinschaft der industriellen und gewerblichen Arbeitgeber- und Arbeitnehmerverbände), which the more progressive elements of the German industrial establishment and the leaders of the socialist labor movement had founded at the height of the November Revolution. In as much as the leaders of the DVP were committed to the preservation of the capitalist economic system, it was a more cooperative and a more social form of capitalism that they sought to save.[55]

The sense of confidence and solidarity that the DVP exuded at Leipzig could not have contrasted more dramatically with the confusion and indecisiveness that existed within the ranks of the DDP. For whereas the Democrats had still not resolved the differences that divided their party with respect to the future of German capitalism, the DVP remained resolute in its defense of the existing economic order. And whereas the Democrats had failed to present a united front against the imposition of the Allied peace terms, the DVP could point with pride to its uncompromising defense of Germany's national honor. Yet for all of the optimism with which Stresemann and the leaders of the DVP viewed their party's immediate future, the party was plagued by a number of nagging problems. If nothing else, the DVP's increasing dependence upon special economic interests intent upon transforming it into an instrument of their own political will did not augur well for the party's ability to pursue an independent course of action. More importantly, the unity that the DVP had forged in the first nine months of 1919 was a unity born of a spirit of opposition and nurtured by advantages that only a party in opposition could enjoy. What might happen to that unity once the party was no longer unencumbered by the burden of responsibility, once it no longer enjoyed the luxury of opposition, remained to be seen.

CHAPTER FOUR

The Swing of the Pendulum

THE SECOND HALF OF 1919 witnessed a sharp swing to the right that extended to virtually every sector of the German bourgeoisie. Although in one sense this was clearly related to the wave of national indignation that swept Germany following the imposition of the Versailles Peace Treaty, in another it reflected the growing uncertainty that surrounded the question of how the social cost of Germany's lost war was to be distributed among the various strata of German society. The importance of this question had been largely obscured by the histrionics that had accompanied the debate over acceptance or rejection of the Allied peace terms. But once the treaty had been signed, it was no longer possible for Weimar's political leaders to ignore the practical consequences of Germany's military defeat and the peace settlement they had just concluded with the Allies. Just as the war had imposed a heavy burden on nearly every sector of German society, so would the postwar peace settlement demand a new round of sacrifices from the German people. The overriding question on Germany's political agenda in the fall and winter of 1919 was how this burden and these sacrifices were to be distributed throughout the German nation as a whole. And this, in turn, raised a second and ultimately more important question, namely, whether or not Germany's new republican institutions were capable of withstanding the political conflict that the resolution of this problem was almost certain to engender.[1]

The leaders of the German Democratic Party were by no means oblivious to the way in which the problem of distributing the social cost of Germany's lost war had become intertwined with the survival of her new republican institutions. On the one hand, no party was more strongly committed to the defense of Germany's new republican order than the DDP. Having just played a central role in the creation of the Weimar Constitution, its leaders were irrevocably committed to a policy of cooperation with the more moderate elements of the German working class in order to ensure the survival of the new constitutional order. On the other hand, the DDP was also a bourgeois party whose middle-class supporters were justifiably concerned about the concessions that the Democrats might have to make in the area of social and economic policy for the sake of their alliance with the Majority Socialists. What this reflected was a fundamental contradiction in the DDP's political priorities that its withdrawal from the government at the height of the crisis over the Versailles Peace Treaty had done little to alleviate. Not only had this failed to prevent ratification of the Versailles Treaty—even its most vociferous opponents conceded that there was no practical alternative to acceptance—but it had also deprived the Democrats of whatever influence they might have had over the formulation and implementation of state economic policy. Now that the government was forced to confront the practical consequences of the new peace settlement, the Democrats were anxious to rejoin the government lest it introduce legislation detrimental to the material interests of those social groups still supporting their party.[2]

On 21 September an overwhelming majority of the Democratic delegation to the National Assembly authorized the party leadership to initiate negotiations with the Center and Majority Socialists on the conditions under which the DDP might reenter the government. In arriving at this decision, the Democrats let their hopes of exercising a moderating influence upon the social and economic policies of the Bauer government override their antipathy towards Erzberger and their distrust of the left wing of the Majority Socialists.[3] Above all else, the Democrats—and particularly the business interests on the party's right wing—were anxious to modify certain features of a government bill that sought to define the future status of the workers' councils that had sprung up in factories throughout the country during the recent revolution.[4] In the negotiations that took place between the DDP and the Bauer government in the last week of September, however, the Majority Socialists refused to make any concessions that might have softened Democratic opposition to the proposed Factory Council Law for fear that this might result in widespread defections on their own party's left wing.[5] This, in turn, produced a political deadlock that was broken only when the Democratic delegation, having consoled themselves with a series of minor victories on tax policy and a number of other issues, voted on 2 October to reenter the government in spite of the fact that no agreement on the controversial Factory Council Law had yet been reached. Although this decision encountered sharp criticism from a handful of deputies on the party's right wing, the vast majority of the delegation felt that the DDP could no longer justify its role as an opposition party and that the arguments for reentering the government clearly outweighed those for remaining in opposition.[6]

The DDP's decision to reenter the national government came at a time when the party was already suffering heavy defections to both the German People's Party and the German National People's Party.[7] Whether or not this gambit would enable the Democrats to halt the erosion of their party's electoral base ultimately depended upon the success with which they were able to allay middle-class anxiety over the social and economic policies of the Weimar Coalition. To be sure, the Democrats had made their reentry into the government contingent upon the acceptance of a number of conditions, including the suspension of wartime economic controls and tax relief for the small business sector.[8] But once the DDP was back in the government, its leaders discovered to their great chagrin that they lacked the leverage to force the Majority Socialists to live up to these commitments. The Democrats' position under Bauer was decidedly weaker than it had been in the Scheidemann government three months earlier. Instead of the three ministries they had held under Scheidemann, the Democrats now had to content themselves with two relatively minor cabinet posts, the Ministry of Interior under Koch-Weser and the Ministry of Justice under Schiffer. Moreover, the Democrats had lost control of the Ministry of Finance to Erzberger, whom none of the Democrats trusted and who was intent upon increasing the tax burden of Germany's propertied classes.[9] None of this, particularly in light of the general unrest that began to spread through the German working class in the fall of 1919, augured well for the DDP's effectiveness as a member of the governmental coalition.[10]

The first test of strength between the Democrats and the other government parties centered not around the Factory Council Law that had attracted so much attention in the negotiations prior to the reorganization of the government, but around plans to impose a special levy upon all forms of private and corporate wealth in Germany. Ostensibly a measure to help control postwar inflation, the National Emergency Levy (*Reichsnotopfer*) represented the cornerstone of Erzberger's reorganization of German finances and was designed to effect a major redistribution of wealth in favor of the industrial working class.[11] This bill would have severely affected the propertied classes that had rallied behind the DDP in the elections to the National Assembly, and it was staunchly opposed by Gothein, Dernburg, and those party members with close ties to the business community.[12] Consequently, when a motion to support the bill carried by a slim two-vote margin at a caucus of the Democratic delegation on the evening of 16 December, the leaders of the delegation decided against invoking party discipline (*Fraktionszwang*) in the vote scheduled to take place on the following day for fear that this would provoke an open rebellion on the party's right wing.[13] In the decisive parliamentary vote on 17 December only thirty-one of the DDP's seventy-five deputies supported the government bill. Not only was nearly half of the Democratic delegation absent when the vote took place, but eight deputies, including such party stalwarts as Gothein and Fischbeck, went so far as to register their opposition to the Reich Emergency Levy by voting against it in open defiance of the delegation leadership.[14]

The DDP's failure to block passage of the Reich Emergency Levy or to modify its more pernicious features did much to reinforce middle-class disenchantment with the party's performance as a member of the Weimar Coalition. Whatever effects this may have had upon the Democratic rank and file, however, were only magnified by the public furor that accompanied the beginning of parliamentary debate on the Factory Council Law at the end of November. Before reentering the government in early October, the leaders of the Democratic delegation to the National Assembly had tried to reassure the party's industrial supporters that they were committed to fundamental changes in the text of the bill.[15] Particularly onerous to both the DDP party leadership and the German business community were provisions allowing for the election of workers' representatives to a company's board of directors and for the review of a firm's financial records by members of the factory council. The leaders of the DDP's business wing were so adamant in their opposition to these features of the bill that they refused to honor the party's pleas for financial assistance as long as its position on the Factory Council Law and related pieces of social and economic legislation remained unclear.[16] Yet for all of the vehemence with which the DDP's business interests fought the bill, the leaders of the party could ill afford to provoke a new cabinet crisis so soon after having reentered the government. To do so, they feared, would permanently destroy their political credibility with the Majority Socialists and Center.[17]

Although the Democrats were eventually able to bring about a series of relatively minor amendments in the text of the Factory Council Law,[18] these changes did little to temper the business community's deep-seated hostility toward the bill. On 11 December the National Federation of German Industry staged a major protest demonstration in Berlin at which it denounced the proposed Factory Council Law as part of a concentrated attack upon the foundations of the free enterprise system.[19] Three days later a heated debate erupted at the DDP party congress in Leipzig when Theodor Vogelstein, Hermann Fischer, and the leaders of the party's business wing openly challenged the official party position that the recent changes in the text of the bill had removed its "poisonous fangs," thereby making it acceptable to all factions in the party.[20] While Erkelenz and the leaders of the DDP's social-liberal wing hailed the Factory Council Law as "a great step toward the democratization of German economic life,"[21] the party's business leaders served quiet notice on the Democratic leadership that failure to oppose the bill in its present form would cause a majority of the DDP's representatives from commerce and industry to leave the party in protest.[22] Last-minute efforts at a compromise that might have satisfied both the Majority Socialists and the DDP's right wing proved futile, and on 18 January 1920—five days after 42 left-wing demonstrators against the bill had been killed and another 105 wounded on the steps of the Reichstag—nearly half of the Democratic deputies were absent from the floor when the decisive vote took place.[23] While these defections were not sufficient to block passage of the bill, the vote only underscored the appearance of confused and indecisive leadership that had plagued the DDP ever since the controversy over the Versailles Peace Treaty earlier that summer.

Even if threats of a general secession on the DDP's right wing failed to materialize, the party's failure to take a clear and unequivocal stand against the Factory Council Law had a profound impact upon the willingness of its supporters in the German business community to underwrite the costs of the DDP's organizational development. Inspired by the exhortations of Naumann, Erkelenz, and the party's more farsighted political leaders, the Democrats had set out to provide themselves with the most modern and sophisticated political organization in all of Germany. The purpose of such an organization was not merely to enhance the party's effectiveness at the polls but, more importantly, to sustain a high degree of political mobilization on the part of the Democratic rank and file in the intervals between elections. Based upon an elaborate network of party confidants or *Vertrauensmänner* at the local and village levels, this organization was to be responsible for reporting changes in local voter attitudes to the national party headquarters in Berlin so that measures could be taken either to exploit these changes or to minimize their impact upon the party's popular support. At the same time, the leaders of the DPP also sought to create an elaborate horizontal structure aimed at integrating special groups such as women and youth more directly into the life of the party. In this respect, the leaders of the DDP envisaged the creation of national organizations for women, youth, and special vocational interests that would be represented by special executive committees attached to the party's national headquarters in Berlin.[24]

By the summer of 1919 the leaders of the DDP could point with pride to a national organization that embraced an estimated 900,000 registered members, more than 2,000 local chapters (*Ortsgruppen*), and 118 full-time party secretaries at the state, provincial, and local levels. The party was strongest in Württemberg, with 49,000 members, while Hamburg, Hesse-Nassau, and Teltow-Beskow in Berlin followed closely behind with slightly fewer than 40,000 members apiece.[25] Originally the Democrats had hoped to finance the costs of maintaining such an organization by contributions and dues from the party's rank-and-file membership without having to rely too heavily upon the support of outside economic interests.[26] It soon became apparent, however, that the demands placed upon party finances by the construction of such an organization greatly exceeded the resources of the DDP's rank and file. Not only had party reserves been badly depleted by direct subsidies to state and local chapters nationwide,[27] but the revenue that the Democrats had hoped to generate from small contributions and annual membership dues of one mark per party member fell considerably short of the amount anticipated.[28] Under these circumstances the leaders of the DDP had no alternative but to turn to the Curatorium for the Reconstruction of German Economic Life, the Hansa-Bund, and other outside economic interests for the financial support they needed to sustain their party's organizational development.[29] The willingness of these interests to support the DDP, however, had cooled significantly in light

of the party's record on matters of social and economic policy, with the result
that they began to attach specific conditions, particularly with respect to the
selection of candidates for the next national elections, to their offers of financial assistance.[30] Not only did this constitute a direct threat to the independence and political integrity of the DDP, but it did little to alleviate a financial
crisis that by the end of the year had forced the leaders of the DDP to
comtemplate a drastic reduction in the scope of their party's activities.[31]

The financial and organizational difficulties that plagued the leaders of the
DDP toward the end of 1919 came at a time when their party was beginning to
experience increasingly heavy defections to the DVP and DNVP on the part of
the independent middle class and small business sector.[32] More than a simple
reaction to the DDP's failure to present a united front against the acceptance of
the Versailles Peace Treaty, these losses stemmed from the deep sense of
betrayal that Germany's propertied classes felt as a result of the party's refusal
to block the passage of legislation detrimental to their own vested interests.
The leaders of the DVP moved quickly to exploit the rift that had developed
between the Democrats and the more traditional elements of the German
middle class by portraying the DDP as an unwitting yet fully culpable acces-
sory to Social Democratic schemes for the socialization of German economic
life.[33] Stresemann and his associates pointed to the DDP's tacit support of Erzberger's reorganization of the German tax system as irrefutable evidence of its
indifference to the plight of the German middle strata and attacked the Reich
Emergency Levy as part of a concerted effort by Erzberger and the Social
Democrats to expropriate Germany's propertied classes.[34] Likewise, the
DDP's alleged flirtation with government socialization schemes in the spring
of 1919 as well as its equivocation on the Factory Council Law were cited as
further examples of its unreliability in matters of social and economic policy.
The DVP, on the other hand, rejected all economic experimentation in favor of
the free enterprise system and the cooperative arrangements that had been
enshrined in the Zentralarbeitsgemeinschaft.[35]

The controversy over socialization in March 1919, the continuation of
wartime economic controls well after the conclusion of peace, and the passage
of the Reich Emergency Levy and Factory Council Law all helped crystallize
middle-class resentment against the Weimar Coalition and the new republican
order that it was in the process of establishing. At the same time, the "stab-in-
the-back" legend provided the German Right with an effective mechanism for
channeling nationalist resentment over the loss of the war and the imposition
of the Versailles Peace Treaty in an increasingly antirepublican direction.
Much of this furor centered around the person of Matthias Erzberger, who had
earned the enmity of the German Right not only for his role in sponsoring the
peace resolution in the summer of 1917 and in accepting the terms of Germany's surrender at Compiègne a year later but also for his policies as minister

of finance in the Bauer government. "Down with Erzberger" became a rallying cry for the antirepublican forces on the German Right as the beleaguered Erzberger tried to salvage what remained of his political reputation by initiating a libel suit against his most unrelenting opponent, the DNVP's Karl Helfferich. When the highly publicized Erzberger-Helfferich trial of early 1920 ended in the latter's exoneration, not only had Erzberger's political career suffered a blow from which it never recovered, but the new republican order had been damaged by its association with the embattled finance minister to the point where it too was in danger of a violent assault from the German Right.[36]

A barometer of antirepublican sentiment in the early years of the Weimar Republic, the crusade against Erzberger bore dramatic testimony to the sharp swing to the right that had taken place in Germany since the summer of 1919. For their own part, the leaders of the DDP felt politically compromised by Erzberger's continued presence in the cabinet, and they were only waiting for the conclusion of his suit against Helfferich before pressing for his removal from office. Democratic antipathy toward Erzberger stemmed both from deep-seated differences over the direction of German tax policy and from the feeling that his failure to defend himself against Helfferich's charges of slander and personal aggrandizement had made him an intolerable liability for Germany's republican cause.[37] Another—and by no means less troublesome—symptom of the revival of Germany's radical Right at the beginning of 1920 was a dramatic resurgence of political anti-Semitism. Much of this was directed against the DDP, whose own leadership cadre included a number of prominent Jews, such as Hugo Preuss, Bernhard Dernburg, and Ludwig Haas. Acting almost as if they were embarrassed by the high visibility that Jews enjoyed within their party, the Democrats responded with a weak counterattack that simply sought to disprove right-wing allegations regarding the extent of Jewish influence within the DDP without ever addressing the larger question of anti-Semitism itself.[38] Stresemann and the leaders of the DVP, on the other hand, were anxious to dissociate themselves from the more virulent forms of anti-Semitism that had surfaced on the radical Right. But the denunciation of anti-Semitism that the DVP managing committee published on 28 January was undercut by the way in which it attributed the resurgence of anti-Semitism in the postwar period to the prominent role that Jews had played in revolutionary movements at home and abroad.[39] Neither liberal party, therefore, was prepared to offer more than token resistance to the wave of anti-Semitism that began to sweep through Germany in the early 1920s.

In the meantime, right-wing efforts to overthrow Germany's republican regime were drawing to a climax. The key figure in these efforts was Wolfgang Kapp, a former Prussian civil servant and co-founder of the German Fatherland Party (Deutsche Vaterlandspartei), who after the end of the war had gravitated to the DNVP without ever aspiring or rising to a position of influence within the party. Instead Kapp joined the renowned German war hero Erich von Ludendorff in October 1919 in founding the National Association (Nationale Vereinigung), an organization created not so much to attract a mass political following as to sow discontent in the ranks of the Reichswehr and right-wing political groups. With Ludendorff's sponsorship, Kapp was able to gain the cooperation of a number of influential army officers, the most important of whom was General Walther von Lüttwitz, commander of all field troops east of the Elbe as well as in Saxony, Thuringia, and Hanover. Assured of Reichswehr support for a military putsch against the Weimar Republic, Kapp and the leaders of the National Association began to cultivate closer ties with right-wing civilian politicians in hopes that they might be persuaded to accept cabinet posts in the government of national concentration that they planned to form upon seizing power. Events drew to a head following the government's decision in late January 1920 to dissolve the volunteer paramilitary units whose existence it had tolerated as a means of repressing the revolutionary threat from the German Left. Spurred into action by government demobilization orders for two marine brigades, the insurgent military units under Lüttwitz entered Berlin on the morning of 13 March and quickly succeeded in occupying all major government offices and installations.[40] In spite of its initial success, however, the putsch was ill conceived, lacked adequate preparation, and collapsed within days of the march on Berlin. The refusal of military authorities in southern and western Germany to cooperate with the Kapp government, a general strike of all workers, civil servants, and white-collar employees called by leaders of the socialist unions on the evening of 13 March, and the refusal of the ministerial bureaucracies in Berlin to cooperate with the putschists all but paralyzed economic life throughout Germany and left Kapp and his supporters with no alternative but to end the insurrection on the best possible terms.[41]

While these developments represented a critical turning point in the early history of the Weimar Republic and foreshadowed many of the problems that were to lead to its eventual demise, they also served to dramatize the differences that existed between the two liberal parties. In their first official reaction to the putsch on the morning of 13 March the leaders of the Democratic Party condemned the insurrection as an act that threatened the security of the German nation and called for an immediate return to the rule of law and order.[42] On the following day, after a meeting with the representatives from the other government parties, the DDP amplified its position by issuing a much fuller statement denouncing the putschists as traitors to the German state and defending the general strike that the socialists had proclaimed the day before as "a concerted protest of the German nation against the frivolous attempt to overthrow the constitution and system of law to which hundreds of thousands of

German civil servants had sworn their loyalty."[43] This position contrasted dramatically with that of the DVP, whose leaders did not hesitate to display open sympathy toward the motives of those who had launched the march on Berlin.[44] In its first official pronouncement on the putsch, the DVP not only refrained from any declaration of support for the legitimate government but attributed the insurrection to the government's failure to call for new elections in accordance with the provisions of the Weimar Constitution. Accepting the putsch as a fait accompli, the leaders of the DVP did not demand the removal of the Kapp regime, but stressed instead the necessity of transforming it into a government resting upon constitutional sanction and capable of attracting a broad spectrum of political support.[45] At the same time, the leaders of the DVP denounced the general strike as an invitation to civil war and demanded its immediate termination as a necessary precondition for the restoration of law and order.[46]

In its internal deliberations during the first two days of the putsch, the DVP was divided between those like Eugen Leidig, Hugo Garnich, and Oskar Maretzky, who favored recognition of the Kapp regime, and those like Rudolf Heinze and Jakob Riesser, who advocated a policy of neutrality, if not outright repudiation of the putschists.[47] Stresemann, who could only have rejoiced at the embarrassment that the putsch had caused for the republican government and the parties that supported it, began to qualify his support of the Kapp regime when not only the hopelessness of its position but also the indisputably reactionary pedigree of its leading exponents became increasingly apparent on the third and fourth days of the putsch.[48] As the collapse of the putsch drew near, Stresemann worked in close contact with representatives from the DNVP and the three government parties to end the crisis with a compromise that would secure the resignations of Kapp and Lüttwitz in return for the reorganization of the national government on the broadest possible basis, the dissolution of the National Assembly and new general elections within the next two months, and the election of the Reich president by direct popular vote rather than by a majority in the National Assembly. What Stresemann hoped to accomplish as a mediator between the Kapp and Bauer governments, therefore, was not so much a return to the state of affairs that had existed before the putsch as the acceptance of conditions by the Bauer government that would have effectively terminated the National Assembly's domination of German political life.[49] With the collapse of the putsch on 17 March in a settlement that embodied much of what Stresemann had strived for, the leaders of the DVP moved quickly to insulate themselves against whatever confusion their initial reaction to the putsch had caused by publishing a second proclamation on the afternoon of 18 March. In contrast to the equivocation that had characterized the party's appeal of 13 March, this proclamation portrayed the DVP as a loyal defender of the Weimar Constitution, whose commitment to the principle of organic development precluded any accommodation with the putschists. While still attributing the insurrection to the policies of the republican government, the statement highlighted the role that the DVP had played in bringing the crisis to a peaceful resolution and appealed for the formation of a united front against the threat of Bolshevism to which the government's call for a general strike had given renewed life.[50]

The appeal of 18 March was carefully designed to divert criticism away from the DVP for its unabashed opportunism during the first days of the putsch and toward the Democrats for their support of the general strike and their responsibility for the social upheaval that threatened to follow in its wake. The discrepancies between this appeal and the one the DVP had published on the first day of the putsch, however, did not escape the attention of the Democrats, who promptly attacked Stresemann and the leaders of the DVP for having accorded de facto recognition to the Kapp regime and then, after the failure of the putsch had become apparent, trying to exploit the situation created by the putsch for their own partisan purposes.[51] But the DDP's ability to capitalize upon the vulnerable situation in which the DVP found itself as a result of its behavior during the Kapp Putsch was severely hampered by the widespread alarm that its own endorsement of the general strike had produced within the ranks of Germany's middle-class electorate. The DDP's vulnerability in this respect became blatantly apparent during the course of negotiations to end the general strike. On 19 March Carl Legien, the leader of the socialist labor unions, presented the government with a set of nine demands whose acceptance constituted a necessary precondition for termination of the strike. Among other things, Legien demanded that those unions that had contributed to the fall of the Kapp regime should be given a decisive hand in the reorganization of the government at both the national and state levels.[52] While the government parties regarded the other eight conditions as relatively harmless, they viewed this particular demand as a radical departure from the principles of parliamentary government enshrined in the Weimar Constitution and vigorously opposed it. In the final analysis, however, the need to terminate the general strike—if for no other reason than to prevent the Communists from using it to promote further civil unrest—clearly overrode all other considerations, and at a marathon session with Legien and his associates on the night of 19–20 March, representatives from the three government parties agreed to use their influence to secure acceptance of the union demands, including a modified version of the controversial first point calling for direct union involvement in the reorganization of the national government.[53]

The agreement announced by Legien and the representatives of the three government parties on the morning of 20 March marked the end of the general strike that had paralyzed Germany for nearly a full week. By the time agreement had been reached, however, the strike had already deteriorated into a series of violent confrontations between forces loyal to the republic and work-ers' armies from the Ruhr intent on overthrowing the Weimar Republic and establishing a dictatorship of the proletariat. The insurrection in the Ruhr evoked the spectre of social revolution and constituted a severe embarrassment to both the Weimar Coalition and the leaders of the socialist labor unions in Berlin.[54] Developments in the Ruhr were particularly distressing to the leaders of the Democratic Party, whose endorsement of the general strike made them culpable, at least in the eyes of many middle-class voters, for the workers' uprising in the Ruhr.[55] Consequently, the Democrats viewed the concessions that Legien had extracted from representatives of the three government parties on the night of 19–20 March with extreme caution. At a meeting of the Democratic delegation to the National Assembly on the morning of 23 March the Democratic minister of interior, Erich Koch-Weser, repudiated the govern-ment parties' agreement with Legien and warned that "democracy as both a party and as a bourgeois ideal would be lost forever" if the DDP acceded to the unions' demands. Should Bauer give in to pressure from the unions for the formation of a workers' government, the DDP would not hesitate to force the resignation of the entire national government and demand new general elec-tions at the earliest possible opportunity.[56]

When the delegation reconvened on the following day, only five deputies, including Gustav Hartmann and Wilhelm Gleichauf from the Hirsch-Duncker trade-union movement and Ernst Remmers from the German Civil Servants' Association, spoke in favor of accepting Legien's nine points.[57] Those depu-ties with close ties to the German business community, on the other hand, were adamant in their opposition to any concessions to the unions and demanded that the DDP dissociate itself as unequivocally as possible from Legien's nine points and the idea of a workers' government.[58] The influence of the DDP's business wing was most heavily felt within the party executive committee, which met on 23 and 25 March to fortify the delegation in its determination to resist union pressure for acceptance of the nine points.[59] While Democratic opposition to the nine points raised serious questions about the future of the Weimar Coalition, the DDP scored a minor triumph of its own when the Bauer government tendered its resignation on 26 March. The Democrats had sought the dismissal of the entire Bauer government ever since the collapse of the putsch, if for no other reason than to thwart union efforts to single out the DDP's Eugen Schiffer for dismissal as minister of justice on account of the role he had played in negotiating an end to the putsch.[60] The chancellorship fell to another Majority Socialist, Hermann Müller-Franken, who over the course of the next several days proceeded to put together a new government based on the Weimar Coalition. The Democrats received four posts in the new government, including the politically sensitive Ministry of Defense, which went to a prominent Bavarian liberal, Otto Gessler.[61] But when Müller, under heavy pressure form the Independent Socialists, approached the Democrats about a commitment to the nine points, they refused to recognize the right of the unions to interfere in the legislative process and categorically rejected Legien's demands.[62]

Although the Kapp-Lüttwitz Putsch ended in a clear and decisive defeat for the insurgents, both the government and the parties supporting it emerged from the ordeal in a seriously weakened state. This was particularly true of the German Democratic Party, which found itself increasingly torn between its commitment to the new republic and the antisocialist fears of those who formed the backbone of its middle-class electorate. While a move away from the party had been evident ever since the socialization debates in the spring of 1919, the DDP's response to the putsch and particularly its endorsement of the general strike only served to confirm middle-class distrust of the party and to intensify the disaffection of those who had originally rallied to its support on the assumption that it represented the last and most effective bulwark against a socialist takeover. Under these circumstances, the hard line taken by the Democrats with respect to Legien's nine points did little to repair the damage that their party's support of the general strike had done to its standing with the German middle class. By the same token, middle-class anxiety over the general strike had made it virtually impossible for the Democrats to capitalize upon Stresemann's trenchant opportunism during the first days of the putsch. Here the Democrats had no choice but to accept the bitter truth that in the public mind the fear of social revolution clearly overshadowed whatever indiscretions Stresemann might have committed against the Weimar Constitution. This, in turn, enabled Stresemann, with an unerring political instinct that left his rivals badly outmaneuvered, to transform what could very easily have been a major fiasco for both himself and his party into a position of remarkable strength. As unconscionable as his behavior during the first days of the putsch may have been, Stresemann nevertheless provided the DVP with effective and decisive leadership that not only shielded it from reprisals for its initial equivocation in regard to the Kapp regime but also enabled it to mobilize middle-class anxiety over the general strike in anticipation of the forthcoming national elections.

CHAPTER FIVE

Democracy in Retreat

THE DEMOCRATS HAD AGREED to serve in the newly constituted Müller government on the condition that general elections be held at the earliest possible opportunity.[1] The elections, which took place on 6 June 1920 in the shadow of the Kapp Putsch and continued conflict in the Ruhr, were to serve as a general referendum on the policies and accomplishments of the Weimar Coalition. The campaign was characterized by a bitter fratricidal conflict between the two liberal parties, as the DVP tried to mobilize middle-class disenchantment with the DDP's performance as a member of the coalition. For the DDP the primary question of the elections was whether or not it could hang on to its mandate as Germany's largest nonconfessional bourgeois party—and thus preserve the delicate balance of democratic forces that had governed the country since the end of the war—in face of the sharp swing to the right that had taken place throughout the country in the second half of 1919. The lines of conflict for the 1920 Reichstag elections thus ran right through the heart of the German liberal movement.

In spite of the optimism with which Koch, Haußmann, and other prominent Democrats greeted the prospect of new general elections, the aggressiveness displayed by the unions in the aftermath of the Kapp-Lüttwitz Putsch as well as the persistence of armed conflict in the Ruhr placed the parties of the Weimar Coalition at a distinct disadvantage. Still, the Democrats campaigned as a loyal member of the Weimar Coalition and stressed the need to continue ties with the Center and Majority Socialists after the end of the campaign.[2] The Democratic goal, as outlined by party chairman Carl Petersen at a meeting of the DDP party council on 17 April, was to secure a majority for the parties of the Weimar Coalition so that the reconstruction of the German state might proceed unhampered by the combined strength of the antirepublican forces on the Right and the Left.[3] In defending the DDP's performance as a member of the Weimar Coalition, however, the Democrats absolved themselves of all responsibility for the outbreak of the November Revolution and highlighted their role in stabilizing conditions after the end of the war. In this respect, the Democrats pointed with pride to the ratification of the Weimar Constitution and the establishment of a new political order in which the frustrations and social tensions of the old Bismarckian Empire could be effectively resolved. But by no means, as party spokesmen constantly reiterated, did the DDP's willingness to cooperate with the Majority Socialists in the reconstruction of the German state imply consensus on social and economic issues. Not only did the DDP remain unequivocally committed to the maintenance of the free enterprise system, but it had consistently used its influence within the Weimar Coalition to restrain the zeal for economic experimentation displayed by its socialist allies.[4] The real purpose of the campaign, as the DDP's Eugen Schiffer emphasized in a much-publicized campaign speech in Magdeburg on 27 April, was therefore not to put an end to the Weimar Coalition but to bring about a change in its internal composition so that the bourgeois elements that had heretofore remained in the minority could assume leadership.[5]

The Democratic campaign was carefully designed to reassure the DDP's middle-class electorate that the party's participation in the Weimar Coalition and its alliance with the Majority Socialists had been necessary to expedite Germany's political stabilization. At the same time, the Democrats took special pains to point out that the general strike that had brought about the collapse of the Kapp-Lüttwitz Putsch was in point of fact not a strike intended to promote the social and economic interests of specific vocational groups but rather a national work stoppage (*Arbeitsruhe*) in which both employers and employees willingly participated. If the protest against the Kapp regime happened to degenerate into armed insurrection in the Ruhr and other parts of the country, responsibility for this turn of events lay not with the legitimate government or with the workers who had rallied to its defense but with the right-wing circles that had instigated the putsch in the first place.[6] The central thrust of the Democratic campaign in the 1920 elections, therefore, was clearly directed against the German Right. The Democrats held right-wing agitation for a restoration of the monarchy responsible for creating the climate in which the Kapp Putsch had taken place,[7] and they further denounced the right-wing parties for their campaign against the so-called "Jewish influence" in German public life. Particularly vulnerable to this sort of agitation by virtue of their party's close identification with the Jewish bourgeoisie, the Democrats denounced the Nationalists for having encouraged such demagoguery and chastised the DVP for its failure to dissociate itself from the Jew-baiting of the radical Right.[8] The net effect of right-wing agitation against the Weimar Republic, claimed the leaders of the DDP, was only to weaken Germany's international standing and undermine prospects for a peaceful revision of the Versailles Treaty. For while the DDP, like its rivals on the German Right, recognized the revision of the Versailles Treaty as the overriding goal of German foreign policy, it differed from the DVP and DNVP in insisting that this could take place only on the basis of international understanding and reconciliation. Only as a politically stable democracy, contended the Democrats, could Germany possibly gain the international confidence necessary for a revision of the treaty.[9]

While the Democratic campaign highlighted the contributions the DDP had made to Germany's political stabilization following the end of the war, Stresemann and the leaders of the DVP structured their campaign around the slogan "From red chains will keep you free/Alone the German People's Party" in a carefully orchestrated attempt to exploit the antisocialist fears of the German middle strata.[10] The DVP's ultimate objective in the 1920 election campaign was not merely to mobilize middle-class dissatisfaction with the DDP's lackluster, if not erratic, performance as a member of the Weimar Coalition, but also to lay the foundation for its own entry into the government on terms that would have effectively ended Social Democratic dominance over Germany's political life. The central thrust of the DVP's campaign, however, was directed not so much against the Majority Socialists, with whom Stresemann was eventually prepared to cooperate, as against the Democrats, whose weakness and vacillation he held responsible for the ascendancy of the socialist Left.[11] While Stresemann thus recognized the necessity of cooperating with the Majority Socialists after the elections had taken place, he insisted that this required the creation of a powerful bourgeois counterweight to Social Democratic influence and called upon Germans of all political affiliations to support the DVP as a "party of national reconstruction" whose cooperation was essential if Germany was ever to recover from the ravages of war and revolution. Only through the genuine cooperation of all social classes within the framework of a government dedicated to the task of national reconstruction, claimed Stresemann in a major policy statement before the Federation of Saxon Industrialists (Verband Sächsischer Industrieller) on 5 May, would it be possible for the state to recover the authority it had lost as a result of the November Revolution and to provide Germany with the leadership necessary for a revision of the Versailles Treaty abroad and economic recovery at home.[12]

The DVP's willingness to cooperate with the Majority Socialists in a government of national reconstruction clearly distinguished it from its major rival on the German Right, the German National People's Party. Equally significant as a point of contrast between the two parties was the DVP's decision to abandon the monarchist cause in light of the disrepute into which it had fallen as a result of the Kapp-Lüttwitz Putsch.[13] For the most part, however, the DVP carefully muted its criticism of the DNVP in favor of a more coordinated campaign against the parties on the Left.[14] Only an isolated pamphlet of dubious origin in which the Nationalists were assailed for their anti-Semitic excesses and their duplicity during the Kapp Putsch seemed to mar the sense of common purpose that characterized the campaigns of the two right-wing parties.[15] But the truce between the two right-wing parties was suddenly broken when a group of prominent Nationalists under the leadership of Siegfried von Kardorff defected to the DVP just seven weeks before the election. A former Free Conservative who had joined the DNVP in December 1918 and had served as chairman of its delegation to the Prussian Constitutional Assembly, Kardorff was critical of the sharp swing to the right that had taken place in the DNVP in the second half of 1919 and had earned the enmity of his party's right wing with a sharp attack against the stab-in-the-back legend during the course of a speech in Berlin in February 1920.[16] Anticipating the defeat of his efforts to free the DNVP from the antirepublican ballast it had accumulated over the course of the previous year and a half, Kardorff approached Stresemann in early 1920 about the possibility of defecting to the DVP. Plans for Kardorff's defection were then finalized when he and two other members of the DNVP's Free Conservative faction—Otto Arendt and Otto von Dewitz—met with Stresemann on 15 April.[17] Two days later the three publicly announced their defection in a statement that attacked "the increasing prominence of extreme right-wing personalities within the DNVP and their influence upon the development of the party." Affirming their unconditional commitment to both the spirit and letter of the Weimar Constitution, Kardorff and his associates heralded the consolidation of all social classes into a genuine *Volksgemeinschaft* as an indispensable prerequisite for the reconstruction of the German fatherland and pledged themselves to work for this goal in concert with all of those, including the Majority Socialists, who shared their respect for the principles of constitutional government.[18]

Stresemann hoped that Kardorff's defection would trigger a major secession on the DNVP's left wing.[19] Although Nationalist defections failed to materialize on the scale for which he had hoped, his party's prospects were bolstered by a similar development on the right wing of the DDP. The DVP had openly solicited the support of right-wing Democrats ever since the middle of 1919, apparently in the hope that dissatisfaction with the party's social and economic policies would eventually alienate its more conservative supporters.[20] Still, it was not until after the DDP's support of the general strike during the Kapp Putsch that anything in the way of a secession on the DDP's right wing took place. On 27 April a group of twenty-seven Berlin Democrats led by Otto Wiemer and Otto Mugdan announced their defection from the DDP to the DVP. Citing the DDP's support of the general strike as an invitation to political and cultural anarchy, the dissidents called for the creation of a large liberal party infused by a strong sense of national feeling and committed to the defense of the free enterprise system.[21] But the effect of this statement, which had been prepared in conjunction with Stresemann and the DVP leadership in the hope of triggering further defections in other parts of the country, was not as profound as Stresemann would have liked. For outside of Berlin and its immediate environs the only place where the secession attracted much support was Leipzig, where on 30 April thirteen right-wing Democrats announced their defection to the DVP.[22] Elsewhere the secession was confined almost exclusively to isolated attacks against the DDP and declarations of solidarity with the DVP.

If the defection of Kardorff and Wiemer lent dramatic support to Stresemann's contention that the DVP was a party of national concentration whose
cooperation was indispensable for the moral and economic regeneration of the
German fatherland,[23] it also placed the Democrats at a severe psychological
disadvantage in their campaign against the DVP.[24] One factor, however, that
kept many Democrats—and particularly those of Jewish descent—from supporting the DVP was the party's ambivalent attitude toward anti-Semitism.[25]
Though Stresemann's wife was Jewish, his own position on anti-Semitism,
outlined in a letter to the Central Association of German Citizens of the Jewish
Faith (Centralverein deutscher Staatsbürger jüdischen Glaubens or CV), was
less than unequivocal. For while Stresemann readily condemned the anti-
Semitic excesses of the radical Right, he also maintained that certain Jewish
institutions such as the *Berliner Tageblatt* had to bear much of the responsibility for the resurgence of anti-Semitism that had taken place in Germany
after the end of World War I. In this respect, Stresemann drew a critical
distinction between those Jews like Theodor Wolff and Rudolf Mosse who
used their influence over public opinion to poison everything associated with
Germany's national greatness and patriotic German Jews such as Max Warburg and Jakob Riesser whose love of nation was beyond question.[26] The
denunciation of anti-Semitism that the DVP managing committee issued in
late January 1920 was colored by precisely this sort of ambiguity and did little
to allay Jewish misgivings about the party.[27] As a result, the DVP remained
unacceptable to Jewish businessmen whose growing uneasiness over the social
and economic policies of the DDP might otherwise have left them favorably
disposed to a change of party affiliation.[28]

The 1920 Reichstag elections took place under the provisions of a new
electoral law that, in contrast to the system of single-member constituencies
prevailing in the Second Empire, was based upon the principle of proportional
representation. According to this law, a party was entitled to one Reichstag
mandate for every 60,000 votes it received in any one of Germany's thirty-five
electoral districts. A party could, however, combine specified districts, such as
Baden and Württemberg or the three Saxon districts, into a multiple constituency (*Wahlkreisverband*) where a combined total of 60,000 votes would suf-
fice for a seat in the Reichstag provided that at least 30,000 votes had been
received in one of the constituent districts. In those districts where the party
had failed to poll the 60,000 votes necessary for a direct mandate, these votes,
along with any surplus votes from districts in which delegates had been
elected, would be counted toward the election of candidates on a special
national slate (*Reichsliste* or *Reichswahlvorschlag*) chosen by the party leadership. The number of delegates a party could elect from its national slate,
however, was limited to the number of direct mandates it had received at the
district level. Designed to inhibit the formation of splinter parties, this provision made it theoretically possible for a party to be denied the full complement

of mandates to which it would have been entitled under a system of absolute proportional representation.[29]

An immediate consequence of the new electoral law was to enhance greatly the role that special interest organizations were able to play in the electoral process. What emerged in the first years of the Weimar Republic, therefore, was an elaborate network of alliances or *Querverbindungen* between organized economic interests and the various bourgeois parties that used them to gain access to the voting public. This, however, meant that the various bourgeois parties found themselves subjected to two different sets of tensions, one horizontal and the other vertical. For in addition to the horizontal tensions that existed beween the different social and economic interests that constituted a party's material base, there were also strong vertical tensions between those special interest organizations with a mass popular base and those that sought to represent the interests of Germany's industrial and agricultural elites. At no point were the conflicts generated by this situation more acute than in the selection of candidates for national election.

The effects of the new electoral law could be seen in the case of both liberal parties. For although both the DDP and DVP were extremely solicitous of those special interest organizations that represented numerically significant sectors of Germany's middle-class electorate, they were also obliged to make major concessions to Germany's industrial elite in order to secure the funding they needed to run their campaigns. This was particularly true of the DDP, whose position on the Reich Emergency Levy and the Factory Council Law had done much to alienate its supporters in the German business community.[30] In December 1919, however, the Democrats succeeded in persuading Carl Friedrich von Siemens, chairman of the Curatorium for the Reconstruction of German Economic Life, to head their party's ticket in Berlin in the Reichstag elections that were scheduled to take place the following spring.[31] Siemens's nomination helped clear the way in January 1920 for a supplemental contribution from the Curatorium to the DDP, although the contribution was subject to conditions designed to strengthen the position of big business within the party.[32] Siemens and his associates were thus able not only to persuade the party's national leadership to authorize the creation of a special advisory committee for commerce and industry[33] but also to secure the nomination of candidates favorably disposed to big business to prominent places on the Democratic ticket for the 1920 elections. Of the first ten candidates nominated to the DDP's national ticket at a meeting of the party executive committee on 2 May, no less than six could be identified as either official or unofficial representatives of the German business community, while three other prominent industrialists—Siemens, Philipp Wieland, and Friedrich Raschig—had been nominated to secure candidacies at the district level.[34]

The favorable treatment accorded to business representatives in the nomination of candidates for the 1920 Reichstag elections was not without negative repercussions upon the DDP's electoral prospects. For in deferring to the wishes of the German business community, the Democratic leadership ran the risk of alienating the working-class and white-collar elements on the party's left wing.[35] Particularly significant was the party's failure to nominate Gustav Schneider, the driving force behind the newly created Federation of Employee Unions (Gewerkschaftsbund der Angestellten or GdA) and a member of the Democratic delegation to the National Assembly, to a secure candidacy on its national ticket. Schneider's nomination to a relatively hopeless position on the DDP's national slate severely hurt the party's chances of capitalizing upon white-collar disillusionment with the Majority Socialists and represented a crucial mistake on the part of the party leadership.[36] The DDP's failure to appreciate the electoral potential of Germany's nascent white-collar class was compounded by the problems it was experiencing with the more traditional elements of the German middle strata. The Democratic position on socialization, the Reich Emergency Levy, and the Factory Council Law had done much to alienate segments of the small business sector, thereby setting a trend that was greatly accentuated by the party's endorsement of the general strike and by what was widely perceived as a policy of deference to the industrial working class.[37] From this perspective, it would have been far more expedient if the DDP had deemphasized its commitment to the Weimar Coalition for the sake of a clearer line of demarcation with regard to the Majority Socialists.[38]

Such a tactic would have helped to reassure not only the independent middle class but also those elements in the German agricultural community that had rallied to the DDP's support in the elections to the National Assembly. Although the Democrats had sought to consolidate their position in the German countryside by espousing a number of programs designed to promote the welfare of the small family farmer,[39] the DDP's failure to bring about an end to government controls over agricultural prices and production, as well as its support of Social Democratic ministers of agriculture in both the Reich and Prussia, had done much to undermine the party's peasant support, with the result that widespread defections had begun to occur throughout the entire party organization by the end of 1919.[40] In February 1920 the leaders of the DDP tried to check their party's deteriorating position within the German agricultural community by publishing a special agrarian program whose central feature was a proposal for a program of agrarian resettlement designed to reverse the migration from countryside to city that had been taking place for the better part of a century.[41] This coincided with a vigorous defense of the DDP's alliance with the German Peasants' League by Karl Böhme, the DBB's secretary general, at the league's national convention in early March 1920.[42] Although Böhme succeeded in winning nearly unanimous approval for a renewal of the alliance in the upcoming Reichstag elections,[43] the dissension caused by the DDP's equivocation in matters of vital concern to the German agricultural community remained fairly widespread among the independent peasantry in central and western Germany.[44]

The DDP's prospects were further hampered by a strain in its relations with the German civil service. In the elections to the National Assembly the DDP had benefited from the strong support it had received from Ernst Remmers and the leaders of the newly founded German Civil Servants' Association.[45] In the meantime, however, ties between the civil service and the three government parties had been severely weakened by postwar inflation and socialist demands for a "democratization" of Germany's governmental bureaucracy. Beset by a spate of civil servant defections to the parties that stood to the right and left of the governmental coalition, the DDP supported a reform of Germany's civil servant salary structure that the Müller government had initiated in late April 1920 in an effort to reward the civil service for its loyalty during the Kapp Putsch and to repair at least some of the damage done to its social and economic position by the inflation.[46] To many civil servants, however, these measures did not go far enough in removing the causes of their social and economic distress and left the DDP and other government parties vulnerable to charges from the German Right that here too they had sacrificed the welfare of the professional civil service to the interests of the German working class.[47]

In the meantime, the leaders of the DVP moved quickly to exploit the problems the Democrats were having with the different sectors of the German middle class by presenting a ticket that was as sociologically heterogeneous as possible. In this respect, they hoped not only to attract the support of specific middle-class constituencies through the nomination of Otto Thiel from the German National Union of Commercial Employees, Albrecht Morath from the German Civil Servants' Association, and Wilhelm Dusche from the German Peasants' League to secure candidacies on their national ticket but also to achieve a breakthrough into the ranks of the nonsocialist working class. In late January 1920 the DVP managing committee authorized the creation of special vocational committees for both the salaried employees and wage laborers. Headed by Thiel and Otto Knebel respectively, these committees were created for the dual purpose of providing more vigorous representation for white-collar and working-class interests at the upper echelons of the party organization and aiding the party in its recruitment of white-collar and working-class members.[48] Although Thiel, as deputy chairman of the 400,000-member United Federation of German Employee Unions (Gesamtverband deutscher Angestelltengewerkschaften), served as an effective advocate for white-collar interests within the DVP,[49] the DVP's labor leaders felt grossly underrepresented within the party's inner councils and protested vigorously against the preferential treatment that the management-controlled "yellow" unions had received at the local levels of the party organization.[50]

The dilemma in which the leaders of the DVP found themselves became increasingly apparent with the nomination of candidates for the 1920 Reichstag elections. Not only did national party leaders have little, if any, direct influence over the selection of candidates at the district level, but their efforts to place working-class representatives prominently on the DVP's national slate of candidates were undercut by the party's financial dependence upon outside economic interests. In its initial deliberations on 17 and 19 April, the DVP's national party leadership decided to reserve the first four places on its national ticket behind Stresemann and a woman candidate, Clara Mende, for two middle-class representatives—Thiel and Morath—and two industrialists—Stinnes and Reinhold Quaatz—with the precise order of their placement to be determined at a later date.[51] When the final composition of the list was established on 2 May, however, Quaatz had been dropped to the eighth position, thereby jeopardizing his chances for election to the Reichstag. This provoked a strong protest from Johannes Flathmann, secretary of the Commission for the Collection, Administration, and Allocation of the Industrial Campaign Fund, who threatened to withhold campaign contributions unless the party honored its commitment to Quaatz.[52] At the same time, the leaders of the Christian trade unions complained bitterly over the fact that Georg Streiter, a prominent Evangelical labor leader, had been placed no higher than twelfth on the DVP's national ticket and therefore stood only a remote chance of being elected.[53] Under mounting pressure from both the labor and business factions within his party, Stresemann took it upon himself to rearrange the order of those who had been nominated to the DVP's national ticket by replacing the seventh-ranking nominee—Heinrich Rippel, editor-in-chief of the *Tägliche Rundschau*—with August Winnefeld of the Union of Christian Mine Workers, who was already assured of election by virtue of his nomination to head the party ticket in South Westphalia.[54] Not only did this materially improve Quaatz's chances of election and thus help placate the group around Flathmann, but the nomination of Winnefeld to a prominent position on the DVP's national ticket was calculated to enhance the party's image with the Christian working class even though Streiter's election remained highly problematic.

In their quest for financial support, both liberal parties demonstrated considerable willingness to accommodate the demands of German big business. Still, the DDP found itself at a severe financial and organizational disadvantage vis-à-vis the DVP. For although the Democrats received over 1 million marks from the Curatorium for the Reconstruction of German Economic Life, the fact that more than two-thirds of this was targeted for Siemens's campaign in Berlin[55] left the party with insufficient funds for its campaign in other parts of the country. By the end of 1919 the DDP had amassed a deficit of more than 200,000 marks, thus leaving its leaders with no choice but to undertake a drastic reduction in the size and scope of organizational activities. In contrast to the 130 full-time employees who had staffed the DDP's national headquarters during the campaign for the National Assembly, the party now employed only about thirty. Similar cuts had taken place at the district and local levels of the DDP's national organization.[56] This stood in sharp contrast to the situation within the DVP, which received over 750,000 marks from the Curatorium[57] in addition to the sums that Flathmann and the leaders of Ruhr heavy industry had placed at its disposal for use in the campaign.[58] Moreover, the large-scale support it had received from the Ruhr over the course of the preceding nine months[59] had made it possible for the DVP not only to rebuild much of its organizational base in Württemberg, Saxony, Thuringia, Schleswig-Holstein, and Pomerania but also to establish entirely new party secretariats in West Prussia, Upper Silesia, and parts of Bavaria. The success of these efforts could be seen in the fact that between October 1919 and April 1920 the DVP was able to increase its number of local chapters throughout the country from 1,063 to 2,181, its number of full-time employees from 91 to 161, and its national membership from 258,606 to an estimated 395,200.[60] Only in the south German states of Baden, Bavaria, and Württemberg were party leaders still seriously plagued by the problems that had resulted from the collapse of the old National Liberal organization during the last months of 1918.[61]

In the struggle between the two liberal parties, the odds were clearly stacked in favor of the DVP. Not only did nationalist indignation over the terms of the Versailles Treaty, lingering uneasiness over the DDP's social and economic policies, and middle-class alarm over the DDP's support of the general strike during the Kapp Putsch place the Democrats at a profound psychological disadvantage relative to the DVP, but Stresemann and his associates were far better prepared—both financially and organizationally—for the rigors of a national campaign. All of this combined to produce a massive shift to the right within Germany's liberal electorate, a shift that saw the Democrats lose more than half of the votes they had received in the elections to the National Assembly and the DVP more than double its popular vote from 1919. What the outcome of the 1920 Reichstag elections revealed for the German liberal parties was a return to the relative strengths of 1912, as the DVP came within a percentage point of equaling the NLP's share of the popular vote eight years earlier. At the same time, the 8.3 percent share of the popular vote that the DDP received in 1920 fell a full four percentage points short of what the Progressive People's Party had received in 1912, so that the overall performance of the German liberal parties—the DVP's success notwithstanding— was significantly weaker in 1920 than it had been in the last national elections of the Second Empire.[62]

In explaining their losses in the 1920 elections, the Democrats cited a variety of factors, including Stresemann's demagoguery, the political immaturity of the German bourgeoisie, the disloyalty of the Berlin press, and the failure of their party organization throughout the country.[63] While all of these explanations no doubt contained an element of truth, they failed to come to terms with the real reasons for the DDP's disastrous performance. What the leaders of the DDP failed to recognize was that the DDP's defeat in the 1920 Reichstag elections stemmed from a fatal contradiction in the party's self-image and basic political orientation. The DDP had originally been founded as a party of bourgeois concentration whose essential purpose was to provide the German bourgeoisie in all its sociological heterogeneity with the strong, effective organization necessary to represent its legitimate social and economic interests within the framework of a parliamentary democracy. At the same time, however, party leaders also conceived of the DDP as a bridge between the bourgeoisie and the industrial working class and categorically rejected the notion that their party should become too closely identified with the interests of any particular social class. In this respect, the Democrats came to espouse a somewhat oversimplified version of Hegel's philosophy of the state that held the state to be above the clash of antagonistic social interests and the institution in which this conflict found its ultimate resolution. This was clearly reflected in the official party program adopted by the DDP at its Leipzig party congress in December 1919 in an attempt to infuse German middle-class liberalism with the social canon of Naumann and his followers. But as the outcome of the 1920 Reichstag elections revealed, this produced a fateful and ultimately irreconcilable contradiction in their party's political profile. Not only had the DDP failed to secure a significant breakthrough into the ranks of the industrial working class, but its constant equivocation on such issues as socialization, Erzberger's tax reform, and the Factory Council Law had profoundly alienated much of the middle class support upon which it ultimately depended.[64]

The DDP's losses were particularly heavy in metropolitan Berlin, where the secession of Wiemer and his associates had crowned the loss of nearly 60 percent of its 1919 electorate. During the Second Empire Berlin had always been a Progressive stronghold, more or less impervious to National Liberal pressure. But with the outcome of the 1920 elections, the DVP had suddenly replaced the DDP as the strongest bourgeois party in the city. The Democrats sustained equally heavy losses in virtually every district north of the Main River. In Pomerania, where the party's internal divisions had led to the nomination of two separate slates of candidates, the DDP lost 142,000 votes, many directly to the DNVP. In Hesse-Nassau the Democrats lost another 149,000 votes, while in Merseburg and South Hanover their losses totaled 92,500 and 75,000 votes respectively. Even in those south German states where the DVP organization was still in the process of being rebuilt, the Democrats suffered surprisingly heavy losses. In Württemberg, where the local ticket was led by Haußmann and industrialist Philipp Wieland, the DDP lost 170,000 votes, or

51.2 percent of what it had received in 1919, while in the neighboring state of Baden a balanced ticket headed by the former National Liberal Hermann Dietrich and the longtime Progressive politician Ludwig Haas lost 110,000 votes, or 48.6 of the DDP's 1919 total. Even in traditional liberal strongholds such as these the DDP was unable to withstand the challenge from the Right.[65]

An exact sociological profile of Democratic losses in the 1920 Reichstag elections is impossible in view of the lack of reliable statistical data from the 1919 elections to the National Assembly. Not only had the boundaries of many districts changed between 1919 and 1920, but published data on the 1919 elections rarely extend to the level where meaningful comparisons with the 1920 elections can be made. Nevertheless, it is possible to offer some general observations about the sociological disposition of those voters who had turned their backs upon the DDP between 1919 and 1920. In the first place, the Democrats seem to have sustained by far their heaviest losses among the more traditional elements of the urban middle class. In 1919 the artisanry and the small business sector had supported the DDP, though by no means unanimously, on the assumption that only it could stem the tide of social revolution that was sweeping the country. By 1920, however, the DDP was no longer perceived in middle-class circles as a bulwark against social revolution but rather as a willing ally in Social Democratic schemes to expropriate the independent middle class.[66] The DDP also seems to have suffered substantial, though decidedly less heavy, losses among elements of the so-called new middle class, namely, among civil servants and white-collar employees. Civil servants were particularly disturbed over the DDP's acquiescence in Social Democratic efforts to "rejuvenate" the bureaucracy by purging it of elements loyal to the old regime, while at the same time the party's failure to nominate the GdA's Gustav Schneider to a secure candidacy on its national ticket had done much to hurt its standing with the organized white-collar movement. In the case of the German peasantry, on the other hand, the DDP's performance varied greatly from district to district, depending in large measure upon the amount of support it received from the German Peasants' League. For the most part, however, the DDP's losses in the countryside seem to have been less severe than in the large urban areas and middle-sized cities.[67]

In their campaign for the 1920 Reichstag elections Stresemann and the leaders of the DVP proved remarkably adept at exploiting the uncertainties that the DDP's performance as a member of the Weimar Coalition had aroused within Germany's middle-class electorate. Having barely survived the 1919 elections to the National Assembly, the DVP more than justified its own separate existence by polling over 3.6 million votes and increasing its parliamentary representation from twenty-five to sixty-two seats. One of the interesting ironies of the election results, however, was that the DVP proved immensely successful in areas like Berlin, Potsdam, Frankfurt an der Oder, and Pomerania, where the National Liberals had never experienced much success, while in former National Liberal strongholds such as Baden and Württemberg the party lagged significantly behind its 1912 performance. What this suggests is that the DVP had not only succeeded in mobilizing many former National Liberals who had defected to the DDP in the winter of 1918–19 but also in attracting the support of those who before the war had voted for either the Progressive or Free Conservative parties. Geographically, the DVP achieved its greatest success north of the Main River in districts such as South Hanover, Berlin, Potsdam I, Hesse-Nassau, and Merseburg, where it more than doubled its popular vote from 1919. Similar successes were recorded in Saxony, Silesia, and Thuringia, districts in which the collapse of the old National Liberal organization had prevented it from fielding a slate of candidates in the elections to the National Assembly. In Thuringia alone the DVP polled over 235,000 votes in the 1920 Reichstag elections, while in the three Saxon districts it recorded a net gain of more than 350,000 votes, thereby surpassing the NLP's performance in 1912. For the same reasons that it is difficult to construct a sociological profile of DDP losses in the 1920 elections, it is also hard to construct one of the DVP electorate. Still, it seems apparent that the People's Party was most successful among the peasantry in north and northwestern Germany; in those urban areas characterized by a disproportionately high percentage of the population employed in business, administration, or the liberal professions; and among academics and pensioners. Within the artisanry and the industrial working class, on the other hand, the DVP seems to have experienced at best marginal success, while its overtures to the Christian labor movement seem to have had no appreciable effect on the outcome of the election. For all intents and purposes, the DVP remained a party of the rural and urban middle classes.[68]

The shift within Germany's liberal electorate from the DDP to the DVP was only one aspect of a more general pattern of electoral polarization that saw all of the government parties sustain heavy losses. Like the DDP, the Majority Socialists lost nearly half of the popular vote it had received in 1919, while the Center, reeling from the defection of its entire Bavarian organization to the Bavarian People's Party (Bayerische Volkspartei or BVP) in January 1920, lost a third of its 1919 popular vote. In place of the commanding majority they had held in the National Assembly, the parties of the Weimar Coalition now controlled only 205 of the 452 seats in the newly elected Reichstag. The big winners in the 1920 elections, on the other hand, were the Independent Socialists, who virtually tripled their vote in the 1919 elections and increased their parliamentary strength from twenty-two to eighty-four seats, and the DVP and DNVP, which were able to capitalize upon heavy defections from the Center and DDP to come within a percentage point of doubling their share of the vote from the 1919 elections. As a referendum on the policies and accomplishments of the Weimar Coalition, the outcome of the 1920 Reichstag elections clearly established the extent of popular disillusionment with the new republican order.

The Search for Stability
1920–1922

The Battle Enjoined

THE OUTCOME OF THE 1920 Reichstag elections held disturbing implications for the future of Germany's parliamentary institutions. As it had
emerged from the elections to the National Assembly, the Weimar party
system offered two possibilities for the formation of a broad parliamentary
coalition. Along one axis were the parties of the Weimar Coalition that accepted the republican system of government and supported—though with
some initial reservations on the part of the DDP—a foreign policy predicated
upon the acceptance of the Versailles Treaty as the precondition for its eventual
revision. The principal obstacle to the maintenance of such a coalition was the
lack of a general consensus between its socialist and nonsocialist members on
questions of social and economic policy. The second axis united those parties
that were committed to the preservation of the free enterprise system, namely,
the two liberal parties, the Center, and the right-wing DNVP. Yet whatever
solidarity these parties may have evinced in defense of the bourgeois economic
order was undermined by fundamental divisions on constitutional and foreign
policy issues. The way in which these two axes intersected with each other
rendered any governmental coalition, whether consisting of the democratic
parties or those that identified themselves with the defense of capitalism,
inherently unstable. As a result, the formation of a coalition government
resting upon the support of a parliamentary majority in the Reichstag might not
always be possible.[1]

The outcome of the June elections had deprived the parties of the Weimar
Coalition of the parliamentary majority that they had enjoyed in the National
Assembly. At the same time, however, the DNVP's uncompromising hostility
toward the new republican order and its intransigence in matters of foreign
policy effectively precluded a reorganization of the government on the basis of
those parties that were committed to the defense of the capitalist economic
system. The only hope of forming a government that rested upon the support
of a majority in the newly elected Reichstag, therefore, lay in extending the
existing governmental coalition either to the Independent Socialists on the Left
or to the DVP on the Right. Of these alternatives, the Majority Socialists
clearly preferred the former, and on 11 June Hermann Müller, to whom Reich
President Ebert had entrusted the task of forming a new government, formally
invited the Independent Socialists to take part in talks aimed at the formation

of a coalition government whose first order of business would be to defend the social and political accomplishments of the November Revolution.[2] When the Independent Socialists responded to Müller's offer with a bitter invective that left no room for compromise, Müller resigned the commission he had received from Ebert, whereupon the Reich president turned to the DVP's Rudolf Heinze in hopes that he might be able to form a majority government stretching from the Majority Socialists to the DVP. These hopes, however, were dealt a quick and fatal blow when on 13 June the Majority Socialists announced that they had no intention of either resurrecting the old governmental coalition or joining a new government in which elements of the German Right were represented.[3] At the same time, the Center's refusal to participate in any government that included representatives from the right-wing DNVP torpedoed whatever hopes Heinze and the leaders of the People's Party might have had of extending the government coaliton to the Right. Unable to organize a government capable of commanding the support of a parliamentary majority, Heinze resigned his mandate on 15 June and withdrew his name from further consideration as a candidate for the chancellorship. Ebert now turned to Carl Trimborn, chairman of the German Center Party, in hopes that he might succeed where Heinze had failed.[4]

Throughout the early stages of the negotiations, the Democratic Party maintained a conspicuously low profile, if for no other reason than to conceal the deep-seated cleavages that had surfaced within its own ranks. Chastened by their party's losses in the recent Reichstag elections, the Democrats were in the midst of reassessing the DDP's political future and had resigned themselves to the fact that their influence upon the course of events in Berlin was negligible. The party's weakness was compounded by the fact that its leaders were unable to agree upon the course of action the DDP should follow in the wake of its defeat at the polls. The leaders of the DDP's right wing, for example, were sympathetic to the establishment of closer political ties to the DVP and supported the creation of a government consisting of the two liberal parties, the Center, and the newly founded Bavarian People's Party on the grounds that such a step would reassure those middle-class voters who had deserted the DDP in the recent Reichstag elections and help prepare the way for an eventual merger of the DDP and DVP into a united liberal party. The leaders of the party's social-liberal wing, on the other hand, remained adamantly opposed to the DDP's participation in any government that included either of the right-wing parties for fear that this would only discredit the DDP in the eyes of those who had supported it at the polls. Not only did they categorically reject the idea of a united liberal party, but they preferred seeing the government in the hands of a right-wing coalition that would allow them to assume the role of the loyal oppositon over becoming part of a minority government in which they would have to share power with the DVP.[5]

In deference to the sharp divisions that existed within their own party, the Democrats were content to let events run their course in hopes that the Majority Socialists might still be persuaded to join the government.[6] It was only after Trimborn met with Carl Petersen, the DDP's national chairman, on the afternoon of 15 June that the Democrats specified the conditions under which they might be willing to enter the government. These demands were necessarily vague and called, among other things, for the unconditional recognition of the Weimar Constitution, the cessation of all agitation for the restoration of the monarchy, and the rejection of any attempt on the part of one social class to establish domination over another. Concrete proposals relative to the conduct of German foreign policy or the reorganization of the German economy were avoided so as not to complicate the task of forming a new government.[7] The publication of these conditions cleared the way for an understanding with the DVP, and on 17 June Stresemann and Heinze informed Trimborn of their party's willingness to enter a government with the DDP and Center so long as this did not entail a retreat from the principles upon which their party had been founded. The only specific condition that they attached to the DVP's participation in such a government was that the conduct of German foreign policy and the reconstruction of German economic life be placed in the hands of competent experts without regard to their party affiliation.[8]

In the meantime Ebert and Trimborn had succeeded in persuading Konstantin Fehrenbach, a sixty-eight-year-old Centrist who had distinguished himself as president of the National Assembly, to assume leadership of the new government. A man of impeccable republican credentials, Fehrenbach was highly respected as a spokesman for the Center's left wing, and his appointment as chancellor was certain to smooth the way for Majority Socialist toleration of the bourgeois minority government that the leaders of the Center, DDP, and DVP were being asked to form. Yet while the leaders of the DDP were willing to accept Fehrenbach as the new chancellor, they were still apprehensive about the prospect of belonging to a government that did not possess the support of a clear majority in the Reichstag. The Democrats made one last effort to secure the cooperation of the Majority Socialists at a meeting with the Reich president on the evening of 17 June, but were frustrated by Ebert's own reluctance to use his influence with the MSPD party leadership on behalf of a government capable of commanding a parliamentary majority.[9] This constituted a severe setback to the DDP's social-liberal faction around Anton Erkelenz and Gertrud Bäumer, and at a meeting of the DDP Reichstag delegation on the morning of 19 June they tried to block the party's entry into the Fehrenbach government by introducing a resolution that would have prevented the DDP from participating in any government in which the Majority Socialists were not also represented. When this resolution was rejected by a 23–7 margin in favor of one that officially sanctioned the DDP's entry into the

Fehrenbach government, Erkelenz issued a thinly veiled threat that raised the spectre of a secession on the party's left wing.[10] Erkelenz and his supporters continued their efforts to block the formation of the Fehrenbach government at a meeting of the DDP party council three days later, but once again they were turned back when the council adopted a resolution officially endorsing the position taken by the delegation at its meeting on 19 June.[11] The last obstacle to the DDP's entry into the Fehrenbach government was thus removed.

Like their Democratic counterparts, the leaders of the DVP were sharply divided over their party's relationship to the Fehrenbach government. As one of the principal victors in the 1920 Reichstag elections, the People's Party entered the negotiations with expectations scarcely capable of fulfillment. In this respect, Stresemann sought not just to secure influential cabinet posts for members of his own party but also to make certain that the Foreign Office and those ministries responsible for Germany's financial and economic reconstruction were placed in the hands of "specialists" free from Social Democratic influence.[12] The fact, however, that the new government was dependent upon the toleration of the Majority Socialists severely limited the extent to which the DVP was able to influence its composition and program. Not only did the chancellor refuse to replace Joseph Wirth, Erzberger's successor at the Ministry of Finance, with someone who might have been more acceptable to the DVP party leadership,[13] but the leaders of the DVP were unable to persuade the government to treat the ministries of Finance, Economics, and Transportation as a single complex whose respective cabinet officers were to be mutually acceptable to each other, a condition that, if accepted, would have forced Wirth's removal from office.[14] By the same token, the DVP's efforts to persuade a prominent representative from the German business community to accept the Ministry of Economics were stymied by a variety of factors, not the least of which was the fact that no industrialist wanted to be held responsible for the concessions Germany would have to make at the upcoming Spa Conference on the matter of coal deliveries to the Allies. For a while it seemed—to be sure, much to the jubilation of those who stood on the DDP's left wing[15]—that efforts to bring the DVP into the cabinet might break down as a result of Social Democratic threats to vote against the new government should it prove too conciliatory with respect to the DVP's demands.[16] Such threats, however, failed to materialize, as the Majority Socialists, having already succeeded in frustrating most of the DVP's objectives, withdrew their remaining demands and agreed to go along with the installation of the new government.

Fehrenbach officially presented his new government on 25 June. The Democrats, clearly the weakest member of the coalition, were represented by Otto Gessler and Erich Koch-Weser, who continued in their previous positions at the ministries of Defense and Interior respectively. The People's Party, on the other hand, was represented not only by Heinze as the minister of justice but also by Ernst Scholz at the Ministry of Economics and Hans von Raumer at the Treasury. Furthermore, the new foreign minister, Walter Simons, also stood close to the DVP, although he remained officially unaffiliated with the party. The remaining five cabinet posts were held by Wilhelm Groener, a military officer with strong republican sympathies who was appointed to the Ministry of Transportation, and four Centrists, the most prominent of whom was the controversial Wirth. Consisting of representatives from the three bourgeois parties that stood between the Majority Socialists and the DNVP, the Fehrenbach government was little more than a caretaker government whose torturous formation and narrow political base clearly reflected its limited political potential. Not only did the Fehrenbach government command the support of less than 40 percent of those who sat in the newly elected Reichstag, but the Majority Socialists, who indicated that they would tolerate the new government at least until the conclusion of the Spa negotiations, were in a position to block the implementation of policies they regarded as detrimental to the welfare of the German working class. The Majority Socialists were thus able to avoid the onus of political responsibility while at the same time retaining what amounted to a virtual veto over the foreign and domestic policies of the new government.[17]

Neither of the two liberal parties were pleased with the outcome of the negotiations that had culminated in the formation of the Fehrenbach government. Not only did the Democrats regard the manner in which the negotiations had been conducted as a departure from the procedure outlined in the Weimar Constitution,[18] but the refusal of the Majority Socialists to accept governmental responsibility had left them with no alternative but to enter a government about which they were less than enthusiastic. Had it been possible, the Democrats would have preferred to join the Majority Socialists in opposition so that their party might have an opportunity to recover from the losses it had sustained in the last Reichstag elections. In the final analysis, however, their sense of responsiblity to the welfare of the nation as a whole prevailed over their party's best interests, and they reluctantly accepted the political sacrifice that participation in the Fehrenbach government entailed.[19] Within the DVP, on the other hand, frustration over the outcome of the negotiations was particularly strong among the industrial interests on the party's right wing. Their dissatisfaction stemmed from a number of factors, not the least of which was the government's lack of independence vis-à-vis the Majority Socialists. Equally disturbing was the presence in the cabinet of three left-wing Centrists—Fehrenbach, Wirth, and Johannes Giesberts. Above all else, Wirth's appointment to the Ministry of Finance meant that Germany's propertied classes could expect little in the way of relief from the oppressive tax policies of his mentor and predecessor, Matthias Erzberger. To many a party member it seemed that the DVP had given up too much and received too little in return for its willingness to enter the government.[20]

The disillusionment that many members of the DVP felt over their party's entry into the Fehrenbach government did not become fully apparent until after the conclusion of the Spa Conference in the middle of July 1920. German hopes that the conference would produce an agreement on reparations consonant with Germany's capacity to pay were undercut from the very outset by the coolness with which the Allies treated the German delegation. The conference nearly broke down when on 10 July Hugo Stinnes, a member of the German delegation and one of Germany's leading coal producers, launched a scathing attack upon the "Siegerwahnsinn" of the Entente in rejecting Allied demands that Germany commit herself to the delivery of 2 million tons of coal per month as partial fulfillment of her reparations obligation.[21] While Stinnes's speech gave vent to the increasing frustration that many Germans felt over their nation's treatment at the hands of the Allies, it also severely complicated the position of the German delegation at Spa and set the scene for a heated confrontation between those like Stinnes who refused to accept Allied demands even at the risk of occupation of the Ruhr and the more moderate members of the German delegation such as Fehrenbach and Raumer who saw no alternative but to submit to Allied pressure. Yet for all the vehemence with which Stinnes attacked Allied reparations demands, the Fehrenbach government in fact had no choice but to accept the Allied terms, with the result that on 16 July it signed a protocol obligating Germany to supply the Allies with 2 million tons of coal per month for the six months beginning 1 August. Although the German government managed to secure minor concessions regarding the price of the coal it was supposed to deliver, this could not erase the fact that for all intents and purposes the Spa Conference represented a severe diplomatic defeat not only for Fehrenbach and the members of the German delegation but also for German heavy industry.[22]

The signing of the Spa Protocol marked the beginning of the rift in German politics over the question of fulfillment. This rift extended deep into the ranks of the DVP, which by virtue of its membership in the Fehrenbach government was obliged to support ratification of the Spa Protocol in spite of mounting opposition throughout the party organization. Within the DVP the sharpest criticism of the Fehrenbach government and its conduct of German foreign policy came from those members of the party with close ties to the Ruhr industrial establishment. The position of heavy industry within the DVP Reichstag delegation had been greatly strengthened by the election of men like Stinnes, Kurt Sorge, and Reinhold Quaatz in the 1920 general elections. The leader of this group was the indefatigable Stinnes, whose political pedigree had been noticeably enhanced by the overwhelmingly positive response which his defiance at Spa had evoked among the party's rank-and-file membership. Stinnes epitomized a new breed of German capitalist, one who openly recognized the necessity of cooperating with the more moderate elements of the socialist labor movement within the framework of institutions like the

Zentralarbeitsgemeinschaft as a way of blocking government schemes for the socialization of the coal and steel industries. Stinnes looked upon politics as little more than an extension of economics and failed to recognize any distinction between the private and public sectors. As one of Germany's leading coal producers, Stinnes did not hesitate to equate Germany's general welfare with the maximum utilization of her productive capacity and insisted that the solution of her postwar economic woes lay in the removal of all restrictions, governmental or otherwise, that interfered with her industrial productivity.[23]

While not even Stinnes's sharpest critics could dispute the therapeutic effect that his speech at Spa had had upon the DVP's rank and file, no one could deny that it had also done much to crystallize antigovernment sentiment throughout the party organization. At a meeting of the DVP leadership on 26–27 July, Carl Cremer, a DVP deputy from Dortmund with close ties to Ruhr heavy industry, attacked the party's performance as a member of the Fehrenbach government and introduced a resolution that would have forced it to leave the government if a series of conditions, including Wirth's dismissal as minister of finance, were not met.[24] Although Stresemann was able to head off this threat by promising to enter into confidential negotiations with the leaders of the government, the episode set the scene for an even more determined assault upon his leadership of the party at a meeting of the DVP Reichstag delegation on 4 August. This time Stresemann's principal antagonist was Reinhold Quaatz, who, like Cremer, enjoyed close ties to heavy industry in the Ruhr. Quaatz attacked the DVP leadership for its failure to appreciate the crucial significance of the Rhine-Ruhr basin for Germany's economic recovery and warned that German heavy industry might be forced "to seek its representation outside the DVP" if its spokesmen were not given a more influential role both within the party and in the various parliamentary committees on which it was represented. To Stresemann, Quaatz's threat of an industrial exodus from the DVP seemed a particularly crude attempt at political extortion, and he responded with a vigorous defense of the party's support of industrial interests that left Quaatz temporarily isolated within the delegation.[25]

Following his altercation with Quaatz before the DVP Reichstag delegation, Stresemann took special pains to reassure both Vögler and Stinnes, neither of whom had attended the meeting, that he did not regard Quaatz's threat as representative of their position, and the episode passed without further incident.[26] The real significance of Quaatz's action, however, lay not so much in its immediate effect upon the DVP's relations with heavy industry as in the fact that it foreshadowed a pattern of increasing conflict within the DVP over the party's attitude toward the Weimar Republic. For while the left wing of the party led by Heinze and supported by Stresemann, Raumer, and Kardorff recognized the imperative of working within the framework of the existing political order, the DVP also contained a powerful right wing represented by

Quaatz, Oskar Maretzky, and Baron Kurt von Lersner that had strong ideological reservations about the republican form of government and sought to establish common cause with the DNVP in its crusade against the republic.[27]
Between those two groups stood a third faction headed by Vögler and Stinnes
that viewed politics in essentially economic terms and whose loyalty to the
Weimar Republic was predicated upon the extent to which it allowed them to
pursue their economic self-interest. The loyalty of this group had already been
severely tested by the outcome of the negotiations at Spa. The next test was to
come with the revival of the socialization question in the fall of 1920.

As part of the agreement that had ended the general strike following the
collapse of the Kapp Putsch, the Müller government had promised to appoint a
new Socialization Commission for the purpose of amending the Coal Socialization Act of March 1919. This law had established the National Coal Council (Reichskohlenrat) and National Coal Association (Reichskohlenverband) as
regulatory agencies designed to bring about a high degree of economic coordination in the coal industry. It was not long, however, before Germany's coal
producers were able to turn this arrangement to their own advantage by transforming the National Coal Council into a state-sponsored cartel with wide-
ranging discretionary powers over price and production levels. While the
shortcomings of this situation became increasingly apparent in the wake of the
acute coal shortage that plagued Europe in the first years after the end of the
war, it was the combined effect of union pressure following the collapse of the
Kapp Putsch and the outcome of the Spa negotiations that drew renewed public
attention to the need for strengthening and revitalizing the regulatory mechanisms established by the Coal Socialization Act of 1919.[28]

To be sure, the leaders of the DVP's industrial wing had hoped that their
party's presence in the Fehrenbach government would prevent the new cabinet
from taking up the socialization question. But these hopes were quickly dashed
by the concessions that the Center and the DDP had attached to the DVP's
entry into the government.[29] With Fehrenbach's subsequent declaration that
his government would support the work of the Socialization Commission and
with the publication of the commission's recommendations in early September, the DVP could no longer avoid facing the issue.[30] It was against the
background of these developments that Vögler asked Stresemann and the
leaders of the the DVP Reichstag delegation to refrain from taking any position
on the socialization question until after they had had an opportunity to confer
with the leaders of the Ruhr coal industry. Vögler defended his request by
explaining that coal producers in the Ruhr felt little could be accomplished by
merely rejecting the recommendations of the Socialization Commission and
were therefore in the process of formulating counterproposals of their own. If
the Reichstag delegation could be persuaded to accept these proposals as the
basis of its own position, concluded Vögler, the political impact of the coal
industry's proposals would be greatly enhanced.[31]

While Stresemann, a staunch defender of the free enterprise system, readily accepted Vögler's recommendations,[32] implementation of this strategy was hampered not only by increasing pressure within the DVP for its withdrawal from the government but also by a desire on the part of the Majority Socialists to return to power. In late August the Majority Socialists let it be known, no doubt with an eye toward the forthcoming confrontation over the socialization question, that they would be willing to enter the Fehrenbach government on the condition that the DVP withdraw. On 2 September Stresemann met with representatives from the other government parties and quickly enlisted their support in blocking Social Democratic efforts to force the DVP out of the Fehrenbach government.[33] On the following day Stresemann, Eugen Schiffer from the DDP, and Eduard Burlage from the Center met with Fehrenbach to voice their concern over the loss of public confidence that his government had suffered since its formation earlier that summer and to underscore their opposition to Social Democratic intrigues against the DVP. While the three were not opposed to the Socialists' return to power, they were adamant that they receive only the number of cabinet posts to which their parliamentary strength entitled them and refused to go along with any reorganization of the Fehrenbach government that might give them disproportionate influence over its policies.[34]

By the end of September the Majority Socialists appeared to have lost all interest in rejoining the government, and the issue seemed dead until the following spring. In the meantime, the conflict within the DVP over its participation in the Fehrenbach government had come to a head. Within the DVP, criticism of the Fehrenbach government focused not merely upon its diplomatic failure at Spa but also upon its general ineffectiveness at home. In this respect, the leaders of the DVP, including Stresemann himself, were particularly disturbed by the government's apparent softness toward the railway unions' demands for greater control over the operations of the national railroad, while the continuation of Erzberger's tax policies by the new finance minister, Joseph Wirth, had produced widespread disgruntlement at the state and local levels of the party's national organization.[35] The situation within the DVP became increasingly tense following the government's decision on 22 September to proceed with the recommendations of the Socialization Commission. Stresemann and the leaders of the DVP were categorically opposed to any scheme for the socialization of German industry that might compromise private ownership of the means of production, and the government's decision to use the recommendations of the Socialization Commission as the basis of its own bill for the nationalization of the coal industry constituted a direct threat to the DVP's position within the national coalition.[36] The DVP Reichstag delegation reiterated the party's opposition to the recommendations of the Socialization Commission at a special meeting in Weimar at the end of the month and issued what amounted to a virtual declaration of war against the socialization

policies of the Fehrenbach government.[37] At the same time, Alfred Gildemeister and Otto Hugo from the DVP's right wing stepped up their attacks
against Stresemann's policies as party chairman and denounced his apparent
willingness to share governmental responsibility with the Majority Socialists
as a betrayal of the principles upon which the DVP had been founded.[38]

Such criticism did little to shake Stresemann's commitment to the existing
governmental coalition. At a critical meeting of the DVP central executive
committee on 5 October Stresemann undertook a vigorous defense of the
policies his party had pursued since the formation of the Fehrenbach government earlier that summer. Specifically, Stresemann cited the role the DVP had
played in removing the civil service and the conduct of German foreign policy
from the arena of partisan political strife as proof of his party's effectiveness in
the national government. Whatever deficiencies the present government might
have, he continued, could not be attributed to the DVP but rather to the failure
of the Majority Socialists and Nationalists to join forces with the parties of the
bourgeois middle in a government of national reconciliation.[39] While the force
of Stresemann's rhetoric helped defuse the antigovernment sentiment that had
been building within the party ever since the conclusion of the Spa negotiations, the socialization question remained unresolved. In this respect, Stinnes
and the leaders of the DVP's industrial wing hoped to counter government
plans for nationalization of the coal industry with recommendations of their
own that entailed a comprehensive reorganization of that industry but left the
existing ownership structure intact. The central element of Stinnes's plan was
the creation of a state-sponsored coal trust that would include representatives
from both producing and consuming interests and have virtually complete
authority to establish its own price and production policies. The fact that the
government's role in determining prices and production levels would be
sharply reduced meant that the principal beneficiaries of such a scheme would
have been the coal producers themselves. Clearly, what Stinnes meant by
socialization had little in common with either the recommendations of the
Socialization Commission or with the position the Fehrenbach government
had taken in its statement of 22 September.[40]

Throughout the remainder of October the DVP used its influence within the
Fehrenbach government to undercut the support that it had originally given to
the recommendations of the Socialization Commission. The first tangible sign
of success came on 25 October when Raumer, as head of the Treasury, opened
the socialization debate in the National Economic Council (Reichswirtschaftsrat) with a statement that the government did not feel itself bound to the
commission's recommendations for the nationalization of the coal industry.[41]
By dissociating the government from the proposals of the Socialization Commission, Raumer was able to broaden the scope of the debate so that Stinnes's
plans for a structural reorganization of the coal industry could be added to the

agenda. Once the debate was no longer confined to the recommendations of the Socialization Commission, the opponents of socialization were able to have the matter referred to an ad hoc committee of the National Economic Council, where, safely removed from public scrutiny, they succeeded in delaying action on the commission's recommendations until the following spring. By then, the government had become increasingly concerned that nationalization of the coal industry would leave it defenseless against Allied pressure for increased coal deliveries as partial fulfillment of Germany's reparations obligations, with the result that it decided to take no further action on the entire matter.[42] Stinnes and the leaders of German heavy industry could hardly have been more pleased with the way in which the DVP had supported their strategy for handling the socialization question. For by helping redefine the parameters within which the socialization debate was to take place, the DVP had helped Stinnes divert public attention from the agenda of the Socialization Commission until pressure for nationalization of the coal industry had abated. At no point during the first years of the Weimar Republic was the alliance between the DVP and heavy industry more apparent or more effective.

These developments underscored the increasingly powerful role that the German industrial establishment had begun to play in the DVP's internal affairs. By no means, however, was Stresemann oblivious to the possible repercussions this might have upon both the DVP's public image and its freedom of action. For, as he confided to his diary in early November 1920, not only did this threaten to reduce the DVP to a position of complete subservience vis-à-vis German industry, but it also endangered the party's position within the intelligentsia and those middle-class elements upon which it depended for the bulk of its popular support.[43] Stresemann's fears, moreover, seemed fully warranted in light of the growing restlessness of the Christian labor leaders on the party's left wing. Much of their uneasiness stemmed from the DVP's apparent ambivalence toward the management-controlled yellow unions that had flourished throughout Germany before being abandoned by industrial leaders as one of the conditions for the creation of the Zentralarbeitsgemeinschaft in November 1918. Forced onto the defensive by their exclusion from the Zentralarbeitsgemeinschaft, the leaders of the yellow unions gravitated toward the DVP, where their presence was deeply resented by those party members with close ties to the Christian labor movement.[44] Though his own sympathies clearly lay with the Christian labor leaders, Stresemann maintained complete neutrality throughout the early stages of this conflict, and at the DVP's Leipzig congress in October 1919 he negotiated a truce between the rival labor movements which he hoped would minimize the effect of their dispute upon the party's national organization.[45]

The driving force behind the yellow labor movement in the immediate postwar period was Fritz Geisler, who, much to Stresemann's consternation, had been elected to the Reichstag on the DVP ticket in the 1920 elections. In the late summer of 1920 Geisler succeeded in consolidating what still remained of the prewar yellow unions into a new organization entitled the National Federation of German Unions (Nationalverband deutscher Gewerkschaften). The purpose of this organization, as Geisler explained in a speech in Hamburg in late August, was to promote Germany's national regeneration by freeing the German working class from the spirit of class self-interest that had come to dominate both the socialist and Christian labor movements.[46] While the central thrust of Geisler's initiative was clearly directed against the Social Democrats, the leaders of the DVP's Christian labor wing felt threatened by their party's increasingly close identification with the yellow unions and took special pains to reassure their own followers of the DVP's neutrality in the conflict between the two labor movements.[47] These efforts, however, were undercut by the appearance of Heinze, Riesser, and several other prominent DVP parliamentarians at the founding ceremonies of Geisler's organization at the end of October 1920. Denouncing this as an open breach of the DVP's neutrality in the conflict between the Christian and yellow labor movements, Wilhelm Gutsche and Otto Knebel from the DVP's newly founded National Workers' Committee (Reichsarbeiterausschuß der DVP) proceeded to sever their ties with the party.[48] Although the personal loyalty that the DHV's Hans Bechly and Otto Thiel felt toward Stresemann kept this from developing into a general secession on the party's left wing, the episode nevertheless signaled the collapse of the DVP's efforts to win the support of the Christian working class and dramatized the political costs associated with its increasing dependence upon German heavy industry.

The DVP's third party congress opened in Nuremberg during the first week of December 1920 against the background of increasing tension over its relationship to the Fehrenbach government. The two tasks confronting the party leadership were to defend the DVP's course of action against those on the party's right wing who regarded any accommodation with the Weimar Republic as a betrayal of the principles upon which the DVP had been founded and to reassure the party's predominantly middle-class constituency that, recent events notwithstanding, the party had not fallen under the domination of German heavy industry. The first of these tasks fell to Stresemann, who in his keynote address on the evening of 3 December insisted that the desperate situation in which the German nation found itself had left the DVP with no alternative but to enter the Fehrenbach government without regard for the effect this might have upon the party's political fortunes. Claiming that the welfare of the nation as a whole took precedence over the DVP's short-term interests, Stresemann defended his party's entry into the national government as an act of patriotic self-sacrifice that had made it possible for the German bourgeoisie to regain power and seal the fate of socialist schemes for the reorganization of German economic life.[49] While Stresemann's speech highlighted the DVP's role in Germany's postwar stabilization, other speakers took it upon themselves to reaffirm the DVP's self-image as a people's party committed to representing the German nation in all of its sociological heterogeneity. It was in this spirit that Otto Thiel, chairman of the DVP's National White-Collar Committee (Reichs-Angestelltenausschuß der DVP), outlined a grandiose social program that envisaged public relief for those who had been hurt by the war, governmental action to stimulate the construction of new homes, and a comprehensive labor law designed to secure social and economic parity for the German worker. Only by healing the cleavages to which war and defeat had given rise, concluded Thiel, would it be possible for the German people to free themselves from the yoke of the Versailles Treaty and regain their rightful place among the nations of the world.[50]

The last day of the Nuremberg congress was devoted to a series of special conferences held by the various vocational and professional committees that had been founded over the course of the previous year and a half. In the summer of 1919 the leaders of the DVP had authorized the creation of special vocational committees not only for workers and white-collar employees but for civil servants, farmers, and the small business sector as well.[51] The purpose of these committees was to enhance the party's effectiveness in soliciting the support of the various social groups upon which the DVP depended for the bulk of its popular support and to provide these groups with more effective representation within the DVP's national organization.[52] While the activities of the DVP's National Workers' Committee were severely hampered by the increasingly prominent role that Geisler and yellow labor union leaders had begun to play in party affairs, both the party's white-collar and civil servant organizations were particularly outspoken in representing the interests of their respective constituencies. At the head of these two organizations stood Otto Thiel and Albrecht Morath, whose affilation with the German National Union of Commercial Employees and German Civil Servants' Association respectively afforded them an excellent opportunity to solidify ties between the DVP and the professional groups they represented. No less significant was the work of the DVP's National Committee for the Artisanry and Small Business (Reichs-Ausschuß der DVP für Handwerk, Kleinhandel und Gewerbe) under the chairmanship of Heinrich Beythien and Robert Havemann. Alarmed by the increasingly desperate economic situation in which the more traditional elements of the German middle class found themselves, Beythien and his colleagues pledged to reverse this process through a more vigorous representation of middle-class interests on the part of the DVP and its parliamentary delegations.[53]

The activity of the various professional committees that the DVP had founded during the first two years of its existence bore ample testimony to the party's sociological heterogeneity and reflected Stresemann's own conception of the DVP as a people's party committed to reconciling the interests of the different social groups that constituted the nation as a whole. Two questions, however, remained unanswered. Given the high degree of interest articulation that had developed within party ranks, would it be possible for the DVP to fuse the diverse and potentially antagonistic interests that constituted its popular base into a dynamic and cohesive force? Or, conversely, would the party's increasingly close identification with the German industrial establishment undermine its sociological heterogeneity and alienate those upon whom it depended for the bulk of its electoral support? It was upon the resolution of these two questions that the fate of the German People's Party ultimately depended.

CHAPTER SEVEN

The Search for Synthesis

JUST AS GOVERNMENTAL POWER to ameliorate the social and economic hardships caused by World War I was severely limited by the hard realities of Germany's postwar economy, so was the government's ability to develop an effective national response to Allied pressure limited by Germany's military weakness and diplomatic isolation. Under these circumstances, a party's participation in the national government invariably saddled it with responsibility for unpopular decisions, which, by adversely affecting the interests of this or that social group, could only have a negative impact on the integrative potential of those parties that chose to enter the government. The difficulties that plagued the DVP in the second half of 1920, therefore, simply recapitulated—though on a somewhat lesser scale—those that the DDP and Center had already experienced as members of the Weimar Coalition. Given the strain that government participation imposed upon a party's integrative potential, it was by no means certain the DVP would ever succeed in integrating into its own organizational structure those middle-class elements that had become disillusioned with the DDP's performance as a member of the Weimar Coalition. By the same token, it remained to be seen whether or not the Democrats would be able to stem the massive defections that had cost their party more than half of its support since the 1919 elections to the National Assembly.

Following the DDP's defeat in the 1920 Reichstag elections, party morale was so low that some members were openly contemplating the possibility of a merger with the DVP.[1] Rather than resign themselves to such a fate, the leaders of the DDP appointed Robert Jansen from the party's central office in Berlin to head a special nine-man committee for the purpose of generating proposals for a thorough overhaul of the DDP's national organization.[2] Based in large part upon the results of a conference of party secretaries held in Passau in July, Jansen's recommendations were submitted to the DDP executive committee in early October. The central thrust of Jansen's report was twofold. First, the party should increase the number of salaried employees at the state and local levels of the DDP's national organization and place them under the direct supervision of the party's national headquarters in Berlin. Secondly, the party should create a series of special auxiliary committees headed by fully salaried party employees for women, youth, and the various socioeconomic groups that the party sought to represent in hopes of integrating them effectively into the DDP's organizational structure.[3]

While Jansen's recommendations were designed to provide the DDP with a modern political apparatus capable of drawing support from a broad spectrum of the German population, they also entailed a financial commitment that greatly exceeded the party's exhausted resources. The business interests that stood on the DDP's right wing, however, were prepared to assume at least a share of the cost involved in modernizing the party organization in return for a greater voice in shaping its social and economic policies.[4] Up to this time, the DDP's business leaders had been repeatedly frustrated in their efforts to gain a more influential position in the Democratic party organization by the general antipathy that many leading Democrats felt toward big business and the political representation of special economic interests. But with the approach of new national elections in the spring of 1920, the leaders of the DDP were forced by the sad state of their party's finances to formalize ties between the DDP and its backers in finance and industry through the creation of a special committee consisting of Hermann Fischer, Robert Kauffmann, Max Kempner, Alexander Prentzel, and Hjalmar Schacht.[5] In a separate development Schacht and Carl Friedrich von Siemens, a prominent industrialist who had been chosen to head the DDP ticket in Berlin, founded a special organization for Democratic businessmen in the Berlin metropolitan area in hopes of increasing their influence within the local DDP.[6] Insisting that the creation of a similar committee at the national level of the DDP organization constituted a prerequisite for their support in the upcoming national elections, Siemens and his associates pressed for authorization to organize the various business interests within the party into a special advisory committee with direct access to the party's national leadership. Given the desperate financial straits in which their party found itself, the Democrats could ill afford to alienate their potential backers in the German business community and officially sanctioned the creation of such a committee at a meeting of the DDP executive committee in late April 1920.[7]

Efforts to organize the DDP's business interests into a separate committee within the Democratic party organization drew to a climax in October 1920 when more than 300 of the party's leading business representatives met in Berlin to found the National Council of the German Democratic Party for Trade, Industry, and Commerce (Reichsausschuß für Handel, Industrie und Gewerbe beim Hauptvorstand der DDP) as a special advisory body to the DDP executive committee. Though ostensibly an organization representing the German business community in all its structural and geographical diversity,[8] this council was heavily weighted in favor of German big business. Not only were the members of the council's executive committee recruited almost exclusively from the leadership of Germany's large industrial and commercial firms,[9] but spokesmen for the artisanry and the small business sector were conspicuously absent from the council's founding ceremonies in Berlin.[10] Although the council's leaders hoped to rectify the situation by co-opting the party's artisan leaders into the council's executive committee, by no means was it certain that they would be able to overcome the deep-seated antipathy that many artisans and small businessmen felt toward German big business. Moreover, the DDP's artisan spokesmen had already taken the first steps toward organizing their followers into a separate organization tentatively named the Democratic Council for the Artisanry and Middle Class (Demokratischer Ausschuß für Handwerk und Mittelstand) under the leadership of Reichstag deputies Franz Bartschat and Wilhelm Kniest.[11] The creation of this committee was clearly designed to help the party stabilize its deteriorating electoral base through the more vigorous representation of middle-class interests within the Democratic party organization. In view of the deepening resentment which the artisanry and independent middle class harbored towards Germany's capitalist elite, it was unlikely that this goal could have been served by co-opting the DDP's artisan and middle-class representatives into its newly created council for trade and industry.

The first test of big business's effectiveness within the Democratic Party came with the reemergence of the socialization question in the fall of 1920. The prominent role that the DDP's Walther Rathenau had played in the deliberations of the Socialization Commmission constituted a source of considerable embarrassment to the leaders of the DDP's business wing, and his proposal for the reorganization of the coal industry, even though it fell far short of socialist demands for full nationalization, was sharply criticized at the founding ceremonies of the DDP's National Council for Trade, Industry, and Commerce in mid-October.[12] Within the DDP Rathenau's most effective critic was Siemens, who had originally sought to unite the bourgeois parties behind a scheme that both recognized the public's ultimate right of ownership to Germany's mineral wealth and sought to postpone nationalization by allowing the state to lease the right to exploit Germany's natural resources to the mining companies themselves.[13] After conferring with the leaders of the DDP's industrial wing, Siemens presented his proposal to the leaders of his own party at a special three-day conference of the DDP Reichstag delegation in Ulm during the last week of September. Like Stinnes and Rathenau, the leaders of the DDP Reichstag delegation were generally dissatisfied with the structure of the German coal industry, and they readily conceded the need for its eventual reorganization.[14] At the same time, they felt that it was imperative for the Fehrenbach government to take some sort of immediate action on the socialization question in order to appease the more moderate elements within the socialist labor movement.

Confronted with the task of reconciling the need to reorganize the German

coal industry with their own ideological commitment to the principles of the
free enterprise system, the leaders of the DDP Reichstag delegation appointed
a six-man socialization committee under the chairmanship of Eugen Schiffer
to try, if possible, to resolve the differences that had developed within the
party on the socialization question.[15] The socialization committee of the DDP
Reichstag delegation met on three occasions in the second half of October. At
no point during the course of its deliberations, however, did a general consensus emerge on the position that the party should take in the upcoming socialization debates.[16] Although the party was ultimately spared the embarrassment
of having to vote on the issue by the success with which Stinnes and the DVP
were able to sidetrack debate in the National Economic Council, the episode
nevertheless revealed just how equivocal the leaders of the DDP had become
in their attitude toward German big business. For in spite of all the success
Fischer, Siemens, and the leaders of the DDP's business wing had experienced
in securing for themselves a more influential position in the party's national
organization, the leaders of the party's left wing remained deeply antipathetic
to their efforts and were adamantly opposed to any policy that might identify
the DDP too closely with the interests of the business community. From their
perspective, the party's immediate task lay in winning the support of the more
moderate elements within the German working class, and they were apprehensive that the DDP's increasingly close identification with the German business
community might jeopardize their efforts in this direction.[17]

Ever since the November Revolution, the leaders of the DDP's left wing had
been actively involved in a concerted effort to organize the nonsocialist and
nonconfessional elements of the German working class into an independent
force within the Democratic party organization.[18] In November 1918 Gustav
Hartmann, soon to become a member of the DDP delegation to the National
Assembly and national chairman of the Hirsch-Duncker Federation of German
Labor Associations, had joined Adam Stegerwald from the Christian labor
movement in founding the German Democratic Trade-Union Federation as an
umbrella organization for all of Germany's nonsocialist unions.[19] A parallel
move had been underway within the German white-collar class since the last
years of the war and had already reached a preliminary climax with the
founding of the Alliance of Clerks' Unions (Arbeitsgemeinschaft der Kaufmännischen Verbände) in October 1916. Following the end of the war and the
formation of the Zentralarbeitsgemeinschaft, the leaders of the German white-
collar movement proceeded to found the Federation of Clerical Employee
Unions (Gewerkschaftsbund der kaufmännischen Angestelltenverbände),
which quickly affiliated itself with Stegerwald's fledgling DDGB.[20] The driving force behind the efforts to create a single trade-union federation for all of
Germany's non-socialist white-collar unions was Gustav Schneider, a member
of the Democratic delegation to the National Assembly and chairman of the

Leipzig-based Federation of German Clerks.[21] But in the summer of 1919, just as preparations for the official founding of the new white-collar union were nearing a conclusion, the leaders of the conservative German National Union of Commercial Employees announced that they were dissociating themselves from the new organization so as not to compromise the integrity of their struggle against the so-called Weimar system.[22] Shortly thereafter, the efforts to consolidate the nonsocialist forces within the German working class suffered a similar fate, as allegedly irreconcilable ideological differences between the Christian and Hirsch-Duncker labor unions led to the collapse of the DDGB.[23]

While these developments clearly revealed the extent to which prewar ideological divisions continued to frustrate the unity and effectiveness of the German labor movement, they did not deter Schneider and his associates from going ahead with their original plan for founding a new white-collar union. In November 1920 they officially founded the Federation of Employee Unions as an umbrella organization for all of those nonsocialist white-collar unions willing to work within the framework of the existing system of government in order to improve the social and economic conditions of Germany's white-collar population.[24] The founding of the GdA marked an important milestone in the DDP's efforts to establish a permanent foothold within the German white-collar movement. For although the GdA professed a policy of bipartisan neutrality and included a handful of Social Democrats among its leaders and national membership, the overwhelming majority of the new organization's leaders were affiliated with the DDP.[25] Moreover, the founding of the GdA coincided with a similar move on the part of the DDP's Anton Erkelenz to transform the Free National Labor Congress (Freiheitlich-nationaler Arbeiter-Kongreß), which he and the leaders of the Hirsch-Duncker unions had founded in the spring of 1918, into a broad-based coalition of labor, white-collar, and civil servant unions with close personal ties to the Democratic party leadership. Negotiations toward that end reached a preliminary climax in March 1920 when the leaders of the GdA, the Federation of German Labor Associations, and a handful of independent civil servant unions agreed to merge, though still preserving their organizational and juridical integrity, into the Free National Ring of German Worker, Employee, and Civil Servant Unions (Freiheitlich-nationaler Gewerkschaftsring deutscher Arbeiter-, Angestellten- und Beamtenverbände or FNG).[26]

With an initial membership of approximately 700,000, the FNG corresponded in terms of its underlying concept and basic organizational principles to the German Trade-Union Federation (Deutscher Gewerkschaftsbund or DGB) that Stegerwald and his associates were in the process of creating for the Christian labor movement. Each of these organizations represented a general coalition of working class, white-collar, and civil servant unions on the basis of a particular ideological orientation, which in the FNG's case was an un-equivocal commitment to the republican form of government as embodied in the Weimar Constitution.[27] From this perspective, therefore, the founding of the FNG in the spring of 1920 must be seen as an attempt on the part of Hartmann, Schneider, and Erkelenz to develop a solid base of organizational support within Germany's working population for the democratic principles to which their party subscribed. Their next task was to integrate the rank-and-file membership of the FNG and its affiliated unions as firmly as possible into the DDP's national organization, if for no other reason than to offset the growing influence of private business interests within the Democratic Party. Here the driving force was Erkelenz, who at the DDP's Nuremberg party congress in December 1920 proceeded to organize the working-class interests on the party's left wing into a special committee of their own called the National Workers' Council of the German Democratic Party (Reichs-Arbeitnehmeraus-schuß der Deutschen Demokratischen Partei). As the council's newly elected chairman, Erkelenz called upon the DDP to fulfill its historic mission as a party of social reconcilation by dedicating itself to the full and equitable integration of the German worker into the social and political fabric of the nation. Rejecting Marxism as a simpleminded panacea for all of Germany's economic ills, Erkelenz exhorted his party to commit itself unequivocally to a program of social and economic reform aimed at the democratization of Germany's economic system through increased rationalization, economic co-determination and self-administration, and expanded employee ownership of the means of production.[28]

The formation, on the one hand, of the DDP's National Council for Trade, Industry, and Commerce and, on the other, of its National Workers' Council bore dramatic testimony to the increasingly high degree of interest articulation that had developed within the Democratic party organization, and it con-fronted party leaders with the urgent need to draft a comprehensive social and economic program for the entire party. This task fell to none other than Walther Rathenau, one of Germany's most prolific intellectual luminaries and the scion of one of the nation's most powerful industrial dynasties. Born in 1867, the elder son of the founder and principal owner of the General Electric Company (Allgemeine Elektrizitätsgesellschaft), Rathenau had distinguished himself in the period before World War I not only as an extremely successful industrial entrepreneur but also as a highly imaginative thinker whose philo-sophical system represented a curious amalgam of the ideas of Hegel and Marx, Nietzsche and Spengler, Friedrich Naumann and Max Weber. The central thrust of Rathenau's social and economic philosophy, developed at length in a series of extended essays written during the war, was that Ger-many's postwar recovery depended upon the total reorganization of her economy and the accelerated rationalization of the nation's productive and distributive processes. This presupposed not only a high degree of coordination between the different sectors of the German economy and increased state intervention in the economic process but also the concentration of economic power in the hands of an enlightened capitalist elite whose role in the economic system was to be determined not by the accidents of inherited wealth and status but by education and merit. While Rathenau clearly recognized the need for removing all artifical barriers to the social mobility of the German working class, he showed little but disdain for the egalitarian utopias of contemporary Marxists and called instead for the creation of an organic "people's state" with an elite accessible to all social classes as its distinguishing feature.[29]

With the outbreak of World War I, Rathenau helped organize the War Raw Materials Department of the Prussian Ministry of War, a department he continued to head until the spring of 1915. Following his father's death a few months later, Rathenau became president of General Electric and continued to support the German war effort with a constant stream of memoranda on the mobilization of the nation's economic resources.[30] Still, for a variety of personal and social reasons, Rathenau remained curiously estranged from those whom he had been called upon to serve. A sentimental monarchist, as he once described himself, Rathenau became progressively disaffected from the rule of Wilhelm II and openly rejoiced at the Kaiser's demise in November 1918. While Germany's defeat and the collapse of the Second Empire no doubt did much to confirm Rathenau's deeply pessimistic cast of mind, these developments also held the promise of new and fruitful avenues of activity. On 16 November 1918 Rathenau tried to gain a wider audience for the ideas he had been expounding since the outbreak of the war by founding a new political organization named the Democratic People's League (Demokratischer Volksbund). As Rathenau explained at the league's founding ceremonies in Berlin, the purpose of this organization was not to become a new political party but rather to unite the German bourgeoisie and mobilize it against the dictatorial aspirations of Germany's socialist Left.[31] The Democratic People's League represented the full spectrum of opinion on Germany's moderate Left, and its founding manifesto carried the signatures of such luminaries as Ernst Troeltsch, Friedrich Naumann, Theodor Heuss, and Adam Stegerwald.[32] The founding of the People's League, however, was marred almost from the outset by the fact that aside from agreement to issue an appeal for the immediate convocation of a National Assembly, there was little in the way of a consensus regarding the new organization's political objectives. With the onset of efforts to found the DDP in the second half of November 1918, the situation within the People's League became increasingly uncertain as many of those who had originally rallied to its support began to dissociate themselves from it for one reason or another.[33] In the meantime, Rathenau had become so discouraged by the lack of public interest in the People's League that he decided to postpone publication of the program that he had begun to draft for its use.[34] Clearly, in view of Rathenau's own equivocation, the organization was no longer viable, and after consulting with his associates in the German electrical industry, he formally initiated its dissolution at a meeting on 26 November.[35]

Hardly more than a brief episode in the history of the German party sytem, the founding and sudden demise of the Democratic People's League reflected both Rathenau's essential estrangement from German party politics and his irresolute style of political leadership. Like many of those who had participated in the League's ill-fated founding, Rathenau subsequently joined the Democratic Party, where he found a home of sorts among the leaders of its left wing. Still, Rathenau's relationship to the party as a whole remained highly problematic. In 1919 he was denied nomination to a secure candidacy in the elections for the National Assembly by the anti-Semetic prejudices of local leaders in Liegnitz, and subsequent efforts to have his name placed on the DDP's national slate met with a similar fate.[36] By the same token, Rathenau was carefully excluded from a role in the leadership of the party, a factor that resulted in his increasing disaffection from it and its political accomplishments. Writing to an acquaintance in the fall of 1919, Rathenau complained bitterly that the DDP was nothing more than "the old Progressive People's Party in republican makeup" and that in its determination to preserve the status quo it had become hopelessly moribund and devoid of ideas.[37] Following the DDP's defeat in the 1920 Reichstag elections, Rathenau emerged as one of the leading voices for a rejuvenation of the party, although his suggestions remained characteristically abstract and vague. Claiming that the era of large-scale capitalism had passed, Rathenau called upon the DDP to accommodate itself to the realities of twentieth-century life by shedding the liberal-individualistic millstone it had inherited from the nineteenth century and becoming a "party of intellect" that found its raison d'être not in the defense of vested class interests but in pointing the way to the future.[38]

Rathenau's selection as one of the DDP's principal spokesmen on economic policy at its Nuremberg party congress in December 1920 attested to the increasingly prominent role he had come to play in German domestic politics after his appointment to the second Socialization Commission earlier that spring. In light of Rathenau's growing influence within the Fehrenbach government, the Democrats could no longer justify denying him a place among the party's notables. At Nuremberg the debate on economic policy was opened by Philipp Wieland, who as chairman of the DDP's National Council for Trade, Industry, and Commerce presented a set of recommendations for Germany's economic recovery that had been drafted by members of the DDP Reichstag delegation with close ties to the German business community. According to Wieland, the key to Germany's economic recovery lay in restoring the purchasing power of the mark and in increasing Germany's industrial and agricultural productivity. This, however, presupposed not only a sharp reduction in the overall level of government spending and the modernization of Germany's industrial infrastructure but also an immediate revision of the provisions of the Versailles Peace Treaty that pertained to Germany's economic life.[39] The general thrust of Wieland's remarks differed sharply from Rathenau's own analysis of the situation. For although both Wieland and Rathenau recognized the central importance of restoring Germany's industrial productivity, Rathenau contended that this required a far-reaching reorganization of the economy and an end to laissez-faire capitalism as it had existed during the nineteenth century. Unlike Wieland, Rathenau did not think that Germany's economic recovery was contingent upon a revision of the Versailles Treaty but insisted that the terms of the treaty left Germany with no alternative but to organize her only remaining asset—namely, her labor potential—as effectively as possible. To accomplish this, Rathenau called for the large-scale concentration of economic power along both vertical and horizontal lines in the form of cooperative associations (*Gemeinschaften*) in which not only those who owned the means of production but also those who belonged to the industrial and clerical work force would be fully represented. The question confronting Germany, concluded Rathenau, was not socialization or no socialization but whether or not she would find her way from the economic anarchy of the nineteenth century to the rationally structured organic economy that represented the wave of the future.[40]

In spite of the standing ovation that Rathenau reportedly received at the conclusion of his speech, his concept of an "organic economy" met with a cool reception from the leaders of the DDP's business wing. Though praising Rathenau for the breadth of his vision, both Otto Keinath from the Central Association of German Wholesalers and Carl Friedrich von Siemens from the Berlin electrical industry cautioned against the temptation to look upon increased organization as a panacea for Germany's economic ills and openly queried whether or not the concept of an organic economy could ever be implemented without fundamentally undermining the position of the private entrepreneur. The sharpest criticism, however, came from Wilhelm Kniest, cochairman of the party's newly created committee for the artisanry and independent middle class, and Hermann Fischer, president of the unabashedly laissez-faire Hansa-Bund. Kniest was particularly concerned about the effect that implementation of Rathenau's proposals might have upon the more traditional elements of the German middle class, while Fischer, in the bitterest polemic of all, assailed Rathenau's plans not only on account of their impracticability but also because they were not fundamentally different from the socialization schemes of Wissell, Mollendorf, and the Majority Socialists. Of the various speakers who addressed the congress on social and economic policy, only Georg Graf from the DDP's National Workers' Council evinced any genuine sympathy for Rathenau's concept of an organic economy, although even his remarks were tempered by the reservation that the concentration of economic power along the lines suggested by Rathenau might inadvertently perpetuate existing economic inequalities unless it was accompanied by measures to democratize Germany's economic structure.[41]

The debate at the Democratic party congress in Nuremberg bore vivid testimony to the lack of an effective consensus within the DDP on the social and economic issues confronting the German people. What militated so decisively against such a consensus were two not unrelated factors. In the first place, many Democrats preferred to ignore the increasingly prominent role that organized economic interests had come to play in the German party system and therefore devoted far too little attention to the task of representing the interests of those social groups upon which the DDP depended for the bulk of its electoral support. This was particularly true of those intellectuals like Wilhelm Cohnstaedt, Richard Frankfurter, and Heinrich Gerland who had played such a crucial role in shaping the DDP's self-image during the first years of its existence. Nowhere, for example, was the disdain with which this group regarded the role of organized economic interests in the German party system more apparent than in Rathenau's appeal for a party of intellect and in his proposal for a reorganization of the economy along lines that ran sharply counter to the vested economic interests of those who constituted the nucleus of the DDP's right wing.[42] Secondly, the Democrats were constantly trying to please too many separate constituencies without any clear conception as to which of these constituencies were most important for the future of the party. As the creation of special vocational committees for industry, labor, and the various sectors of the German middle class clearly revealed, the second half of 1920 witnessed a dramatic increase in the degree of interest articulation and representation within the Democratic party organization. This, however, posed a severe threat to the long-term stability of the DDP. For not only did it run counter to the general antipathy of the party's intellectual leaders toward the increasingly prominent role of organized economic interests in German political life, but they were, as the outcome of the debate at Nuremberg indicated, unable to provide a satisfactory ideological basis upon which the reconcilation of these interests might take place. As a response to the problem of integrating the diverse and potentially antagonistic interest groups that constituted the DDP's material base into an effective and durable political coalition, Rathenau's speech was woefully inadequate and only reflected the combination of diffidence and disdain with which all too many party leaders approached the entire question of interest representation.[43] Given the increasingly desperate plight in which many of those who had previously supported the DDP found themselves toward the end of 1920, this did not bode well for the future of the party.

CHAPTER EIGHT

Can the Middle Hold?

ON 20 NOVEMBER 1920 Adam Stegerwald caused a political sensation when he capped his keynote address at the tenth national congress of the Christian trade-union movement in Essen with an appeal for the creation of a new political party whose program was to be organized around four central concepts: German, Christian, democratic, and social.[1] Coming from one of Germany's foremost Catholic politicians, Stegerwald's appeal for the creation of a socially heterogeneous, interconfessional Christian people's party reflected the growing anxiety of many of Germany's more responsible political leaders over the way in which the German party system had developed since the founding of the Weimar Republic. In a more immediate sense, however, Stegerwald's appeal was directly related to three specific developments that threatened to destroy the network of political alliances or *Querverbindungen* that he and his supporters in the newly founded German Trade-Union Federation had managed to build up since the end of the war. The first and clearly most ominous of these was the growing possibility that the German Center Party might suddenly fall apart as a result of the bitter internal conflict that had erupted between its left and right wings. The Center's demise as a viable political force seemed to be foreshadowed not only by the dissolution of the parliamentary coalition between the Center and the Bavarian People's Party in January 1920 but also by the emergence of the Christian People's Party (Christliche Volkspartei) in the Rhineland and northern Bavaria and the outspoken sympathy of conservative Catholic circles for the right-wing DNVP. By the same token, the DVP's increasingly close ties to the management-controlled yellow labor unions had led to a serious deterioration of its relations with the Christian trade-union movement, as the secession of Wilhelm Gutsche and a handful of his associates from the DVP in early November 1920 clearly revealed. Similarly, the sharp swing to the right that had taken place within the German National People's Party at the time of the Kapp Putsch threatened not only to undercut the influence that the DNVP's Christian-social wing had played in the party's early development but also to drive a sharp ideological wedge between the Protestant and Catholic wings of the Christian labor movement.[2]

It was against the background of these developments that Stegerwald and the leaders of the German Trade-Union Federation decided to undertake a reform and reorganization of the German party system. At the heart of their efforts lay an eight-page memorandum entitled "Arbeiterbewegung und Politik," which the leaders of the Christian labor movement had prepared in September 1920 for the purpose of internal discussion and orientation. This document stressed the increasingly important role that the Christian trade-unions had come to play in postrevolutionary Germany as well as the extremely difficult situation in which the political fragmentation of the Christian labor movement had placed the leaders of the DGB and its affiliated unions. To remedy this situation, the memorandum proposed the creation of a "genuine people's party" that would be at least as large as the Majority Socialists and whose primary purpose would be to help the Christian unions win back the support of those workers who had gone over to the socialist labor movement since the outbreak of the war in 1914. Yet in spite of its strong working-class orientation, such a party should not be merely a workers' party but should embrace all of those who, regardless of confession or social class, were prepared to cooperate in the reconstruction of Germany on a Christian, national, democratic and social basis. Still, the consolidation of the "constructive" elements from the Protestant and Catholic camps into an interconfessional Christian people's party could only take place on the basis of the Center itself. To reform and rejuvenate the Center so that it could serve as the crystallization point around which such a party could coalesce was, the memorandum concluded, the historic task with which the Christian labor movement found itself confronted.[3]

While the ideas contained in this memorandum were fully consistent with the goals Stegerwald had espoused before the outbreak of the war, the intensity with which he began to pursue the creation of an interconfessional party in the fall of 1920 was directly related to the possibility that the Center might fall under the permanent domination of Erzberger and the leaders of its extreme left wing. Such a development would have been totally unacceptable to the profoundly conservative Stegerwald, who became increasingly anxious to develop an alternative base of operation for himself and the Christian labor movement should Erzberger succeed in gaining control of the party. Stegerwald's hopes that the Center might be persuaded to go along with his project, however, were soundly rebuffed at a meeting of the party's national committee in late October, at which time Joseph Wirth, an Erzberger protégé who had served as minister of finance since the previous spring, denounced the idea of a new political party as "downright grotesque."[4] Undaunted by the opposition of his party colleagues, Stegerwald forged ahead with his plans to use the congress that the Christian trade unions were scheduled to hold in Essen at the end of November as the forum from which he would issue his appeal for a reform and consolidation of the German party system. His speech, entitled "Die christliche Arbeiterschaft und die Lebensfragen des deutschen Volkes," opened with a panoramic description of the crisis in which Christian Europe found itself and ended with a dramatic appeal for the creation of a Christian-national people's party capable of transcending the social and confessional cleavages that had become such a prominent feature of Germany's political landscape. Inasmuch as neither the Catholic nor the Protestant sector of the population was sufficiently strong to create such a party, it was only through the consolidation of the constructive elements from both camps into a new middle party that the social, economic, and cultural rehabilitation of the German people could ever take place.[5]

Although Stegerwald's speech may have come as a disappointment to those who had hoped that he would use the Essen congress to announce the founding of a new political party, the leaders of the Christian trade-union movement quickly incorporated his recommendations into a resolution on the German party system that was subsequently known as the "Essen Program." To facili-tate implementation of this resolution, Stegerwald's associates also approved a number of specific measures, including the creation of a special newspaper for the Christian labor movement and the formation of a parliamentary action committee whose primary responsibility would be to coordinate the activity of Reichstag deputies who belonged to the Christian labor movement and lay the foundation for the founding of a new political party along the lines proposed by Stegerwald.[6] Outside of the Christian labor movement, however, the response to Stegerwald's appeal was less than encouraging. Not only was the DHV's Otto Thiel forced to defend his role in the preparation of Stegerwald's speech at a meeting of the DVP managing committee on 1 December, but at the party's Nuremberg congress a few days later he explicitly denied speculation that Stegerwald was planning to found a new political party.[7] At the same time Stresemann scrupulously avoided any mention of Stegerwald's Essen speech in his keynote address at the Nuremberg congress and confined his remarks to a general appeal for an end to the confessional schism that had frustrated Germany's quest for national unity for nearly four centuries.[8] Equally dis-heartening was the reaction to Stegerwald's speech within the right-wing DNVP, where the idea of an interconfessional Christian people's party elicited a negative response from both the leadership of the DNVP's newly created National Catholic Committee (Reichskatholikenausschuß der Deutschnatio-nalen Volkspartei) and spokesmen for white-collar and working-class elements on the party's left wing.[9]

Although the promulgation of Stegerwald's Essen Program may have pro-duced little in the way of tangible results,[10] it nevertheless brought the state of acute flux in which the German party system found itself following the 1920 Reichstag elections into dramatic focus. This state of flux was also reflected in the doubts that many prominent Democrats began to have about their own party's future. Following the DDP's disastrous performance in the 1920

Reichstag elections, the leaders of the party's right wing had openly discussed the possibility of a merger with the DVP, and in October 1920 several Saxon Democrats had actually approached Stresemann in hopes of negotiating a merger between the state organizations of their respective parties.[11] The heavy losses suffered by the DDP in the Saxon state elections on 14 November 1920 lent renewed credence to fears regarding the party's future and stimulated a revival of interest in a merger with the DVP.[12] In late November a regional party from northern Germany calling itself the Schleswig-Holstein State Party (Schleswig-Holsteinische Landespartei) officially petitioned the leaders of both the DDP and DVP on behalf of a united liberal ticket for the Prussian Landtag elections that were scheduled to take place early the following year. But when this issue was first discussed at a meeting of the DDP party council on 27 November and then again three days later at a caucus of the Democratic Reichstag delegation, it encountered strong opposition from the leaders of the party's left wing on grounds that this would discredit the DDP in the eyes of precisely those social strata upon whose support its electoral success ultimately depended.[13] At the same time, however, the leaders of the DDP's right wing—and in particular those with close ties to middle-class interest organizations such as the German Peasants' League and the Hansa-Bund—spoke strongly in favor of closer ties with the DVP and prevailed upon the party's national leadership at a meeting of the DDP executive committee on 3 December to issue at least a tentatively favorable response to the initiative from Schleswig-Holstein.[14]

As these developments clearly indicated, the Democrats were deeply divided over the DDP's future relations with the DVP. Of the party's national leaders, only Heinrich Gerland openly espoused a merger of the DDP and DVP into a united liberal party, and his efforts to stimulate discussion on the issue at the DDP's Nuremberg congress in December 1920 met with characteristic silence.[15] Still, many party leaders, including party chairman Carl Petersen, were deeply concerned about the DDP's long-term future and envisioned its eventual absorption into a comprehensive political coalition stretching, as Petersen put it in imitating Naumann's famous slogan from the early 1900's, "from Scheidemann to Stresemann."[16] Within the German People's Party, on the other hand, there was little interest in a one-sided merger with the DDP, although even among its members schemes for a far-reaching realignment of the German party system enjoyed a surprising measure of support. On 13 December Siegfried von Kardorff from the DVP Reichstag delegation and Arthur Freundt, the private secretary of industrialist Albert Vögler, met with Stresemann to discuss the creation of a new political party that would encompass elements from all of Germany's nonsocialist parties. The presence of Freundt indicated that this proposal carried not only Vögler's approval but also the imprimatur of Vögler's political mentor, Hugo Stinnes.

To be headed by a four-man directorate consisting of Stresemann, Stegerwald, Petersen, and the DNVP national chairman, this party would be based upon the principles that Stegerwald had enunciated at Essen and would include Stegerwald and Franz Behrens from the leadership of the Christian labor movement as well as prominent industrialists like Siemens, Stinnes, and the DNVP's Alfred Hugenberg. Responsibility for conducting the negotiations that were to culminate in the founding of the new party was to be in the hands of Stinnes and Stegerwald, who would first assure themselves of the cooperation of their respective associates before proceeding further.[17]

As bizarre as Kardorff's proposal for a new political party embracing elements as disparate as Stegerwald, Stinnes, and Hugenberg may have been, both it and the debate within the DDP about a merger with the DVP underscored the state of uneasiness with which the leaders of Germany's more moderate bourgeois parties viewed the development of the German party system during the first years of the Weimar Republic. From this perspective, therefore, Stegerwald's appeal for the creation of a socially comprehensive, interconfessional Christian people's party must be seen as both a symptom and a preliminary diagnosis of the structural weaknesses that were eventually to culminate in the dissolution and collapse of the Weimar party system. At the heart of this problem lay the inability of those parties that were prepared to work within the framework of the Weimar Constitution to achieve effective integration of the diverse and increasingly antagonistic social and economic interests that constituted their material base. The problem of political integration was apparent from the very founding of the Weimar Republic and could be seen not only in the severe internal crises experienced by both the DDP and the German Center Party during the first years of the republic but also in the failure of the German People's Party to absorb those Democrats who had become disillusioned with the DDP's performance as a member of the Weimar Coalition into its own organizational structure. At no point in the early history of the Weimar Republic were the integrational deficiencies of the German liberal parties more apparent than in the Prussian Landtag elections of 20 February 1921.

Like the Reich, Prussia had been governed by the parties of the Weimar Coalition since the elections to the Prussian Constitutional Assembly in late January 1919. When the Reichstag elections of June 1920 revealed that the coalition no longer enjoyed the confidence of the German electorate, however, the Prussian government came under increasingly heavy pressure from both the DVP and DNVP to dissolve the Prussian Landtag and schedule new state elections at the earliest opportunity. But when new elections were finally set for the middle of February, not only the DDP and Center but also the DVP found themselves forced onto the defensive by a particularly sharp attack from the leaders of the German Right. In opening the DNVP campaign at a rally in

Berlin's Philharmonic Hall on 9 January 1921, party chairman Oskar Hergt took special pains to include the DVP in a general condemnation of the Fehrenbach government and cited in particular its failure to block acceptance of the Spa accord as a sign of its unreliability in matters of Germany's national interest. By the same token, the DVP was also held responsible for the continuation of Erzberger's tax policies under the new minister of finance, Centrist Joseph Wirth, and for the government's failure to schedule new Prussian elections as soon as possible. All of this, concluded Hergt, suggested that the DVP was unwilling to pursue any course of action that might jeopardize the possibility of a coalition with the Majority Socialists at some point in the near future. And this, to his way of thinking, constituted nothing less than a betrayal of the mandate that the DVP had received in the June 1920 Reichstag elections.[18]

As Hergt's speech indicated, the leaders of the DNVP looked upon the Prussian state elections of February 1921 as a general referendum on the Fehrenbach government and the policies it had pursued since assuming office in the summer of 1920. Issues of foreign policy, as well as those of domestic policy, figured prominently in the Nationalist arsenal against Fehrenbach and the parties supporting his government. Of the three government parties, the DDP found itself in the most vulnerable position at the time of the Prussian elections. Still recoiling from their losses in the 1920 Reichstag elections, the Democrats were extremely pessimistic about their prospects in Prussia and feared that the upcoming state elections might bring an electoral catastrophe even more devastating than the one they had suffered the previous summer.[19] The party's position was particularly desperate in view of the fact that the Majority Socialists, upon whose cooperation the Democrats had staked their political future, persistently refused to join it and the other middle parties in a government of national reconciliation. As long as the Majority Socialists refused to enter a coalition with the German middle parties, then the DDP, as the chief exponent of such a coalition, was severely handicapped in its efforts to defend itself against the polemics of the German Right. Throughout the fall and early winter of 1920, the DDP party chairman Carl Petersen repeatedly appealed for the Majority Socialists to join the DDP, DVP, and Center in a government of the German middle stretching "from Scheidemann to Stresemann."[20] But much to his constant chagrin, the Majority Socialists remained adamant in their refusal to join a government coalition in which the DVP was also represented.

As a campaign slogan for the 1921 Prussian state elections, Petersen's appeal "from Scheidemann to Stresemann" was singularly ineffective and failed to take into cognizance the increasingly powerful antisocialist sentiment that was spreading through certain sectors of the German bourgeoisie. In general, the Democratic campaign was altogether lacking in originality and seemed ill suited to stem the flow of defections that had plagued the party since the spring and early summer of 1919. Of the four central issues around which the Democrats chose to organize their campaign, only their strong stand in favor of rural resettlement actually addressed the material interests of the DDP's potential electorate, while the other three—municipal government, school policy, and the relationship between the Reich and Prussia—were essentially political in nature and tended to ignore the growing significance that the German middle strata had come to attach to their own material self-interest.[21] This stood in sharp contrast to the campaign conducted by the DVP. For whereas the Democrats chose to relegate questions of social and economic self-interest to secondary status, the leaders of the DVP focused their campaign upon specific socioeconomic strata, first by highlighting what their party had done for those strata during the past legislative period and then by nominating representatives from those strata to prominent positions on the party's slate of candidates.[22] The effect of this strategy was not only to enhance the DVP's appeal among middle-class elements disillusioned with the DDP's performance as a member of the Weimar Coalition but also to insulate the party against the efforts of special interest organizations like the Central Association of German Home and Property Owners' Organizations (Zentralverband der Deutschen Haus- und Grundbesitzervereine) to mobilize the more traditional elements of the German middle class on behalf of a new political party.

The DDP's failure to devote sufficient attention to the material interests of the German middle strata was to prove particularly costly in term of its effectiveness within the independent middle class and small peasantry. While both of these groups were embittered by the continuation of wartime economic controls and by increasing state interference in the ecomonic process, the artisanry and small business sector also felt themselves to be the target of a discriminatory tax policy that severely impaired their ability to recover from the effects of the war. In addition to complaining about the general increase in taxation that had occurred since the end of the war, spokesmen for the independent middle class cited special taxes on sales and capital gains as well as the small business tax that state and municipal authorities had begun to impose throughout the country as instances of an ill-conceived policy that, if unchecked, could lead to the economic destruction of the German middle class.[23] Disgruntlement with the DDP was not, however, confined to the urban middle classes but also extended to the countryside, where the leaders of the German Peasants' League were in the process of reassessing their ties to the Democratic Party. In 1920 the leaders of the DBB had renewed their electoral alliance with the DDP only after a heated internal conflict that did not bode well for the future of relations between the two organizations. While relations between the DDP and DBB were already strained by the slow pace at which wartime controls over agricultural prices and production were being lifted,[24] the situation in Prussia was complicated by the fact that the Democrats belonged to a government in which the Majority Socialists occupied the all-important Ministry of Agriculture, with the result that the DDP was held responsible for the discriminatory treatment that the peasantry had allegedly suffered at the hands of the Prussian government.[25] Even though the Democrats tried to salvage what remained of their position in the countryside by publishing a special agrarian program for the Prussian state elections,[26] relations between government and peasantry in Prussia had become so strained by the beginning of 1921 that, in what amounted to a dramatic reversal of the policy pursued in the 1920 Reichstag elections, the leaders of the German Peasants' League decided not to renew their alliance with the DDP and entered the campaign for the Prussian Landtag elections without endorsing any particular political party.[27]

While the DVP's close identification with the material welfare of the German middle class tended to insulate it against many of the problems that plagued the Democratic campaign, the party nevertheless had to defend itself against a particularly vigorous offensive on the part of the right-wing DNVP.[28] The leaders of the DVP tried to counter this campaign by stressing themes such as Prussia's national calling and Prussia's historic mission at the party's "Prussian Day" in Potsdam on 9–10 January 1921.[29] At the same time, Stresemann publicly chastised the Nationalists for their refusal to join the DVP and other government parties in a "national unity front" designed to embrace all of those, including the Majority Socialists, who were prepared to set aside their domestic differences for the sake of greater national solidarity in the conduct of German foreign policy.[30] This was a theme to which Stresemann would return more and more frequently following the reception in late January of a new Allied note setting Germany's reparations bill at 242 billion gold marks and outlining a payment schedule that was to extend over the next forty-two years. Claiming that this demanded the formation of a "war cabinet" embracing all of those who had rallied behind the German war effort in the fall of 1914, the leaders of the DVP approached not only the parties that supported the Fehrenbach government but also the Majority Socialists and the DNVP about the possibility of extending the cabinet to both the Left and the Right.[31] But while Stresemann's proposal for the creation of a national unity front as a means of mobilizing domestic opposition to Allied reparations demands met with general support from the leaders of the DDP, it encountered outright rejection from both the Majority Socialists and the DNVP.[32] Seizing upon the DNVP's refusal to participate in the formation of such a front as a sign of its unreliability in matters of Germany's national interest, Stresemann and the leaders of the DVP publicly assailed the Nationalists for having placed short-term electoral gains before the need for national unity in the face of Allied pressure.[33]

Hergt's refusal to join the People's Party in the formation of a national unity front stretching from the DNVP to the Majority Socialists came as a severe disappointment to the industrial interests on the DVP's right wing. In spite of the fact that the two right-wing parties had grown further and further apart following the formation of the Fehrenbach government, Vögler and the leaders of the DVP's right wing still hoped that the creation of such a front might reverse this trend and prepare the way for the reestablishment of closer political ties between the DVP and DNVP.[34] At the same time, however, the DVP found its financial resources for the Prussian campaign sharply limited by the general opposition of influential sectors within the German industrial establishment to the idea of closer collaboration with the Social Democrats. In an attempt to supplement the 1.3 million marks that the DVP had received from the Curatorium for the Reconstruction of German Economic Life,[35] Stresemann and his associates not only appealed directly to the leaders of German heavy industry for assistance in meeting the rising costs of maintaining their party's national organization but also demonstrated a remarkable willingness to accommodate the wishes of heavy industry in the nomination of candidates for the Prussian Landtag elections.[36] But the coal and steel interests that dictated the policies of the more conservative Commission for the Industrial Campaign Fund were so incensed over the DVP's apparent willingness to join the Majority Socialists in the creation of a national unity front that in the allocation of funds for use in the Prussian campaign they began to discriminate against the DVP in favor of the DNVP.[37] While the precise effect this may have had upon the outcome of the election is not clear, the fact nevertheless remains that the overall effectiveness of the DVP's Prussian campaign was handicapped by the discriminatory financing policies of Germany's more conservative industrial magnates.

Whereas the Democrats were content to structure their campaign around issues that were essentially Prussian in scope and focus, neither the DVP nor the DNVP was the least bit reluctant to inject national issues into the Prussian campaign. The DVP's agitation on behalf of a national unity front, for example, was carefully designed to undercut the effectiveness of Nationalist propaganda against the Fehrenbach government and the parties that supported it. In the final analysis, however, neither this nor the Democrats' appeal for the creation of a front from Scheidemann to Stresemann was able to prevent the Nationalists from scoring a decisive victory at the polls on 20 February. As far as the bourgeois parties were concerned, the most noteworthy features of the election outcome were the continued decline of the German Democratic Party and the surprisingly heavy losses sustained by the People's Party. The DDP lost 16.9 percent of the popular vote it had received in the 1920 Reichstag elections, and the DVP saw its share of the popular vote reduced by 8.7 percent. At the same time, the Nationalists were able to increase their popular vote by 17.2 percent, thereby accounting for more than 95 percent of the combined losses of the two liberal parties. What this indicated was that the swing to the right that had manifested itself so vividly in the DDP's heavy losses to the DVP and DNVP in the 1920 Reichstag elections had now begun to embrace the People's Party as well. The DVP's losses, for example, were heaviest in those districts such as Berlin (− 19.8 percent), Potsdam II (− 18 percent), Frankfurt an der Oder (− 16.8 percent), and Pomerania (− 27.7 percent) where the Nationalists had recorded their strongest gains. The DDP's losses, on the other hand, tended to be more evenly distributed throughout the state. Only in five districts—Frankfurt an der Oder (− 30.6 percent), Pomerania (− 26.3 percent), Liegnitz (− 26.3 percent), Hanover-East (− 30 percent), and Düsseldorf-West (− 35.5 percent)—were Democratic losses significantly higher than the statewide average of 16.9 percent, while in five other districts the Democrats were able to hold their losses to less than ten percent of their party's 1920 total. Still, the Democrats saw their share of the popular vote shrink to a pitiful 6.2 percent, while the People's Party, though handicapped by its association with the Fehrenbach government, at least managed to poll 14.2 percent and remained a formidable force in Prussian politics. In both cases, the principal beneficiary of the liberal parties' disappointing performance at the polls was the German National People's Party, which, with 19.1 percent of the total popular vote, now stood behind the Majority Socialists as the second largest party in the Prussian Landtag.[38]

The outcome of the Prussian Landtag elections bore dramatic witness to the increasing disillusionment of the German electorate with both the DDP and DVP and foreshadowed the difficulties that each was to experience over the course of the next several years. Not only did the election results confirm the continued decline of the German Democratic Party, but more significantly they also revealed the failure of the People's Party to attract and retain the support of those middle-class voters who had become disenchanted with the DDP over the course of the previous two years. Originally attracted to the DVP, these voters were now in the process of moving even further to the Right.[39] In assessing their party's performance in the Prussian elections, however, the leaders of the DVP tended to ignore the losses they had suffered since the 1920 Reichstag elections and took solace in the fact that, though a member of the government, their party had managed to escape the fate that befell the DDP following its overwhelming victory in the elections to the National Assembly. Whatever losses the DVP did sustain were attributed to deficiencies in its party organization, the loss of its privileged position as an opposition party, and the demagoguery of the DNVP.[40] In contrast to the apparent equanimity with which the leaders of the DVP accepted their party's losses, the Democrats were genuinely alarmed at the outcome of the Prussian elections. For not only did it seem their efforts to reorganize the DDP following its defeat in the 1920 Reichstag elections had been woefully inadequate, but the election results did much to exacerbate the differences that separated the party's left and right

wings. The party's more conservative leaders regarded the DDP's close identification with the Social Democrats as the principal cause of its electoral
collapse and argued that only a complete and unequivocal break with the
socialist Left would enable it to survive as a viable political force.[41] The
leaders of the DDP's left wing, on the other hand, attributed their party's losses
to the wave of antisocialist sentiment that was currently sweeping the German
middle class and urged the party leadership to resist pressure for a break with
the Majority Socialists for fear that this might drive a permanent wedge
between the socialist working class and the new republican order.[42] Under the
shock of defeat, the unity of the party began to unravel.

A further consequence of the Prussian election was that it severely weakened the position of the Fehrenbach government and led to renewed pressure
from both the Left and Right for a reorganization of the cabinet. Under these
circumstances, efforts to form a new government in Prussia became inextricably linked to a reorganization of the national government under Fehrenbach.
Although a continuation of the Weimar Coalition in Prussia was still techni-
cally possible, both the Center and the DDP felt that this was no longer
feasible in light of the election results and favored a solution whereby the
Majority Socialists would join the national government at the same time that
the Prussian government was broadened to include the DVP.[43] The leaders of
the DVP, on the other hand, were opposed to any solution that might result in a
"one-sided extension" of the Fehrenbach government to the Left and revived
their proposal for the creation of a national unity front stretching from the
Majority Socialists to the DNVP as an alternative to proposals for the reorganization of the Prussian and national governments on the basis of the "Great
Coalition."[44] Regarding the creation of such a front as a national necessity in
view of the impasse that had developed in Germany's reparations negotiations
with the Allies, Stresemann requested that the formation of the new government in Prussia as well as the reorganization of the Fehrenbach government be
postponed until after he had had an opportunity to explore the idea of a
national unity front with the leaders of the DNVP and Majority Socialists.[45]
Though skeptical about the ultimate success of such a move, the Democrats
readily supported Stresemann's request,[46] and on 2 March he, along with two
other members of the DVP Reichstag delegation, met with Hergt, Helfferich,
and Count Kuno von Westarp from the DNVP national leadership in an
attempt to establish the conditions under which they might be willing to
participate in the formation of such a front. In sharp contrast to the position
they had taken during the Prussian campaign, the Nationalists now indicated
that they were prepared to join the Majority Socialists and the parties supporting the Fehrenbach government in the formation of a national unity front along
the lines suggested by Stresemann should developments on the international
scene warrant such a step.[47]

On March 7 Hermann Müller, chairman of the Social Democratic delegation to the Reichstag, ended all speculation about the formation of a national unity front when he announced that under no circumstances would his party participate in a government in which the People's Party was also represented.[48] Two days later Allied troops occupied Düsseldorf, Duisburg, and Ruhrort in an attempt to pressure a reluctant German government into accepting a long-term settlement of the reparations question. With these two developments, negotiations to form a new government in Prussia reached an impasse that was not to be broken for another six weeks. In the meantime, both the parties and the process by which the government was being formed came under increasingly sharp criticism. When the impasse was finally broken in the middle of April, the final result could hardly have been less reassuring to the defenders of Germany's fledgling parliamentary democracy. For whereas the various parties from the Majority Socialists to the DNVP were able to agree upon Adam Stegerwald as the new Prussian minister president, his own efforts to form a broad-based coalition government capable of commanding a parliamentary majority were repeatedly frustrated by the intransigence of the Social Democrats, DVP, and DNVP. As a result, only the Center and the DDP were willing to enter the government that he finally presented to the Landtag on 22 April.[49] In the final analysis, the net effect of the Prussian cabinet crisis and the manner in which it was eventually resolved was only to undermine public confidence in Germany's new republican order and to lend renewed credence to those who maintained that the parliamentary system was incapable of providing Germany with the effective political leadership she so sorely needed in her hour of national distress.

CHAPTER NINE

The Politics of Frustration

THE INABILITY OF THE Weimar party system to generate stable parliamentary majorities did much to compromise its legitimacy even in the eyes of the republic's most devoted adherents. With the Allied occupation of Düsseldorf, Duisberg, and Ruhrort in early March 1921, however, the problem of forming stable parliamentary coalitions was complicated by the intrusion of what was commonly referred to as the national question. Both the DDP and DVP had used nationalism as a common denominator upon which the diverse and potentially antagonistic social and economic interests that constituted their material base could unite. But as the DDP's experience during the conflict over the ratification of the Versailles Peace Treaty clearly revealed, nationalism was a highly volatile issue, as capable of dividing a party as it was of uniting it. At no point during the first years of the Weimar Republic was the destabilizing effect of nationalism upon the integrative potential of the two liberal parties more apparent than in the seven months that stretched from the occupation of the three cities on the right bank of the Rhine in the spring of 1921 to the partition of Upper Silesia in the fall of that year.

Allied action on the right bank of the Rhine made it impossible for the Fehrenbach government to continue ignoring Allied pressure for a settlement of the reparations question as it had done during its first nine months in office. At the same time, however, the Allied decision to cross the Rhine had also done much to stiffen German opposition to an accommodation with the Entente. Not only did leaders of the DVP find themselves under increasingly heavy pressure from their party's rank-and-file membership for a strong response to Allied demands on reparations and disarmament,[1] but the Democrats, who were far more favorably disposed to Fehrenbach's continuance in office than the DVP, criticized the government's passivity in foreign affairs and urged it to adopt a firmer position in its negotiations with the Entente.[2] Reluctant in the light of such sentiment to accept the terms that the Allies had presented at London early in March, Fehrenbach pinned his hopes of remaining in office on American mediation in his country's dispute with the Entente. But when the Harding administration announced that it did not look upon the German counterproposal of 25 April as an acceptable basis for discussion with the Allies, Fehrenbach's position became untenable, and on 4 May he announced his government's resignation despite Democratic entreaties that it remain in office.[3]

As the hopelessness of Fehrenbach's position became more and more apparent, Stresemann began to lay the foundation for the formation of a new
government with himself as chancellor. Like its predecessor, the government
Stresemann hoped to form would be a minority government consisting of
representatives from the DDP, DVP, and Center. But unlike its predecessor,
Stresemann's prospective government would exchange the toleration of the
Majority Socialists for that of the right-wing DNVP, whose leaders had assured him of their support should he be called upon to form a new government.
By the same token, Stresemann also hoped to entice one or more prominent
German industrialists into joining his cabinet.[4] But whatever plans Stresemann may have had for forming a new government were dealt a shattering
blow when on 5 May the Allied Supreme Council in London sent Germany an
ultimatum that threatened occupation of the entire Ruhr basin if Germany did
not accept an Allied schedule of payment of reparations that set Germany's
total obligation at 132 billion gold marks. The ultimatum was to expire on the
morning of 11 May, at which time occupation of the Ruhr would commence.[5]

While all of the German parties from the Independent Socialists to the
Nationalists were unanimous in their condemnation of the London Ultimatum,
the consequences of rejecting the ultimatum were far from clear. Above all
else, the Germans feared that rejection of the Allied ultimatum would lead not
only to the occupation of the Ruhr but also to the loss of Upper Silesia, where
on 3 May an uprising had broken out under the leadership of the Polish
nationalist Wojcieck Korfanty.[6] Faced with the possible loss of Upper Silesia
and the threat of Allied action in the Ruhr, the parliamentary delegations of the
Center and two socialist parties decided by overwhelming majorities to vote
for acceptance of the London Ultimatum, thereby virtually assuring it of a
Reichstag majority in favor of acceptance. This turn of events spelled the
collapse of Stresemann's hopes that he might be asked to form a new government with himself at its helm. For how could Stresemann, who was publicly
committed to a policy of firmer resistance to Allied demands, assume the
leadership of a government whose first item of business would be acceptance
and implementation of the London Ultimatum?

On 8 May Stresemann informed the leaders of the other government parties
that he could not assume responsibility for the formation of a new government
if that also meant that he and his party would have to vote for the unconditional
acceptance of the London Ultimatum. In hopes of salvaging what still remained of his chances at the chancellorship, Stresemann suggested that he be
authorized to approach the British in an attempt to secure concessions that
might make it posssible for him to support acceptance of the ultimatum in the
Reichstag. Above all else, Stresemann sought specific guarantees regarding
the suspension of Allied sanctions in the Ruhr and the future of Upper Silesia
in addition to a general declaration that Germany's reparations obligations

under the Versailles Treaty were not, as the terms of the Allied ultimatum seemed to imply, unlimited.[7] Ignoring the coolness with which the leaders of the Center received his suggestion, Stresemann proceeded to the British embassy in Berlin, where he delivered his proposal early the following day. Whatever hopes Stresemann might have had of softening the Allied position, however, proved vain, for it was not until the day after expiration of the 11 May deadline that the British government indicated its willingness to go along with Stresemann's recommendations for a clarification of the ultimatum.[8]

By delaying their response until after the ultimatum had expired, the British effectively sealed the fate of Stresemann's bid for the chancellorship, and on 10 May he read a statement on behalf of the DVP Reichstag delegation indicating that it would vote against acceptance of the London Ultimatum. As reasons for the DVP's position, Stresemann cited the catastrophic effect that acceptance of the ultimatum would have upon Germany's precarious economic situation as well as the Allies' failure to provide any guarantees regarding the future of Upper Silesia.[9] By no means, however, did Stresemann's position enjoy the undivided support of his own colleagues in the DVP. At a heated caucus of the DVP Reichstag delegation on the evening of 9 May, six members of the delegation—Heinze, Kardorff, Raumer, Thiel, Katharina von Obheim, and Werner von Rheinbaben—announced that they were not prepared to accept the consequences to which rejection of the Allied ultimatum might lead and indicated that they would vote in favor of its acceptance in the Reichstag. Then, when the decisive parliamentary vote took place on the evening of 10 May, these six were joined by eight other members of the delegation, who instead of voting against the London Ultimatum manifested their dissatisfaction with Stresemann's political course by absenting themselves from the parliamentary chamber at the moment the critical vote was taken.[10] All of this pointed to the existence of a substantial minority within the DVP Reichstag delegation that had begun to substitute a more realistic approach to the conduct of German foreign policy for the facile jingoism of Germany's nationalist Right.

If the conflict over acceptance or rejection of the London Ultimatum produced a sharp split within the ranks of the DVP, it produced an even sharper one among the Democrats. Ever since the DDP's ill-fated attempt in the summer of 1919 to place itself at the head of the movement of national protest against the Versailles Peace Treaty, a small yet highly influential group within the Democratic leadership had pressed for a fundamental reassessment of the DDP's position on matters of foreign policy. At the head of this group stood Erich Koch-Weser, Eugen Schiffer, and party chairman Carl Petersen, and what they hoped to do was to replace the emotional nationalism that had characterized the party's fight against Versailles with a more realistic approach to Germany's diplomatic situation. Since such an outlook ran strongly counter to the prevailing sentiment within both the Democratic delegation to the Reichstag and the party organization as a whole, the conflict over the London Ultimatum was to serve as yet another test of the DDP's internal cohesiveness. When the Democrats first discussed the ultimatum at a meeting of the Reichstag delegation on 5 May, Conrad Haußmann immediately challenged suggestions that the Democrats should become more circumspect in their responses to Allied demands by urging the party to establish itself as the nucleus around which all of those who rejected the ultimatum could unite.[11] Resuming his offensive at a subsequent meeting of the delegation four days later, Haußmann contended not only that the terms of the ultimatum exceeded Germany's economic capacity for fulfillment but also that by extending the schedule for payment of reparations over the next thirty years the Allies had unilaterally revised the terms of the Versailles Treaty in a move of dubious legal validity. Moreover, Haußmann argued that those who supported acceptance of the ultimatum had greatly overestimated the consequences that would result from its rejection and maintained that the persistence of the postwar economic crisis would work in favor of moderation on the part of the Allies.[12]

Haußmann's arguments against acceptance of the Allied ultimatum found strong support in virtually all sectors of the party. Fearful of the impact that acceptance of the ultimatum might have upon Germany's economic situation, the leaders of the DDP's business wing were quick to rally to Haußmann's support. Even more surprising, however, was the strong backing Haußmann received from Erkelenz, Bäumer, and those who regarded themselves as the heirs to Naumann's national-social legacy. By the same token, the *Realpolitiker* who recognized compliance with the terms of the London Ultimatum as the only basis for the future conduct of German foreign policy also included prominent spokesmen from both wings of the party. The advocates of acceptance included not only men from the DDP's left wing, like Walther Schücking, a renowned pacifist who had led the party's crusade against ratification of the Versailles Treaty in the summer of 1919, and historian Walter Goetz, but also Defense Minister Otto Gessler and the former treasurer Georg Gothein, both of whom actively supported Koch-Weser and Schiffer in their efforts to reorient the DDP in the direction of a more realistic assessment of Germany's foreign policy prospects.[13] With the lines of disagreement cutting across all of the social and ideological cleavages within the party, it proved impossible to maintain unity, and in the decisive caucus on the evening of 9 May the delegation split 16–12 in favor of rejecting the ultimatum. In the Reichstag vote on the following night twenty-one members of the delegation voted for rejection and seventeen for acceptance of the Allied ultimatum.[14]

The fact that nearly half of the Democratic delegation was willing to accept the London Ultimatum bore visible testimony to the process of political maturation that had taken place at the upper echelons of the party leadership. Still, the party's failure to present a unified front in the vote on the ultimatum left it exposed to charges of indecisiveness and unreliability in matters of Germany's national interest. The damage this did to the DDP's political credibility was compounded by the confused and uncertain policy the party pursued in the negotiations to form a new government. Ideally, the Democrats would have preferred to see the Fehrenbach government remain in office.[15] Reich President Ebert, on the other hand, did not regard the Fehrenbach government as suitable for the implementation of the Allied ultimatum and therefore rejected a Democratic proposal that it remain in office with the explanation that the Allies would not honor Fehrenbach's signature on a document accepting the terms of the London Ultimatum. As it became clear on the night of 9 May that neither the DVP nor a majority in the DDP was prepared to vote for acceptance of the Allied ultimatum, Ebert called upon Centrist Joseph Wirth to form a new government, which he hoped would possess the credibilty necessary to accept and implement the terms of the Allied ultimatum. Such a government would be drawn from those parties prepared to vote for acceptance of the ultimatum in the Reichstag.[16]

At forty-two, the youngest person ever to assume the office of chancellor, Wirth was a politician of impeccable republican credentials who stood on the extreme left wing of the German Center Party and enjoyed the full confidence of both Ebert and the leaders of the Majority Socialist delegation to the Reichstag.[17] His appointment as chancellor in the spring of 1921 was predicated above all else upon his willingness to accept and implement the terms of the London Ultimatum. A political realist who held little sympathy for the histrionics of the nationalist Right, Wirth was convinced that even if fulfillment of the London Ultimatum was not possible in light of Germany's weakened economic condition, compliance was still necessary to demonstrate Germany's good faith and create an environment in which the revision of Versailles might take place. Having already served for more than a year as finance minister, Wirth was also fully aware of the far-reaching changes that implementation of the London Ultimatum would necessitate in Germany's domestic tax structure. In this respect, Wirth was determined that Germany's reparations burden should be distributed as equitably as possible among the various strata of German society, whereby he not only envisaged new property and income taxes but also encouraged Social Democratic schemes for the "seizure of real assets" (*Erfassung der Sachwerte*) through the partial nationalization of industrial stocks and bonds as a means of tapping those forms of wealth whose value had not been materially affected by the decline of the mark since the beginning of the war.[18]

Wirth's appointment as chancellor ran into strong opposition from both the DDP and DVP. Much of the animus toward Wirth stemmed from his close association with Erzberger, and the leaders of the two liberal parties tended to look upon the Wirth government as little more than an Erzberger government in disguise.[19] Moreover, liberal politicians were fearful that Wirth's dependence upon the Social Democrats would lead him to implement the terms of the London Ultimatum by means of fiscal legislation detrimental to the propertied interests that their parties represented.[20] While the People's Party was quick and unequivocal in its denunciation of the Wirth government and instructed its Reichstag deputies not to take part in any negotiations aimed at bringing the DVP into the government,[21] the Democrats were divided between those like Schiffer and Petersen who were prepared to enter the government in order to prevent new elections from being called and those like Koch-Weser who opposed the DDP's entry into the government on the grounds that without the DVP the Democrats would be too weak to sustain themselves against the Center and Majority Socialists.[22] In the initial stages of the negotiations to form a new government the DDP's antipathy toward Wirth prevailed over its fear of new elections, and on 10 May the party's Reichstag delegation rejected an invitation to join the government that Wirth was in the process of organizing by a decisive two-to-one margin.[23] Although the Democrats subsequently softened their position by allowing Gessler to remain in the Cabinet as minister of defense, this did not satisfy Wirth, who, under heavy pressure from the leaders of his own party, informed the Democrats on the afternoon of 10 May that he would abandon his efforts to form a new government if they persisted in their refusal to let a second Democrat, namely Schiffer, join his cabinet as the minister of justice. This was accompanied by threats from Ebert that he would resign the presidency if a new government had not been formed by the time the Reichstag began its deliberations later that evening. The Democrats were simply unable to withstand pressure of this magnitude, and at an emergency session held less than an hour before the convocation of the Reichstag the DDP delegation agreed by a 16–12 margin to let Schiffer enter the government in what constituted a dramatic reversal of the position it had taken earlier in the day.[24]

The Democrats defended their decision to participate in the formation of the Wirth government as an act of political self-sacrifice in which they had placed the welfare of the nation as a whole before the best interests of their party.[25] Still, the fact that the Democrats had arrived at this decision only after having voted first to reject the Allied ultimatum and then not to join the Wirth government created considerable confusion throughout the party organization.[26] And this confusion was not alleviated by Wirth's decision to appoint the DDP's Walther Rathenau as his minister of reconstruction in late May 1921. For while Rathenau's appointment should have strengthened the DDP's ties to the Wirth government, Rathenau himself was something of an outsider as far as the DDP was concerned and did not belong to the inner circle of Democratic party leaders. His appointment, therefore, constituted something of an embarrassment to the party leadership by appearing to tie the DDP all the more closely to the Wirth government without giving it any greater influence over the formulation and execution of its policies.[27] To compensate for their lack of influence over the policies of Wirth and his associates, the Democrats would have liked to entice the DVP into joining the government, but they were unable to overcome Stresemann's deep-seated hostility toward the new chancellor.[28] Nonetheless, Stresemann was quick to appreciate the difficult situation in which the Democrats found themselves and carefully refrained from an open polemic that might have forced them out of the government for fear that this might lead to new elections in which the Majority Socialists would score major gains.[29] The DVP also agreed not to support a Nationalist motion of no-confidence in the Wirth government, thereby sparing the government the ordeal of an open parliamentary challenge and saving the Democrats from the embarrassment of another split in the Reichstag.[30]

For his own part, Wirth was willing to drop his support of Social Democratic schemes for the seizure of real assets so as not to alienate the more moderate bourgeois elements that might still be won over to the support of his foreign policy.[31] At the same time, however, his own government remained deeply divided over the details of his tax program, and his failure to outline precisely how he intended to raise the revenue necessary to meet Allied reparations demands did much to shake international confidence in his ability to carry through the domestic reforms upon which the fate of his foreign policy ultimately rested. The position of the Wirth government was further weakened by the fact that acceptance of the London Ultimatum had led to a resumption of the inflationary spiral that had already produced a dramatic devaluation of the German mark.[32] The leaders of the DVP were particularly fearful that a further deterioration in the purchasing power and exchange value of the mark might radicalize those middle-class elements upon which their party depended for the bulk of its popular support, with the result that they began to pursue the possibility of entering the Wirth government with increased interest. At the very least, this would afford them an opportunity to help shape the government's tax program, in which case they were fully prepared to go along with government proposals for the increased taxation of propertied wealth in order to fulfill the terms of the London Ultimatum. This, in the eyes of Stresemann and other DVP moderates, was clearly preferable to the inflation and the incalculable damage it threatened to inflict upon their party's rank and file.[33]

By giving Germany her first majority government since the demise of the Weimar Coalition, the DVP's entry into the Wirth government in the fall of 1921 would have done much to renew public confidence in the principles of parliamentary democracy. Efforts to broaden the government's parliamentary base, however, were temporarily interrupted by news of Erzberger's brutal assassination on 24 August. In giving vent to the deep-seated anger that he felt at the murder of his friend and former mentor, Wirth launched into a bitter attack against the German Right that did much to offend the more conservative elements within the DVP.[34] In an attempt to repair the damage that Erzberger's assassination had done to their party's prospects of entering the government, the leaders of the DVP issued a series of public statements reaffirming their loyalty to the Weimar Constitution and their willingness to defend it against the use of force from both the Left and the Right.[35] Stresemann was fearful that Erzberger's assassination might provoke a sharp swing to the left on the part of the Wirth government, and conciliatory gestures like this were clearly designed to avert such a danger and to maintain lines of communication with Wirth and his supporters.[36]

If Stresemann hoped to minimize the impact of Erzberger's assassination upon his party's chances of entering the government, then Wirth, on the other hand, had good reasons of his own for hoping that an accommodation with the DVP might still be possible. Acting primarily on his own initiative, Wirth had approached the leaders of the German industrial establishment in the summer of 1921 about the possibility of using industry's credit abroad to guarantee an international loan that would make it possible for the German government to raise the money necessary to fulfill the terms of the London Ultimatum. The London Ultimatum had done much to depress the exchange value of the German mark by stipulating that reparations payments, insofar as they were not to take place in kind, were to be made in foreign currencies. Wirth hoped to get around the problems that such a stipulation posed to the stability of the German mark by offering the German industrial establishment substantial tax benefits in return for its help in securing an international loan of 1.5 billion gold marks that was to be used in paying the next reparations installment due in January 1922. Seeing in Wirth's proposal an opportunity to undercut government plans for the seizure of industrial assets, the leaders of the German industrial establishment indicated their willingness—first in the summer of 1921 and then later at a meeting of the presidium and executive committee of the National Federation of German Industry on 13 September—to assist the Wirth government in meeting the next payment deadline. While no political conditions were attached to industry's willingness to help float the government loan, it was generally understood that the DVP would be invited to join the national government as a guarantee against any sudden shift to the left.[37]

From the very outset, the fate of the industrial credit action was inseparably intertwined with that of the DVP's efforts to enter the Wirth government. This, however, presupposed a general understanding between the DVP and other government parties on the scope and nature of the proposed tax reform. In this respect, the Majority Socialists were insistent that the DVP commit itself in advance to the possibility of heavier property taxes and the eventual seizure of real assets.[38] An item of further concern was the DVP's persistent failure to make an unequivocal declaration of loyalty to the republican form of government, although here the Democrats were willing to accept a simple statement recognizing the Weimar Constitution as the basis of all German law in lieu of a programmatic endorsement of the republic as the ideal form of government for the German people.[39] Ultimately, however, the decision as to whether or not negotiations aimed at bringing the DVP into the government were to take place lay with the Majority Socialists, who up to this point had demonstrated little enthusiasm for either the industrial credit action or proposals to broaden the basis of the governmental coalition. On the other hand, many socialist leaders had become so disenchanted with the DDP's erratic performance as a coalition partner that their opposition to collaboration with the DVP had begun to soften in the hope that it might become the party they had hoped the DDP would be. This set the scene for a dramatic reversal of strategy at the party congress held by the Majority Socialists in Görlitz in the third week of September. In what represented a radical departure from their standing refusal to participate in a government in which the DVP was also represented, the Majority Socialists adopted a resolution affirming their willingness to cooperate with any party that accepted certain minimal demands related to the consolidation and expansion of what had already been achieved in the area of social and economic reform. That this resolution was adopted with the German People's Party in mind was made abundantly clear by the arguments with which the Majority Socialists defended their sudden volte-face.[40]

The Democrats hailed the Görlitz resolution as one of the most significant developments of the postwar period and immediately renewed their appeal for the creation of a comprehensive political front reaching from Scheidemann to Stresemann.[41] Within the People's Party, on the other hand, the situation was somewhat more clouded. For while political moderates like former economics minister Hans von Raumer shared Stresemann's conviction that the long-term political advantages to be gained by joining the government far outweighed whatever concessions the DVP might have to make in tax and economic policy,[42] the manufacturing and commercial interests that constituted the nucleus of the DVP's right wing were extremely evasive when it came to governmental proposals for new taxes that might increase the costs of production.[43] Moreover, the DVP also included men like Stinnes and Vögler who were opposed to any encumbrance of industrial assets for the payment of reparations and therefore rejected the very objectives of the industrial credit action that Wirth had discussed with the leaders of the National Federation of German Industry in early September. Although Stinnes and his supporters remained virtually isolated in the deliberations that took place within the RDI during the first half of September, their position within the DVP afforded them an excellent opportunity to obstruct implementation of the industrial credit action by sabotaging Stresemann's efforts to reach an accommodation with the Wirth government.[44]

The first meeting between representatives from the government and the

DVP took place on 28 September in the presence of Reich President Ebert. General agreement was quickly reached on most important issues, as the DVP conceded the necessity of speeding up collection of the Reich Emergency Levy and introducing new taxes aimed at Germany's propertied wealth. In addition, the DVP indicated a general willingness to go along with proposals for the seizure of real assets if such an action was necessary to stabilize the mark and fulfill Germany's reparations obligations.[45] On the same day, the general membership of the National Federation of German Industry met in Munich to approve the basic outlines of the tentative agreement its leaders had reached with Wirth on the use of industrial credit to float an international loan that would enable the German government to meet the next installment in the schedule of reparations payments established by the London Ultimatum.[46] When negotiations between the government and the DVP were resumed on 3 October, however, serious complications developed as the Social Democrats began to press for the seizure of real assets as a guarantee against the possibility, if not the likelihood, that the industrial credit action might fail.[47] Although Stresemann, in reporting back to his party later that afternoon, took special pains to minimize the differences that had surfaced in his negotiations with the government,[48] the incident nevertheless touched upon the Achilles' heel of Wirth's efforts to reach an accommodation with the DVP.

As Stresemann explained in a letter to industrialist Carl Duisberg, the DVP's entry into the government was necessary to prevent the Social Democrats from reestablishing themselves as the dominant force in Germany's political life. By entering the government, the DVP would not only make it impossible for the Social Democrats to outvote the nonsocialist members of the cabinet but would also keep the Center and DDP from slipping under the control of elements sympathetic to socialist proposals for social and economic reform. In both cases, the bourgeois element in German politics would be decisively strengthened.[49] Yet even as Stresemann was writing these lines the chances that the DVP might enter the government were being profoundly affected by developments beyond his control. In the spring of 1921 the League of Nations had conducted a plebiscite in the former Prussian province of Upper Silesia in order to determine whether its inhabitants would prefer remaining in Germany or becoming part of the new Polish republic. Although the outcome of the plebiscite made the partition of the province inevitable, the issue remained unsettled until early September 1921 when the League commissioned a panel of experts to draft a boundary line for partition of the province. When details of the report were forwarded to the Supreme Council of the League of Nations on 12 October, German fears that it would result in the loss of the province's industrial areas proved fully vindicated. For the report drew a boundary line through the province's so-called industrial triangle that placed three-fourths of the mines and ore deposits of Upper Silesia as well as most of the area's industrial installations under Polish sovereignty. With the official acceptance of this report three day later by the Allied Council of Ambassadors, the partition of Upper Silesia and the transfer of its industrial wealth from German to Polish hands became final, although it was not until 20 October that the German government received the terms of the Allied decision.[50]

The Allied decision over Upper Silesia provoked a storm of protest throughout Germany that both complicated Wirth's efforts to reorganize his government and placed the future of the industrial credit action in immediate jeopardy. Moreover, the partition of Upper Silesia drove a deep wedge within the government between those like Rathenau who felt that Wirth had no choice but to honor his oft-repeated pledge to resign in the event of an unfavorable decision on Upper Silesia and the Majority Socialists who wanted to avoid a cabinet crisis so that they could proceed with their plans for a reform of the German tax system.[51] Feeling that the Wirth government should resign as a protest against the Allied partition of Upper Silesia was widespread within both liberal parties, where resentment over Upper Silesia combined with opposition to the government's tax policies to produce a strong bloc of anti-government sentiment. At a conference of Democratic party leaders on 13 October, the tone was set by Haußmann, Gothein, and Keinath from the party's right wing, all of whom argued that it would be impossible for the Wirth government to remain in office should the decision on Upper Silesia—whose terms were not yet known—prove incompatible with Germany's national interest. Only the calmer and more patient voices of Rathenau, Schiffer, and party chairman Petersen kept the Democrats from forcing the issue with a public resolution that might have caused the Wirth government even further embarrassment.[52]

Within the DVP the situation was even more threatening. On 17 October Kurt Sorge, president of the National Federation of German Industry and a member of the DVP Reichstag delegation, wrote to Stresemann that the fate of the industrial credit action could only be negatively affected by an unfavorable decision in the Upper Silesian question. At the same time Sorge cautioned Stresemann against making a final decision on the DVP's entry into the government as long as the identity of the new chancellor and the program he intended to pursue were still uncertain. While Sorge did not preclude the possibility of participating in a government with Wirth as chancellor, his remarks made it clear that he and the industrial interests for which he spoke regarded Wirth's reappointment as chancellor as politically undesirable in light of the stunning defeat which his foreign policy had suffered in the Upper Silesian question.[53] At a meeting of the DVP Reichstag delegation on the following day, an overwhelming majority of the delegation rejected any suggestion of a compromise with Wirth and made the DVP's entry into the government conditional upon his resignation as chancellor. Only Raumer was willing to accept Wirth's reappointment as head of the government, but he was completely isolated in the face of the vigorous offensive launched by Stinnes and the anti-Wirth forces on the DVP's right wing.[54]

When the Reichstag reconvened after its summer recess on 20 October, the prospects for a break in the deadlock that had developed in the negotiations to form a new government were dealt a severe blow by the arrival of the Allied note containing the final details of the plan for the partition of Upper Silesia. With the arrival of the Allied note, discussion within the DDP—as within the DVP—began to focus more and more upon the person of Wirth.[55] For while the Democrats were generally more favorably disposed toward Wirth than were the leaders of the DVP, they regarded the way in which the Allies had partitioned Upper Silesia as such an affront to Germany's national honor that only the resignation of the entire Wirth government could possibly express the sense of national indignation to which the Allied action had given rise. By the same token, a majority of the Democratic delegation to the Reichstag also argued that under no circumstances should Wirth be reappointed as chancellor since this would only undercut whatever significance his resignation was supposed to carry as an act of moral protest.[56] When the Democrats notified the other government parties of their position on the afternoon of 22 October, the situation of the Wirth government became untenable, as both the DDP and Center agreed that only by resigning could Wirth lend the German protest the moral and political force it needed to convince world opinion of the injustice Germany had suffered at Allied hands. The resignation of the Wirth government was also necessary in order to clear the way for the DVP's entry into the government coalition.[57]

With two of the three parties that supported his government urging him to step down, Wirth submitted his resignation in a letter to Reich President Ebert on the evening of 22 October. At this point, the DDP Reichstag delegation prepared a lengthy statement condemning the Allied partition of Upper Silesia as an open violation of the Versailles Treaty and setting down the conditions under which it would be willing to reenter the government. As their most important single condition, the Democrats stipulated that under no circumstances should the German government undertake any action that might be construed as recognition of the legality of the Allied action in Upper Silesia. Should the government choose to comply with the Allied request for a German commissar to help regulate the economic aspects of the partition, this should be done under official protest against the manner in which the Allies had violated both the spirit and letter of the Versailles Peace Treaty.[58] After presenting their terms to Ebert on the morning of 23 October, the leaders of the DDP met with Stresemann and Adolf Kempkes from the DVP leadership to determine whether or not they were still interested in joining the government. This meeting produced an immediate agreement between the leaders of the two liberal parties first with respect to the desirability of broadening the existing government coalition and secondly with respect to the need for an official German protest to the Allied action in Upper Silesia.[59]

On the following day, representatives from the three government parties and the DVP met with Ebert to formulate the program upon which the new government was to be formed. The discussion focused on three main issues, namely, the form of the German protest against the Allied action in Upper Silesia, the seizure of real assets in the event that the industrial credit action failed to produce the revenue neccessary to fulfill the terms of the London Ultimatum, and the person of the new chancellor. On the first of these points, the four parties were able to agree on the text of a note protesting the Allied partition of Upper Silesia as a violation of the Versailles Peace Treaty, although the DVP and Majority Socialists remained at odds as to the precise form such a protest should take. On the second point, both the DDP and the DVP were willing to go along with Social Democratic demands for the seizure of real assets on the twofold condition that this was done to stabilize the mark and to meet Germany's reparations obligations. Under no circumstances would either of the liberal parties countenance the seizure of real assets for the purpose of redistributing Germany's national wealth. With respect to the third item, Ebert proposed that Wirth succeed himself as chancellor and refused to back down in the face of strong objections from the leaders of the two liberal parties.[60]

The outcome of the meeting with Ebert on the evening of 24 October indicated that whereas the two liberal parties were prepared to make concessions on tax and economic policy in order to bring a government of the so-called Great Coalition into existence, they remained profoundly estranged from Wirth and the Majority Socialists with respect to the national question. Frustration with the outcome of the meeting was particularly strong within the DVP, where party leaders regarded a vigorous response to the Allied partition of Upper Silesia—one, in fact, bordering on open defiance—as a *conditio sine qua non* for any compromise they might be asked to make on the sensitive issues of tax and economic policy. In this respect, the leaders of the DVP were especially distressed by the decision of Ebert, Wirth, and the Majority Socialists to appoint a special commissar for economic negotiations with Poland on the grounds that this automatically implied acceptance of the Allied decision on Upper Silesia. Since in their eyes the minimal conditions for their party's entry into the government had not been met, the leaders of the DVP announced after an emergency meeting of the Reichstag delegation on the night of 24 October that they had no choice but to reject the terms of the agreement that had been drafted in Ebert's office earlier that evening and officially withdrew from all further negotiations to form a new government.[61] In formally communicating this decision to the presidential palace the following morning, Stresemann employed nationalistic rhetoric that placed the Democrats in an extremely delicate situation.[62] Their position was further complicated by an indiscretion in the DVP press designed to discredit the Majority Socialists in the eyes of those who had been outraged by the Allied action in Upper Silesia. The net effect of these developments was to make it virtually impossible for the Democrats, particularly in light of the tremendous emotional significance that they attached to the Upper Silesian question, to join a government in which the Majority Socialists were also represented.[63]

The failure of the two liberal parties to resolve their differences with the Majority Socialists cleared the way for Wirth's reappointment as chancellor on the afternoon of 25 October. The "cabinet of personalities" that Wirth presented on the following morning, however, was virtually the same as the one that had resigned four days earlier and included the three Democratic ministers—Gessler, Rathenau, and Schiffer—who had served in his previous government. This constituted a direct affront to the leaders of the DDP, and at a meeting of the DDP Reichstag delegation later that afternoon they adopted a resolution introduced by Haußmann that explicitly enjoined party members from joining the new government.[64] Although the delegation subsequently softened this position by allowing Gessler, upon whose retention both Ebert and Wirth placed considerable weight, to continue in his previous capacity as minister of defense, this decision simply reflected the lack of a politically suitable successor for the highly sensitive post Gessler had held and did not signal a change in the DDP's attitude toward the Wirth government.[65] The delegation refused to make a similar exception in the case of Rathenau, who, though privately critical of the party's decision not to support the Wirth government, agreed to respect party discipline and spare it further embarrassment.[66] Schiffer, on the other hand, failed to exercise similar discretion when, much to the chagrin of his party's more nationalistic elements, he agreed to serve as the German plenipotentiary for Upper Silesia, thereby robbing the DDP's resignation from the government of much of its significance.[67]

The DDP's refusal to join the Wirth government revealed the extent to which the party's commitment to the principles of parliamentary democracy was being undercut by the wave of intense national feeling that imposition of the London Ultimatum and the partition of Upper Silesia had produced throughout the party organization. For in following the DVP into opposition against the Wirth government, the Democrats found themselves pursuing a policy that was dictated not by their long-term goal of stabilizing the Weimar Republic but by highly charged emotional arguments of uncertain political effect. At no point in the party's history was the disjuncture between the force of national feeling and the dictates of political reason more poignant than in the fall of 1921. Within the DVP, on the other hand, the Upper Silesian crisis provided the leaders of the party's right wing with the pretext they needed to block the DVP's entry into a government whose first item of business would have been to introduce new taxes detrimental to the social and economic interests they represented. Here the identity of feeling and interest was much more complete than it had been in the DDP. Moreover, the collapse of efforts to bring the DVP into the government also cleared the way for a concerted counteroffensive on the part of those within the National Federation of German Industry who opposed the industrial credit action that Wirth had discussed with the RDI leadership earlier that fall. Not only had the DVP's entry into the government constituted an implicit precondition for industry's willingness to participate in the project, but the failure of Wirth's efforts to broaden the basis of his coalition had left his government so weakened that industry no longer had to fear the seizure of industrial assets.[68] The crisis of German parliamentarism that had become apparent with the formation of the first Wirth government in the spring of 1921 had entered a new and more ominous phase.

CHAPTER TEN

From Opposition to Accommodation

THE WEAKNESS OF THE Wirth government in the fall and winter of 1921 was a direct consequence of the policies pursued by the two liberal parties during the Upper Silesian crisis. By the same token, the failure of the liberal parties to support the Wirth government had also done much to undermine their own integrative potential and to exacerbate the cleavages that already existed within their ranks. All of this contributed to a general disenchantment not only with the republican form of government but also with those parties whose equivocation in the critical days of October 1921 had left the Wirth government in such a weakened state. Eager to take advantage of the sense of national indignation to which acceptance of the London Ultimatum and the partition of Upper Silesia had given rise, the leaders of the antirepublican German Right launched a major political offensive that sought to discredit the foreign and domestic policies of the Wirth government and to polarize the German party system into two mutually antagonistic camps.

Nationalist agitation against the Wirth government and the German middle parties drew to a preliminary climax at the DNVP's Munich party congress in early September 1921 when Martin Spahn, a prominent political historian who stood on the right wing of the Center, announced his defection to the DNVP and called for the creation of a greater German Right.[1] On the following day Karl Helfferich, a Nationalist deputy whose role in bringing about Erzberger's political demise had earned him widespread notoriety, launched into a bitter attack against the policy of fulfillment in which he charged that Wirth's interest in increasing taxes was nothing less than part of an overall strategy to finance German reparation payments through the expropriation of Germany's propertied classes. Helfferich was thus trying to lay the inflation and the increasing distress that the German middle strata had begun to experience in the early 1920s at the doorstep of the Wirth government and the architects of fulfillment.[2]

Much to Stresemann's regret, the DNVP's agitation for the creation of a greater German Right had resulted in a marked deterioration of its relations with the DVP.[3] While Stresemann rejected Nationalist appeals for the creation of such a bloc as incompatible with Germany's need for political stability and a "politics of reason,"[4] the recent conflicts over the London Ultimatum and the partition of Upper Silesia had done much to polarize the DVP into a left wing led by Raumer, Kardorff, and Heinze that regretted its decision not to enter the Wirth government and a right wing led by Stinnes, Vögler, and Quaatz that privately sympathized with the Nationalist campaign against the policy of fulfillment.[5] As the conflict drew to a head during the crisis over Upper Silesia, the second of these two factions was joined by a third group headed by Alfred Gildemeister of Bremen and Walter Dauch of Hamburg, both of whom were irreconcilably opposed to the DVP's participation in any government in which the Majority Socialists were also represented.[6] Stresemann, on the other hand, remained convinced that the key to solving Germany's political crisis lay in the formation of a broad-based coalition government stretching from the DVP to the Social Democrats, and he was infuriated at the way in which the group around Gildemeister and Dauch consistently tried to block any accommodation with the Majority Socialists. Complaining bitterly of a "Fronde" against his leadership of the party, Stresemann warned that it was up to the DVP to decide whether it was still capable of pursuing an independent policy of its own or had become a mere flunky for the right-wing DNVP.[7]

Although the crisis within the DVP temporarily abated with the party's refusal to participate in the formation of the second Wirth government, the differences that had given rise to the crisis remained unresolved. With the approach of the DVP's fourth national congress in Stuttgart in the first week of December, the situation within the party became increasingly tense in the wake of reports that efforts to broaden the basis of the Wirth government were about to be resumed.[8] At a closed meeting of the DVP central executive committee on the eve of the congress, a floor fight nearly erupted when Gildemeister demanded that the party leadership refrain from uttering so much as a single word on the possibility of the DVP's entry into the government.[9] In the general debate that took place on the first day of the congress, however, the leaders of the DVP's right wing were careful to avoid an open attack against Stresemann and the policies he represented. The only dissenting voice, in fact, came not from the party's right wing but from Fritz Kaiser, a member of the DVP delegation to the Saxon Landtag and a spokesman for the party's left wing. Deploring the lack of a clear and consistent course of action on the part of the DVP Reichstag delegation, Kaiser criticized the role the party had played in the collapse of the Fehrenbach government as an example of the way in which it had repeatedly squandered its influence and disappointed its followers ever since its victory in the 1920 Reichstag elections. Kaiser concluded his remarks by calling upon the DVP to decide once and for all whether it was a party of opposition, in which case it should take its place alongside the DNVP on the antirepublican German Right, or a party genuinely prepared to accept the mantle of governmental responsibility.[10]

Although Kaiser's remarks were directed not so much against Stresemann as against the DVP Reichstag delegation, they clearly reflected the growing uneasiness that existed within certain sectors of the party. In his keynote address on the evening of 1 December Stresemann tried to divert attention away from the sources of party disunity to those questions of national policy upon which he felt all party members could agree. Specifically Stresemann sought to articulate the sense of national resentment to which the most recent Allied action had given rise and called for the revision of the Versailles Peace Treaty as the first step toward the restoration of a viable European order. By the same token, Stresemann attributed the economic difficulties that all of the victorious powers were experiencing to the terms of the treaty and stressed the international significance of reintegrating Germany into the world economy. It was only toward the end of his speech that Stresemann turned to the questions of domestic policy that had proven so damaging to party unity. And here his comments were marked by some very significant concessions to his party's right wing. For while he characterized the DVP as "a party of the *Volksge-meinschaft*" and reaffirmed its willingness to form a coalition government with the Social Democrats, he stipulated that this could only take place on two conditions, namely, that the leadership of such a government lay in bourgeois hands and that the formation of such a government entail no sacrifice of the DVP's national principles.[11] Stresemann was thus able to placate some of his more vociferous critics on the party's right wing, lay the groundwork for a reconciliation with the group around Gildemeister and Dauch, and isolate those like Quaatz and Eduard Stadtler who remained irreconcilably opposed to his leadership of the party. The Stuttgart congress thus ended in what contemporary political analysts interpreted as an unequivocal personal triumph for Stresemann and the politics of moderation.[12]

If Stresemann's skill as a rhetorician and party tactician prevented the divisions within the DVP from erupting into an open conflict, the DDP by contrast seemed to be drifting from crisis to crisis without any clear idea of the direction in which it was supposed to be headed. The lack of unity that had plagued the party first in the vote on the London Ultimatum and then during the formation of the second Wirth government had done much to undermine public confidence in the DDP and to exacerbate the divisions that already existed within party ranks. Much of the difficulty, as the leaders of the DDP's left wing bitterly complained, stemmed from the fact that the Reichstag delegation elected in June 1920 stood considerably further to the right than the majority of those who sat on the party's national executive councils.[13] The uneasiness that the leaders of the DDP's left wing felt over the party's drift to the right could be seen in the proposal that Anton Erkelenz made at the height of the crisis over the London Ultimatum for the creation of a new "republican democratic people's party" embracing all of those forces, bourgeois as well as proletarian, that were unequivocally committed to the defense of Germany's new republican order. The rationale behind Erkelenz's proposal was that only through the creation of such a party would it be possible for Germany to forge the domestic consensus necessary to fulfill the terms of the London Ultimatum.[14] While Erkelenz's proposal met with little enthusiasm from the Democratic leadership,[15] the left wing of the DDP continued to air the possibility of a new republican party throughout the summer and early fall of 1921, if for no other reason than to counter the growing sentiment on the party's right wing for a merger with the DVP.[16]

With Erzberger's assassination in the late summer of 1921, the need for closer political ties among the parties that supported the republican form of government seemed more urgent than ever.[17] It was against the background of these developments that the leaders of the DDP's left wing launched a concerted campaign to regain control of the party and to halt its slow drift to the right. This campaign was spearheaded by Wilhelm Cohnstaedt from the editorial staff of the influential *Frankfurter Zeitung*. At the height of the November Revolution, the *Frankfurter Zeitung* had thrown its full support behind the newly founded Democratic Party in hopes that it, as a bridge between the bourgeoisie and working class, would join the Social Democrats in establishing the social and political foundations of a truly humane democratic order.[18] But as it became increasingly apparent during the course of 1919–20 that the DDP was unwilling to embrace Social Democratic proposals for a fundamental reorganization of German economic life, the newspaper did not hesitate to criticize the party for having failed to live up to the expectations that had accompanied its founding. Cohnstaedt and his associates were particularly distressed by the fact that the DDP seemed to be moving closer and closer to the DVP on issues such as the Factory Council Law and socialization of the coal industry.[19] The paper also found fault with the DDP's failure to close ranks behind the policy of fulfillment as articulated by Wirth and Rathenau and criticized the party's reluctance to join the second Wirth government as another sign of its weakness vis-à-vis the DVP.[20] Needless to say, this sort of criticism did not find favor with the leaders of the DDP, who resented the disloyalty of the democratic press and the complications it created for the party.[21]

In late August 1921 Cohnstaedt approached Erkelenz in an attempt to enlist his cooperation in a plan to regenerate the DDP and return it to the principles upon which it had been founded. Contending that the leaders of the DDP Reichstag delegation had moved so far to the right that they no longer represented the party as a whole, Cohnstaedt wanted to introduce a motion of no-confidence in the Reichstag delegation at the next party congress scheduled to take place in Bremen the second week of November. Once this motion had passed, the party's social-liberal faction headed by Erkelenz would propose the creation of a special subcommittee to act as a liaison between the Reichstag delegation and the party executive committee. By empowering this committee with a suspensive veto over the actions of the delegation, Cohnstaedt sought to subordinate the delegation to the will of the party executive committee. Since the left wing of the party was more strongly represented on the executive committee than in the Reichstag delegation, Cohnstaedt also proposed the election of a social-liberal to the chairmanship of the DDP executive committee and urged Erkelenz to stand for election.[22]

While Erkelenz concurred with Cohnstaedt's assessment of the situation within the party, he was reluctant in light of his responsibilities as leader of the Hirsch-Duncker trade-union movement to challenge Petersen for the chairmanship of the party executive committee.[23] For his own part, Erkelenz had grown increasingly disenchanted with the general direction in which the DDP seemed to be moving and recognized the need to provide the German worker with more effective representation at the upper echelons of the party organization if the growing influence of the DDP's business wing was to be held in check. This was necessary, as Erkelenz claimed in a speech at the second annual congress of the party's National Workers' Council in September 1921, not only to revitalize the DDP but also to strengthen the social and political foundations of Germany's new republican order.[24] From this perspective, Erkelenz could only have been heartened by the initial success of his efforts to organize the working-class and white-collar elements on the DDP's left wing into a force sufficiently powerful to prevent the party from falling under the domination of outside economic interests. By the end of 1921 the DDP's National Workers' Council, which he had helped found at the end of the previous year, had established chapters in virtually every large German city and could claim the support of more than 11,000 registered members.[25] This provided Erkelenz with an organizational base that no other Democratic party leader could match and from which he and his associates, should they choose to do so, could launch an effective bid for control of the party.

It was not until the middle of October that Erkelenz finally set aside his reservations about becoming more actively involved in the DDP's internal affairs and agreed to go along with Cohnstaedt's suggestion that he challenge Petersen for the chairmanship of the DDP executive committee. Erkelenz conceived of his candidacy as the first step toward reshaping the DDP as a genuinely democratic party capable of competing with the Social Democrats for the political loyalties of Germany's civil servants, white-collar employees, and workers. While this would require the party to turn its back upon the great mass of Germany's private entrepreneurs, small businessmen, and peasants, Erkelenz believed that the Democrats would be able to offset whatever losses they might suffer in these quarters by pursuing a clearer and more resolute course of action at the national level.[26] What Erkelenz envisaged, therefore, amounted to nothing less than a total transformation of the DDP's social and political profile, a transformation that, if successful, would have seen the party abandon its position in the middle of Germany's political spectrum to take its place alongside the Social Democrats on the German Left.

From Erkelenz's perspective the major obstacle to his plans for a revitalization of the DDP lay in the party's financial dependence upon the business interests that constituted the nucleus of its right wing and were so effectively represented within the party organization by the Hansa-Bund's Hermann Fischer.[27] Following the creation of the DDP's National Council for Trade, Industry, and Commerce in October 1920, the leaders of the party's business wing had collected over 120,000 marks for use in rebuilding the party's national organization.[28] Attached to this support, however, were expectations and conditions that the leaders of the DDP's left wing were frequently reluctant to meet. In the campaign for the Berlin city elections in the fall of 1921, for example, the leaders of the DDP's business wing had threatened to withhold financial support from the DDP if it did not join the DVP, DNVP, and Center in the creation of a united bourgeois front.[29] In an attempt to undercut the influence Fischer enjoyed by virtue of his control over party finances, Cohnstaedt and Erkelenz hoped to enlist the support of Walther Rathenau—if not to spearhead the offensive that they planned to launch at Bremen,[30] then at least to help organize a special fund for use by the leaders of the party's left wing in their efforts to regain control of the party.[31] Openly critical of the DDP's failure to enter the second Wirth government,[32] Rathenau heartily endorsed the plans of the party's left wing and, though somewhat skeptical about the eventual outcome of such an undertaking, agreed to support the political offensive it planned to undertake at the party's upcoming congress.[33] Buoyed by Rathenau's declaration of support, the leaders of the DDP's left wing intensified their efforts on behalf of Erkelenz's candidacy in confidence that his election would ensure the change in the party's political course that they so desperately sought.[34]

The DDP's Bremen party congress opened on 11 November 1921 against a background of increased factional strife and amid hopes that party unity could be restored. On the eve of the congress the leaders of the DDP's social-liberal faction held a special caucus at which they decided to lay the groundwork for Erkelenz's election to the chairmanship of the DDP executive committee by introducing a motion of no-confidence in the policies of the Reichstag delegation.[35] On the following day Rathenau set the stage for an open confrontation between the party leadership and the DDP's left wing when, in his keynote address on "Die Erfüllungsproblem und die deutsche Wirtschaft," he publicly criticized the leaders of the DDP Reichstag delegation for the confused and erratic policy they had pursued during the Upper Silesian crisis. Rathenau chastised the delegation in particular for the way in which it had functioned as a "branch" of the German People's Party and denounced its decision to withdraw from the Wirth government as an ill-conceived move that only weakened

the German government at a moment of acute national crisis.[36] The leaders of
the DDP's left wing were quick to take advantage of the opening provided by
Rathenau's speech, and in the debate that followed first Preuß and then
Erkelenz attacked Petersen and the leaders of the Reichstag delegation for
having compromised the ideals upon which the DDP had been founded by
pursuing a policy designed to curry favor with the DVP.[37]

The conflict drew to a head on the second day of the congress when the
leaders of the DDP's social-liberal faction introduced a resolution that expressed a lack of confidence in the policies of the Reichstag delegation. This
prompted a sharp response from the party's national leaders, who came to the
delegation's defense with a tersely worded resolution reaffirming complete
confidence in it and the policies it represented.[38] With the dividing lines so
sharply drawn, party leaders began to fear that the acceptance of either resolution might trigger a secession on one or the other wing of the party. In an
attempt to prevent this, Petersen and the Democratic party leadership held an
emergency caucus with representatives from the faction around Erkelenz and
Cohnstaedt in an attempt to hammer out a compromise that might still salvage
the unity of the party. According to the terms of this compromise, the two
resolutions on the floor of the congress were to be withdrawn in favor of a third
resolution that reaffirmed the DDP's unequivocal commitment to the republican principles upon which it had been founded, called for the reorganization of
the national government on the broadest possible basis, and expressed renewed confidence in the Democratic delegation to the Reichstag as a result of
the frank and open discussion that had taken place at the congress.[39] What
made this resolution acceptable to the leaders of the party's left wing was the
stamp of approval that Petersen and the DDP Reichstag delegation reluctantly
gave to Erkelenz's election to the chairmanship of the party executive committee. This arrangement, however, found little favor with the leaders of the
DDP's business wing, who immediately tried to sabotage Erkelenz's election
by threatening Petersen with the loss of financial support. Fearing that they had
already given away too much, the social-liberals refused to back down on
Erkelenz's election, and for a while it seemed as if the agreement they had just
reached with the party leadership might fall apart. It was only when the social-
liberals agreed to accept Fischer as Erkelenz's deputy that the leaders of the
DDP's business wing relented and agreed to go along with Erkelenz's election.[40] The unity of the party had been salvaged, but the divisions within the
party remained as sharp as ever.

The leaders of the DDP moved quickly to implement the compromise they
had reached with the party's left wing for fear that it might once again fall
apart. Following the formal adoption of the compromise resolution and
Petersen's reelection as DDP chairman on the afternoon of 12 November,
Petersen proposed that Erkelenz be elected to the chairmanship and Fischer to

the deputy chairmanship of the party executive committee. This followed by acclamation, and the elements of the compromise were firmly in place.[41] Yet while party leaders were obviously relieved that an open floor fight had been avoided, the fact nevertheless remained that the DDP was no closer to a resolution of the problems that had given rise to the crisis than it had been before the congress. For instead of healing the divisions within the party, the outcome of the Bremen congress had done much to polarize the Democratic Party into a left wing that complained bitterly of a conspiracy on the part of the DDP's business interests to sabotage the Bremen compromise[42] and a right wing that regarded the social-liberals as a minority faction intent upon imposing its will on the party as a whole.[43]

With their appeal at Bremen for the reorganization of the national government on the broadest possible basis, the Democrats took what appeared to be the first step toward their eventual reentry into the Wirth government. While this appeal gave rise to immediate speculation regarding Rathenau's return to national office, the leaders of the DDP hoped that their initiative would culminate in the appointment of a new government stretching from the Majority Socialists to the DVP. In this respect, the leaders of the DDP's business wing were particularly anxious to secure the DVP's entry into the government in order to offset Social Democratic pressure for a tax reform that would involve the seizure of real assets as a means of redistributing Germany's national wealth. The defeat of the industrial credit action by Hugenberg, Stinnes, and their supporters in the National Federation of German Industry in November 1921 had made it imperative for the government and the Reichstag to develop new sources of revenue to meet Allied reparations demands. At the same time, Allied willingness to consider a moratorium on the payment of reparations was predicated upon the reorganization of German finances and a reform of the German tax code. While, under these circumstances, virtually every sector of the Democratic Party was resigned to increased taxation of Germany's propertied wealth, the party's business leaders, along with Petersen and the leadership of the DDP Reichstag delegation, sought to minimize Social Democratic influence on the government's tax program and to prevent the adoption of measures they regarded as confiscatory in nature. From this perspective, therefore, the Democrats looked upon the creation of a broad parliamentary coalition based upon the parties of the German middle as an essential precondition for the solution of Germany's fiscal crisis.[44]

In their hopes that it might still be possible to form a new national government based upon the Great Coalition, the Democrats were heartened by the course of recent events in Prussia. Since the state elections in February 1921, Prussia had been ruled by a minority government headed by Adam Stegerwald and composed of representatives from the DDP and Center. In the fall of 1921 efforts to reorganize the Prussian government had taken place in conjunction

with negotiations at the national level to bring the DVP into the Wirth government. But whereas the negotiations in the Reich had come to an abrupt end
amid the furor that followed the Allied partition of Upper Silesia, in Prussia
they resulted in the formation of a new government in which not only the
Center and DDP but also the Majority Socialists and DVP were represented.[45]
At Bremen the Democrats took credit for having served as midwife to the birth
of the Great Coalition in Prussia and expressed the hope that Prussia might
serve as an example for the nation as a whole.[46] But the situation in the Reich
was infinitely more complex than it had been in Prussia. For not only did the
final shape of the government tax bill constitute a matter of potentially serious
disagreement between the Majority Socialists and the other government parties, but the conflict over the policy of fulfillment had assumed an intensity at
the national level that was largely missing from state politics.

In the fall of 1921 the leaders of the DVP had been prepared to make
substantial concessions on tax policy in order to expedite their party's entry
into the national government, but efforts toward this end had completely
broken down following the crisis over Upper Silesia. At the DVP's Stuttgart
party congress in December 1921 Stresemann had left the door open to a
resumption of negotiations aimed at the formation of the Great Coalition in the
Reich. But in the preliminary discussions that took place during the first two
weeks of December, Stresemann seemed unsure of himself and was reluctant
to undertake any action that might provoke the wrath of his party's right wing.
Even moderates like Hans von Raumer who had previously endorsed the
DVP's entry into the Wirth government were now wavering in their willingness to assume governmental responsibility under conditions that did not
augur well for the future of their party.[47] At a heated meeting of the DVP
Reichstag delegation on 15 December the leaders of the party's left wing—
Kardorff, Heinze, and Obheim—found themselves virtually isolated as Stresemann, having apparently reached a private understanding with Stinnes on the
previous day, gave in to his party's right wing and outlined a much harder
position than the DVP had previously taken in its negotiations with the Wirth
government.[48] Specifically, the DVP renounced interest in the Economics
Ministry, which was in need of a major administrative overhaul, and demanded in addition to the Finance Ministry another important portfolio such as
the vice-chancellorship, the Ministry of Interior, or the Foreign Office. At the
same time the DVP reiterated its refusal to support the policy of unconditional
fulfillment.[49]

With the hardening of the DVP's position in the second half of December,
efforts to broaden the basis of the second Wirth government came to a temporary standstill. Attention now shifted to the question of tax reform, where the
Democrats had already begun to intensify their efforts on behalf of an accommodation with the DVP.[50] The situation was further complicated by the Allies'

refusal to consider Germany's request for a moratorium on the payment of reparations for the duration of 1922 as long as the Wirth government had not submitted a tax and stabilization program by 28 January. Under these circumstances representatives from the Majority Socialists, the Center, and the two liberal parties met almost continuously between 18 and 26 January to hammer out the details of a tax compromise that would be assured of majority support in the Reichstag. During the course of the negotiations, the DDP and DVP were not only able to persuade the Social Democrats to drop their demands for a new tax on postwar increases of wealth but also succeeded in extracting significant concessions with respect to the maximum rate on the new property tax and the method by which the value of landed capital was to be assessed. In return the Social Democrats were able to win support for the accelerated collection of the Reich Emergency Levy and for the imposition of a compulsory loan (*Zwangsanleihe*) against propertied wealth that was to serve as a political surrogate for the seizure of real assets.[51] In the final analysis, however, the Social Democrats seemed to have surrendered more than they received, and the tax compromise that Wirth presented to the Reichstag on 26 January[52] represented a modest triumph for the two liberal parties in that they were able to block Social Democratic efforts to use the reform as a means of redistributing Germany's national wealth. Given the fact that Allied pressure had made a reorganization of Germany's tax structure inevitable, the two liberal parties were quick to claim credit for the fact that they had succeeded in modifying those provisions of the tax program that in their eyes entailed an unacceptable sacrifice for Germany's propertied classes.[53]

Although the DVP had not made support of the compromise contingent upon its entry into the government, it was widely assumed, particularly within the two liberal parties, that agreement on the tax compromise would quickly lead to the reorganization of the Wirth government on the basis of the Great Coalition.[54] Efforts to bring the DVP into the government, however, were torpedoed by two critical developments at the end of January 1922. The first of these was the appointment of Rathenau as Germany's foreign minister on 31 January. Rathenau's return to national office had been predicted ever since the DDP's Bremen party congress in November 1921, although in light of his outspoken independence[55] Democratic party leaders were intent upon retaining complete freedom of action should he decide to join the government on his own.[56] Rathenau's political capital, however, had risen considerably since his personal diplomatic triumph at the Cannes Conference in early January, with the result that the Democrats now began to close ranks behind him in anticipation of his reentry into the government.[57] Within the DVP, on the other hand, Rathenau was widely regarded as the architect of unconditional fulfillment, and party leaders hoped to block his return to national office by attaching "conditions of a material and personal nature" to their support of the tax compromise.[58] When Wirth proceeded to appoint Rathenau as head of the German Foreign Ministry in apparent defiance of the DVP, the party responded with a tersely worded communiqué in which it denounced Rathenau's appointment as an act of disloyalty toward the DVP and warned that its support of the tax compromise was in jeopardy.[59]

If Rathenau's appointment as German foreign minister temporarily strained relations between the DVP and the Wirth government, then a second and far more damaging development was the civil servant strike that erupted in the state-owned railway system in late January 1922. The steady decline in the purchasing power of the German mark through the second half of 1921 had produced widespread unrest among Germany's railway workers, and in December a nationwide railway strike had been averted only by granting cost-of-living increases that were retroactive to the first of October. Less than a month later, however, Germany found herself confronted with a second railway strike, this time on the part of railway officials who were encouraged by the settlement that the railway workers had reached with the government. The government responded to this new threat by issuing a presidential emergency decree that denied civil servants the right to strike and threatened those who participated in such actions with legal consequences. But when this failed to break the strike, Wirth turned to the leaders of organized labor for their assistance in bringing the strike to an end. Through their mediation Wirth was able to persuade the leadership of the German Civil Servants' Association to repudiate the strike in spite of the fact that it had been called by one of its affiliates, the National Union of German Railway Officials (Reichsgewerkschaft der deutschen Eisenbahnbeamten). In the face of growing opposition from within his own government, Wirth then proceeded to work through the leaders of the German Civil Servants' Association and Germany's major trade-union federations to negotiate an end to the strike and a return to work on the morning of 8 February.[60]

Wirth's handling of the railway officials' strike in early February 1922 drove a sharp wedge not only between his government and the DVP but also between the two liberal parties. For whereas both the DDP and DVP condemned the strike as an illegal breach of the contract binding the civil servant to the state, they differed sharply in their views as to who was responsible for the strike and how it should have been resolved. In general, the Democrats regarded the strike as an unfortunate consequence of the changes that had taken place in the social and economic status of the civil service since the beginning of the war. While the Democrats were critical of the government for its general insensitivity to the plight of the professional civil servant, they supported Wirth's efforts to end the strike through conciliation rather than confrontation and even interceded on behalf of the striking railway officials in order to expedite an end to the crisis.[61] The DVP, on the other hand, sought to capitalize upon the widespread unrest that the strike had caused within civil servant circles by assigning responsibility for the crisis to the Majority Socialists and the Wirth government. Without going so far as to endorse the specific demands of the striking railway officials, the DVP portrayed the strike as an act of desperation that could have been averted had the government taken appropriate action to check the social and economic decline of the state civil service.[62] By the same token, the DVP criticized the Wirth government for having accepted the mediation of the Social Democrats and for having reached an accommodation with representatives from the striking railway officials' union despite promises that it would not negotiate with the union until after the strike had ended.[63]

Motivated in part by the need to placate its own civil servant constituency, the DVP's criticism of the way in which the Wirth government had handled the railway strike signaled the collapse of efforts to reorganize the national government along the lines of the Great Coalition. Not only did a meeting between representatives from the potential coalition partners on the morning of 10 February reveal persistent differences of opinion with respect to the tax compromise,[64] but in the parliamentary debate later that afternoon the DVP introduced a motion of no-confidence in Wirth's performance as chancellor.[65] The purpose of this somewhat bizarre ploy was to exploit the differences that Wirth's handling of the railway strike had created within the ranks of his own cabinet and to force Wirth's removal from office without at the same time irrevocably destroying the DVP's chances of entering a government based upon the Great Coalition. By this time, Wirth found himself facing no less than four separate no-confidence motions, and to clarify the situation he asked the Reichstag for a positive vote of confidence that would determine his government's parliamentary standing once and for all.[66] This was something of a calculated risk since the three parties that supported his government commanded only 220 out of 459 votes in the Reichstag, and the outcome of the vote was by no means certain. But in the final analysis abstentions from the Independent Socialists and the Bavarian People's Party were sufficient to provide the government with a clear 220–185 victory on 15 February.[67]

Immediately following Wirth's victory in the Reichstag, the DVP released a communiqué announcing that it would no longer participate in efforts to reorganize the national government on the basis of the Great Coalition.[68] While Stresemann remained committed to the Great Coalition in principle, the conditions he had outlined for the DVP's entry into the government in his keynote address at Stuttgart in early December 1921 had not been met. As the DVP's reaction to Rathenau's appointment as Germany's foreign minister and to the government's handling of the railway strike clearly revealed, the party was not prepared to accept governmental responsibility under conditions that might identify it too closely with either the policy of fulfillment or Wirth's softness toward the striking railway officials. Disagreements on these matters, however, did not prevent the DVP from cooperating with the Wirth government in its efforts to find a solution to Germany's deepening fiscal crisis.[69] When negotiations on the tax compromise were resumed in the second week of March, the DVP presented the government with a petition specifying the "personal and material guarantees" necessary for its support in the Reichstag. These demands were designed to ensure fiscal responsibility on the part of the Berlin government and enjoyed such strong support with the leaders of the other parties that Wirth agreed to accept them as guidelines for his government's fiscal policies. The leaders of the DVP were thus able to claim credit not only for having demonstrated their willingness to accept material sacrifices for the sake of Germany's national welfare but also for having modified those provisions of the government tax program that might have proven detrimental to the interests they represented.[70] As a result, whatever reservations the DVP might have had about supporting the tax compromise were quickly set aside, and the government's tax program, including the controversial compulsory loan against Germany's propertied wealth, passed the Reichstag in a series of parliamentary votes during the first week of April.[71]

The passage of the tax compromise in the spring of 1922 represented the major domestic accomplishment of the Wirth government. As Wirth explained in his official interpellation before the Reichstag on 26 January, the compromise was designed to create an international climate in which revision of the London Ultimatum could take place and to check the downward slide in the exchange value of the German mark.[72] The value of the mark had fallen steadily since the imposition of the London Ultimatum in the spring of 1921, and the tax compromise in the spring of 1922 represented the last grand effort to stem the fall of the mark before the onset of the hyperinflation that summer. Yet whatever counterinflationary effect the compromise was supposed to have was undercut by three factors. In the first place, the revenue generated by the new taxes was woefully inadequate to cover the deficit that had developed in the German budget by the end of 1921, a fact that stemmed in no small measure from the success with which the two liberal parties had been able to whittle away at specific provisions of the compromise. Secondly, the stabilization of the mark presupposed substantial cuts in the general level of government spending. Not only did the Wirth government's dependence upon the Majority Socialists make it politically difficult to implement cuts that might hurt the German working class, but the outcome of the railway officials' strike in February 1922 meant that the government would be spending more, not less, on salaries and wages during the upcoming fiscal year. Clearly, Wirth and his socialist allies were unwilling to accept the political costs that fiscal stability entailed. Thirdly, the success of the 1922 tax compromise as a counterinflationary measure presupposed some sort of accommodation with the Allies on the reparations question. Indeed, the primary impulse behind the tax compromise had been Allied pressure for a balanced budget as a precondition for a moratorium on the payment of reparations. But as the outcome of the Genoa Conference on European reconstruction in the spring of 1922 was to reveal, the Allies were not yet prepared to negotiate a reduction in Germany's reparations burden. As a result, none of the preconditions for a stabilization of the mark in the spring of 1922 was to materialize, with the result that the door to a further depreciation of the mark had been left dangerously open.[73]

While the economic impact of the 1922 tax compromise may have been negligible, its political significance was not. Gratified by the tangible results that cooperation with the DVP had brought, the Democrats hoped that agreement on the tax compromise would soon lead to a reorganization of the Wirth government on the basis of the Great Coalition, thereby providing Germany with the domestic consensus she so desperately needed in order to accomplish her foreign policy objectives.[74] It was, however, precisely in the area of foreign policy that the People's Party found itself in strongest disagreement with the Wirth government. For while the leaders of the DVP had gone along with the tax compromise in order to help the Wirth government meet Allied reparations demands, they remained openly critical of the policy of fulfillment and continually exhorted the government to adopt a firmer stance in its negotiations with the Entente.[75] Moreover, the leaders of the DVP—and particularly those on its right wing—felt that now that their party had accomplished its objectives with respect to Wirth's tax program, there was no longer any reason for them to enter the government and share the odium of fulfillment.[76] The cynicism that lay behind this strategy did not augur well for the future of Germany's republican institutions.

CHAPTER ELEVEN

To the Defense of the Republic

WITH THE PASSAGE OF the tax compromise in the spring of 1922, attention shifted to foreign policy, where Wirth and Rathenau were still hopeful of an understanding with the Allies on the reparations question. But chances of an international agreement on reparations and related economic matters had already received a sharp setback with the appointment of Raymond Poincaré, an uncompromising Germanophobe, as French prime minister in January 1922. The immediate effect of Poincaré's appointment was to stiffen Allied opposition to Germany's request for a moratorium on the payment of reparations for the remainder of the year, and in late March the Allies demanded that Germany impose a new round of taxes as a precondition for favorable action on her petition for a moratorium. Had the Wirth-Rathenau government acceded to this ultimatum, it would almost certainly have meant the collapse of the tax compromise it had just negotiated between the DVP and the three government parties. Frustrated by increasing Allied intransigence, the German government responded with a resounding rejection of the ultimatum, in which the DVP and Bavarian People's Party readily joined. Consequently, the international conference that was scheduled to meet in Genoa during the second week of April in an attempt to develop a multinational strategy for coping with the problems of Europe's economic reconstruction was doomed to failure before it even met. The Rapallo agreement that Germany signed with Soviet Russia on 16 April 1922 only served to dramatize the impasse that had developed in Germany's relations with the Entente.[1]

As attention shifted from domestic politics to international diplomacy, partisan political strife temporarily abated. The unequivocal rejection with which the Wirth government had responded to Allied demands for a new round of taxes had done much to blunt nationalist agitation from the Right and to strengthen the government's position among those who had previously criticized it for weakness toward the Allies. This, in turn, provided the two liberal parties with a brief respite for regrouping and reorganizing their forces. The problems confronting the German Democratic Party in the spring of 1922 were well-nigh overwhelming. Not only had the party's position during the railway officials' strike earlier that year severely strained its relations with both its own civil servant organization and the Hirsch-Duncker unions,[2] but the DDP's peasant following was on the verge of rebellion as a result of the party's apparent reluctance to press for an end to the controlled economy in agriculture.[3] Moreover, the Democrats were beset by severe financial difficulties that stemmed from declining revenues and from the rapidly rising costs of maintaining a national organization.[4] As one of his first tasks as chairman of the DDP executive committee, Erkelenz had set out to rejuvenate his party's national organization by scheduling a membership drive for the last week of March. This drive was timed to coincide with the Genoa Conference on European reconstruction so that the DDP would be in a position to capitalize upon the diplomatic triumph that the Democrats expected the conference to bring.[5] At the same time, the leaders of the DDP also decided to hold a special congress for their party's civil servant representatives in an effort to repair the damage that the DDP's opposition to the railway officials' strike had done to its relations with the professional civil service.[6]

While the Democrats struggled valiantly to maintain their party's national organization in the face of increasingly unfavorable circumstances, the situation within the DVP remained surprisingly calm. Not only did the DVP's role as an opposition party tend to insulate it from many of the problems that plagued the DDP, but the internal dissension that had once threatened to split the DVP into two irreconcilable camps had lost much of its vehemence. Even Stresemann's decision to soften his party's criticism of the Wirth government until after the conclusion of the Genoa Conference had met with general approval from the leaders of the DVP's right wing.[7] Though not overly optimistic about the eventual outcome of the conference, Stresemann had no desire to undercut the German position at Genoa and exercised considerable restraint in his criticism of Wirth throughout the month of April.[8] By the same token, Stresemann supported the treaty which Germany signed with the Soviet Union at Rapallo as a necessary countermeasure to Allied intransigence in the reparations question, and he foresaw potential benefits for both Germany's economy and her domestic tranquility from her rapprochement with Russia.[9]

In spite of his party's vulnerability to pressure from the German Right, Stresemann continued to moderate his criticism of the Wirth government even after the failure of the Genoa Conference had led to an intensification of Nationalist agitation against the policy of fulfillment.[10] By this time, however, the consensus within the DVP had begun to weaken. When ill health forced Stresemann to leave Berlin in the middle of May in order to undergo treatment at a sanitorium in the Harz Mountains, the leaders of the DVP's right wing took advantage of his absence to persuade the Reichstag delegation to join the DNVP in a vote of no-confidence against the Wirth government and the negotiations it had just concluded with the Allied reparations commission in Paris.[11] For Stresemann this turn of events was doubly disturbing. For not only did it signal a lack of political maturity on the part of his own colleagues, but, more importantly, it made his support of the Wirth government awkward and increasingly difficult.[12]

The political calm that had descended upon Germany in the spring of 1922 was suddenly shattered on the morning of 24 June when right-wing terrorists assassinated Walther Rathenau on his way to the German Foreign Office. Right-wing terrorism had been on the rise ever since the beginning of the year, and Rathenau's murder sent a shock wave that reverberated throughout Germany and the international community. Particularly distraught over Rathenau's death was Wirth, who as chancellor had come to rely more and more upon the remarkable and indeed unique talents of the murdered foreign minister. In a highly emotional speech in the Reichstag on the day after Rathenau's assassination, Wirth responded with a bitter invective against the German Right and called upon all of those who deplored this latest act of violence to unite in defense of the republic. Concluding his speech with words that captured the outrage felt by those who had placed their faith in Germany's new republican order, Wirth pointed to the seats normally occupied by the DNVP and proclaimed: "There stands the enemy who pours his venom into a nation's wounds. There stands the enemy—and on this point there can be no doubt: this enemy stands on the Right."[13]

To Stresemann, Rathenau's assassination came as a severe personal shock. For although he had never been particularly close to the murdered foreign minister and might even have been jealous of the fame he enjoyed at home and abroad, Stresemann condemned the use of violence in the most unequivocal terms and called for immediate action against those who had been responsible for Rathenau's death. Moreover, Stresemann was deeply concerned about the effect that Rathenau's murder might have upon the slow and arduous process of Germany's political stabilization. In this respect, several considerations were paramount in Stresemann's mind. In the first place, the DVP had been making its own separate peace with the Wirth government, and Stresemann feared that Wirth's highly charged attack against the Right foreshadowed a polarization of Germany's political life that might make further accommodation impossible. Stresemann also feared that Rathenau's murder might precipitate a sharp swing to the left that would greatly increase the influence of Germany's working-class parties over the policies of the national government. The impending merger of the Majority and Independent Socialists as well as the general strike by Communist, socialist, and nonsocialist unions on the day of Rathenau's funeral seemed to lend credence to precisely such a fear.[14] Furthermore, the Emergency Decree for the Defense of the Republic, which Wirth enacted by virtue of presidential authority on the night of Rathenau's murder, seemed directed almost exclusively against right-wing parties and organizations.[15]

Stresemann's principal objective in the crisis that followed Rathenau's assassination was to prevent a sharp swing to the left on the part of the Wirth government that might jeopardize future collaboration between it and the DVP. This, in turn, made it imperative that the DVP support the Law for the Defense of the Republic, which the Wirth government was preparing for use against right-wing extremist organizations throughout the country. While the government bill came far short of meeting the demands made by the socialist unions on 27 June, it still went substantially beyond the emergency decree that had just been enacted and contained provisions that neither the DVP nor the two bourgeois government parties were anxious to endorse. Moreover, the fact that in its initial drafts the bill seemed to be directed almost exclusively against the threat of extremist activity on the Right constituted a deficiency that the leaders of the DVP found particularly objectionable.[16]

As the Reichsrat concluded its deliberations on the bill in the first week of July, Stresemann took it upon himself to address the Reichstag in a speech that was to serve as a litmus test of his loyalty to the Weimar Republic. Just as Heinze and Kahl had done before him,[17] Stresemann indicated that the DVP was fully prepared to support government legislation aimed at protecting established political authority against attempts to subvert it by force and terrorism. But in order to soften the bill's obvious ideological overtones and to make it more palatable to those like himself who still felt a strong attachment to the symbols and institutions of the old imperial order, Stresemann proposed that the goal of the bill should not be defense of the republic but defense of the constitution. Then, to dispel any doubts regarding his own loyalty to the Weimar Constitution, Stresemann coupled this recommendation with his most unequivocal and specific endorsement of the republican form of government.

> With respect to the question of monarchy or republic, the decisive factor is whether or not one is prepared to cooperate in this state and with this state. We all know that for the forseeable future the reconstruction of Germany is possible only on the basis of the existing republican constitution if we do not want to dig our own graves by civil war and internal laceration. There is for us, therefore, no choice but to cooperate as sincerely as possible not only in the legislative process as a whole—as we have already done on repeated occasions—but in the passage of this specific law, regardless of whether, as in the case of the Reich, we remain outside the government or, as in Prussia and other German states, we belong to the government.[18]

Though qualified and clearly motivated by tactical considerations, Stresemann's endorsement of the republican form of government was more than a mere act of expediency. In point of fact, Stresemann had been moving toward acceptance of the Weimar Republic ever since he had first recognized at the time of the Fehrenbach government that the republic could be used as effectively by defenders of the status quo as by those who sought to change it. Like Thomas Mann, who also used Rathenau's assassination as the occasion for announcing his conversion to republicanism,[19] Stresemann had come to realize not only that it was possible to work within the framework of the new republican order but also that not to do so was to invite chaos and barbarism. Stresemann's willingness in the summer of 1922 to defend the Weimar Republic against the terrorism of the radical Right, therefore, was not the result of a superficial conversion motivated by purely tactical considerations but represented the culmination of an evolutionary process that extended over the previous two years.[20] In fact, there is good reason to believe that Stresemann might have openly embraced the republican form of government much earlier had it not been for fear of losing his party's right wing. Even then, his defense of the republic in the wake of Rathenau's assassination came as a surprise to many of his colleagues and did much to confuse his supporters at the local levels of the DVP organization.[21]

Though criticized by members of his own party, Stresemann's endorsement of the republican form of government and his willingness to support a modified version of the Law for the Defense of the Republic was warmly received by the leaders of the two nonsocialist government parties. Under heavy pressure from the Social Democrats to broaden the basis of the Wirth government through inclusion of the Independent Socialists, the Center and DDP hoped to keep the government from falling under socialist domination by bringing the DVP into the governmental coalition. Stresemann's public endorsement of the Weimar Constitution in his Reichstag speech of 5 July did much to remove whatever reservations the two parties may have had about the DVP's entry into the government, and on the following day they formally invited the People's Party to participate in negotiations aimed at bringing it into the national government.[22] While the leaders of the DVP were quick to accept this invitation,[23] the Social Democrats responded by threatening to leave the government, thereby forcing new national elections, if such negotiations took place. Given the excited state of public opinion following Rathenau's murder, the leaders of the Center and DDP feared that new elections would produce a dramatic swing to the left, with the result that they had no choice but to retract their invitation to the DVP.[24] In the meantime, efforts to bring the Independent Socialists into the government had also broken down as a result of a fundamental disagreement on the nature and purpose of the Law for the Defense of the Republic. For a while it seemed as if the two socialist parties might still try to force a dissolution of the Reichstag, but as the consequences of such a step became clear, they decided instead to coordinate their policies within the Reichstag through the creation of a formal alliance between their respective parliamentary delegations. Having failed to secure the Independents' entry into the government, the Social Democrats apparently hoped that the creation of such an alliance would enable the socialist parties to bring greater pressure to bear upon the policies of Wirth and his government.[25]

The creation of a formal parliamentary alliance between the two socialist parties on 14 July represented an important step toward their eventual unification at Nuremberg in September 1922. To the leaders of the German middle parties, this development seemed particularly ominous and underscored the need for closer political ties among the various nonsocialist parties that supported the Weimar Republic. On 15 July the leaders of the German Center Party invited the two liberal parties to form a parliamentary coalition similar to the one just forged between the two socialist parties. Within the Center the initiative came from Adam Stegerwald and Heinrich Brauns, both of whom were fearful of the effect a further polarization of Germany's political life might have upon their party and the Christian labor movement.[26] Stegerwald and Brauns had long advocated the creation of an interconfessional Christian people's party as a means of checking the forces of political polarization that were at work within the German party system, and they looked upon the creation of a parliamentary alliance among the three middle parties as a partial realization of this goal. By tying the DVP to the other middle parties, the creation of such an alliance also promised to strengthen the bourgeois presence in the Wirth government and to prevent it from falling under the domination of the newly united socialist Left.[27]

The Center's proposal for the creation of a parliamentary alliance in defense of the Weimar Constitution met with a warm response from the leaders of the two liberal parties. Within the DVP not only Stresemann but also Stinnes and the leaders of the party's industrial wing looked upon the creation of such an alliance as a check on the growing influence of Germany's socialist Left and as a preliminary step toward the DVP's eventual reentry into the government.[28] And within the Democratic Party all but four members of the DDP Reichstag delegation approved of their party's participation in negotiations aimed at the creation of a parliamentary alliance along the lines suggested by the Center.[29] Formal negotiations began on 17 July and culminated two days later in an announcement that the DDP, DVP, and Center had agreed to form a parliamentary coalition to be called the Alliance of the Constitutional Middle (Arbeitsgemeinschaft der verfassungstreuen Mitte). At the same time, however, the three parties took special pains to reassure the leaders of the socialist Left that this action was not directed against the parliamentary alliance they had formed only days before. On the contrary, the primary purpose of the alliance between the three bourgeois parties was to help stabilize Germany's political life on the basis of the Weimar Constitution and to expedite the handling of parliamentary business.[30]

While the leaders of the DDP Reichstag delegation hailed the formation of the Alliance of the Constitutional Middle as a positive step toward the stabilization of Germany's new republican order,[31] the leaders of the party's left wing saw it as part of a continuing conspiracy by the DDP's national leadership to rob them of the fruits of the victory they had won at the Bremen congress in November 1921. Rathenau's death had already deprived the DDP's left wing of its most articulate and influential spokesman, and its leaders now feared a further loss of influence as a result of the DDP's alliance with the DVP and Center. Erkelenz was incensed over the way in which the leaders of the Reichstag delegation had managed to circumvent his authority as chairman of the party executive committee and feared that the creation of the new parliamentary alliance was merely the prelude to an eventual merger of the DDP and DVP.[32] Equally outspoken in their opposition to the new parliamentary alliance were the leaders of the DDP's working-class and civil servant organizations, but neither they nor Erkelenz's supporters were unable to marshal sufficient support within the party's executive councils to force revocation of the agreement with the Center and DVP.[33] Their isolation within the party notwithstanding, the more intransigent elements on the DDP's left wing were determined to take the issue before the Democratic party congress that was scheduled to meet in Elberfeld in the second week of October.[34] But with the collapse of efforts to bring the DVP into the government in the late summer of 1922, Erkelenz decided to abandon his crusade against the new parliamentary alliance so as not to jeopardize his chances of being reelected to the chairmanship of the DDP executive committee.[35] Without Erkelenz's active participation, efforts to force a confrontation at Elberfeld quickly evaporated, and the congress proceeded to adopt a resolution expressing "satisfaction" with the performance of the Reichstag delegation and its elected leaders.[36]

In the eyes of the Democratic party leadership, the Elberfeld party congress in the fall of 1922 represented a pleasant contrast to the last such meeting at Bremen in the fall of 1921. For whereas the Bremen congress had been marred by an open rift between the party's left and right wings, Elberfeld offered a picture of tranquility with little outward sign of the internal divisions that continued to plague the party. This stemmed in no small measure from the fact that the left wing of the party had lost much of the aggressiveness that it had displayed the previous year at Bremen. Not only were the leaders of the DDP's left wing still recoiling from the shock of Rathenau's death, but without Rathenau's leadership they were reluctant to jeopardize the gains they had made at Bremen by renewing their offensive against the policies of the party leadership and the DDP Reichstag delegation. In contrast to Bremen, the Elberfeld congress was marked both by the absence of open political strife and by the apparent resurgence of the DDP's right wing.

The first day of the congress was devoted to a discussion of foreign policy issues in a somewhat transparent attempt to obscure the social and economic cleavages that had developed within the party by reaffirming the DVP's commitment to the "primacy of foreign policy." Speeches by Bernhard Falk from Cologne on the situation in the occupied territories and Ernst Siehr from Königsberg on the status of the German minorities in Eastern Europe were clearly designed to evoke an emotional response to those national issues on which the left and right wings of the party found themselves in essential agreement.[37] The reascendancy of the party's right wing became even more apparent on the second day of the congress when Otto Keinath from the Central Association of German Wholesalers reported on the economic policies of the Reichstag delegation. Categorically rejecting a fiscal solution to Germany's economic problems and reiterating the delegation's opposition to economic experimentation of any sort, Keinath struck a decidedly conservative note when he attributed Germany's economic problems and the fall of her currency to reparations and a sharp decline in labor productivity. Keinath's conclusion that the key to Germany's economic recovery lay not merely in reducing her reparations burden but, more importantly, in restoring labor productivity to prewar levels could only have come as a direct slap in the face to the leaders of the DDP's left wing.[38]

If the creation of the Alliance of the Constitutional Middle and the outcome of the Elberfeld party congress revealed the extent to which the right wing of the DDP had managed to regain control of the party, developments within the DVP indicated a general consensus at the upper echelons of the party organization in support of the policies Stresemann had pursued since the beginning of the spring.[39] Within the DVP Reichstag delegation the only noteworthy opposition to Stresemann's political course came from Reinhold Quaatz and Fritz Geisler, both of whom preferred the establishment of closer ties with the right-wing DNVP to the parliamentary alliance with the DDP and Center. Geisler's opposition was at least partially rooted in the fact that the initiative for the creation of the parliamentary alliance of the DVP, DDP, and Center had come from Stegerwald and the leadership of the Christian labor movement. As chairman of the rival National Federation of German Unions, Geisler was particularly incensed by an article that Otto Thiel, a member of the DVP Reichstag delegation and an influential functionary in the German National Union of Commercial Employees, had published in early August 1922 asserting that there was no room for representatives of the management-controlled yellow unions within any of the parties that belonged to the new parliamentary alliance.[40] Citing this as evidence of the party's capitulation to the Christian labor unions and as a breach of the neutrality that the DVP had promised to maintain in the conflict between the Christian and yellow labor movements, Geisler demanded that the party take disciplinary action against Thiel and that Stresemann provide spokesmen from the yellow unions with an opportunity to respond to Thiel's charges in the official party press.[41]

Stresemann, who by this time had begun to lose patience with the intrigues of the yellow trade-union movement,[42] might not have been overly concerned about Geisler's agitation were it not also for the fact that the DVP's participation in the Alliance of the Constitutional Middle as well as his own willingness to support a modified version of the Law for the Defense of the Republic had produced widespread unrest at the local levels of the party's national organization. Moreover, the DVP's public admission that the restoration of the monarchy no longer lay within the realm of immediate possibility had left many of its more conservative supporters deeply confused about its long-range political objectives.[43] In an attempt to take advantage of the growing uneasiness that existed within certain sectors of the DVP, Geisler publicly attacked Stresemann's leadership of the party with an article in which he exhorted the DVP to repudiate its alliance with the DDP and Center for the sake of a new parliamentary coalition with the right-wing DNVP. Failure to do so, he threatened, would result in the loss of the party's popular base and its demise as a viable political force.[44] Infuriated by both the tone and substance of Geisler's article, Stresemann despaired of further collaboration with the yellow labor movement, and at a meeting of the DVP central executive committee in Breslau in late September 1922 he sided openly with the party's Christian labor leaders in a debate on the trade-union question. The committee handed the leaders of the yellow labor unions a further setback when it formally endorsed the Alliance of the Constitutional Middle as a step toward overcoming the social and political cleavages that had become so deeply entrenched in the fabric of Germany's national life.[45] Isolated within the party and embittered by their treatment at the hands of Stresemann and the DVP's national leadership, Geisler and those of his associates who still belonged to the party began an exodus from the DVP that was to lead them over the course of the next several years into ever increasing dependence upon the right-wing DNVP.[46]

The defection of Geisler and the leaders of the yellow labor movement was only part of the price that the DVP had to pay for its defense of the republic in the summer of 1922. A far more significant price—and one the DDP had to pay as well—was the virtual collapse of its state organization in Bavaria. In Bavaria, as in most of southern Germany, the outbreak of the November Revolution had led to a brief consolidation of liberal forces on the basis of the German Democratic Party. The Bavarian DDP, however, stood considerably to the right of the national party, and its leaders were often openly critical of the policies of their colleagues at Weimar and Berlin during the first years of the postwar period.[47] Their relative independence from the policies of their party's national leadership, however, enabled the Bavarian Democrats to escape the state and national elections in the summer of 1920 with significantly lighter losses than those suffered by Democrats in the rest of the country. But unlike the Reich, where the DVP had emerged as the principal beneficiary of the DDP's defeat at the polls, the Bavarian political scene was characterized by the existence of two regional parties—the Bavarian People's Party, which had dissolved its last ties to the Center earlier in the year, and a radical farmers' party known as the Bavarian Peasants' League—that proved remarkably successful in attracting the support of disgruntled Democratic voters. The DVP, on the other hand, had yet to recover from the collapse of its state organization in the November Revolution and was unable to take advantage of the DDP's electoral predicament.[48]

As a result of its defeat in the 1920 Landtag elections, the Bavarian DDP was obliged to relinquish one of its two seats in the government that had been formed under the leadership of the BVP's Gustav von Kahr in the wake of the Kapp Putsch.[49] The DDP's position in the Kahr government, however, became increasingly problematic when, in the fall of 1920, the BVP adopted a political program that constituted a direct challenge to the Reich's claims of sovereignty over Bavarian affairs. Consequently, when the Wirth government began to take action against right-wing extremist organizations in Bavaria and other parts of the country following Erzberger's assassination in the summer of 1921, relations between the Reich and Bavaria became increasingly strained. This, in turn, placed the leaders of the Bavarian DDP—and particularly Eduard Hamm, the party's lone representative in the Kahr government—in an extremely difficult situation as they tried, though without great success, to bring the crisis to a quick resolution.[50] The conflict had immediate repercussions upon the Bavarian DDP, where the particularist sympathies of local party members clashed sharply with the efforts of the central government in Berlin to establish its sovereignty over state government authorities in Munich.[51] By the same token, the leaders of the Bavarian DDP were distressed by the triumph of the party's left wing at Bremen in November 1921 and took particular umbrage at the adoption of a resolution characterizing the DDP as "an outspoken republican party." Such a resolution, complained the leaders of the Bavarian DDP, only revealed the insensitivity of the party's national leadership to the problems that continued to haunt their efforts to establish the DDP as a viable force in Bavarian politics.[52]

The threat that Bavarian particularism posed to the future of the two liberal parties did not become fully apparent until after Rathenau's assassination in the summer of 1922. The Law for the Defense of the Republic contained provisions that the Bavarian press and the leaders of the Bavarian Right were quick to denounce as a violation of Bavarian sovereignty. This pressure, which was fueled by the antirepublican sentiment of influential sectors of the Bavarian bourgeoisie, made it impossible for the Bavarian government, now in the hands of the BVP's Count Hugo von Lerchenfeld, to support the law without fundamental changes in the sections that infringed upon Bavarian sovereignty. When the law was passed over strenuous Bavarian objections on 21 July 1922, the Lerchenfeld government responded three days later by issuing its own Decree for the Defense of the Constitution of the Republic and declared the Reich's Law for the Defense of the Republic invalid for the state of Bavaria.[53] Throughout the crisis Hamm and the leaders of the Bavarian DDP had tried to mediate between state and Reich authorities in hopes of averting an open conflict.[54] But Lerchenfeld's action represented a breach of the Weimar Constitution that no responsible Democrat could countenance, and on 24 July Hamm tendered his resignation from the Bavarian government with the full support of the state executive committee of the Bavarian DDP.[55]

The conflict between the Reich and Bavaria in the summer of 1922 exacted a heavy toll upon the Bavarian DDP. The party's state organization had already suffered a number of resignations as a result of the way in which the DDP's national leadership had supposedly capitulated to Wirth's demands for expanded authorization to combat right-wing radicalism in Bavaria and other parts of the country.[56] With the DDP's support of the Law for the Defense of the Republic and Hamm's resignation from the Lerchenfeld government, what had begun as a trickle of defections became a flood that left the party's Bavarian organization in a complete shambles.[57] In the meantime, the leaders of the DVP were all too eager to take advantage of the rift that had materialized between the rank and file of the Bavarian DDP and the party's national leadership in Berlin. But here too a fundamental and ultimately irreconcilable split had developed between the DVP's state and national leaders. For although Stresemann, like Hamm, had sought to mediate on behalf of an understanding between the Reich and Bavarian governments,[58] he found it impossible to countenance Lerchenfeld's breach of the Weimar Constitution and fully sympathized with the reasons that had led Hamm to resign from the Bavarian government.[59] Moreover, Stresemann's reluctant and admittedly qualified support of the Law for the Defense of the Republic as well as the DVP's decision to join the Center and DDP in the Alliance of the Constitutional Middle found little favor with the more conservative leaders of the Bavarian DVP. On 23 July the state executive committee of the Bavarian DVP adopted a formal resolution that disavowed the steps that had been taken by the party's national leadership in defense of Germany's new republican order and expressed full support for the Lerchenfeld government in its struggle to preserve Bavarian sovereignty.[60] Even though this action did not have the full support of local party leaders in much of the state, the damage it did to the DVP's position in Bavarian politics proved irreparable.

This series of events dealt the Bavarian liberal movement a blow from which it never recovered. Over the course of the next year and a half, whatever support the DDP and DVP had enjoyed in Bavaria at the time of the 1920 Landtag elections evaporated, and the two parties were all but swept away by the strong swing to the right that determined the outcome of the next state elections in the spring of 1924.[61] The collapse of the Bavarian liberal movement, however, was only one instance of the way in which the critical days of June and July 1922 served as a watershed in the history of political liberalism during the Weimar Republic. Not only had Rathenau's assassination robbed the DDP's left wing of its most articulate and dynamic spokesman, but the shock of Rathenau's murder had prompted Stresemann to come to the republic's defense in a series of moves that left many of those on his party's right wing bewildered and embittered. Moreover, the formation of the Alliance of the Constitutional Middle by those parties that had rallied to the defense of the existing political order initiated a period of closer cooperation between the two liberal parties that was to continue until the spring of 1924. Yet, while this no doubt helped to stabilize the German middle during a period of increasing political turmoil, Rathenau's assassination had also done much to destroy international confidence in Germany's ability to master the political and economic problems that faced her. This, in turn, led to renewed pressure on the German mark and to an intensification of the inflationary forces that already existed within the German economy. As a result, the leaders of the German liberal parties suddenly found themselves confronted with a myriad of new problems, not the least of which were the virtual collapse of their parties' national organizations and the traumatic demoralization, if not radicalization, of those social forces upon which the German liberal movement had always depended for the bulk of its popular support. The crisis of Weimar liberalism and the crisis of the German middle class had become inseparably intertwined.

PART THREE

Between Ruin and Reconstruction
1922–1924

CHAPTER TWELVE

Democracy in Dissolution

THE FIRST YEARS OF THE Weimar Republic stood under the shadow of the German inflation. More than any other single event, it was the great inflation of the early 1920s that destroyed the social foundations of the Weimar Republic and made the rise of National Socialism ultimately possible.[1] Within the German liberal parties the impact of the inflation was essentially threefold. First of all, it greatly accelerated the disintegration of the predominantly middle-class social base upon which the two liberal parties rested, thereby continuing a process that had begun with the industrialization of Germany in the nineteenth century and had been intensified by the social and economic hardships of World War I. Secondly, the inflation did much to exacerbate the social and economic antagonisms that had emerged within the German liberal electorate and to create new antagonisms where none had previously existed. In this respect, the inflation superimposed a pattern of social and economic conflict upon the political and ideological divisions that had already surfaced within the German liberal parties, with the result that their integrative potential, already compromised by factors unrelated to the inflation, was further weakened. Thirdly, the two liberal parties found themselves confronted with mounting financial difficulties that severely hampered the effectiveness of their national organizations and made it increasingly difficult, if not impossible, for them to contain the forces of social and political disintegration that the inflation had unleashed.[2]

As strange as it may seem, the inflation played a relatively subordinate role in the thinking of Germany's liberal leadership through the late summer and early fall of 1921. Even though the leaders of the two liberal parties frequently had to deal with secondary manifestations of the inflation such as the rising costs of maintaining a political organization or the need to adjust salaries to keep pace with the rising cost of living, for the most part they remained preoccupied, if not obsessed, with questions of foreign policy. It was not the inflation but the Spa Conference, the London Ultimatum, and the partition of Upper Silesia that caught and held their attention. To be sure, few liberals went so far as to share Rathenau's view that the inflation helped insulate Germany from the effects of the economic crisis that had descended upon the other countries of the industrialized world and therefore had long-term political benefits that outweighed the short-term hardship it was causing various sectors of German society.[3] Still, most seemed prepared to accept depreciation of the mark to the level at which it had stabilized in the spring of 1920 as the regrettable, though unavoidable, price Germany had to pay for losing the war, while others entertained illusions that it might still be possible to restabilize the mark at its prewar level. Whatever their motives, the leaders of the German liberal parties remained willing, if not unwitting, partners in the "inflation consensus" that surfaced in Germany between March 1920 and May 1921.[4]

All of this began to change with the resumption of the inflationary spiral in the spring of 1921. For the first time, the leaders of the German liberal parties became openly concerned about the effect the inflation was beginning to have upon the various social and economic groups from which they drew the bulk of their support.[5] By November 1921 Rathenau was publicly decrying the inflation and warning that Germany's current economic boom was merely the fever of a victim who seemed to be in glowing health but in reality was consuming the last reserves of his bodily strength.[6] The fact, however, that the second wave of inflation in the summer and fall of 1921 coincided with acceptance of the London Ultimatum led Germany's liberal leaders to misunderstand the causes of the inflation and to attribute it almost entirely to Allied diplomatic machinations.[7] Moreover, the close connection between the resumption of the inflation in the spring of 1921 and acceptance of Allied reparations demands made it possible for the leaders of the German Right to blame the inflation on the misguided efforts of Germany's republican leadership to fulfill the terms of the London Ultimatum. By equating fulfillment with the proletarization of the German people, Helfferich and his associates within the German National People's Party were able to mobilize the anguish of those hurt by the inflation into an emotionally effective campaign against both the architects of German foreign policy and the system of government that had made that foreign policy possible.[8]

With the renewed depreciation of the mark in the summer of 1921, the plight of the German liberal parties—and particularly that of the German Democratic Party—became increasingly critical. In general, the DDP was hit much harder by the inflation than the rival German People's Party, which was spared the brunt of middle-class frustration over the deepening economic crisis by virtue of the fact that it was not a member of the national government between May 1921 and November 1922. For the DDP, however, the second wave of inflation in the summer and fall of 1921 came just as the party seemed to be recovering from the devastating losses it had suffered in the Reichstag elections of June 1920 and the Prussian Landtag elections of February 1921. In the Berlin municipal elections of October 1921, for example, the DDP recorded a modest gain of approximately 8,000 votes while the DVP, on the other hand, suffered a loss of nearly 20,000 votes. In the Brunswick state elections three months later, the DDP improved upon its performance in the last state elections of

May 1920 by more than 6,500 votes as the result of a special electoral alliance it had concluded with a local farmers' organization, the League of Agricultural Tenants and Small Peasants (Verband landwirtschaftlicher Pächter und Kleinbauern). Even set against the party's losses in Thuringia and Baden, these results were sufficient to belie the popular impression that the DDP was moribund and beyond recovery.[9]

If the outcome of regional elections in Germany in late 1921 and early 1922 indicated that the Democrats might have succeeded in halting their party's decline, any hopes for a long-term improvement in the DDP's political fortunes were quickly destroyed by the progressive deterioration of the German mark following acceptance of the London Ultimatum. The immediate problem confronting the leaders of the DDP was one of financing the party's national organization during a period of acute monetary instability. In an attempt to avoid becoming overly dependent on support from outside economic interests, the Democrats had originally sought to finance their party's activities through the regular collection of dues from the DDP's rank-and-file membership. But even the relatively moderate rate of inflation in the immediate postwar period made rational budgetary procedures extremely difficult, so that by the end of 1919 party leaders were complaining about the havoc that the rising costs of paper, postage, and other essentials had played with party finances.[10] Although the problem temporarily abated with the relative stabilization of the mark in the spring of 1920, the Democrats were never able to achieve their goal of financial independence from outside economic interests. The general failure of the DDP's local organizations to collect membership dues and forward them to Berlin created such a large deficit in the party's operating budget that party leaders were left with no alternative but to turn to sources outside the party. In 1920, for example, membership dues were sufficient to cover only about a tenth of the DDP's operating expenses, while nearly 1 million marks had to be raised from outside sources.[11]

By the fall of 1921 the DDP's financial plight had become so desperate that party leaders had to borrow more than 100,000 marks in order to cover the deficit that the inflation had produced in the DDP's operating budget.[12] Addressing party leaders on the eve of the Bremen congress in November 1921, party treasurer Hermann Fischer warned his fellow Democrats that if the DDP did not take immediate steps to resolve its financial difficulties, it might as well close up shop for the coming political year.[13] As a temporary expedient, the DDP party council approved a 50 percent increase in annual membership dues to twenty-four marks, a third of which was to be forwarded to Berlin to help cover the operating expenses of the party's national headquarters.[14] At the same time, appeals to the DDP's backers in the financial and business communities succeeded in raising the money the party needed to pay off the debts it had contracted during the course of 1921.[15] This, however, did little to solve the specific problems that the inflation presented to the leaders of the DDP. Not only did party employees begin to clamor for salary increases to help them keep pace with the rising cost of living,[16] but the budgetary process itself was thrown into complete chaos by the inflation's effects on the DDP's operating expenses. For 1922 party leaders had projected a budget of 2.4 million marks for the DDP's national headquarters in Berlin. Actual costs, however, exceeded 7.7 million marks. Although over half of the resulting deficit was to be covered through the generosity of the DDP's backers in finance and industry, party leaders were so severely strapped for funds that by the end of 1922 they had no alternative but to begin cutting back on the size of the party's national organization.[17]

The DDP's precarious financial situation in 1921 and 1922 was further complicated by the widespread disaffection the inflation had produced between the DDP and the various social groups from which it recruited its popular support. At the heart of the problem lay the DDP's inability to provide effective political representation for the diverse and increasingly antagonistic social groups that constituted its material base. Frustration with the DDP was particularly pronounced within three social groups: the independent middle class, the peasantry, and the civil service. Of these three groups, the independent middle class had been the first to become estranged from the DDP. The party's failure to take a strong stand against government socialization schemes at the Weimar National Assembly and its subsequent role in securing passage of the Reich Emergency Levy had produced a strong move away from the DDP on the part of the independent middle class as early as the end of 1919 and had cost it heavily in the June 1920 Reichstag elections.[18] This began a trend that was to continue over the course of the next several years and that party leaders belatedly tried to arrest through a more vigorous representation of middle-class interests in connection with the tax compromise of 1922.[19] But the party's continued ambivalence toward middle-class interests was underscored by a characteristic split in the DDP Reichstag delegation on a vote to create a special rent tax in early March 1922. Ostensibly designed to generate capital for the construction of new homes, the bill represented only one more example of continuing governmental control over the housing industry and was vigorously opposed by organized housing interests throughout the country. While an overwhelming majority of the Democratic delegation joined the DVP, DNVP, and BVP in voting against the bill, a handful of deputies led by Anton Erkelenz and Gertrud Bäumer sided with the two socialist parties and a sizable majority in the Center to secure its passage, thereby lending further credence to the arguments of those who claimed that the DDP was unreliable in its defense of middle-class interests.[20]

Charges that the Democrats were unreliable in their defense of middle-class economic interests were not confined to the more traditional elements of the urban middle class but had become widespread among the small and middle-sized peasantry as well. Relations between the DDP and the German Peasants' League, the party's principal liaison to the German agricultural community, had deteriorated steadily since they first entered into an alliance for the 1919 elections to the National Assembly. Although the Peasants' League had renewed the alliance prior to the 1920 Reichstag elections, it did so only after a bitter internal struggle in which Karl Böhme, the DBB's general secretary and a member of the Democratic delegation to the National Assembly, fended off a series of attacks from those within the DBB who preferred closer ties to the more conservative DVP. In the 1921 Prussian Landtag elections the DBB withheld its endorsement from the DDP as a sign of its dissatisfaction with the party's failure to dissociate itself from the policies pursued by Social Democrat Otto Braun as the Prussian minister of agriculture.[21] As a member of the DDP's right wing, Böhme not only criticized the party for its lack of independence vis-à-vis the Social Democrats but favored the cultivation of closer ties with the DVP and the eventual creation of a united liberal party.[22] At the same time, Böhme harbored a deep resentment against the metropolitan Democratic press and the influence it allegedly exercised over the policies of the DDP.[23]

A major source of Böhme's dissatisfaction with the DDP was its equivocation on the question of government controls over agricultural prices and production. The acute food shortage following the end of World War I had left the German government with little choice but to continue the wartime system of agricultural price and procurement controls into the immediate postwar period. The continuation of these controls, however, was deeply resented by Germany's agricultural producers, who demanded an immediate end to the controlled economy (*Zwangswirtschaft*) and a return to a free market in agriculture.[24] Böhme and the leaders of the DBB were particularly outspoken in the struggle for a free economy, and in August 1920 they recorded their first triumph when representatives from the DDP, DVP, DNVP, and Center voted to suspend government controls over the beef and potato industries.[25] Efforts to deregulate the grain industry, on the other hand, encountered stiff resistance from the SPD and Center, both of which feared the effects that a dramatic rise in the price of bread might have upon the urban working class. Consequently, when efforts to dismantle government controls over the grain industry were resumed in the summer of 1921, the Wirth government responded by establishing a dual market structure that required agricultural producers to meet mandatory delivery quotas at fixed prices at the same time that it permitted them to sell production in excess of these quotas on the open market at whatever price it might bring.[26]

Though conceived of as a transitional step toward the eventual restoration of a free market in the grain industry, the proposed grain levy (*Getreideumlage*) met with almost universal condemnation from agricultural interest organizations, including the German Peasants' League.[27] By no means insensitive to this sort of pressure, the Democrats proceeded to break with the other government parties and joined the DVP, DNVP, and BVP in an unsuccessful effort to block passage of the bill when it came before the Reichstag in June 1921.[28] With the renewed depreciation of the mark and the resultant rise in consumer prices over the course of the next six months, however, it soon became apparent that the dual market structure established by the grain levy bill was both patently unfair to Germany's grain producers and totally inadequate to the task of maintaining stable bread prices. As a result, the DDP found itself at one and the same time under heavy attack from consumer organizations for having supported a reduction in delivery quotas[29] and under pressure from the German Peasants' League for a fundamental reorientation of the party's social and economic policies that would strengthen its commitment to the productive forces in German society.[30] The situation exploded at a meeting of the DDP executive committee on 22 January 1922 when Böhme deplored the increasingly hopeless situation in which the party found itself, castigated the party leadership for its subservience to the "asphalt Democrats" on the DDP's left wing, and called for the immediate creation of a united liberal party through a merger with the DVP. While Böhme's frustration was understandable in light of the economic difficulties facing Germany's small and middle-sized grain producers, his attacks did little to ingratiate himself with the leaders of the party and prompted counterallegations that the DBB was trying to turn the DDP into an instrument of its own economic self-interest. All of this underscored Böhme's growing isolation within the party and the danger of an eventual rupture between the DDP and DBB.[31]

The DBB's loyalty to the Democratic Party was severely tested by the decision to renew the grain levy bill in the summer of 1922. By then a wide gap had developed between the price a farmer received for grain delivered to the government and what he might be able to get for grain he sold on the open market. Agricultural interest organizations, including the German Peasants' League, were adamant in their opposition to the existing system of mandatory delivery quotas and demanded its immediate revocation and the total restoration of the free market in agriculture.[32] At the same time, the agitation surrounding government efforts to renew the grain levy system afforded the DBB's rivals in the German agricultural community, especially the conservative National Rural League (Reichs-Landbund or RLB), an excellent opportunity to attack the DBB's alliance with the DDP as a betrayal of the small peasant producer.[33] In the early summer of 1922 it seemed as if the entire system was about to be dismantled as representatives from all of the bourgeois parties, including the Center and DDP, voted in committee against its extension in spite of the sharp increase in consumer food prices that this would almost certainly entail. The situation changed dramatically, however, with Rathenau's assassination on 24 June 1922. Faced with the threat of new national elections in which they could be held responsible for the increase in bread prices, the leaders of the DDP went behind Böhme's back to reach a compromise with the Center and Social Democrats that renewed the grain levy for the forthcoming year but exempted peasants with holdings of ten hectares or less from its provisions.[34] While this stipulation benefited the DDP's small peasant supporters in northwestern Germany and overcame whatever objections they might have had to an extension of the grain levy system,[35] it did little to appease Böhme's own supporters in the DBB, the vast majority of whom owned holdings in excess of ten hectares and therefore remained adamantly opposed to the compromise that the DDP had reached with the other government parties.[36] This did not augur well for the unity of the party, and in the decisive vote on the renewal of the grain levy on 1 July 1922 the Democratic delegation split with eighteen in favor, five opposed, and seventeen abstaining.[37]

Although the DDP's role in the passage and extension of the grain levy bill did much to strain already weakened ties between the party and the German Peasants' League, another social group upon which the DDP depended for a large part of its support stood to benefit from the government regulation of the grain industry, namely the professional civil service. From the first days of the Weimar Republic the DDP had worked in close cooperation with the newly founded German Civil Servants' Association to preserve the professional civil service and ensure its loyalty to Germany's new republican order. A major step in this direction was the reform of Germany's civil service salary structure that the DDP helped implement in April 1920 and that sought to eliminate some of the more glaring inequities caused by the depreciation of the mark since the end of the war. Among other things, this law reduced the number of civil service classifications from over fifty to thirteen, narrowed the gap between the upper and lower ends of the salary scale, and provided for the payment of special cost-of-living supplements in the event that the inflation continued.[38] At the same time, the leaders of the DDP also took steps to organize civil servants who belonged to their party into a special organization called the National Council of German Democratic Civil Servants (Reichsausschuß der Deutschen demokratischen Beamten) under the chairmanship of Gerhard Vogt. The purpose of this organization, whose official founding took place at the DDP's Nuremberg party congress in December 1920,[39] was not only to enhance the party's effectiveness in recruiting civil servant support but also to keep party leaders abreast of issues directly affecting the social and economic welfare of the state civil service.[40] By the time of the Bremen party congress in the fall of 1921, Vogt and his followers had established liaison groups in over a hundred cities and had built up an elaborate network of 2,819 confidants or *Vertrauensmänner* attached to more than a thousand of the party's local chapters.[41]

Within the DDP the National Council of German Democratic Civil Servants stood on the party's left wing, where Vogt and his associates joined forces with Erkelenz and the leaders of the DDP's National Workers' Council in common cause against the DBB's efforts to block renewal of the grain levy. These efforts, however, were subordinate to the broader goal of providing civil servants with a forum within the Democratic party organization for the defense of their social and economic interests. As domestic prices began to climb again in the summer of 1921, the DDP's civil servant spokesmen responded with a vigorous campaign at the upper echelons of the party organization for a new round of adjustments in civil servant salaries. This agitation reached a climax at the Bremen party congress in November 1921 when the National Council of German Democratic Civil Servants adopted a sixteen-point program for a reform of Germany's civil service salary structure.[42] Although the Reichstag proceeded to approve salary adjustments for higher government officials in November 1921 and January 1922, this brought little relief to civil servants in the middle and lower ranges of the salary scale. Threats of a civil service strike became increasingly widespread during the winter of 1921–22 before culminating in a nationwide work stoppage by government railway officials in the first week of February.[43] When the leaders of the DDP sided with the government in denouncing the strike as a breach of the civil servant's contract with the state,[44] their stand severely tested the loyalties of those civil servants who belonged to the party and threatened to trigger a general secession among its supporters in the state civil service.[45]

Even though Democratic mediation played a major role in bringing the strike to a quick and peaceful end, the situation within the party remained highly volatile. Not only did the strike dramatize the radicalizing effect of the inflation on the German civil service, but the position taken by the DDP during the strike had given rise to widespread doubts about the sincerity of its commitment to the social and economic welfare of the professional civil servant. In an attempt to repair the damage the strike had done to the DDP's relations with the professional civil service, Vogt and the leaders of the National Council of German Democratic Civil Servants scheduled a conference of the party's civil servant representatives for the third week of April, to which Erich Koch-Weser and other prominent Democrats were invited to speak.[46] The Democrats also revived proposals for the introduction of a sliding salary scale for civil servants so that their salaries could be adjusted automatically to fluctuations in the cost of living. Only a self-activating mechanism such as this, they argued, could provide civil servants with the economic security to which they were rightfully entitled and protect the state against a repeat of the strike that had just taken place.[47]

In general, the Democrats were less hesitant about identifying themselves with the interests of the civil service than they were in the case of the peasantry and independent middle class. Not only did this help protect the DDP against large-scale defections by disgruntled civil servants, but it also reflected the influence that civil servant spokesmen were able to exercise at the upper echelons of the party organization. The party's deference to civil service interests could also be seen in the debate that surrounded the recommendations of the DDP's business wing for a reorganization of Germany's economic structure. By no means had the manufacturing and retailing interests that constituted the nucleus of the DDP's right wing succeeded in escaping the ravages of the inflation. In this respect, the party's business leaders complained that the loss in purchasing power experienced by nearly every sector of German society as a result of the inflation had led to a dramatic decline in domestic consumption. At the same time, they charged that antiprofiteering laws making it illegal to base prices on replacement or reproduction costs had destroyed the profitability of many commercial enterprises. To help rectify this situation, the leaders of the DDP's business wing called for a sharp reduction in spending at all levels of government and the introduction of a unified tax structure limiting the taxation powers of local and municipal authorities. Arguing that a currency reform would be of little consequence without a reduction of Germany's reparations burden, the DDP's business spokesmen only underscored what the leaders of the German business community had been saying for some time, namely that the key to Germany's economic recovery was not fiscal but political and lay in the wholesale reorganization of her domestic economic structure.[48]

In early August, Philipp Wieland, chairman of the DDP's National Council for Trade, Industry, and Commerce and a presidial member of the National Federation of German Industry, wrote to Hermann Bücher, the RDI's executive secretary, to suggest that the two organizations cooperate more closely in the formulation of economic policy and in dealing with economic questions that came before the Reichstag.[49] Wieland's suggestion came just weeks after the leaders of the RDI had appointed a special committee consisting of Albert Vögler, Hans von Raumer, Paul Silverberg, and a number of other prominent industrialists for the purpose of drafting a comprehensive program for Germany's economic recovery. Although the committee's work was permanently interrupted by the occupation of the Ruhr in January 1923, its drafts served as the basis of the program the RDI adopted in 1925 and contained the elements of an official ideology for Germany's industrial elite.[50] As the RDI began work on its program in the late summer and fall of 1922, parallel efforts were under way within the DDP's National Council for Trade, Industry, and Commerce, where Wieland and his associates unveiled a series of proposals that bore a remarkable resemblance to the program under discussion in the RDI. Both drafts proceeded from the assumption that a currency reform aimed at stabilizing the mark would be ineffective as long as the reparations question remained unsettled. Since Allied intransigence on the reparations question ruled out a fiscal solution to Germany's economic problems, both the RDI and the group around Wieland concentrated their attention upon a structural reorganization of the German economic system as the key to Germany's economic recovery. Here the central assumption was that if Germany could put her own economic house in order, it would be possible to refute Allied arguments that Germany was using the economic crisis at home to escape her financial obligations abroad. Both drafts also identified the need to increase economic productivity as the key to solving Germany's economic problems and therefore advocated the immediate elimination of all governmental restrictions that interfered with the goal of full productivity. Specifically, this entailed not only an end to all government controls over industry and agriculture but also an end to the eight-hour day, the major social achievement of the November Revolution. In the area of fiscal policy, on the other hand, this meant the adoption of a balanced budget and a sharp reduction in the tax burden that the private economic sector had been forced to assume. This, in turn, presupposed drastic cuts in spending at all levels of government and a corresponding decrease in the size of the state civil service.[51]

Wieland presented the program that he and the executive committee of the DDP's National Council for Trade, Industry, and Commerce had drafted to the DDP Reichstag delegation on 10 November 1922, whereupon it was approved and subsequently published as the delegation's official position on the question of economic recovery.[52] The publication of this program with the imprimatur of the DDP Reichstag delegation, however, provoked a storm of protest from the party's civil service spokesmen, who complained not only that they had been excluded from any sort of meaningful role in drafting the program but also that the program favored the party's large capitalistic interests at the expense of those who constituted the bulk of its rank-and-file support.[53] No doubt Vogt and his associates in the National Council of German Democratic Civil Servants were most disturbed by the provisions in the delegation's program that called for a reduction in the size of Germany's civil bureaucracy and a reorganization of the state-owned railway system. At a meeting of the DDP party council on 26 November, Vogt joined forces with Heinrich Dahl from the DDP's National Workers' Council to introduce a resolution that called upon the party to reject the economic program of its Reichstag delegation and refer the task of formulating such a program to a special commission in which the party's civil servant and working-class constituencies were also represented. The DDP party council stood considerably to the left of the Reichstag delegation, and in the ensuing debate the delegation's critics clearly outnumbered its supporters. As a result the meeting ended with the adoption of a resolution that transferred responsibility for drafting an economic program for the party as a whole to a special commission constituted more or less along the lines suggested by Vogt and Dahl. While party leaders were careful not to embarrass the delegation by publicly disavowing the program it had published earlier in the month, this did little to soften the effects of the defeat that the delegation and the party's business wing had suffered at the hands of the ideologues in control of the DDP party council.[54]

The failure of the DDP party council to approve the economic program that the Reichstag delegation had drafted in close cooperation with the party's business leaders was significant in several respects. In the first place, the decision to refer the delegation's program to committee effectively killed it as the occupation of the Ruhr in 1923 suddenly made all efforts at economic stabilization superfluous. This turn of events only added to the frustration that the leaders of the DDP's business wing already felt over developments within the party. The party's business leaders had been pressing for the adoption of an economic program for nearly three years, and the action of the DDP party council seemed only one more instance of the general inability of those who sat in the party's executive councils to address themselves to the economic problems that were slowly but surely destroying the social fabric of the Democratic Party. Moreover, the rebuff that the leaders of the DDP's business wing had experienced at the hands of the party council threatened the DDP with a loss of financial support from its backers in the business community at a time when the DDP was almost totally dependent upon contributions from sources outside the party. More importantly, however, the DDP's failure in the fall and early winter of 1922 to adopt an economic program for the party as a whole bore dramatic testimony to the disintegrative effect of the German inflation on the party's predominantly middle-class social base. By intensifying the degree of interest articulation and conflict at all levels of the party organization, the inflation had made it all but impossible for the leaders of the DDP to discover some sort of common ground upon which the diverse and increasingly antagonistic social and economic groups that constituted their party's material base might be reconciled. As its social base continued to fragment under the impact of the inflation, the German Democratic Party stood on the verge of total dissolution.

CHAPTER THIRTEEN

An Uneasy Equilibrium

IN ITS INITIAL STAGES the inflation seems to have had less of an effect upon the German People's Party than it had upon the DDP. Although both parties were exposed to the same general pressures as a result of the inflation, the fact that the DVP did not belong to the national government between May 1921 and November 1922 helped insulate it from much of the frustration that the German middle strata felt about their deteriorating social and economic position. Moreover, the DVP had always been more consistent in its representation of middle-class interests than the DDP, and its national organization was in much better financial shape than that of the rival Democratic Party. Yet while all of this seemed to augur well for the DVP's continued effectiveness at least during the more moderate stages of the inflation, the party was to become increasingly divided between those like Stresemann who genuinely deplored the effect the inflation was having upon the DVP's predominantly middle-class social base and those like Stinnes who, in their determination to use the inflation to secure specific social, economic, and political objectives, were essentially indifferent to the increasingly desperate plight in which the German middle class found itself. Not only did this seriously handicap the DVP in its efforts to formulate a strategy for combating the inflation, but over the course of time it magnified the differences that separated Stresemann from the leaders of his party's right wing to the point where compromise was no longer possible. As the inflation continued and its ravages became more apparent, the situation within the DVP grew more and more volatile until that party too was threatened with dissolution into its constituent social and economic interests.

Stresemann was quick to identify himself and the DVP with the plight of the German middle class. It is, however, unlikely that Stresemann ever fully comprehended the magnitude or complexity of the crisis in which the German middle class found itself. For all intents and purposes, Stresemann thought of the inflation in essentially political terms. Just as the causes of the inflation were political, so it would require a political solution to bring the inflation under control. The principal culprits in Stresemann's explanation of what had happened to the German middle class were Erzberger, the Social Democrats, and the Entente. Speaking at a regional party congress in Lüdenscheid on 18 September 1921, Stresemann charged that the proletarization of the German middle class was not an accident but the result of a carefully orchestrated policy on the part of Erzberger and his socialist allies to reduce all of those who opposed their vision of a socialized Germany to an amorphous mass of economically dependent men and women. But this, continued Stresemann, only complemented what the Entente was hoping to achieve with the London Ultimatum, namely the proletarization of the entire German nation. And once again it was the German middle class that was being asked to bear the brunt of such a policy. "If," Stresemann queried,

> we ask ourselves who has suffered the most from the devaluation of the currency that the lost war and revolutionary mismanagement have left in their wake, then we must answer the intellectual and commercial middle class. More than any other group in our society, this class has the right to rise up in rebellion against the kind of proletarization to which it has been subjected. I cannot regard as healthy a nation in which a large mass of economically dependent men and women on one hand stands opposed to a socialized Germany on the other. Even Germany cannot survive under such a strain. To see to it that this patiently suffering middle class is preserved must, it seems to me, be the guiding principle of our current policy.[1]

To underscore Stresemann's personal commitment to the social and economic welfare of the German middle class, the leaders of the DVP formulated a series of specific proposals designed to alleviate much of the distress that different sectors of the German middle class were experiencing as a result of the inflation. The mechanism through which this took place was the elaborate edifice of vocational and professional committees (*Fachausschüsse*) that the party had developed since 1919 as a means not only of increasing its effectiveness within the various social groups that served as the backbone of its popular support but also of providing those groups with a forum for articulating their special interests within the framework of the DVP party organization. In June 1921, for example, the party's committees for white-collar employees, agriculture, the small business sector, teachers, artisans, and workers held special conventions of their own in conjunction with a meeting of the DVP central executive committee in Hamburg.[2] And in late August the DVP's civil servants' committee held a convention in Berlin that was attended by over 200 delegates, including Stresemann and the leaders of the party's delegations in the Reichstag and Prussian Landtag.[3] Still, the leaders of the DVP were concerned about the effect this sort of activity might have upon the overall unity of their party, and in November 1921 they adopted a set of guidelines that governed the activity of the DVP's vocational committees and defined their relationship to the party as a whole. According to these guidelines, the party's vocational committees were to be placed under the supervision of the DVP managing committee and were to be completely dependent upon the DVP party organization for the funds they needed to conduct their activities. Under no circumstances were the DVP's vocational and professional committees to have financial assets or resources seperate from those of the party.[4]

This stood in sharp contrast to the way in which the Democrats had failed to establish effective control over the activity of their party's professional and vocational committees. For although the National Council of German Democratic Civil Servants, the DDP's National Workers' Council, and related organizations within the DDP received regular subsidies from the Democratic party headquarters in Berlin,[5] they were financially autonomous and had the right, if not the responsibility, to raise funds from their rank-and-file membership. As a result, the DDP's vocational committees enjoyed much greater independence from the party organization than did their counterparts in the DVP, so much so, in fact, that they could, if sufficiently motivated, criticize the party in public or pursue a course of action detrimental to the best interests of the party as a whole. Whereas this situation tended to strengthen the disintegrative forces at work within the Democratic party organization, the tight controls that the DVP placed upon the activities of its vocational committees helped protect the party against the threat that the overly vigorous representation of special economic interests posed to its internal cohesiveness and stability.

Of the two liberal parties, the DVP had always been considerably more effective in its efforts to attract and retain the support of the more traditional elements of the German middle class. Not only had the DVP succeeded in establishing itself as a champion of the independent middle class at the Weimar National Assembly,[6] but the DDP's participation in a governmental coalition in which the Social Democrats were also represented made it at least implicitly culpable for the implementation of economic policies detrimental to the best interests of the artisanry and small business sector. While the Democrats had repeatedly compromised themselves with concessions to the Social Democrats on questions of fiscal and economic policy, the leaders of the DVP could point with pride to the role they had played in dismantling government controls over Germany's middle-class economy and in blocking the introduction of new taxes they regarded as harmful to the economic vitality of the independent middle class.[7] But the DVP's ability to influence governmental policy toward the middle class diminished markedly with the installation of the Wirth government in the spring of 1921. In July 1921, for example, the DVP was unsuccessful in its efforts to end government controls over the housing industry and to block the imposition of a special rent tax whose proceeds were to be used to finance the construction of new housing.[8] No less exasperating was the party's inability to prevent local and municipal governments throughout the country from introducing a special business tax (*Gewerbesteuer*) in an attempt to compensate for the loss of revenue they had suffered as a result of the reorganization of German finances under Erzberger.[9] Complaining that these measures only discriminated against the most productive elements of the German economy, the leaders of the DVP called for tax relief and a return to unrestricted free enterprise as the key to rehabilitating Germany's middle-class economy and as the first step toward fulfilling the promise to protect and preserve the independent middle class enshrined in Article 164 of the Weimar Constitution.[10]

The DVP's commitment to the social and economic welfare of the independent middle class notwithstanding, the party lacked the leverage necessary to provide the artisan and small businessman with the relief they needed in order to survive the deepening economic crisis. To be sure, the party had been able to secure minor concessions beneficial to the small business sector as a result of its involvement in passing the 1922 tax compromise. At the same time, however, efforts to bring about an end to government controls over the housing industry had been repeatedly frustrated by the lack of support that such a project enjoyed within the ranks of the parties backing the government. In light of its general failure to provide the more traditional elements of the German middle class with the tangible support to which they felt entitled, the DVP found itself increasingly vulnerable to defections to special interest parties that promised to provide the independent middle class with more effective representation than it had received from the DVP and other nonsocialist parties. The appeal of special interest parties had first manifested itself in the Prussian Landtag elections of February 1921, when organized housing interests had run their own slate of candidates in an open challenge to the DVP and other nonsocialist parties. In the Baden state elections later that fall the DVP's efforts to reestablish itself as a viable political force in southwest Germany were undercut by the success of special interest parties such as the Economic Association of the German Middle Class (Wirtschaftliche Vereinigung des deutschen Mittelstandes) and the Baden Rural League (Badischer Landbund) in mobilizing the more traditional elements of the German middle class.[11] If unchecked, such a development could easily lead to the party's dissolution into its constituent social and economic interests.

If the DVP proved less than successful in providing the more traditional elements of the German middle class with the effective political representation they needed to survive the deepening economic crisis, its record with respect to Germany's burgeoning white-collar population and her professional civil service was somewhat more reassuring. The DVP's success in representing the interests of its white-collar and civil servant constituencies, however, stemmed not so much from any sort of preferential treatment on its part as from the alliances or *Querverbindungen* that its white-collar and civil servant representatives had established across party lines with their counterparts in the different government parties. As the DVP's most prominent spokesman for the German salaried employee, Otto Thiel was able to enlist the support of his colleagues in the German National Union of Commercial Employees and the German Trade-Union Federation in securing the passage of legislation beneficial to the group he represented. The same was true of the DVP's Albrecht Morath, who as the party's chief spokesman for the professional civil service was able to work through the German Civil Servants' Association to provide the civil service with a measure of relief from the hardship it was experiencing as a result of the inflation. The DVP's spokesmen for the commercial and independent middle class, on the other hand, lacked politically effective allies within the government parties and tended to look upon the industrial interests that sat on the DVP's right wing as their principal source of support both within and outside the party.[12] This, however, only underscored their essential isolation from the avenues of power in the early Weimar Republic and reflected the frustration that they felt at having to compete for patronage within a system that from their perspective was still dominated by the socialist working class.

The DVP's principal accomplishment on behalf of the salaried employee was a comprehensive reform of the national white-collar insurance program that Stresemann and the leaders of the prewar National Liberal Party had guided through the Reichstag in 1911. In the summer of 1920 Thiel and his associates waged a successful struggle to preserve the system's integrity in the face of Social Democratic efforts to merge it with the existing system of disability insurance. The following December the DVP introduced legislation that would have expanded the white-collar insurance program's coverage and adjusted benefits to meet increases in the cost of living. When these measures threatened to exhaust the program's pension fund, Thiel and the leaders of the DVP's social-liberal wing worked in close conjunction with representatives from the Christian and liberal white-collar unions to insure the system's financial solvency by forcing an 80 percent reduction in the size of its administrative staff.[13] Yet in spite of Thiel's unquestioned accomplishments on behalf of the salaried employee, relations between the DVP and the German white-collar movement remained tenuous at best. For not only had the party failed to provide Wilhelm Fecht from the liberal Federation of Employee Unions with a secure candidacy for the 1921 Prussian Landtag elections,[14] but within the more conservative German National Union of Commercial Employees to which Thiel belonged the inflation had done much to activate the latent antipathy the union leadership had always harbored toward the capitalist economic system.[15] Moreover, Thiel's vote for acceptance of the London Ultimatum in May 1921 had prompted charges from the antilabor elements on the DVP's right wing that in breaking with the rest of the Reichstag delegation to support acceptance of the ultimatum he had yielded to pressure from the antinational elements in control of the Christian labor movement.[16] None of this bode particularly well for the future of the DVP's alliance with the more conservative elements of the German white-collar movement.

The antipathy that Thiel and his associates in the leadership of the German National Union of Commercial Employees felt toward the capitalist economic interests on the DVP's right wing had become widespread among the party's civil servant spokesmen as well.[17] Here, as in the case of the DDP, the tension between the DVP's civil servant and business wings stemmed from the fact that the latter's proposals for economic recovery almost invariably included provisions for a dramatic reduction in the size of the German civil service. Yet in spite of the general irritation with which the party's industrial leaders viewed the enormous expansion of Germany's civil bureaucracy during and after the war, Stresemann and the leaders of the DVP were anxious to prevent the civil service from falling under the influence of the working-class parties on Germany's socialist Left. As a member of the Fehrenbach government, the DVP had actively supported efforts to soften the inflation's effects upon government employees through a comprehensive reform of Germany's civil service salary structure.[18] Following its resignation from the government in the spring of 1921, the DVP sharply criticized the Wirth government for the inadequacy of its own efforts to protect the civil servant against the effects of the inflation and warned that failure to adjust civil servant salaries to meet increases in the cost of living could only lead to the radicalization of the entire civil servant movement.[19]

The outbreak of the railway officials' strike in the first week of February 1922 seemed to vindicate the DVP in its criticism of the Wirth government.[20] For although the leaders of the DVP categorically rejected the notion that the civil servant enjoyed the same right to strike as the industrial wage earner, they also portrayed the strike as an act of desperation on the part of loyal government officials who had been pushed to the wall by the government's persistent refusal to recognize the seriousness of their plight.[21] In this respect, the DVP criticized the Wirth government not only for having failed to approve supplemental salary payments that, if implemented, could have prevented the outbreak of the strike in the first place, but also for having entered into indirect negotiations with representatives from the striking railway officials' union in order to bring the strike to an end. So infuriated were the leaders of the DVP by Wirth's handling of the strike that they introduced a motion of no-confidence in the chancellor when the issue was debated before the Reichstag in the middle of February.[22] At the same time, Stresemann and his associates took steps to solidify their position vis-à-vis the civil service by reviving earlier proposals for the introduction of a sliding salary scale that would automatically adjust civil servant salaries to fluctuations in the cost of living. By providing the civil service with the economic security it needed to maintain its standard of living in the face of mounting domestic prices, the leaders of the DVP hoped to stem the forces of social and political radicalization that had begun to gain the upper hand within the civil service movement.[23]

A fourth major social group to which the DVP addressed itself during the early years of the Weimar Republic was the independent peasantry. The DVP's efforts to win the support of peasants and farmers who had formerly patronized the National Liberal Party had been severely handicapped, however, by the defection of Böhme and his associates in the leadership of the German Peasants' League to the rival DDP. Within the DBB, however, there still remained a handful of officials headed by William Dusche and Friedrich Harte who were loyal to the DVP and who sought to sabotage Böhme's alliance with the DDP. Although their efforts to pressure the Peasants' League into adopting a neutral stance in the 1920 Reichstag elections had failed to generate much support among the leaders of the DBB's Prussian affiliate, the DDP's reluctance to support an end to government controls over agricultural prices and production was to provide them with an opening they were quick to exploit.[24] Yet, as more and more farmers became disenchanted with the agricultural policies of the early Weimar governments, the leaders of the DVP became increasingly concerned that these farmers, in rebelling against the parties of the Weimar Coalition, might bypass the DVP in favor of the right-wing German National People's Party or one of the regional agrarian parties that had surfaced in Bavaria, Württemberg, Thuringia, and other parts of the country. Reinforcing these fears was the vigorous offensive that the DNVP and its supporters in the newly founded National Rural League had recently unleashed throughout the German countryside.[25]

The principal figure in the DVP's efforts to contain the conservative tide that threatened to sweep the German countryside in the first years of the Weimar Republic was Karl Hepp, a DVP Reichstag deputy from Hesse-Nassau and a prominent official in the leadership of the National Rural League. Following the end of the war Hepp had played an active role in efforts to organize the small and middle-sized farmers of western and central Germany into a new agricultural interest organization called the German Rural League (Deutscher Landbund). This action was directed first and foremost against the large landowning interests from east of the Elbe River that had dominated the Agrarian League ever since its founding in 1893 and whose policies had frequently discriminated against the interests of the small and middle-sized farmers in places like Hepp's own district of Hesse-Nassau. But the revolutionary upheaval of the immediate postwar period made the existence of two such organizations impractical, and after more than a year of negotiations the German Rural League merged with the Agrarian League on 1 January 1921 to form the National Rural League with an initial membership of well over 2 million, thus making it the largest agrarian organization in all of Germany.[26] Within the RLB Hepp was one of the few who did not belong to the German National People's Party, and he frequently came under attack from the more conservative members of the RLB leadership for his ties to the DVP. Still, as a token of the RLB's bipartisan neutrality, Hepp was elected to one of its two presidencies at the first RLB convention in March 1921.[27]

Hepp stood on the extreme right wing of the DVP and harbored a deep-seated antipathy toward the Weimar Republic and the basic principles of parliamentary government. As the DVP's principal liaison within the National Rural League and as the leader of the RLB's so-called liberal wing, Hepp sought to organize the small and middle-sized farmers from central and southwestern Germany into a force sufficiently powerful to offset the influence of those East Elbian Junkers who had formerly been in control of the Agrarian League and who now belonged to the right-wing DNVP.[28] In public appearances for the DVP, Hepp quickly established himself as an outspoken opponent of the controlled economy in agriculture, and he categorically rejected the grain levy system when it was first proposed by the Ministry of Agriculture in the spring of 1921.[29] Here he not only reiterated his party's unequivocal commitment to the restoration of the free market in agriculture but also attacked the notion widely held in agrarian circles that the DVP was the party of big business and therefore had nothing to offer the small farmer.[30] Hepp's vigorous advocacy of the DVP notwithstanding, the party encountered formidable obstacles in its efforts to develop a firm foothold within the German agricultural community. Most of the RLB's regional affiliates had remained under the control of those with close ties to the DNVP, and the agitation of regional agrarian parties such as the Baden Rural League had attracted considerable support away from the DVP in spite of DVP efforts to brand such parties as auxiliaries or *Hilfstruppen* of the DNVP.[31] Whether or not Hepp and the leaders of the DVP would eventually succeed in containing the Nationalist tide that seemed to be sweeping the German countryside during the first years of the Weimar Republic remained to be seen.

By no means was the internal disintegration of the German People's Party as advanced as that of the DDP. Whereas by the end of 1922 the Democratic Party stood on the verge of a complete financial and organizational collapse, Stresemann and the leaders of the DVP had managed to achieve an uneasy equilibrium between the various interest groups that constituted their party's social base. As a result, the DVP's performance in state and local elections through 1921–22 revealed some slippage, but by no means were its losses as severe as those suffered by the DDP.[32] Moreover, the DVP found itself in much better financial shape than the DDP thanks to the generous support it had received from its backers in business and finance.[33] Particularly significant in this respect was the massive assistance that Stresemann received from Carl Duisberg and the leaders of the German chemical industry in his efforts to provide the DVP with a daily newspaper in the German capital. Stresemann had long complained that the lack of such an organ placed the DVP at a serious disadvantage vis-à-vis the other bourgeois parties, all of which enjoyed the support of influential daily newspapers in the metropolitan Berlin area. In an attempt to remedy this deficiency, Stresemann turned to Duisberg and his associates in the German chemical industry for their support in launching a new Berlin daily entitled *Die Zeit*.[34] Anxious to strengthen party moderates and offset the dominant influence that heavy industry seemed to be gaining within the DVP, the leaders of the German chemical industry responded favorably to Stresemann's request and agreed to underwrite the founding of the new paper in November 1921 to the extent of 2 million marks.[35]

While the leaders of the DVP had succeeded in achieving at least a tenuous equilibrium between the various interest groups that constituted their party's material base, the maintenance of this equilibrium presupposed an immediate end to the inflation and a permanent stabilization of the German mark. Stresemann himself was acutely aware of the disintegrative effect that the inflation had had upon his party's predominantly middle-class social base, and his willingness to support the government's tax compromise in the spring of 1922 had been predicated upon the assumption that this would help stabilize the mark and bring a return to normal economic conditions. In this respect, however, Stresemann found himself separated from the heavy industrialists on the DVP's right wing by a fundamental difference of opinion over the way in which the mark was to be stabilized. For while Stresemann and other party leaders were anxious to halt the inflation at the earliest possible moment so as to minimize its effects upon the DVP's rank and file, the faction around Stinnes and Vögler was determined to attach political conditions to the stabilization of the mark that would eliminate many of the most important social achievements of the November Revolution. Speaking before the National Economic Council on 9 November, Stinnes rejected stabilization at any cost and outlined a series of conditions that would have to be met before any permanent stabilization of the mark could be expected. The central assumption upon which Stinnes based his argument was that efforts to stabilize the mark were doomed as long as they were not accompanied by an increase in industrial productivity. To achieve increased productivity, Stinnes not only demanded that the government ban all strikes and wage conflicts for the period immediately following stabilization of the mark but also proposed the temporary suspension of the eight-hour day until Germany had achieved a favorable balance of trade and a fiscal surplus sufficient to pay the interest and amortization on the international loan she needed to stabilize the mark and meet her reparations obligations.[36]

While the primary significance of Stinnes's speech lay in the fact that it signaled an intensification of heavy industry's struggle against the social legacy of the November Revolution, it also presaged the beginning of a conflict within the DVP between those like Stresemann who sought an end to the inflation before it had completely destroyed their party's social base and those like Stinnes who were determined to use the inflation as a means of accomplishing specific social and political objectives. Though only in its infancy, the cleavage that had developed along these lines was to prove far more destructive of party unity than the effects of the inflation itself. As long as the DVP remained in opposition, the possibility of an open rupture seemed remote. But as the pressure of events in the fall of 1922 began to push the DVP toward a return to governmental responsibility, the situation within the party became increasingly volatile. For the DVP and the industrial interests that stood behind it, the moment of truth was drawing near.

CHAPTER FOURTEEN

The Descent into Chaos

ON 23 OCTOBER 1922 the Reichstag adjourned for a three week recess amid signs of mounting political unrest. The steady decline of the mark since Rathenau's assassination and the upcoming visit of the Allied Reparations Commission in the first week of November combined to create a climate of growing uneasiness that was compounded by the relentless and often scurrilous attacks that the German Right continued to level against the "Weimar System" and the parties generally identified with it.[1] Moreover, the formal unification of the two socialist parties at Nuremberg in September 1922 had greatly strengthened the working-class component of Wirth's government coalition so that the bourgeois members of his cabinet began to clamor for a reorganization of the government and the inclusion of the German People's Party. Against the background of these developments Wirth decided to use the parliamentary recess in the fall of 1922 to make one last attempt to bring the DVP back into the government. Should he fail, Wirth was prepared to accept the consequences and resign from office. Should he succeed, the reorganization of his government would be followed by a dramatic new initiative in the reparations question and firm measures to stabilize the mark.[2]

If Wirth was interested in establishing closer ties with the DVP in order to avoid becoming overly dependent upon the Social Democrats, Stresemann and the leaders of the DVP were no less interested in joining his government. Since the spring of 1922 the DVP had demonstrated considerable willingness to support the Wirth government in securing the passage of unpopular domestic measures such as the tax compromise in March and April and the Law for the Defense of the Republic in July. More than anything else, it was Wirth's softness toward the Allies and the policy of unconditional fulfillment that stood in the way of closer relations between Wirth and the DVP. At the Breslau meeting of the DVP central executive committee in late September 1922 the party had taken the first step toward its eventual reentry into the government by formally endorsing the Alliance of the Constitutional Middle that the leaders of its Reichstag delegation had concluded with the DDP and the Center following Rathenau's assassination earlier that summer.[3] Equally significant as an indication of the DVP's eagerness to join the government was its refusal to join the DNVP in a campaign to block the extension of Ebert's term of office as Reich president.[4] Originally the leaders of the DVP had hoped that it might be possible to postpone new presidential elections until some point in the future when political passions would not be running so high.[5] But when this ploy failed, the leaders of the DVP proceeded to outrage their supporters on the party's right wing by joining the Social Democrats and the other government parties in voting to extend Ebert's term of office for another two-and-a-half years by means of a special exemption from the provisions of the Weimar Constitution.[6] Although this shift to the middle produced widespread dissension on the DVP's right wing, it was a risk that Stresemann and the party's more moderate leaders were willing to run so as not to jeopardize their chances of rejoining the government.[7]

While the initiative for a reorganization of the government along the lines of the Great Coalition came from Wirth, it received strong encouragement from the Alliance of the Constitutional Middle. Created in July 1922 as a bourgeois counterweight to the parliamentary coalition between the two socialist parties, the Alliance brought representatives from the three middle parties together under its auspices for the first time on 20 October. The alliance readily endorsed the DVP's entry into the government and began to make preparations for the formation of a bourgeois minority government should the newly unified Social Democratic Party refuse to share governmental responsibility with the DVP.[8] Contrary to all expectations, however, the Social Democrats showed little inclination to provoke a cabinet crisis with the visit of the Allied Reparations Commission so near at hand, and they carefully refrained from making a reorganization of the government contingent upon any conditions that the leaders of the three middle parties might find unacceptable.[9] Representatives from the DVP, DDP, and Center met again on 27 October to draft a program for economic recovery that they hoped would serve as the basis for a compromise with the Social Democrats despite unresolved differences as to precisely how the economic situation was to be stabilized. Whereas the Socialists argued that the Reichsbank should use its gold reserves to stabilize the mark before any changes in the existing wage structure could be considered, spokesmen for the Alliance of the Constitutional Middle contended that the use of the Reichsbank's gold reserves to stabilize the mark would be ineffective as long as it was not accompanied by economic reforms aimed at increasing industrial productivity. In this respect, the three middle parties were in essential agreement that the eight-hour day constituted one of the major obstacles to an increase in industrial productivity, and they recommended the adoption of a flexible wage structure in which compensation would be determined not by the number of hours spent on the job but by the productivity of one's labor. Other measures the three middle parties agreed on as preconditions for stabilizing the mark included a balanced budget, a reduction in the size of the civil bureaucracy, and a reform of the German tax system.[10]

Although the Social Democrats were willing to concede the necessity of increasing industrial productivity, they looked upon attacks against the eight-hour day with considerable apprehension, and on 30 October the leaders of the SPD Reichstag delegation issued a warning that under no circumstances would they countenance changes in the length of the work day as a condition for remaining in the government.[11] Efforts to reconcile the differences that had developed between the Social Democrats and the Alliance of the Constitutional Middle, however, continued throughout the recess and eventually led to a softening of the SPD's position on the eight-hour day.[12] But the prospects of a political compromise between the Social Democrats and the parties of the bourgeois middle began to unravel almost as soon as agreement on the measures necessary to stabilize the mark had been reached. The leaders of the DVP were particularly incensed by the decision of the Wirth government to petition the Allied Reparations Commission for a moratorium on the payment of reparations instead of pressing the German case for a reduction of her reparations burden, a maneuver that they criticized as another example of the government's weakness toward the Allies.[13] At the same time, Stinnes's attack against the eight-hour day in the National Economic Council on 9 November only added to the deep-seated reservations that the Social Democrats already had about sharing governmental responsibility with the DVP.[14] Consequently, when Wirth resumed his efforts to reorganize his government on the basis of the Great Coalition following the departure of the Allied Reparations Commission on 10 November, he found himself no closer to his goal than he had been when the Reichstag first adjourned.[15]

The crisis drew to a head on 13 and 14 November. Deeply distrustful of the DVP, the Social Democrats were willing to participate in a reorganization of the Wirth government as long as this only meant adding men with backgrounds in business and finance to his cabinet, but not if it entailed the DVP's formal entry into the government. While this might have been sufficient to satisfy Wirth, it fell far short of what the leaders of the DVP had been expecting from the negotiations, and on 13 November they informed Wirth that under no circumstances would they go along with a reorganization of the national government that did not involve their party's acceptance into the cabinet as a full and responsible member of the governmental coalition.[16] When, early the following day, representatives from the Alliance of the Constitutional Middle came out in unanimous support of the DVP's demands for a place in the national government,[17] Wirth made this the basis of his own position and formally asked the Social Democrats whether or not they were prepared to share governmental responsibility with the DVP in a cabinet of the Great Coalition. Alarmed as much by the tone as by the content of Wirth's ultimatum, the SPD Reichstag delegation voted on 14 November to reject the DVP's entry into the government by an overwhelming 150–20 margin.[18] His hopes of the Great Coalition effectively dashed, Wirth tendered his resignation as chancellor in a meeting with Ebert later that evening.

Although the Social Democrats and the Alliance of the Constitutional Middle were able to agree upon the terms of the fiscal and economic program that Wirth had submitted to the Allies on 13 November,[19] it proved impossible to translate this into a durable and politically effective government coalition. The SPD's deep-seated distrust of heavy industry as well as its concern for the survival of the recent merger between the two socialist parties made the Social Democrats extremely apprehensive about sharing governmental responsibility with the DVP. Yet while primary responsibility for the failure of Wirth's efforts to reorganize his government lay with the Social Democrats, it is also clear that the DVP—and particularly the industrial interests on its right wing—sought to saddle the SPD with responsibility for implementing unpopular social and economic policies aimed at increasing labor productivity.[20] Under these circumstances, the leaders of the DVP not only anticipated the SPD's withdrawal from the governmental coalition but were fully prepared to take the lead in forming a bourgeois minority government based upon the Alliance of the Constitutional Middle should negotiations with the Social Democrats break down. But Stresemann's hopes that he might be asked to form a new government were blocked by Ebert, who apparently feared that this would give the DVP and the industrialists behind it too great an influence over the formulation of national policy.[21] When the Center, still smarting from the way in which the Social Democrats had treated Wirth, declined to nominate one of its own members as a candidate for the chancellorship,[22] Ebert proceeded to overlook Stresemann in order to commission Wilhelm Cuno, the politically unaffiliated head of the Hamburg-America Shipping Line (Hamburg-Ameri-ka-Packetfahrt Aktiengesellschaft), with the task of forming a new government.

Following his nomination as Wirth's successor on 16 November, Cuno set out to organize a government based upon essentially the same parties Wirth had struggled to bring together. But when the Social Democrats made their participation in such a government conditional upon the acceptance of demands that neither Cuno nor the Alliance of the Constitutional Middle were prepared to accept, Ebert interceded with the parties in question to secure their consent to the formation of a government that was not bound by formal ties to the parties supporting it. Cuno's efforts to organize a government free from formal political commitments to the various parties in the Reichstag continued over the next several days before culminating in the presentation of a new government on the morning of 22 November. Although Cuno and five of his ministers were politically unaffiliated, his claim that the new cabinet stood above parties was undercut almost from the outset by the fact that the rest of his cabinet had been recruited from the three parties that belonged to the Alliance of the Constitutional Middle. In addition to the DDP's Otto Gessler and two Centrists who had been carried over from the previous government, the new cabinet included two members of the DVP, Rudolph Heinze and

Johann Becker, at the Justice and Economic ministries respectively and Democrat Rudolf Oeser at the Ministry of Interior. Cuno's assertions to the contrary, his new cabinet clearly derived the bulk of its support from the Alliance of the Constitutional Middle and the moderate bourgeois parties that had coalesced to form it in the aftermath of Rathenau's assassination.[23]

Having pledged himself to regard the fiscal and economic program contained in the German reparations note of 13 November as the basis of his government's own economic program, Cuno received an overwhelming vote of confidence from the Reichstag on 22 November as all of Germany's major political parties except the Communists rallied behind his cabinet. The two major problems facing the Cuno government were the fall of the mark and reparations. Since Rathenau's assassination in the summer of 1922, the exchange value of the German mark had fallen from a dollar quotation of 75 in July to 1,711 at the end of November.[24] The Reichsbank, however, was unwilling to use its gold reserves to help stabilize the mark as long as the reparations question remained unsettled. Immediately upon his installation in office, therefore, Cuno undertook a major diplomatic initiative aimed at winning Allied support for a reduction of Germany's reparations burden and a moratorium on the payment of reparations. But Cuno's efforts to create a climate in which a revision of Germany's reparations burden might take place were repeatedly frustrated by Poincaré, who not only blocked a favorable response to the German reparations note at a conference of Allied prime ministers in London during the second week of December but also seemed intent upon using Germany's failure to fulfill her reparations obligations as a pretext for seizing the Ruhr. When the Allied Reparations Commission proceeded to declare Germany in default on the delivery of reparations in kind—first on 22 December 1922 and then again on 9 January 1923—Poincaré had all the justification he felt he needed, and on 11 January French and Belgian troops began to occupy the Ruhr.[25]

The occupation of the Ruhr in January 1923 constituted a national crisis every bit as traumatic as the loss of the war itself. Indeed, to many Germans it seemed as if the French move into the Ruhr was merely a continuation of the war by different means, and the sense of national solidarity to which it gave rise was as real as that of August 1914. Under these circumstances, the DDP and DVP were quick to join the other major parties in rallying to the support of the Cuno government and the policy of passive resistance it announced on 13 January. Though supported by virtually every sector of German society, the policy of passive resistance placed a severe strain upon Germany's already weakened finances and did much to intensify the inflationary pressures at work in the German economy. Within days of the occupation, the German government began to organize a massive relief program for the occupied territories. Under this program the government not only provided unemployment benefits to those who had lost their jobs as a result of the occupation but also assumed responsibility for a large share of the wages paid to industrial workers in the occupied territories. The only way such programs could be financed was through massive deficit spending, an expedient that combined with the lack of international confidence in the German economy to push the mark to a record low quotation of 44,000 to the dollar at the end of January.[26] As the mark continued to deteriorate through the first half of February, the government found itself under increasingly heavy pressure from organized labor to stabilize the mark,[27] and in the middle of February the Reichsbank reluctantly began to use its gold reserves in a desperate attempt to prevent a total collapse of the currency. As a result, the exchange value of the mark temporarily stabilized at 25,000 marks to the dollar for a period of approximately eight weeks from the end of February through the middle of April. By the end of this period, however, it became apparent that efforts to save the mark were doomed to failure as long as the policy of passive resistance continued, and on 18 April the government abandoned its support of the mark amid reports that the Stinnes concern had begun to make large-scale purchases of foreign currencies.[28] Over the course of the next six weeks the mark fell another sevenfold, so that by the end of June 1923 it required 150,000 to purchase just one dollar.

As the mark resumed its fateful decline in the spring of 1923, the financial situation of the two liberal parties became increasingly desperate. This was particularly true in the case of the DDP, where the formation of the Alliance of the Constitutional Middle had given rise to grave doubts about the party's future as an independent political force.[29] In an attempt to cover the deficit in their party's operating budget, the Democrats increased membership dues to seventy-five marks per month for 1923 and required each of the DDP's thirty-five district organizations to forward fifty marks for each registered member to the party's central headquarters in Berlin before the end of January. Since the DDP had 209,530 registered members at the end of 1922,[30] this should have produced more than 10 million marks—or approximately 14,000 gold marks —for the party's immediate use.[31] Of this amount, however, less than 1 million marks was ever forwarded to the party's national headquarters, as the DDP's district organizations either underreported their membership, pleaded financial exigency, or simply failed to respond to their party's appeal for help.[32] The party's financial plight was further complicated by the growing unwillingness of German big business to commit its resources to the maintenance of the DDP's national organization. Not only was the DDP specifically excluded from the benefits of a special collection organized by the Commission for the Industrial Campaign Fund on behalf of the DVP and DNVP,[33] but the Curatorium for the Reconstruction of German Economic Life, which had given the DDP 182,300 marks in 1922, withheld all support from the Democrats through the first half of 1923.[34] As a result, the leaders of the DDP were left with no alternative but to curtail their subsidies to the party's local and district organizations and to initiate a drastic reduction in the size of their Berlin staff.[35]

The effect of this situation on the DDP's national organization was catastrophic. In reviewing the state of the party organization at a meeting of the DDP executive committee in early March 1923, the DDP's secretary general, Werner Stephan, painted a uniformly distressing picture of the situation in which the party found itself.[36] The lack of funds led to a virtual cessation of the party's publishing activities and to the financial collapse of its own publishing house, the Verlag Neuer Staat.[37] Of the DDP's thirty-five district organizations, seven were without a secretary, five were staffed entirely by volunteers, and two were on the verge of closing. The party's organizational collapse was most apparent in the countryside, where Stephan estimated that if new elections were held, the DDP would enter the campaign with no organizational support whatsoever in Pomerania, Brandenburg, Upper Silesia, Thuringia, northern Westphalia, and southern Bavaria.[38] Equally distressing was the lethargy of the DDP's vocational and professional committees. Of the various committees the DDP had created since the summer of 1920 to enhance its effectiveness within specific social and professional groups, only the party's National Council for Trade, Industry, and Commerce was able to sustain any sort of activity through the first part of 1923. And it, lamented the party's national leaders, seemed more intent upon raising funds for its own use than helping the party as a whole.[39] The DDP's National Workers' Council, on the other hand, was virtually moribund as a result of inadequate financial support and the illness of its secretary general, Heinrich Dahl, while the National Council of German Democratic Civil Servants had managed to stave off financial ruin only by virtue of the fact that its chairman, Gerhard Vogt, was willing to work on a volunteer basis. Yet even in the case of those committees that were blessed with effective leadership, the lack of funds had forced a sharp cutback in the scope of their activities.[40]

By the middle of May the DDP's organizational collapse had become so acute that a handful of Democratic deputies secretly approached Stresemann about the possibility of merging their two parties or, should that prove impossible, joining the DVP themselves. While Stresemann was fully prepared to accept those Democrats who agreed to work on the basis of the DVP program into the party, he had no interest in a merger of the two liberal parties, with the result that the project died amid Democratic denials that such overtures had ever taken place.[41] Still, this did not mean that the German People's Party had succeeded in escaping the forces of social and economic disintegration that had already done so much to destroy the DDP as a viable political force. For although the DVP's role as an opposition party throughout most of 1921 and 1922 as well as the support it had received from its backers in finance and industry had helped shield it from the initial ravages of the inflation, by the end of 1922 it too had begun to experience severe financial difficulties as a result of the fall of the mark.[42] Moreover, the inflation had seriously undermined the financial integrity of *Die Zeit*, which Stresemann had founded in November 1921 in an attempt to provide the DVP with a daily newspaper in Berlin.[43] Much of the DVP's financial weakness, however, stemmed from the niggardliness and unreliability of its backers in heavy industry. For in sharp contrast to its popular image as the party of big business and industry, the DVP had never received the kind of support from heavy industry that the public associated with it. Hugo Stinnes, for example, continued to limit his contributions to the party to 10,000 marks a year even after the inflation had rendered such an amount worthless.[44] And the 50,000 marks the DVP received from Paul Reusch, general director of the Gutehoffnungshütte in Oberhausen, at the end of February 1923[45] were worth less than two dollars on the international exchange. Under these circumstances, it could have come as no surprise to Stresemann that when he approached Stinnes for a donation on behalf of *Die Zeit* in the summer of 1923, the self-styled "Merchant of Mulheim" characteristically responded that for the moment his firm had no need of additional advertising.[46]

To compensate for his party's lack of support from German heavy industry, Stresemann began to cultivate closer ties with Carl Duisberg and the leaders of the newly founded cartel of German chemical firms known as I.G. Farben (Interessengemeinschaft Farbenindustrie). In general, the leaders of the German chemical industry were more favorably disposed to the Weimar Republic than their counterparts in heavy industry, and they were anxious to offset the predominant influence that Stinnes and his associates seemed to have gained within the DVP. When Stresemann approached Duisberg and his associates in December 1922 for a contribution of 15 million marks to help *Die Zeit*,[47] they responded by creating a special commission to represent their political interests within the DVP and the other nonsocialist parties with Wilhelm Ferdinand Kalle, a member of the DVP Prussian Landtag delegation and an outspoken champion of Stresemann's political course, as its unofficial chairman.[48] Known as the "Kalle Committee," this commission was subsequently expanded to include Paul Moldenhauer from the DVP Reichstag delegation, Hermann Hummel from the DDP, and Clemens Lammers from the Center in addition to several members of I.G. Farben's board of directors, the most influential of whom were Duisberg from the Bayer Dye Manufacturers (Farbenfabrik Bayer A.G.) and Carl Bosch of the Baden Aniline and Soda Manufacturers (Badische Anilin- und Soda-Fabrik).[49] In February 1923 Kalle arranged a contribution of 10 million marks from the directors of I.G. Farben as part of a financial package to help save *Die Zeit* that also included donations from the leading Berlin banks and the machine-manufacturing industry.[50] But as Stresemann himself readily conceded, even this support would be of little avail as long as the inflation continued its destructive course.

In spite of the obvious difficulties that Cuno's failure to stabilize the mark had created for the two liberal parties, both continued to support his government and its policy of passive resistance in the Ruhr. While in the case of the DDP this was a function of the general paralysis that had descended upon the Democratic leadership in the first half of 1923, in the case of the DVP it stemmed from Stresemann's reluctance to provoke a cabinet crisis at a time when he himself was not yet prepared to assume the reins of power. Moreover, whatever reservations Stresemann may have had about the Cuno government at the time of its formation[51] had been almost completely dispelled by the firmness of Cuno's response to the occupation of the Ruhr.[52] By the middle of March, however, the unanimity that had prevailed within the DVP during the initial stages of the Ruhr crisis had begun to evaporate in the face of increasing industrial opposition to the policies of the Cuno government.[53] Though a prominent industrialist in his own right, Cuno was regarded as something of an outsider by the leaders of German heavy industry, and his own conception of Germany's political priorities differed substantially from that of Stinnes and his associates. Specifically, Stinnes disagreed with the basic assumption of Cuno's political program, namely that Germany should undertake efforts of her own to stabilize the mark without waiting for the Allies to make concessions on the reparations question. In a lengthy conversation with Stresemann on the morning of 19 March, Stinnes registered his growing opposition to Cuno's political course by criticizing his efforts to support the mark as a threat to German industry's competitive advantage on the world market. By the same token, Stinnes insisted that resistance in the Ruhr was doomed to failure and urged Germany to take action to resolve the crisis by negotiations before the situation ended in complete catastrophe. In this repect, Stinnes conceded that it would probably be necessary for Germany to mortgage the nation's "real assets" as part of any definitive reparations settlement but stipulated that such an arrangement would have to include an end to the controlled economy and revocation of the eight-hour day as preconditions for industry's cooperation in any such agreement.[54]

Within a month of Stresemann's conversation with Stinnes, the Cuno government was forced to abandon its efforts to support the mark. This was accompanied by a significant shift in Stresemann's own views on the struggle in the Ruhr, a shift that may have been at least partially motivated by Stinnes's pessimistic assessment of the situation in the occupied territories. Addressing the Reichstag on 17 April—the day before the government announced the cessation of its efforts to support the mark—Stresemann took special pains to reaffirm his support of the Cuno government in the face of increasingly heavy criticism in the press and parliament. The real significance of Stresemann's speech, however, lay not so much in his continued support of the Cuno government as in his apparent willingness to consider negotiations with the French as a means of ending the crisis in the Ruhr. Stresemann suggested that the reparations question should be reexamined in the light of Germany's capacity to pay so as to facilitate negotiation of an international loan for the purpose of stabilizing the mark. At the same time, Stresemann proposed that Germany should explore the possibility of negotiations with the Entente in order to avoid a catastrophe in the Ruhr.[55] In view of the government's increasing dependence upon the DVP, Cuno could ill afford to ignore the thrust of Stresemann's remarks, and on 2 May his government transmitted a note to the signatories of the Versailles Treaty, the Vatican, and concerned neutral governments in which he proposed to fix Germany's reparations burden at 30 billion gold marks and offered to raise this sum through an international loan guaranteed by a mortgage on Germany's industrial assets. In return, the French would have to evacuate the Ruhr and restore the situation in the Rhineland to what it had been before the occupation.[56]

In French and Belgian circles the German reparations offer of 2 May was quickly perceived as a weakening of the German position, and they emphatically rejected the note on 6 May. In the meantime, the terms of the German note had also come under strong criticism from nearly all of Germany's political parties for having given away too much to those responsible for the debacle in the Ruhr. When the British response on 13 May dashed whatever hopes Cuno may have had of driving a wedge between the Allies, his government's position became virtually untenable, and attention began to focus almost immediately upon Stresemann as his successor to the chancellorship.[57] The crisis drew to a head in late May when the National Federation of German Industry attached all but impossible conditions to the use of industrial assets as a guarantee for an international loan that would have made it possible for the German government to fulfill the terms of the reparations proposal outlined in its note of 2 May.[58] With the Cuno government on the brink of collapse, Stresemann met with the chancellor on the evening of 26 May in an attempt to dissuade him from resigning and then with representatives from the Alliance of the Constitutional Middle to devise a formula that might enable the Cuno government to remain in office in spite of the apparent rebuff it had just received at the hands of German industry. At Stresemann's urging, the leaders of the three middle parties quickly closed ranks behind the beleaguered chancellor, and in a three-hour meeting with Cuno on the morning of 28 May they succeeded in persuading him to remain in office. Then, to counter whatever negative effects publication of the RDI's statement of conditions may have had on the domestic political situation, the Alliance released a statement that hailed the RDI's statement as a sign of industry's willingness to participate in a solution of the reparations problem without, however, making any reference to the difficulties this statement had created for the government.[59]

Had it not been for Stresemann's intitiative, the Cuno government would almost certainly have fallen in the last days of May 1923. By persuading the embattled chancellor to remain in office and by rallying the parties of the Alliance of the Constitutional Middle to the support of the Cuno government, Stresemann not only managed to avoid a cabinet crisis at a time when it might have had severe repercussions on Germany's position in the Ruhr, but he also succeeded in postponing his own succession to the chancellorship until a more auspicious moment had arrived. In the meantime, the immediate task was to help create an international climate conducive to ending the crisis in the Ruhr, a goal that would not have been served by a change of governments in Berlin. Yet while much of Stresemann's cautious behavior in the spring of 1923 stemmed from his reluctance to assume office under conditions that did not augur well for the success of his policies, it also revealed the process of political maturation he had undergone since the early days of the Weimar Republic. No longer the recalcitrant monarchist whose opportunism had led him to the brink of illegality at the time of the Kapp Putsch, Stresemann had not only made his separate peace with the Weimar Republic but was fully prepared to place himself, his incomparable political talents, and his party at the republic's service and defense. And if the circumstances that existed in the spring of 1923 dictated postponing his bid for power, he was willing to pay this price so that the full force of his leadership might not be prematurely exhausted in the pursuit of unattainable goals. Confident that his hour in Germany's political life was drawing near, Stresemann had only to wait until conditions for his succession to power were right.

CHAPTER FIFTEEN

Stresemann's Hundred Days

BY THE BEGINNING OF August 1923 the position of the Cuno government was no longer tenable. Not only had the value of the mark fallen nearly twentyfold since the first of June, but the diplomatic initiative that Cuno had so ceremoniously launched with the German reparations note of 2 May had all but evaporated in the face of French intransigence and British indifference. At the same time, the sense of national solidarity to which the occupation of the Ruhr had originally given rise was beginning to show signs of severe strain. In the last weeks of July a wave of strikes and rioting had swept through the Ruhr and parts of unoccupied Germany, and the Social Democrats, ever sensitive to the plight of the German working class, were beginning to waver in their support of passive resistance. More ominous still were the growing strength of the radical Left in Saxony and Thuringia and the emergence of separatist movements in Bavaria and the Rhineland that posed an open threat to the unity of the Reich. In a word, Germany seemed on the verge of a total national collapse as the summer of 1923 entered its final month.

Even as the demise of the Cuno government seemed to be drawing near, Stresemann and the leaders of the German People's Party continued to support it in spite of growing public frustration over its lack of tangible success. At the same time, however, Stresemann and his associates began to lay the foundation for a change of leadership by hinting at their willingness to share governmental responsibility with the Social Democrats. At a meeting of the DVP central executive committee in early July, Eugen Leidig from the party's delegation to the Prussian Landtag launched into a vigorous defense of the DVP's cooperation with the Social Democrats in Prussia, where a government of the Great Coalition had been in office since the fall of 1921. Stresemann returned to the same theme when in his own remarks he portrayed the DVP as a party of the *Volksgemeinschaft* whose goal was to unite all of the forces in German society, proletarian as well as bourgeois, that were prepared to set aside their partisan political differences for the sake of victory in the Ruhr.[1] Still, there were disquieting signs within the DVP, as even the party's more responsible leaders began to complain about the general inactivity of the Cuno government in the second half of July.[2] Among those who were particularly outspoken in their criticism of the chancellor was Hans von Raumer, a member of the DVP's left wing who urged Stresemann to enter into direct negotiations with the Social Democrats to work out the details of a social and economic program that would serve as the basis for their entry into the government. Specifically, Raumer maintained that such a program should address itself to the questions of tax reform, the eight-hour day, reduction of the civil service, and the role of organized labor in the formulation of national economic policy. Only after agreement had been reached on issues such as these, contended Raumer, would it be feasible to proceed with the installation of a new government based upon the Great Coalition.[3]

The crisis surrounding the future of the Cuno government came to an abrupt head when on 27 July *Germania*, the national organ of the German Center Party, published a blistering attack that represented a virtual call for Cuno's resignation as chancellor.[4] Stresemann, who had played an instrumental role in preventing the collapse of the Cuno government in May, could not help but agree with the general thrust of *Germania*'s attack, and he immediately returned to Berlin to prepare for a change of government and to lay the foundation for what he hoped would be his appointment to the chancellorship. Among those with whom Stresemann met upon his return to Berlin was Hermann Müller, chairman of the Social Democratic Reichstag delegation. Though reluctant to speak for his party as a whole, Müller stressed that under no circumstances could Germany afford the luxury of a prolonged cabinet crisis and indicated his tentative support for the SPD's entry into a government of the Great Coalition.[5] Still, the unsettled situation within the SPD as well as the fact that the British had not yet responded to the latest German note of 7 June made Stresemann reluctant to press for Cuno's resignation. For the moment he preferred to bide his time and continue to support the government.[6]

When the Reichstag reconvened in the second week of August, Stresemann tried to defuse the crisis with a speech in which he not only endorsed the policies of the Cuno government but also sought to reassure the Social Democrats about his own political credentials by publicly affirming his support of the republican system of government.[7] At a meeting of the DVP Reichstag delegation on the following day, Stresemann succeeded in persuading his colleagues to stand behind the Cuno government as long as the chancellor chose to remain in office but to seek a government based upon the Great Coalition with a nonsocialist as chancellor should the cabinet fall.[8] But with the government's announcement on 11 August that it had failed to soften French opposition to the German reparations proposals, the fundamental weakness of Germany's diplomatic position became so painfully apparent that the SPD Reichstag delegation adopted a resolution calling for Cuno's resignation and the formation of a new government on the broadest possible basis.[9] This effectively sealed the fate of the Cuno government, which on the following morning announced its intention to resign pending the formation of a new government. Anxious to avoid a protracted cabinet crisis, Ebert promptly acted upon the recommendation of the Alliance of the Constitutional Middle and entrusted Stresemann with the formation of a new government based upon the parties of the Great Coalition.[10] Buttressed by the strong support that his candidacy received from the three middle parties, Stresemann worked through the night of 12–13 August to reach an accommodation with the Social Democrats that would be amenable to the more conservative elements of his own party. Within the SPD Stresemann's candidacy received strong support not only from Müller but also from the man whom he had tapped for the Ministry of Finance, Rudolf Hilferding, and at a heated meeting of the Social Democratic Reichstag delegation on the morning of 13 August they were able to persuade their colleagues, though only by an 83–39 vote, to enter the new government.[11] After overcoming further difficulties with respect to Gessler's reappointment as minister of defense and after interceding on the SPD's behalf in a conflict with the Center over control of the Ministry of Interior, Stresemann was able to present Ebert with his cabinet on the evening of 13 August, whereupon the formal transfer of power took place.[12]

The speed with which Stresemann was able to form his government obscured the fragile political foundation upon which it rested. Particularly controversial was Stresemann's appointment of Hilferding as the new minister of finance. For although Hilferding possessed Stresemann's full confidence, the appointment of the former Independent Socialist to such a critical post aroused the deepest suspicions of those who sat on the DVP's right wing and met with little enthusiasm within the SPD Reichstag delegation, where Hilferding was still regarded as something of an outsider. Moreover, the appointment of the DVP's Hans von Raumer, a longtime advocate of closer cooperation with the Social Democrats, to head the Ministry of Economics did little to assuage the apprehension of those within the DVP who feared that the formation of the Stresemann cabinet signaled the beginning of yet another assault against the free enterprise system.[13] Consequently, when the Reichstag met on 14 August to provide the new government with a vote of confidence, neither the Social Democrats nor the DVP were able to maintain a united front. Within the SPD a group of forty left-wing deputies issued a statement announcing their opposition to the Great Coalition, and in the vote that took place on 14 August no less than forty-five socialist deputies stayed away from the Reichstag as a gesture of their dissatisfaction with the recent course of events.[14] Within Stresemann's own party, on the other hand, opposition to the new government was so strong that twenty-two members of the DVP Reichstag delegation—including Becker, Dauch, Gildemeister, Hepp, Moldenhauer, Quaatz, and Vögler—were absent when the crucial vote took place.[15] Even though the new cabinet managed to survive its first parliamentary challenge with little difficulty, the beginning of Stresemann's chancellorship, for his party as well as his government, could hardly have been less auspicious.

The next hundred days were to prove among the most tumultuous in the history of the young republic. A firm believer in the primacy of foreign policy, Stresemann began his term of office with the premise that stabilization of the mark and a return to economic normalcy at home constituted indispensable prerequisites for an active foreign policy and that the first task of his government should therefore be to secure the domestic preconditions necessary for diplomatic success in the Ruhr.[16] At the same time, Stresemann also believed that an end to the crisis in the Ruhr was possible only on the basis of direct negotiations with the French, something the Cuno government had assiduously tried to avoid.[17] Before overtures to the French stood any chance of success, however, it was necessary for Germany to put her own economic house in order. With this in mind, the Stresemann government entertained a series of proposals in the second half of August aimed at stabilizing the mark. In this respect, Hilferding favored a plan that would stabilize the mark through the state seizure of foreign currency accounts, increased taxation, and a dramatic reduction in the volume of money in circulation. All of this would eventually culminate in the creation of a new currency based upon gold.[18] Although these proposals received initial support from the Social Democrats and the other government parties,[19] they encountered stiff opposition not only from the DNVP's financial expert, Karl Helfferich, but also within the cabinet itself from Minister of Agriculture Hans Luther. As a result, Hilferding's proposals never made it out of the cabinet.[20]

As the mark continued its precipitous decline in the first weeks of September, Stresemann and the leaders of his government came to the reluctant conclusion that stabilization of the currency was impossible as long as the government continued to support passive resistance in the Ruhr. For Stresemann this amounted to a fundamental reversal of the position he had taken upon assuming the chancellorship. For whereas he had earlier maintained that the success of German foreign policy depended upon political and economic stability at home, he now came to realize that the solution to Germany's mounting domestic difficulties presupposed an end to the conflict in the Ruhr.[21] Stresemann's reassessment of Germany's political situation was reinforced by ominous signs from the occupied territories indicating that the policy of passive resistance was in danger of collapse.[22] Under these circumstances Stresemann felt that he had no choice but to begin preparations for an end to passive resistance, and on 12 September he informed his party's Reichstag delegation that the state of German finances made continuation of the struggle in the Ruhr impossible. Although most of Stresemann's colleagues were willing to accept his reading of the situation, Vögler and Quaatz immediately accused the government of capitulation in the Ruhr and denounced the idea of direct negotiations with the French as an admission of defeat.[23] As spokesmen for Ruhr heavy industry, their views were representative of the general sentiment that existed at the local levels of the DVP organization in the occupied territories, where party leaders were extremely concerned about the effect of nationalist agitation on the DVP's rank-and-file support and feared that an end to passive resistance would trigger massive defections to the DNVP and other right-wing groups.[24]

As Stresemann made final preparations for the termination of passive resistance in the Ruhr, the situation within the German People's Party became increasingly tense. On 24 September the leaders of the party's district organization in Franconia registered their disapproval of Stresemann's political course by severing their ties with the DVP and reconstituting themselves as the National Liberal State Party of Bavaria (Nationalliberale Landespartei Bayern).[25] At a heated meeting of the DVP Reichstag delegation on the following morning, the leaders of the party's right wing resumed their attack against the decision to terminate passive resistance and called upon the delegation to disavow the chancellor if he continued his efforts to reach a separate accommodation with the French. Particularly vehement in his denunciation of the Stresemann government was Vögler, who attacked the chancellor for having failed to implement the economic reforms that were necessary for the conduct of a successful and vigorous foreign policy. When the delegation proceeded to adopt a resolution that explicitly rejected the resumption of negotiations with the French, it placed itself on a collision course with Stresemann's conduct of foreign policy and openly challenged his authority as leader of the party.[26]

The official termination of passive resistance on the morning of 26 September sent reverberations throughout the entire DVP organization. From Hamburg to Hesse, local party officials complained about the effect the decision to end passive resistance was having on the DVP's rank-and-file support.[27] The situation was particularly threatening in the Ruhr, where one prominent industrialist—Paul Reusch from the Gutehoffnungshütte in Oberhausen—was so incensed by Stresemann's decision that he immediately declared his resignation from the party.[28] By no means, however, was resentment over the termination of passive resistance limited to representatives of the Ruhr industrial establishment. The leaders of the party's district organizations in the Ruhr and Westphalia, the vast majority of whom did not support Stresemann's decision, found themselves deluged with so many resignations from local party members that they began to fear for the very survival of the party organization.[29] No less ominous was the situation in Bavaria, where the refusal of the Bavarian government to recognize the legality of the federal state of emergency that the Stresemann cabinet had declared throughout the state on 26 September in anticipation of the public uproar over the termination of passive resistance had driven a sharp wedge between the Bavarian DVP and state government officials.[30]

While the termination of passive resistance created serious problems for the leaders of the DVP's national organization, it also triggered a severe crisis within the DVP Reichstag delegation, where Stresemann's opponents on the party's right wing had temporarily succeeded in gaining the upper hand. In the last week of September Germany's right-wing press, including papers that stood close to the industrial interests on the DVP's right wing, leveled a general broadside against the SPD in an attempt to discredit it as a member of the governing coalition. By no coincidence, this broadside came just as the government was about to begin work on a comprehensive enabling act that would give it the emergency authorization necessary to deal with issues such as the conflict in the Ruhr, separatist movements in Bavaria and the Rhineland, and stabilization of the mark.[31] The fact that the Social Democrats were to be actively involved in formulating and implementing these measures aroused the suspicion of the industrial interests on the DVP's right wing, and they immediately sought to sabotage Stresemann's relations with the SPD by persuading the DVP Reichstag delegation to make its support of the proposed enabling act contingent upon the acceptance of conditions to which few Social Democrats were likely to agree. At the same time, the leaders of the DVP's right wing—particularly Stinnes and his associates—also began to cultivate closer ties with the DNVP and Reichswehr in preparation for a putsch that would replace the Stresemann government with a military dictatorship under the direction of General Hans von Seeckt, the enigmatic chief of the German high command. In the balance hung not merely the unity of the DVP but the survival of the Weimar Republic itself.[32]

At a meeting between the government and representatives of the government parties on the morning of 2 October, Ernst Scholz, Stresemann's successor as chairman of the DVP Reichstag delegation, triggered the crisis that had been building on the party's right wing by announcing that under no circumstances would his party be willing to give the government the emergency authorization it sought as long as it remained constituted in its present form. Although he approved in principle of the proposed enabling act, Scholz insisted that a complete reorganization of the government represented a *conditio sine qua non* for his party's willingness to go along with such a measure and urged Stresemann to initiate negotiations with the DNVP in an attempt to reorganize his cabinet on the broadest possible basis. At the same time, Scholz maintained that the proposed enabling act should not, as the Social Democrats had argued, be restricted to questions of financial policy but should be expanded in scope to include, among other things, provisions for a change in the length of the work day.[33] While Stresemann himself may have come to the conclusion that a break with the Social Democrats was unavoidable, he clearly did not want the onus for such a break placed at the doorstep of his own party, and he regarded Scholz's impetuousness as an embarrassment to himself and the DVP. Whatever hopes Stresemann may have had that the crisis would blow

over were completely shattered when, after a heated meeting of the DVP
Reichstag delegation later that afternoon, Raumer submitted his resignation as
minister of economics in response to demands that both he and his socialist
counterpart, Hilferding, leave the government.[34] Of all those who belonged to
the DVP's national leadership, Raumer was the most dedicated advocate of
cooperation with the Social Democrats, and his resignation represented a
severe setback to those who still hoped to salvage the existing governmental
coalition.

At this point the only hope of salvaging the Great Coalition lay in a
compromise on the eight-hour day. Although Stresemann was able to unite his
cabinet behind a compromise in the proposed enabling act that provided for an
increase in the length of the work day as long as this did not endanger the
health of the worker,[35] the parties supporting his government remained deeply
and irreconcilably divided on precisely how the changes in the length of the
work day were to be implemented.[36] The fate of the Stresemann government
was effectively sealed on the morning of 3 October, when the SPD Reichstag
delegation rejected by a 61–54 vote the compromise that the cabinet had
agreed on the night before. At the heart of this stand lay the Social Democrats'
refusal to sanction the government's efforts to improve industrial productivity
by increasing the length of the work day.[37] In the meantime, the DVP Reichstag delegation had met to express its support of the government compromise
and to reaffirm the position it had taken throughout the crisis, namely that
authorization to increase the length of the work day should be incorporated
into the government's enabling act. The delegation then adopted a resolution
expressing full confidence in Stresemann's performance as chancellor and
stating that his retention as chancellor offered the only hope for finding a way
out of the current crisis. Of the deputies attending the meeting, only Stinnes
refused to support the resolution.[38]

Reluctant to defy his own party after it had given him such a strong vote of
confidence, Stresemann tendered his resignation as chancellor in a meeting
with President Ebert on the evening of 3 October. Although Stresemann no
doubt agreed with Scholz and the leaders of the DVP Reichstag delegation that
the length of the work day had to be increased in order to improve industrial
productivity,[39] ultimate responsibility for the collapse of his government lay
with the heavy industrial interests on the DVP's right wing that were determined to force the Social Democrats out of the national government. But if the
collapse of the Great Coalition was to serve as the signal for a right-wing
putsch aimed at installing Seeckt as Germany's military dictator, the plans for
such a putsch failed to materialize in the period immediately following the
resignation of Stresemann's government.[40] While this might be attributed in
part to inadequate planning or Seeckt's lack of political resolve, a factor of no
less significance was the speed with which Ebert acted to end the crisis and

restore the authority of the central government in Berlin. For instead of accepting Stresemann's resignation as chancellor, Ebert immediately commissioned him with the task of forming a new government that, it was hoped, would have sufficient parliamentary strength to force the enabling act through the Reichstag. Despairing of further collaboration with the Social Democrats, the leaders of the DVP Reichstag delegation had entered into exploratory negotiations with the German Nationalists in an attempt to determine under what conditions they might be willing to enter the government.[41] But their hopes of replacing the SPD with the DNVP as their party's coalition partner suffered an irreversible setback when the DNVP announced that under no circumstances would it enter a government with Stresemann as its chancellor.[42]

At this point the leaders of the DVP resigned themselves to the creation of a bourgeois minority government with the DDP and Center, a prospect that few of them viewed with any enthusiasm.[43] While Stresemann still hoped to win Nationalist support by filling the cabinet posts formerly held by the Social Democrats with specialists or *Fachminister* who, though nominally unaffiliated, stood close to the DNVP,[44] both the Democrats and the Center continued to press for the maintenance of the Great Coalition and offered to mediate between the DVP and SPD on the question of the eight-hour day. The deadlock was finally broken when much to Stresemann's surprise the Social Democrats agreed to a temporary suspension of the eight-hour day for the purpose of economic recovery on the condition that this was not to be regarded as a permanent change in the length of the normal work day. At the same time, the socialists stipulated that any changes in the length of the work day should not be implemented under the auspices of the proposed enabling act but through a separate bill to be brought before the Reichstag at the earliest possible opportunity.[45] As fragile as this agreement may have been, it nevertheless cleared the way for a continuation of the existing governmental coalition. In the final analysis, however, the cabinet that Stresemann presented on the morning of 6 October was decidedly more conservative in tone and composition than its predecessor had been. For not only had Stresemann appointed a conservative, Count Gerhard von Kanitz, to the Ministry of Agriculture in an apparent attempt to win the support of the moderate Right, but Hans Luther, a prominent municipal politician from the Ruhr who enjoyed close ties to German heavy industry, had moved over from the Ministry of Agriculture to replace Hilferding as minister of finance.[46] Even though the Great Coalition had managed to survive the collapse of the first Stresemann cabinet, the influence that the Social Democrats were able to exercise over the formulation and implementation of national policy in the new government had been sharply curtailed.

Although the second Stresemann cabinet was clearly more conservative than the first, the heavy industrialists on the DVP's right wing remained profoundly disaffected from the new government. Obviously anticipating the formation of a right-wing government that would not stand in the way of their efforts to restore industrial productivity, Stinnes and his associates in the Ruhr coal industry had already taken unilateral steps aimed at the abrogation of the eight-hour day in coal mines throughout the occupied parts of the region. The compromise that Stresemann and the Social Democrats had reached on the length of the work day, however, placed the legality of this action, which was supposed to take effect with the full approval of occupation authorities on 8 October, in serious doubt and forced Stinnes and the Ruhr coal producers to beat a hasty retreat in the face of united opposition from the German labor movement.[47] Stinnes vented his rage over this turn of events in a series of demands that he sent to Stresemann on 7 October and that subsequently found their way into the Berlin press.[48] The profound cleavage that had developed between Stresemann and the leaders of the DVP's industrial wing could be seen not only in Stinnes's heightened interest in the possibility of a right-wing military dictatorship but, more immediately, in their refusal to support the enabling act that the Stresemann government presented to the Reichstag in the second week of October. Much to Stinnes's dismay, Stresemann remained faithful to the compromise that he and the Social Democrats had reached on the question of the eight-hour day, and he adamantly refused to include provisions for a change in the length of the work day among the issues to be dealt with under the auspices of the enabling act.[49] To signal their dissatisfaction with the government's apparent lack of independence vis-à-vis the Social Democrats, no less than twelve DVP deputies—including Stinnes, Quaatz, Sorge, and Vögler—were absent when the preliminary vote on the emergency powers clause of the enabling act took place on 11 October. When the entire bill came up for a final vote two days later, Stinnes and his colleagues officially abstained, although they yielded to party discipline and were present for the vote in order to help secure the quorum necessary for parliamentary action.[50]

Acting on the basis of the emergency authorization it had received from the Reichstag on 13 October, the Stresemann cabinet proceeded to enact a comprehensive fiscal and tax program designed to lay the foundation for an eventual stabilization of the mark. In the meantime, however, the government found itself confronted with another crisis that was to prove every bit as divisive as the conflict over the eight-hour day. Since the beginning of the year, extremist elements on the Left and Right had become increasingly active in Saxony, Thuringia, and Bavaria. The situation was particularly threatening in Bavaria, where state authorities refused to recognize the sovereignty of the republican government in Berlin and where local rightists were on the verge of an open rebellion against the Reich. As relations between the Reich and

Bavaria continued to deteriorate following the termination of passive resistance in the Ruhr, Stresemann's minister of defense, Democrat Otto Gessler, began to contemplate a move against the left-wing governments in Saxony and Thuringia as a means of appeasing rightist forces in his home state of Bavaria. The situation in Saxony became increasingly critical following the appointment of two Communist ministers to the state government in the first week of October, and on 17 October the Reichswehr began to occupy Saxony and Thuringia in order to prevent the complete breakdown of law and order. When the situation continued to deteriorate in spite of Social Democratic mediation between the Reich and the state government in Saxony, Stresemann instructed Rudolf Heinze, a member of the DVP Reichstag delegation whom he had recently appointed federal commissar in Saxony, to depose the Saxon state government on the morning of 29 October. While this action met with immediate approval from the bourgeois members of the Stresemann cabinet, the Social Democrats—and particularly their minister of the interior, Wilhelm Sollmann—complained bitterly about the chancellor's partiality toward the Right and threatened to withdraw from the government if he did not take similar action against the right-wing government in Bavaria. This threat played directly into the hands of Gessler, who was anxious to force the Social Democrats out of the government in order to clear the way for an accommodation with the Bavarians. When Stresemann and the other nonsocialist members of his cabinet supported Gessler in his refusal to take action against the Bavarian government, the Social Democrats felt that they could no longer support a government that demonstrated such partiality toward the Right, and on 2 November they announced their resignation from the Stresemann cabinet.[51]

The collapse of the Great Coalition in the first days of November 1923 threatened Germany with the complete paralysis of her parliamentary institutions and led to the revival—this time with Ebert's tentative approval—of plans for the establishment of a military dictatorship. In the meantime, however, Ebert asked Stresemann to continue as chancellor at the head of a bourgeois minority government resting upon the support of the DDP, DVP, and Center. While Stresemann readily accepted this commission and secured the approval of his cabinet for a continuation of the government as a minority coalition at a meeting of his ministers on the afternoon of 5 November,[52] the position of his government remained extremely weak. Not only did its lack of a parliamentary majority mean that it could govern only so long as the Reichstag was not in session, but it had lost its emergency powers due to a provision of the enabling act of 13 October that automatically terminated its emergency authorization with any change in the composition of the government. Moreover, Stresemann found himself confronted with a virtual mutiny within the DVP Reichstag delegation.[53] While the leaders of the DVP's right wing

welcomed the collapse of the Great Coalition, they were perplexed by Stresemann's determination to continue as head of a minority government and hoped
to pressure him into accepting Nationalist ministers into his cabinet in spite of
public statements by the DNVP that it would not enter a government with
Stresemann as chancellor. When Stresemann announced at a stormy meeting
of the DVP Reichstag delegation on 5 November that he considered Nationalist conditions for entering the government unacceptable and that he had no
intention of issuing them an invitation,[54] the leaders of the DVP's right wing—
Gildemeister, Dauch, Hepp, and the unflappable Quaatz—responded at a
meeting of the delegation on the following day with an angry attack against
Stresemann's performance as chancellor. Particularly malicious were unfounded allegations by Kurt von Lersener and Oskar Maretzky that in Seeckt's
own words Stresemann had lost the confidence of the Reichswehr. Only a last-
minute appearance by Stresemann succeeded in defusing the situation and
forestalling action on a resolution introduced by Gildemeister that would have
authorized Scholz as chairman of the DVP Reichstag delegation to enter into
direct negotiations wih the DNVP.[55] The attack continued when the delegation
convened on 9 November, although by this time Stresemann's supporters had
managed to regroup to block passage of a resolution that might have been
construed as a repudiation of the chancellor in favor of one that simply urged
him to issue a public invitation to the DNVP and Bavarian People's Party to
join a united bourgeois coalition under his leadership.[56]

The collapse of Hitler's ill-fated Beer Hall Putsch in Munich on 9 November
1923 did much to stem the tide of anti-Stresemann sentiment that had been
building on the DVP's right wing and had a sobering effect upon his critics
within the DVP Reichstag delegation. In a delegation caucus on 11 November
the leaders of the anti-Stresemann fronde found themselves virtually isolated
as Scholz and other party moderates refused to participate in their intrigues
against the chancellor.[57] On the following day Stresemann announced the
appointment of the DVP's Karl Jarres, the highly respected lord mayor of
Duisburg and a politician of impeccable conservative credentials, to the Ministry of Interior in an obvious attempt to placate his critics on the DVP's right
wing and win the support of the DNVP. In the meantime, Stresemann had also
begun to receive emphatic declarations of support from the leaders of the
party's district and local organizations,[58] while the spokesmen for the DVP's
Prussian Landtag delegation complained bitterly about the split that had developed between it and the Reichstag delegation.[59] All of this helped set the scene
for the decisive victory that Stresemann scored over his opponents on the
DVP's right wing at a meeting of the central executive committee on 18
November. By an overwhelming 206–11 margin the committee, by far the
largest and most authoritative body within the DVP party organization,
adopted a resolution that reiterated its full confidence in Stresemann's perfor-

mance as chancellor and ruled out any change in the leadership of the government as injurious to Germany's diplomatic interests. To underscore the lack of support the dissidents enjoyed at the district and local levels of the party's national organization, the resolution stressed that under no circumstances should Stresemann be sacrificed for the sake of a new government coalition and exhorted the delegation to provide the chancellor with the unqualified support he so richly deserved.[60]

Chastened by the vehemence of Stresemann's counterattack before the DVP central executive committee and isolated by the strong vote of confidence the chancellor had received from the committee, the leaders of the anti-Stresemann faction within the DVP Reichstag delegation were left with no alternative but to support the government when the Reichstag reconvened on 20 November.[61] But while Stresemann was able to rally his party, including its recalcitrant right wing, for one last parliamentary challenge, he was not able to overcome the deep-seated resentment that the government's action in central Germany had produced within the ranks of the SPD. Still embittered by the partiality that the government had shown the Bavarian Right while deposing left-wing governments in Saxony and Thuringia, the Social Democrats introduced a motion of no-confidence in the Stresemann government, which, though uncertain of passage itself, obliged the chancellor to ask the Reichstag for a positive vote of confidence.[62] In the decisive test of strength that took place on 23 November, the Social Democrats joined the Communists, the Bavarian People's Party, the DNVP, and the fledgling German Racist Freedom Party (Deutschvölkische Freiheitspartei or DVFP) in depriving the government of its parliamentary mandate, thereby prompting the reprimand from Ebert that while the reasons for their action would soon be forgotten, they would live to regret the consequences of their stupidity for the next ten years.[63] In the meantime, Stresemann had suffered the ignominy of being the first chancellor in the history of the Weimar Republic to be forced from office by a formal vote of the Reichstag.

In spite of its ignominious demise, the Stresemann government had nevertheless distinguished itself as the most vigorous and effective government of the postwar period. In the scant hundred days Stresemann had been in office, he and his cabinet had succeeded in leading Germany from the brink of ruin to the threshold of recovery. Not only had the Stresemann government ended passive resistance in the Ruhr and taken the initial steps toward stabilizing the mark, but it had been forced to deal with a myriad of problems that threatened nothing less than the very survival and unity of the Reich. Throughout all of this, Stresemann never once wavered in his commitment to the republican form of government, and his adamant refusal to do anything that might permanently damage the prospects of cooperation with the Social Democrats testified to his emergence as a statesman of truly national stature. In retrospect

Stresemann's hundred days as chancellor may seem little more than an apprenticeship for the following six years he was to spend as Germany's foreign minister. The price that he had to pay for his newly won status, however, was high. His policies as chancellor had cost him the support of many of his former associates in the German business community, had driven a wedge deep into the ranks of his own party, and had earned him the kind of right-wing abuse that had formerly been reserved for the likes of Erzberger, Wirth, and Rathenau. If for Stresemann effective political leadership entailed the courage to accept responsibility for unpopular decisions that placed the welfare of the nation as a whole before partisan political interests, he could only have been deeply pained by the fact that so few of his colleagues were willing to share the burden of responsibility that history had placed upon his shoulders.

CHAPTER SIXTEEN

In the Shadow of Stabilization

IN MANY ESSENTIAL RESPECTS, the stabilization of the mark in the winter of 1923–24 proved every bit as destructive of Weimar democracy as the runaway inflation of the early 1920s. Not only did the various measures that the German government took to stabilize the mark inflict additional and in some cases unexpected economic hardship upon those social strata that had already been hurt by the inflation, but the very manner in which the mark was stabilized did much to compromise the legitimacy of the German party system as it had developed during the early years of the Weimar Republic. This, in turn, had profound repercussions within both the DDP and DVP, which of all of Germany's political parties were most closely associated with the pluralistic multiparty system that Germany had developed since the founding of the Second Empire. The German liberal parties were compromised both by the way they had abdicated responsibility for the formulation and implementation of the government's stabilization program and by their failure to protect middle-class economic interests during the stabilization process. The fate of Weimar liberalism had thus become inextricably intertwined with the deepening legitimacy crisis that plagued the German party system through the second half of the 1920s.[1]

The initial steps to stabilize the mark had been taken by the Stresemann government in October and November 1923. The termination of passive resistance in the Ruhr, a series of drastic budget cuts in late October, and finally the currency reforms of 15 November all represented significant steps toward the restoration of financial stability in Germany. Following Stresemann's resignation at the end of November the task fell to a new government headed by Centrist Wilhelm Marx. The negotiations that led to the formation of the Marx government were extremely arduous and did little to reassure those whose faith in parliamentary democracy had already been shaken by the political convulsions of the early 1920s. Initially, Reich President Ebert had asked the DVP's Siegfried von Kardorff to assume responsibility for the formation of a new government, but his candidacy had run into strong opposition from the DNVP and was quickly dropped. Ebert then turned to Adam Stegerwald, who proceeded to win tentative approval from all of the parties from the Democrats to the German Nationalists. But Stegerwald's efforts to form a new government broke down when the DNVP made its participation contingent upon a reorganization of the state government in Prussia, a demand that neither the Center nor the DDP was prepared to meet. By the same token, the DNVP refused to accommodate requests from the Center and the two liberal parties for an unequivocal commitment to the basic guidelines of Stresemann's foreign policy. A final round of negotiations on the afternoon of 29 November failed to break the deadlock, whereupon Ebert, having despaired of installing a government capable of commanding a parliamentary majority in the Reichstag, commissioned Marx to form a minority government consisting of representatives from the three middle parties and the Bavarian People's Party.[2]

The fact that the Marx government lacked a clear parliamentary majority meant that it would have to circumvent the Reichstag in the implementation of its stabilization program. Though dedicated republicans who believed in the basic principles of parliamentary government, neither Ebert nor Marx was willing to entrust the task of stabilizing the mark to a representative parliament where every stabilization proposal would be at the mercy of special economic interests. Moreover, quick and decisive action was necessary to restore governmental authority at home and abroad, a consideration that precluded relying upon the slow and measured procedures of conventional parliamentary rule. Yet while even the Social Democrats recognized that stabilization could not take place according to established parliamentary procedures, they were reluctant to leave the task of stabilizing the mark to a government over which they had no effective control and insisted that measures designed to protect the prerogatives of parliament be incorporated into the enabling act that the Reichstag passed on 8 December. This led to the creation of a special fifteen-man committee consisting of representatives from all of the major parties to review the specific legislative decrees by which the government sought to stabilize the mark. The responsibilities of this committee, however, were purely advisory in nature, and it never fulfilled any of the expectations that had led to its formation. As a result, the German Reichstag—as well as the various political parties that constituted it—was effectively excluded from any sort of meaningful control over the form and substance of the government's stabilization program.[3]

The principal architect of the government's stabilization program was Hans Luther, a former municipal politician from the Ruhr who had served as Stresemann's minister of agriculture before succeeding the SPD's Rudolph Hilferding as head of the Finance Ministry in early October 1923. Politically unaffiliated, Luther shared little of the concern that the leaders of Germany's political parties felt over the social impact of stabilization. Moreover, the fact that Luther enjoyed close ties to the Ruhr industrial establishment precluded a stabilization settlement that might have damaged the interests of Germany's propertied classes. As far as Luther was concerned, the immediate task was to achieve a balanced budget through a sharp reduction in the general level of government spending and a modest increase in taxation. Then and only then would it be possible to reform the currency and stabilize the mark.[4] As finance minister under Marx, Luther took advantage of the special emergency powers contained in Article 48 of the Weimar Constitution to enact the first of three emergency tax decrees on 7 December in an effort to develop new sources of state revenue. On the following day the Reichstag passed a new enabling act that provided the Marx government with the emergency authorization Luther needed to complete the work he had begun under Stresemann. It was under the auspices of this act that the Marx government proceeded to enact two further emergency tax decrees, the first on 19 December 1923 and the second just before the expiration of the government's emergency powers on 15 February 1924.[5]

Although its ostensible purpose was to tax increases in private and corporate wealth that had resulted from the inflation, Luther's tax program proceeded from the assumption that Germany's propertied interests—and particularly industry and agriculture—had already been taxed to the limit of their economic capacity and were therefore incapable of generating the revenue that the government so sorely needed.[6] To be sure, the government did agree to incorporate into the Third Emergency Tax Decree of 14 February 1924 a 2 percent tax on industrial profits resulting from the inflation, but this seemed insignificant in comparison to the tax burden that homeowners and private businessmen were being asked to bear. Since the inflation had made it possible for private homeowners to liquidate the mortgages and other debts against their property at a fraction of their original value, the Marx government felt justified in imposing a special tax on rents as a means of tapping the gains that middle-class homeowners had recorded during the inflation.[7] At the same time, the Marx government transferred authority to levy a general sales tax to the state governments as part of a compromise that saw the Reich assume responsibility for the collection of income and property taxes throughout the country. Just as the rent tax fell heavily upon the shoulders of Germany's middle-class homeowners, the sales tax that the states were now empowered to collect imposed a heavy burden upon the retail sector of Germany's middle-class economy and did much to arouse middle-class opposition to the stabilization program of 1923–24.[8]

Although middle-class homeowners and private businessmen were irate over the increasingly heavy tax burden with which they found themselves saddled, the most controversial feature of the Third Emergency Tax Decree was its handling of the revaluation issue. On 28 November 1923 the German Supreme Court had ruled that the government's refusal to recognize any distinction between the gold mark in which prewar financial transactions had been conducted and the devalued paper mark with which current financial obligations were being liquidated was incompatible with the principles of "equity and good faith" contained in Article 242 of the German civil code. Since this decision raised the spectre that every revaluation dispute could be taken to court where it would be settled according to its individual merits and the debtor's ability to make financial restitution, the Marx government began work on a bill aimed at establishing the general guidelines under which the revaluation of those paper mark assets that had been destroyed by the inflation was to take place. In spite of strong opposition from the tightfisted Luther, Marx and his associates drafted a bill that allowed for the revalorization of mortgages and other private debts at 15 percent of their original gold mark value. All government debts such as war bonds, however, were exempted from revaluation until after a final settlement of the reparations question had taken place.[9]

Inasmuch as the tax and revaluation provisions of the Third Emergency Tax Decree were certain to arouse widespread opposition within the German middle class, the government was fearful that when the Reichstag convened in the middle of February, it would succumb to public pressure and try to amend those provisions of the decree that posed an unacceptable burden for specific social groups. Since this would have only undermined the integrity and ultimate effectiveness of the government's stabilization program, Marx and the members of his cabinet hoped that the leaders of the government parties could be persuaded to go along with an extension of the government's emergency powers beyond their expiration on 15 February. The Democrats had strong reservations not only about the social consequences of the government's stabilization program but also about the constitutional implications of the way in which the mark had been stabilized and therefore refused to support a new enabling act or any extension of the government's emergency powers.[10] By the same token, neither the Social Democrats nor the German Nationalists were willing to support a government motion that would avert a parliamentary debate on the Third Emergency Tax Decree. When negotiations broke down in the first week of March, Ebert realized that the gulf between parliament and the government had become too great for effective political action, and he reluctantly authorized dissolution of the Reichstag. New elections were set for the first week of May.[11]

The call for new elections found both liberal parties badly divided and ill prepared for the rigors of a national campaign. Not only had the inflation severely ravaged both their national organizations and the social strata upon which they were politically dependent, but the political battles of the last several months had done much to exacerbate the divisions that already existed within the ranks of Germany's liberal leadership. Stresemann's policies as chancellor had caused widespread dissension not only within his own party but within the DDP as well. For the most part, the DDP had been much more reliable in its support of the Stresemann government than the chancellor's own party. The decision to end passive resistance in the Ruhr had, in sharp contrast to its reception within the DVP, won almost unanimous approval from the Democratic party leadership.[12] Moreover, Stresemann's refusal to break with the Social Democrats when he reorganized his government in early October 1923 received strong support from the leaders of the DDP Reichstag delegation, who hoped to maintain the existing governmental coalition as long as possible.[13] It was, therefore, not until the last week of October, when the crisis in Bavaria and Saxony threatened to wreck what still remained of the Great Coalition, that the Democrats began to waver in their support of the Stresemann government. The Democrats were particularly distressed by Stresemann's lack of initiative with respect to the situation in Bavaria, and on 25 October the DDP Reichstag delegation registered its disapproval of his Bavarian policy by adopting a resolution that called upon the national government "to proceed with all energy" against the renegade state government under the leadership of Kahr and Lossow. At the same time, the Reich's decision to intervene in Saxony came under sharp attack from the leaders of the DDP, particularly when this resulted in the collapse of the Great Coalition on 2 November.[14]

As Stresemann's position became increasingly uncertain, the tension that had been building within the DDP ever since the formation of his government exploded into open view. Party unity had already been severely shaken by a bitter exchange between Petersen and Koch-Weser at a meeting of the DDP Reichstag delegation on 25 October.[15] The resignation of the Social Democrats from the Stresemann cabinet in early November set off another round of fighting within the DDP Reichstag delegation as Gessler and the leaders of the party's right wing tried to marshal support for the Reich's intervention against the left-wing government in Saxony.[16] At the same time, the DDP's support of the rump cabinet that Stresemann tried to patch together following the collapse of the Great Coalition came under heavy fire from the leaders of the DDP's left wing, who demanded that Stresemann, Luther, Gessler, and Jarres be replaced by new ministers whose republican credentials were beyond question.[17] By the end of the year disaffection on the DDP's left wing had become so widespread that in late December a handful of left-wing intellectuals led by Karl Vetter and including such luminaries as Thomas Mann, Curt von Ossietzky, and Fritz von Unruh announced the founding of a new political party known as the Republican Party of Germany (Republikanische Partei Deutschlands or RPD). This party, which espoused an unequivocal commitment to the republican form of government, sought to establish itself as a viable political force between the DDP and SPD and directed its appeal to Democrats who felt betrayed by their party's turn to the right.[18]

By the end of 1923 the situation within the DDP had become so explosive that a change of leadership was necessary to quell the mutiny that had erupted throughout the party organization. Fortunately, Petersen's election as lord mayor of Hamburg in early January 1924 provided him with a convenient pretext for resigning the party chairmanship, thereby sparing the DDP the spectacle of a bitter leadership fight. In the ensuing struggle for control of the party, Koch-Weser easily prevailed over Gessler and Hermann Hummel, both candidates of the party's right wing, and was officially chosen as Petersen's successor at a meeting of the DDP party council on 27 January.[19] A professional civil servant whose rise in Prussian municipal politics before the outbreak of World War I had been nothing short of meteoric, Koch-Weser had already distinguished himself as minister of interior in the Bauer government. Identifying himself with the national-social tradition inspired by the late Friedrich Naumann at the turn of the century, Koch-Weser evoked Naumann's vision of a national democracy as the basis upon which the reconstruction of the German state should take place in his keynote address at the DDP's Weimar party congress in early April. By the same token, Koch-Weser reiterated his commitment to Petersen's conception of a strong German middle and stressed his willingness to cooperate with the Social Democrats within the framework of the Great Coalition, in his eyes the only permanent solution to Germany's political woes.[20]

Although Koch-Weser's election had the immediate effect of preventing further defections on the DDP's disgruntled left wing,[21] the Democrats remained deeply divided as they began their campaign for the May 1924 Reichstag elections. This, however, was no less true of the German People's Party, where Stresemann's hundred days as chancellor had produced a veritable rebellion on the party's right wing. The fact that the party's district organization in Franconia, having already seceded from the DVP to reconstitute itself as the National Liberal State Party of Bavaria, planned to take part in both the Bavarian and national elections that were scheduled for the spring of 1924[22] was only one indication of the organizational malaise that existed in many quarters of the party. For his part, Stresemann was concerned that his conflict with the DVP Reichstag delegation might spill over into the party's national organization. By no means had the ill feeling between Stresemann and the leaders of the DVP's right wing abated since the collapse of his government, and the anti-Stresemann forces within the DVP Reichstag delegation were determined to force a showdown over the DVP's future political course. The issue at stake, argued Bremen's Alfred Gildemeister in a particularly aggressive letter from early December 1923, was whether the DVP would commit itself to a policy of bourgeois unification, seek a return of the Great Coalition without the German Nationalists, or work for a consolidation of the middle with alternating alliances to the Left and the Right.[23]

Angered by the way Stresemann had attacked them in the official DVP press, the leaders of the anti-Stresemann forces marshaled their strength for a decisive showdown at a meeting of the DVP Reichstag delegation on 12 January 1924.[24] Here Gildemeister and his associates proceeded to draft a resolution that blamed the Social Democrats for the collapse of the Great Coalition and identified the formation of a new coalition stretching from the middle to the Right as the DVP's immediate goal. The resolution specifically stressed the importance of winning over the DNVP to a policy of constructive cooperation and combating the negativism that had characterized that party's recent political behavior.[25] But Stresemann, who remained deeply embittered over the way in which the leaders of his party's Reichstag delegation had conducted their own negotiations with the Nationalists while he was still chancellor,[26] was offended not merely by the language of the resolution but also by its virtual endorsement of a coalition with the DNVP. At Stresemann's insistence and over the vehement objection of his archnemesis Reinhold Quaatz, the delegation agreed to submit the resolution to its executive commit-tee for editorial revision.[27] This committee met on 21 January and made substantive as well as stylistic changes in the text of the resolution, the most important of which was to replace the passage calling for the creation of a coalition stretching from the middle to the Right with a somewhat less explicit statement stressing the need for a viable bourgeois coalition. Not only were all specific references to the DNVP deleted from the resolution, but the consoli-dation of all "state-supporting" bourgeois forces was equated with the Great Coalition as a different yet complementary path to the DVP's ultimate goal of a genuine *Volksgemeinschaft*.[28]

Although a majority of the delegation agreed to accept the changes that had been made in its resolution of 12 January, the leaders of the DVP's right wing were irate over the way their resolution had been robbed of its original mean-ing and attacked Stresemann for meddling in the delegation's affairs. Strese-mann's handling of the matter only reinforced their determination to force a change in the direction in which their party seemed to be headed, and on 12 March they announced the founding of a new organization within the DVP called the National Liberal Association (Nationalliberale Vereinigung or NLV).[29] The impulse behind the founding of the NLV came from a group of DVP deputies who stood under the nominal leadership of industrialist Hugo Stinnes. Stinnes's immediate animus toward Stresemann stemmed in large part from a letter that Albert Morath, a member of the DVP Reichstag delegation and the party's chief spokesman for the German civil servant movement, had written to Stinnes in the second week of February in an attempt to dissuade him from standing for reelection to the Reichstag.[30] Although Morath had under-taken this step without informing Stresemann, Stinnes attributed authorship of the letter to the DVP party chairman and launched into a new round of tirades against his leadership of the party.[31] By the first week of March, Stinnes and his associates had come to the conclusion that it was impossible for him to remain in the party, although the precise form that his break from the DVP should take remained unsettled. One of the options under consideration was to split the DVP in two by organizing a secession on the party's right wing.[32]

Although illness kept Stinnes from becoming directly involved in the negotiations that led to the founding of the NLV, seven other members of the DVP Reichstag delegation, including such close Stinnes associates as Quaatz and Albert Vögler, were present when the organization was officially launched on 12 March.[33] Over the course of the next several days they were joined by four more members of the delegation, including the leaders of the party's agrarian wing, Karl Hepp and Friedrich Döbrich.[34] The presence of Hepp and Döbrich notwithstanding, the NLV was dominated by the industrial and business interests that constituted the nucleus of the DVP's right wing. Not only were fully four-fifths of the twenty-five party members who attended the NLV's founding ceremonies either directly or indirectly related to the Ruhr industrial establishment, but the founders of the NLV also included Alfred Gildemeister and Carl Piper, two DVP deputies with close ties to north German commercial interests, as well as Kurt Sorge, president of the National Federation of German Industry.[35] With the exception of Quaatz, Oskar Maretzky, and possibly one or two others, however, none of those involved in the founding of the NLV desired a break with the DVP. Speaking at the NLV's first public demonstration on 26 March, Gildemeister insisted that the goal the founders of the NLV had set for themselves was not to hurt or split the DVP but to return it to the principles upon which it had been founded. In this respect, Gildemeister defended the resolution adopted by the DVP Reichstag delegation on 12 January as an attempt to lay the foundation for the creation of a broad bourgeois front in the upcoming election campaign and for the formation of a new government that would no longer require the support or cooperation of the socialist Left.[36]

Stresemann's reaction to the founding of the NLV was quick and decisive. Meeting under his leadership on 13 March, the DVP party executive committee adopted a resolution that expressly denounced the existence of a separate organization within the party as incompatible with its solidarity and political effectiveness.[37] Although this resolution met with vehement opposition from Gildemeister and the leaders of the NLV,[38] they were unable to prevent Stresemann from referring the matter to the DVP executive committee, where he was assured of majority support.[39] When the DVP central executive committee reaffirmed this resolution on the eve of the party's Hanover congress later in the month, the dissidents around Quaatz and Gildemeister were left with no choice but to dissolve the NLV or face expulsion from the party. While Ernst Scholz, chairman of the DVP Reichstag delegation, and other party moderates were able to intercede with Gildemeister and his supporters on behalf of a compromise with the party leadership,[40] their efforts with Quaatz and the more intractible of Stresemann's opponents on the DVP's extreme right wing proved futile. Rejecting a compromise that would have made it possible for them to remain in the party, Quaatz and his associates hoped instead to provoke a general secession on the DVP's right wing with the slogan "Out of the Stresemann-Party."[41]

The outcome of the DVP's Hanover party congress on 29–30 March 1924 represented an unequivocal triumph for Stresemann and his conception of the DVP as a party of the *Volksgemeinschaft*. Not only had the congress and its executive organs rallied to Stresemann's support in his struggle with the leaders of the NLV, but he had succeeded in restoring party unity in the face of Quaatz's efforts to organize a secession on the DVP's right wing. Although Quaatz and his associates continued to press their attacks against Stresemann and promptly reconstituted the NLV as a bipartisan organization free to support its own candidates or candidates from other parties in the forthcoming national elections,[42] the NLV was unable to achieve a significant breakthrough into the DVP's national organization. The only exception was in northern Bavaria, where the local party organization was already in a state of virtual collapse. In Vögler's district of South Westphalia, on the other hand, the furor over his involvement in the NLV was so great that he was obliged to resign as honorary chairman of the local party organization and withdraw as a candidate for reelection to the Reichstag.[43] Stinnes's sudden death on 10 April only added to the confusion that the leaders of the NLV were experiencing in the wake of Stresemann's counteroffensive at Hanover. The NLV's fate as an independent political force was effectively sealed in late April when Quaatz and Moritz Klönne, a prominent Ruhr industrialist who had formerly belonged to the DVP, accepted candidacies on the DNVP's national ticket.[44]

In the campaign for the 1924 Reichstag elections both the DVP and DDP made a valiant effort to recapture the middle-class support they had lost during the inflation. The DVP's Hanover party congress had opened under the motto "The Middle Class in Its Struggle for Survival" and was carefully orchestrated to reiterate the DVP's unwavering commitment to the social and economic welfare of the German middle class.[45] In his keynote address on the second day of the congress, Stresemann launched into a spirited defense of the government's stabilization program as the only possible course available to the German government in its efforts to end the inflation. Absolving the cabinets headed first by him and then by Marx of any responsibility for the misery in which the German middle class found itself, Stresemann blamed the inflation upon the short-sightedness of the German working class and called upon the middle class to accept the sacrifices it had been forced to make as a part of the price that Germany had to pay in order to regain her national freedom.[46] At the same time, Stresemann and the leaders of the DVP supplemented this ploy with a series of specific recommendations for the social and economic rehabilitation of the German middle class, recommendations that if successfully implemented would modify essential components of the government's stabilization program. Not only did the leaders of the DVP reject the revaluation provisions of the Third Emergency Tax Decree as inherently unjust and in need of revision, but they also called for a more equitable salary structure for Germany's professional civil service, the relaxation of credit for small business and agriculture, and an end to government controls over the housing industry.[47] Though unwilling to go so far as to demand the outright appeal of the government's stabilization program, the leaders of the DVP clearly sought to modify those of its features that entailed an unacceptable burden for their party's middle-class supporters.

Like Stresemann and his associates, the leaders of the DDP were far more attentive to the material welfare of the German middle class in the May 1924 Reichstag elections than they had been in previous campaigns. On 28 February the DDP's Erich Koch-Weser opened his party's campaign with a speech in which he called for a program of internal reparations aimed at helping those who had been hurt by the inflation.[48] Several days later another prominent Democrat, Hermann Fischer, reiterated his party's commitment to the social and economic rehabilitation of the German middle class and identified lower taxes, an end to government economic controls, and a return to the free enterprise system as the keys to middle-class economic recovery.[49] But aside from demands for a more effective and equitable revaluation of the private savings that had been destroyed by the inflation,[50] Democratic proposals for the rehabilitation of the middle class remained vague and ill defined. Indeed, by the beginning of April the DDP had begun to move from an explicit identification with the social and economic plight of the German middle class to a more general identification with the welfare of the nation as a whole. In a comprehensive review of the DDP's social and economic policy at the party's national congress in Weimar, Fischer scarcely mentioned the plight of the middle class—and then only in meaningless platitudes that offered the form, but not the substance, of a genuine commitment to middle-class economic interests.[51] By the same token, the speeches delivered by Erkelenz, Ludwig Haas, and Emmy Beckmann on the final day of the congress all focused on broad national issues such as the preservation of Germany's national culture and the struggle for a revision of the Versailles Treaty.[52] While this reflected the congenital uneasiness that many Democrats felt with regard to the representation of special economic interests, in the more immediate context it represented a subtle attempt to divert attention away from the DDP's failure to protect middle-class economic interests during the inflation by highlighting national policy issues upon which all segments of the German middle class could presumably agree.

In their efforts to recapture the middle-class support they had lost during the early 1920s, the two liberal parties were severely handicapped by their complicity in the implementation of a stabilization program whose net effect was to place the social cost of stabilizing the mark upon the back of Germany's beleaguered and badly traumatized middle class.[53] Germany's civil servant leaders were particularly infuriated by the measures the Stresemann government had taken in November 1923 to reduce the size of the state civil service, and their supporters had already begun to abandon the more moderate bourgeois parties in favor of the DNVP and those that stood to its right. The liberal parties were also hurt by the decision of the Reichsbank to order a severe restriction of credit in April 1924, a measure that forced a record number of middle-class businesses into bankruptcy and produced widespread unemployment among skilled workers and white-collar employees throughout the country.[54] No less distressing was the situation in the countryside, where lingering resentment over the controlled economy in agriculture combined with a poor harvest and the disappearance of cheap credit to produce a massive shift to the right in the political loyalties of the German peasantry. Not only did the leaders of the German Peasants' League fail to give the DDP the unequivocal endorsement they had given it in 1919 and 1920, but the more conservative rural organizations that had supported the DVP at the time of the last Reichstag elections were in the process of affiliating themselves with the renegade National Liberal Association. Only the Catholic peasantry in the Rhineland and Westphalia remained immune from a development that threatened Germany's republican parties with the complete loss of their rural support.[55]

At the heart of the problems that faced the German liberal parties in the spring of 1924 was the virtual collapse of their national party organizations. The inflation had forced the closure of all but three of the DDP's thirty-five district headquarters, and the call for new elections had come before party leaders had had sufficient opportunity to repair the damage the inflation had done to the lower levels of their party's national organization.[56] The situation within the DVP was somewhat better, although party leaders had to contend with the fact that eleven of the DVP's district organizations were without a full-time secretary, while six others were without any staff whatsoever.[57] Furthermore, efforts to rebuild liberal party organizations in time for the May elections were severely hampered by the lack of adequate funds. Not only had the inflation inflicted severe economic hardship upon those social strata from which the German liberal parties had traditionally received a significant portion of their financial support, but outside economic interests were no longer as generous with contributions as they had been before the inflation. In the case of the DDP, for example, the Central Association of German Wholesalers had made its contribution of 250,000 marks contingent upon the nomination of lobbyist Otto Keinath to a secure place on the DDP's national slate only to reduce its contribution to a mere 50,000 marks when other political considerations led the Democrats to demote Keinath from fourth to fifth place on their party's national ticket. Of the party's major benefactors, only the Eastern Society (Ostgesellschaft) and the Federation of Employee Unions honored their commitments of 30,000 and 25,000 marks respectively without hesitation, while even the Central Association of German Citizens of the Jewish Faith and other Jewish circles failed to support the DDP as vigorously as they had done in the past.[58]

Stresemann too was embittered over the way in which his party had been treated by its erstwhile financial backers, and only through personal appeals to his friends and former associates in the German business community was he able to finance the DVP's election campaign.[59] To complicate the situation even further, the Commission for the Collection, Administration, and Allocation of the Industrial Campaign Fund had effectively collapsed during the latter stages of the inflation, and with the illness and eventual death of its longtime secretary general, Johannes Flathmann, it disappeared from the political scene in early 1924. Although its place was quickly taken by an ad hoc committee organized by Vögler in the early spring of 1924,[60] this committee actually stood much closer to the DNVP than to either of the liberal parties and did not hesitate to support candidates from the renegade National Liberal Association against those of the DVP in Berlin and other parts of the country.[61] The Curatorium for the Reconstruction of German Economic Life, on the other hand, decided to increase its influence over the policies of the parties it supported by funneling all contributions through specifically designated trustees or *Vertrauensmänner* who alone were responsible for their disposition during the campaign. Although the DVP and DDP still received well over half of the 650,000 marks that the Curatorium collected for use in the campaign,[62] this resulted in a serious loss of autonomy vis-à-vis the Curatorium and was bitterly resented by both Stresemann and the leaders of the DDP.[63]

If there was one bright spot in Stresemann's search for financial backing, it was the generous and unconditional support he received from the German chemical industry. At the end of 1922 Carl Duisberg and the leaders of the chemical industry had created a special committee under the chairmanship of the DVP's Wilhelm Ferdinand Kalle in an attempt to offset the influence of Ruhr heavy industry. Openly critical of the policies pursued by Stinnes and his supporters during the recent political crisis,[64] Duisberg had not only welcomed the formation of the Stresemann government but began to funnel money from his associates in the chemical industry to the more moderate bourgeois parties through the auspices of the Kalle Committee. The principal beneficiary of this arrangement was the DVP, which began to receive annual contributions of 200,000 marks in addition to equivalent sums at the time of national or state elections. The DDP and Center, on the other hand, received annual donations of 30,000 and 50,000 marks respectively as well as special campaign contributions in the vicinity of 50,000 to 70,000 marks apiece.[65] Even this, however, was not sufficient to compensate the two liberal parties for the loss of revenue they had suffered from the general disaffection of Germany's economic elite and still left them desperately short of the funds needed to rebuild their national organizations.

Their supporters traumatized by the inflation and embittered over the way in which the mark had been stabilized, their organizations decimated by the collapse of the mark and by rampant internal strife, and their finances suffering from the fickleness of German big business, the German liberal parties went down to a devastating defeat in the May 1924 Reichstag elections. The Democrats, who had already suffered heavy losses in the last national elections four years earlier, lost another 678,000 votes and saw their representation in the Reichstag slip from thirty-nine to twenty-five deputies. All told, Democratic losses amounted to 29.1 percent of the party's 1920 vote. Aside from Berlin, where the large-scale infusion of industrial money in support of Siemens's candidacy had enabled the Democrats to recapture some of the support they had lost in 1920, the DDP lost heavily in virtually every part of the country. The DDP's losses were particularly heavy in the three Bavarian districts, where the conflict with the Reich had led to the loss of over two-thirds of its 1920 electorate, and in Frankfurt an der Oder, Mecklenburg, Magdeburg, and Merseburg, where its losses amounted to nearly half of the vote it had received four years earlier.[66] In explaining their party's losses, the leaders of the DDP were quick to cite not only the poor state of party finances and the collapse of their party organization throughout much of the country but also the effects of the government's stabilization program upon significant sectors of the Democratic electorate. In this respect, they were particularly distressed by the loss of civil servant support to right-wing political parties and the defection of former supporters in the peasantry and urban middle class to splinter parties that placed primary emphasis upon the representation of special economic interests.[67] Reduced to their common denominator, the DDP's losses in the May 1924 Reichstag elections underscored both the increasing fragmentation of the party's electoral base and the difficulties that lay before the party if it was to reestablish itself as a major force in Germany's political life.

Stresemann and the leaders of the DVP, on the other hand, were relieved that their party's losses in the May elections were not more severe than they eventually proved to be. For although the DVP had lost more than 1.2 million votes—or 31.3 percent of what it had received four years earlier—along with twenty of its sixty-five seats in the Reichstag, Stresemann readily conceded that had the elections taken place six weeks earlier, his party would have suffered a far more devastating defeat.[68] Like the Democrats, the leaders of the DVP were quick to attribute their party's losses to the unpopularity of the measures that the government had taken to stabilize the mark. In this respect, party officials cited the loss of civil servant support to the right-wing DNVP as well as the DVP's virtual collapse in the countryside as part of the price it had to pay for its role in restoring economic order. The latter development was particularly distressing. The DVP owed much of its success in the 1920 Reichstag elections to the strong support it had received from local farm organizations in the central and southwestern parts of Germany. In the spring of 1924, however, an alliance that the National Liberal Association had concluded with farm organizations in Hesse, Thuringia, Baden, and Württemberg polled nearly 600,000 votes, all but 240,000 of which came at the expense of the DVP. As a perplexed Otto Hugo observed at a meeting of the DVP central executive committee in early July, only the artisanry and more traditional elements of Germany's economic middle class had remained loyal to the party.[69]

Nowhere was the plight of the two liberal parties more desperate than in Bavaria, where their share of the popular vote had declined from 14.1 percent in 1919 to a mere 3.5 percent in 1924. The collapse of Bavarian liberalism stemmed from a variety of factors, not the least of which were the strength of Bavarian particularism and the rise of political radicalism on the extreme Right. Both the DDP and DVP had been direct casualties of the conflict that had erupted between the Reich and Bavaria in the early 1920s. The damage this conflict had done to their state party organizations was compounded by the storm of protest that accompanied Stresemann's decision to terminate passive resistance in the Ruhr. Anti-Stresemann sentiment assumed an even more ominous tone when the DVP party chairman, acting in his capacity as Reich chancellor, invoked presidential emergency powers to declare a state of national emergency in Bavaria in an attempt to suppress the agitation of the Bavarian Right. The subsequent crisis, which culminated in the abortive Beer Hall Putsch on the night of 8–9 November 1923, caught the two liberal parties in a vicious political crossfire that drove those liberals who resented federal intervention in Bavarian affairs into the ranks of the BVP and those who decried the weakness of Germany's national government into the arms of Hitler and the Bavarian Right. In the state elections that took place on 6 April 1924 the DDP and DVP were all but swept away by a massive swing to the right that not only anticipated the outcome of the national elections that had been set for the following month but foreshadowed what was to happen in the next confrontation between liberalism and right-wing radicalism at the beginning of the 1930s.[70]

Between them, the two liberal parties saw their share of the electorate slip from 22.9 percent in 1919 and 22.2 percent in 1920 to a disappointing 14.9 percent in 1924. In the Reich as well as in Bavaria, this was accompanied by a dramatic increase in the strength of Germany's antirepublican Right.[71] Not only was the DNVP able to improve upon its performance in the 1920

Reichstag elections by more than 1.3 million votes and thus emerge from the election as the second strongest party in the Reichstag, but the German Racist Freedom Party, a crude coalition of right-wing racist groups that had temporarily replaced the outlawed Nazi Party, received nearly 2 million votes and won thirty-two parliamentary seats. Both parties had conducted vigorous campaigns against the government's stabilization program from the winter of 1923–24 in an attempt to capitalize upon the political frustration of social groups that had been hurt by the Third Emergency Tax Decree.[72] The gains of the antirepublican Right, however, were complemented by a second development that was to have even greater long-term impact, namely the breakthrough of special interest parties into the ranks of Germany's middle-class electorate. All told, middle-class and agrarian splinter parties received more than 8 percent of the popular vote in the May 1924 Reichstag elections. This development foreshadowed a fundamental realignment of the German party system in which traditional, ideologically oriented "people's parties" like the DDP and DVP were displaced by special interest parties that no longer sought to represent the nation as a whole but rather specific sectors of the German middle strata. In the final analysis, this was to constitute a far more serious threat to the future of the two liberal parties and the stability of the Weimar party system than the success of the radical Right.[73]

PART FOUR

Stabilization and Fragmentation
1924–1928

CHAPTER SEVENTEEN

A Return to Normalcy?

THE SECOND HALF OF THE 1920s offered a confused and often contradictory picture of Germany's political realities. On the surface, the period appeared to be one of social, political, and economic stability. Stresemann's diplomatic successes at London, Locarno, and Geneva did much to enhance Germany's international prestige and lent the Weimar Republic a sense of national self-esteem that had been noticeably absent during the first years of its existence. At the same time, the influx of foreign capital under the auspices of the Dawes Plan made it possible for the German economy to recover from the deep depression that had followed the stabilization of the mark in the winter of 1923–24. Similarly, influential economic interest organizations such as the National Federation of German Industry and the National Rural League seemed to have reconciled themselves to the republic and were apparently prepared to pursue their objectives within the framework of Germany's new republican order. By the same token, the Communists seemed resigned to the fact that German capitalism had entered a period of temporary stabilization, while the radical Right found itself in a state of complete disarray following Hitler's abortive Beer Hall Putsch in the fall of 1923. Even in the cultural arena, where the millenarian impulse so characteristic of early German expressionism had given way to the stark realism of the "New Objectivity," it was possible to detect a shift in aesthetic sensibilities that was directly related to the stabilization of Germany's bourgeois capitalist order.

While all of this seemed to suggest that the collective national trauma that Germany had experienced since the end of the war was finally drawing to a close, the air of stability and confidence exuded by the Weimar Republic throughout the second half of the 1920s was in fact highly misleading. For although the immediate trauma of defeat and economic dislocation may have receded into the deeper recesses of Germany's national consciousness, her political culture remained profoundly scarred by the damage that the inflation and subsequent stabilization of the mark had inflicted upon the social bases of German politics. Moreover, the authoritarian manner in which the mark had been stabilized had not only discredited those parties that had acquiesced in the implementation of the government's stabilization program, but it had also severely compromised the legitimacy of the German party system as it had developed during the early years of the Weimar Republic. As the structural weakness of Weimar democracy became increasingly apparent during the second half of the 1920s, the Weimar party system found itself in the midst of a profound legitimacy crisis that was no longer confined to its traditional critics on the Right but extended deep into the ranks of those parties that had always identified themselves most closely with the principles of representative government.[1]

The legitimacy crisis that plagued the Weimar party system in the second half of the 1920s had at least four specific manifestations. The first of these was the continued decline of the two parties that identified themselves most closely with the pluralistic party system that had developed in Germany since the middle of the previous century, namely the German Democratic Party and the German People's Party. Closely related to this development was the emergence of middle-class splinter parties that manifested if not an explicit, then at least an implicit, antipathy to the German party system as it had evolved during the early years of the Weimar Republic.[2] By the same token, the deepening legitimacy crisis of the Weimar party system could be seen in the increasingly prominent role of economic interest organizations such as the National Federation of German Industry and the National Rural League. Their position in Germany's political life had been greatly enhanced by the decisive role they played in the ratification of the Dawes Plan, and in the subsequent parliamentary disputes over tariffs, revaluation, social welfare, and civil servant salary reform they asserted themselves with such vigor that contemporary political pundits began to complain openly about the "tyranny of special economic interests."[3]

At no point, however, were the structural problems that plagued Weimar parliamentarism in the second half of the 1920s more apparent than in the cabinet negotiations that followed the May 1924 Reichstag elections.[4] The four parties that supported the Marx government—the Center, the Bavarian People's Party, and the two liberal parties—commanded scarcely a third of the seats in the Reichstag, while the Social Democrats had been so severely chastened by their experiences as a member of Stresemann's Great Coalition that they had little desire for a return to power. Under these circumstances, the DNVP's strong performance at the polls would have assured it of a leading role in any future government were it not for the fact that its fierce opposition to the recommendations of the Dawes Committee had given rise to serious doubts about its reliability in matters of German foreign policy. Stresemann, however, was anxious to secure a broad parliamentary mandate for acceptance of the Dawes recommendations and hoped that at least the more moderate elements within the DNVP could be won over to the support of his foreign policy.[5] Moreover, the idea of a "bourgeois bloc" with the DNVP enjoyed strong support on the DVP's right wing, where no less a luminary than Karl Jarres, the minister of interior in the Marx cabinet and one of the party's most influential spokesmen, could be numbered among its advocates.[6] In marked contrast to the DVP, however, both the Center and the DDP were extremely wary of the Nationalists' apparent willingness to make concessions on foreign policy issues as a way of easing themselves into power, and they viewed Nationalist suggestions that the task of forming a new government be entrusted to the former head of the German navy, Great Admiral Alfred von Tirpitz, with particular skepticism. Consequently, when the Nationalists fueled these misgivings by refusing to commit themselves to the Dawes recommendations as the basis for the future conduct of German foreign policy, negotiations between the DNVP and the four government parties threatened to break down completely.[7]

At this point the DVP Reichstag delegation tried to break the deadlock that had developed in the government's negotiations with the DNVP by formally demanding the dismissal of the Marx cabinet.[8] Yet while this deprived the government of its parliamentary mandate and forced Marx to submit his cabinet's resignation to the Reich president, Ebert ignored Nationalist demands that they be entrusted with the task of forming a new government and proceeded to reappoint Marx to the position he had just resigned. At the same time, Stresemann enlisted the cooperation of the British and American ambassadors in an attempt to overcome Nationalist opposition to the Dawes recommendations, while the three principal government parties—the BVP being the lone exception—continued to stress their commitment to the basic principles of Stresemann's foreign policy.[9] But the second round of negotiations that began with Marx's reappointment on 28 May proved no more successful than the first. For although Stresemann was willing to step down as foreign minister if this would facilitate an accommodation with the DNVP, the Nationalists not only held firm to the so-called Tirpitz solution but also made their participation in a new national government contingent upon a reorganization of the state government in Prussia. By the same token, they still refused to provide the DVP and other government parties with specific guarantees regarding the Dawes recommendations. All of this tended to confirm suspicions that the Nationalists were not genuinely interested in sharing governmental responsibility if this also meant having to share the onus for acceptance and ratification of the Dawes recommendations, and on 31 May the government formally broke off its negotiations with the DNVP. Three days later Marx announced the formation of a new government that, aside from the fact that the Bavarian People's Party was no longer represented in it, was essentially unchanged from the one it was replacing.[10]

The collapse of efforts to bring the DNVP into the government in the late spring of 1924 was symptomatic of the problems that were to plague the Weimar Republic over the course of the next six years and lent renewed credence to the polemics of right-wing political pundits who disparaged the

Weimar party system as both the source and symbol of Germany's national fragmentation. Though understandably concerned over the implications of this deadlock for the future of Germany's parliamentary institutions, the Democrats were actually relieved that they had been spared a decision that might have split their party. For whereas the leaders of the DDP recognized the necessity of forcing the DNVP to accept responsibility for implementation of the Dawes recommendations, they were willing to enter a government in which the Nationalists were represented only if they could be certain that control of the government would remain in the hands of the three middle parties. In this respect, the Democrats were particularly critical of the way in which the DVP Reichstag delegation seemed to be pursuing its own partisan objectives without regard for its commitments to the other government parties.[11] Not only had the DVP Reichstag delegation refused to join the DDP and Center in renewing the Alliance of the Constitutional Middle,[12] but the DVP's decision to press for the dismissal of the Marx government undercut the common platform that the three middle parties had formulated as the basis of their negotiations with the Nationalists. At the same time, the leaders of the DDP were extremely uneasy about their party's prospects as the only bourgeois party in opposition to a predominantly bourgeois government. As Koch-Weser confided to his diary in the middle of May: "Should a government led by the German Nationalists come into existence, then it would be very difficult for us. With the collapse of our press and our organization thoughout the country, we could hardly have the strength as the only bourgeois party to carry on an effective opposition."[13]

The uncertainty that existed within the ranks of the DDP became all too apparent at an emergency meeting of the party executive committee on 26 May.[14] In a heated debate that lasted for more than four hours the party split between those on its right wing who argued that the DDP could ill afford to permit the formation of a bourgeois government with the DNVP in which it was not represented and those on the party's left wing who were adamantly opposed to the DDP's participation in a coalition government with the Nationalists as long as adequate guarantees regarding that government's domestic and foreign policies had not been secured. Particularly outspoken in their opposition to a coalition with the Nationalists were Wilhelm Cohnstaedt, Gertrud Bäumer, Ludwig Haas, Walther Schücking and Theodor Tantzen, as well as Hermann Fischer and Hermann Hummel from the party's right wing, while Eduard Hamm, Carl Friedrich von Siemens, Heinrich Gerland and Eugen Schiffer all supported the DDP's entry into a coalition government with the DNVP. Citing recent developments in Bavaria, where the Social Democrats' withdrawal from the state government had made it possible for right-wing separatists to gain power, Hamm warned his colleagues against relinquishing power before it was absolutely necessary and stressed the advantages to be gained by forcing the Nationalists to accept the basic guidelines of German foreign policy as articulated by Stresemann.[15] But Hamm's arguments failed to allay the mounting animosity that the leaders of the DDP's left wing felt toward the Nationalists, and the meeting ended in a deadlock that could have split the party right down the middle had not the DNVP's intransigence led to a breakdown of its negotiations with the other government parties.

Neither Stresemann nor the leaders of the DDP expected the newly elected Reichstag to last for more than a few months. The constellation of parties within the Reichstag was simply too unstable to permit a parliamentary resolution of the problems that confronted the German people. The issue that eventually brought about the dissolution of the Reichstag was essentially the same one that had dominated the negotiations to form a new government in May, namely the need to bring the DNVP into the cabinet in order to secure a domestic consensus that would assure parliamentary approval of the agreement that Germany was about to conclude with the Entente in London. Named after the American vice-president who had served as chairman of the committee that drafted it, the Dawes Plan was essential to Germany's economic recovery since it authorized international loans amounting to 800 million marks. In return, Germany would have to accept an Allied plan for the payment of reparations and agree to reorganize certain national assets, such as the state railway system, as public entities.[16] This was essentially the same plan the DNVP's Karl Helfferich had denounced as a "second Versailles" before his untimely death in a train accident on 24 April. But now the Nationalists found themselves under increasingly heavy pressure from the National Federation of German Industry, the National Rural League, and other special interest organizations that stood to benefit from the expected influx of foreign capital, with the result that party unity began to disintegrate.[17] As a further inducement to the Nationalists, the DVP Reichstag delegation publicly offered to use all the means at its disposal to secure the DNVP's entry into the government if the party proved willing to accept its share of responsibility for the implementation of the London accord.[18]

When the Nationalist delegation split by a 52–48 margin in the decisive vote on 29 August and thereby assured ratification of the Dawes Plan by the necessary two-thirds majority, Stresemann found himself under heavy pressure from the DVP's right wing to honor the commitment the party's Reichstag delegation had made to the Nationalists. But the fact that those Nationalists who supported ratification of the Dawes Plan had come under heavy attack from the DNVP's state and local organizations made Stresemann extremely reluctant to pursue the matter until the situation within the DNVP had been clarified.[19] Consequently, it was not until the end of September that the leaders of the DVP Reichstag delegation resumed their efforts to bring the Nationalists into the government.[20] Even then, Marx was still extremely apprehensive about the diplomatic implications of the DNVP's entry into the government, and at a ministerial conference on 1 October he announced that he intended to invite not only the DNVP but also the Social Democrats to participate in negotiations aimed at broadening the basis of his governmental coalition. But the Nationalists, who clearly preferred remaining in opposition to joining a coalition with the Social Democrats, were conveniently spared the public onus for the collapse of negotiations when on 9 October the leaders of the SPD Reichstag delegation rejected the idea of a coalition government stretching from their party to the DNVP and withdrew from further deliberations. This cleared the way for an accommodation with the Nationalists, who on the following day agreed not only to recognize the Weimar Constitution as legally binding upon themselves and their party but also to accept the Dawes Plan and all of its provisions as irrevocable facts of Germany's political life. At this point, only an unresolved difference of opinion regarding Germany's bid for membership in the League of Nations seemed to stand in the way of the DNVP's entry into the government.[21]

While the Nationalists were prepared to accept the conditions the cabinet had attached to their entry into the government, both the Center and the DDP had strong reservations about a one-sided extension of the government to the Right and publicly committed themselves to the maintenance of the existing governmental coalition at meetings of their respective Reichstag delegations on the afternoon of 14 October.[22] Angered by this turn of events, the DVP Reichstag delegation met later that evening and issued a statement that castigated the other government parties for their lack of resolve and rejected a continuation of the existing coalition government as "practically impossible."[23] Although the Center subsequently modified its position to sanction an extension of the existing government coalition to the Right as long as the Democrats remained in the government, the leaders of the DDP remained adamant in their refusal to participate in a coalition government in which the Nationalists were also represented.[24] Koch-Weser's position, outlined in an article he had written for the *Berliner Tageblatt* in the middle of September, was that although acceptance of the Dawes recommendations had been possible in the present Reichstag, the strength of the radical parties and the DNVP's unreliability in matters of foreign policy made their implementation an impossibility. A dissolution of the Reichstag, new elections, and more stable parliamentary relations were therefore essential if the provisions of the Dawes Plan were to be implemented.[25] But as the government's negotiations with the DNVP drew to a climax in the second week of October, the situation within the DDP became increasingly volatile. Not only were party leaders anxious to avoid new elections that might find them forced onto the defensive,[26] but opposition to Koch-Weser's tactics had begun to crystallize on the DDP's right wing around Defense Minister Otto Gessler. Gessler's allies, who included

Hamm, Schiffer, and Gerland, argued that it was necessary to force the Nationalists into assuming responsibility for the implementation of the Dawes Plan and criticized the party leadership for its inability to pursue a course of action independent of the Social Democrats.[27]

The first sign of a split within the DDP Reichstag delegation came on 16 October when Karl Böhme, secretary general of the German Peasants' League and a prominent spokesman for the party's right wing, resigned from the DDP and defected to the German People's Party.[28] This, however, was only the prelude to a far more serious explosion that was to come at a meeting of the DDP Reichstag delegation on the afternoon of 20 October. Two days earlier Marx had informed Koch-Weser that while he had no intention of abandoning his efforts to bring the DNVP into the government, he considered Gessler's retention as minister of defense essential and fully intended to ask the Reich president to dissolve the Reichstag if the Democrats made it impossible to remain in office. Since the Reichstag was scheduled to reconvene on 21 October, Marx set five o'clock on the afternoon of the twentieth as the deadline for the DDP's decision.[29] In the critical meeting of the DDP Reichstag delegation that took place just before the expiration of Marx's deadline, Gessler's supporters introduced two resolutions, the first of which called upon the delegation to abandon its opposition to the DNVP's entry into the government. Such a government, the resolution declared, should be judged on the basis of its accomplishments and not according to an inflexible formula that categorically ruled out cooperation with the Nationalists.[30] After this resolution had been defeated by a one-sided vote, Schiffer introduced a second resolution that would have permitted Gessler to remain in office even though the Democrats refused to support the government to which he belonged.[31] This too was rejected, whereupon the delegation proceeded to adopt by an overwhelming 26–5 margin a resolution that not only reaffirmed the DDP's opposition to a reorganization of the Marx government but explicitly barred any member of the delegation from serving in a government to which the DDP did not belong.[32]

Upon learning of the DDP's decision, Marx dissolved the Reichstag and scheduled new elections for 7 December 1924. In the meantime, the leaders of the DDP found themselves facing the threat of a major secession on the party's right wing. On 21 October Schiffer, Gerland, and Otto Keinath, along with two members of the Democratic delegation to the Prussian Landtag, announced their resignation from the party. Gessler, Hamm, and another DDP Reichstag deputy from Bavaria, Georg Sparrer, were expected to join the secession as soon as they had consulted with the leaders of their state party organization.[33] In an open letter to the Democratic party leadership, Schiffer and his associates claimed that the recent crisis within the DDP was only the latest example of its failure to fulfill its historic mission as a party of liberal and bourgeois concentration. The DDP had been founded as a united liberal party in which all of those elements willing to cooperate in the construction of the German state on a truly liberal and democratic basis could unite. Not only had the DDP's reluctance to pursue any course of action that might offend the Social Democrats driven more and more of its middle-class supporters from the party, but this had now reached a point where noncollaboration with the DNVP had become a cardinal principle of the DDP's political creed.[34]

Whatever hopes Schiffer and his associates may have had of igniting a general secession on the DDP's right wing all but collapsed when Gessler and Hamm failed in their efforts to interest the leaders of the Bavarian DDP in the founding of a new liberal party.[35] Frustrated by this turn of events, Schiffer joined industrialist Carl Friedrich von Siemens, another member of the DDP's right wing who had recently resigned his seat in the Reichstag to assume the chairmanship of the German National Railway Corporation (Deutsche Reichsbahn-Gesellschaft),[36] and five other representatives of Germany's liberal establishment in announcing the founding of the Liberal Association (Liberale Vereinigung or LV) on 28 October 1924.[37] Dedicated to overcoming what Schiffer later described as "the cancer [*Krebschaden*] of German liberalism, its splintering,"[38] the Liberal Association compared itself to the German National Association of 1859 and insisted that its goal was not to found a new political party but to put an end to the historic cleavage that had existed within the German liberal movement ever since its inception at the beginning of the nineteenth century. Claiming that this goal could be properly served only through a merger of existing liberal parties, the founders of the Liberal Association abstained from taking part in the Reichstag elections that had been scheduled for the first week of December and simply urged their sympathizers to support candidates who were prepared to fight for the concept of liberal unity within their respective political parties.[39] Its professions of political neutrality to the contrary, the central thrust of the LV's pronouncements during the course of the campaign was directed against the DDP, whose alleged failure as a party of liberal concentration had made the founding of the Association necessary.[40]

Koch-Weser and the leaders of the DDP looked upon Schiffer and his associates as renegades who had deserted their party in the heat of battle, and they denounced the founding of the Liberal Association as part of a conspiracy to inflict even further damage upon the DDP.[41] This contrasted sharply, as one might expect, with the position of Stresemann, who hoped that the recent crisis within the DDP might enable his own party to score a decisive breakthrough into the ranks of the Democratic electorate.[42] But Stresemann's hopes that a full-fledged secession might develop on the DDP's right wing failed to materialize when former National Liberals such as Hermann Dietrich, Philipp Wieland, Bernhard Falk, and Peter Stubmann all rallied to the defense of their party.[43] By the same token, Friedrich Wachhorst de Wente tried to isolate the damage caused by Böhme's defection to the DVP by reaffirming his loyalty as president of the German Peasants' League to the DDP at a meeting of the party executive committee on 21 October,[44] while Hamm, who as minister of economics in the Marx cabinet had been particularly critical of the DDP's efforts to block the DNVP's entry into the government, used his influence with the leaders of the DDP's Bavarian organization to smooth over the differences that had surfaced in their relations with the party's national leadership.[45] Even the leaders of the DDP's business wing began to raise money for the party's use in the upcoming campaign in spite of the fact that many of them were still deeply dissatisfied with the stance the party had taken during the recent cabinet crisis.[46]

The national party congress that the leaders of the DDP held in Berlin on 1– 2 November 1924 manifested a degree of internal unity that was virtually unprecedented in the party's short history. In the keynote address on the second day of the congress, Koch-Weser defended the policies the DDP had pursued for the past five years as an indispensable contribution to Germany's political and economic stabilization and claimed that the ratification of the Dawes Plan marked the beginning of a new era in Germany's postwar history. At the same time, Koch-Weser launched into a sharp attack against Stresemann and the leaders of the DVP for having provoked a cabinet crisis at a time when there was no pressing need for a reorganization of the government and openly challenged the DVP's contention that the Nationalists had undergone some sort of "inner change" as a result of their vote on the Dawes Plan.[47] The main thrust of Koch-Weser's speech was clearly directed against the DVP and the German Right. Not only was this line of attack designed to insulate the DDP against the danger of further defections to the DVP, but it enabled the party to reestablish its position among those social groups that had formerly constituted the nucleus of the DDP's left wing.

Inasmuch as the DDP's poor showing in the May 1924 Reichstag elections had stemmed from its failure to devote sufficient attention to the problems of specific social groups such as the civil service and white-collar class, party leaders now found themselves under heavy pressure from the representatives of both groups to rectify this deficiency in the selection of candidates for the December elections.[48] Threatened by what amounted to a virtual mutiny on the part of the DDP's civil servant and white-collar supporters, party leaders had no choice but to give in to these demands, with the result that they nominated first Gustav Schneider, chairman of the Federation of Employee Unions, and then Otto Schuldt, a civil servant representative, to secure positions on the DDP's national slate of candidates. Similar concessions were made to the party's artisan and peasant interests with the nomination of master plumber Franz Bartschat and farm specialist Heinrich Rönneburg to positions on the national ticket that assured them of at least a good chance of being elected.[49] As a result, the DDP entered the campaign for the December 1924 elections with a social profile that was both more clearly defined and more highly diversified than it had been at the time of the spring elections.

At no time since the DVP's entry into the Fehrenbach government in the summer of 1920 had battle lines between the two liberal parties been more sharply drawn than in the campaign for the December 1924 Reichstag elections. The bitter recriminations between the two party chairmen over the question of the DVP's moral responsibility for Rathenau's assassination were only symptomatic of the deep gulf that had developed between the two liberal parties in the fall and winter of 1924.[50] But if the leaders of the DDP approached the upcoming elections with renewed self-confidence and a greater display of unity than they had shown in some time, the same could be said of Stresemann and his associates in the German People's Party. For not only had Stresemann's efforts to bring the DNVP into the government done much to placate his critics on the DVP's right wing,[51] but the leaders of the National Liberal Association, which had caused Stresemann so much difficulty in the spring elections, were anxious to settle their differences with the DVP party leadership.[52] Moreover, funds from its former supporters in the Ruhr had begun to flow once again into the DVP's campaign coffers, though not necessarily in the amounts to which the party had been accustomed and invariably subject to conditions regarding their disposition.[53] All of this augured well for the DVP's performance in the upcoming elections and contributed in no small measure to Stresemann's hopes of scoring substantial gains at the expense of both the DDP and the DNVP.

Stresemann's campaign rhetoric was carefully designed to subordinate domestic political issues—and particularly those of a divisive nature—to the overriding goal of Germany's liberation from the shackles of Versailles. To be sure, the DVP continued to address itself to special economic interests and, like the DDP, made a concerted effort to recapture the support of the civil service, artisanry, and other middle-class elements that had deserted it over the course of the past several years.[54] But, for the most part, Stresemann conceived of the election as a referendum on the foreign policy he had pursued for the preceding fifteen months, and he consistently warned his supporters against placing so much emphasis on their material interests that they lost sight of the fact that politics was and would always remain a struggle over ideals.[55] Nowhere was Stresemann's commitment to the "primacy of foreign policy" more apparent than in his keynote address at the DVP's Dortmund party congress on 14 November 1924. In a speech that was directed as much at the Democrats and German Nationalists as at his own party faithful, Stresemann prefaced his review of the events that had led up to the dissolution of the Reichstag with an appeal for a "national Realpolitik" that rested upon a broad domestic consensus that transcended existing party lines and was free from nationalistic illusions about the true extent of German power. The negotiations with the DNVP were therefore designed not only to wean the more responsible elements within the DNVP from the illusions of the radical Right but also to forge a stable domestic consensus for the conduct of German foreign policy. For, as Stresemann was to reiterate throughout his speech, it was only on the basis of such a consensus that Germany would be able to continue down the road to national liberation that had begun with the Treaty of London and the French agreement to evacuate the Ruhr.[56]

Though sharply critical of Stresemann's domestic policies, the leaders of the DDP were not hesitant to claim a share of the credit for his recent diplomatic successes and to hail the benefits that Germany could expect to receive from the Treaty of London as the fruits of a Democratic foreign policy.[57] Much of the campaign, however, was dominated by a domestic issue that threatened to nullify whatever benefits the two liberal parties hoped to reap from their identification with Stresemann's success at the conference table. The revaluation provisions of the Third Emergency Tax Decree had aroused widespread resentment on the part of those private investors who had been dispossessed by the inflation, but efforts to revise or modify those provisions had been stymied by the political deadlock that existed in the Reichstag following the elections in the spring of 1924. The call for new elections in the fall of 1924 found the leaders of the revaluation movement deeply divided over the strategy they should pursue in the forthcoming campaign and led to a further fragmentation of their efforts on behalf of a revision of the Third Emergency Tax Decree. This manifested itself first of all in the founding of the German Revaluation and Recovery Party (Deutsche Aufwertungs- und Aufbaupartei) in Berlin on 1 November under the leadership of Reinhard Wüst from Halle in Saxony.[58] Several days later a similar party calling itself the Revaluation and Reconstruction Party (Aufwertungs- und Wiederaufbau-Partei) was founded under the sponsorship of the Berlin and Hamburg chapters of the Protective Association of Mortgagees and Savers for the German Reich (Hypotheken-Gläubiger- und Sparer-Schutzverband für das Deutsche Reich), which had been created at the end of 1922 as a national umbrella organization for all of those private investors who had been dispossessed by the inflation.[59]

By no means, however, was this activity sanctioned by the national leadership of the Mortgagees and Savers' Protective Association, which at a meeting of its executive committee on 6 November voted against the founding of a new political party in favor of continued cooperation with the established parties that seemed most likely to support its demands for a full and equitable revaluation of paper mark assets that had been destroyed by the inflation.[60] Ever sensitive to pressure of this sort, the Democrats had already taken steps to recoup the losses they had suffered the previous spring by coming out in support of significantly higher revalorization percentages than those provided for in the Third Emergency Tax Decree,[61] while the DVP, which had hoped to bring the DNVP into the government so that a settlement of revaluation and related economic problems might be possible, presented the electorate with a detailed six-point program recommending higher revalorization percentages for all categories of indebtedness.[62] But neither party was prepared to support the Mortgagees and Savers' Protective Association's demands for a total revaluation of paper mark assets that had been destroyed by the inflation. Nor were they willing to provide representatives from the revaluation movement with guaranteed candidacies for the upcoming Reichstag elections. As a result, the Mortgagees and Savers' Protective Association chose to withhold its endorsement from the two liberal parties. Both the DNVP and the so-called National Socialist Freedom Movement (Nationalsozialistische Freiheitsbewegung), on the other hand, proved amenable to the association's demands and received its unconditional support.[63]

The revaluation question was significant in several respects. Not only did it enable the Nationalists to shift the focus of the campaign away from their alleged unreliability in matters of foreign policy to the much safer ground of German domestic politics, but it left the two liberal parties hard pressed to defend themselves against charges from the Mortgagees and Savers' Protective Association and other middle-class interest organizations that they had abandoned the German middle class in its moment of need. As a result, Stresemann's hopes that the German electorate might return to its senses and chastise the Nationalists for their failure to support his program of national Realpolitik failed to materialize. Much to his dismay, the outcome of the 7 December 1924 Reichstag elections resulted in another—and in this case totally unexpected—victory for the DNVP, which managed to increase its share of the popular vote by more than half a million votes and the size of its parliamentary delegation by eight seats. But the fact that the parties that supported his foreign policy also emerged from the election considerably strengthened made it difficult for him or the leaders of the DNVP to interpret the outcome of the election as a repudiation of his accomplishments as German foreign minister. The Social Democrats, for example, polled nearly 1.8 million more votes than they had received in the May elections and increased their representation in the Reichstag from 100 to 131 seats, while the Center recorded less dramatic gains of approximately 200,000 votes and four Reichstag mandates. Even the two liberal parties were able to reverse the losses that they had suffered in the spring, scoring moderate gains that amounted to slightly more than 600,000 votes and ten seats in parliament. The big losers in the campaign, on the other hand, were the radical parties on the Left and Right, as both the Communists and the National Socialist Freedom Movement suffered losses in the vicinity of 1 million votes apiece.[64] If anything, the outcome of the elections suggested a relaxation of political tensions throughout the Reich and temporarily strengthened those forces that had come to support the Republic. Whether or not this would lead to a more permanent stabilization of Germany's parliamentary system remained to be seen.

For the most part, the leaders of the German liberal parties had good reason to be satisfied with the outcome of the campaign. The Democrats, for example, derived particular satisfaction from the fact that their party's popular vote had increased by nearly 16 percent between the May and December elections, while in Prussia, where Landtag elections had taken place on the same day as the national elections, the DDP received 50,000 more votes than it had received in the last state elections in February 1921. Heartened by their party's strong gains in Berlin, Baden, and Bavaria, the Democrats were relieved that the DDP had succeeded in breaking the long string of electoral setbacks it had suffered over the preceeding five years, and they hailed the outcome of the December elections as the beginning of a new period of growth and expansion for the DDP.[65] The undisguised sense of relief with which the Democrats received the election results, however, contrasted markedly with the mood in the DVP. For although the People's Party had improved upon its popular vote in the May elections by more than 13 percent, Stresemann and his associates had entered the campaign with hopes that large-scale defections from the DDP and DNVP might enable the DVP to win back the pivotal position it had held in 1920. Not only did these defections fail to materialize on a scale sufficient to provide the DVP with the unequivocal electoral triumph for which Stresemann had hoped, but the DVP, like the DDP, was severely hurt by the continued success of special interest parties within Germany's middle-class electorate. An alliance of middle-class splinter parties headed by the Bavarian Peasant and Middle-Class League (Bayerischer Bauern- und Mittelstandsbund) amassed over 1 million votes in the December elections and elected seventeen deputies to the Reichstag. Regional agrarian parties in Württemberg, Baden, Hesse, and several other parts of the country attracted an additional half million votes and won another eight seats in parliament, while the German-Hanoverian Party (Deutsch-Hannoversche Partei or DHP), a single-issue party with virtually no appeal outside of Hanoverian Prussia, collected no less than 260,000 votes. Even the fledgling revaluation parties, founded on the eve of the election and with no national organization whatsoever, polled 116,000 votes.[66] A barometer of middle-class disaffection from the established bourgeois parties, the continued appeal of special interest parties such as these injected an element of increasing instability into the Weimar party system and rendered the outcome of the December Reichstag elections highly ambiguous.

CHAPTER EIGHTEEN

A House Divided against Itself

WITH THE END OF THE inflation and the reestablishment of international confidence in Germany's economic future, Germany entered a period of economic and political stabilization that was to continue until the onset of the great depression at the end of the 1920s. This, in turn, lent credence to the popular feeling that Germany had entered a period of normalcy and stability and that even if life was not going to be as sweet as it had been before the war, things were not going to be as chaotic or as feverish as they had been for the past six years. But, as a closer examination of the period between 1924 and 1929 reveals, Germany's political culture was plagued by persistent problems that did much to belie the popular feeling of normalcy and stability. The most perplexing of these was the inability of Germany's parliamentary system to generate a durable domestic consensus upon which the definition, articulation, and pursuit of Germany's national interest could take place.

By the middle of the 1920s the Weimar party system offered two possibilities for the formation of a broad parliamentary coalition capable of commanding a majority in the Reichstag. On the one hand, it was theoretically possible to achieve a parliamentary majority in the Reichstag through the creation of a coalition that included all of the forces, bourgeois as well as socialist, that supported Stresemann's policy of conciliation with the Entente. But this constellation of forces, which had crystallized in support of the Stresemann government in the late summer of 1923, was plagued by fundamental and ultimately irreconcilable differences over social and economic policy. Having been severely chastened by their experiences as a member of Stresemann's Great Coalition, the Social Democrats were content to spend the entire period from 1924 to 1928 in opposition, while the industrial interests on the DVP's right wing remained intractibly opposed to any concessions on social and economic policy that might facilitate the SPD's entry into the national government. A second possibility lay in the consolidation of all of the forces that shared a basic commitment to the preservation of the free enterprise system and that sought to free German capitalism from the various obstacles the November Revolution had placed in its path. But this coalition, which would have included the German Nationalists, was beset by deep-seated and ultimately irreconcilable disagreements over constitutional and foreign policy issues, so that in the final analysis its viability was no less problematic than that of the first.[1]

The failure of Germany's parliamentary system to generate a viable domestic consensus for the conduct of national policy was directly related to the fragmentation of Weimar party politics, a fact that did much to compromise the legitimacy of the Weimar party system in the eyes of Germany's liberal leadership. In confidential remarks at a meeting of government leaders on 19 December 1924, Defense Minister Otto Gessler argued that the persistent failure of efforts to form a government capable of commanding a parliamentary majority was not just a government crisis but a constitutional crisis that could be remedied only through a fundamental reform of the Weimar Constitution. Specifically, Gessler complained that the Weimar Constitution had given Germany a parliament that might work with two or three parties but not with fifteen. With the cabinet almost totally dependent upon the will of the Reichstag, the proliferation of parties within the Reichstag had made it impossible for Germany's political leaders to form any sort of lasting consensus upon which the cabinet could base its policies. At the same time, the Reich president, whose election by the entire nation was supposed to serve as a plebiscitarian counterweight to the factionalism of the Reichstag, had been stripped of his powers to the point where his office was purely ceremonial in nature, while the Reichsrat had developed into nothing more than a college for the one-sided representation of states' interests against those of the Reich as a whole. Arguing that the religious, economic, social, and regional divisions among the German people had rendered the existing constitutional structure unworkable, Gessler insisted that only an immediate overhaul of the Weimar Constitution could prevent the complete paralysis of state authority. If the government failed to undertake a reform of the Weimar Constitution by legal means, it would only be a matter of time before others less concerned with the legality of their methods would attempt the task.[2]

While Gessler's remarks constituted a remarkably astute analysis of the political impasse that Germany had reached by the middle of the 1920s, the leaders of the German liberal movement were severely handicapped in their efforts to formulate an effective response to this situation by the open rift that had developed between the two liberal parties. German liberalism was truly a house divided against itself following the December 1924 Reichstag elections, and at no point was this more apparent than during the negotiations to form a new government in the winter of 1924–25. Although the Democrats, whose refusal to enter a government in which the DNVP was also represented had triggered the most recent cabinet crisis, readily conceded that the outcome of the December elections made it impossible for the present government to remain in office,[3] the ferocity of the campaign and the DVP's apparent turn to the right had made them even less inclined to share governmental responsibility with the Nationalists than they had been before the elections. At the same time, Democratic hopes that the Social Democrats' strong gains in the December elections might lead to the formation of the Great Coalition were effectively torpedoed by Stresemann and the leaders of the DVP Reichstag delegation. The outcome of the recent Reichstag elections had only strengthened Stresemann in his conviction that it was essential to bring the Nationalists into the government so that they could no longer disdain responsibility for Germany's foreign policy or for the unpopular measures that might be necessary to solve her domestic problems. Not only did this preclude a return to the Great Coalition that he had headed in the early summer and fall of 1923, but it also meant that maintenance of the existing governmental coalition was out of the question.[4]

On 10 December the DVP executive committee handed the government a resolution in which it called for the resignation of the existing cabinet and for the creation of a new government coalition in which the DNVP was represented.[5] Five days later the Marx government submitted its resignation, whereupon the Reich president commissioned Stresemann with the task of forming a new government. While Stresemann had no intention of exchanging his post at the foreign office for the chancellorship, his advocacy of a coalition with the Nationalists made him the logical choice for such a task. But Stresemann's efforts on behalf of a coalition with the DNVP suffered a sharp setback when first the DDP and then the Center refused to participate in a bourgeois government with the Nationalists, and on 17 December he resigned the commission he had received from Ebert.[6] As the crisis dragged on through the Christmas recess, Stresemann and the leaders of the DVP began to lean more and more heavily toward the creation of a "cabinet of experts" that included representatives from the DNVP and other nonsocialist parties without, however, being formally bound to any of the parties that belonged to it.[7] Although the Democrats remained adamantly opposed to such a suggestion, the proposal found tentative support within the Center, where the leaders of the party's right wing had begun to gain the upper hand. But efforts on the part of the Center's Wilhelm Marx to form a cabinet of experts consisting merely of representatives from the DDP, Center, and ministerial bureaucracy were again torpedoed by the leaders of the DVP Reichstag delegation, who on 7 January 1925 denounced such a solution as nothing more than a "disguised cabinet of the middle" and reiterated their previous position that only a government that commanded a firm bourgeois majority in the Reichstag could possibly solve the myriad of problems facing the German people.[8] This left Marx, who was publicly opposed to his party's participation in a bourgeois coalition with the Nationalists, no choice but to abandon his efforts to form a new government, and on 9 January he, like Stresemann before him, resigned the commisson with which Ebert had entrusted him.[9]

Following Marx's failure to break the political deadlock that had developed in Berlin, Stresemann suggested that Finance Minister Hans Luther be allowed to try his hand at forming a new government. Six days later Luther presented the Reichstag with a cabinet that included three members of the DNVP, as well as representatives from the DVP, Center, and Bavarian People's Party. This government, however, differed from all preceding Weimar governments by virtue of the fact that it was not bound by any formal commitments to the parties belonging to it. While those ministers with close party affiliations— Stresemann from the DVP, Heinrich Brauns from the Center, Martin Schiele from the DNVP, and Karl Stingl from the BVP—were supposed to function as unofficial liaisons between the government and their respective political parties, the cabinet itself was formally independent from the parties to which its members belonged and was not bound by any demands they might make upon it.[10] Perfectly consistent with Luther's conception of himself as a "politician without a party," this represented an authoritarian response to the parliamentary crisis in which Germany had found herself at the end of 1924 and aroused strong misgivings within both the Center and DDP on account of its radical departure from accepted parliamentary practice. But the Center, whose left wing was temporarily neutralized by factors unrelated to the cabinet negotiations, was unwilling to press the issue and merely made Brauns's participation in such a government contingent upon Gessler's retention as minister of defense. As a result, responsibility for the success or failure of Luther's efforts to form a new government came to rest in the reluctant hands of the DDP.[11]

The situation in which the leaders of the DDP found themselves in January 1925 was complicated by a variety of factors. In the first place, the leaders of the DDP's left wing were deeply embarrassed by the policies that Gessler had recently pursued in Saxony and Bavaria, and they were unwilling to pay for his retention in office with another sacrifice of their principles.[12] But Koch-Weser and his associates had just gone through one crisis involving the party's right wing, and they were anxious to avoid a crisis over Gessler that would almost certainly be more damaging to party unity than the one they had recently experienced with Schiffer.[13] Moreover, for all of the reservations the Democrats may have had about the composition of the Luther government or about the way in which it had come into being, their strong and unconditional support of Stresemann's foreign policy precluded any blanket condemnation of the new government and forced them to be far more circumspect in their treatment of it than they might otherwise have been. All of this bespoke compromise, and on 21 January Koch-Weser announced that the Democratic delegation would abstain in the vote of confidence on the government's program that was scheduled to take place the following day.[14] Even though party leaders insisted that this was not to be interpreted as a demonstration of confidence in the Luther government and coupled their announcement with a sharp attack against the DVP for the unsteady course it had pursued ever since the formation of the Stresemann government,[15] the decision to abstain found little favor with the leaders of the DDP's left wing, where four members of the delegation—Walther Schücking, Adolf Korell, Otto Schuldt, and Ernst Lemmer—refused to heed the call for party unity and left the Reichstag just as the decisive vote was about to take place.[16]

The principal architect of the Luther government was Stresemann, who had worked quietly, yet steadily, to bring the DNVP into the government ever since he first assumed the chancellorship in the late summer of 1923. Stresemann's determination to bring the Nationalists into the government was motivated as much by his belief that cooperation with the DNVP was essential for the stabilization of Germany's new republican order as it was by his desire to win at least the more responsible elements within the DNVP over to the support of his foreign policy. In this respect, Stresemann hoped that the DNVP's entry into the government would not only educate the Nationalists about the practical limits under which all German politicians were forced to operate but would help free them from the nationalistic illusions that had become so deeply entrenched on the party's right wing.[17] But as compelling as these arguments may have appeared to Stresemann, they had little effect upon the Democrats, who harbored a lingering distrust of the DNVP and deplored its entry into the national government as a grievous mistake for both domestic and diplomatic reasons. Even though tactical considerations had led the Democrats to abstain in the vote of confidence on 22 January, they remained strongly opposed to the Luther government and continued to censure Stresemann for having risked Germany's political future by bringing the Nationalists into the government.[18]

The rift that had developed between the two liberal parties over the DNVP's role in government carried over into the elections for a new Reich president in the spring of 1925. Even before his untimely death on 28 February 1925, Ebert had let it be known that he had little desire to run for reelection, with the result that the various factions within the German bourgeoisie had begun to jockey for position long before the campaign actually began. As the weakest of these groups, the DDP favored a joint campaign by the parties of the Weimar Coalition and initially proposed that Walter Simons, president of the German Supreme Court and Ebert's legal successor as Reich president, be nominated as a republican unity candidate.[19] When the Social Democrats sabotaged this proposal on 7 March by opting to support one of their own members in the preliminary election that was scheduled to take place later in the month, the Democrats recommended that all of Germany's major political parties, including the SPD and DNVP, unite behind Simons's candidacy in order to avoid arousing the old class antagonisms that existed throughout the German nation.[20] This suggestion was directed not so much against the Social Democrats as against the Loebell Committee, a bipartisan organization of bourgeois parties and interest groups that had constituted itself on 12 February under the chairmanship of Friedrich von Loebell, president of the National Citizens Council (Reichsbürgerrat), for the purpose of electing a nonsocialist president.[21] But the Loebell Committee, to which neither the DDP nor the Center belonged, had already settled upon the DVP's Karl Jarres as its choice for president and was very close to a formal announcement on his behalf.[22] Still, the members of the Loebell Committee could not ignore the fact that Jarres, who stood on his party's extreme right wing, was unlikely to attract much support from the parties to the left of the DVP, and at a meeting on 11 March a representative from an alliance of special interest parties known as the Economic Association (Wirtschaftliche Vereinigung) proposed that the committee switch its support from Jarres to Gessler. This proposal met with a warm response from the DDP and Center, whose leaders indicated that they would be willing to join forces with the Loebell Committee if it nominated Gessler for the presidency.[23]

As one of the three men whom the Loebell Committee had originally considered, Gessler enjoyed strong support within both the DVP and DNVP, where his reputation as a political conservative had earned him a measure of respect. Moreover, Gessler had the added advantage of being both a Catholic and a Democrat and would certainly fare better in any national campaign than the decidedly more conservative Jarres. Yet while the leaders of the Loebell Committee were initially prepared to endorse Gessler as their candidate for the presidency, his nomination ran into strong and unexpected opposition from several quarters. The leaders of the DDP's left wing were particularly critical of the policies Gessler had pursued at the Ministry of Defense and resented the way in which he had virtually ignored the party at the time of his appointment to the Luther government earlier in the year. But Koch-Weser's vigorous defense of Gessler's candidacy at a meeting of the DDP party council on the morning of 12 March persuaded many of those who had originally opposed his nomination to change their minds, with the result that the party voted to endorse his candidacy by a one-sided 185–15 margin.[24] A far more serious obstacle to Gessler's nomination, however, was Stresemann's fear that the election of someone so closely identified with the Reichswehr would seriously jeopardize the security pact that he was in the process of negotiating with the French.[25] Stresemann immediately prevailed upon the Center to delay its endorsement of Gessler's candidacy until the afternoon of 12 March, by which time he would have had an opportunity to consult with the leaders of his own party. But when the DVP Reichstag delegation met on the morning of 12 March to discuss the candidate question, it coupled its affirmation of support for Jarres with a qualifying statement indicating that in the interests of electing a bourgeois Reich president it was prepared to endorse Gessler if all of Germany's bourgeois parties agreed to unite in support of his candidacy.[26] Rebuffed by the leaders of his own delegation, Stresemann took his case to the DVP national committee, which overrode the Reichstag delegation's decision from earlier that morning and issued an unequivocal endorsement of Jarres's candidacy.[27] This, combined with the fact that both the Center and the Nationalists were beginning to have reservations of their own about Gessler's candidacy, effectively destroyed any chance the Democratic defense minister had of receiving the nomination and cleared the way for Jarres's official endorsement as a candidate for the Reich presidency at a meeting of the Loebell Committee on the afternoon of 12 March.[28]

Stresemann's role in sabotaging Gessler's candidacy for the Reich presidency left the leaders of his own party's Reichstag delegation in a state of complete bewilderment[29] and led to a further deterioration of his relationship with Koch-Weser and the leaders of the DDP.[30] The strain that had developed in relations between the two parties was obvious throughout the campaign for the preliminary electoral skirmish that took place on 29 March. Whereas the DVP readily supported Jarres as the endorsed candidate of the Loebell Committee, strategic considerations made it impossible for the Democrats to support either Wilhelm Marx or Otto Braun, the candidates of the Center and Social Democrats respectively. This left the Democrats with no alternative but to nominate a candidate of their own, particularly if they wanted to keep their predominantly Protestant electorate from voting for Jarres.[31] With the more prominent Democrats unwilling to run in what was clearly a hopeless cause, the DDP turned to Willy Hugo Hellpach, a relatively obscure academic who had served as minister president of Baden since the end of 1922.[32] The choice of Hellpach proved particularly unfortunate, not only because it gave him an inflated sense of his own importance to the party but, more importantly, because he lacked the national political profile necessary to make his campaign credible. Moreover, the DDP was extremely short of funds and was unable to mobilize the resources it had had at its disposal for the December 1924 Reichstag elections. As a result, Hellpach's candidacy attracted about 350,000 fewer votes than the DDP had received in the last national elections. Jarres, on the other hand, emerged from the campaign as the most popular candidate, with more than 10 million votes to his credit. But this amounted to less than 40 percent of the total popular vote and was insufficient to provide Jarres with the absolute majority required by the Weimar Constitution for the election of the Reich president. A runoff election in which the winner was to be determined by a mere plurality was set for the last week of April.[33]

Once again the various bourgeois parties began to jockey for position in anticipation of their next skirmish at the polls. The Bavarian People's Party, which had not supported Jarres in the preliminary election and was unlikely to support him should he choose to run again, immediately called for the nomination of a candidate behind whom all of Germany's bourgeois parties could unite. This appeal met with a particularly warm response from the leaders of the DDP, who still entertained hopes that it might be possible to nominate either Simons or Gessler as a republican unity candidate.[34] But these hopes were shattered when the Center and Social Democrats announced without ever having consulted the Democratic party leadership that they would support Marx in the runoff election that was scheduled for 26 April. At the same time, efforts to revive Gessler's candidacy met with unyielding opposition from the more conservative members of the Loebell Committee, who were prepared to renominate Jarres even though his candidacy now appeared hopeless.[35] Under these circumstances, the leaders of the DDP were left with no alternative but to declare their support for Marx and to affiliate themselves with the so-called People's Bloc (Volksblock) that the Center and SPD had begun to organize on his behalf.[36] Though defended by most party leaders as a step that would help stabilize Germany's republican order if it resulted in Marx's election, this decision aroused profound misgivings, if not open dissent, among a handful of Democrats who looked upon Marx's election as a direct threat to the cultural and educational policies for which the DDP had always stood. Forced to choose between the need for republican unity in the face of a united German Right and the need to keep the German school system free of church interference, the Democrats were able to marshal only grudging support for Marx's candidacy and entered the campaign with their ranks badly divided.[37]

By this time, the leaders of the Loebell Committee—or National Bloc (Reichsblock), as it was now known—had also begun to reassess their candidate's prospects in the upcoming runoff election. Candidates representing the three parties that belonged to the People's Bloc had received more than 13 million votes in the preliminary campaign, and it was unlikely that Jarres, even with defections from the DDP, could overcome that deficit. In their search for a new candidate capable of winning the BVP's endorsement and mobilizing nonvoters throughout the country, the more conservative members of the Loebell Committee began to focus more and more closely upon the person of retired war hero Paul von Hindenburg as a replacement for Jarres. Though reluctant to run for the presidency, Hindenburg agreed to become a candidate if all the parties belonging to the National Bloc were prepared to support his candidacy. The news that the Loebell Committee might drop Jarres in favor of Hindenburg, however, came as a bitter shock to Stresemann, who had precisely the same sort of reservations about Hindenburg as he had about Gessler. But Stresemann, who thought that the DVP's reaffirmation of support for Jarres would be sufficient to discourage Hindenburg from running, made a fundamental miscalculation when he failed to send a personal emissary to the former field marshal's home in Hanover to underscore his party's opposition to Hindenburg's candidacy.[38] As a result, the Nationalists were able to persuade Hindenburg to keep his candidacy alive, and at the decisive meeting of the Loebell Committee on the afternoon of 8 April they pressed their case for his nomination with increasing vigor. The committee's inability to reach a decision so irritated Jarres that during the course of the meeting he withdrew his name from further consideration, thereby clearing the way for a unanimous endorsement of Hindenburg's candidacy by the various parties, including the BVP and DVP, that belonged to the National Bloc.[39]

Stresemann's failure to prevent Hindenburg's nomination for the Reich presidency in April 1925 represented one of the most serious mistakes of his political career. Deeply disturbed by the diplomatic implications of Hindenburg's possible election, Stresemann withheld his personal endorsement of the old field marshal until the last week of the campaign and then couched it in such cautious terms that his reservations were immediately apparent.[40] Moreover, the DVP maintained a conspicuously low profile throughout the campaign, leaving as much as possible to the DNVP and the various patriotic organizations that had rallied so enthusiastically to Hindenburg's candidacy. Whereas Stresemann's coolness toward Hindenburg's candidacy had little effect upon the enthusiasm with which his party's rank-and-file membership embraced the war hero's decision to run, the Democrats were plagued by widespread defections to the National Bloc following the announcement that Hindenburg had agreed to stand for election. Although the only prominent party member who publicly endorsed Hindenburg's candidacy was Ernst Müller-Meiningen, a conservative Bavarian Democrat who proceeded to leave the DDP in protest against its decision to support Marx,[41] anticlerical and antisocialist feeling was so strong in certain quarters of the party that the Democrats were powerless to hold their erstwhile followers in line. In Leipzig, for example, the DDP's cooperation with the Center and SPD under the aegis of the People's Bloc triggered a major secession on the part of local schoolteachers who regarded this as a betrayal of the cultural and educational policies for which the Democrats had always stood. In other parts of the country the Democrats had to contend with a highly emotional campaign by the Lutheran Church and its auxiliary organizations to discredit Marx's candidacy with slogans such as "Protestants, Do Not Betray Your Faith!"[42] But if confessional prejudice made it difficult for the Democrats to mobilize their predominantly Protestant electorate on behalf of Marx's candidacy, the fact that Marx was a Catholic had little effect upon conservative Bavarians who shared his religion but resented his close ties to the Social Democrats. In the final analysis, it was precisely the combination of Protestant reluctance to support a candidate who was closely identified with the cause of political Catholicism and conservative Catholic aversion to Social Democracy that provided Hindenburg, the very symbol of Prussian conservatism and militarism, with the margin of victory on 26 April.[43]

Athough Stresemann was deeply concerned over the diplomatic repercussions of Hindenburg's election, he consoled himself with the hope that this might facilitate the DNVP's reconciliation with the Weimar Republic. But these hopes were abruptly shattered in October 1925 when the DNVP resigned from the Luther government in a mood of nationalistic frenzy over the security pact that Germany had just initialed with France, Belgium and Italy at Locarno.[44] Although this turn of events had little effect upon the eventual ratification of the Locarno accords, it represented a dramatic setback to Stresemann's policy of stabilizing the republic from the Right.[45] By the same token, Jarres and the more conservative elements on the DVP's right wing deplored the effect of the DNVP's resignation from the Luther government upon the incipient consolidation of the German Right that had begun with the formation of the Loebell Committee during the recent presidential campaign.[46] The Democrats, on the other hand, viewed the DNVP's refusal to support the Locarno agreements as further evidence of the Nationalists' unreliability in matters of foreign policy and entertained renewed hopes that the failure of Stresemann's opening to the Right might lead to a resumption of efforts on behalf of a coalition with the Social Democrats.[47]

Negotiations to form a new government were postponed until after the formal ratification of the Locarno treaties in late November 1925, at which time the Nationalists joined the Communists and National Socialists in voting against the new security pact. Initial discussions in the first week of December revealed strong support for the Great Coalition in both the Center and DDP, and on 14 December Koch-Weser was officially commissioned with the task of forming a new government. But Hindenburg, who privately favored the retention of Luther as the head of a bourgeois minority government with friendly ties to the DNVP, formulated his instructions to Koch-Weser in such a way that his authorization to negotiate was limited solely to the creation of a government based upon the Great Coalition. Should Koch-Weser fail in his efforts to bring such a government into existence—as Hindenburg fully expected—the responsibility for forming a new government would then revert to someone else, presumably Luther.[48]

Although Koch-Weser had profound reservations about the conditions that Hindenburg had attached to his efforts to form a new government, he could hardly decline the mandate that the Reich president had offered him and immediately tried to establish some sort of common ground upon which the Social Democrats and the DVP could agree.[49] Much to his surprise, Koch-Weser quickly discovered that the People's Party, which had originally made its participation in a government of the Great Coalition contingent upon the publication of a comprehensive economic program to which all of the government parties were formally bound,[50] was far more flexible in its attitude toward the Great Coalition than were the Social Democrats. For whereas the DVP seemed willing to make a number of important concessions in order to facilitate an agreement with the SPD, the Social Democrats, no doubt sensitive to the severe unemployment that had descended upon Germany since the stabilization of the mark, insisted upon an increase in unemployment benefits and a reduction of taxes for lower income groups as the price Germany's middle parties had to pay for their entry into the government. But when Koch-Weser tried to incorporate these demands into the platform upon which he hoped to base his government, the Social Democrats rejected his efforts as inadequate, a position that contrasted sharply with the DVP's cautious acceptance of Koch-Weser's program. As Koch-Weser himself observed, the Social Democrats had little desire to forgo the advantages of remaining in opposition for the dubious honor of sitting in a government whose policies they could not control. By the morning of 17 December, Koch-Weser recognized the futility of further contacts with the Social Democrats, and he resigned the mandate to form a new government that he had received from Hindenburg three days earlier.[51]

Koch-Weser was every bit as bewildered by the rebuff he had suffered at the hands of the Social Democrats as Stresemann had been two months earlier by the Nationalists' decision to bolt the Luther government. There was, as contemporary political analysts quickly noted, a curious irony in the problems that first Stresemann and then Koch-Weser had experienced in their respective efforts to bring the DNVP and SPD into the government. Still, this did not deter Koch-Weser from his ultimate goal of a government based on the Great Coalition, and on 19 December—just two days after his own bid for the chancellorship had ended in failure—he wrote to Marx and urged the Center to join the DDP in pressuring the Social Democrats into a resumption of negotiations. The DDP party chairman even suggested that the two parties threaten to withdraw from the Great Coalition in Prussia if the Social Democrats refused to abandon their opposition to such a government in the Reich.[52] This proposal coincided in large measure with sentiment within the Center, where a majority of the Reichstag delegation was strongly opposed to participation in a minority government under Luther or anybody else.[53] On 10 January 1926 the Center's delegations to the Reichstag and Prussian Landtag publicly urged a resumption of negotiations aimed at the formation of the Great Coalition in the Reich, whereupon Hindenburg agreed to give Koch-Weser and the Center's Konstantin Fehrenbach four days to reach agreement with the Social Democrats. This initiative, however, ended in failure two days later, when the Social Democrats voted against participating in a coalition government with the DVP by virtually the same margin as they had rejected such an offer in December.[54]

The definitive collapse of negotiations to form a government based upon the Great Coalition in January 1926 left the Center and DDP with no alternative but to enter a bourgeois minority government under Luther. Not only did this outcome coincide with the general strategy that the presidential entourage had pursued throughout the crisis, but Luther, unlike Koch-Weser, was given a free hand to organize the government as he saw fit. But instead of intervening directly in the negotiations to form a new government, Luther inexplicably held back and simply let the different parties that were willing to support his government decide among themselves how the various posts within his cabinet were to be allocated.[55] All of this represented a critical departure from established parliamentary procedure and gave rise to growing concern within Democratic circles about the implications of Hindenburg's intervention in the cabinet negotiations during the winter of 1925–26 for the future development of Weimar democracy.[56] The Democrats' uneasiness over this turn of events was further intensified by the fact that Koch-Weser's appointment as Luther's minister of interior encountered such vehement opposition from the leaders of the Bavarian People's Party that he had to be dropped in favor of the Democratic mayor of Dresden, Wilhelm Külz. The Democrats were particularly incensed over Luther's failure to intercede on Koch-Weser's behalf, and for a while it seemed as if the party might not approve the appointment of Külz and Peter Reinhold, who had been slated for the Ministry of Finance, to the Luther cabinet. The impasse was broken only when Koch-Weser argued at a meeting of the DDP Reichstag delegation on 19 January that his person should not stand in the way of a solution to the cabinet crisis that had plagued Germany for the better part of two months and urged his colleagues to set aside their reservations about the Luther government in order to help bring the crisis to an end. When the ensuing tally revealed that only seven of the sixteen Democratic deputies were prepared to heed Koch-Weser's appeal, Erkelenz promptly switched his vote to create a deadlock that prevented the delegation from coming out in opposition to the Luther government. Not only did this make it possible for Luther to proceed with the appointment of Külz, Reinhold, and Gessler, but Koch-Weser's willingness to step down as a candidate for the Ministry of Interior set an example for the rest of the delegation, which at his urging agreed to support the Luther government in the vote of confidence that was set for the following week.[57]

On 28 January 1926 the second Luther government survived its first test of strength in the Reichstag, thereby putting an end to the cabinet crisis that had all but paralyzed the German government since the ratification of the Locarno accords two months earlier. The manner in which this crisis was eventually resolved, however, was hardly reassuring for the future of Weimar parliamentarism. Of the 440 deputies participating in the vote, only 160 chose to support the government, while another 130, including most of the Social Democratic delegation, provided the government with its margin of victory by officially abstaining. The Nationalists, upon whom both Luther and Stresemann had set their hopes for a conservative stabilization of the Weimar Republic, remained adamant in their opposition to Stresemann's foreign policy and joined the Communists and National Socialists in voting against the new government.[58] As members of the government coalition, however, the two liberal parties demonstrated an almost unprecedented degree of party discipline in coming to

Luther's support. Only two members of the DVP Reichstag delegation—Alfred Gildemeister and Karl Hepp—missed the crucial vote,[59] while the Democrats, having once been so close to denying Luther the support of their party, quickly closed ranks behind a government about whose manner of formation and ultimate effectiveness they could only have harbored the gravest of misgivings.[60]

With the installation of the second Luther government in January 1926, the deep rift that had developed between the two liberal parties as a result of Stresemann's opening to the Right suddenly closed. The DNVP's decision to bolt the Luther government following the conclusion of the Locarno accords had severely chastened Stresemann in his hopes that the Nationalists might be won over to the support of the Weimar Republic. By the same token, the SPD's stubborn refusal to participate in a government based upon the Great Coalition had done much to disabuse the Democrats of their faith in the political acumen of the socialist leadership. Out of these disappointments emerged a greater awareness of the common heritage and purpose that the two liberal parties shared. The most obvious manifestation of this was the willingness of both Koch-Weser and Stresemann to share the spotlight at a special social function held by the Liberal Association in Berlin on 1 February 1926 to celebrate the new spirit of liberal unity that had expressed itself in the formation of the second Luther government. Over 500 representatives of Germany's liberal elite were in attendance, including the chancellor, the three Democratic members of his cabinet, Postal Minister Rudolph Krohne from the DVP, and three members of the Prussian government, as well as nearly fifty current or former members of the Reichstag.[61] The mood in which the demonstration took place was perhaps best expressed by Koch-Weser, who compared the two liberal parties to two brothers in search of brides, who, after unsuccessful courtships to the Left and the Right, had returned home to share their disappointments with each other. While Koch-Weser's careful choice of gender suggested that there could never be a marriage between the two, his analogy was immediately appreciated by Stresemann, who added that in "making the necessities of the state prevail over one-sided interests" the DDP and DVP were truly two sons of the same mother.[62]

CHAPTER NINETEEN

The Middle Class in Revolt

THE MOST PERSISTENT PROBLEM that plagued the leaders of the German liberal parties in the second half of the 1920s was the increasing disaffection of the German middle class and the formation of middle-class splinter parties intended to furnish middle-class economic interests with more effective political representation than either the DDP or DVP were capable of providing. This development had been greatly intensified by the general course of social and economic development during the Weimar Republic. Not only had the runaway inflation of the early 1920s done much to exacerbate the social and economic antagonisms that already existed within the German middle strata, but the sporadic economic recovery that Germany experienced in the second half of the decade bypassed economically and politically signifi-cant sectors of the German middle class. In the case of the so-called new middle class, where the principal effect of the inflation had been to narrow the income gap between the salaried employee and the industrial wage earner, the position of the white-collar worker following the stabilization of the mark in 1923–24 was severely hurt by the influx into the labor market of those who had been dispossessed by the inflation. This development coincided with the widespread introduction of office equipment and led to a dramatic reduction in the demand for white-collar services that made it possible for unscrupulous employers to impose arbitrary salary cuts upon their office and sales personnel and to dismiss those employees whose age, high salary, or inadequate profes-sional training made them an economic liability. The net effect of these factors was to produce an abnormally high rate of unemployment among white-collar employees who were either over forty years of age or had not yet perfected a trade. Nor was the position of the civil servant appreciably better. Not only was the civil service still reeling from the cuts that the government had made in the size of Germany's civil administration in the course of its efforts to stabilize the mark, but civil servant salaries continued to lag behind those of other professional groups until the fall of 1927, when the Reichstag passed a comprehensive reform of Germany's civil service salary structure. These factors combined with the repeated attacks of organized labor against the privileged professional status of the civil bureaucracy to create an element of lingering insecurity within civil servant circles that did much to frustrate their reconciliation with the Weimar state.[1]

Germany's economic recovery in the second half of the 1920s also bypassed those social groups that constituted the nucleus of Germany's so-called old middle class. The situation in the countryside was particularly desperate as a result of factors that were only partly related to the way in which the mark had been stabilized, and it continued to deteriorate over the course of the next decade. Like the farmer, both the artisan and the small businessman had also been severely hurt by the restrictive credit policies that the Reichsbank had adopted in the spring of 1924. Not only had this forced an unprecedented number of marginal middle-class enterprises into bankruptcy during the first year of stabilization, but the private credit institutions that traditionally provided the small business sector with inexpensive, long-term loans had all but collapsed during the inflation. As a result, artisans and small businessmen were left with no alternative but to turn to the considerably more expensive industrial capital market for the credit they needed to maintain inventories and to rationalize their productive facilities. The vitality of the small business sector was further hampered by a 20 percent decline in Germany's per capita consumption since the outbreak of the war and by a special business tax that a number of state governments had imposed under the powers relegated to them by the Third Emergency Tax Decree. All of these factors—Germany's diminished per capita consumption, the scarcity of long-term credit, and a discriminatory tax policy—combined with the increasing rationalization of Germany's economic structure to prevent the independent middle class from recovering the privileged position it had held before the war and to push both the artisan and the small businessman in an increasingly antidemocratic direction.[2]

Even before the outbreak of the world economic crisis at the end of the 1920s, the leaders of Germany's liberal establishment spoke openly of a revolt of the German middle class and warned of the disastrous consequences this would have for the existing party system.[3] The two liberal parties, however, were severely hampered in their efforts to develop an effective response to this situation by the fact that they continued to conceive of themselves as *Gesamtinteressenparteien*, that is, as parties that sought to represent the German nation in all of its sociological heterogeneity and therefore refused to give primacy to the interests of any particular social group. This was particularly true of the DDP, whose defense of middle-class economic interests was consistently undercut by its conception of itself as a *Verfassungspartei* whose primary responsibility was to defend the integrity of the Weimar Constitution.[4] By the same token, Stresemann's emphasis upon the primacy of foreign policy was essentially an attempt to divert attention away from the material losses the DVP's middle-class supporters had suffered since the outbreak of World War I to those larger national issues upon which all sectors of Germany's middle-class electorate could presumably agree.[5] In the final analysis, it was precisely this sort of ideological ambiguity that left the two liberal parties so vulnerable to the agitation of special interest parties that sought to mobilize the more disgruntled elements of the German middle class by promising them more effective representation than either the DDP or DVP was capable of providing.

The first group to break away from the established bourgeois parties to form a political party of its own was the independent middle class. Here the initial impulse came from a handful of Berlin artisans who, under the leadership of master baker Hermann Drewitz, had run their own slate of candidates in the elections for the Charlottenburg city council on 23 February 1919. This ticket, known as the Electoral Association of Economic Professions (Wahlvereinigung der wirtschaftlichen Berufe), went on to score a modest victory, winning over 8,900 votes and electing four deputies to the city council. Drewitz and his associates proceeded to organize themselves into a local political party called the Business Alliance for City and State (Wirtschaftsbund für Stadt und Land) in the spring of 1920. The alliance ran its own slate of candidates in Berlin and several other districts in the June 1920 national elections and polled nearly 90,000 votes. Heartened by further gains in the Charlottenburg and Berlin municipal elections later that summer, the movement's representatives from Berlin, Breslau, Mecklenburg, and Pomerania met in Charlottenburg from 11 to 13 September 1920 to discuss the founding of a national middle-class party. Although the delegates were by no means united in their views on the founding of a new political party, Drewitz and his supporters eventually prevailed, and on 12 September they formally reconstituted themselves as the Business Party of the German Middle Class (Wirtschaftspartei des deutschen Mittelstandes or WP).[6]

It was not long before the new party began to attract the attention of influential interest groups within the German middle class. German home-owners were particularly frustrated by the continuation of government controls over the housing industry and felt directly threatened by socialist demands for a land reform that would radically restructure existing property relations.[7] In the fall of 1920 the Prussian chapter of the Central Association of German Home and Property Owners' Organizations, a powerful national lobby with more than half a million members, approached the DDP and other bourgeois parties with the proposal that its representatives be given special consideration in the nomination of candidates for the forthcoming Prussian state elections.[8] But the response of the various bourgeois parties—and particularly that of the DVP[9]—proved uniformly disappointing, with the result that on 3 January 1921 the leaders of the Prussian Home and Property Owners' Organizations threw their full support behind the Business Party and began to raise funds for its use in the Prussian elections that had been scheduled for the following month.[10] The principal architect of this alliance was Johann Victor Bredt, a former German Nationalist who had left the DNVP following its involvement in the Kapp Putsch in the spring of 1920. But Bredt's efforts to marshal support for the new party in Prussia's western provinces met with strong opposition from DNVP loyalists who held executive positions in the local Home and Property Owners' Organizations. As a result, the WP's decision to establish a chapter in the Rhineland and Westphalia met with a cool reception from precisely those forces that had helped found the party in Berlin. With only the rudiments of a party organization outside of Berlin and its immediate environs, the leaders of the WP experienced little success in their efforts to lure organized homeowners in the other parts of Prussia away from the more established bourgeois parties.[11]

The only other social group whose support the founders of the Business Party actively sought in the campaign for the 1921 Prussian state elections was the artisanry. The fact that many artisans were also homeowners established an identity of interests that the leaders of the WP hoped to translate into a permanent political alliance. Like the homeowners, the artisans felt threatened by the Socialization Commission's repeated forays against the private ownership of the means of production, and they were adamantly opposed to the new taxes the National Assembly had authorized in the fall of 1919 and to the continuation of government controls over German economic life. But the WP's hopes of securing a breakthrough into the ranks of the organized artisanry received a sharp setback when the National Federation of the German Artisanry (Reichsverband des Deutschen Handwerks) adopted a resolution at its Jena congress in September 1920 that explicitly rejected the founding of a new middle-class party.[12] The Jena resolution was a clear reaffirmation of the nonpartisan principles upon which the federation had been founded and reflected fears that too close an identification with any political party would undermine the effectiveness with which it was able to represent artisan interests in the Reichstag. While the leaders of the federation readily conceded that their influence within the existing bourgeois parties was not what they had hoped it would be, they also argued that a one-sided alliance with the Business Party or any similar constellation of middle class forces would only isolate the artisanry from the larger political parties upon whose support the passage of legislation essential for its economic welfare ultimately depended.[13]

The same fears were shared by the leaders of the Christian Middle Class (Christlicher Mittelstand), an organization that middle-class conservatives from the predominantly Catholic parts of the Rhineland had founded in February 1920 in an attempt to strengthen their position within the Center and other nonsocialist parties. Although the founders of the Christian Middle Class were outspoken in their criticism of the economic policies that the Center had supported as a member of the Weimar Coalition, they too stressed the vocational rather than political solidarity of the German middle class and explicitly rejected the creation of a special middle-class party well before the WP had been founded.[14] In spite of a lack of support from organizations like the

Christian Middle Class and the National Federation of the German Artisanry, the WP went on to collect more than 192,000 votes in the Prussian state election of February 1921 and elected four deputies to the Landtag. This represented a significant accomplishment in view of the fact that the party's success was confined almost exclusively to those areas where it had received the support of the local Home and Property Owners' Organizations. In Berlin and the two adjacent Potsdam districts, for example, the WP received 4.5 percent of the popular vote and trailed the DDP by only a few percentage points. Organizational footholds had also been established in Pomerania, Silesia, and Hesse-Nassau, although in each of these areas the WP's share of the popular vote was generally about half of what it had been in and around Berlin.[15]

These successes, as well as the WP's strong showing in the Mecklenburg Landtag elections on 13 March 1921, gave the leaders of the Business Party ample reason to be pleased with the progress their party had made since its founding six months earlier. Their next step was to formulate a program that would help legitimize the WP in the eyes of the social groups upon whose support its future ultimately depended. The rudimentary program that party leaders outlined at the WP's first national congress in Breslau in the first week of April 1921 had two essential components. The first of these was an unequivocal identification with the material interests of the two social groups that had come together to form the party, although even here a certain contradiction could be detected between the artisans' demands for protection against the "excesses of free competition" and the homeowners' demands for the restoration of "economic freedom" in the housing industry. In general, however, the leaders of the WP espoused a classical liberal program calling for an end to all state interference in the free enterprise system, tighter controls over the activity of large cartels and monopolies, and the establishment of a balanced budget through a sharp reduction in the general level of government spending. The leaders of the WP supplemented this with a conservative cultural program that stressed the sanctity of Christian culture in the church, school, and family in hopes that this would provide the spiritual cement necessary to fuse the German middle class into a cohesive political force.[16]

The WP's success in the Prussian and Mecklenburg state elections notwithstanding, the leaders of the National Federation of the German Artisanry remained strongly opposed to the idea of a national middle-class party and urged their followers to continue their efforts within the more established bourgeois parties such as the DVP, DNVP, and Center.[17] But the general course of social and economic development during the early years of the Weimar Republic severely strained relations between the artisanry and the various bourgeois parties to which it had entrusted the defense of its vital interests. Not only were artisans frustrated by the failure of the parties for which they had voted in 1920 to prevent the Fehrenbach and Wirth governments from saddling them with new taxes that only added to the mounting production costs they were already experiencing as a result of the inflation, but the government's efforts to control profiteering and price-gouging during the hyperinflation of 1922–23 aroused widespread indignation throughout the small business sector.[18] By the same token, German homeowners were irate over the government's persistent failure to end its controls on the housing industry. Although the inflation had made it possible for many homeowners to liquidate mortgages and other debts against their property on extremely favorable terms, the continuation of government rent controls prevented them from taking advantage of the acute housing shortage that existed in Germany after the end of the war. The Reichstag's decision in June 1921 to impose a special rent tax on all housing constructed prior to 1 July 1918 aroused resentment from organized housing interests throughout the country, as did the special law for the protection of renters that the Reichstag passed in the early summer of 1923.[19] The net effect of these developments was to intensify middle-class disaffection from those parties that could be held responsible for the government's action and to strengthen the WP's appeal as a defender of middle-class economic interests.

As the inflation continued its hectic course during the first half of the 1920s, the Business Party was able to break out of the isolation in which it had found itself at the time of the Prussian elections. In March 1921 the Cologne Middle-Class Association (Mittelstandsvereinigung Köln) switched its affiliation from the pro-Center Christian Middle Class, which it had helped found in February of the previous year, to the Berlin Middle-Class Cartel (Berliner Mittelstands-kartell) under the leadership of the WP's Hermann Drewitz.[20] At the same time, the party also succeeded in winning the support of the Bavarian Peasants' League, a kindred organization that had run its own slate of candidates in state and national elections ever since it first appeared on the political scene in the 1890s. On 9 July 1922 representatives from the WP, the Cologne Middle-Class Association, and the Bavarian Peasants' League met in Weimar to announce that they had formed a national political alliance and would cooperate in future national elections.[21] Although the Peasants' League insisted upon retaining its organizational integrity and never went so far as to reconstitute itself as the WP's Bavarian chapter, this agreement marked the beginning of a cooperative arrangement that was to continue for the next six years.

While the social and economic turmoil of the German inflation provided the Business Party with its initial breakthrough into the ranks of the German middle class, its appeal as a party of middle-class protest was further enhanced by the terms under which the mark was stabilized in the winter of 1923–24. Homeowners and artisans alike were incensed over the Third Emergency Tax Decree, which not only continued the rent tax that organized housing interests already found so detestable but left the small business tax (*Gewerbesteuer*), which state and municipal authorities had come to rely upon as their chief source of revenue, essentially intact. Moreover, the sharp restriction of credit that the Reichsbank ordered on 7 April 1924 inflicted severe economic hardship upon the small business sector and forced many an artisan and independent retailer into bankruptcy.[22] In the campaign for the May 1924 Reichstag elections the leaders of the Business Party were quick to translate middle-class resentment over the way in which the mark had been stabilized into a general referendum against the parties that had been either directly or indirectly involved in the stabilization process. Not only did leaders of the WP denounce the new taxes instituted by the government since the beginning of the 1920s as part of a concerted effort to expropriate the German middle class, but they portrayed the existing bourgeois parties as the pawns of powerful economic interests whose own welfare was inimical to that of the independent middle class. Only by uniting behind the WP's slogan of "Middle Class, Awake!" would it be possible for the artisan, the homeowner, and the small businessman to defend their vital interests against those elements in Germany's economic life that threatened to squeeze them out of existence.[23]

Throughout the campaigns for the May and December 1924 Reichstag elections, the leaders of the WP sought to mobilize the latent anticapitalist feeling that had always existed within the German middle class and that the runaway inflation of the early 1920s had done much to inflame. At the same time, the WP preyed upon middle-class fears of proletarization and attacked the social legacy of the November Revolution as a direct threat to the survival of the German middle class. The effectiveness of such an appeal was clearly reflected in the outcome of the May elections, in which the WP and other middle-class splinter parties collected an alarming 15 percent of the national popular vote. Aside from the proto-Nazi German Racist Freedom Party, the most successful of these parties was the WP, whose alliance with the Bavarian Peasants' League attracted nearly 700,000 votes and elected ten deputies to the Reichstag. Of this total, the WP and its regional affiliates outside of Bavaria could claim more than 490,000 votes for themselves in spite of the fact that the party failed to run a slate of candidates in Schleswig-Holstein, Hanover, Westphalia, and parts of Saxony. The WP was able to remedy this situation in Saxony and several other key districts in the December Reichstag elections, with the result that its share of the popular vote grew from 1.8 to 2.3 percent. At the same time, the national ticket that the WP had formed with the Bavarian Peasants' League collected more than 1 million votes in the December elections and increased the number of deputies it sent to the Reichstag from ten to seventeen.[24]

Immediately after the May 1924 Reichstag elections Anton Fehr, the BBB's chief parliamentary spokesman, approached the leaders of the Business Party about the formation of a parliamentary coalition for the newly elected Reichs-tag.[25] Officially known as the Economic Association, this alliance was subse-quently expanded to include the German-Hanoverian Party, a regional party which had received over 300,000 votes in the May elections, and served as the basis of an agreement that the three parties were to conclude for the December 1924 Reichstag elections.[26] The most important consequence of the WP's success in the May 1924 elections, however, was a pronounced softening in the opposition of organized artisan interests to the idea of a national middle-class party. In marked contrast to the strong stand they had taken against the creation of such a party in the fall of 1920, the leaders of the National Federation of the German Artisanry expressed qualified support at their Berlin congress in late May 1924 for the idea of a single party that embraced not merely the artisanry but all elements of Germany's commercial middle class. Although federation leaders still remained adamantly opposed to the creation of a special party for the artisanry itself and took great pains to reaffirm their traditional policy of bipartisan neutrality toward all of Germany's nonsocialist parties, they could no longer ignore the growing sentiment within certain quarters of the artisan movement for a break with the more established bour-geois parties.[27] Immediately after the dissolution of the Reichstag in October 1924, the federation petitioned the various bourgeois parties for their positions on a series of questions related to the future of the artisan movement. The federation was anxious to determine not only which of these parties were prepared to give representatives from the artisan movement preferential treat-ment in the nomination of candidates for the forthcoming national elections but also whether or not they were willing to support its demands for special legislation aimed at improving the social and economic status of the German artisanry.[28]

In spite of the economic difficulties it had experienced during the war and the early years of the Weimar Republic, the artisanry was not so much a declining social class as a determined and self-conscious status group intent upon recapturing the privileged position it had held before the advent of industrial capitalism.[29] A clear indication of this was the increased vigor with which artisan leaders in the second half of the 1920s began to press their demands for a structural reorganization of the German economy. Unlike so-cialist schemes for massive state intervention in the economic process, these demands were rooted in the long tradition of corporatist social thought that had developed during the course of the previous century as a reaction to the disintegration of traditional European society under the impact of industrial capitalism. The social and economic turmoil following the end of the war had done much to stimulate a revival of corporatist sentiment among those social groups that felt most directly threatened by the demise of the old order. This was particularly true of the German artisanry, whose leaders began to embrace corporatist proposals for the reorganization of the economy with increasing enthusiasm.[30] Of the various nonsocialist parties, none was prepared to identify itself as unequivocally with the interests of the German artisanry as the Business Party. As a result, the second half of the 1920s witnessed a strong influx of artisans who had formerly voted for one of the more established bourgeois parties into the ranks of the WP. Artisan interests, for example, were able to gain almost complete control over the local party organization in Hamburg,[31] while in Saxony and Thuringia the WP's rapid growth between 1924 and 1928 stemmed in no small measure from the strong support it received from the leaders of local artisan organizations.[32]

This development was to have a profound impact not only upon the WP's social composition but upon its ideological orientation as well. In its initial programmatic statement from November 1922, the WP had espoused a classical liberal position, with primary emphasis upon the defense of middle-class economic interests within the framework of the existing economic order.[33] But with the strong influx of organized artisans into their party during the second half of the 1920s, the leaders of the WP could no longer ignore the appeal of corporatist ideas among the more traditional elements of the German middle class, and in the fall of 1925, after changing their party's name to the National Party of the German Middle Class (Reichspartei des deutschen Mittelstandes),[34] they began deliberation on a new party program in hopes of enhancing the WP's ideological profile. The fruit of these deliberations was a new set of guidelines that party leaders presented at the WP's Görlitz party congress in the summer of 1926. The work of Saxon party leader Walther Wilhelm, the "Görlitzer Richtlinien" reaffirmed the WP's loyalty to the republican form of government only to undercut whatever significance this was supposed to have by also calling for a revision of the Weimar Constitution aimed at freeing governmental authority from the excesses of popular sovereignty. The most salient feature of the new party program, however, remained the way in which it sought to reformulate the traditional demands of homeowners, artisans, and small businessmen in the language of German corporatism.[35]

With the adoption of the "Görlitzer Richtlinien" in the summer of 1926, the Business Party completed its transformation from a party serving as little more than an agent for organized housing interests into one that claimed to represent the German middle class in all of its sociological heterogeneity. In point of fact, however, the WP's appeal was directed almost exclusively at the so-called old middle class and ignored other middle-class groups such as civil servants and white-collar employees. One group for which the WP held little or no appeal was the mass of middle-class investors who had been dispossessed by the runaway inflation of the early 1920s and who had just begun to band together in the struggle for a revision of the revaluation provisions of the Third Emergency Tax Decree. As the representative of private homeowners who had used the inflation to liquidate the mortgages and other debts that had accumulated against their property on extremely favorable terms, the WP was adamantly opposed to any change in the existing revaluation legislation that might increase the financial liability of those upon whom it depended for the bulk of its organized support.[36] To Germany's countless thousands of dispossessed savers, it must have seemed more than a little ironic that the WP was surpassed only by the Communists and Social Democrats in the vehemence with which it, as a party claiming to represent the entire middle class, rejected their demands for a full and equitable restoration of the paper mark assets that had been destroyed by the inflation.

Germany's small investors took the first step toward the creation of a new political party in the spring of 1922 when a handful of private savers in Stuttgart formed the Alliance against Profiteering and High Prices (Bund gegen Wücherer and Teuerung). By the end of the year the campaign for a full and equitable revaluation of mortgages and other paper mark assets had become so widespread that a national organization known as the Protective Association of Mortgagees and Savers for the German Reich was founded in Berlin under the joint chairmanship of F. W. Fudickar and Erwin Kühn.[37] Receiving the bulk of its support from pensioneers, civil servants, unemployed women and widows, white-collar employees, and the liberal professions, the Mortgagees and Savers' Protective Association sought to put an end to the repayment of mortgages and other financial obligations in devalued currency and to bring about a revaluation of debts that had already been liquidated in this manner. The movement scored its first major triumph in November 1923 when the German Supreme Court struck down the government's contention that there was no difference between the gold mark in which prewar financial transactions had been conducted and the devalued paper mark with which current financial obligations were being liquidated as being incompatible with the principles of "good faith and equity" contained in Article 242 of the German civil code.[38] Yet, while this decision forced the German government to recognize the legal basis upon which the demands of the revaluation movement rested, the revaluation provisions of the Third Emergency Tax Decree provided little in the way of immediate relief to those who had been dispossessed by the inflation and were bitterly denounced by spokesmen for small investors throughout the country.[39]

The deep-seated bitterness that Germany's middle-class investors felt as a result of the government's handling of the revaluation question contributed in no small way to the dramatic gains of both the DNVP and the German Racist Freedom Party in the May 1924 Reichstag elections. At the same time, a splinter group known as the Militant League of Beggars (Kampfbund der Geusen) that addressed itself almost exclusively to those elements of the German middle class that had been dispossessed by the inflation received nearly 60,000 votes in the May elections.[40] In the December elections its place was taken by two new revaluation parties—the German Revaluation and Recovery Party and the Revaluation and Reconstruction Party—which polled a combined total of approximately 120,000 votes in spite of the fact that neither enjoyed the support of the national leadership of the Mortgagees and Savers' Protective Association.[41] In the meantime, the association had decided to offer its support in the upcoming national elections to those parties that agreed to nominate representatives from the revaluation movement to secure positions on their own slate of candidates. After consulting with the leaders of all of Germany's nonsocialist parties, the association endorsed the Center, the DNVP, and the German Racist Freedom Party, while withholding its support from the two liberal parties, neither of which were willing to make the desired concessions.[42]

The German Nationalists' success in the December 1924 Reichstag elections stemmed in no small measure from their relentless exploitation of the revaluation issue. Not only had the DNVP made vague promises for a full restoration of paper mark assets destroyed by the inflation, but it had also succeeded in securing the cooperation of Georg Best, a prominent Darmstadt jurist who had played a major role in preparing the decision handed down by the German Supreme Court on 28 November 1923. But the close relationship that had developed between the DNVP and the Mortgagees and Savers' Protective Association in the December elections was severely shaken by the party's decision in January 1925 to enter a national government headed by the one person whom the leaders of the revaluation movement held most directly responsible for the plight of the small investor, Finance Minister Hans Luther. For his own part, Luther was concerned that a far-reaching revaluation of war bonds and other governmental obligations would impede Germany's economic recovery, and he approached a revision of the revaluation provisions of the Third Emergency Tax Decree with the greatest of reluctance. As the government procrastinated on the revaluation question through the first months of 1925, both the Democrats and the Social Democrats, neither of whom belonged to the Luther government, assailed the Nationalists for their demagoguery in the revaluation issue and denounced their party for its failure to live up to the campaign promises it had made a year earlier.[43] Under increasingly heavy fire from the opposition, the government reached a compromise with the DNVP and the other government parties that established 25 percent of the original gold mark value as the revalorization percentage for mortgages and other private debts, 15 percent for industrial obligations, and 5 percent—a figure the Reichstag later reduced to 2.5 percent for assets that had changed hands since 1 July 1920—for war bonds and other forms of government indebtedness. To insure that this did not jeopardize Germany's economic recovery, the compromise also placed a moratorium on the settlement of private revaluation claims until January 1932, while the repayment of government obligations was to take place in the form of annuities that were to extend over the next thirty years.[44]

The government's revaluation bill fell far short of meeting the demands that had emerged from the ranks of the revaluation movement and provoked a storm of protest from revaluation organizations throughout the country. When the details of the bill were finally released in early May 1925, the DNVP came under a new round of attacks from the DDP and Social Democrats for having wooed the support of those who had been hurt by the inflation only to turn its back on them once it had attained power.[45] In the meantime, the situation within the DNVP had reached crisis proportions when Best, who had been elected to the Reichstag as part of an agreement between the DNVP and the Mortgagees and Savers' Protective Association, resigned from the DNVP Reichstag delegation in protest against its decision on 13 May to accept the compromise that had been worked out between the government and the parties that had supported it. Unfazed by these developments, the DNVP and other government parties forced the controversial law through the Reichstag on 16 July without ever giving the Social Democrats, the DDP, or even the dissidents within their own ranks an opportunity to modify the provisions they found most objectionable.[46]

Deeply embittered by the way the government and the parties supporting it had ignored their demands for a full and equitable restoration of paper mark assets destroyed by the inflation, the leaders of the revaluation movement appointed a special commission headed by Adolf Bauser, a secondary schoolteacher from Nagold in Württemberg, for the purpose of exploring the possibility of founding a new political party with the various revaluation organizations in other parts of the country. Bauser traveled extensively throughout Germany in the first half of 1926, meeting with leaders from the Coalition of Revaluation Organizations (Arbeitsgemeinschaft der Aufwertungsorganisationen), the fledgling Cultural and Constitutional State Party (Kultur- und Rechtsstaatspartei) in Saxony, and a host of similar organizations in an attempt to lay the foundation for the creation of a new political party that would redress the injustice Germany's small investors had suffered at the hands of the government, the Reichstag, and the more established bourgeois parties. Bauser's efforts received strong support from the Mortgagees and Savers' Protective Association, which in early 1926 had officially renamed itself the Savers' Association for the German Reich (Sparerbund für das Deutsche Reich), and drew to a successful conclusion with the founding of the National Party for People's Justice and Revaluation (Reichspartei für Volksrecht und Aufwertung), more popularly known as the People's Justice Party (Volksrechtspartei or VRP), at a special convention of the Savers' Association in Erfurt on 28–29 August 1926.[47]

According to its founders, the People's Justice Party was not a mere interest party concerned soley with recovering what the small investor had lost as a result of the inflation but rather a party of principle whose ultimate purpose was to bring about a return to the concepts of right and justice that lay at the very foundation of German culture. More specifically, the VRP denounced the manner in which successive governments since the end of the war had trampled upon the rights of the small investor as an affront to the moral foundations upon which the authority of the German state ultimately rested. While the leaders of the party manifested a strong antipathy toward the republican form of government, they reserved their sharpest criticism for those vested economic interests that had profited from the inflation and were now intent upon using their control of the more established bourgeois parties to prevent those who had been hurt by the inflation from securing a redress of their grievances. Arguing that the domination of powerful economic interests had robbed the existing system of government of its moral legitimacy, the founders of the VRP focused their appeal upon the renter, the pensioner, the war veteran—in short, upon those marginal elements in German society that felt most directly threatened by the prospect of proletarization and whose lack of political cohesiveness had left them defenseless in the bitter social conflict that had developed in Germany since the end of the war. It was, the leaders of the VRP contended, only through the consolidation of these elements on the basis of the People's Justice Party, a party uncompromised by the politics of the past, that the moral as well as social regeneration of the German nation could take place.[48]

The founding of the People's Justice Party in the late summer of 1926 was carefully timed to coincide with the opening of the campaign for the Saxon Landtag elections on 31 October 1926. Here the VRP's chief rival for the votes of the disaffected middle class was the Business Party, which had supported the 1925 revaluation law only in return for a relaxation of government rent controls and a promise to reduce, if not eliminate, the house rent tax.[49] Although the two parties appealed to fundamentally different sectors of the German middle class, both were sharply critical of the way in which the German party system had developed since the founding of the Weimar Republic and routinely portrayed the Reichstag and the parties that controlled it as the pawns of special economic interests. Yet while the agitation of middle-class splinter parties such as the WP and VRP represented a direct threat to the electoral prospects of both liberal parties and the DNVP, it also ran counter to efforts on the part of other elements within the Saxon bourgeoisie to unite the various bourgeois parties into an antisocialist front for the upcoming state elections. Here the initial impulse came from patriotic organizations such as the Stahlhelm, the Young German Order (Jungdeutscher Orden), and the Viking League (Bund Wiking) under the leadership of the former Kapp

Putschist Hermann Ehrhardt, although it quickly passed into the more respectable hands of the Saxon State Citizens' Council (Sächsischer Landbürgerrat) and a host of state economic interest organizations.[50] Although these efforts to form an antisocialist front eventually collapsed when the WP refused to go along with an arrangement that used the results of the December 1924 Reichstag elections to determine the placement of candidates on the proposed unity ticket, they nevertheless revealed the existence of a strong centripetal potential within the Saxon bourgeoisie that ran directly counter to the increasing fragmentation of the Weimar party system.

The Saxon Landtag elections in the fall of 1926 represented a critical moment in the dissolution of the Weimar party system. Not only did the three traditional nonconfessional parties—the DDP, DVP, and DNVP—lose nearly 40 percent of the votes they had received in the December 1924 Reichstag elections, but the WP and VRP received more than a quarter of all nonsocialist votes cast. The DDP, which portrayed itself as a stabilizing force in Saxon politics and highlighted the role it had played in Saxony's return to normalcy after the tumultuous events of 1922–23,[51] tended to ignore the material issues that had come to preoccupy the German middle class and lost a shocking 42.5 percent of its 1924 vote. The DVP, whose leaders had tried to counter the appeal of special-interest parties by pointing to their own advocacy of middle-class economic interests,[52] suffered similar, though less severe, losses amounting to 28.3 percent of what it had received in 1924. The most surprising aspect of the Saxon election results, however, was the resounding defeat suffered by the DNVP. Plagued by lingering resentment over its role in the passage of the 1925 revaluation legislation, the DNVP was unable to shake the VRP's charges that it was nothing more than the party of big agriculture and big business and sustained massive losses among those petty bourgeois elements that had rallied to its support in 1924. The People's Justice Party, on the other hand, proved remarkably adept in establishing itself, in the words of the DNVP's Walther Rademacher, as a "rallying point for all of those disgruntled elements . . . that because of their background were either unwilling or unable to support the Socialists or the Communists."[53] Yet while the VRP collected more than 98,000 votes and elected four deputies to the new Saxon parliament, its success was eclipsed by that of the Business Party. Attracting support from the more affluent elements of the Saxon middle class and benefiting from the unofficial support it received from artisan and homeowner organizations throughout the state,[54] the WP emerged from the elections with more than 237,000 votes—or nearly twice as many as it had received in Saxony in the December 1924 Reichstag elections and an impressive 10.1 percent of all votes cast—and claimed ten seats in the newly elected Landtag.[55]

The dramatic gains that the two middle-class splinter parties recorded in the 1926 Saxon Landtag elections constituted a direct threat to the future of the

German liberal movement and a stinging indictment of the ideological foundations upon which the Weimar party system rested. The outcome of the Thuringian Landtag elections on 30 January 1927 was not substantially different, as
the WP and VRP received 9.4 and 2.7 percent of the popular vote respectively.[56] The leaders of the German liberal parties could no longer afford to
look upon these developments with equanimity. For at stake lay not merely the
future of their own political parties but the very survival of Germany's parliamentary institutions. As a perplexed Stresemann was to write for the
Deutsche Stimmen in early December 1926:

> The most distressing thing about the present situation in Germany is the
> tendency to overemphasize the purely economic and vocational aspect of
> the political struggle. Should the principle behind the Business Party
> triumph, then the political fabric of Germany's national life would soon
> fragment to the point where we would have agricultural groups here,
> industrial groups there, the civil servants and white-collar employees
> somewhere else. But in the midst of all this, the spiritual cement neces-
> sary to fuse these elements into a dynamic and organic whole would be
> sadly missing.[57]

CHAPTER TWENTY

Overtures to Reform

THE FOUNDING OF THE Business Party of the German Middle Class in the early 1920s and the National Party for People's Justice and Revaluation in the summer of 1926 represented attempts on the part of the urban middle classes to salvage their declining social and economic fortunes through the creation of new political parties that placed primary, if not exclusive, emphasis upon the representation of middle-class economic interests. The success that these parties experienced in the second half of the 1920s served as an effective barometer of middle-class disaffection from the existing political system and represented an intensification of the legitimacy crisis that had plagued the Weimar party system since the stabilization of the mark in the winter of 1923–24. Not only did the challenge of special interest parties like the WP and VRP entail an explicit repudiation of the ideological foundations upon which the Weimar party system had always rested, but the difficulties that surrounded the formation of the Marx and Luther governments in 1925–26 had given rise to increasing doubts within Germany's liberal leadership about the future of the governmental system in whose birth it had played such a prominent role. As it became increasingly apparent that the fragmentation of German party politics constituted a major obstacle to the definition and articulation of Germany's national interest, even those who identified themselves most closely with the principles of representative government began to entertain proposals for a reform and reorganization of the German party system.

The period between 1924 and 1928 witnessed the emergence of at least four proposals for a reform of the Weimar party system, each with its own specific ideological orientation and implications for the future development of German parliamentarism. The first of these came from the ranks of the Business Party, which sought to reorganize the German party system along corporatist and vocational lines.[1] The strong emphasis that this proposal placed upon the political representation of class and vocational interests, however, contrasted sharply with the more or less explicit ideological orientations of the other three proposals. The Liberal Association, for example, sought to revitalize Weimar parliamentarism through a renewal of the German liberal movement and the creation of a united liberal party. But the association's efforts to overcome the historic schism that had existed within the German liberal movement ever since the middle of the nineteenth century prompted two counterproposals in the summer of 1926 from groups that did not share its basic commitment to the values of political and economic liberalism. Taking their cue from the Liberal Association's campaign for a united liberal party, the leaders of the DVP and DNVP delegations to the Prussian State Council (Preußischer Staatsrat) took what they hoped would be the first step toward the consolidation of the German Right by issuing an appeal for the creation of a parliamentary coalition between their respective parties in the Reichstag and Prussian Landtag. But this initiative, which would have had far-reaching implications for both the domestic and foreign policies of the Weimar Republic, was immediately countered by former chancellor Joseph Wirth, who proceeded to call for the establishment of closer ties between the DDP, Center, and Social Democrats under the aegis of a new organization named the Republican Union (Republikanische Union).

The proliferation of proposals for a reform and reorganization of the German party system represented tangible evidence of the deepening legitimacy crisis in which the Weimar party system found itself during the second half of the 1920s. The emergence of these proposals was also directly related to the crisis of Weimar liberalism and the continued weakness of the German liberal parties in the period immediately preceding the outbreak of the world economic crisis. Symptoms of weakness were particularly evident in the case of the DDP, where hopes that the party's gains in the December 1924 Reichstag elections signaled a reversal of its political fortunes never materialized. Although the collapse of the DDP's national organization during the hyperinflation of 1922–23 had made it impossible for party officials to maintain an accurate record of the party's national membership, the Democrats estimated at the end of 1925 that the DDP had approximately 135,000 members, a figure that they asserted was considerably higher than that of either the DVP or WP.[2] But this figure, based on Democratic claims that an estimated 50,000 people had joined the DDP following the secession of Schiffer and his associates in the fall of 1924,[3] fell more than 35 percent short of the 209,500 members that party leaders maintained the DDP had had in the fall of 1922.[4] Moreover, preparations for the recruitment campaign the Democrats had planned for the third week of March 1925 had been completely disrupted by the news of Ebert's death, with the result that the DDP found itself committing resources that could have been better used to build up its national organization to the election of a new Reich President. With its finances already strained by the campaign for the December 1924 Reichstag elections,[5] the DDP now had to spend more than 80,000 marks—or about a third of its operating budget for 1925—on the two presidential campaigns, leaving it with a debt of approximately 20,000 marks that continued to plague it for the remainder of the year.[6]

It was not until the spring and early summer of 1926 that Hermann Fischer, the DDP's treasurer, was able to liquidate the debt that the party had accumulated over the course of the previous two years by appealing to the generosity of its backers in finance and industry.[7] Still, the party found itself desperately short of the funds needed to maintain an effective national organization. The operating budget for the party's national headquarters in Berlin for 1926 and 1927 averaged less than 150,000 marks per year, and in certain parts of the country the DDP district organizations were so short of funds that they could no longer afford to hire a full-time party secretary.[8] The party's organizational malaise was most apparent in central and western Germany, where a series of reverses in state and municipal elections had cost the DDP a third of the votes it had received in the December 1924 Reichstag elections. In October 1925, for example, the Democrats lost more than 30 percent of their 1924 vote in the Berlin municipal elections,[9] thereby setting a trend that was to repeat itself over the course of the next year and a half in Mecklenburg, Lübeck, Saxony, and Thuringia. This was accompanied by a 12 percent decline in the DDP's national membership between its Breslau party congress in 1925 and its Hamburg party congress in the spring of 1927. The party's losses were particularly severe in the three Saxon districts (20 percent), Westphalia (25 percent), and Lübeck (33 percent), while in Berlin party officials estimated that approximately a quarter of those who had belonged to the DDP at the end of 1925 had left it by the beginning of 1927.[10]

The Democrats attributed their party's decline in 1925–26 to a combination of several factors, not the least of which were their own organizational ineptitude, the electoral apathy of the German middle class, and the increasing popularity of special interest parties like the WP and VRP.[11] The party's predicament was compounded by a series of policy decisions that had the effect of alienating elements on both its left and right wings. In May 1926 the DDP triggered a major cabinet crisis that culminated in the collapse of the second Luther government when it refused to go along with a proposal that would have permitted Germany's diplomatic missions to display not only the new republican flag with its historic black, red, and gold colors but also the modified version of the old imperial banner that served as Germany's commercial flag.[12] The irritation that leaders of the party's right wing felt over this turn of events was hardly assuaged when a month later the DDP party leadership refused to dissociate itself from the referendum that the Social Democrats and Communists introduced for the uncompensated expropriation of Germany's dynastic houses by leaving the decision to support or reject the referendum to the discretion of individual party members.[13] The DDP's failure to take a stand against the principle of expropriation without compensation did much to discredit the party in the eyes of its more conservative supporters and prompted the resignation of at least one prominent Democrat, Reichsbank president Hjalmar Schacht, as a protest against its swing to the left.[14] While both of these developments led to increasing uneasiness on the DDP's right wing, the party was torn by a third crisis at the end of 1926 when only twelve of the DDP's thirty Reichstag deputies voted for the so-called "Law against Trash and Filth," which Wilhelm Külz, the Democratic minister of interior, had introduced in the Reichstag.[15] Designed to bring the proliferation of pornography and obscene literature under state control, this law met with such vehement opposition from the metropolitan Democratic press that its passage in December 1926 provoked the resignation of another prominent party member in the person of Theodor Wolff, editor in chief of the influential *Berliner Tageblatt* and a self-styled spokesman for the DDP's left wing.[16]

The net effect of these three crises was to produce a further erosion of the DDP's middle-class support and to weaken what integrative potential it still possessed following the runaway inflation of the early 1920s. In dissecting their party's social composition, the Democrats estimated that the DDP recruited the bulk of its support more or less equally from three social groups: civil servants, workers and white-collar employees, and the commercial middle class.[17] Although the DDP was able to record marginal gains in 1925 and 1926 among the first two groups,[18] these gains were more than offset by the heavy losses the party sustained among the commercial middle class as a result of its failure to oppose the referendum for the uncompensated expropriation of Germany's royal families.[19] By the end of 1926 party leaders had become so distressed by the DDP's loss of middle-class support that they briefly considered drafting a new economic program that would have tied the party more closely to middle-class economic interests. But as it became clear during the course of the subsequent deliberations that there was no longer any common ground upon which the DDP's divergent and increasingly antagonistic social and economic interests might be reconciled, these efforts were abandoned in the face of strong opposition not only from the ideological purists on the party's left wing but also from Hermann Fischer, president of the Hansa-Bund and one of the DDP's leading spokesmen for the interests of the German business sector.[20]

In sharp contrast to the dissension and increasingly frequent defections that plagued the DDP throughout much of 1925–26, the German People's Party offered a picture of relative harmony and stability. Control of the DVP Reichstag delegation, which had caused Stresemann so much difficulty between 1920 and 1924, now lay in the hands of party moderates who supported his foreign and domestic policies.[21] At the same time, the role Stresemann had played in bringing the DNVP into the government had done much to placate the leaders of his party's right wing, virtually all of whom rallied to his support following the Nationalists' decision to leave the Luther government in the fall of 1925.[22] Stresemann and the DVP also stood to benefit from the election of Carl Duisberg from the Bayer chemical concern to the presidency of the National Federation of German Industry in January 1925. Though politically unaffiliated, Duisberg had been one of Stresemann's most loyal supporters during the gloomy days of 1922–23, and his election as president of the RDI signaled a new willingness on the part of Germany's industrial elite to collaborate with the Weimar state. Not only did Duisberg bring men of a distinctly more liberal outlook into positions of influence within the RDI leadership, but he was firmly committed to working within the existing system of government and made the establishment of closer ties to industry spokesmen within the various nonsocialist parties one of his first priorities as president of the RDI.[23] Yet while these developments contributed to at least a temporary relaxation of tension between Stresemann and the leaders of his party's industrial wing, the DVP continued to experience financial difficulties throughout most of 1925–26 and was unable to gain access to the industrial funds that had now fallen under the control of the DNVP's Alfred Hugenberg.[24]

The most critical problem confronting the leaders of the DVP in the second half of the 1920s was that of maintaining peace between the different social groups that constituted their party's material base. The two years following the stabilization of the mark were characterized by a general contraction of the German economy, as profits, productivity, and employment plummeted to alarming levels in the winter of 1925–26. While this stemmed in large part from the measures that the government had taken to stabilize the mark in the winter and spring of 1924, industry analysts were quick to blame Germany's deteriorating economic situation upon a wage and salary structure that prevented her industry from being competitive in the world market.[25] Such sentiment was particularly strong on the DVP's right wing, where Otto Hugo and spokesmen for the party's business interests began to press for a fundamental reform of the existing wage structure. Suggestions to this effect, however, provoked an angry response from Hans Bechly, chairman of the German National Union of Commercial Employees and a member of the DVP central executive committee. Speaking at a conference of the DVP's National White-Collar Employee Committee in December 1925, Bechly lashed out against Hugo for having misrepresented the causes of Germany's economic distress and called upon the DVP to free itself from this sort of rhetoric so that it might establish itself as a genuine people's party capable of appealing to all strata of German society, including the wage earners who currently supported the two working-class parties.[26] Bechly's remarks were followed by an exchange of open letters that threatened to develop into an open split within the DVP's national organization before party officials in Berlin intervened to bring it to an end.[27] Nevertheless, the episode remained symptomatic of the tension that existed between the DVP's industrial wing and the various middle-class groups forming the backbone of the party's rank-and-file electorate and left the DVP increasingly vulnerable to defections on the part of its predominantly middle-class electorate that not even Stresemann's popularity as Germany's foreign minister could stem.[28]

As the decline of the two liberal parties continued more or less unabated throughout the second half of the 1920s, the leaders of Germany's liberal establishment began to take an increasingly active interest in proposals for the creation of a united liberal party. The movement to create such a party had a long history of its own, dating back at least as far as Friedrich Naumann's turn-of-the-century campaign for the creation of a united liberal party embracing both the various strands of German Progressivism and the National Liberals. But the collapse of negotiations between Stresemann and the founders of the DDP in the fall and winter of 1918 had dealt the movement for liberal unity a blow from which it never recovered, and in the period between 1918 and 1924 activity on behalf of a united liberal party was limited to occasional and mostly inconsequential outbursts by Heinrich Gerland, Karl Böhme, and other members of the DDP's right wing in support of a merger with the DVP. It was not until the founding of the Liberal Association in the fall of 1924, therefore, that these efforts received any sort of sustained organizational support. Originally founded by a handful of disgruntled Democrats who had left the DDP in protest against its refusal to participate in a coalition government with the German Nationalists, the Liberal Association constituted itself under the chairmanship of Eugen Schiffer on 27 November 1924 as an organization seeking, like the German National Association of 1859 before it, to serve the greater cause of German national unity by putting an end to the historic schism within the ranks of the German liberal movement.[29]

Claiming from the outset that they had no intention of founding a new political party, the leaders of the Liberal Association refrained from taking part in the campaign for the December 1924 Reichstag elections in hopes that it might be possible to undertake a more concerted initiative in support of a united liberal party once the elections were over.[30] Upon conclusion of the campaign, representatives from the Liberal Association met with the leaders of the two liberal parties in an attempt to repair the damage that the recent campaign had done to the unity of the German liberal movement and to enlist their support on behalf of closer political and organizational ties between their respective parties. But in neither party did these overtures meet with a particularly warm response. Koch-Weser and the leaders of the German Democratic Party looked upon Schiffer and the founders of the Liberal Association as renegades who had deserted the DDP in the heat of battle and denounced the founding of the LV as part of a conspiracy to inflict still further damage upon the party.[31] Stresemann, on the other hand, had initially shown some willingness to cooperate with the Liberal Association, though not so much from a genuine interest in the idea of a united liberal party as from the hope that the association, after having first strengthened itself by further defections at the expense of the DDP, might eventually merge with his own party.[32] But when the Democrats began to attack the first Luther government, in whose formation the DVP party chairman had played such a decisive role, Stresemann's interest in the Liberal Association quickly cooled, with the result that he actively discouraged his followers from having anything to do with it.[33]

By the end of February 1925 the Liberal Association's relations with the two parties it hoped to unite had become so strained that Schiffer decided to break off all further contacts. At the same time, the association's efforts to build up a strong national organization had come to a virtual standstill, a state of affairs that Schiffer attributed not so much to public indifference to the idea of a united liberal party as to the LV's own lethargy.[34] In an attempt to remedy this situation, the leaders of the Liberal Association decided to hold a national convention that would coincide with the publication of the first issue of the group's official organ, a journal entitled *Wille und Weg*.[35] On 16 May 1925 approximately one hundred representatives of Germany's liberal establishment met in the main chamber of the National Economic Council to celebrate the Liberal Association's official founding. The principal speakers were Schiffer, who spoke briefly on the essence of liberalism, and industrialist Carl Friedrich von Siemens, who delivered a concise survey of the German economic situation. They were followed by the famous historian Friedrich Meinecke, who called for a merger of the DDP and DVP and urged the association to concentrate its attention upon the cultural values the two liberal parties held in common so that this might serve as the basis upon which the creation of a united liberal party could take place. The final two speakers were Otto Fischbeck, a member of the DDP Reichstag delegation, and Hermann von Richter, a member of the DVP delegation to the Prussian Landtag who had served as the state minister of finance from 1921 to 1925. Both took special pains to stress that the Liberal Association had no intention of founding a new political party alongside those that already existed and that it sought to pursue its goal of a united liberal party by working with and not against the leadership of the existing liberal parties.[36]

Aside from Schiffer, the most prominent member of the Liberal Association was Siemens, who himself had recently resigned from the DDP Reichstag delegation in order to accept the chairmanship of the German National Railway Corporation. The participation of Siemens was of more than merely symbolic significance, since he also served as the association's treasurer during the first year and a half of its existence and financed many of its operations, including the publication of its journal, out of his own pocket.[37] But the massive support that the LV received from Siemens during the first year or so of its existence could not compensate for the lack of interest and outright resentment that it had encountered from the leaders of the two liberal parties. Resentment was particularly strong on the DDP's left wing, where the decision of three Democratic deputies—Fischbeck, Julius Kopsch, and Georg Sparrer—to join the Liberal Association prompted the DDP Reichstag delegation to adopt a resolution that prohibited other members of the delegation from affiliating themselves with the new organization.[38] The situation was no less discouraging in the DVP, where an overwhelming majority of the party's Reichstag delegation remained irreconcilably opposed to the creation of a united liberal party[39] and where Stresemann continued to discourage party members and officials of the DVP's national organization from becoming too deeply involved in the association's activities.[40]

Stresemann and the leaders of the DVP were particularly resentful of the way in which the founders of the Liberal Association had tried to usurp the liberal heritage upon which their own party had been founded. Anxious to reaffirm their party's liberal pedigree, the leaders of the DVP devoted a special meeting of the party's central executive committee on 23–24 May 1925 to a repudiation of the ideological assumptions behind the founding of the Liberal Association. The keynote speaker was Otto Most, a member of the DVP Reichstag delegation who insisted that liberalism and democracy were mutually exclusive concepts that had as little in common as liberalism and conservatism. Tending to identify democracy with Social Democracy, Most argued that the democratic principle of mass rule was altogether incompatible with the liberal ideal of the individual personality. The most important problem confronting the present generation of Germany's liberal leadership, therefore, was to defend the freedom and integrity of the individual against the tyranny of the masses.[41] The practical implications of Most's remarks were spelled out on the following day when Stresemann squelched all rumors about a possible merger of the DVP with either the DDP or DNVP by insisting that these schemes would only deprive the People's Party of the pivotal position it currently held in German domestic politics.[42] The meeting then concluded with the adoption of a resolution that underscored the DVP's role as custodian of the national and liberal traditions formerly associated with the prewar National Liberal Party and reiterated its refusal to participate in efforts that might lead to its merger with another political party.[43]

Most's argument that liberalism and democracy represented mutually exclusive political ideologies constituted an unequivocal repudiation of the ideal of liberal unity as propagated by the founders of the Liberal Association and underscored the association's political isolation during the first year of its existence. The situation suddenly changed, however, in the fall of 1925, when the DNVP withdrew from the first Luther government in protest against the Locarno treaties that Germany had just concluded with France and Belgium. Operating on the assumption that both the DDP and DVP would be represented in any new government that might be formed, the leaders of the Liberal Association immediately launched a campaign aimed at the formation of a parliamentary alliance or *Arbeitsgemeinschaft* between the Reichstag delegations of the two liberal parties.[44] In this respect, the association approached not only the DDP and DVP but also the fledgling Business Party, whose national chairman, Hermann Drewitz, agreed to cooperate in efforts to bring the three parties closer together.[45] This was accompanied by a change in LV leadership that led to an immediate improvement in its relations with the two liberal parties. In December 1925 the sixty-five-year-old Schiffer asked to be relieved of his responsibilities as chairman of the Liberal Association and proposed that the office he was vacating be replaced by a dual chairmanship held jointly by Fischbeck and Richter from the DDP and DVP respectively. A third chairmanship would be held open for the WP's Drewitz, should he too be willing to serve.[46] Although Drewitz eventually declined, the replacement of Schiffer by Fischbeck and Richter removed the greatest single obstacle to cooperation between the association and the DDP and made it possible for Democrats like Koch-Weser who sought to improve relations between the two liberal parties to become more actively involved in the Liberal Association's affairs.[47]

Immediately after the formation of the second Luther government in January 1926, the Liberal Association invited the chancellor and the leaders of the DDP, DVP, and WP to take part in a special banquet that its Berlin chapter had planned for 1 February. After privately conferring with each other, Stresemann and Koch-Weser agreed to participate in the banquet on the condition that their attendance was not to be construed as a sign of support for the association's efforts to create a united liberal party or a parliamentary alliance between the two liberal parties in the Reichstag.[48] The banquet, held in Berlin's fashionable Deutsche Gesellschaft 1914, proved an unequivocal success and marked the high point in the LV's brief appearance on Germany's political stage. Not only did the function attract more than five hundred representatives of Germany's liberal elite, but the podium was graced by a long list of luminaries that included the DVP's Wilhelm Kahl, Koch-Weser, Stresemann, Drewitz, and Luther, in addition to Fischbeck and Richter. The recurrent theme of their remarks was that the two liberal parties were, in Stresemann's words, sons of the same mother and that they shared a common heritage and a common purpose that belied the superficial differences currently separating them.[49] Even the largely ceremonial character of these remarks could hardly dispel the fact that as a demonstration of liberal unity the evening in the Deutsche Gesellschaft 1914 was unprecedented in the annals of the German liberal movement.

Although neither Stresemann nor Koch-Weser was prepared to commit himself to the creation of a united liberal party, each agreed to cooperate with the Liberal Association in its efforts to foster greater understanding between their respective parties.[50] Stresemann's willingness to cooperate with the Liberal Association stood in sharp contrast to the position he had taken at the meeting of the DVP central executive committee in May 1925 and was no doubt related to his disappointment over the recent behavior of the DNVP. But the leaders of the Liberal Association were unable to translate Stresemann's good will into any sort of permanent political commitment as relations between the two liberal parties soured in the second half of 1926. The role that the DDP played in bringing about the collapse of the second Luther government revived much of the animosity that had existed between the two liberal parties for most of the previous year and dealt a serious blow to the LV's efforts on behalf of closer cooperation between the DDP and DVP.[51] The association's relations with the DDP were further strained when the LV passed a resolution at its second annual convention in Berlin on 11 June 1926 that denounced the referendum for the uncompensated expropriation of Germany's dynastic houses as a violation of private property and called upon its supporters throughout the country to boycott the referendum at the polls.[52] The leaders of the DDP's left wing were so infuriated by Fischbeck's public endorsement of the association's position that only Koch-Weser's personal intervention at a convention of the DDP's Berlin organization in early July prevented the adoption of a resolution officially censuring party members who refused to sever their ties to the Liberal Association.[53]

The difficulties that plagued the Liberal Association during the second half of 1926 could also be seen in its relationship with the German People's Party, where the prevailing sentiment was not in favor of closer ties to the Democrats but for closer cooperation with its neighbor to the right, the German National People's Party. This became apparent in the wake of an action initiated by the DVP's Karl Jarres in conjunction with Baron Wilhelm von Gayl from the DNVP in the summer of 1926. The two men, both held in high esteem by conservative circles throughout the country, had shared the leadership of a special *Arbeitsgemeinschaft* between their respective parties in the Prussian State Council for the past five years. Acting independently of the parties to which they belonged, they proposed the formation of a similar coalition in the Reichstag and Prussian Landtag on the assumption that such a step would help strengthen the conservative, national, and Christian element in Germany's political life.[54] This proposal, which took the form of a private letter to the leaders of the two parties before it was released to the press in the first week of July, met with a particularly warm response from the leaders of the DNVP, who were interested in the formation of such a coalition because it might improve their chances of reentering the government. By the same token, spokesmen for conservative special interest organizations such as the National Rural League looked upon the establishment of closer political ties between the DVP and DNVP as a conservative response to the Liberal Association and its agitation for a united liberal party.[55]

Although the authors of the Gayl-Jarres initiative did not seek to bring about a merger of their respective political parties, the implementation of their proposal would have had a profound impact upon the future of the German party system, with potentially disastrous consequences for the DVP. This, however, seemed to escape the attention of Scholz, Gildemeister, and the leaders of the DVP's right wing, whose initial response, though somewhat more guarded than that of the DNVP, was generally positive.[56] But whatever support the Gayl-Jarres initiative received from this corner of the party was more than offset by the strong opposition it encountered from the leaders of the DVP's delegation to the Prussian Landtag and the party's national organization. The party's more moderate leaders were concerned not only that the formation of a parliamentary alliance with the DNVP would rob the DVP of the influence it currently enjoyed as an independent party of the middle but also that this might precipitate a sharp swing to the left within the DDP and Center.[57] For his own part, Stresemann refrained from taking a public stand against the proposal for fear of the effect this might have upon the Nationalists' willingness to reenter the government.[58] Consequently, it was not until the very end of July that Stresemann outlined his objections to the proposed alliance in a long letter to Jarres. Here Stresemann argued that a close political alliance with the DNVP would deprive the DVP of the pivotal position it had held in German domestic politics since the beginning of the decade and would force it, as the smaller of the two parties, to resign from the national government. Secondly, Stresemann feared that the establishment of a parliamentary alliance with the DNVP would provoke a sharp swing to the left within the Center and lead to the reestablishment of the Weimar Coalition as the arbiter of Germany's poltical future. And lastly, Stresemann expressed concern that implementation of the Gayl-Jarres proposal might provoke a secession on the DVP's left wing and lead to the founding of a new liberal party under the leadership of someone like the DVP's own Wilhelm Kahl.[59]

Stresemann's fears that the implementation of the Gayl-Jarres proposal might drive the Center into the arms of the DDP and Social Democrats were directly related to the uncertain situation that had existed within the Center since the formation of the first Luther government in January 1925. Much of this uncertainty centered around the person of Joseph Wirth, the mercurial ex-chancellor whose opposition to the social and economic policies of the Luther government had led him to resign from the Center Reichstag delegation in August 1925.[60] While the collapse of the first Luther government in the fall of 1925 paved the way for a quick reconciliation between Wirth and his party's national leadership, the threat of a split within the party remained imminent in view of Wirth's concern over the Center's continued drift to the right. It was against the background of these developments that Wirth decided to use the agitation for a parliamentary alliance between the DVP and DNVP as the occasion for undertaking an initiative of his own, and on 20 July he issued a public appeal calling for the creation of a Republican Union consisting of those forces in the parties of the Weimar Coalition that were unequivocally committed to the preservation and defense of Germany's republican institutions.[61]

Wirth's initiative was designed to draw the Social Democrats out of the political isolation in which their stand in support of the uncompensated expropriation of Germany's dynastic families had left them. At the same time, it represented a direct response not only to the Liberal Association's campaign for the founding of a united liberal party, but also to the Gayl-Jarres proposal for the creation of a parliamentary alliance between the DVP and DNVP. But the action was poorly prepared and met with general skepticism from the leaders of the DDP, where only Ludwig Haas, a highly regarded member of the party's left wing and an outspoken opponent of the campaign for liberal unity, seemed willing to associate himself with the project.[62] Although they supported Wirth's ultimate goal of closer ties between Germany's republican parties, Koch-Weser and the more moderate leaders of the DDP were concerned that their participation in the proposed Republican Union might force the DVP into even greater dependence upon the DNVP, thereby nullifying their policy of a strong German middle.[63]

Wirth's appeal for the consolidation of Germany's democratic Left under the auspices of the Republican Union seemed to presage precisely that swing to the left that Stresemann had feared and that had caused such uneasiness among the supporters of the Gayl-Jarres initiative. But their efforts to counter this development by broadening the scope of their action to include all "state-supporting" parties and by inviting the Center to participate in the proposed parliamentary alliance met with little enthusiasm from the Center's national leadership, which rejected both Wirth's appeal for a consolidation of the democratic Left and the Gayl-Jarres initiative in favor of the party's traditional commitment to a strong political middle.[64] The final blow to the Gayl-Jarres initiative, however, came from an entirely unexpected direction. Speaking at the annual convention of the National Federation of German Industry in early September 1926, Paul Silverberg created a virtual sensation when he proposed the formation of a new national government in which not only the "state-supporting" bourgeois parties but also the Social Democrats were to be represented.[65] Whatever his motives, Silverberg's appeal for the creation of a government that included the SPD came as a rude shock to those who looked upon implementation of the Gayl-Jarres proposal as the first step toward the establishment of an antisocialist bloc and effectively killed whatever interest there may still have been within the DVP for the idea of a parliamentary alliance with the DNVP.[66] With its prospects for implementation rapidly eroding, the proposal was then decisively defeated in October 1926 when the DVP's Cologne party congress unanimously adopted a resolution reaffirming Stresemann's concept of an independent and liberal German People's Party.[67]

All of this activity threatened to exhaust the vitality that efforts to reform and reorganize the German party system had demonstrated earlier in the year. Nowhere was this more apparent than in the case of the Liberal Association, which found itself increasingly isolated from the very parties it had hoped to unite. Particularly distressing to the leaders of the Liberal Association was the outcome of the Saxon Landtag elections on 31 October 1926. Not only did the heavy losses that the two liberal parties suffered at the polls underscore the continued decline of the German liberal movement, but they also afforded the leaders of the DDP's left wing a new pretext for launching still another round of attacks against the association and the concept of a united liberal party.[68] While Koch-Weser was once again able to prevent the party's left wing from passing a resolution that would have obliged all party members to sever their ties with the association, he himself had become so discouraged by the lack of progress the movement for liberal unity had made since the beginning of the year that he was reluctant to become more actively involved in its affairs.[69] Even more exasperating was the impasse that had developed in the Liberal Association's relationship with the Business Party. The interest that Drewitz and other party leaders had taken in the movement for liberal unity at the beginning of the year had cooled markedly in the wake of the WP's impressive performance in the Saxon elections. This coincided with a fundamental shift in the WP's ideological orientation away from the liberal principles that had characterized the party's earliest programmatic statements to the corporatism of the "Görlitzer Richtlinien" from the summer of 1926. As a result, the association's efforts to establish closer relations with the WP's national leadership in the fall and early winter of 1926 met with mounting indifference.[70]

With the formation of the fourth Marx cabinet in January 1927, the two liberal parties once again found themselves in opposition to each other. This turn of events had disastrous implications for the future of the Liberal Association, which by the middle of the summer had become so moribund that Siemens and his associates were on the verge of withdrawing all financial support.[71] The only place where the Association seemed to be making any progress at all was in Bavaria, where in January 1927 a state chapter had been founded under the chairmanship of Karl Hammerschmidt, a former Democratic deputy to the Bavarian Landtag.[72] Still, whatever gains the association had been able to record in this corner of the country failed to compensate for its stagnation at the national level. The LV's third national convention in Berlin on 22 March was a particularly bland affair, with not a single liberal politician of national stature on the program.[73] By the end of the year, the association's lethargy had become so pervasive that not even its most ardent supporters could help but lament its apparent demise. As Hammerschmidt himself asked in an article written for *Wille und Weg* in the summer of 1928, "What remains of the fine speeches that Kahl, Koch-Weser, Stresemann, Drewitz, Luther, and Fischbeck gave before a truly outstanding audience in the 'Deutsche Gesellschaft' on the evening of 1 February 1926?" Only disappointments.[74]

CHAPTER TWENTY-ONE

Revolt in the Countryside

THE AGITATION FOR A reform and reorganization of the German party system served as an effective barometer of the deepening legitimacy crisis in which the institutions of Weimar democracy found themselves during the second half of the 1920s. At the same time, these efforts were all directly related to the continued decline of the German liberal parties and bore convincing testimony to the uncertainty that these developments had caused within the ranks of Germany's liberal elite. Yet as the outcome of the efforts clearly revealed, the growing awareness of the need for a reorganization of the German party system had not produced a consensus as to the precise form this reorganization should take. As a result, the leaders of Germany's liberal establishment were unable to formulate any sort of concerted response to the increasing fragmentation of the Weimar party system and to the threat that the emergence of special interest parties such as the Business Party and the People's Justice Party posed to the future of their own political parties.

By the end of the 1920s the dissolution of the Weimar party system had spread from the urban middle classes to the German countryside. The farmer had never been particularly well integrated into the political fabric of Germany's national life. Not only did his loyalties tend to be more regional than national in character, but the imposition of government controls over agricultural prices and production during the course of World War I had done much to intensify his inherent antipathy toward Berlin and centralized political authority. Moreover, regional agrarian parties had existed in Bavaria, Württemberg, and other parts of the country ever since the agricultural crisis of the mid-1890s.[1] The most important of these was the Bavarian Peasants' League, a radical populist party that had run its own slate of candidates in state and national elections ever since its founding in 1893. With its incipient anti-capitalism and ingrained antipathy toward the industrial and agricultural elites of Wilhelmine Germany, the BBB appealed to precisely those same petty bourgeois elements that in other parts of the country had supported the various liberal parties, and its success, perhaps best reflected by the fact that in the 1898 Reichstag elections it received 18 percent of the Bavarian vote, helped acccount for the relative weakness of the Bavarian liberal movement before 1914.[2] The founding of the BBB represented a populist response to the increasingly difficult situation in which the Bavarian peasantry found itself at the end of the nineteenth century, and the success with which it was able to mobilize peasant anxiety over the deteriorating agricultural situation both alarmed and impressed conservative rural elites. In Württemberg, for example, the local chapter of the conservative Agrarian League tried to emulate the BBB's methods of political mobilization by founding its own political party, entitled the Württemberg Peasants and Wine Growers' League (Württembergischer Bauern- und Weingärtnerbund or WBWB). But unlike the BBB, which retained complete independence from other political parties and stood on the left of Bavaria's political spectrum, the WBWB was dominated by conservative landowners who were implacably opposed to any liberalization of Germany's political life and were anxious to prevent the emergence of a radical populist movement like the BBB among the local peasantry.[3]

The formation of parties like this—not only in Bavaria and Württemberg but also in Hesse, Thuringia, and other parts of the country—underscored the inadequate integration of the German farmer into the institutional fabric of Germany's political life. Only in predominantly Catholic areas, where the Center received strong organizational support from the Association of German Christian Peasant Unions (Vereinigung der christlichen deutschen Bauernvereine), and in Prussia's eastern provinces, where the Agrarian League worked hand in hand with the German Conservative Party, were Germany's national political parties able to achieve effective integration of organized agrarian interests into their own political movements. In the southwestern, central, and northern parts of the country, ties between organized agriculture and the more ideologically oriented national parties remained extremely tenuous right up until the collapse of the Second Empire. In the January 1919 elections to the National Assembly, however, virtually all of Germany's major agricultural interest organizations closed ranks behind the various nonsocialist parties in an attempt to hold the forces of social and political upheaval that had been unleashed by the November Revolution in check. Not only did the archconservative Agrarian League throw the full weight of its organization and influence behind the newly formed German National People's Party, but the Christian peasant unions overcame whatever reservations they might have had about the Center's swing to the left during the last years of the war to support it in the elections to the National Assembly. By the same token, the German Peasants' League, which had been founded in 1909 by farm leaders with close ties to the prewar National Liberal Party, entered into a close electoral alliance with the German Democratic Party on the assumption that it represented the best bulwark against the twin dangers of social revolution and feudal reaction.[4] Of Germany's major agricultural interest organizations, only the Bavarian Peasants' League, which had briefly allied itself with the Independent Socialists in overthrowing the Wittelsbach monarchy, chose to run its own slate of candidates in the campaign for the National Assembly.[5]

The network of alliances or *Querverbindungen* that had developed after the end of World War I between Germany's nonsocialist parties and the different sectors of the German agricultural community were severely strained by the general course of German economic development during the first half of the 1920s. By the end of 1924 German agriculture stood on the brink of a complete economic collapse. For while the runaway inflation of the early 1920s had made it possible for the agricultural community to liquidate over 80 percent of its prewar debt, not only the inflation but also the stabilization of the mark in the winter of 1923–24 had exacted a heavy toll upon German agriculture. In the first place, the new currency was to be created from the proceeds of a compulsory mortgage or *Zwangshypothek* that the government levied against all landed property, agricultural as well as industrial, in November 1923. Farmers, including those who had already marketed their 1923 harvests at prices denominated in devalued paper marks, were required to pay this mortgage, as well as their property and income taxes for 1923, in funds whose value was tied to gold or some other stable monetary base. The financial burden that this entailed for small peasant proprietors throughout the country was compounded by the fact that the Reichsbank's decision to curtail credit in the spring of 1924 had led to the collapse of the private credit cooperatives that had traditionally provided them with the capital they needed for the purchase of seed, fertilizer, and farm machinery on relatively inexpensive terms. This development, which left the small farmer with no alternative but to turn to the larger and more expensive credit market that had been organized to meet the capital needs of commerce and industry, combined with a dramatic increase in the prices of fertilizer, machinery, and other farm necessities and the virtual collapse of international farm prices to plunge German agriculture into a deep depression that was to last well into the next decade.[6]

The reluctance with which the first governments of the Weimar Republic went about the task of dismantling wartime controls over agricultural prices and production did much to aggravate relations not only between the German Peasants' League and the DDP but also between the Christian peasant unions and the Center.[7] At the same time, relations between the DVP and the more conservative elements of the agricultural community had come under an increasingly heavy strain of their own. When the National Rural League had been founded at the beginning of 1921, the DVP's Karl Hepp was elected as one of the RLB's two national presidents in an effort to establish at least the appearance of parity between the large landowners from east of the Elbe River and the small and middle-sized farmers of central and western Germany.[8] In campaigning for the DVP, Hepp took special pains to dispel the notion that the DVP was the party of big business and therefore had nothing to offer the small farmer.[9] But Hepp's relations with the DVP had become increasingly strained following Stresemann's appointment to the chancellorship in the late summer of 1923. Not only was Hepp adamantly opposed to Stresemann's willingness to head a government in which the Social Democrats were also represented,[10] but in the spring of 1924 he, along with Karl Friedrich Döbrich from the Thuringian Rural League (Thüringer Landbund or TLB), joined the leaders of the DVP's right wing in founding the National Liberal Association in an attempt to change the direction in which the party was headed.[11] In the May 1924 Reichstag elections the Thuringian Rural League as well as Hepp's own organization in Hesse-Nassau joined the NLV in an electoral alliance that polled nearly 600,000 votes and elected ten Reichstag deputies, all of whom subsequently affiliated themselves with the DNVP Reichstag delegation.[12] Although Hepp remained loyal to the DVP and was reelected to the Reichstag on its ticket in December 1924, party leaders could only bemoan the loss of what had once been a promising foothold in the German countryside.[13]

In the meantime, relations between the German Peasants' League and the DDP had continued to deteriorate to the point that in October 1924 Karl Böhme, the DBB's secretary general and a member of the DDP Reichstag delegation, announced his resignation from the party and defected to the German People's Party. A former National Liberal who had gone over to the DDP in the fall of 1918, Böhme had become increasingly critical of the DDP's farm policy throughout the early 1920s and took advantage of the furor that had been created by the party's refusal to share governmental responsibility with the DNVP to announce his defection to the DVP.[14] In the final analysis, however, Böhme's defection stemmed from fears that the commercial interests on the DDP's right wing would prevent the party from supporting the DBB's demands for a selective agricultural tariff when Germany regained her tariff autonomy in January 1925. When the question of an agricultural tariff had first been raised in the summer of 1924, the leaders of the DDP's business wing had voiced strong opposition to any tariff that might increase the costs of production or provoke retaliatory measures by Germany's trading partners.[15] Confronted by a determined alliance of free-trade forces that spanned both wings of the party, Böhme was convinced that the DDP no longer had anything to offer the German farmer and went over to the DVP in hopes that it would support the DBB in its efforts to secure the passage of a tariff on dairy and meat products.[16] In spite of the fact that many of the DBB's leading officials, including its president, Friedrich Wachhorst de Wente, refused to follow Böhme's lead and quickly reaffirmed their loyalty to the DDP,[17] the episode dramatized the widening gulf that had opened up between the DDP and the small peasant proprietors whom it had wooed so effectively in 1919 and 1920.

In the eyes of organized agricultural interests, the debate over German tariff policy in the first half of 1925 served as the litmus test of a party's commitment to the welfare of the German farmer. The "most favored nation" status that Germany had been required to grant the various Allied powers at Versailles was scheduled to expire in January 1925, and agricultural as well as industrial interest organizations were anxious to gain a voice in shaping the general guidelines under which future tariff agreements with Germany's trade partners were to be negotiated. These guidelines were contained in a special tariff bill that the first Luther government had drafted with the direct involvement of the DVP and DNVP in the spring of 1925. This bill, which rested upon a basic compromise aimed at achieving tariff parity between the industrial and agricultural sectors of the German economy, sought to establish minimum tariffs on a wide range of agricultural imports as well as to exclude foreign competitors from the domestic market for industrial goods.[18] As one of the principal architects of the compromise upon which the proposed tariff legislation rested, the DVP defended the bill not only on account of the undeniable benefits it held for German industry but also because of the protection it supposedly afforded the beleaguered German farmer.[19] But the bill ran into strong opposition from the Social Democrats and DDP, who denounced it as a pact between big business and big agriculture at the expense of the consuming public. The commercial interests on the DDP's right wing were particularly concerned over the effect the proposed industrial tariffs would have upon German export markets and demanded that all tariffs on raw materials and unfinished products be stricken from the bill, lest they result in higher production costs for the artisan and small manufacturer. The Democrats were also quick to champion the cause of the small peasant proprietor, whose livelihood from the sale of meat and dairy products was threatened by the government's plans to introduce a tariff on imported feed grains. But the DDP's efforts to modify features of the proposed tariff bill that they found particularly objectionable met with little success, with the result that the party officially abstained in the decisive parliamentary vote on 12 August 1925.[20]

The DDP's reluctance to support the government's tariff bill in the summer of 1925 led to another round of attacks by Böhme and his associates in the leadership of the German Peasants' League.[21] This time, however, the main casualty of Böhme's offensive was not the DDP but the German Peasants' League. For as Böhme intensified his attacks against the DDP during the course of 1925, a severe split developed within the ranks of his own organization between himself and those like Wachhorst de Wente who had remained loyal to the DDP.[22] The crisis within the DBB drew to a head in August 1926 when Böhme was forced to resign as its secretary general amid allegations of embezzlement and financial impropriety. Not only did this leave the league on the verge of complete financial ruin, but Böhme's resignation was followed in February 1927 by the defection of a large part of the DBB's Berlin staff to the rival National Rural League and the loss of more than half of the DBB's 18,000 members by the middle of the year.[23] The DBB's decline was irreversible, and in October 1927 what still remained of its national organization merged with the Bavarian Peasants' League and an association of twelve regional peasant unions known as the National Federation of Small and Middle-Sized Agricultural Enterprises (Reichsverband landwirtschaftlicher Klein- und Mittelbetriebe) in the form of a new agricultural pressure group known as the German Peasantry (Deutsche Bauernschaft or DBS).[24]

With an initial membership of approximately 200,000, the German Peasantry represented a loose coalition of fifteen independent peasant unions, the largest of which was the 30,000-member Bavarian Peasants' League. The preeminence of the BBB could be seen in the fact that Anton Fehr, without question its most prominent national politician, was elected to the chairmanship of the new organization's executive committee. Espousing a policy of nonpartisan neutrality with respect to all political parties, the German Peasantry stood to the left of center and was clearly the most progressive of the agricultural interest organizations that surfaced in Germany after World War I. Its primary objective was to strengthen the economic position of the small family farmer, and it was strongly opposed to the preferential treatment that large grain producers received with the adoption of the 1925 tariff bill.[25]

Anxious to repair the damage that Böhme's defection to the DVP had done to their party's ties with Germany's small and middle-sized farmers, the Democrats moved quickly to take advantage of peasant disenchantment with the 1925 tariff bill. In January 1925 the DDP appointed a special committee under the chairmanship of Reichstag deputy Heinrich Rönneberg for the purpose of providing the party with a comprehensive agrarian program that would enable it to recapture the rural support it had lost since the beginning of the decade.[26] This program, whose basic objectives were outlined by Rönneberg and his associates at the DDP's National Peasant Congress (Reichsbauerntag) in January 1927, placed primary emphasis upon the economic emancipation and rehabilitation of the small peasant and family farmer. To achieve this, the program called for a series of specific reforms that included greater protection for the rights of the tenant farmer and elimination of the land tax (*Landsteuer*) for small and middle-sized agricultural producers. Although the program also envisaged a selective agricultural tariff aimed at providing dairy and livestock farmers with more effective protection from the import of finished food products, tariff protection for wheat, corn, and other feed grains was ruled out on the grounds that this only benefited Germany's large landholders at the expense of higher production costs for the small peasant. The most radical feature of the proposed farm program, however, was a recommendation for increasing the number of small farm holdings through the expropriation and resettlement of large landed estates that were no longer economically viable.[27]

Although the proposal for agricultural resettlement aroused strong opposition among the more conservative elements of the party, the Democrats went ahead with the publication of their new farm program in early 1928 after making several minor modifications designed to placate those who opposed its more radical features.[28] By this time, however, the situation in which many German farmers had found themselves following the stabilization of the mark had become even more desperate. In the first place, whatever benefits the agricultural sector was supposed to have reaped from the return to protectionism in the summer of 1925 had been undercut by the bilateral trade treaties that the German Foreign Office had negotiated between 1925 and the end of 1926 in an attempt to develop new markets for Germany's surplus industrial production.[29] Moreover, the 1925 tariff bill had done little to help the small farmer, who found himself confronted with mounting production costs and a domestic market saturated with imported meat and dairy products. The failure of the government's protectionist policies became fully apparent in the winter of 1927–28, when the bottom fell out of domestic pork prices and peasants, particularly in the north and north central parts of the country, took to the streets in protest. Peasant unrest drew to a dramatic climax on 28 January 1928, when more than 140,000 farmers, artisans, and small shopkeepers from Schleswig-Holstein demonstrated against high taxes, high interest rates, and foreign imports.[30] This was followed by similar, though less impressive, demonstrations in Thuringia, Württemberg, and other parts of the country, as conservative rural elites tried to contain the wave of peasant discontent to which the deepening agricultural crisis had given rise.[31] These developments were particularly alarming to the leaders of the DNVP, which of all the established bourgeois parties was most heavily dependent upon peasant support, and in February 1928 they rushed forward with an emergency farm program whose central features were provisions for tax relief, credit assistance, and tighter controls over the import of pork and other meat products.[32]

It was against the background of these developments that the first steps toward the creation of a national agrarian party were taken. Here the initial impulse came from Fehr and the leaders of the Bavarian Peasants' League. Ever since its involvement in the Bavarian revolution of 1918–19, the BBB had moved more and more to the political center under the leadership of Fehr and other party moderates like Georg Eisenberger, the chairman of its state organization. As the BBB shifted its attention away from questions of national policy to the social and economic issues that were pressing so heavily upon the Bavarian peasantry, it changed its name in November 1922 to the Bavarian Peasant and Middle-Class League in an attempt to extend its influence into the towns and small cities that dotted the Bavarian countryside.[33] At the same time, the leaders of the BBB sharply attacked the "Draconian" measures that the national government had taken to stabilize the mark in 1923–24, and in the campaign for the May 1924 Reichstag elections they demanded the immediate repeal of those facets of the government's stabilization program that posed an unacceptable burden to Germany's rural and urban middle classes.[34] A further indication of the BBB's political reorientation in the early 1920s was the electoral alliance it concluded with the Business Party of the German Middle Class for the May and December 1924 Reichstag elections. Not only did this provide the BBB with its greatest electoral success since the end of the war, but from 1924 to 1928 this alliance continued in the form of a special parliamentary coalition known as the Economic Association, in which the BBB, WP, and German-Hanoverian Party were all represented.[35]

By the middle of the 1920s the democratic radicalism that inspired the BBB's founding at the end of the previous century had been largely eclipsed by the exigencies of interest politics. Still, the leaders of the Bavarian Peasants' League remained deeply committed to the republican form of government and evinced none of the disdain for democratic institutions that characterized the more conservative agrarian organizations. In state politics, where the BBB had sought to promote closer ties between the two liberal parties and the Bavarian People's Party, the virtual collapse of the Bavarian liberal movement between 1922 and 1924 had forced the BBB into increasing dependence upon the BVP. Though clearly dictated by the necessities of Bavarian politics, the alliance with the bastion of Bavarian conservatism proved particularly unpopular with the leaders of the BBB's left wing, who in 1926–27 resumed their populist agitation against the status quo in Bavaria and the Reich. But while the incipient radicalization of the BBB's left wing had little effect upon the league's place in Bavarian political life, it heralded an end to the national political alliance that Fehr and his associates had concluded with the Business Party and conservative middle-class groups from other parts of the country in the first half of the 1920s. The BBB's decision to participate in the founding of the German Peasantry in the fall of 1927 and Fehr's willingness to accept election to the chairmanship of the DBS's executive committee marked the beginning of still another reorientation in the BBB's political development, one which in this case would lead to the creation of a national peasants' party.[36]

Speaking at a demonstration of the Silesian Peasants' League (Schlesischer Bauernbund) in Breslau on 12 February 1928, Fehr announced that the BBB would present a full national slate of candidates under the name German Peasants' Party (Deutsche Bauernpartei or DBP) in the Reichstag elections that were scheduled to take place later that spring.[37] Fehr's announcement came in response to an appeal that the leaders of the Silesian Peasants' League had issued in August of the preceeding year for the creation of a national peasants' party, and it marked the end of the BBB's alliance with the Business Party.[38] In making such an announcement, however, Fehr no doubt assumed that the newly founded German Peasantry would serve as the new party's organizational base. But these plans ran into strong opposition from peasant spokesmen with close ties to the DDP, who used their influence within the German

Peasantry to undercut Fehr's position as the DBS's national chairman. As a result, the DBS dissociated itself from the efforts to found a new agrarian party and reaffirmed its policy of nonpartisan neutrality at an emergency meeting of its executive committee on 22 March. This was accompanied by Fehr's resignation as chairman of the German Peasantry's national organization in favor of Emil Marth, an undistinguished Pomeranian farmer with little in the way of national political ambitions.[39] Undaunted by this turn of events, Fehr and the other five members of the BBB's delegation to the Reichstag formally reconstituted themselves as the German Peasants' Party and proceeded with their plans to run a national slate of candidates in the upcoming Reichstag elections.[40]

The founding of the German Peasants' Party in the spring of 1928 aroused widespread apprehension not only among the leaders of the DDP but also within the ranks of Germany's conservative agrarian elite. But while Germany's more conservative farm leaders were fearful that the founding of the German Peasant's Party foreshadowed a further radicalization of the German countryside, they were deeply divided as to how they should respond to the disorienting effect that the deepening agricultural crisis had had upon Germany's rural population. Much of the difficulty stemmed from the decentralized structure of the National Rural League, the principal bastion of agrarian conservatism in the Weimar Republic since its founding in January 1921. For unlike the highly centralized and Junker-dominated Agrarian League that had preceded it, the National Rural League was a loose federation of state and regional farm organizations, all of which were legally and corporatively independent of the RLB's central headquarters in Berlin.[41] Moreover, several of the RLB's regional affiliates—most notably those in Thuringia and Württemberg—had run their own slate of candidates in virtually every state and national election since the founding of the Weimar Republic and exercised considerably more influence over their local constituencies than the RLB itself. Citing the success they had had with their own slate of candidates in recent state and national elections, the leaders of the Thuringian Rural League petitioned the RLB's national leadership in November 1927 to run its own slate of candidates in the Reichstag elections that were scheduled to take place early the following year.[42] This proposal, however, encountered fierce opposition from RLB leaders with close ties to the DNVP, and it was shelved at a meeting of the RLB executive committee on 14 December 1927 in favor of a resolution that left the question of electoral strategy to the discretion of the RLB's state and regional affiliates.[43]

The subsequent demonstration by 36,000 Thuringian peasants in Rudolstadt on 7 February 1928 and Fehr's announcement five days later that the Bavarian Peasants' League would present a national slate of candidates in the upcoming Reichstag elections convinced the leaders of the Thuringian Rural League that they could no longer afford to wait for the official sanction of the RLB leadership in Berlin. On 17 February Franz Hanse and Karl Friedrich Döbrich from the Thuringian Rural League joined Wilhelm Dorsch from the Hessian Rural League (Hessischer Landbund) in announcing that they had decided to sever their ties with the DNVP, in whose Reichstag delegation they had sat from 1924 to 1928, as a prelude to the founding of a new agrarian party known as the Christian-National Peasants and Farmers' Party (Christlich-nationale Bauern- und Landvolkpartei or CNBLP).[44] While the leaders of the right-wing DNVP were extremely apprehensive that this presaged a further radicalization of the German peasantry and feared that the CNBLP might join forces with Fehr and the founders of the German Peasants' Party,[45] the impulse that lay behind the founding of the CNBLP was profoundly conservative and had little in common with the radical populism of the Bavarian Peasants' League. As Ernst Höfer, chairman of the Thuringian Rural League, explained in an article written shortly after the CNBLP's founding, the party to which he and his associates had given birth was essentially an attempt to contain the wave of agrarian unrest that was sweeping the country by providing farmers throughout the country with the effective political representation they needed in order to survive the deepening agricultural crisis. Insofar as all of Germany's nonsocialist parties had consistently sacrificed the welfare of farmers to that of other vocational groups, only the consolidation of the German agricultural community into a united agrarian party could possibly hold the radicalization of the German countryside in check.[46]

The fact that the three principals involved in the founding of the CNBLP—Hanse, Döbrich, and Dorsch—were all former members of the DNVP Reichstag delegation gave rise to immediate allegations that the new party was nothing but a Nationalist ploy created for the sole purpose of duping unwitting peasants into voting for candidates who, once they had been elected, would promptly rejoin the DNVP.[47] The new party's credibility was greatly enhanced, however, when the three former Nationalists were joined several days later by Karl Hepp, a member of the DVP Reichstag delegation and an agrarian leader of truly national stature.[48] Having served as one of the RLB's two national presidents since the organization's founding in 1921, Hepp had long sought to organize the small and middle-sized farmers from central and southwestern Germany into a force sufficiently powerful to prevent the RLB from falling under the domination of the large landowning interests from east of the Elbe.[49] But Hepp's ties to the DVP, already strained in the spring of 1924 by his membership in the National Liberal Association, had been severely weakened by Stresemann's refusal during the 1925 tariff debates to support tariff protection for the wine-growing interests upon which he, as a Reichstag deputy from Hesse-Nassau, was politically dependent.[50] Like most of Germany's agricultural leaders, Hepp was also extremely critical of the way in which German trade policy between 1925 and 1927 had consistently favored the interests of the export industry over those of the farmer.[51] Hepp's decision to leave the DVP in the spring of 1928, therefore, represented an act of protest not only against Stresemann's foreign policy but also against the predominant position that organized business interests had managed to gain within both the DVP Reichstag delegation and the executive councils at the head of the party's national organization.

The founding of the Christian-National Peasants and Farmers' Party took place with Hepp's full cooperation in the Thuringian capital of Weimar on 8 March 1928.[52] In their struggle to organize the German agricultural community into a united agrarian party, however, the founders of the CNBLP encountered strong opposition from both the leaders of the DNVP and their allies within the National Rural League.[53] In view of Hepp's position as one of the RLB's two national presidents, this posed a severe threat to the RLB's internal solidarity and raised the danger of an open split between those RLB affiliates that supported the DNVP and CNBLP respectively. In its initial response to the founding of the CNBLP, the RLB executive committee had taken special pains to reaffirm its policy of nonpartisan neutrality with respect to all political parties and had left the decision to support or reject the CNBLP to the discretion of its regional affiliates throughout the country.[54] This decision met with strong criticism from the leaders of the DNVP, who began to press the National Rural League for a stronger and less equivocal stand against the new party.[55] At the same time, the leaders of the DNVP tried to halt the spread of the new party by entering into electoral alliances with the RLB's organizational affiliates in those parts of the country where the CNBLP had not yet established itself.[56] But when these tactics failed to deter the founders of the CNBLP from expanding their party's campaign into areas where local farm leaders had remained loyal to the DNVP, the fragile truce that the leaders of the National Rural League had negotiated between the two parties in February 1928 collapsed into an open conflict that threatened to destroy the nonpartisan foundations upon which the RLB had always rested.[57]

The emergence of agrarian splinter parties in the spring of 1928 constituted an important chapter in the dissolution of the Weimar party system. This development was a direct response to the deepening economic crisis in which German agriculture found itself following the stabilization of the mark and bore dramatic testimony to the increasing disaffection of Germany's rural electorate from the various parties through which it had traditionally sought to achieve its social and economic objectives. The long-range implications of this for the future of the Weimar party system, however, were far from clear. For although the founders of the DBP and CNBLP evinced a certain antipathy toward the way in which the German party system had developed since the founding of the Weimar Republic, they also recognized the necessity of working within the existing system of government in order to provide their respective constituencies with the effective political representation they needed to survive the worsening agricultural situation. From this perspective, therefore, the formation of agrarian splinter parties in the spring of 1928 offered grounds for hope that the political pragmatism that had manifested itself in their founding might triumph over the unyielding ideological opposition that Germany's more conservative agrarian spokesmen had demonstrated toward the Weimar Republic. Yet, at the same time, the emergence of the DBP and CNBLP had a destabilizing effect upon the Weimar party system as a whole and greatly accelerated the internal disintegration of Germany's more established bourgeois parties. While this development posed the greatest threat to the DNVP, neither of the liberal parties could escape its implications. For not only did the founding of the German Peasants' Party present a direct challenge to the tenuous hold that the DDP still had over the small family farmer in the north and north central parts of the country, but the defection of Hepp to the CNBLP threatened the German People's Party with the loss of its already badly decimated agrarian wing.

CHAPTER TWENTY-TWO

The Challenge of Interest Politics

AS THE FORMATION OF SPECIAL interest parties in the second half of the 1920s clearly revealed, the dissolution of the Weimar party system was well under way long before the world economic crisis descended upon Germany in the fall of 1929. The emergence of the Business Party and the People's Justice Party in the cities and of the German Peasants' Party and the Christian-National Peasants and Farmers' Party in the countryside bore dramatic testimony to the increasing fragmentation of Germany's middle-class electorate and threatened all of Germany's more established bourgeois parties, including the Center and DNVP, with dissolution into their constituent social and economic interests. Nowhere was the threat that the challenge of interest politics posed to the future of the Weimar party system more apparent than in the campaign for the Reichstag elections of 20 May 1928.

The 1928 Reichstag elections took place in a climate of economic and political stability, a factor that should have worked to the advantage of the parties identified with the existing system of government. But the economic prosperity of the late 1920s was deceptive in the sense that it had passed over significant segments of the German population and never translated into the permanent economic recovery for which Germany's political leaders had hoped. Unemployment remained disturbingly high throughout the second half of the 1920s, as a persistent shortage of investment capital continued to frustrate Germany's general economic recovery. It was not until the appointment of the DDP's Peter Reinhold as the minister of finance in the second Luther cabinet that the German government began to employ countercyclical policies as a means of stimulating economic growth and reducing unemployment.[1] Still, the psychological trauma of the inflation and a sense of betrayal over the way in which the mark had been stabilized remained deeply entrenched in those social strata upon which Germany's more traditional bourgeois parties had always depended for the bulk of their electoral support. Neither this nor the fact that they had been obliged to accept responsiblity for unpopular domestic measures such as the revaluation law or the 1925 tax reform augured well for those parties that had served more or less continually in the national government since the end of the great inflation.

The two liberal parties entered the campaign for the May 1928 Reichstag elections in disagreement on many of the fundamental questions that confronted the German electorate. After a brief period of cooperation in the third Marx cabinet from June to December 1926, the DDP had again refused to participate in the formation of a government in which the right-wing DNVP was also represented. Efforts to broaden the base of the existing governmental coalition had begun in late October as representatives from the three government parties—the DVP, DDP, and Center—met with spokesmen for both the Nationalists and the Social Democrats in an attempt to reach agreement on the policies necessary to combat the mounting unemployment that Germany's economic stagnation had left in its wake.[2] While both the Democrats and the Center hoped that this would lead to the formation of a new government based upon the Great Coalition, the leaders of the DVP's right wing were apprehensive that such a development might result in a new round of social legislation inimical to the interests of German free enterprise.[3] The uneasiness with which the leaders of the DVP's right wing viewed the prospect of a coalition with the Social Democrats erupted into public view at a party rally in Insterburg in early December when Ernst Scholz, chairman of the DVP Reichstag delegation, publicly attacked the SPD for its position on questions of social and military policy and reiterated his personal commitment to the formation of a bourgeois coalition with the DNVP.[4] Scholz's speech was immediately perceived as a "declaration of war" by the Social Democratic press and effectively ended the SPD's unofficial support of the Marx government. Stresemann, who was in Geneva at the time of Scholz's speech, was irritated over this turn of events and tried to repair the damage it had done to the government's prospects of political survival upon his return to Berlin on 14 December. Stresemann's hopes of a reconciliation with the Social Democrats, however, were immediately shattered when Philipp Scheidemann, the SPD's expert on military affairs, disclosed a long list of German violations of the Versailles Peace Treaty, including secret military collaboration with Soviet Russia, in a sensational speech before the Reichstag on 16 December.[5] Not only did Scheidemann's revelations eliminate the Social Democrats as a potential coalition partner for the DVP, but on the following day the SPD Reichstag delegation introduced a motion of no-confidence in the Marx government, which, much to Stresemann's dismay, the Nationalists allowed to pass.[6] With the subsequent resignation of the Marx government, Germany suddenly found herself mired in her third "Christmas crisis" in as many years.

In early January 1927 the DVP's Julius Curtius tried to break the political stalemate that had developed in Berlin by entering into direct negotiations with the DNVP. But Curtius's efforts to organize a new government with Nationalist participation ended in failure as the Center steadfastly refused to share governmental responsibility with the DNVP for fear that this would drive the Catholic working class into the arms of the Social Democrats.[7] The Center began to waver, however, when Marx was asked to pick up where Curtius had failed and when the leaders of the DNVP agreed to accept the guidelines that the Center Reichstag delegation had adopted on 21 January as the basis upon which the new government was to be formed. With the thaw in relations between the DNVP and Center, Stresemann found himself caught on the horns of an increasingly uncomfortable dilemma. As Germany's foreign minister, Stresemann preferred a continuation of the previous governmental coalition and feared that the DNVP's entry into the government might weaken his chances of an agreement with the French on the evacuation of the Rhineland.[8] As chairman of the German People's Party, on the other hand, Stresemann could ill afford to ignore the growing sentiment within the ranks of his own party for a coalition with the DNVP. Scholz was unrelenting in his efforts as chairman of the DVP Reichstag delegation to bring about a coalition with the Nationalists, and on 19 January the delegation announced that it would not support a return of the previous governmental coalition until all efforts to reach an accommodation with the DNVP had been exhausted.[9]

While pressure from the DVP's right wing left Stresemann with no choice but to go along with the Nationalists' entry into the government, he hoped to offset the influence that the Center and DNVP would be able to exercise over the government's social and economic policies by inducing either the Democrats or the coalition of special interest groups known as the Economic Association to join the cabinet. But the Democrats, whose leaders were adamantly opposed to the cultural and educational policies of the new government,[10] were prepared to enter it only if they received two cabinet posts, a demand neither Marx nor the leaders of the DNVP were willing to consider. Consequently, when the DDP Reichstag delegation met on 27 January to take a position on the government Marx was in the process of forming, it voted unanimously to dissociate itself from the creation of the new government and to oppose it when it was presented to the Reichstag.[11] The first casualty of this decision was the DDP's Otto Gessler, whose credibilty as Germany's minister of defense had already been seriously compromised by Scheidemann's revelations in the Reichstag. Fearful that Scheidemann's disclosures might lead to a reform of the Reichswehr if the Defense Ministry were placed in less reliable hands, Hindenburg appealed to Gessler to continue as Germany's minister of defense in spite of the strong stand the Democrats had taken against the new government. Anxious to spare his party any further embarrassment, Gessler quietly resigned from the DDP on 28 January in what to all outward appearances was a perfectly amicable parting of the ways.[12]

Gessler's resignation gave the Democrats a free hand to attack the new government when it was presented to the Reichstag in the first week of February 1927. In addition to Marx, Stresemann, Gessler, and Curtius, the cabinet included four Nationalists—Martin Schiele, Walther von Keudell, Oskar Hergt, and Wilhelm Koch—as well as Heinrich Brauns and Heinrich

Köhler from the Center and Georg Schatzel from the BVP. Koch-Weser seized
upon the DNVP's presence in the new government as grounds for challenging
the credibility of its commitment to the republican system of government and
cited the Nationalists' inability to offer an unequivocal statement in support of
the Weimar Republic as clear proof of the duplicity with which they had
entered the government.[13] Yet for all of their rhetoric about the DNVP's lack
of sincerity in entering the government, the Democrats were less than consistent in their own attitude toward the new Marx cabinet. In differentiating their
position from that of the SPD, the Democrats rejected the idea of opposition
for its own sake in order to support those government programs that benefited
the social and economic interests upon which they were politically dependent.
In April 1927, for example, the DDP initially supported a government bill
aimed at regulating the length of the workday before finally rejecting it on the
grounds that it failed to set a minimum rate for overtime compensation.[14] A
month later the Democrats cooperated with the government in securing the
passage of a bill that replaced the relief program in effect since the end of the
inflation with a comprehensive system of unemployment compensation to
which both labor and management were required to contribute.[15] Finally, the
DDP went along with a reform of Germany's civil servant salary structure that
the government introduced in the fall of 1927 in an attempt to rectify some of
the more persistent salary inequities that had resulted from the inflation.[16] In
each case, the Democrats had tempered their opposition to the Marx government with a sober dose of interest politics.

The balance between cooperation and opposition that the leaders of the DDP
tried to strike in their relations with the Marx government did much to confuse
the party's ideological identity and only aggravated the legitimacy crisis that
had plagued it since the end of the great inflation. Following their defeat in the
1926 Saxon Landtag elections, the Democrats had hoped to salvage their
party's declining electoral fortunes by identifying themselves more closely
with the material interests of their middle-class electorate. In January 1927 the
DDP held a special congress for the commercial middle class in what was both
a sustained attack against the agitation of the Business Party and a reaffirmation of its own commitment to the future of Germany's middle-class
economy.[17] Two weeks later the Democrats held a similar congress for the
party's peasant supporters, at which time Heinrich Rönneburg presented the
general outlines of a comprehensive new farm program geared to the social
and economic interests of the small family farmer.[18] But these efforts, which
represented the DDP's first tentative steps toward the formulation of a new
economic program that would have tied it more closely to middle-class economic interests, encountered strong opposition from the ideological purists on
the party's left wing and were quickly abandoned as it became clear that there
was no longer any sort of common ground upon which those interests might be

reconciled with each other.[19] To atone for their failure to develop an economic program linking the DDP more closely to the representation of middle-class economic interests, the Democrats sought instead to identify themselves even more explicitly with what they perceived as Germany's national interest. At the DDP's Hamburg party congress in April 1927, the Democrats called for a fundamental reform of Germany's federal structure and dedicated themselves to the creation of what they termed "the greater German unitary state."[20] Essentially an attempt to resuscitate the strong nationalistic impulse that had been at work in the DDP during the first years of its existence, the appeal for the creation of a "unitary state" became a central feature of the DDP's campaign for the 1928 Reichstag elections, as party leaders tried to compensate for their apparent coolness to middle-class economic interests by highlighting those national issues upon which all sectors of the party's middle-class electorate could presumably agree.[21]

Although the leaders of the DVP had always been less inhibited in their solicitation of middle-class economic interests than their counterparts in the DDP, the inflation and subsequent stabilization of the mark had done much to intensify the general level of interest antagonism within their party as well. The situation within the DVP was further complicated by the fact that representatives of the German industrial establishment had become so firmly entrenched on the party's right wing that it was vulnerable to charges from the WP and VRP that it was nothing more than the pawn of big business. Using his visibility as Germany's foreign minister to maximum advantage, Stresemann had tried to counter the effect that these developments had had upon his party's predominantly middle-class electorate by reaffirming the national traditions with which the DVP had always identified itself. But while Stresemann, like the Democrats, was not averse to using nationalism as a means of compensating his party's middle-class supporters for the material losses they had suffered during the first half of the decade, his party's nationalist appeal was supplemented by a renewed emphasis upon liberalism and the ideological traditions upon which it, as the postwar successor of the old National Liberal Party, had been founded.[22] The DVP's Hanover party congress in March 1927, for example, was an elaborate celebration of the sixtieth anniversary of the NLP's founding, in which the leaders of the DVP not only paid homage to the memory of Rudolph Bennigsen and hailed the role their predecessors had played in the creation of Bismarck's Second Empire but also reaffirmed their commitment to the national and liberal values for which the old party had stood.[23]

The increased emphasis that Stresemann and the leaders of the DVP began to place upon their party's liberal legacy was both an attempt to counter the appeal of middle-class splinter parties and an implicit challenge to the cultural and educational policies of the Marx cabinet. The formation of the Marx government in January 1927 had been based upon a series of compromises between the Center and DNVP which, among other things, envisaged the introduction of a new school law that would authorize the establishment of denominational schools throughout the Reich.[24] This proposal, which reached the cabinet in the summer of 1927 in the form of a bill drafted by the Nationalist minister of interior, Walther von Keudell, represented a clear repudiation of the educational policies that the two liberal parties had espoused since the founding of the Weimar Republic and aroused widespread indignation throughout the German liberal establishment. This development was particularly distressing to the leaders of the German People's Party, who found themselves under increasingly heavy pressure from their partners in the governing coalition to support the bill in the interest of governmental solidarity.[25] At the same time, both the Liberal Association and the DDP began to mobilize liberal sentiment against the proposed bill in hopes that this might strengthen the DVP in its resolve to block its passage.[26] With the rejection of the Keudell bill by the Reichsrat on 14 October, attention shifted to the Reichstag, where it was no longer possible to avert a break between the DVP and its partners in the Marx government. On 27 November the DVP central executive committee reiterated its opposition to any change in the national school system that sought to abolish the privileged status that Article 174 of the Weimar Constitution had accorded nondenominational common schools in those parts of Germany where they were already established. By the same token, the DVP categorically rejected those sections of the proposed school bill that threatened the integrity of academic instruction or the authority of the state in educational matters.[27]

The strong stand that Stresemann and the leaders of the DVP took against the Keudell school bill in the fall of 1927 was a clear and unequivocal reaffirmation of the liberal principles upon which the party had been founded. But the DVP's hopes of modifying what it saw as the most offensive provisions of the bill were frustrated by the obstinance of the Center, whose leaders steadfastly refused to countenance any change in the language of the Keudell bill that might make it acceptable to the DVP. The Center's inflexibility was directly related to the storm of protest that its support of the recent reform of Germany's civil servant salary structure had aroused among the party's traditional supporters in the independent middle class and Christian labor movement. By evoking memories of the Center's *Kulturkampf* against liberalism in the first years of the Second Empire, the leaders of the party hoped to conceal the social divisions that had opened up beneath them and to find a cause around which all Catholics, regardless of their social class, could rally.[28] This tactic precluded any sort of compromise with the DVP on the substance of the proposed school bill, with the result that the governing coalition officially collapsed in the middle of February 1928. New elections were set for 20 May after the government parties heeded a presidential request that the cabinet be given an opportunity to pass a budget and complete other vital business before the Reichstag was dissolved.

The call for new elections in the spring of 1928 found the German liberal parties in a defensive frame of mind that did not augur well for their prospects at the polls. From the outset, the Center Party tried to saddle the DVP with responsibility for the collapse of the Marx government and waged a vigorous campaign against the corrosive effect of political liberalism on the spiritual foundations of Germany's national life.[29] By the same token, the DNVP tried to capitalize upon the disgruntlement that the DVP's vigorous defense of nondenominational common schools had produced among the more conservative elements of Germany's Lutheran population. But for the Nationalists the conflict over the national school law was only the external reason for the collapse of the Marx government. The real reason, as Nationalist speakers continued to remind their audiences throughout the campaign, was a fundamental disagreement within the government over the conduct of German foreign policy. From this perspective, therefore, ultimate responsibility for the demise of the Marx government lay with Stresemann, who, in his determination to bring about a coalition with the Social Democrats so that he could continue his career as foreign minister, had deliberately provoked a break with the Right. In this way, the Nationalists were able to relate the collapse of the Marx government to the broad national issues that had always obsessed them and to establish not only the struggle against the policy of fulfillment but also anti-Marxism as the central themes of their campaign.[30]

The most serious challenge the two liberal parties had to face in the campaign for the 1928 Reichstag elections, however, came not from the Center or DNVP but from the various special interest parties that had appeared on the scene since the end of the great inflation. The most aggressive of these was the Business Party, which had recorded an impressive string of victories in state and municipal elections throughout the second half of the 1920s. Not only could the WP point with pride to its record of accomplishment on behalf of artisans, homeowners, and small businessmen in states like Saxony and Thuringia, where its success at the polls had been sufficient to propel it into power,[31] but it proved remarkably adept at mobilizing middle-class sentiment against the social and economic policies of the more established bourgeois parties. On 18 March the Cartel for the Independent Middle Class (Kartell des selbständigen Mittelstandes), an ostensibly nonpartisan organization under the chairmanship of the WP's Hermann Drewitz, sponsored a series of mass demonstrations throughout the country under the slogan "Middle Class in Need." This initiative reached a climax in Berlin, where several thousand demonstrators closed their shops and marched through the streets in protest against high taxes, government rent controls, and excessive government ex-

penditures.[32] This was combined with a sharp attack against the more traditional bourgeois parties for having betrayed the vital interests of the middle
class. The WP was particularly critical of the DDP on account of its long
history of collaboration with the Social Democrats, the "mortal enemy" of the
German middle class. The WP also attacked the Democrats for their failure to
maintain a united front with the other bourgeois parties in the struggle against
the small business tax in the Prussian Landtag in 1924, while the DDP's failure
to cooperate in efforts to bring about an end to government controls over the
housing industry was cited as further evidence of the party's indifference to
middle-class economic interests.[33] Although the WP was somewhat more
restrained in its treatment of the DVP, it took special pains to dissociate itself
from Stresemann's foreign policy and denounced the party for its heavy dependence upon German heavy industry. By the same token, the WP assailed the
Nationalists for their close ties to organized agriculture and the Center for its
relationship with the Christian trade unions in what amounted to a general
indictment of the German party system as it was presently constituted.[34]

In their attacks against the traditional bourgeois parties, both the Business
Party and its chief rival for the votes of the disaffected middle class, the
People's Justice Party, evinced if not an explicit then certainly an implicit
antipathy to the German party system as it had developed since the early years
of the Weimar Republic. Not only were the other bourgeois parties denounced
as the pawns of special economic interests whose welfare was inimical to that
of the German middle class, but the fragmentation of the German party system
was held directly responsible for the inability of the middle class to sustain
itself against the two blocs that had come to dominate Weimar politics—
namely big business and organized labor. But whereas the Business Party
concentrated its efforts upon homeowners, artisans, and small businessmen—
in short, upon those elements of the middle class that had come through the
inflation with their wealth relatively intact[35]—the VRP appealed to those
marginal elements in German society to whom the trauma of proletarization
had suddenly become very real. By striking a note of moral indignation over
the fate they had suffered at the hands of the Weimar state, the VRP hoped to
galvanize pensioners, renters, war veterans, widows and the countless thousands of small investors whose savings had been destroyed by the inflation into
a force sufficiently powerful to free Germany's political life from the domination of the anonymous plutocratic forces that had been responsible for the
revaluation settlement of 1925.[36]

The revolt of the independent middle class was paralleled by similar developments in the German countryside. The mass demonstrations that farmers
from Schleswig-Holstein to Württemberg had staged in the first months of
1928 under the slogan "Agriculture in Need" signaled a radicalization of
Germany's rural population that threatened to eclipse anything the leaders of

the WP and VRP had hoped to incite in the urban middle class. Though motivated by fundamentally different ideological tenets, the leaders of the German Peasants' Party and the Christian-National Peasants and Farmers' Party each hoped to check the wave of social and political unrest that was sweeping the German agricultural community by providing it with more effective political representation than it had been receiving from the more established bourgeois parties. Speaking at a party rally in early May, the CNBLP's Karl Hepp denounced the recent reform of Germany's civil servant salary structure as another example of the way in which the DVP and other bourgeois parties had consistently sacrificed the welfare of the German farmer to the interests of other social groups.[37] At the same time, the founders of the CNBLP attacked the DNVP for its failure to use its influence as a member of the national government first in 1925 and then again in 1927–28 to secure the adoption of an agricultural tariff capable of providing the German farmer with adequate protection against foreign imports.[38] In their attacks against the more established bourgeois parties, both the DBP and CNBLP evinced much of the same antipathy toward the Weimar party system that had already manifested itself in the campaign propaganda of the WP and VRP. This was particularly evident in the case of the CNBLP, whose leaders characteristically punctuated their campaign speeches with obligatory diatribes against the "party haggling [Parteiwirtschaft] of Weimar democracy" and called for a fundamental reorganization of the German state along vocational and corporatist lines.[39] The same sentiment could also be seen in the election manifestoes of the Bavarian Peasant and Middle-Class League, where it combined with a strong dose of anticapitalism to produce appeals for an end to the "party machinations of large capital, trusts, and concerns."[40]

The manipulation of antisystem sentiment by the leaders of the various middle-class splinter parties posed a problem for campaign strategists for the two liberal parties that they could ill afford to ignore. In this respect, both the DDP and DVP not only deprecated the role that special economic interests had come to play in Germany's national life but challenged the effectiveness with which special interest parties like the WP and VRP were able to represent the interests of those social groups for which they supposedly stood.[41] More importantly, the leaders of the liberal parties tried to shift the campaign's central focus away from issues of economic self-interest to broader questions of national policy capable of transcending the social and economic cleavages that had developed within the ranks of Germany's middle-class electorate. The Democrats, for example, chose to structure their campaign around such national issues as the evacuation of the Rhineland, the establishment of a better understanding with Germany's European neighbors, the defense of the republican system of government against dictatorial schemes from the Left and Right, and the creation of a unitary national state aimed at ending the revenue losses caused by the duplication of governmental functions at the state and national levels. Other issues on which the Democrats sought to focus their campaign included a defense of liberal cultural policies with reference to the recent conflict over the national school bill and a reform of Weimar's electoral law that would place the individual candidate and not his party at the center of the electoral process.[42] Economic issues, on the other hand, played a conspicuously subordinate role in Democratic propaganda for the 1928 elections. For although the Democrats did not hesitate to defend their party's record in promoting the welfare of specific social groups such as the white-collar class, the civil service, the peasantry, or even the independent middle class,[43] they nevertheless hoped to elevate the campaign to a higher plane by placing primary emphasis upon issues of a political rather than economic nature.[44]

If the DDP hoped to divert voter attention away from the economic issues that the special interest parties had thrust into the center of the campaign, the same could be said, though to a somewhat lesser extent, of the German People's Party. To be sure, the leaders of the DVP had always been far more consistent in their support of middle-class economic interests than their counterparts in the DDP, and they could point with pride to the role they had played in securing the passage of legislation beneficial to the social groups represented by their party. Still, they were extremely concerned about the inroads that the Business Party had made into the ranks of the DVP's middle-class electorate and feared that Hepp's recent defection to the CNBLP might result in the loss of what remained of their party's badly decimated agrarian wing.[45] To counter the threat of special interest parties like the WP and CNBLP, party strategists tried to capitalize upon Stresemann's popularity as German foreign minister with slogans such as "What are the other candidates to you / You'll vote like Gustav Stresemann too."[46] At the same time, they drew special attention not only to the role the DVP had played in the passage of the white-collar insurance program in the summer of 1927 and the civil servant salary reform later that fall but also to the party's persistent efforts on behalf of a tax reform that would reduce the financial burden of Germany's commercial middle class.[47] Nevertheless, the DVP's support for the controversial revaluation law in the summer of 1925, its failure to press for an end to the rent tax and other government controls over the housing industry, and the preferential treatment that the German export industry had received in the various trade treaties that Stresemann had negotiated since the beginning of 1925 had done much to alienate the party's potential supporters in the urban and rural middle classes.

The success with which the DDP and DVP could fend off the attacks of special interest parties depended not only upon their ability to divert voter attention away from social and economic issues on which they felt particularly vulnerable but also upon the effectiveness of their national organizations. The

Democrats had originally envisioned a comprehensive campaign effort embracing not only conventional devices such as public rallies, illustrated fliers, and marches by republican organizations but also relatively sophisticated techniques of mass agitation such as films, loudspeakers, and recordings.[48] But while the campaign the DDP had planned for the 1928 Reichstag elections was as modern in conception as that of any other political party, its success presupposed the existence of a strong national organization capable of sustaining a concerted propaganda effort over an extended period of time. Although the Democrats had launched a campaign to revitalize their party's national organization at a conference of the party's regional secretaries in Bad Eilsen in the fall of 1927,[49] party leaders were unable to solve the financial woes that had perenially plagued the DDP since the beginning of the 1920s. The DDP had formed a special finance committee in the summer of 1927, but efforts to raise the money necessary for the party's modernization foundered on the reluctance of the DDP's financial backers to contribute more than they were already accustomed to giving.[50] As the party's financial difficulties persisted into the spring of 1928, the leaders of the DDP were forced to enter the campaign with an organization incapable of supporting the massive propaganda effort that they had orginally envisioned.

Though cast in the mold of a classical *Honoratiorenpartei* to a far greater extent than the DDP, the People's Party started the campaign for the 1928 Reichstag elections with both its organization and its finances in substantially better shape than those of the DDP. Not only had all but a few of the DVP's district organizations succeeded in liquidating most of the debt they had accumulated over the course of the past four years,[51] but in the spring of 1927 the leaders of the Ruhr industrial establishment had begun to provide the DVP and DNVP with semiannual contributions of 50,000 marks apiece to finance the operations of their respective national organizations.[52] In early 1928 a group of twelve Ruhr industrialists known as the "Ruhrlade" established a special fund in the name of Friedrich Springorum, director of the Hoesch Iron and Steel Works (Eisen- und Stahlwerke Hoesch A.G.) in Dortmund, to finance candidates from the various bourgeois parties in the upcoming Reichstag elections.[53] Although efforts to centralize the allocation of industrial campaign funds for the 1928 Reichstag elections in the hands of the Ruhrlade proved impracticable,[54] big business contributed more than 1,350,000 marks to individual candidates and the leaders of various bourgeois parties for use in the 1928 campaign. Of the major contributions that the Ruhrlade, the Curatorium, the chemical industry's Kalle Committee, and various banks placed at the disposal of the bourgeois parties for use in the campaign, more than half— or approximately 730,000 marks—went either to the DVP's national headquarters in Berlin or to candidates seeking election on the DVP ticket, whereas the Nationalists and Democrats had to content themselves with 327,000 and

209,000 marks respectively.[55] While this may have provided the DVP with an initial advantage in its rivalry with the DDP and other middle parties, it also favored the nomination of industrial candidates at the district level of the DVP's national organization in such a way that the party's integrity as a spokesman for middle-class economic interests was severely compromised.[56]

In spite of the relatively generous support they received from the industrial establishment, neither the DVP nor any other of Germany's traditional bourgeois parties was able to withstand the assault of special interest parties in the May 1928 Reichstag elections. Widely hailed as a triumph for Germany's republican forces, the outcome of the elections was characterized by a sharp swing to the left that saw both the Social Democrats and Communists score impressive gains at the polls. At the same time, all of the established bourgeois parties, including the Center and DNVP, sustained heavy losses. Yet contrary to the general impression created by a superficial analysis of the election results, the losses suffered by the more established bourgeois parties stemmed not so much from defections to the two working-class parties as from a combination of middle-class voter apathy and the appeal of special interest parties like the WP and CNBLP. Voter abstention reached a record high in the 1928 Reichstag elections as more than one-fourth of all eligible voters failed to go to the polls. In the meantime, middle-class splinter parties had captured nearly 12 percent of the popular vote, or more than twice as much as they had received in the last national elections in December 1924. Not only did the Business Party more than double the popular vote it had received four years earlier and increase its representation in the Reichstag from eleven to twenty-three deputies, but the Christian-National Peasants and Farmers' Party and the German Peasants' Party received a combined total of more than 1 million votes and elected seventeen deputies to the Reichstag. By the same token, the People's Justice Party polled nearly half a million votes in the 1928 Reichstag elections, although peculiarities of the Weimar electoral law prevented the VRP from receiving the full complement of parliamentary mandates to which it would have been entitled under a system of absolute proportional representation. All told, more than 830,000 votes—enough to have elected an additional fourteen deputies had they gone to one of the larger political parties—were cast for parties that, as a result of their small size, failed to receive so much as a single mandate.[57]

Between them, the two liberal parties lost a total of more than 700,000 votes and saw their share of the popular vote decline from 16.2 percent in December 1924 to 13.5 percent in 1928. In the DDP's case, this amounted to the loss of 21.7 percent of its December 1924 vote and seven of its thirty-two seats in the Reichstag. In explaining their party's disappointing performance at the polls, the Democrats were quick to concede that the broad national issues around which they had tried to structure their campaign no longer excited the imagination of Germany's middle-class electorate. As Koch-Weser lamented at a meeting of the DDP's executive committee on 14 June, neither the party's campaign for a reform of Germany's federal structure nor its vigorous defense of liberal principles during the recent conflict over the national school bill had struck a responsive chord with the DDP's potential supporters.[58] In their failure to gauge the mood of the electorate, the Democrats had not only alienated significant sectors of the German middle class but had left themselves vulnerable to the agitation of special interest parties. The party's losses were disproportionately heavy in southwest Germany where a particularly high rate of voter abstention made itself felt, in Silesia where the German Peasants' Party scored significant gains among the local peasant population, and in Schleswig-Holstein where the Business Party made its first appearance in a national campaign. By the same token, the DDP suffered losses significantly higher than those it suffered in other parts of the country throughout central Germany and, with the exception of Cologne-Aachen, on the left bank of the Rhine, while in Berlin it lost virtually a third of the vote it had received four years earlier.[59] Although the specific reason may have differed from one district to another, the common denominator underlying all of these losses was the apathy and demoralization that more than a decade of unrelenting economic hardship and political impotence had produced within the ranks of the DDP's middle-class electorate.[60]

The same factors were also responsible for the unexpectedly heavy losses sustained by the German People's Party. The leaders of the DVP had originally entered the campaign with hopes of scoring major gains at the expense of the DNVP, whose two stints in the government had done much to nullify its appeal as an opposition party. Moreover, Stresemann had hoped that his diplomatic triumphs abroad would translate into electoral success at home as more and more voters recognized the wisdom of his foreign policy. But for Stresemann and his associates, this proved to be a fatal misreading of the electoral mood, as the DVP lost more than 300,000 votes and saw its strength in the Reichstag slip from fifty-one to forty-five deputies. In reflecting upon his party's defeat at the polls, Stresemann was quick to bemoan the low rate of voter participation throughout the country.[61] While there was a clear correlation between voter abstention and the DVP's poor showing in several of the areas where the party suffered its heaviest losses, a factor of perhaps even greater significance was the success of special interest parties. For example, the DVP lost nearly 94,000 votes in the three Saxon districts, where it and the other bourgeois parties had been the target of a particularly aggressive campaign by the Business Party since the middle of the decade. It lost another 32,000 votes in Hesse-Nassau, where Hepp's defection to the CNBLP had cost it the support of small and middle-sized farmers throughout the district. Although the DVP actually managed to improve upon its performance in the December 1924 elections in nine of Germany's thirty-five election districts, the success of special interest parties like the WP and CNBLP combined with the apathy about which Stresemann had complained to inflict losses of between 10 and 15 percent in traditional party strongholds such as Brunswick, Thuringia, and the Palatinate. Accordingly, the DVP's net losses in the Reich as a whole amounted to 12.1 percent of its December 1924 vote.[62]

The outcome of the 1928 Reichstag elections revealed the extent to which Germany's middle-class voter was motivated not by nationalism or ideology, but by economic self-interest. By no means, however, was this phenomenon confined to Germany's liberal electorate as both the DNVP and Center sustained suprisingly heavy losses of their own. In the DNVP's case, these were particularly devastating, with the party losing nearly 2 million votes—or 31 percent of what it had received in the last national elections—and 30 of its 103 seats in the Reichstag. Like the leaders of the two liberal parties, the Nationalists were also quick to complain about the "materialistic attitude of broad sectors of the German nation" and deplored the preference that all too many of their former voters had shown for special-interest parties like the WP and CNBLP.[63] Nor was the Center able to escape this trend. In contrast to the modest gains it had registered in each of the 1924 Reichstag elections, in May 1928 the Center lost over 400,000 votes—or 9.9 percent of its December 1924 vote—and six of its sixty-seven deputies. Unlike the other established bourgeois parties, however, the Center was generally successful in retaining the support of its rural voters. Still, it experienced surprisingly heavy losses in predominantly urban areas, where its support of the 1927 civil servant salary reform had severely damaged its standing with both the more traditional elements of the Catholic middle class and the Christian labor movement. As a result, both the WP and the Social Democrats were able to register significant gains at the Center's expense.[64]

Although the 1928 Reichstag elections had taken place in a climate of relative economic and political stability and had returned a republican majority for the first time since 1919, the outcome of the elections could hardly have been more disturbing to supporters of Germany's republican regime. The gains that special interest parties registered at the expense of the more traditional, ideologically oriented bourgeois parties indicated that the German party system was in an advanced stage of structural disintegration and that a reform of the Weimar party system was essential to the survival of the republic. This, in turn, was accompanied by a dramatic intensification of the legitimacy crisis that had plagued the Weimar party system ever since the stabilization of the mark at the end of 1923–24. For just as the emergence of special interest parties in the second half of the 1920s implicitly challenged the legitimacy of a system that had failed to provide adequate protection for the material interests of Germany's middle-class electorate, now even those most strongly committed to the preservation of Germany's republican institutions were beginning to question the legitimacy of a system whose increasing fragmentation threatened to make the definition and articulation of Germany's national interest impossible.

PART FIVE

At the Crossroads
1928–1930

CHAPTER TWENTY-THREE

Liberal Unity in Revival and Eclipse

THE 1928 REICHSTAG ELECTIONS constituted a watershed in the history of Weimar liberalism. Not only were the leaders of the DVP and DDP alarmed at the severity of the losses their parties had suffered at the polls, but the outcome of the election was to instill new life in the movement for a united liberal party. Characterized by repeated appeals for a regeneration of German liberalism and a reform of the German party system, the next two years were to determine whether or not liberalism would survive as a viable force in Germany's political life. This period was also to witness the death of Germany's most prominent liberal statesman, the outbreak of the world economic crisis, and a sharp swing to the right within all of Germany's nonsocialist parties. At the same time, the collapse of the Great Coalition and the appointment of the Brüning government in the spring of 1930 brought the chronic crisis of German parliamentarism to a dramatic climax and underscored the need for a reform and reorganization of the Weimar party system if effective representative government was to survive. For the leaders of the German liberal movement, their "hour of destiny," as a lead editorial in the *Kölnische Zeitung* from the summer of 1928 so aptly put it, had arrived.[1]

The outcome of the 1928 Reichstag elections came as a bitter shock to the leaders of the German liberal establishment and prompted them to reexamine the situation in which their movement found itself. The first to address this problem, however, was not a spokesman for either of the two liberal parties but Theodor Wolff, the factious and controversial editor of the *Berliner Tageblatt*. In an editorial that appeared on the front page of the *Tageblatt* exactly one week after the election, Wolff appealed for the creation of a united republican party under the joint leadership of Stresemann, Joseph Wirth, and an unnamed Democrat. Embracing the progressive elements from the DVP, DDP, and Center, this party would seek to unite the German bourgeoisie into a solid phalanx capable of cooperating with the Social Democrats on the basis of complete parity.[2] Wolff's appeal, however, had little in common with the idea of a united liberal party and met with immediate skepticism from the leaders of the two liberal parties. Particularly outspoken in his criticism of Wolff's proposal was the DDP's Erich Koch-Weser, who dismissed the idea of a united republican party as a utopian fantasy that bore no relation to the realities of Weimar politics and publicly reaffirmed his own preference for the establishment of closer ties between the existing liberal parties.[3]

Of greater immediate impact than Wolff's proposal was the revival of the Liberal Association. Since the formation of the fourth Marx government in January 1927, the Liberal Association had languished on the periphery of Germany's political life. The association's annual convention, which took place in Berlin in the second week of March 1927, was a particularly bland affair that paled in comparison to the elaborate celebration that Stresemann and the leaders of the DVP had organized for the same weekend to commemorate the sixtieth anniversary of the founding of the National Liberal Party.[4] In an attempt to overcome its increasing isolation from the two parties that it had originally hoped to unite, the Liberal Association tried to focus attention on the cultural values that all liberals, regardless of their party affiliation, presumably held in common by launching a vigorous attack against the national school bill introduced by the Marx-Keudell government in the fall of 1927.[5] At the same time, the association tried, though without success, to negotiate an alliance between the DDP, DVP, Business Party, and Bavarian Peasants' League for the Bavarian state elections that were scheduled to take place in early 1928[6] and sponsored the creation of a Liberal Club as a counterpart to the fashionable Herrenklub of Germany's conservative political elite.[7]

The collapse of the Marx government in the spring of 1928 and the defeat of the two liberal parties in the May Reichstag elections provided the leaders of the Liberal Association with a fresh opportunity to break out of the isolation that had plagued their efforts for the past year and a half. It was with this in mind that the LV decided to abolish the dual chairmanship that the DDP's Otto Fischbeck and the DVP's Ernst Richter had held since the end of 1925 in favor of a single chairmanship to be held by an individual unencumbered by close ties to either of the two liberal parties. The person whom the leaders of the Liberal Association selected for this post was August Weber, a former National Liberal who had gone over to the DDP in the winter of 1918.[8] Since his retirement from national political life at the end of 1918, Weber had turned his attention to the German business world, where he had prospered both as a small industrialist and as a private landowner. Weber's brand of liberalism, therefore, tended to be highly pragmatic and emphasized the need to protect those social strata upon which the German liberal movement depended for the bulk of its material support—namely the artisan, the peasant, the merchant, and the civil servant—as the first priority of liberal social policy. For Weber, the future of German liberalism depended upon a clear recognition of its class character and a reaffirmation of its historic commitment to the social and economic welfare of those upon whose support it ultimately rested.[9]

Under Weber's tutelage, the Liberal Association moved quickly to take advantage of the shock wave that the outcome of the 1928 Reichstag elections had sent through the two liberal parties. The association's immediate goal was to bring about the formation of a parliamentary coalition or *Fraktionsgemein-*

schaft between the DDP and DVP as a first step toward the eventual creation of a united liberal party.[10] Before his election to the chairmanship of the Liberal Association became official, Weber entered into exploratory negotiations with the leaders of the two liberal parties and was rewarded by promises of cooperation from both Stresemann and Koch-Weser. Not only did the two liberal leaders express a general willingness to cooperate with the LV in its efforts to foster better relations between their respective parties, but they agreed to serve along with the DVP's Wilhelm Kahl as the association's honorary cochairmen.[11] This gesture of support was underpinned by the fact that Karl Trucksaeß and Werner Stephan, the managing secretaries of the DVP and DDP respectively, also agreed to serve on the Liberal Association's executive committee.[12] All of this testified to the sobering effect the outcome of the 1928 Reichstag elections had had upon the leadership of the German liberal movement and encouraged the association in its hopes that "the electoral misfortunes of the two liberal parties might translate into the good fortune of liberalism itself."[13]

It was in this spirit that the leaders of the Liberal Association decided to hold a special "Liberal Day" in the Reichstag on the afternoon of 1 July. The purpose of this convention was to bring prominent personalities from all walks of life together in an impressive demonstration for the idea of a united liberal party.[14] But while Weber was successful in lining up the support of influential liberal newspapers such as the *Kölnische Zeitung,* the *Deutsche Allgemeine Zeitung,* and the *Berliner Börsen-Courier,*[15] his efforts to secure the cooperation of prominent representatives from the two liberal parties proved generally disappointing. At a meeting of the DVP Reichstag delegation on 28 June, Paul Moldenhauer spoke out strongly against the Liberal Association and urged the adoption of a resolution that dissociated the DVP from the agitation for a united liberal party. Moldenhauer's recommendation received strong support from Ernst Scholz, who as chairman of the DVP Reichstag delegation argued that the party was still bound by the resolution that the DVP central executive committee had adopted in May 1925 identifying the German People's Party as the only legitimate heir to the national and liberal traditions of the old NLP. While Scholz conceded that this did not necessarily preclude the formation of a parliamentary coalition between the DDP and DVP, he insisted that a merger of the two liberal parties was completely out of the question. Consequently, members of the delegation were free to join the association or participate in its so-called Liberal Day, but only so long as the association did not engage in any activity that might lead to the founding of a new political party.[16]

The situation within the German Democratic Party was equally frustrating. For although Koch-Weser had come to the conclusion after the 1928 Reichstag elections that Germany could no longer afford the luxury of two liberal parties, his decision to serve along with Stresemann and Kahl as one of the Liberal

Association's honorary cochairmen had evoked sharp criticism from the leaders of the DDP's left wing.[17] The party's most persistent critic of liberal unity
was Anton Erkelenz, who not only declined Weber's invitation to participate in
the association's Liberal Day but bemoaned the confusion that the agitation for
a united liberal party had caused within the very parties the association sought
to unite.[18] The situation within the party threatened to reach crisis proportions
at a meeting of the DDP executive committee on 14–15 June, as Peter Stubmann, Richard Frankfurter, and Georg Bernhard—all respected leaders of the
party's left wing—challenged Koch-Weser's pessimistic prognosis of the
DDP's political future and demanded that he immediately dissociate himself
from the campaign for a united liberal party.[19] The conflict carried over into
the DDP Reichstag delegation, where Koch-Weser was hard pressed to prevent
the passage of a resolution that expressly prohibited any member of the
delegation from participating in the association's Liberal Day.[20] By this time
Koch-Weser had become so distressed by the persistence with which the
leaders of the DDP's left wing attacked his involvement in the Liberal Association that he decided to excuse himself from the festivities it had planned for
1 July.[21]

Although many of Germany's leading liberal politicians were discouraged
from taking part in the association's Liberal Day, the demonstration still
attracted the presence of over 400 representatives of Germany's liberal elite,
including such luminaries as the new minister of defense, Wilhelm Groener,
and the vice-president of the Reichstag, Siegfried von Kardorff. The keynote
speaker was the DVP's Wilhelm Kahl, who read a telegram from the ailing
Stresemann that expressed his full support for the association's efforts on
behalf of a better understanding between the liberal parties.[22] Kahl was followed by a host of speakers who tended to concentrate upon one of two
problems. Some, like Rochus von Rheinbaben and Johannes Schröder, addressed themselves to the problem of the younger generation and lamented the
fact that the German liberal movement seemed to have lost the support of those
between twenty-five and forty years of age. It was only by appealing to the
idealism and political imagination of the younger generation, they said, that
the movement for liberal unity could ever succeed. But exhortations to this
effect were overshadowed by a fundamental difference of opinion that surfaced
in the debate over social and economic policy. For whereas historian Friedrich
Meinecke contended that the "great liberal party of the future" must be "social-
minded" and strive to represent the nation in all of its social and economic
diversity, Weber insisted that the success of the German liberal movement
ultimately depended upon the extent to which it was able to protect the material
interests of those social groups from which it had traditionally recruited the
bulk of its popular support. To Weber, the havoc that first the war and then the
inflation had wrought upon the classes that formed the social backbone of the

German liberal movement required a fundamental reorientation in liberal social policy and a redefinition of liberalism's relationship to the material interests of its predominantly middle-class supporters.[23]

The differences of opinion that had surfaced in the debate between Meinecke and Weber represented the two horns of a dilemma that had plagued the German liberal movement ever since the middle of the previous century. Could a party of the liberal bourgeoisie represent, promote, and defend its own social interests and yet at the same time work for the reconciliation of conflicting social interests within the framework of the state without compromising the welfare of those it sought to represent? Or, in other words, could a united liberal party be both bourgeois and social at the same time? The resolution that the Liberal Association released at the conclusion of its Liberal Day, however, left this question essentially unresolved, calling merely for a "social liberalism that guaranteed the free development of the individual personality" and denouncing the welfare state for "having suffocated the individual's sense of personal responsibility in a feeling of riskless complacency." On the question of social and economic policy, the resolution confined itself to a general condemnation of state socialism for having destroyed the more traditional elements of the German middle class at the same time that it had consigned those who belonged to Germany's new middle class of civil servants and white-collar employees to a position of permanent social and economic dependence.[24] The very vagueness with which the association approached the plight of the German middle class was itself symptomatic of the uneasiness that Meinecke and other liberals who subscribed to an idealistic theory of the state felt about the representation of material economic interests.

Encouraged by the generally favorable response that their campaign for a united liberal party had found in the liberal press, the leaders of the Liberal Association envisaged a wide range of activities for the summer of 1928 that would enable their organization to broaden its base of popular support. Among the specific measures the Association had in mind were the appointment of a special committee for the purpose of drafting a comprehensive social and economic program and the creation of a separate organization for the younger generation. More importantly, the association also decided, in what amounted to a dramatic departure from its previous policy, to proceed with the formation of state and local chapters throughout the country. Except in Bavaria, where a state organization had been founded in January 1927, the LV had been careful to refrain from such activity for fear that it might be interpreted as a prelude to the founding of a new political party. Now, in the wake of the severe losses that the two liberal parties had suffered in the 1928 Reichstag elections, all such scruple had suddenly vanished. The success of these projects, however, required considerable sums of money that the association did not have at its disposal. Weber himself estimated that at least an additional 30,000 marks would be necessary for the association to fulfill its goals through the summer and early fall of 1928. If the association failed to raise this money, Weber warned, it would have no alternative but to curtail its activities just as the movement for liberal unity seemed to be gaining momentum.[25]

While financial difficulties continued to plague the leaders of the Liberal Association for the remainder of the year, a more serious problem—and one upon which the success of their efforts to create a united liberal party ultimately depended—was the lack of cooperation from the DDP and DVP. The cacophony of protest that had greeted Koch-Weser's initial overtures on behalf of a united liberal party had done little to assuage the deep-seated pessimism he felt about the future of his own party, and he remained determined to cooperate with the association insofar as that was compatible with his position as DDP party chairman. In this respect, Koch-Weser was joined by other prominent Democrats such as Hermann Dietrich, who had just been appointed minister of agriculture in the new national government, and Peter Reinhold, who had served as finance minister throughout most of 1926.[26] Even Carl Petersen, the DDP's national chairman from 1919 to 1924, recognized the hopelessness of the situation in which his party currently found itself and lent his name to the ranks of those who supported the creation of a united liberal party.[27] But the willingness of Koch-Weser and his associates to participate in the founding of a united liberal party was contingent upon a clarification of the situation within the DVP. For while Koch-Weser's relations with Stresemann had undergone such a remarkable improvement over the previous four years that they now found themselves in essential agreement on most of the basic issues confronting their respective parties,[28] the Democrats remained deeply suspicious of the elements on the DVP's right wing and were adamantly opposed to their inclusion in a united liberal party.[29]

Like Koch-Weser, Stresemann too had become discouraged about the future of the German liberal movement and privately conceded that the time when Germany could afford the luxury of two liberal parties had passed. Shortly after the association's Liberal Day, Stresemann informed Weber of his willingness to cooperate with the LV and volunteered to assist him in organizing a series of informal dinners aimed at bringing the leaders of the two liberal parties closer together.[30] Stresemann's willingness to become more actively involved in the association's efforts to foster closer relations between the two liberal parties was directly related to a deterioration of the situation within his own party's Reichstag delegation. The outcome of the 1928 Reichstag elections had greatly strengthened the position of the industrial interests on the DVP's right wing, and they were determined to use their influence within the DVP Reichstag delegation to block their party's participation in a coalition government with the Social Democrats. On 12 June the SPD's Hermann Müller had been entrusted with the task of forming a new government based on the parties of the Great Coalition, but his efforts to reach an accommodation with the DVP had been repeatedly frustrated by the intransigence of Scholz and the leaders of the DVP Reichstag delegation. A complete breakdown of negotiations seemed imminent when on 13 June the DVP delegations to the Reichstag and Prussian Landtag issued a joint communiqué that made their party's participation in the Great Coalition in the Reich contingent upon a reorganization of the state government in Prussia.[31] When Otto Braun, the Social Democratic minister president of Prussia, refused to go along with the DVP's demands that it be invited to join the Prussian government, Müller's efforts to form a new government based upon the Great Coalition were officially abandoned on the morning of 22 June.[32]

Stresemann was convalescing in Bühlerhöhe near Baden-Baden when he received news of the way in which Scholz and the leaders of the DVP Reichstag delegation had sabotaged Müller's efforts to form a new government. Distressed by the obstinance of his own party's right wing, Stresemann tried to break the deadlock that had developed in Berlin by sending Müller a telegram in which he proposed that the new government be organized as a "cabinet of personalities" without formal commitments to the parties which were represented in it.[33] While Stresemann's initiative cleared the way for the subsequent installation of a new government consisting of representatives from the SPD to the DVP, his "Shot from Bühlerhöhe" triggered a virtual rebellion within the DVP Reichstag delegation. At a meeting of the delegation's executive committee on the morning of 26 June, Scholz declared that Stresemann's interference in the delegation's affairs had made it impossible for him to continue as its chairman, but he was eventually dissuaded from resigning by repeated declarations of solidarity from other members of the committee.[34] That evening a group of veteran deputies under the leadership of Alfred Zapf met in Scholz's absence to fashion a compromise that would repair the damage that Stresemann's telegram to Müller had done to his relations with the delegation.[35] This resulted in three resolutions that, much to the disappointment of Stresemann's more intransigent opponents on the DVP's right wing, were subsequently approved at a meeting of the delegation on the afternoon of 27 June. While the first of these merely reaffirmed the delegation's confidence in Scholz's performance as its chairman and commended him for the role he had played in the recent cabinet negotiations, the second chastised Stresemann—by implication if not by name—by stressing that effective leadership of the party presupposed consultation and close cooperation with the delegation and its duly elected leadership. The third resolution, which like the second was adopted only after a bitter struggle between Stresemann's supporters and his opponents on the DVP's right wing, approved the participation of Stresemann and the DVP's Julius Curtius in Müller's cabinet of personalities, but reserved the delegation's right to support or reject the new government as it saw fit.[36]

Though conceived in a spirit of compromise, the three resolutions that the DVP Reichstag delegation adopted at its caucus on the afternoon of 27 June represented a direct challenge to Stresemann's control of the party and underscored the growing rift that had developed between him and the leaders of the delegation. Refusing to submit to what he called the "tyranny of the delegation,"[37] Stresemann responded with a vigorous defense of his position as party leader that drew heavily upon traditional liberal values. The essence of Stresemann's liberalism was rooted in his belief that the individual and his sense of personal responsibility constituted the ultimate foundation of all political activity. According to Stresemann, it was his responsibility and his alone to decide as the DVP's duly elected chairman whether or not he was to serve in a particular government. Under no circumstances did the delegation or any other body within the party have the right to usurp that responsibility. In attaching its own conditions to the DVP's entry into the government, however, the delegation was trying to subvert Stresemann's freedom to act according to his own sense of responsibility by subordinating him to the demands of the organization as a whole. To Stresemann, this represented a radical departure from the concept of individual responsibility that lay at the heart of the German liberal tradition and a fateful step toward the creation of a democracy that was no longer liberal, but merely formal, in character.[38]

The DVP Reichstag delegation steadfastly refused to modify the language of the three resolutions it had adopted on 27 June in spite of Stresemann's threats to resign from the party if this were not done. At the same time, Scholz was able to placate Stresemann by persuading all but the party's most intractible opponents of the Great Coalition to join the other government parties in supporting Müller's cabinet of personalities in its initial vote of confidence on 5 July. Still, Stresemann remained deeply embittered over the way in which the delegation had sought to sabotage his leadership of the party and began to prepare a series of organizational reforms that would prevent the recurrence of a similar crisis in the fall.[39] Stresemann also began to take a more active interest in the efforts to bring about a reform and realignment of the German party system. But here Stresemann was thinking not so much in terms of a one-sided merger with the DDP as of a broader realignment of political forces that, he hoped, would ultimately include the left wing of the DNVP as well. "What looms before me," Stresemann wrote to Scholz as the crisis within the DVP Reichstag delegation began to abate, "is the ideal of a large bourgeois-liberal party that will embrace not only the reasonable elements from the Democratic Party, but also the left wing of the German Nationalists. . . ."[40] "If we could ever succeed in absorbing the left wing of the German Nationalists and the right wing of the Democrats," he mused in a similar vein in a letter to his old friend Rudolph Schneider, "then we would finally have the large bourgeois party we have always needed to counterbalance the Center."[41]

Stresemann's ruminations from the summer of 1928 reflected his growing awareness of the need for a fundamental realignment of the German party system and for the consolidation of those moderate bourgeois forces willing to cooperate on the basis of the existing form of government. The unfortunate irony of this situation, however, was not only that the recent conflict between Stresemann and the DVP Reichstag delegation had done much to dampen whatever interest Koch-Weser and his associates had shown in the idea of a united liberal party[42] but also that Stresemann's failing health as well as his desire to preserve peace within his party made him extremely wary of undertaking any sort of overt initiative on behalf of the Liberal Association's efforts to foster closer relations between the two liberal parties.[43] While this made it possible for Weber to blame his own organization's lack of progress since the early summer of 1928 upon Stresemann's indecisiveness as leader of the DVP, a far more immediate problem was the LV's inability to solve the financial difficulties that had plagued it for the first four years of its existence. Not only did the ambitious agenda that the association had set for itself following the defeat of the two liberal parties in the 1928 Reichstag elections presuppose substantially more operating capital than the association had at its disposal, but Weber's hopes that his reputation as an economic expert would provide the association with easy access to the financial resources of big business remained essentially unfulfilled. As a result, the association was unable to sustain the momentum the Liberal Day had generated and was forced to curtail virtually all of the activities it had planned for the rest of the summer.[44] By the following spring the Liberal Association had become so moribund that even Stresemann, having just weathered another conflict with the party's right wing, could only lament its virtual disappearance from the German political scene.[45]

The eclipse of the Liberal Association in the fall and early winter of 1928 was only one more symptom of the general malaise that gripped Germany's liberal institutions in the second half of the 1920s. This was accompanied by a sharp swing to the right within all of Germany's nonsocialist parties that threatened to overwhelm what still remained of the liberal movement. Essentially a reaction against the Social Democratic victory in the 1928 Reichstag elections, this swing manifested itself not only in the resurgence of the DVP's right wing and its challenge to Stresemann's control of the party, but also in the election of Alfred Hugenberg and Ludwig Kaas as national party chairmen of the DNVP and Center respectively. Hugenberg stood on the DNVP's extreme right wing, and his election to the party's national chairmanship in October 1928 signaled the definitive collapse of Stresemann's hopes that the Nationalists might still be won over to the support of the Weimar Republic. By the same token, the infamous "Fürstenwald Hate Declaration" that Elhard von Morozo-wicz of the Stahlhelm, a right-wing veterans' organization with an estimated

225,000 members, directed against the so-called Weimar system in September 1928 bore dramatic testimony to the renewed vigor of the forces that were to triumph with Hugenberg's election a month later. Although Stresemann had sought to maintain good relations with the Stahlhelm after its rise to national prominence in the second half of the 1920s, he realized that the Fürstenwald Hate Declaration made future cooperation impossible and urged those of his colleagues in the DVP Reichstag and Prussian Landtag delegations who still belonged to the veterans' organization to sever their ties as expeditiously as possible in hopes that this might trigger a general secession on the part of DVP members throughout the country.[46] Even Scholz, himself a member of the Stahlhelm, conceded that a break with the organization could no longer be avoided, and on 2 October he helped secure passage of a resolution in the DVP Reichstag delegation deploring the recent developments within the Stahlhelm and declaring that membership in it was no longer compatible with membership in the delegation.[47]

Appalled by the increasing radicalism of the German Right, Stresemann hoped to attract the support of those DNVP moderates who found it impossible to accept Hugenberg's leadership of the party by initiating a thorough reform of the DVP's national organization. While Stresemann's immediate objective was to strengthen the powers of the party chairman and the party executive committee so that a recurrence of the crisis that had erupted in the summer of 1928 would not be possible, he also sought to reduce the influence of the industrial interests that formed the nucleus of the DVP's right wing by providing the party's middle-class, white-collar, and working-class elements with a greater voice in the conduct of party affairs. Not only would this make the DVP more appealing to the more moderate elements within the DNVP, but it would also help attract the support of the younger generation and the great legion of middle-class voters who had become so profoundly alienated from the existing middle parties.[48] This goal received particularly strong support from Otto Thiel, who, as the party's chief liaison with the German white-collar movement, had become increasingly concerned that the DVP might fall under the domination of the industrial interests on the party's right wing. Thiel saw a clear parallel between his own position in the DVP and the recent attempts on the part of Hugenberg's supporters within the DNVP to have Walther Lambach, like himself an important official in the German National Union of Commercial Employees, expelled from the party for publicly questioning its commitment to monarchism at a time when realistic prospects for the restoration of the monarchy no longer existed.[49] Hopeful that it might be possible for the DVP to win the support of white-collar and working-class elements within the DNVP that felt threatened by Hugenberg's election to the party chairmanship, Thiel circulated a set of recommendations designed to curtail the influence of the party's industrial wing and transform the DVP from a one-sided interest party into a genuine *Volkspartei* capable of attracting support from all sectors of society.[50]

Stresemann won approval for his proposed reform of the DVP's national organization at a special meeting of the party's central executive committee in late November 1928, and a special sixteen-member committee under the chairmanship of Stresemann's longtime associate Adolf Kempkes was assigned the task of making preliminary recommendations for a reform of the party.[51] Before Stresemann and his supporters had an opportunity to act on any of these proposals, however, the party was convulsed by another internal crisis that both dramatized the need for organizational reform and struck at Stresemann's leadership of the party. In November 1928 Müller had reopened negotiations with the Center in an attempt to transform his government from a cabinet of personalities into a government of the Great Coalition. The leaders of the DVP Reichstag delegation seized upon this as an opportunity not only to renew their party's demands for a place in the Prussian government but also to attach new conditions in the area of tax and fiscal policy to their continued support of the Müller cabinet. The negotiations were further complicated by the fact that the recent election of prelate Ludwig Kaas to the chairmanship of the German Center Party had done much to heighten the differences that had always separated the Center and DVP on issues of cultural policy. Consequently, a serious deadlock threatened to develop when the leaders of the Prussian Center Party refused to go along with the DVP's demands for a reorganization of the Prussian government.[52] As it became clear that the most the Center was prepared to offer was a promise to reorganize the Prussian government after its own demands for a greater role in the Müller cabinet had been satisfied, the DVP Reichstag delegation voted unanimously to reject the Center's offer at a meeting on the afternoon of 5 February 1929.[53] On the following day the lone Centrist minister in the Müller cabinet resigned, thereby ending his party's support of the national government.

Although Stresemann held the Center and not the leaders of his own party's Reichstag delegation responsible for the stalemate that had developed in Berlin, he was greatly distressed by the collapse of the government coalition, particularly since he regarded political stability at home as essential to the success of the negotiations that he was about to begin in Paris for a revision of the Dawes Plan.[54] But just as it appeared that he might persuade Kaas and Otto Braun, the Social Democratic minister president of Prussia, to soften their opposition to the DVP's entry into the Prussian government,[55] the business interests on his party's right wing began to make difficulties of their own by adopting a resolution against new taxes at a meeting of the DVP's National Council for Commerce and Industry on the morning of 21 February.[56] Stresemann found himself almost completely isolated when, at a heated meeting of the DVP Reichstag delegation later that afternoon, representatives of the party's business wing joined forces with the leaders of the Prussian DVP to reject Braun's offer of a seat in the Prussian government.[57] Confronted by a determined majority that seemed intent upon sabotaging his efforts to reach a compromise with the Center and SPD, Stresemann scheduled an emergency meeting of the DVP central executive committee for 26 February in hopes that it, the most powerful body in the DVP party organization, would provide the mandate he needed to override the opposition to the existing governmental coalition that had surfaced in the party's parliamentary delegations.

The meeting of the DVP central executive committee on 26 February 1929 was to prove one of the bitterest experiences of Stresemann's long political career. He opened the meeting with a speech that was unquestionably one of the finest rhetorical performances of his life. Contending that Germany found herself in the midst of a severe parliamentary crisis that was much more than a mere crisis of confidence in the existing government, Stresemann returned to themes that he had first enunciated at the time of his conflict with the DVP Reichstag delegation in the summer of 1928. According to Stresemann, German parliamentarism had degenerated into a caricature of itself, as political parties and their parliamentary delegations tried to usurp the right of parliament itself to appoint and recall members of the government. What this represented was simply another manifestation of the fundamental evil of modern political life, namely the displacement of the individual by the organization. With reference to the current political crisis, Stresemann reminded his colleagues that special economic interests should not take precedence over the welfare of the nation as a whole and denounced the use of obstructionist tactics that threatened to undermine the vitality of Germany's parliamentary institutions. What Germany needed, argued Stresemann in conclusion, was a reform of parliamentarism, a reform that would insure "that the spirit of partisanship finds its limits in the necessities of German history, that it [parliament] overcomes the tendency toward the formation of formal rather than genuine majorities, and that, if all this fails on account of the parties themselves, then the call will sound: *res venit ad triaros* and responsible leaders will find the strength to govern, that is, to assume the leadership."[58]

Stresemann's speech represented a vigorous reaffirmation of the individualistic values that lay at the heart of his political creed. Yet for all of its passion and eloquence, Stresemann's speech had little impact upon his critics in the DVP central executive committee, many of whom treated him with open disrespect.[59] First Ernst Stendel from the DVP delegation to the Prussian Landtag, then Walther Jänecke and Hans Zehle from the DVP's "Central German Coalition," and finally Otto Hugo as one of the party's leading spokesmen for Ruhr economic interests assailed the Müller government for its mismanagement of German finances and denounced the efforts to transform the cabinet of personalities into a government of the Great Coalition with formal political commitments from the various government parties. As the mutiny against Stresemann's leadership of the party continued to build, Hugo introduced a resolution that tied the formation of the Great Coalition in the Reich to a reorganization of the Prussian state government and barred the DVP from entering any national government that refused to meet its demands for a sharp reduction in the level of government spending. Sensing that an embarrassing defeat was at hand, Stresemann retired with Scholz and the less intransigent of his opponents to fashion a compromise that both reaffirmed the DVP's commitment to the establishment of the Great Coalition and underscored its unwavering opposition to any tax increase. Anxious not to jeopardize the victory they had just won, Hugo and his supporters abandoned their offensive against Stresemann and accepted the compromise resolution that the party leadership offered as a substitute for the one introduced by Hugo.[60]

Although Stresemann had managed to salvage both the unity of his party and the government coalition, he remained deeply depressed over the situation within the DVP and began to contemplate his withdrawal from active political life. As the stalemate continued into the second and third weeks of March,[61] Stresemann gave vent to his frustration over his party's behavior in a series of letters to his closest associates within the DVP. Complaining that the DVP wanted out of the government so that it could pursue a policy of "national opposition" in the style of the Stahlhelm and Hugenberg, Stresemann suggested that it might be better for him to resign from the party so that it could be free to mimic the petty chauvinism of the radical Right.[62] Particularly revealing was the long letter he wrote to the party patriarch Wilhelm Kahl. Conceding the existence of a profound split between himself and the rest of the party, Stresemann argued that the DVP was "no longer a party of Weltanschauung, but a party of industrial interests." Not only had the triumph of special economic interests led to the virtual eclipse of the DVP's liberal ideals, but, more tragically, it had prevented the party from fulfilling the mission that history had thrust upon it. "I wanted to be," wrote Stresemann in words that mirrored his disillusionment, "the bridge between the old and new Germanies. And, to be sure, a part of our party has also recognized this as its historical mission. But others can only play the old gramophone records and want to hear the same old melodies over and over again."[63]

The embarrassment that Stresemann suffered at the hands of his party's right wing only strengthened his conviction that a reform and realignment of the German party system was essential to the survival of effective parliamentary government. His speech before the DVP central executive committeee represented a bitter indictment of the way in which German parliamentarism had developed since the founding of the Weimar Republic and reflected the growing disenchantment that the leaders of the German liberal movement had come to feel toward the system of government in whose establishment they had played such a prominent role. The defeat of the two liberal parties in the 1928 Reichstag elections, the difficulties that had accompanied the formation of the Müller government later that summer, and the parliamentary stalemate that had devloped in the spring of 1929 all bore dramatic testimony to the deepening crisis of Germany's liberal order and underscored the need for a reform of Weimar parliamentarism that would free it from the destructive grip of special economic interests. But the leaders of the German liberal movement seemed too exhausted—one might even say too compromised—by the burden of responsibility to provide the spark that might kindle such a reform. From where, then, might that spark come?

CHAPTER TWENTY-FOUR

The Mission of the Younger Generation

IN HIS SPEECH BEFORE the DVP central executive committee on 26 February 1929 Stresemann touched briefly upon one of the most perplexing problems confronting the leaders of Germany's liberal parties. "One of the worst signs of the current situation," he remarked toward the close of his speech, "is the fact that our youth has remained aloof from party life."[1] By no means, however, was this problem confined to Stresemann's own party. For by the middle of the 1920s the alienation of bourgeois youth from all forms of political activity had become a prominent feature of Germany's political culture. This represented the culmination of a process that had begun during the last decades of the Second Empire with the emergence of a youth movement that rejected the social and moral conventions of Wilhelmine Germany in hopes of investing life with a deeper meaning through fellowship and communion with nature. Though avowedly apolitical in its initial manifestations such as the *Wandervögel*, the German youth movement was generally contemptuous of the way in which Germany had developed since the founding of the Second Empire and espoused a disdain for modern political life that was inspired by the *völkisch* ideas of Paul de Lagarde and Julius Langbehn. With the approach of war, the movement became increasingly politicized, although attempts to unite the older members of the youth movement under the aegis of the Free German Youth (Freideutsche Jugend) in a common crusade for the reformation of German public life were doomed to failure by the lack of an adequate ideological consensus. Yet in spite of its general aloofness from the social and political institutions of Wilhelmine Germany, the German youth movement remained fervently nationalistic and received the call to arms in the summer of 1914 with an enthusiasm that was to prove suicidal.[2]

For all intents and purposes, the outbreak of World War I marked the end of the German youth movement. The unbridled enthusiasm with which Germany's bourgeois youth greeted the declaration of war quickly dissolved into the dark despair of trench warfare. But if the reality of war shattered apocalyptic visions of a new Germany in which the hypocrisy and artificiality of the past were to be swept away in the heat of battle, disillusionment was soon compounded by the bitterness of defeat.[3] Many of those who had served at the front found it difficult to make the adjustment to civilian life after the end of the war and experienced a general sense of anomie that was only heightened by the collapse of the Second Empire and the revolutionary turmoil of the postwar period. But much to their dismay, the war and revolution had done little to dislodge the traditional patriarchies in politics and business, with the result that they soon found avenues for advancement in these fields all but closed.[4] At the same time, efforts to revive the German youth movement in more or less the form in which it had existed before the war failed, in large part because of the sharp ideological divisions that defeat and revolution had produced in the ranks of Germany's bourgeois youth.[5] Despairing of modern life and hoping to recapture the excitement and camaraderie they had experienced at the front, disaffected veterans, including many who had been active in the prewar youth movement, began to regroup in a new form of organization called the *Bund*. But whereas the *Wandervögel* had allowed its members the freedom necessary for self-discovery and personal development, the *Bund* was much more rigid in its basic organizational concept and demanded the complete subordination of the individual to the welfare of the group as a whole. Loyalty and obedience to the leader constituted the basic principles upon which the *bündisch* movement of the postwar period ultimately rested.[6]

Although many of the *Bünde* that flourished in Germany after the end of World War I abstained from partisan political activity as much as possible, those that became politically involved professed little loyalty to the republican system of government. If the programs of the more politically active *Bünde* had any sort of common denominator, it resided in a vague commitment to the *Volksgemeinschaft* as an alternative to the fragmented and atomized character of modern political life. Parliamentary democracy was held responsible for having intensified the social, confessional, and regional antagonisms that existed within the German nation, and political parties were dismissed as manifestations of the national divisiveness that accompanied the introduction of parliamentary government.[7] By the same token, the *Bünde* also criticized the triumph of egoism in the economic sphere and espoused a clear preference for the return to some sort of precapitalist economic order. Based upon the "front experience" and what the leaders of the *Bünde* fondly referred to as the "socialism of the trenches," such an order would be cooperative rather than competitive, organic rather than mechanical, and collectivist rather than individualist. Though assuredly anticapitalist in its basic orientation, the socialism of the *Bünde* had little in common with Marxism, which they categorically rejected on account of its invitation to class warfare and a philosophy of history that denied the spiritual bases of human life. Like liberalism, parliamentarism, and capitalism, Marxism was simply another manifestation of the materialistic poison that had spread throughout Germany since the end of the previous century and from which Germany would have to free herself if she was ever to make the *Volksgemeinschaft* a reality.[8]

Long before the *Bünde* had begun to supplant the youth movement as the focal point for the political activity of the younger generation, the Democrats had made a concerted effort to integrate the German youth movement—or at least those elements within it with which they felt an ideological affinity—into their party's own organizational structure. By appealing to the idealism that had played such an important role in the German youth movement before the outbreak of the war, the Democrats hoped that the movement's disaffection from the old political order could be translated into support for the new. In April 1919 the DDP held a Democratic Youth Day in Berlin, and three months later, on the occasion of its first national party congress, it founded the National League of German Democratic Youth Clubs (Reichsbund Deutscher Demokratischer Jugendvereine) under the chairmanship of Max Weißner.[9] A sister organization known as the National League of Democratic Students (Reichsbund Demokratischer Studenten) was subsequently established under the chairmanship of Wilhelm Mommsen for university matriculants throughout the country.[10] The DDP's efforts to establish a foothold in the German youth movement were frustrated, however, by the antipathy that those who had formerly belonged to the Free German Youth felt toward partisan political activity of any sort, and a major conflict ensued between the Free Germans and those who sought to bring about a reformation of German public life by working through the DDP. Following the secession of the Free Germans from the National League of German Democratic Youth Clubs in late 1922, the latter organization chose Ernst Lemmer, a young trade-union secretary from the Free National Ring of German Worker, Employee, and Civil Servant Unions, as its new chairman in a move designed to strengthen its ties to the DDP.[11] Elected to the Reichstag in the fall of 1924, the twenty-six-year-old Lemmer stood on the DDP's extreme left wing with regard to every major issue except pacifism and was firmly committed to the proposition that the younger generation should become more actively involved in the struggle for the Weimar Republic. But despite Lemmer's vigorous efforts to repair the damage that the schism between the Free Germans and the Young Democrats had done to his movement's national organization, membership in the National League of German Democratic Youth Clubs had declined from an estimated 12,000 at the beginning of the Weimar Republic to less than 2,300 by the middle of 1927.[12] Democratic hopes of establishing a major organizational foothold within the German youth movement had clearly failed to materialize.

While a number of prominent Democrats like Lemmer, Gertrud Bäumer, and Heinrich Landahl had all made their way from the German youth movement to the DDP, the DVP's image as the party of industrial capitalism severely hampered its efforts to recruit the support of those who had been active in the youth movement before the outbreak of World War I. Moreover, the defection of the Young Liberal movement to the DDP in November and December 1918 had left the DVP without a suitable youth organization of its

own. In an attempt to rectify this situation, the DVP founded a special organization known as the Youth Group of the German People's Party (Jugendgruppe
der Deutschen Volkspartei) in the summer of 1919.[13] Rechristened the Hindenburg League—Youth Group of the German People's Party (Hindenburgbund—Jugendgruppe der Deutschen Volkspartei) in the summer of 1929,[14]
this organization stood under the leadership of former naval captain Ernst
Hintzmann and appealed, as both its name and leadership suggest, to the more
nationalistic elements of the younger generation.[15] In the final analysis, however, neither this nor the special organization that the DVP created for university students in 1925 proved particularly effective in winning the support of the
younger generation. At no point was this more painfully apparent than in the
1928 Reichstag elections, when the failure of more than 10 million eligible
voters to go to the polls contributed directly to the DVP's electoral difficulties.[16] Stresemann perceived a direct relationship between the defeat of the
more established bourgeois parties and their inability to attract the support of
the younger generation, and in the reform of the DVP's national organization
that he undertook in the fall of 1928 he made improving the party's effectiveness among the generation between twenty and forty years of age one of his
highest priorities. Looking upon the younger generation as an ally in his
struggle against the industrial interests that had become so deeply entrenched
on the DVP's right wing, Stresemann publicly exhorted it to become more
actively involved in Germany's political life so that it might serve as a bulwark
against the rising tide of interest politics.[17]

Stresemann's efforts to rejuvenate the DVP coincided with a spontaneous
revival of political activism on the part of Germany's liberal youth. In February 1928 a group of young journalists, academics, and businessmen from
Cologne founded the February Club (Februar-Klub) in an attempt to forge a
closer bond between their generation and the political system from which it
had been all but excluded. The initiative for the founding of the February Club
came from Engelbert Regh, chairman of the DVP district organization in
Cologne-Aachen.[18] Regh and the founders of the February Club were adamantly opposed to the increasingly prominent role that special economic
interests had come to play in Germany's national life, and they regarded
themselves as the vanguard of a movement that sought to rejuvenate the
German party system by freeing it from the destructive grip of economic self-
interest.[19] The February Club enjoyed particularly close ties to the *Kölnische
Zeitung*, one of Germany's most prestigious liberal papers, and in the campaign for the 1928 Reichstag elections it published two unsigned manifestos
calling upon the younger generation to support the DVP.[20] By the end of 1928
the February Club had succeeded in expanding its base of operations throughout much of western Germany with the emergence of affiliated chapters in
Bonn, Duisburg, Düsseldorf, and two other cities in the Rhine-Ruhr basin.[21]

This, however, was accompanied by an increased strain in its relations with the DVP. The leaders of the February Club were frustrated by the DVP's failure to take their movement seriously, and at a meeting of the Cologne February Club in December 1928 Josef Winschuh, one of the movement's most capable leaders, chastised Regh and the local DVP leadership for their lack of genuine interest in the efforts of the younger generation.[22] At the same time, the leaders of the February Club began to take a more active interest in the efforts to create a united liberal party and invited August Weber, chairman of the Liberal Association, to address their organization in early January 1929.[23]

In December 1928 another Young Liberal club calling itself the Quirites was founded in Berlin under the chairmanship of Theodor Eschenburg, a twenty-six-year-old historian who had already caught Stresemann's attention as a future political leader. Although Eschenburg himself belonged to the DVP, the Quirites espoused a policy of complete neutrality with respect to the various political parties and merely sought, as Eschenburg explained in a letter to the DDP's Hermann Dietrich, "to bring the younger generation into closer contact with the generation currently in power and thus make its own modest contribution to the creation of a genuine political community in Germany."[24] Over the course of the next several months similar organizations sprang up in southwest Germany, where the liberal tradition had its deepest historical roots. In March 1929 a group of young Stuttgart lawyers, businessmen, and schoolteachers with close ties to the DVP founded a Young Liberal club so that they might be able to discuss current political issues in a freer and less inhibited atmosphere than they found at official party meetings.[25] This coincided with the creation of a sister organization in Freiburg known as the League for the Regeneration of Political Life (Bund zur Erneuerung des politischen Lebens) under the chairmanship of Cesar Ley, a local journalist with close ties to the DDP's Dietrich.[26] Though motivated by a somewhat different set of ideological concerns, the founding of the Heidelberg Coalition for Young German Politics (Heidelberger Arbeitsgemeinschaft für jungdeutsche Politik) by a group of young academics under the spiritual tutelage of sociologist Alfred Weber served as a further indication of the revival of political interest that was taking place within the younger generation in the spring of 1929.[27]

By far the most important of the Young Liberal groups to surface in the spring of 1929 was the Front 1929. Like the Quirites, the Front 1929 drew its membership almost exclusively from the ranks of Berlin's bourgeois intelligentsia. But whereas the Quirites chose to maintain a low profile and concentrated their efforts primarily upon the cultivation of closer informal ties between the younger generation and established political figures like Stresemann, Koch-Weser, and Dietrich, the Front 1929 sought to establish itself as the crystallization point around which all of those who were genuinely interested in the reform of German public life could unite. The leader of the Front

1929 was Baron Rochus von Rheinbaben, the author of a popular biography of Stresemann and a longtime member of the Liberal Association. Like Rheinbaben, most of those who belonged to the Front 1929 had been active in the movement for liberal unity since the middle of the 1920s, and the founding of the new organization in early March 1929 had taken place with the foreknowledge and encouragement of the Liberal Association's national leadership.[28] The true spirit behind the founding of the Front 1929, however, was Stresemann. Not only were Stresemann and Rheinbaben personal friends of long standing, but the former had become so embittered over his recent treatment at the hands of the DVP's right wing that he agreed to cooperate with the Front in its campaign for a reform of German public life and actively encouraged it to work for the creation of a comprehensive bourgeois party that would also include the more moderate elements on the DNVP's left wing.[29]

The program published by the founders of the Front 1929 in the summer of 1929 was characteristically vague and contained little that had not already been mentioned by the February Club in its manifestoes of the previous year. Like the February Club, the Front 1929 called for a reform of Germany's federal structure that would strengthen the authority of the central government and an electoral reform that would place the individual and not his party at the center of the electoral process. At the same time, the Front urged the creation of a second legislative chamber organized along vocational or corporatist lines. Not only would this free parliament from the pressure of special economic interests, but it would also provide Germany's beleaguered middle classes with the means for securing more effective representation for their own vital interests. The central element of the program with which Rheinbaben and his associates announced the founding of the Front 1929, however, was their commitment to a reform and reorganization of the German party system. Claiming that all of Germany's political parties, including the Center and Social Democrats, found themselves in various stages of internal disintegration, the Front 1929 sought to instill the German party system with the spirit of the younger generation in hopes that its idealism and devotion to the welfare of the state as a whole might serve as the rallying point for the creation of a comprehensive bourgeois party embracing all of those who, regardless of their party affiliation, sought to free German public life from the poison of economic self-interest.[30]

In its agitation for a reform and reorganization of the German party system, the Front 1929 clearly envisaged something far more ambitious than the merger of the DDP and DVP into a united liberal party. In the informal negotiations that they conducted with various political leaders in the spring of 1929, Rheinbaben and his associates met not only with representatives from the two liberal parties but also with spokesmen for the anti-Hugenberg wing of the DNVP. The most enthusiastic response, however, came from the DDP,

where Koch-Weser, Dietrich, and Lemmer all took an active interest in the
aspirations of the Front 1929 and, in Dietrich's case, even helped finance its
operations through the spring and summer of 1929.[31] The Front 1929 also
succeeded in attracting the support of representatives from the Christian trade
unions, the German National Union of Commercial Employees, the Hansa-
Bund, and various Catholic youth groups throughout the country.[32] But whatever encouragement Rheinbaben and his supporters received from these quarters was offset by the strong opposition their efforts on behalf of a united
bourgeois party encountered within the ranks of the DVP. For although Stresemann continued to support the younger generation in its efforts to bring about a
reform and realignment of the German party system, Scholz and the leaders of
the DVP's right wing remained deeply suspicious of the agitation for a new
political party and urged Stresemann to dissociate himself from it as unequivocally as possible.[33] To the leaders of the Front 1929, this meant that the only
hope of overcoming opposition of Scholz and his associates lay in the establishment of closer ties with the anti-Hugenberg elements on the DNVP's left
wing so that the leaders of the DVP, encircled by proponents of bourgeois
unity, would be left with no alternative but to modify their position on the
question of a united bourgeois party.[34]

In its efforts to organize support for the creation of a united bourgeois party
stretching from the Democrats to the left wing of the DNVP, the Front 1929 did
not limit its efforts to the leaders of Germany's existing political parties but
also made a concerted effort to win the cooperation of the various groups that
claimed to represent the so-called younger generation. Not only did the
Freiburg League for the Regeneration of Political Life vote to reconstitute
itself as the local chapter of the Front 1929 at its first public meeting in the
middle of March,[35] but on 15 March the leaders of the west German February
Club movement agreed to a coalition or *Arbeitsgemeinschaft* with the Front
1929 whereby the club's various affiliates throughout the Rhine-Ruhr basin
would function as local chapters for the Front.[36] By far the most significant
support that the Front 1929 received from the ranks of the younger generation
did not, however, come from the Young Liberal movement but from the Young
German Order under the leadership of its enigmatic high master, Artur
Mahraun. Mahraun had been directly involved in the deliberations that led up
to the founding of the Front 1929, and in early March he and Rheinbaben
published an exchange of letters affirming their mutual commitment to a
regeneration of German public life and their willingness to cooperate in the
creation of a comprehensive *staatsbürgerliche* front free from the corruption
of economic self-interest.[37]

Founded in the social and political chaos that followed the end of World War
I, the Young German Order had grown from a small band of veterans pressed
into temporary service on Germany's eastern front in the first half of 1920 into

one of the country's largest and most influential paramilitary organizations.[38] Like most of the *Bünde* that surfaced in Germany during the first years after the end of the war, the Young German Order evinced a deep-seated antipathy toward the existing political order and conceived of itself as a revolutionary movement that, like the *Wandervögel* before it, claimed to embody a new will, a new way of life, and a new form of social organization seeking to break through the sterile bonds of a society that had outlived its usefulness.[39] At the heart of this vision lay the concept of the *Volksgemeinschaft*, which to Mahraun and his associates was rooted in the front experience and envisaged the creation of a new political order in which the historic cleavages between bourgeois and worker, Protestant and Catholic, monarchist and republican would all dissolve in the spirit of self-sacrifice and love of nation that had prevailed at the front. In reality, however, the *Volksgemeinschaft* of which Mahraun and his followers spoke so passionately offered little more than a utopian vision of an idealized organic society that had supposedly disappeared with the triumph of bourgeois capitalism. The impulse that lay at the heart of this vision was decidedly antimodern and appealed primarily to those elements in German society whose material existence had been most directly threatened by the rapid pace of economic modernization since the last decades of the previous century. For all intents and purposes, the Young German ideology remained the response of a declining social class that tried to compensate for its loss of economic substance by escaping into a fantasy world of brother-hoods and neighborhoods, romantic concepts that bore little relation to the hard realities of the late 1920s.[40]

The publication of Mahraun's *Das jungdeutsche Manifest* in December 1927 marked the beginning of a critical new period in the history of the Young German Order. Representing the most elaborate statement of Mahraun's politi-cal philosophy, *Das jungdeutsche Manifest* assailed the "partyism" that had come to dominate German public life as the source and symbol of Germany's national fragmentation and outlined a program for the peaceful evolution of the Weimar Republic into a higher and more perfect form of democracy based upon the principle of the *Volksgemeinschaft*. Mahraun's notion of the *Volksge-meinschaft*, however, was explicitly antiliberal in that it demanded that the self-interest of the individual be sacrificed to the welfare of the nation as a whole and espoused a hierarchical political order in which rank was not based upon wealth or inherited social status but upon one's innate leadership ability. Yet for all of the disdain Mahraun may have felt toward the bourgeois liberal order, he and his associates categorically rejected schemes for its forcible overthrow and accepted the existing form of government as the foundation upon which their ideal of the democratic *Volksstaat* was to be erected. It was precisely Mahraun's willingness to pursue his goals within the framework of the existing system of government as well as his vigorous defense of Stresemann's foreign policy that set the Order apart from the other patriotic associations that dotted Germany's political landscape in the second half of the 1920s. By the same token, Mahraun reserved his sharpest criticism for the "anonymous plutocratic forces" that had supposedly gained control of the German Right and called for the creation of a second legislative chamber organized along vocational lines as a means of freeing Germany's national life from the corrosive grip of organized economic interests.[41]

The practical implications that Mahraun's call to arms held for the future of the Weimar Republic were not immediately clear. In the 1928 Reichstag elections, for example, the Young German Order instructed its estimated 200,000 members to abstain from voting on the grounds that this might compromise the integrity of their struggle against the system that they had pledged to reform.[42] But the aloofness that Mahraun and his associates tried to maintain toward German party politics through the spring and summer of 1928 was shaken by two events that only confirmed their misgivings about the political maturity of the so-called national movement. The first of these was the infamous Fürstenwald Hate Declaration, which Stahlhelm leader Elhard von Morozowicz issued against the Weimar Republic at a rally in early September. But whatever this may have done to arouse the apprehension of Mahraun and his associates regarding the political maturity of Germany's largest veterans' organization[43] was quickly overshadowed by their revulsion at the subsequent election of film and press magnate Alfred Hugenberg to the DNVP party chairmanship a month later. Not only did Hugenberg more than any other politician of the Weimar Republic personify those anonymous plutocratic forces that Mahraun had reviled so unsparingly in *Das jungdeutsche Manifest*, but his election further confirmed Mahraun's contention that the German party system was in the advanced stages of internal dissolution. The only way out of the malaise in which the German party system found itself, argued Mahraun in a spate of publications that followed Hugenberg's triumph, was through the revitalization and consolidation of the German middle into a strong, united front capable of defending the state against the twin dangers of world plutocracy and Bolshevism. Yet while one of Mahraun's prime motives in proposing such a project was to provide the anti-Hugenberg elements on the DNVP's left wing with a new base from which they could continue their service to the state, the "new front" to which Mahraun was constantly referring cut through all of the existing political parties, separating those who supported the younger generation in its crusade for a reformation of German public life from those like Hugenberg and his associates who still practiced the politics of class conflict.[44]

The first concrete step toward the creation of a broad national front along the lines proposed by Mahraun was taken at a meeting of the High Chapter (*Hochkapital*) of the Young German Order on 26–27 January 1929. In response to Mahraun's appeal that the disintegration of the existing party system made it necessary for the Order to take the initiative in providing responsible national leaders with a more reliable organizational base from which they could continue their political activity, the High Chapter adopted a resolution calling for the preparation of a People's National Action (Volksnationale Aktion) aimed at consolidating the various elements that constituted Germany's national middle into a new and more comprehensive political front.[45] Over the course of the next six weeks Mahraun met repeatedly with representatives from the various bourgeois parties in an attempt to win their support for the creation of such a front. But even Koch-Weser, who privately sympathized with the Order's crusade against "partyism" and applauded its efforts to become more actively involved in the practical political sphere, was appalled by its obscurantism and lack of a clear political program.[46] Similarly, the leaders of the DNVP's young conservative faction, upon whose cooperation Mahraun had placed such great hopes, regarded the Order's unabashed romanticism as wholly unsuited for concrete political action and remained skeptical about its offer of support.[47] About the only real encouragement that Mahraun received in his initial overtures during February and early March 1929 came from disillusioned Democrats like Lemmer and Willy Hellpach, the leaders of the Christian-national trade-union wing within the DNVP, and spokesmen for the younger generation such as Rheinbaben and Winschuh. Otherwise Mahraun and his associates could find little reason to be satisfied with the results of their negotiations.[48]

Confusion over the motives that lay behind the Order's decision to launch the People's National Action in the first months of 1929 mounted in the wake of rumors that this foreshadowed the founding of a new political party in which not only Mahraun but even Koch-Weser and Stresemann might be involved. Efforts on the part of Mahraun and his associates to dispel this confusion were largely unsuccessful and produced little more than restatements of the need to consolidate the so-called national middle into a united front against world plutocracy and Bolshevism.[49] This situation was particularly disconcerting to the leaders of the DVP, who followed the close relationship that had developed between Mahraun and Rheinbaben's Front 1929 with growing concern. Moreover, the February Club's decision to conclude an alliance with the Front 1929 in the middle of March was accompanied by a severe strain in its relationship with the DVP. A trip to Berlin earlier in the month and a series of private talks with Rheinbaben, the DVP's Julius Curtius, and Otto Bornemann from the Young German Order had convinced the leaders of the February Club movement that aside from Stresemann the leaders of the DVP were generally indifferent to the aspirations of the younger generation.[50] Relations between the February Club and the DVP were brought to the point of an open break when on 17 March the *Kölnische Zeitung*, the party's leading organ in the

Rhineland and a staunch supporter of the Young Liberal movement, published a lead editorial that concluded a sympathetic discussion of the younger generation's efforts to rejuvenate the German party system by calling upon Stresemann to place himself at the head of the movement to found a united middle party free from the influence of outside economic interests.[51] The net effect of this development was only to harden the opposition that Scholz and the leaders of the DVP's right wing already expressed toward the political pretensions of the younger generation.[52]

In spite of the displeasure that he felt at seeing his name mentioned in connection with speculation about the founding of a new political party, Stresemann continued to support the efforts of the younger generation and refused to be pressured by the leaders of his party's right wing into repudiating its campaign for a reform and rejuvenation of the German party system.[53] What Stresemann found particularly encouraging about the Front 1929 and the People's National Action was that the younger generation had been shaken from its political apathy and was beginning to make a positive contribution of its own to a solution of the problems confronting the German state.[54] The danger, however, was that the impulse that had manifested itself in the younger generation's campaign for a reform of the German party system might gravitate beyond the orbit of the established political parties, in which case Mahraun and his associates might choose to found a new political party of their own. This was something Stresemann and the leaders of the DVP desperately wanted to prevent, and in December 1928 they appointed Josef Hardt, a secondary school teacher from Lobau in Saxony, to the chairmanship of a special committee responsible for formulating recommendations aimed at integrating the younger generation more firmly into the party's organizational structure.[55] It was against the background of these developments that one of Hardt's associates, Frank Glatzel from the Düsseldorf February Club, proposed the creation of a special organization for the DVP's younger members that, though financially and organizationally autonomous from the party apparatus, would seek to provide the younger generation with a greater voice in the DVP's internal affairs. Specifically, Glatzel hoped that the creation of such an organization would initiate an internal reform and rejuvenation of the DVP so that it might serve as the crystallization point for the creation of a united bourgeois party.[56]

After a preliminary meeting in Berlin on 26 March, Hardt and Glatzel met with a number of the DVP's more active younger members in Eisenach on 21 April to finalize plans for the creation of a special organization for party members who were between twenty-five and forty years of age.[57] The fact, however, that the organization they had in mind would pursue its goals in alliance with the DVP encountered strong opposition within the February Club from those like Winschuh who feared that such an arrangement would only compromise the integrity of the younger generation's efforts to reform the existing party system. But Winschuh's efforts to keep the February Club movement from identifying itself too closely with the DVP or any other political party were thwarted in early May when club members with close ties to the DVP succeeded in securing the passage of a resolution that committed it to pursuing its objectives within the framework of the German People's Party. Although this resulted in Winschuh's resignation as chairman of the movement's west German organization and the secession of several club members affiliated with the *Kölnische Zeitung*, it represented a clear triumph for those like Glatzel and the DVP's Engelbert Regh who hoped to channel the idealism and energy of the younger generation into a reform of the DVP.[58]

These hopes came a step closer to realization with the official founding of the Reich Association of Young Populists (Reichsgemeinschaft junger Volksparteiler or RjV) in Weimar on 26 May 1929. As Glatzel explained in his keynote address at the RjV's founding ceremonies, the purpose of this organization was to infuse the DVP with the spirit of the younger generation so that it might succeed in attracting the support of those elements throughout the country that had become thoroughly disillusioned with the existing party system. In this respect the Reich Association of Young Populists hoped to forge a close alliance between all of the forces within the DVP that sought to renew its commitment to the *Volksgemeinschaft* and free it from the domination of outside economic interests. Only then, Glatzel concluded, would the German People's Party be able to fulfill its historic mission as the crystallization point for the "great state party of the national middle."[59]

As a former activist in the German youth movement, Glatzel was ideally suited to serve as a bridge between the younger generation and the existing party system. Moreover, Glatzel's close ties to the German National Union of Commercial Employees suggested the existence of at least a tacit alliance between the younger generation and the DVP's white-collar wing against the predominant position that big business had come to occupy at the upper levels of the party's national organization. But Glatzel's hopes that it might be possible to rebaptize the People's Party in the spirit of the younger generation ran counter to the direction in which Mahraun and the leaders of the Young German Order seemed to be moving. On 2 June the High Chapter of the Young German Order decided to proceed with the plans it had made at the beginning of the year to hold three mass demonstrations in the summer and early fall of 1929.[60] The first of these was scheduled to take place in Dortmund in the middle of June under the motto "From the Bourgeois State to the People's State" and supposedly sought to liquidate the fruitless yet emotionally charged conflict between republicans and monarchists over the colors of the German flag.[61] Those whom Mahraun personally invited to participate in the demonstration represented an impressive cross-section of Germany's political elite.

In addition to Stresemann and Koch-Weser, the list of invited guests included Curtius and Otto Thiel from the DVP, Dietrich and Hellpach from the DDP, Walther Lambach and Hans-Erdmann von Lindeiner-Wildau from the left wing of the DNVP as well as a sizable contingent from the Christian and Hirsch-Duncker trade-union movements. Of the more than fifty nationally known political figures whom Mahraun invited, no less than a dozen, including eight members of the Reichstag, belonged to the DNVP, a fact that attested to the Young German leader's abiding interest in providing the anti-Hugenberg elements on the Right with a forum from which they could continue their political activity.[62]

The Dortmund demonstration opened on the evening of 15 June with a panel discussion by Gustav Schneider from the Federation of Employee Unions, Fritz Baltrusch from the Christian-national labor movement, and a spokesman for the German National Union of Commercial Employees on the relationship between capital and labor in the democratic *Volksstaat* of the future. But the high point of the demonstration came on the following morning in Dortmund's Westphalia Hall when more than 15,000 members of the Young German Order marched across a stage bedecked in the black-white-red of Imperial Germany and the black-red-gold of the Weimar Republic in what represented a symbolic end to the historic conflict between monarchist and republican over the ideal form of government for the German people.[63] Yet for all of the significance that Mahraun attached to the liquidation of this conflict for the evolution of the Weimar Republic into the democratic *Volksstaat* of the future, the fact nevertheless remained that none of the more prominent Nationalists whom he had invited to Dortmund was present to take part in the Order's symbolic reconciliation of the old and new Germanys. With the exception of a small contingent of Christian trade unionists headed by Baltrusch and the DHV's Karl Dudey, the Nationalists were virtually unrepresented at the rally in Dortmund. Mahraun's strongest and most visible support, therefore, came not from disaffected Nationalists in search of a new political home but from prominent Democrats such as Koch-Weser, Lemmer, and Schneider, all of whom publicly affirmed their commitment to the long-range goals the Order had set for itself. A similar declaration of support came from Stresemann, who though in Madrid at the time of the demonstration, relayed his best wishes for its success through Ernst Hintzmann, leader of the DVP's Hindenburg youth cadre.[64]

If for no other reason, the Dortmund rally was significant for the way in which it suddenly projected Mahraun and the People's National Action into the limelight of national politics. No longer was it possible, as Lemmer wrote for the *Vossische Zeitung* a week after the demonstration, for the established political parties to ignore the younger generation and its demands for a reform and rejuvenation of the German party system. But, as Lemmer continued, it was also incumbent upon Mahraun and his associates to clarify their own objectives so that cooperation with reform-minded elements in the existing bourgeois parties might be facilitated.[65] A further indication of the increased seriousness with which Germany's political leaders began to take the aspirations of Mahraun and the Young German leadership were the words of high praise that the DNVP's Gustav Hülser had for the People's National Action at the first national congress of the Christian-Social Reich Union (Christlich-soziale Reichsvereinigung) in the first week of August. This organization, which had been founded in the immediate aftermath of Hugenberg's election to the Nationalist party chairmanship in the fall of 1928, was a focal point of anti-Hugenberg sentiment within the DNVP and was on the verge of breaking away from the party if a change in its leadership did not take place. Hülser, himself a member of the Young German Order and a longtime friend of Mahraun's, took special pains to praise the goals of the People's National Action and to stress the extent to which they coincided with those of his own Christian-social movement.[66]

Throughout the remainder of the summer and early fall of 1929, Mahraun and his associates devoted themselves to clarifying the goals that had inspired the inception of the People's National Action. The most elaborate statement of these goals was the Dresden Proclamation, which the leaders of the People's National Action released in early September. Prompted by demands for greater clarity and specificity, this document outlined a comprehensive seven-point program for domestic regeneration that covered everything from proposals for federal and electoral reform to the creation of a second legislative chamber concerned exclusively with economic matters.[67] Yet in spite of their efforts to establish some sort of common ground upon which they and the leaders of the existing political parties could meet, Mahraun and his associates were inspired by an impulse that remained profoundly alien to the hard realities of Weimar party politics. *Bund* and party represented two radically different species of political organization, and there was considerable skepticism on both sides as to whether they could ever be reconciled to each other.[68] The crucial question confronting Stresemann, Koch-Weser, and the leaders of the German liberal parties, therefore, was whether or not the impulse that had manifested itself in the appeals of the younger generation for a reform and rejuvenation of the German party system could be accommodated within the framework of the existing political system. If not, then only a further splintering of Germany's already badly fragmented bourgeois party system could be expected.

The last years of the Weimar Republic witnessed a sharp reaction against the increasingly prominent role that organized economic interests had come to play in Germany's national life since the beginning of the 1920s. This reaction drew much of its impetus from the idealism of the younger generation and sought to reassert the primacy of the national and political moment in German public life over the purely economic. The Young German Order's crusade against "partyism" and the Young Liberal movement's appeal for a reform and rejuvenation of the German party system, however, represented an assault upon the legitimacy of the Weimar party system of even greater consequence than that of special interest parties. For just as the stabilization of the mark in the winter of 1923–24 had initiated a legitimacy crisis that manifested itself in the emergence of middle-class splinter parties that placed the representation of special economic interests before the welfare of the nation as a whole, the younger generation was now challenging the legitimacy of a system whose increasing fragmentation along lines of economic self-interest severely undermined the ability of Germany's republican institutions to define and articulate the national interest. Not only did this represent a dramatic intensification of the legitimacy crisis that had plagued the Weimar party system since the middle of the 1920s, but it underscored the close connection that existed in the minds of Germany's liberal leadership between a reform of the German party system and the survival of effective parliamentary government.

CHAPTER TWENTY-FIVE

A Legacy Unfulfilled

THE STABILIZATION OF THE Weimar Republic from 1924 to 1928 took place through the co-optation of conservative economic interest groups such as the National Federation of German Industry and the National Rural League into the political fabric of Weimar parliamentarism. By the end of the 1920s, however, a strong reaction against the increasingly prominent role that organized economic interests had come to play in German political life began to materialize within the ranks of the younger generation and the so-called national movement. The efforts of Mahraun and his associates in the Young Liberal movement to free the German party system from the tyranny of economic self-interest was only one aspect of a more generalized assault against the influence that organized economic interests had gained in return for their help in stabilizing Germany's embattled republican order. In its more virulent forms such as the Fürstenwald Hate Declaration, which the Stahlhelm issued in September 1928, this represented nothing less than an attempt to destroy the basis upon which the co-optation of conservative economic interests into the political fabric of the Weimar Republic had taken place.

The principal figure in the radicalization of the German national movement at the end of the 1920s was Alfred Hugenberg, the newly elected chairman of the German National People's Party. Between 1918 and 1924 Hugenberg had supported a variety of right-wing organizations, including elements from the Christian labor movement, in hopes that this might culminate in the creation of a movement of national concentration or *Sammlung* sufficiently powerful to overthrow the hated Weimar system. But the split in the DNVP Reichstag delegation in the August 1924 vote on the Dawes Plan meant that many of those upon whose support Hugenberg had originally counted were prepared to betray the national cause for the sake of short-term economic gains.[1] Hugenberg was not beholden to any of the conservative economic interest groups that had come to dominate Germany's political development during the second half of the 1920s, and indeed his life's mission was to subvert the role they had played in Weimar's political stabilization. Summed up most epigrammatically by his slogan "Bloc or Mush?," the first item on Hugenberg's political agenda was to transform the DNVP from a sociologically heterogeneous reservoir of Christian, national, and conservative sentiment into a strong, compact bloc "fused together by the iron hammer of Weltanschauung." This was to be accomplished by purging the DNVP of those special economic interests that had been responsible for the split in the vote on the Dawes Plan and for seducing the party into entering the government in 1925 and again in 1927. At the same time, Hugenberg and his associates sought to pulverize the more moderate bourgeois parties such as the DDP, DVP, and Center by polarizing the German party system into two mutually antagonistic and irreconcilable camps. Then and only then, they believed, would it be possible to free Germany from the Marxist poison that was slowly but surely sapping her national vitality.[2]

Hugenberg took the first step toward the second of these objectives in the late spring of 1929 when he gathered the DNVP, the Stahlhelm, and a number of other right-wing organizations, including the still benign National Socialist German Workers' Party (Nationalsozialistische Deutsche Arbeiterpartei or NSDAP), into the National Committee for the German Referendum against the Young Plan (Reichsausschuß für das deutsche Volksbegehren gegen den Young-Plan). The ostensible purpose of this committee was to mobilize public opinion against the new reparations agreement that Stresemann had been negotiating with the Allies since the beginning of the year. Its ulterior motive, however, was to subvert those parties that had publicly identified themselves with Stresemann's policy of conciliation toward the French and were now prepared to support ratification of the Young Plan. This, in turn, would enable Hugenberg as the self-proclaimed leader of the German national movement to free Germany from the morass of parliamentarism in which she was mired and to reassert the primacy of Germany's national interest over the army of special economic interests that had come to dominate her public life.[3]

The implications that Hugenberg's campaign against the Young Plan held for the future of the German liberal movement were ominous. Not only was the entire crusade directed against the foreign policy achievements of Germany's leading liberal politician, but it threatened to submerge the two liberal parties in a sea of nationalist fury aimed at the very foundations of the Weimar Republic. It was against the background of these developments that Stresemann and Koch-Weser met in Vitznau on 22 September to discuss the formation of a "Bloc of National Consciousness" as the focal point around which all of those who objected to the misuse of the word "national" by Hugenberg and the leaders of Germany's radical Right could unite. In this respect, Stresemann was particularly intrigued by the words of high praise that Koch-Weser had for Mahraun and the Young German Order and responded enthusiastically to his suggestion that it might serve as a *bündisch* counterweight to the more radical elements in the so-called national movement. This bloc would also serve as a forum for domestic reform and seek to foster closer personal ties between the leaders of the German middle parties. Although both Stresemann and Koch-Weser agreed that participation in this bloc should in no way whatsoever infringe upon the organizational integrity or freedom of action of the parties that chose to join it, they clearly hoped that the experience of working together might lead to the establishment of permanent organizatonal ties between the participating parties. The two agreed to continue their talks after they had returned to Berlin, and Koch-Weser offered to bring Mahraun to one of their next meetings so that the precise role the Young German Order might play in their plans for the creation of the proposed bloc could be explored in greater detail.[4]

Koch-Weser's conversation with Stresemann at Vitznau underscored the two men's growing awareness of the need for closer ties between the two liberal parties if they were to withstand the challenge of Germany's radical Right. Stresemann's interest in the project was prompted in no small measure by his uncertainty over the situation within his own party. For although the leaders of the DVP had quickly closed ranks in support of his foreign policy by dissociating themselves in no uncertain terms from Hugenberg's call for a referendum against the Young Plan,[5] the industrial interests on his party's right wing had yet to reconcile themselves to the domestic alliances required for the conduct of Stresemann's foreign policy. The conflict over compulsory arbitration that the Ruhr steel industry had provoked in the fall of 1928 marked the beginning of a period of increased militancy on the part of Germany's industrial leadership and did much to harden sentiment against the Great Coalition on the DVP's right wing. Moreover, industry's hopes that adoption of the Young Plan might bring at least a measure of relief from the high taxes that had plagued Germany's capacity for capital accumulation were all but dashed by the concessions the Müller government was forced to make during the latest round of negotiations at The Hague. Compounding the bitterness that the leaders of the German industrial establishment felt over the outcome of the Hague negotiations was the fact that the state unemployment insurance program enacted in 1927 was on the verge of a complete financial collapse and would soon be bankrupt if employer contributions were not increased. All of this placed an increasingly heavy strain on the DVP's relations with the Müller government.[6]

The crisis was inadvertently triggered by a speech that Ernst Scholz, chairman of the DVP Reichstag delegation, delivered at a party rally in Königsberg on 4 September. In expressing disappointment over the concessions Germany had been forced to make at The Hague, Scholz insisted that the Young Plan would be economically feasible only if it was accompanied by a fiscal reform aimed at increasing Germany's capacity for capital accumulation.[7] Though by no means intended as a break between himself and his party's official position, Scholz's Königsberg speech encouraged the industrial interests on the DVP's right wing to intensify their agitation against government plans to rescue the existing system of unemployment insurance by increasing employer contributions. The government hoped to break the deadlock by combining a reform aimed at eliminating many of the program's more serious abuses with an increase in employer and employee contributions effective through the end of March 1931. Fearful that a government crisis would seriously weaken Germany's bargaining position during the final rounds of the Young Plan negotiations, Stresemann's supporters within the DVP Reichstag delegation pressed for acceptance of the government compromise.[8] But the Federation of German Employer Associations (Vereinigung der deutschen Arbeitgeberverbände) prevailed upon their agents within the DVP Reichstag delegation to oppose the new levy, with the result that a deadlock serious enough to force Stresemann to interrupt his convalesence at Vitznau ensued.[9]

Ignoring his doctor's advice, Stresemann returned to Berlin on 25 September in a desperate attempt to prevent his party from bolting the governmental coalition. He met with the DVP Reichstag delegation on the morning of 27 September, at which time Thiel, Kardorff, and Carl Cremer tried in vain to overcome the objections of the party's right wing to an increase in employer contributions to the unemployment insurance program.[10] With spokesmen for the party's industrial wing insistent that only a substantial reduction in the program's benefits would erase its mounting budgetary deficit, the government compromise seemed doomed to defeat. With the final vote scheduled for 3 October, the DVP Reichstag delegation held two marathon sessions on the preceding day, during which Stresemann and his supporters were finally able to persuade a slim majority within the delegation to abstain from voting on the unemployment insurance bill.[11] This represented a crucial victory for Stresemann's efforts to keep the Great Coalition alive and a bitter setback for the business interests on the DVP's right wing. But the strain had taken its toll upon the ailing foreign minister. Unable to attend the delegation's afternoon session, Stresemann found it necessary to retire to his Berlin residence in an attempt to gather his strength. Later that night, after conferring with several of his associates, Stresemann suffered a massive stroke that rendered him unconscious and left his right side paralyzed. Early the next morning he suffered a second stroke and died immediately. At the age of fifty-one, Germany's leading liberal statesman had died.

Stresemann's death created a void in the ranks of Germany's liberal leadership into which no one was capable of stepping. Not only did it deprive the German liberal movement of the one person who might have been able to unite it through the sheer force of personality, but it came just as he was beginning to recognize the need for an end to the historic schism within the liberal camp. It was under the cloud of Stresemann's death that the Democratic Party held its eighth national congress from 4–6 October in Mannheim, a citadel of south German liberalism. In the keynote address on the first day of the congress, Koch-Weser paid a touching tribute to the fallen foreign minister and briefly alluded to their plans for the creation of a bloc of national consciousness as a way of protesting the abuse of genuine national sentiment by the German Right. Koch-Weser then turned to one of Stresemann's favorite themes, the crisis of German parliamentarism. "The Weimar constitution," Koch-Weser argued, "is good. But what the parties have made of it is a mockery." The historical mission of the DDP, he continued, had not been fulfilled with the ratification of the constitution. The spirit that had originally inspired the drafting of the Weimar Constitution was moribund. It was the task of the DDP, Koch-Weser concluded, to revitalize that spirit through a program of vigorous domestic reform touching upon every aspect of political life. Only after such a program had been completed would the DDP be in a position to claim that its historic mission had been fulfilled.[12]

By referring to their recent conversation at Vitznau, Koch-Weser was laying claim to Stresemann's fallen mantle in hopes that the shock of his death might prompt all of those who embraced a politics of reason and self-restraint to close ranks behind his own party's political banner. The precise direction in which he and his associates proposed to take the DDP emerged more clearly during a speech that Hermann Dietrich delivered later that evening on the question of Germany's economic future. Dietrich had served as minister of agriculture since the formation of the Müller government and was widely known as a staunch and articulate spokesman for the peasant middle class.[13] Using the recent conflict over unemployment insurance as his point of departure, Dietrich maintained that it was no longer possible to ignore the power of either organized labor or big business. The tremendous concentration of economic power that had taken place throughout Germany since the outbreak of World War I had given birth to economic forces so powerful that they threatened to draw all economic activity into their orbit. This process, continued Dietrich, worked to the great disadvantage of Germany's urban and rural middle classes, which, caught between the growing power of organized labor and big business, found themselves threatened with economic annihilation. In their economic distress, these elements had become increasingly disaffected from the republican form of government, with some going so far as to reject it altogether. The only way in which the loyalty of these elements to the existing form of government could be assured was through their economic rehabilitation. But—and herein lay the political nub of Dietrich's speech—the increasing fragmentation of Germany's middle-class interest structure had robbed those elements that found themselves caught in the squeeze between labor and big business of the political cohesiveness they needed for the defense of their vital interests.[14]

The high point of the DDP's Mannheim party congress came on the following evening when Gustav Stolper, a highly respected economist and journalist, delivered a major programmatic speech on the social and economic Weltanschauung of German democracy. If Dietrich's speech had been a call for the German middle classes to unite behind the DDP in defense of their social and economic interests, Stolper's speech was an attempt to define the "spiritual goal" toward which the realignment of the German middle should be heading.[15] Although it clearly bore the stamp of his distinctive genius, Stolper's speech represented the collective labors of a special committee that the Democrats had appointed in the wake of their disastrous performance in the 1928 Reichstag elections for the purpose of providing the DDP with a comprehensive social and economic program.[16] The central feature of Stolper's program was an unequivocal commitment to the capitalist economic system. "That capitalism and only capitalism," stated Stolper toward the end of his speech, "is capable of generating the maximum of material wealth—and with it the greatest possible happiness for the individual—has been more than amply demonstrated by the course of economic development over the last hundred years." The emancipation of the worker, therefore, was not so much an economic as a technological problem that could be solved most effectively on the basis of a partnership between capital and labor within the framework of the existing economic system. The crucial question confronting the architects of German social policy was no longer the need to protect the worker against the vicissitudes of industrial capitalism, but rather the economic rehabilitation of the German middle classes. Here Stolper was demanding nothing less than a total reorientation of German social policy:

> Before the war the object of German social policy had been the industrial worker and no one else. But now there are other sectors of the population that deserve the support of the government to the same extent that the worker once required it. Here we are thinking in the first place of the army of suffering peasants and of the severely threatened middle classes. Oppressed by taxes, welfare costs, and rising interest rates, these elements find themselves caught in a squeeze from two sides: the capitalist and the proletariat. At their side stand the growing mass of clerical and technical employees who lack the organization and combativeness to look after their own interests as effectively as the industrial proletariat can do with its powerful unions.[17]

The key to Stolper's program for the economic rehabilitation of the German middle classes lay in a reform of Germany's tax structure and a sharp reduction in the general level of government spending.[18] The strong emphasis that Stolper placed on the need to facilitate the process of capital accumulation represented a fundamental shift in the DDP's social and economic philosophy that found immediate approval from the business interests on the party's right wing and immediate approbation from the leaders of the social-liberal faction that constituted the nucleus of its left wing. Meeting separately in Heidelberg on the afternoon of 3 October, spokesmen for the DDP's National Council for Trade, Industry, and Commerce hailed the new economic program as a reaffirmation of the party's commitment to the free enterprise system and an unequivocal repudiation of socialist schemes for "economic democracy." By the same token, they praised its stress upon tax reform and reduced government spending as renewed proof of the DDP's historic concern for the social and economic welfare of the German middle class.[19] Erkelenz and the leaders of the DDP's left wing, on the other hand, were already deeply distressed at the way in which Dietrich's policies as minister of agriculture had consistently favored the urban and rural middle classes at the expense of the industrial worker,[20] and they criticized Stolper's emphasis upon the problem of capital accumulation as a strategy for economic recovery that sacrificed the interests of the small businessman, worker, and white-collar employee to those of finance and industry.[21] The sharpest criticism came from the Young Democrats' Hans Muhle, who broke the silence that Stolper's other critics had maintained at the Mannheim congress to publicly assail the vigor with which he had defended the capitalist economic system as a betrayal of the DDP's commitment to the social and political emancipation of the German worker.[22]

If the promulgation of Stolper's economic program represented a decisive shift to the right in the DDP's social and economic philosophy, the uneasiness that the leaders of the DDP's left wing felt over this turn of events was compounded by their loss of influence at the highest echelons of the Democratic party organization. A nervous disorder that had plagued Erkelenz for the better part of a year led to his virtual exclusion from any sort of meaningful role in his party's internal affairs. The frustration Erkelenz felt over his increasing isolation within the party expressed itself in a series of private attacks against the Hansa-Bund for conspiring to take control of the DDP and against Koch-Weser for wanting to establish a one-man dictatorship of his own.[23] Powerless to check his party's drift to the right, Erkelenz despaired of contesting his exclusion from the party leadership and submitted his resignation as chairman of the DDP executive committee shortly before the Mannheim congress convened.[24] But Koch-Weser's plans to combine Erkelenz's post with his own position as chairman of the DDP party council encountered unexpected opposition from two groups, one of which supported Dietrich and the other Prussian Finance Minister Hermann Höpker-Aschoff, at a meeting of the party leadership on the morning before the new officers were to be elected. Both groups felt that Koch-Weser lacked the dynamism necessary to lead the DDP out of the impasse in which it found itself and favored the election of a new party leader with greater personal charisma. In the final analysis, however, it was decided to leave the chairmanship in Koch-Weser's hands in light of the fact that his conversations with Stresemann had given him a mandate to explore the possibility of a merger with the DVP and other middle parties that neither Dietrich nor Höpker-Aschoff could claim.[25]

Koch-Weser's reelection took place without complication at a meeting of the full congress on the afternoon of 5 October. Not only did this amount to a tacit endorsement of whatever initiative he might take on behalf of a united liberal party, but the other offices within the Democratic leadership were filled by party members who also sympathized with the campaign for a reform and realignment of the German party system. Oskar Meyer, chairman of the DDP Reichstag delegation and a longtime advocate of liberal unity, and Ernst Lemmer, the national leader of the Young Democratic movement, were chosen to serve as Koch-Weser's vice-chairmen in the DDP executive committee. The selection of Lemmer was particularly significant in that it represented part of a concerted effort by the Democratic leadership to attract the support of the younger generation and coincided with the appointment of fifteen of the party's younger members to seats on the DDP executive committee. Of the four party members elected to deputy chairmanships in the DDP party council, both Willy Hellpach and Gertrud Bäumer had publicly endorsed the younger generation's campaign for a rejuvenation of the German party system, while a third, the Hansa-Bund's Hermann Fischer, had been a leading figure in the Young Liberal movement before the outbreak of the war.[26] All of this was designed to sustain the impression that the Democrats had tried to create throughout the congress, namely that with Stresemann's death Germany had entered a period of profound uncertainty in which the DDP had received a new historical mission.[27]

The Mannheim congress represented a dramatic watershed in the history of the German Democratic Party. Koch-Weser's revelations about his conversation with Stresemann, a new economic program that was immediately hailed as a Magna Carta for the creation of a united liberal party, and internal reforms that greatly expanded the role of the younger generation were all designed to catapult the DDP into the leadership of the movement for bourgeois unity. These efforts were rewarded when just days after the conclusion of the congress Josef Winschuh, the former chairman of the Cologne February Club, requested a meeting with Koch-Weser so that they might discuss the implications of what had transpired at Mannheim.[28] Koch-Weser responded to Winschuh's inquiry not only by granting him an interview but also by preparing a statement outlining how he hoped to accomplish a reform of the existing party system. Convinced that the inertia of party bureaucracies and vested economic interests made a merger of existing party organizations impossible, Koch-Weser advocated the founding of an entirely new party capable of attracting a broad base of popular support from the DDP to the left wing of the DNVP. Preparations for the founding of such a party, including the task of drafting a new party program, should be placed in the hands of a special committee consisting of prominent personalities recruited not merely from the leadership of the existing bourgeois parties but also from the ranks of those who stood outside the confines of partisan political life. After thorough preparation on its own, this committee would direct its appeal for the creation of a united middle party to the German people at large in hopes that the popular response to such an appeal would be sufficiently enthusiastic to override the self-perpetuating stasis of existing party bureaucracies.[29]

Two days after his conversation with Winschuh on 21 October, Koch-Weser met with Julius Curtius, Hans Luther, and Wilhelm Kahl from the left wing of the DVP.[30] In his overtures to the DVP, Koch-Weser actively sought the cooperation of those elements within the DVP that had remained loyal to Stresemann's political course, but he was not interested in an accommodation with the industrial interests on the party's right wing. Curtius was generally regarded as the principal heir to the liberal legacy that Stresemann had culti- vated so assiduously within the DVP. But Curtius, who otherwise might have been favorably disposed to Koch-Weser's project, found himself so overbur- dened following his appointment as Stresemann's successor at the Foreign Office that he was unable to provide Koch-Weser with the active support he needed for the success of his venture. The same was true of Luther, who had only joined the party in the fall of 1927 and declined to become actively involved in Koch-Weser's efforts to found a united middle party on the grounds that he was not yet a bona fide member of the DVP.[31] This left Koch- Weser and his principal collaborator in the project, the Liberal Association's August Weber, with no alternative but to pin their hopes on the patriarchal Wilhelm Kahl. As a longtime member of the Liberal Association, Kahl clearly sympathized with the initiative Koch-Weser had taken. But at the same time his own sense of party loyalty was so strong that he was reluctant to undertake any action on behalf of a united middle party without first securing the consent of his colleagues in the DVP Reichstag delegation.[32] On 27 November Sieg- fried von Kardorff, himself frustrated by his party's lack of initiative in the matter of bourgeois concentration, tried to prod the DVP into action by calling for the creation of a parliamentary alliance or *Arbeitsgemeinschaft* embracing all of Germany's moderate bourgeois parties at a convention of the DVP Association for Trade and Industry (Vereinigung für Handel und Industrie der Deutschen Volkspartei) in Berlin.[33] The following day Kahl informed the DVP Reichstag delegation of the discussions that had taken place since Strese- mann's death and requested permission to represent the DVP in future negotia- tions with Koch-Weser. But neither Kardorff's public appeal nor Kahl's mea- sured discretion could overcome the deep-seated antipathy that the vast majority of those who sat in the DVP Reichstag delegation felt toward the idea of closer political ties with the DDP, and they steadfastly refused to give Kahl the authorization he sought on the grounds that this threatened to compromise the delegation's own freedom of action.[34]

By the end of November Koch-Weser's hopes that he might be able to carry the project he and Stresemann had first conceived at Vitznau to some sort of successful conclusion had collapsed in disappointment. Responsibility for the collapse of these efforts, however, lay not so much with Koch-Weser or the DDP as with the leaders of Stresemann's party. But the DVP's indifference to the growing pressure for a reform and realignment of the German party system posed a serious threat to the future of its own relations with the Young German Order and the various Young Liberal clubs that had formed throughout the country since the spring of the previous year. At a confidential meeting of the High Chapter of the Young German Order on 12–13 October, Mahraun declared that Stresemann's recent death and Hugenberg's referendum against the Young Plan had so altered the domestic political situation that the Order could no longer postpone its plans for the founding of a new political party.[35] Three weeks later Mahraun issued a public appeal calling upon the German people to support the creation of a new organization called the People's National Reich Association (Volksnationale Reichsvereinigung or VNR) as the crystallization point around which a "great party of national regeneration" could form.[36] In defending the creation of the VNR as a response to the lack of public confidence in the existing party system, Mahraun claimed that the mechanical fusion of existing party organizations could never eliminate the "partyism" that had become such a despicable feature of Germany's political life. To the contrary, only the emergence of a genuine popular movement with roots that extended to every corner of the nation could possibly satisfy the deep-seated longing that the German people felt for an end to the superficial political divisions within its ranks.[37]

Although Mahraun and his associates took great pains to deny charges that the founding of the VNR was simply a prelude to the creation of another political party,[38] their actions threatened to drive a permanent wedge between the DVP and the Young Liberal groups that had assembled on its left wing. The leaders of the Front 1929 were already miffed by the DVP's refusal to support its efforts on behalf of a united liberal ticket in the Berlin municipal elections scheduled to take place in the middle of November.[39] By the same token, the general cynicism that Mahraun, Rheinbaben, and Winschuh felt toward the existing party system represented an increasingly serious obstacle to the aspirations of Frank Glatzel and his supporters in the Reich Association of Young Populists. Though shaken by Stresemann's death, the leaders of the RjV remained convinced that the consolidation of the German middle could take place only on the basis of the DVP, and they responded to the news of Stresemann's passing by redoubling their efforts on behalf of closer ties between the various Young Liberal groups that had surfaced on the DVP's left wing.[40] But an agreement that Glatzel had reached in early November with the leaders of the west German February Club movement set off such a storm of protest among the latter's rank-and-file membership that it was never implemented. At the heart of this dispute lay the deep misgivings that the February

Club harbored toward the DVP and its failure to take the concerns and aspirations of the younger generation seriously.[41] Efforts to repair relations between the RjV and the February Club at a special convention held later in the month at Eisenach collapsed in a sea of ill feeling as Glatzel and his associates refused to accommodate the February Club by softening their commitment to the DVP.[42]

The success of Glatzel's efforts to forge closer organizational ties between the DVP and the reform-minded elements on the party's left wing ultimately depended upon the person whom the DVP chose to succeed Stresemann as its party chairman. The obvious choice of the DVP's younger elements was Curtius, but he had effectively removed himself as a candidate for the party chairmanship by agreeing to take Stresemann's place at the Foreign Ministry. Far less acceptable to the leaders of the Young Liberal movement was Scholz, whose close ties to German industry, record of opposition to the movement for bourgeois unity, and apparent indifference to the aspirations of the younger generation hardly recommended him as a suitable successor for the DVP party chairmanship.[43] Moreover, Scholz was still recuperating from the abdominal surgery he had undergone earlier in the fall, and it was uncertain whether or not he possessed the stamina to provide the DVP with the vigorous leadership it so desperately needed. Distressed by the lack of suitable candidates for the party chairmanship, the leaders of the DVP's district organizations in Brunswick, Hanover, and Göttingen began to organize a draft in support of the one man who in their opinion possessed the energy and political vision to lead the DVP out of the dead end in which it found itself, namely former chancellor Hans Luther.[44]

Although the mere mention of his possible candidacy met with enthusiastic approval from spokesmen for both the DVP's industrial and white-collar constituencies,[45] Luther was extremely reluctant to become involved in the struggle for the party chairmanship and agreed to become a candidate only if Scholz's health made it impossible for him to assume the responsibilities of the office.[46] Luther's disclaimer, however, failed to deter his more ardent backers, the most determined of whom was Walter Jänecke from the *Hannoverscher Kurier*, from announcing their support of his candidacy at a meeting of party officials in Leipzig in late November.[47] This was the first time that the possibility of Luther's candidacy had been mentioned publicly, and it led to a number of inquiries from the RjV and other interested circles regarding his willingness to accept the party chairmanship.[48] But as it became clear that Scholz's health would permit him to assume the responsibilities of the chairmanship, Luther disavowed any interest in becoming party chairman and officially informed Adolf Kempkes from the DVP's national headquarters that he wished to have his name withdrawn from consideration as a possible candidate.[49] Kempkes, in turn, read Luther's statement at a meeting of the DVP national committee on 2 December, after which the committee passed a unanimous resolution recommending Scholz's election as party chairman when the DVP central executive committee met later in the month. Efforts on the part of the DVP's left wing to check Scholz's influence as party chairman through the creation of a special vice-chairmanship to be held presumably by one of its own members were subsequently turned back by Scholz's supporters.[50]

Scholz's endorsement by the DVP national committee virtually assured his election as party chairman at the next meeting of the DVP central executive committee. This represented a severe setback to the leaders of the DVP's left wing, and they protested bitterly over their exclusion from a meaningful role in the party's internal affairs. In a long letter to the members of the DVP executive committee, Glatzel expressed his dismay over this turn of events and argued that only the consolidation of the "national middle" around a reformed and rejuvenated DVP could possibly counter the increasing resignation that both the German middle classes and the younger generation felt about the development of the German party system. Conceding that the withdrawal of Curtius and Luther had left Scholz as the only logical choice for the party chairmanship, Glatzel proposed the creation of a special vice-chairmanship responsible for organizational matters and recommended Eduard Dingeldey, a Reichstag deputy from Hesse-Darmstadt, for the post.[51] But Glatzel's entreaties fell on deaf ears when the DVP central executive committee met on 14 December to elect a new party chairman. Neither his proposal for the creation of a special vice-chairmanship nor the suggestion by Brunswick's Hermann Schmidt that the party leadership be placed in the hands of a triumvirate consisting of Scholz, Luther, and Kahl received the slightest consideration from Scholz's supporters. The frustration the leaders of the DVP's left wing felt over the way things had developed manifested itself in the fact that in the voting for the party chairmanship no less than 25 of the 181 voting delegates abstained, while 3 others cast their ballots for candidates whose names had not been placed in nomination. Even the wide margin by which Scholz was subsequently chosen could not conceal the lack of enthusiasm with which the DVP's more liberal elements greeted his election.[52]

Scholz's election to the DVP party chairmanship in December 1929 represented a decisive triumph for the conservative business and industrial interests on the party's right wing. This, in turn, coincided with an intensification of the DVP's attacks against the fiscal policies of the Müller government, as the leaders of the party's right wing tried to sabotage the Great Coalition in favor of a bourgeois government that might be more amenable to the special economic interests they represented.[53] The implications these developments held for the prospects of a united liberal party were not lost upon the leaders of the DDP. Speaking at a meeting of the DDP executive committee on 13 December, Koch-Weser conceded that little was to be gained through a merger of the two liberal parties and reiterated his conviction that only the founding of an entirely new party could generate the psychological momentum necessary to fuse the German middle into a dynamic and cohesive force.[54] Koch-Weser's own commitment to the creation of such a party, however, had been complicated by a resurgence of activity on the DDP's left wing. At Mannheim an opposition group had begun to form around Hermann Landahl, Ferdinand Friedensburg, and Normann Koerber in reaction to the party's drift to the right under Koch-Weser and Dietrich. In November this group formally constituted itself as the Social Republican Circle (Sozialrepublikanischer Kreis) at a private conference in the small Saxon town of Probstzella. Its leadership quickly passed into the hands of Lemmer, Hans Muhle, and Friederich Mewes, all of whom enjoyed close ties to the Hirsch-Duncker labor movement and the Young Democrats. Adamantly opposed to any realignment of the German party system that might compromise the DDP's political and organizational integrity, the Social Republican Circle rejected the idea of a united liberal party on the grounds that it would only harden existing class lines at the expense of the German worker and dedicated itself to an internal reform of the DDP aimed at strengthening its social and republican character.[55]

The hardening of lines between the DDP and DVP in the wake of Stresemann's death was only one more symptom of the general sclerosis that afflicted the German party system at the end of the 1920s. A far more ominous symptom of this affliction was the dramatic rise of the National Socialist German Workers' Party in the second half of 1929. Over the course of three regional elections in different parts of the country, the NSDAP achieved what amounted to a major breakthrough into the ranks of the German middle class. On 27 October the NSDAP received 7 percent of the vote in elections to the Baden state parliament. Three weeks later it scored an equally impressive triumph when it polled 5.4 percent of the vote in the Prussian municipal elections. And in the Thuringian Landtag elections on 8 December the party surpassed the 10 percent barrier for the first time in its history, with 11.3 percent of the popular vote.[56] What the outcome of these elections revealed was that the NSDAP was well on its way to establishing itself as a party of middle-class protest long before the full impact of the world economic crisis had been felt. While much of this is to be attributed to the innovations Hitler and the Nazi leadership had introduced in the areas of political organization and mass propaganda, the dramatic take-off of National Socialism in the second half of 1929 could never have taken place were it not for the fact that all of Germany's traditional bourgeois parties, with the notable exception of the

Center and its counterpart in Bavaria, found themselves in a state of advanced internal dissolution. The alarming success with which the Nazis were able to penetrate the ranks of Germany's middle-class parties lent a new sense of urgency to liberal efforts to reform and rejuvenate the Weimar party system. For the leaders of the German liberal parties, the moment of decision was drawing near.

CHAPTER TWENTY-SIX

An Opening on the Right?

AS 1929 DREW TO AN uncertain and troubled close, Germany's political landscape was suddenly shattered by an event that held profound implications for the future of the movement for a united bourgeois party. On 3–4 December twelve members of the DNVP Reichstag delegation, including such party stalwarts as G. R. Treviranus and Hans-Erdmann von Lindeiner-Wildau as well as the leadership of its Christian-social faction, officially seceded from the Nationalist Party after having failed to reverse the course that Hugenberg had set for it upon his election to the party chairmanship in October 1928. Triggered by a conflict over the language of the referendum Hugenberg had initiated against the Young Plan in the summer of 1929, the secession had its origins in Hugenberg's determination to purge the DNVP of the elements that had compromised the integrity of its struggle against the Weimar system by seducing it into entering the national government in 1925 and 1927. Hugenberg's determination to discredit those Nationalists whom he held responsible for the DNVP's two experiments at government participation drew much of its impetus from the radical nationalism of patriotic associations such as the Stahlhelm and the Pan-German League (Alldeutscher Verband) and sought to mobilize the antisystem sentiment that had become so deeply entrenched at the local levels of the DNVP's national organization. By the end of 1929 Hugenberg's control of the DNVP's national organization was so firm that not only had Treviranus and his associates despaired of forcing a change in the party chairmanship, but they had begun to make preparations for what they hoped would develop into a major secession on the party's left wing.[1]

Following their exodus from the DNVP, the twelve secessionists proceeded to join the nine deputies from the fledgling Christian-National Peasants and Farmers' Party in forming a special parliamentary alliance known as the Christian-National Coalition (Christlich-nationale Arbeitsgemeinschaft) with Treviranus as its chairman.[2] While this expedient provided the secessionists with official status as a parliamentary delegation, Treviranus and his associates hoped that it would pave the way for the establishment of more permanent political ties between the various groups that had broken away from the DNVP. In this respect, their immediate objective was to create a loose federation of moderate conservative forces tentatively called the "German Right" as the first step toward their eventual consolidation in a new conservative party to the left of Hugenberg's DNVP.[3] These efforts, however, were frustrated from the very outset, as neither the former Nationalists who had affiliated themselves with the Christian-National Peasants and Farmers' Party nor the leaders of what had once been the DNVP's Christian-social faction were interested in closer political ties with the other groups that had broken away from the DNVP. Just as Karl Hepp and the leaders of the CNBLP took special pains to stress that the Christian-National Coalition was nothing more than a practical expedient dictated by the parliamentary weakness of the two groups,[4] the Christian-socials rejected the idea of close ties with groups of a different ideological persuasion for fear that this might compromise the purity of their own crusade for a Christian regeneration of German political life.[5]

By the beginning of 1930 the efforts to consolidate the various groups that had broken away from the DNVP into a united German Right had drawn to a complete standstill. Uncertain as to whether or not these efforts should be continued, Treviranus called a meeting of the twelve secessionists and their political advisers for the afternoon of 9 January for the purpose of presenting them with a clear "either-or" option.[6] The DHV's Max Habermann opened the meeting by suggesting that Treviranus's proposal for a loose federation of moderate conservative forces in the form of a united "German Right" should be shelved in favor of a new political party embracing all those who had been forced out of the DNVP. This proposal came under immediate fire, however, from Emil Hartwig, who as a Christian-social categorically rejected any arrangement that might compromise his own movement's ideological and organizational integrity. The overall sentiment against such an arrangement was so strong that by the end of the meeting only four of the twelve secessionists were prepared to go along with something even as modest as Treviranus's proposal for a federation of anti-Hugenberg conservatives.[7] Abandoned by their former allies in agriculture and the Christian-social labor movement, the young conservatives were left with no alternative but to found their own political organization called the People's Conservative Association (Volkskonservative Vereinigung or VKV). This organization, as Treviranus insisted in his keynote address at its official founding on 28 January, did not conceive of itself as a political party in any sense of the word but rather as a nonpartisan association of moderate conservative forces seeking to realize what the Christian-National Coalition already represented in microcosm, namely the unification of all conservative forces from the peasantry, artisanry, working class, and intelligentsia that were prepared to serve the state on the basis of the existing form of government.[8]

The fragmentation of Germany's moderate Right into an agrarian, a Christian-social, and a young conservative wing dealt a severe blow to the movement for bourgeois unity at the same time that it underscored the need for greater political cohesiveness on the part of the moderate bourgeois forces that stood to the left of the DNVP. Mahraun's campaign for a consolidation of the German middle had been inspired in large part by hopes that it might be possible to reach some sort of accommodation with the anti-Hugenberg forces on the left wing of the DNVP. Although Mahraun and his associates could derive a measure of satisfaction from the willingness of Fritz Baltrusch and a handful of lesser known Nationalists, including some with close ties to the Christian trade-union movement, to attach their signatures to the public appeal issued by the People's National Reich Association on 28 January,[9] the fact that none of the twelve deputies who had seceded from the DNVP was willing to identify himself with their campaign for a consolidation of the German middle remained a source of bitter disappointment.[10] By the same token, Glatzel and the leaders of the Reich Association of Young Populists looked upon the former Nationalists as potential allies in their campaign for a regeneration of German political life but were fearful that the founding of the People's Conservative Union and the appeal that Mahraun and his supporters had issued on behalf of the People's National Reich Association portended a further splintering of the Weimar party system.[11]

Nor was the gravity of the situation lost upon the leaders of Germany's industrial establishment. Many of Germany's more politically astute industrialists had long favored the consolidation of those parties that were unequivocally committed to the defense of the capitalist economic system. The appeal of such an idea to Germany's industrial elite had been greatly enhanced by the conflict between industry and the Müller government that had erupted in the fall of 1929 over the questions of unemployment insurance and fiscal reform. The publication in December 1929 of a comprehensive program of social and economic reform by the National Federation of German Industry under the title *Aufstieg oder Niedergang?* marked the beginning of an intensified industrial offensive against the social and economic policies of the Great Coalition. This program, which proceeded from the contention that implementation of the Young Plan presupposed a thorough reform of Germany's tax and financial structure, was accompanied by an appeal for the "concentration of all constructive forces" in the struggle for fiscal and economic sanity.[12] It was with this in mind that the RDI's president, Carl Duisberg, in what amounted to a radical departure from the federation's traditional abstention from partisan political activity, gave the anti-Hugenberg forces within the DNVP 20,000 marks to assist them in the founding of a new political party.[13] For the most part, however, the leaders of the German industrial establishment placed little faith in the efforts to create a new political party, favoring instead the creation of a strong anti-Marxist front through either a merger or a federation of the various groups that stood between Hugenberg and the left wing of the DDP.[14]

The specific goals behind the RDI's appeal for the concentration of all constructive forces became increasingly clear in the first three months of 1930.

By the end of January the compromise on tax and fiscal policy that the DVP Reichstag delegation had half-heartedly accepted in the middle of December had collapsed with the publication of the final terms of the Young Plan. At this point, the leaders of the DVP's right wing began to mobilize their supporters at the district and local levels of the party's national organization in an attempt to pressure the Reichstag delegation and the DVP's two cabinet officers, Paul Moldenhauer and Julius Curtius, into leaving the government if it did not meet industry's demands for tax and fiscal reform.[15] But Ernst Scholz, the DVP's newly elected national chairman, was reluctant to provoke a cabinet crisis before the Young Plan had been ratified, and at a critical meeting of the DVP Reichstag delegation on 10 February he succeeded in winning approval for still another compromise aimed at forestalling a break with the government.[16] Scholz also hoped that a postponement of the cabinet crisis would allow him to undertake some sort of initiative in the matter of bourgeois concentration, so that once the Young Plan had been ratified, Germany's bourgeois parties would have sufficient leverage to force the formation of a new government more favorably disposed to industry's reform program.[17] The change that had taken place in Scholz's thinking on the question of bourgeois unity was apparent from his suggestion at a meeting of the DVP national committee on 2 March that perhaps the time for a realignment in the basic configuration of German party politics had arrived. Though deferring the creation of a united bourgeois party to some point in the distant future, Scholz proposed that the "state-supporting" bourgeois parties—and here he was referring to the Democrats, the Christian-National Coalition, and the Business Party, in addition to his own DVP—test their ability to work together in the form of a parliamentary *Arbeitsgemeinschaft* concerned with securing passage of the various financial and economic reforms necessary for implementation of the Young Plan. Should cooperation in the realm of practical politics prove successful, it would be appropriate for the parties in question to explore the possibility of more permanent organizational ties.[18]

As Scholz's ruminations on the possibility of a parliamentary coalition between the "state-supporting" bourgeois parties revealed, the movement for bourgeois unity as defined by the leaders of the DVP was inseparably related to the struggle for a reform of Germany's financial and economic structure. In this respect, the business community demanded that the deficit in the national budget caused by the mounting cost of Germany's unemployment insurance program should be liquidated through a drastic reduction in the general level of government spending without imposing new burdens on commerce and industry that might inhibit the process of capital accumulation or encourage the flight of domestic capital abroad.[19] When the tax and fiscal program that the government presented to the Reichstag on 6 March failed to reduce taxes and spending to a level sufficient to satisfy the demands of German business, this provoked a storm of protest from business organizations throughout the country, including the National Federation of German Industry and the Federation of German Employer Associations.[20] The immediate effect of this offensive was to intensify pressure from the DVP's right wing for a break with the Müller government and to isolate Moldenhauer as the cabinet officer responsible for the formulation of the government program within the DVP Reichstag delegation.[21] On 6 March the DVP Reichstag delegation rejected a compromise that its own ministers in the Müller government had helped fashion. In anticipation of the DVP's withdrawal from the coalition, the other government parties formed a rump cabinet to oversee ratification of the Young Plan and await the outcome of the DVP party congress scheduled to meet in Mannheim in the fourth week of March.[22]

With the approach of the DVP's Mannheim congress, the leaders of the Young Liberal movement hoped to persuade Scholz and the party's national leadership to use the congress as a forum for undertaking some sort of public initiative on behalf of a united bourgeois party. On 16 March representatives from the Reich Association of Young Populists, the Front 1929, and the west German February Clubs met in Koblenz to draft a letter to Scholz urging him to dedicate himself to the goal of bourgeois concentration both in his keynote address at Mannheim and in an official party resolution.[23] On the following day spokesmen for the three groups that had met in Koblenz took part in an informal luncheon that August Weber and Wilhelm Kahl had organized on behalf of the Liberal Association at Berlin's fashionable Hotel Continental.[24] The purpose of this meeting was to explore the possibility of closer political ties between the parties of the middle and moderate Right, and the participants included Koch-Weser, Treviranus, the DVP's Otto Thiel, the WP's Gotthard Sachsenburg, and a sizable contingent from the Young Liberal movement. Koch-Weser opened the discussion by attributing the general ineffectiveness of Germany's parliamentary system to the fragmentation of the bourgeois middle and went on to propose the formation of a special commission to enter into exploratory negotiations about the founding of a new middle party with the leaders of the various bourgeois parties. Koch-Weser's suggestion prompted an immediate response from Treviranus, who argued that such an undertaking would be effective only if it were directed toward specific political goals and not toward something as nebulous as bourgeois concentration. Consequently, Treviranus concluded, the creation of a parliamentary *Arbeitsgemeinschaft* concerned with practical political matters such as tax and fiscal reform seemed a far more appropriate response to the problem of bourgeois unity than the creation of a new political party. This, however, met with little enthusiasm from the spokesmen for the younger generation, who were quick to reject the idea of a parliamentary coalition between the existing bourgeois parties as a wholly inadequate response to the increasingly powerful longing of the German nation for an end to the superficial political divisions within its ranks.[25]

Although the meeting in the Hotel Continental on the afternoon of 17 March failed to produce a consensus regarding the precise form bourgeois unity should take, it nevertheless formed an important part of the background to the DVP's eighth national congress, which opened in Mannheim five days later amid rumors that the party was about to bolt the Müller government. Scholz's own thinking on the various options that stood before the DVP was profoundly influenced by a long conversation he had with former chancellor Hans Luther on the eve of the congress. Luther, who had figured prominently in all the speculation about the formation of a new national government and the creation of a new middle party, urged Scholz to refrain from initiating a break with the Great Coalition so that the onus for such a step would ultimately lie with the Social Democrats and not with the DVP. At the same time, Luther encouraged Scholz to take a strong stand in favor of a reform of Germany's federal structure—one of Luther's pet projects ever since his election as chairman of the League for the Regeneration of the Reich (Bund zur Erneuerung des Reiches) in early 1928—and even hinted that Scholz might use the congress as a forum for announcing a bold new initiative in the matter of bourgeois concentration.[26]

The extent of Luther's influence upon the DVP party chairman could be seen in the keynote speech that Scholz delivered at Mannheim on the morning of 22 March. For at the same time that Scholz emphatically reaffirmed his party's demands for a thorough reform of Germany's financial and economic structure, he proclaimed, to the great dismay of the DVP's right wing, "that a government against or even without the Social Democrats was simply not possible for an extended period of time." Though equivocal at best, Scholz's endorsement of the Great Coalition served as the point of departure for a no less surprising statement on the matter of bourgeois concentration. Maintaining that cooperation with the Social Democrats was feasible only if Germany's moderate bourgeois parties came together into a strong, compact bloc of their own, Scholz proclaimed that the DVP should take upon itself the task of strengthening the bourgeois middle so that it could defend itself against the radical parties on the Left and Right. "With this goal in mind," continued Scholz, "I direct to all of those bourgeois parties that share our goal for positive and constructive cooperation an appeal for a closer union [*Zusammenschluß*]—a union that under certain circumstances does not have to stop at existing party lines."[27]

If Scholz's endorsement of the Great Coalition came as a sharp disappointment to those on the DVP's right wing who had hoped that the Mannheim congress would produce a break with the Social Democrats,[28] his appeal for closer ties between the parties of the bourgeois middle was immediately hailed by spokesmen for the Young Liberal front as a bold and unselfish step toward the goal of a united middle party.[29] The real significance of Scholz's appeal, however, did not become fully apparent until the resignation of the Müller government on 27 March, just four days after the conclusion of the Mannheim congress. Although formal responsibility for the collapse of the government lay with the SPD Reichstag delegation for having withdrawn its confidence in the chancellor at a caucus earlier that morning, Müller's resignation represented the culmination of a course that the leaders of the DVP had pursued since Stresemann's death in the fall of 1929. Scholz's reaffirmation of support for the principle of the Great Coalition at Mannheim was little more than a tactical ploy designed to force the Social Democrats into making a break that the DVP itself actively sought. The leaders of the DVP no doubt hoped that Müller's resignation would pave the way for the formation of a new government that would be more amenable to their demands for fiscal reform, and they were disappointed when Luther, around whom much of the speculation in the DVP had centered, removed himself as a candidate for the chancellorship in order to succeed Hjalmar Schacht as president of the Reichsbank. This, in turn, cleared the way for the nomination of Heinrich Brüning, who as chairman of the Center Reichstag delegation had figured prominently in the Reichswehr's plans for a change of government since the preceding winter. Although he would have preferred to postpone assumption of power until a more propitious moment and had in fact worked to keep the Müller government in office through the recent crisis, Brüning accepted Hindenburg's call to the Reich Chancellery and within a matter of days succeeded in organizing a new government that stretched from the DDP to the left wing of the DNVP.[30]

Brüning's appointment as chancellor had profound implications both for the development of the German party system and for the future of Weimar democracy. As a young secretary for the German Trade-Union Federation immediately after the end of World War I, Brüning had played a major role in drafting the appeal for an interconfessional Christian people's party that his mentor, Adam Stegerwald, had delivered at the Essen congress of the Christian trade-union movement in November 1920. When Brüning assumed the chancellorship some ten years later, the ideals of the Essen Program were still very much at the heart of his attitude toward the Weimar party system.[31] From this perspective Brüning welcomed the idea of the consolidation of the various groups behind his government into some sort of "state-supporting" bourgeois conservative party, and he actively encouraged Scholz in his efforts to forge closer ties between the parliamentary delegations of the nonsocialist parties to the left of Hugenberg's DNVP.[32] Brüning's immediate objective, however, was to win the cooperation of the German Right, either by persuading Hugenberg to abandon his policy of unconditional opposition or by inducing the more moderate elements in the DNVP to bolt the party. The key figure in Brüning's strategy was Martin Schiele, a prominent Nationalist deputy who had played a central role in the efforts to organize the German agricultural community into a national agrarian lobby known as the Green Front (Grüne

Front). Brüning hoped that Schiele's appointment as minister of agriculture would encourage the leaders of the DNVP's agrarian wing to support his government. At the same time, however, it raised the spectre of a second and even more damaging secession from the DNVP should Hugenberg remain intractible in his opposition. Moreover, Brüning was fully prepared—and Reich President von Hindenburg had given him the necessary authorization—to implement his policies by means of the presidential emergency powers contained in Article 48 of the Weimar Constitution in the event that a Reichstag majority failed to materialize.[33]

The formation of the Brüning government in the spring of 1930 lent renewed impetus to the efforts at bourgeois concentration. Although Brüning was not bound by formal commitments to the various parties that supported his government, his cabinet included representatives from every major political group from the DDP to the DNVP. The DVP was represented, as it had been in the previous cabinet, by Curtius and Moldenhauer at the Foreign Office and Finance Ministry respectively, while Dietrich, who had moved over to the Ministry of Economics to accommodate Schiele's appointment as minister of agriculture, was the lone Democrat in the new cabinet. The cabinet also included Treviranus from the fledgling Christian-National Coalition and Johann Victor Bredt from the Business Party, as well as Stegerwald and Joseph Wirth from the chancellor's own party.[34] The fact that all of the major parties from the left wing of the DNVP to the Democrats were now lined up in support of the national government afforded Scholz a unique opportunity to act upon the pledge he had made at Mannheim. Still, the first official talks did not take place until the third week of April, when Scholz met with Koch-Weser, Lindeiner-Wildau, and the WP's Hermann Drewitz to discuss the possibility of an electoral truce in the event of new national elections.[35] The four party leaders were to meet on three more occasions over the course of the next six weeks, although the discussion no longer dealt with the question of electoral strategy but centered around Scholz's proposal for the creation of a parliamentary alliance consisting of those groups, excluding the Center and Bavarian People's Party, that supported the Brüning government.[36]

Scholz's efforts to forge a parliamentary alliance between the various non-Catholic parties that supported the Brüning government received strong encouragement from the industrial interests on his own party's right wing. Not only would such an arrangement strengthen the antisocialist forces in the Reichstag, but industry also hoped that it would enable its parliamentary representatives to exercise a decisive influence upon the fiscal and economic policies of the Brüning cabinet.[37] Strong resistance to Scholz's efforts on behalf of a bourgeois parliamentary alliance, however, came from the DDP, where party leaders found themselves embroiled in a bitter internal conflict over the DDP's future political course. The conflict had erupted in the wake of a decision by the leaders of the Württemberg DDP in January 1930 to go along with the local DVP in entering the state government headed by conservative Nationalist Wilhelm Bazille in a move that local party leaders hailed as a practical application of liberal unity.[38] The entry of the Württemberg Democrats into the Bazille government came less than three months after a similar exercise in liberal unity in the neighboring state of Baden, where the DDP had resigned from a coalition government with the Center and Social Democrats in order to join the DVP in a self-proclaimed "liberal opposition."[39] In each case, this turn of events had severe repercussions upon the local DDP organizations and did much to discredit the concept of liberal unity as espoused by Koch-Weser and his supporters in the party's national leadership.

The situation within the DDP was further complicated by the bizarre behavior of Willy Hugo Hellpach, a member of the DDP Reichstag delegation who had been the Democratic candidate for the Reich presidency in 1925. An enthusiastic supporter of the Front 1929 and Young German Order, Hellpach praised the initiative that the leaders of the Württemberg DDP had shown in entering the Bazille government as a "decisive break with the sterile and outmoded stereotypes of the past" and chastised the DDP's national leadership for its own timidity in the matter of bourgeois concentration.[40] The sharp rebuff that the leaders of the Württemberg Democrats received at the hands of the DDP executive committee in early February only confirmed Hellpach's fears that the DDP and other bourgeois parties lacked the capacity for self-regeneration. In a lengthy article in the *Neue Zürcher Zeitung* Hellpach claimed that the German liberal parties had defaulted in the matter of bourgeois unity, thereby allowing the initiative to pass into the hands of the new conservative movements that were emerging from the ruins of the DNVP.[41] Hellpach's article represented a stinging indictment of German liberalism and only aggravated the difficulties that he was already having with the DDP's national leadership on account of his defense of the Württemberg Democrats. By the beginning of March Hellpach had become so distressed over the situation in the DDP that he decided to make one last attempt to shock it out of its lethargy. Citing the DDP's inactivity in the matter of bourgeois unity as only the last and most striking example of its inability to respond to the myriad of problems that had come to weigh so heavily upon the German people, Hellpach resigned his seat in the Reichstag along with his other party offices in an open letter to the chairman of the DDP Reichstag delegation.[42]

Hellpach continued to agitate for the creation of a united bourgeois party throughout the remainder of the spring. Yet for all of its melodrama, the resignation of his Reichstag mandate failed to evoke the response upon which he had been counting. Within the DDP only Wolfgang Jänicke, a leading government official from Potsdam, sympathized with the motives that had prompted Hellpach to resign, while outside of the party expressions of support were confined to Luther and Lindeiner-Wildau.[43] At the same time, the leaders of the DDP's left wing tried to counter whatever effect Hellpach's resignation was supposed to have upon the party faithful by intensifying their agitation against the establishment of closer political ties with the more conservative bourgeois parties, either in the form of a parliamentary alliance as proposed by Scholz or that of a united bourgeois party as proposed by Hellpach. The vigor with which the DDP's left wing pressed its attack against the idea of bourgeois unity in whatever form it might assume was directly related to its frustration over the party's participation in the Brüning government. Dietrich's decision to enter the Brüning government after only a minimum of consultation with other party leaders was deeply resented by the DDP's left wing, whose spokesmen not only criticized the preferential treatment he had shown toward peasant and middle-class economic interests during his tenure as minister of agriculture but also feared that Brüning was about to embark upon a right-wing experiment that might seriously weaken the foundations of Weimar democracy.[44] Two members of the DDP's left wing, Lemmer and Erkelenz, had such strong reservations about the new government that at a meeting of the DDP Reichstag delegation on 28 March they refused to support it in any vote of confidence that might take place.[45] Still, Dietrich's popularity with the Democratic rank and file precluded the vast majority of the delegation, including those deputies who may not have agreed with his decision to enter the government, from disavowing him for fear of the repercussions this might have upon the party's national organization. By the same token, the Democrats were reluctant to entertain the possibility of new national elections without the benefit of Dietrich's full support. As a result, the leaders of the DDP felt that they had no real choice but to support the Brüning government in its first parliamentary test on 3 April.[46]

The DDP's decision to support the Brüning government did much to inflame the crisis that had been developing within the party since the beginning of the year and led to a new round of attacks against its involvement in the movement for bourgeois unity. Fueled by a particularly determined offensive in the editorial columns of the *Berliner Tageblatt*,[47] this crisis came to a head at a meeting of the DDP party council in late May 1930. By this time, Scholz and the leaders of the other bourgeois parties had grown impatient with the DDP's equivocation on the formation of a parliamentary alliance and were pressing the Democrats for a definitive answer.[48] At the same time, Koch-Weser was under increasingly heavy pressure from Mahraun and the leaders of the Young German Order to dissociate himself from the "pseudo-concentration of the propertied bourgeoisie" and join the People's National Reich Association in its crusade for a truly comprehensive concentration of the German middle.[49] Consequently, when Scholz, Lindeiner-Wildau, and Drewitz pressed Koch-Weser one last time for a response to the proposal for a parliamentary alliance

at a meeting of the four party leaders on 20 May, the Democratic party
chairman was unable to give them the answer they sought and asked them to
wait until after the DDP party council had had an opportunity to discuss the
matter at its next caucus on 25 May.[50]

The meeting of the DDP party council opened in Halle against the background of a bitter conflict between the party's left and right wings over the
question of its involvement in the efforts to create a united bourgeois party.
Led by Heinrich Landahl and Normann Koerber, the Social Republican Circle
cast off the veil of obscurity that had surrounded the first months of its
existence to assume leadership of the efforts to reform and rejuvenate the DDP
so that the creation of a new middle party along the lines proposed by Hellpach
would no longer be necessary.[51] At the same time, Hellpach refused to let the
fact that the People's Conservatives no longer seemed interested in the creation
of a united bourgeois party divert him from his ultimate goal of *volksbürgerliche* concentration on the broadest possible basis.[52] But while Koch-Weser
and most of his associates in the DDP party leadership agreed with Hellpach
that a sweeping realignment of the German party system was essential for the
survival of effective parliamentary government, the agitation of the Social
Republican Circle and the threat of a secession on the DDP's left wing made it
impossible for them to endorse Hellpach's appeal for the creation of a new and
comprehensive bourgeois middle party as vigorously as they might otherwise
have done. After a lengthy and acrimonious debate in which the leaders of the
DDP's left wing assailed the idea of a united bourgeois party as a betrayal of
the social and republican principles upon which the party had been founded,
Koch-Weser and his supporters prevailed upon Hellpach to accept a compromise resolution that both stressed the social and republican character of the
DDP's commitment to bourgeois concentration and made its participation in
the movement for bourgeois unity contingent upon a thorough reform and
rejuvenation of the DDP's own national organization. Though soundly rejected by leaders of the DDP's left wing, this resolution received Hellpach's
full support and won approval by an overwhelming 118–25 margin.[53]

At a meeting of the DDP Reichstag delegation on 27 May, Koch-Weser gave
a detailed report of the negotiations that had taken place between himself and
the leaders of the other bourgeois parties since the formation of the Brüning
government and asked whether or not the creation of a parliamentary alliance
along the lines proposed by Scholz was consistent with the resolution that the
DDP party council had adopted at Halle.[54] The answer, as a statement that the
delegation released three days later clearly indicated, was a resounding no,
since in the DDP's eyes the "mere addition of existing parties or parliamentary
delegations" neither constituted a sufficient response to the need for a realignment of the German party system nor adequately secured the political
principles for which the DDP had always stood.[55] In the meantime, Scholz's

efforts to forge a parliamentary alliance between the various non-Catholic parties supporting the Brüning government had run into strong opposition from spokesmen for the agrarian wing of the Christian-National Coalition, with the result that Lindeiner-Wildau was left with no choice but to announce his group's withdrawal from the proposed parliamentary alliance at a meeting of the four party leaders on the morning of 28 May. Though initially inclined to go ahead with the plans for a parliamentary alliance even if the Democrats dropped out, Scholz and Drewitz saw no point to a coalition that consisted only of their two parties, and, upon hearing Lindeiner-Wildau's announcement, they abandoned all further efforts.[56]

The collapse of Scholz's efforts to form a parliamentary alliance drew a sigh of relief from Mahraun and his associates in the leadership of the People's National Reich Association. Although its leaders continued to insist that the VNR had no intention of organizing itself as a new political party, the two liberal parties reacted to the news of its founding at the end of January 1930 with concern that this foreshadowed the emergence of yet another party in Germany's badly fragmented political middle. These fears were hardly allayed when Mahraun proclaimed at the VNR's first national congress in April 1930 that a genuine concentration of the German middle could never take place on the basis of the existing political parties or through their merger into some sort of united bourgeois party.[57] The antiestablishment character of the VNR's approach to the question of bourgeois unity became even more apparent in the wake of the caustic attacks that Mahraun and his associates directed against Scholz's campaign for closer ties between the existing bourgeois parties.[58] These attacks assumed increasingly ominous overtones with the dissolution of the Saxon Landtag on 20 May. Alarmed at the sympathetic response that the People's National Action had evoked at the local levels of their party's national organization, the leaders of the DVP hoped to dissuade the VNR from entering the campaign for the state elections that had been scheduled for the fourth week of June. But by the time Scholz was able to reach Mahraun on the morning of 21 May, the Young German leader had already begun to notify the VNR's local chapters throughout the country that the situation in Saxony had deteriorated to such an extent that the VNR might have to intervene in the campaign.[59] Mahraun's prophecy fulfilled itself on the following day when the executive committee of the VNR's Saxon organization announced that it had decided to enter its own slate of candidates in the forthcoming state elections and would therefore be in no position to consider an alliance with other political groups.[60]

The VNR's decision to enter the Saxon state elections in the early summer of 1930 came as a severe blow to the leaders of the Young Liberal movement and did much to strain their faith in a reform and rejuvenation of the DVP. This was particularly true of the west German February Club, whose leaders reacted to the impasse in which the movement for bourgeois unity found itself by sending Scholz a sharply worded letter in which they exhorted him to redouble his efforts to realize the goals he had set for himself at Mannheim.[61] The disaffection of the Young Liberal movement, however, was only one of the problems that plagued the DVP on the eve of the Saxon state elections. A far more serious problem was the dispute that had erupted within the party over the policies of one of its two representatives in the Brüning government, Finance Minister Paul Moldenhauer. In March Moldenhauer had sought to cover the mounting deficit in the national budget through the introduction of a special head tax or *Bürgersteuer* on all adult citizens but had dropped the idea in the face of strong opposition from the commercial and industrial interests on the DVP's right wing. Confronted by a further deterioration of Germany's financial situation over the spring of 1930, Moldenhauer sought to reintroduce the idea in the form of a special 3 percent levy called the *Notopfer der Festbesoldeten* on the salaries of all government employees. This proposal, however, ran into strong criticism not only from the leaders of the DVP's business wing but, more importantly, from spokesmen for the various civil servant organizations that the DVP depended upon for a large share of its electoral support. These two factions joined forces at a meeting of the DVP Reichstag delegation on 16 June to secure approval for a series of demands that amounted to a virtual repudiation of Moldenhauer's policies as minister of finance and made the party's continued support of the Brüning government highly uncertain. Reluctant to follow Brüning's advice and publicly disavow the action of his party, Moldenhauer tendered his resignation at a meeting of the cabinet two days later.[62]

The Moldenhauer affair left the DVP vulnerable to charges from Mahraun and his associates that it was indeed nothing but an agent of special economic interests. No less damaging was the way in which the leaders of the VNR were able to exploit the discrepancy that existed between the DVP's portrayal of itself as a foe of political extremism and its participation in a government in the neighboring state of Thuringia, where Wilhelm Frick, a prominent member of the Nazi heirarchy, served as minister of the interior.[63] Yet while these factors combined to inflict upon the DVP losses that Scholz, as its national chairman, could only describe as "catastrophic,"[64] by no means was the DVP the only party to emerge from the Saxon state elections on 22 June 1930 with its ranks decimated. For whereas the DVP lost more than 130,000 votes—or nearly 40 percent of what it had received in the last state elections in May 1929—and saw its representation in the Landtag slip from thirteen to eight mandates, its losses were still proportionately less than those sustained by Hugenberg's DNVP. Reeling from one wave of defections after another, the DNVP lost over 40 percent of its 1929 vote and more than 60 percent of what it had received in the October 1926 Landtag elections. With a mere 4.8 percent of the popular vote, the DNVP was scarcely more than a splinter party itself. At the same time, however, those parties that had been the first to benefit from the decline of the more traditional, ideologically oriented bourgeois parties—namely the Business Party, the People's Justice Party, and the Christian-National Peasants and Farmer's Party—were unable to capitalize upon the electoral catastrophe that befell the DVP, DNVP, and to a lesser extent the DDP. On the contrary, all three parties experienced reverses that indicated that perhaps the appeal of special interest parties had peaked.[65]

Who, then, were the principal victors in the Saxon state elections of 22 June 1930? Modest gains were recorded by the People's National Reich Association and the Christian-Social People's Service (Christlich-sozialer Volksdienst or CSVD), both of whom were making their first appearance in Saxony and therefore contributed to the sharp increase in voter participation that character-ized the elections. But even then, the VNR and CSVD received only 39,000 and 55,000 votes—or about 1.5 and 2.1 percent of the popular vote—respec-tively and could hardly have accounted for the heavy losses sustained by the other bourgeois parties. The principal victor in the 1930 Saxon Landtag elec-tions, therefore, was not any of the more moderate bourgeois parties that had hoped to establish themselves somewhere to the left of Hugenberg's DNVP but rather that paragon of right-wing radicalism, the National Socialist Ger-man Workers' Party. In what was only the latest and most impressive in a long string of electoral triumphs dating back to the last Saxon elections in the spring of 1929, the NSDAP virtually tripled the number of votes it had received the previous year and increased the size of its parliamentary delegation from five to fourteen deputies. With more than 375,000 votes—or 14.4 percent of the popular vote—the NSDAP had succeeded in establishing itself as the largest non-Marxist party on the Saxon political landscape.[66] What the outcome of the Saxon Landtag elections indicated was that the movement for bourgeois unity, whether in the form propagated by Koch-Weser or Scholz or Mahraun, was in danger of being outflanked by an ultimately more radical approach to the problem of bourgeois concentration taken by the Nazi Party.

CHAPTER TWENTY-SEVEN

Concentration or Splintering?

ON 18 JULY 1930 Chancellor Heinrich Brüning dissolved the Reichstag and called for new elections after Hugenberg's followers in the DNVP joined the Social Democrats, Communists, and National Socialists in revoking the emergency powers that the government had used to enact its fiscal program two days earlier. Brüning's call for new elections came against the background of a deepening economic crisis that had become increasingly acute with the Wall Street panic of October 1929. The Great Depression of the early 1930s, however, was only the last in a series of economic catastrophes to hit Germany in less than two decades and represented part of a continuum that also included the war and the runaway inflation of the immediate postwar period. Even the brief stabilization of the German economy from 1924 to 1929 was a mixed blessing to German society as a whole and did little to alleviate the pattern of social and economic distress that had plagued the German middle classes ever since the outbreak of World War I. The principal effect of the Great Depression, therefore, was only to exacerbate the deep-seated anxieties that the German middle strata already felt as a result of their declining social and economic position and to heighten the longing that existed within middle-class circles for an end to the superficial political divisions within their ranks.[1]

The German middle strata had always possessed a potential cohesiveness by virtue of their fear of proletarization, their antipathy toward big business and organized labor, and their subjective identification with a system of social values rooted in the status-conscious society of the Second Empire. With the outbreak of the world economic crisis and the increasing fragmentation of the Weimar party system, the task of translating this potential into political reality became the overriding issue of German domestic politics. At no point was the urgency with which the leaders of Germany's bourgeois parties addressed themselves to the question of bourgeois concentration more apparent than in the immediate aftermath of Brüning's call for new elections. Yet what militated so decisively against the efforts to forge a higher degree of political cohesiveness among the various nonsocialist parties to the left of the DNVP was first of all the increasing fragmentation of Germany's middle-class interest structure and secondly the existence of not one but a multitude of schemes for bourgeois concentration. The fate of the movement for bourgeois unity in the summer of 1930, therefore, was ultimately decided by the fact that these schemes cut across each other in such a way that they rendered the implementation of any particular scheme impossible. This, in turn, only added to the confusion that already existed within Germany's middle-class electorate and left the established bourgeois parties increasingly vulnerable to the threat of Nazi penetration.

The leaders of the two liberal parties responded to the situation that had been created by the dissolution of the Reichstag in dramatically different fashions. The DVP's disastrous performance in the Saxon Landtag elections had convinced Scholz and other party leaders that only the establishment of closer political ties among the parties to the left of Hugenberg's DNVP could arrest the decline of the bourgeois middle and overcome middle-class indifference toward the established bourgeois parties.[2] Scholz was particularly interested in the possibility of closer ties with the various groups that had broken away from the DNVP, and on the afternoon of 21 July he met with Count Kuno von Westarp, Hugenberg's predecessor as Nationalist party chairman and the leader of a second secession from the DNVP three days earlier. Dismissing the founding of a united bourgeois party as impracticable in light of the short time that remained before the election, Scholz proposed the formation of a bourgeois unity ticket embracing the various groups from the Democrats to Westarp and his associates on Germany's moderate Right. The purpose of such a ticket, Scholz explained, would be to marshal support for Brüning's domestic reforms, to protect the state against the resurgence of radicalism on left and right, and to create a strong bourgeois counterweight to the influence of Social Democracy.[3] Although Westarp's response was noncommittal, Scholz proceeded on the following day to send Brüning and the leaders of the DDP, Business Party, and Christian-National Coalition an open letter inviting them to take part in conversations aimed at satisfying the "strong yearning for consolidation of all state-supporting forces" that had made itself felt in broad sectors of the German populace.[4]

Scholz's initiative received strong, albeit skeptical, encouragement from the leaders of the German industrial establishment. Germany's industrial leadership had long deplored the disunity of the bourgeoisie as a source of its own weakness vis-à-vis organized labor and looked upon the establishment of closer ties among the parties to the left of the DNVP as a means of offsetting Social Democratic dominance in the Reichstag.[5] Here the principal impetus came from a group of conservative Ruhr industrialists led by Paul Reusch and Fritz Springorum, two of the more politically active members of the Ruhrlade, which had been founded on Reusch's initiative as the "secret cabinet" of Ruhr heavy industry in late 1927. For the most part, Reusch and his associates were critical of the political course Hugenberg had pursued since his election to the DNVP party chairmanship, and they were fully prepared to help Westarp in his efforts to organize the various elements that had broken away from the DNVP into a new conservative party.[6] At the same time, however, they hoped the new party that Westarp and his supporters were in the process of founding would join the DVP and other moderate bourgeois parties in some sort of alliance for the Reichstag elections that were scheduled to take place in September. It was precisely with this in mind that Reusch and his associates in the Ruhrlade threatened to withhold financial support from any party, including the Center and DNVP, that refused to participate in a political truce for the duration of the campaign.[7]

Industrial pressure notwithstanding, the initial response to Scholz's invitation of 22 July was hardly encouraging. Westarp, for example, was so preoccupied with the task of organizing the various groups that had broken away from the DNVP into a new political party called the Conservative People's Party (Konservative Volkspartei or KVP) that he regarded Scholz's appeal for the consolidation of all "state-supporting" forces as an unwanted distraction from his immediate objective.[8] Still, the founders of the Conservative People's Party were desperately short of funds and could ill afford to turn their backs upon the contributions that Reusch and his associates were prepared to make if they only agreed to some sort of electoral alliance with the other moderate bourgeois parties. Consequently, when Westarp and his supporters met with representatives from the German business community shortly before the KVP's official founding on the afternoon of 23 July, they took special pains to stress that while they had little interest in a merger with other political parties, they were not opposed to an agreement aimed at minimizing interparty animosity during the campaign. Nor did Westarp and his associates rule out the possibility of a parliamentary coalition or *Fraktionsgemeinschaft* between the various non-Catholic parties that supported the Brüning government once the elections were over.[9] But Westarp's willingness to participate in an electoral truce with the other bourgeois parties to the left of the DNVP did not extend to either of the other two parties that had emerged from the ruins of the DNVP's left wing. On 20 July the leaders of the Christian-Social People's Service voted overwhelmingly to enter the upcoming campaign with its own slate of candidates, and on the following weekend the party's national executive committee explicitly rejected the idea of an electoral alliance with other political parties for fear that this would compromise the unique confessional orientation that lay at the heart of the CSVD's political program.[10] By the same token, the leaders of the Christian-National Peasants and Farmers' Party remained adamant in their opposition to any agreement with other political groups that might weaken the appeal they intended to make along class and vocational lines and cautiously avoided any reference to Scholz's proposal in the election appeal the CNBLP issued on 23 July.[11] The same was also true of the Business Party, where Drewitz casually dismissed Scholz's proposal at a meeting of the WP leadership on 24 July as only the most recent in a long string of attempts to salvage what still remained of Germany's traditional bourgeois parties.[12]

As in the case of the parliamentary alliance he had proposed the previous spring, Scholz's appeal for the consolidation of all "state-supporting" bourgeois forces encountered strong resistance from the leaders of the DDP. Opening his party's campaign in Berlin on 23 July, Koch-Weser criticized Scholz's proposal as a premature initiative that lacked the necessary consensus on such fundamental issues as federal reform, tariff policy, and foreign affairs.[13] Yet while the Democrats had little interest in an accommodation with the more conservative bourgeois parties, they could hardly afford to be saddled with the public onus for the collapse of efforts to form such an alliance.[14] Consequently, the Democrats were left with no alternative but to participate in the initial stages of the negotiations while hoping all along that other difficulties would force an end to Scholz's efforts. At the same time, the Democrats instructed Ernst Lemmer, a member of the DDP's left wing who had been on good terms with the Young German leadership ever since the spring of 1929, to approach Mahraun about the possibility of an alliance of their own.[15] This overture came at a particularly opportune moment, for not only were the Democrats greatly impressed by the performance of Mahraun's People's National Reich Association in Saxony, but the leaders of the VNR were already making preparations to enter the forthcoming national campaign with their own slate of candidates.[16] The fact, however, that the VNR possessed neither the organization nor the experienced political leadership to conduct a national campaign made its leaders more amenable to an alliance with the Democrats than the latter had expected, with the result that negotiations between representatives from the two groups began in earnest on the evening of 23 July.[17]

As representatives from the DDP and People's National Reich Association met over the course of the next four days, agreement proved far more extensive than the leaders of the two organizations had originally expected. The Democrats, who had intensified their contacts with the Young Germans at the beginning of the year in hopes that closer political ties might eventually develop,[18] were represented by Koch-Weser, Lemmer, Gertrud Bäumer, and Oskar Meyer, while Mahraun and his principal associate in the leadership of the Young German Order, Otto Bornemann, took part on behalf of the VNR. While the Democrats were hopeful that the VNR, with its youthful idealism and selfless devotion to the state, might provide the spiritual cement necessary to fuse the German middle into a dynamic political force,[19] Mahraun and his associates were anxious to sustain the momentum that had been generated by the VNR's performance in the Saxon state elections and hoped that an alliance with the DDP would enable them to overcome their lack of a national organization. Neither the Democrats nor the Young Germans, however, believed that the conclusion of an electoral alliance would be sufficient to overcome the apathy and factionalism of the German middle, with the result that their discussion began to focus more and more on the possibility of founding an entirely new party. A serious deadlock, however, developed when Mahraun, reluctant to accept the entire Democratic Party into the new organization, proposed that the DDP continue to exist as a separate home for all of those "state-supporting" elements on Germany's bourgeois Left that might not be suitable for membership in the new party. It was only when Koch-Weser threatened to break off negotiations if the new party was not open to all members of the DDP, including those on its extreme left wing, that Mahraun acceded, though only on the condition that the party be extended to the right at the earliest possible opportunity.[20]

Precisely what Mahraun meant by an extension of the party to the right was not immediately clear. Although Mahraun was pleased by the decision of Fritz Baltrusch, Arthur Adolf, Erich Glimm, and a handful of former Nationalists with close ties to the Christian labor movement to join the new party, this was hardly sufficient to avoid the stigma he feared would result from the absorption of the entire DDP. Ideally Mahraun would have liked an accommodation with the young conservatives around Treviranus and Lindeiner-Wildau, but with the founding of the Conservative People's Party that was no longer a realistic possibility. Consequently, the founders of the new party began to turn their attention to the DVP, where they hoped to take advantage of the split that had developed between Scholz and the leaders of his party's left wing. In this respect, they not only hoped to win the support of prominent DVP parliamentarians like Julius Curtius, Otto Thiel, and Eduard Dingeldey[21] but also to secure a major breakthrough into the ranks of the various Young Liberal groups that had assembled on the party's left wing. The frustration that these elements felt over the situation in the DVP had already manifested itself in a sharply worded letter that the leaders of the February Club had sent to Scholz following the VNR's decision to enter the Saxon Landtag elections earlier that summer,[22] and there was every reason for Koch-Weser and his associates to believe that they could be won over to the support of the party they were in the process of founding.

Immediately after the dissolution of the Reichstag, the leaders of an amorphous group calling itself the Young Front for Political Concentration (Junge Front der staatspolitischen Sammlung) had invited the leaders of the DDP, DVP, and Business Party to a meeting on the afternoon of 26 July for the purpose of developing a coordinated strategy for the upcoming campaign.[23] Founded in April 1930 and headed by the February Club's Josef Winschuh, this group included representatives from the Young German Order, the People's Conservative Association, the Front 1929, and several lesser-known organizations, and it sought to bring together all of those within the younger generation who, regardless of party affiliation or ideological persuasion, were committed to the ideal of a united and socially progressive bourgeois party.[24] From the very outset, however, the discussion was marked by a sharp divergence of opinion between those like Koch-Weser who argued that such an effort should include only groups that shared a common ideological heritage and those like Frank Glatzel who maintained that any such action should take place on the broadest possible basis without regard for outmoded ideological distinctions such as liberal and conservative. When Koch-Weser went so far as to propose—without, however, giving any indication of the far-reaching agreement that he had just reached with the VNR—the creation of a united middle party, the proposal was immediately rejected by the DVP's Adolf Kempkes on the grounds that the technical difficulties involved in such an undertaking could not be solved in the short time that still remained before the election. His party, therefore, would not be able to take part in such a project.[25]

The discussion was continued without Kempkes but in the presence of a delegation from the People's National Reich Association at a second meeting later that evening. To the general astonishment of Winschuh and his associates, Koch-Weser broke the news of the agreement that had just been reached between the DDP and VNR and asked which of the groups from the Young Front were prepared to join them in their efforts to consolidate the German *Staatsbürgertum* into a united political party dedicated to the preservation of the state against the radicalism of the Left and the Right. But whereas Glatzel and his associates from the RjV criticized Koch-Weser's unorthodox methods and tried to secure a postponement of the new party's founding so that they might have an opportunity to consult with the leaders of the DVP, not only Winschuh, but also Rochus von Rheinbaben from the Front 1929 and Theodor Eschenburg from the Quirites had become so frustrated by the DVP's indifference to the aspirations of the younger generation—and particularly by Scholz's failure to attend the meeting they had held earlier in the day—that after a period of initial hesitation they decided to cast their lot with the new party.[26]

Over the course of the next thirty-six hours Koch-Weser made a determined effort to secure the cooperation of the leaders of the DVP's left wing. These overtures took place behind the backs of Scholz and the DVP party leadership. At no time between their first meeting on 23 July and the official founding of the new party on 28 July did Koch-Weser, Mahraun, or any of their associates try to establish contact with Scholz or the DVP's central headquarters in Berlin since, on the basis of their own experience, nothing was to be accomplished through direct negotiations with the DVP as long as a man like Scholz remained at its helm.[27] Under these circumstances, Koch-Weser hoped that the close personal ties he had cultivated over the last two years with Kahl, Curtius, and other members of the DVP's left wing would enable him to overcome the inertia of existing party bureaucracies.[28] But when Koch-Weser informed Kahl of the plans to found a new party on the evening of 26 July, the DVP patriarch replied that while he fully sympathized with the efforts to consolidate the German middle, his own sense of party loyalty prevented him from supporting the new party without first consulting his own party leadership. Likewise, Dingeldey was so offended by the way in which Koch-Weser had operated behind the backs of his own party's leaders that he too rallied to the defense of the DVP.[29] Whatever hopes Koch-Weser may have originally had of securing a major breakthrough into the ranks of the DVP's left wing had been all but dashed before the founding of his own party ever took place.

After five days of exhaustive negotiations, Koch-Weser, Mahraun, and Winschuh formally announced the founding of the German State Party (Deutsche Staatspartei or DStP) at a press conference on the morning of 28 July.[30] From the outset, the founders of the State Party took special pains to stress that the DStP was not a merger of existing political parties but an entirely new party that sought to mobilize the German middle into a dynamic political force capable of freeing the state from the tyranny of outside economic interests.[31] It was in this spirit that the founders of the DStP issued a special appeal to the younger generation and received declarations of support from the National Federation of German Democratic Youth, the Front 1929, and the leaders of the west German February Club movement.[32] Of the various organizations that claimed to speak in the name of the younger generation, only the Reich Association of Young Populists refused to identify itself with the State Party. Although Glatzel and the leaders of the RjV sympathized with the goals of the new party and could ill afford to repudiate it in view of their own campaign for a united middle party, they denounced the way in which the State Party had been founded as an attempt to destroy the unity and political effectiveness of their own political party.[33] Having already reached an agreement with Scholz by which his election to the Reichstag had been assured, Glatzel maintained that the cause of bourgeois unity could best be served by an accommodation between the DVP and State Party and urged his followers to use all of their influence within the DVP to soften its stand against the new party.[34]

The founding of the German State Party on 28 July 1930 came as an unexpected shock not only to the leaders of the DVP but also to Koch-Weser's colleagues in the leadership of the DDP. Koch-Weser had kept the circle of those who knew about his negotiations with the VNR intentionally small, and he had given his colleagues only an inkling of what was actually afoot when the DDP executive committee met to discuss election strategy on the afternoon of 25 July.[35] Koch-Weser's failure to consult with the proper party organs before going ahead with the founding of the DStP provoked a storm of protest on the party's left wing, where trade-union secretary Anton Erkelenz shocked his colleagues by announcing his defection to the Social Democrats.[36] The danger that this might develop into a major secession on the DDP's left wing, however, quickly evaporated when Hans Muhle, Hermann Schäfer, and the leaders of the Social Republican Circle rallied to the defense of the new party at a crucial meeting of the DDP party council on 30 July. This group, consisting for the most part of younger party members who had attached themselves to Lemmer's political star, was attracted to the Young German Order's political idealism and regarded the founding of the DStP as the beginning of a frontal assault against the role that organized capitalist interests had come to play in German public life. At the same time that their enthusiasm for the new party did much to minimize the possibility of a mass exodus on the DDP's left wing, the strong support that the State Party received from Hellpach, Stolper, and Oskar Meyer effectively blunted the criticism of those on the party's right wing who not only resented the high-handed manner in which the founding of the DStP had taken place but criticized Koch-Weser's failure to reach an accommodation with the DVP.[37]

Though confused and in some cases embittered by Koch-Weser's fait accompli, the DDP party council was left with no choice but to go along with the agreement Koch-Weser had reached with Mahraun and the leaders of the VNR two days earlier. Within the DVP, on the other hand, the mood was even more turbulent. Speaking at a meeting of the DVP national committee on 31 July, Scholz leveled a stinging indictment against the founders of the State Party for having negotiated behind his back with members of his own party and denounced the merger between the Democrats and the VNR as a one-sided distortion of the ideal of bourgeois concentration propagated by himself and the leaders of the DVP.[38] The sharp rebuff that Scholz handed the founders of the DStP had immediate repercussions within the Reich Association of Young Populists, where Glatzel was struggling desperately to hold his followers in line. Anxious to prevent the question of the State Party from disrupting the convention the RjV was scheduled to hold in Kassel on 3 August, Glatzel not only had those members of the RjV who had joined the DStP or belonged to the Young German Order summarily expelled from the organization before the convention took place but also blocked the RjV's representatives from Frankfurt, Lübeck, and Berlin from introducing a resolution in support of a reconciliation between the DVP and the State Party.[39] As a result, Glatzel faced little or no opposition in securing the passage of a resolution at Kassel that denounced the founding of the DStP as incompatible with its own conception of bourgeois unity and called upon the founders of the DStP to join the DVP in the creation of a truly comprehensive middle party.[40]

Much of the rancor that Scholz and his supporters felt toward the founders of the State Party stemmed from the fact that the creation of the DStP had cut across their own, admittedly more modest, efforts at bourgeois concentration.[41] The first meeting between representatives from the various groups to which Scholz had addressed his appeal of 22 July did not take place until the afternoon of 30 July, by which time the State Party was already two days old. When Scholz's inquiry as to which of these groups were prepared to join the DVP in the creation of a united middle party evoked a cool response from

Treviranus, Drewitz, and Koch-Weser, he broached the possibility of an electoral truce for the duration of the campaign and proposed the publication of a
joint election appeal in support of the reform program that Brüning had just
begun to implement under the mantle of Reich President von Hindenburg. At
the same time, Scholz alluded to the need for closer parliamentary cooperation
between the various parties that supported the Brüning government, presumably in the form of a parliamentary *Arbeitsgemeinschaft* once the elections
were over.[42] When these proposals met with no objections from the leaders of
the other three parties, a second meeting was scheduled for the afternoon of 31
July, whereupon Koch-Weser announced that the State Party would not take
part in the publication of a joint election appeal and was therefore withdrawing
from further negotiations directed toward that end. Undaunted by Koch-
Weser's announcement, Scholz and the other party leaders agreed to continue
their efforts at another meeting on the following day. Here the DVP, WP, and
KVP were joined by the CNBLP's Günther Gereke, who agreed to join the
other three parties in the publication of a special election appeal under the
name "Hindenburg Program" that committed them to the implementation and
defense of Brüning's domestic reforms. The DVP's Adolf Kempkes was then
commissioned to draft the text of the proposed appeal so that it could be
presented at the next scheduled meeting of the four parties on 7 August.[43]

Surprised by the vehemence with which Scholz and the leaders of the DVP
had denounced the founding of the State Party, Koch-Weser tried to assuage
the hard feelings that had developed between their two parties by writing a
personal letter to the DVP party chairman in which he suggested that they set
aside their differences so that negotiations aimed at a merger of the DVP and
DStP might begin. Skeptical that anything could be accomplished as long as
Scholz remained at the helm of the DVP, Koch-Weser concluded his overture
by proposing that they both withdraw from the leadership of the new party and
leave it in the hands of those less scarred by the skirmishes of the past.[44] In
light of the heavy fire that Scholz had drawn from the German liberal press for
his uncompromising rejection of the State Party, he could hardly reject Koch-
Weser's proposal out of hand and agreed to a meeting between himself and the
DStP's Hermann Höpker-Aschoff on the afternoon of 7 August.[45] Yet for all of
Scholz's apparent interest in an understanding with the State Party, his meeting
with Höpker-Aschoff was doomed to failure from the very outset. Scholz
opened the meeting by proposing the unilateral absorption of the State Party
into the DVP, in which case he would step down as its chairman and the DVP
would change its name to the somewhat awkward amalgam of German People's (State) Party (Deutsche Volks[Staats-]partei). When Scholz defended
such an arrangement on the grounds that it did not close the door to a further
extension of the party to the right, Höpker-Aschoff rejected it not only because
of the subordinate status it offered the DStP but, more importantly, because it

was animated by an antisocialist bias that would only exacerbate the social antagonisms already dividing the German people. What Höpker-Aschoff sought, as he explained in an article for the *Kölnische Zeitung* several days later, was the consolidation of the "Freies Bürgertum"—that is, white-collar employees, artisans, independent businessmen, intellectuals, and professionals—into a united liberal party that could take its place alongside the SPD, Center, and conservative Right as one of the four pillars of the German party system.[46] Scholz, on the other hand, refused to recognize Höpker-Aschoff's distinction between liberal and conservative and rejected his proposal for a merger of the DVP and DStP as a distortion of the ideal of bourgeois concentration that he and his party had been propagating since the DVP's Mannheim party congress earlier that spring.[47]

The outcome of the meeting between Scholz and Höpker-Aschoff on the afternoon of 7 August signaled the collapse of efforts to create a united liberal party through a merger of the DVP and DStP.[48] At the same time, Scholz's efforts to negotiate an electoral truce between the various non-Catholic parties that supported the government were drawing to an equally disappointing conclusion. When Scholz and the leaders of the WP, KVP, and CNBLP had last parted company on 1 August, it had been with the understanding that they would meet in six days to approve the text of a joint appeal they planned to issue in support of the reform program popularly associated with the name of Reich President von Hindenburg. But before the details of this arrangement could be finalized, a number of ultimately insoluble problems developed. Drewitz and the leaders of the Business Party, for example, had come under increasingly heavy pressure from the party's district and local organizatons to dissociate themselves from the entire action and to refrain from all ties with other bourgeois parties.[49] At the same time, the leaders of the newly founded Conservative People's Party were anxious to avoid any policy that might identify their party too closely with the DVP and made their participation in Scholz's joint election appeal contingent upon the cooperation of their allies in the Christian-National Peasants and Farmers' Party. But whereas Gereke and Minister of Agriculture Martin Schiele, the chief architects of the CNBLP's alliance with the KVP, were prepared to cooperate with the other bourgeois parties under the auspices of the Hindenburg Program, the forces around Karl Hepp and CNBLP party chairman Ernst Höfer were adamantly opposed to the concept of bourgeois unity and refused to countenance any accommodation between the CNBLP and the other parties to the left of Hugenberg's DNVP.[50]

The next meeting between the leaders of the four parties that had initially agreed to conduct their campaign under the banner of the Hindenburg Program was scheduled to take place immediately after the meeting between Scholz and Höpker-Aschoff on the afternoon of 7 August. Gereke opened the meeting with an announcement that he had been unable to persuade the leaders of his party to go along with the action that had been proposed by Scholz and that the CNBLP was therefore withdrawing from the joint appeal. While the KVP's Lindeiner-Wildau responded to Gereke's announcement by asking for a recess so that he might consult with the leadership of his own party, the WP's Gotthard Sachsenberg argued that the withdrawal of the CNBLP made it impossible for the WP, as the only remaining vocational party, to go ahead with the project. The strain that had developed in relations between the DVP and DStP, however, made it difficult for Scholz to agree to a postponement of the final decision on the outside chance that either the WP or CNBLP might reconsider its position. Under these circumstances, the leaders of the four parties agreed that there was no point to continuing their efforts on behalf of a truce in the forthcoming election campaign.[51]

The collapse of Scholz's efforts to negotiate an electoral truce between the moderate bourgeois parties to the left of the DNVP came as a bitter disappointment to the group around Reusch and Springorum. On 8 August representatives from the Ruhrlade met with Treviranus, Westarp, and Gereke, along with a handful of lesser-known politicians from the Center and moderate Right, in Springorum's Berlin offices. At the urging of Springorum and his associates, Treviranus and his supporters agreed to resume the efforts at bourgeois concentration that the collapse of Scholz's negotiations on the previous day had left in such disarray. The State Party, however, would be excluded from such an undertaking because of the negative attitude its leaders had consistently manifested toward the idea of bourgeois unity.[52] Two days later Treviranus publicly invited the leaders of the other three parties back to the negotiating table in hopes that their shared sense of responsibility toward the state would prove stronger than the sectarian issues that divided them.[53] At the same time, the group around Reusch and Springorum used its financial resources to soften the WP's opposition to a joint appeal with the DVP and KVP. Not only did Sachsenberg receive a campaign contribution of 20,000 marks in return for his efforts on behalf of bourgeois unity, but Reusch and his associates held out the prospect of further aid if the WP agreed to go along with the creation of a united bourgeois ticket for the upcoming elections.[54] Not even the leaders of the WP could afford to turn their backs upon support of this magnitude, with the result that on 18 August Drewitz and Sachsenberg agreed, though without consulting any of the responsible organs within their party, to join the DVP and KVP in issuing a joint election appeal that pledged them to set aside their differences for the sake of a united effort on behalf of the domestic reforms initiated by Hindenburg. At Scholz's suggestion, publication of the appeal was delayed until 21 August so that an effort to secure the signatures of the Christian-Social People's Service and German State Party might be made.[55]

As a response to the need for greater political cohesiveness among the "state-supporting" elements of the German bourgeoisie, the joint appeal that the DVP, KVP, and WP issued in support of the Hindenburg Program on 21 August 1930 was woefully inadequate. At no point since the founding of the Weimar Republic had conditions for the creation of a united middle party been more favorable or the need for such a party more evident than in the period immediately following Brüning's call for new elections in the summer of 1930. For all of its obvious shortcomings, the founding of the German State Party represented a concerted attempt to fuse the democratic and progressive elements of the German bourgeoisie into a united middle party that, had it materialized according to the dreams of its founders, might have prevented—or at least impeded—the sharp swing to the right that characterized Germany's political development from 1930 to 1933. It was, for all practical purposes, the last attempt to consolidate the German middle on the basis of a democratic and socially progressive platform that offered the slightest prospect of success. The fate of the State Party, however, was in large part decided by the fact that its founding cut across a second, more modest attempt at bourgeois concentration on the part of the leaders of the DVP. This, in conjunction with the fact that the founders of the State Party had made secret overtures to prominent representatives of the DVP's left wing, so infuriated the leaders of the People's Party that an accommodation between the two liberal parties became impossible. Under these circumstances, the joint appeal issued by the DVP, KVP, and WP remained little more than an empty gesture that offered the appearance but not the substance of bourgeois unity.

Appeals for a reform and realignment of the German party system had become an increasingly prominent feature of Germany's political landscape in the two years since the last national elections in the spring of 1928. The net effect of this agitation, however, was only to arouse popular expectations that none of Germany's more moderate bourgeois parties was capable of satisfying. The failure of the liberal parties to develop a coherent response to the growing pressure for a higher degree of bourgeois political cohesiveness severely compromised whatever legitimacy they still possessed in the eyes of the social groups that had traditionally supported them. As the German liberal parties entered the campaign for the 1930 national elections, their inability to satisfy the longing for unity to which the deepening economic crisis and the increasing fragmentation of the Weimar party system had given rise left them defenseless against the more radical schemes for bourgeois concentration that had surfaced on the German Right.

CHAPTER TWENTY-EIGHT

Defeat and Demoralization

IN THE DEBATE THAT PRECEDED the dissolution of the Reichstag on 18 July 1930, the DDP's Hermann Dietrich warned that the decisive question facing the German nation was whether it was merely an agglomeration of private interests or a *Staatsvolk* capable of recognizing the identity of its own welfare with that of the state as a whole.[1] Dietrich's speech brought the paralytic effect that the increasing fragmentation of the Weimar party system had had upon the authority of the state and its ability to cope with the deepening economic crisis into dramatic focus. At the same time, it reflected the growing frustration that not only influential sectors of Germany's elite but also increasingly large segments of her middle-class electorate felt about the inability of Weimar's parliamentary institutions to produce a viable domestic consensus upon which effective national leadership might be based. Appeals for the creation of a united liberal party, for a rejuvenation and reorganization of the German party system, and for greater bourgeois cohesiveness in the face of Marxism all represented different responses to the crisis of bourgeois hegemony as it had developed in Germany at the beginning of the 1930s. But as the tortuous and ultimately futile course of negotiations in the period following the dissolution of the Reichstag clearly revealed, Germany's bourgeois leadership was no longer capable of articulating a coherent response to the deepening crisis in which the Weimar state found itself on the eve of the 1930 Reichstag elections. Nor was it able to satisfy the increasingly powerful longing for a higher degree of political solidarity that the fragmentation of the bourgeois party system and the deteriorating economic situation had produced within the ranks of Germany's middle-class electorate.[2]

The dissolution of the Weimar party system was already well advanced when Brüning issued his call for new elections in the summer of 1930. As far as the parties of the middle and moderate Right were concerned, the most pressing question was whether or not they could sustain themselves as individual entities now that efforts at bourgeois concentration had brought such meager results. Much of the campaign between the two liberal parties, therefore, focused on the question of responsibility for the collapse of the negotiations that had taken place in the wake of Brüning's call for new elections. In this respect, the leaders of the DVP were quick to assail the founders of the State Party for having sabotaged the admittedly more modest efforts at bourgeois concentration that Scholz had initiated with his appeal of 22 July.[3] By the same token, they portrayed the founding of the State Party as a marriage of desperation between the Democrats and Young Germans and insisted that the new party was nothing but the old DDP under a new name. Or, as one DVP pun so aptly put it: "An old cook [Koch], a new stew/The German State Party through and through!"[4] To justify this position in the face of widespread criticism from their party's rank-and-file membership, the leaders of the DVP cited the differences that separated the two parties on the question of cooperation with the Social Democrats as the principal reason for their refusal to join the DStP in the creation of a united liberal party.[5] Not only were Scholz and his supporters deeply suspicious of the State Party's commitment to a policy of constructive cooperation with the Social Democrats, but their own interest in the concept of bourgeois concentration was rooted in their desire to exclude the SPD from any sort of meaningful role in Germany's political future.

The vehemence with which Scholz and the leaders of the DVP attacked the concept of bourgeois concentration as it had manifested itself in the founding of the German State Party came as a sharp rebuff to elements within the German bourgeoisie that still nurtured hopes of a united liberal party.[6] This was particularly true in Württemberg, where the leaders of the two liberal parties agreed on 10 August to run a single slate of candidates in the forthcoming Reichstag elections without first consulting their respective superiors in Berlin.[7] A similar agreement was concluded shortly thereafter in the neighboring state of Baden, where on 9 August Dietrich had approached the DVP's Julius Curtius with the proposal that they place themselves at the head of a joint ticket in their own home state.[8] Anxious to avoid another fait accompli in Schleswig-Holstein, the DVP's national headquarters in Berlin interceded with the leaders of the local party organization there to block the conclusion of an agreement similar to those that had just been reached between the two liberal parties in Baden and Württemberg.[9] Although it was eventually the State Party and not the DVP that broke off negotiations in Schleswig-Holstein, the interference of the DVP's national headquarters was deeply resented by the local party leadership and only dramatized the gulf that had developed between the party's national leaders and its rank-and-file membership on the question of bourgeois unity.[10]

The polemics over the question of responsibility for the failure of bourgeois unity quickly exhausted whatever enthusiasm the founding of the German State Party had evoked within the ranks of Germany's middle-class electorate. Still, the leaders of the State Party were anxious to capitalize upon the widespread disaffection that Scholz's equivocation in the matter of bourgeois concentration had produced among the DVP's rank and file and insisted that only the creation of an entirely new party—not the merger of existing party organizations—could possibly overcome the lassitude and factionalism that more than a decade of political impotence had produced within the German middle. Characterizing their party as a "self-help organization" for all of those who placed the welfare of the state before their own private interests, the founders of the State Party were particularly vehement in denouncing not only the various special interest parties that had surfaced in Germany since the middle of the 1920s but also the DVP and DNVP for having capitulated to the rising tide of interest politics.[11] By the same token, the leaders of the DStP categorically rejected the concept of bourgeois unity as promulgated by the leaders of the DVP on the grounds that this would only exacerbate the social and economic cleavages that already existed within the German nation. The only beneficiaries of such an arrangement would be the special economic interests that had used their control of the DVP to subvert the DStP's efforts at *staatsbürgerliche* concentration on the broadest possible basis.[12] Fearful that accommodation with the more established bourgeois parties would only compromise their own party's appeal as a new political entity, the leaders of the State Party declined Scholz's invitation to join the DVP, KVP, and Business Party in publishing a joint appeal in support of the Hindenburg Program in the second half of August.[13]

The feud with Scholz severely handicapped the DStP in its efforts to legitimize itself as a party of national concentration. An even more serious obstacle to the party's effectiveness in the campaign for the 1930 Reichstag elections was the increasing friction between old-line Democrats and the leaders of the Young German Order. Although the DDP party council had endorsed the founding of the State Party by an overwhelming margin at its meeting on 30 July, the alliance with the Young German Order was particularly unpopular in such traditional Democratic strongholds as Baden, Württemberg, and Hamburg.[14] But Erkelenz's defection to the SPD was an option few Democrats, including those who had been most outspoken in their opposition to the founding of the State Party, were willing to follow. For the pacifist elements that had traditionally stood on the DDP's left wing the only way out of the dilemma in which their party's merger with the Young German Order had placed them was to found a new organization of their own known as the Union of Independent Democrats (Vereinigung Unabhängiger Demokraten) under the chairmanship of Ludwig Quidde, president of the German Peace Society, at a special convention in Nuremberg on 3 August. Outside of Quidde and other dissident Democrats such as Georg Bernhard and Hellmuth von Gerlach, the union's major source of support came from the leaders of the Young Democratic movement in Nuremberg, Berlin-Brandenburg, and Hamburg. The founders of the new organization were particularly critical of the slow drift to the right that had taken place within the DDP since the 1928 Reichstag elections and hoped to establish themselves as the point around which erstwhile Democrats who refused to accept the founding of the State Party could coalesce. Recognizing that their organization lacked the resources to mount an effective campaign in the short time that still remained before the election, the renegade Democrats refrained from running their own slate of candidates. At the same time, however, they encouraged their supporters to vote for the democratic party of their choice so as to weaken the chances of the antirepublican parties that stood at the extremes of Germany's political spectrum.[15]

The founding of the German State Party had an equally disquieting effect upon the DDP's Jewish supporters. Of all the bourgeois parties, the DDP had always been the clear favorite of the German Jewish community's estimated 200,000 voters, about half of whom had supported the party with varying degrees of loyalty ever since its founding in 1918. The highly visible role that Wolff, Rathenau, Preuss, and other prominent Jews had played in the DDP's early development, however, had left the party vulnerable to agitation from anti-Semitic circles intent upon discrediting it as the pawn of "Jewish finance capital" or the party of the "metropolitan Jewish press." The fact that their party had always served as such a convenient target for anti-Semitic propaganda may have had something to do with the residual antipathy that many leading Democrats, including Koch-Weser and Dietrich, harbored toward those features of Germany's postwar development with which Jews were popularly associated.[16] Although this rarely translated into anything serious enough to threaten the DDP's Jewish support, the alliance with the Young German Order in the summer of 1930 aroused widespread apprehension within those Jewish circles that had traditionally voted Democratic. To many Jews, the Young German Order was part of the same basic milieu that had spawned the Stahlhelm and NSDAP, and they took particular offense at a paragraph in the Order's statutes that barred them from membership in the organization. Mahraun, who had no sympathy for the more virulent forms of anti-Semitic prejudice that had erupted on Germany's radical Right, tried to reassure the DDP's Jewish supporters by issuing a statement in the first week of August that denounced anti-Semitism as a form of cultural barbarism.[17] The fact, however, that Mahraun bracketed his condemnation of racial hatred with a reaffirmation of the Order's commitment to the defense of Germany's Christian culture undercut whatever palliative effect it and similar statements by Koch-Weser and other party leaders were supposed to have upon the DDP's Jewish electorate. Jewish concerns about the new party were only reinforced by the strong opposition that the nomination of Jewish candidates, perhaps best illustrated by the case of Gustav Stolper, encountered from the Young Germans in one district after another.[18]

The dispute over the selection of candidates was only one of the problems that plagued the unity of the DStP during the first months of its existence. At the outset, leadership of the DStP lay in the hands of an ad hoc fifteen-member action committee consisting of five representatives each from the DDP, VNR, and the Young Liberal faction that had formerly stood on the DVP's left wing. As long as Koch-Weser had served as the DDP's principal representative in the DStP action committee, the Young Germans had little reason to complain about the cooperation of the Democrats. But following the collapse of his negotiations with Scholz in the first week of August, Koch-Weser had delegated his responsibilities as the DDP's chief liaison with the VNR to Höpker-Aschoff, a man who had little sympathy for the Order's unabashed romanticism. Not only did Höpker-Aschoff infuriate the leaders of the VNR by proposing a merger between the DStP and DVP in his conversation with Scholz on 7 August, but a week later he threatened to resign from the action committee if Stolper were not allowed to head the DStP ticket in Hamburg.[19] At the same time, the conflict between the Democrats and Young Germans over the selection of candidates for the upcoming election had assumed such an intensity that not one of the candidates proposed by the VNR was accepted without a bitter fight from the leaders of the local DDP organization.[20] Although the leaders of the VNR eventually expressed satisfaction with all but a handful of the candidates selected to head the DStP ticket at the district level, the friction that had developed between them and old-line Democrats did much to dampen their enthusiasm for the new party and severely impaired the DStP's effectiveness in the campaign for the September 1930 Reichstag elections.

The difficulties that the DStP experienced in the nomination of candidates for the September elections carried over into the deliberations on the party program, where the unresolved tension between the liberalism of old-line Democrats like Dietrich, Stolper, and Höpker-Aschoff and the romanticism of the Young German Order continue to frustrate efforts to achieve party unity.[21] The major programmatic statement issued by the DStP on 22 August under the title "Manifesto of the German State Party" did little more than reformulate traditional Democratic objectives such as federal and electoral reform in the vocabulary of the German youth movement and was characteristically vague on questions of social and economic policy. Aside from a general appeal for the creation of a "social capitalism" in which the needs of the economy were to be reconciled with the welfare of the state as a whole, all the document had to offer on the crisis in which the German middle class found itself was a demand for more effective protection against those economic forces that threatened it with extinction through the large-scale concentration of economic power.[22] The way in which this statement conveniently ignored the specific problems that were pressing so heavily upon the German middle class contrasted sharply with how the political pragmatists around Dietrich and Stolper sought to structure their party's campaign. For them the key to the DStP's success at the polls lay in winning the support of those lower middle-class elements in the cities and countryside that the outbreak of the world economic crisis had done so much to radicalize. At the heart of their appeal for the support of the middle class lay an unequivocal commitment to its economic rehabilitation through a comprehensive fiscal and administrative reform aimed at reducing the tax burden with which it had been saddled.[23] For Mahraun and his associates, on the other hand, whatever hopes the State Party had of winning mass support lay not so much in an appeal to middle-class economic interests as in the articulation of an entirely new style of political leadership, one that, in the words of Gertrud Bäumer, a Democrat who had become particularly enamored of the Young German Order, combined the qualities of magic, Eros, and a sense of values rooted in the people.[24] What this represented was a clear retreat from the values of political liberalism as traditionally espoused by the leaders of the DDP into the naive, if not murky, romanticism of the German youth movement.

If the State Party was unable to articulate a coherent response to the increasing desperation of the German middle strata, the DVP found itself confronted by a situation that was every bit as threatening. Since the last general elections in the spring of 1928, the DVP's national organization had experienced the loss of an estimated 38,000 members, while over the same period of time the number of its local chapters had declined by nearly 15 percent to slightly more than 2,000.[25] At the heart of the DVP's organizational malaise lay its inability to reconcile the divergent interests of the various social and economic groups that constituted its material base. By the beginning of the 1930s the DVP drew the overwhelming bulk of its support from three principal groups: civil servants, white-collar employees, and independent businessmen. But, as a bitter exchange between representatives from the party's white-collar and business wings at a meeting of the DVP central executive committee on 4 July 1930 revealed, the deepening economic crisis placed a severe strain upon relations that even in the best of times were somewhat less than amicable.[26] The situation within the DVP was further complicated by the fact that Brüning's plans for balancing the national budget envisaged a general reduction in the salaries of all state civil servants. Spokesmen for the DVP's civil servant wing were in fact so incensed over Brüning's plans for restoring fiscal responsibility that they joined the party's business leaders in forcing Moldenhauer's resignation as minister of finance.[27] The tension within the party had hardly abated when Brüning proceeded to incorporate a 2.5 percent reduction in civil servant salaries into the special emergency decree that he issued on 26 July.[28]

The problem of maintaining party unity in the face of the deepening economic crisis became all too apparent at a special conference that the leaders of the DVP held in the Reichstag on 25 July for the purpose of formulating a unified position on the social and economic issues they expected to dominate the campaign. What emerged from this conference was a clear picture of the conflicting objectives of the three major groups that constituted the DVP's social base. Whereas spokesmen for the business interests on the DVP's right wing—Carl Cremer, Curt Hoff, and Otto Keinath—pressed the case for tax breaks that would facilitate the process of capital formation, Albrecht Morath spoke out as the party's chief liaison with the German Civil Servants' Association against any budget cuts that might affect the already precarious position of Germany's civil bureaucracy. Morath, however, conveniently ignored the fact that if significant cuts were not to be made in either the size or salaries of the civil service, only a general retrenchment in the area of social welfare could possibly achieve the reduction in taxes that the leaders of the DVP's business wing thought essential for Germany's economic recovery. But this suggestion encountered vigorous opposition from Otto Thiel, who argued on behalf of the DVP's white-collar wing that any cuts in social welfare would only inflict additional and unjustified hardship upon those who had already lost their jobs as a result of the depression. If anything, concluded Thiel, existing social welfare programs should be expanded in order to cope with the effects of the deepening economic crisis.[29]

If the social and economic fragmentation of Germany's middle-class electorate constituted one of the major problems facing the German liberal parties in the campaign for the 1930 Reichstag elections, a second and no less perplexing problem was the increasing disaffection of Germany's industrial elite. Germany's industrial leaders had grown increasingly frustrated with the plethora of political parties that had surfaced in Germany during the second half of the 1920s, and they had hoped that the call for new elections in the summer of 1930 might lead to the establishment of closer political ties between the various nonsocialist parties to the left of Hugenberg's DNVP.[30] It was this consideration that led Eduard Hamm, a former Democratic deputy from Bavaria and the executive secretary of the German Chamber of Industry and Commerce (Deutscher Industrie- und Handelstag), to praise the founding of the State Party as a first step toward the eventual consolidation of the liberal bourgeoisie in a united middle party.[31] But Hamm's enthusiasm for the new party was not shared by Paul Reusch and the leaders of German heavy industry, who were so frustrated by the way in which the founding of the DStP had sabotaged their efforts to forge an electoral alliance between the various non-Catholic bourgeois parties to the left of the DNVP that they decided to exclude it from any funds they might allocate for use in the campaign.[32] By the same token, the Curatorium for the Reconstruction of German Economic Life decided, in a move that mirrored its growing disillusionment over the way in which the German party system had developed since the early 1920s, to curtail its future operations. Confronted with the prospect of a new national campaign in which the movement for bourgeois unity had been reduced to a shambles, the Curatorium decided at a meeting of its executive committee on 28 August to raise no new funds but merely to allocate those already at its disposal. Under the terms of this arrangement the DNVP, DVP, State Party, and Conservative People's Party would each receive 24,000 marks directly from the Curatorium.[33] While the various firms that still belonged to the Curatorium were free to supplement these sums with individual contributions of their own, the amount of money that the Curatorium allocated to the two liberal parties for use in the 1930 campaign was only about one-fourth of what it had provided in 1928.

Both the DVP and DStP suffered from the fact that the general level of industrial financing in the campaign for the 1930 elections was markedly lower than it had been in previous national campaigns. The shortfall was crucial not only because of what the two parties were to waste in unproductive polemics against each other but also because the campaign found them engaged in a bitter two-front war against special interest parties on the one hand and National Socialism on the other. The Business Party, whose leaders refused to honor the electoral truce that national party chairman Hermann Drewitz had concluded with the leaders of the DVP and Conservative People's Party on 21 August,[34] tried to compensate for its relative ineffectiveness as a member of the Brüning government by waging a particularly aggressive campaign against the more established bourgeois parties. In this respect, the WP not only denounced the two years during which the DVP had shared governmental responsibility with the Social Democrats as a betrayal of the German middle class but held the State Party responsible for all of the sins that its predecessor, the DDP, had committed against middle-class economic interests during the twelve years of its existence.[35] But whatever aggressiveness the WP may have manifested toward the two liberal parties in its campaign for the 1930 elections was eclipsed by that of the National Socialist German Workers' Party. Claiming that an improvement in Germany's economic situation was impossible as long as she continued to pay tribute to the Allies, the Nazis condemned all of the parties from the Social Democrats to those that had emerged from the ruins of the DNVP's left wing as traitors to the national cause and held them publicly responsible for the catastrophic situation in which Germany found herself. The Nazis reserved their sharpest words, however, for the Young German Order, branding Mahraun and his associates as "Young-Deutschen" and denouncing them for their scandalous marriage to the DDP, the "typical party of Jewish finance capital." At the same time, the Nazis characterized the DVP as the "stirrup holder" for Social Democracy and singled out Stresemann, Moldenhauer, and Curtius as the three archtraitors responsible for betraying the German nation to the red menace.[36]

Underlying all of these charges was the common theme that the German middle parties, including the Center and those that had formed to the left of the DNVP, should be destroyed with all possible ruthlessness so that the final confrontation between Left and Right, between Marxism and the "national opposition," could take place. Yet in spite of the fact that the Nazis had made them the principal target of their campaign, the parties of the middle and moderate Right were slow to recognize the extent to which the Nazi movement constituted a genuine threat to their very existence. This was particularly true of the DVP, which was so concerned about establishing a sharp front vis-à-vis the DStP and Social Democrats that it completely underestimated the severity of the Nazi challenge.[37] Symptomatic of the way in which the DVP tried to contend with the Nazi threat was a pamphlet written by Gotthart Heribert, who attributed Nazi successes to the radicalizing effect of Social Democratic policies upon the German middle strata and dismissed the Nazi brand of socialism as little more than a "blind hatred of capitalism born of envy, a primitive socialism, which for that very reason was all the more dangerous."[38] In a similar vein, the WP's Heinrich Albert Hömberg tried to highlight the social radicalism of the Nazi movement by publishing a compilation of excerpts from the speeches and writings of prominent Nazi leaders that documented their thoroughly contemptuous, if not Bolshevistic, attitude toward the basic values of middle-class society.[39] Of all the major non-Catholic bourgeois parties, however, none was more consistent in its condemnation of Nazism nor devoted more resources to exposing its true nature than the DStP. For whereas the anti-Nazism of the DVP and WP was almost invariably overshadowed by their hostility toward Social Democracy, the DStP was quick to identify the NSDAP as its principal antagonist in the campaign for the 1930 Reichstag elections and openly questioned the sincerity of the DVP's campaign against Nazism in light of its willingness to share governmental responsibility with the NSDAP in Thuringia.[40]

Between 18 August and 14 September the NSDAP held no less than 30,000 separate demonstrations in virtually every corner of the Reich. As the campaign wound to a conclusion, such Nazi notables as Joseph Goebbels, Hermann Göring, Gregor Strasser, R. Walter Darré, and Ritter von Epp, as well as the untiring Hitler, spoke at every conceivable opportunity in a campaign that was articulated with the greatest possible precision and sustained by an organization without equal in all of Germany.[41] It was an assault with which none of the more moderate bourgeois parties could possibly contend, and it provided the Nazis with an electoral victory that surpassed the predictions of even the most astute political observer. Ending up with more than 18 percent of the total popular vote, the NSDAP received the support of nearly 6.5 million voters and elected a startling 107 deputies to the Reichstag. Coupled with strong gains by the Communists, the Nazi victory bore dramatic testimony to the increasing polarization of the German party system and signaled the virtual demise of the German middle as a viable political force. The dilemma of the middle was further compounded by the proliferation of regional and special interest parties, which, buoyed by a second wave of defections from the DNVP, went on to poll approximately 14 percent of the popular vote. Of the more established bourgeois parties, only the Center and Bavarian People's Party were able to withstand the combined onslaught of middle-class splinter parties and the NSDAP. For the DVP, DNVP, and German State Party, the outcome of the elections was an unmitigated disaster.[42]

Hopes that the State Party might establish itself as a viable alternative to the radicalism of the NSDAP collapsed completely in the wake of the elections. Not only had the DStP failed to achieve a major breakthrough into the ranks of the DVP's left wing, but old-line Democrats had been so offended by the DDP's merger with the Young German Order that they had turned their backs upon the State Party in utter dismay. In key Democratic strongholds such as Baden and Württemberg, for example, the founding of the DStP had produced such widespread disenchantment that the artisanry and independent middle class—social groups that constituted the backbone of the DDP's local support—began to transfer their allegiance to the Business Party and Christian-Social People's Service.[43] Not even the unity ticket that the State Party had concluded with the local leaders of the DVP could shield it from losses amounting to more than 20 percent of the vote the DDP had received in the two states in the last national elections. By the same token, the founding of the DStP had driven many longtime Democratic supporters in Hamburg, a district in which the Young German Order was virtually nonexistent, into the arms of the Social Democrats without attracting any new support from the VNR.[44] Only in Dresden-Bautzen and East Hanover, where the VNR possessed a strong grass-roots organization, and in Cologne-Aachen, where an endorsement from the *Kölnische Zeitung* helped the party achieve a significant breakthrough into the ranks of the local DVP, was the State Party able to improve substantially upon the DDP's performance two years earlier.[45] In those areas where Mahraun's followers failed to receive special consideration in the selection of candidates, however, the support that the DStP had received from the Young German Order proved a source of major disappointment. In the eyes of one embittered Democrat, it seemed that no less than half of those who belonged to the Order had voted for the NSDAP in preference to the party that the leadership of their own movement had helped create.[46]

The net effect of these developments was to cost the State Party approximately one-fifth of the votes that the DDP had received in the 1928 Reichstag elections as well as five of the twenty-five seats that the Democrats had held in the last national parliament. Still, these losses were considerably less than those sustained by its major rival, the German People's Party. Of the 2.7 million votes it had received in 1928, the DVP lost more than a million, as well as a third of its forty-five seats in the Reichstag. Distributed more or less evenly throughout the country, its losses were heaviest in traditional DVP strongholds such as Chemnitz-Zwickau, Thuringia, and the Palatinate, where it failed to retain so much as half of the support it had received two years earlier.[47] Shocked by the outcome of the election, the leaders of the DVP were unable to attribute their party's poor performance at the polls to any single factor. While some, like Walter Schnell, the DVP district chairman in Halle-Merseburg, cited the DVP's equivocation in the matter of bourgeois concentration as the primary reason for its electoral debacle,[48] those with close ties to German heavy industry blamed the DVP's weakness at the polls upon its coalition with the Social Democrats, the Moldenhauer affair, and Curtius's lackluster performance as German foreign minister.[49] For others, such as the DHV's Otto Thiel, however, the real reason behind the DVP's slow but steady decline since the beginning of the decade lay in the fact that its increasingly close identification with big business had severely compromised its character as a people's party, thereby alienating the various middle-class interests upon which the DVP depended for the bulk of its electoral support. First the worker, then the artisan and small peasant, and now the white-collar employee and civil servant, explained Thiel at a convention of the Reich Association of Young Populists a month after the election, had been left with no alternative but to leave the party in frustration over the way in which it had capitulated to the wishes of industry and big business.[50]

The outcome of the September 1930 Reichstag elections bore vivid testimony to the continued decline of the German liberal movement. Since the beginning of the decade, the liberal parties' share of the popular vote had fallen from 23 and 22.2 percent in the 1919 and 1920 national elections respectively to 13.5 percent in May 1928 and 8.4 percent in September 1930. This, coupled with shock over the magnitude of the Nazi victory, sent reverberations throughout the German liberal establishment and created a state of virtual panic within the two liberal parties. The situation was particularly volatile within the German State Party, where relations between the Democrats and Young Germans had begun to break down during the course of the campaign.[51] According to the agreement upon which the founding of the DStP had been based, Koch-Weser was to serve as the new party's parliamentary leader and Mahraun as the head of its national organization. This arrangement, however, was jeopardized from the very outset when Höpker-Aschoff, Stolper, and a group of old-line Democrats who had never fully reconciled themselves to the merger with the VNR succeeded in blocking Koch-Weser's election as chairman of the DStP Reichstag delegation at the delegation's first caucus on the morning of 17 September.[52] Relations between the two groups were further strained when Mahraun, acting in his self-proclaimed capacity as national leader (*Reichsführer*) of the DStP, unilaterally tried to revise the guidelines that the DStP action committee had approved on 19 September for the party's future organizational development. In this respect, Mahraun and his associates were particularly incensed over a provision in the agreement that conferred automatic membership in the DStP upon all members of the DDP and VNR who did not express wishes to the contrary.[53] Then, to aggravate the situation even further, the DDP executive committee passed a resolution on 27 September explicitly urging all party members to join the DStP, so that, in the words of Oskar Meyer, it might be suffused with the spirit of the old DDP. At the same time, the group around Höpker-Aschoff prevailed upon the leaders of the DDP to postpone the formal dissolution of their party until after the fate of the State Party had been decided.[54]

In their determination to sabotage the alliance between the DDP and the People's National Reich Association, Höpker-Aschoff and his supporters were aided by the inexperience and political naivete of the Young Germans, whose refusal to compromise on what they regarded as matters of principle only undermined whatever support they still enjoyed within the DDP. Moreover, Mahraun's ability to strike a compromise that might have kept the party from falling apart was severely limited by the widespread disgruntlement that the alliance with the Democrats had produced within the ranks of his own movement.[55] In the last week of September the Young Germans had begun to attack the Democrats in the open, even going so far as to denounce Stolper for "economic high treason" and to demand that all members of the DStP Reichstag delegation refrain from accepting appointments to corporate directorships. It was against the background of these attacks that representatives from the two groups—Höpker-Aschoff, Meyer, Bäumer, and August Weber for the DDP and Mahraun, Baltrusch, and Bornemann for the VNR—met for more than seven hours on 2 October in one last attempt to break the impasse that had developed in relations between their organizations.[56] Negotiations, however, broke down when Mahraun rejected a proposal from Höpker-Aschoff that would have created a unified national organization by transferring all authority for organizational decisions to a special executive committee in which he would be obliged to share the chairmanship with a representative from the DDP. Mahraun also took exception to a proposal for the absorption of the Democratic party organization into the DStP on the grounds that this would give the Democrats a disproportionately large share of delegates at the national congress that the State Party was scheduled to hold later that fall.[57]

Following the collapse of negotiations on 2 October, Mahraun sent a letter to the members of the DStP Reichstag delegation in which he warned that the solidarity of the delegation had been jeopardized by the DDP's efforts to take over the State Party and sharply denounced Democratic characterizations of the DStP as a party of the bourgeois Left.[58] At the same time, Mahraun sent a second circular to the leaders of the VNR and Young German Order in which he dismissed the State Party as an alliance of expediency (*Zweckverband*) to which they no longer owed any special allegiance. Not only did Mahraun characterize the People's National Reich Association as an "independent column of troops" whose relationship to the DStP would depend upon the way in which the party behaved, but he specifically instructed his supporters to refrain from any activity that did not directly benefit the VNR.[59] None of this augured well for the future of the party when the DStP action committee met on 7 October to see if a modus vivendi between the Democrats and VNR might still be achieved. After another marathon session during which it became clear that not even those who had come over to the DStP from the DVP were prepared to support the VNR's proposal for a reorganization of the DStP, Mahraun introduced a resolution that sought to remove Höpker-Aschoff and Meyer from the leadership of the new party on the grounds that they stood in irreconcilable opposition to the principles upon which it had been founded. When this resolution was rejected by both the Democratic and Young Liberal factions in the action committee, Mahraun declared that further negotiations were pointless and announced the VNR's secession from the DStP.[60]

Ultimate responsibility for the break between the People's National Reich Association and the German State Party lay as much with the Young Germans as it did with the group of old-line Democrats around Höpker-Aschoff and his associates. For while it is true that Höpker-Aschoff and his supporters did their best to obstruct implementation of the understanding that Koch-Weser had reached with the Young Germans prior to the founding of the State Party, it is also clear that the inflexibility of Mahraun and his followers did much to alienate the support of Democrats like Bäumer, Meyer, and Lemmer who in July and August had thrown the full weight of their political reputation behind the alliance with the VNR.[61] At the heart of the crisis, however, lay not so much the petty ideological differences that Mahraun cited in defense of the VNR's decision to leave the DStP as the fact that the leaders of the Young German Order, having been schooled in the authoritarianism of Germany's antiparliamentary Right, were congenitally incapable of making the sort of political compromises necessary to hold the party together. Unable to admit their own responsibility for the collapse of the State Party, the Young Germans remained profoundly alienated from the system of government that they had hoped to rescue from the demagoguery of the radical Right and retreated back into the murky world of antisystem politics from which they had originally emerged.[62] For the Democrats, on the other hand, the failure of their short-lived fling with political romanticism was no less traumatic. Not only were the Democrats distressed by the fact that the secession of the VNR had reduced the size of the DStP Reichstag delegation from twenty to fourteen deputies— thereby leaving it one short of the minimum needed for representation in the Reichstag's various parliamentary committees—but Koch-Weser and his immediate entourage were so demoralized by the way in which the founding of the State Party had ended that they felt obliged to withdraw from its leadership. For Koch-Weser, whose critics demanded that he resign his seat in the Reichstag in addition to his position as Democratic party chairman, this meant the end of a long and distinguished political career.[63]

The Young German secession from the German State Party in the first week of October 1930 dealt the left wing of the German liberal movement a blow from which neither it nor the movement for liberal unity ever recovered. What had begun as a bold and dramatic attempt to revitalize the German liberal movement—and, along with it, Germany's faltering parliamentary democracy—by infusing it with the spirit and idealism of the younger generation had ended in a shattering psychological defeat for both the leaders of the German liberal parties and their allies in the younger generation. The agitation for the creation of a united liberal party before the 1930 Reichstag elections had done little more than arouse expectations on the part of Germany's middle-class electorate that neither the Democrats nor their rivals in the DVP could satisfy. Just as the founding of the German State Party struck many Democrats as a particularly peculiar form of the unity in which they had been encouraged to believe, so the bitter invectives that Scholz heaped upon the founders of the DStP during the early stages of the campaign deeply offended many middle-class liberals. Combined with the pathetic fate the State Party was to suffer in the aftermath of the election, the net effect of these developments was to discredit liberalism as the ideological axis around which the German bourgeoisie could coalesce. For all intents and purposes, liberalism had exhausted itself as a viable force in the political life of the Weimar Republic.

PART SIX

In the Shadow of Nazism
1930–1933

CHAPTER TWENTY-NINE

Changing the Guard

ON 17 OCTOBER THOMAS MANN, a proud and self-acclaimed son of the German bourgeoisie, delivered a lecture in Berlin's Beethoven Hall in which he abandoned the all too familiar terrain of art, literature, and philosophy to reflect upon the implications of the Nazi triumph at the polls. For Mann, who only recently had declined an invitation from Koch-Weser to sign a manifesto on behalf of the German State Party,[1] such excursions into the realm of practical politics were indeed rare. In 1922 it had taken the shock of Rathenau's assassination for Mann to break his silence on everyday politics and issue a stirring defense of the Weimar Republic as the only true steward of the humanistic values that Goethe and his generation had implanted so deeply in the culture of the German bourgeoisie. Now, under the impact of a development he found no less disturbing, Mann called upon the German bourgeoisie to join him at the side of the Social Democrats in defense of those values against the "eccentric barbarity," the "epileptic ecstasy," and the "mass narcosis" of Nazism. Although Mann was careful not to neglect the role that economic despair had played in the rise of Nazism, he preferred to see the "mass convulsions," the "hectic baying," and the "frenzied repetition of monotonic catchwords" to which much of Germany had fallen victim as part of a deeper spiritual crisis extending to the very foundations of German bourgeois culture, a crisis so profound in its implications and impact that only the Social Democrats could be counted upon to defend the values upon which that culture had been based.[2]

Though colored by his admittedly eclectic view of German history, Mann's "appeal to reason" from the fall of 1930 reflected the deep-seated uneasiness that the outcome of the September Reichstag elections had produced throughout the ranks of Germany's liberal establishment. Not only had the radical parties on both the left and the right of Germany's political spectrum experienced unprecedented success in exploiting the anxiety, bitterness, and general disorientation that the outbreak of the world economic crisis had left in its wake, but the two liberal parties—both self-styled custodians of political reason—were in the process of being pushed to the periphery of Germany's national life. In a broader sense, however, Mann's lecture—and particularly his appeal on behalf of Social Democracy—was only symptomatic of the more general crisis that plagued Germany's ruling classes during the last years of the

Weimar Republic. The outcome of the 1930 Reichstag elections had made it increasingly difficult, if not impossible, for the German bourgeoisie to organize and maintain its hegemony over Germany's political life on the basis of the existing party system. Although the crisis of bourgeois hegemony had existed in a more or less latent form ever since the founding of the Weimar Republic, it was only with the outbreak of the world economic crisis and the radicalization of those lower middle-class elements upon which the more traditional bourgeois parties had depended for the bulk of their electoral support that the crisis became acute. More specifically, the formation of middle-class splinter parties and the rise of National Socialism as a mass party of middle-class protest pointed to a fundamental breakdown in the mechanisms by which Germany's ruling classes had traditionally exercised their political hegemony within the framework of Weimar's fledgling parliamentary democracy.[3]

Just as the collapse of the Müller government in the spring of 1930 indicated that the Social Democrats were no longer willing to share governmental responsibility on terms dictated by the DVP's industrial wing, so Brüning's increasingly frequent recourse to Article 48 underscored the lack of a viable domestic consensus upon which enactment of his government program might take place. Brüning had originally hoped that it would be possible to implement his program on the basis of a parliamentary majority that included elements from the left wing of the DNVP. His hopes, however, that the anti-Hugenberg elements that had seceded from the DNVP might reestablish themselves as a moderate conservative force upon which he could base his own political future had been dealt a severe blow by the outcome of the 1930 Reichstag elections. Not only were government officials alarmed at the magnitude of the Nazi victory, but the more moderate conservative parties upon which Brüning had set his hopes emerged from the elections with only forty Reichstag mandates among them. Particularly disappointing was the performance of the Conservative People's Party, which managed to elect only four deputies on the basis of a platform that stressed its support for Brüning's political program, while the Christian-National Peasants and Farmers' Party and the Christian Social People's Service—the other two parties that had splintered off from the DNVP's left wing—came away from the September elections with nineteen and fourteen deputies respectively. Assuming that all of the parties between the Social Democrats and DNVP supported his government, Brüning could count upon the support of only about 200 deputies in the newly elected Reichstag, a figure that left the government far short of the 368 mandates at the disposal of the four parties that opposed it.[4]

Given the configuration of political forces that emerged from the 1930 Reichstag elections and the continued intransigence of Germany's radical Right, Brüning was left with no practical alternative to the use of Article 48.

This was particularly true insofar as the political strategy to which Brüning had committed himself entailed severe economic hardships for the broad masses of the German people and therefore presupposed a high degree of independence from the pressures of the Reichstag if it was to be successfully implemented. The central element of the program that Brüning presented to the Reichstag on 16 October 1930 was a fiscal and economic reform that provided for a balanced budget, a sharp reduction in the overall level of government spending, the simplification of Germany's administrative apparatus, and a tax policy that would not interfere with Germany's productive capabilities or her capacity for capital formation.[5] Underlying this program, however, were two strategic objectives that went considerably beyond the parameters of fiscal and economic reform. For not only did Brüning look upon a reform of German finances as a necessary prerequisite for a revision of the Young Plan and a liquidation of Germany's reparations burden by international agreement, but he also sought to depress domestic price levels to the point where Germany would find herself in a commanding position on the world market once economic normalcy had been restored. Inasmuch, however, as both of these goals were predicated upon a thorough reform of German finances, Brüning was determined to carry out such a program regardless of its domestic consequences and had no intention, at least from the fall of 1930 on, of implementing it through the Reichstag, where special economic interests would have an opportunity to emasculate it. From this perspective, the use of Article 48 and the systematic disenfranchisement of the Reichstag were necessary corollaries to Brüning's deflationary fiscal policy.[6]

No chancellor since Luther could claim the confidence of Germany's industrial elite to the same extent as Brüning when the newly elected Reichstag met for the first time in October 1930. With few exceptions, the most notable of which was Fritz Thyssen of the United Steel Works (Vereinigte Stahlwerke), the leaders of the industrial establishment warmly supported Brüning's plans for a reform of German finances as well as his wage and reparations policies.[7] The most difficult political problem confronting Germany's industrial leadership, particularly in the aftermath of the 1930 Reichstag elections, was to create a domestic consensus with sufficient cohesiveness to secure passage of Brüning's program in the Reichstag. Ideally, Reusch and his associates in the Ruhrlade would have preferred a merger of the various parties that stood between the NSDAP and Center—that is, including the DNVP and excluding the German State Party—into a united bourgeois party, but their experiences in the period preceding the 1930 elections led them to discount such a possibility in the foreseeable future. Still, the Ruhrlade hoped that it might yet be possible to persuade the leaders of the more moderate bourgeois parties to conclude a *Fraktionsgemeinschaft* in support of reforms that industry deemed necessary for Germany's economic recovery. Even without the DNVP or DStP, such a coalition would still have included nearly one hundred Reichstag deputies, thereby providing industry with the strong parliamentary base it so sorely needed.[8]

Industry's hopes of uniting the various parties between the DNVP and Center into some sort of parliamentary alliance capable of commanding the support of a hundred or more Reichstag deputies presupposed a degree of cohesiveness and an identity of interests that simply did not exist. This became abundantly clear in the course of negotiations that Count Kuno von Westarp, the former Nationalist party chairman who had helped found the ill-fated Conservative People's Party in July 1930, conducted with representatives from the other moderate bourgeois parties in the immediate aftermath of the September Reichstag elections. Not only did these efforts enjoy strong support within both the DVP and the Conservative People's Party,[9] but prominent industrialists such as Paul Silverberg and Albert Vögler were fully prepared to use their influence on behalf of closer ties between the parties of the middle and moderate Right.[10] But the prospects of such a coalition received a devastating blow when first the Christian-National Peasants and Farmers' Party and then the Business Party indicated that they might not support the Brüning government in the forthcoming vote of confidence and were therefore withdrawing from the efforts to form a parliamentary alliance with the DVP and other middle parties. All that remained of the efforts to organize a parliamentary alliance in support of the Brüning government when the Reichstag convened on 18 October was a purely technical *Fraktionsgemeinschaft* between the Conservative People's Party and the Christian-Social People's Service, an arrangement of minimal political significance that merely enabled the two parties to attain the minimum of fifteen mandates necessary for representation on the Reichstag's parliamentary committees.[11]

Following the collapse of efforts to consolidate the moderate bourgeois parties between the Center and DNVP into a united parliamentary front, the leaders of the German State Party approached the DVP Reichstag delegation about the possibility of a parliamentary alliance between the two liberal parties. The secession of the People's National Reich Association in the first week of October had cost the DStP six of its twenty seats in the Reichstag, thus leaving it one short of the number required for recognition as an official Reichstag delegation. The State Party had made its first overtures in the direction of the DVP almost immediately after the VNR secession but had lost interest when it seemed that the anti-Brüning forces on the DVP's right wing might try to force Curtius's resignation as Brüning's foreign minister.[12] When negotiations between the DVP and DStP were resumed on a somewhat more intensive level in the third week of October, the initial indications were encouraging insofar as the DVP had ceased its intrigues against the Brüning government and was genuinely interested in an accommodation with the State

Party. But just as the leaders of the two liberal parties were about to finalize an agreement establishing a technical *Fraktionsgemeinschaft* between their Reichstag delegations, their efforts were suddenly torpedoed by an irate Ernst Scholz, who interrupted a brief convalescence in the outskirts of Berlin to take part in the final stages of the negotiations. Still in a state of pique over the way in which the founding of the DStP had undercut his own efforts at bourgeois concentration, Scholz announced, to the great dismay of all involved, that he had no intention of doing the State Party such a favor and offered only to accept the fourteen DStP deputies into the DVP delegation as special guests or *Hospitanten*. This proposal, however, was totally unacceptable to the leaders of the State Party not only on account of the manner in which it had been presented but, more importantly, because it sought to deprive the DStP of its parliamentary identity at a time when the party was still trying to legitimize itself in the eyes of its supporters. When subsequent efforts on the part of Dietrich and other DStP leaders failed to soften Scholz's position, negotiations between the two parties were formally broken off on 20 October.[13]

The failure of Germany's moderate bourgeois parties to close ranks behind the Brüning government in the fall of 1930 was only one more symptom of the way in which the fragmentation of the German party system aggravated the crisis of bourgeois hegemony during the last years of the Weimar Republic. This crisis was further reflected in the fact that the only thing that saved Brüning from defeat in the vote of confidence that took place in the Reichstag on 18 October was the decision of the Social Democrats to tolerate his government on the assumption that it represented less of an evil than the right-wing elements that stood to profit from its demise.[14] While this development may have been welcomed in certain quarters as a sign of Brüning's willingness to seek parliamentary sanction for his fiscal and economic programs, Social Democratic toleration of the Brüning government was to remain a heavy liability that seriously compromised the chancellor's standing with the more conservative elements of Germany's bourgeois elite. This was particularly true of German heavy industry, where Vögler and his associates were to redouble their efforts on behalf of a rapprochement between Brüning and the DNVP's Alfred Hugenberg in hopes that this might keep the chancellor from becoming too heavily dependent upon the Social Democrats.[15] As this episode clearly revealed, the tacit alliance that had developed between Brüning and the leaders of the SPD Reichstag delegation in the fall of 1930 severely strained the chancellor's relations to the capitalist economic interests that had originally rallied so enthusiastically to the support of his government.

The crisis of bourgeois hegemony could also be seen, though with less immediate impact, in the myriad problems that continued to plague the German liberal parties in the aftermath of the September Reichstag elections. For the leaders of the German State Party, the immediate task was to repair the damage that the secession of the People's National Reich Association had done to the morale and credibility of their party. After a moment of initial uncertainty in which several party leaders briefly weighed the possibility of a merger with the DVP,[16] the initiative was taken by Hermann Dietrich, who at a meeting of the DDP executive committee on 16 October succeeded in convincing his colleagues that the efforts to establish the DStP as an entirely new political party should be continued.[17] In that this entailed the dissolution of the DDP and the absorption of all but its extreme left wing into the DStP, Dietrich and his associates were particularly anxious to retain the cooperation of the Young Liberals around Josef Winschuh, Rochus von Rheinbaben, and Theodor Eschenburg in hopes that this would prevent the DStP from being stigmatized as nothing but a continuation of the old DDP. In this respect, however, the leaders of the State Party had to contend with the widespread disenchantment that the Young German secession had produced within the ranks of those Young Liberal forces that had originally rallied to the DStP's support. In the case of the west German February Club movement, for example, disillusionment over developments within the State Party was so strong that on 12 October Josef Winschuh, the movement's official representative in Berlin and one of the DStP's original founders, advised his supporters to withdraw from the State Party at the earliest possible opportunity.[18] Desperate to avert a second secession from the DStP, Dietrich and his associates went to great lengths to reassure Winschuh that in both program and leadership the new party was fundamentally different from the now-defunct DDP. Convinced that these reassurances were indeed sincere, Winschuh reversed his decision to leave the State Party and agreed to accept both the party vice-chairmanship and the Reichstag mandate that had become available through Koch-Weser's political retirement.[19]

Although the Young Liberals never constituted more than a small minority in the DStP, their presence nevertheless lent a degree of credence to the State Party's claim that it was not a mere continuation of the old DDP but rather an entirely new political party. This claim was further substantiated by the determination of those who had taken control of the DStP to exclude the pacifist and radical democratic elements on the DDP's extreme left wing from any sort of meaningful role in the new party.[20] The future of this group clouded the agenda of the special party congress that the Democrats held on 8–9 November 1930 in Hanover for the purpose of formally dissolving their party and transferring its assets and organization to the DStP. When the dissolution of the DDP was officially proposed at the DDP party congress on the afternoon of 8 November, Willy Braubach from the Union of Independent Democrats denounced the move as the prelude to a merger with the DVP and assailed Winschuh as an archreactionary in the employ of capitalist economic interests. In a similar, though less aggressive, vein Ludwig Quidde from the German

Peace Society and Wilhelm Heile from the League for European Understanding (Verband für europäische Verständigung) pleaded with the Democrats "to
leave the DDP alive" so that the brand of "national pacifism" they represented
might still have a political home.[21] Their entreaties, however, proved to no
avail, as all but a handful of the 334 delegates at Hanover voted to approve the
DDP's dissolution and absorption into the State Party.[22] Undaunted by this turn
of events, the elements around Braubach and Quidde refused to join the State
Party and retired three weeks later to Kassel, where they founded the Radical
Democatic Party (Radikaldemokratische Partei) as the focal point around
which all who had been left homeless by the demise of the DDP might
coalesce.[23] The founding of this party, which never succeeded in breaking out
of its political isolation, was but one more manifestation of the disastrous
splintering of liberal forces in the Weimar Republic.

Having shorn themselves of the pacifist and radical democratic elements
that had formerly stood on the DDP's extreme left wing, the group around
Dietrich, Höpker-Aschoff, and Oskar Meyer followed the DDP's dissolution
on 8 November with the official founding of the German State Party the next
day. The ideological basis upon which the DStP sought to legitimize itself was
a heightened commitment to the authority and welfare of the state. As
Dietrich, who had been chosen to head the new party at a meeting of the DDP
executive committee on the morning of 8 November,[24] stressed in his keynote
speech at the DStP's founding ceremonies on the following day, the outcome
of the recent Reichstag elections had created a situation in which the state
found itself besieged by mass radical parties that rejected the existing economic order. The dangers this posed to the German nation, continued Dietrich,
were compounded by the fact that some of Germany's bourgeois parties stood
in open opposition to the existing form of government, while others, like the
Business Party and People's Party, either subscribed to a code of unconditional
interest politics or sought to oppress the working class with appeals against
Marxism. What the state needed to survive, therefore, was a new class of
citizens or *Staatsbürger* who were willing to place the interests of the state and
its struggle for survival above all other concerns. "We want to educate the
citizen," concluded Dietrich, "to become a true member of the state and to
serve that which as the embodiment of his nationhood is the presupposition
and guarantee for the existence of every individual. . . . Our ideal is a free,
powerful and social German national state. It is for this that we fight!"[25]

By no means was the strong emphasis that Dietrich placed upon the role and
function of the state inconsistent with the basic tenets of the German liberal
tradition. Still, this represented a subtle but nonetheless fundamental shift in
the DStP's ideological orientation away from many of the principles with
which its predecessor had become historically identified. This shift was most
apparent in the sections of Dietrich's speech that dealt with cultural policy. For

not only did Dietrich blame the state of spiritual confusion in which Germany currently found herself on the excesses to which the freedoms of speech and press had given rise, but he went so far as to complain that in the area of cultural and intellectual life the liberal age had come to an end.[26] What this suggested was a dramatic retreat from the cultural pluralism to which much of the old DDP had subscribed and an underlying antipathy to the modernist culture that in many circles had become synonymous with Weimar. The shift to a more conservative position could also be seen in the statist themes that Winschuh enunciated in the course of his speech on the question of political regeneration, while the appeal by Erich Obst, a former Young Democrat and an economic geographer from Hanover, for "an active German foreign policy" evoked images of national indignation reminiscent of the early 1920s.[27] The DStP's more aggressive stance on matters of Germany's national interest combined with its unabashed statism to give it a decidedly more conservative profile than its predecessor had possessed.

Of the various parties that actively supported the Brüning cabinet, none—with the obvious exception of the Center—was more firmly committed to the policies of the Brüning government than the German State Party. For in spite of the reservations they may have had about Schiele's farm program or Brüning's inclination to circumvent established parliamentary procedures through the use of Article 48, the leaders of the DStP staunchly defended Brüning's deflationary fiscal policies as the "bitter medicine" that Germany had to take in order to find her way out of the depression.[28] The DStP's support of the Brüning government, however, did little to enhance its popularity with the broad masses of the German people and only aggravated the problems party leaders were already experiencing in their efforts to establish the DStP as a viable political force. The most nagging of these problems was the credibility crisis the DStP had suffered with the secession of Mahraun and his associates at the beginning of October. Not only had hopes that the party's Hanover congress might dispel this crisis been rudely shattered when Willy Hellpach, a former Democratic Reichstag deputy who had helped spearhead the movement for bourgeois unity, used the ceremonies at Hanover to announce his resignation from the DStP,[29] but by the beginning of 1931 it had become apparent that in Rhineland, Westphalia, and other parts of the country many, if not most, of those who had formerly belonged to the DDP were extremely hesitant about becoming involved in the new party.[30] By the same token, many of the DDP's auxiliary organizations, such as the National League of German Democratic Youth, had all but collapsed during the formation of the State Party and would have to be built anew if they were to be of service to the DStP.[31] All of this combined with the heavy psychological toll under which the leaders of the State Party were already laboring as a result of the deepening economic crisis to produce a mood of growing resignation and pessimism about the future of the party.[32]

The uncertainty that surrounded the future of the German liberal movement in the aftermath of the 1930 Reichstag elections extended deep into the ranks of both liberal parties. Like their counterparts in the DStP, the leaders of the German People's Party were deeply shocked by the magnitude of the defeat their party had suffered at the polls. With losses that amounted to more than a third of its 1928 vote, the DVP entered a period of increasing uncertainty, as its leaders tried not only to ascertain the reasons for its electoral decline but also to devise a strategy that might enable the German bourgeoisie to preserve its political preeminence in the face of an increasingly radicalized electorate.[33] It was against the background of these developments that a group of party functionaries under the leadership of Walther Schnell, chairman of the DVP district organization in Halle-Merseberg, decided to take matters into its own hands. On 17 September Schnell sent Scholz a sixteen-page letter in which he argued that the very fate of the German bourgeoisie depended upon its consolidation into a single political party and urged the DVP party chairman not to allow his party's petty interests to interfere with the greater goal of bourgeois concentration. In this respect, Schnell dismissed the efforts to form an alliance between the parliamentary delegations of the existing bourgeois parties as a hopelessly inadequate response to the crisis in which the German bourgeoisie found itself and warned that these parties, the DVP included, were all in danger of being swept away by more radical efforts at bourgeois unity if they failed to heed the mood of the people. "What I therefore see as the most important task of our party leadership," concluded Schnell, "is to take these matters into its own hands and, if need be, offer itself as a clear and unequivocal sacrifice so that the German People's Party will be at the center of activity and not simply one of the obstacles to be overrun by the revival and reorientation of the bourgeoisie."[34]

After having informed Scholz and the DVP's national leadership of his intentions, Schnell took the first concrete step in pursuit of his goal when he invited party officials from all parts of the country, as well as members of the DVP Reichstag delegation who might be interested in his project, to a special conference in Berlin's Hapsburger Hof on the evening of 23 September.[35] With few exceptions, those who took part in the discussion at the Hapsburger Hof readily supported Schnell's contention that by itself the formation of a parliamentary coalition between the DVP and other moderate bourgeois parties was an inadequate response to the need for bourgeois unity and agreed that only the consolidation of the various parties from the DStP to the People's Conservatives in a united bourgeois party could possibly provide the German bourgeoisie with the stable parliamentary base it needed to make its influence felt in the Reichstag. In this respect, Schnell and his associates recommended the cultivation of closer contacts between themselves and the local leaders of the other bourgeois parties as a means of underpinning efforts at the national level to form a parliamentary alliance between the moderate bourgeois parties.

Not only would this improve the chances for success in Berlin, but more importantly it would transform the struggle for bourgeois unity into a genuine popular movement with organized support from below.[36]

For all the urgency that Schnell attached to his initiative, he was anxious not to antagonize Scholz or the party's national leaders and continually reassured them that what he had in mind was consistent with the best interests of both the DVP and the various circles that supported it. Indeed, Schnell and his associates clearly sought to pursue their objectives in conjunction with the DVP's national leadership and hoped that the meeting of the DVP central executive committee that had been set for 26 October would commit the party to the strategy they had formulated at the meeting in the Hapsburger Hof.[37] But these hopes received a sharp setback when the party's national leaders decided on 20 October to postpone the meeting of the central executive committee around which Schnell and his supporters had planned much of their strategy. Regarding this as a sign of Scholz's flagging interest in their efforts, Schnell and the leaders of the DVP district organizations that supported his project immediately petitioned for a meeting of the DVP executive committee on 2 November.[38] At the same time, they sought to undercut Scholz's authority as party chairman through the creation of a deputy party chairmanship with responsibility for the modernization of the DVP party organization and the implementation of Schnell's strategy for the creation of a united bourgeois party. This proposal was justified on the grounds that Scholz's responsibilities as chairman of the DVP Reichstag delegation left him little time for the task of reorganizing the party or for conducting the arduous negotiations necessary to lay the foundation for the creation of a united bourgeois party. The fact that Scholz was frequently ill and had suffered a relapse of the stomach problems that had required surgery the previous fall only lent added credence to the rationale that Schnell and his supporters offered in defense of their proposal.[39]

On 2 November the DVP national council chose Eduard Dingeldey, a forty-four-year-old lawyer from Darmstadt and a member of the DVP Reichstag delegation since 1928, to serve as Scholz's deputy party chairman.[40] The selection of Dingeldey was propitious in several respects. In the first place, Dingeldey strongly supported the movement for bourgeois unity, having been among the first in the party to openly champion the idea of closer ties with the other nonsocialist parties.[41] Secondly, Dingeldey had long encouraged the younger generation to become more actively involved in the affairs of the DVP and was popular with the reform-minded elements that had coalesced on the party's left wing behind Frank Glatzel and the Reich Association of Young Populists.[42] Moreover, Dingeldey had served as chairman of the DVP district organization in South Hesse ever since the beginning of the 1920s and possessed the practical experience necessary to carry out the organizational reforms that the group around Schnell deemed essential to the DVP's survival.

Not only did Dingeldey belong to the inner circle of those party officials who had rallied around Schnell in the immediate aftermath of the DVP's defeat in the September elections, but on most political issues—and particularly on the question of cooperation with the Social Democrats—he was sufficiently conservative to win the support of all but the most incorrigible of those who stood on the party's right wing. Although Dingeldey conceded that the tactical situation in which the Brüning government found itself following the elections had left it with no alternative but to accept the support of the Social Democrats, he also insisted that in the long run the implementation of Brüning's fiscal and economic program would be impossible as long as the chancellor remained dependent upon socialist support. Under these circumstances, the government should make every effort to secure the cooperation of the National Socialists, if for no other reason than to expose their demagoguery and political opportunism. Distressed by the success with which the Nazis had been able to mobilize the anxiety and despair of an economically uprooted middle class, Dingeldey maintained that one of the most important tasks confronting the DVP in the aftermath of the September elections was to transform the revolutionary forces that had found a temporary home in the NSDAP into a "constructive component of the state."[43]

With Dingeldey's appointment as the DVP deputy party chairman, the initiative that Schnell and his associates had originally taken in the matter of bourgeois concentration passed into the hands of the party's national leadership. But the understanding upon which Dingeldey's election had been based threatened to fall apart when Scholz, who had been convalescing in Locarno since the middle of October, refused to accept the division of labor that was to go along with the creation of the deputy party chairmanship. Though sharply critical of Scholz's leadership of the party, Schnell and his associates had been prepared to leave him in formal control of the party as long as he agreed to grant Dingeldey the authority and freedom of movement he needed to fulfill his mandate as the party's deputy chairman. When Scholz insisted, however, that ultimate authority for reorganizing the party and conducting negotiations aimed at the creation of a united bourgeois party lay with him and could not be delegated to the deputy party chairman, the forces around Schnell began to press for his removal from the party chairmanship.[44] Scholz continued to receive strong support from the industrial interests on the DVP's right wing,[45] but any inclination he may have had to carry his fight for the party chairmanship to the DVP central executive committee evaporated following a visit by Dingeldey in Locarno in the first week of November. Citing ill health as his reason, Scholz informed the DVP executive committee on 11 November of his decision to step down as party chairman and recommended that Dingeldey be installed as his successor when the committee met later in the month.[46]

Although the leaders of the DVP's right wing continued to have reservations about Dingeldey's succession to the party chairmanship, Scholz's recommendation undercut whatever plans they may have had for blocking his election and cleared the way for his installation as the new party chairman at a meeting of the DVP central executive committee on 30 November. At the same time, the committee elevated Scholz to the party's honorary chairmanship in a gesture designed not only to spare the former party chairman unnecessary embarrassment but also to dispel rumors of discord in the party.[47] Dingeldey's election represented a major triumph for the reform-minded elements on the DVP's left wing and met with strong approval from Glatzel and the leaders of the Reich Association of Young Populists. Not only did the program that Dingeldey outlined in his maiden speech as DVP party chairman underscore his commitment to a sweeping reform of Germany's political system,[48] but his election aroused hopes that progress toward the long-awaited goal of a reform and reorganization of the German party system, a goal the RjV had proclaimed ever since its founding in the spring of 1929, might be resumed.[49]

Notwithstanding the enthusiasm with which Glatzel and his associates greeted Dingeldey's election to the DVP party chairmanship, this turn of events did not signify a dramatic shift to the left in the policies of the DVP but merely confirmed the slow drift to the right that had been underway in the party since the summer of 1928. In point of fact, Dingeldey felt no great loyalty toward the Brüning government and believed that the DVP could fulfill its historic mission as a party of bourgeois concentration only after it had freed itself from the burden of governmental responsibility.[50] By the same token, the sharp rebuff that Dingeldey handed Dietrich and the leaders of the State Party in his acceptance speech before the DVP central executive committee on 30 November indicated that the new DVP chairman was not so much interested in improving relations between the two liberal parties as in cultivating closer ties with the German Right.[51] None of this augured particularly well for the future of the DVP's relationship to the Weimar Republic.

At no point since the founding of the Weimar Republic did the forces of German liberalism seem in greater disarray than at the end of 1930. The left wing of the German liberal movement had yet to recover from the trauma that had accompanied the founding of the German State Party, and its leaders, their ranks badly decimated by the loss of men like Koch-Weser and Erkelenz, struggled desperately to contain the pessimism and resignation that had become rampant in the DStP's national organization. At the heart of their problems lay a crisis of credibility that the Young German secession in October 1930 had done much to exacerbate and the party's official founding a month later little to resolve. The situation in which the DStP found itself in the fall of 1930 contrasted dramatically with that of the rival German People's Party. Not only had the DVP survived the recent election campaign with its national organization essentially intact, but the transfer of power from Scholz to

Dingeldey had been accomplished with a minimum of disruption and hard feeling. Moreover, Dingeldey's election had given rise to new hopes that the DVP might still establish itself as the crystallization point around which a dynamic and comprehensive party of bourgeois concentration could form. Yet for all the promise that Dingeldey's election seemed to hold for the future of the DVP, the direction in which he proposed to take the party only threatened to drive the wedge between the two wings of the German liberal movement even deeper. At a time when conservative political pundits were proudly proclaiming the end of the liberal era, the German liberal parties entered a period of deepening estrangement not only from each other but also from the sectors of Germany's economic elite that had historically sought to use them as instruments of their political hegemony.

CHAPTER THIRTY

In the Grip of the Depression

THE YEAR 1931 WAS ONE of deep and unremitting economic crisis. Germany's increasing dependence upon short-term foreign loans as a source of investment capital had left her economy particularly vulnerable to a major crisis. The withdrawal of foreign capital, which had begun on a limited scale in the second half of 1928, assumed critical proportions with the Wall Street crash of October 1929. Although this temporarily abated with the introduction of Brüning's austerity program in the spring of 1930, the outcome of the 1930 Reichstag elections had done little to restore international confidence in Germany's political stability and triggered an even more frantic run on her already weakened capital reserves. The flight of foreign capital in the fall and winter of 1930–31, in turn, created a severe credit squeeze that only aggravated the liquidity problems German big business was already experiencing as a result of the sharp decline in the market for manufactured goods. Under these circumstances, firms that had come to rely upon short-term foreign loans as a source of investment capital were left with no alternative but to cut back production and reduce the size of their work force. The number of unemployed workers, which had stood at around 3 million when Brüning first assumed office, had climbed to more than 4.4 million by the end of the year and was to reach nearly 5.3 million in the spring of 1931. Not only did this place a severe strain on state finances and force the Brüning government into adopting even more drastic austerity measures, but it further undermined international confidence in Germany's credit worthiness and accelerated the flight of foreign capital. The crisis reached a dramatic, if not sensational, climax when the collapse of the Austrian Credit Institute in May 1931 produced a run on Germany's capital reserves that threatened many of the country's leading financial institutions with insolvency and forced the Brüning government to declare a bank holiday on 14 and 15 June.[1]

To Brüning the deepening economic crisis was essentially a fiscal problem that could only be solved through a balanced budget and a drastic reduction in the general level of government spending. Yet while Brüning defended his government's austerity program on the grounds that it was necessary to restore Germany's credit worthiness in the eyes of the international banking community, he also sought to use the deepening domestic crisis as a means of reopening the reparations question and bringing about a revision of the Young

Plan. Convinced that a liquidation of Germany's reparations obligation was essential to her long-term economic stability, Brüning was quick to rationalize the short-term economic hardship that his austerity program had inflicted upon certain socioeconomic strata as the price that Germany had to pay in order to regain her freedom at home and abroad.[2] Since Brüning also realized that such a program could never be enacted through the Reichstag where special economic interests would have an opportunity to dismantle the provisions they found most repugnant, the chancellor embarked upon a policy of disenfranchising the Reichstag through the use of Article 48 as part of a silent constitutional reform that also encompassed the creation of a "unitary federal state" and—if one takes Brüning's memoirs at face value—the restoration of the monarchy.[3] The essence of Brüning's fiscal and economic program, therefore, was contained in four massive emergency decrees (*Notverordnungen*) that were enacted between December 1930 and December 1931 without ever having been submitted to the Reichstag for parliamentary approval. Only twice, in February 1931 and again in February 1932, did Brüning call upon the Reichstag to fulfill its constitutional responsibilities, and in both cases it was to approve the budget in accordance with conditions that Germany's international creditors had attached to the extension of new short-term credits.[4]

The implications these developments held for the stability of the German party system were essentially twofold. In the first place, Brüning's determination to exclude the Reichstag and the parties that constituted it from any sort of meaningful role in the formulation of his fiscal and economic program severely compromised whatever legitimacy they still possessed in the eyes of their traditional electorates. In this respect, the events of 1930–32 recapitulated the legitimacy crisis that the Weimar party system had experienced with the stabilization of the mark in the winter of 1923–24, though over a much more extended period of time and against the background of an international banking crisis that precluded new infusions of foreign capital. Secondly, the net effect of Brüning's deflationary policy was to exacerbate the domestic economic crisis and radicalize those social strata upon which the more moderate bourgeois parties depended for the bulk of their electoral support. This was particulary true in the case of civil servants, who experienced salary cuts of approximately 20 percent between December 1930 and February 1932 and who began to gravitate in increasingly large numbers to the radical parties on the extreme right of Germany's political spectrum.[5] White-collar employees, on the other hand, were often the first to lose their jobs during a period of economic retrenchment, so that by 1932 more than 520,000 of their number— or an estimated 13.6 percent of Germany's white-collar work force—had joined the ranks of the unemployed. At the same time, the small business sector was reeling from a 30 percent decline in retail sales since the beginning of 1930, while the number of bankruptcies between 1930 and 1931 increased by 20 percent.[6] Even in small towns, where the middle classes may have been able to shield itself from the more pernicious effects of the depression, mass unemployment and the public idleness that went with it evoked a spectre of social revolution that quickly eroded existing political loyalties.[7]

Under these circumstances, the coalition of moderate bourgeois parties that had supported Brüning in the spring and early summer of 1930 began to fall apart. The first party to bolt the coalition was the Christian-National Peasants and Farmers' Party.[8] The general ineffectiveness of the Brüning-Schiele farm program following its enactment in April 1930 severely undercut the position of Germany's more moderate farm leaders and created a situation in the 1930 Reichstag elections that the parties of the radical Right were quick to exploit. The leaders of the CNBLP were particularly disturbed by the fact that in many parts of the country their party had run a distant third behind the DNVP and NSDAP in its bid for the loyalty of the German farmer. Determined to reverse the direction in which their party seemed to be headed, the anti-Brüning forces on the CNBLP's right wing scored a decisive victory at a meeting of the CNBLP Reichstag delegation on 1 October 1930 by securing the passage of a resolution that chastised the government for its lack of initiative in the reparations question and called for its reorganization as a government of national concentration in which all right-wing parties, including the National Socialists, would be invited to participate.[9] When Brüning failed to heed these demands, the leaders of the CNBLP Reichstag delegation responded by supporting right-wing motions of no-confidence and voted against the government's request for a parliamentary recess after all of these motions had been defeated.[10] In the meantime, Schiele had been forced to resign as managing president of the National Rural League in the first of a series of events that effectively stripped the CNBLP of whatever influence it had enjoyed within Germany's largest agricultural interest organization.[11] Although the leaders of the CNBLP continued to oppose the Brüning government and voted against the emergency decree that it presented to the Reichstag in early December 1930, party unity was far too fragile to withstand the radicalizing effect that the combination of economic distress and Nazi propaganda had had upon Germany's rural population, and on 10 February 1931 Heinrich von Sybel, Albrecht Wendhausen, and two other CNBLP deputies joined the DNVP and NSDAP in walking out of the Reichstag in a move that brought the split that had been developing within the party since the September elections into acute focus.[12]

By the spring of 1931 the CNBLP had all but ceased to exist as a viable political force. The same was true of Germany's only other national agrarian party, the German Peasants' Party. Since its founding in the spring of 1928, the German Peasants' Party had rested upon a loose alliance of small peasant unions from the north and northwestern parts of Germany with the Bavarian

Peasants' League, a powerful force in state politics ever since the turn of the century. The loss of more than 140,000 votes and two Reichstag mandates in the 1930 Reichstag elections, however, had done much to exacerbate the differences that separated the northern and Bavarian wings of the party. As a mood of general resignation spread throughout the party in the aftermath of its defeat at the polls, the leaders of the Bavarian Peasants' League tried to salvage what still remained of their political position by joining the CNBLP in a special parliamentary coalition called the German Rural Folk (Deutsches Landvolk).[13] The formation of this alliance, however, met with strong criticism from the northern wing of the party, and in December 1930 August Hillebrand, the only DBP deputy elected outside of Bavaria, proceeded to affiliate himself with the German State Party in a step that meant the virtual end of the German Peasants' Party as a national political entity.[14] Not only had the Bavarian Peasants' League failed to establish itself as the crystallization point around which a national peasants' party could form, but the differences that separated the DBP's northern and southern wings had proven too great to bridge.

The fate that befell Germany's two most important agrarian splinter parties was paralleled by an equally bitter and divisive conflict within the ranks of the country's only other vocational party, the Business Party of the German Middle Class. The leaders of the WP were particularly distressed by the fact that whatever gains their party had recorded through the expansion of its electoral base into Württemberg, Hesse, and the Rhineland had been more than offset by disproportionately heavy losses in the areas where it had experienced its first success.[15] Party leaders were quick to blame the WP's electoral stagnation upon its decision to enter the government in the spring of 1930, and they began to extricate themselves from the government coalition almost as soon as the election results were known. The party's move to the right could be seen not only in its refusal to support or tolerate any government that was either directly or indirectly dependent upon the Social Democrats but also in its efforts to force a reorganization of the Brüning government that reflected the results of the September elections.[16] Anti-Brüning sentiment was particularly strong in Saxony and Thuringia, where local party leaders tried to force Johann Victor Bredt, the WP's lone representative in the Brüning cabinet, to leave the government just as the Reichstag was about to convene in the third week of October. Although the WP Reichstag delegation eventually agreed under pressure from the presidential palace to permit Bredt's retention as a special *Fachminister* in the national cabinet,[17] relations between the WP and the Brüning government continued to deteriorate to the point that by the end of November not even party chairman Hermann Drewitz, until then one of Bredt's strongest supporters, could defuse the pressure that had built up within the party for a break with the chancellor.[18]

Following a particularly heated meeting of the WP national committee on 24 November, Bredt deferred to the pressure from his party's right wing and requested that he be relieved of his responsibilities as minister of justice. Hopeful that the WP might reverse itself as it had done on 13 October, Brüning postponed taking action on Bredt's request until 4 December, when the party's decision to introduce a motion of no-confidence against his government ended all hopes of a reconciliation.[19] In the meantime, a bitter conflict for control of the party had erupted between Drewitz and his opponents on the WP's right wing. Signs that such a conflict was brewing had become visible in early November when Otto Colosser, a WP deputy from Berlin who had distinguished himself as an effective party propagandist, resigned his post as the WP's deputy party chairman in protest against Drewitz's "one-man dictatorship" over the party's internal affairs.[20] Encouraged by the leaders of the party's Saxon organization, Colosser rejected efforts at reconciliation and intensified his attacks against the party chairman by accusing him of using party funds for his own personal gain.[21] When the WP national committee refused to support Colosser's allegations of financial impropriety and initiated expulsion proceedings against the renegade deputy,[22] the leaders of the WP's three Saxon district organizations demanded that Drewitz relinquish the party leadership until he had been cleared of the charges against him. When he refused, the three Saxon organizations declared their secession from the national party on 14 January 1931. At the same time, Colosser announced his resignation from the WP and refused to appear before the special party court that had been convened for the purpose of expelling him from the party.[23]

By the spring of 1931 the Business Party of the German Middle Class found itself on the verge of a complete organizational collapse. The leaders of the WP struggled desperately to repair the damage the conflict between Drewitz and Colosser had done to their party's national organization, but they were repeatedly frustrated by new demands for Drewitz's resignation.[24] Unshaken in his determination to retain control of the party, Drewitz decided to take his case before the national party congress the WP was scheduled to hold in Hanover during the last weekend of April. Buoyed by the strong support he received from Bredt, Ladendorff, and Sachsenberg, Drewitz was able to withstand the opposition's attacks against his leadership of the party and won reelection to the party chairmanship by a three-to-one margin. In the meantime, Drewitz's supporters sought to appease his critics on the WP's right wing, including the leaders of the three Saxon district organizations that had returned to the fold in time to take part in the Hanover congress, by offering them an expanded role in the party's executive councils.[25] All of this, however, proved of little avail, as the controversy over Drewitz's alleged improprieties continued to rage throughout the summer of 1931 until finally he was left with no choice but to surrender the party chairmanship in order to prevent another secession even more damaging than the one that had taken place in January. With its national organization decimated by defections in one part of the country after another, the WP was no longer capable of providing the German middle class with the effective political representation it needed to survive the deepening economic crisis.[26]

As the collapse of the WP and CNBLP clearly revealed, special interest parties proved particularly vulnerable to the disintegrative forces that had been unleashed by the outbreak of the Great Depression. Having traditionally legitimized themselves through the representation of special economic interests, these parties were incapable of sustaining themselves during a period of deepening economic crisis in which the classical methods of interest representation were no longer effective. Consequently, the collapse of special interest parties during the early stages of the depression was far more precipitous than that of the more established, ideologically oriented bourgeois parties. To be sure, the depression had done much to undermine the integrative potential of the two liberal parties and to radicalize the social strata upon which they depended for the bulk of their popular support. Nevertheless, both the State Party and the People's Party had managed to avoid the bitter leadership crises that had proven so devastating to the WP and CNBLP and were thus able to survive the early stages of the depression without the massive organizational collapse that had taken place in the case of the special interest parties. On the contrary, both the DStP and the DVP were hopeful that the crises that the special interest parties had experienced in the winter and spring of 1931 might work to their own advantage.

Of all the various parties that stood between the Center and DNVP, none was more firmly committed to the Brüning government nor more adamantly opposed to efforts aimed at bringing the NSDAP into the cabinet than the German State Party. In sharp contrast to the strong sentiment that the outcome of the September Reichstag elections had produced within the CNBLP, WP, and DVP in favor of an accommodation with the NSDAP, the leaders of the State Party dismissed hopes that the Nazis might be enticed into entering the government as illusory and continued to denounce them in the sharpest possible terms.[27] In this respect, the leaders of the DStP hoped that the crisis that had recently erupted within the WP, as well as the general uncertainty that seemed to grip the DVP, might provide their party with renewed access to middle-class circles that had deserted the DDP during the course of the 1920s. It was no doubt with this in mind that Dietrich urged his colleagues at a meeting of the DStP managing committee on 17 December 1930 to intensify their agitation among the more traditional elements of the rural and urban middle classes.[28] But whatever hopes Dietrich and his associates may have had of regaining the support of the peasantry and artisanry were frustrated by a variety of factors, not the least of which was Dietrich's close identification with the increasingly unpopular policies of the Brüning government. When pressed by the leaders of the DStP's national organization to provide them with a program capable of attracting the masses,[29] Dietrich's response was characteristically feeble. Writing to Hermann Schäfer at the helm of the DStP organization in Cologne, Dietrich replied that at the present the party's only course of action was "to defend the reforms of the present government as the basis upon which the salvation of the German people was to take place."[30] But, as DStP Reichstag deputy Josef Winschuh observed in a letter to Dietrich at the beginning of February, passive support for the government was no substitute for the active measures the party had to take in order to attract new followers.[31]

Disgruntlement over the condition in which the party found itself throughout the first part of 1931 was particularly strong in the DStP Reichstag delegation, where August Weber, the delegation chairman, complained bitterly about Dietrich's insensitivity to the effects of his policies as minister of finance upon the party's morale and organizational development.[32] Party leaders were distressed not only by their inability to convince homeowners and small businessmen that the DStP was genuinely committed to the social and economic welfare of the independent middle class[33] but also by the uneasiness that rumors of a new round of cuts in salaries and social benefits were causing among civil servants who had remained loyal to the party.[34] A further index of the party's organizational malaise was the fact that throughout the country anywhere from 30 to 60 percent of those who belonged to the DDP in the summer of 1930 had failed to join the DStP by the spring of 1931.[35] In Cologne, for example, local party officials estimated that the DStP's "march to the right" had cost it the support of more than half of those who had formerly belonged to the DDP,[36] while in Hanover the situation was so desperate that Erich Obst, the DStP district chairman and one of the principal speakers at the party's founding ceremonies the previous November, all but recommended that the party concede defeat and dissolve itself.[37] The only bright spot in the DStP organization in the spring of 1931 was Hamburg, where local party leaders had already reached a high level of activity in anticipation of the municipal elections that were scheduled to take place later that fall.[38]

The German State Party never recovered from the organizational malaise that plagued it through the first half of 1931. The leaders of the DStP were repeatedly frustrated in their efforts to instill new life into the party organization both by their close identification with the Brüning government and by the widespread demoralization that the deepening economic crisis had produced among the social strata from which their party had traditionally recruited the bulk of its support.[39] At the same time, the party's financial situation was so desperate that many of its local and regional offices were threatened with closure,[40] while Weber and the party treasurer Hermann Fischer were experiencing more and more difficulty in raising the money necessary to underwrite the operating costs of its national headquarters in Berlin.[41] Yet while all of this left the DStP incapable of defending itself against the wave of social and political radicalism that was sweeping the country, the most devastating blow to the party's prospects of survival came in the form of the Second Emergency Decree for the Protection of the Economy and Finance (*Notverordnung zur Sicherung der Wirtschaft und Finanzen*) that the Brüning government enacted on the basis of the president's emergency powers on 5 June 1931. Designed to eliminate the mounting deficit that had appeared in the national budget during the first half of the year, the emergency decree provided for a wide range of cuts in government spending at the same time that it introduced a special "crisis tax" and increased existing taxes on sugar and mineral oil. To help justify the hardship this entailed for the different strata of German society, Brüning combined its promulgation on 5 June with the publication of a *Tribut-aufruf* in which he called upon Germany's international creditors to honor the sacrifices the German people had been asked to make by granting them relief from their country's "intolerable" reparations burden.[42]

The emergency decree of 5 June 1931 aroused vociferous opposition in virtually every sector of German society. Anxious to exploit the ground swell of antigovernment sentiment that promulgation of the decree left in its wake, the German Right intensified its agitation against the Brüning cabinet and demanded the immediate suspension of its emergency powers.[43] This proved particularly damaging to the German State Party, whose ability to defend itself against the attacks of the German Right was severely compromised by the fact that its national chairman was also Brüning's minister of finance. Although the DStP Reichstag delegation was quick to defend the government against the polemics of the more conservative bourgeois parties and promised to meet with the chancellor in an attempt to modify the features of the decree it found most objectionable,[44] its leaders remained privately critical of the psychological effect that publication of the decree had had upon the German people and complained bitterly about the government's failure to consult with them prior to its promulgation.[45] At the same time, the storm of protest with which the organized artisanry had greeted publication of the decree[46] effectively dashed the DStP's hopes of securing a major breakthrough into the ranks of the middle-class circles that had been left politically homeless by the collapse of the Business Party and completely undercut any benefit it had hoped to reap from the defection of two WP deputies, Otto Colosser and Otto Dannenberg, earlier in the summer.[47] No less alarming was the impact of the decree upon the DStP's supporters in the new middle class. Spokesmen for the DStP's civil servant wing dutifully reported the bitterness that the government's decision to reduce civil servant salaries had produced within the ranks of the professional bureaucracy, and they urged the party leadership to intercede with the government in an attempt to soften the provisions of the emergency decree that constituted an unacceptable sacrifice for the already beleaguered civil servant.[48] In a similar vein, the Federation of Employee Unions protested vehemently against the loss in income that would result from the government's plan to shorten the work week without increasing hourly compensation and warned that only a more equitable distribution of the social burden of combating the depression would help stem the tide of bitterness and frustration that was currently spreading through the ranks of Germany's white-collar population.[49]

While the reaction against the emergency decree of 5 June 1931 may have dealt a severe blow to whatever hopes Dietrich and his associates held for the resurgence of the German State Party, it also did much to aggravate the divisions that had surfaced within the German People's Party following its defeat in the 1930 Reichstag elections. When Dingeldey assumed leadership of the DVP in early December 1930, he inherited a party that was already deeply divided over its relationship to the Brüning government. Not only were the leaders of the DVP's right wing generally disenchanted with the program Brüning had presented to the Reichstag in October 1930, but they were extremely critical of the performance of their party's own Julius Curtius as Brüning's foreign minister.[50] Consequently, when the government enacted the first of its four Emergency Decrees for the Protection of the Economy and Finance in early December, the leaders of the DVP's right wing had sought to tie their party's support of the decree to a reorganization of the cabinet that would remove Curtius, Dietrich, and the Center's Joseph Wirth from office. These efforts, however, failed to receive the support of a majority in the DVP Reichstag delegation, with the result that the party continued to support the Brüning government in spite of Dingeldey's deepening resentment over the way in which the chancellor had virtually excluded the parties that supported his cabinet from any sort of meaningful role in the formulation of government policy.[51]

Dingeldey's support of the Brüning government during the first months of his tenure as DVP party chairman was tempered by his concern that the chancellor had become so heavily dependent upon the Social Democrats that he could no longer carry his program of fiscal and economic reform to a successful conclusion. Anxious to free the government from all socialist influence, Dingeldey actively pursued the establishment of closer relations with the leaders of the "national opposition" in hopes that the cabinet's political base might be expanded to include the more responsible elements on the German Right. It was no doubt with this in mind that the DVP agreed to join the other parties to the right of the DStP and Center in supporting a referendum for the dissolution of the Prussian Landtag that the Stahlhelm was to initiate in the spring of 1931.[52] But Dingeldey's hope that the parties of the national opposition could be persuaded to adopt a more responsible attitude toward the Brüning government received a severe blow when the DNVP and NSDAP walked out of the Reichstag on 10 February 1931 in a demonstration designed to dramatize their contempt for what still remained of Germany's parliamentary system. To Dingeldey, this turn of events was significant in two respects. Not only did it underscore the loss of authority that Germany's parliamentary institutions had suffered since Brüning first began to rely upon Article 48 as a means of enacting his government program, but it had a sobering effect upon Dingeldey's initial optimism regarding the political maturity of Hitler and his allies on the radical Right.[53]

Following the secession of the national opposition from the Reichstag in February 1931, Dingeldey became much less restrained in his criticism of the forces that had gathered around Hitler and Hugenberg. Speaking before the DVP central executive committee in the middle of April, Dingeldey characterized the National Socialist movement as "a great danger for the psychic forces of the German nation" and chastised it for the way in which it had tried "to obscure the truth with the language of hate and the dream of an uncertain future."[54] Yet for all the vehemence with which Dingeldey attacked the parties of the national opposition for their flight from political responsibility, he remained deeply concerned about the inroads that they—and particularly the NSDAP—had made into his own party's electoral base. Convinced that only a party with the appeal and dynamism of National Socialism could prevent the German bourgeoisie from falling under the seductive sway of Nazi demagoguery, Dingeldey sought to reverse the DVP's declining fortunes by transforming it into a vibrant force capable of serving as the pole around which the various elements of a demoralized and badly splintered bourgeoisie could unite. It was with this in mind that the DVP executive committee published a special action program under the title "Kampfziele der Deutschen Volkspartei" at the conclusion of its meeting on 19 April. Ostensibly a reaffirmation of the DVP's commitment to the values of political, economic, and cultural liberalism, this program sought to reformulate traditional liberal goals in the language and rhetoric of the German Right. On the question of individual rights, for example, the "Kampfziele" pledged the DVP to defend the rights of "the ethically responsible individual"—that is, one whose individuality was grounded in faith and religiosity—against revolution, socialism, and materialism in what amounted to a curious, if not illiberal, redefinition of the individual and his place in society. By the same token, the program called for a reform of the Weimar Constitution that would strengthen the powers of the Reich president at the same time that it eliminated the excesses of parliamentarism, and in the area of cultural policy it stressed the need for a more diligent cultivation of the religious and national values that lay at the heart of Germany's Christian culture. Only in those sections of the program that dealt with fiscal and economic policy did the program offer more than token tribute to the DVP's liberal pedigree.[55]

A clear retreat from the unabashed defense of liberal principles that had characterized Stresemann's tenure as party chairman, the "Kampfziele" can only be understood as an attempt on the part of the DVP to accommodate itself to the sharp swing to the right that had taken place in Germany's political culture with the onset of the Great Depression. Perhaps the most telling indictment of the DVP's action program as a statement of liberal principles was the fact that it received strong support from precisely those elements on the party's left wing that enjoyed close ties to the German National Union of Commercial Employees, a reservoir of antiliberal, nationalist, and conservative sentiment ever since the founding of the Weimar Republic.[56] But whatever impetus Dingeldey and the leaders of the DVP hoped to receive from the publication of the program was quickly dissipated by the dissension over their party's continued support of the Brüning government. Party leaders were already distressed by the concessions the chancellor had made to the Social Democrats on the question of royalty taxes during the budgetary debates earlier that spring,[57] and they feared that Germany's deteriorating financial situation through the first half of 1931 would result in a new round of tax increases and social cutbacks harmful to the interests of the groups that still supported their party.[58] The concerns that Dingeldey outlined to Brüning in a long letter in the middle of May,[59] however, had little effect upon the final configuration of the emergency decree that Brüning enacted into law on 5 June. Not only did Brüning disregard Dingeldey's advice that he delay publication of the decree until after he had concluded his talks with the British at Chequers, but the decree contained provisions for a reduction of civil servant salaries and an increase in the national sales tax that struck directly at the economic interests of the groups whose support was vital for the future of the DVP.

Dingeldey was distressed over the way in which the chancellor had chosen to ignore his party's recommendations regarding the emergency decree of 5 June 1931. Speaking at a DVP rally in Dortmund on the same day that the decree was promulgated, Dingeldey assailed the new tax levies and the cuts in civil servant salaries as a "retreat to the policies of the past" and deplored the way in which the chancellor had tried to appease the German Left by reinstating the forty-hour workweek. At the same time, however, the DVP party chairman was careful to temper his criticism of the emergency decree with affirmations of his continued high regard for the person of the chancellor and called upon Brüning to restore public confidence in his leadership of the government by severing all ties to the SPD.[60] Although Dingeldey's attacks against the policies of the Brüning government received immediate support from the elements on the DVP's right wing that had long sought to force a reorganization of the national government, his efforts to separate his personal opinion of the chancellor from his criticism of the emergency decree revealed the uneasiness that not only he but also significant sectors of his party felt about its new political course. Consequently, when the DVP Reichstag delegation met on 11 June to vote on the demands of the opposition parties for an immediate convocation of the Reichstag, no less than thirteen of the twenty-eight deputies present refused to go along with their party chairman in supporting a motion for convocation.[61]

Commanding the support of scarcely half of those who sat in the DVP Reichstag delegation, the decision to join the opposition parties in pressing for an immediate convocation of the Reichstag represented a dramatic reversal of the course Dingeldey had steered since his election to the DVP party chairmanship at the end of the previous year. At the same time, it dealt a severe blow to Brüning's efforts to contain the storm of protest that had been unleashed by the promulgation of the emergency decree. Adamantly opposed to demands both for modifications in the text of the decree and for a reorganization of his government, Brüning was anxious to avoid a confrontation with the Reichstag that might weaken his government's position on the eve of his negotiations with the British.[62] In an attempt to reverse the stand that the DVP had taken two days earlier in favor of reconvening the Reichstag, Brüning met with Dingeldey and industrialist Albert Vögler on the morning of 13 June. Not only did Brüning express tacit support for the eventual reorganization of his cabinet as a "government of national defense," but he also agreed to entertain proposals from the DVP for a "relaxation" of the existing system of wage and salary arbitration in what amounted to an obvious bid for the support of the party's industrial wing.[63] Coming on the heels of an urgent appeal that Hans Luther, president of the Reichsbank and himself a member of the DVP, had made to Dingeldey only the day before,[64] these overtures were designed to mute the antigovernment sentiment that had surfaced within the DVP following promulgation of the emergency decree and to lay the foundation for another reversal of course by the DVP party chairman.

As the government intensified its efforts to prevent the Reichstag from being called back into session, the threat of an open split between the DVP's left and right wings became increasingly acute. At a meeting of the DVP national committee on 12 June, a motion introduced by Curtius seeking to reverse the stand the party's Reichstag delegation had taken the day before was narrowly defeated in a vote that saw the committee almost evenly divided.[65] In his efforts to force a reversal of Dingeldey's political course, Curtius received strong support from Wilhelm Ferdinand Kalle, an influential DVP deputy with close ties to the Frankfurt chemical industry. Speaking as one of the party's longtime financial backers, Kalle urged Dingeldey to repair the damage that the party's decision to call for the convocation of the Reichstag had done to his relations with the chancellor and warned that continuation of the anti-Brüning course would leave him and his friends with no alternative but to leave the party.[66] As pressure mounted, Dingeldey began to show signs of weakening when, at a meeting of the DVP Reichstag delegation on the evening of 15 June, he alluded to the gravity of the situation in which the Reich found itself and urged his colleagues to place the concerns of the state as a whole before those of the special economic interests that had deluged the party with petitions of their own.[67] At the same time, the leaders of the DVP's right wing continued to mobilize their supporters at the local and district levels of the party's national organization in an attempt to block any move in the direction of an accommodation with the government.[68]

Responsibility for reconvening the Reichstag lay in the hands of a special parliamentary committee known as the Council of Elders (Ältestenrat). With this body scheduled to meet later that afternoon, the DVP Reichstag delegation met on the morning of 16 June to determine how its representatives in the Council of Elders should be instructed to vote. In what amounted to a stunning reversal of the position he had taken five days earlier, Dingeldey urged the delegation to revise its resolution of 11 June in light of two factors: the potentially devastating effect that the premature convocation of the Reichstag would have upon the already precarious state of German finances and the reassurances that he had received from the chancellor regarding the eventual reorganization of his cabinet. Although Dingeldey's recommendation came under immediate attack from the leaders of the party's industrial wing, at least five of those who had supported the first resolution on 11 June reversed their position, with the result that the delegation agreed by an 18–9 margin to withdraw its support for a convocation of the Reichstag.[69] When the Council of Elders met later in the day to vote on reconvening the Reichstag, the DVP's reversal helped provide the chancellor with the votes he needed to block convocation of both the Reichstag and its budget committee. Not only had Brüning succeeded in blocking parliamentary debate of the emergency decree, but another nail had been driven into the coffin of German parliamentarism.

The DVP's decision first to oppose and then to support the Brüning government caused widespread confusion throughout the party organization and did much to discredit Dingeldey's leadership of the party in the eyes of those who stood on its extreme right wing.[70] Hard pressed to defend the DVP's two policy reversals in the space of just five days, Dingeldey argued that the original resolution of 11 June was essentially an attempt to provide the chancellor with the freedom of movement he needed to reorganize his government and undertake a dramatic new intiative at home and abroad. Once assurances to this effect had been received, the DVP could no longer assume responsibility for perpetuating a government crisis that led to a further deterioration of national finances and therefore reversed its initial position so that Brüning might have an opportunity to act upon the hopes that the DVP had placed in his willingness to break with the bankrupt policies of the past.[71] Though essentially an accurate reflection of the concerns that had moved the DVP party leadership during the first two weeks of June 1931, the tortured logic of Dingeldey's argument bore dramatic testimony to the difficult situation in which Brüning's deflationary fiscal policies and authoritarian style of government had placed the DVP and the rest of Germany's moderate bourgeois parties. For not only had Brüning's deflationary policies done much to radicalize the social strata from which the DVP, DStP, and other moderate bourgeois parties recruited the bulk of their popular support, but his preference for Article 48 over established parliamentary procedures severely compromised whatever legitimacy Germany's parliamentary institutions still possessed in the eyes of the country's beleaguered and demoralized middle-class electorate. The more Brüning undercut and usurped the legislative prerogatives of the Reichstag, the more voters he inadvertently drove into the ranks of Germany's radical parties.

CHAPTER THIRTY-ONE

The Storm from the Right

BY THE MIDDLE OF 1931 economic crisis and political impotence had combined to destroy what little credibility Germany's more moderate bourgeois parties still possessed in the eyes of the German electorate. Only the German Center Party and its Bavarian counterpart, the Bavarian People's Party, had succeeded in insulating themselves against the forces of social and political disintegration that the outbreak of the world economic crisis had unleashed upon the other nonsocialist parties to the left of the DNVP. Having staked their existence upon the representation of material economic interests, both the Business Party and the Christian-National Peasants and Farmers' Party—not to mention the smaller middle-class splinter parties that had surfaced since the middle of the 1920s—found it increasingly difficult to sustain themselves during a period of acute economic contraction and entered a sharp decline that not even their break with the Brüning government could reverse. The plight of the German liberal parties, on the other hand, was compounded by the fact that neither the the DStP nor the DVP had severed its ties to the Brüning government, although in the case of the latter there were signs that a break might be imminent. Unable to shake the stigma that their support of the Brüning government had produced in the eyes of those who had borne the brunt of its deflationary policies, the two liberal parties were powerless to prevent their supporters from being driven into the arms of the radical Right.

As the principal beneficiary of the crisis in which Germany's more moderate bourgeois parties found themselves during the first half of 1931, Germany's radical Right had pursued a course of political destabilization and polarization since its ill-fated crusade against the Young Plan in the summer and fall of 1929. The net effect of this agitation was essentially twofold in that it not only complicated the situation of the Brüning government but posed a serious threat to the internal stability and cohesiveness of the more moderate bourgeois parties as well. Yet for all its hostility toward the existing system of government, the so-called "national front" was by no means of a single mind about how its goal of polarizing the nation was to be achieved. For whereas the DNVP and NSDAP both sought to polarize the nation through the annihilation of the various parties that stood between them and the socialist Left, the leaders of the Stahlhelm hoped to create a broad national front that included not only the DNVP and NSDAP but also the very parties that Hugenberg and

Hitler had slated for destruction. In short, the leaders of the Stahlhelm were far more committed to achieving their objectives in cooperation with the more moderate bourgeois parties than either the DNVP or NSDAP.[1]

The leaders of the Stahlhelm took the first concrete step toward their goal of consolidating the various groups to the right of the Center and DStP into a national front when they announced at the eleventh annual National Front Soldiers' Congress (*Reichsfrontsoldatentag*) in Koblenz at the beginning of October 1930 that they would introduce a popular referendum in Prussia for the dissolution of the state parliament. Frustrated by the predominant position the Social Democrats had held in Prussia ever since the founding of the Weimar Republic, the Stahlhelm hoped to strike a blow in the struggle against Marxism by forcing new elections that would reflect the change in the national mood that had taken place since 1928.[2] Although preliminary negotiations with the DNVP, Business Party, Christian-National Peasants and Farmers' Party, and National Rural League revealed a general consensus in favor of the proposed referendum, Hitler showed little enthusiasm for the entire project and refused to commit the NSDAP in spite of the strong support the Stahlhelm's proposal had evoked from other Nazi leaders.[3] The DVP was formally invited to join the coalition that supported the proposed referendum on 8 November, but at a meeting with representatives from the Stahlhelm and other prospective participants four days later, Adolf Kempkes from the DVP's national headquarters in Berlin refused to commit his party as long as the involvement of the National Socialists remained uncertain.[4] Skeptical about the proposed action's prospects of success, Hugenberg met with Hitler on two separate occasions—first on 4 December 1930 and then again on 3 February 1931—in an attempt to secure a definitive commitment of support from the Nazi leadership.[5] When these overtures proved of no avail, the leaders of the Stahlhelm decided to wait no longer and officially announced on 4 February 1931 that they would proceed with their plans for a referendum on the dissolution of the Prussian Landtag.[6]

As a nonpartisan veterans' organization whose 300,000 members were drawn from all of the parties to the right of center, the Stahlhelm was ideally suited to the task of consolidating the German Right into a unified political force. Its hopes that the various parties on the Right might rally behind its crusade for a dissolution of the Prussian Landtag, however, were frustrated not only by the equivocation of the Nazi leadership but also by the threat that the exodus of the national opposition from the Reichstag on 10 February posed to the collaboration of the more moderate bourgeois parties such as the DVP and Business Party.[7] The DVP's position was particularly delicate in light of the fact that the secession was directed against a national government that it still supported and in which it was represented. But the Stahlhelm's fears that this might put an end to the DVP's participation in its plans for the Prussian referendum were quickly allayed when Dingeldey, speaking before a group of 150 DVP and DNVP businessmen on 11 February, reaffirmed his party's commitment to the struggle against socialism and hailed the proposed referendum as a major contribution to this struggle.[8] At the same time, the six DVP district organizations in the Rhineland and Westphalia joined the Stahlhelm and all of its allies except the NSDAP in the formation of a regional nonpartisan committee to oversee and coordinate the referendum campaign in the Rhine-Ruhr basin.[9] To be sure, the leaders of the DVP were careful to stress that their party's support of the referendum did not affect its relationship to the Brüning government and tried to defend their decision to collaborate with the Stahlhelm as an attempt to loosen the ties that had developed between it and the more radical right-wing parties.[10] But this strategy backfired when both the DNVP and NSDAP began to use the campaign for the dissolution of the Prussian Landtag as an opportunity to strike out against the Brüning government and the parties that still supported it. This, in turn, did much to exacerbate the tensions that already existed within the DVP over the question of its relationship to the Brüning government at the same time that it thwarted the Stahlhelm's goal of a united national front.[11]

If the referendum for the dissolution of the Prussian Landtag jeopardized the internal cohesiveness of the DVP, it also paralyzed efforts on the part of political moderates to reconstitute the German middle as a viable political force. Although the concept of a united middle party had been severely compromised by the recriminations that had followed the founding of the German State Party, the longing for the establishment of closer political and organizational ties between the parties of the middle and moderate Right was far from dead. Nowhere was this to be seen more clearly than in the initiative undertaken by a group of municipal politicians from Kassel in the first months of 1931 in support of the principle of bourgeois unity. On 15 January 1931 twenty-six Kassel politicians representing every faction from the Radical Democrats to the Conservative People's Party and the Christian-Social People's Service met in the home of city executive Ferdinand Friedensburg to discuss the possibility of closer ties among their parties.[12] Encouraged by the positive response that their initiative had evoked at both the municipal and national level, Friedensburg and his associates decided to establish a "state-bourgeois coalition of the middle" (*staatsbürgerliche Arbeitsgemeinschaft der Mitte*) with a permanent office in Berlin.[13] The new organization was scheduled to make its public debut with a special ceremony in the capital on 25 March, and invitations were sent out to more than fifty representatives of Germany's political and economic elite, including such luminaries as Hans Luther, Otto Gessler, Eduard Hamm, Roland Brauweiler from the Federation of German Employer Associations, and Abraham Frowein from the National Federation of German Industry, as well as two representatives from the German labor movement, Fritz Baltrusch from the United Federation of Christian Trade Unions and Friedrich Mewes of the Federation of Employee Unions.[14] The meeting, however, proved to be a bitter disappointment to those who had gone to so much trouble to organize it. For not only did many of those who had been invited decline to attend for one reason or another, but the referendum that the Stahlhelm had just introduced in Prussia found the participants so sharply divided that Friedensburg, himself a member of the State Party and an opponent of the referendum, despaired of further action in support of a united middle party until after the referendum had taken place.[15]

The fate of Friedensburg's efforts, modest though they admittedly were, bore ample testimony to the discord that the referendum for the dissolution of the Prussian Landtag had sown within the ranks of Germany's moderate bourgeois elite. The dividing line between those who supported and those who rejected the referendum ran right through the heart of the German liberal movement and pitted the DVP against the DStP in what was but one more instance of the deepening schism between the two liberal parties. As long as this continued, efforts to check the spread of National Socialism through the creation of a united middle party remained hopelessly stalled. In the meantime, the situation within the DVP continued to deteriorate under the steady barrage of abuse that the more radical elements within the referendum coalition directed against the Brüning government and the parties supporting it. This barrage reached an almost deafening crescendo following the DVP's decision in June 1931 to reverse the position it had initially taken in the aftermath of the Second Emergency Decree in favor of an immediate reconvocation of the Reichstag. The steady deterioration of Germany's economic situation through the remainder of the summer, the general ineffectiveness of German foreign policy following President Hoover's proposal for a moratorium on the payment of reparations and related international debts, and the collapse of the Darmstadt National Bank on 13 July 1931 all led to a further erosion of the government's popularity and exposed the parties that supported it to a new round of attacks from the radical Right. Within the DVP the effect of this situation was essentially twofold in that it not only produced a severe strain in the party's ties to the more radical elements within the referendum coalition[16] but also greatly intensified the antigovernment sentiment that existed on the DVP's right wing.[17]

The leaders of the DVP's right wing were particularly distressed over Brüning's failure to live up to the promise he had supposedly made to Dingeldey for a reorganization of his government in return for the DVP's support during the cabinet crisis that had followed promulgation of the Second Emergency Decree in early June 1931.[18] In this respect, the leaders of the DVP's right wing hoped to translate the widespread opposition that various provisions of the emergency decree had encountered at the local and district

levels of the party's national organization into a mandate for a reorganization
and extension of the government to the Right. Though by no means unsympa-
thetic to this general strategy, Dingeldey and the party's national leaders,
including those with close ties to the Ruhr industrial establishment, were
reluctant to press for a change in the government at the height of the banking
crisis for fear that this would only accelerate the withdrawal of short-term
foreign credits from Germany's already beleaguered financial markets.[19] A
further problem lay in the fact that neither Hugenberg nor Hitler had manifested much interest in joining the Brüning government or forming a new
government with the DVP and the other parties that stood to the right of center.
Spokesmen for the DVP's right wing had approached Hugenberg on several
occasions during the summer of 1931, but their efforts to lay the foundation
for the formation of a new governmental coalition with the DNVP and NSDAP
had been largely unsuccessful.[20] At the same time, Dingeldey's own conversation with Hitler on 28 July revealed that while the Nazi leader was prepared to
accept the DVP's help in overthrowing the Brüning government, he was
characteristically vague regarding the program or personnel of the government
he planned to put in its place.[21] The DVP's last hopes for a change in the
attitude of the radical Right toward the idea of a coalition government with the
more moderate bourgeois parties vanished when Hugenberg took special pains
to reassure Hitler following his meeting with Reich President Hindenburg on 1
August that he had no intention of abandoning the common goals to which
they had dedicated themselves as leaders of Germany's national opposition.[22]
Under these circumstances, Dingeldey and his associates had no choice but to
continue their support of the Brüning government in spite of the increasing
skepticism with which they viewed its prospects of success.

   On 9 August the referendum for the dissolution of the Prussian Landtag
drew to a close, falling about 4 million signatures short of the 13.5 million it
needed to take effect. The last week of the referendum, however, was marked
by an incident that drew national attention to the debilitating effect the agitation of the radical Right was having on the situation within the DVP. On 4
August Count Alexander zu Dohna, a one-time member of the DVP delegation
to the Weimar National Assembly and a highly respected member of the
party's left wing, published an article in the *Kölnische Zeitung* in which he
publicly criticized the strong endorsement the DVP executive committee had
given to the referendum for the dissolution of the Prussian Landtag.[23] Over the
course of the next several days, Dohna's stance received support from two
other members of the DVP's left wing, party patriarch Wilhelm Kahl and
former Reichstag deputy Fritz Mittelmann, with Kahl going so far as to hail
nonsupport of the referendum a "patriotic duty."[24] This development infuriated
the leaders of the DVP's right wing, who complained that such antics only
endangered the unity of the party and left it defenseless against the agitation of

the more radical elements within the referendum coalition.[25] Although Kahl subsequently tried to defuse the situation by publicly reaffirming his full and unqualified support of Dingeldey's leadership of the party, the issue continued to rankle the more nationalistic elements on the DVP's right wing, where the venerable Kahl was roundly denounced for having stabbed his party in the back.[26]

Immediately after the failure of the referendum for the dissolution of the Prussian Landtag, the leaders of the DVP's left wing urged Dingeldey to reassume the initiative in the matter of bourgeois concentration.[27] For Dingeldey, however, the entire question of bourgeois unity had become so intimately intertwined with the future of the Brüning government that he saw no point in undertaking any action on behalf of a united bourgeois party until after the cabinet's fate had been decided. Not only did the dividing line between those who supported and opposed the Brüning government run through the heart of the very elements Dingeldey and his associates hoped to unite, but the uncertainty that surrounded the chancellor's political survival precluded any sort of effective action in the matter of bourgeois unity.[28] Dingeldey's reservations, however, only reflected the situation within his own party, where another assault against the policies of the Brüning government was beginning to take shape. The tension that had been building within the DVP since the promulgation of the Second Emergency Decree earlier that summer approached a critical level following the government's decision in early September to abandon its plans for a customs union project with Austria. The principal architect of this project was the DVP's own Julius Curtius, who as Brüning's foreign minister had hoped to achieve a major diplomatic triumph that would help stabilize his government's position at home. The proposed customs union, however, encountered strong opposition from the French, who proceeded to use the deepening financial crisis in central Europe to force the Austrians into abandoning the project.[29] Curtius had been a favorite target of the DVP's right wing ever since he had succeeded Stresemann as head of the German Foreign Office in the fall of 1929. With the collapse of the customs union project in the fall of 1931, even Dingeldey pleaded with Curtius to spare himself, his party, and his government further embarrassment by stepping down as Brüning's foreign minister.[30]

If the furor over Curtius and the uncertainty surrounding the fate of the Brüning government made it impossible for Dingeldey to undertake any sort of meaningful action in the matter of bourgeois unity, the leaders of the German State Party were anxious to fill the void. Appalled by the increasing polarization of German political life, the leaders of the DStP hoped that the defeat of the referendum for the dissolution of the Prussian Landtag would clear the way for a new initiative in the matter of bourgeois unity that would enable them, among other things, to take advantage of the split that had developed between the left and right wings of the DVP.[31] Here, however, the initiative came not from Dietrich, who had become so overburdened by the demands of his cabinet post that he was no longer capable of running the party,[32] but from August Weber, chairman of the DStP Reichstag delegation, and Wilhelm Abegg, a high-ranking Prussian civil servant who belonged to the DStP. At the end of August, Abegg approached Hans Schlange-Schöningen, a former DNVP moderate who had gone over to the Christian-National Peasants and Farmers' Party at the beginning of 1930 and one of Brüning's strongest supporters on the German Right, in an attempt to organize some sort of concerted action between the parties of the middle and moderate Right when the Reichstag reconvened on 13 October. With Schlange's support, a meeting was arranged with Weber, who in the wake of Dietrich's preoccupation with Germany's deepening fiscal crisis had assumed all but formal leadership of the DStP. Though skeptical about their chances of success, the three agreed to broaden their efforts to include representatives from the other bourgeois parties in the twofold aim of strengthening Brüning's position in the Reichstag and increasing the influence of the middle and moderate Right over the government's legislative program.[33]

Although Abegg and his associates received strong encouragement from Brüning's confederates in the Reich Chancellery,[34] they suffered a severe and in many ways prophetic setback when Ernst Scholz, Dingeldey's predecessor as the DVP's national party chairman, declined to participate in their project on the grounds that its primary objective should not be to support but to overthrow the existing government.[35] Scholz's response underscored the difficulties that efforts to consolidate the German middle into any sort of united political front invariably faced. Abegg and his associates, however, refused to let this deter them from their original goal, and in the last two weeks of September they met with representatives from the DVP, the Christian-Social People's Service, the Christian-National Peasants and Farmers' Party, and the all but defunct People's Conservative movement on three separate occasions in Berlin's fashionable Deutsche Gesellschaft 1914.[36] At the second meeting on 21 September, Schlange made an impassioned plea for closer cooperation on behalf of the Brüning government that succeeded in overcoming the reservations of conservatives like Count Westarp about the prominent role that the State Party and its representatives had played in the early stages of the negotiations. As a result, the group agreed to a two-stage strategy that envisaged both the publication of a petition calling upon the parties of the middle and moderate Right to close ranks behind the national government and the presentation of a joint statement in support of the Brüning government in the opening session of the Reichstag on 13 October.[37] But when reports of this agreement were leaked to the public—first in a speech by Gustav Hülser at the CSVD's national congress in Leipzig[38] and then in a greatly exaggerated form in the

Berliner Tageblatt[39]—the conservatives around Westarp became increasingly uneasy, until finally Wolfgang Hauenschild-Tscheidt from the CNBLP withdrew from the project just prior to the next scheduled meeting on 29 September. This meeting, as could be expected, ended in a virtual impasse that left little hope for anything more elaborate than a purely nonbinding joint declaration on 13 October.[40]

What ultimately spelled the collapse of the efforts to consolidate the various parties between the Center and DNVP into a united parliamentary front prior to the reopening of the Reichstag in October 1931 was the sharp swing to the right that had taken place within the DVP since the beginning of the summer. For while Thiel and Glatzel from the DVP's left wing actively supported the efforts to unify the parties of the middle and moderate Right behind the policies of the Brüning government,[41] the industrial interests that constituted the nucleus of the party's right wing were intent upon using the collapse of the Austro-German customs union project to force Curtius's resignation as German foreign minister in hopes that this might clear the way for a reorganization and extension of the national government to the Right.[42] Uncertain as to the course the DVP should pursue once the Reichstag had been called back into session, Dingeldey hoped that the formation of closer political ties between the parties of the middle and moderate Right would enable them to regain a measure of influence over the course of events in Berlin.[43] But unlike the group around Weber and Schlange-Schöningen, Dingeldey was no longer prepared to give the chancellor his unqualified support. Speaking at a DVP election rally in Hamburg on 24 September, Dingeldey not only repeated his call for a reorganization of the national government but indicated that his party's willingness to support the chancellor was predicated upon his ability to undertake the reforms necessary for Germany's economic recovery. Foremost among the reforms Dingeldey had in mind was a thorough overhaul of the existing system of wage and salary arbitration, a project that enjoyed strong support among the industrial interests on his party's right wing.[44]

On 3 October Curtius announced his resignation as Brüning's foreign minister, thereby removing the last obstacle that stood in the way of the DVP's break with the government. Over the course of the next several days Brüning tried desperately to prevent the DVP's defection from the governmental coalition by offering cabinet posts to Ernst Scholz and other prominent party members.[45] In the meantime, however, the DVP party leadership had come under increasingly heavy pressure from influential sectors within the Ruhr industrial establishment for a clear and irrevocable break with the Brüning government.[46] This, in combination with the severe losses the DVP had suffered in the Hamburg senate elections on 27 September and the news that the radical Right was about to launch another offensive against the Brüning government, helped create an atmosphere of panic at the upper echelons of the DVP party organization that made continuation of the previous political course impossible. Consequently, when the new cabinet that Brüning presented to the public on 9 October differed only slightly from the one he had just dismissed, the last vestige of hope that Dingeldey might come out in support of the Brüning government quickly vanished. Frustrated by the way in which the chancellor had ignored his party's demands for an extension of the government to the Right, Dingeldey denounced the second Brüning cabinet as even weaker than the one it had replaced and immediately recommended that the party withdraw its support from the government. This recommendation was then accepted over the vigorous objections of the party's left wing at a series of meetings with the DVP executive committee, the DVP national council, and the DVP Reichstag delegation on 9–10 October.[47]

The DVP's decision in the fall of 1931 to withdraw its support from the Brüning government represented a critical turning point in the history of the party. Not only did this turn of events spell the collapse of efforts on the part of Abegg, Weber, and Schlange-Schöningen to unite the parties of the middle and moderate Right behind the policies of the Brüning government, but it also did much to blur the lines that separated the DVP from the more radical parties on the German Right. This latter point was particularly significant in light of the undisguised sympathy that many of those on the DVP's right wing felt for the establishment of closer ties with the forces of the national opposition. On 11 October the leaders of the DNVP, NSDAP, Stahlhelm, National Rural League, and a host of similar right-wing organizations held a mass demonstration in the small resort town of Bad Harzburg in what was supposed to mark the beginning of a major new offensive aimed at the overthrow of the Brüning government.[48] Dingeldey's own reaction to this latest maneuver on the part of the radical Right was characteristically equivocal. For although the DVP party chairman continued to chastise the leaders of the national opposition for their refusal to share the burden of governmental responsibility and tried to dissuade members of his own party's right wing from taking part in the Harzburg rally, he was also quick to affirm his willingness to enter into an alliance with the national opposition on the basis of mutual respect and political prudence.[49] This sort of ambivalence, particularly after the DVP had joined the ranks of those parties that were seeking to bring about the fall of the Brüning government, made it extremely difficult for Dingeldey to hold his party in line. Undeterred by Dingeldey's words of caution, two DVP Reichstag deputies, former Reichswehr Commander in Chief Hans von Seeckt and retired naval officer Ernst Hintzmann, attended the Harzburg demonstration, while Carl Schmid and Erich von Gilsa, the one a present and the other a former member of the DVP Reichstag delegation, sent congratulatory telegrams.[50]

It was against the background of these developments that the Reichstag reconvened on 13 October. The next four days were to determine whether

Brüning possessed sufficient parliamentary support to continue his present political course or would go down to defeat at the hands of the "Harzburg Front." In the meantime, the situation within the DVP continued to deteriorate as the leaders of the party's left wing began to rebel against Dingeldey's new political course. The first sign that a crisis was brewing came on 10 October when Hans von Eynern, a member of the DVP delegation to the Prussian Landtag and one of the party's most respected moderates, resigned from the DVP in protest against Dingeldey's move to the right.[51] On the same day a substantial minority in the DVP Reichstag delegation spoke out against Dingeldey's decision to terminate his party's support of the Brüning government, giving rise to widespread speculation that perhaps as many as seven deputies would not go along with the rest of the delegation in voting against the chancellor. In addition to Curtius and Kahl, this group included Siegfried von Kardorff, Wilhelm Ferdinand Kalle, and Rudolf Schneider, as well as the delegation's only representatives from the party's white-collar wing, Frank Glatzel and Otto Thiel.[52] The possibility that such a large contingent from the delegation might actually vote for Brüning alarmed the leaders of the DVP's right wing, who demanded that Dingeldey take disciplinary action, including possible expulsion from the party, against those members of the delegation who refused to follow the party's new political course.[53] Dingeldey, however, was concerned that such a move might precipitate a general secession on the party's left wing, and at his urging the delegation adopted a resolution shortly before the decisive vote on the afternoon of 16 October that removed the threat of sanctions against those deputies who continued to support the chancellor.[54] In the ensuing vote five members of the DVP Reichstag delegation—Thiel, Glatzel, Kalle, Kahl, and Kardorff—proceeded to cast their ballots with the government, while four others, including Curtius and Brüning's former finance minister Paul Moldenhauer, failed to take part in the vote. Of the DVP's thirty Reichstag deputies, only twenty-one supported their party chairman in his break with the government.[55]

In his first test of strength with the forces of the Harzburg Front, Brüning managed to eke out a narrow yet decisive victory by a margin of twenty-five votes. The margin of victory, however, was provided not by the defection of men like Kardorff, Kahl, and Kalle but by an unexpected reversal on the part of the Business Party. Instead of abating as party leaders had hoped, the crisis that had forced the WP's withdrawal from the Brüning government in the fall of 1930 had grown progressively worse as a result of the allegations of financial impropriety that surrounded the WP's national party chairman, Hermann Drewitz. Not even Drewitz's reelection to the party chairmanship by an overwhelming majority of the delegates at the WP's Berlin party congress in April 1931[56] or the WP's frontal assault against the fiscal and economic policies of the Brüning government[57] could stem the steady erosion of the

WP's popular support. The crisis within the party reached a climax in early August 1931 when the WP's three district organizations in Saxony seceded from the party to reconstitute themselves as the Saxon Business Party (Sächsische Wirtschaftspartei).[58] This development made it virtually impossible for Drewitz to continue as party leader, and on 18 August he relinquished responsibility for the conduct of party affairs to Johann Victor Bredt, the WP's most highly respected public figure and a former member of the Brüning cabinet.[59] Bredt's appointment as the WP's acting chairman while Drewitz was forced to defend himself in court against a civil suit arising from his involvement in the collapse of a special middle-class bank in Berlin cleared the way for a reconciliation with the Saxon Business Party, and on 8 September the WP's three Saxon district organizations officially rejoined the party.[60]

The scars that the Drewitz affair left on the WP's national organization made party leaders wary of the prospect of new national elections. Following the reconvocation of the Reichstag on 13 October, Drewitz and Jakob Mollath, chairman of the WP Reichstag delegation, met with both Brüning and the leaders of the national opposition in an attempt to determine the party's future political course. As a result of these conversations, the leaders of the WP quickly concluded that whereas the chancellor was prepared to make certain concessions with respect to the protection of middle-class economic interests, neither Hitler nor Hugenberg was willing to provide any assurances about the composition and program of the government they planned to install once Brüning had been forced from office. Consequently, when the Center indicated that under no circumstances would it join the NSDAP and DNVP in forming a new right-wing government, the leaders of the WP Reichstag delegation threw their full support behind the chancellor in an attempt to avert the political chaos that his fall from power was certain to invite.[61] With the defection of the DVP, the WP's sudden, though not entirely unexpected, reversal was to prove decisive in enabling the chancellor to survive the political challenge that the forces of the Harzburg Front had directed against his government. The effect of the WP's decision upon its national organization was both immediate and devastating. On 17 October Hugo Weber, a former member of the Saxon state government and one of the four men who had been chosen to run the party following Drewitz's political disgrace, gave vent to the bitterness he felt over the WP's decision to support the Brüning government by declaring his resignation as the party's first vice-chairman. In the meantime, a virtual mutiny had erupted at the local levels of the WP's national organization, as one local chapter after another either dissolved itself, seceded from the party, or transferred its allegiance to the Radical Middle-Class Party (Radikale Mittelstandspartei) that disgruntled middle-class activists had founded in Frankfurt at the end of September.[62] All of this created a situation that the leaders of the Harzburg Front were able to exploit with consummate skill, both by denouncing the WP as a traitor to the cause of the national opposition and by imploring its members to join their ranks.[63]

The net effect of the WP's decision to support the Brüning government in the fall of 1931 was to accelerate the party's internal disintegration and to drive the overwhelming bulk of its rank-and-file membership into the arms of the radical Right. By the end of 1931 the Business Party was effectively dead as a political force. Nor was the situation within the German People's Party appreciably better. For although the DVP's national organization was still essentially intact, the party's break with the Brüning government had aroused widespread opposition on the DVP's left wing at the same time that it had encouraged the leaders of the party's right wing to seek even closer ties with the forces of the national opposition.[64] Of all the nonsocialist and nonconfessional parties that stood to the left of the DNVP and NSDAP, only the German State Party had emerged from the crisis surrounding the formation of the second Brüning cabinet unscathed. Not only had the DStP given the chancellor its full and unequivocal support throughout his confrontation with the radical Right, but it regarded Brüning's triumph in the Reichstag as a vindication of its own political course.[65] Moreover, the leaders of the State Party hoped to take advantage of the confusion that the most recent altercation over the fate of the Brüning government had created within the WP and DVP. In this respect, the leaders of the DStP were heartened by the decision of still another WP parliamentarian, Prussian Landtag deputy Adolf Leonhardt, to join their party in late October 1931.[66] By the same token, they hoped to exploit the split that had developed in Württemberg and other parts of the country between the DVP's rank and file and those DVP deputies who had gone along with Dingeldey's new political course.[67]

For all of the optimism that the leaders of the DStP were able to read into the events of October 1931, however, it was not the German State Party but the National Socialist German Workers' Party that emerged as the principal beneficiary of the crisis that had accompanied the reorganization of the Brüning government. For instead of abating as Germany's more moderate political leaders had hoped, the appeal of National Socialism had grown steadily in the period since the last national elections in the fall of 1930. In a series of state and local elections in various parts of the country over the course of the preceding year, the NSDAP had consistently polled between 25 and 40 percent of the popular vote, with its strongest gains coming in areas that were predominantly agricultural and Protestant.[68] The outcome of the Hessian Landtag elections on 15 November 1931 was to offer further proof of the NSDAP's growing appeal. In Hesse, as in other parts of the country, the parties of the middle and moderate Right fell easy prey to the NSDAP, which tallied 37.1 percent of the popular vote and increased its representation in the Hessian Landtag from one to twenty-seven seats. Dingeldey, who had hoped that his party's break with the Brüning government would insulate it against the attacks of the radical Right,[69] saw the DVP go down to a resounding defeat in which it lost all but one of its seven seats in the Landtag. The DStP, on the other hand, lost four of the five seats that the now-defunct Democratic Party had won in the last state elections, while the Hessian Rural League, a regional agrarian party with national ties to the CNBLP, held on to only two of its nine parliamentary mandates. More importantly, the fact that the DNVP lost two of its three seats in the Landtag indicated that, far from being able to control the forces it had helped set in motion, it too was in danger of being swept away by the storm from the Right.[70]

Between the Fronts

THE FORMATION OF THE second Brüning government in the fall of 1931 underscored the dramatic shift to the right that had taken place in Germany since the outbreak of the great depression. Stemming as much from the radicalizing effect that the deepening economic crisis had had upon Germany's middle-class electorate as from the machinations of Germany's conservative elites, this development was to reach a preliminary climax in the smashing victory that the NSDAP recorded in a series of state and local elections on 24 April 1932. Not only did the outcome of the elections represent a stunning rejection of Weimar democracy and erase the last vestige of legitimacy it still possessed in the eyes of the German people, but it effectively sealed the fate of the Brüning government and set the stage for the chancellor's dismissal a month later. In the meantime, the German liberal parties drifted from crisis to crisis, unable to formulate any sort of coherent response to the increasingly desperate situation in which the country found itself in the winter of 1931–32. For all intents and purposes, liberalism had exhausted itself as a viable force in German political life, a fact confirmed by the virtual annihilation of the two liberal parties on 24 April and by their effective exclusion from the corridors of power in Berlin.

The German liberal parties remained deeply divided on a myriad of issues, not the least of which was the fate of the Brüning government. For whereas the leaders of the DStP continued to support the Brüning government as the republic's last line of defense against the radical Right, Dingeldey and the leaders of the DVP had just broken with the chancellor in hopes that this would lead to the formation of a new national government in which the forces of the national opposition were represented. Underlying this split was a fundamental difference of opinion regarding the nature and significance of the Nazi movement. With few exceptions, the leaders of the DStP were outspoken and uncompromising foes of National Socialism. By far the party's most ambitious attack against the Nazi movement came in the form of a small book that Theodor Heuss, himself a member of the DStP Reichstag delegation, published in the winter of 1931–32 under the title *Hitlers Weg*. In what was both a remarkably dispassionate analysis of the origins and appeal of Nazism and a vigorous defense of Germany's republican institutions, Heuss took special pains to stress the role of racism and anti-Semitism in the Nazi program and dismissed the Nazi quest for a new order as an atavistic revolt against the modern world. The appeal of Nazism, Heuss argued, had less to do with the originality of its program than with Hitler's ability to exploit the discontent of those who had become disoriented by Germany's military defeat and a decade of economic hardship. At the heart of Nazism, therefore, lay a curious anomaly, namely its ability to mobilize the deepest and most irrational impulses within man through the use of techniques that represented the epitome of political rationality—in other words, its ability to rationalize the irrational.[1]

Heuss's analysis of Nazism was characterized—and some have said marred —by its mixture of scholarly detachment and irony. In many respects, it paled in comparison with the impassioned denunciation of Nazism that August Weber, chairman of the DStP Reichstag delegation, delivered from the floor of the Reichstag in February 1932. Here, to the constant jeering of the Nazi delegation, Weber proceeded to denounce the Nazis as a party of political thugs who had willingly embraced violence and murder as a means of accomplishing their ends.[2] Weber's bitter invective, however, contrasted sharply in tone and content with the ambivalence that characterized the DVP's attitude toward the NSDAP. For although Dingeldey and his associates remained openly critical of both Nazi racism and the confusion that surrounded the NSDAP's social and economic program, they were also anxious to align themselves with the forces of the national opposition in hopes of reversing their party's declining electoral fortunes and moderating the radicalism of Hitler and his allies in the Harzburg Front. To the dismay of the more conservative elements on the DVP's right wing, Dingeldey was actually more interested in an understanding with the NSDAP than in an alliance with the Nationalists,[3] and in the campaign for the Hessian Landtag elections he had proposed to Hitler that their two parties suspend polemics against each other for the sake of a united front against the parties of the Weimar Coalition.[4] None of this, however, sat well with the leaders of the DVP's left wing, who criticized their party's courtship of the NSDAP as a radical departure from the strong anti-Nazi stand it had taken in the campaign for the 1930 Reichstag elections.[5]

The dissension over Dingeldey's courtship of the NSDAP was only one indication of the deep split that had developed within the DVP by the end of 1931. The party's break with the Brüning government had produced widespread disaffection on the DVP's left wing, where in late October a group of dissidents had coalesced under the leadership of Wilhelm Kunz, a prominent Berlin lawyer, and Count Alexander zu Dohna, a professor of law at the University of Bonn and a former member of the DVP delegation to the Weimar National Assembly. This group, which consisted of from forty-five to sixty members, met repeatedly between the end of October and the beginning of December 1931 in an attempt to return the DVP to the political course it had

pursued under the leadership of its late founder and chairman, Gustav Stresemann. The Kunz-Dohna faction was particularly resentful of the increasingly
prominent role Ruhr heavy industry had come to play in the DVP's internal
affairs and hoped that it might be possible to initiate a reform of party finances
that would end the DVP's dependence upon outside economic interests. At the
same time, Kunz and his supporters remained adamantly opposed to Dingeldey's overtures to the radical Right, arguing that the DVP should dedicate
itself instead to the cultivation of closer ties with the various middle-class
splinter parties that stood between the Center and DNVP.[6]

On 6 November Kunz, DVP Reichstag deputy Frank Glatzel, and two other
members of the dissident faction met with Dingeldey to reassure the DVP
chairman of their loyalty to the party and to enlist his support for their efforts to
revitalize the party in the spirit of Stresemann. This meeting, however, proved
a bitter disappointment for the forces around Kunz and Dohna. For although
Dingeldey readily conceded that Kunz and his supporters were acting in what
they thought to be the best interests of the party, he was extremely reluctant to
become involved in an open confrontation with the DVP's industrial wing for
fear that this might trigger a major secession from the party.[7] Dingeldey's
reluctance to challenge the party's industrial wing, in turn, had a chilling effect
upon the DVP's relations with the leadership of the German National Union of
Commercial Employees, an influential white-collar union that had consistently
supported the DVP ever since the earliest days of the Weimar Republic. At the
heart of this strain lay Dingeldey's refusal to commit the DVP to the publication of a new social program endorsing the principle of compulsory arbitration
in wage and salary disputes between labor and management and reaffirming
the special legal status of labor unions like the DHV in the collective bargaining process.[8] To Hans Bechly, the DHV's national chairman and a member of
the DVP central executive committee, this only confirmed his fears that the
DVP had fallen under the domination of its industrial wing and that there was
little, if any, room within it for the salaried employee. In a particularly blunt
letter that he wrote to Dingeldey at the end of November, Bechly warned that if
the DVP could not at least grant the German labor movement the legal
recognition to which it was entitled, he no longer saw any future for the party
as far as his union was concerned.[9]

Frustrated by Dingeldey's apparent indifference to the concerns they had
voiced over their party's political future, the leaders of the DVP's left wing
decided to plead their case before the DVP central executive committee at its
next scheduled meeting in early December 1931.[10] The possibility of an open
confrontation with the DVP's left wing, however, produced an immediate
hardening in Dingeldey's attitude toward the dissidents and prompted charges
of disloyalty to himself and the party.[11] At the same time, the industrial
interests on the DVP's extreme right wing began to clamor for a purge of the

elements that had opposed the party's new political course and hoped that the DVP central executive committee would commit the party to the establishment of closer ties with the more conservative elements in the national opposition.[12] None of this augured well for either the unity of the party or the aspirations of its left wing when the DVP central executive committee met in Hanover on 6 December. Dingeldey opened the meeting with a vigorous defense of the DVP's break with the Brüning government in which he assailed the chancellor's fiscal and economic policies as the factor most singly responsible for the radicalization of the German bourgeoisie. The controversy that the party's new political course had aroused within the DVP Reichstag delegation, Dingeldey continued, was a regrettable, though fully understandable, price that he and the DVP party leadership had to pay for the strength of their political convictions. Although the tone of Dingeldey's remarks were clearly conciliatory, the dissidents on the DVP's left wing were given little opportunity to present their views in the discussion that followed. Only Friedrich Caspari from the Kunz-Dohna group and Otto Thiel from the DHV dared subject themselves to the gauntlet of abuse that Ernst Hintzmann, Otto Hembeck, and the leaders of the DVP's right wing had prepared for them. The extent of their isolation within the party became all too painfully apparent when they could muster only 14 of 344 votes against a resolution that reiterated the DVP's unequivocal opposition to the Brüning government and its commitment to the formation of a new government resting upon "the broad national forces of the German people."[13]

The outcome of the meeting of the DVP central executive committee on 6 December 1931 represented a decisive, if not devastating, defeat for the left wing of the party. The leaders of the DVP's left wing were distraught not only by the intolerance with which the rest of the party—and particularly those on its extreme right wing—had received their views but also by the way in which Hintzmann, Hembeck, and their associates had used the meeting to propagate the idea of a merger with the DNVP.[14] Rejecting such a goal as totally incompatible with the spirit in which Stresemann had founded the party, the leaders of the Kunz-Dohna group began to weigh the possibility of a general secession from the party.[15] It was against the background of these developments that Fritz Mittelmann, another member of the DVP's left wing who was in the process of being expelled from the party for having publicly criticized its swing to the right,[16] proposed the creation of a new German National Association, which like its namesake from 1859 would embrace the political views of all "positive-minded" bourgeois circles from the People's Conservatives around Westarp to die-hard liberals like the DStP's August Weber.[17] The purpose of such an organization, as Dohna explained in a letter to Kunz in the middle of December, would be to consolidate those elements of the German bourgeoisie that had not yet succumbed to the "psychosis of National Socialism" into a united political front capable of protecting the existing political order and providing the chancellor with the domestic support he needed to free himself from the influence of Social Democracy.[18]

Though of little immediate consequence, the plans for the creation of a second German National Association revealed the extent to which a significant segment of the DVP's left wing had become disaffected from Dingeldey and the rest of the party. While Dingeldey continued to defend his break with the Brüning government, he remained sensitive to the concerns of his party's left wing and clearly hoped to dissuade its leaders from leaving the DVP.[19] It was no doubt with this in mind that Dingeldey began to seek closer political and organizational ties with the leaders of the other moderate bourgeois parties. Dingeldey had met with representatives from the various middle-class splinter parties that stood to the left of the DNVP on several occasions through the spring and summer of 1931, and in late November he had Albrecht Morath from the DVP Reichstag delegation make discreet overtures in the direction of the DStP's August Weber on the assumption that "the hour of the party and floor leaders had arrived."[20] Over the course of the next six weeks, Dingeldey was to meet with the leaders of the Business Party, the Christian-National Peasants and Farmers' Party, and the Conservative People's Party on at least three separate occasions. What emerged from these discussions was a proposal from the WP's Gotthard Sachsenberg to reconstitute the various parties that stood between the Center and the DNVP as a Christian-national bloc organized along corporatist lines and consisting of four independent social groups: the peasantry, the commercial middle class, the Christian working class, and the bourgeoisie. As the first step toward the creation of such a bloc, the WP proposed the formation of a single parliamentary delegation under Westarp's chairmanship as well as a joint effort in the forthcoming campaign for the Prussian state elections.[21]

Although he remained skeptical about its prospects for success, Dingeldey was willing to go along with the project and thought ultimately in terms of a merger of his own DVP with the WP, the CNBLP, the People's Conservatives, and those members of the DStP who were willing to take part in such a project without the official sanction of their party leadership.[22] That Dingeldey would even consider such a step reflected not only his growing uncertainty about the DVP's political future but also his desire to check the influence of the forces on its extreme right wing. Ever since the meeting of the DVP central executive committee in Hanover, Dingeldey had found himself under increasingly heavy pressure from the leaders of his party's right wing to enter into a close alliance with the forces of the national opposition. In this respect, Dingeldey's chief antagonist was Erich von Gilsa, a former DVP Reichstag deputy in the employ of the Gutehoffnungshütte's Paul Reusch and the party's chief liaison to the Stahlhelm.[23] On 5 January 1932 Gilsa had Dingeldey meet with the leaders of the six DVP district organizations from the Rhine-Ruhr basin in an attempt to pressure the party's national leadership into opening negotiations with the DNVP's Alfred Hugenberg. Gilsa's ultimate objective was to force a merger of the DVP and DNVP into a united right-wing party capable of retaining the support of those who otherwise might fall under the sway of National Socialism.[24] It was in the very same spirit that Heinrich Mahnken, the Stahlhelm's district leader for the Rhineland and Westphalia, sent an ultimatum to the chairmen of the DVP's six west German district organizations demanding that their party undertake concrete steps aimed at a merger with the DNVP or suffer the consequences in the upcoming elections to the Prussian Landtag.[25]

Dingeldey responded to the growing pressure for a merger with the DNVP with a vigorous defense of the DVP's political integrity at a heated six-and-a-half-hour meeting of the party's Rhenish-Westphalian *Arbeitsgemeinschaft* on 28 January. Responsibility for the failure to create a united German Right along the lines suggested by Gilsa and the Stahlhelm, argued Dingeldey, lay not with the leadership of his party but with Hugenberg and his refusal to accept anything less than the total absorption of the DVP in the DNVP party apparatus. In the debate that followed, all but one of the six DVP district organizations at the meeting—the lone exception being the organization from South Westphalia—came around to support Dingeldey's position.[26] Dingeldey's remarks, however, only strengthened Gilsa in his conviction that the DVP party chairman was not genuinely interested in the cultivation of closer political ties with the DNVP, and on the following day he announced his resignation from the DVP as a way of protesting its weak and irresolute leadership.[27] At the same time, the Stahlhelm intensified its agitation against the DVP as Mahnken urged his supporters to leave the party in retaliation for its abandonment of the national cause.[28] It was against the background of these developments that Otto Hembeck and Ludwig Schultz from the DVP district organization in South Westphalia sent shock waves that reverberated throughout the party when they proposed at a regional convention in Dortmund on 26 February that the entire district organization secede from the DVP and go over to the DNVP intact. When efforts at mediation failed, Hembeck and his supporters went ahead with their plans and formally announced the secession of the DVP's South Westphalian organization in the first week of March. Although many of the party's local leaders in the district refused to join the secession, Dingeldey's hopes of isolating the crisis collapsed when influential party members such as Albert Hueck, a former DVP Reichstag deputy with close ties to Ruhr coal interests, and Hermann Klingspor, chairman of the DVP's Westphalian youth organization, also left the party.[29]

The events in South Westphalia dealt a damaging blow to the DVP's prospects in the forthcoming Prussian elections and accelerated the disintegration of the party's right wing. Throughout the crisis, Ruhr heavy industry strongly supported the efforts of Gilsa, Hembeck, and associates to force a merger of the DVP and DNVP into a united bourgeois party, although in the case of Reusch and Gustav Krupp von Bohlen und Halbach this was accompanied by an equally strong desire to force Hugenberg's removal from the DNVP party chairmanship.[30] Dingeldey, on the other hand, was determined to preserve the DVP's political integrity vis-à-vis the radical Right and took special pains to differentiate between its "purely objective" criticism of the Brüning government and the blanket condemnation of the Weimar system that characterized the antigovernment polemics of the Harzburg Front.[31] Consequently, when the Reichstag reconvened in late February to consider the government's budget proposal for the coming fiscal year, Dingeldey had the DVP introduce a separate motion of no-confidence in the Brüning government as a way of highlighting its independence from the parties of the Harzburg Front.[32] At the same time, Dingeldey tried to counter the growing sentiment for a merger with the DNVP on the DVP's right wing by adopting a harsher line toward the elements of the party that had opposed its break with the Brüning government. Fearful that another split like the one that had materialized in the Reichstag delegation the previous October would result in a major secession on the party's right wing,[33] Dingeldey moved that all members of the delegation who were not otherwise excused for reasons of health or business should be required under penalty of expulsion from the delegation to support the party's motion of no-confidence in the Brüning government in the decisive vote scheduled for the afternoon of 26 February.[34] When Julius Curtius and Siegfried von Kardorff, two of the left wing's most highly respected spokesmen, refused to heed this warning and deliberately missed the crucial vote on the fate of the Brüning government, they were forthwith expelled from the delegation.[35]

Throughout all of this, Dingeldey continued his efforts to establish closer political and organizational ties with the other moderate bourgeois parties between the Center and DNVP. But, as Dingeldey wrote to a colleague shortly after the reconvocation of the Reichstag, this presupposed complete unanimity in all of the major political questions that confronted the German nation.[36] This condition automatically excluded the German State Party, which had once again set aside its reservations about the Brüning government to support it in its most recent confrontation with the radical Right. To be sure, the leaders of the DStP continued to criticize the social effects of the government's austerity program and privately chastised the chancellor for the weakness of his response to the threat of Nazism.[37] But, as in the past, the prospect of a right-wing government in which the DNVP and NSDAP were sure to hold the upper hand held little attraction for the leaders of the State Party, who voted unanimously in support of the Brüning government as a clearly preferable alternative to a cabinet of the Harzburg Front.[38] Similar considerations were also decisive in the case of the Business Party, whose parliamentary leaders ignored the effects of right-wing agitation on their party's national organization to support the chancellor in the decisive vote on 26 February.[39] The consequences of this decision were devastating. For not only did the WP's decision to support the Brüning government effectively dash whatever hopes Dingeldey had of unifying the parties of the middle and moderate Right, but more importantly it virtually destroyed what still remained of the WP's badly decimated national organization. The defection of Hugo Weber and Hermann Kaiser, the leaders of the Saxon Business Party, to the DNVP earlier in the month only typified the havoc that the WP's continued support of the Brüning government had wrought upon its national organization.[40]

About the only issue upon which Germany's moderate bourgeois parties could agree in the winter and spring of 1932 was the need to reelect the aging Paul von Hindenburg to a second term as Reich president. Originally, both the DStP and DVP, as well as the other nonsocialist parties to the left of the DNVP, had hoped to avoid a presidential election through a parliamentary extension of Hindenburg's term of office. Dingeldey, in fact, had even gone so far as to meet with Hitler in early January in an unsuccessful bid for the NSDAP's cooperation in securing the Reichstag's approval for such an extension.[41] With the collapse of these overtures in the second week of January, the two liberal parties supported efforts to draft the Reich president for a second term of office, albeit for entirely different reasons. Though at first less than enthusiastic about the prospect of Hindenburg's candidacy, Dietrich and the leaders of the DStP came to regard his reelection as essential for the survival of the Weimar Republic, particularly after Hitler declared his candidacy for Hindenburg's post in the third week of February.[42] For Dingeldey and the leaders of the DVP, on the other hand, Hindenburg's candidacy provided their party with an excellent opportunity to embellish its image as a party of political responsibility whose opposition to the Brüning government was qualitatively different from the antisystem polemics of the radical Right.[43] As a result, cooperation between the two liberal parties on behalf of the Hindenburg campaign was severely handicapped by their radically divergent attitudes toward the Brüning government. In Leipzig, for example, plans to have Dietrich kick off the local campaign were nearly scuttled when the DVP threatened to lead a secession of the more conservative bourgeois parties from the nonpartisan Hindenburg Committee if such a prominent member of the national government was allowed to speak.[44]

Whatever their motives for supporting Hindenburg might have been, both the DStP and DVP were relieved when the Reich president won reelection in the runoff ballot on 10 April. To be sure, the leaders of the two liberal parties were hopeful that the effect of Hindenburg's victory might carry over into their campaign for the state and local elections scheduled to take place two weeks later in Prussia, Bavaria, Württemberg, and other parts of the country. Such optimism, however, was hardly justified in light of the financial and organizational difficulties that plagued the two liberal parties in the spring of 1932. The State Party, for example, entered the campaign for the April elections beset by a plethora of problems, not the least of which was the lingering resentment that the leaders of its left wing—and particularly those with close ties to the DStP's civil servant wing—felt about the party's continued support of the Brüning government.[45] The leaders of the DStP were particularly concerned about the role that Ernst Lemmer, Bruno Hauff, and other members of the party's left wing had played in launching new political movements such as the Iron Front (Eiserne Front) and the Republican Action (Republikanische Aktion) for fear that this would lead to a further fragmentation of the DStP's already weakened resources.[46] At the same time, the DStP's own organization had all but collapsed under the weight of Nazi intimidation and financial crisis. Not only did local party officials who had openly supported Hindenburg's candidacy in the recent presidential elections find themselves the target of Nazi terror, but the sources of funding upon which the DStP had traditionally depended had all but dried up in the wake of the depression and the general frustration that the business community felt toward the fiscal and economic policies of the Brüning government. About the only parts of the country where the DStP national organization was still relatively intact were Hamburg, Baden, and Württemberg.[47]

By no means were the organizational and financial difficulties that confronted the DStP in the spring of 1932 unique to it. The contradiction that had been implicit in the DVP's decision to support Hindenburg at the same time that it continued to oppose Brüning became increasingly apparent during the course of the campaign and left the party vulnerable to defections on both its left and right wings. The split that had emerged within the DVP Reichstag delegation over the party's break with the Brüning government had produced sharp divisions throughout the DVP's national organization and had brought the party to the brink of a complete organizational collapse in several parts of the country. The situation was particularly threatening in the six district organizations from the Rhine-Ruhr basin, where efforts to force a merger with the DNVP and the defection of Hembeck, Hueck, and Klingspor had cost the DVP between 15 and 25 percent of its organized membership.[48] In Hesse and parts of southwest Germany, on the other hand, the DVP's break with Brüning had done much to alienate local party leaders who questioned the wisdom of trying to force the chancellor's removal from office before a suitable replacement had been found.[49] In the meantime, a lack of sufficient operating funds had forced the DVP's vocational committees to curtail many of their activities, while key auxiliary organizations like the Reich Association of Young Populists and the Hindenburg Youth were in danger of being torn apart by the conflict between the party's left and right wings.[50] None of this augured well for the DVP's prospects in the Prussian and other state elections that had been set for the last Sunday in April.

The plight of the German middle parties in the spring of 1932 was compounded by the fact that their most important financial backers were no longer prepared to support them in the manner to which they had become accustomed. This was particularly true of the Curatorium for the Reconstruction of German Economic Life, which had decided to dissolve itself and liquidate its assets following the collapse of the movement for bourgeois unity in the summer of 1930.[51] Consequently, when representatives from the DVP, DStP, and other moderate bourgeois parties approached the Curatorium for financial assistance in the spring of 1932, their appeals fell on deaf ears.[52] In the meantime, leaders of the Ruhr industrial establishment were threatening to withhold funds from parties that refused to cooperate in the forthcoming campaign. On 18 March Baron Tilo von Wilmowsky, the brother-in-law of Gustav Krupp von Bohlen und Halbach and a moderate conservative who bitterly opposed Hugenberg's leadership of the DNVP, approached Siemens, Reusch, I.G. Farben's Carl Bosch, and three prominent Ruhr industrialists— Paul Silverberg, Fritz Springorum, and Albert Vögler—with the proposal that they tie their contributions for the spring 1932 campaign to the conclusion of some sort of electoral alliance between the various bourgeois parties to the left of the NSDAP and the right of the Center and Bavarian People's Party. Wilmowsky's proposal carried the imprimatur of his brother-in-law, who as president of the National Federation of German Industry hoped that pressure of this sort might ultimately lead to the creation of a united bourgeois party capable of preventing the German bourgeoisie from falling even further under the influence of Nazism.[53] But Krupp's hopes of success presupposed a general consensus on the part of Germany's industrial elite that simply did not exist. For whereas Siemens, as the founder and former chairman of the now-defunct Curatorium for the Reconstruction of German Economic Life, remained adamant in his refusal to support any party in the upcoming election campaign, Reusch and Springorum found themselves in sharp disagreement over the need to force Hugenberg's removal from the DNVP party chairmanship so that the German bourgeoisie might unify on the basis of the Nationalist party organization. As it became apparent that these differences were irreconcilable, hopes for some sort of concerted industrial action on behalf of a united bourgeois front in the state elections that had been set for 24 April quickly evaporated.[54] Industrial antipathy toward the existing bourgeois parties, however, remained unchanged.

All of the parties from the DStP to the DNVP were hurt by the sharp reduction in the level of industrial support for their campaigns in the state elections that took place in Prussia, Bavaria, and other parts of the country on 24 April 1932. Aside from the fact that the division between those who supported and those who opposed Hugenberg's leadership of the DNVP continued to frustrate industry's efforts on behalf of a united bourgeois party, the major obstacle to the conclusion of an alliance among the more moderate bourgeois parties in the spring of 1932 was the DVP's Dingeldey. For although the DVP was virtually at the end of its financial resources and could therefore ill afford to ignore industrial pressure for some sort of united bourgeois front,[55] Dingeldey made his party's participation in the formation of a Prussian electoral bloc contingent upon the inclusion of Hugenberg and the DNVP.[56] Not only did this constitute a condition that none of the more moderate bourgeois parties—and particularly the DStP—were likely to accept, but it also presumed that an accommodation with Hugenberg might be possible. Hugenberg's own antipathy to such a project became immediately apparent when on 30 March he offered to accept candidates from the parties to the right of the Center on his own party's ticket for the Prussian Landtag on the twofold condition that all *Reststimmen*—or votes that these parties did not need for the election of their own candidates—would go to the DNVP and that the deputies who were elected through this arrangement would subsequently affiliate themselves as guests or *Hospitanten* with the DNVP Landtag delegation.[57] To Dingeldey and the leaders of the DVP, the conditions that Hugenberg attached to his offer of cooperation with the less radical bourgeois parties were tantamount to a virtual capitulation to the DNVP, and they rejected them in emphatic and unequivocal terms.[58] At the same time, the collapse of Dingeldey's efforts to include the DNVP in a united bourgeois front for the Prussian Landtag elections also meant the DVP's withdrawal from the negotiations to form an electoral alliance between the more moderate bourgeois parties that stood to the left of the DNVP.

Undaunted by Dingeldey's refusal to participate in their efforts, the leaders of the Business Party, the Christian-National Peasants and Farmers' Party, and an amorphous group calling itself the "Young Right" went ahead with their plans to form a loose electoral alliance for the Prussian campaign. But this alliance, which bore the name National Front of German Estates (*Nationale Front deutscher Stände*) and was headed by Count Kuno von Westarp from the defunct Conservative People's Party,[59] was hopelessly inadequate as a response to the virtual collapse of the German party system and only underscored the inability of the parties of the middle and moderate Right to free themselves from the outmoded formulas of the past. In the meantime, the DStP and DVP entered the campaign without the benefit of an electoral alliance, either between themselves or with the other parties to the left of the DNVP. Hoping to unite "all bourgeois strata in the struggle against radicalism,"[60] the leaders of the State Party directed the central thrust of their campaign against the elements on Germany's radical Right whose agitation against Brüning and the Weimar system posed such a serious threat to the authority of the state. In this respect, the leaders of the DStP deplored the fragmentation of the German middle and attacked the more moderate bourgeois parties for their failure to unite in defense of the existing political order.[61] But whereas the DStP made the radical Right—and particularly the NSDAP—the principal target of its campaign, Dingeldey and his associates sought above all else to destroy the commanding position that the parties of the Weimar Coalition had held in Prussia ever since the founding of the republic. To be sure, the leaders of the DVP continued to chastise the radical Right for its refusal to share the burden of political responsibility and tried to warn the German bourgeoisie against the danger of falling under the spell of Nazism. But admonitions of this sort paled in comparison to the vehemence with which the DVP attacked the parties of the Weimar Coalition for their role in dispossessing and radicalizing the German middle class.[62] By striking a blow against the "Prussian system," Dingeldey hoped to unite the German bourgeoisie behind the "banner of National Liberalism," so that when the long-awaited change of governments in Berlin took place, the DVP would be sufficiently powerful to moderate the excesses of the national opposition.[63]

To no one's great surprise, the outcome of the state elections on 24 April 1932 bore dramatic and indisputable testimony to the electoral collapse of the German liberal movement.[64] In Prussia, the largest of the German states, the DVP lost approximately two-thirds of the popular vote it had received in the 1930 Reichstag elections, while the DStP saw its electoral strength cut in half. In terms of parliamentary strength, this translated into a loss of thirty-three of forty seats for the DVP and twenty of twenty-two for the DStP. For all intents and purposes, liberalism had been eliminated as a force in Prussian politics, as the NSDAP and those parties that were implacably opposed to the liberal parliamentary order now commanded 250 of the 423 seats in the Prussian Landtag. In Bavaria, where political liberalism had all but disappeared from the scene in the early 1920s, neither the DStP nor the DVP was able to win so much as a single mandate, while in the neighboring state of Württemberg the State Party—in contrast to the all but defunct DVP—was able to hold on to two of its four parliamentary seats. The only exception to the general pattern of liberal electoral collapse was Hamburg, where the DStP, by virtue of a particularly energetic campaign against the NSDAP,[65] actually succeeded in increasing its share of the popular vote since the last municipal elections in September 1931 from 8.7 to 11.3 percent. Elsewhere, however, the picture that greeted the leaders of the two liberal parties on the day after the election was one of unmitigated defeat.

The outcome of the April 1932 elections effectively sealed the fate of the Brüning government, and on 27 May the chancellor tendered his resignation after a stormy session with Hindenburg in which the Reich president refused to give him the emergency authorization he needed for another confrontation with the Reichstag. Brüning's failure as chancellor was the direct, if not inescapable, consequence of a series of fundamental contradictions that lay at the heart of his political program. In the first place, Brüning's efforts to replace the German party state with an authoritarian *Beamtenstaat* was fundamentally incompatible with a deflationary fiscal policy that inflicted severe economic hardship upon the individual civil servant. By the same token, Brüning was committed by the terms under which he had assumed office to a program of agricultural subsidies that ran counter to the central thrust of his chancellorship, namely to reduce the overall level of government spending so that Germany's international creditors might be more amenable to a renegotiation of the Young Plan and the liquidation of her reparations burden. Similarly, Brüning's hope of transforming the Reichsrat into a paraparliamentary counterweight to the Reichstag was all but doomed to failure by his increasing infringement upon the financial autonomy of the very state governments that sat in the Reichsrat. And last but not least, whatever hopes Brüning may have had of "taming" the National Socialists were undercut by the effects of a fiscal and economic program that struck at virtually every sector of German society and inadvertently drove broad segments of Germany's midle-class electorate into the ranks of the Nazi movement. To hope, as Brüning seems to have done, that all of these contradictions would somehow be suspended—or, to use the German word, *aufgehoben*—by the liquidation of Germany's reparations burden was at best illusory and at worst a fragile premise for the conduct of national policy.

CHAPTER THIRTY-THREE

Liberalism's Dying Gasp

AT THE HEART OF THE electoral collapse of the two liberal parties in the spring of 1932 lay an intangible factor that all but defies careful historical analysis, namely the spiritual and moral exhaustion of the German bourgeoisie. The combination of war, defeat, revolution, the humiliation of Versailles, and nearly two decades of uninterrupted economic distress had produced a sense of spiritual malaise with which Weimar's political leaders were incapable of coping and that left the German bourgeoisie ripe for seduction by the facile formulas and relentless dynamism of the Nazi movement. At the same time, the longing for an end to the superficial political divisions that had consistently frustrated the German bourgeoisie in what it had come to regard as a struggle for social and economic survival had become more and more pronounced. But, as the outcome of the elections on 24 April 1932 so clearly revealed, liberalism was no longer capable of serving as the ideological basis upon which the German bourgeoisie in all of its sociological diversity could unite. In the eyes of most Germans, liberalism was little more than a remnant of the past, discredited both by its identification with special economic interests and by its failure to protect the interests of those who had traditionally supported it. It was unity that the German bourgeoisie demanded in its hour of need, and it was unity that the German liberal parties had consistently failed to provide. And so the pendulum of German politics continued its swing to the right, a swing hastened by the failure of the German liberal parties to provide any sort of effective response to the longing for unity to which the deepening economic crisis and the increasing fragmentation of the German party system had given rise.

The outcome of the April 1932 elections lent new impetus to the efforts to create a united middle party. Within the German State Party despair over the outcome of the elections was so great that party leaders began to question its very existence. As Oskar Meyer put it at a meeting of the DStP managing committee on 28 April, "the State Party had a patriotic duty to die as quickly as possible" so that a new party, one with a stronger bourgeois profile, might take its place without being seen as "a continuation of the old party in disguise."[1] Dingeldey and his associates in the German People's Party had also come to the conclusion that their party's only chance of survival—and in Dingeldey's eyes the German bourgeoisie's only chance of survival as well—lay in establishing itself at the head of a new movement for bourgeois unity.[2] The idea of a united middle party enjoyed a broad base of support within the DVP, stretching from the white-collar elements on the party's left wing to men like Wilhelm Ferdinand Kalle, an influential member of the DVP Reichstag delegation who had served as the party's liaison to the German chemical industry for more than a decade.[3] Still, Dingeldey and his associates were apprehensive that leadership of the movement for bourgeois unity might slip from their grasp. Consequently, in the first week of May, Wilhelm Fecht from the DVP's national headquarters in Berlin drafted an elaborate plan for the reorganization of the German middle that was predicated upon the DStP's exclusion from any role in the founding of a new party.[4] The DVP may have wanted unity, but only on its own terms.

As the leaders of the German liberal parties groped for a response to their crushing defeat in the spring elections of 1932, they found themselves under increasingly heavy pressure from bourgeois circles outside the confines of existing party life to put forward some sort of initiative in the matter of bourgeois unity. On 30 April Ferdinand Friedensburg, a former Democrat whose earlier efforts on behalf of bourgeois unity had ended in failure, published a lead article in the *Berliner Tageblatt* calling for the consolidation of the DStP, DVP, and WP along with the minuscule People's Justice Party into a united bourgeois party capable of checking the penetration of National Socialism into the ranks of the German middle strata.[5] Friedensburg's initiative found immediate resonance in Königsberg, where in early April a group espousing similar goals and calling itself the National Reich Club (Nationaler Reichsklub or NRK) had been founded under nonpartisan leadership embracing all the groups from the DStP to the People's Conservatives.[6] Neither of these efforts, however, was quite as ambitious as the plan for bourgeois concentration that emerged from the ranks of the Hansa-Bund for Commerce, Trade, and Industry. Following the Nazi successes in the 1930 Reichstag elections, the Hansa-Bund had launched a vigorous propaganda campaign under the slogan "Economic Freedom against Economic Need" in an attempt to rescue the liberal-capitalist economic order from the collectivist tendencies that had surfaced at both extremes of the political spectrum.[7] In early April 1932, after the first presidential campaign had revealed widespread middle-class sympathy for the NSDAP's anticapitalist rhetoric, the Hansa-Bund founded the Central Office for Bourgeois Politics (Zentralstelle für bürgerliche Politik) under the direction of Ernst Mosich in an effort to intensify its agitation within the German middle strata. With the financial resources of the Hansa-Bund at its disposal, this organization was committed to "a realignment of Germany's political fronts with an eye toward restoring a strong bourgeois influence on politics and legislation" and sought to promote the goal of a united middle party by fostering closer relations between representatives from the various groups constituting the German bourgeoisie.[8]

Tentative negotiations between representatives from the middle parties to the right of the DStP took place throughout the month of May but were invariably frustrated by the general uncertainty that surrounded the still-unsettled fate of the Brüning government.[9] Nor was the situation made any easier by the dismissal of the Brüning government on 31 May and the subsequent dissolution of the Reichstag by his successor, Franz von Papen. Although Brüning's removal from office was hardly unexpected, the call for new elections injected a note of even greater urgency into the efforts to unify the German bourgeoisie and upset the timetable upon which the earlier negotiations had been based. Moreover, the two liberal parties were divided, as they had been in the case of the Brüning government, in their attitudes toward the new cabinet. While Hermann Fischer and those DStP leaders with close ties to the German business community may have felt a certain sense of relief at no longer having to bear the brunt of Brüning's interventionist economic policies,[10] Dietrich and the vast majority of the party's leaders were extremely critical of the social composition of Papen's "cabinet of barons" and sought to mobilize antigovernment sentiment in the campaign for the Reichstag elections that had been set for the end of July with slogans like "People against Junkers!" and "Middle Class Awake!"[11] The DVP, on the other hand, was more favorably disposed to the new government in spite of the fact that it, like the DStP, had not been consulted during the negotiations that had led to its installation and harbored reservations of its own about the government's aristocratic social profile. The leaders of the DVP were also critical of the fact that the new government had not made a serious effort to bring the National Socialists into the cabinet so that they might have an opportunity to demonstrate their capacity for constructive political action. While Dingeldey and his supporters were anxious to put some distance between themselves and the Papen government, they clearly regarded it as preferable to its predecessor and refrained from the antigovernment polemics that characterized the DStP's campaign in the summer of 1932.[12]

The fact that the two liberal parties were divided on the question of the Papen government did not augur well for the prospects of a united bourgeois front for the forthcoming national elections. Efforts to found a united bourgeois party began almost immediately after the dissolution of the Reichstag and showed signs of promise until the DVP, fearful that the undertaking was about to slip from its control, attached conditions to its participation in the project that made it impossible for the DStP to take part.[13] On 5 June the DVP executive committee tried to sabotage the DStP's participation in the founding of a new middle party by making its own involvement contingent upon the extension of similar overtures in the direction of Hugenberg's DNVP, the establishment of a sharp front against the Social Democrats, and the adoption of a positive attitude toward the newly installed Papen government.[14] The efforts to create a united middle party had also come under increasingly heavy fire within the DStP, where such party stalwarts as Ernst Lemmer, Gustav Stolper, and Theodor Heuss all voiced strong objections to their party's absorption in a new political combination that included the more conservative middle parties.[15] The prospects of an accommodation between the two liberal parties were further damaged when Dietrich, who up until this point had remained aloof from all of the deliberations about the founding of a new party, indicated at a meeting of the DStP leadership on the morning of 9 June that he would have nothing to do with the creation of a united middle party.[16] When Carl Schmid, a DVP Reichstag deputy from South Düsseldorf who stood on the party's extreme right wing, resigned from the DVP in protest against its involvement in the efforts to create a united middle party,[17] this only reinforced Dingeldey's determination to force a break with the State Party. At a meeting with representatives from the DStP, WP, and People's Conservatives on the evening of 9 June, Dingeldey refused to take part in the creation of a united bourgeois party unless efforts were also made to secure the cooperation of Hugenberg and the DNVP. At the same time, Dingeldey refused to participate in any project that adopted "a one-sided combat stance [*Kampfstellung*] against National Socialism."[18] When their protests that this would make an effective campaign against the National Socialists impossible proved to be of no avail, the DStP's Carl Petersen and August Weber realized that the preconditions for a concentration of the bourgeois middle along democratic lines no longer existed and announced their withdrawal from all further negotiations.[19]

The outcome of the meeting on the evening of 9 June spelled the collapse of efforts to create a united middle party in time for the Reichstag elections at the end of July. For although Hugo Eckener, Wilhelm Solf, and a handful of highly respected but politically unaffiliated representatives of Germany's bourgeois elite tried to inject new life into the movement for bourgeois unity by inviting more than 200 of their peers to a special convention in Berlin's Deutsche Gesellschaft 1914 on the evening of 14 June,[20] the withdrawal of the State Party had immediate repercussions not only upon the grass-roots support for the efforts to create a united bourgeois party that had surfaced in East Prussia, Hesse-Kassel, and other parts of the country[21] but also upon the willingness of the Hansa-Bund, I.G. Farben, and other potential benefactors to support the project.[22] By the morning of 13 June the situation had become so hopeless that Eckener cabled Solf and asked to be excused from the proceedings that had been scheduled for the following evening.[23] At the same time, Mosich informed Dingeldey that although he continued to support the principle of bourgeois concentration, he had decided not to affiliate himself with the new party even if the meeting on 14 June should have positive results.[24] This meant, much to Dingeldey's chagrin, that the financial support Mosich had indicated might be available from the Hansa-Bund, I.G. Farben, and other sources in the German business community would no longer be forthcoming.[25] It also meant that the convention that Solf and his associates planned to hold in the Deutsche Gesellschaft 1914 had no chance of success and would turn out to be, in the words of the DStP's Theodor Heuss, "a total bust."[26]

While it is doubtful that the creation of a united middle party would have materially affected the outcome of the 31 July Reichstag elections, the episode is nevetheless significant for what it reveals about the poverty of Germany's liberal leadership in the last years of the Weimar Republic. Interested in the movement for bourgeois unity only insofar as it might be of benefit to his own party, Dingeldey deliberately sabotaged what were essentially nonpartisan efforts to reconstitute the German middle as an independent political force so that his own party could establish itself as the crystallization point around which a united bourgeois party might form. By making the DVP's participation in the creation of such a party contingent upon the acceptance of conditions that the leaders of the State Party were almost certain to reject, Dingeldey sought to exclude the only other party capable of challenging the DVP's claim to leadership from any sort of meaningful role in the process of bourgeois consolidation. Moreover, Dingeldey seems to have conceived of the consolidation of the German middle not as an end in itself but as the prelude to an accommodation with the DNVP and the formation of a united bourgeois bloc embracing all of those elements that stood between the Center and NSDAP.[27] Not only Solf and Eckener—both of whom stood close to the DStP—but other bourgeois moderates as well were deeply resentful of having been used for what the KVP's Hans-Erdmann von Lindeiner-Wildau denounced as "a polishing up [*Auflackierung*] of the DVP," and one by one they dissociated themselves from the efforts to create some sort of united bourgeois front for the forthcoming Reichstag elections.[28] Once again the leaders of the German liberal parties—and in particular the leaders of the DVP—had failed to satisfy the deep-seated longing for unity that had begun to pulse throughout the German bourgeoisie in the wake of the deepening economic crisis, thus leaving the German bourgeoisie with no alternative but to turn elsewhere if that longing was to be satisfied.

Though essentially unfazed by the collapse of the efforts to create a united middle party, Dingeldey assumed a posture of indignant concern that enabled him to saddle the DStP, Mosich, or anyone else who might serve his purpose with responsibility for the failure of bourgeois unity.[29] Much of this, however, was part of a ploy that Dingeldey used at a meeting of the DVP central executive committee on 20 June to obtain authorization to take "any and all measures necessary for the preservation of the National Liberal heritage."[30]

Armed with what amounted to a blank check for anything that might improve the DVP's electoral prospects, Dingeldey proceeded to conclude an alliance with Hugenberg and the leaders of the DNVP for the forthcoming national elections.[31] Although Dingeldey insisted that this alliance was purely technical in nature and infringed in no way whatsoever upon his party's political integrity, this turn of events had a devastating impact upon what remained of the DVP's left wing, where an accommodation with the "socially reactionary" Hugenberg was seen as tantamount to a betrayal of the National Liberal legacy for which Stresemann and the founders of the DVP had stood. On 2 July Carl Cremer, a member of the DVP Reichstag delegation who had quietly opposed Dingeldey's turn to the right, announced his resignation from the DVP[32] in a step that was to be followed over the next several days by Hans Bechly, Frank Glatzel, and Otto Thiel from the German National Union of Commercial Employees. With the exodus of Bechly and his associates, the party's last remaining link to the German white-collar movement had been destroyed.[33]

Throughout all of this the leaders of the DStP remained hopeful that the dissolution of the DVP's left wing might bolster their own party's chances at the polls. Following the fiasco in the Deutsche Gesellschaft 1914, representatives from the DStP met privately with spokesmen from both the Business Party and the left wing of the DVP to see if anything might be salvaged from the wreck that Dingeldey had made of the movement for bourgeois unity.[34] Neither these nor the DStP's negotiations with the Center and Social Democrats about the possibility of an agreement similar to the one the DVP had concluded with the DNVP, however, proved successful, with the result that the State Party was left with no alternative but to enter the campaign for the 1932 Reichstag elections without the benefit of any sort of electoral alliance.[35] A further consequence of the failure of the movement for bourgeois unity in the summer of 1932 was the virtual disappearance of all financial support from outside economic interests. Miffed by the failure of its own efforts to stimulate the creation of a united bourgeois party, the Hansa-Bund declined to raise funds for the DStP, DVP, or any other political party in the campaign for the July elections,[36] while Carl Friedrich von Siemens, at one time a leading source of financial support for Germany's moderate bourgeois parties, held fast to his decision from the spring of 1932 not to honor any of the requests for financial assistance that he received from the existing bourgeois parties.[37] By the same token, the anti-Hugenberg elements around Krupp and Reusch were so distressed by the failure of their efforts to force a change in the DNVP party leadership that they showed little inclination to support any of the parties—and particularly the DNVP—that were competing in the July 1932 elections.[38] Although the DVP's alliance with the DNVP provided it with access to the funds that Fritz Springorum, the Ruhr's unofficial treasurer, had placed at the disposal of General Kurt von Schleicher,[39] neither it nor the DStP possessed the resources necessary for the sort of campaign that would have enabled them to withstand the assault of Germany's radical Right.

The central and recurrent theme in the DStP's campaign for the July 1932 Reichstag elections was the need to defend Germany's republican institutions against the three-headed hydra of feudal reaction, National Socialism, and constitutional overthrow. Of Germany's various bourgeois parties, none, including the Center, was more resolute in its defense of the Weimar Republic than the German State Party. Though reserving much of its scorn for the role that the Brüning and Papen governments played in undermining the social and political foundations of the Weimar Republic, the DStP wasted no time in identifying the NSDAP as the single most deadly threat to Germany's republican order and denounced it not only for having allied itself with the Communists in a campaign to subvert the authority of the state but also for its dictatorial aspirations and contempt for basic human values.[40] At the same time, the DStP tried to reassure its Jewish voters that the lack of an electoral alliance with one of the larger republican parties did not mean that their votes against Nazism would go uncounted if they chose to support the DStP.[41] This was accompanied by an equally disingenuous attempt to remind the German middle class of the benefits it had supposedly received from the fiscal and economic policies of the Brüning-Dietrich government.[42] Such claims, however, only dramatized the essentially defensive nature of the DStP's campaign in the summer of 1932 and did little to assuage the resentment that had surfaced within middle-class circles as a result of Brüning's deflationary fiscal policy.

Whereas the State Party rejected the Papen government in harsh and unequivocal terms, the DVP was more or less obliged by the terms of its agreement with the DNVP to adopt if not a positive, then at least a tolerant, attitude toward the new cabinet. Although Dingeldey and his associates had convinced themselves that the alliance with Hugenberg was necessary in order to gain access to industrial campaign funds and prevent the defection of potential DVP voters to the larger right-wing parties,[43] their agreement with the DNVP severely compromised the credibility of the DVP's commitment to the republican form of government and alienated those on the party's left wing who regarded themselves as the heirs to Stresemann's political legacy. The DVP's public support of Papen's strike against the Prussian state government on 20 July 1932[44] only dramatized the problematic nature of its commitment to the Weimar Constitution and prompted at least one more prominent party member, former Reichstag deputy Curt Hoff, to leave the DVP in dismay over its refusal to take the last remaining step and merge with the DNVP.[45] As the differences between the two parties became more and more blurred, the leaders of the DVP tried to legitimize their party's existence as a separate political entity by resuscitating the national and liberal traditions with which it had always identified itself. At the same time, Dingeldey took special pains to reassure the party faithful that the alliance with the DNVP was "purely technical" in nature and had no effect whatsoever upon the DVP's political and organizational integrity. What supposedly united the two parties was not so much a common ideological bond as a determination to prevent the return of a government that was either based or dependent upon the parties of the Weimar Coalition and to defend the existing economic order against the socialistic tendencies that had surfaced at the extremes of Germany's political spectrum.[46]

The outcome of the 31 July 1932 Reichstag elections left little doubt about the almost total collapse of the German middle. Whereas the non-Catholic middle parties had received 21.9 percent of all votes cast in the last national elections in September 1930, their share of the 1932 popular vote had dropped to a mere 4.8 percent. On an individual basis, this translated into losses of 58 percent for the Christian-Social People's Service, 71.9 and 72.4 percent for the DStP and DVP respectively, and 89.3 and 91.0 percent respectively for Germany's two largest special interest parties, the Business Party and the Christian-National Peasants and Farmers' Party. This was accompanied by massive gains on the part of the NSDAP, which polled over 13.7 million votes—or 37.4 percent of the total popular vote—and increased its strength in the Reichstag from 107 to 230 seats. Of Germany's nonsocialist parties, only the Center and Bavarian People's Party were able to withstand the Nazi juggernaut, while even the DNVP, an outspoken opponent of Nazi radicalism throughout the campaign, lost approximately one-tenth of the votes it had received in 1930 and saw its parliamentary representation reduced from forty-one to thirty-seven deputies.[47]

Although the DStP received over 370,000 votes in the July 1932 Reichstag elections, the lack of an electoral alliance with one of the larger republican parties prevented it from receiving the full complement of mandates to which it would have been entitled under a system of absolute proportional representation. Since the Weimar electoral law limited the number of deputies a party could elect from its national slate of candidates to the number of direct mandates it had received at the district level, the DStP was able to secure the election of only four deputies—Dietrich, Heuss, Lemmer, and Stolper—instead of the six it would have received had all of its votes counted. Only the DStP's relatively strong position in traditional liberal strongholds such as Hamburg and Baden-Württemberg enabled it to elect any candidates at all. The DVP, on the other hand, would have received only two seats in the Reichstag had it not been for its alliance with the DNVP. For although the DVP polled more than 436,000 votes, the only place where it could muster sufficient strength for a direct mandate was Saxony, where industrialist Rudolf Schneider was reelected to the Reichstag. The alliance with the DNVP, on the other hand, made it possible for the DVP to count all of its votes toward the election of Dingeldey and five other DVP candidates who had been suitably placed on the DNVP's national ticket. As a result, the DVP emerged from the elections with a total of seven seats in the Reichstag.

Though not entirely unexpected, the outcome of the July 1932 Reichstag elections came as a bitter shock to the leaders of the German State Party and triggered another round of debates over the party's continued existence. Resignation over the DStP's political future was particularly strong on the party's right wing, where a group of former DStP deputies headed by August Weber and Oskar Meyer decided to force the issue by threatening to resign from the party if it did not dissolve itself at the earliest possible opportunity.[48] Even Dietrich had begun to despair of keeping the party alive, and at a meeting of the DStP managing committee on 2 September he announced his resignation as the party's national chairman and expressed his own doubts about the DStP's ability to survive as an independent political entity. Still, in deference to the strong sentiment that party officials in Baden, Württemberg, and Hamburg had voiced in support of the DStP's continued existence, the committee agreed to postpone any decision affecting its future until after the south German Democrats had had an opportunity to discuss the matter at the conference they were scheduled to hold in Bietigheim in two days.[49] The tone of the Bietigheim conference was set by Reinhold Maier, the Württemberg minister of economics who underscored the strong stand that the conference was to take against the DStP's dissolution by outlining the new goals to which the party should dedicate itself.[50] The resolution that the Bietigheim conference subsequently adopted in favor of the State Party's continued existence received strong support from the leaders of the Hamburg party organization and led the DStP executive committee to override the decision the party's managing committee had reached nine days earlier in favor of the DStP's dissolution. The committee then proceeded to replace the managing committee with a special fifteen-member *Arbeitsausschuß* and entrusted it with responsibility for rebuilding the party's national organization. At the same time, it decided to fill the vacancy that had been created by Dietrich's resignation as the DStP's national chairman with a three-man directorate consisting of Dietrich, Maier, and Hamburg's Carl Petersen.[51]

The DStP's decision to ignore the growing pressure from within its own ranks for its immediate dissolution took on added significance in light of continued efforts to bring about the creation of a united middle party. Following the collapse of the movement for bourgeois unity in the campaign for the July Reichstag elections, Solf and his associates had joined forces with a group known as the Committee for the Formation of a Political Middle (Zwölfer-Ausschuß zur Bildung einer politischen Mitte) to found a new organization called the German National Association (Deutscher Nationalverein or DNV) at a convention in Berlin on 18 September.[52] Like its namesake of 1859, the German National Association of 1932 did not conceive of itself as a new political party but rather as a nonpartisan organization committed to the consolidation of all who, regardless of their present party affiliation, shared a basic belief in the values of individual freedom and constitutional government. Whereas previous attempts at bourgeois concentration had all originated with the leaders of existing political parties and were therefore doomed to failure, the founders of the National Association maintained that the movement for bourgeois unity could succeed only if it were rooted in the German masses.[53] In the meantime, the DNV hoped to serve as a new political home for those who had been left homeless by the demise of the German middle parties, a fact reflected in the predominant position that former members of the DVP's left wing held in the new organization's leadership. Although the chairmanship of the National Association rested in the hands of the DStP's Eberhard Wildermuth, no less than half of the DNV's fifteen-member executive committee, as well as its two vice-chairmen, Count Alexander zu Dohna and Otto Ziebell, had previously belonged to the DVP.[54] Efforts to broaden the DNV's political base by attracting the support of prominent conservative moderates such as Hans Schlange-Schöningen, however, foundered on the antipathy of the People's Conservatives toward the DNV's alleged "democratic ballast,"[55] while Paul Moldenhauer and other established DVP politicians declined to affiliate themselves with the DNV on account of the prominent role that former DVP leaders such as Cremer, Glatzel, and Hans von Eynern had played in its founding.[56]

Although the leaders of the National Association had no intention of trying to found a new party until an appropriate organizational substructure had been created, they still hoped to mediate between the existing bourgeois parties on behalf of an "election cartel" for the Reichstag elections that had become necessary with the dissolution of the Reichstag on 12 September.[57] But whereas the negotiations in June 1932 had at least offered some prospect of success until Dingeldey's intrigues led to the disaffection of both the DStP and the People's Conservatives, those in September seemed doomed to failure from the very outset. A preliminary meeting held on 17 September at the instigation of the VRP's Adolf Bauser produced little in the way of tangible results as the State Party refused to participate in anything more elaborate than a joint national slate with completely independent tickets at the district level.[58] At the same time, Dingeldey and the leaders of the DVP dismissed the idea of closer ties with the other middle parties in favor of continued cooperation with the DNVP. In this respect, Dingeldey and his associates were no longer content with a mere renewal of the technical *Listenverbindung* that had existed between the two parties in the previous campaign but hoped that Hugenberg could be persuaded to join the DVP, the Stahlhelm, and various business

organizations in the formation of a broad-based *Rechtsblock* embracing all of
the groups that stood behind the Reich president and the program that the
Papen government had proclaimed in his name.[59] Much to Dingeldey's chagrin, this idea met with utter indifference from Hugenberg, who steadfastly
refused to commit himself to anything more than a renewal of the DVP's
Listenverbindung with the DNVP.[60]

Just as Dingeldey's overtures to the German Right foundered on Hugenberg's lack of interest in anything more elaborate than a renewal of his party's
alliance with the DVP, so the efforts to consolidate what still remained of the
German middle parties into a united front for the forthcoming Reichstag
elections foundered on Dingeldey's preference for an accommodation with the
DNVP. On 23 September Wildermuth invited Dingeldey, Dietrich, and the
leaders of the other non-Catholic bourgeois parties to the left of the DNVP to a
meeting the following morning in hopes that the DNV might still be able to
prevent the electoral alliances that the DVP and DStP were reportedly on the
verge of concluding with the DNVP and Social Democrats respectively.[61] But
this initiative, as well as all subsequent efforts on the part of Bauser and the
leaders of the smaller middle parties, was doomed to failure when Dingeldey
failed to show the slightest sign of interest.[62] In the meantime, the leaders of
the DStP had intensified their negotiations with the Social Democrats in hopes
that an accommodation similar to the one the DVP was in the process of
concluding with the DNVP might still be possible. When these negotiations
were broken off in the first week of October, the State Party was left with no
alternative but to go it alone as it had done in the previous election.[63]

The leaders of the State Party opened their campaign with a major rally in
Mannheim on 2 October. At the heart of the rally lay the concept of "national
democracy," by which the leaders of the DStP tried to resuscitate the nationalistic impulse that had played such a crucial role in the history of the German
liberal movement. Though essentially a restatement of classical liberal tenets
in language compatible with the increasingly nationalistic mood of Germany's
middle-class electorate, the concept of national democracy entailed not only a
reaffirmation of the DStP's commitment to the republican form of government
but also a series of recommendations aimed at strengthening the authority of
Germany's representative institutions. These recommendations had nothing in
common with the more radical proposals for a reform of the Weimar Constitution that had emerged from the ranks of the Papen government. For while the
leaders of the State Party may have found it expedient to soften their criticism
of Papen's economic program, they remained adamantly opposed to right-
wing schemes that sought to disenfranchise parliament for the sake of an
authoritarian state based upon the person of the Reich president. The key to
Germany's social, economic, and political recovery lay not in dismantling
what still remained of the existing constitutional order, according to State

Party leaders, but in restoring the vital link between nationalism and democracy that had inspired its founding.[64]

If the DStP continued to defend the existing constitutional order against its detractors on the moderate as well as the radical Right, Dingeldey and the leaders of the DVP found their freedom of action severely limited by the terms of their understanding with the DNVP and began to dissociate themselves from the existing political order in favor of a campaign that was more in tune with the rhetoric of the German Right. In a major programmatic speech before the DVP central executive committee in Erfurt on 9 October, Dingeldey hailed the "liquidation of the Weimar system" as an historical fact that the DVP had anticipated some thirteen years earlier with its vote against ratification of the Weimar Constitution. As an alternative to the "alien [*volksfremdes*] system" and the "rule of unbridled parliamentary democracy" to which the framers of the Weimar Constitution had given birth, Dingeldey called for a fundamental reform of the existing governmental system that would free the state from the control of the masses and strengthen the powers of the Reich president. The deficiencies of the existing constitutional order, in turn, were directly responsible for the rise of National Socialism, whose leaders had only compounded the crisis in which the German state found itself by choosing the path of mass demagoguery over that of responsible political leadership. Seeking to capitalize upon the widespread disillusionment that many of those who had flocked to the Nazi banner in July felt about the NSDAP's recent political course, Dingeldey chastised Hitler for his refusal to accept a share of governmental responsibility and called upon the German bourgeoisie to rally behind the DVP in support of the one man whose name was synonymous with the struggle to rejuvenate the state, Reich President Paul von Hindenburg.[65]

Throughout the campaign for the November 1932 Reichstag elections both the DStP and the DVP hoped that middle-class disenchantment with Nazi radicalism would lead to a revival of their own electoral fortunes. Neither party, however, possessed the resources necessary to achieve a serious breakthrough into the ranks of the Nazi electorate. This was particularly true of the State Party, which was unable to finance its campaign even in a traditional liberal stronghold such as Württemberg without going into debt.[66] The DVP, on the other hand, continued to receive small donations from some of its longtime supporters in the Ruhr, but experienced considerable difficulty in tapping the financial resources of larger industrial concerns.[67] Though still divided over the question of Hugenberg's political future, Germany's industrial leaders favored the creation of a united German Right on the basis of the DNVP party organization and therefore had only a passing interest in supporting any of the smaller bourgeois parties that stood between it and the Center.[68] At the same time, the DVP's swing to the right following the collapse of the Brüning government had cost the party much of the support it had traditionally received

from the chemical industry.[69] Although the DVP still found itself in a decidedly better financial situation than the DStP, its own resources had been so
heavily drained by the spate of defections on its left and right wings that it was
no longer capable of mounting an effective national campaign.

The outcome of the 6 November 1932 Reichstag elections confirmed what
the leaders of the two liberal parties had been claiming throughout the campaign, namely that many of those who had voted for the NSDAP in July had
become disenchanted with the obstructionist tactics of the Nazi leadership and
were no longer prepared to condone them with their support at the polls. For
although the NSDAP was still the largest party with 33.1 percent of the
popular vote, it had lost more than 2 million votes—or 14.9 percent of what it
had received in July—and saw its representation in the Reichstag slip from 230
to 196 seats. The principal beneficiary of the Nazi defeat was the DNVP,
which polled nearly a million more votes than it had received three months
earlier and increased the size of its Reichstag delegation from thirty-seven to
fifty-two deputies. The DNVP's electoral gains were matched by those of the
DVP, which, much to Dingeldey's satisfaction, improved upon its performance in the July elections by more than 225,000 votes and gained four seats
in the Reichstag for a total of eleven. The DStP, on the other hand, was far less
fortunate, as it and the other parties popularly associated with the Weimar
system—the Social Democrats and Center—experienced a disconcerting defeat at the polls. For the State Party this was particularly devastating in that it
not only lost more than 30,000 votes—or 9 percent of its July total—but failed
to hold on to its direct mandate in Hamburg and therefore returned only two
deputies to the Reichstag. Even if Germany's middle-class voters had become
alarmed at the NSDAP's dictatorial aspirations, they were not yet prepared, as
the outcome of the elections clearly revealed, to return to the fold of the
republican parties.[70]

By the middle of 1932 the demise of the non-Catholic middle had become a
well-established fact of German political life. At the same time, the rallying
point around which the German bourgeoisie could coalesce in defense of what
it perceived as its vital interests had shifted decisively, if not irrevocably, to the
right. This state of affairs stemmed not only from the radicalizing effect of the
deepening economic crisis on Germany's middle-class electorate but also from
the inability of Germany's moderate bourgeois parties to establish any sort of
common ground upon which their followers might unite. The critical position
in the efforts to create a united middle party was held by the DVP, where the
dividing line between those who sought to consolidate the German bourgeoisie
in defense of the existing constitutional order and those who sought to create a
united German Right with an outspoken antidemocratic and antisocialist character ran right through the middle of the party. The situation within the DVP
was further complicated by the fact that the industrial interests that constituted

the nucleus of its right wing consistently blocked any rapprochement between the DVP and the other middle parties that might have led to a stabilization of Germany's beleaguered parliamentary system. Not only did this severely limit Dingeldey's freedom of action in his relations with the other middle parties, but from 1930 on Germany's industrial elite began to withhold funds from parties that refused to go along with its particular concept of bourgeois concentration. The net effect of this was only to accelerate the internal disintegration of Germany's non-Catholic middle parties and to create a situation that enabled the NSDAP to establish itself as the comprehensive bourgeois party of concentration (*Sammelpartei*) for which the German middle class had been longing.

CHAPTER   THIRTY-FOUR

An Ignominious End

IN SPITE OF THE SEVERE blow that the outcome of the November 1932 Reichstag elections had dealt to the momentum of the Nazi movement, the situation in Berlin seemed no nearer a resolution than it had been before the dissolution of the Reichstag. The position of the Papen government remained extremely weak. Not even the fact that the DVP and DNVP, the two parties most closely identified with the goals and rhetoric of the Papen government, had won almost twenty more seats in the Reichstag than they had had in the previous legislative period could compensate for Papen's failure to win the support of the two parties upon which the fate of his chancellorship ultimately rested, the NSDAP and Center. Relations between Hitler and Papen had been severely strained since the NSDAP had rejected the chancellor's offer of a role in his government earlier that summer, and a new round of negotiations in the third week of November did little to soften Nazi opposition to the Papen regime. At the same time, Papen's hopes of a reconciliation with the Center were frustrated by the lingering resentment that the party's leaders felt toward the chancellor as a result of the role he had played in the demise of his predecessor. As it became increasingly clear that neither the Center nor the NSDAP was prepared to abandon its opposition to the Papen government, the chancellor was left with no alternative but to tender his resignation so that the search for a new government capable of commanding a parliamentary majority might begin.[1]

The search for Papen's successor continued for nearly two weeks before Hindenburg and the presidential entourage eventually settled on General Kurt von Schleicher, a professional military officer who had served as Papen's minister of defense.[2] An enigmatic figure who had managed to shun the political limelight until his appointment to the Papen government, Schleicher shared little of his predecessor's enthusiasm for a radical reform of the Weimar Constitution aimed at dismantling what still remained of Germany's representative institutions. At the same time, however, Schleicher had grown weary of trying to create a stable parliamentary majority on the basis of the existing party system and sought instead to base his government upon an alliance of labor unions extending from the General German Trade-Union Federation on the right wing of the SPD to the more moderate elements that had coalesced on the NSDAP's left wing under the leadership of Gregor Strasser. The cement with which Schleicher hoped to hold this alliance of ideologically disparate working-class groups together was a program of public works (*Arbeitsbe-schaffung*) designed to alleviate the widespread unemployment that the world economic crisis had left in its wake. Although Schleicher, like Papen, felt a reform of the Weimar Constitution was ultimately necessary to restore the authority of the state, his first item of business was not constitutional reform but putting an end to unemployment.[3]

Although they may have had some reservations about Schleicher's ultimate political objectives, the leaders of the German State Party gave a sigh of relief at the demise of the Papen government and greeted the appointment of the new chancellor with cautious optimism.[4] Still, the situation in which the party found itself was nothing short of desperate. Not only were Dietrich and Maier, the party's lone representatives in the Reichstag, so embarrassed by the DStP's defeat in the November elections that they renamed themselves the South German Democrats (Süddeutsche Demokraten),[5] but their efforts to hold the party together met with strong opposition from a group within the party around the former chairman of the DStP Reichstag delegation, August Weber. On the eve of the November elections Weber and five other former Reichstag deputies—Wolfgang Jänicke, Marie-Elizabeth Lüders, Oskar Meyer, Peter Reinhold, and Baron Hartmann von Richthofen—had informed Dietrich that if a national party congress were not convened within the next four weeks for the explicit purpose of initiating the DStP's dissolution, they would leave the party.[6] When the DStP *Arbeitsausschuß* discussed the matter at its first meeting after the elections, however, neither Weber's call for the convocation of a special party congress nor his appeal for the DStP's dissolution met with much support.[7] Still, the leaders of the DStP were anxious to avert a break with the Weber faction and appointed Carl Petersen, by far the most skillful mediator of the three men who shared the DStP party chairmanship, to meet with the dissidents. Although Weber and Richthofen remained steadfast in their resolve to the leave the party, Petersen not only succeeded in persuading them not to publicize their break with the party but managed to dissuade Lüders and Meyer from following their example.[8]

Throughout all of this, Dietrich and his associates were sustained in their determination to keep the DStP alive by the hope that the appointment of the Schleicher government signaled a change in the political climate that would lead to a revival of Germany's more moderate bourgeois parties.[9] Their attitude of passive resignation contrasted sharply with the inflated sense of self-importance with which Dingeldey began to flaunt his party's recent success at the polls. As the leader of Germany's largest middle-class splinter party, Dingeldey aspired to a role in German political life that belied his party's numerical weakness. Not only did he continue to support Papen even after the chancellor's position had become hopeless, but once Papen's fate had been decided, he immediately ingratiated himself with Schleicher by encouraging him to accept the chancellorship.[10] At the same time, Dingeldey tried to increase his party's political leverage by joining the Christian-Social People's Service, the German Peasants' Party, and the German-Hanoverian Party in the formation of a technical parliamentary coalition or *Fraktionsgemeinschaft* that consisted of a total of twenty Reichstag deputies.[11] Yet while this might have helped enhance the DVP's parliamentary profile, it also alienated the DNVP and jeopardized renewal of the electoral alliance that had served the DVP so well in the last two Reichstag elections.[12]

Nowhere was Dingeldey's pretentiousness more apparent than in his attitude toward the efforts to reconstitute the German middle as an independent political force. After the November elections the leaders of the German National Association had intensified their efforts on behalf of a united middle party on the grounds that none of the splinter parties to the left of Hugenberg's DNVP was capable of recapturing the support of the middle-class elements that had become disillusioned with National Socialism.[13] Although Wildermuth hoped to pursue his goal with a minimum of friction with the existing middle parties and repeatedly disclaimed any intention of wanting to found a new splinter party alongside those that already existed,[14] his efforts were continually frustrated by the deep-seated suspicion that his agitation for the creation of a united bourgeois party had aroused among the leaders of the surviving middle parties. In early November Wildermuth had sought to win the DStP's Carl Petersen over to the cause of a united middle party, but he was unable to dispel the skepticism the leaders of the State Party felt about the ultimate success of his efforts to consolidate the German middle on the basis of a democratic platform.[15] By the middle of the month, Wildermuth had become so discouraged by the DStP's lack of interest in his project that he, like Weber a month later, resigned from the party in exasperation.[16] At the same time, the general antipathy of Dingeldey and his associates toward the National Association had been greatly reinforced not only by their party's recent success at the polls but also by the sharp attack that the DNV's Frank Glatzel had directed against his former party in the final days of the campaign.[17] Consequently, it was not until after the political situation had temporarily stabilized with the formation of the Schleicher government that Wildermuth was able to arrange a meeting with the DVP party chairman. Even then, Dingeldey did not share Wildermuth's sense of urgency in the matter of bourgeois concentration and responded to the suggestion that he enter into exploratory talks with spokesmen from the People's Conservatives, WP, and DStP with the observation that these groups hardly had anything left to offer in the way of popular or electoral support.[18]

Although Wildermuth's conversation with Dingeldey ended with mutual assurances that both would do their best to avoid friction between their organizations, the DVP chairman had no intention of cooperating with the National Association and refused to allow DVP functionaries who might have been interested in the creation of a united middle party to hold office in the DNV's national organization.[19] Dingeldey's refusal to offer more than lip service in support of Wildermuth's campaign for a united middle party stemmed ultimately from his determination to establish the DVP as the dominant force on Germany's moderate Right, a goal that would only have been jeopardized by the existence of such a party. For his part, Wildermuth hoped to force the DVP into reassessing its attitude toward the creation of a united middle party by cultivating closer ties with the leaders of Germany's moderate Right. On 23 December Wildermuth had a long conversation with Hans Schlange-Schöningen, a prominent conservative moderate who urged the National Association to begin preparations for new national elections by consolidating all nonreactionary, non-Catholic, and nonsocialist elements on a single national ticket.[20] By the same token, Wildermuth could only have been encouraged by the apparent willingness of G. R. Treviranus, recently elected to the chairmanship of the People's Conservative Association in a move that greatly strengthened that organization's more political-minded elements, to assist the National Association in its efforts to secure a foothold on the German Right.[21]

Although Wildermuth and his associates were encouraged by the success of their overtures to Schlange-Schöningen, Treviranus, and the anti-Hugenberg forces on Germany's moderate Right, relations between the National Association and the two liberal parties remained highly problematic. Not only had the National Association's inactivity in the campaign for the November Reichstag elections done much to reinforce the doubts that the leaders of the State Party felt about the sincerity of the DNV's commitment to a consolidation of the German middle,[22] but Dingeldey and his associates were deeply resentful of the lack of self-restraint that the DNV had demonstrated in soliciting support for the concept of a united middle party among the DVP rank and file.[23] It was only with the imminent demise of the Schleicher government in the second half of January 1933 that the prospects for some sort of an accommodation between the parties of the middle and moderate Right began to improve. Hugenberg's irritation over the technical *Fraktionsgemeinschaft* that Dingeldey had concluded with the Christian-Social People's Service and German-Hanoverian Party made it increasingly unlikely that the DNVP would renew its electoral alliance with the DVP in the event of new national elections. While the leaders of the DVP still hoped that it might be possible to renew the alliance that had served them so well in the last two national elections,[24] they now began to explore the possibilities of an accommodation with the DStP and other middle parties as a safeguard against their party's almost certain annihilation should it be forced to enter a new national campaign alone.[25] Wilder-

muth, in the meantime, hoped to capitalize upon the DVP's momentary isolation and took steps to repair the damage that the DNV's agitation for a united
bourgois party had done to relations between their two organizations.[26]

The modest gains that the National Association had made in its efforts to
bring the parties of the middle and moderate Right closer together were soon
overwhelmed by the pace of events in Berlin. Schleicher's hopes of basing his
government on a coalition of ideologically disparate working-class elements
stretching from the free trade unions to the left wing of the NSDAP had been
doomed from the outset. Schleicher was unable to assuage the deep-seated
misgivings that the leaders of the ADGB had about his long-range social and
political objectives, and the disclosure of his negotiations with Strasser produced such a furor within the NSDAP that the latter resigned all of his posts in
the party organization. At the same time, Schleicher's willingness to share
governmental responsibility with leaders from organized labor, as well as
the interventionist overtones of his social and economic program, alarmed
Germany's industrial leadership and severely damaged whatever chances he
might have had of winning the support of influential business interests. As
Schleicher's position became increasingly desperate after the beginning of the
new year, the leaders of the national opposition began to lay the foundations
for a new governmental coalition organized along the lines of the erstwhile
Harzburg Front. Schleicher's fate was sealed when first the National Rural
League and then the DNVP broke with the government in the third week of
January. Although he still enjoyed the support of the Center and other middle
parties, Schleicher was unceremoniously dumped on 28 January, when the
Reich president, under heavy pressure from the East Elbian Junkers as well as
from members of his own entourage, refused to go along with the chancellor's
request for authorization to dissolve the Reichstag.[27] The final stage in the
liquidation of Germany's parliamentary system had begun.

Two days later the formation of a new government with Hitler as its chancellor and Papen as its vice-chancellor was officially announced. The Hitler-
Papen government rested upon a coalition between the NSDAP and representatives of Germany's conservative elite in which the latter had been led to
believe that they had gained the upper hand over the Nazi dynamo and could
use it in the stabilization of their own social, economic, and political power.[28]
This turn of events—and particularly the dissolution of the Reichstag and the
call for new elections issued by the government on its first day in office—
caught the leaders of the German liberal movement by surprise. Even Dingeldey, who had long supported efforts to co-opt the NSDAP into accepting a
share of governmental responsibility, was distressed by the way in which the
new government had come into existence and warned against a new wave of
economic experimentation that might jeopardize Germany's long-term economic recovery. In confidential remarks before the DVP national committee

on 5 February, Dingeldey tried to reassure his associates that a genuine concentration of Germany's national forces could never succeed without the participation of the DVP and voiced concern over the government's lack of a clear idea of what it wanted to do with the economy.[29] While Dingeldey's enthusiasm for the new government was clearly muted by his disappointment that the DVP had not been asked to join it, the leaders of the German State Party, on the other hand, remained resolute in their defense of the republican system and refused to recognize the new government as a legitimate claimant to state power. At a major rally on the eve of Hitler's installation as chancellor, the leaders of the DStP called for a "government of democratic authorities" and denounced the intrigues that were taking place behind the backs of the German people as a breach of established parliamentary prerogatives.[30] When the Hitler-Papen government was officially presented on the following day, their deepest fears were confirmed.

Although the two liberal parties reacted to the formation of the Hitler-Papen government in characteristically different fashions, both were alarmed by the call for new elections in the first week of March. Not only did this come at a time when neither liberal party was prepared for the rigors of a new national campaign, but the differences that had surfaced in the two parties' attitudes toward the new government precluded the possibility of close cooperation in the forthcoming campaign. Two days after the installation of the new government, Wildermuth, working in close cooperation with the leaders of the DStP, invited representatives from the eight splinter parties that stood between the Center and DNVP to a meeting in the Hotel Continental on the morning of 5 February so that they might explore the possibilities of a "common effort in the forthcoming Reichstag elections."[31] This effort, however, was doomed to failure from the start. For whereas Wildermuth and his associates maintained that the forthcoming campaign could be waged "only as a full-scale assault against the National Socialists,"[32] Dingeldey sought to affiliate his party with the progovernment forces that had begun to coalesce in the Combat Front Black-White-Red (Kampffront Schwarz-Weiß-Rot) under the leadership of Papen, Hugenberg, and the newly appointed minister of labor, Franz Seldte from the Stahlhelm.[33] Consequently, when Wildermuth met with spokesmen from the various middle-class splinter parties on the morning of 5 February, the DVP immediately torpedoed efforts to organize an "election cartel" between the parties of the middle and moderate Right by refusing to participate in any project in which the DStP was also involved.[34] Not even in the death throes of the Weimar Republic were the two liberal parties able to agree upon a common course of action.

Following the collapse of Wildermuth's efforts to unite what remained of the so-called bourgeois middle, the leaders of the State Party turned first to the Center and then to the Bavarian People's Party in search of an alliance that would salvage as many antigovernment votes as possible. When the two Catholic parties balked at such an arrangement for fear that it would drive their more conservative supporters into the arms of the government parties, the DStP proceeded over the strenuous objections of the party's local leaders in Baden, Württemberg, and Hamburg to conclude an alliance with the Social Democrats.[35] According to the terms of this alliance, any votes that the SPD and DStP did not use in the election of candidates at the district level would be transferred to a joint national ticket from which the State Party would receive one Reichstag mandate for every 60,000 votes it had contributed. In this way, the DStP was assured of the same number of deputies it would have received under a system of absolute proportional representation.[36] In the meantime, Dingeldey had sought to enlist Papen's support in his efforts to have the DVP included in the Combat Front Black-White-Red that the vice-chancellor was in the process of forming with Hugenberg and Seldte.[37] But Papen, who had promised to intercede with Hugenberg on Dingeldey's behalf, was unable to soften the hard stand the DNVP national chairman had taken against a renewal of his party's alliance with the DVP. Abandoned by the DNVP, Dingldey sought to salvage what still remained of his party's rapidly diminishing electoral prospects by joining the Christian-Social People's Service and the German Peasants' Party in the creation of the Christian-National Election Bloc (Christlich-nationaler Wahlblock), an alliance that Dingeldey alternately characterized as the "left wing of the national front" and "one of the three great pillars of the national revolution."[38]

Throughout the campaign, the DVP tried desperately to legitimize itself as a member of the national front. Speaking before the party faithful in Darmstadt on 19 February, Dingeldey criticized the leaders of the new government for defining the concept of national concentration too narrowly and warned that their goal of a truly comprehensive national government was unattainable without the participation of those liberal forces that had traditionally formed the backbone of the German national movement.[39] The need to strengthen these elements so that they might assume their rightful place alongside the DNVP and NSDAP in a truly comprehensive government of national concentration was all the more apparent in light of the confusion that surrounded the government's economic program. In this respect, the leaders of the DVP not only expressed concern over the inflationary impact of the government's public works program but warned against giving agricultural economic interests preferential treatment in the formulation of German trade policy.[40] While these remarks were designed to arouse middle-class apprehension over the thrust and fairness of government economic policy, the DVP also sought to solidify its own position with the urban middle classes by committing itself as unequivocally as possible to a series of specific recommendations for the social and economic rehabilitation of the artisanry, housing industry, and small business sector.[41] The DVP staked its last hopes of political survival on the uncertain loyalty of the German middle class.

As the campaign progressed, the differences that separated the DVP and the government on questions of economic and trade policy became more and more pronounced.[42] Still, the DVP's willingness to identify itself with the government's appeal for the concentration of all national forces stood in sharp contrast to the vehemence with which the leaders of the State Party tried to portray the new government as the tool of social and political reaction. Sustained by the hope that the divisions within the government would somehow give Germany's democratic forces one last chance,[43] the leaders of the DStP refused to surrender "so much as a single inch of the republican line" and called upon the "freedom-loving bourgeoisie in town and country" to help defend the existing constitutional order against the "unholy alliance" of Hitler, Hugenberg, and Papen.[44] Party leaders were particularly critical of the government's efforts to polarize the German people into two mutually antagonistic camps, one national and anti-Marxist and the other Marxist and antinational. What the DStP offered as an antidote to the forces that were in the process of tearing the nation apart was the "will to national democracy" that had saved the nation from dissolution in 1918 and would do so again in the current political crisis. The answer to Germany's political woes lay not in the polarization of the nation into two irreconcilable camps but in its consolidation across class lines in defense of the republican institutions that had served it so well for the past fourteen years.[45]

Neither the DStP's defense of Weimar's political accomplishments nor the DVP's efforts to ingratiate itself with the leaders of the new government offered adequate protection against the ruthlessness with which Hitler and his associates were able to exploit the dramatic change that had taken place in the popular psyche with the installation of the new regime. If the last months of 1932 had witnessed the erosion of popular support for the Nazi movement, the trend had clearly been reversed by the excitement that accompanied the appointment of the Hitler-Papen cabinet. Moreover, Papen's own hopes of holding the Nazi steamroller in check by calling forth a new "national movement with a Christian-conservative character" had been shattered by Hugenberg's refusal to accept the DVP and other bourgeois splinter parties into the Combat Front Black-White-Red except on conditions that would have been tantamount to the end of their independent political existence.[46] In their efforts to secure an absolute majority for the forces that stood behind the government, Hugenberg and the leaders of the DNVP seemed more intent upon crushing the parties of the middle and moderate Right than upon preventing a Nazi victory at the polls. Not only did Hugenberg soften the anti-Nazi line he had taken in the last national elections, but he sought to drive a wedge between the DVP party leadership and its rank-and-file membership by appealing to the nationalistic instincts of the latter. If the government was to achieve its goal of an absolute majority, this was not to be accomplished by broadening the base of the existing governmental coalition but through the annihilation of those parties that stood to the left of the DNVP.[47]

In addition to whatever psychological advantage the government forces enjoyed going into the campaign, they also held a decisive advantage in terms of their material resources. Though not directly involved in the series of events that had led up to the installation of the Hitler-Papen government, the leaders of the German industrial establishment had been alarmed by the policies of the Schleicher government and were anxious to regain some measure of influence over the course of events in Berlin. On 20 February approximately twenty-five representatives of Germany's largest and most powerful industrial firms met in the Berlin residence of the NSDAP's Hermann Göring in response to an invitation from the future Nazi warlord. After a lengthy introductory statement in which Hitler scarcely concealed his dictatorial aspirations,[48] first Göring and then Hjalmar Schacht appealed to the assembled throng for assistance in providing the government with the funds it needed to score a decisive victory at the polls. Reassured by Hitler's profession of faith in the free enterprise system, Germany's industrial leaders proceeded to establish a war chest of 3 million marks that was to be administered by Schacht and divided between the NSDAP and the Combat Front according to a three-to-one ratio.[49] Not only did this arrangement place the more moderate government forces around Hugenberg and Papen at a distinct disadvantage vis-à-vis the NSDAP in the allocation of industrial campaign funds, but both the DVP and its allies in the Christian-National Bloc found themselves denied access to the funds that industry had placed at Schacht's disposal. The DVP subsequently received 10,000 marks from the Siemens Electrical Works, as well as several smaller donations from its supporters in the Ruhr,[50] but this generosity did not extend to the German State Party, which even in the eyes of industrial moderates like Siemens had lost all vestige of political credibility.[51] In the final analysis, neither of the German liberal parties possessed the material resources necessary to withstand the effects of the government's propaganda campaign.

The immediate and most obvious consequence of the government campaign effort was a dramatic increase in the number of voters who took part in the election. All told, nearly 4 million more voters went to the polls in the March 1933 Reichstag elections than the previous November. Most of these, it can be safely assumed, voted for the NSDAP, which managed to increase its popular vote by nearly 6 million and its representation in the Reichstag from 196 to 288 seats. Although the Combat Front Black-White-Red failed to improve upon the DNVP's performance in the last national elections and entered the Reichstag with the same number of seats the DNVP had had during the previous legislative session, government forces still received 51.9 percent of the popular vote and now controlled 340 of the 647 seats in the Reichstag. At the same time, the Christian-National Election Bloc that the DVP had concluded with the Christian-Social People's Service and German Peasant's Party failed to shield its members from severe losses of their own. In spite of efforts to attach itself to the forces behind the government, the DVP lost more than a third of the 660,000 votes it had received in the November elections and saw its strength in the Reichstag reduced from eleven to two mandates. The Christian-Social People's Service, on the other hand, managed to retain four of the five seats it had won in the last national elections, while the German Peasants' Party garnered enough votes in Bavaria to secure two mandates of its own. Not only had Dingeldey's efforts to establish the Christian-National Election Bloc as one of the three great pillars of the national revolution ended in failure, but the frustration that he and the leaders of the DVP felt over the outcome of the elections was compounded by the fact that the State Party had succeeded in increasing its parliamentary representation from two to five seats in spite of a slight decline in its popular vote. Although the DStP received nearly 100,000 fewer votes than the DVP, its alliance with the Social Democrats had enabled it to overtake the DVP as the bourgeois splinter party with the largest delegation in the Reichstag. This, however, was a point of little consolation to the leaders of the DStP.[52]

The outcome of the 1933 Reichstag elections had a demoralizing effect upon the leaders of the two liberal parties and left their will to resist the establishment of the Nazi dictatorship severely weakened. The paralysis of will that gripped the German liberal movement in the immediate aftermath of the March elections, however, stemmed not so much from the shock of its defeat at the polls as from the skill with which Hitler and his associates were able to manipulate the national sentiment of those who were still nominally in charge of the two liberal parties. This, along with the ever-present threat of physical violence, accounted for the extreme passivity with which Germany's liberal leadership greeted Hitler's efforts to liquidate the last vestiges of the old republican order. The final test of liberal principle was the vote on the Enabling Act that Hitler presented to the Reichstag when it reconvened on 22 March. This bill, which the leaders of the Nazi movement had drafted without consulting their coalition partners, essentially asked the Reichstag to suspend the Weimar Constitution for the next four years so that the government might have a free hand in undertaking whatever it deemed necessary for Germany's political and economic recovery. Passage of this bill, particularly in the form in which it reached the floor of the Reichstag, would have been tantamount to the Reichstag's capitulation to the forces of the radical Right and to the abdication of its historic role in shaping Germany's political future.[53]

Although the Enabling Act required a two-thirds majority in the Reichstag before it could take effect, neither of the two liberal parties was large enough to have any appreciable effect upon the outcome of the vote. Whatever significance this vote held for the two liberal parties, therefore, was more symbolic than substantive. Having already cast its lot with the "forces of national concentration" that had come together to form the Hitler-Papen government, the DVP remained oblivious to the ultimate implications of the government bill and blithely supported it in the belief that the government should be given every opportunity to demonstrate what it could do about solving the myriad problems that confronted the German people. Throughout all of this, Dingeldey, who had entered a Swiss sanitorium in the middle of March and was therefore not in direct contact with developments in Berlin, labored under the delusion that the current government coalition was incapable of solving these problems and that it was only a matter of time until it would give way to political moderates like himself and the leaders of the Center Party.[54] Whether the result of his political isolation or of his congenital naivete about the true nature of the Nazi phenomenon, Dingeldey's optimism was not shared by the leaders of the DStP, who realized that passage of the Enabling Act meant the definitive collapse of their political hopes. While the government's appeals for national unity made it difficult for the leaders of the State Party to vote against the bill, they hoped to modify its more odious features through a formal amendment in the Reichstag. In this respect, Dietrich was fully apprised of Brüning's efforts to persuade Hugenberg to go along with an amendment that would severely limit the scope of the proposed bill.[55] When these efforts, however, collapsed as the result of a threatened revolt within the DNVP against Hugenberg's leadership of the party, the five DStP Reichstag deputies—Dietrich, Heuss, Lemmer, Maier, and Heinrich Landahl—were left with the choice of either supporting the bill or joining the Social Democrats in opposing it. When the DStP delegation met on the morning of 23 March to formulate its course of action, both Dietrich and Heuss advocated opposing the bill, but they were outvoted by their three colleagues. In the interests of party unity Dietrich and Heuss agreed to go along with the delegation majority in voting for the Enabling Act in the decisive vote later that afternoon.[56]

Whereas the DVP's decision to support the Enabling Act was motivated by little more than the desire to curry favor with the government, the leaders of the DStP had convinced themselves that Hitler and his associates were determined to do whatever they wanted to do regardless of what happened to the bill in the Reichstag. By helping secure passage of the Enabling Act, the leaders of the State Party hoped that if the government could be prevented from having to violate the Weimar Constitution, it might be possible to contain the "national revolution" within constitutional bounds.[57] Though feeble at best, this hope stemmed not so much from a misreading of Nazi intentions—the leaders of the DStP, for example, took special pains to criticize the government for its failure to incorporate provisions guaranteeing civil liberties, the integrity of the judi-

ciary and civil service, and the freedom of art and scholarship into the text of
the Enabling Act[58]—as from the sense of utter futility that gripped them when
they stood face to face with the destruction of their life's work. By the same
token, the leaders of the State Party were immobilized by the tremendous
psychological pressure to which they, as representatives of a political tradition
that had always placed primary emphasis upon the unity and welfare of the
nation as a whole, had been subjected by the government's constant appeals
for national solidarity. No bill, as Dietrich testified before the Württemberg
Landtag after the end of World War II, had ever provoked such a demonstration of support from the party's rank-and-file membership as had the Enabling
Act in the spring of 1933.[59] Given the ever-present threat of physical violence
and the DStP's reluctance to be the only bourgeois party to vote against the
bill, the party's capitulation does not seem all that surprising.

The passage of the Enabling Act removed the last legal obstacle to the
establishment of the Nazi dictatorship and set the scene for the final chapter in
the destruction of the German liberal parties. The purge of the civil bureaucracy that the new regime initiated in April 1933 forced those government
officials who still belonged to the two liberal parties to choose between the loss
of their jobs and the renunciation of their party membership. The DStP's
alliance with the Social Democrats at the time of the last Reichstag elections
left its members particularly vulnerable to this sort of pressure and provided
the government with the pretext it needed to intensify its agitation against the
party. Still, when the DStP executive committee met on 14 May to discuss the
party's future, spokesmen for only four of the twenty-nine district organizations represented at the meeting supported the party's unconditional dissolution.[60] In an attempt to forestall the inevitable, the leaders of the State Party
tried to ingratiate themselves with the ruling authorities by expressing their
solidarity not only with the declaration on foreign policy Hitler delivered to the
Reichstag on 16–17 May[61] but also with the *Gleichschaltung* of the German
labor movement and the speed with which the government was able to dismantle the last remnants of Germany's Bismarckian federal structure.[62] None of
this, however, proved of much avail. The DStP's last hopes of a future in the
new Nazi state were irretrievably shattered when the ban that the government
had placed on all Social Democratic political activity was extended to the State
Party. Anticipating their fate at the hands of a hostile government, the leaders
of the DStP took matters into their own hands and announced their party's
official dissolution in a terse, two-sentence statement on 28 June 1933.[63]

The dissolution of the German State Party preceded that of the German
People's Party by only a few days. In the case of the DVP, however, the fate of
the party was decided more by internal disaffection than by external pressure.
Immediately after the passage of the Enabling Act, Otto Hugo, along with
Dingeldey one of the DVP's two deputies in the Reichstag and a leading

spokesman for the business interests on the party's right wing, argued that the time for the DVP's orderly demise had come so that he and his associates in the business community could join the NSDAP in hopes of strengthening the more moderate procapitalist forces in the party.[64] Hugo's suggestion, however, encountered immediate opposition from Dingeldey, who had become increasingly disenchanted with the Hitler government during his convalescence in Switzerland and was anxious to prevent what still remained of the DVP from becoming submerged in the rising tide of German Fascism. When the DVP national committee came to Dingeldey's defense with a resolution that reaffirmed the party's continued political existence,[65] Hugo was so incensed that he not only resigned his offices in the DVP party organization but met with Hitler on 5 April to negotiate an agreement whereby members of the DVP could join the NSDAP.[66] Acting on Hugo's initiative, the DVP district organizations in the Rhineland and Westphalia announced their dissolution three days later in a series of resolutions that called upon their supporters to join the NSDAP.[67] The decisive showdown came at a meeting of the DVP central executive committee on 23 April, at which time Dingeldey and his supporters prevailed over those who sought to force the party's dissolution, albeit by a margin so narrow that it could hardly have been interpreted as a vote of confidence in the DVP's political future.[68] Although the party had ceased to exist in much of the country as a result of Hugo's defection, it was not until after Hugenberg's resignation from the Hitler cabinet and the DNVP's official dissolution on 27 June that Dingeldey conceded the hopelessness of his party's position and announced its dissolution in a two-paragraph statement on 4 July.[69]

Hardly noteworthy in and of itself, the disappearance of the German liberal parties in the summer of 1933 was but one more facet of the massive shift to the right that had taken place in German political life during the last years of the Weimar Republic. The fate of Weimar democracy—and particularly in the critical years from 1930 to 1933—was determined by the fact that the crystallization point around which the German middle strata could unite had been pushed inexorably to the right until finally the more moderate efforts at bourgeois concentration were outflanked and overwhelmed by the one party that embodied the most radical approach to the problem of bourgeois unity, the NSDAP. The force with which this shift took place stemmed from a variety of factors, not the least of which was the radicalizing effect of the deepening economic crisis upon the social strata that had traditionally supported the more moderate bourgeois parties. At the same time, the failure of Germany's parliamentary leaders to develop a coherent and effective strategy for combating the depression undermined the last vestiges of public confidence in Germany's republican institutions and transformed the legitimacy crisis that had plagued the Weimar party system since the middle of the previous decade into a crisis of the German state. As parliamentary democracy gave way to government by decree, the two liberal parties found themselves excluded from any sort of meaningful role in the legislative process until they, like the other remnants of the hated Weimar system, could be swept from the historical stage with impunity.

Final Reflections

THE TWO LIBERAL PARTIES had ceased to be a factor in German political life long before their formal dissolution in the summer of 1933. By no means, however, is the failure of the German liberal movement in the Weimar Republic to be dismissed simply as a consequence of German liberalism's historic failures in the nineteenth century or as the product of some supposed deformity in Germany's social and political development. Such an argument would not only rob the history of Weimar liberalism of much of its urgency and inherent drama, but it would also ignore the specific and often historically contingent factors that did so much to destroy the vitality of the German liberal parties beween 1918 and 1933. While this is not to deny the role that long-range historical forces played in determining the fate of the Weimar liberal parties, it is to insist upon closer attention to the ways in which these forces became manifest in order to strike a better balance between the notions of contingency and continuity in our understanding of what happened to the German liberal parties and the political order whose fate they ultimately shared.

The failure of Weimar liberalism stemmed from a variety of factors so closely intertwined that it becomes difficult to disentangle one from another. The first of these was the perpetuation of the historic schism within the German liberal movement. At no point since the National Liberal secession from the German Progressive Party in 1866–67 had conditions for the creation of a united liberal party been more favorable than they were in the fall and winter of 1918. The failure to create such a party, however, had more to do with the personal animosity that Stresemann and the self-styled founders of the DDP felt toward each other than with historical necessity or inevitability. The emergence of the DVP alongside the DDP severely frustrated the legitimation of Germany's new republican order and set the scene for a particularly bitter fratricidal conflict during the first years of the Weimar Republic in which Stresemann and his associates tried to transform nationalist indignation over the terms of the Versailles Peace Treaty and middle-class anxiety over the legacy of the November Revolution into a general indictment of the so-called Weimar system. Although the ferocity of this split abated with Stresemann's move to the center in the second half of the 1920s, the existence of two liberal parties undercut the effectiveness with which the leaders of the German liberal movement were able to represent the material interests of their predominantly middle-class constituencies and ultimately prevented the formation of a united liberal front against the threat that the resurgence of the radical Right posed to the survival of the Weimar Republic. Never were the two liberal parties further apart than in their attitudes and policies toward National Socialism.

A second factor that played a crucial role in determining the fate of Weimar liberalism was the so-called national question. Nationalism was deeply ingrained in the German liberal tradition, and it is by no means an historical accident that both the DDP and DVP relied upon nationalism as a means of integrating the divergent and potentially antagonistic social and economic forces that constituted their material base into some sort of coherent political force. But nationalism in the Weimar Republic was a two-edged sword whose ultimate effect was to harm rather than strengthen the integrative potential of the two liberal parties. In the summer of 1919, for example, the conflict over acceptance or rejection of the Versailles Peace Treaty produced an open split within the Democratic Party between those who recognized that Germany had no alternative but to accept the Allied peace terms and those who sought to project the DDP into the leadership of the movement of national opposition to the treaty's ratification and implementation. This scenario repeated itself in the spring of 1921 when the Democratic delegation to the Reichstag split in the vote to accept or reject the reparations demands contained in the London Ultimatum. And then in the fall of 1921 the Democrats sowed further confusion in the ranks of their followers by leaving the government in protest against the Allied partition of Upper Silesia only to reenter virtually the same government three months later.

The cumulative effect of all this was to discredit the Democratic Party in the eyes of those who were indignant over Germany's treatment at the hands of the Allies and to compromise the credibility of its appeals to German national sentiment. At the same time, the conflict over the conduct of German foreign policy also retarded the process by which the German People's Party eventually came to accept the Weimar Republic. In the spring of 1921 Stresemann had been fully prepared to accept the chancellorship and might very well have done so had the Allies been willing to accept some modifications in the terms of the London Ultimatum. By the same token, the Allied partition of Upper Silesia in October 1921 brought efforts to form a government of the Great Coalition consisting of the Majority Socialists, the Center, and the two liberal parties to an immediate halt. In both cases, these developments were accompanied by acute internal crises within the DVP that did much to undermine Stresemann's effectiveness as the party's national leader. Nor did this problem abate with Stresemann's appointment to the chancellorship in the summer of 1923. Not only did Stresemann's decision to terminate passive resistance provoke a storm of protest on the DVP's right wing, but his pursuit of a diplomatic understanding with the very powers that had defeated Germany in

World War I left him and his party exposed to charges of having betrayed the national cause. Even though the liberal parties proceeded to close ranks behind the basic principles of Stresemann's foreign policy in the second half of the 1920s, the controversy between 1919 and 1924 over the extent to which Germany should attempt to fulfill the terms of the Versailles Treaty extended deep into the ranks of the liberal parties and severely compromised their credibility among the more nationalistic elements of Germany's liberal electorate.

A third factor that figured prominently, if not decisively, in the decline of the German liberal movement was the general course of social and economic development during the Weimar Republic. Both the DDP and DVP conceived of themselves as *Gesamtinteressenparteien*, that is, as sociologically hetero-geneous people's parties that sought to represent the welfare of the nation as a whole rather than the interests of any specific social group. The net effect of the war, the runaway inflation of the early 1920s, the government's stabiliza-tion program in 1923–24, and the outbreak of the world economic crisis at the end of the decade, however, was to heighten the degree of interest articulation and antagonism among those social groups that constituted the backbone of Germany's liberal electorate to such a degree that by the end of the 1920s all of Germany's nonsocialist parties, including the DDP and DVP, were threatened with dissolution into their constituent social and economic interests. More-over, the fact that the two liberal parties had been virtually excluded from any sort of meaningful role in the stabilization of the mark severely compromised their legitimacy in the eyes of the social groups that had been asked to bear the brunt of the government's stabilization program and severely damaged their chances of recovery during Germany's brief return to normalcy in the second half of the 1920s.

By the second half of the 1920s the decline of the Weimar liberal parties had become irreversible. This was particularly true in the case of the DDP, where the hopes with which its leaders had greeted the founding of the Weimar Republic had been all but shattered by the wave of national indignation that swept Germany following publication of the Allied peace terms in the late spring of 1919. This, along with the party's constant equivocation on ques-tions of social and economic policy, dealt the DDP a blow from which it never recovered and helped trigger the mass defection of the party's middle-class electorate that materialized first in the June 1920 Reichstag elections and then again in the February 1921 elections to the Prussian Landtag. The loss of middle-class support was then intensified by the bitter conflict that accompa-nied imposition of the London Ultimatum in May 1921 and the Allied partition of Upper Silesia five months later. Still, there is evidence to suggest that the party might have succeeded in reversing its decline had it not been for the resumption of the inflationary spiral in the second half of 1921 and the onset of the hyperinflation in the summer of 1922. The final blow came with the enactment of the government's stabilization program in the winter of 1923–24. Not only was the mark stabilized in a highly authoritarian manner that violated the very principles of parliamentary democracy to which the DDP had committed itself, but the party's inability to protect its predominantly middle-class supporters against the effects of the government's stabilization program only dramatized its unreliability as a defender of middle-class economic interests. In spite of the modest gains it recorded in the December 1924 Reichstag elections, one can safely conclude that with the hyperinflation of 1922–23 and the stabilization of the mark in the winter of 1923–24 the decline of the German Democratic Party had become irreversible.

Developments in the German People's Party followed a similar, though not necessarily identical, pattern. Slow to reconcile themselves to the establishment of the new republican order, the leaders of the DVP moved quickly to translate middle-class disenchantment with the DDP's performance as a member of the governmental coalition into a general indictment of the Weimar Republic. Several factors, however, prevented the DVP from integrating middle-class voters who had become disillusioned with the DDP into its own organizational structure. The first of these was the estrangement that the DVP's increasingly close identification with heavy industry produced in its relations with the various social groups from which the party recruited the bulk of its popular and electoral support. This was then intensified by the disintegrative effect that the runaway inflation of the early 1920s had upon the DVP's middle-class electorate and national organization. Underlying both of these developments, however, was a third factor, namely the heavy price Stresemann and his associates had to pay for their willingness to share the burden of governmental responsibility. This problem, which first manifested itself in the wake of the DVP's decision to enter the Fehrenbach government in the summer of 1920, reached an explosive climax in the hundred days of Stresemann's chancellorship when the industrial interests on the DVP's right wing tried to organize what they hoped would develop into a general secession from the party. As this episode clearly revealed, government responsibility entailed responsibility for unpopular decisions in the areas of both domestic and foreign policy that not only the leaders of the DVP's right wing but a significant segment of the party's middle-class electorate proved unwilling to bear. Even though the DVP emerged from the May and December 1924 Reichstag elections in substantially better shape than the rival DDP, the party remained deeply divided along social, economic, and ideological lines. Conflicts over tariffs, revaluation, tax reform, civil servant salaries, social policy, and—most dramatically—unemployment insurance were conflicts that pitted one part of the party against another. In the final analysis, only Stresemann's national stature and extraordinary talents as a political leader kept the DVP from falling apart much earlier than it actually did. When death removed Stresemann from the political scene in the fall of 1929, it was only a matter of time until the leaders of the DVP's right wing gained control of the party, thereby sounding its death knell as a viable force in Germany's political life.

The decline of the German liberal parties in the second half of the 1920s was only one manifestation of the deepening legitimacy crisis that plagued the Weimar party system in the wake of the currency stabilization of 1923–24. Other facets of this crisis included the increasing prominence of conservative economic interest organizations such as the National Federation of German Industry and the National Rural League, recurrent parliamentary stalemates that inhibited the formation of governments resting upon a stable majority in the Reichstag, intermittent appeals for a reform and realignment of the Weimar party system, and, last but not least, the emergence of middle-class splinter parties that no longer sought to represent the welfare of the nation as a whole but addressed themselves to the interests of specific social groups. By the end of the 1920s the penetration of organized economic interests into the political sphere and the fragmentation of the Weimar party system along lines of economic self-interest had reached such a point that the leaders of the German liberal movement had begun to despair about the fate of the system of government in whose establishment they had played such a prominent role. Liberal appeals between 1924 and 1930 for a reform and reorganization of the German party system, however, only underscored the deepening legitimacy crisis in which the Weimar party system had found itself since the stabilization of the mark in 1923–24 and aroused expectations on the part of Germany's middle-class electorate that neither the Democrats nor the leaders of the DVP were capable of fulfilling. The net effect of these appeals was to further disrupt already weakened patterns of voter identification within Germany's liberal electorate and to create a situation that Hitler and the leaders of the Nazi movement were able to exploit with consummate skill.

The failure of the movement for liberal unity in the summer of 1930 greatly accelerated the internal disintegration of the two liberal parties and left their supporters all but defenseless against the appeal of National Socialism. At the same time, the antisocial character of Brüning's fiscal and economic program did much to radicalize the very social strata upon which the liberal parties depended for the bulk of their popular support, while the chancellor's determination to undercut the legislative prerogatives of the Reichstag effectively deprived the liberal parties of whatever legitimate function they may have possessed in the eyes of the electorate. Moreover, the disintegration of the two liberal parties was intensified by the increasing indifference of Germany's industrial elite. Germany's industrial leadership had supported the liberal parties handsomely during the first years of the Weimar Republic, no doubt in an attempt to construct an effective bourgeois bulwark against the tide of social and political revolution that seemed to be sweeping the country. But the leaders of the German industrial establishment were frustrated by how little they were able to accomplish through their control of party finances, and in their frustration many began to turn away from the parties they had originally supported. Not only did Germany's industrial leadership fail to pursue a policy that might have helped stabilize the existing party system, but by withholding funds from those parties that did not submit to its demands, it inadvertently accelerated their internal disintegration and helped create the conditions under which Germany's antiparliamentary Right could come to power.

All of these factors—the legacy of schism within the German liberal movement, the destabilizing effect of the so-called national question upon the two liberal parties, the general course of social and economic development during the Weimar Republic, the increasingly prominent role of organized economic interests in German political life, the failure of liberal efforts to create a united bourgeois party, and the increasing disaffection of Germany's industrial elite —combined to destroy German liberalism as a viable force in Weimar political life. Although it would be imprudent to focus exclusively upon any one of these factors, the role of social and economic development remains crucial to any understanding of the failure of Weimar liberalism. The cumulative effect of the war, the inflation, stabilization, and the outbreak of the world economic crisis was to create a Hobbesian state of *bellum omnium contra omnes* in which the social fabric of German liberalism was effectively destroyed. Although the dissolution of the German middle class as a homogeneous social force was well under way before the outbreak of World War I, it required a series of national catastrophes—catastrophes that were indeed unique in modern German history—to destroy the social base of the German liberal movement and produce the massive psychological trauma that led to the end of the Weimar Republic.

The failure of the German liberal parties during the Weimar Republic and the collapse of the political order with which they had become so closely identified were not, as this study has consistently argued, predetermined by the weight of historical tradition or by the litany of failure that inscribed the history of German liberalism in the nineteenth century. On the contrary, the founding of the Weimar Republic marked the culmination of a revival of liberal forces that had begun under Naumann's nimbus at the beginning of the twentieth century and that set the stage for what the more progressive elements of Germany's liberal bourgeoisie regarded as a moment of unprecedented promise. Although Weimar liberals admittedly operated within a tradition that may have limited their vision and that may not have been entirely compatible with their conception of the perfect polity, in the final analysis it was not that tradition but the sheer weight of the problems with which they had to contend that turned their hopes to bitter ashes. The legacy of Germany's military defeat and the symbolic identification of that defeat with the establishment of the Weimar Republic, Allied intransigence from the imposition of the Versailles Peace Treaty to the occupation of the Ruhr, and the devastating course of Germany's social and economic development in the early 1920s all combined to create an environment in which the seed of liberal democracy could hardly take root, let alone flourish. By the time the republic had finally begun to stabilize itself in the second half of the 1920s, political liberalism and the values for which it stood had become so thoroughly discredited in the eyes of many of its former supporters that it no longer offered a viable alternative to the rising tide of interest politics that had begun to transform the landscape of German political life. Consequently, when the outbreak of the world economic crisis and the onslaught of National Socialism threatened to sweep away the last vestiges of Germany's liberal order, the toll that more than a decade of internecine conflict, demoralizing electoral defeats, and unremitting economic distress had taken upon the vitality of Germany's liberal parties became painfully apparent. Lacking the spiritual as well as the material resources to withstand the challenge of Nazism, the German liberal parties passed into obscurity with little more than token resistance.

Notes

ABBREVIATIONS

In addition to the abbreviations used in the text, the following abbreviations are used in the notes.

AA	Politisches Archiv des Auswärtigen Amts, Bonn
Abt.	Abteilung
ACDP	Archiv für Christlich-Demokratische Politik der Konrad Adenauer-Stiftung, Sankt Augustin bei Bonn
AHR	*American Historical Review*
BA	Bundesarchiv, Koblenz
BA-MA	Bundesarchiv-Militärarchiv, Freiburg im Breisgau
BTB	*Berliner Tageblatt*
CEH	*Central European History*
DAZ	*Deutsche Allgemeine Zeitung*
DPK	*Demokratische Partei-Korrespondenz*
DS	*Deutsche Stimmen*
FZ	*Frankfurter Zeitung*
GLA	General Landesarchiv
GSA	Geheimes Staatsarchiv, Berlin-Dahlem
HA	Historisches Archiv
HA/GHH	Historisches Archiv der Gutehoffnungshütte, Oberhausen
HSA	Hauptstaatsarchiv
HZ	*Historische Zeitschrift*
JCH	*Journal of Contemporary History*
JMH	*Journal of Modern History*
KZ	*Kölnische Zeitung*
LA	Landesarchiv
NL	Nachlaß
NLC	*Nationalliberale Correspondenz*
SA	Staatsarchiv
SAA	Siemens Archiv Akte
StA	Stadtarchiv
VfZ	*Vierteljahrshefte für Zeitgeschichte*
WA	Werksarchiv
ZSg	Zeitgeschichtliche Sammlung
ZSA	Zentrales Staatsarchiv der Deutschen Demokratischen Republik, Potsdam

INTRODUCTION

1. For a general survey of the literature on the German question, see Theodore S. Hamerow, "Guilt, Redemption, and Writing German History," *AHR* 88 (1983): 53–72.

2. Ralf Dahrendorf, *Society and Democracy in Germany* (Garden City, 1967), pp. 33–64.

3. James J. Sheehan in a book review, *JMH* 48 (1976): 564–67.

4. In particular, see Hans-Ulrich Wehler, *Das deutsche Kaiserreich 1871 bis 1918* (Göttingen, 1973).

5. David Blackbourn and Geoff Eley, *The Peculiarities of German History: Bourgeois Society and Politics in Nineteenth-Century Germany* (Oxford, 1984), pp. 1–35. On the debate that Blackbourn and Eley have sparked, see James N. Retallack, "Social History with a Vengeance? Some Reactions to H. U. Wehler's 'Das Deutsche Kaiserreich,'" *German Studies Review* 7 (1984): 423–50, and Roger Fletcher, "Recent Developments in West German Historiography: The Bielefeld School and Its Critics," ibid., pp. 451–80. For an excellent discussion of postwar German historiography, see the introduction by Georg Iggers in *The Social History of Politics: Critical Perspectives in West German Historical Writing since 1945*, ed. Georg Iggers (Leamington Spa, 1985), pp. 1–48.

6. Blackbourn and Eley, *Peculiarities of German History*, pp. 178–205.

7. Ibid., p. 33.

8. Geoff Eley, "What Produces Fascism: Preindustrial Traditions or a Crisis of a Capitalist State?," *Politics and Society* 12 (1983): 53–82.

9. Dahrendorf, *Society and Democracy*, p. 400. For a further example of the exaggerated claims regarding the explanatory utility of illiberalism, see the introduction in Fritz Stern, *The Failure of Illiberalism: Essays on the Political Culture of Modern Germany* (New York, 1972), pp. xi–xliv.

10. Konrad H. Jarausch, "Illiberalism and Beyond: German History in Search of a Paradigm," *JMH* 55 (1983): 268–84.

11. For a survey of the secondary literature on the history of Weimar liberalism, see Lothar Albertin, "Liberalismus in der Weimarer Republik," *Neue Politische Literatur* 19 (1974): 220–34, and Konstanze Wegner, "Linksliberalismus im wilhelminischen Deutschland und in der Weimarer Republik," *Geschichte und Gesellschaft* 4 (1978): 120–38, as well as James C. Hunt, "The Bourgeois Middle in German Politics, 1871–1933: Recent Literature," *CEH* 11 (1978): 83–106. See also Jürgen C. Hess and E. van Steensel van der Aa, *Bibliographie zum deutschen Liberalismus* (Göttingen, 1981), pp. 121–36.

12. For the most balanced discussion of why liberalism failed in the Weimar Republic, see Jürgen C. Hess, "Die Desintegration des Liberalismus in der Weimarer Republik," in *Auf dem Weg zum modernen Parteienstaat. Zur Entstehung, Organisation und Struktur politischer Parteien in Deutschland und den Niederlanden*, ed. Hermann W. von der Dunk and Horst Lademacher (Kassel, 1986), pp. 249–72.

13. For an overview of these developments, see Larry Eugene Jones, "The Dissolution of the Bourgeois Party System in the Weimar Republic," in *Social Change and Political Development in Weimar Germany*, ed. Richard Bessel and E. J. Feuchtwanger (London, 1981), pp. 268–88.

14. Leonard Krieger, *The German Idea of Freedom: History of a Political Tradition* (Chicago, 1957), pp. 86–139.

15. This point has been persuasively argued first by Theodore S. Hamerow, *Restoration, Revolution, Reaction: Economics and Politics in Germany, 1815–1871* (Princeton, 1958), pp. 58–64, and more recently by James J. Sheehan, "Liberalism and Society in Germany, 1815–1848," *JMH* 45 (1973): 583–604. On the social origins of the German liberal movement, see James J. Sheehan, *German Liberalism in the Nineteenth Century* (Chicago, 1978), pp. 19–34, as well as the collection of essays in Wolfgang Schieder, ed., *Liberalismus in der Gesellschaft des deutschen Vormärz* (Göttingen, 1983).

16. Lothar Gall, "Liberalismus und 'bürgerliche Gesellschaft.' Zu Charakter und Entwicklung der liberalen Bewegung in Deutschland," *HZ* 220 (1975): 324–56.

17. Hans Mommsen, "Die Auflösung des Bürgertums seit dem späten 19. Jahrhundert," in *Bürger und Bürgerlichkeit im 19. Jahrhundert*, ed. Jürgen Kocka (Göttingen, 1987), pp. 288–315. See also Sheehan, *Liberalism*, pp. 239–57, as well as Theodor Schieder, "Die Krise des bürgerlichen Liberalismus. Ein Beitrag zum Verhältnis von politischer und gesellschaftlicher Verfassung," in *Staat und Gesellschaft im Wandel unserer Zeit. Studien zur Geschichte des 19. und 20. Jahrhunderts*, ed. Theodor Schieder (Munich, 1958), pp. 58–88.

18. David Blackbourn, "The *Mittelstand* in German Society and Politics, 1871–1914," *Social History*, no. 4 (1977): 409–33.

19. Sheehan, *Liberalism*, pp. 51–68. See also Dieter Langewiesche, "Die Anfänge der deutschen Parteien. Partei, Fraktion und Verein in der Revolution von 1848/49," *Geschichte und Gesellschaft* 11 (1985): 324–61.

20. Sheehan, *Liberalism*, pp. 108–19. For further details, see Heinrich August Winkler, *Preußischer Liberalismus und deutscher Nationalstaat. Studien zur Geschichte der Deutschen Fortschrittspartei 1861–1866* (Tübingen, 1964), pp. 91–125, and Gerhard Eisfeld, *Die Entstehung der liberalen Parteien in Deutschland 1858–70. Studien zu den Organisationen und Programmen der Liberalen und Demokraten* (Hanover, 1969), pp. 59–197.

21. Sheehan, *Liberalism*, pp. 121–40, 181–218. The secondary literature on German liberalism in the Second Empire is quite extensive. On the NLP, see Hermann Block, *Die parlamentarische Krisis der Nationalliberalen Partei 1879–80* (Hamburg, 1930), and Dan S. White, *The Splintered Party: National Liberalism in Hesse and the Reich, 1867–1918* (Cambridge, Mass., 1976), as well as the shorter contributions by Gustav Schmidt, "Die Nationalliberalen—eine regierungsfähige Partei? Zur Problematik der inneren Reichsgründung 1870–1878," in *Die deutschen Parteien vor 1918*, ed. Gerhard A. Ritter (Düsseldorf, 1973), pp. 208–23, and Heinrich August Winkler, "Vom linken zum rechten Nationalismus. Der deutsche Liberalismus in der Krise von 1878/79," *Geschichte und Gesellschaft* 4 (1978): 5–28. On the various left-wing liberal parties, see Gustav Seeber, *Zwischen Bebel und Bismarck. Zur Geschichte des Linksliberalismus in Deutschland 1871–1893* ([East] Berlin, 1965). See also Felix Rachfahl, "Eugen Richter und der Linksliberalismus im neuen Reiche," *Zeitschrift für Politik* 5 (1912): 261–374. Also useful are Konstanze Wegner, *Theodor Barth und die Freisinnige Vereinigung. Studien zur Geschichte des Linksliberalismus im wilhelminischen Deutschland (1893–1910)* (Tübingen, 1968), as well as Klaus Simons, *Die würt-*

*tembergischen Demokraten. Ihre Stellung und Arbeit im Parteien- und Verfassungs-
system in Württemberg und im Deutschen Reich 1890–1920* (Stuttgart, 1969), and
James C. Hunt, *The People's Party in Württemberg and Southern Germany, 1890–1914*
(Stuttgart, 1975).

22. Sheehan, *Liberalism*, pp. 221–38. See also Alfred Milatz, "Die linksliberalen
Parteien und Gruppen in den Reichstagswahlen 1871–1912," *Archiv für Sozialgeschichte* 12 (1972): 272–92.

23. Thomas Nipperdey, "Die Organisation der bürgerlichen Parteien in Deutschland
vor 1918," *HZ* 185 (1958): 559–70. See also Theodor Schieder, "Die Theorie der Partei
im älteren deutschen Liberalismus," in Schieder, *Staat und Gesellschaft*, pp. 110–32.

24. Sheehan, *Liberalism*, pp. 159–77, 258–65. For a general overview of these
developments, see Gerhard Schulz, "Über Entstehung und Formen von Interessengruppen in Deutschland seit dem Beginn der Industrialisierung," *Politische Vierteljahresschrift* 2 (1961): 124–54, and Hans-Jürgen Puhle, "Parlament, Parteien und Interessenverbände 1890–1914," in *Das kaiserliche Deutschland. Politik und Gesellschaft
1870–1918*, ed. Michael Stürmer (Düsseldorf, 1970), pp. 340–77.

25. In this respect, see the extremely useful study by Dirk Stegmann, *Die Erben
Bismarcks. Parteien und Verbände in der Spätphase des Wilhelminischen Deutschlands. Sammlungspolitik 1897–1918* (Cologne, 1970).

26. Sigmund Neumann, *Die deutschen Parteien. Wesen und Wandel nach dem Krieg*
(Stuttgart, 1932), p. 52.

27. Stegmann, *Erben Bismarcks*, pp. 59–130.

28. For further details, see the divergent interpretations in Volker R. Berghahn, *Der
Tirpitz Plan. Genesis und Verfall einer innenpolitischen Krisenstrategie unter Wilhelm
II* (Düsseldorf, 1971), pp. 11–20, and Geoff Eley, "Sammlungspolitik, Social Imperialism, and the Navy Law of 1898," *Militärgeschichtliche Mitteilungen* 11 (1974): 29–
63.

29. For the text of Naumann's appeal, see his speech in *Protokoll über die Verhandlungen des Nationalsozialen Vereins (Vierter Vertretertag) zu Göttingen vom 1.–4.
Oktober 1899* (Berlin-Schöneberg, [1899]), pp. 32–40.

30. On Naumann's early thought and career, see Werner Conze, "Friedrich Naumann. Grundlagen und Ansatz seiner Politik in der nationalsozialen Zeit (1895 bis
1903)," in *Schicksalswege deutscher Vergangenheit. Beiträge zur geschichtlichen
Deutung der letzten hundertfünfzig Jahre*, ed. Walther Hubatsch (Düsseldorf, 1950),
pp. 355–86. For a general overview of Naumann's intellectual development, see Walter
Struve, *Elites against Democracy: Leadership Ideals in Bourgeois Political Thought,
1890–1933* (Princeton, 1973), pp. 78–113, as well as Wolfgang J. Mommsen, "Wandlungen der liberalen Idee im Zeitalter des Imperialismus," in *Liberalismus und imperialistischer Staat. Der Imperialismus als Problem liberaler Parteien in Deutschland
1890–1914*, ed. Karl Holl and Günther List (Göttingen, 1975), pp. 109–47.

31. In particular, see Theodor Barth and Friedrich Naumann, *Die Erneuerung des
Liberalismus. Ein politischer Weckruf* (Berlin, 1906).

32. Friedrich Naumann, "Klassenpolitik des Liberalismus," in *Friedrich Naumann,
Werke*, 6 vols. (Cologne and Opladen, 1964–68), 4:258–62.

33. Ursula Büttner, "Vereinigte Liberale und Deutsche Demokraten in Hamburg
1906–1930," *Zeitschrift des Vereins für Hamburgische Geschichte* 63 (1977): 1–34.

34. Werner Link, "Der Nationalverein für das liberale Deutschland (1907–1918)," *Politische Vierteljahresschrift* 5 (1964): 422–44.

35. For further information on these negotiations, see Ludwig Elm, *Zwischen Fortschritt und Reaktion. Geschichte der Parteien der liberalen Bourgeoisie in Deutschland 1893–1918* ([East] Berlin, 1968), pp. 156–69, 203–9, as well as the valuable study by Beverly Heckart, *From Bassermann to Bebel: The Grand Bloc's Quest for Reform in the Kaiserreich, 1900–1914* (New Haven, 1974), pp. 26–33, 64–68, 122–24.

36. Friedrich Naumann, "Die Leidensgeschichte des deutschen Liberalismus," in *Werke*, 4:299.

37. For example, see Curt Köhler, *Der Jungliberalismus. Eine historisch-chronologische Darstellung* (Cologne, 1912). For further information on the Young Liberals and their place within the NLP, see Heckart, *From Bassermann to Bebel*, pp. 38–43, as well as the unpublished dissertation by George F. Mundle, "The German National Liberal Party, 1900–1914. Political Revival and Resistance to Change" (Ph.D. dissertation, University of Illinois, 1975), pp. 76–104.

38. Heckart, *From Bassermann to Bebel*, pp. 211–87. On the split within the NLP, see Stegmann, *Erben Bismarcks*, pp. 305–16, and Mundle, "National Liberal Party," pp. 226–318.

39. On the founding and goals of the Hansa-Bund, see Siegfried Mielke, *Der Hansa-Bund für Gewerbe, Handel und Industrie 1909–1914. Der gescheiterte Versuch einer antifeudalen Sammlungspolitik* (Göttingen, 1976), pp. 11–44. See also Stegmann, *Erben Bismarcks*, pp. 176–95.

40. For further details, see George Vascik, "The German Peasants' League and the Revival of National Liberalism," paper delivered before the German Studies Association in St. Louis, Mo., 18 Oct. 1987.

41. For further information, see Heckart, *From Bassermann to Bebel*, pp. 186–92, as well as the detailed study by Jürgen Bertram, *Die Wahlen zum Deutschen Reichstag vom Jahre 1912. Parteien und Verbände in der Innenpolitik des Wilhelminischen Reiches* (Düsseldorf, 1964), pp. 69–79, 101–7, 212–41.

42. Bertram, *Wahlen*, pp. 205–21, 243–49.

43. Heckart, *From Bassermann to Bebel*, pp. 211–87. On the split within the NLP, see Stegmann, *Erben Bismarcks*, pp. 305–16, and Mundle, "National Liberal Party," pp. 226–318.

44. Gustav Schmidt, "Parlamentarisierung oder 'Präventive Konterrevolution'? Die deutsche Innenpolitik im Spannungsfeld zwischen konservativer Sammlungsbewegungen und latenter Reformbestrebungen 1907–1914," in *Gesellschaft, Parlament und Regierung. Zur Geschichte des Parlamentarismus in Deutschland*, ed. Gerhard A. Ritter (Düsseldorf, 1974), pp. 249–74.

45. For further details, see Geoff Eley, *Reshaping the German Right: Radical Nationalism and Political Change after Bismarck* (New Haven and London, 1980), pp. 316–34.

CHAPTER ONE

1. On the social effects of the war, see Jürgen Kocka, *Klassengesellschaft im Krieg. Deutsche Sozialgeschichte 1914–1918* (Göttingen, 1973), pp. 65–95, as well as the more specialized studies by Andreas Kunz, *Civil Servants and the Politics of Inflation in Germany, 1914–1924* (Berlin, 1986), pp. 94–131, and Robert G. Moeller, *German Peasants and Agrarian Politics, 1914–1924: The Rhineland and Westphalia* (Chapel Hill, 1986), pp. 43–67.

2. For example, see Friedrich Naumann, *Der Kaiser im Volksstaat* (Berlin-Schöneberg, 1917).

3. On the crisis within the NLP, see Hartwig Thieme, *Nationaler Liberalismus in der Krise. Die nationalliberale Fraktion des Preußischen Abgeordnetenhauses 1914–1918* (Boppard am Rhein, 1963), pp. 93–121.

4. On the debate over war aims and the passage of the "Peace Resolution," see Klaus Epstein, *Matthias Erzberger und das Dilemma der deutschen Demokratie* (Berlin and Frankfurt am Main, 1962), pp. 204–36. For the FVP's policies during the July crisis, see Friedrich von Payer, *Von Bethmann-Hollweg bis Ebert. Erinnerungen und Bilder* (Frankfurt am Main, 1923), pp. 23–38, as well as the incisive article by Stuart T. Robson, "German Left Liberals and the First World War," in *Canadian Historical Association. Historical Papers Presented at the Annual Meeting Held at Ottawa, June 7–19, 1967*, pp. 216–34.

5. For example, see Friedrich Naumann, *Der Weg zum Volksstaat* (Berlin, [1918]), as well as Payer, *Von Bethmann-Hollweg bis Ebert*, pp. 113–72.

6. NLP, Reichsgeschäftsstelle, "Die Einigungsverhandlungen mit der Fortschrittlichen Volkspartei—Gründung der Deutschen Volkspartei," 22 Nov. 1918, BA: ZSg 1-47/7 (8). For the most detailed treatment of the efforts to create a united liberal party in the fall of 1918, see Lothar Albertin, *Liberalismus und Demokratie am Anfang der Weimarer Republik. Eine vergleichende Analyse der Deutschen Demokratischen Partei und der Deutschen Volkspartei* (Düsseldorf, 1972), pp. 45–72. See also the recent study by Bruce B. Frye, *Liberal Democrats in the Weimar Republic: The History of the German Democratic Party and the German State Party* (Carbondale, 1985), pp. 45–54.

7. On these developments, see the entries for 11–13 Nov. 1918, in Theodor Wolff, *Tagebücher 1914–1919. Der Erste Weltkrieg und die Entstehung der Weimarer Republik in Tagebüchern, Leitartikeln und Briefen des Chefredakteurs am "Berliner Tageblatt" und Mitbegründers der "Deutschen Demokratischen Partei,"* ed. Bernd Sösemann, 2 vols. (Boppard am Rhein, 1984), 2:649–53, as well as the galley proofs of an unpublished article by Richard Frankfurter, "Zur Geschichte der Deutschen Demokratischen Partei und ihres Programms," [Dec. 1918], BA: NL Richthofen, 18/12–22. For the best analysis of Wolff's intentions, see Modris Eksteins, *The Limits of Reason: The German Democratic Press and the Collapse of Weimar Democracy* (Oxford, 1975), pp. 31–45. Somewhat less perceptive is the biographical study by Gotthard Schwarz, *Theodor Wolff und das "Berliner Tageblatt." Eine liberale Stimme in der deutschen Politik 1906–1933* (Tübingen, 1969), pp. 79–96. See also the account in Werner Stephan, *Aufstieg und Verfall des Linksliberalismus. Geschichte der Deutschen Demokratischen Partei* (Göttingen, 1973), pp. 13–17.

8. On the plight of the Progressives, see Fischbeck to Gothein, 18 and 21 Nov. 1918, BA: NL Gothein, 20/39–42.

9. Circular letter by Gothein, 13 Nov. 1918, HSA Stuttgart, NL Haußmann, 114. See also Gothein to Hirschfeld, 15 Nov. 1918, BA: NL Gothein, 22/202.

10. On developments in Württemberg, see the detailed memorandum by Haußmann, 29 Nov. 1918, HSA Stuttgart, NL Haußmann, 101, as well as the letter from Wieland to Haußmann, 21 Nov. 1918, ibid.

11. For the text of Wolff's appeal and a list of its signatories, see Otto Nuschke, "Wie die Deutsche Demokratische Partei wurde, was sie leistete und was sie ist," in *Zehn Jahre Deutsche Republik. Ein Handbuch für republikanische Politik*, ed. Anton Erkelenz (Berlin-Zehlendorf, 1928), pp. 25–26. For an indication of Progressive reluctance to sign the appeal, see Haußmann's undated reply to Wieland's letter of 21 Nov. 1918, HSA Stuttgart, NL Haußmann, 101.

12. For example, see Marwitz to Stresemann, 12 Nov. 1918, BA: R 45 II/1/1.

13. On Stresemann's contacts with the Progressives, see the notations in his desk calendar, 15–16 Nov. 1918, AA: NL Stresemann, 3171/201/166101, as well as his letters to Stubmann and Wieland, 15 Nov. 1918, ibid., 3069/187/134553–54, 134556–57. For the best analysis of Stresemann's role in these negotiations, see Wolfgang Hartenstein, *Die Anfänge der Deutschen Volkspartei 1918–1920* (Düsseldorf, 1962), pp. 7–47, and Henry Ashby Turner, Jr., *Stresemann and the Politics of the Weimar Republic* (Princeton, 1963), pp. 3–26. See also the account that Stresemann published anonymously in DVP, Reichsgeschäftsstelle, ed., *Die Entstehung der Deutschen Volkspartei* (Berlin, 1919).

14. For example, see Stresemann to Brüss, 25 Nov. 1918, AA: NL Stresemann, 3069/187/134605–9.

15. In this respect, see Hugo to Stresemann, 15 Nov. 1918, AA: NL Stresemann, 3069/187/134545–48, and Flathmann to Friedberg, 18 Nov. 1918, BA: R 45 II/1/59–63.

16. For example, see Wieland to Stresemann, 13 Nov. 1918, AA: NL Stresemann, 3069/187/134519–22, and Weber to Stresemann, 15 Nov. 1918, BA: R 45 II/1/13–14.

17. Stresemann to Brüss, 25 Nov. 1918, AA: NL Stresemann, 3069/187/134605–9.

18. DVP, Reichsgeschäftsstelle, *Entstehung der Deutschen Volkspartei*, pp. 5–7. See also Stresemann's handwritten notes on the meeting of 18 Nov. 1918, AA: NL Stresemann, 3069/187/134581–82, as well as the extremely revealing correspondence between Stresemann and Fischbeck, 4–15 July 1922, ibid., 3110/247/138864–69, 143870–76.

19. For the Progressives' reaction, see Fischbeck to Gothein, 18 Nov. 1918, BA: NL Gothein, 20/39–40.

20. DVP, Reichsgeschäftsstelle, *Entstehung der Deutschen Volkspartei*, pp. 7–8. See also Fischbeck to Gothein, 21 Nov. 1918, BA: NL Gothein, 20/41–42, and Gothein to Haußmann, 25 Nov. 1918, HSA Stuttgart, NL Haußmann, 114.

21. Stresemann, telegram to Brandenburg, Schindler, Falk, Rose, Loewry, and Boehm, 19 Nov. 1918, BA: R 45 II/1/79.

22. NLP, Reichsgeschäftsstelle, "An die Parteifreunde!," 25 Nov. 1918, AA: NL Stresemann, 3069/187/134604.

23. For further information, see Richthofen, "Politische Aufzeichnungen, insbe-

sondere über meine Beziehungen zu Dr. Gustav Stresemann," Mar. 1947, BA: NL Richthofen, 20a.

24. On developments in Württemberg, see the memorandum by Haußmann, 29 Nov. 1918, HSA Stuttgart, NL Haußmann, 101, as well as Wieland to Stresemann, 30 Nov. 1918, AA: NL Stresemann, 3069/187/134627–29. On the situation in Bavaria, see Pius Dirr, "Zur Geschichte der Deutschen Volkspartei in Bayern," *Der Waffenschmied* 2, nos. 1/2 (Jan.–Feb. 1919): 1–8.

25. Brüss to Stresemann, 27 Nov. 1918, BA: R 45 II/1/133–42.

26. See Stresemann's handwritten notes of a meeting with Marwitz, Fischer, and other NLP leaders, 23 Nov. 1918, AA: NL Stresemann, 3069/187/134593–96.

27. Görnandt, Thissen, and Kauffmann to the DDP, 30 Nov. 1918, BA: R 45 II/1/167–73. See also Köhler (Hansa-Bund) to Stresemann, 28 Nov. 1918, ibid., 155.

28. For example, see Vogelstein to Gothein, 26 Nov. 1918, BA: NL Gothein, 32/85–88, as well as the entry for 3 Dec. 1918, in Wolff, *Tagebücher*, 2:667.

29. Stresemann to Brüss, 3 Dec. 1918, BA: R 45 II/1/178–81.

30. For the text of Friedberg's statement, see Nuschke, "Deutsche Demokratische Partei," pp. 28–29. On the meeting of 2 Dec. 1918, see Leidig's report in DVP, Reichsgeschäftsstelle, *Entstehung der Deutschen Volkspartei*, pp. 17–20, as well as his later account in "Der Übergang von der Nationalliberalen Partei zur Deutschen Volkspartei," in *Deutscher Aufbau. Nationalliberale Arbeit der Deutschen Volkspartei*, ed. Adolf Kempkes (Berlin, 1927), pp. 7–15.

31. For an indication of Stresemann's reaction, see the entry in his desk calendar for 3 Dec. 1918: "Friedberg vollzieht Kapitulation vor demokratischer Partei," AA: NL Stresemann, 3171/201/166104.

32. For further information, see Hartenstein, *Anfänge der Deutschen Volkspartei*, pp. 71–72.

33. Marwitz to Stresemann, 6 Dec. 1918, BA: R 45 II/1/189–91.

34. Resolution of the Hanoverian NLP, 6 Dec. 1918, BA: R 45 II/1/197.

35. *Schulthess' europäischer Geschichtskalender* 59 (1918): 571–72. See also the minutes of the official founding of the DVP, 15 Dec. 1918, BA: R 45 II/1/227–37.

36. Nuschke, "Deutsche Demokratische Partei," p. 30.

37. Johannes Rathje, *Deutsche Volkspartei oder Deutsche Demokratische Partei?* (Berlin-Zehlendorf, [1919]), pp. 15–16.

38. "Wahlaufruf," in *Allgemeine Werbeflugschriften der Deutschen demokratischen Partei* (Berlin-Zehlendorf, 1918), pp. 1–4.

39. Minutes of the DDP executive committee, 7 Jan. 1919, BA: R 45 III/15/12–28. See also Stephan, *Linksliberalismus*, pp. 37–38.

40. Stephan *Linksliberalismus*, p. 37.

41. Ernst Portner, "Der Ansatz zur demokratischen Massenpartei im Deutschen Linksliberalismus," *VfZ* 13 (1965): 150–61. For further details, see Frye, *Liberal Democrats*, pp. 55–70, and Peter M. Bowers, "The Failure of the German Democratic Party, 1918–1930" (Ph.D. dissertation, University of Pittsburgh, 1973), pp. 20–37.

42. "An unsere nationalliberale Parteifreunde," 15 Dec. 1918, in *Werbeflugschriften der Deutschen demokratischen Partei*, pp. 5–7.

43. "An unsere jungliberale Freunde," n.d., in *Werbeflugschriften der Deutschen*

demokratischen Partei, pp. 8–9. See also Bruno Marwitz, *Deutsche Demokratie und nationaler Liberalismus*, Deutsch-demokratische Ziele, no. 6 (Berlin, 1919).

44. In this respect, see the appeal from the DBB executive committee, "Männer und Frauen vom Deutschen Bauernbund," and the speech by Böhme from 28 Nov. 1918, in *Deutscher Bauernbund* 10, no. 11 (30 Nov. 1918): 81–86, and "Die Politik des Deutschen Bauernbundes," ibid., no. 13 (23 Dec. 1918): 97–98. See also Karl Böhme, *Der Bauernstand in Knechtschaft und Freiheit* (Berlin, 1924), pp. 112–16, as well as the more recent monograph by Martin Schumacher, *Land und Politik. Eine Untersuchung über politische Parteien und agrarische Interessen 1914–1923* (Düsseldorf, 1978), pp. 432–39.

45. Minutes of the DDP managing committee, 5 Dec. 1918, BA: R 45 III/9/6. See also "An das Landvolk," n.d., in *Werbeflugschriften der Deutschen demokratischen Partei*, pp. 10–14.

46. In this respect, see "An alle Beamten im Reichs-, Staats- und Gemeindedienst," n.d., in *Werbeflugschriften der Deutschen demokratischen Partei*, pp. 15–19, as well as Albertin, *Liberalismus und Demokratie*, pp. 131–33, and Kunz, *Civil Servants and the Politics of Inflation*, pp. 151–56.

47. Albertin, *Liberalismus und Demokratie*, pp. 141–42. For further information, see Heinz-Jürgen Priamus, *Angestellte und Demokratie. Die nationalliberale Angestelltenbewegung in der Weimarer Republik* (Stuttgart, 1979), pp. 153–60.

48. This point has been convincingly argued for the city of Frankfurt by Günter Hollenberg, "Bürgerliche Sammlung oder sozialliberale Koalition? Sozialstruktur, Interessenlage und politisches Verhalten der bürgerlichen Schichten 1918/19 am Beispiel der Stadt Frankfurt am Main," *VfZ* 29 (1979): 392–430.

49. For example, see Hartmann's speech at the official founding of the DDGB, 20 Nov. 1918, in *Zweck und Ziele des Deutsch-demokratischen Gewerkschaftsbundes*, Schriften des Deutsch-demokratischen Gewerkschaftsbundes, no. 1 (Berlin, 1919), pp. 8–14.

50. For further details, see Rennie William Brantz, "Anton Erkelenz, the Hirsch-Duncker Trade Unions, and the German Democratic Party" (Ph.D. dissertation, Ohio State University, 1973), pp. 65–66.

51. On the Curatorium's general objectives, see Siemens to Ziegler, 11 June 1919, SAA: NL Siemens, 4/Lf 646. For further information on the Curatorium's activities in the elections for the National Assembly, see Albertin, *Liberalismus und Demokratie*, pp. 167–74.

52. Siemens to Deutsch, 2 Jan. 1919, SAA: NL Siemens, 4/Lf 646.

53. Undated memorandum on the Curatorium's expenditures for the elections for the National Assembly, SAA: NL Siemens, 4/Lf 646.

54. Hartenstein, *Anfänge der Deutschen Volkspartei*, pp. 49–54. For examples of Stresemann's campaign rhetoric, see Gustav Stresemann, *Von der Revolution bis zum Frieden von Versailles. Reden und Aufsätze* (Berlin, 1919), pp. 47–89. On the differences between liberalism and democracy, see also Eugen Leidig, *Liberalismus und Demokratie* (Berlin, 1919), as well as Wilhelm Kahl, "Der Liberalismus der Deutschen Volkspartei," in *Volk und Reich der Deutschen*, ed. Bernhard Harms, 3 vols. (Berlin, 1929), 2:88–103.

55. Gustav Stresemann, *Deutsche Gegenwart und Zukunft. Vortrag gehalten in Stuttgart am 18. November 1917* (Stuttgart, 1917), pp. 27–29.

56. Gustav Stresemann, "Das alte und neue Deutschland," 19 Dec. 1918, in Gustav Stresemann, *Reden und Schriften. Politik—Geschichte—Literatur 1897–1926*, ed. Rochus von Rheinbaben, 2 vols. (Berlin, 1926), 1:238.

57. "Aufruf der Deutschen Volkspartei," 18 Dec. 1918, in *Die deutschen Parteiprogramme*, ed. Felix Salomon, 3 vols. (Leipzig, 1926), 3:18–22.

58. For a detailed, though somewhat misleading, account of these efforts, see Eric Dorn Brose, *Christian Labor and the Politics of Frustration in Imperial Germany* (Washington, 1985), pp. 361–70. See also John K. Zeender, "German Catholics and the Concept of an Interconfessional Party, 1900–1922," *Journal of Central European Affairs* 23 (1964): 424–39, and William L. Patch, Jr., *Christian Trade Unions in the Weimar Republic, 1918–1933: The Failure of "Corporate Pluralism"* (New Haven, 1985), pp. 35–45.

59. In this respect, see Baltrusch to Stresemann, 12 Dec. 1918, AA: NL Stresemann, 3068/183/134018–19, and Gutsche to Stresemann, 14 Dec. 1918, ibid., 134088–91.

60. Leidig to Stinnes, 3 Jan. 1919, ACDP: NL Stinnes, 002/3.

61. Hartenstein, *Anfänge der Deutschen Volkspartei*, pp. 63–66.

62. For the most detailed analysis of the liberal parties' performance in the elections for the National Assembly, see Albertin, *Liberalismus und Demokratie*, pp. 138–44. On the DDP specifically, see Bowers, "Failure of the German Democratic Party," pp. 37–45.

63. In addition to Albertin, *Liberalismus und Demokratie*, pp. 138–44, see Hartenstein, *Anfänge der Deutschen Volkspartei*, pp. 67–73. For a valuable regional study of the DVP's performance, see Ursula Schelm-Spangenberg, *Die Deutsche Volkspartei im Lande Braunschweig. Gründung, Entwicklung, soziologische Struktur, politische Arbeit* (Brunswick, 1964), pp. 19–20, 40–48.

64. In this respect, see Gerhard A. Ritter, "Kontinuität und Umformung des deutschen Parteiensystems 1918–1920," in *Entstehung und Wandel der modernen Gesellschaft. Festschrift für Hans Rosenberg zum 65. Geburtstag*, ed. Gerhard A. Ritter (Berlin, 1970), pp. 342–76.

65. This point has been persuasively argued in the short essay by Lothar Albertin, "German Liberalism and the Foundation of the Weimar Republic: A Missed Opportunity?," in *German Democracy and the Triumph of Hitler*, ed. Anthony Nichols and Erich Matthias (London, 1971), pp. 29–46. For a less sanguine appraisal of liberalism's prospects in the postwar period, see Jürgen C. Hess, "Gab es eine Alternative? Zum Scheitern des Linksliberalismus in der Weimarer Republik," *HZ* 223 (1976): 638–54.

CHAPTER TWO

1. For a persuasive argument to this effect, see Stuart T. Robson, "German Left Liberals and the First World War," in *Canadian Historical Association. Historical*

Papers Presented at the Annual Meeting Held at Ottawa, June 7–19, 1967, pp. 229–34.

2. In this respect, see Gerhard Schulz, "Räte, Wirtschaftsstände und die Transformation des industriellen Verbandswesens am Anfang der Weimarer Republik," in *Gesellschaft, Parlament und Regierung. Zur Geschichte des Parlamentarismus in Deutschland*, ed. Gerhard A. Ritter (Düsseldorf, 1974), pp. 355–66.

3. Gerhard A. Ritter, "Kontinuität und Umformung des deutschen Parteiensystems 1918–1920," in *Entstehung und Wandel der modernen Gesellschaft. Festschrift für Hans Rosenberg zum 65. Geburtstag*, ed. Gerhard A. Ritter (Berlin, 1970), pp. 367–68.

4. For an excellent statement of Naumann's views in the immediate postwar period, see Friedrich Naumann, *Demokratie als Staatsgrundlage. Vortrag, gehalten am 4. März 1919 in der Stadtkirche in Jena*, Demokratische Reden, no. 5 (Berlin, 1919). For an indication of his personal antipathy towards the Wolff-Weber group, see Naumann's letter to Hohmann, 25 Nov. 1918, quoted in Theodor Heuss, *Friedrich Naumann. Der Mann, das Werk, die Zeit* (Stuttgart and Berlin, 1937), p. 592.

5. See Gertrud Bäumer, *Soziale Erneuerung. Amtliches Stenogramm der Rede in der Nationalversammlung vom 21. Februar 1919*, Demokratische Reden, no. 3 (Berlin, 1919).

6. In addition to Rennie William Brantz, "Anton Erkelenz, the Hirsch-Duncker Trade Unions, and the German Democratic Party" (Ph.D. dissertation, Ohio State University, 1973), see Attila A. Chanady, "Anton Erkelenz and Erich Koch-Weser: A Portrait of Two German Democrats," *Historical Studies: Australia and New Zealand* 12 (1967): 491–505.

7. For example, see Friedrich von Payer, *Anno 1848* (Frankfurt am Main, 1923).

8. For an indication of the attitudes of this group, see Wieland to Reusch, 26 and 30 Jan. 1919, HA/GHH: NL Reusch, 30019390/29.

9. Sigmund Neumann, *Die deutschen Parteien. Wesen und Wandel nach dem Kriege* (Stuttgart, 1932), p. 47.

10. Gothein to Haußmann, 25 Nov. 1918, HSA Stuttgart, NL Haußmann, 114.

11. Fischbeck to Haußmann, 1 Dec. 1918, HSA Stuttgart, NL Haußmann, 114.

12. *BTB*, 2 Dec. 1918, no. 615.

13. Minutes of the DDP managing committee, 13 Dec. 1918, BA: R 45 III/9/17.

14. Wolff to Fischbeck, [Apr. 1919], HSA Stuttgart, NL Haußmann, 102. See also Fischbeck's report at the meeting of the DDP managing committee, 25 Apr. 1919, BA: R 45 III/9/98.

15. DDP, Reichsgeschäftsstelle, ed., *Bericht über die Verhandlungen des 1. Parteitages der Deutschen Demokratischen Partei abgehalten in Berlin vom 19. bis 22. Juli 1919* (Berlin, 1919), p. 237.

16. Minutes of the DDP party council, 28 Sept. 1919, BA: R 45 III/10/11–15.

17. DDP, Reichsgeschäftsstelle, ed., *Bericht über die Verhandlungen des 2. außerordentlichen Parteitages der Deutschen Demokratischen Partei, abgehalten in Leipzig vom 13.–15. Dezember 1919* (Berlin, [1920]), pp. 8–9.

18. For a somewhat more sympathetic assessment of Petersen's qualities as a political leader, see Erich Lüth, "Carl Petersen—Wegbereiter des Bündnisses zwischen

Bürger und Arbeiter in Hamburg," in Erich Lüth and Hans-Dieter Loose, *Bürgermeister Carl Petersen 1868–1933* (Hamburg, 1971), pp. 1–28.

19. Wilhelm Ziegler, *Die deutsche Nationalversammlung 1919/1920 und ihr Verfassungswerk* (Berlin, 1932), p. 42. On the negotiations that led to the formation of the Scheidemann government, see Payer's report before the Democratic delegation to the National Assembly, 7 and 10 Feb. 1919, in Petersen's diary, SA Hamburg, NL Petersen, 62.

20. See the memoir by Erich Koch-Weser on the Weimar National Assembly, 13 Feb. 1919, BA: NL Koch-Weser, 17, subsequently published by Günter Arns, "Erich Koch-Wesers Aufzeichnungen vom 13. Februar 1919," *VfZ* 17 (1969): 96–115.

21. Friedrich Naumann, *Die Demokratie in der Nationalversammlung. Rede gehalten in der deutschen Nationalversammlung am 13. Februar 1919*, Demokratische Reden, no. 1 (Berlin, 1919).

22. Eugen Schiffer, *Deutschlands Finanzlage nach dem Kriege. Rede gehalten in der deutschen Nationalversammlung am 15. Februar 1919* (Berlin, 1919).

23. Notes on the meeting of the DDP delegation to the National Assembly, 1 Mar. 1919, HSA Stuttgart, NL Haußmann, 25. See also the minutes of the DDP delegation, 2 Mar. 1919, NL Baum (Yale University Archives, Holborn Papers, box 1). For a fuller statement of Haußmann's views, see his speech, "Demokratie und Mittelstand," 16 Apr. 1919, HSA Stuttgart, NL Haußmann, 102, reprinted in Conrad Haußmann, *Aus Conrad Haußmanns politischer Arbeit* (Frankfurt am Main, 1923), pp. 81–86.

24. Ziegler, *Nationalversammlung*, pp. 54–60. In this respect, see Lothar Döhn, "Wirtschafts- und Sozialpolitik der Deutschen Demokratischen Partei und der Deutschen Volkspartei," in *Sozialer Liberalismus*, ed. Karl Holl, Günter Trautmann, and Hans Vorländer (Göttingen, 1986), pp. 90–95, and Hartmut Schustereit, *Linksliberalismus und Sozialdemokratie in der Weimarer Republik. Eine vergleichende Betrachtung der Politik von DDP und SPD 1919–1930* (Düsseldorf, 1975), pp. 56–62.

25. Entry in Koch-Weser's diary, 6 Mar. 1919, BA: NL Koch-Weser, 16/23.

26. Minutes of the DDP delegation to the National Assembly, 5 Mar. 1919, NL Baum.

27. Entry in Koch-Weser's diary, 6 Mar. 1919, BA: NL Koch-Weser, 16/23.

28. Werner Stephan, *Aufstieg und Verfall des Linksliberalismus. Geschichte der Deutschen Demokratischen Partei* (Göttingen, 1973), pp. 70–74. See also Rudolf Ißberner, ed., *Demokratisches ABC-Buch* (Berlin, [1920]), pp. 153–55, as well as the discussion in Brantz, "Erkelenz," pp. 78–82.

29. Entry in Koch-Weser's diary, 11 Mar. 1919, BA: NL Koch-Weser, 16/71.

30. Ibid., 16/87–89.

31. Wieland to Reusch, 22 Apr. 1919, HA/GHH: NL Reusch, 30019390/29.

32. Friedrich von Payer, *Demokratie und Mehrheitsregierung. Etatsrede, Weimar, 11. April 1919* (Weimar, 1919).

33. Minutes of the DDP executive committee, 12–13 Apr. 1919, BA: R 45 III/15/81–110. See also Stephan, *Linksliberalismus*, pp. 74–77.

34. For example, see Wieland to Payer, 28 May 1919, BA: NL Payer, 12/192.

35. The text of these speeches are to be found in Robert Friedberg, Conrad Haußmann, and Ludwig Quidde, *Der Entwurf des Friedensvertrages. Reden gehalten in der Nationalversammlung vom 12. Mai 1919 sowie in der Preußischen Landesversamm-*

lung vom 13. Mai 1919 (Berlin, 1919). For the most detailed analyses of the Democratic response to the allied peace terms, see Lothar Albertin, *Liberalismus und Demokratie am Anfang der Weimarer Republik. Eine vergleichende Analyse der Deutschen Demokratischen Partei und der Deutschen Volkspartei* (Düsseldorf, 1972), pp. 324–44, and more recently Jürgen C. Hess, *"Das ganze Deutschland soll es sein." Demokratischer Nationalismus in der Weimarer Republik am Beispiel der Deutschen Demokratischen Partei* (Stuttgart, 1978), pp. 76–111.

36. Minutes of the DDP executive committee, 18 May 1919, BA: R 45 III/15/149–59.

37. Albertin, *Liberalismus und Demokratie*, pp. 324–33.

38. See Haußmann's remarks at a meeting of the DDP delegation to the National Assembly, 4 June 1919, HSA Stuttgart, NL Haußmann, 59, as well as the entry in Koch-Weser's diary, 3 June 1919, BA: NL Koch-Weser, 16/153–55.

39. Haußmann to Hieber, 12 June 1919, HSA Stuttgart, NL Haußmann, 59.

40. Klaus Epstein, *Matthias Erzberger und das Dilemma der deutschen Demokratie* (Berlin and Frankfurt am Main, 1962), pp. 354–68.

41. Walther Schücking, *Annehmen oder Ablehnen? Rede in der Fraktion der Demokratischen Partei zu Weimar am 19. Juni 1919* (n.p., [1919]). On Schücking's position within the party, see Detlef Acker, *Walther Schücking (1971–1935)* (Münster, 1970), pp. 115–22, and Karl Holl, "Pazifismus oder liberaler Neu-Imperialismus? Zur Rolle der Pazifisten in der Deutschen Demokratischen Partei 1918–1930," in *Imperialismus im 20. Jahrhundert. Gedenkschrift für George W. Hallgarten*, ed. Joachim Radkau and Imanuel Geiss (Munich, 1976), pp. 171–95.

42. Minutes of the DDP delegation to the National Assembly, 19 June 1919, HSA Stuttgart, NL Haußmann, 59.

43. Ibid. See also Friedrich von Payer, *Von Bethmann-Hollweg bis Ebert. Erinnerungen und Bilder* (Frankfurt am Main, 1923), pp. 295–98.

44. Minutes of the DDP delegation to the National Assembly, 19 June 1919, HSA Stuttgart, NL Haußmann, 59. For Erkelenz's position, see his handwritten notes from 19 June 1919, BA: NL Erkelenz, 84/128–31.

45. Epstein, *Erzberger*, pp. 360–61.

46. Minutes of the DDP delegation to the National Assembly, morning and afternoon sessions, 20 June 1919, HSA Stuttgart, NL Haußmann, 59.

47. For Haußmann's role in these developments, see the letter to his son, 24 June 1919, in *Aus Haußmanns politischer Arbeit*, pp. 177–80.

48. Minutes of the DDP delegation to the National Assembly, 21 [incorrectly dated 20] June 1919, HSA Stuttgart, NL Haußmann, 59.

49. Minutes of the meeting of the minority faction of the Democratic delegation, 21 June 1919, BA: NL Erkelenz, 84/144–47. See also Erkelenz to Duensing, 24 June 1919, ibid., 84/76.

50. Statement signed by Erkelenz, Gleichauf, Remmers, and Schneider, 22 June 1919, BA: NL Erkelenz, 84/176.

51. Eduard Heilfron, ed. *Die Deutsche Nationalversammlung im Jahre 1919 in ihrer Arbeit für den Aufbau des neuen deutschen Volksstaates*, 9 vols. (Berlin, 1919–20), 4:2731–37. See also Eugen Schiffer, "Die Stellung der Deutschen Demokratischen Partei in der Friedensfrage," *Der Waffenschmied* 2, no. 5 (July 1919): 4–9.

52. Stephan, *Linksliberalismus*, pp. 86–87.

53. Minutes of the DDP delegation to the National Assembly, 23 June 1919, HSA Stuttgart, NL Haußmann, 59.

54. For further details, see Payer, *Von Bethmann-Hollweg bis Ebert*, pp. 298–304.

55. Haußmann to Hieber, 30 June 1919, HSA Stuttgart, NL Haußmann, 115.

56. For example, see Bernstorff to Schiffer, 29 June 1919, BA: NL Schiffer, 6/60–62.

57. Schiffer, "Das erste Jahr nach der Revolution," *Das demokratische Deutschland* 1, no. 48 (9 Nov. 1919): 1085–1101. For the most detailed study of the DDP's role in drafting the Weimar Constitution, see Ernst Portner, *Die Verfassungspolitik der Liberalen 1919. Ein Beitrag zur Deutung der Weimarer Reichsverfassung* (Bonn, 1973).

58. Gerland, "Was müssen wir vom Parteitag fordern?," *Das demokratische Deutschland* 1, no. 31 (13 July 1919): 723–44.

59. DDP, Reichsgeschäftsstelle, *Bericht über die Verhandlungen des 1. Parteitages*, pp. 58–62, 64–69.

60. For the text of this resolution as well as Hartmann's supporting arguments, see ibid., pp. 220–30.

61. Ibid., pp. 219–29.

CHAPTER THREE

1. For a fuller discussion of Stresemann's social and political values, see Larry Eugene Jones, "Gustav Stresemann and the Crisis of German Liberalism," *European Studies Review* 4 (1974): 141–63. The literature on Stresemann is far too extensive for detailed citation here. For further information, see the comprehensive bibliography by Martin Walsdorff, *Bibliographie Gustav Stresemann* (Düsseldorf, 1972).

2. On Stresemann's career as a lobbyist in Saxony, see Donald K. Warren, *The Red Kingdom of Saxony: Lobbying Grounds for Gustav Stresemann, 1901–1909* (The Hague, 1964).

3. Gustav Stresemann, "Friedrich Naumann," in Gustav Stresemann, *Reden und Schriften. Politik—Geschichte—Literatur 1897–1926*, ed. Rochus von Rheinbaben, 2 vols. (Berlin, 1926), 1:244–45. See also "Kreise um den jungen Stresemann," *KZ*, 9 Oct. 1929, no. 353a.

4. For example, see the essays reprinted in Gustav Stresemann, *Wirtschaftspolitische Zeitfragen* (Dresden, 1910), pp. 103–42.

5. "Stresemann und die Jungliberalen," *KZ*, 4 Oct. 1929, no. 546b.

6. Gustav Stresemann, *Neue Zeiten. Rede am 27. März 1917 im Reichstag* (Berlin, 1917).

7. In this respect, see Stresemann's speech in *Durch deutschen Sieg zum deutschen Frieden. Fünf Reden zur Lage gehalten am 19. Januar 1917 in der Versammlung des "Unabhängigen Ausschusses für einen Deutschen Frieden" im Sitzungssaale des Abgeordnetenhauses zu Berlin* (Berlin, 1917), pp. 31–42.

8. For example, see Stresemann to Hugo, 15 Nov. 1918, AA: NL Stresemann, 3069/187/134572–74, and Stresemann to Brüss, 3 Dec. 1918, BA: R 45 II/1/179–81.

9. Wolfgang Hartenstein, *Die Anfänge der Deutschen Volkspartei 1918–1920* (Düsseldorf, 1962), pp. 67–73.

10. Ibid., p. 75.

11. Lothar Albertin, *Liberalismus und Demokratie am Anfang der Weimarer Republik. Eine vergleichende Analyse der Deutschen Demokratischen Partei und der Deutschen Volkspartei* (Düsseldorf, 1972), pp. 145–48.

12. For further details, see Hartenstein, *Anfänge der Deutschen Volkspartei*, pp. 107–12.

13. Gustav Stresemann, *Weimar und die Politik* (Berlin, 1919), pp. 5–7. See also Stresemann to Riesser, 1 Feb. 1919, AA: NL Stresemann, 3079/202/136987–88, and Stresemann to Boehm, 3 Feb. 1919, ibid., 137017–22.

14. Stresemann, "Preußen und Deutschland in der neuen Verfassung," *DS* 31, no. 12 (23 Mar. 1919): 185–90.

15. Stresemann's speech in DVP, Reichsgeschäftsstelle, ed., *Bericht über den ersten Parteitag der Deutschen Volkspartei am 13. April 1919 in den akademischen Rosensälen in Jena* (Berlin, 1919), pp. 15–16.

16. DVP, Reichsgeschäftsstelle, ed. *Grundsätze der Deutschen Volkspartei. Beschlossen auf dem Parteitag in Leipzig am 19. Oktober 1919 der Deutschen Volkspartei* (Berlin, 1931), pp. 4–5.

17. Kahl, "Grundfragen der Verfassung," in *Deutscher Aufbau. Nationalliberale Arbeit der Deutschen Volkspartei*, ed. Adolf Kempkes (Berlin, 1927), pp. 25–34.

18. See Heinze's report in DVP, Reichsgeschäftsstelle, ed., *Bericht über den zweiten Parteitag der Deutschen Volkspartei am 18., 19. und 20. Oktober 1919 im Kristallpalast in Leipzig* (Berlin, 1920), pp. 34–35, as well as Wilhelm Kahl, *Die Deutsche Volkspartei und das Reich*, Flugschriften der Deutschen Volkspartei, no. 14 (Berlin, 1919).

19. Gustav Stresemann, *Die Deutsche Volkspartei und ihr politisches Programm. Rede auf dem Leipziger Parteitag der Deutschen Volkspartei am 18. Oktober 1919*, Flugschriften der Deutschen Volkspartei, no. 11 (Berlin, 1919), pp. 16–21.

20. Stresemann to Schmidgall, 24 Mar. 1919, AA: NL Stresemann, 3088/206/137629–31.

21. Gustav Stresemann, "Das bittere Ende," in Gustav Stresemann, *Von der Revolution bis zum Frieden von Versailles. Reden und Aufsätze* (Berlin, 1919), pp. 172–80.

22. Otto Hugo, *Der Mittelstand und die Deutsche Volkspartei* (Berlin, 1919), pp. 18–20. See also Beythien, "Gedanken über den Mittelstand," *DS* 31, no. 39 (28 Sept. 1919): 662–66.

23. In particular, see Alexander Backhaus, *Aufgaben der Landwirtschaft und ihre Vertretung durch die Deutsche Volkspartei* (Berlin, 1919), and Wilhelm Dusche, *Die Deutsche Volkspartei und die Landwirtschaft* (Berlin, 1919), as well as the monograph by Martin Schumacher, *Land und Politik. Eine Untersuchung über politische Parteien und agrarische Interessen 1914–1923* (Düsseldorf, 1978), pp. 454–60.

24. For example, see Bechly, "Angestelltenbewegung und parlamentarische Regierung," *DS* 30, no. 47 (24 Nov. 1918): 778–81.

25. See Otto Thiel, "Die Deutsche Volkspartei," in *Jahrbuch für Deutschnationale Handlungsgehilfen 1921* (Hamburg, [1921]), pp. 63–73.

26. Minutes of the DVP managing committee, 1–2 May 1919, BA: R 45 II/50/33–37.

27. *Die Deutsche Volkspartei und die Beamten,* Flugschriften der Deutschen Volkspartei, no. 13 (Berlin, 1919).

28. Hartenstein, *Anfänge der Deutschen Volkspartei,* pp. 64–66.

29. Paul Gustav Reinhardt, *Die Deutsche Volkspartei und ihre Ziele. Vortrag gehalten am 27. Mai 1919 in der Aula des Nikolaigymnasiums in Leipzig* (Leipzig, [1919]).

30. DVP, Landesverband Baden, ed., *Entstehung und Entwicklung der Deutschen Volkspartei (Deutschen liberalen Volkspartei) im ersten Revolutionsjahr. Aufklärungsschrift* (Heidelberg, [1919]), pp. 11–14.

31. Curtius to Stresemann, 24 June 1919, AA: NL Stresemann, 3088/207/137842–44.

32. On developments in the Württemberg liberal movement, see Gottlob Egelhaaf, "Mein Rückkehr zur nationalliberalen Partei," *Schwäbischer Merkur,* 17 Sept. 1919, no. 428, and Hieber, "Zur parteipolitischen Lage," *Stuttgarter Neues Tageblatt,* 12–14 Oct. 1919, nos. 517–21. On the founding and early history of the Württemberg DVP, see Gottlob Egelhaaf, *Lebens-Erinnerungen,* ed. Adolf Rapp (Stuttgart, 1960), pp. 147–50.

33. See Garnich's report in DVP, Reichsgeschäftsstelle, *Bericht über den zweiten Parteitag* pp. 53–61.

34. According to an internal report prepared in the spring of 1920, the DVP had a total of 258,600 members in October 1919 and 395,200 in April 1920. The most active DVP organizations were those in Dortmund-Arnsberg—with more than 70,000 members—Brunswick, and Oldenburg. See "Bericht über die Entwicklung der Organisation," [May 1920], BA: R 45 II/52/185–87.

35. For further details, see Adolf Kempkes, "Die Organisation der Deutschen Volkspartei," in *Deutscher Aufbau,* ed. Kempkes, pp. 16–24.

36. See Garnich's report on party finances at a meeting of the DVP managing committee, 1–2 May 1919, BA: R 45 II/50/37–47.

37. Leidig to the Curatorium for the Reconstruction of German Economic Life, 5 Jan. 1919, SAA: NL Siemens, 4/Lf 646.

38. See Stresemann's remarks at a meeting of the executive committee of the DVP delegation to the National Assembly, 22 Mar. 1919, AA: NL Stresemann, 3088/206/137709–11.

39. Stresemann to W. von Siemens, 10 Mar. 1919, AA: NL Stresemann, 3079/202/137135–38.

40. Handwritten note dated 17 May [?] 1919, on the original of Stresemann's letter to Siemens from 10 Mar. 1919: "Von Herrn W. Siemens telefonisch mit Dr. Stresemann besprochen. Mitgeteilt, daß Unterstützung nicht gewährt werden kann." SAA: NL Siemens, 4/Lf 646.

41. Flathmann to Stresemann, 12 and 21 Mar. 1919, AA: NL Stresemann, 3088/206/137640, 137704–7.

42. For further details, see Lothar Döhn, *Politik und Interesse. Die Interessen-struktur der Deutschen Volkspartei* (Meisenheim an Glan, 1970), pp. 99–108.

43. Stresemann to Flathmann, 28 Mar. 1919, AA: NL Stresemann, 3088/206/137681–82.

44. Garnich's report on party finances before the DVP managing committee, 1–2 May 1919, BA: R 45 II/50/83–89.

45. Minutes of the meeting of the Curatorium for the Reconstruction of German Economic Life, 9 May 1919, SAA: NL Siemens, 4/Lf 646.

46. Borsig to Siemens, 10 July 1919, SAA: NL Siemens, 4/Lf 646.

47. Vögler to Stinnes, 15 Oct. 1919, ACDP: NL Stinnes, 002/1. For further details, see Horst Romeyk, "Die Deutsche Volkspartei in Rheinland und Westfalen 1918–1933," *Rheinische Vierteljahrsblätter* 39 (1975): 206–8.

48. In this respect, see Vögler to Sorge, 15 Oct. 1919, ACDP: NL Stinnes, 002/1, and Flathmann to Stinnes, 23 Oct. 1919, ibid., 002/4, as well as Flathmann to Kuhbier, 27 Oct. 1919, AA: NL Stresemann, 3088/208/138010–11.

49. For an indication of such sentiment, see the speech by Oskar Hergt, *Gegenwart und Zukunft der Deutschnationalen Volkspartei. Rede auf dem Parteitag der Deutsch-nationalen Volkspartei in Berlin am 12. und 13. Juli 1919*, Deutschnationale Flug-schrift, no. 21 (Berlin 1919), p. 9. For the most detailed discussion of the efforts to merge the DVP and DNVP, see Hartenstein, *Anfänge der Deutschen Volkspartei*, pp. 131–42.

50. Stresemann to Schmidgall, 24 Mar. 1919, AA: NL Stresemann, 3088/206/137629–31.

51. DVP, Reichsgeschäftsstelle, *Bericht über den ersten Parteitag*, p. 30.

52. Minutes of the DVP managing committee, 29 June 1919, BA: R 45 II/50/151–55.

53. Stresemann, *Deutsche Volkspartei und ihr politisches Programm*, pp. 22–23. See also Curtius, "Die deutschnationale Volkspartei, ihre Zusammensetzung, Grund-sätze, Taktik nach dem Berliner Parteitag vom 12. und 13. Juli 1919," *DS* 31, no. 41 (19 Oct. 1919): 708–17.

54. DVP, Reichsgeschäftsstelle, *Grundsätze der Deutschen Volkspartei*, pp. 4–5. See also the speech by Kahl in DVP, Reichsgeschäftsstelle, *Bericht über den zweiten Parteitag*, pp. 102–7.

55. For a fuller discussion of the DVP's social and economic program, see Vögler's speech in DVP, Reichsgeschäftsstelle, *Bericht über den zweiten Parteitag*, pp. 107–19. See also Lothar Döhn, "Wirtschafts- und Sozialpolitik der Deutschen Demokratischen Partei und der Deutschen Volkspartei," in *Sozialer Liberalismus*, ed. Karl Holl, Günter Trautmann, and Hans Vorländer (Göttingen, 1986), pp. 90–91.

CHAPTER FOUR

1. On the changing political climate in 1919 and early 1920, see Charles S. Maier, *Recasting Bourgeois Europe: Stabilization in France, Germany, and Italy in the De-cade after World War I* (Princeton, 1975), pp. 138–46, 158–73.

2. For the best discussion of the events surrounding the DDP's reentry into the government, see Lothar Albertin, *Liberalismus und Demokratie am Anfang der Weimarer Republik. Eine vergleichende Analyse der Deutschen Demokratischen Partei und der Deutschen Volkspartei* (Düsseldorf, 1972), pp. 355–60, and Rennie William Brantz, "Anton Erkelenz, the Hirsch-Duncker Trade Unions, and the German Democratic Party" (Ph.D. dissertation, Ohio State University, 1973), pp. 105–10.

3. Entries in Koch-Weser's diary, 20–21 Sept. 1919, BA: NL Koch-Weser, 16/259–63. See also the minutes of the DDP Reichstag delegation, 21 Sept. 1919, BA: NL Erkelenz, 84/174–75.

4. In particular, see Waldstein's report before the DDP party council, 28 Sept. 1919, BA: R 45 III/10/16–20. See also Erkelenz, "Betriebsräte und Demokratie," *Das demokratische Deutschland* 1, no. 39 (7 Sept. 1919): 885–89. For the background of this conflict, see Maier, *Recasting Bourgeois Europe*, pp. 158–64.

5. See Schiffer's statement at a meeting of the DDP delegation to the National Assembly, 28 Sept. 1919, BA: NL Erkelenz, 84/177–78, as well as the entries in Koch-Weser's diary, 26 and 29 Sept. 1919, BA: NL Koch-Weser, 16/163–71. See also Petersen's letter to his wife, 19 Sept. 1919, SA Hamburg, NL Petersen, 20.

6. Minutes of the DDP delegation to the National Assembly, 2 Oct. [incorrectly dated 2 Sept.] 1919, HSA Stuttgart, NL Haußmann, 25. See also the minutes of the delegation's meetings on 1–2 Oct. 1919, NL Baum (Yale University Archives, Holborn Papers, box 1). For a defense of the DDP's decision to reenter the government, see Petersen, "Zur Neubildung des Kabinetts," *Das demokratische Deutschland* 1, no. 44 (12 Oct. 1919): 988–96.

7. See Schiffer's remarks at a meeting of the DDP delegation to the National Assembly, 21 Sept. 1919, NL Baum, as well as the debate at the meeting of the DDP party council, 28 Sept. 1919, BA: R 45 III/10/20–28.

8. Report by Waldstein, 28 Sept. 1919, BA: R 45 III/10/18–19.

9. For a further indication of the anti-Erzberger sentiment within the DDP, see the remarks by Waldstein and Hoff at the meeting of the DDP party council, 28 Sept. 1919, BA: R 45 III/10/19–22.

10. For an indication of the DDP's early difficulties in the Bauer government, see the letter from Petersen to his wife, 26 Oct. 1919, SA Hamburg, NL Petersen, 20.

11. For further details, see Klaus Epstein, *Matthias Erzberger und das Dilemma der deutschen Demokratie* (Berlin and Frankfurt am Main, 1962), pp. 381–91, as well as the detailed analysis by Peter-Christian Witt, "Finanzpolitik und sozialer Wandel in Krieg und Inflation," in *Industrielles System und politische Entwicklung in der Weimarer Republik. Verhandlungen des Internationalen Symposiums in Bochum vom 12.–17. Juni 1973*, ed. Hans Mommsen, Dietmar Petzina, and Bernd Weisbrod (Düsseldorf, 1974), pp. 395–426.

12. Conrad Haußmann, *Schlaglichter. Reichstagsbriefe und Aufzeichnungen*, ed. Ulrich Zeller (Frankfurt am Main, 1924), pp. 297–99.

13. Minutes of the DDP delegation to the National Assembly, 16 Dec. 1919, NL Baum.

14. Werner Stephan, *Aufstieg und Verfall des Linksliberalismus. Geschichte der Deutschen Demokratischen Partei* (Göttingen, 1973), pp. 136–39. See also Rudolf Ißberner, ed., *Demokratisches ABC-Buch* (Berlin, [1920]), pp. 132–38.

15. Entry in Koch-Weser's diary, 26 Sept. 1919, BA: NL Koch-Weser, 16/265.

16. Siemens to Fischer, 7 Nov. 1919, SAA: NL Siemens, 4/Lf 646.

17. See the debate at the meeting of the DDP delegation to the National Assembly, 24–25 Nov. 1919, HSA Stuttgart, NL Haußmann, 25.

18. In this respect, see Weinhausen, "Demokratische Politik beim Rätegesetz," *Die Hilfe* 25, no. 47 (4 Dec. 1919): 690–92, as well as Raschig's report in DDP, Reichsgeschäftsstelle, ed., *Bericht über die Verhandlungen des 2. außerordentlichen Parteitages der Deutschen Demokratischen Partei, abgehalten in Leipzig vom 13.–15. Dezember 1919* (Berlin, [1920]), pp. 85–88. For further details, see Maier, *Recasting Bourgeois Europe*, pp. 161–62.

19. *Protestkundgebung der deutschen Industrie gegen das Betriebsrätegesetz, Berlin, 11. Dezember 1919*, Veröffentlichungen des Reichsverbandes der deutschen Industrie, no. 9 (Berlin, 1920).

20. DDP, Reichsgeschäftsstelle, *Bericht über die Verhandlungen des 2. außerordentlichen Parteitages*, pp. 103–4, 111–14.

21. Erkelenz, "Wirtschaftliche Selbstverwaltung," in Anton Erkelenz, *Moderne Sozialpolitik* (Berlin, 1926), pp. 50–59.

22. Undated letter from Köhler, appended to a letter from Gwardowski to the members of the presidium of the Democratic Club, 23 Dec. 1919, SAA: NL Siemens, 4/Lf 555.

23. Wilhelm Ziegler, *Die deutsche Nationalversammlung 1919/1920 und ihr Verfassungswerk* (Berlin, 1932), pp. 207–12. The account in Stephan, *Linksliberalismus*, pp. 153–57, is factually inaccurate. For a detailed breakdown of the Democratic vote on the Factory Council Law, see Ißberner, *Demokratisches ABC-Buch*, pp. 24–29.

24. For further details, see DDP, Reichsgeschäftsstelle, ed., *Niederschrift über die Tagung der Parteisekretäre der Deutschen demokratischen Partei am 17. und 18. Mai 1919 im Anwaltshause in Berlin* (Berlin, [1919]). See also Erkelenz, "Betrachtungen zur Organisation der Partei," *Die Hilfe* 25, no. 47 (20 Nov. 1919): 658–60.

25. Report by Nuschke in DDP, Reichsgeschäftsstelle, ed., *Bericht über die Verhandlungen des 1. Parteitages der Deutschen Demokratischen Partei abgehalten in Berlin vom 19. bis 22. Juli 1919* (Berlin, 1919), pp. 9–17.

26. Erkelenz, "Parteifinanzen," *Die Hilfe* 25, no. 49 (4 Dec. 1919), 692–93.

27. Minutes of the DDP managing committee, 9 Aug. 1919, NL Baum.

28. Financial report by Fischer before the DDP party council, 12 Dec. 1919, BA: R 45 III/10/52–64.

29. Minutes of the DDP managing committee, 5 Sept. 1919, BA: R 45 III/9/135–39. See also Fischer to Siemens, 5 Nov. 1919, SAA: NL Siemens, 4/Lf 646, as well as Schacht to Gothein, 11 and 21 Nov. 1919, BA: NL Gothein, 30/27–29.

30. Siemens to Fischer, 7 Nov. 1919, SAA: NL Siemens, 4/Lf 646.

31. Financial report by Fischer before the DDP party council, 12 Dec. 1919, BA: R 45 III/10/52–64.

32. Kopsch to Stresemann, 26 Dec. 1919, AA: NL Stresemann, 3088/208/138158–61.

33. Hugo, "Die Bilanz von Weimar," *DS* 31, no. 36 (31 Aug. 1919): 585–95.

34. Gustav Stresemann, *Rede zu Magdeburg am 3. November 1919* (Magdeburg, [1919]), pp. 19–23. See also Johannes Becker, *Die neuen Steuern. Vortrag gehalten in*

Hamburg am 5. Oktober 1919, Hamburger Flugschriften, no. 1 (Hamburg, [1919]), and Jakob Riesser, *Das Reichsnotopfer und die Deutsche Volkspartei. Rede in der Nationalversammlung vom 9.12.19*, Flugschriften der Deutschen Volkspartei, no. 18 (Berlin, 1919), pp. 6–12.

35. *Das Betriebsrätegesetz, die Parteien und wirtschaftliche Berüfe*, Flugschriften der Deutschen Volkspartei, no. 21 (Berlin, 1920), pp. 6–15.

36. On the crusade against Erzberger and the political repercussions of the Erzberger-Helfferich trial, see Epstein, *Erzberger*, pp. 392–414, and John G. Williamson, *Karl Helfferich, 1872–1924. Economist, Financier, Politician* (Princeton, 1977), pp. 291–302, 312–27.

37. In this respect, see Quidde to Dirr, 26 Feb. 1920, and Jansen to the Bavarian DDP, 28 Feb. 1920, both in StA Munich, NL Dirr, 7.

38. Ißberner, *Demokratisches ABC-Buch*, pp. 43–44. For a more detailed discussion of this problem, see Bruce B. Frye, "The German Democratic Party and the 'Jewish Problem' in the Weimar Republic," *Year Book of the Leo Baeck Institute* 21 (1976): 143–72.

39. Resolution of the DVP managing committee, 28 Jan. 1920, AA: NL Stresemann, 3091/220/140063.

40. On the preparations for the putsch, see Johannes Erger, *Der Kapp-Lüttwitz Putsch. Ein Beitrag zur deutschen Innenpolitik 1919/20* (Düsseldorf, 1967), pp. 85–107, and Harold J. Gordon, *The Reichswehr and the German Republic, 1919–1926* (Princeton, 1957), pp. 90–143, as well as the recent study by James Diehl, *Paramilitary Politics in Weimar Germany* (Bloomington and London, 1977), pp. 67–74.

41. Erger, *Kapp-Lüttwitz Putsch*, pp. 171–219.

42. Robert Jansen, *Der Berliner Militärputsch und seine politischen Folgen* (Berlin, [1920]), pp. 20–21. See also Theodor Heuss, *Kapp-Lüttwitz. Das Verbrechen gegen die Nation* (Berlin, 1920).

43. Jansen, *Militärputsch*, p. 23.

44. For a detailed analysis of the DVP's response to the Kapp-Lüttwitz putsch, see Wolfgang Hartenstein, *Die Anfänge der Deutschen Volkspartei 1918–1920* (Düsseldorf, 1962), pp. 149–93. For a particularly critical analysis of Stresemann's conduct during the putsch, see Henry Ashby Turner, Jr., *Stresemann and the Politics of the Weimar Republic* (Princeton, 1963), pp. 47–67. For the reaction of the industrial interests which stood behind the DVP, see Gerald D. Feldman, "Big Business and the Kapp Putsch," *CEH* 4 (1971): 99–130.

45. Statement by the DVP leadership, 13 Mar. 1920, in Gustav Stresemann, *Die Märzereignisse und die Deutsche Volkspartei* (Berlin, 1920), p. 27.

46. See the speech by Kahl, 14 Mar. 1920, in *Kapp-Putsch und Bolschewismus in der Nationalversammlung. Vier Reden der Führer der Deutschen Volkspartei*, Flugschriften der Deutschen Volkspartei, no. 16 (Berlin, 1920), pp. 29–35.

47. Minutes of a meeting of the DVP leadership on the afternoon of 13 Mar. 1920, AA: NL Stresemann, 3090/217/139543–53.

48. See Stresemann's remarks at the meeting of the DVP party leadership, 13 Mar. 1920, AA: NL Stresemann, 3090/217/139549–50, and again at a meeting on the morning of 14 Mar. 1920, ibid., 139554–56.

49. Particularly revealing with respect to the DVP's objectives during the last stages

of the putsch are the minutes of the meeting of the DVP leadership, 15 Mar. 1920, AA: NL Stresemann, 3090/217/139562–71. On Stresemann's role as a mediator, see Hartenstein, *Anfänge der Deutschen Volkspartei*, pp. 170–78, and Turner, *Stresemann*, pp. 58–63.

50. Statement of the DVP delegation to the National Assembly, 18 Mar. 1920, in Stresemann, *Märzereignisse*, pp. 27–28.

51. In this respect, see the speeches in Ludwig Haas and Robert Friedberg, *Die Deutsche Demokratische Partei und der Kapp-Putsch. Zwei Reden deutschdemo-kratischer Parteiführer* (Berlin, 1920), pp. 6–13, 36–42, and Jansen, *Militärputsch*, pp. 30–32.

52. For further details, see Hartmut Schustereit, *Linksliberalismus und Sozial-demokratie in der Weimarer Republik. Eine vergleichende Betrachtung der Politik von DDP und SPD 1919–1930* (Düsseldorf, 1975), pp. 81–91, and Heinrich Potthoff, *Gewerkschaften und Politik zwischen Revolution und Inflation* (Düsseldorf, 1979), pp. 261–87.

53. Jansen, *Militärputsch*, pp. 48–49.

54. On the political repercussions of the Ruhr insurrection, see Werner T. Angress, "Weimar Coalition and Ruhr Insurrection, March–April 1920: A Study of Government Policy," *JMH* 29 (1957): 1–20.

55. On the fears of DDP leaders, see the entry in Koch-Weser's diary, 19 Mar. 1920, BA: NL Koch-Weser, 25/105–7.

56. See Koch-Weser's remarks at a meeting of the DDP delegation to the National Assembly, 23 Mar. 1920, HSA Stuttgart, NL Haußmann, 25.

57. See the debate at the meetings of the DDP delegation to the National Assembly, 23–24 Mar. 1920, HSA Stuttgart, NL Haußmann, 25, and NL Baum. See also the entry in Koch-Weser's diary, 24 Mar. 1920, BA: NL Koch-Weser, 27/41–43.

58. In this respect, see Wieland to Reusch, 11 Apr. 1920, HA/GHH: NL Reusch, 30019390/29, as well as the article by Gothein, "Die acht Pünkte," *BTB*, 2 Apr. 1920, no. 152.

59. Minutes of the DDP executive committee, 23 Mar. 1920, BA: R 45 III/16/21–23.

60. Statement by the DDP on the resignation of the Bauer government in *DPK*, 26 Mar. 1920, no. 63. On the controversy over Schiffer's negotiations with the putschists, see the entries in Koch-Weser's diary, 19 and 25 Mar. 1920, BA: NL Koch-Weser, 25/107–9, and 27/49–53.

61. On the DDP's role in these negotiations, see the report by Payer before the DDP delegation to the National Assembly, 24 Mar. 1920, HSA Stuttgart, NL Haußmann, 25, as well as the protocol of these meetings in NL Baum. On Gessler's appointment as minister of defense, see the minutes of the DDP delegation, 23 Mar. 1920, HSA Stuttgart, NL Haußmann, 25.

62. See Haas's statement before the National Assembly, 29 Mar. 1920, in Haas and Friedberg, *Deutsche Demokratische Partei und Kapp-Putsch*, p. 25. On the DDP's relations with the government, see Payer's report to the DDP delegation to the National Assembly, 28 Mar. 1920, HSA Stuttgart, NL Haußmann, 25, as well as the entry in Koch-Weser's diary, 29 Mar. 1920, BA: NL Koch-Weser, 27/65. See also Ißberner, *Demokratisches ABC-Buch*, pp. 82–85.

CHAPTER FIVE

1. Statement of the DDP delegation to the National Assembly in *DPK*, 26 Mar. 1920, no. 63.

2. Conrad Haußmann, "Zusammenarbeit," in Eduard David, Johannes Giesberts, and Conrad Haußmann, *Warum brauchen wir eine Regierung der Mitte? Drei Beiträge* (Berlin, 1920), pp. 11–13.

3. Minutes of the DDP party council, 17–18 Apr. 1920, BA: R 45 III/10/112–13.

4. Carl Petersen, *Zum Wahlkampf! Rede gehalten am 24. April 1920 in Görlitz* (Berlin, [1920]), pp. 3–12, 16–19. See also Ferdinand Hoff, *Politische Zeit- und Streitfragen in demokratischer Beleuchtung. Ein Wort zur Aufklärung für die kommenden Wahlen* (Berlin, [1920]), pp. 3–32, 73–82.

5. Eugen Schiffer, *Von der Nationalversammlung zum Reichstag. Rede gehalten am 26. April 1920 in Magdeburg* (Berlin, [1920]), p. 23.

6. Ibid., pp. 10–11. See also Petersen's remarks before the DDP party council, 17–18 Apr. 1920, BA: R 45 III/10/110–13.

7. Petersen, *Wahlkampf*, pp. 12–15. See also Hoff, *Streitfragen*, pp. 33–43, and Schiffer, *Nationalversammlung*, pp. 16–17.

8. Hoff, *Streitfragen*, pp. 43–55.

9. Petersen, *Wahlkampf*, pp. 20–22. See also Walther Schücking, *Auf dem Weg zur deutschen Demokratie* (Berlin, [1920]), pp. 11–12.

10. For a detailed analysis of the DVP's strategy in the 1920 campaign, see Wolfgang Hartenstein, *Die Anfänge der Deutschen Volkspartei 1918-1920* (Düsseldorf, 1962), pp. 203–11.

11. See Stresemann's speech before the DVP central executive committee, 18 Apr. 1920, reported in *NLC*, 18 Apr. 1920, no. 83, as well as his address in the DVP Reich Club, 29 May 1920, ibid., 31 May 1920, no. 117.

12. Stresemann, "Der Wiederaufbau Deutschlands und die Industrie," in *Bericht über die 16. Hauptversammlung des Verbandes Sächsischer Industrieller am 5. Mai 1920*, Veröffentlichung des Verbandes Sächsischer Industrieller, no. 32 (Dresden, 1920), pp. 93–121.

13. Rauch to Curtius, 16 Apr. 1920, AA: NL Stresemann, 3089/213/138854–57.

14. For the DVP's official attitude toward the DNVP, see the letter from Stresemann and Schütz to the DVP district chairmen, 11 Mar. 1920, BA: R 45 II/52/236–37, as well as Stresemann to Sthamer, 4 Feb. 1920, AA: NL Stresemann, 3091/220/140084–86.

15. A. W. Kroschel, *Das Deutschnationale Gewissen* (Berlin, 1920).

16. For the most detailed discussion of the Kardorff defection, see Hartenstein, *Anfänge der Deutschen Volkspartei*, pp. 195–99. For further details, see Lewis Hertzman, *DNVP: Right-Wing Opposition in the Weimar Republic, 1918–1924* (Lincoln, 1963), pp. 112–17. For Kardorff's position within the DNVP, see the memorandum entitled "Richtlinien für eine Erweiterung des Programms der Deutschnationalen Volkspartei," n.d., BA: NL Kardorff, 16/3–14, as well as Kardorff's letter to Hergt, 23 Feb. 1920, AA: NL Stresemann, 3091/221/140215–17.

17. Stresemann's memorandum of a meeting with Arendt, Dewitz, Kardorff, and Jordan (DDP), 15 Apr. 1920, AA: NL Stresemann, 3089/213/138848. For a detailed

statement of Kardorff's reasons for leaving the DNVP, see his letters to Neuhaus, 19 and 29 Apr. 1920, ibid., 3091/221/140222–34.

18. Statement by Arendt, Dewitz, and Kardorff, n.d., appended to Kardorff's letter to Stresemann, 17 Apr. 1920, BA: NL Kardorff, 13/145–47.

19. Stresemann's remarks before the DVP managing committee, 17 Apr. 1920, BA: R 45 II/53/89–93.

20. For example, see the two articles by Johannes Fuch, "Die Zukunft der Deutschen Demokratischen Partei und die Nationalliberalen," *DS* 31, no. 29 (20 July 1919): 489–92, and "Rechtsdemokraten und Deutsche Volkspartei," ibid., no. 37 (14 Sept. 1919): 617–21.

21. This correspondence has been reproduced in *Die Demokratische Partei ist als Verräterin des Bürgertums und Mittelstandes entlarvt* (Berlin, [1920]), pp. 3–9.

22. Ibid., pp. 14–30.

23. See Stresemann's remarks at a DVP rally in Berlin, 9 May 1920, in *KZ*, 10 May 1920, no. 430, as well as Rauch, "v. Kardorff, Wiemer, Stresemann," *DS* 32, no. 19 (9 May 1920): 305–8.

24. Werner Stephan, *Aufstieg und Verfall des Linksliberalismus. Geschichte der Deutschen Demokratischen Partei* (Göttingen, 1973), pp. 169–70.

25. For example, see the complaints in Riesser to Stresemann, 19 Dec. 1919, AA: NL Stresemann, 3088/208/138134.

26. Stresemann to the Central Association of German Citizens of the Jewish Faith, 28 Jan. 1920, AA: NL Stresemann, 3091/220/140060–62. For further information on Stresemann's attitude toward anti-Semitism, see his letter to Berckemeyer, 3 Apr. 1920, ibid., 3090/217/139606–09, as well as the manuscript of an apparently unpublished article entitled "Die wirklichen Ursachen des Antisemitismus," 22 Apr. 1920, ibid., 3091/222/140370–74. The account in Felix Hirsch, *Stresemann. Ein Lebensbild* (Göttingen, 1978), pp. 114–15, is misleading.

27. Resolution adopted by the DVP managing committee, 28 Jan. 1920, AA: NL Stresemann, 3091/220/140063.

28. Berckemeyer to Stresemann, 20 Mar. 1920, AA: NL Stresemann, 3090/217/139604–5.

29. For the text of the Weimar electoral law, see Alfred Milatz, *Wähler und Wahlen in der Weimarer Republik* (Bonn, 1965), pp. 41–51.

30. Siemens to Fischer, 7 Nov. 1919, SAA: NL Siemens, 4/Lf 646.

31. Siemens to the chairman of the DDP, Bezirksverband Berlin, 8 Dec. 1919, SAA: NL Siemens, 4/Lf 555.

32. Siemens to Fischer, 27 Jan. 1920, SAA: NL Siemens, 4/Lf 646.

33. For further information, see Siemens to Kauffmann, 9 Apr. 1920, as well as DDP Reichsgeschäftsstelle to Kauffmann, 30 Apr. 1920, both in SAA: NL Siemens, 4/Lf 555.

34. Minutes of the DDP executive committee, 2 May 1920, BA: R 45 III/16/31–34. See also Fischer to Siemens, 19 Apr. 1920, SAA: NL Siemens, 4/Lf 646.

35. See Erkelenz's remarks at the meeting of the DDP executive committee, 2 May 1920, BA: R 45 III/16/34.

36. Stephan, *Linksliberalismus*, p. 171.

37. In this respect, see the report of the meeting of the DDP precinct committee for

Stuttgart, 24 Mar. 1920, HSA Stuttgart, NL Haußmann, 103, as well as Marwitz to Siemens, 15 May 1920, SAA: NL Siemens, 4/Lf 555.

38. Gerland to Frankfurter, 18 May 1920, BA: NL Gerland, 7.

39. In this respect, see Otto Pautsch, *Demokratie und Landwirtschaft. Vortrag gehalten am 30. März 1919 auf dem Parteitage des Brandenburgischen Provinzialverbandes der Deutschen demokratischen Partei* (Berlin-Zehlendorf, [1919]), as well as Oeser, "Demokratie und Landwirtschaft," *Das demokratische Deutschland* 1, no. 12 (1 Mar. 1919): 274–78.

40. For an example of the DDP's equivocation on the controlled economy in agriculture, see Pautsch, "Demokratie und Landwirtschaft," *Das demokratische Deutschland* 1, no. 22 (10 May 1919), 507–12. On peasant dissatisfaction with the DDP, see Böhme's remarks before the DDP party council, 28 Sept. 1919, BA: R 45 III/10/21.

41. *DPK*, 18 Feb. 1920, no. 40.

42. Böhme, "Die Bundespolitik. Rede gehalten auf der Vertretertagung des Deutschen Bauernbundes am 6. März 1920," in *Politisches ABC. Taschenbuch für Bauernbündler*, ed. Deutscher Bauernbund (Berlin, 1920), pp. 146–68. See Böhme's speech, "Entstehung und Politik des Deutschen Bauernbundes," 9 Dec. 1919, in *Deutscher Bauernbund* 12, no. 1 (2 Jan. 1920): 2–10.

43. *DPK*, 8 Mar. 1920, no. 56. The alliance was officially approved at a meeting of the DDP executive committee on 25 Mar. 1920. See BA: R 45 III/16/22.

44. For example, see Ernst Remmers, *Der Beamte in Volksstaat* (Berlin, 1919). For further information, see Lothar Albertin, *Liberalismus und Demokratie am Anfang der Weimarer Republik. Eine vergleichende Analyse der Deutschen Demokratischen Partei und der Deutschen Volkspartei* (Düsseldorf, 1972), pp. 131–33, and Andreas Kunz, *Civil Servants and the Politics of Inflation in Germany, 1914–1924* (Berlin, 1986), pp. 152–53.

45. Carl Delius, *Deutsche Demokratische Partei und Beamtenbesoldung* (Berlin, 1920). See also Kunz, *Civil Servants and the Politics of Inflation*, pp. 187–204.

46. Ibid., pp. 207–9.

47. For example, see the minutes of the DDP precinct committee for Stuttgart, 24 Mar. 1920, HSA Stuttgart, NL Haußmann, 103.

48. Minutes of the DVP managing committee, 28 Jan. 1920, BA: R 45 II/51/165–67.

49. For example, see Thiel, "Die deutsche Privatangestellten-Bewegung," *DS* 32, no. 17 (25 Apr. 1920): 273–81.

50. See Knebel to Stresemann, 30 Oct. 1919, BA: R 45 II/50/433–34, as well as Thiel's remarks before the DVP managing committee, 28 Jan. 1920, ibid., 51/166.

51. Memorandum on the meetings of the DVP election committee, 17 and 19 Apr. 1920, AA: NL Stresemann, 3089/213/138917–20. See also Flathmann to Stinnes, 19 Apr. 1920, ACDP: NL Stinnes, 002/4.

52. Flathmann to Stresemann, 4 May 1920, AA: NL Stresemann, 3089/212/138646–51.

53. Behrens to Stresemann, 4 May 1920, AA: NL Stresemann, 3089/212/138839–40.

54. Hartenstein, *Anfänge der Deutschen Volkspartei*, pp. 220–23.

55. Curatorium for the Reconstruction of German Economic Life to the DDP, 31

May 1920, SAA: NL Siemens, 4/Lf 646.

56. Report by Fischer before the DDP party council, 12 Dec. 1919, BA: R 45 III/10/52–64.

57. In this respect, see the letters from Kempkes, Campe, and Garnich to Siemens, 28 Apr. 1920, and from Garnich to the Curatorium for the Reconstruction of German Economic Life, 3 June 1920, both in SAA: NL Siemens, 4/Lf 646.

58. For an indication of such support, see Flathmann to Hugenberg, 16 June 1920, BA: NL Hugenberg, 15/37.

59. For example, see Vögler to Stresemann, 9 Sept. 1919, AA: NL Stresemann, 3088/207/137905–6, and Vögler to Hugenberg, 8 Dec. 1919, BA: NL Hugenberg, 49/36–38.

60. "Bericht über die Entwicklung der Organisation," [May 1920], BA: R 45 II/52/ 185–87. For further information, see the minutes of a meeting between Stresemann, Vögler, Garnich, Schütz, and Freundt, 11 Jan. 1920, AA: NL Stresemann, 3091/220/ 140012, as well as the report on the meeting of the DVP organizational and recruitment committee, 23 Jan. 1920, ibid., 140056–58.

61. Curtius's remarks before the DVP managing committee, 17 Apr. 1920, AA: NL Stresemann, 3089/213/138887.

62. For a general analysis of the outcome of the 1920 Reichstag elections, see Charles S. Maier, *Recasting Bourgeois Europe: Stabilization in France, Germany, and Italy in the Decade after World War I* (Princeton, 1975), pp. 171–72, and Gerhard A. Ritter, "Kontinuität und Umformung des deutschen Parteiensystems 1918–1920," in *Entstehung und Wandel der modernen Gesellschaft. Festschrift für Hans Rosenberg zum 65. Geburtstag*, ed. Gerhard A. Ritter (Berlin, 1970), pp. 367–76.

63. In this respect, see Heile, "Die Reichstagwahlen," *Die Hilfe* 26, no. 24 (10 June 1920): 354–56, and Erkelenz, "Lehren aus der Wahl," ibid., nos. 27–28 (5 and 15 July 1920): 406–7, 419–20, as well as Jansen's report in DDP, Reichsgeschäftsstelle, ed., *Bericht über die Verhandlungen des 2. ordentlichen Parteitages der Deutschen Demokratischen Partei, abgehalten in Nürnberg, 11.–14. Dezember 1920*, (Berlin, [1921]), pp. 14–19.

64. Ernst Portner, "Der Ansatz zur demokratischen Massenpartei im Deutschen Linksliberalismus," *VfZ* 13 (1965): 156–61.

65. For a more detailed analysis of the Democratic performance in the 1920 Reichstag elections, see Stephan, *Linksliberalismus*, pp. 173–75; Albertin, *Liberalismus und Demokratie*, pp. 153–58; and Peter M. Bowers, "The Failure of the German Democratic Party, 1918–1930" (Ph.D. dissertation, University of Pittsburgh, 1973), pp. 84–89.

66. On the political behavior of the independent middle class during the Weimar Republic, see Heinrich August Winkler, *Mittelstand, Demokratie und Nationalsozialismus. Die politische Entwicklung von Handwerk und Kleinhandel in der Weimarer Republik* (Cologne, 1972), pp. 121–39.

67. Albertin, *Liberalismus und Demokratie*, pp. 157–58.

68. Ibid., pp. 153–58. See also Hartenstein, *Anfänge der Deutschen Volkspartei*, pp. 237–51, as well as W. St. [Wolfgang Stresemann], "Betrachtungen zum Wahlergebnis," *DS* 32, no. 34 (22 Aug. 1920): 570–73.

CHAPTER SIX

1. M. Rainer Lepsius, "From Fragmented Party Democracy to Government by Emergency Decree and National Socialist Takeover: Germany," in *The Breakdown of Democratic Regimes: Europe*, ed. Juan J. Linz and Alfred Stephan (Baltimore, 1978), pp. 42–43.

2. Heinrich August Winkler, *Von der Revolution zur Stabilisierung. Arbeiter und Arbeiterbewegung in der Weimarer Republik 1918 bis 1924* (Berlin and Bonn, 1984), p. 360.

3. Ibid., pp. 361–63.

4. Rudolf Morsey, *Die Deutsche Zentrumspartei 1917–1923* (Düsseldorf, 1966), pp. 329–30. See also the minutes of the meeting of the Center Reichstag delegation, 16 June 1920, in Rudolf Morsey and Karsten Ruppert, eds., *Die Protokolle der Reichstagsfraktion der Deutschen Zentrumspartei 1920–1925* (Mainz, 1981), pp. 3–6.

5. Minutes of the DDP executive committee, 10 June 1920, BA: R 45 III/16/44–51.

6. Remarks by Schiffer in *DPK*, 12 June 1920, no. 124.

7. Statement by Petersen, ibid. 16 June 1920, no. 127.

8. *NLC*, 17 May 1920, no. 131.

9. See the detailed report of Ebert's meeting with representatives from the DDP, MSPD, and Center on the evening of 17 June 1920, in Haußmann's diary, HSA Stuttgart, NL Haußmann, 150.

10. See the entry in Haußmann's diary, 19 June 1920, HSA Stuttgart, NL Haußmann, 150. For the text of Erkelenz's resolution, see the minutes of the DDP Reichstag delegation, 19 June 1920, BA: NL Erkelenz, 136.

11. Minutes of the DDP party council, 22 June 1920, in Lothar Albertin, ed., *Linksliberalismus in der Weimarer Republik. Die Führungsgremien der Deutschen Demokratischen Partei und der Deutschen Staatspartei 1918–1933* (Düsseldorf, 1980), pp. 132–34. See also *DPK*, 23 June 1920, no. 133.

12. See Stresemann's remarks before the DVP managing committee, 16 June 1920, AA: NL Stresemann, 3090/215/139212–13.

13. Protocol of a conversation between the Reich Chancellery and the DVP's Johann Becker, 22 June 1920, in *Akten der Reichskanzlei: Das Kabinett Fehrenbach. 25. Juni 1920 bis 4. Mai 1921*, ed. Peter Wulf (Boppard am Rhein, 1972), pp. 6–7.

14. Protocol of a conversation with Heinze, Stresemann, and Quaatz, 23 June 1920, ibid., pp. 9–10.

15. For example, see the remarks by Erkelenz and Grund at a meeting of the DDP Reichstag delegation, 23 June 1920, BA: NL Erkelenz, 136.

16. Protocol of a conversation with Stresemann, Heinze, Quaatz, and Vögler, 24 June 1920, in *Das Kabinett Fehrenbach*, ed. Wulf, p. 12.

17. Winkler, *Von der Revolution zur Stabilisierung*, pp. 363–64.

18. Statement by Petersen in *DPK*, 16 June 1920, no. 127.

19. Petersen to his wife, 24 June 1920, SA Hamburg, NL Petersen, 20.

20. For an indication of the divisions that existed within the DVP, see the minutes of a joint meeting of the DVP Reichstag delegation, managing committee, and Prussian Landtag delegation, 26–27 July 1920, BA: R 45 II/53/367–92.

21. Peter Wulf, *Hugo Stinnes. Wirtschaft und Politik 1918–1924* (Stuttgart, 1979), p. 206.

22. On the background and course of the negotiations at Spa, see Charles S. Maier, *Recasting Bourgeois Europe: Stabilization in France, Germany, and Italy in the Decade after World War I* (Princeton, 1975), pp. 203–7.

23. For an excellent characterization of Stinnes's views on politics, see ibid., pp. 209–12.

24. Minutes of the DVP Reichstag delegation, managing committee, and Prussian Landtag delegation, 26–27 July 1920, BA: R 45 II/53/367–92.

25. Memorandum on the meeting of the DVP Reichstag delegation, 4 Aug. 1920, AA: NL Stresemann, 3090/214/139093–98.

26. Stresemann to Vögler, 5 Aug. 1920, and Stresemann to Stinnes, 5 Aug. 1920, AA: NL Stresemann, 3090/214/139101–3. See also Stinnes to Stresemann, 7 Aug. 1920, ibid., 139113–15, as well as Stresemann's reply of 16 Aug. 1920, ibid., 3088/209/138174–75.

27. Minutes of the DVP Reichstag delegation, managing committee, and Prussian Landtag delegation, 26–27 July 1920, BA: R 45 II/53/367–92.

28. Maier, *Recasting Bourgeois Europe*, pp. 140–42, 212–13. For further details, see Peter Wulf, "Die Auseinandersetzung um die Sozialisierung der Kohle in Deutschland 1920/21," *VfZ* 25 (1977): 46–98, as well as the relevant chapter in Wulf, *Stinnes*, pp. 221–41.

29. Entry in Koch-Weser's diary, 26 June 1920, BA: NL Koch-Weser, 27/155.

30. For further details, see Wulf, "Sozialisierung der Kohle," pp. 57–61.

31. Vögler to Stresemann, 28 Aug. 1920, AA: NL Stresemann, 3088/209/138193–94.

32. Stresemann to Vögler, 31 Aug. 1920, AA: NL Stresemann, 3088/209/138212.

33. See Schiffer's remarks at a meeting of representatives from the DDP, DVP, and Center Reichstag delegations, 2 Sept. 1920, AA: NL Stresemann, 3171/141/165754, as well as Schiffer's memorandum of 2 Sept. 1920, BA: NL Schiffer, 4/68. See also Stresemann to Kardorff, 10 Sept. 1920, BA: NL Kardorff, 13/158–59.

34. See Stresemann's remarks before the DVP managing committee, 13 Sept. 1920, BA: R 45 II/53/435–37, as well as his letter to Obheim, 8 Sept. 1920, AA: NL Stresemann, 3088/209/138287–89.

35. Stresemann to Riesser, 10 Sept. 1920, AA: NL Stresemann, 3088/209/138264–65. See also Stresemann's remarks before the DVP managing committee, 13 Sept. 1920, BA: R 45 II/53/433. For an indication of the dissension at the local levels of the DVP party organization, see Dingeldey to Stresemann, 10 Sept. 1920, AA: NL Stresemann, 3088/209/138292–97, and Bickes and Hammer (DVP Württemberg) to Stresemann, 10 Sept. 1920, ibid., 138309–10.

36. For the government's deliberations on the socialization question, see the minutes of the ministerial conference, 22 Sept. 1920, in *Das Kabinett Fehrenbach*, ed. Wulf, pp. 189–93.

37. *NLC*, 4 Oct. 1920, no. 218.

38. See the entry in Stresemann's diary, 1 Oct. 1920, AA: NL Stresemann, 3171/141/165851, as well as the note on the meeting in Weimar, 30 Sept.–1 Oct. 1920, ibid., 165759.

39. *NLC*, 5 Oct. 1920 (special edition). See also the entry in Stresemann's diary on the meeting of the DVP central executive committee, 5 Oct. 1920, AA: NL Stresemann, 3091/218/139787–97.

40. For further details, see Wulf, *Stinnes*, pp. 231–38. See also the report of Stinnes's speech before the National Economic Council at a meeting of the DVP industrial committee, 26 Oct. 1920, AA: NL Stresemann, 3171/141/165781–88.

41. Wulf, "Sozialisierung der Kohle," p. 76.

42. Ibid., pp. 76–96.

43. Entry in Stresemann's diary, 3 Nov. 1920, AA: NL Stresemann, 3171/141/ 165789.

44. Minutes of the DVP managing committee, 1–2 May 1919, BA: R 45 II/50/101– 5.

45. Thiel's remarks before the DVP managing committee, 28 Jan. 1920, BA: R 45 II/51/166.

46. Fritz Geisler, *Die nationale, wirtschaftsfriedliche Gewerkschaftsbewegung beim Wiederaufbau Deutschlands. Rede gehalten im National-Klub von 1919 in Hamburg am 31. August 1920* (Hamburg, [1920]), pp. 39–40.

47. Kloth, "Deutsche Volkspartei und Arbeitnehmerschaft," *DS* 32, no. 40 (3 Oct. 1920): 661–66.

48. Büttemeyer to Kloth, 9 Nov. 1920, BA: R 45 II/54/297.

49. Gustav Stresemann, *Deutsche Volkspartei und Regierungspolitik. Rede gehalten auf dem 3. Parteitag der Deutschen Volkspartei in Nürnberg am 3. Dezember 1920*, Flugschriften der Deutschen Volkspartei, no. 26 (Berlin, 1921), pp. 3–14.

50. Otto Thiel, *Die sozialen Aufgaben des Wiederaufbaues. Rede gehalten auf dem Nürnberger Parteitag am 4. Dezember 1920*, Flugschriften der Deutschen Volkspartei, no. 30 (Berlin, 1921). See also Thiel, "Die Sozialpolitik der Deutschen Volkspartei," *DS* 33, no. 2 (9 Jan. 1921): 29–32, and no. 3 (16 Jan. 1921): 40–48.

51. *NLC*, 6 Dec. 1920, no. 268.

52. Kempkes, "Die Organisation der Deutschen Volkspartei," in *Deutscher Aufbau. Nationalliberale Arbeit der Deutschen Volkspartei*, ed. Adolf Kempkes (Berlin, 1927), pp. 20–21.

53. Heinrich Beythien, *Der gewerbliche Mittelstand und die Deutsche Volkspartei. Rede, gehalten im Reichstag am 1.12.1920*, Flugschriften der Deutschen Volkspartei, no. 29 (Berlin, 1921).

CHAPTER SEVEN

1. See the debate at the meeting of the DDP executive committee, 10 June 1920, BA: R 45 III/16/44–51.

2. Minutes of the DDP party council, 12 June 1920, BA: R 45 II/16/52–53.

3. See Jansen's report on the DDP party organization in DDP, Reichgeschäftsstelle, ed., *Bericht über die Verhandlungen des 2. ordentlichen Parteitages der Deutschen Demokratischen Partei, abgehalten in Nürnberg, 11.–14. Dezember 1920* (Berlin, [1921]), pp. 16–21. See also *Der Demokrat* 1, no. 1 (14 Oct. 1920): 2–6, and the minutes of the DDP executive committee, 17 Oct. 1920, BA: R 45 III/16/66.

4. Memorandum of a meeting of DDP businessmen, 13 July 1920, SAA: NL Siemens, 4/Lf 555.

5. Minutes of the DDP executive committee, 27 Feb. 1920, BA: R 45 III/16/16. See also Kauffmann's remarks in DDP, Reichsausschuß für Handel, Industrie und Gewerbe beim Hauptvorstand der Deutschen Demokratischen Partei, ed., *Protokoll der Gründungsversammlung des Reichsausschusses für Handel, Industrie und Gewerbe beim Hauptvorstand der DDP vom 16. Oktober 1920* (Berlin, [1920]), p. 7.

6. Siemens and Zeitlin to the members of the provisional executive committee of the Metropolitan Berlin Chapter of the DDP's Association for Trade, Industry, and Commerce, 15 Apr. 1920, SAA: NL Siemens, 4/Lf 555.

7. DDP Reichsgeschäftsstelle to Kauffmann, 30 Apr. 1920, SAA: NL Siemens, 4/Lf 555.

8. See the "Richtlinien" presented by Kauffmann in DDP, Reichsausschuß für Handel, Industrie und Gewerbe beim Hauptvorstand der Deutschen Demokratischen Partei, *Protokoll der Gründungsversammlung*, pp. 9–10.

9. See Bunzel's remarks, ibid., p. 19.

10. See the discussion on the role of the artisanry, ibid., pp. 12–15.

11. *Der Demokrat* 1, no. 1 (14 Oct. 1920): 4.

12. See the speeches by Vogelstein, Fischer, and Siemens, in DDP, Reichsausschuß für Handel, Industrie und Gewerbe beim Hauptvorstand der Deutschen Demokratischen Partei, *Protokoll der Gründungsversammlung*, pp. 21–46, 55–58.

13. Siemens to Vögler, 21 Sept. 1920, BA: NL Silverberg, 135/38–47.

14. Haußmann to Koch-Weser, 10 Oct. 1920, HSA Stuttgart, NL Haußmann, 115.

15. Rudolf Ißberner, ed., *Demokratisches ABC-Buch* (Berlin, [1920]), pp. 156–57.

16. Minutes of the socialization committee of the DDP Reichstag delegation, 20, 27, and 29 Oct. 1920, BA: NL Gothein, 69/71–89. See also Koch-Weser's remarks in DDP, Reichsausschuß für Handel, Industrie und Gewerbe beim Hauptvorstand der Deutschen Demokratischen Partei, *Protokoll der Gründungsversammlung*, pp. 52–55.

17. Erkelenz to Gerland, 15 Sept. 1920, BA: NL Erkelenz, 127.

18. For the best discussion of these efforts, see Rennie William Brantz, "Anton Erkelenz, the Hirsch-Duncker Trade Unions, and the German Democratic Party" (Ph.D. dissertation, Ohio State University, 1973), pp. 122–27, 141–47.

19. See Hartmann's speech at the DDGB's official founding, 20 Nov. 1918, in *Zweck und Ziele des Deutsch-demokratischen Gewerkschaftsbundes*, Schriften des Deutsch-demokratischen Gewerkschaftsbundes, no. 1 (Berlin, 1919), pp. 8–14.

20. For further information, see Gewerkschaftsbund der Angestellten, ed., *Epochen der Angestellten-Bewegung 1774–1930* (Berlin, 1930), pp. 138–51, 164–73, as well as the recent secondary monograph by Heinz-Jürgen Priamus, *Angestellte und Demokratie. Die nationalliberale Angestelltenbewegung in der Weimarer Republik* (Stuttgart, 1979), pp. 72–82.

21. See Gustav Schneider, *Die Kraft der Angestellten, der Rätegedanke, die Eineits-Gewerkschaft. Betrachtungen über die Zukunft der Angestellten-Bewegung* (Leipzig, [1919]).

22. On the DHV's withdrawal from the efforts to create a national federation of white-collar unions, see Iris Hamel, *Völkischer Verband und nationale Gewerkschaft. Der Deutschnationale Handlungsgehilfen-Verband 1893–1933* (Hamburg, 1967), pp. 171–75.

23. Theodor Böhme, *Die christlich-nationale Gewerkschaft. Ihr Werden, Wesen und Wollen* (Stuttgart, 1930), p. 85.

24. Gewerkschaftsbund der Angestellten, *Epochen der Angestellten-Bewegung*, pp. 174–85, 217–21.

25. For the best statement of Gustav Schneider's political views, see his *Der Angestellte im demokratischen Volksstaat*, Flugschriften aus der Deutschen Demokratischen Partei, no. 4 (Leipzig, 1920), and *Staat und Gewerkschaft*, Schriftenfolge des Gewerkschaftsbundes der Angestellten, no. 8 (Berlin, [1921]).

26. Brantz, "Erkelenz," pp. 144–45.

27. Erkelenz, "Zweck und Ziele des Gewerkschaftsringes," in *1. Freiheitlich-nationaler Kongreß des Gewerkschaftsringes deutscher Arbeiter-, Angestellten- und Beamtenverbände 27. bis 29. November 1920 in Berlin*, ed. Ernst Lemmer ([Berlin, 1930]), pp. 12–33. See also Erkelenz, "Der Gewerkschaftsring," *Die Hilfe* 26, no. 41 (25 Nov. 1920): 628–29.

28. DDP, Reichs-Arbeitnehmerausschuß, ed., *Die Gründungstagung des Reichs-Arbeitnehmerausschusses der Deutschen Demokratischen Partei am 10. Dezember auf dem 2. ordentlichen Parteitag zu Nürnberg* (Berlin, [1921]), pp. 6–8.

29. The secondary literature on Rathenau is both extensive and uneven. For the best discussion of Rathenau's philosophical ideas and the influences that helped shape them, see Peter Berglar, *Walther Rathenau. Seine Zeit, sein Werk, seine Persönlichkeit* (Bremen, 1970), pp. 71–224. Also helpful is the sensitive essay by James Joll, "Walther Rathenau: Prophet without a Cause," in James Joll, *Intellectuals in Politics: Three Biographical Essays* (London, 1960), pp. 59–129, while a provocative analysis of Rathenau's social and political thought is to be found in Walter Struve, *Elites against Democracy: Leadership Ideals in Bourgeois Political Thought, 1890–1933* (Princeton, 1973), pp. 149–85.

30. For the details of Rathenau's life, see Harry Kessler, *Walther Rathenau: His Life and Work* (New York, 1930).

31. Rathenau, "Rede in der Versammlung zur Schaffung eines demokratischen Volksbundes," 16 Nov. 1918, in Walther Rathenau, *Gesammelte Reden* (Berlin, 1924), pp. 27–38. See also Kessler, *Rathenau*, pp. 248–50. By far the most detailed account of the brief history of the Democratic People's League is Hans Martin Barth, "Der demokratische Volksbund. Zu den Anfängen des politischen Engagements der Unternehmer der Berliner Elektroindustrie im November 1918," *Jahrbuch für die Geschichte Mittel- und Ostdeutschlands* 16/17 (1968/69): 254–66.

32. Barth, "Volksbund," pp. 254–55.

33. Ibid., pp. 256–57. See also the revealing letter from Siemens to Rathenau, 25 Nov. 1918, SAA: NL Siemens, 4/Lf 669.

34. Kessler, *Rathenau*, pp. 249–50.

35. Rathenau to Siemens, 26 Nov. 1918, and Rathenau to Bosch, 27 Nov. 1918, in Walther Rathenau, *Politische Briefe* (Dresden, 1929), pp. 217–21.

36. Kessler, *Rathenau*, pp. 250–51.

37. Rathenau, *Politische Briefe*, pp. 263–65.

38. Walther Rathenau, *Demokratische Entwicklung. Vortrag im Demokratischen Klub zu Berlin am 28. Juni 1920* (Berlin, 1920), pp. 26–28.

39. DDP, Reichgeschäftsstelle, *Bericht über die Verhandlungen des 2. ordentlichen*

Parteitages, pp. 106–24. See also "Leitsätze für die Wirtschaft," ibid., pp. 320–22. On the formulation of these recommendations, see the minutes of the business faction of the DDP Reichstag delegation, 28 Oct. 1920, SAA: NL Siemens, 4/Lf 555.

40. DDP, Reichsgeschäftsstelle, *Bericht über die Verhandlungen des 2. ordentlichen Parteitages*, pp. 125–40. See also Rathenau, *Gesammelte Reden*, pp. 123–49.

41. DDP, Reichsgeschäftsstelle, *Bericht über die Verhandlungen des 2. ordentlichen Parteitages*, pp. 141–52, 165–76.

42. In this respect, see Mosich, "Demokratie und Wirtschaft," *Das demokratische Deutschland* 3, no. 3 (23 Jan. 1921): 53–56.

43. Typical of such an attitude is Theodor Heuss, "Die Deutsche Demokratische Partei," in *Volk und Reich der Deutschen*, ed. Bernhard Harms, 3 vols. (Berlin, 1929), 2:104–21.

CHAPTER EIGHT

1. Adam Stegerwald, *Deutsche Lebensfragen. Vortrag gehalten auf dem 10. Kongreß der christlichen Gewerkschaften Deutschlands am 21. November 1920 in Essen* (Cologne, 1920), pp. 34–55.

2. For further details, see Larry Eugene Jones, "Adam Stegerwald und die Krise des deutschen Parteiensystems. Ein Beitrag zur Deutung des 'Essener Programms' vom November 1920," *VfZ* 27 (1979): 1–29, as well as William L. Patch, Jr., *Christian Trade Unions in the Weimar Republic, 1918–1933: The Failure of "Corporate Pluralism"* (New Haven, 1985), pp. 63–75. On the situation within the Center, see Rudolf Morsey, *Die Deutsche Zentrumspartei 1917–1923* (Düsseldorf, 1966), pp. 360–78.

3. "Arbeiterbewegung und Politik. Als Manuskript gedrückt für die Führer der christlich-nationalen Arbeiterbewegung," Sept. 1920, ACDP: NL Stegerwald.

4. Notes on the meeting of the Center national committee, 31 Oct.–1 Nov. 1920, BA: NL ten Hompel, 16.

5. Stegerwald, *Lebensfragen*, pp. 52–53.

6. Ibid., pp. 58–59.

7. On Thiel's defense of the "Essen Program," see his remarks at the meeting of the DVP managing committee, 1 Dec. 1920, BA: R 45 II/54/83–85, as well as his speech before the DVP's National White-Collar Committee, 5 Dec. 1920, in *NLC*, 6 Dec. 1920, no. 268.

8. Gustav Stresemann, *Deutsche Volkspartei und Regierungspolitik. Rede gehalten auf dem 3. Parteitag der Deutschen Volkspartei in Nürnberg am 3. Dezember 1920*, Flugschriften der Deutschen Volkspartei, no. 26 (Berlin, 1921), pp. 19–20.

9. For the Nationalist response, see Emil Kloth, *Parteien und Gewerkschaften* (Berlin, [1928]), p. 15.

10. On the fate of the "Essen Program," see Jones, "Stegerwald," pp. 21–27.

11. Entries in Stresemann's diary for 10 and 14 Oct. 1920, AA: NL Stresemann, 3171/142/165852.

12. On the outcome of the Saxon Landtag elections in Nov. 1920, see *Der Demokrat* 1, no. 6 (25 Nov. 1920): 95–98.

13. For further details, see the minutes of the DDP party council, 27 Nov. 1920, BA:

R 45 III/10/137–46, and the minutes of the DDP Reichstag delegation, 30 Nov. 1920, HSA Stuttgart, NL Haußmann, 25, as well as the entry in Koch-Weser's diary, 30 Nov. 1920, BA: NL Koch-Weser, 27/333.

14. Minutes of the DDP executive committee, 3 Dec. 1920, BA: R 45 III/16/78–79. See also Werner Stephan, *Aufstieg und Verfall des Linksliberalismus. Geschichte der Deutschen Demokratischen Partei* (Göttingen, 1973), pp. 187–89.

15. Gerland to Schiffer, 6 Dec. 1920, BA: NL Schiffer, 6/29–30.

16. See Petersen's remarks before the DDP executive committee, 3 Dec. 1920, BA: R 45 III/16/81–83, as well as Petersen, "Die deutsche Mitte," *Der Demokrat* 1, no. 2 (21 Oct. 1920): 22–26.

17. Memorandum from 14 Dec. 1920 of a conversation on the day before between Stresemann, Kardorff, and Freundt, AA: NL Stresemann, 3090/216/139371.

18. Oskar Hergt, *Auf zum Preußenkampf! Aus der Rede am Sonntag, den 9. Januar 1921, in der Philharmonie in Berlin*, Deutschnationale Flugschrift, no. 83 (Berlin, 1921), pp. 4–13.

19. For example, see the remarks of Böhme and Wachhorst de Wente from the DBB, 3 Dec. 1920, BA: R 45 III/16/85–87.

20. Petersen's speech before the DDP party council, 27 Nov. 1920, BA: R 45 III/10/137–40, and before the DDP executive committee, 3 Dec. 1920, ibid., 16/81–83.

21. In this respect, see Dominicus's speech in DDP, Reichsgeschäftsstelle, ed., *Bericht über die Verhandlungen des Preußenausschusses der Deutschen Demokratischen Partei am 28. November 1920 in Hannover* (Berlin, [1920]), pp. 11–25, as well as the report in *Der Demokrat* 1, no. 7 (2 Dec. 1920): 110–14.

22. In this respect, see the letter from the DVP managing committee to the party's Prussian district organizations, 28 Dec. 1920, BA: R 45 II/9/83–87, as well as DDP, Reichsgeschäftsstelle, ed., *Die Deutsche Volkspartei in der Preußischen Landesversammlung*, (Berlin, 1921), pp. 67–77.

23. For example, see E. H. Meyer, *Die Stellung des gewerblichen Mittelstandes nach den neuen Steuergesetzen. Vortrag gehalten auf Veranlassung der Handelskammer Berlin am 3. März 1921*, Zeit- und Streitfragen des deutschen Handwerks, no. 4 (Hanover, 1921), pp. 11–23.

24. For further details, see Karl Böhme, *Der Bauernstand in Knechtschaft und Freiheit* (Berlin, 1924), pp. 117–18, and Rudolf Ißberner, ed., *Demokratisches ABC-Buch* (Berlin, [1920]), pp. 183–85.

25. See Böhme's remarks in DDP, Reichsgeschäftsstelle, ed., *Bericht über die Verhandlungen des 2. ordentlichen Parteitages der Deutschen Demokratischen Partei, abgehalten in Nürnberg, 11.–14. Dezember 1920* (Berlin, [1921]), pp. 153–65.

26. DDP, Reichsgeschäftsstelle, *Bericht über die Verhandlungen des Preußenausschusses*, pp. 16–18.

27. *Deutscher Bauernbund* 13, no. 3 (21 Jan. 1921): 17–18.

28. See Kardorff to Stresemann, 10 Jan. 1921, BA: NL Kardorff, 13/168.

29. *NLC*, 10–11 Jan. 1921, nos. 7–8. See also Otto Boelitz, *Der nationale und kulturelle Beruf Preußens. Rede auf dem ersten Preußentag der Deutschen Volkspartei in Potsdam am 9. Januar 1921* (Berlin, 1922).

30. *NLC*, 17 Jan. 1921, no. 13.

31. Ibid., 2 Feb. 1921, no. 27.

32. For the details of these negotiations, see DVP, Reichsgeschäftsstelle, ed., *Die Bemühungen der Deutschen Volkspartei um die Bildung einer nationalen Einheitsfront* (Berlin, [1921]), pp. 1–5. See also Petersen to Stresemann, telegram, 3 Feb. 1921, AA: NL Stresemann, 3095/238/142728–29, and Haußmann to Koch-Weser, 2 Feb. 1921, HSA Stuttgart, NL Haußmann, 115, as well as Stresemann's letters to Hergt, 3 and 10 Feb. 1921, AA: NL Stresemann, 3094/237/142456–58, 142503–4.

33. [Stresemann], "Zur Frage der nationalen Einheitsfront," *DS* 33, no. 8 (20 Feb. 1921): 113–17.

34. Vögler to Hugenberg, 10 Feb. 1921, BA: NL Hugenberg, 49/8.

35. Undated memorandum of a conversation between Siemens and Vögler in the spring of 1921, SAA: NL Siemens, 4/Lf 646. Of the 3.9 million marks that the Curatorium allocated for use in the Prussian campaign, the DDP and DNVP received 1.1 million marks each and the DVP 1.3 million marks. The remaining 400,000 marks were distributed among various women's political clubs.

36. See the correspondence between Sorge and Kempkes, 4–6 Jan. 1921, BA: R 45 II/9/105–9.

37. Hugenberg to Vögler, 7 Feb. 1921, and to Cremer, 7 Feb. 1921, BA: NL Hugenberg, 49/9–10. See also Hugenberg to Flathmann, 11 and 17 Jan. 1921, ibid., 13/145–46, and Flathmann to Hugenberg, 7 and 10 Feb. 1921, ibid., 20/60–64. For further details, see Heidrun Holzbach, *Das "System Hugenberg." Die Organisation bürgerlicher Sammlungspolitik vor dem Aufstieg der NSDAP* (Stuttgart, 1981), pp. 70–98.

38. The statistics upon which this analysis was based were taken from Preußisches Statistisches Landesamt, ed., *Die Wahlen zum Preußischen Landtag am 20. Februar 1921 und 19. November 1922* (Berlin, 1924), pp. 4–5, 94–97. For further details, see Dietrich Orlow, *Weimar Prussia 1918–1925: The Unlikely Rock of Democracy* (Pittsburgh, 1986), pp. 19–20, 27–28, 30.

39. Heile, "Die preußischen Wahlen," *Die Hilfe* 27, no. 8 (25 Feb. 1921): 82–83.

40. Wolfgang Stresemann, "Preußenwahlen und Deutsche Volkspartei," *DS* 33, no. 10 (6 Mar. 1921): 145–52. See also the entry in Stresemann's diary, 21 Feb. 1921, AA: NL Stresemann, 3094/237/142503–4.

41. Wieland to Payer, 19 Mar. 1921, BA: NL Payer, 14/32–34.

42. See the minutes of the DDP executive committee, 26–27 Feb. 1921, BA: R 45 III/17/6–9, 12–18.

43. On the efforts to form a new government in Prussia in the spring of 1921, see Robert Jansen, *Die Regierungsbildung in Preußen* (Berlin, [1921]). See also the account in Orlow, *Weimar Prussia*, pp. 77–81.

44. See the memorandum of Stresemann's conversation with Fehrenbach, 21 Feb. 1921, as well as the minutes of the meeting between representatives of the Center, DDP, and DVP, 22 Feb. 1921, AA: NL Stresemann, 3094/237/142496–502.

45. Stresemann to Schiffer, 24 Feb. 1921, BA: NL Schiffer, 6/127.

46. Schiffer to Stresemann, 25 Feb. 1921, BA: NL Schiffer, 6/128.

47. Memorandum of a conversation between spokesmen for the DVP and DNVP, 2 Mar. 1921, AA: NL Stresemann, 3094/237/142533–36. See also Hergt to Stresemann, 25 Feb. 1921, ibid., 143520–21.

48. See Stresemann's report to the DVP managing committee, 8 Mar. 1921, AA: NL Stresemann, 3094/237/142551–53.

49. For further details, see Jansen, *Regierungsbildung*, pp. 14–15. For the DVP's position, see the statement from 9 Mar. 1921, AA: NL Stresemann, 3094/237/142566–69.

CHAPTER NINE

1. Rauch to Stresemann, 30 Mar. 1921, AA: NL Stresemann, 3094/237/142250–52. See also the debate at the meeting of the DVP managing committee, 8 Mar. 1921, ibid., 142551–65.

2. Minutes of the DDP Reichstag delegation, 7 Mar. 1921, HSA Stuttgart, NL Haußmann, 25.

3. On the last days of the Fehrenbach government, see the entries in Koch-Weser's diary, 23 Apr.–5 May 1921, BA: NL Koch-Weser, 27/459–87.

4. For the fullest discussion of Stresemann's efforts to form a new government in the spring of 1921, see Henry Ashby Turner, Jr., *Stresemann and the Politics of the Weimar Republic* (Princeton, 1963), pp. 84–88.

5. Stresemann's memorandum on the period from 23 Apr.–1 May 1921, AA: NL Stresemann, 3094/234/141927–29. See also the list of prospective cabinet members in Stresemann's own handwriting, ibid., 141963.

6. Entry in Koch-Weser's diary, 9 May 1921, BA: NL Koch-Weser, 27/511.

7. Memorandum by Stresemann entitled "Ultimatum, deutsche Volkspartei und Regierungsbildung," [July 1921], AA: NL Stresemann, 3094/235/141983–85.

8. F. R. [Felix Rauch], "Deutsche Volkspartei, Ultimatum und Regierung Wirth," *DS* 33, no. 23 (5 June 1921): 361–67.

9. *NLC*, 11 May 1921, no. 106.

10. *Stenographische Berichte über die Verhandlungen des Reichstags*, 349:3652–56. For their motives, see the statements by Heinze, Rheinbaben, Kardorff, and Thiel at a meeting of the DVP central executive committee, 11 June 1921, in a special edition of *NLC*, 11 June 1921. For an indication of the sentiment of the DVP's right wing, see Quaatz, "Die Kapitulation vom 10. Mai," *Deutsche Zeitung*, 26 May 1921, no. 238.

11. Minutes of the DDP Reichstag delegation, 5 May 1921, HSA Stuttgart, NL Haußmann, 63. See also the entry in Koch-Weser's diary, 5 May 1921, BA: NL Koch-Weser, 27/485–89.

12. Minutes of the DDP Reichstag delegation, 9 May 1921, HSA Stuttgart, NL Haußmann, 63. For a full litany of the arguments that Haußmann cited in defense of his position, see the manuscript of his speech, "Das deutsche Volk hätte das Ultimatum von London vom 5. Mai 1921 nicht annehmen sollen," before the Stuttgart DDP, 21 May 1921, ibid., 102.

13. Minutes of the DDP Reichstag delegation, evening of 9 May 1921, HSA Stuttgart, NL Haußmann, 63.

14. DDP, Reichsgeschäftsstelle, ed., *Ultimatum und Regierungsbildung. Die Haltung der Deutschen Demokratischen Partei* (Berlin, [1921]), pp. 47–48. See also Külz,

"Das Ultimatum und die Demokratische Partei," *Das demokratische Deutschland* 3, nos. 19/20 (15 May 1921): 425–28.

15. *Der Demokrat* 2, no. 19 (12 May 1921): 369–73.

16. On the formation of the Wirth government, see Ernst Laubach, *Die Politik der Kabinette Wirth 1921–1922* (Lübeck and Hamburg, 1968), pp. 21–31, as well as Rudolf Morsey, *Die Deutsche Zentrumspartei 1917–1923* (Düsseldorf, 1966), pp. 379–86.

17. For a brief characterization of Wirth, see Laubach, *Kabinette Wirth*, pp. 26–29.

18. For further details, see Charles S. Maier, *Recasting Bourgeois Europe: Stabilization in France, Germany, and Italy in the Decade after World War I* (Princeton, 1975), pp. 249–55. See also Joseph Wirth, *Reden während der Kanzlerschaft* (Berlin, 1925), pp. 39–65.

19. Entry in Koch-Weser's diary, 13 May 1921, BA: NL Koch-Weser, 27/522.

20. For example, see Stubmann, "Von der Ökonomik des Ultimatums," *Das demokratische Deutschland* 3, no. 22 (5 June 1921): 481–87, and Becker, "Ultimatum und Reichsfinanzen," *DS* 33, no. 26 (26 June 1921): 426–33.

21. Stresemann and Runkel to the members of the DVP Reichstag delegation, 12 May 1921, AA: NL Stresemann, 3094/235/142110. Such sentiment was particularly strong among the industrial interests that constituted the nucleus of the DVP's right wing. See Sorge to Stresemann, 13 May 1921, ibid., 142119–20.

22. Entry in Koch-Weser's diary, 13 May 1921, BA: NL Koch-Weser, 27/519–20. See also Petersen's speech before the DDP executive committee, 13 June 1921, BA: R 45/III/17/46.

23. Entry in Koch-Weser's diary, 13 May 1921, BA: NL Koch-Weser, 27/520.

24. Ibid., 521–23. See also DDP, Reichsgeschäftsstelle, *Ultimatum und Regierungsbildung*, pp. 19–21.

25. *Der Demokrat* 2, no. 19 (12 May 1921): 369–73.

26. In particular, see the criticism that was directed at the DDP Reichstag delegation at a meeting of the DDP executive committee, 13 June 1921, BA: R 45 III/17/46–49.

27. On Rathenau's appointment, see Laubach, *Kabinette Wirth*, pp. 34–37, and David Felix, *Walther Rathenau and the Weimar Republic: The Politics of Reparations* (Baltimore, 1971), pp. 64–66.

28. See the minutes of the DDP Reichstag delegation, 1 and 3 June 1921, HSA Stuttgart, NL Haußmann, 25. See also Stresemann's defense of the DVP's refusal to enter the Wirth government at a meeting of the DVP central executive committee, 11 June 1921, in a special edition of *NLC*, 11 June 1921.

29. [Stresemann], "Reichsregierung und Preußenregierung," *DS* 33, no. 24 (12 June 1921): 377–80.

30. Note by Stresemann, 4 June 1921, AA: NL Stresemann, 3109/232/141586–87.

31. Wirth, *Reden*, pp. 109–30. See also the cabinet minutes of 29 June 1921, in *Akten der Reichskanzlei: Die Kabinette Wirth I und II. 10. Mai 1921 bis 26. Oktober 1921. 26. Oktober 1921 bis 22. November 1922*, ed. Ingrid Schulze-Bidlingmaier, 2 vols. (Boppard am Rhein, 1973), 1:115–19.

32. For further details, see Maier, *Recasting Bourgeois Europe*, pp. 249–53.

33. On the deliberations within the DVP leadership, see Leidig to Stresemann, 21

Aug. 1921, and Stresemann to Leidig, 7 Sept. 1921, AA: NL Stresemann, 3109/231/
141378–88. On the efforts of the DVP's left wing to influence party policy, see Heinze
to Kardorff, 26 July 1921, BA: NL Kardorff, 10/33–34, and Raumer to Kardorff, 29
July 1921, ibid., 12/86–90. For a detailed analysis of the efforts to form a government
of the "Great Coalition" in the fall of 1921, see Lothar Albertin, "Die Verantwortung
der liberalen Parteien für das Scheitern der großen Koalition im Herbst 1921," *HZ* 205
(1967): 566–627.

34. Wirth, *Reden*, pp. 181–87. For the DVP's reaction, see Hepp to Stresemann, 4
Sept. 1921, AA: NL Stresemann, 3109/231/141458–60.

35. *NLC*, 5 Sept. 1921, no. 185. See also Stresemann, "Vor wichtigen Entscheidungen," *Vossische Zeitung*, 18 Aug. 1921, no. 404.

36. Stresemann to Hepp, 8 Sept. 1921, AA: NL Stresemann, 3109/231/141157–58.
See also the memorandum of Stresemann's conversation with Ebert, 31 Aug. 1921,
ibid., 141422–26.

37. For further details, see Albertin, "Verantwortung," pp. 580–83, and Maier,
Recasting Bourgeois Europe, pp. 249–53.

38. See Müller-Franken's remarks at a meeting of the leaders of the government
parties, 13 Sept. 1921, in *Die Kabinette Wirth*, ed. Schulze-Bidlingmaier, 1:256–58.

39. *Der Demokrat* 2, no. 37 (15 Sept. 1921): 709–10.

40. Albertin, "Verantwortung," pp. 583–85. For a fuller discussion of the Görlitz
congress and its significance in the development of the MSPD, see Heinrich August
Winkler, *Von der Revolution zur Stabilisierung. Arbeiter und Arbeiterbewegung in der
Weimarer Republik 1918 bis 1924* (Berlin and Bonn, 1984), pp. 434–54.

41. Petersen, "Die Politik der Mitte," *BTB*, 25 Sept. 1921, no. 452.

42. Raumer to Stresemann, 18 Sept. 1921, AA: NL Stresemann, 3109/230/141144–
48.

43. See the minutes of the DVP National Committee for Trade and Industry, 7 July
and 6 Sept. 1921, BA: R 45 II/60/79–107.

44. For further details, see Peter Wulf, *Hugo Stinnes. Wirtschaft und Politik 1918–
1924* (Stuttgart, 1979), pp. 271–76.

45. Memorandum of a meeting between representatives from the government and
the DVP, 28 Sept. 1921, in *Die Kabinette Wirth*, ed. Schulze-Bidlingmaier, 1:292–93.
See also the proposals that the DVP formulated for the government program, 28 Sept.
1921, AA: NL Stresemann, 3109/230/141249–50. On the situation within the DVP,
see Riesser to Stresemann, 29 Sept. 1921, ibid., 141251.

46. Wulf, *Stinnes*, pp. 275–76.

47. Minutes of the meeting of party leaders from the MSPD, Center, DDP, and DVP,
3 Oct. 1921, in *Die Kabinette Wirth*, ed. Schulze-Bidlingmaier, 1:297–302.

48. Minutes of the DVP managing committee, 3 Oct. 1921, AA: NL Stresemann,
3109/230/141263–69. See also Arning to Stresemann, 15 Oct. 1921, ibid., 3093/225/
140545–49.

49. Stresemann to Duisberg, 15 Oct. 1921, AA: NL Stresemann, 3093/225/140551–
53.

50. Laubach, *Kabinette Wirth*, pp. 93–97.

51. Cabinet minutes of 10 and 12 Oct. 1921, in *Die Kabinette Wirth*, ed. Schulze-
Bidlingmaier, 1:311–17. See also Felix, *Rathenau*, p. 103.

52. Minutes of a meeting of the DDP leadership, 13 Oct. 1921, BA: R 45 III/17/63–69. See also Haußmann's notes on the meeting, as well as the draft of his letter to Wirth, 13 Oct. 1921, both in HSA Stuttgart, NL Haußmann, 64. For further details, see Albertin, "Verantwortung," pp. 592–601, and Jürgen C. Hess, *"Das ganze Deutschland soll es sein." Demokratischer Nationalismus in der Weimarer Republik am Beispiel der Deutschen Demokratischen Partei* (Stuttgart, 1978), pp. 140–42.

53. Sorge to Stresemann, 17 Oct. 1921, AA: NL Stresemann, 3093/225/140554–61. See also Gildemeister, "Illusions-Politik!," *Das Bayernblatt* 1, no. 29 (22 Oct. 1921): 1–2.

54. Rauch to Arning, 20 Oct. 1921, AA: NL Stresemann, 3093/225/140586–89.

55. Petersen to his wife, 20–21 Oct. 1921, SA Hamburg, NL Petersen, 20.

56. Ibid. See also the minutes of the DDP Reichstag delegation, 20–21 Oct. 1921, HSA Stuttgart, NL Haußmann, 64.

57. Minutes of the meeting of the interfractional committee, 22 Oct. 1921, in *Die Kabinette Wirth*, ed. Schulze-Bidlingmaier, 1:335–37. See also Haußmann's notes on this meeting, HSA Stuttgart, NL Haußmann, 64. The DDP had finalized its position at a meeting of the Reichstag delegation earlier that morning.

58. Friedrich Weinhausen, *Demokraten und Oberschlesische Krisis* (Berlin, [1921]), pp. 7–9.

59. Ibid., pp. 9–10. See also the text of the agreement between Kempkes, Koch-Weser, Petersen, and Stresemann, 23 Oct. 1921, AA: NL Stresemann, 3093/225/140615.

60. On the meeting with Ebert on 24 Oct. 1921, see the detailed report by Petersen and Koch-Weser before the DDP Reichstag delegation, 25 Oct. 1921, HSA Stuttgart, NL Haußmann, 64. See also Petersen, "Die oberschlesische Entscheidung und die gegenwärtige Krise," *Das demokratische Deutschland* 3, no. 45 (10 Nov. 1921): 989–96.

61. *NLC*, 25 Oct. 1921, no. 224. For a tortured defense of the DVP's position, see Kempkes, "Zur politischen Lage," *DS* 33, no. 44 (30 Oct. 1921): 713–17.

62. Stresemann to Ebert, 25 Oct. 1921, AA: NL Stresemann, 3093/225/140622–23.

63. Minutes of the DDP Reichstag delegation, 25 Oct. 1921, HSA Stuttgart, NL Haußmann, 64. See also Weinhausen, "Warum die Demokraten aus der Regierung ausgetreten sind," *Der Demokrat* 2, no. 43 (27 Oct. 1921): 842–44.

64. Minutes of the DDP Reichstag delegation, 26 Oct. 1921, HSA Stuttgart, NL Haußmann, 64. On the composition of the second Wirth government, see Laubach, *Kabinette Wirth*, pp. 105–7.

65. See Schücking's statement in the Reichstag, 26 Oct. 1921, quoted in Weinhausen, *Demokraten*, p. 13.

66. Rathenau to Koch-Weser, 31 Oct. 1921, BA: NL Koch-Weser, 74/37–39, reprinted in Walther Rathenau, *Politische Briefe* (Dresden, 1929), pp. 315–17.

67. See the criticism of Schiffer's action in Hamm to Schiffer, 28 Oct. 1921, BA: NL Schiffer, 6/123–24.

68. For further details, see Albertin, "Verantwortung," pp. 607–10; Maier, *Recasting Bourgeois Europe*, pp. 262–66; and Wulf, *Stinnes*, pp. 280–93.

CHAPTER TEN

1. Martin Spahn, *Der Weg zur deutschen Rechten. Rede auf dem dritten Parteitag der Deutschnationalen Volkspartei in München am 2. September 1921*, Deutschnationale Flugschrift, no. 115 (Berlin, 1921).

2. Karl Helfferich, *Die Lage der deutschen Finanzen. Rede auf dem 3. deutschnationalen Parteitag in München am 3. September 1921*, Deutschnationale Flugschrift, no. 121 (Berlin, 1921). For a more thorough discussion of Helfferich's polemics against the Wirth government, see John G. Williamson, *Karl Helfferich, 1872–1924. Economist, Financier, Politician* (Princeton, 1977), pp. 344–64.

3. For example, see Stresemann to Hergt, 23 June and 16 Aug. 1921, AA: NL Stresemann, 3109/233/141834–35, 141838–40, as well as Hilger to Stresemann, 28 Aug. 1921, ibid., 141851–52.

4. Stresemann, "Rechtsblock oder Politik der Mitte?," *NLC*, 16 Sept. 1921, no. 194.

5. For an indication of Stinnes's hostility to the policy of fulfillment, see his scathing indictment of the Wiesbaden agreement which Rathenau had concluded with France on the payment of reparations in kind in Stinnes to Rathenau, 19 Oct. 1921, AA: NL Stresemann, 3093/225/140573–75.

6. For further details, see Stresemann to Stahlknecht, 21 Oct. 1921, AA: NL Stresemann, 3093/225/140590, and Rose to Stresemann, 21 and 28 Oct. 1921, ibid., 140591–92, 140595–98.

7. Stresemann to Rose, 22 Oct. 1921, AA: NL Stresemann, 3093/225/140593–94.

8. Entry in Stresemann's diary, 21 Nov. 1921, in Gustav Stresemann, *Vermächtnis. Der Nachlaß in drei Bänden*, ed. Henry Bernhard, 3 vols. (Berlin, 1932–33), 1:21.

9. *Vossische Zeitung*, 2 Dec. 1921, no. 567.

10. Speech by Kaiser before the DVP party congress in Stuttgart, 1 Dec. 1921, AA: NL Stresemann, 3093/229/141108–15. See also the report in the *Vossische Zeitung*, 2 Dec. 1921, no. 567.

11. Stresemann, "Die politische Lage. Rede auf dem Parteitag der Deutschen Volkspartei in Stuttgart am 1. Dezember," *DS* 33, no. 51 (18 Dec. 1921): 845–59.

12. *Vossische Zeitung*, 2 Dec. 1921, no. 567. See also Biermann of the DVP organization in Bremen to Stresemann, 3 Dec. 1921, AA: NL Stresemann, 3093/225/140668–69.

13. Cohnstaedt to Payer, 23 Aug. 1921, BA: NL Payer, 14/55–56.

14. Erkelenz's handwritten draft of the new party's political program, 3 May 1921, BA: NL Erkelenz, 136. See also Erkelenz, "Wie schafft man eine Erfüllungsmehrheit?," *Die Hilfe* 27, no. 19 (5 July 1921): 291–92.

15. See the entry in Koch-Weser's diary, 13 May 1921, BA: NL Koch-Weser, 27/524–27, as well as Haußmann's notes on the meeting of the DDP Reichstag delegation, 11 May 1921, HSA Stuttgart, NL Haußmann, 25.

16. For example, see the articles by Cohnstaedt, "Deutsche Mittelpartei," *FZ*, 10 July 1921, no. 504, and "Erfüllungsmehrheit und Parteifragen," *Die Hilfe* 27, no. 22 (5 Aug. 1921): 340–41, as well as Erkelenz, "Tendenz der Parteientwicklung," ibid., no. 26 (25 Sept. 1921): 403–5.

17. Erkelenz to Gunkel, 8 Sept. 1921, BA: NL Erkelenz, 17/31.

18. For an analysis of the editorial policies of the *Frankfurter Zeitung*, see Modris Eksteins, "The Frankfurter Zeitung: Mirror of Weimar Democracy," *JCH* 6 (1971): 3–28, as well as the more exhaustive study of the German liberal press during the early years of the Weimar Republic by Werner Becker, *Demokratie des sozialen Rechts. Die politische Haltung der Frankfurter Zeitung, der Vossischen Zeitung und des Berliner Tageblatts 1918–1924* (Göttingen, 1971), pp. 53–118. For the most detailed discussion of these developments, see Rennie William Brantz, "Anton Erkelenz, the Hirsch-Duncker Trade Unions, and the German Democratic Party" (Ph.D. dissertation, Ohio State University, 1973), pp. 153–63.

19. See Cohnstaedt's remarks before the DDP party council, 27 Nov. 1920, BA: R 45 III/10/141.

20. Becker, *Demokratie des sozialen Rechts*, pp. 88–89.

21. Wieland to Payer, 19 Mar. 1921, BA: NL Payer, 14/32–34. See also Payer to Cohnstaedt, 26 Aug. 1921, ibid., 58–63, as well as Sparrer's remarks before the DDP executive committee, 11 Sept. 1921, in Lothar Albertin, ed., *Linksliberalismus in der Weimarer Republik. Die Führungsgremien der Deutschen Demokratischen Partei und der Deutschen Staatspartei 1918–1933* (Düsseldorf, 1980), p. 190.

22. Cohnstaedt to Erkelenz, 25 Aug. 1921, BA: NL Erkelenz, 16/281–82. See also Cohnstaedt to Payer, 23 Aug. and 2 Sept. 1921, BA: NL Payer, 14/55–56, 64–67.

23. Erkelenz to Cohnstaedt, 1 Sept. 1921, BA: NL Erkelenz, 17/5–6.

24. Anton Erkelenz, *Die Aufgaben der Arbeitnehmer im demokratischen Staat. Rede auf der Tagung des Reichs-Arbeitnehmerausschusses der D.D.P. am 18. September 1921 zu Berlin*, Schriften des Reichs-Arbeitnehmerausschusses der Deutschen Demokratischen Partei, no. 1 (Berlin, [1921]), pp. 17–23.

25. See Dahl's report in DDP, Reichs-Arbeitnehmerausschuß, ed., *Bericht über die Verhandlungen des 2. ordentlichen Tagung des Reichs-Arbeitnehmerausschusses der Deutschen Demokratischen Partei, abgehalten am 17. und 18. September 1921 in Berlin* (Berlin, [1921]), pp. 5–11, and Jansen's report in DDP, Reichsgeschäftsstelle, ed., *Bericht über die Verhandlungen des 3. (ordentlichen) Parteitages der Deutschen Demokratischen Partei, abgehalten in Bremen vom 12. bis. 14. November 1921 in den Gesamträumen des Parkhauses (Bürgerpark)* (Berlin, [1921]), pp. 11–13.

26. Erkelenz to Cohnstaedt, 16 Oct. 1921, BA: NL Erkelenz, 136.

27. Ibid. See also Cohnstaedt to Erkelenz, 19 Oct. 1921, ibid., 17/88–90.

28. For example, see Petersen and Fischer to Siemens, 13 Jan. 1921, and Fischer to Siemens, 17 July 1921, both in SAA: NL Siemens, 4/Lf 555.

29. Becker to Siemens, 27 Sept. 1921, SAA: NL Siemens, 4/Lf 555. See also the letters from the Hansa-Bund, Ortsverband Groß-Berlin, to Siemens, 9 Sept. 1921, and from Kopsch to Siemens, 24 Sept. 1921, ibid.

30. Erkelenz to Rathenau, 28 Oct. 1921, BA: NL Erkelenz, 17/100–101.

31. Cohnstaedt to Rathenau, 3 Nov. 1921, BA: NL Erkelenz, 17/111–14.

32. Rathenau to Koch-Weser, 31 Oct. 1921, BA: NL Koch-Weser, 74/37–39, reprinted in Walther Rathenau, *Politische Briefe* (Dresden, 1929), pp. 315–17.

33. Cohnstaedt to Erkelenz, 31 Oct. 1921, BA: NL Erkelenz, 17/106. See also Rathenau to Erkelenz, 31 Oct. 1921, ibid., 17/104–5, reprinted in Rathenau, *Politische Briefe*, pp. 317–18.

34. Cohnstaedt to Erkelenz, 7 Nov. 1921, BA: NL Erkelenz, 17/21.

35. Ibid.

36. For the text of Rathenau's speech, see DDP, Reichsgeschäftsstelle, *Bericht über die Verhandlungen des 3. Parteitages*, pp. 34–50, as well as Walther Rathenau, *Gesammelte Reden* (Berlin, 1924), pp. 331–57. See also Werner Stephan, *Aufstieg und Verfall des Linksliberalismus. Geschichte der Deutschen Demokratischen Partei* (Göttingen, 1973), pp. 200–201.

37. DDP, Reichsgeschäftsstelle, *Bericht über die Verhandlungen des 3. Parteitages*, pp. 51–52, 63–72.

38. Ibid., p. 74.

39. For the text of this resolution, see ibid., pp. 82–83.

40. On the details of this compromise, see Cohnstaedt to Payer, 23 Nov. 1921, BA: NL Payer, 14/77–78.

41. DDP, Reichsgeschäftsstelle, *Bericht über die Verhandlungen des 3. Parteitages*, pp. 82–83. See also Stubmann, "Bremer Nachklang," *Das demokratische Deutschland* 3, no. 46 (17 Nov. 1921): 1013–19, as well as Stephan, *Linksliberalismus*, p. 206.

42. For example, see Cohnstaedt to Erkelenz, 28 and 29 Nov. 1921, BA: NL Erkelenz, 17/171, 176.

43. Gerland to Eggeling, 17 Nov. 1921, BA: NL Gerland, 6.

44. See the debate at the meeting of the DDP party council, 4 Dec. 1921, in Albertin, *Linksliberalismus*, pp. 231–33. See also Otto Keinath, Gustav Schneider, and Hermann Fischer, *Der Kampf um die neuen Steuern. Referate, gehalten im Parteiausschuß der D.D.P. am 4.12.21*, ed. Reichsgeschäftsstelle der Deutschen Demokratischen Partei (Berlin, [1922]). For the general background of this debate, see Charles S. Maier, *Recasting Bourgeois Europe: Stabilization in France, Germany, and Italy in the Decade after World War I* (Princeton, 1975), pp. 266–68.

45. For the details of these negotiations, see the official Democratic account by Robert Jansen, *Die große Koalition in Preußen* (Berlin, [1921]), as well as Dietrich Orlow, *Weimar Prussia 1918–1925: The Unlikely Rock of Democracy* (Pittsburgh, 1986), pp. 83–87.

46. Stephan, *Linksliberalismus*, pp. 201–3.

47. Raumer to Stresemann, 14 Dec. 1921, AA: NL Stresemann, 3093/229/141136–38.

48. Rauch to Kilburger, 16 Dec. 1921, AA: NL Stresemann, 3093/227/140838–39.

49. Stresemann to Becker, 18 Dec. 1921, and Stresemann to Bretschneider, 19 Dec. 1921, AA: NL Stresemann, 3093/227/140855–56, 140862–63.

50. Petersen to Spahn, 11 Jan. 1922, BA: NL Erkelenz, 18/35–36.

51. For further details, see Maier, *Recasting Bourgeois Europe*, pp. 269–70, and Ernst Laubach, *Die Politik der Kabinette Wirth 1921–1922* (Lübeck and Hamburg, 1968), pp. 145–48. For the DVP's position during the negotiations, see the letter from Jakob Riesser to his son, 29 Jan. 1922, BA: NL Riesser (Kleine Erwerbung 549), 1/5.

52. Joseph Wirth, *Reden während der Kanzlerschaft* (Berlin, 1925), pp. 258–60.

53. See Fischer, "Die Demokraten und das Steuerkompromiß," *Der Demokrat* 3, no. 5 (2 Feb. 1922): 70–73.

54. For example, see Petersen, "Steuerkompromiß und Regierungsbildung," *Hamburger Fremdenblatt*, 2 Feb. 1922, no. 56.

55. For example, see Rathenau to Nuschke, 16 Jan. 1922, in Rathenau, *Politische Briefe*, pp. 323–24.

56. Petersen to Wirth, 11 Jan. 1922, BA: NL Erkelenz, 18/33–34.

57. Petersen to his wife, 21 Jan. 1922, SA Hamburg, NL Petersen, 20. See also Petersen's remarks before the DDP executive committee, 22 Jan. 1922, BA: R 45 III/18/21. On Rathenau's accomplishments at Cannes, see David Felix, *Walther Rathenau and the Weimar Republic: The Politics of Reparations* (Baltimore, 1971), pp. 120–23.

58. Riesser to his son, 29 Jan. 1922, BA: NL Riesser (Kleine Erwerbung 549), 1/5. See also Johann Becker, *Steuerkompromiß und Deutsche Volkspartei*, Flugschriften der Deutschen Volkspartei, no. 41 (Berlin, 1922), pp. 28–30.

59. *Schulthess' europäischer Geschichtskalender* 63 (1922): 14–15. On the situation within the DVP, see Riesser to his son, 16 Feb. 1922, BA: NL Riesser (Kleine Erwerbung 549), 1/6–7. For the DDP's reaction to these developments, see Petersen, "Steuerkompromiß und Regierungsbildung."

60. For further details, see Andreas Kunz, *Civil Servants and the Politics of Inflation in Germany 1914–1924* (Berlin, 1986), pp. 281–329.

61. *Die Deutsche Demokratische Partei und der Beamtenstreik* (Berlin, [1922]), pp. 15–36.

62. Albrecht Morath, *Nachrevolutionäre Beamtenpolitik*, Flugschriften der Deutschen Volkspartei, no. 42 (Berlin, 1922), pp. 3–10.

63. Ibid., pp. 16–17. See also Riesser to his son, 16 Feb. 1922, BA: NL Riesser (Kleine Erwerbung 549), 1/6–7.

64. See the minutes of a meeting between Wirth and representatives from the government parties and DVP, 10 Feb. 1922, BA: NL ten Hompel, 16/14–17, as well as Koch-Weser's undated notes from Jan.–Feb. 1922, BA: NL Koch-Weser, 139.

65. For the text of this resolution, see DVP, Reichsgeschäftsstelle, ed., *Wahlhandbuch 1924* (Berlin, 1924), pp. 44–45. See also Schoch, "Kanzler Wirth und Deutsche Volkspartei," *Das Bayernblatt* 2, no. 7 (18 Feb. 1922): 1–3.

66. Wirth, *Reden*, p. 297.

67. *Stenographische Berichte über die Verhandlungen des Reichstags* 352:5884–86. For further details, see Kunz, *Civil Servants and the Politics of Inflation*, pp. 338–39, and Laubach, *Kabinette Wirth*, pp. 155–57.

68. *Das Bayernblatt* 2, no. 7 (18 Feb. 1922): 1. See also Stresemann to Rose, 1 Mar. 1922, AA: NL Stresemann, 3110/242/143223–24.

69. See Raumer to Stresemann, 23 Feb. 1922, AA: NL Stresemann, 3095/242/143210–13.

70. DVP, Reichsgeschäftsstelle, *Wahlhandbuch 1924*, pp. 45–46.

71. Laubach, *Kabinette Wirth*, pp. 157–59.

72. Wirth, *Reden*, pp. 249–63.

73. On the reasons for the failure of German fiscal policy during the early years of the Weimar Republic, see Peter-Christian Witt, "Finanzpolitik und sozialer Wandel in Krieg und Inflation," in *Industrielles System und politische Entwicklung in der Weimarer Republik. Verhandlungen des Internationalen Symposiums in Bochum vom 12.–17. Juni 1973*, ed. Hans Mommsen, Dietmar Petzina, and Bernd Weisbrod (Düsseldorf, 1974), pp. 416–24.

74. For example, see Pohlmann, "Das Steuerkompromiß," *Die Hilfe* 38, no. 8 (15 Mar. 1922): 117–18, and Mosich, "Grundsätzliches zur Frage der Großen Koalition," *Das demokratische Deutschland* 4, no. 9 (3 Mar. 1922): 193–98.

524 Notes to Pages 147–50

75. Stresemann, "Die Deutsche Volkspartei und die Reparationsforderungen der Entente," *DS* 34, no. 14 (2 Apr. 1922): 210–22. See also Riesser to his son, 30 Mar. 1922, BA: NL Riesser (Kleine Erwerbung 549), 1/10–11.

76. Osius to Stinnes, 10 Mar. 1922, ACDP: NL Stinnes, 022/3.

CHAPTER ELEVEN

1. On the diplomatic situation in the spring of 1922, see Charles S. Maier, *Recasting Bourgeois Europe: Stabilization in France, Germany, and Italy in the Decade after World War I* (Princeton, 1975), pp. 281–86. On German foreign policy at Genoa and Rapallo, see David Felix, *Walther Rathenau and the Weimar Republic: The Politics of Reparations* (Baltimore, 1971), pp. 127–46, and Carole Fink, *The Genoa Conference: European Diplomacy, 1921–1922* (Chapel Hill, 1984), pp. 177–208, 232–57.

2. In this respect, see Vogt to Petersen, 2 Feb. 1922, BA: NL Erkelenz, 127, and Vogt to Erkelenz, 7 Mar. 1922, ibid., 19/32–33.

3. For an indication of peasant unrest within the DDP, see Böhme's remarks before the DDP executive committee, 22 Jan. 1922, BA: R 45 III/18/22–25.

4. On the DDP's financial plight in the spring of 1922, see Fischer's report before the DDP executive committee, 22 Jan. 1922, BA: R 45 III/18/28–30, as well as the report from Jansen and Kuhle to Erkelenz, 28 Jan. 1922, BA: NL Erkelenz, 110.

5. Erkelenz to Siemens, 14 Jan. 1922, SAA: NL Siemens, 4/Lf 555.

6. Vogt to the DDP executive committee, 7 May 1922, BA: NL Erkelenz, 19/32–33.

7. Stresemann to Behn, 11 May 1922, AA: NL Stresemann, 2110/246/143679–80.

8. Stresemann to Raumer, 29 Apr. 1922, AA: NL Stresemann, 3110/243/143331–32.

9. Stresemann to Bücher, 29 Apr. 1922, AA: NL Stresemann, 3110/243/143344–46.

10. For a defense of the DVP's position in the spring of 1922, see Stresemann's letter to Prince Reuss, 9 May 1922, AA: NL Stresemann, 3110/246/143653–55.

11. DVP, Reichsgeschäftsstelle, ed. *Wahlhandbuch 1924* (Berlin, 1924), pp. 46–47. On developments within the DVP Reichstag delegation, see Riesser to his son, 28 May 1922, BA: NL Riesser (Kleine Erwerbung 549), 1/14–15, as well as Morath to Stresemann, 2 June 1922, AA: NL Stresemann, 3110/246/143728–32, and Raumer to Stresemann, 20 June 1922, ibid., 310/247/143773–79.

12. Stresemann to Obheim, 22 June 1922, AA: NL Stresemann, 3110/247/143780–84.

13. Joseph Wirth, *Reden während der Kanzlerschaft* (Berlin, 1925), p. 406.

14. For the best insight into Stresemann's thinking in the period following Rathenau's assassination, see his letters to Becker, 10 July 1922, AA: NL Stresemann, 3096/248/143927–28, and to Crown Prince Wilhelm, 21 July 1922, ibid., 143999–4004. On the situation within the DVP Reichstag delegation, see Riesser to his son, 27 June 1922, BA: NL Riesser (Kleine Erwerbung 549), 1/17–18. See also Henry Ashby Turner, Jr., *Stresemann and the Politics of the Weimar Republic* (Princeton, 1963), pp. 97–100.

15. For further information, see Gotthard Jasper, *Der Schutz der Republik. Studien zur staatlichen Sicherung der Demokratie in der Weimarer Republik 1922–1930* (Tübingen, 1963), pp. 56–59.

16. On the details of the government bill, see ibid., pp. 69–76.

17. Ibid., pp. 77–83.

18. Gustav Stresemann, *Schutz der Verfassung*, Flugschriften der Deutschen Volkspartei, no. 43 (Berlin, 1922), p. 12.

19. Thomas Mann, *Von deutscher Republik. Rede, gehalten am 15. Oktober 1922 im Beethovensaal zu Berlin* (Berlin, 1922).

20. This point has been argued most persuasively by Turner, *Stresemann*, pp. 110–13. For a dissenting viewpoint, see Annelise Thimme, "Gustav Stresemann. Legende und Wirklichkeit," *HZ* 181 (1956): 305–7.

21. For example, see Schrott-Matern to Stresemann, 8 July 1922, AA: NL Stresemann, 3096/248/143919–22.

22. Marx and Koch-Weser to the executive committee of the DVP Reichstag delegation, 6 July 1922, BA: NL Erkelenz, 136. See also *NLC*, 7 July 1922, no. 128. On efforts to broaden the base of the Wirth government following Rathenau's assassination, see Rudolf Morsey, *Die Deutsche Zentrumspartei 1917–1923* (Düsseldorf, 1966), pp. 457–67.

23. *NLC*, 8 July 1922, no. 129.

24. For further information, see the letter from Riesser to his son, 13 July 1922, BA: NL Riesser (Kleine Erwerbung 549), 1/22–23.

25. Heinrich August Winkler, *Von der Revolution zur Stabilisierung. Arbeiter und Arbeiterbewegung in der Weimarer Republik 1918 bis 1924* (Berlin and Bonn, 1984), pp. 486–501.

26. On Stegerwald and the origins of this proposal, see Thiel to Stresemann, 29 June 1922, AA: NL Stresemann, 3110/247/143838–39.

27. Stegerwald, "Vom Partei- und Koalitionswesen," *Germania*, 18 July 1922, no. 396. See also Adam Stegerwald, *Zusammenbruch und Wiederaufbau* (Berlin, 1922), pp. 16–25. For Brauns's point of view, see his two articles, "Deutschlands innenpolitisches Elend," *Germania*, 16 July 1922, no. 393, and "Die Verfassungspartei," ibid., 18 July 1922, no. 395, both reprinted in Heinrich Brauns, *Katholische Sozialpolitik im 20. Jahrhundert. Ausgewählte Aufsätze und Reden*, ed. Hubert Mockenhaupt (Mainz, 1976), pp. 101–7.

28. For the DVP's official response to the Center's proposal, see *NLC*, 17 July 1922, no. 135. For Stresemann's defense of closer political ties with the Center and DDP, see his speech before the DVP organization in Elberfeld, 22 July 1922, AA: NL Stresemann, 3096/248/144055–59, as well as his letter to Stinnes, 21 July 1922, ibid., 3096/249/144079–81.

29. Erkelenz, confidential circular no. 12 to the leaders of the DDP national organization, 17–18 July 1922, SAA: NL Siemens, 4/Lf 555.

30. DVP, Reichsgeschäftsstelle, *Wahlhandbuch 1924*, pp. 51–52. For details of the negotiations, see Petersen to Erkelenz, 28 July 1922, BA: NL Erkelenz, 127, and Erkelenz to Cohnstaedt, 2 Aug. 1922, ibid., 21/20–21.

31. In this respect, see Petersen's remarks before the DDP executive committee, 19 July 1922, BA: R 45 III/18/69, as well as Petersen, "Die Politik der Mitte," *Berliner*

Montagspost, 17 July 1922, no. 25, and Külz, "Die parlamentarische Arbeitsgemeinschaft," *Das demokratische Deutschland* 4, no. 40 (29 Sept. 1922): 937–42.

32. Erkelenz to Petersen, 24 July 1922, BA: NL Erkelenz, 20/247, and 1 Aug. 1922, ibid., 127. See also Rennie William Brantz, "Anton Erkelenz, the Hirsch-Duncker Trade Unions, and the German Democratic Party" (Ph.D. dissertation, Ohio State University, 1973), pp. 195–200.

33. Minutes of the DDP executive committee, 27 Sept. 1922, and the DDP party council, 8 Oct. 1922, in Lothar Albertin, ed., *Linksliberalismus in der Weimarer Republik. Die Führungsgremien der Deutschen Demokratischen Partei und der Deutschen Staatspartei 1918–1933* (Düsseldorf, 1980), pp. 273–76. See also Vogt to the DDP executive committee, 31 July 1922, BA: R 45 III/18/75, and Dahl to the labor representatives in the DDP party council, 20 Aug. 1922, BA: NL Erkelenz, 21/89.

34. Cohnstaedt to Erkelenz, 31 Aug. and 6 Sept. 1922, BA: NL Erkelenz, 21/111, 113.

35. Brantz, "Erkelenz," pp. 199–200. See also Erkelenz to Petersen, 12 Sept. 1922, BA: NL Erkelenz, 21/150–52, and Erkelenz to Liebig, 25 Sept. 1922, ibid., 21/180.

36. DDP, Reichsgeschäftsstelle, ed., *Bericht über die Verhandlungen des 4. ordentlichen Parteitages der Deutschen Demokratischen Partei, abgehalten in Elberfeld am 9. und 10. Oktober 1922 in den Gesamträumen der Stadthalle*, (Berlin, [1922]), pp. 59–60.

37. Ibid., pp. 8–10, 12–16.

38. Ibid., pp. 47–56.

39. In this respect, see Stinnes to Stresemann, 25 July and 7 Aug. 1922, AA: NL Stresemann, 3096/249/144084–86, 144123–25, as well as Stresemann to Dingeldey, 12 Aug. 1922, ibid., 3096/250/144197–200.

40. Thiel, "Wirtschaftliche Vereinigungen und politische Entwicklungsmöglichkeiten," *DS* 34, no. 32 (6 Aug. 1922): 501–7.

41. Geisler to Stresemann, 25 Aug. 1922, BA: R 45 II/37/133–35.

42. Stresemann to Kirschner, 1 Sept. 1922, AA: NL Stresemann, 3096/252/144303–8.

43. Dingeldey to Stresemann, 7 Aug. 1922, AA: NL Stresemann, 3096/250/144162–68.

44. Geisler, "Eine Warnung an die Deutsche Volkspartei," *Das freie Wort*, 10 Sept. 1922, no. 37.

45. *NLC*, 25 and 28 Sept. 1922, nos. 164–65. See also Stresemann to Helle, 15 Sept. 1922, AA: NL Stresemann, 3096/251/144378–79, and Otto Thiel, "Deutsche Volkspartei," in *Internationales Handwörterbuch des Gewerkschaftswesens*, ed. Ludwig Heyde, 2 vols. (Leipzig, 1931–32), 1:347–49.

46. In this respect, see Geisler to Heyl von Herrensheim, 6 Dec. 1922, BA: NL Dingeldey, 72/103. The final break between Geisler and the DVP did not materialize until the early spring of 1923. See *NLC*, 15 Mar. 1923, no. 22.

47. For example, see Ernst Müller-Meiningen, *Aus Bayerns schwersten Tagen. Erinnerungen und Betrachtungen aus der Revolutionszeit* (Berlin and Leipzig, 1924), pp. 247–48. For further information on the history of Bavarian liberalism during the early years of the Weimar Republic, see Joachim Riemann, "Der politische Liberalismus in der Krise der Revolution," in *Bayern im Umbruch. Die Revolution von 1918, ihr*

Voraussetzungen, ihr Verlauf und ihre Folgen, ed. Karl Bosl (Munich, 1969), pp. 165–99.

48. *Süddeutsche Demokratische Korrespondenz*, 9 June 1920, no. 128.

49. Müller-Meiningen, *Aus Bayerns schwersten Tagen*, pp. 244–50.

50. For example, see Hamm to Kahr, 31 Aug. 1921, BA: NL Gessler, 53/1–4, and Hamm to Wirth, 1 Sept. 1921, NL Hamm. On the background of this conflict, see Jasper, *Schutz der Republik*, pp. 34–56, and Werner Zimmermann, *Bayern und das Reich 1918–1923. Der bayerische Föderalismus zwischen Revolution und Reaktion* (Munich, 1953), pp. 79–125.

51. Hamm to Erkelenz, 16 Sept. 1921, NL Hamm.

52. See Hammerschmidt to Erkelenz, 29 Nov. 1921, BA: NL Erkelenz, 17/177, and Dirr to the DDP executive committee, 2 Dec. 1921, StA München, NL Dirr, 37. For the offending resolution, see DDP, Reichsgeschäftsstelle, ed., *Bericht über die Verhandlungen des 3. (ordentlichen) Parteitages der Deutschen Demokratischen Partei, abgehalten in Bremen vom 12. bis. 14. November 1921 in den Gesamträumen des Parkhauses (Bürgerpark)* (Berlin, [1921]), pp. 55–56.

53. For further details, see Ernst Laubach, *Die Politik der Kabinette Wirth 1921–1922* (Lübeck and Hamburg, 1968), pp. 263–69, and Jasper, *Schutz der Republik*, pp. 92–100.

54. For example, see Hamm to Lerchenfeld, 22 July 1922, NL Hamm, as well as Hamm's lengthy memorandum, "Aufzeichnungen über die bayerische Krise," 24 July 1922, BA: NL Erkelenz, 127.

55. *Süddeutsche Demokratische Korrespondenz*, 26 July 1922, no. 170.

56. For example, see Hammerschmidt to Erkelenz, 9 July 1922, and Dirr to Erkelenz, 13 and 18 July 1922, all in BA: NL Erkelenz, 127.

57. Dirr to Hamm, 16 Apr. 1923, NL Hamm.

58. Stresemann to Lerchenfeld, 11 July 1922, AA: NL Stresemann, 3096/248/143935–40.

59. Stresemann to Hamm, 1 Aug. 1922, AA: NL Stresemann, 3096/250/144145–46.

60. *Das Bayernblatt* 2, no. 31 (14 Aug. 1922): 2–4.

61. Bürger, "Die bayerischen Wahlen," *DS* 36, no. 8 (20 Apr. 1924): 122–26. See also Stresemann to Schoch, 9 Apr. 1924, AA: NL Stresemann, 3159/89/171932–33.

CHAPTER TWELVE

1. For the most valuable history of the German inflation, see Carl-Ludwig Holtfrerich, *Die deutsche Inflation 1914–1923. Ursachen und Folgen in internationaler Perspektive* (Berlin and New York, 1980). On the political aspects of the inflation, see Agnete von Specht, *Politische und wirtschaftliche Hintergründe der deutschen Inflation 1918–1923* (Bern, 1982). The short-term political consequences of the inflation have yet to be examined in all of their complexity, but for a preliminary effort in this direction, see Gerald D. Feldman, "Bayern und Sachsen in der Hyperinflation 1922–23," *HZ* 238 (1984): 569–609. On the social effects of the inflation, see Charles S. Maier, *Recasting Bourgeois Europe: Stabilization in France, Germany, and Italy in the*

Decade after World War I (Princeton, 1975), pp. 359–64; Constantino Bresciani-Turroni, *The Economics of Inflation: A Study of Currency Depreciation in Post-War Germany, 1914–1923*, trans. Millicent E. Sayers (London, 1937), pp. 286–333; and Karsten Laursen and Jorgen Pedersen, *The German Inflation 1918–1923* (Amsterdam, 1964), pp. 72–122, as well as the still-useful contemporary analysis by Franz Eulenberg, "Die sozialen Wirkungen der Währungsverhältnisse," *Jahrbücher für Nationalökonomie und Statistik* 122 (1924): 748–94.

2. Much of this and the following chapter has been taken from my forthcoming article, "Democracy and Liberalism in the German Inflation. The Crisis of a Political Movement, 1918–1924," in one of the next volumes in the series Beiträge zu Inflation und Wiederaufbau in Deutschland und Europa 1914–1924.

3. See Rathenau's remarks from 24 Jan. 1921, quoted in Holtfrerich, *Inflation*, p. 207.

4. On the concept of an "inflation consensus," see Charles S. Maier, "The Politics of Inflation in the Twentieth Century," in *The Political Economy of Inflation*, ed. Fred Hirsch and John H. Goldthorpe (Cambridge, Mass., 1978), pp. 37–72. On the situation in Germany, see Gerald D. Feldman, "The Political Economy of Germany's Relative Stabilization during the 1920/21 World Depression," in *Die deutsche Inflation. Eine Zwischenbilanz/The German Inflation Reconsidered: A Preliminary Balance*, ed. Gerald D. Feldman et al. (Berlin and New York, 1982), pp. 180–206.

5. For example, see Leidig to Stresemann, 25 Aug. 1921, AA: NL Stresemann, 3109/231/141378–86.

6. Rathenau before the DDP party congress in Bremen, 11 Nov. 1921, quoted in Maier, *Recasting Bourgeois Europe*, p. 359.

7. For example, see Stresemann to Zschorer, 5 Aug. 1922, AA: NL Stresemann, 3096/250/144158–59.

8. In particular, see Karl Helfferich, *Die Politik der Erfüllung* (Munich, 1922), pp. 81–97.

9. For further information, see Jansen's report in DDP, Reichsgeschäftsstelle, ed., *Bericht über die Verhandlungen des 3. (ordentlichen) Parteitages der Deutschen Demokratischen Partei, abgehalten in Bremen vom 12. bis. 14. November 1921 in den Gesamträumen des Parkhauses (Bürgerpark)* (Berlin, [1921]), pp. 18–19, and Werner Stephan, *Aufstieg und Verfall des Linksliberalismus. Geschichte der Deutschen Demokratischen Partei* (Göttingen, 1973), p. 222. On the outcome of the Berlin municipal elections, see Wolfgang Stresemann, "Die Stadtverordnetenwahlen," *DS* 33, no. 44 (30 Oct. 1921): 717–20.

10. See Fischer's report to the DDP party council on the state of party finances, 12 Dec. 1919, BA: R 45 III/10/54–64.

11. Fischer's report from 11 Dec. 1920, in DDP, Reichsgeschäftsstelle, ed., *Bericht über die Verhandlungen des 2. ordentlichen Parteitages der Deutschen Demokratischen Partei, abgehalten in Nürnberg, 11.–14. Dezember 1920* (Berlin, [1921]), pp. 22–26.

12. See the DDP's financial balance for 1921, appended to the letter from Jansen and Kuhle to Erkelenz, 28 Jan. 1922, BA: NL Erkelenz, 110.

13. See Fischer's statement before the DDP executive committee, 10 Nov. 1921,

BA: R 45 III/17/95–96, and to the DDP party council, 11 Nov. 1921, ibid., 11/78–79.

14. Minutes of the DDP party council, 11 Nov. 1921, BA: R 45 III/81–82. See also Erkelenz, "Parteifinanzen und Parteiorganisation," *Der Demokrat* 2, no. 50 (15 Dec. 1921): 977–80.

15. Jansen to Erkelenz, 18 and 27 Apr. 1922, BA: NL Erkelenz, 19/189–90, 204–6.

16. Erkelenz to the Association of DDP Party Employees, 6 Apr. 1922, BA: NL Erkelenz, 19/167–70.

17. For the DDP's budget and financial balance for 1922, see BA: NL Erkelenz, 110. For further information, see Fischer's circular of 18 Oct. 1922, SAA: NL Siemens, 4/Lf 555, as well as his report before the Elberfeld party congress in DDP, Reichsgeschäftsstelle, ed., *Bericht über die Verhandlungen des 4. ordentlichen Parteitages der Deutschen Demokratischen Partei, abgehalten in Elberfeld am 9. und 10. Oktober 1922 in den Gesamträumen der Stadthalle*, (Berlin, [1922]), pp. 67–68.

18. For example, see Kopsch to Stresemann, 26 Dec. 1919, AA: NL Stresemann, 3088/208/138158–61.

19. In this respect, see Fischer, "Die Demokraten und das Steuerkompromiß," *Der Demokrat* 3, no. 5 (2 Feb. 1922): 70–73, as well as the report of the conference held by the DDP's Council for the Middle Class in Berlin, 27 Nov. 1922, ibid., no. 51 (20 Dec. 1922): 630–31.

20. For the details of this vote, see the letter from the DDP Reichsgeschäftsstelle to Schücking, 26 Mar. 1922, BA: NL Schücking, 49. For the official party position, see Max Bahr, *Das Reichsmietengesetz* (Berlin, [1922]).

21. For further details, see Martin Schumacher, *Land und Politik. Eine Untersuchung über politische Parteien und agrarische Interessen 1914–1923* (Düsseldorf, 1978), pp. 445–53.

22. Karl Böhme, *Der Bauernstand in Knechtschaft und Freiheit* (Berlin, 1924), p. 118. See also Böhme, "Demokratie und Volkspartei," *Deutscher Bauernbund* 12, no. 39 (13 Nov. 1920): 323–24.

23. Böhme to Siemens, 1 Apr. 1921, SAA: NL Siemens, 4/Lf 555.

24. For a more detailed discussion of this problem, see Robert G. Moeller, "Winners as Losers in the German Inflation: Peasant Protest over the Controlled Economy, 1920–1923," in *Die deutsche Inflation/The German Inflation*, ed. Feldman et al., pp. 255–88.

25. *Deutscher Bauernbund* 12, no. 30 (20 Aug. 1920): 251. See also DDP, Reichsgeschäftsstelle, ed., *D.D.P. und Landwirtschaft*, Materialen zur demokratischen Politik, no. 84 (Berlin, 1924), pp. 2–3.

26. Moeller, "Winners as Losers," pp. 274–78.

27. See Böhme's speech before the DBB's national congress in Berlin, 28 May 1921, in *Deutscher Bauernbund* 13, no. 23 (10 June 1921): 187–93.

28. DDP, Reichsgeschäftsstelle, *D.D.P. und Landwirtschaft*, p. 3. See also *Deutscher Bauernbund* 13, no. 24 (17 June 1921): 199–200.

29. Erkelenz, "Zwangswirtschaft und Brotpreis," *Der Demokrat* 2, no. 31 (4 Aug. 1921): 601–4.

30. Böhme to Siemens, 4 Jan. 1922, SAA: NL Siemens, 4/Lf 555.

31. Minutes of the DDP executive committee, 22 Jan. 1922, BA: R 45 III/18/18–

530 *Notes to Pages 167–71*

30. See also Böhme's keynote address at a DBB congress in Berlin, 17 Feb. 1922, in *Deutscher Bauernbund* 14, no. 9 (3 Mar. 1922): 57–63, as well as Tantzen to Erkelenz, 10 Mar. 1922, BA: NL Erkelenz, 127.

32. For the DBB's position, see Böhme's speech from late May 1922 in *Deutscher Bauernbund* 14, no. 22 (2 June 1922): 166–68.

33. For example, see Josef Kaufhold, *Die Sünden der Demokratischen Partei und des Deutschen Bauernbundes an die Landwirtschaft*, Deutschnationale Flugschrift, no. 134 (Berlin, 1922).

34. On the outlines of this compromise, see DDP, Reichsgeschäftsstelle, *D.D.P. und Landwirtschaft*, pp. 4–8. On the political background of this compromise, see Gotthard Jasper, *Der Schutz der Republik. Studien zur staatlichen Sicherung der Demokratie in der Weimarer Republik 1922–1930* (Tübingen, 1963), pp. 77–78. On the divisions which this issue created within the DDP, see Cohnstaedt to Erkelenz, 19 June 1922, BA: NL Erkelenz, 20/55.

35. Rönneburg to Erkelenz, 26 June 1922, BA: NL Erkelenz, 127.

36. On Böhme's predicament, see Erkelenz to Tantzen, 19 June 1922, BA: NL Erkelenz, 20/56.

37. *Der Demokrat* 2, nos. 33/34a (6 Sept. 1922): 502.

38. Karl Delius, *Deutsche Demokratische Partei und Beamtenbesoldung* (Berlin, [1920]), pp. 3–7.

39. *Der Demokrat* 1, no. 11 (30 Dec. 1920): 181.

40. See Gerhard Vogt, ed., *Handbuch für die Mitglieder des Reichsausschusses der deutschen demokratischen Beamten, für Vorsitzende der Ortsbeamtenausschüsse und Vertrauenspersonen* (Berlin, 1925), pp. 5–6.

41. Organizational report by Jansen in DDP, Reichsgeschäftsstelle, *Bericht über die Verhandlungen des 3. Parteitages*, p. 13.

42. *Der Demokrat* 2, no. 47 (24 Nov. 1921): 930–32. See also Vogt, "Was erwarten die Beamten vom Parteitage?," ibid., no. 44 (3 Nov. 1921): 859–61, as well as Vogt's speech, "Lebensfragen der Beamtenschaft," in DDP, Reichsgeschäftsstelle, *Bericht über die Verhandlungen des 3. Parteitages*, pp. 127–29. For an indication of civil servant unrest within the DDP, see Keller to Erkelenz, 27 Aug. 1921, BA: NL Erkelenz, 26/286.

43. For a Democratic analysis of the conditions that led to the outbreak of the strike, see DDP, Reichsgeschäftsstelle, ed., *Die Deutsche Demokratische Partei und der Beamtenstreik* (Berlin, n.d. [1922]), pp. 15–18.

44. Ibid., pp. 28–29.

45. Vogt to Petersen, 2 Feb. 1922, BA: NL Erkelenz, 127.

46. Vogt to the DDP executive committee, 7 Mar. 1922, BA: NL Erkelenz, 19/32–33.

47. Delius, "Die neueste Besoldungsregelung," *Der Demokrat* 3, no. 16 (20 Apr. 1922): 249–55. See also Schuldt's recommendations for a reform of Germany's civil servant salary structure at the DDP's Civil Servant Day in Berlin, 22–23 Apr. 1922, ibid., no. 17 (27 Apr. 1922): 269–73, as well as Karl Delius, *Die Stellung der Beamtenschaft im neuen Staat* (Berlin, [1922]).

48. In this respect, see Fischer's speech in Hermann Fischer and Oskar Meyer, *Die Politik des Hansa-Bundes. Programmreden gehalten auf der Haupt-Versammlung des*

Hansa-Bundes in Nürnberg vom 5. bis 7. Mai 1922 (n.p., [1922]), pp. 9–24, and Keinath's address at the DDP's Elberfeld party congress in DDP, Reichsgeschäftsstelle, *Bericht über die Verhandlungen des 4. Parteitages*, pp. 47–56.

49. See the correspondence between Wieland and Bücher, 5–15 Aug. 1922, appended to Bücher to Siemens, 15 Aug. 1922, SAA: NL Siemens, 4/Lf 555.

50. For further details, see Gerald D. Feldman, *Iron and Steel in the German Inflation, 1916–1923* (Princeton, 1977), pp. 319–27.

51. For the program drafted by Wieland and his associates in the DDP, see the resolution of the DDP's National Council for Trade, Industry, and Commerce, n.d., appended to Mosich to Siemens, 8 Nov. 1922, SAA: NL Siemens, 4/Lf 736. On the details of the RDI's draft, see Feldman, *Iron and Steel*, pp. 321–27.

52. *Deutscher Geschichtskalender* 38 (1922): A, 287–88.

53. Vogt to the DDP Reichstag delegation, 20 Nov. 1922, BA: NL Erkelenz, 22/185.

54. Minutes of the DDP party council, 26 Nov. 1922, BA: R 45 III/11/201–06.

CHAPTER THIRTEEN

1. *NLC*, 21 Sept. 1921, no. 197. See also Leidig to Stresemann, 25 Aug. 1921, AA: NL Stresemann, 3109/231/141378–86.

2. *NLC*, 14 June 1921, no. 132.

3. Ibid., 2, 5, and 6 Sept. 1921, nos. 183, 185–86.

4. Minutes of the DVP managing committee, 2 Nov. 1921, AA: NL Stresemann, 3093/225/140643–44. See also Adolf Kempkes, "Die Organisation der Deutschen Volkspartei," in *Deutscher Aufbau. Nationalliberale Arbeit der Deutschen Volkspartei*, ed. Adolf Kempkes (Berlin, 1927), pp. 20–21.

5. See the budget and balance sheets for the DDP from 1921, 1922, and 1923, BA: NL Erkelenz, 110.

6. See also Otto Hugo, *Der Mittelstand und die Deutsche Volkspartei* (Berlin, 1919).

7. Heinrich Beythien, *Der gewerbliche Mittelstand und die Deutsche Volkspartei. Rede, gehalten im Reichstag am 1.12.1920*, Flugschriften der Deutschen Volkspartei, no. 21 (Berlin, 1921).

8. Maretzky, "Die Zwangswirtschaft im Wohnungswesen und die Reichsmietsteuern," *NLC*, 4 July 1921, no. 149.

9. See Scholz, "Steuerproblem und Mittelstand," *Deutsche Handels-Warte* 10, no. 6 (Mar. 1922): 145–48, and Most, "Einzelhandel und Gewerbesteuer," ibid., 11, no. 3 (Feb. 1923): 56–62.

10. Heinrich Beythien, *Die Lage des gewerblichen Mittelstandes*, Flugschriften der Deutschen Volkspartei, no. 39 (Berlin, 1922).

11. DVP, Landesverband Baden, to Dingeldey, 10 Nov. 1921, BA: NL Dingeldey, 20/114.

12. See the letter [from Zapf?] to Vögler, 7 Oct. 1922, BA: NL Zapf, 7.

13. Thiel, "Sozialpolitik," in *Deutscher Aufbau*, ed. Kempkes, pp. 213–15. For further details, see Thiel, "Die Angestelltenversicherung und der Reichstag," *NLC*, 11

June 1921, no. 130, and Thiel, "Der Weg der deutschen Sozialversicherung," *DS* 33, no. 44 (30 Oct. 1921): 722–28.

14. For further details, see the correspondence between the DVP national headquarters in Berlin and the DVP office in Frankfurt am Main, 20–29 Dec. 1920, BA: R 45 II/9/69–70, 91–92.

15. For example, see Max Habermann, *Die neue Ordnung von Kapital und Arbeit. Vortrag gehalten auf der Tagung des Ausschusses des Deutschen Handlungsgehilfentages am 22. Mai 1921* (Hamburg, 1921), pp. 52–56. See also Döhn, *Politik und Interesse*, pp. 132–39, 148–53.

16. In this connection, see Thiel to Stresemann, 1 Aug. 1921, AA: NL Stresemann, 3109/232/141646–47, and the DVP office in Frankfurt am Main to Stresemann, 6 Aug. 1921, ibid., 141679–80, as well as Arning to Stresemann, 17 May and 3 June 1921, ibid., 3109/233/141751–55.

17. For example, see Morath to Stinnes, 9 Feb. 1924, AA: NL Stresemann, 3159/88/171663–65.

18. Morath, "Beamtenfragen im Reichstage," *NLC*, 1 Sept. 1920, no. 192. See also ibid., 18 Dec. 1920, no. 279.

19. See the reports by Morath and Wollbrandt at the DVP's National Civil Servant Day as well as the resolutions that the convention adopted on the high cost of living (*Teuerung*) in *NLC*, 2 and 5 Sept. 1921, nos. 183–85.

20. Morath, "Zum Streikrecht der Beamten," *DS* 33, no. 5 (30 Jan. 1921): 65–69.

21. Albrecht Morath, *Nachrevolutionäre Beamtenpolitik*, Flugschriften der Deutschen Volkspartei, no. 42 (Berlin, 1922), pp. 3–9.

22. Scholz, "Innere Entwicklung im Reiche," in *Deutscher Aufbau*, ed. Kempkes, pp. 37–38.

23. Morath, "Beamtenbesoldung und gleitender Skala," *NLC*, 6 Mar. 1922, no. 45.

24. See Westermann's report as chairman of the DDP's National Council for Agriculture, 12 June 1921, in the *NLC*, 14 June 1921, no. 132.

25. Martin Schumacher, *Land und Politik. Eine Untersuchung über politische Parteien und agrarische Interessen 1914–1923* (Düsseldorf, 1978), pp. 454–66.

26. For further details, see Jens Flemming, *Landwirtschaftliche Interessen und Demokratie. Ländliche Gesellschaft, Agrarverbände und Staat 1890–1925* (Bonn, 1981), pp. 161–97, 229–37.

27. *NLC*, 5 Mar. 1921, no. 54. Hepp's private papers have been deposited in the Zentrales Staatsarchiv der Deutschen Demokratischen Republik in Potsdam, but were unavailable for the purposes of this investigation.

28. For Hepp's political views, see his letter to Stresemann, 4 Sept. 1921, AA: NL Stresemann, 3109/231/141458–60.

29. Karl Hepp, *Lage und Aufgaben der deutschen Landwirtschaft. Nach einem Vortrag gehalten in Darmstadt am 1. April 1921 auf dem Parteitag der Deutschen Volkspartei in Hessen*, Aufklärungsschriften der Deutschen Volkspartei in Hessen, no. 13 (Darmstadt, 1921), pp. 9–11. On the DVP's opposition to the controlled economy in agriculture, see Dusche, "Die Volksernährung und der Abbau der Zwangswirtschaft," *NLC*, 11–12 Oct. 1920, nos. 224–25, and Schönrock, "Die Landwirtschaftspolitik der Deutschen Volkspartei," in *Deutscher Aufbau*, ed. Kempkes, pp. 150–52.

30. Karl Hepp, *Ernährung und Landwirtschaft*, Flugschriften der Deutschen Volkspartei, no. 40 (Berlin, 1922), pp. 3–8, 14–16.

31. DVP, Landesverband Baden, to Dingeldey, 10 Nov. 1921, BA: NL Dingeldey, 20/114. For the DVP's view of such parties, see DVP, Landesverband Baden, ed. *Badische Politik 1918–1921. Wahlhandbuch der Deutschen liberalen Volkspartei (Landesverband Baden der Deutschen Volkspartei)* (Heidelberg, [1921]), pp. 61–64.

32. On the state of the DVP's national organization during the early stages of the German inflation, see Garnich's reports before the DVP's Nuremberg party congress in Dec. 1920, BA: R 45 II/26/255–69, and the Stuttgart party congress in Dec. 1921, in the *NLC*, 1 Dec. 1921, no. 250, as well as the annual report for 1921 on the DVP organization in Darmstadt, [15 July 1922], BA: NL Dingeldey, 16/73–76.

33. For an indication of such support, see Riesser to Stresemann, 11 Aug. 1922, AA: NL Stresemann, 3096/250/144192, and Vögler to Kempkes, 26 Sept. 1922, ACDP: NL Stinnes, 001/4.

34. Stresemann to Duisberg, 15 Oct. 1921, WA Bayer, Autographen-Sammlung Duisberg.

35. See the letter from the Farbwerke vorm. Meister Lucius und Brüning to the directors of I. G. Farben, 30 Nov. 1921, WA Bayer, 4B/20. On the political motives behind this decision, see Kalle and Lymans [?] to the directors of I. G. Farben, 2 Jan. 1922, ibid.

36. Hugo Stinnes, *Mark-Stabilisierung und Arbeitsleistung. Rede gehalten am 9. November 1922 im Reichswirtschaftsrat* (Berlin, 1922). For further details, see Gerald D. Feldman, *Iron and Steel in the German Inflation, 1916–1923* (Princeton, 1977), p. 332, and Peter Wulf, *Hugo Stinnes. Wirtschaft und Politik 1918–1924* (Stuttgart, 1979), p. 434.

CHAPTER FOURTEEN

1. For example, see Max Wallraf, *Die deutschen Parteien am Scheidewege. Rede auf dem vierten deutschnationalen Reichsparteitage in Görlitz am 28. Oktober 1922*, Deutschnationale Flugschrift, no. 139 (Görlitz, 1922), pp. 3–12.

2. In this respect, see Wirth's remarks at a cabinet meeting, 23 Oct. 1922, in *Akten der Reichskanzlei: Die Kabinette Wirth I und II. 10. Mai 1921 bis 26. Oktober 1921. 26. Oktober 1921 bis 22. November 1922*, ed. Ingrid Schulze-Bidlingmaier, 2 vols. (Boppard am Rhein, 1973), 2:1136–37, as well as his remarks at a meeting of the Center Reichstag delegation, 24 Oct. 1922, BA: NL ten Hompel, 16.

3. *NLC*, 25 Sept. 1922, no. 164.

4. Memorandum of a conversation between Kempkes, Hergt, and Westarp, 6 Oct. 1922, AA: NL Stresemann, 3096/252/144428–30.

5. Draft of a resolution by the DVP executive committee, 13 Oct. 1922, AA: NL Stresemann, 3096/252/144490.

6. *Stenographische Berichte über die Verhandlungen des Reichstags*, 357:8937.

7. On the dissension within the DVP over its failure to oppose the extension of Ebert's term of office, see the DVP, Landesverband Bremen, to Stresemann, 8 Oct.

1922, AA: NL Stresemann, 3096/252/144453–54, and Moldenhauer to Stresemann, 16 Oct. 1922, ibid., 144504–7.

8. Riesser to his son, 22 Oct. 1922, BA: NL Riesser (Kleine Erwerbung 549), 1/29–30.

9. Riesser to his son, 25 Oct. 1922, BA: NL Riesser (Kleine Erwerbung 549), 1/31–32.

10. Riesser to his son, 28 Oct. 1922, BA: NL Riesser (Kleine Erwerbung 549), 1/33. See also ten Hompel's notes on the meeting of the Alliance of the Constitutional Middle, 27 Oct. 1922, BA: NL ten Hompel, 16, and Stresemann's notes on Raumer's reports to the DVP Reichstag delegation, 28 Oct. 1922, AA: NL Stresemann, 3096/252/144534.

11. *Schulthess' europäischer Geschichtskalender* 63 (1922): 136–37.

12. See the memorandum by ten Hompel, "Die letzten Wochen der Kanzlerschaft Wirth," [Nov.–Dec. 1922], BA: NL ten Hompel, 15.

13. Riesser to his son, 5 Nov. 1922, BA: NL Riesser (Kleine Erwerbung 549), 1/34–35.

14. Ten Hompel, "Die letzten Wochen der Kanzlerschaft Wirth," [Nov.–Dec. 1922], BA: NL ten Hompel, 16. See also Gerald D. Feldman, *Iron and Steel in the German Inflation, 1916–1923* (Princeton, 1977), pp. 332–33.

15. See the outcome of Wirth's conversation with representatives from the SPD, DDP, DVP, BVP, and Center, 10 Nov. 1922, in *Die Kabinette Wirth*, ed. Schulze-Bidlingmaier, 2:1163–64. See also Riesser to his son, 11 Nov. 1922, BA: NL Riesser (Kleine Erwerbung 549), 1/37–38.

16. Stresemann to Wirth, 13 Nov. 1922, AA: NL Stresemann, 3097/253/144571–72.

17. Brauns's remarks at a meeting of the Center Reichstag delegation, 17 Nov. 1922, appended to ten Hompel, "Die letzten Wochen der Reichskanzlerschaft Wirth," [Nov.–Dec. 1922], BA: NL ten Hompel, 16.

18. Heinrich August Winkler, *Von der Revolution zur Stabilisierung. Arbeiter und Arbeiterbewegung in der Weimarer Republik 1918 bis 1924* (Berlin and Bonn, 1984), pp. 500–501.

19. Ernst Laubach, *Die Politik der Kabinette Wirth 1921–1922* (Lübeck and Hamburg, 1968), pp. 306–7.

20. In this respect, see Moldenhauer to Stresemann, 16 Oct. 1922, AA: NL Stresemann, 3096/252/144504–7, and Faehre to Stresemann, 17 Oct. 1922, ibid., 144519–23, as well as Riesser to his son, 11 Nov. 1922, BA: NL Riesser (Kleine Erwerbung 549), 1/37–38.

21. See Stresemann to Dingeldey, 4 Dec. 1922, AA: NL Stresemann, 3097/253/144661–62.

22. Rudolf Morsey, *Die Deutsche Zentrumspartei 1917–1923* (Düsseldorf, 1966), 489–90.

23. On the DVP's involvement in the formation of the Cuno government, see Cuno to Stresemann, 12 Dec. 1922, AA: NL Stresemann, 3097/253/144636–38. For further information, see Hermann J. Rupieper, *The Cuno Government and Reparations, 1922–1923: Politics and Economics* (The Hague, 1979), pp. 13–30.

24. Carl-Ludwig Holtfrerich, *Die deutsche Inflation 1914–1923. Ursachen und Folgen in internationaler Perspektive* (Berlin and New York, 1980), p. 15.

25. For further details, see Rupieper, *Cuno and Reparations*, pp. 42–96, and Charles S. Maier, *Recasting Bourgeois Europe: Stabilization in France, Germany, and Italy in the Decade after World War I* (Princeton, 1975), pp. 272–304.

26. Memorandum on the collapse of the mark, 30 Jan. 1923, in *Akten der Reichskanzlei: Das Kabinett Cuno. 22. November 1922 bis 12. August 1923*, ed. Karl-Heinz Harbeck (Boppard am Rhein, 1968), pp. 206–7. See also Rupieper, *Cuno and Reparations*, pp. 97–107, and Maier, *Recasting Bourgeois Europe*, pp. 357–59, 364–66.

27. See the petition from the DGB to Cuno, 7 Feb. 1923, in *Das Kabinett Cuno*, ed. Harbeck, pp. 228–31.

28. For further details, see Rupieper, *Cuno and Reparations*, pp. 107–12, and Maier, *Recasting Bourgeois Europe*, pp. 366–67.

29. Bonn to Fischer, 25 July 1922, BA: NL Erkelenz, 127.

30. For further details, see Fischer's report to the DDP party council, 18 Oct. 1922, BA: R 45 III/11/183a–86, as well as Fischer to Siemens, 2 Nov. 1922, SAA: NL Siemens, 4/Lf 646.

31. Minutes of the DDP party council, 26 Nov. 1922, BA: R 45 III/11/190–94. For the DDP membership figure, see Fischer's report to the DDP party council, 18 Oct. 1922, ibid., 184.

32. See the report on the DDP's finances appended to the minutes of the DDP executive committee, 8 Mar. 1923, BA: R 45 III/19/16–17.

33. In this connection, see Mosich to Siemens, 5 Feb. 1923, SAA: NL Siemens, 4/Lf 555, and Siemens to the DDP's National Council for Trade, Industry, and Commerce, 7 Feb. 1923, ibid., 4/Lf 514.

34. Minutes of the meeting of the Curatorium, 15 June 1923, SAA: NL Siemens, 4/Lf 646.

35. Kuhle to Erkelenz, 19 Feb. 1923, BA: NL Erkelenz, 110.

36. Stephan, "Bericht über den Stand der Organisation," [8 Mar. 1923], BA: R 45 III/19/18–24.

37. For further details, see Kuhle to Erkelenz, 26 Jan. 1923, BA: NL Erkelenz, 23/111–13.

38. Stephan, "Bericht über den Stand der Organisation," [8 Mar. 1923], BA: R 45 III/19/23–24.

39. For example, see Flinsch to Siemens, 10 Apr. 1923, SAA: NL Siemens, 4/Lf 555.

40. Stephan, "Bericht über den Stand der Organisation," [8 Mar. 1923], BA: R 45 III/19/20–21.

41. In this respect, see Stresemann to the DVP, Ortsgruppe Nordhausen, 12 May 1923, AA: NL Stresemann, 3098/259/145521, as well as the relevant documents from late May 1923, ibid., 3097/254/144770–72. For the Democratic reaction to these developments, see the minutes of the DDP executive committee, 27 May 1923, BA: R 45 III/19/27–28, as well as Vogt, "Gegen die liberale Einheitspartei," *Vossische Zeitung*, 9 June 1923, no. 270.

42. For example, see the minutes of the financial committee of the DVP district

536 *Notes to Pages 191–93*

organization in South Westphalia, 26 Oct. and 11 Dec. 1922, HSA Düsseldorf, NL Klingspor, 1, as well as Stresemann to Riesser, 31 Jan. 1923, AA: NL Stresemann, 3097/256/145094–95.

43. On the financial status of *Die Zeit*, see Stresemann to Jordan, 1 Mar. 1922, AA: NL Stresemann, 3095/242/143235–37, and Stresemann to Stinnes, 13 May 1922, ibid., 3110/246/143686–88.

44. Stresemann to Bömers, 19 Oct. 1922, AA: NL Stresemann, 3096/252/144515–18.

45. Reusch to the DVP Berlin, 27 Feb. 1923, HA/GHH: NL Reusch, 30019390/0.

46. Stinnes to Stresemann, 31 Aug. 1922, AA: NL Stresemann, 3159/87/144760–65.

47. Stresemann to Kalle, 19 Dec. 1922, AA: NL Stresemann, 3097/253/144760–65. See also Kalle to Duisberg, 27 Dec. 1922, WA Bayer, Autographen-Sammlung Duisberg.

48. Duisberg to Wolff, 29 Jan. 1923, WA Bayer, Autographen-Sammlung Duisberg. For Kalle's political views and relationship to Stresemann, see his unpublished memoirs from 1933, "Es war einmal. Erinnerungen an die Zeit von 1870 bis 1932," pp. 27–42. I am grateful to the late Felix Hirsch for having placed these memoirs at my disposal.

49. On the composition of the "Kalle Committee," see Moldenhauer, "Politische Erinnerungen," BA: NL Moldenhauer, 1/136. For further information, see Peter Hayes, *Industry and Ideology: I.G. Farben in the Nazi Era* (Cambridge, 1987), pp. 48–52.

50. Kalle to Stresemann, 13 Feb. 1923, AA: NL Stresemann, 3097/256/145135–38. For further details on the arrangements to save *Die Zeit*, see Duisberg to Kalle, 3 Jan. 1923, WA Bayer, Autographen-Sammlung Duisberg, as well as Litwin to Stresemann, 23 Mar. 1923, AA: NL Stresemann, 3098/257/145267–70.

51. For example, see Stresemann to Dingeldey, 4 Dec. 1922, AA: NL Stresemann, 3097/253/144661–62.

52. In this respect, see Stresemann, "Ruhraktion und politische Lage," *DS* 35, no. 6 (20 Mar. 1923): 97–110. See also Stresemann to Bürger, 8 Jan. 1923, AA: NL Stresemann, 3097/256/145027–29, and to Uebel, 8 Jan. 1923, ibid., 145030–31. For further information, see Henry Ashby Turner, Jr., *Stresemann and the Politics of the Weimar Republic* (Princeton, 1963), pp. 105–10, and Alfred E. Cornebise, "Gustav Stresemann and the Ruhr Occupation: The Making of a Statesman," *European Studies Review* 2 (1972): 43–67.

53. See Stresemann to Reincke-Bloch, 25 Jan. 1923, AA: NL Stresemann, 3097/256/145080–82.

54. Stresemann's memorandum of a conversation with Stinnes, 19 Mar. 1923, AA: NL Stresemann, 3098/257/145243–45. For further information, see Feldman, *Iron and Steel*, pp. 332–35, 351–57, 385–89.

55. Cornebise, "Stresemann and the Ruhr," pp. 50–52. For the text of this speech, see Gustav Stresemann, *Reden und Schriften. Politik—Geschichte—Literatur 1897–1926*, ed. Rochus von Rheinbaben, 2 vols. (Berlin, 1926), 2:43–58.

56. Rupieper, *Cuno and Reparations*, pp. 147–52.

57. Stresemann to Bandhahn, 17 May 1923, AA: NL Stresemann, 3098/258/145482–84.

58. RDI to the Reich Chancellor, 25 May 1923, in *Das Kabinett Cuno*, ed. Harbeck,

pp. 508–13. For further information, see Rupieper, *Cuno and Reparations*, pp. 152–63.

59. The text of this statement is to be found in BA: R 43 I/37/77. On Stresemann's efforts to prevent the fall of the Cuno government, see his letter to Rose, 30 May 1923, AA: NL Stresemann, 3098/259/145584–86, as well as the entries in his diary, 23–28 May 1923, in Gustav Stresemann, *Vermächtnis. Der Nachlaß in drei Bänden*, ed. Henry Bernhard, 3 vols. (Berlin, 1932–33), 1:65.

CHAPTER FIFTEEN

1. *NLC*, 8 July 1923, no. 59.

2. Leidig to Stresemann, 18 July 1923, AA: NL Stresemann, 3098/260/145698–701. See also Raumer to Stresemann, 25 July 1923, ibid., 145774–79.

3. Raumer to Stresemann, 23 July 1923, AA: NL Stresemann, 3098/260/145649–52.

4. On the situation within the Center, see Rudolf Morsey, *Die Deutsche Zentrumspartei 1917–1923* (Düsseldorf, 1966), pp. 509–15.

5. On Stresemann's conversation with Müller, see his letters to Kempkes, 29 July 1923, AA: NL Stresemann, 3098/260/145780–84, and to Leidig, 29 July 1923, ibid., 145788–90.

6. Stresemann to Jänecke, 1 Aug. 1923, AA: NL Stresemann, 3098/260/145835–37.

7. Henry Ashby Turner, Jr., *Stresemann and the Politics of the Weimar Republic* (Princeton, 1963), p. 108. For a summary of this speech, see Gustav Stresemann, *Vermächtnis. Der Nachlaß in drei Bänden*, ed. Henry Bernhard, 3 vols. (Berlin, 1932–33), 1:76–77.

8. Declaration by Stresemann before the DVP Reichstag delegation, 10 Aug. 1923, AA: NL Stresemann, 3159/87/171264–65.

9. Heinrich August Winkler, *Von der Revolution zur Stabilisierung. Arbeiter und Arbeiterbewegung in der Weimarer Republik 1918 bis 1924* (Berlin and Bonn, 1984), p. 600.

10. For further details, see the minutes of the meeting of the Alliance of the Constitutional Middle, 12 Aug. 1923, in *Akten der Reichskanzlei: Das Kabinett Cuno. 22. November 1922 bis 12. August 1923*, ed. Karl-Heinz Harbeck (Boppard am Rhein, 1968), pp. 738–46.

11. Winkler, *Von der Revolution zur Stabilisierung*, p. 602.

12. Turner, *Stresemann*, pp. 109–10. For further details, see Stresemann's own account in the pamphlet he anonymously coauthored with Henry Bernhard, *Das Kabinett Stresemann* (Berlin, 1924), pp. 3–9, as well as the introduction by Karl Dietrich Erdmann and Martin Vogt in *Akten der Reichskanzlei: Die Kabinette Stresemann I und II. 13. August bis 6. Oktober 1923. 6. Oktober bis 30. November 1923*, ed. Karl Dietrich Erdmann and Martin Vogt, 2 vols. (Boppard am Rhein, 1978), 1:xxi–xxvii.

13. For heavy industry's attitude toward the formation of the Stresemann government, see Gerald D. Feldman, *Iron and Steel in the German Inflation, 1916–1923* (Princeton, 1977), pp. 393–96.

14. Winkler, *Von der Revolution zur Stabilisierung*, p. 602.

15. *Stenographische Berichte über die Verhandlungen des Reichstags*, 361:11871–73. Of the 22 DVP deputies who missed the vote, only five had been excused for legitimate reasons. For further details, see Roland Thimme, *Stresemann und die Deutsche Volkspartei 1923–1925* (Lübeck and Hamburg, 1961), p. 36.

16. Gustav Stresemann, *Die Wille zur Verständigung. Rede vor dem "Deutschen Industrie- und Handelstag" am 24. August 1923* (Berlin, [1923]), pp. 2–7.

17. For Stresemann's critique of Cuno's foreign policy, see his letter to Jänecke, 1 Aug. 1923, AA: NL Stresemann, 3098/260/145835–37.

18. For further details, see Martin Vogt, "Rudolf Hilferding als Finanzminister im ersten Kabinett Stresemann," in *Historische Prozesse der deutschen Inflation 1914 bis 1924. Ein Tagungsbericht*, ed. Otto Busch und Gerald D. Feldman (Berlin, 1978), pp. 127–58, as well as Karl-Bernhard Netzband and Hans Peter Widmaier, *Währungs- und Finanzpolitik in der Ära Luther 1923–1925* (Tübingen, 1964), pp. 19–20.

19. Memorandum by Bäumer on a meeting of party leaders with representatives from the Stresemann government, 22 Aug. 1923, BA: NL Erkelenz, 27/141–43.

20. Minutes of the cabinet meeting, 7 Sept. 1923, in *Die Kabinette Stresemann*, ed. Erdmann and Vogt, 1:204–13. See also Netzband and Widmaier, *Währungs- und Finanzpolitik*, p. 20.

21. Memorandum by Stresemann, 7 Sept. 1923, in Stresemann, *Vermächtnis*, 1:108–14. See also Alfred E. Cornebise, "Gustav Stresemann and the Ruhr Occupation: The Making of a Statesman," *European Studies Review* 2 (1972): 57–63.

22. For example, see Walter Kamper, *Die Rheinlandkrise des Herbstes 1923. Ein politischer Überblick* (Frankfurt am Main, 1925), pp. 36–38.

23. Minutes of the DVP Reichstag delegation, 12 Sept. 1923, AA: NL Stresemann, 3159/87/171304–11.

24. See the report on the attitude of the parties in the Ruhr, 15 Sept. 1923, in *Die Kabinette Stresemann*, ed. Erdmann and Vogt, 1:284–89.

25. *Deutscher Geschichtskalender* 47 (1923): II:A, 158–61.

26. Minutes of the DVP Reichstag delegation, 25 Sept. 1923, AA: NL Stresemann, 3159/87/171326–31.

27. For example, see the letters from Rose to Stresemann, 26 Sept. 1923, AA: NL Stresemann, 3159/87/171334–36, and from Dingeldey to Stresemann, 26 Sept. 1923, ibid., 3111/267/146914–16.

28. Reusch to Blumberg, 26 Sept. 1923, HA/GHH: NL Reusch, 30019393/0.

29. Schultz to Stresemann, 3 Oct. 1923, AA: NL Stresemann, 3159/87/171363–66.

30. For a fuller discussion of the situation in Bavaria, see below, chap. 16.

31. For further details, see the minutes of the cabinet meeting, 30 Sept. 1923, and of the ministerial conference, 1 Oct. 1923, in *Die Kabinette Stresemann*, ed. Erdmann and Vogt, 1:410–15, 417–31.

32. For an excellent discussion of this crisis and its impact upon the DVP, see Günter Arns, "Die Krise des Weimarer Parlamentarismus im Frühherbst 1923," *Der Staat* 8 (1969): 181–216. On the situation in the DVP, see the confidential report that the DVP national headquarters in Berlin sent to party secretaries throughout the country in the first week of October 1923, AA: NL Stresemann, 3159/87/171337–43. On Stinnes's involvement in Seeckt's plans for a military dictatorship, see Peter Wulf, *Hugo Stinnes. Wirtschaft und Politik 1918–1924* (Stuttgart, 1979), pp. 452–65.

33. Minutes of a meeting between the government and the leaders of the government parties, 2 Oct. 1923, in *Die Kabinette Stresemann*, ed. Erdmann and Vogt, 1:436–44.

34. Raumer to Stresemann, 2 Oct. 1923, ibid., p. 446. See also the report from the DVP national headquarters to party secretaries throughout the country, [ca. 3 Oct. 1923], AA: NL Stresemann, 3159/87/171337–43.

35. Stresemann, *Vermächtnis*, 1:141. See also the minutes of the cabinet meeting, 2 Oct. 1923, in *Die Kabinette Stresemann*, ed. Erdmann and Vogt, 1:447–52.

36. Note by Erkelenz on a meeting of representatives from the government parties, 2 Oct. 1923, BA: NL Erkelenz, 28/108–9.

37. Stresemann, *Vermächtnis*, 1:143. See also Winkler, *Von der Revolution zur Stabilisierung*, pp. 625–32.

38. Report from the DVP national headquarters to party secretaries throughout the country, [ca. 3 Oct. 1923], AA: NL Stresemann, 3159/87/171337–43. See also *NLC*, 3 Oct. 1923, no. 91.

39. Stresemann to Schultz, 9 Oct. 1923, AA: NL Stresemann, 3159/87/171367–69.

40. For a discussion of possible factors, see Arns, "Krise des Weimarer Parlamentarismus," pp. 203–14.

41. Minutes of the executive committee of the DVP Reichstag delegation, 3 Oct. 1923, BA: R 45 II/66/6.

42. Albrecht Philipp, *Von Stresemann zu Marx. Sechs Monate deutschnationaler Politik (August 1923–Januar 1924)*, Deutschnationale Flugschrift, no. 146 (Berlin, 1924), pp. 12–16.

43. Riesser to his son, 4 Oct. 1923, BA: NL Riesser (Kleine Erwerbung 549), 1/61.

44. Turner, *Stresemann*, pp. 121–22.

45. For the details of this compromise, see Stresemann to Schultz, 9 Oct. 1923, AA: NL Stresemann, 3159/87/171367–69, as well as the memorandum by ten Hompel, "Kabinettskrisis in den ersten Oktober-Tagen 1923," n.d., BA: NL ten Hompel, 15.

46. Stresemann, *Vermächtnis*, 1:145–46.

47. For a more detailed discussion of these developments, see Feldman, *Iron and Steel*, pp. 405–17, and Stinnes, *Wulf*, pp. 446–49, as well as the lengthy article by Gerald D. Feldman and Irmgard Steinisch, "Die Weimarer Republik zwischen Sozial- und Wirtschaftsstaat. Die Entscheidung gegen den Achtstündentag," *Archiv für Sozialgeschichte* 20 (1980): 387–400.

48. Stinnes to Stresemann, 7 Oct. 1923, AA: NL Stresemann, 3105/2/154192–94.

49. Stresemann to Stinnes, 11 Oct. 1923, AA: NL Stresemann, 3105/2/154226–28.

50. *Stenographische Berichte über die Verhandlungen des Reichstags*, 361:12152–54. See also the letter from Riesser to his son, 13 Oct. 1923, BA: NL Riesser (Kleine Erwerbung 549), 1/61.

51. On the Saxon crisis, see Donald B. Pryce, "The Reich Government versus Saxony, 1923: The Decision to Intervene," *CEH* 10 (1977): 112–47. On the situation in Bavaria, see Werner Zimmermann, *Bayern und das Reich 1918–1923. Der bayerische Föderalismus zwischen Revolution und Reaktion* (Munich, 1953), pp. 134–49. For Stresemann's response to these developments, see Bernhard, *Kabinett Stresemann*, pp. 15–22. On the situation within the SPD, see Winkler, *Von der Revolution zur Stabilisierung*, pp. 648–64.

52. Ministerial conference, 5 Nov. 1923, in *Die Kabinette Stresemann*, ed. Erdmann

and Vogt, 2:965–69. See also Turner, *Stresemann*, pp. 129–31, and Wulf, *Stinnes*, pp. 452–65.

53. For a careful and detailed analysis of this conflict, see Turner, *Stresemann*, pp. 131–41.

54. Stresemann's remarks before the DVP Reichstag delegation, 5 Nov. 1923, AA: NL Stresemann, 3159/87/171435–36. For the DNVP's position, see Scholz's remarks on his negotiations with the DNVP leadership, ibid., 171432–33, as well as Philipp, *Von Stresemann zu Marx*, pp. 21–23.

55. Minutes of the DVP Reichstag delegation, 6 Nov. 1923, AA: NL Stresemann, 3159/87/171437–39.

56. Minutes of the DVP Reichstag delegation, 9 Nov. 1923, AA: NL Stresemann, 3159/87/171465–70. For the text of this resolution, see BA: R 45 II/38/77–78.

57. Minutes of the DVP Reichstag delegation, 10 Nov. 1923, AA: NL Stresemann, 3159/87/171474–79. See also the statement that Scholz released on the meeting of the DVP Reichstag delegation on the previous day, ibid., 3111/267/146957.

58. For example, see Dingeldey to Stresemann, 9 Nov. 1923, AA: NL Stresemann, 3111/267/146950–54.

59. Campe and Kalle to Stresemann, 20 Nov. 1923, AA: NL Stresemann, 3159/87/171489–92.

60. *NLC*, 19 Nov. 1923, no. 115.

61. Minutes of the DVP Reichstag delegation, 19 Nov. 1923, AA: NL Stresemann, 3159/87/141484–88.

62. Stresemann's remarks at a cabinet meeting, 22 Nov. 1923, in *Die Kabinette Stresemann*, ed. Erdmann and Vogt, 2:1162.

63. Entry in Stresemann's diary, 23 Nov. 1923, in Stresemann, *Vermächtnis*, 1:245.

CHAPTER SIXTEEN

1. For further details, see Larry Eugene Jones, "In the Shadow of Stabilization: German Liberalism and the Legitimacy Crisis of the Weimar Party System, 1924–30," in *Die Nachwirkungen der Inflation auf die deutsche Geschichte 1924–1933*, ed. Gerald D. Feldman (Munich, 1985), pp. 21–41.

2. For the DDP's position during these negotiations, see "Erklärung zum Kabinett Stegerwald," 29 Nov. 1923, BA: NL Erkelenz, 136. See also the letter from Riesser to his son, 26 Nov. 1923, BA: NL Riesser (Kleine Erwerbung 549), 1/65–66, and Albrecht Philipp, *Von Stresemann zu Marx. Sechs Monate deutschnationaler Politik (August 1923–Januar 1924)*, Deutschnationale Flugschrift, no. 146 (Berlin, 1924), pp. 23–32.

3. Michael Stürmer, *Koalition und Opposition in der Weimarer Republik 1924–1928* (Düsseldorf, 1967), pp. 33–38. For a liberal response to these developments, see Stubmann, "Die Krisis der deutschen Innenpolitik," *Deutsche Einheit* 6, no. 1 (5 Jan. 1924): 1–6.

4. Hans Luther, *Feste Mark—Solide Wirtschaft. Rückblick auf die Arbeit der Regierung während der Wintermonate 1923/24* (Berlin, 1924), pp. 5–13.

5. Karl-Bernhard Netzband and Hans Peter Widmaier, *Währungs- und Finanzpolitik in der Ära Luther 1923–1925* (Tübingen, 1964), pp. 118–20, 137–223.

6. Luther, *Feste Mark—Solide Wirtschaft*, pp. 14–36.

7. For further details, see Peter-Christian Witt, "Inflation, Wohnungszwangswirtschaft und Hauszinssteuer. Zur Regelung von Wohnungsbau und Wohnungsmarkt in der Weimarer Republik," in *Wohnen im Wandel. Beiträge zur Geschichte des Alltages in der bürgerlichen Gesellschaft*, ed. Lutz Niethammer (Wuppertal, 1979), pp. 396–99.

8. Netzband and Widmaier, *Währungs- und Finanzpolitik*, pp. 177–90, 196–203.

9. Luther, *Feste Mark—Solide Wirtschaft*, pp. 37–48. For further details, see Larry Eugene Jones, "Inflation, Revaluation, and the Crisis of Middle-Class Politics, 1923–28," *CEH* 12 (1979): 148–52.

10. Fischer, "Bericht über die 3. Steuernotverordnung," [Feb. 1924], BA: NL Dietrich, 70/264–73. See also Koch-Weser's remarks at a meeting of government party leaders, 14 Feb. 1924, in *Akten der Reichskanzlei: Das Kabinett Marx I und II. 30. November 1923 bis 3. Juni 1924. 3. Juni 1924 bis 15. Januar 1925*, ed. Günter Abramowski, 2 vols. (Boppard am Rhein, 1973), 1:363.

11. Stürmer, *Koalition und Opposition*, pp. 37–38.

12. Memoranda by Koch-Weser, 21 and 24 Sept. 1923, BA: NL Koch-Weser, 139. See also the minutes of the DDP executive committee, 22 Sept. 1923, BA: R 45 III/19/41–42.

13. Memorandum by Koch-Weser, 6 Nov. 1923, BA: NL Koch-Weser, 139.

14. Memorandum by Koch-Weser, 5 Oct. 1923, BA: NL Koch-Weser, 139.

15. Stephan to Erkelenz, 27 Oct. 1923, BA: NL Erkelenz, 125.

16. Memorandum by Koch-Weser, 6 Nov. 1923, BA: NL Koch-Weser, 139.

17. Vogt to Erkelenz, 16 Nov. 1923, BA: NL Erkelenz, 29/45–46. For the DDP's attitude toward Stresemann's rump cabinet, see Petersen to Stresemann, 7 Nov. 1923, AA: NL Stresemann, 3105/4/154543–46.

18. "Politische Erneuerung! Aufruf der Republikanischen Partei Deutschlands," [Jan. 1924], BA: NL Erkelenz, 126. See also Vogt to Petersen, 16 Dec. 1923 and 3 Jan. 1924, ibid., as well as Republikanische Partei Deutschlands, Wahlkreisverband Leipzig, "Kundgabe an die Wähler und Wählerinnen im Wahlkreis Leipzig!," [Apr. 1924], Bayerisches Hauptstaatsarchiv, Munich, Abt. V, Flugblätter-Sammlung, F233.

19. Minutes of the DDP party council, 27 Jan. 1924, BA: R 45 III/12/62.

20. Speech by Koch-Weser, "Die Deutsche Demokratische Partei im Kampfe für Reich und Volk (Rückblick und Ausblick)," in DDP, Reichsgeschäftsstelle, ed., *Bericht über die Verhandlungen des 5. ordentlichen Parteitages der Deutschen Demokratischen Partei, abgehalten in Weimar am 5. und 6. April 1924* (Berlin, [1924]), pp. 9–17. For a characterization of Koch-Weser's capabilities and shortcomings as a party leader, see Attila Chanady, "Erich Koch-Weser and the Weimar Republic," *Canadian Journal of History* 7 (1972): 51–63, and Werner Stephan, *Acht Jahrzehnte erlebtes Deutschland. Ein Liberaler in vier Epochen* (Düsseldorf, 1983), pp. 188–22.

21. For example, see Erkelenz's reaction to the new party in his letter to Vetter, 31 Jan. 1924, BA: NL Erkelenz, 126.

22. "Wahlprogramm der Nationalliberalen Landespartei Bayerns (Beschlossen vom

ersten Landesvertretertag in Nürnberg am 17. Februar 1924)," Bayerisches Haupt-staatsarchiv, Munich, Abt. V, Flugblätter-Sammlung, F84.

23. Gildemeister to Stresemann, 8 Dec. 1923, AA: NL Stresemann, 3159/88/171536–39.

24. Gildemeister to Kardorff, 8 Jan. 1924, BA: NL Kardorff, 9/106. See also Gildemeister to Stresemann, 18 Dec. 1923, AA: NL Stresemann, 3159/88/171571–74.

25. For the original text of this resolution, see "Stellung der Reichstagsfraktion der Deutschen Volkspartei zur 'Großen Koalition,' " 12 Jan. 1924, AA: NL Stresemann, 3159/89/171766–67.

26. Stresemann to Gildemeister, 19 Dec. 1923, AA: NL Stresemann, 3159/88/171540–42.

27. Undated memorandum from Feb.–Mar. 1924 entitled "Betrifft: Geheimrat Dr. Quaatz," AA: NL Stresemann, 3111/267/147061–68. For Quaatz's views, see Quaatz, "Abbau des Parlamentarismus," *Der Tag*, 18 Dec. 1923, no. 284.

28. Minutes of the executive committee of the DVP Reichstag delegation, 21 Jan. 1924, BA: R 45 II/66/13. For the final version of this resolution, see DVP, Reichs-geschäftsstelle, ed., *Wahlhandbuch 1924* (Berlin, 1924), pp. 166–68.

29. *NLC*, 13 Mar. 1924, no. 37. See also Quaatz, "Die nationalliberale Vereinigung der D.V.P.," *Der Tag*, 15 Mar. 1924, no. 65.

30. Morath to Stinnes, 9 Feb. 1924, ACDP: NL Stinnes, 002/7.

31. For example, see the two drafts of a letter from Stinnes to Scholz, n.d., appended to Humann to Osius, 25 Feb. 1924, ACDP: NL Stinnes, 002/7, as well as the entry in Quaatz's diary, 5 Mar. 1924, BA: NL Quaatz, 16. For a fuller discussion of Stinnes's disgruntlement with Stresemann's political leadership, see Peter Wulf, *Hugo Stinnes. Wirtschaft und Politik 1918–1924* (Stuttgart, 1979), pp. 519–23.

32. Humann to Osius, 6 Mar. 1924, ACDP: NL Stinnes, 002/7.

33. Report on the founding of the NLV, 12 Mar. 1924, AA: NL Stresemann, 3159/89/171762–63. See also the entries in Quaatz's diary, 12–13 Mar. 1924, BA: NL Quaatz, 16.

34. See the entry in Quaatz's diary, 15 Mar. 1924, BA: NL Quaatz, 16, as well as the circular from Quaatz to the members of the NLV, 15 Mar. 1924, AA: NL Stresemann, 3159/89/171760–61.

35. On the NLV's connections to Ruhr heavy industry, see Roland Thimme, *Strese-mann und die Deutsche Volkspartei 1923–1925* (Lübeck and Hamburg, 1961), pp. 50–55, and Wulf, *Stinnes*, pp. 524–25.

36. Alfred Gildemeister, *Was wir wollen! Rede auf der Tagung der Nationalliberalen Vereinigung der Deutschen Volkspartei am Mittwoch, den 26. März 1924* ([Berlin, 1924]), pp. 3–9. See also the report in the *Berliner Börsen-Zeitung*, 26 Mar. 1924, no. 146.

37. *NLC*, 17 Mar. 1924, no. 30.

38. Gildemeister to Stresemann, 14 Apr. 1924, AA: NL Stresemann, 3159/88/171714–15.

39. Entry in Quaatz's diary, 13 Mar. 1924, BA: NL Quaatz, 16.

40. DVP, Reichsgeschäftsstelle, *Wahlhandbuch 1924*, pp. 169–70. See also the undated memorandum from the spring of 1924 on the negotiations with the NLV, BA: R

45 II/39/41–42, as well as Dingeldey to Heyl zu Herrensheim, 1 Apr. 1924, BA: NL Dingeldey, 72/134–36.

41. Entries in Quaatz's diary, 28 Mar. and 2 Apr. 1924, BA: NL Quaatz, 16.

42. In this respect, see Schultz to Westermann, 11 Apr. 1924, HSA Düsseldorf, NL Klingspor, 1/89–93, as well as the circular from Maretzky on behalf of the National Liberal Election Committee (Nationalliberaler Wahlausschuß), 16 Apr. 1924, AA: NL Stresemann, 3159/89/171873–74.

43. Faehre to Stresemann, 24 May 1924, AA: NL Stresemann, 3160/90/172019–24.

44. *DAZ*, 23 Apr. 1924, no. 190.

45. Invitation to the DVP's Hanover party congress, 29–30 Mar. 1924, BA: R 45 II/28/1.

46. Stresemann, "Durch Opfer und Arbeit zur Freiheit," 30 Mar. 1924, in Gustav Stresemann, *Reden und Schriften. Politik—Geschichte—Literatur 1897–1926*, ed. Rochus von Rheinbaben, 2 vols. (Berlin, 1926), 2:180–83.

47. See the speeches by Dusche, Beythien, Morath, and Düringer at the DVP's Hanover party congress, 29 Mar. 1924, in a special supplement to the *Hannoverscher Kurier*, 29 Mar. 1924, no. 152, in BA: R 45 II/28/147–59.

48. Erich Koch-Weser, *Gegen eine neue Inflation! Für die Einheit des Reiches und die Autorität der Reichsregierung! Für innere Reparation! Gegen den Mißbrauch der Wirtschaftsfreiheit! Rede in der Reichstagssitzung vom 28. Februar 1924* (Berlin, [1924]), pp. 1–3.

49. Hermann Fischer, *Gegen eine neue Inflation! Für Revision der Beamtenabbauverordnung! Für Hebung des Mittelstandes! Gegen die Münchener Hochverräter! Rede in der Reichstagssitzung vom 7. März 1924* (Berlin, [1924]), pp. 4–8.

50. Hermann Dietrich, *Was wird aus den Sparguthaben?* (Karlsruhe, 1924), pp. 6–12.

51. Hermann Fischer, *Volk, Staat und Wirtschaft. Vortrag auf dem Parteitag der Deutschen Demokratischen Partei 5. April 1924* (Berlin, [1924]), pp. 27–29.

52. DDP, Reichsgeschäftsstelle, *Bericht über die Verhandlungen des 5. Parteitages*, pp. 55–119.

53. For example, see DDP, Verein Nürnberg, to the DDP Reichsgeschäftsstelle, 8 Feb. 1924, BA: NL Erkelenz, 126.

54. For further details, see Thomas Childers, *The Nazi Voter: The Social Foundations of Fascism in Germany, 1919–1933* (Chapel Hill, 1983), pp. 64–66, 91–97. On the plight of the civil service, see Andreas Kunz, *Civil Servants and the Politics of Inflation in Germany 1914–1924* (Berlin, 1986), pp. 377–82.

55. On the NLV's tactics in the May 1924 elections, see the report attached to Stocksieck's letter to Stresemann, 3 May 1924, AA: NL Stresemann, 3159/89/171922–24. On the Catholic peasantry, see Moeller, *German Peasants and Agrarian Politics, 1914–1924: The Rhineland and Westphalia* (Chapel Hill, 1986), pp. 143–53.

56. Erkelenz to Koch-Weser, 23 Feb. 1924, BA: NL Koch-Weser, 139. For further details, see Kuhle to Erkelenz, 27 Aug. 1923, BA: NL Erkelenz, 27/117–18, and Kuhle to Jansen, 24 Oct. 1923, ibid., 28/173–75, as well as the remarks by Fischer and Erkelenz before the DDP executive committee, 22 Sept. 1923, BA: R 45 III/19/39–41.

57. Minutes of the DVP managing committee, 8 Jan. 1924, BA: R 45 II/57/69–70.

58. "Rechenschaftsbericht der Reichsgeschäftsstelle für die Reichstagswahlen 1924," 25 July 1924, BA: NL Gerland, 8. For further details, see Werner Schneider, *Die Deutsche Demokratische Partei in der Weimarer Republik 1924–1930* (Munich, 1978), pp. 71–74.

59. For example, see Stresemann to Boehm, 7 Apr. 1924, BA: Kleine Erwerbung 557, as well as Stresemann to Soberheim, 22 Apr. 1924, AA: NL Stresemann, 3159/89/171903–4.

60. Memorandum from Wiskott, 18 Mar. 1924, HA/GHH: Allgemeine Verwaltung, 400106/83.

61. Raumer to Vögler, 29 Apr. 1924, BA: NL Kardorff, 14/19–22. See also E. Stinnes to Thomas, 7 Apr. 1924, ACDP: NL Stinnes, 002/7.

62. Meeting of the Curatorium for the Reconstruction of German Economic Life, 11 Apr. 1924, SAA: NL Siemens, 4/Lf 736.

63. For example, see Stresemann to Riesser, 26 Mar. 1924, AA: NL Stresemann, 3159/89/171778–79, as well as Fischer to Siemens, 17 Apr. 1924, SAA: NL Siemens, 4/Lf 555, and Stephan to Erkelenz, 30 Apr. 1924, BA: NL Erkelenz, 31/90–91.

64. Duisberg to Weinberg, 24 Sept. 1923, WA Bayer: NL Duisberg, 4B/20.

65. See the depositions from Pfeiffer and Kalle, 8 Sept. 1947, StA Nürnberg, Bestand KV-Prozesse, Fall 6, Nr. X 3.

66. *Der Demokrat* 5, nos. 18/19 (19 June 1924): 193–97, and nos. 24/25 (7 Aug. 1924): 229–31.

67. For example, see Ißberner, "Frische Lehren des Wahlkampfes," *Der Demokrat* 5, no. 12 (8 May 1924): 153–55, and Erkelenz, "Nüchterne Wahlbetrachtungen," ibid., 5, nos. 14/15 (22 May 1924): 173–76. For further information, see "Reichstagswahl vom 4. Mai 1924: Der Wahlausfall in Baden," [May 1924], BA: NL Dietrich, 217/411–28, and Wolf to Gothein, 9 May 1924, BA: NL Gothein, 18/90.

68. Stresemann to Jarres, 9 May 1924, AA: NL Stresemann, 3160/90/171964–69.

69. Remarks by Hugo before the DVP central executive committee, 7 July 1924, BA: R 45 II/39/351–53. See also Wolfgang Stresemann, "Das Ergebnis der Reichstagswahlen," *DS* 36, no. 9 (5 May 1924): 146–50, as well as "Das Wahlergebnis," [May 1924], HSA Düsseldorf, NL Klingspor, 1/38–40.

70. Bürger, "Die bayerischen Wahlen," *DS* 36, no. 8 (20 Apr. 1924): 122–26. See also Stephan, "Die Parteibewegung in den verschiedenen Gegenden Deutschlands," *Die Hilfe* 30, no. 11 (1 June 1924): 173–76.

71. Stephan, "Die Parteibewegung in Deutschland seit der Revolution," *Die Hilfe* 30, no. 10 (15 May 1924): 168–70.

72. Childers, *Nazi Voter*, pp. 83–87.

73. Thomas Childers, "Inflation, Stabilization, and Political Realignment in Germany 1924 to 1928," in *Die deutsche Inflation. Eine Zwischenbilanz/The German Inflation Reconsidered: A Preliminary Balance*, ed. Gerald D. Feldman et al. (Berlin and New York, 1982), pp. 409–31.

CHAPTER SEVENTEEN

1. For an overview of this problem, see Larry Eugene Jones, "In the Shadow of Stabilization: German Liberalism and the Legitimacy Crisis of the Weimar Party System, 1924–30," in *Die Nachwirkungen der Inflation auf die deutsche Geschichte 1924–1933*, ed. Gerald D. Feldman (Munich, 1985), pp. 21–41.

2. In this respect, see Thomas Childers, "Interest and Ideology: Anti-System Politics in the Era of Stabilization, 1924–28," in *Die Nachwirkungen der Inflation*, ed. Feldman, pp. 1–20.

3. For example, see Hans Roger, *Die uns regieren. Kritische Streifzüge durch Parlament, Parteien und Presse* (Magdeburg, [1927]), pp. 50–91.

4. For further details, see Michael Stürmer, *Koalition und Opposition in der Weimarer Republik 1924–1928* (Düsseldorf, 1967), pp. 38–49.

5. Stresemann to Hembeck, 13 May 1924, AA: NL Stresemann, 3160/90/171986–88.

6. Statement by Jarres in a ministerial conference, 16 May 1924, in *Akten der Reichskanzlei: Das Kabinett Marx I und II. 30. November 1923 bis 3. Juni 1924. 3. Juni 1924 bis 15. Januar 1925*, ed. Günter Abramowski, 2 vols. (Boppard am Rhein, 1973), 1:642.

7. See the minutes of a conversation between representatives from the DNVP and the government parties, 21 and 23 May 1924, BA: NL Erkelenz, 136.

8. DVP, Reichsgeschäftsstelle, ed., *Nachtrag zum Wahlhandbuch 1924* (Berlin, 1924), pp. 23–24.

9. See the statement drafted by the Center, DDP, and DVP on 20 May 1924 and released to the press following the resignation of the Marx cabinet, in *Die Kabinette Marx I und II*, ed. Abramowski, 1:659, n. 1.

10. Marx's statement at a ministerial conference, 31 May 1924, ibid., 1:671–72. The DVP was represented in the second Marx government by Stresemann and Jarres, and the DDP by Gessler, Hamm, and Rudolf Oeser. Aside from the fact that Curt Joel had replaced the BVP's Erich Emminger as the minister of justice, the second Marx government was unchanged from the one that had been in office since December 1923.

11. See the remarks by Erkelenz and Koch-Weser before the DDP executive committee, 21 May 1924, BA: R 45 III/19/73–78.

12. Resolution of the DVP Reichstag delegation, 14 May 1924, in *NLC*, 15 May 1924, no. 76.

13. Entry in Koch-Weser's diary, 15 May 1924, BA: NL Koch-Weser, 31/3.

14. Minutes of the DDP executive committee, 26 May 1924, BA: R 45 III/19/84–93.

15. See the draft of Hamm's letter to Cohnstaedt, 19 May 1924, NL Hamm.

16. Charles S. Maier, *Recasting Bourgeois Europe: Stabilization in France, Germany, and Italy in the Decade after World War I* (Princeton, 1975), p. 486, n. 7.

17. Stürmer, *Koalition und Opposition*, pp. 49–58. On the situation in the DNVP, see Lewis Hertzman, *DNVP: Right-Wing Opposition in the Weimar Republic, 1918–1924* (Lincoln, 1963), pp. 204–39.

18. *NLC*, 1 Sept. 1924, no. 145. See also the memorandum of Stresemann's conver-

sation with Curtius and Zapf from the DVP Reichstag delegation, 24 Aug. 1924, AA: NL Stresemann, 3119/15/156931–32.

19. Stresemann to Campe, 8 Sept. 1924, AA: NL Stresemann, 3119/15/157093–96.

20. *NLC*, 25 Sept. 1924, no. 157. For further details, see Curtius, "Politische Umschau: Der Kampf um eine Mehrheitsregierung," *DS* 36, no. 21 (5 Nov. 1924): 339–46.

21. Stürmer, *Koalition und Opposition*, pp. 73–78.

22. DVP, Reichsgeschäftsstelle, *Nachtrag zum Wahlhandbuch 1924*, pp. 98–99.

23. Ibid., pp. 99–100.

24. Resolution by the DDP Reichstag delegation, 15 Oct. 1924, in *DAZ*, 16 Oct. 1924, no. 488. See also Erkelenz to Tantzen, 16 Oct. 1924, BA: NL Erkelenz, 33/67.

25. Koch-Weser, "Vor neuen Entscheidungen," *BTB*, 14 Sept. 1924, no. 438.

26. Heuss to Koch-Weser, 1 Oct. 1924, BA: NL Heuss, 58.

27. In this respect, see Gessler to Heuss, 31 Oct. 1924, BA: NL Heuss, 79.

28. Böhme to Koch-Weser, n.d., in *Deutscher Bauernbund* 16, no. 42 (16 Oct. 1924): 349–50.

29. Marx to Koch-Weser, 18 Oct. 1924, BA: NL Koch-Weser, 87/53–54.

30. Resolution I signed by Schiffer, Keinath, Gerland, Gessler, and Sparrer, 20 Oct. 1924, BA: NL Schiffer, 23/96.

31. Resolution II signed by Schiffer, Gerland, Keinath, Sparrer, and Kopsch, 21 [*sic*] Oct. 1924, BA: NL Schiffer, 23/96.

32. *KZ*, 21 Oct. 1924, no. 744. See also the entry in Koch-Weser's diary, 20 Oct. 1924, BA: NL Koch-Weser, 31/31–32.

33. Statement by Schiffer, Keinath, and Gerland, n.d., BA: NL Schiffer, 23/209. See also *KZ*, 22 Oct. 1924, no. 748.

34. *KZ*, 23 Oct. 1924, no. 751. For the most exhaustive accounts of the reasons behind the secession, see Gerland, "Mein Austritt aus der Demokratischen Partei," *Fränkischer Kurier*, 19 and 20 Nov. 1924, nos. 322–23, as well as Gerland's open letter to Koch-Weser, 25 Oct. 1924, in *KZ*, 28 Oct. 1924, no. 764, and Schiffer's open letter to Baumgartner, 8 Nov. 1924, in *FZ*, 11 Nov. 1924, no. 844. Also of interest are Gerland's letter to his sister, 24 Oct. 1924, BA: NL Gerland, 45, and Schiffer's letter to Tantzen, 19 Dec. 1924, BA: NL Schiffer, 23/35–36.

35. Rothenbücher to Erkelenz, 29 Oct. 1924, BA: NL Erkelenz, 128.

36. Siemens to Koch-Weser, 30 Sept. 1924, SAA: NL Siemens, 4/Lf 514.

37. "Aufruf der Liberalen Vereinigung," [28 Oct. 1924], SAA: NL Siemens, 4/Lf 697.

38. Eugen Schiffer, *Ein Leben für Liberalismus* (Berlin, 1951), pp. 234–35.

39. On the LV's strategy during the campaign for the Dec. 1924 elections, see Gerland, "Die Liberale Vereinigung und ihre Ziele," *KZ*, 23 Nov. 1924, and Schiffer, "Die Wahlen und die Liberale Vereinigung," *Schöneberger Morgenzeitung*, 4 Dec. 1924, no. 43, as well as the manifesto of the Liberal Association, 27 Nov. 1924, SAA: NL Siemens, 4/Lf 697.

40. In particular, see Schiffer, "Deutsche Demokratische Partei und Liberale Vereinigung," *Hamburgischer Korrespondent*, 6 Nov. 1924, no. 521, as well as the "Aufruf der Liberalen Vereinigung," [28 Oct. 1924], SAA: NL Siemens, 4/Lf 697.

41. DDP, Reichsgeschäftsstelle, ed., *Die Liberale Vereinigung*, Materialien zur demokratischen Politik, no. 120 (Berlin, 1924), pp. 13–22.

42. Stresemann to Wappes, 4 Nov. 1924, AA: NL Stresemann, 3160/91/172285–86.

43. Werner Stephan, *Aufstieg und Verfall des Linksliberalismus. Geschichte der Deutschen Demokratischen Partei* (Göttingen, 1973), p. 277.

44. Minutes of the DDP executive committee, 21 Oct. 1924, BA: R 45 III/16/96–97.

45. Hamm to Dirr, 5 Nov. 1924, NL Hamm.

46. Mosich to Koch-Weser, 3 Nov. 1924, BA: NL Erkelenz, 128.

47. Erich Koch-Weser, *Gerade aus—nicht rechts, nicht links! Rede auf dem demokratischen Parteitag am 2. November 1924 zu Berlin* (Berlin, [1924]), pp. 1–6. See also *Der Demokrat* 5, nos. 36–37 (Nov. 6, 1924): 297–300, and Stephan, *Linksliberalismus*, pp. 278–79.

48. For further details, see Delius to Erkelenz, 27 Oct. 1924; Lemmer to Erkelenz, 29 Oct. 1924; and Thal to Erkelenz, 30 Oct. 1924, all in BA: NL Erkelenz, 128, as well as the *Handbuch für die Mitglieder des Reichsausschusses der deutschen demokratischen Beamten, für Vorsitzende der Ortsbeamtenausschüsse und Vertrauenspersonen*, ed. Gerhard Vogt (Berlin, 1925), pp. 28–29.

49. Stephan, *Linksliberalismus*, pp. 279–80.

50. For example, see the exchange in *NLC*, 3 Dec. 1924, no. 201, as well as the postelection correspondence between Stresemann and Koch-Weser, 12 Dec. 1924–3 Jan. 1925, AA: NL Stresemann, 3160/91/172407–8, 172421–27; 3160/92/172442–46, 172452–54, 172472.

51. In this respect, see Hugo's remarks before the DVP central executive committee, 7 July 1924, BA: R 45 II/39/345–49.

52. Zapf to Stresemann, 24 Oct. 1924, AA: NL Stresemann, 3160/90/172213–14.

53. For example, see Curtius to Reusch, 31 Oct. 1924, and Woltmann to Curtius, 6 Nov. 1924, both in HA/GHH: Allgemeine Verwaltung, 400106/83.

54. For example, see Morath, "Die Deutsche Volkspartei und die Beamten," *KZ*, 29 Nov. 1924, no. 843, and *Beamtenpolitik der Deutschen Volkspartei*, Flugschriften der Deutschen Volkspartei, no. 58 (Berlin, 1924), as well as *Mittelstandspolitik der Deutschen Volkspartei*, Flugschriften der Deutschen Volkspartei, no. 55 (Berlin, 1924).

55. *KZ*, 13 Oct. 1924, no. 724.

56. Gustav Stresemann, *Nationale Realpolitik. Rede auf dem 6. Parteitag der Deutschen Volkspartei in Dortmund am 14. November 1924*, Flugschriften der Deutschen Volkspartei, no. 56 (Berlin, 1924), pp. 9–11, 17–19.

57. For example, see Hjalmar Schacht, *Zwölf Monate demokratischer Politik. Rede am 4. November 1924 in Dessau* (Berlin, [1924]), pp. 4–6.

58. See "Aufruf der 'Aufwertungs- und Aufbaupartei' " and the official announcement of the party's founding, both dated 1 Nov. 1924 and appended to an official party circular from 9 Nov. 1924, GSA Berlin-Dahlem, ZSg XII/IV, no. 220. For the party's basic orientation, see Reinhard Wüst, *Im Aufwertungskampf für Wahrheit und Recht gegen "Luthertum" und "Marxismus." Eine gemeinverständliche Auseinandersetzung*

mit den Trugschlüssen und Schlagworten der Aufwertungsgegnern (Halle, 1924).

59. See "Wahlaufruf u. Programm der Aufwertungs- und Wiederaufbau-Partei," n.d., GSA Berlin-Dahlem, ZSg, XII/IV, no. 220.

60. *Die Aufwertung*, 7 Nov. 1924, no. 7.

61. See the letter from Stephan, DDP general secretary, to the Savers' Association, 29 Oct. 1924, in *Die Demokratie und die Aufwertung*, Materialien zur demokratischen Politik, no. 112 (Berlin, 1924), p. 10, as well as Külz, "Die Demokratische Partei und die Aufwertung der öffentlichen Anleihen," 24 Nov. 1924, BA: NL Dietrich, 294/86–87. See also the entry in Koch-Weser's diary, 19 Nov. 1924, BA: NL Koch-Weser, 31/43.

62. Wunderlich, "Aufwertung und Fürstenauseinandersetzung," in *Deutscher Aufbau. Nationalliberale Arbeit der Deutschen Volkspartei*, ed. Adolf Kempkes (Berlin, 1927), pp. 192–202, as well as Wunderlich's speech before the DVP's Dortmund party congress, 13 Nov. 1924, BA: R 45 II/29/163–99, and Stresemann, *Nationale Realpolitik*, pp. 39–42.

63. *Die Aufwertung*, 28 Nov. 1924, no. 27.

64. Heino Kaack, *Geschichte und Struktur des deutschen Parteiensystems. Ein Handbuch* (Opladen, 1971), pp. 97–100.

65. *Der Demokrat* 10, nos. 42/43 (18 Dec. 1924): 358–63. See also Stephan, *Linksliberalismus*, pp. 280–81.

66. Kaack, *Parteiensystem*, p. 100.

CHAPTER EIGHTEEN

1. Above all else, see M. Rainer Lepsius, "From Fragmented Party Democracy to Government by Emergency Decree and National Socialist Takeover: Germany," in *The Breakdown of Democratic Regimes: Europe*, ed. Juan J. Linz and Alfred Stephan (Baltimore, 1978), pp. 35–46.

2. Minutes of a ministerial conference, 19 Dec. 1924, BA: NL Gessler, 50/60–63, reprinted in Otto Gessler, *Reichswehrpolitik in der Weimarer Zeit*, ed. Kurt Sendtner and with an introduction by Theodor Heuss (Stuttgart, 1958), pp. 498–500.

3. Koch-Weser to Gessler, 9 Dec. 1924, BA: NL Koch-Weser, 139, and Koch-Weser to Hamm, 9 Dec. 1924, NL Hamm.

4. Stresemann's remarks at a ministerial conference, 10 Dec. 1924, in *Akten der Reichskanzlei: Das Kabinett Marx I und II. 30. November 1923 bis 3. Juni 1924. 3. Juni 1924 bis 15. Januar 1925*, ed. Günter Abramowski, 2 vols. (Boppard am Rhein, 1973), 2:1219–20. See also the manuscript of an article by Stresemann, "Zur Regierungskrise," 24 Dec. 1924, AA: NL Stresemann, 3120/18/157792–806.

5. Dingeldey to Heyl zu Herrensheim, 13 Dec. 1924, BA: NL Dingeldey, 72/159–60.

6. Riesser to his son, 17 Dec. 1924, BA: NL Riesser (Kleine Erwerbung 549), 1/84.

7. Stresemann to Retzmann, 26 Dec. 1924, AA: NL Stresemann, 3120/18/157822–23.

8. *NLC*, 7 Jan. 1925, no. 4.

9. Minutes of the Center Reichstag delegation, 9 Jan. 1925, in Rudolf Morsey and Karsten Ruppert, eds., *Die Protokolle der Reichstagsfraktion der Deutschen Zentrumspartei 1920–1925* (Mainz, 1981), p. 551.

10. Hans Luther, *Politiker ohne Partei. Erinnerungen* (Stuttgart, 1960), pp. 315–18.

11. Entry in Koch-Weser's diary, 13 Jan. 1925, BA: NL Koch-Weser, 32/35–37.

12. For example, see Tantzen to Erkelenz, 30 Jan. 1925, BA: NL Erkelenz, 90/179.

13. Erkelenz's remarks before the DDP executive committee, 2 Feb. 1925, in Lothar Albertin, ed., *Linksliberalismus in der Weimarer Republik. Die Führungsgremien der Deutschen Demokratischen Partei und der Deutschen Staatspartei 1918–1933* (Düsseldorf, 1980), pp. 334–35.

14. For example, see Erich Koch-Weser, *Wider den Rechtsblock. Rede im Reichstag, am 21. Januar 1925* (Berlin, [1925]), pp. 7–8.

15. Ludwig Haas, *Die deutsche Demokratie und das Kabinett Luther. Reichstags-Rede vom 22. Januar 1925* (Berlin, [1925]), pp. 1–8.

16. Werner Stephan, *Aufstieg und Verfall des Linksliberalismus. Geschichte der Deutschen Demokratischen Partei* (Göttingen, 1973), pp. 284–85.

17. For a detailed analysis of Stresemann's relations with the DNVP, see Robert P. Grathwohl, *Stresemann and the DNVP: Reconciliation or Revenge in German Foreign Policy, 1924–1928* (Lawrence, 1980).

18. Erkelenz to Wildermuth, 30 Jan. 1925, BA: NL Erkelenz, 90/176–78.

19. Koch-Weser to his fiancée, 8 Mar. 1925, BA: NL Koch-Weser, 32/53–55. See also the circular from Erkelenz, Koch-Weser, and Fischer to the members of the DDP national organization, 9 May 1925, BA: R 45 III/33/43–47, as well as Werner Schneider, *Die Deutsche Demokratische Partei in der Weimarer Republik 1924–1930* (Munich, 1978), pp. 108–13.

20. Erkelenz to the leaders of the Center, DNVP, DVP, BVP, SPD, Loebell Committee, and Business Party, 9 Mar. 1925, BA: NL Erkelenz, 130.

21. For further details, see Loebell, "Die Verhandlungen des Loebell-Ausschusses," *Der Deutschen-Spiegel. Politische Wochenschrift* 2, no. 13 (27 Mar. 1925): 581–87. On the formation and composition of the Loebell Committee, see Roland Thimme, *Stresemann und die Deutsche Volkspartei 1923–1925* (Lübeck and Hamburg, 1961), pp. 109–11, and Hans-Jochen Hauss, *Die erste Volkswahl des deutschen Reichspräsidenten. Eine Untersuchung ihrer verfassungspolitischen Grundlagen, ihrer Vorgeschichte und ihres Verlaufes unter besonderer Berücksichtigung des Anteils Bayerns und der Bayerischen Volkspartei* (Kallmünz, 1965), pp. 41–43.

22. Loebell to Jarres, 9 Mar. 1925, BA: NL Jarres, 23.

23. Koch-Weser and Erkelenz, "Zu den Verhandlungen über die Aufstellung des Reichswehrministers Gessler als Kandidat für das Amt des Reichspräsidenten," [14 Mar. 1925], BA: NL Koch-Weser, 147.

24. Entry in Koch-Weser's diary, 15 Mar. 1925, BA: NL Koch-Weser, 32/73–81.

25. For Stresemann's reasons, see his letter to Gessler, 11 Mar. 1925, BA: NL Gessler, 9/62–64, reprinted in Gessler, *Reichswehrpolitik*, pp. 506–7. For the most detailed accounts of Stresemann's opposition to the Gessler candidacy, see Thimme, *Stresemann und die Deutsche Volkspartei*, pp. 116–21, and Henry Ashby Turner, Jr., *Stresemann and the Politics of the Weimar Republic* (Princeton, 1963), pp. 193–95.

26. *Die Zeit*, 13 Mar. 1925, no. 100. See also Riesser to his son, [Mar. 1925], BA: NL Riesser (Kleine Erwerbung 549), 1/90.

27. *Die Zeit*, 13 Mar. 1925, no. 100. See also the report of this meeting in AA: NL Stresemann, 3160/92/172588–89.

28. On the collapse of Gessler's candidacy, see the statement by Koch-Weser and Erkelenz, [14 Mar. 1925], BA: NL Koch-Weser, 147, as well as the entry in Koch-Weser's diary, 15 Mar. 1925, ibid., 32/73–81.

29. For example, see Kardorff to Stresemann, 13 Mar. 1925, AA: NL Stresemann, 3160/92/172585–87.

30. Koch-Weser to his fiancée, 13 Mar. 1925, BA: NL Koch-Weser, 32/59–61.

31. For a highly colorful, yet less than objective account of Hellpach's candidacy, see Willy Hellpach, *Wirken in Wirren. Lebenserinnerungen. Eine Rechenschaft über Wert und Glück, Schuld und Sturz meiner Generation*, 2 vols. (Hamburg, 1949), 2:252–75.

32. Vogt, "Zum Wahlergebnis vom 29. März," *Der Demokrat* 6, no. 7 (9 Apr. 1925): 181–82.

33. Hauss, *Volkswahl*, pp. 72–77.

34. Ibid., pp. 81–82.

35. In this respect, see Rheinbaben to Bredt, 25 Mar. 1925, in Johann Victor Bredt, *Erinnerungen und Dokumente von Joh. Victor Bredt 1914 bis 1933*, ed. Martin Schumacher (Düsseldorf, 1970), pp. 347–49.

36. Remarks by Koch-Weser before the DDP party council, 5 Apr. 1925, in Albertin, *Linksliberalismus*, pp. 342–43. See also circular no. 33 from the DDP national headquarters, 7 Apr. 1925, BA: R 45 III/33/49–54.

37. For example, see the dissenting comments by Hellpach before the DDP executive committee, 2 Apr. 1925, and by Fischer, Cohnstaedt, and Willenberg at a meeting of the DDP party council, 5 Apr. 1925, in Albertin, *Linksliberalismus*, pp. 341–48, as well as "Bericht über die zweite Reichspräsidentenwahl," [Apr.–May 1925], BA: NL Erkelenz, 111/146–50.

38. Turner, *Stresemann*, pp. 196–97; Hauss, *Volkswahl*, pp. 85–95.

39. In this connection, see Curtius's notes on the meeting of the Loebell Committee, 8 Apr. 1925, BA: R 45 II/11/217–25, and Jarres to Stresemann, 15 Apr. 1925, AA: NL Stresemann, 3163/23/158731, as well as the discussion of Hindenburg's nomination by Andreas Dorpalen, *Hindenburg and the Weimar Republic* (Princeton, 1964), pp. 64–75.

40. Stresemann, "Deutsche Volkspartei und Reichspräsidentenwahl," *Die Zeit*, 19 Apr. 1925, no. 160.

41. Müller-Meiningen and Stolz to Koch-Weser, 9 Apr. 1925, BA: NL Erkelenz, 36/37a.

42. "Bericht über die zweite Reichspräsidentenwahl," [Apr.–May 1925], BA: NL Erkelenz, 111/146–50.

43. For further details, see John K. Zeender, "The German Catholics and the Presidential Election of 1925," *JMH* 35 (1963): 366–81, and Karl Holl, "Konfessionalität, Konfessionalismus und demokratische Republik—zu einigen Aspekten der Reichspräsidentenwahl von 1925," *VfZ* 17 (1969): 254–75.

44. For further details, see Turner, *Stresemann*, pp. 203–18, and Grathwohl, *Stresemann and the DNVP*, pp. 102–44.

45. For example, see Stresemann to Keudell, 27 Nov. 1925, AA: NL Stresemann, 3146/32/160613–15.

46. Jarres to Treviranus, 31 Oct. 1925, BA: NL Jarres, 54.

47. See the entry in Koch-Weser's diary, 21 Nov. 1925, BA: NL Koch-Weser, 32/157–61, as well as his speech, "Erstrebtes und Erreichtes," at the DDP's Breslau party congress, 4–6 Dec. 1925, in *Der Demokrat* 6, no. 17 (27 Dec. 1925): 536–43.

48. See Hindenburg's comments in a conversation with Scholz, 7 Dec. 1925, in *Akten der Reichskanzlei: Die Kabinette Luther I und II. 15. Januar 1925 bis 20. Januar 1926. 20. Januar 1926 bis 17. Mai 1926*, ed. Karl-Heinz Minuth, 2 vols. (Boppard am Rhein, 1977), 2:986. For further information on the intervention of Hindenburg's entourage in the cabinet negotiations in the winter of 1925–26, see Michael Stürmer, *Koalition und Opposition in der Weimarer Republik 1924–1928* (Düsseldorf, 1967), pp. 135–46, 288–90, and Dorpalen, *Hindenburg*, pp. 98–101.

49. Entry in Koch-Weser's diary, 7 Dec. 1925, BA: NL Koch-Weser, 32/167–69.

50. Koch-Weser's "Richtlinien" for the formation of a government based on the "Great Coalition," [18 Dec. 1925], BA: NL Koch-Weser, 32/219–27.

51. Minutes of the executive committee of the DVP Reichstag delegation, 9 Dec. 1925, BA: R 45 II/66/60–62.

52. Entry in Koch-Weser's diary, 18 Dec. 1925, BA: NL Koch-Weser, 39/209–17.

53. Koch-Weser to Marx, 19 Dec. 1925, BA: NL Koch-Weser, 100. See also the correspondence between Koch-Weser and Haas, 21–31 Dec. 1925, ibid.

54. Marx to Koch-Weser, 24 Dec. 1925, BA: NL Koch-Weser, 100.

55. Entry in Koch-Weser's diary, 30 Jan. 1926, BA: NL Koch-Weser, 34/3–5.

56. Koch-Weser's remarks before the DDP party council, 24 Jan. 1926, in Albertin, *Linksliberalismus*, p. 363.

57. Dietrich to Dees, 26 Jan. 1926, BA: NL Dietrich, 79/64–65. See also the entry in Koch-Weser's diary, 30 Jan. 1926, BA: NL Koch-Weser, 34/11–13.

58. In this respect, see Luther's memorandum of a conversation with Hindenburg, Westarp, and Schiele, 28 Jan. 1926, BA: NL Luther, 362.

59. Entry in Stresemann's diary, 28 Jan. 1926, in Gustav Stresemann, *Vermächtnis. Der Nachlaß in drei Bänden*, ed. Henry Bernhard, 3 vols. (Berlin, 1932–33), 2:386–87.

60. Stephan, *Linksliberalismus*, p. 318.

61. *Vossische Zeitung*, 3 Feb. 1926, no. 29.

62. For the text of Koch-Weser's and Stresemann's remarks, see [Liberale Vereinigung], *Die Liberale Vereinigung* (Berlin, [1926]), pp. 10–14.

CHAPTER NINETEEN

1. For a general survey of the economic development of the German middle classes during the Weimar Republic, see Herman Lebovics, *Social Conservatism and the Middle Classes in Germany, 1914–1933* (Princeton, 1969), pp. 13–48. See also Konrad H. Jarausch, "The Crisis of the German Professions, 1918–33," *JCH* 20 (1985): 379–98. On the problems of the white-collar class, see Jürgen Kocka, "Zur Problematik der deutschen Angestellten 1914–1933," in *Industrielles System und politische Entwicklung in der Weimarer Republik. Verhandlungen des Internationalen Symposiums in Bochum vom 12.–17. Juni 1973*, ed. Hans Mommsen, Dietmar Petzina, and Bernd Weisbrod (Düsseldorf, 1974), pp. 792–811, as well as Heinz-Jürgen Priamus,

Angestellte und Demokratie. Die nationalliberale Angestelltenbewegung in der Weimarer Republik (Stuttgart, 1979), pp. 19–33. For the state civil service during the early years of the Weimar Republic, see Andreas Kunz, *Civil Servants and the Politics of Inflation 1914–1924* (Berlin, 1986).

2. For a general survey of this problem, see Heinrich August Winkler, "From Social Protectionism to National Socialism: The German Small-Business Movement in Comparative Perspective," *JMH* 48 (1976): 1–18.

3. For example, see the exchange between Dauch and Moldenhauer, both members of the DVP Reichstag delegation, in *Der künftige Kurs der deutschen Sozialpolitik. Verhandlungen des Wirtschaftspolitischen Ausschusses des Hansa-Bundes für Gewerbe, Handel und Industrie, Berlin, 4. Dezember 1926*, Flugschriften des Hansa-Bundes, no. 8 (Berlin, 1927), pp. 59–63.

4. Werner Schneider, *Die Deutsche Demokratische Partei in der Weimarer Republik 1924–1930* (Munich, 1978), pp. 46–57.

5. In this respect, see not only Henry Ashby Turner, Jr., *Stresemann and the Politics of the Weimar Republic* (Princeton, 1963), pp. 179–81, but also the incisive essay by Lewis Hertzman, "Gustav Stresemann: The Problem of Political Leadership in the Weimar Republic," *International Review of Social History* 5 (1960): 370–71.

6. On the founding and early history of the WP, see Hermann Drewitz, "Die politische Standesbewegung des deutschen Mittelstandes vor und nach dem Kriege," in *Jahrbuch der Reichspartei des deutschen Mittelstandes 1929*, ed. Reichspartei des deutschen Mittelstandes (n.p., [1929]), pp. 19–23, as well as the detailed monograph by Martin Schumacher, *Mittelstandsfront und Republik. Die Wirtschaftspartei— Reichspartei des deutschen Mittelstandes 1919–1933* (Düsseldorf, 1972), pp. 31–34.

7. Franz Jörissen, *Hausbesitz und Mittelstand. Nach einem Vortrag gehalten auf dem Verbandstage des Zentralverbandes deutscher Haus- und Grundbesitzer-Vereine Köln a. Rhein 1921*, Schriften des Zentralverbandes der Haus- und Grundbesitzer-Vereine Deutschlands, no. 22 (Spandau, 1921).

8. Seyfart to the DVP, Landesverband Preußen, 18 Nov. 1920, BA: R 45 II/9/37, and to the DVP Reichsgeschäftsstelle, 17 Dec. 1920, ibid., 61–62.

9. Seyfart to Bredt, 13 Jan. 1921, NL Bredt.

10. Seyfart, confidential circular to the Home Owners' Organization in Prussia, Jan. 1921, NL Bredt. See also Martin Schumacher, "Hausbesitz, Mittelstand und Wirtschaftspartei in der Weimarer Republik," in *Industrielles System und politische Entwicklung*, ed. Mommsen, Petzina, and Weisbrod, pp. 829–30.

11. Johann Victor Bredt, *Erinnerungen und Dokumente von Joh. Victor Bredt 1914 bis 1933*, ed. Martin Schumacher (Düsseldorf, 1970), pp. 163–66.

12. *Das Deutsche Handwerksblatt* 14, no. 10 (Oct. 1920): 229. See also Herfürth, "Handwerk und Mittelstandsbewegung," ibid., no. 11 (Nov. 1920): 231–32.

13. Vogel, "Die Organisation des Handwerks und die politischen Parteien," ibid., 15, no. 2 (15 Jan. 1921): 17–20.

14. See the remarks by the organization's founder and first chairman, Leo Schwering, in Christlicher Mittelstand, Generalsekretariat, ed., *Christlicher Mittelstand. Mittelstandstagung für das westliche Deutschland am 24. und 25. Februar 1920 im Vortragssaal der Bürgergesellschaft zu Köln* (Cologne, [1920]), p. 40. See also Schumacher, *Mittelstandsfront*, pp. 35–42.

15. Preußisches Statistisches Landesamt, ed., *Die Wahlen zum Preußischen Land-*

tag am 20. Februar 1921 und 19. November 1922 (Berlin, 1924), pp. 4–5, 94–97.

16. See the speeches by Drewitz, Bredt, Ladendorff, and Holzamer in Wirtschafts-partei des deutschen Mittelstandes, Generalsekretariat, ed., *Verhandlungen des 1. Parteitages der Wirtschaftspartei des deutschen Mittelstandes zu Breslau vom 23., 24. und 25. April 1921* (Berlin, [1921]), pp. 22–28, as well as Bredt, *Erinnerungen und Dokumente*, pp. 169–71.

17. Rosenhauer, "Der Mittelstand und die Mittelstandspartei," *Das Deutsche Hand-werksblatt* 15, no. 9 (1 May 1921): 129–30.

18. For further information, see the paper presented by Gerald D. Feldman, "Coping with Inflation: The Controlled Economy, Anti-Profiteering Laws, and the Social Classes," at a seminar of the Lehrman Institute, New York City, 13 Apr. 1982.

19. Schumacher, "Hausbesitz, Mittelstand und Wirtschaftspartei," pp. 825–29. See also Peter-Christian Witt, "Inflation, Wohnungszwangswirtschaft und Hauszinssteuer. Zur Regelung von Wohnungsbau und Wohnungsmarkt in der Weimarer Republik," in *Wohnen im Wandel. Beiträge zur Geschichte des Alltages in der bürgerlichen Gesell-schaft*, ed. Lutz Niethammer (Wuppertal, 1979), pp. 390–99, and Dan P. Silverman, "A Pledge Unredeemed: The Housing Crisis in Weimar Germany," *CEH* 3 (1970): 112–39.

20. Schumacher, *Mittelstandsfront*, pp. 42–43.

21. *Der Mittelstand*, 16 July 1922, no. 25. See also Drewitz, "Standesbewegung," p. 23, and Bredt, *Erinnerungen und Dokumente*, p. 174.

22. For further details, see Karl-Bernhard Netzband and Hans Peter Widmaier, *Währungs- und Finanzpolitik in der Ära Luther 1923–1925* (Tübingen, 1964), pp. 227–31. See also *Deutsche Handels-Warte* 12, no. 10 (May 1924): 288–91.

23. In particular, see the WP's election appeal for the May 1924 Reichstag elections as well as the speeches by Drewitz, Bredt, and Ladendorff at the WP's Berlin party congress, 22–24 Mar. 1924, in Wirtschaftspartei des deutschen Mittelstandes, Partei-vorstand, ed., *Handbuch der Wirtschaftspartei des deutschen Mittelstandes für die Reichstags- und Gemeindewahlen 1924* (Berlin, [1924]), pp. 2–5, 10–20, 25–29.

24. Heino Kaack, *Geschichte und Struktur des deutschen Parteiensystems. Ein Handbuch* (Opladen, 1971), pp. 97–100. For further information, see Bredt, *Erinne-rungen und Dokumente*, pp. 175–77, as well as the statistical tables in Schumacher, *Mittelstandsfront*, pp. 222–23.

25. Fehr to Bredt, 9 May 1924, NL Bredt.

26. Protocol of an agreement between Fehr (BBB), Hempe and Alpers (DHP), and Bredt and Dannenberg (WP), 5 Nov. 1924, NL Bredt.

27. See in particular the remarks by Meusch, Thierkopf, and Würm in Reichsver-band des deutschen Handwerks, ed., *Stenographischer Bericht über die Verhand-lungen der 2. (24.) Vertreterversammlung des Deutschen Handwerks- und Gewerbe-kammertages und der 5. Vollversammlung des Reichsverbandes des deutschen Hand-werks am 27. und 28. Mai in Berlin* (Hanover, 1924), pp. 12–16, 33–35.

28. "Das Handwerk und die Wahlen," [Oct. 1924], BA: NL Dietrich, 219/241.

29. This point has been persuasively argued by Frank Domurad, "The Politics of Corporatism: Hamburg Handicraft in the Late Weimar Republic, 1927–1933," in *Social Change and Political Development in Weimar Germany*, ed. Richard Bessel and E. J. Feuchtwanger (London and New York, 1981), pp. 174–206.

30. Meusch, "Die Berufsstandspolitik des Handwerks," *Das Deutsche Handwerks-*

blatt 18, no. 13 (1 July 1924): 193–98. For a discussion of corporatist thought in the Weimar Republic, see Domurad, "Politics of Corporatism," pp. 175–87, and Lebovics, *Social Conservatism*, pp. 109–12.

31. Domurad, "Politics of Corporatism," pp. 188–89.

32. For example, see *Der Mittelstand*, 15 Jan. 1927, no. 2.

33. See the text of the "Richtlinien der Wirtschaftspartei des Deutschen Mittelstandes" from Nov. 1922, in Reichspartei des deutschen Mittelstandes, *Jahrbuch der Reichspartei des deutschen Mittelstandes 1929*, pp. 144–46.

34. Bredt, *Erinnerungen und Dokumente*, p. 181.

35. Reichspartei des deutschen Mittelstandes, ed., *Die Satzungen und Görlitzer Richtlinien der Reichspartei des deutschen Mittelstandes e.V. (Wirtschaftspartei)* (Berlin, [1929]), pp. 18–31. See also Bredt, "Das politische Parlament und die berufsständischen Vertretungen," in *Volk und Reich der Deutschen*, ed. Bernhard Harms, 3 vols. (Berlin, 1929), 2:282–300.

36. Johann Victor Bredt, *Hypothetken-Aufwertung* (Munich, [1924]).

37. The best source of information on the early history of the revaluation movement is a speech by Adolf Bauser, "Die Geschichte des Aufwertungskampfes," at a convention held by the Reich Party for People's Justice and Revaluation in Stuttgart, 5–6 Mar. 1927, in *Für Wahrheit und Recht. Der Endkampf um eine gerechte Aufwertung. Reden und Aufsätze*, ed. Adolf Bauser (Stuttgart, 1927), pp. 5–11. Much of the following has been excerpted from Jones, "Inflation, Revaluation, and the Crisis of Middle-Class Politics: A Study in the Dissolution of the German Party System, 1923–28," *CEH* 12 (1979): 149–68.

38. On the legal aspects of the revaluation question, see David Southern, "The Impact of the Inflation: Inflation, the Courts and Revaluation," in *Social Change and Political Development*, ed. Bessel and Feuchtwanger, pp. 55–76, and Michael Hughes, "Economic Interest, Social Attitudes, and Creditor Ideology: Popular Responses to Inflation," in *Die deutsche Inflation. Eine Zwischenbilanz/The German Inflation Reconsidered: A Preliminary Balance*, ed. Gerald D. Feldman et al. (Berlin and New York, 1982), pp. 385–408.

39. For example, see Reinhard Wüst, *Das Aufwertungsproblem und die 3. Steuernotverordnung. Eine gemeinverständliche Betrachtung* (Halle, 1924).

40. Bauser, "Geschichte des Aufwertungskampfes," p. 7.

41. Kaack, *Parteiensystem*, pp. 99–100.

42. *Die Aufwertung*, 28 Nov. 1924, no. 24.

43. In this respect, see Hermann Dietrich, *Gegen die Ausbeutung des Mittelstandes zugunsten des Großkapitals. Für eine gerechte Entschädigung aller Kriegs- und Inflationsgeschädigten. Rede im Reichstag am 20. Februar 1925* (Berlin, [1925]).

44. Protocol of a meeting between the government and representatives from the government parties, 18 Mar. 1925, in *Akten der Reichskanzlei: Die Kabinette Luther I und II. 15. Januar 1925 bis 20. Januar 1926. 20. Januar 1926 bis 17. Mai 1926*, ed. Karl-Heinz Minuth, 2 vols. (Boppard am Rhein, 1977), 1:185–97.

45. In this respect, see Hermann Dietrich, *Aufwertung und Deutsche Demokratische Partei. Der Wahlschwindel der Deutschnationalen. Rede gehalten im Deutschen Reichstag am 8. Mai 1925* (Berlin, [1925]).

46. See the correspondence between Best and the DNVP party leadership in *Der*

Endkampf um die Aufwertung, Deutschnationale Flugschrift, no. 219 (Berlin, 1925), pp. 27–32, as well as Best, "Das Kompromiß in der Aufwertungsfrage und seine Väter," *Die Aufwertung*, 12 June 1925, no. 23.

47. Bauser, "Notwendigkeit, Aufgaben und Ziele der Volksrechtspartei," in *Für Wahrheit und Recht*, ed. Bauser, pp. 90–91.

48. On the goals and ideological orientation of the VRP, see ibid., pp. 92–95, and Posadowsky-Wehner, "Ansprache, gehalten auf der Reichsdelegiertentagung des Sparerbundes zu Erfurt am 28. August 1926," in Adolf von Posadowsky-Wehner, *Die Enteignung des Gläubiger-Vermögens. Eine Sammlung von Aufsätzen* (Berlin, [1928]), pp. 42–46. For the official party program presented at the VRP's delegate congress in Nov. 1926 and formally adopted at Naumburg in Sept. 1927, see "Programm der Volksrechts-Partei (Reichspartei für Volksrecht und Aufwertung) VRP," n.d., BA: ZSg 1/261 (1).

49. See Jörissen's remarks at a meeting between government officials and representatives of the government parties, 18 Mar. 1925, in *Die Kabinette Luther*, ed. Minuth, 1:187–88.

50. On the course of these negotiations, see Frank to Stresemann, 24 Aug. 1926, with the protocol of a meeting in Dresden, 22 Aug. 1926, AA: NL Stresemann, 3161/96/173213–17, and Dieckmann to Stresemann, 24 and 28 Aug. 1926, ibid., 173221–24, as well as Arthur Graefe, *3 Jahre Aufbaupolitik. Zu den Sachsenwahlen 1926*, ed. Sächsische Wahlkreisverbände der Deutschen Volkspartei (Dresden, 1926), pp. 59–62.

51. "Vom Klassenstaat zum Volksstaat. Vier Jahren sächsischer Politik 1922–1926," [Oct. 1926], Bayerisches Hauptstaatsarchiv, Munich, Abt. V, Flugblätter-Sammlung, F 62/1926.

52. Stresemann to Kaiser, 27 Oct. 1926, AA: NL Stresemann, 3162/97/173325–34.

53. Memorandum by Rademacher, "Zur Frage der Aufwertung," 19 Nov. 1926, NL Westarp.

54. Dieckmann to Stresemann, 30 Sept. [*sic*; Oct] 1926, AA: NL Stresemann, Col. U. 2/299.

55. *Wirtschaft und Statistik* 6, no. 21 (18 Nov. 1926): 783–84.

56. Ibid., no. 3 (Feb. 1927): 155–56. See also *Der Demokrat* 8, no. 3 (10 Feb. 1927): 35.

57. Stresemann, "Die Gegenwartsaufgaben des nationalen Liberalismus," *DS* 38, no. 23 (5 Dec. 1926): 553–58.

CHAPTER TWENTY

1. For example, see Bredt, "Berufsgedanke und Parteireform," *KZ*, 10 Feb. 1930, no. 81a.

2. In this respect, see Stephan's report at the DDP's Breslau party congress, 6 Sept. 1925, BA: R 45 III/5/119–33, and Erkelenz, "Organisatorisches," *Der Demokrat* 7, no. 1 (7 Jan. 1926): 2–4. For a regional breakdown of the DDP's national membership, see DDP, Reichsgeschäftsstelle, ed., *Organisationshandbuch der Deutschen Demo-*

kratischen Partei (Berlin, 1926), pp. 438–39. For further information, see Werner Schneider, *Die Deutsche Demokratische Partei in der Weimarer Republik 1924–1930* (Munich, 1978), pp. 222–30.

3. Circular from the DDP Reichsgeschäftsstelle, 1 Dec. 1924, BA: R 45 III/ 32/102.

4. Report by Fischer to the DDP party council, 18 Oct. 1922, BA: R 45 III/11/184.

5. In this respect, see the letters from Erkelenz to Mendelsohn, 15 Jan. 1925; to Retzlaff, 31 Jan. 1925; and to Kahn, 31 Jan. 1925, all in BA: NL Erkelenz, 90.

6. See Stephan's report at a meeting of the DDP organization committee, 5 May 1925, BA: R 45 II/24/8–9, as well as Stephan to Erkelenz, 31 July and 22 Sept. 1925, BA: NL Erkelenz, 130, and Fischer to Erkelenz, 20 Mar. 1926, ibid., 132. For further information, see the balance sheet for the DDP Reichsgeschäftsstelle, 1 Jan.–31 Dec. 1925, ibid., 110.

7. Werner Stephan, *Die Deutsche Demokratische Partei im Berichtsjahr 1926. Jahresbericht der Reichsparteileitung* (n.p., [1927]), p. 10. See also Fischer to Dietrich, 13 July 1926, BA: NL Dietrich, 77/82–85.

8. For the DDP's budget, see Fischer's report at the Hamburg party congress, 24 Apr. 1927, BA: R 45 III/6/297–301, and the report of the revision committee, [Apr. 1927], ibid., 402–6. The DDP's budget for 1927 can be found in BA: NL Erkelenz, 111.

9. Stephan to Erkelenz, 26 Oct. 1925, BA: NL Erkelenz, 37/161–62.

10. Stephan, *Deutsche Demokratische Partei im Berichtsjahr 1926*, pp. 6–9.

11. Ibid., pp. 3–7.

12. For the DDP's role in this crisis, see the entry in Koch-Weser's diary, 6–7 May 1926, BA: NL Koch-Weser, 34/127–57. For further details, see Michael Stürmer, *Koalition und Opposition in der Weimarer Republik 1924–1928* (Düsseldorf, 1967), pp. 146–51.

13. *Der Demokrat* 7, no. 11 (3 June 1926): 231–33. See also the minutes of the DDP executive committee, 20 May 1926, BA: R 45 III/20/21–26, and Erkelenz to Bruckmann, 2 June 1926, BA: NL Erkelenz, 39/139–41.

14. *Der Demokrat* 7, no. 12 (17 June 1926): 247–48. See also Welcker to Erkelenz, 9 Aug. 1926, BA: NL Erkelenz, 129.

15. For further information, see the report in *Der Demokrat* 7, no. 23 (9 Dec. 1926): 393–95, as well as the correspondence between Bäumer and Koch-Weser, 8–10 Feb. 1927, BA: NL Koch-Weser, 36/67–75.

16. For further details, see Karl Holl, "Der Austritt Theodor Wolffs aus der Deutschen Demokratischen Partei," *Publizistik* 16 (1971): 294–302. See also Koch-Weser, "Zwei Austritte," *Der Demokrat* 7, no. 24 (23 Dec. 1926): 411–13.

17. Report by Stephan before the DDP's Breslau party congress, 6 Sept. 1925, BA: R 45 III/5/129.

18. Schneider to Hummel, 26 Oct. 1926, BA: NL Erkelenz, 124.

19. Stephan, *Deutsche Demokratische Partei im Berichtsjahr 1926*, p. 9.

20. Fischer to Koch-Weser, 18 June 1927, BA: NL Erkelenz, 43/241. On the fate of these efforts, see the minutes of the DDP executive committee, 21 June 1927, BA: R 45 III/20/89–100, as well as the entry in Koch-Weser's diary, 21 June 1927, BA: NL Koch-Weser, 36/159–61.

21. See the report on the situation within the DVP Reichstag delegation that Morath sent Stresemann, 26 Jan. 1925, AA: NL Stresemann, 3160/92/122510–14.

22. For example, see Jarres to Treviranus, 31 Oct. 1925, BA: NL Jarres, 54, as well as the minutes of the DVP central executive committee, 22 Nov. 1925, BA: R 45 II/40/29–235.

23. In this respect, see Duisberg to Silverberg, 13 Mar. 1925, BA: NL Silverberg, 259/13–18. On Duisberg's election and its political implications, see Bernd Weisbrod, *Schwerindustrie in der Weimarer Republik. Interessenpolitik zwischen Stabilisierung und Krise* (Wuppertal, 1978), pp. 217–26.

24. Detailed information on the DVP's finances for the period from 1924 to 1928 is virtually nonexistent. For an indication of the party's financial difficulties, see Stresemann to Boehm, 8 Feb. 1925 and 5 Mar. 1926, BA: Kleine Erwerbung 557, 1/68–71, as well as Kempkes to Reusch, 3 Mar. 1925, HA/GHH: NL Reusch, 400101293/14.

25. Weisbrod, *Schwerindustrie*, pp. 301–22.

26. Excerpt from Bechly's speech at the convention of the DVP's National White-Collar Employee Committee, 13 Dec. 1925, appended to Thiel's circular of 18 Dec. 1925, BA: R 45 II/58/447–55.

27. See Trucksaeß to Bechly, 17 Apr. 1926, BA: R 45 II/58/503, as well as the correspondence between Bechly and Hugo, 14 Jan.–2 Feb. 1926, ibid., 465–68, 477, 487–90.

28. This point has been stressed by Otto Thiel, *Wie kommen wir zu einer großen Deutschen Volkspartei? Vortrag, geh. auf der Tagung der Reichsgemeinschaft junger Volksparteiler in Berlin am 26. Oktober 1930* (n.p., [1930]), pp. 5–7.

29. Protocol of the founding of the LV, 27 Nov. 1924, SAA: NL Siemens, 4/Lf 697. For the most detailed treatment of the Liberal Association, see Larry Eugene Jones, "'The Dying Middle': Weimar Germany and the Failure of Bourgeois Unity, 1924–1930" (Ph.D. dissertation, University of Wisconsin, 1970), pp. 44–145.

30. Schiffer, "Die Wahlen und die Liberale Vereinigung," *Schöneberger Morgenzeitung*, 4 Dec. 1924, no. 43.

31. DDP, Reichsgeschäftsstelle, ed., *Die Liberale Vereinigung*, Materialien zur demokratischen Politik, no. 120 (Berlin, 1924), pp. 13–22.

32. Draft of a letter from Stresemann to Hammerschmidt, 4 Nov. 1924, AA: NL Stresemann, 3111/267/147072–73.

33. Remarks by Prentzel before the LV managing committee, 9 and 16 Feb. 1925, SAA: NL Siemens, 4/Lf 697.

34. Schiffer to Siemens, 26 Feb. 1925, SAA: NL Siemens, 4/Lf 697.

35. Minutes of the LV managing committee, 2 Mar. 1925, SAA: NL Siemens, 4/Lf 697. See also Becker to Marcks, 7 Mar. 1925, and Becker to Brandenburg, 24 Mar. 1925, ibid.

36. For the stenographic record of this demonstration, see Liberale Vereinigung, *Mitglieder- und Vertreterversammlung zu Berlin im Gebäude des Reichswirtschaftsrats am 16. Mai 1925* (Berlin-Charlottenburg, [1925]). See also Gerland, "Die Einigung des Liberalismus," *Berliner Börsen-Zeitung*, 23 Mar. 1925, no. 238, and R. B. [Richard Bahr], "Die Liberale Vereinigung," *Wille und Weg* 1, no. 5 (1 June 1925): 116–20.

37. Detailed information on Siemens's role in financing the publication of the LV's journal is to be found in SAA: NL Siemens, 4/Lf 556.

38. Stephan, circular to DDP party officials, 15 May 1925, BA: R 45 III/33/55–56. See also Erkelenz to Koch-Weser, 26 May 1925, BA: NL Erkelenz, 36/204–5.

39. Meeting of the executive committee of the DVP Reichstag delegation, 9 May 1925, BA: R 45 II/66/41–42.

40. Stresemann to Rose, telegram, 18 May 1925, AA: NL Stresemann, 3161/93/172759.

41. Otto Most, "Der liberale Gedanke in der Deutschen Volkspartei," in Otto Most, Gustav Stresemann, and Wilhelm Kahl, *Deutscher Liberalismus. Reden in der Sitzung des Zentralvorstandes der Deutschen Volkspartei am 23. Mai 1925 in Berlin* (Berlin, 1925), pp. 5–23. See also the entry in Stresemann's diary, 25 May 1925, in Gustav Stresemann, *Vermächtnis. Der Nachlaß in drei Bänden*, ed. Henry Bernhard, 3 vols. (Berlin, 1932–33), 2:301–3.

42. *NLC*, 25 May 1925, no. 98.

43. Most, Stresemann, and Kahl, *Deutscher Liberalismus*, p. 3.

44. Rheinbaben and May to Siemens, 3 Dec. 1925, SAA: NL Siemens, 4/Lf 697, and to Dietrich, 3 Dec. 1925, BA: NL Dietrich, 73/127.

45. Report by Fischbeck before the LV managing committee, 14 Dec. 1925, SAA: NL Siemens, 4/Lf 697. On the WP's attitude toward the LV, see Colosser's remarks at a meeting of the LV organization for West Berlin, 7 Dec. 1925, BA: NL Dietrich, 73/121–25.

46. Meeting of the LV managing committee, 14 Dec. 1925, SAA: NL Siemens, 4/Lf 697.

47. Koch-Weser to Erkelenz, 30 Jan. 1926, BA: NL Erkelenz, 133. See also circular no. 5 from the DDP Reichsgeschäftsstelle, 6 Feb. 1926, ibid., 112.

48. Entry in Koch-Weser's diary, 5 Feb. 1926, BA: NL Koch-Weser, 34/19.

49. For the text of their speeches, see [Liberale Vereinigung], *Die Liberale Vereinigung* (Berlin, n.d. [1926]). See also the *Vossische Zeitung*, 3 Feb. 1926, no. 29, and Mittelmann, "Der liberale Gedanke marschiert!," *Wille und Weg* 1, no. 22 (15 Feb. 1926): 539–41.

50. Entry in Koch-Weser's diary, 1 Mar. 1926, BA: NL Koch-Weser, 34/39.

51. *Wille und Weg* 2, no. 6 (15 June 1926): 144.

52. Ibid., p. 143.

53. Entry in Koch-Weser's diary, 8 July 1926, BA: NL Koch-Weser, 34/275. See also Koch-Weser to Fischbeck, 12 June 1926, ibid., 241.

54. Gayl and Jarres to Stresemann, 30 June 1926, BA: R 45 II/3/7–11.

55. In this respect, see Westarp to Gayl, 5 July 1926, NL Westarp, as well as Gayl to Jarres, 2 July and 26 Aug. 1926, both in BA: NL Jarres, 37.

56. For example, see Gayl to Jarres, 2 July 1926, BA: NL Jarres, 37, as well as Gildemeister, "Arbeitsgemeinschaft der Rechten," *KZ*, 13 July 1926, no. 512, and Dingeldey, "Die Arbeitsgemeinschaften der Bürgerlichen," *Rheinisch-Westfälische Zeitung*, 29 July 1926, no. 521.

57. See Campe to Stresemann, 7 July 1926, BA: R 45 II/3/15–16, and Kempkes to Jarres, 15 July 1926, BA: NL Jarres, 37.

58. Stresemann to Campe, 13 July 1926, AA: NL Stresemann, 3161/95/173091–93.

59. Stresemann to Jarres, 30 July 1926, BA: R 45 II/3/37–49.

60. On the tension between Wirth and the leaders of the Center Party, see Josef

Becker, "Joseph Wirth und die Krise des Zentrums während des IV. Kabinetts Marx (1927–1928)," *Zeitschrift für die Geschichte des Oberrheins* 109 (1961): 361–482.

61. Wirth, "Ziel und Wege deutscher Politik" und "Wille und Ziele," in Joseph Wirth, ed., *Der Aufbruch. Republikanische Flugschriften* (Berlin and Frankfurt am Main, 1926), pp. 7–22.

62. Haas, "Die Einheitsfront der Republikaner" and "Liberalismus und Republikanische Union," in ibid., pp. 30–32, 63–66.

63. For the reaction of the DDP's national leadership, see Koch-Weser, "Republikanische Einigung," *Die Hilfe* 32, no. 17 (1 Sept. 1926): 348–52, and Stephan, "Die 'Republikanische Union,'" *Deutsche Einheit* 8, no. 33 (14 Aug. 1926): 769–72, as well as the record of Koch-Weser's conversation with Stresemann, 19 Aug. 1926, BA: NL Koch-Weser, 34/325. See also the entry in Koch-Weser's diary, 30 July 1926, ibid., 285, as well as his circular to the members of the DDP Reichstag delegation, 13 Aug. 1926, ibid., 297–301.

64. Georg Schreiber, "Innenpolitik des Reiches," *Politisches Jahrbuch 1926*, ed. Georg Schreiber (Mönchen-Gladbach, 1927), pp. 79–82. For the overtures to the Center, see Treviranus, "Weg mit den Scheuklappen," *Berliner Börsen-Zeitung*, 23 July 1926, no. 337, as well as Treviranus to Jarres, 18 Aug. 1926, BA: NL Jarres, 37.

65. Weisbrod, *Schwerindustrie*, pp. 246–72.

66. Jarres to Loebell, 6 Sept. 1926, BA: NL Jarres, 37. See also Scholz, "Innere Entwicklung und Deutsche Volkspartei," *KZ*, 1 Oct. 1926, no. 732.

67. Stresemann, *Vermächtnis*, 2:419.

68. See the minutes of the DDP executive committee, 6 Nov. 1926, BA: R 45 III/20/36–41, and of the DDP party council, 28 Nov. 1926, ibid., 13/97–109, as well as the entry in Koch-Weser's diary, 30 Nov. 1926, BA: NL Koch-Weser, 34/357.

69. Entry in Koch-Weser's diary, 19 Aug. 1926, BA: NL Koch-Weser, 34/335–37.

70. See Rheinbaben's remarks at a meeting of the LV managing committee, 19 Nov. 1926, SAA: NL Siemens, 4/Lf 697, and Rheinbaben to Stresemann, 16 Dec. 1926, AA: NL Stresemann, 3162/97/173884–86.

71. Siemens to Schiffer, 28 July 1927, SAA: NL Siemens, 4/Lf 556.

72. Liberale Vereinigung, *Liberale Politik im neuen Staate. Leitsätze, Vorträge und Ansprachen* (Munich, 1927). See also Hammerschmidt, "Die Liberale Vereinigung in Bayern," *Wille und Weg* 2, no. 19 (1 Jan. 1927): 475–79.

73. *KZ*, 23 Mar. 1927, no. 219.

74. Hammerschmidt, "Enttäuschungen," *Wille und Weg* 4, no. 5 (1 June 1928): 107–10.

CHAPTER TWENTY-ONE

1. Arno Panzer, "Parteipolitische Ansätze der deutschen Bauernbewegung bis 1933," in *Europäische Bauernparteien im 20. Jahrhundert*, ed. Heinz Gollwitzer (Stuttgart and New York, 1977), pp. 524–42. See also Hans-Jürgen Puhle, *Politische Agrarbewegungen in kapitalistischen Industriegesellschaften. Deutschland, USA und Frankreich im 20. Jahrhundert* (Göttingen, 1975), pp. 29–103. The following chapter is based in large part upon Larry Eugene Jones, "Crisis and Realignment: Agrarian

Splinter Parties in the Late Weimar Republic, 1928–33," in *Peasants and Lords in Modern Germany: Recent Studies in Agricultural History*, ed. Robert G. Moeller (London, 1986), pp. 198–232.

2. On the founding and early history of the BBB, see Puhle, *Agrarbewegungen*, pp. 62–63, as well as the more recent articles by Heinz Haushofer, "Der Bayerische Bauernbund (1893–1933)," in *Europäische Bauernparteien*, ed. Gollwitzer, pp. 562–82, and Ian Farr, "Populism in the Countryside: The Peasant Leagues in Bavaria in the 1890's," in *Society and Politics in Wilhelmine Germany*, ed. Richard J. Evans (London and New York, 1978), pp. 136–59.

3. James C. Hunt, "The 'Egalitarianism' of the Right: The Agrarian League in Southwest Germany, 1893–1914," *JCH* 10 (1975): 513–30.

4. Martin Schumacher, *Land und Politik. Eine Untersuchung über politische Parteien und agrarische Interessen 1914–1923* (Düsseldorf, 1978), pp. 387–439.

5. Bayerischer Bauernbund, Hauptgeschäftsstelle, ed., *Der Bayerischer Bauernbund im Jahre 1919*, Flugschriften des Bayerischen Bauernbundes, no. 1 (Munich, [1919]).

6. For a general survey of the German agricultural crisis in the mid-1920s, see Harold James, *The German Slump: Politics and Economics, 1924–1936* (Oxford, 1986), pp. 246–59. On the specific impact of the inflation, see Jonathan Osmond, "Peasant Farming in South and West Germany during War and Inflation 1914 to 1924: Stability or Stagnation?," in *Die deutsche Inflation. Eine Zwischenbilanz/The German Inflation Reconsidered: A Preliminary Balance*, ed. Gerald D. Feldman et al. (Berlin and New York, 1982), pp. 289–307, and Robert G. Moeller, *German Peasants and Agrarian Politics, 1914–1924: The Rhineland and Westphalia* (Chapel Hill, 1986), pp. 95–115.

7. For further details, see Robert G. Moeller, "Winners as Losers in the German Inflation: Peasant Protest over the Controlled Economy, 1920–1923," in *Die deutsche Inflation/The German Inflation*, ed. Feldman et al., pp. 255–88.

8. *NLC*, 5 Mar. 1921, no. 54.

9. Karl Hepp, *Ernährung und Landwirtschaft*, Flugschriften der Deutschen Volkspartei, no. 40 (Berlin, 1922), pp. 3–8, 14–16.

10. See Hepp's remarks before the DVP Reichstag delegation, 5 and 9 Nov. 1923, AA: NL Stresemann, 3159/87/171446, 171468.

11. Report by Quaatz, 15 Mar. 1924, AA: NL Stresemann, 3159/89/171760–61.

12. Heino Kaack, *Geschichte und Struktur des deutschen Parteiensystems. Ein Handbuch* (Opladen, 1971), p. 98. On the NLV's tactics in the May 1924 elections, see the report attached to Stocksieck's letter to Stresemann, 3 May 1924, AA: NL Stresemann, 3159/89/171922–24.

13. Remarks by Hugo before the DVP central executive committee, 7 July 1924, BA: R 45 II/39/351–53.

14. Böhme to Koch-Weser, n.d., in *Deutscher Bauernbund* 16, no. 42 (16 Oct. 1924): 349–50.

15. Gothein, "Schutzzölle oder Ermässigung der Produktionskosten?," *Deutsche Einheit* 6, no. 27 (5 July 1924): 633–37. See also Hamm to Weiß, 30 July 1924, NL Hamm.

16. Böhme, *Bauernstand*, pp. 122–24.

17. Statement by Wachhorst de Wente before the DDP executive committee, 21 Oct. 1924, BA: R 45 III/19/96–97.

18. For further details, see Michael Stürmer, *Koalition und Opposition in der Weimarer Republik 1924–1928* (Düsseldorf, 1967), pp. 98–107, as well as the more specialized study by Dirk Stegmann, "Deutsche Zoll- und Handelspolitik 1924/5–1929 unter besonderer Berücksichtigung agrarischer und industrieller Interessen," in *Industrielles System und politische Entwicklung in der Weimarer Republik. Verhandlungen des Internationalen Symposiums in Bochum vom 12.–17. Juni 1973*, ed. Hans Mommsen, Dietmar Petzina, and Bernd Weisbrod (Düsseldorf, 1974), pp. 499–513.

19. In this respect, see Rudolf Schneider, *Warum brauchen wir die Zollvorlage? Rede gehalten im Reichstag am 24. Juni 1925*, Flugschriften der Deutschen Volkspartei, no. 65 (Berlin, 1925), and DVP, Reichsgeschäftsstelle, ed., *Die Reichspolitik. Überblick über die wichtigsten Vorgänge der Reichspolitik vom Januar bis September 1925* (Berlin, [1925]), pp. 37–47.

20. See Meyer's remarks before the DDP executive committee, 16 June 1925, in Lothar Albertin, ed., *Linksliberalismus in der Weimarer Republik. Die Führungsgremien der Deutschen Demokratischen Partei und der Deutschen Staatspartei 1918–1933* (Düsseldorf, 1980), pp. 351–52, as well as Felix Raschig, *Zolltarifvorlage und Deutsche Demokratische Partei* (Berlin, 1925).

21. For example, see Karl Böhme, *Der nationale Liberalismus und die Bauern*, Flugschriften der Deutschen Volkspartei, no. 69 (Berlin, 1927), pp. 22–27.

22. Remarks by Wachhorst de Wente before the DDP executive committee, 10 Oct. 1925, BA: R 45 III/19/120–22.

23. For a highly colored account of these events, see Karl Böhme, *Zum Streit der landwirtschaftlichen Organisationen! Ein Wort zur Abwehr* (Leipzig, [1928]), pp. 3–19.

24. Lübke and Müller to the Reich Chancellery, 1 Oct. 1927, BA: R 43 I/1301/2–3. See also Wachhorst de Wente's remarks in Deutsche Demokratische Partei, Preußische Landtagsfraktion, ed., *Preußen-Tag der Deutschen Demokratischen Partei am 22. und 23. Oktober 1927 in Berlin (Stenographischer Bericht)* (Berlin, 1927), p. 50.

25. "Aufbau und Ziele der Deutschen Bauernschaft," n.d., appended to Lübke to Kaiser, 20 Feb. 1932, BA: NL Kaiser, 221.

26. DDP, Reichsgeschäftsstelle, circular from 28 Feb. 1925, BA: NL Erkelenz, 111/125–27. See also Tantzen to Erkelenz, 30 Jan. 1925, ibid., 90/183–85, and Rönneburg, "Die Deutsche Demokratische Partei und die Landwirtschaft," *Der Demokrat* 6, no. 20 (15 Oct. 1925): 442–45, and no. 21 (5 Nov. 1925): 457–60.

27. *Der Demokrat* 8, no. 3 (10 Feb. 1927): 36–45.

28. Rudolf Lantzsch, *Die Agrarpolitik der Deutschen Demokratischen Partei*, Schriftenreihe für politische Werbung, no. 8 (Berlin, 1928).

29. For further details, see Dieter Gessner, *Agrarverbände in der Weimarer Republik. Wirtschaftliche und soziale Voraussetzungen agrarkonservativer Politik vor 1933* (Düsseldorf, 1976), pp. 46–81.

30. Hans Beyer, *Die Agrarkrise und die Landvolkbewegung in den Jahren 1928–1932. Ein Beitrag zur Geschichte "revolutionärer" Bauernbewegung zwischen den beiden Weltkriegen* (Itzehoe, 1962).

31. On the demonstrations in Thuringia and Württemberg, see *Der Thüringer Land-*

bund 9, no. 12 (11 Feb. 1928): 1, and Württembergischer Bauern- und Weingärtner-bund, ed., *Der württembergische Bauernfreund. Ein Wegweiser und Jahrbuch für unseren bäuerlichen und gewerblichen Mittelstand für das Jahr 1929* (Stuttgart, [1929]), pp. 90–91.

32. Kuno von Westarp, *Bauernnot—Volksnot. Das Arbeitsprogramm des Reichstages und das landwirtschaftliche Programm der Deutschnationalen Volkspartei*, Deutschnationale Flugschrift, no. 317 (Berlin, 1928).

33. *Der Bündler* 4, no. 49 (3 Dec. 1922): 2.

34. See Fehr's speeches from the spring of 1924, ibid., 6, no. 4 (27 Jan. 1924): 2–3, and no. 11 (16 Mar. 1924): 1–3. See also Jonathan Osmond, "A Second Agrarian Mobilization? Peasant Associations in South and West Germany, 1918–24," in *Peasants and Lords*, ed. Moeller, pp. 184–85.

35. In this respect, see Fehr to Bredt, 9 May 1924, as well as the protocol of an agreement between the BBB, DHP, and WP, 5 Nov. 1924, both in NL Bredt.

36. Puhle, *Agrarbewegungen*, pp. 85–87.

37. Hiltmann, "Tatsachen und Probleme der Bauernbewegung," *Die grüne Zukunft* 1, nos. 1–2 (Oct.–Nov. 1928): 2–5, 18–24. For the text of Fehr's speech, see *Bayer. Bauern- und Mittelstandsbund*, 22 Feb. 1928, no. 5.

38. Remarks by Koch-Weser and Wachhorst de Wente at a meeting of the DDP executive committee, 6 Mar. 1928, BA: R 45 III/20/127–29.

39. *Deutsche Bauernzeitung* 2, no. 14 (1 Apr. 1928): 157–58, and no. 16 (15 Apr. 1928): 181–83.

40. Hiltmann, "Tatsachen und Probleme," p. 24.

41. Puhle, *Agrarbewegungen*, p. 84.

42. Resolution from the TLB executive committee, 24 Nov. 1927, appended to a circular from the RLB presidium, 23 Dec. 1927, NL Weilnböck.

43. Report on the meeting of the RLB executive committee, 14 Dec. 1927, NL Weilnböck.

44. *Thüringer Landbund* 9, no. 15 (22 Feb. 1928): 1.

45. Stauffenberg to Westarp, 24 Feb. 1928, NL Westarp.

46. Höfer, "Zur Gründung der Christlich-Nationalen Bauernpartei," *Thüringer Landbund* 9, no. 20 (21 Mar. 1928): 1. See also Dorsch, "Zur Gründung der Christlich-Nationalen Bauern- und Landvolkpartei," ibid., no. 32 (21 Apr. 1928): 1, and Baum, "Was will die Christlich-Nationale Bauern- und Landvolkpartei?," *Nassauische Bauern-Zeitung*, 5 May 1928, no. 105.

47. Lantzsch, "Bauernparteien?," *Der Demokrat* 9, no. 6 (18 Mar. 1928): 164–65.

48. Kempkes to Stresemann, 24 Feb. 1928, AA: NL Stresemann, 3162/99/173883–89.

49. Hepp to Stresemann, 4 Sept. 1921, AA: NL Stresemann, 3109/231/141458–60.

50. Hepp to Stresemann, 24 May 1925, AA: NL Stresemann, 3161/93/172762–63.

51. See Hepp's speech in Reichs-Landbund, e.V., ed., *Der 8. Reichs-Landbund-Tag. Die Reden der Präsidenten und des Ernährungsministers Schiele* (Berlin, [1928]), pp. 8–9.

52. *Thüringer Landbund* 9, no. 20 (10 Mar. 1928): 1.

53. In this respect, see Schmidt-Stettin to Hepp, 26 Mar. 1928, and Richthofen to Hepp, 15 Apr. 1928, both in NL Weilnböck, as well as Westarp to Alvensleben, 14 Apr.

1928, NL Westarp. See also Lothar Steuer, *Die deutsche Landwirtschaft und die politischen Parteien. Eine Wahlkampfbetrachtung* (Kassel, 1928), pp. 12–15.

54. *Der Reichs-Landbund* 8, no. 8 (25 Feb. 1928): 101.

55. Westarp to Wilmowsky, 23 Feb. 1928, NL Westarp.

56. In this respect, see the protocol of an agreement between the Bavarian Rural League (Bayerischer Landbund) and the Bavarian DNVP, 3 Mar. 1928, NL Weilnböck, as well as Hilpert to Westarp, 4 Mar. 1928, and Lüttichau to Westarp, 24 Mar. 1928, both in NL Westarp.

57. Feldmann to Höfer, 27 Mar. 1928, NL Westarp. See also Hopp to the RLB presidium, 8 May 1928, NL Weilnböck.

CHAPTER TWENTY-TWO

1. Harold James, *The German Slump: Politics and Economics, 1924–1936* (Oxford, 1986), pp. 43–44. See also Peter Reinhold, *Deutsche Finanz- und Wirtschaftspolitik. Rede gehalten am 23. April 1927 in Hannover* (Leipzig, 1927), pp. 8–16.

2. For further details, see Michael Stürmer, *Koalition und Opposition in der Weimarer Republik 1924–1928* (Düsseldorf, 1967), pp. 162–81.

3. *NLC*, 7 Dec. 1926, no. 201. See also the memorandum by Bernhard, 10 Dec. 1926, AA: NL Stresemann, 3162/97/173381–82.

4. Memorandum by Stresemann, [Dec. 1926–Jan. 1927], AA: NL Stresemann, 3167/48/163462–66.

5. For further details, see Hans W. Gatzke, *Stresemann and the Rearmament of Germany* (Baltimore, 1954), pp. 72–76.

6. Stresemann to Hintzmann, 5 Jan. 1927, AA: NL Stresemann, Col. U3/299.

7. See the minutes of the Center Reichstag delegation, 11–14 Jan. 1927, in Rudolf Morsey, ed., *Die Protokolle der Reichstagsfraktion und des Fraktionsvorstandes der Deutschen Zentrumspartei 1926–1933* (Mainz, 1969), pp. 80–88. See also *NLC*, 11 and 15 Jan. 1927, nos. 7 and 10, as well as Curtius's own account of his efforts to form a new government in Julius Curtius, *Sechs Jahre Minister der deutschen Republik* (Heidelberg, 1948), pp. 45–50.

8. Stresemann to Marx, 14 Jan. 1927, AA: NL Stresemann, 3167/49/163560–66.

9. *NLC*, 20 Jan. 1927, no. 14.

10. Entry in Koch-Weser's diary, 26 Jan. 1927, BA: NL Koch-Weser, 36/17–23.

11. Entry in Koch-Weser's diary, 27 Jan. 1927, BA: NL Koch-Weser, 36/25–31.

12. Entry in Koch-Weser's diary, 29 Jan. 1927, BA: NL Koch-Weser, 36/45–47. See also Gessler to Koch-Weser, 28 Jan. 1927, BA: NL Gessler, 9/72, reprinted in Otto Gessler, *Reichswehrpolitik in der Weimarer Zeit*, ed. Kurt Sendtner and with an introduction by Theodor Heuss (Stuttgart, 1958), p. 502, as well as Koch-Weser to Bruckmann, 18 Feb. 1927, BA: NL Heuss, 381.

13. Erich Koch-Weser, *Die Deutsche Demokratische Partei in der Opposition. Rede bei der Beratung der Regierungserklärung am Freitag, 4. Februar 1927* (Berlin, [1927]), pp. 1–4.

14. In this respect, see Oswald Riedel, ed., *Das ABC der DDP* (Berlin, 1927), p. 27.

15. Ibid., pp. 25–26.

16. Schuldt, "Die neue Besoldung," *Der Demokrat* 8, no. 18 (29 Sept. 1927): 377–79.

17. Proceedings of the DDP's Middle-Class Congress (Reichsmittelstandstag der DDP), 16 Jan. 1927, BA: R 45 III/36/48–51.

18. *Der Demokrat* 8, no. 3 (10 Feb. 1927): 36–45.

19. On the fate of these efforts, see the minutes of the DDP executive committee, 21 June 1927, BA: R 45 III/20/89–100, as well as the entry in Koch-Weser's diary, 21 June 1927, BA: NL Koch-Weser, 36/157–61.

20. In this respect, see Erich Koch-Weser and Hermann Luppe, *Der großdeutsche Einheitsstaat. Das Ziel und der Weg. Die Verhandlungen des Hamburger Parteitages der Deutschen Demokratischen Partei*, ed. Reichsgeschäftsstelle der DDP (Berlin, [1927]).

21. See Koch-Weser's speech before the DDP party council, 29 Apr. 1928, BA: R 45 III/13/164–67, as well as Erich Koch-Weser, *Einheitsstaat und Selbstverwaltung* (Berlin, 1928).

22. For example, see Stresemann, "Die Gegenwartsaufgaben des nationalen Liberalismus," *DS* 38, no. 23 (Dec. 5, 1926): 553–58. For a recent treatment of this problem, see Stephen G. Fritz, "The Search for *Volksgemeinschaft*: Gustav Stresemann and the Baden DVP, 1926–1930," *German Studies Review* 7 (1984): 249–80.

23. DVP, Reichsgeschäftsstelle, ed., *60 Jahr-Feier der Nationalliberalen Partei am 19. und 20. März 1927 in Hannover* (Berlin, [1927]).

24. For further details, see Günther Grünthal, *Reichsschulgesetz und Zentrumspartei in der Weimarer Republik* (Düsseldorf, 1968), pp. 196–207.

25. Ibid., pp. 229–37.

26. Liberale Vereinigung, *Zum Reichsschulgesetz. Kundgebung zum Entwurf eines Reichsschulgesetzes am 23. Oktober 1927* (Berlin, 1927), pp. 5–26. See also Pachnicke, "Die Liberale Vereinigung und die Schule," *Wille und Weg* 3, no. 15 (1 Nov. 1927): 353–55.

27. *Berliner Stimmen* 5, no. 12 (Dec. 1927): 2. See also Stephen G. Fritz, "'The Center Cannot Hold.' Educational Policies and the Collapse of the Democratic Middle in Germany: The School Bill Crisis in Baden, 1927–1928," *History of Education Quarterly* 25 (1985): 413–37.

28. Ellen L. Evans, "The Center Wages *Kulturpolitik*: Conflict in the Marx-Keudell Cabinet of 1927," *CEH* 2 (1969): 139–58.

29. For example, see Reichsgeneralsekretariat der Deutschen Zentrumspartei, ed., *Der Liberalismus. Die Deutsche Demokratische Partei/Die Deutsche Volkspartei* (Berlin, 1928).

30. Alfred Hanemann, *Materialien für deutschnationale Wahlredner* (Freiburg im Breisgau, 1928), pp. 1–9.

31. For example, see Walther Heym, *Die Vertretung des gewerblichen Mittelstandes durch den 3. Landtag von Thüringen* (Rudolstadt, 1926), pp. 36–80.

32. *Kölner Nachrichten*, 24 Mar. 1928, no. 12.

33. Ibid., 21 Apr. 1928, no. 16. See also Reichspartei des deutschen Mittelstandes, ed., *Wahrheiten. 1928 Wahlhandbuch der Reichspartei des deutschen Mittelstandes (Wirtschaftspartei)* (Berlin, 1928), pp. 58–65.

34. *Kölner Nachrichten*, 14 Apr. 1928, no. 15.

35. For example, see "Mittelstand. Die Entscheidung ist da!," [May 1928], BA: ZSg 1–176 (1), as well as the appeal directed to "Handwerk, Gewerbe, Hausbesitz," in Reichspartei des deutschen Mittelstandes, *Wahrheiten*, pp. 161–72.

36. For example, see Bauser, "Auf zur Wahl!," *Deutsches Volksrecht*, 19 May 1928, no. 40, as well as the "Wahlaufruf der Volksrechts-Partei," ibid., 16 May 1928, no. 39.

37. *Nassauische Bauern-Zeitung*, 10 May 1928, no. 109.

38. Baum, "Was will die Christlich-Nationale Bauern- und Landvolkpartei?," *Nassauische Bauern-Zeitung*, 5 May 1928, no. 105.

39. In this respect, see the *Nassauische Bauern-Zeitung*, 22 Mar. 1928, no. 60, as well as "Bauer höre! Das Programm der Christlich-Nationalen Bauern- und Landvolkpartei," [1928], NL Weilnböck.

40. "Der Bayerische Bauern- und Mittelstandsbund ruft auf!," [1928], Bayerisches Hauptstaatsarchiv, Munich, Abt. V, Flugblätter-Sammlung, F64.

41. For example, see DDP, Reichsgeschäftsstelle, ed., *Die Deutsche Wirtschaftspartei*, Materialien zur demokratischen Politik, no. 132 (Berlin, 1927), and Hünzinger, "Die Steuerdemagogie der Wirtschaftspartei," *Der Demokrat* 9, no. 4 (23 Feb. 1928): 102–4, as well as DVP, Reichsgeschäftsstelle, ed., *Wahlhandbuch 1928* (Berlin, 1928), pp. 141–74.

42. In this respect, see Koch-Weser's speech, "Sieben Ziele für den neuen Reichstag," before the DDP party council, 29 Apr. 1928, BA: R 45 III/13/164–67, as well as Hans Ehlermann, *Der Wahlkampf 1928 (Einführung und Überblick)*, Schriftenreihe für politische Werbung der DDP, no. 1 (Berlin, 1928), pp. 3–6, and "Wahlaufruf der Deutschen Demokratischen Partei," *Der Demokrat* 9, no. 9 (10 May 1928): 253–56.

43. For example, see Hans Reif, *Mittelstandspolitik*, Schriftenreihe für politische Werbung der DDP, no. 9 (Berlin, 1928), and Rudolf Lantzsch, *Die Agrarpolitik der Deutschen Demokratischen Partei*, Schriftenreihe für politische Werbung der DDP, no. 8 (Berlin, 1928).

44. In this respect, see Erkelenz, "Die Aufgaben der deutschen Demokratie," *Der Demokrat* 9, no. 5 (8 Mar. 1928): 129–31, and Koch-Weser, "Worum es geht," ibid., 9, no. 9 (10 May 1928): 257–61.

45. For example, see the remarks by Hembeck, Hollmann, and Winnefeld at a meeting of the DVP managing committee, 8 Dec. 1927, BA: R 45 II/58/559–79, as well as Kempkes to Stresemann, 24 Feb. 1928, AA: NL Stresemann, 3162/99/173883–89.

46. For examples of the DVP's identification with middle-class economic interests, see DVP, Reichsgeschäftsstelle, *Wahlhandbuch 1928*, pp. 269–312, 339–49.

47. Quoted by Henry Ashby Turner, Jr., *Stresemann and the Politics of the Weimar Republic* (Princeton, 1963), p. 236.

48. Minutes of the DDP executive committee, 6 Mar. 1928, BA: R 45 III/20/125–31. See also Werner Stephan, *Parteiorganisation im Wahlkampf* (Berlin, [1928]), pp. 11–21.

49. Stephan to Erkelenz, 20 June 1927, BA: NL Erkelenz, 127.

50. For example, see Kempner to Erkelenz, 7 Dec. 1927, BA: NL Erkelenz, 130. For further information on the DDP's financial situation, see the minutes of the DDP finance committee, 3 Mar. 1928, BA: R 45 III/24/69–70, and Stephan to Erkelenz, 9

May 1928, BA: NL Erkelenz, 48/232, as well as the correspondence between Fischer and Siemens, 2 Mar.–4 May 1928, SAA: NL Siemens, 4/Lf 646.

51. Kempkes's report before the DVP managing committee, 8 Dec. 1927, BA: R 45 II/58/561.

52. The details of the arrangement insofar as it pertained to the DVP are unclear. For a reference to its existence, see Wilmowsky to Krupp, 15 Dec. 1927, HA Krupp, FAH 23/502.

53. Haniel to Reusch, 6 Mar. 1928, HA/GHH: NL Reusch, 40010124/11. On the policies and composition of the Ruhrlade, see Henry Ashby Turner, Jr., "The *Ruhrlade*: Secret Cabinet of Heavy Industry in the Weimar Republic," *CEH* 3 (1970): 195–228.

54. Siemens to Bücher, 11 Apr. 1928, SAA: NL Siemens, 4/Lf 646.

55. In this respect, see the documents prepared for use at the Curatorium's meeting on 2 Nov. 1928, SAA: NL Siemens, 4/Lf 646, as well as the vague data on contributions from the German chemical industry contained in the deposition by Ernst Pfeiffer, 8 Sept. 1947, StA Nürnberg, Bestand KV-Prozesse, Fall 6, Nr. X 3.

56. For example, see Kempkes to Stresemann, 24 and 29 Feb. 1928, AA: NL Stresemann, 3162/99/173883–89, 173909–12, and Bernhard to Stresemann, 28 Feb. 1928, ibid., 173894–905.

57. Heino Kaack, *Geschichte und Struktur des deutschen Parteiensystems. Ein Handbuch* (Opladen, 1971), pp. 103–4. The unpublished dissertation by Virgil Creekmore, Jr., "The German Reichstag Elections of 1928" (Ph.D. dissertation, Tulane University, 1968), is seriously deficient in the sense that it makes no mention of the impact that the emergence of special interest parties in the second half of the 1920s had upon the outcome of the elections. For a valuable corrective, see Thomas Childers, "Inflation, Stabilization, and Political Realignment in Germany 1924 to 1928," in *Die deutsche Inflation. Eine Zwischenbilanz/The German Inflation Reconsidered: A Preliminary Balance*, ed. Gerald D. Feldman et al. (Berlin and New York, 1982), pp. 424–31, and Jerzy Holzer, *Parteien und Massen. Die politische Krise in Deutschland 1928–1930* (Mainz, 1975), pp. 13–48.

58. Koch-Weser's remarks before the DDP executive committee, 14 June 1928, BA: R 45 III/20/178–79. For similar views, see Weber, "Welche Frage beherrscht den Wahlkampf?," *DAZ*, 27 May 1928, nos. 243–44, and Erkelenz, "Die Auswirkungen des Parlamentarismus auf den Volkswillen," *Die Hilfe* 34, no. 11 (1 June 1928): 245–47.

59. Stephan, "Der demokratische Stimmenverlust," *Der Demokrat* 9, nos. 11/12 (14 June 1928): 309–14.

60. For example, see Frech to Dietrich, 29 May 1928, BA: NL Dietrich, 221/49–59.

61. Stresemann to Havemann, 2 June 1928, AA: NL Stresemann, 3163/100/174111–13.

62. For a detailed analysis of the DVP's electoral losses, see *KZ*, 13 June 1928, no. 320a.

63. Westarp's remarks at a meeting of the DNVP Reichstag delegation, 14 June 1928, BA: NL Schmidt-Hannover, 35. For further information, see Lothar Steuer, *Die deutschnationale Wahlniederlage vom 20. Mai 1928. Ihre Ursachen, Zusammenhänge, Folgerungen* (Anklam, 1928), pp. 16–20, as well as the memorandum from the German National Workers' League (Deutschnationaler Arbeiterbund) to Westarp, 12

June 1928, NL Westarp. On the party's losses in Saxony, see Rademacher to Westarp, 21 Mar. 1928, ibid.

64. For further details, see the valuable regional study by Günter Plum, *Gesell-schaftsstruktur und politisches Bewußtsein in einer katholischen Region 1928–1933. Untersuchung am Beispiel des Regierungsbezirks Aachen* (Stuttgart, 1972), pp. 27–31.

CHAPTER TWENTY-THREE

1. *KZ*, 13 June 1928, no. 320a.

2. T. W. [Theodor Wolff], "Am Füsse der Pyramide," *BTB*, 27 May 1928, no. 248. See also T. W., "Antwort auf viele Fragen," ibid., 10 June 1928, no. 271, as well as the entry for 30 May 1928, in Ernst Feder, *Heute sprach ich mit . . . Tagebuch eines Berliner Publizisten 1926–1932*, ed. Cecile Löwenthal-Hensel and Arnold Paucker (Stuttgart, 1971), pp. 180–81.

3. Koch-Weser, "Die Folgerungen aus dem Wahlkampf," *Vossische Zeitung*, 13 June 1928, no. 140. See also Koch-Weser's remarks before the DDP executive committee, 14 June 1928, BA: R 45 III/20/177–82.

4. *KZ*, 23 Mar. 1927, no. 219. See also the minutes of the LV managing committee, 14 and 27 Jan., 21 Feb., and 8 Mar. 1927, all in SAA: NL Siemens, 4/Lf 697.

5. Liberale Vereinigung, *Zum Reichsschulgesetz. Kundgebung zum Entwurf eines Reichsschulgesetzes am 23. Oktober 1927* (Berlin, 1927), pp. 5–26.

6. Hammerschmidt, "Die Liberale Vereinigung vor den Wahlen," *Wille und Weg* 3, no. 17 (1 Dec. 1927): 405–6. For further information, see Liberale Vereinigung Bayern, "Vorschläge für Richtlinien zur einer Wahlgemeinschaft bei der bayerischen Landtagswahl 1928," n.d., as well as the letters from the Bavarian chapter of the Liberal Association to the LV's national headquarters in Berlin, 14 Oct. 1927, in SAA: NL Siemens, 4/Lf 697.

7. See the correspondence between Rheinbaben and Stresemann, 25–27 Feb. 1928, AA: NL Stresemann, 3149/65/165127–31.

8. Minutes of the LV managing committee, 5 June 1928, SAA: NL Siemens, 4/Lf 697. Unfortunately Weber's unpublished memoirs, "Rückblick und Ausblick (1871–1956)," BA: Kleine Erwerbung 384, were written without the benefit of original documents when the author was over eighty years old and are therefore of only marginal value to the historian.

9. For example, see Weber's speech in Liberale Vereinigung, *Liberaler Tag im deutschen Reichstag, Berlin, den 1. Juli 1928* (Dresden, 1928), pp. 50–54.

10. Rheinbaben to Stresemann, 12 June 1928, AA: NL Stresemann, 3163/101/174133–35. See also Rochus von Rheinbaben, *Liberale Politik im neuen Reiche* (Karlsruhe, 1928), pp. 5–12.

11. Entry in Koch-Weser's diary, 22 June 1928, BA: NL Koch-Weser, 37/141–43.

12. Weber's report before the LV managing committee, 5 June 1928, SAA: NL Siemens, 4/Lf 697.

13. Remarks by Schiffer before the LV executive committee, 5 June 1928, SAA: NL Siemens, 4/Lf 697.

14. In this respect, see Weber to Siemens, 6 June 1928, SAA: NL Siemens, 4/Lf

697, and Weber to Dietrich, 7 June 1928, BA: NL Dietrich, 111/106, as well as Weber, "Aufruf der Liberalen Vereinigung," June 1928, ibid., 106/208–9.

15. Weber's report before the LV managing committee, 5 June 1928, SAA: NL Siemens, 4/Lf 697.

16. Minutes of the DVP Reichstag delegation, 28 June 1928, BA: R 45 II/67/99. See also the interview with Scholz in the *Neue Freie Presse*, 15 July 1928, no. 22928.

17. For example, see Cohnstaedt to Koch-Weser, 7 June 1928, BA: NL Erkelenz, 131.

18. Erkelenz to Weber, 18 June 1928, BA: NL Erkelenz, 49/80. See also Erkelenz, "Das deutsche Parteiensystem," *Die Hilfe* 39, no. 12 (15 June 1928): 272–73, and "Konzentration und Rationalisierung des Parteiwesens," *Der Demokrat* 9, nos. 11–12 (14 June 1928): 315–17.

19. Minutes of the DDP executive committee, 14–15 June 1928, BA: R 45 III/20/ 172–75, 182–84.

20. In this connection, see the bulletin from Stephan to the members of the DDP executive committee, 28 June 1928, BA: NL Erkelenz, 49/111.

21. *FZ*, 1 July 1928, no. 486.

22. Liberale Vereinigung, *Liberaler Tag*, p. 10.

23. Ibid., pp. 27–29, 34–36, 50–54.

24. Ibid., pp. 54–56.

25. Minutes of the LV executive committee, 6 July 1928, SAA: NL Siemens, 4/Lf 697.

26. For example, see Dietrich to Weber, 5 July 1928, BA: NL Dietrich, 106/212, and Reinhold to Stresemann, 6 June 1928, AA: NL Stresemann, 3163/100/174107.

27. Petersen to Gessler, 17 July 1928, BA: NL Gessler, 18/237–38, reprinted in Otto Gessler, *Reichswehrpolitik in der Weimarer Zeit*, ed. Kurt Sendtner and with an introduction by Theodor Heuss (Stuttgart, 1958), p. 503.

28. For example, see the correspondence between Koch-Weser and Stresemann, 16–25 June 1928, AA: NL Stresemann, 3174/68/167019–22, 167937.

29. In this connection, see the entries in Koch-Weser's diary for 18 Dec. 1925, BA: NL Koch-Weser, 32/211–15, and 5 Feb. 1926, ibid., 34/19.

30. Stresemann to Weber, 5 July 1928, AA: NL Stresemann, 3164/105/175126–27.

31. Minutes of the DVP Reichstag delegation, 13 June 1928, BA: R 45 II/67/86–88. For further information, see Henry Ashby Turner, Jr., *Stresemann and the Politics of the Weimar Republic* (Princeton, 1963), pp. 238–44, and Helga Timm, *Deutsche Sozialpolitik und der Bruch der großen Koalition im März 1930* (Düsseldorf, 1952), pp. 82–89.

32. On the course of these negotiations through the third week of June 1928, see the undated memorandum by Müller, BA: R 43 I/1308/111–17, reprinted in *Akten der Reichskanzlei: Das Kabinett Müller II. 28. Juni 1928 bis 27. März 1930*, ed. Martin Vogt, 2 vols. (Boppard am Rhein, 1970), 1:1–3.

33. Stresemann to Müller-Franken, telegram, 23 June 1928, AA: NL Stresemann, 3174/68/167893.

34. Minutes of the executive committee of the DVP Reichstag delegation, 26 June 1928, BA: R 45 II/66/113–19.

35. Morath to Stresemann, 30 June 1928, AA: NL Stresemann, 3163/101/174198–207.

36. *DAZ*, 28 June 1928, nos. 295–96. See also the minutes of the DVP Reichstag delegation, 27 June 1928, BA: R 45 II/67/97–98, as well as Scholz to Stresemann, 28 June 1928, AA: NL Stresemann, 3163/101/174188–89.

37. Stresemann to Kempkes, 2 July 1928, AA: NL Stresemann, 3163/101/174265–67.

38. In this respect, see Stresemann to the DVP Reichstag delegation, 30 June 1928, AA: NL Stresemann, 3161/101/174233–38, and to Scholz, 30 June 1928, ibid., 174209–11. For a further elaboration of this theme, see the manuscript of Stresemann's article, "Persönlichkeit, Politik und Organisation," 31 Dec. 1928, AA: NL Stresemann, 3175/75/168882–87.

39. Turner, *Stresemann*, pp. 254–56.

40. Stresemann to Scholz, 19 July 1928, AA: NL Stresemann, 3163/102/174329–41.

41. Stresemann to Schneider, 11 July 1928, AA: NL Stresemann, 3163/101/174305–6.

42. Stephan to Erkelenz, 18 July 1928, BA: NL Erkelenz, 49/156–57.

43. In this respect, see the entry in Koch-Weser's diary, 3 Sept. 1928, BA: NL Koch-Weser, 37/241, and DDP, Reichsgeschäftsstelle, circular no. 29, 11 Sept. 1928, BA: R 45 III/41/61–66.

44. Weber's report before the LV executive committee, 6 Sept. 1928, SAA: NL Siemens, 4 Lf/697.

45. Stresemann to Zöphel, 15 Apr. 1929, AA: NL Stresemann, 3164/105/174941–44.

46. Stresemann to Kempkes, 23 Sept. 1928, AA: NL Stresemann, 3163/102/174412–13, and to Scholz, 26 Sept. 1928, ibid., 174418–20. For further details, see Volker R. Berghahn, *Der Stahlhelm. Bund der Frontsoldaten 1918–1935* (Düsseldorf, 1966), pp. 113–14.

47. Minutes of the executive committee of the DVP Reichstag delegation, 2 Oct. 1928, BA: R 45 II/66/125–38. See also Scholz to Stresemann, 1 Oct. 1928, AA: NL Stresemann, 3163/102/174429, and Schoch, "Stahlhelm, Deutsche Volkspartei und Volksbegehren," *DAZ*, 19 Oct. 1928, nos. 489–90.

48. Stresemann to Zapf, 23 Oct. 1928, AA: NL Stresemann, 3163/102/174478–80.

49. Speech by Thiel, reported in the *Berliner Stimmen* 6, no. 3 (19 Jan. 1929): 2. On the political implications of the Lambach affair, see Larry Eugene Jones, "Between the Fronts: The German National Union of Commercial Employees from 1928 to 1933," *JMH* 48 (1976): 462–82.

50. Thiel, "Denkschrift über die Reorganisation der Deutschen Volkspartei," 31 Dec. 1928, appended to Thiel's letter of 5 Jan. 1929 to the members of the DVP executive committee, BA: NL Jarres, 41. See also Thiel, "Volkspartei oder Klassenpartei?," *DS* 41, no. 3 (5 Feb. 1929): 71–76.

51. For further details, see the minutes of the DVP managing committee, 5 Dec. 1928, AA: NL Stresemann, 3164/103/174572–77, and of the first meeting of the DVP organization committee, 20 Dec. 1928, ibid., 174587–88.

52. Minutes of the Center Reichstag delegation, 5 Feb. 1929, in Rudolf Morsey, ed., *Die Protokolle der Reichstagsfraktion und des Fraktionsvorstandes der Deutschen Zentrumspartei 1926–1933* (Mainz, 1969), pp. 265–66. For a fuller discussion of this crisis, see Timm, *Sozialpolitik*, pp. 118–24, and Larry Eugene Jones, "'The Dying Middle': Weimar Germany and the Failure of Bourgeois Unity, 1924–1930" (Ph.D. dissertation, University of Wisconsin, 1970), pp. 181–203.

53. Minutes of the DVP Reichstag delegation, 5 Feb. 1929, BA: R 45 II/67/124–26. See also DVP, Reichsgeschäftsstelle, confidential bulletin no. 6, 6 Feb. 1929, AA: NL Stresemann, 3164/103/174626–28.

54. Stresemann's remarks before the DVP Reichstag delegation, 18 Feb. 1929, BA: R 45 II/67/127.

55. On Stresemann's efforts to reach an accommodation with Kaas and Braun, see the correspondence between Kaas and Stresemann, 10–19 Feb. 1929, AA: NL Stresemann, 3175/77/169171–73, 169210–15, and 3101/302/151936–41, as well as the account in Otto Braun, *Von Weimar zu Hitler* (New York, 1940), pp. 272–73.

56. Report of the meeting of the DVP National Council for Commerce and Industry, 21 Feb. 1929, BA: R 45 II/60/281–84.

57. Minutes of the DVP Reichstag delegation, 21 Feb. 1929, BA: R 45 II/67/128–29.

58. Stresemann's speech before the DVP central executive committee, 26 Feb. 1929, AA: NL Stresemann, 3164/103/174673–90. For abridged versions of this speech, see Gustav Stresemann, *Vermächtnis. Der Nachlaß in drei Bänden*, ed. Henry Bernhard, 3 vols. (Berlin, 1932–33), 3:428–33, and Stresemann, "Die Krise des Parlamentarismus," *DS* 41, no. 5 (5 Mar. 1929): 134–41.

59. Memorandum by Bernhard, 27 Feb. 1929, AA: NL Stresemann, 3164/104/174694–97.

60. Minutes of the DVP central executive committee, 26 Feb. 1929, BA: R 45 II/43/26–49, 75–83, 125–30. For the resolution adopted at the conclusion of the meeting, see *NLC*, 27 Feb. 1929, no. 43.

61. In this respect, see Curtius to Stresemann, 14 and 16 Mar. 1929, AA: NL Stresemann, 3175/77/169343–45, 169348–51, and Cremer to Stresemann, 23 Mar. 1929, ibid., 3164/104/174823–29.

62. For example, see Stresemann to Kempkes, 11 Mar. 1929, AA: NL Stresemann, 3175/77/169303–07, and Stresemann to Curtius, 11 Mar. 1929, ibid., 169313–16.

63. Stresemann to Kahl, 13 Mar. 1929, AA: NL Stresemann, 3164/104/174722–33.

CHAPTER TWENTY-FOUR

1. Speech by Stresemann before the DVP central executive committee, 26 Feb. 1929, AA: NL Stresemann, 3164/103/174673–90.

2. For further details, see Walter Z. Laqueur, *Young Germany: A History of the German Youth Movement*, with an introduction by R. H. S. Crossman (New York, 1962), pp. 3–38, 66–73. On the political implications of generational conflict in the Weimar Republic, see Hans Mommsen, "Generationskonflikt und Jugendrevolte in der Weimarer Republik," in *"Mit uns zieht die neue Zeit." Der Mythos Jugend*, ed. Thomas

Koebner, Rolf-Peter Janz, and Frank Trommler (Frankfurt am Main, 1985), pp. 50–67, and Elisabeth Domansky, "Politische Dimensionen von Jugendprotest und Generationenkonflikt in der Zwischenkriegszeit in Deutschland," in *Jugendprotest und Generationenkonflikt in Europa im 20. Jahrhundert. Deutschland, England, Frankreich und Italien im Vergleich*, ed. Dieter Dowe (Brunswick and Bonn, 1986), pp. 113–37.

3. Ibid., pp. 89–98.

4. Robert Michels, *Umschichtungen in den herrschenden Klassen nach dem Kriege* (Stuttgart and Berlin, 1934), pp. 99–102.

5. Laqueur, *Young Germany*, pp. 99–129.

6. Ibid., pp. 155–66.

7. Felix Raabe, *Die bündische Jugend. Ein Beitrag zur Geschichte der Weimarer Republik* (Stuttgart, 1961), pp. 103–15. For the most detailed and useful treatment of paramilitary *Bünde* in the postwar period, see James M. Diehl, *Paramilitary Politics in Weimar Germany* (Bloomington, 1977).

8. In this respect, see the insightful contemporary assessment by Georg Schroeder, "Der Sozialismus der nationalen Jugend," *Der Arbeitgeber. Zeitschrift der Vereinigung der Deutschen Arbeitgeberverbände* 20, no. 8 (15 Apr. 1930): 218–20, and Josef Winschuh, "Bündische Bewegung und Sozialpolitik," *Soziale Praxis. Zentralblatt für Sozialpolitik und Wohlfahrtspflege* 39, no. 24 (12 June 1930): 561–65.

9. For further details, see Herbert Kugelmann, *Die deutschdemokratische Jugendbewegung. Ihre Ziele und Bestrebungen* (Berlin-Zehlendorf, 1919), pp. 7–10, 54–57, as well as the essay by Hans-Otto Rommel, "Die Weimarer Jungdemokraten," *Liberal* 13 (1971): 915–24.

10. In this respect, see Mommsen, "Demokratische Arbeit an den Hochschulen. Zum Jenaer Studententag am 6. und 7. Oktober," *Der Demokrat* 2, no. 40 (6 Oct. 1921): 769–71.

11. Aside from some scattered items on the 1922 Young Democratic congress in Jena, Lemmer's unpublished Nachlaß in the Archiv für Christlich-Demokratische Politik, Sankt Augustin bei Bonn, contains little on the activities of the Young Democrats. Nor is Lemmer's own autobiography, *Manches war doch anders . . . Erinnerungen eines deutschen Demokraten* (Frankfurt am Main, 1968), particularly helpful for a history of the movement. For an indication of its general political orientation under his leadership, see Lemmer, "Ein Nachwort zu Bamberg. Die Führertagung der jungen Demokratie," *BTB*, 22 Oct. 1926, no. 499.

12. Werner Stephan, *Die Deutsche Demokratische Partei im Berichtsjahr 1926. Jahresbericht der Reichsparteileitung* (n.p., [1927]), pp. 24–26.

13. DVP, Reichsgeschäftsstelle, ed. *Deutsche Jugend—Deutsche Volkspartei*, Jugend-Schriften der Deutschen Volkspartei, no. 5 (Berlin, 1924).

14. *Berliner Stimmen* 6, no. 25 (22 June 1929): 2–3.

15. For the Hindenburg League's ideological orientation, see Hindenburgbund, Jugendgruppe der Deutschen Volkspartei, ed. *Staatsbürgerliche Jugendbildung. Unsere Reichsschulungswoche in Braunlage/Harz vom 22. bis 27. April 1930* (Berlin, [1930]), 3–14.

16. Contemporary literature on the problem is quite extensive. For example, see Ziegler, "Die übersprungene Generation," *DS* 40, no. 12 (20 June 1928): 357–62, and Stephan, "Die 'Führerkrise' oder Generationswechsel in der Politik," *Wille und Weg* 4,

no. 16 (15 Nov. 1928): 378–81, as well as lengthier discussions of this question in Richard Wolff, *Ideenkrisis—Parteienwirrwarr. Eine historisch-politische Betrachtung* (Berlin, 1931), pp. 66–78, and Arthur Dix, *Die deutschen Reichstagswahlen 1871–1930 und die Wandlungen der Volksgliederung* (Tübingen, 1930), pp. 32–37.

17. Stresemann, "Die deutsche Jugend," *NLC*, 29 Dec. 1928, no. 235.

18. Invitation from Regh, 31 Jan. 1928, BA: NL Sieling (Kleine Erwerbung 484), 1. For a more detailed treatment of the February Club, see Karl-Hermann Beeck, "Die Gründung der Deutschen Staatspartei im Jahre 1930 im Zusammenhang der Neuordnungsversuche des Liberalismus" (Ph.D. dissertation, Cologne, 1957), pp. 16–54, and Larry Eugene Jones, " 'The Dying Middle': Weimar Germany and the Failure of Bourgeois Unity, 1924–1930" (Ph.D. dissertation, University of Wisconsin, 1970), pp. 215–55.

19. Remarks by Winschuh at the first meeting of the Cologne February Club, 10 Feb. 1928, BA: NL Sieling (Kleine Erwerbung 484), 1. See also Regh, "Der Februar-Klub," *Frankfurter Nachrichten*, 31 Mar. 1929, no. 90.

20. "Jugend und Wahlen," *KZ*, 14 May 1928, no. 266, and "Die deutsche Generation zwischen 20 und 40," ibid., 19 May 1928, no. 275b.

21. February Club circular dated 1 Feb. 1929, BA: NL Sieling (Kleine Erwerbung 484), 1.

22. Minutes of the Cologne February Club, 11 Dec. 1928, BA: NL Sieling (Kleine Erwerbung 484), 1.

23. *KZ*, 8 Jan. 1929, no. 16.

24. Eschenburg to Dietrich, 19 Dec. 1929, BA: NL Dietrich, 123/147–48. For further information on the Quirites, see the report by Mansfeld at an editorial conference of the *Kölnische Zeitung*, 4 Dec. 1930, in "Büchner Protokolle. Redaktionssitzungen der Kölnischen Zeitung 22. März 1929 bis 2. Dezember 1935."

25. DVP, Wahlkreisverband Württemberg, to the DVP Reichsgeschäftsstelle, 13 Mar. 1929, BA: R 45 II/5/9–10.

26. Ley to Dietrich, 25 Feb. 1929, BA: NL Dietrich, 239/1.

27. On the Heidelberg Coalition for Young German Politics, see Kind's report at a meeting of the action committee of the February Club, 28 Apr. 1930, BA: NL Sieling (Kleine Erwerbung 484), 2. For a general survey of this activity, see Josef Winschuh, "Die Rolle der Sozialpolitik in den neuen politischen Strömungen," *Die Arbeitgeber* 20, no. 8 (15 Apr. 1930): 214–18.

28. Wolff to Becker, 25 Mar. 1929, BA: NL Becker, 56.

29. On Stresemann's relationship to the Front 1929, see Mansfeld's report, 22 Mar. 1929, "Büchner-Protokolle," and the memorandum of Stresemann's remarks during a conversation with Rheinbaben and Stein, 26 Apr. 1929, AA: NL Stresemann, 3164/105/174987–88.

30. Rheinbaben, " 'Front 1929' und ihr Gedankenkreis," *Frankfurter Nachrichten*, 31 Mar. 1929, no. 90. See also "Richtlinien der Front 1929," n.d., BA: NL Koch-Weser, 101/103.

31. For example, see Rheinbaben to Dietrich, 18 June 1929, BA: NL Dietrich, 239/45.

32. For the most detailed record of the negotiations in the spring of 1929, see

Rheinbaben to Stresemann, 23 Mar. 1929, AA: NL Stresemann, 3176/78/169430–35. See also Mansfeld's remarks, 22 Mar. 1929, "Büchner-Protokolle."

33. Scholz to Stresemann, 20 Mar. 1929, AA: NL Stresemann, 3164/104/174786–87.

34. Freund to Dietrich, 14 Apr. 1929, BA: NL Dietrich, 239/33–35.

35. Ley to Dietrich, 17 Mar. 1929, BA: NL Dietrich, 239/3.

36. *KZ*, 21 Mar. 1929, no. 158.

37. *Der Jungdeutsche*, 7 Mar. 1929, no. 50.

38. On the early history of the Young German Order, see the autobiographical reminiscences in Artur Mahraun, *Gegen getarnte Gewalten* (Berlin, 1928), pp. 6–10. Though extensive, the secondary literature on the history of the Order tends to be uncritical. For the most balanced treatment, see Diehl, *Paramilitary Politics*, pp. 95–100, 169–73, 222–76. Less satisfactory is the standard history by Klaus Hornung, *Der Jungdeutsche Orden* (Düsseldorf, 1958). On the Order's activities during the late 1920s, see the useful contributions by Alexander Kessler, *Der Jungdeutsche Orden in den Jahren der Entscheidung (I) 1928–1930* (Munich, 1975), and *Der Jungdeutsche Orden auf dem Wege zur Deutschen Staatspartei* (Munich, 1980).

39. Pastenaci, "Der Jungdeutsche Orden und die Jugendbewegung," *Süddeutsche Monatshefte* 23, no. 9 (June 1926): 177–80.

40. For the most comprehensive statement of Young German ideology, see Artur Mahraun, *Parole 1929* (Berlin, 1929), pp. 3–34. For the most detailed analysis of Mahraun's thought, see Ernst Maste, *Die Republik der Nachbarn. Die Nachbarschaft und der Staatsgedanke Artur Mahrauns* (Giesen, 1957). The antiliberal character of Young German ideology is most apparent in Reinhard Höhn, *Der bürgerliche Rechtsstaat und die neue Front* (Berlin, 1929). See also the brief discussion of Mahraun's ideas in Diehl, *Paramilitary Politics*, pp. 222–27.

41. Artur Mahraun, *Das jungdeutsche Manifest* (Berlin, 1927), pp. 7–10, 95–107, 139–42, 197–203.

42. Mahraun, *Gegen getarnte Gewalten*, pp. 207–8.

43. See Bornemann's remarks before the 18th High Chapter of the Young German Order, 29–30 Sept. 1928, BA: R 161/12.

44. Artur Mahraun, *Die neue Front. Hindenburgs Sendung* (Berlin, 1928), pp. 87–105. See also Mahraun, "Gedanken über die Politik des Jungdeutschen Ordens im Jahre 1928," *Der Meister* 4, no. 4 (Jan. 1929): 152–53.

45. Protocol of the 19th High Chapter of the Young German Order, 26–27 Jan. 1929, BA: R 161/12. See also Mahraun, "Volksnationale Aktion," *Der Meister* 4, no. 6 (Mar. 1929): 243–54.

46. Entry in Koch-Weser's diary, 27 Feb. 1929, BA: NL Koch-Weser, 39/11–13.

47. Schroeder, "Auseinandersetzungen mit dem Jungdo," *Der Ring* 2, no. 44 (3 Nov. 1929): 849–51.

48. With the exception of Mansfeld's report, 22 Mar. 1929, "Büchner-Protokolle," no record of the Order's negotiations in the spring of 1929 has survived. The foregoing account has drawn heavily upon the personal recollections of Otto Bornemann, Ernst Lemmer, Wilhelm Ridder, and G. R. Treviranus, as well as the wealth of information that Erich Eggeling supplied in his letter of 18 Sept. 1967.

49. Protocol of the 20th High Chapter of the Young German Order, 24–25 Mar. 1929, BA: R 161/12.

50. Handwritten minutes of the meeting of the February Club's action committee, 15 Mar. 1929, BA: NL Sieling (Kleine Erwerbung 484), 1. See also Mansfeld's report, 22 Mar. 1929, "Büchner-Protokolle."

51. *KZ*, 17 Mar. 1929, no. 150.

52. For example, see Scholz to Stresemann, 20 Mar. 1929, AA: NL Stresemann, 3164/104/174786–87, and Moldenhauer to Stresemann, 4 Apr. 1929, ibid., 3164/105/ 174933–36.

53. Stresemann to Scholz, 26 Mar. 1929, AA: NL Stresemann, 3164/104/174863– 67.

54. Stresemann to Zöphel, 15 Apr. 1929, AA: NL Stresemann, 3164/105/174941– 44, and Stresemann to Hellpach, 17 Apr. 1929, ibid., 174954–56. See also the text of Stresemann's interview with Börner from the *Deutsche Führerbriefe*, Apr. 1929, ibid., 174995–5000.

55. Goepel, "Entwicklung und Stand der politischen Reformsbestrebungen der jungen Generation," *Hochschulblätter der Deutschen Volkspartei*, May 1929, no. 30, in BA: R 45 II/6/11–14.

56. Glatzel to Winschuh, 25 Mar. 1929, BA: R 45 II/69/417–19. See also the handwritten draft of a lecture by Sieling, 17 Feb. 1930, BA: NL Sieling (Kleine Erwerbung 484), 2.

57. Memorandum of a conversation in the Hotel Fürstenhof, Eisenach, 21 Apr. 1929, BA: R 45 II/6/1–9. See also Hardt and Glatzel to Kempkes, 17 May 1929, ibid., 5/17–21.

58. For further details, see Regh to Kempkes, 15 May 1929, BA: R 45 II/4/19–21, and Moldenhauer to Stresemann, 24 May 1929, AA: NL Stresemann, 3164/105/ 175076–79, as well as the report in *KZ*, 17 May 1929, no. 267.

59. See the abbreviated text of Glatzel's speech at Weimar, "Zusammenschluß junger Volksparteiler," n.d., BA: R 45 II/6/19–31, as well as his article, "Was will die Reichsgemeinschaft junger Volksparteiler?," *Niedersächsisches Wochenblatt* 36, no. 12 (22 June 1929). See also the report in *KZ*, 27 May 1929, no. 284, as well as Meier, "Das Ergebnis von Weimar," *DS* 41, no. 11 (5 June 1929): 321–29, and Reichsgemeinschaft junger Volksparteiler, *Aufmarsch und Ziel* (Lobau, [1929]), pp. 24–37.

60. Protocol of the 21st High Chapter of the Young German Order, 1–2 June 1929, BA: R 161/12.

61. Mahraun to Stresemann, 4 June 1929, AA: NL Stresemann, 3177/81/170105–6, and Mahraun to Baltrusch, 4 June 1929, BA: NS 26/858.

62. "Verzeichnis der geladenen Ehrengäste," appended to Mahraun's letter to Stresemann, 4 June 1929, BA: NL Stresemann, 3177/81/170107–10.

63. *Der Jungdeutsche*, 18 June 1929, no. 139.

64. Ibid. See also Stresemann to Mahraun, 11 June 1929, AA: NL Stresemann, 3171/81/170111.

65. Lemmer, "Hinein in die Politik," *Vossische Zeitung*, 22 June 1929, no. 148.

66. *Der Jungdeutsche*, 6 Aug. 1929, no. 181. See also Hülser, "Christlich-soziale Realpolitik," *Der Deutsche*, 24 July 1929, no. 171, and "Christlich-sozialer Aufbruch," *Der Jungdeutsche*, 30 July 1929, no. 175.

67. *Der Jungdeutsche*, 1 and 3 Sept. 1929, nos. 204–5.
68. For example, see Heuss, "Parteien und Bünde," *Wille und Weg* 4, no. 2 (15 Apr. 1928): 40–46.

CHAPTER TWENTY-FIVE

1. For the most perceptive analysis of Hugenberg's political strategy, see Heidrun Holzbach, *Das "System Hugenberg." Die Organisation bürgerlicher Sammlungspolitik vor dem Aufsteig der NSDAP* (Stuttgart, 1981), pp. 65–136. On Hugenberg's election to the DNVP party chairmanship, see John A. Leopold, *Alfred Hugenberg: The Radical Nationalist Campaign against the Weimar Republic* (New Haven, 1977), pp. 27–54.
2. For an indication of Hugenberg's political agenda, see Alfred Hugenberg, *Klare Front zum Freiheitskampf. Rede gehalten auf dem 9. Reichsparteitag der Deutschnationalen Volkspartei in Kassel am 22. November 1929*, Deutschnationale Flugschrift, no. 339 (Berlin, 1929).
3. On the formation of this committee, see Leopold, *Hugenberg*, pp. 55–67, and Volker R. Berghahn, *Der Stahlhelm. Bund der Frontsoldaten 1918–1935* (Düsseldorf, 1966), pp. 122–31, as well as the extremely informative dissertation by Elizabeth Friedenthal, "Volksbegehren und Volksentschied über den Young-Plan und die deutschnationale Sezession" (Ph.D. dissertation, Tübingen, 1957), pp. 36–51.
4. Entry in Koch-Weser's diary, 27 Nov. 1929, BA: NL Koch-Weser, 101/125–31. See also Stresemann to Koch-Weser, 17 Sept. 1929, AA: NL Stresemann, 3178/86/171118–19.
5. Resolution of the DVP national committee, 30 Sept. 1929, BA: R 45 II/63/17.
6. For further details, see Ilse Maurer, *Reichsfinanzen und große Koalition. Zur Geschichte des Reichskabinetts Müller (1928–1930)* (Bonn and Frankfurt am Main, 1973), pp. 68–79.
7. Speech by Scholz, reported in *DAZ*, 6 Sept. 1929, nos. 410–11.
8. Curtius to Stresemann, 20 Sept. 1929, AA: NL Stresemann, 3178/86/171177–79.
9. For the objectives of the DVP's right wing, see Gilsa to Reusch, 12 and 24 Sept. 1929, HA/GHH: NL Reusch, 400101293/9.
10. Minutes of the DVP Reichstag delegation, 27 Sept. 1929, BA: R 45 II/67/159–60. See also Gilsa to Reusch, 28 Sept. 1929, HA/GHH: NL Reusch, 400101293/9.
11. Minutes of the DVP Reichstag delegation, 2 Oct. 1929, BA: R 45 II/67/159–67.
12. Speech by Koch-Weser at the DDP's Mannheim party congress, 4 Oct. 1929, BA: R 45 III/7/17–55. See also *Der Demokrat* 10, no. 20 (20 Oct. 1929): 486–96.
13. Hermann Dietrich, *Ein Jahr Agrarpolitik* (Berlin, 1929). For a detailed discussion of Dietrich's policies as minister of agriculture, see Adelheid von Saldern, *Hermann Dietrich. Ein Staatsmann der Weimarer Republik* (Boppard am Rhein, 1966), pp. 45–83.
14. Speech by Dietrich at the DDP's Mannheim party congress, 4 Oct. 1929, BA: R 45 III/7/57–79. See also *Der Demokrat* 10, no. 20 (20 Oct. 1929): 497–500.
15. Stolper to Reemtsa, 19 Oct. 1929, BA: NL Stolper, 44.

16. Minutes of the DDP executive committee, 14–15 June 1928, BA: R 45 III/20/195–98.

17. Gustav Stolper, *Die wirtschaftlich-soziale Weltanschauung der Demokratie. Programmrede auf dem Mannheimer Parteitag der Deutschen Demokratischen Partei am 5. Oktober 1929* (Berlin, 1929), pp. 27–30.

18. Ibid., pp. 10–17, 22–24.

19. In this respect, see DDP, Reichsausschuß für Handel, Industrie und Gewerbe und Reichsmittelstandsausschuß, ed., *Heidelberger Tagung des Reichsausschusses für Handel, Industrie und Gewerbe und des Reichsmittelstandsausschusses der Deutschen Demokratischen Partei 3. Oktober 1929* (Berlin, [1929]), pp. 9–14, 29–45, as well as Ernst Mosich, *Materialien zur Finanzreform*, Druckschriften des Hansa-Bundes für Gewerbe, Handel und Industrie, n.s., no. 2. (Berlin, 1929).

20. Erkelenz to Stolper, 16 Sept. 1929, BA: NL Erkelenz, 54/43–54.

21. Bernhard to Koch-Weser, 11 Oct. 1929, BA: NL Stolper, 44.

22. Muhle, "Zum jungdemokratischen Wirtschaftsprogramm," *Der Herold der deutschen Jungdemokratie* 10, no. 10 (Oct. 1929): 146–47.

23. For example, see Erkelenz to Haas, 23 Feb. 1929, and Erkelenz to Bäumer, 18 Mar. 1929, both in BA: NL Erkelenz, 133.

24. Erkelenz to Lange, 27 Sept. 1929, BA: NL Erkelenz, 54/106, and Erkelenz to Cohnstaedt, 1 Oct. 1929, ibid., 54/119–22.

25. Report by Mansfeld, 8 Oct. 1929, "Büchner-Protokolle. Redaktionssitzungen der Kölnischen Zeitung 22. März 1929 bis 2. Dezember 1935."

26. Ibid. See also Haas's report on the recommendations of the DDP nominating committee, 5 Oct. 1929, BA: R 45 III/7/245–46, as well as Werner Stephan, *Aufstieg und Verfall des Linksliberalismus. Geschichte der Deutschen Demokratischen Partei* (Göttingen, 1973), pp. 416–17.

27. Hellpach's closing speech at the DDP's Mannheim congress, 6 Oct. 1929, BA: R 45 III/7/254–55. See also Weber, "Die Sendung der Mitte," *KZ*, 20 Oct. 1929, no. 576a, and Höpker-Aschoff, "Die Lage der Mittelparteien nach dem Mannheimer Parteitag," *Der Beobachter. Ein Volksblatt aus Schwaben*, 2 Nov. 1929, no. 44.

28. Winschuh to Koch-Weser, 9 Oct. 1929, BA: NL Koch-Weser, 101/83.

29. Koch-Weser, "Aufzeichnung für die Besprechung am 18. Oktober 1929," BA: NL Koch-Weser, 101/91–101. To date this meeting, see the memorandum of Winschuh's telephone call, n.d., ibid., 101/84.

30. To establish the date of Koch-Weser's meetings with Curtius, Luther, and Kahl, see the handwritten note dated "Mittwoch," BA: NL Koch-Weser, 101/37, as well as the entry in his diary for 23 Oct. 1929, ibid., 101/107.

31. Entry in Koch-Weser's diary, 23 Oct. 1929, BA: NL Koch-Weser, 101/107. See also Weber to Jänicke, 1 Nov. 1929, BA: NL Jänicke, 26.

32. See Weber to Koch-Weser, 21 Nov. 1929, BA: NL Koch-Weser, 101/110, and Kahl to Koch-Weser, 24 Nov. 1929, ibid., 101/122–23.

33. *Hannoverscher Kurier*, 28 Nov. 1929, no. 557. See also Kardorff, "Das Gebot der Stunde," *Berliner Börsen-Zeitung*, 16 Oct. 1929, no. 483.

34. Minutes of the DVP Reichstag delegation, 28 Nov. 1929, BA: R 45 II/67/173.

35. Protocol of the 23d High Chapter of the Young German Order, 12–13 Oct. 1929, BA: R 161/12.

36. Mahraun, "Aufruf an alle!," 1 Nov. 1929, BA: NS 26/875.

37. Artur Mahraun, *Der Aufbruch. Sinn und Zweck der Volksnationalen Reichs-vereinigung* (Berlin, 1930), pp. 36–40, 46–57.

38. Mahraun, "Volksnationale Reichsvereinigung," *Der Meister* 5, no. 2 (Nov. 1929): 49–64.

39. For further details, see Rheinbaben to Stresemann, 18 and 28 Sept. 1929, AA: NL Stresemann, 3178/86/171122–26, and 3165/106/175316–17, as well as Stein to Koch-Weser, 24 Sept. and 15 Oct. 1929, BA: NL Koch-Weser, 101/77–81, 89.

40. RjV, circular no. 3, 18 Oct. 1929, BA: R 45 II/6/113–17. See also Glatzel, "Die Parteikrise und die junge Generation," *Landauer Anzeiger*, 28 Oct. 1929, no. 252.

41. For further details, see Wichterich to Sieling, 13 Nov. 1929, BA: NL Sieling (Kleine Erwerbung 484), 1.

42. Regh to Sieling, 30 Nov. 1929, BA: NL Sieling (Kleine Erwerbung 484), 1. See also RjV, circular no. 6, 9 Dec. 1929, BA: R 45 II/6/139–47.

43. Glatzel to the members of the DVP executive committee, 11 Dec. 1929, BA: NL Jarres, 40.

44. Meeting of the executive committee of the DVP district organization in Hannover, 21 Nov. 1929, StA Braunschweig, GX6/637.

45. For example, see Bretschneider to Thiel, 8 and 22 Nov. 1929, both in StA Braunschweig, GX6/605, as well as Reusch to Gilsa, 9 Nov. 1929, HA/GHH: NL Reusch, 400101293/4.

46. Luther to Jänecke, 11 Oct. 1929, BA: NL Luther, 296.

47. On the meeting in Leipzig, see the memorandum of a conversation between Luther and Jänecke, 26 Nov. 1929, BA: NL Luther, 296, and Jänecke to Thiel, 27 Nov. 1929, ibid., 363.

48. Dieckmann to Luther, 28 Nov. 1929, BA: NL Luther, 363.

49. Luther to Kempkes, 30 Nov. 1929, StA Braunschweig, GX6/605. See also the memorandum of a conversation between Luther, Hardt, and Schroeder, 30 Nov. 1929, BA: NL Luther, 363.

50. Memorandum on the meeting of the DVP national committee, 3 Dec. 1929, appended to the letter from Luther to Reusch, 4 Dec. 1929, HA/GHH: NL Reusch, 400101290/29.

51. Glatzel to the members of the DVP executive committee, 11 Dec. 1929, BA: NL Jarres, 40.

52. Minutes of the DVP central executive committee, 14 Dec. 1929, BA: R 45 II/44/135–67, 405.

53. In this respect, see the minutes of the DVP Reichstag delegation, 10–14 Dec. 1929, BA: R 45 II/67/175–89, as well as the remarks by Jänecke, Kuhbier, and Hugo before the DVP central executive committee, 14 Dec. 1929, ibid., 44/247–57, 279–301. For further details, see Maurer, pp. 95–101, and Bernd Weisbrod, *Schwerindustrie in der Weimarer Republik. Interessenpolitik zwischen Stabilisierung und Krise* (Wuppertal, 1978), pp. 467–71.

54. Minutes of the DDP executive committee, 13 Dec. 1929, BA: R 45 III/21/105–6.

55. On the formation of this group, see Mansfeld's report, 8 Oct. 1929, "Büchner-Protokolle," as well as the report in *KZ*, 26 Apr. 1930, no. 266. For its basic political

goals, see the remarks by Muhle, Mewes, and Lemmer before the DDP executive committee, 13 Dec. 1929, BA: R 45 III/21/107–8, as well as Lemmer to Schücking, 26 Apr. 1930, BA: NL Schücking, 50.

56. The literature on the Nazi breakthrough in 1929–30 is both voluminous and growing. For the most recent contributions to an understanding of this problem, see Jerzy Holzer, *Parteien und Massen. Die politische Krise in Deutschland 1928–1930* (Mainz, 1975), pp. 49–63, as well as the valuable regional studies by Donald R. Tracey, "The Development of the National Socialist Party in Thuringia, 1924–1930," *CEH* 8 (1975): 23–50; Ellsworth Faris, "Takeoff Point for the National Socialist Party: The Landtag Election in Baden, 1929," *CEH* 8 (1975): 140–71; Jeremey Noakes, *The Nazi Party in Lower Saxony, 1921–1933* (Oxford, 1971), pp. 108–46; and Geoffrey Pridham, *Hitler's Rise to Power: The Nazi Movement in Bavaria, 1923–1933* (London, 1973), pp. 78–145. On the social bases of the Nazi breakthrough, see Thomas Childers, *The Nazi Voter: The Social Foundations of Fascism in Germany, 1919–1933* (Chapel Hill, 1983), pp. 119–91.

CHAPTER TWENTY-SIX

1. The secondary literature on the crisis within the DNVP is quite extensive. In addition to the unpublished dissertation by Elizabeth Friedenthal, "Volksbegehren und Volksentschied über den Young-Plan und die deutschnationale Sezession" (Ph.D. dissertation, Tübingen, 1957), pp. 36–147, and John A. Leopold, *Alfred Hugenberg: The Radical Nationalist Campaign against the Weimar Republic* (New Haven, 1977), pp. 27–83, see Attila A. Chanady, "The Disintegration of the German National People's Party, 1924–1930," *JMH* 39 (1967): 65–91, and David P. Walker, "The German Nationalist People's Party: The Conservative Dilemma in the Weimar Republic," *JCH* 14 (1979): 627–47.

2. *Aufruf und Gründung*, Volkskonservative Flugschriften, no. 1 (Berlin, 1930), pp. 4–5. See also Hans-Erdmann von Lindeiner-Wildau, *Erneuerung des politischen Lebens. Reichstagsrede gehalten am 13. Dezember 1929*, Schriften der Deutschnationalen Arbeitsgemeinschaft, no. 1 (Berlin-Charlottenburg, 1929).

3. Entry in Passarge's diary, 5 Jan. 1930, BA: NL Passarge, 2/9. See also Treviranus, "Das Fähnlein der Zwölf," *Das Staatsschiff* 1, no. 5 (16 Jan. 1930): 176–78.

4. For example, see the report of Hepp's speech in Münster in late Feb. 1930 in *Der Landbürger* 5, no. 6 (16 Mar. 1930): 83. For further details, see Larry Eugene Jones, "Crisis and Realignment: Agrarian Splinter Parties in the Late Weimar Republic, 1928–33," in *Peasants and Lords in Modern Germany: Recent Studies in Agricultural History*, ed. Robert G. Moeller (London, 1986), pp. 207–10.

5. Bausch, "Was fordert die politische Lage von uns?," *Christlicher Volksdienst*, 25 Jan. 1930, no. 4.

6. Entry in Passarge's diary, 5 Jan. 1930, BA: NL Passarge, 2/10.

7. Entry in Passarge's diary, 12 Jan. 1930, BA: NL Passarge, 2/13–18. On the DHV's involvement in these efforts, see Larry Eugene Jones, "Between the Fronts: The German National Union of Commercial Employees from 1928 to 1933," *JMH* 48

(1976): 469–72, and Iris Hamel, *Völkischer Verband und nationale Gewerkschaft. Der Deutschnationale Handlungsgehilfenverband 1893–1933* (Hamburg, 1967), pp. 218–31.

8. G. R. Treviranus, *Auf neuen Wegen,* Volkskonservative Flugschriften, no. 2 (Berlin, 1930), pp. 3–8. On the founding of the VKV, see Erasmus Jonas, *Die Volkskonservativen 1928–1933. Entwicklung, Struktur, Standort und staatspolitische Zielsetzung* (Düsseldorf, 1965), pp. 57–60.

9. Bornemann, "Die volksnationale Aktion," *Der Jungdeutsche,* 29 Jan. 1930, no. 24.

10. In particular, see Bornemann, "Persönlicher Brief an alle Großmeister!," n.d., reproduced in an internal communiqué from the Jungdeutscher Orden, Großballei Westdeutschland, 31 Jan. 1930, BA: R 161/59.

11. Glatzel, "Volksnationale Aktion und Volkskonservative Vereinigung," in RjV, circular no. I/2, 3 Feb. 1930, BA: R 45 II/6/149–57. See also RjV, circular no. III/9, 19 Mar. 1930, StA Braunschweig, GX6/612.

12. *Aufstieg oder Niedergang? Deutsche Wirtschafts- und Finanzreform 1929. Eine Denkschrift des Präsidiums des Reichsverbandes der Deutschen Industrie,* Veröffentlichung des Reichsverbandes der Deutschen Industrie, no. 49 (Berlin, 1929), pp. 45–46. See also Duisberg's closing remarks at the RDI's extraordinary membership convention, 19 Dec. 1929, WA Bayer, 62/10.9c.

13. See the correspondence between Duisberg and Alvensleben, 28 Nov.–3 Dec. 1929, WA Bayer, Autographen-Sammlung Duisberg.

14. For example, see Wilmowsky to Krupp, 22 Nov. 1929, HA Krupp, FAH 23/503.

15. On the activities of the DVP's right wing, see Gilsa to Reusch, 25 Jan. and 5 Feb. 1930, HA/GHH: NL Reusch, 400101293/4. For further details, see Ilse Maurer, *Reichsfinanzen und große Koalition. Zur Geschichte des Reichskabinetts Müller (1928–1930)* (Bonn and Frankfurt am Main, 1973), pp. 108–21, and Bernd Weisbrod, *Schwerindustrie in der Weimarer Republik. Interessenpolitik zwischen Stabilisierung und Krise* (Wuppertal, 1978), pp. 472–77.

16. Gilsa to Reusch, 11 Feb. 1930, HA/GHH: NL Reusch, 400101293/4.

17. For an indication of Scholz's thinking on the matter of bourgeois concentration, see Kahl to Luther, 3 Feb. 1930, BA: NL Luther, 363.

18. Speech by Scholz before the DVP national committee, 2 Mar. 1930, BA: R 45 II/32/25–27.

19. For industry's position, see Kastl to Moldenhauer, 8 Feb. 1930, HA/GHH: NL Reusch, 400101293/10.

20. Declarations of the RDI and six other business organizations, 6 Mar. 1930, WA Bayer, Autographen-Sammlung Duisberg. See also the memorandum of Herle's conversation with Moldenhauer, 8 Mar. 1930, ibid.

21. Moldenhauer to Duisberg, 10 Mar. 1930, WA Bayer, Autographen-Sammlung Duisberg.

22. For further details, see Maurer, *Reichsfinanzen,* pp. 129–39.

23. Report by Mansfeld, 25 Mar. 1930, "Büchner-Protokolle. Redaktionssitzungen der Kölnischen Zeitung 22. März 1929 bis 2. Dezember 1935." The conference can be dated from an invitation of 11 Mar. 1930 in BA: NL Sieling (Kleine Erwerbung 484), 2.

24. Weber to Koch-Weser, 13 Mar. 1930, BA: NL Koch-Weser, 101/145.

25. An undated protocol of this meeting, apparently prepared by a member of the RjV in Aug. 1930, has been preserved in StA Braunschweig, GX6/612. For Koch-Weser's position, see his "Material zu einem Programm für die neu zu gründende Partei der Mitte," [Apr. 1930], BA: NL Koch-Weser, 101/149–59.

26. Report by Mansfeld, 25 Mar. 1930, "Büchner-Protokolle."

27. Minutes of the DVP's Mannheim party congress, 21–23 Mar. 1930, BA: R 45 II/31/131–55. See also the report of Scholz's speech in DVP, Reichsgeschäftsstelle, ed., *8. Reichsparteitag der Deutschen Volkspartei in Mannheim vom 21. bis 23. März 1930* (Berlin, [1930]), pp. 3–6.

28. Correspondence between Gilsa and Reusch, 23–25 Mar. 1930, HA/GHH: NL Reusch, 400101293/4.

29. *KZ*, 24 Mar. 1930, no. 165b.

30. On the formation of the Brüning government, see Brüning's own account in Heinrich Brüning, *Memoiren 1918–1934* (Stuttgart, 1970), pp. 145–68, as well as the collection of documents published by Rudolf Morsey, "Neue Quellen zur Geschichte der Reichskanzlerschaft Brünings," in *Staat, Wirtschaft und Politik in der Weimarer Republik. Festschrift für Heinrich Brüning*, ed. Ferdinand A. Hermens and Theodor Schieder (Berlin, 1967), pp. 207–32. On the political implications of this development, see the provocative essay by Werner Conze, "Die Krise des Parteienstaates in Deutschland 1929/30," *HZ* 178 (1954): 47–83.

31. Leo Schwering, "Stegerwald und Brünings Vorstellungen über Parteireform und Parteiensystem," in *Staat, Wirtschaft und Politik*, ed. Hermens and Schieder, pp. 23–40.

32. For an indication of Brüning's attitude on the question of bourgeois concentration, see his letter to Pünder, 22 Apr. 1930, BA: NL Pünder, 30/53–57.

33. For a critical reassessment of Brüning's strategy and objectives as chancellor, see Hans Mommsen, "Heinrich Brüning als Reichskanzler: Das Scheitern eines Alleingangs," in *Wirtschaftskrise und liberale Demokratie. Das Ende der Weimarer Republik und die gegenwärtige Situation*, ed. Karl Holl (Göttingen, 1978), pp. 16–45.

34. On the composition of the Brüning government, see Brüning, *Memoiren*, pp. 165–68.

35. DVP, Reichsgeschäftsstelle, circular no. 2, 25 Apr. 1930, ZSA: DVP/225/168.

36. On the general course of these negotiations, see Gilsa to Reusch, 1 May 1930, HA/GHH: NL Reusch, 400101293/4, and Erkelenz to Voss, 15 May 1930, BA: NL Erkelenz, 126.

37. Hugo, "Der Ruf nach Sammlung," *Königsberger Allgemeine Zeitung*, 17 May 1930, no. 229.

38. Maier, "Wege und Ziele der liberalen und demokratischen Einigung," *Stuttgarter Neues Tageblatt*, 24 Jan. 1930, no. 38. For the most detailed account of the DDP's entry in the Württemberg government, see Hopf to the DDP national headquarters, 22 Jan. 1930, BA: NL Koch-Weser, 104/11–19.

39. For further details, see Stahl, "Die Regierungsbildung in Baden," *Der Demokrat* 10, no. 24 (20 Dec. 1929): 619–20, and Wolf, "Nach der Mitte sammeln! Das badische Beispiel," *DS* 41, no. 24 (20 Dec. 1929): 749–53.

40. Hellpach to Bruckmann, 25 Jan. 1930, BA: NL Koch-Weser, 104/83.

41. Hellpach, "Konservative Demokratie," *Neue Zürcher Zeitung*, 4 Feb. 1930, no. 218.

42. Hellpach to Meyer, 3 Mar. 1930, GLA Karlsruhe, NL Hellpach, 257.

43. In this respect, see Jänicke to Hellpach, 5 Mar. 1930, GLA Karlsruhe, NL Hellpach, 284, and Hellpach to Jänicke, 28 Mar. 1930, BA: NL Jänicke, 56.

44. Erkelenz to Dietrich, 19 Mar. 1930, BA: NL Erkelenz, 126.

45. Entry for 28 Mar. 1930, in Ernst Feder, *Heute sprach ich mit . . . Tagebuch eines Berliner Publizisten 1926–1932*, ed. Cecile Löwenthal-Hensel and Arnold Paucker (Stuttgart, 1971), pp. 252–53.

46. See Koch-Weser's remarks before the DDP party council, 25 May 1930, BA: R 45 III/14/46–51, as well as Rexrodt, "Das Kabinett Brüning und die D.D.P.," *Der Demokrat* 11, no. 8 (20 Apr. 1930): 177–79, and Külz, "Die demokratische Partei und das Kabinett Brüning," *Die Hilfe* 36, no. 16 (19 Apr. 1930): 401–3.

47. For example, see Feder, "Hintergründe," *BTB*, 24 Apr. 1930, no. 194, and Grzimek, "Neue Parolen," ibid., 29 Apr. 1930, no. 200, as well as the entries for 24 Apr.–2 May 1930, in Feder, *Heute sprach ich mit. . .*, pp. 257–59.

48. Gilsa to Reusch, 17 May 1930, HA/GHH: NL Reusch, 400101293/4.

49. Mahraun to Koch-Weser, 23 Apr. 1930, BA: NL Koch-Weser, 101/165–66.

50. Gilsa to Reusch, 21 May 1930, HA/GHH: NL Reusch, 400101293/4.

51. In this respect, see Voss, "Kann die Deutsche Demokratische Partei eine Partei der Massen werden? Denkschrift über die Möglichkeit einer Reaktivierung der Partei und einer Erneuerung ihrer Taktik," [Apr. 1930], BA: NL Heile, 23, as well as the correspondence between Voss and Erkelenz, 7–8 May 1930, BA: NL Erkelenz, 58/39–42, 49–52. See also Erkelenz to Cohnstaedt, 19 May 1930, ibid., 143–44.

52. Hellpach, "Klares Nein," *KZ*, 18 May 1930, no. 271a. See also Hellpach's correspondence with Dingeldey, 13–28 May 1930, BA: NL Dingeldey, 96/214–16, and with Lindeiner-Wildau, 20 May–12 June 1930, GLA Karlsruhe, NL Hellpach, 257.

53. Minutes of the DDP party council, 25 May 1930, BA: R 45 III/14/44–79.

54. Erkelenz to Bäumer, 9 June 1930, BA: NL Erkelenz, 58/228–30.

55. "Arbeitsgemeinschaft der Mittelparteien?," *Der Demokrat* 11, no. 11 (5 June 1930): 258. See also Koch-Weser to Scholz, 9 July 1930, BA: NL Koch-Weser, 105/116–18.

56. See Scholz's statements before the DVP Reichstag delegation, 28 May 1930, BA: R 45 II/67/240–41, and the DVP central executive committee, 4 July 1930, ibid., 46/75–77, as well as the official statement in *NLC*, 31 May 1930, no. 105. For the position of the People's Conservatives, see Lindeiner-Wildau to Hellpach, 20 May 1930, GLA Karlsruhe, NL Hellpach, 257, and Blank to Reusch, 17 July 1930, HA/GHH: NL Reusch, 4001012024/7, as well as Lindeiner-Wildau, "Wandlungen im Parteileben," *Volkskonservative Stimmen*, 7 June 1930, no. 9.

57. See Mahraun's speech in Volksnationale Reichsvereinigung, *Der erste Reichsvertretertag am 5. und 6. April 1930* (Berlin, 1930), pp. 50–52.

58. For example, see Pastenaci, "Die Deutsche Volkspartei und wir," *Der Jungdeutsche*, 25 Mar. 1930, no. 71, and "Sammlungsparole," ibid., 23 Apr. 1930, no. 94.

59. Mahraun to the VNR's local chapters, 21 May 1930, BA: NS 26/875. On the contacts between the DVP and Mahraun, see DVP, circular no. 5, 28 May 1930, ZSA: DVP/225/160–64.

60. *KZ*, 24 May 1930, no. 282.

61. West German February Club to Scholz, 22 May 1930, BA: NL Sieling (Kleine Erwerbung 484), 2. See also the minutes of the February Club's action committee, 28 Apr. 1930, as well as the club's correspondence with Regh, 22–28 Apr. 1930, ibid.

62. For further information, see Moldenhauer to Scholz, 12 June 1930, BA: R 45 II/69/157–59, and Gilsa to Reusch, 17 June 1930, HA/GHH: NL Reusch, 400101293/4, as well as the sections from Moldenhauer's memoirs in Ilse Maurer und Udo Wengst, eds., *Politik und Wirtschaft in der Krise 1930–1932. Quellen zur Ära Bruning*, with an introduction by Gerhard Schulz, 2 vols. (Düsseldorf, 1980), 1:205–12, 243–46.

63. Remarks by Dieckmann before the DVP national committee, 3 July 1930, BA: R 45 II/32/221.

64. Minutes of the DVP central executive committee, 4 July 1930, BA: R 45 II/46/43.

65. "Die Wahlen zum Landtag im Freistaat Sachsen am 22. Juni 1930," *Wirtschaft und Statistik* 10 (1930): 695–96.

66. Ibid.

CHAPTER TWENTY-SEVEN

1. A social history of the German depression has yet to be written. For a provocative step in this direction, see Rudolf Vierhaus, "Auswirkungen der Krise um 1930 in Deutschland. Beitrag zu einer historisch-psychologischen Analyse," in *Die Staats- und Wirtschaftskrise des Deutschen Reiches 1929/33*, ed. Werner Conze and Hans Raupach (Stuttgart, 1967), pp. 155–75. See also Peter Wulf, "Die Mittelschichten in der Krise der Weimarer Republik 1930–1933," in *Wirtschaftskrise und liberale Demokratie. Das Ende der Weimarer Republik und die gegenwärtige Situation*, ed. Karl Holl (Göttingen, 1978), pp. 89–102.

2. Scholz's remarks before the DVP central executive committee, 4 July 1930, BA: R 45 II/46/75–77.

3. Blank to Reusch, 21 July 1930, HA/GHH: NL Reusch, 4001012024/7. See also Scholz's remarks before the DVP national committee, 31 July 1930, BA: R 45 II/32/247–49.

4. DVP, Reichsgeschäftsstelle, ed., *Mit Hindenburg für Deutschlands Rettung!* (printed as a manuscript, Berlin, [1930]), pp. 24–26.

5. For an indication of such sentiment, see the speeches by Duisberg and Wieland before the RDI central committee, 23 May 1930, WA Bayer, 62/10.5.

6. For example, see Blank to Reusch, 21–24 July 1930, HA/GHH: NL Reusch, 4001012024/7.

7. Blank to Springorum, 29 July 1930, HA/GHH: NL Reusch, 4001012024/7. For further information on the politics of the Ruhrlade, see Henry Ashby Turner, Jr., "The *Ruhrlade*: Secret Cabinet of Heavy Industry in the Weimar Republic," *CEH* 3 (1970): 195–228, and Reinhard Neebe, *Großindustrie, Staat und NSDAP 1930–1933. Paul Silverberg und der Reichsverband der Deutschen Industrie in der Krise der Weimarer Republik* (Göttingen, 1981), pp. 73–76.

8. Blank to Reusch, 21 July 1930, HA/GHH: NL Reusch, 4001012024/7. On the

founding of the KVP, see Erasmus Jonas, *Die Volkskonservativen 1928–1933. Entwicklung, Struktur, Standort und staatspolitische Zielsetzung* (Düsseldorf, 1965), pp. 79–86.

9. *Berliner Börsen-Courier*, 24 July 1930, no. 340. See also Blank to Reusch, 24 July 1930, HA/GHH: NL Reusch, 4001012024/7.

10. *Christlicher Volksdienst*, 26 July 1930, no. 30, and 2 Aug. 1930, no. 31.

11. *Der Landbürger* 5, no. 15 (2 Aug. 1930): 255.

12. *Kölner Nachrichten*, 2 Aug. 1930, no. 31.

13. *Der Demokrat* 9, nos. 14/15 (5 Aug. 1930): 339.

14. Report by Meyer before the DDP executive committee, 25 July 1930, BA: R 45 III/22/77–79.

15. Lemmer's remarks at a meeting in the Democratic Club, Berlin, 6 Oct. 1930, BA: NL Jänicke, 56.

16. Mahraun to Baltrusch, 22 July 1930, BA: NS 26/875.

17. There is no record of the negotiations that led to the founding of the German State Party in the summer of 1930. The best account of these negotiations is to be found in Werner Stephan, *Aufstieg und Verfall des Linksliberalismus. Geschichte der Deutschen Demokratischen Partei* (Göttingen, 1973), pp. 439–53. For the best secondary treatments, see Bruce B. Frye, *Liberal Democrats in the Weimar Republic: The History of the German Democratic Party and the German State Party* (Carbondale, 1985), pp. 155–77, and the unpublished dissertation by Karl-Hermann Beeck, "Die Gründung der Deutschen Staatspartei im Jahre 1930 im Zusammenhang der Neuordnungsversuche des Liberalismus" (Ph.D. dissertation, Cologne, 1957), pp. 141–50. For further information, see Attila A. Chanady, "The Dissolution of the German Democratic Party in 1930," *AHR* 73 (1968): 1445–49, and Erich Matthias and Rudolf Morsey, "Die Deutsche Staatspartei," in *Das Ende der Parteien 1933*, ed. Erich Matthias and Rudolf Morsey (Düsseldorf, 1960), pp. 31–39. On the role of the Young Germans, see Alexander Kessler, *Der Jungdeutsche Orden in den Jahren der Entscheidung (I) 1928–1930* (Munich, 1975), pp. 102–14.

18. For example, see the minutes of the DDP managing committee, 28 Jan. 1930, BA: R 45 III/23/1–3, as well as Werner Stephan, *Acht Jahrzehnte erlebtes Deutschland. Ein Liberaler in vier Epochen* (Düsseldorf, 1983), pp. 177–78.

19. In this respect, see Bäumer's remarks before the DDP executive committee, 25 July 1930, BA: R 45 III/22/84–85, as well as her letter to Erkelenz, 31 July 1930, BA: NL Erkelenz, 112.

20. Koch-Weser's remarks before the DDP party council, 30 July 1930, BA: R 45 III/14/103–8. See also the minutes of the VNR national executive committee, 26 July 1930, BA: NS 26/875.

21. In this respect, see Bornemann, "Die Gründung der Deutschen Staatspartei," 5 Sept. 1930, BA: R 45 III/59/32–33, as well as the report in *NLC*, 30 July 1930, no. 145. For an indication of what the founders of the DStP hoped to achieve, see the circular from Koch-Weser, Meyer, and Lemmer, 27 July 1930, BA: R 45 III/44/25, as well as the exchange of telegrams between Koch-Weser and Foehr, 26 July 1930, BA: NL Koch-Weser, 105/23–25.

22. Croon, Rodens, and Sieling to Scholz, 22 May 1930, BA: NL Sieling (Kleine Erwerbung 484), 2.

23. Report by Winschuh before the action committee of the February Club movement, 2 Aug. 1930, reported in the *Kölner Tageblatt*, 5 Aug. 1930, no. 391. See also Rheinbaben, "Der erste Schritt: Ein praktischer Vorschlag zur Parteireform," *Berliner Börsen-Courier*, 24 July 1930, no. 339.

24. On the founding and goals of the Young Front, see the memorandum from Rodens to the action committee of the February Club movement, [Apr. 1930], as well as the debate at the meeting of the action committee, 28 Apr. 1930, both in BA: NL Sieling (Kleine Erwerbung 484), 2.

25. A protocol of this meeting has been preserved in the StA Braunschweig, GX6/612.

26. Ibid. On the RjV's position, see Glatzel's remarks before the DVP national committee, July 31, 1930, BA: R 45 II/32/295–307, as well as his article, "Die jungen Volksparteiler und die Staatspartei," *Berliner Börsen-Courier*, 1 Aug. 1930, no. 354. See also Winschuh, "Junge Generation vor die Front!," *Kasseler Tageblatt*, 3 Aug. 1930, no. 212, and Eschenburg, "Die Deutsche Staatspartei," *Berliner Börsen-Courier*, 29 July 1930, no. 347.

27. Petersen to Koch-Weser, 29 July 1930, BA: NL Koch-Weser, 105/71–72.

28. For example, see Koch-Weser to Curtius, 28 July 1930, BA: NL Koch-Weser, 105/45–46.

29. *NLC*, 30 July 1930, no. 145. See also Dingeldey's statement before the DVP national council, 31 July 1930, BA: R 45 II/32/329–31.

30. *KZ*, 28 July 1930, no. 408.

31. Artur Mahraun, *Die Deutsche Staatspartei. Eine Selbsthilfeorganisation deutschen Staatsbürgertums* (Berlin, 1930), pp. 8–29.

32. In this respect, see the reports in the *Berliner Börsen-Courier*, 31 July 1930, no. 351; *KZ*, 1 Aug. 1930, no. 416; and *Kölner Tageblatt*, 5 Aug. 1930, no. 391, as well as the statement of the February Club, 29 July 1930, BA: NL Sieling (Kleine Erwerbung 484), 2.

33. *Frankfurter Nachrichten*, 31 July 1930, no. 210.

34. *Berliner Börsen-Courier*, 31 July 1930, no. 351. On the agreement between Scholz and Glatzel, see Kruspi to the RjV local chairmen, 8 Aug. 1930, BA: R 45 II/6/221–23, and Glatzel to Scholz, 12 Aug. 1930, ibid., 5/41–49.

35. Koch-Weser's speech before the DDP executive committee, 25 July 1930, BA: R 45 III/22/80–83.

36. Erkelenz to Koch-Weser, 29 July 1930, BA: NL Erkelenz, 132.

37. Minutes of the DDP party council, 30 July 1930, BA: R 45 III/14/108–27. For an indication of the outrage certain party leaders felt over the founding of the DStP, see the letters from Dechamps to Koch-Weser and the DDP party council, 29 July 1930, BA: NL Koch-Weser, 105/73–89.

38. Minutes of the DVP national committee, 31 July 1930, BA: R 45 II/32/249–55. See also *NLC*, 2 Aug. 1930, no. 148.

39. *Berliner Börsen-Courier*, 5 Aug. 1930, no. 359. For indications of the unrest that existed within the RjV, see the open letter from Heide to Scholz, ibid., no. 360, and the appeal from Bente to the DVP youth organizations, ibid., 12 Aug. 1930, no. 372.

40. *KZ*, 4 Aug. 1930, no. 421.

41. For example, see Gilsa to Reusch, 29 July 1930, HA/GHH: NL Reusch, 400101293/4, and Jarres to Lucas, 12 Aug. 1930, BA: NL Jarres, 45.

42. A protocol of this meeting, erroneously dated 23 July and reconstructed from memory by a member of the RjV, can be found in the StA Braunschweig, GX6/612. For further information on this meeting, see Koch-Weser's remarks before the DDP party council, 30 July 1930, BA: R 45 III/14/119–23, and Scholz's remarks before the DVP national committee, 31 July 1930, BA: R 45 II/32/255–63, as well as the statement in *NLC*, 1 Aug. 1930, no. 147.

43. Westarp, "Bericht über die Verhandlungen mit der DVP wegen Zusammenwirkens für das Hindenburg Programm," [Aug. 1930], NL Westarp.

44. Koch-Weser to Scholz, 1 Aug. 1930, BA: NL Koch-Weser, 105/133–35.

45. In this respect, see the memorandum of a phone call from Koch-Weser to the DDP headquarters, 6 Aug. 1930, as well as Koch-Weser to Stephan, 6 Aug. 1930, both in BA: NL Koch-Weser, 105/213–15.

46. Höpker-Aschoff, "Freies Bürgertum," *KZ*, 13 Aug. 1930, no. 440.

47. For the most detailed report of this meeting, see DVP, Reichsgeschäftsstelle, circular no. 11, 9 Aug. 1930, ZSA: DVP/225/143–46. For Scholz's position, see his articles "Der Sinn des Zusammenschlusses," *DAZ*, 9 Aug. 1930, nos. 365–66, and "Was ich will," *KZ*, 10 Aug. 1930, no. 433. See also DVP, Reichsgeschäftsstelle, *Mit Hindenburg*, pp. 27–28.

48. Dietrich, "Der schwarze Donnerstag," *DAZ*, 9 Aug. 1930, nos. 365–66.

49. For example, see the resolution adopted by the WP district organization in Cologne-Aachen in the *Kölner Nachrichten*, 9 Aug. 1930, no. 32.

50. In this respect, see the report of Höfer's speech in St. Goarshausen, 27 July 1930, in the *Nassauische Bauern-Zeitung*, 29 July 1930, no. 173, and of Hepp's speech in Usingen, 28 Aug. 1930, ibid., 30 Aug. 1930, no. 200.

51. Westarp, "Bericht über die Verhandlungen mit der DVP," NL Westarp.

52. Blank to Reusch, 9 Aug. 1930, HA/GHH: NL Reusch, 4001012024/7.

53. *KZ*, 12 Aug. 1930, no. 437. See also Treviranus, "Gemeinsame Verantwortung," *DAZ*, 12 Aug. 1930, nos. 369–70.

54. Blank to Springorum, 13 Aug. 1930, HA/GHH: NL Reusch, 4001012024/7.

55. For the text of this appeal, see *NLC*, 22 Aug. 1930, no. 162. For further information, see Scholz's statement before the DVP central executive committee, 24 Aug. 1930, BA: R 45 II/47/49–57.

CHAPTER TWENTY-EIGHT

1. *Stenographische Berichte über die Verhandlungen des Reichstags*, 428:6513–17.

2. For some provocative thoughts along these lines, see David Abraham, "Constituting Bourgeois Hegemony: The Bourgeois Crisis of Weimar Germany," *JMH* 51 (1979): 417–33.

3. "Warum scheiterte die bürgerliche Sammlung?," 15 Aug. 1930, and "Wie wurde und was will die Staatspartei?," [Aug.–Sept. 1930], both in LA Schleswig, NL Schifferer, 27a. For the most detailed defense of the DVP's position in its negotiations

with the DStP, see DVP, Reichsgeschäftsstelle, ed. *Stichworte für den Wahlkampf 1930* (Berlin, 1930), pp. 38–51.

4. Ibid., p. 41.

5. *KZ*, 15 Aug. 1930, no. 433.

6. For example, see Lucas to Jarres, 11 Aug. 1930, BA: NL Jarres, 45.

7. *KZ*, 12 Aug. 1930, no. 437.

8. In this respect, see the exchange of telegrams between Dietrich and Curtius, 9–10 Aug. 1930, BA: NL Dietrich, 255/89–93.

9. Transcript of a telephone conversation between Kempkes and Macht (DVP Schleswig-Holstein), 14 Aug. 1930, LA Schleswig, NL Schifferer, 27g.

10. On the collapse of these efforts, see the minutes of the meeting between representatives from the DVP and DStP district organizations in Schleswig-Holstein, 14 Aug. 1930, as well as the communiqué from the DVP Schleswig-Holstein to the DStP Schleswig-Holstein, 18 Aug. 1930, both in LA Schleswig, NL Schifferer, 27a.

11. DStP, ed., *Spiegel der Parteien*, Materialien zur demokratischen Politik, no. 151 (Berlin, [1930]), pp. 15–46. For further information on the DStP campaign, see Bruce B. Frye, *Liberal Democrats in the Weimar Republic: The History of the German Democratic Party and the German State Party* (Carbondale, 1985), pp. 163–70.

12. Mahraun, *Staatspartei*, pp. 25–29.

13. *KZ*, 22 Aug. 1930, no. 458.

14. For example, see Hieber to Koch-Weser, 29 July 1930, BA: NL Koch-Weser, 105/93, as well as Hans Robinsohn, "Erinnerungsbericht über die Umwandlung der Deutsch-Demokratischen Partei zur Deutschen Staatspartei in Hamburg im Sommer 1930," 20 Apr. 1971, SA Hamburg, Handschriften-Sammlung 1233.

15. For further details, see Quidde, "Absage an die Deutsche Staatspartei," *Das Tagebuch* 11, no. 32 (9 Aug. 1930): 1255–61, and Stündt, "Die alte Fahne treu! Von Gründung, Zweck und Ziel der Vereinigung unabhängiger Demokraten," *Das Echo der jungen Demokratie* 12, nos. 8/9 (Aug.–Sept. 1930): 111–17, as well as the sensitive article by Karl Holl, "Pazifismus oder liberaler Neo-Imperialismus? Zur Rolle der Pazifisten in der Deutschen Demokratischen Partei," in *Imperialismus im 20. Jahrhundert. Gedenkschrift für George W. F. Hallgarten*, ed. Joachim Radkau and Imanuel Geiss (Munich, 1976), pp. 171–95.

16. Bruce B. Frye, "The German Democratic Party and the 'Jewish Problem' in the Weimar Republic," *Year Book of the Leo Baeck Institute* 21 (1976): 143–72.

17. *Der Jungdeutsche*, 6 Aug. 1930, no. 181.

18. For further details, see Stolper to Höpker-Aschoff, 13 Aug. 1930, and Stolper to Landahl, 22 Aug. 1930, both in BA: NL Stolper, 44, and Friedensburg to Höpker-Aschoff, 15 Aug. 1930, BA: NL Friedensburg, 25/160–61, as well as the bulletin from the Young German leadership to the leaders of the VNR, 16 Aug. 1930, BA: NS 26/875. For further information on Jewish attitudes toward the founding of the DStP, see P. B. Wiener, "Die Parteien der Mitte," in *Entscheidungsjahr 1932. Zur Judenfrage in der Endphase der Weimarer Republik*, ed. Werner E. Mosse (Tübingen, 1965), pp. 292–97.

19. Erich Eggeling, *Partei oder Bewegung? Der jungdeutsche Kampf um die Staatspartei* (Berlin, 1930), pp. 12–17.

20. For example, see the minutes of the DDP executive committee, 12 and 20 Aug. 1930, BA: R 45 III/22/88–102.

21. For example, see Stolper to Wolff, 12 Sept. 1930, BA: NL Stolper, 44.

22. *Der Demokrat* 11, no. 17 (5 Sept. 1930): 381–85.

23. For example, see the text of Stolper's speech, "Finanzpolitik und Mittelstand," [Aug.–Sept. 1930], BA: NL Stolper, 44, and DStP, *Entwurf einer Wahlrede für bäuerliche Versammlungen* (Berlin, [1930]), as well as the report of Dietrich's speech in Karlsruhe, 4 Aug. 1930, in *Der Demokrat* 11, no. 16 (20 Aug. 1930): 361–64.

24. Gertrud Bäumer, *Sinn und Form geistiger Führung* (Berlin, 1930), pp. 7–33.

25. Manuscript of Kempkes's report on the state of the party organization at the DVP Mannheim congress, [Mar. 1930], BA: R 45 II/31/331–37.

26. Minutes of the DVP central executive committee, 4 July 1930, BA: R 45 II/46/189–201. See also the two letters from Thiel to the members of the DVP central executive committee, 14 and 26 July 1930, ibid., 69/427–31, 435–39.

27. Moldenhauer to Scholz, 12 June 1930, BA: R 45 II/69/157–59. See also the resolution adopted by the DVP Reichstag delegation against the proposed levy on civil servant salaries, 16 June 1930, BA: NL Zapf, 42, as well as the excerpts from Moldenhauer's unpublished memoirs in Ilse Maurer and Udo Wengst, eds., *Politik und Wirtschaft in der Krise 1930–1932. Quellen zur Ära Brüning*, with an introduction by Gerhard Schulz, 2 vols. (Düsseldorf, 1980), 1:205–12, 243–46.

28. Hans Mommsen, "Die Stellung der Beamtenschaft in Reich, Ländern und Gemeinden in der Ära Bruning," *VfZ* 21 (1973): 154.

29. DVP, Reichsgeschäftsstelle, ed., *Die finanziellen und sozialpolitischen Probleme bei der Reichstagswahl 1930. Rede der Reichstagsabgeordneten Dr. Cremer, Dr. Hoff, Keinath, Morath und Thiel, gehalten bei einer volksparteilichen Tagung am 25. Juli 1930 im Reichstage* (printed as a manuscript, Berlin, 1930), pp. 3–44.

30. For example, see the circular to the membership of the Bavarian Industrialists' Federation (Bayerischer Industriellen-Verband), 19 Aug. 1930, HA/GHH: Allgemeine Verwaltung, 400106/104.

31. Hamm to Reusch, 28 July 1930, HA/GHH: NL Reusch, 40010123/25.

32. In this respect, see Reusch to Hamm, 2 Aug. 1930, HA/GHH: NL Reusch, 4001023/25, and Reusch to Weinlig, 16 Sept. 1930, ibid., 400101293/10.

33. In this respect, see Witzleben's memorandum on the meeting of the Curatorium's executive committee, 28 Aug. 1930, as well as his letter to Borsig, 1 Sept. 1930, both in SAA: NL Siemens, 4/Lf 646.

34. *Kölner Nachrichten*, 30 Aug. 1930, no. 35. For further details, see Blank to Reusch, 28 Aug. 1920, HA/GHH: NL Reusch, 4001012024/7.

35. Reichspartei des deutschen Mittelstandes, ed., *Unsere Arbeit und unsere Gegner. 1930 Wahlhandbuch der Reichspartei des deutschen Mittelstandes (Wirtschaftspartei)* (Berlin, 1930), pp. 175–84, 197–203.

36. Goebbels, "Außerordentliches Rundschreiben der Reichspropagandaleitung zur Vorbereitung des Wahlkampfes am 14. September 1930," 23 July 1930, BA: NL Streicher, 24. See also Goebbels, "Das patriotische Bürgertum," *Nationalsozialistische Monatshefte* 1, no. 5 (Aug. 1930): 223–29.

37. For example, see "Der Sinn des Wahlkampfes," Nachrichtendienst Nr. 17 des

Landesverbandes Schleswig-Holstein der Deutschen Volkspartei, 12 Aug. 1930, LA Schleswig, NL Schifferer, 27a.

38. Gotthart Heribert, *Hitler und sein Evangelium. Ein Wort an alle* (Berlin, [1930]). See also DVP, Reichsgeschäftsstelle, ed., *Der Wolf ohne Schafspelz. Oder: Was das deutsche Volk sich alles bieten läßt!* (Cologne, [1930]).

39. H. A. Hömberg, *Hitlerpartei oder Wirtschaftspartei—Phrase oder Vernunft? Eine Sammlung national-sozialistischer Pressestimmen und Ansprüchen von Führern der N.S.D.A.P.* (Recklinghausen, [1930]). See also Reichspartei des deutschen Mittelstandes, *Unsere Arbeit und unsere Gegner*, pp. 123–29.

40. DStP, *Spiegel der Parteien*, pp. 3–22, 26–28.

41. For the most detailed account of the Nazi campaign, see David A. Hackett, "The Nazi Party in the Reichstag Elections of 1930" (Ph.D. dissertation, University of Wisconsin, 1971), pp. 195–331.

42. For the most detailed analyses of the 1930 election results, see ibid., pp. 332–89; Jerzy Holzer, *Parteien und Massen. Die politische Krise in Deutschland 1928–1930* (Mainz, 1975), pp. 64–103; Thomas Childers, *The Nazi Voter: The Social Foundations of Fascism in Germany* (Chapel Hill, 1983), pp. 118–91; and Alfred Milatz, "Das Ende der Parteien im Spiegel der Wahlen 1930 bis 1933," in *Das Ende der Parteien 1933*, ed. Erich Matthias and Rudolf Morsey (Düsseldorf, 1960), pp. 744–58.

43. In this respect, see the letters from the DStP organization in Pforzheim to Dietrich, 19 Sept. 1930, BA: NL Dietrich, 256/38–40, as well as Hopf to Heuss, 20 Sept. 1930, and the detailed summary prepared by the Württemberg DDP, 24 Sept. 1930, both in BA: NL Heuss, 57. See also Frye, *Liberal Democrats*, pp. 170–71.

44. Stolper to Landahl, 16 Sept. 1930, BA: NL Stolper, 44.

45. Rexrodt, "Die Reichstagswahlen und die D.D.P.," *Der Demokrat* 11, no. 18 (20 Sept. 1930): 414–17.

46. Heuss to Hopf, 12 Oct. 1930, BA: NL Heuss, 57.

47. Milatz, "Ende der Parteien," p. 750.

48. Schnell to Scholz, 17 Sept. 1930, BA: NL Dingeldey, 42/9–20.

49. For example, see Gilsa to Scholz, 16 Sept. 1930, HA/GHH: NL Reusch, 400101293/4, and Klingspor to Hintzmann, 23 Sept. 1930, HSA Düsseldorf, NL Klingspor, 4.

50. Otto Thiel, *Wie kommen wir zu einer großen Deutschen Volkspartei? Vortrag gehalten auf der Tagung der Reichsgemeinschaft junger Volksparteiler in Berlin am 26. Oktober 1930* (printed as a manuscript, n.p., [1930]), pp. 1–7.

51. The literature on the Young German secession is extensive, though often highly subjective. For the Young German side of the argument, see Eggeling, *Partei oder Bewegung?*, pp. 12–33, and Alexander Kessler, *Der Jungdeutsche Orden in den Jahren der Entscheidung (I) 1928–1930* (Munich, 1975), pp. 134–66. For the Democratic perspective, see Werner Stephan, *Aufstieg und Verfall des Linksliberalismus. Geschichte der Deutschen Demokratischen Partei* (Göttingen, 1973), pp. 467–77. The most balanced accounts are to be found in Karl-Hermann Beeck, "Die Gründung der Deutschen Staatspartei im Jahre 1930 im Zusammenhang der Neuordnungsversuche des Liberalismus" (Ph.D. dissertation, Cologne, 1957), pp. 177–86; Attila A. Chanady, "The Dissolution of the German Democratic Party in 1930," *AHR* 73 (1968): 1449–52; and Frye, *Liberal Democrats*, pp. 173–75.

52. See the postscript to Stolper's letter to Landahl, 16 Sept. 1930, BA: NL Stolper, 44.

53. Eggeling, *Partei oder Bewegung?*, pp. 20–21.

54. Minutes of the DDP executive committee, 27 Sept. 1930, BA: R 45 III/22/108–34.

55. For example, see Mahraun's remarks before the VNR executive committee, 17 Oct. 1930, BA: NS 26/875.

56. Rexrodt to Koch-Weser, Lemmer, and Stephan, 2 Oct. 1930, BA: NL Koch-Weser, 107/47–48.

57. Höpker-Aschoff, Meyer, and Rexrodt, circular no. 19 to the DDP party organization, 9 Oct. 1930, BA: R 45 III/44/105–12. See also Eggeling, *Partei oder Bewegung?*, pp. 26–27, and Jänicke's memorandum on his conversation with Meyer, 9 Oct. 1930, BA: NL Jänicke, 56.

58. Mahraun to Koch-Weser, 3 Oct. 1930, BA: NL Koch-Weser, 107/49–50.

59. Circular from Mahraun to the leaders of the VNR and the Young German Order, 3 Oct. 1930, BA: NS 26/875.

60. Notes on the meeting of the DStP action committee, 7 Oct. 1930, BA: NL Stolper, 116. For further information, see the circular from Meyer to the DDP party organization, 7 Oct. 1930, BA: R 45 III/44/103–4, as well as Eggeling, *Partei oder Bewegung?*, pp. 29–33, and Meyer, "Der Bruch in der Staatspartei," *Der Demokrat* 11, no. 20 (20 Oct. 1930): 461–63.

61. For example, see Lemmer to Kluthe, 15 Oct. 1930, BA: NL Kluthe, 12/46–47.

62. For example, see the protocol of the 27th High Chapter of the Young German Order, 12 Dec. 1930, BA: R 161/12.

63. On the circumstances surrounding Koch-Weser's resignation, see Jänicke's protocol of a meeting in the Democratic Club, 6 Oct. 1930, BA: NL Jänicke, 56, as well as Stolper's notes on the same meeting, BA: NL Stolper, 116. For further information, see Meyer to Koch-Weser, 11 Oct. 1930, BA: NL Koch-Weser, 110/63–68, as well as Koch-Weser's own letters to Ehlermann, 8 Oct. 1930, ibid., 5–7, and to Schiedmantel, 11 Oct. 1930, BA: NL Schücking, 50.

CHAPTER TWENTY-NINE

1. Mann to Koch-Weser, 7 July [*sic*; Aug.] 1930, BA: NL Koch-Weser, 105/255.

2. Thomas Mann, *Deutsche Ansprache. Ein Appell an die Vernunft. Rede, gehalten am 17. Oktober 1930 im Beethovensaal zu Berlin* (Berlin, 1930), pp. 11–31.

3. David Abraham, *The Collapse of the Weimar Republic: Political Economy and Crisis* (Princeton, 1981), pp. 301–13.

4. For the government's reaction to the election results, see the memorandum by Pünder, 16 Sept. 1930, BA: NL Pünder, 134/228–30.

5. Heinrich Brüning, *Das Programm der Reichsregierung. Rede im Reichstage am 16. Oktober 1930* (Berlin, 1930), pp. 3–10, 13–14.

6. For further details, see Hans Mommsen, "Staat und Bürokratie in der Ära Brüning," in *Tradition und Reform in der deutschen Geschichte. Gedenkschrift für Waldemar Besson*, ed. Gotthard Jasper (Frankfurt, 1976), pp. 81–137, and Peter-

Christian Witt, "Finanzpolitik als Verfassungs- und Gesellschaftspolitik. Überlegungen zur Finanzpolitik des Deutschen Reiches in den Jahren 1930 bis 1932," *Geschichte und Gesellschaft* 8 (1982): 386–414.

7. For a more detailed analysis of industry's relationship to the Brüning government in the fall and winter of 1930, see Reinhard Neebe, *Großindustrie, Staat und NSDAP 1930–1933. Paul Silverberg und der Reichsverband der Deutschen Industrie in der Krise der Weimarer Republik* (Göttingen, 1981), pp. 78–89, and Henry Ashby Turner, Jr., *German Big Business and the Rise of Hitler* (Oxford, 1985), pp. 124–27, 158–65.

8. In this respect, see Haniel to Reusch, 15 Oct. 1930, HA/GHH: NL Reusch, 4001012000/3a, and Silverberg to Jarres, 17 Oct. 1930, BA: NL Jarres, 45.

9. Silverberg to Jarres, 17 Oct. 1930, BA: NL Jarres, 45.

10. For example, see Dryander to Jarres, 8 and 10 Oct. 1930, and Jarres to Silverberg, 14 Oct. 1930, all in BA: NL Jarres, 45.

11. For further details, see Westarp, "Meine Verhandlungen zwischen dem 18. Juli und 18. Oktober 1930," [Oct. 1930], NL Westarp, as well as Larry Eugene Jones, "Sammlung oder Zersplitterung? Die Bestrebungen zur Bildung einer neuen Mittelpartei in der Endphase der Weimarer Republik 1930–1933," *VfZ* 25 (1977): 269–71.

12. Heuss to Hopf, 12 Oct. 1930, BA: NL Heuss, 57. See also Scholz's remarks at a meeting of the DVP Reichstag delegation, 10 Oct. 1930, BA: R 45 II/67/271.

13. Heuss to Hopf, 20 Oct. 1930, BA: NL Heuss, 57. See also the entries in Jänicke's diary, 20–21 Oct. 1930, BA: NL Jänicke, 56.

14. For the Social Democratic position, see Vorstand der SPD, *Jahrbuch der Sozialdemokratie für das Jahr 1930* (Berlin, [1931]), pp. 20–23.

15. Memorandum by Pünder, 26 Nov. 1930, BA: R 45 I/1021/144–47.

16. Stephan to Koch-Weser, 11 Oct. 1930, BA: NL Koch-Weser, 107/55–58.

17. Minutes of the DDP executive committee, 16 Oct. 1930, BA: R 45 III/22/139–64.

18. Minutes of a meeting of the friends and members of the February Club, Cologne, 19 Oct. 1930, BA: NL Sieling (Kleine Erwerbung 484), 2.

19. Höpker-Aschoff's report at a meeting of the DDP executive committee, 16 Oct. 1930, BA: R 45 III/22/146–47. See also Winschuh's statement at a meeting of the friends and members of the February Club, Cologne, 25 Oct. 1930, BA: NL Sieling (Kleine Erwerbung 484), 2, as well as his letter to Dingeldey, Oct. 1930, BA: NL Dingeldey, 39/1.

20. Remarks by Höpker-Aschoff at a meeting of the DDP executive committee, 8 Nov. 1930, BA: R 45 III/22/176.

21. Remarks by Braubach, Heile, and Quidde at the DDP's Hanover party congress, 8 Nov. 1930, BA: R 45 III/8/27–30, 38–40, 43–45.

22. *Blätter der Staatspartei* 11, no. 22 (20 Nov. 1930): 524.

23. Stündt, "Die neue linke greift an! Zum Gründungsparteitag der Radikaldemokratischen Partei in Kassel," *Das Echo der jungen Demokratie* 12, nos. 11/12 (Nov.–Dec. 1930): 161–64. See also Radikaldemokratische Partei, Reichsgeschäftsstelle, ed., *Radikale Demokratie!* (Berlin, [ca. 1930–31]). For a brief history of the party, see Burkhard Gutleben, "Radikaldemokratische Partei—aufrechte Liberale ohne Erfolg," *Liberal* 28 (1986): 65–75.

24. On the circumstances surrounding Dietrich's election, see the minutes of the DDP executive committee, 8 Nov. 1930, BA: R 45 III/22/178–80.

25. Hermann Dietrich, *Ziele und Aufgaben der Staatspartei. Rede, gehalten auf dem Gründungsparteitag der Deutschen Staatspartei, Hannover, den 9. November 1930* (Berlin, [1930]).

26. Ibid., p. 3.

27. *Blätter der Staatspartei* 11, no. 22 (20 Nov. 1930): 530–32, 535–39. Aside from the cursory treatment in Bruce B. Frye, *Liberal Democrats in the Weimar Republic: The History of the German Democratic Party and the German State Party* (Carbondale, 1985), pp. 178–94, the only serious histories of the DStP are Erich Matthias and Rudolf Morsey, "Die Deutsche Staatspartei," in *Das Ende der Parteien 1933*, ed. Erich Matthias and Rudolf Morsey (Düsseldorf, 1960), pp. 31–97, and Jürgen C. Hess, "Wandlungen im Staatsverständnis des Linksliberalismus der Weimarer Republik 1930–1933," in *Wirtschaftskrise und liberale Demokratie. Das Ende der Weimarer Republik und die gegenwärtige Situation*, ed. Karl Holl (Göttingen, 1978), pp. 46–88.

28. Weber, "Die Aufgaben der Staatspartei im neuen Reichstage," *Der Demokrat* 11, no. 20 (20 Oct. 1930): 459–61.

29. Hellpach to Meyer, n.d., GLA Karlsruhe, NL Hellpach, 257. See also Hellpach, "Meine Trennung von der Staatspartei," *Hannoverscher Kurier*, 9 Nov. 1930, no. 527.

30. Schäfer to Dietrich, 13 Jan. 1931, BA: NL Dietrich, 255/195–97.

31. For example, see Jaeger to Dietrich, 9 Dec. 1930, BA: NL Dietrich, 245/35–38.

32. For example, see Neven's report on his conversation with Höpker-Aschoff, 4 Dec. 1930, "Büchner-Protokolle. Redaktionssitzungen der Kölnischen Zeitung 22. März 1929 bis 2. Dezember 1935," as well as Weber to Jänicke, 2 Jan. 1931, BA: NL Jänicke, 26, and Friedensburg to the Kassel DStP, 23 Jan. 1931, BA: NL Friedensburg, 25/174.

33. On the history of the DVP during the last years of the Weimar Republic, see Hans Booms, "Die Deutsche Volkspartei," in *Das Ende der Parteien*, ed. Matthias and Morsey, pp. 521–39; and Werner Methfessel, "Die Deutsche Volkspartei am Ende der Weimarer Republik" (Ph.D. dissertation, Jena, 1966). An abbreviated version of Methfessel's dissertation has been published as *Der Weg in den Abgrund. Zur Geschichte der Deutschen Volkspartei 1930–1933*, ed. Sekretariat des Zentralvorstandes der Liberal-Demokratischen Partei Deutschlands ([East Berlin], 1978).

34. Schnell to Scholz, 17 Sept. 1930, BA: NL Dingeldey, 42/9–20. See also Schnell, "Volksbürgerliche Sammlung," *DAZ*, 12 Oct. 1930, no. 475–76.

35. Circular from Schnell, 19 Sept. 1930, BA: NL Dingeldey, 42/1–3.

36. Report on the meeting of the DVP party leaders in Berlin, 23 Sept. 1930, StA Braunschweig, GX6/637.

37. Schnell to Scholz, 8 Oct. 1930, BA: NL Dingeldey, 42/25–26.

38. Petition to the DVP executive committee, 21 Oct. 1930, BA: NL Dingeldey, 31/2.

39. For the rationale behind this move, see Dingeldey to Schnell, 28 Oct. 1930, 31/7, and Dingeldey to Scholz, 28 Oct. 1930, BA: NL Dingeldey, 31/11–12.

40. *NLC*, 4 Nov. 1930, no. 214.

41. For example, see Dingeldey, "Zusammenschluß der Mitte," *KZ*, 27 Apr. 1930, no. 229a.

42. For example, see Glatzel to Dingeldey, 12 Dec. 1930, BA: NL Dingeldey, 53/46–47.

43. Eduard Dingeldey, *Die Deutsche Volkspartei seit dem 14. September 1930. Rede in der Sitzung des Reichsausschusses der Deutschen Volkspartei am 2. November 1930* (Berlin, [1930]), pp. 3–12. See also the text of Dingeldey's speech before the DVP central executive committee, 30 Nov. 1930, in *NLC*, 2 Dec. 1930, no. 234.

44. For further details, see Dingeldey to Dauch, Hembeck, and Strauss, 4 Nov. 1930, BA: NL Dingeldey, 31/25–29, as well as the responses from Schnell, 5 Nov. 1930, ibid., 101/3–5; Jänecke, Nov. 6, 1930, ibid., 31/36–37; Dauch, 6 Nov. 1930, ibid., 31/38–40; and Jochmus, 7 Nov. 1930, ibid., 31/42–43.

45. For example, see Gilsa to Reusch, 30 Oct. 1930, HA/GHH: NL Reusch, 400101293/4.

46. *DAZ*, 19 Nov. 1930, nos. 539–40. See also Scholz to Dingeldey, 11 Nov. 1930, BA: NL Dingeldey, 31/48–49.

47. *NLC*, 2 Dec. 1930, no. 234.

48. Ibid.

49. In this respect, see Glatzel to Dingeldey, 12 Dec. 1930, BA: NL Dingeldey, 53/46–47, as well as Glatzel, "Um die Zukunft der Partei," in *Die Reichsgemeinschaft* 1, nos. 5–6 (Dec. 1930): 1–3.

50. See the text of Dingeldey's speech, "Die Partei und die politischen Aufgaben unserer Zeit," 26 Oct. 1930, BA: NL Dingeldey, 53/21–26.

51. *NLC*, 2 Dec. 1930, no. 234.

CHAPTER THIRTY

1. The literature on the outbreak and course of the German depression has become quite extensive. By far the most authoritative study of the German depression is the recent book by Harold James, *The German Slump: Politics and Economics, 1924–1936* (Oxford, 1986). On the causes of the depression, see also T. Balderston, "The Origins of Economic Instability in Germany, 1924–1930: Market Forces versus Economic Policy," *Vierteljahresschrift für Sozial- und Wirtschaftsgeschichte* 69 (1982): 488–514, and "The Beginning of the Depression in Germany, 1927–1930: Investment and the Capital Market," *Economic History Review* 26 (1983): 395–415. On the German banking crisis, see the standard history by Karl Erich Born, *Die deutsche Bankenkrise 1931. Finanzen und Politik* (Munich, 1967). On the social consequences of the depression, see the collection of essays by Peter Stachura, ed., *Unemployment and the Great Depression in Weimar Germany* (New York, 1986). For an excellent regional study of the depression, see Ursula Büttner, *Hamburg in der Staats- und Wirtschaftskrise 1928–1931* (Hamburg, 1982).

2. In this respect, see the speech by Brüning, "Deutschlands dringendste Aufgaben," 5 Feb. 1931, in Heinrich Brüning and Julius Curtius, *Um Deutschlands Zukunft. Zwei Reden* (Berlin, 1931), pp. 6–8.

3. See Werner Conze, "Die Reichsverfassungsreform als Ziel der Politik Brünings," *Der Staat* 11 (1972): 209–17, and more recently Peter-Christian Witt, "Finanzpolitik als Verfassungs- und Gesellschaftspolitik. Überlegungen zur Finanzpolitik des

Deutschen Reiches in den Jahren 1930 bis 1932," *Geschichte und Gesellschaft* 8 (1982): 386–414.

4. For the most detailed treatment of Brüning's fiscal and economic policies, see Horst Sanmann, "Daten und Alternativen der deutschen Wirtschafts- und Finanzpolitik in der Ära Brüning," *Hamburger Jahrbuch für Wirtschafts- und Gesellschaftspolitik* 10 (1965): 109–40. On the political consequences of Brüning's program, see Werner Jochmann, "Brünings Deflationspolitik und der Untergang der Weimarer Republik," in *Industrielle Gesellschaft und politisches System. Beiträge zur politischen Sozialgeschichte*, ed. Dirk Stegmann, Bernd-Jürgen Wendt, and Peter-Christian Witt (Bonn, 1978), pp. 97–112.

5. For further details, see Hans Mommsen, "Die Stellung der Beamtenschaft in Reich, Ländern und Gemeinden in der Ära Brüning," *VfZ* 21 (1973): 151–65.

6. Thomas Childers, *The Nazi Voter: The Social Foundations of Fascism in Germany, 1919–1933* (Chapel Hill, 1983), pp. 211–13, 233–35. For further information, see Heinrich August Winkler, *Mittelstand, Demokratie und Nationalsozialismus. Die politische Entwicklung von Handwerk und Kleinhandel in der Weimarer Republik* (Cologne, 1972), pp. 140–46.

7. For example, see William Sheridan Allen, *The Nazi Seizure of Power: The Experience of a Single German Town, 1922–1945*, 2d ed. (New York, 1984), pp. 69–90.

8. For further details, see Larry Eugene Jones, "Crisis and Realignment: Agrarian Splinter Parties in the Late Weimar Republic, 1928–33," in *Peasants and Lords in Modern Germany: Recent Studies in Agricultural History*, ed. Robert G. Moeller (London, 1986), pp. 216–19.

9. *Nassauische Bauern-Zeitung*, 3 Oct. 1930, no. 229. See also H. Sieber, "Rechtskurs," ibid., 14 Oct. 1930, no. 238.

10. For example, see Hepp, "Gebot der Stunde," *Nassauische Bauern-Zeitung*, 23 Oct. 1930, no. 246.

11. *Reichs-Landbund* 10, no. 43 (25 Oct. 1930): 507. For further details, see Wilmowsky to Krupp, 28 Oct. 1930, HA Krupp, FAH 23/504, as well as the report in the *Nassauische Bauern-Zeitung*, 25 Oct. 1930, no. 248.

12. *Der Landbürger* 6, no. 4 (16 Feb. 1931): 54–55. For further information on the split within the CNBLP, see *KZ*, 12 Feb. 1931, no. 84, and *Nassauische Bauern-Zeitung*, 14 Feb. 1931, no. 37, as well as the article by Gereke, "Landwirtschaft und Opposition," ibid., 17 Feb. 1931, no. 39.

13. *Bayer. Bauern- und Mittelstandsbund*, 3 Dec. 1930, no. 6.

14. Hillebrand, "Neue Fraktionsbildungen im Reichstag," *Die grüne Zukunft* 3, nos. 11/12 (Nov.–Dec. 1930): 133.

15. For example, see Stein to Bredt, 17 Sept. 1930, NL Bredt. For further details, see Martin Schumacher, *Mittelstandsfront und Republik. Die Wirtschaftspartei—Reichspartei des deutschen Mittelstandes 1919–1933* (Düsseldorf, 1972), pp. 222–23.

16. Resolution adopted by the WP national committee, 26 Sept. 1930, BA: R 45 I/1308/625. See also *Kölner Nachrichten*, 4 Oct. 1930, no. 40.

17. For further details, see Johann Victor Bredt, *Erinnerungen und Dokumente von Joh. Victor Bredt 1914 bis 1933*, ed. Martin Schumacher (Düsseldorf, 1970), pp. 252–55, as well as Pünder's memorandum from 13 Oct. 1930, BA: R 43 I/1308/627.

18. Drewitz to Bredt, 21 Nov. 1930, NL Bredt.

19. Bredt, *Erinnerungen und Dokumente*, pp. 259–64. See also Bredt to Brüning, 25 Nov. 1930, BA: R 43 I/1308/629, as well as Pünder's memoranda from 25 Nov. and 3 Dec. 1930, ibid., 633, 637–38.

20. *Hannoverscher Kurier*, 2 Nov. 1930, no. 515.

21. *Hannoverscher Kurier*, 29 Dec. 1930, no. 606. See also Colosser, "Zur Aufklärung in Sachen Drewitz-Colosser," [Feb. 1931], BA: ZSg 103/935/62–68.

22. *Kölner Nachrichten*, 10 Jan. 1931, no. 2.

23. *Hannoverscher Kurier*, 15 Jan. 1931, no. 23.

24. For example, see Ernst Horneffer, *Die Krise der Wirtschaftspartei* (Leipzig, [1931]), pp. 13–14.

25. *Hannoverscher Kurier*, 28 Apr. 1931, no. 195.

26. For further details, see Hans Klett, *Der Untergang des Mittelstandes. Der Zerfall der Wirtschaftspartei* (Berlin, [1931]), pp. 14–50.

27. For example, see Nuscke to Dietrich, 31 Dec. 1930, BA: NL Dietrich, 246/179–82, and "Lemmer im Reichstag gegen die Nationalsozialisten!," 9 Feb. 1931, ibid., 243/185–86.

28. Minutes of the DStP managing committee, 17 Dec. 1930, BA: R 45 III/51/20–21.

29. For example, see Schäfer to Dietrich, 27 Feb. 1931, BA: NL Dietrich, 247/87–89.

30. Dietrich to Schäfer, 3 Mar. 1931, BA: NL Dietrich, 247/83–85.

31. Winschuh to Dietrich, 6 Feb. 1931, BA: NL Dietrich, 247/399–40.

32. Weber to Jänicke, 2 Jan. 1931, BA: NL Jänicke, 26.

33. Scheuermann to Fischer, 19 Mar. 1931, BA: NL Dietrich, 247/51–55.

34. Vogt to Dietrich, 2 May 1931, BA: NL Dietrich, 244/357.

35. Lüders to Dietrich, 3 Apr. 1931, BA: NL Dietrich, 245/167–73.

36. Schäfer to Dietrich, 27 Feb. and 30 Apr. 1931, BA: NL Dietrich, 247/87–89, and 244/307.

37. Obst to Dietrich, 24 Apr. 1931, BA: NL Dietrich, 246/199–201.

38. Landahl to Dietrich, 26 Jan. 1931, BA: NL Dietrich, 243/365–67. For further information on the state of the DStP organization in the spring of 1931, see the detailed reports filed by Lüders to Dietrich, 23 Feb.–5 Apr. 1931, ibid., 245/157–73, 211–25.

39. Weber to Jänicke, 7 Apr. 1931, BA: NL Jänicke, 26. See also Moeller (DStP Rostock) to Dietrich, 30 May 1931, BA: NL Dietrich, 246/85–89.

40. For example, see Vogtland to Dietrich, 28 May 1931, BA: NL Dietrich, 244/153–54.

41. In this respect, see Weber to Jänicke, 23 Mar. 1931, BA: NL Jänicke, 26, and Fischer to Dietrich, 21 Apr. 1931, BA: NL Dietrich, 247/7–9.

42. Heinrich Brüning, *Memoiren 1918–1934* (Stuttgart, 1970), p. 278. For a detailed exposition of the emergency decree, see Adam Stegerwald, *Die Notverordnung vom 5. Juni 1931. Ihr Hintergrund, Wesen und Ziel* (Berlin, 1931).

43. See the resolutions of the DNVP Reichstag delegation, 21 July 1931, in *Unsere Partei* 9, no. 15 (1 Aug. 1931): 190.

44. DStP, Reichsgeschäftsstelle, circular no. 5, 10 June 1931, BA: R 45 III/60/56–61.

45. In this respect, see Weber's remarks in *Stenogramm der Verhandlungen des Wirtschaftspolitischen Ausschusses der Hansa-Bundes für Gewerbe, Handel und Industrie, Berlin, am 17. und 18. Juni 1931* (Berlin, 1931), as well as Weber's lengthy memorandum to Dietrich, 13 July 1931, BA: NL Dietrich, 309/21–142.

46. For example, see the petition from the National Federation of the German Artisanry to Brüning, 4 July 1931, BA: R 43 I/2370/288–98. For further information, see Winkler, *Mittelstand*, pp. 140–46.

47. On the defection of Colosser and Dannenburg, see Dietrich to Külz, 19 June 1931, BA: NL Dietrich, 242/43–44, as well as the report in *Blätter der Staatspartei* 1, nos. 12/13 (15 July 1931): 272.

48. In this respect, see Funke to Barteld, 6 June 1931, appended to Barteld to Dietrich, 9 June 1931, BA: NL Dietrich, 242/7–11, and Vogt and Schuldt to Dietrich, 9 June 1931, ibid., 247/341–42, as well as Vogt, "Die Notverordnung," *Der Beamtenfreund. Organ des Reichsbeamtenausschusses der Deutschen Staatspartei* 7, no. 6 (25 June 1931): 41–42.

49. For example, see the GdA petitions to Brüning, 29 June and 2 July 1931, BA: R 43 I/2370/201–2, 253–62.

50. Minutes of the DVP Reichstag delegation, 10 and 16 Oct. 1930, BA: R 45 II/67/271–75, 279–84.

51. In this respect, see the minutes of the DVP Reichstag delegation, 3–4 Dec. 1930, BA: R 45 II/67/291–95, as well as Gilsa to Reusch, 5 Dec. 1930, HA/GHH: NL Reusch, 400101293/4. For an indication of the uneasiness within the DVP national organization, see the letter from the Brunswick district organization to the DVP national headquarters, 6 Dec. 1930, StA Braunschweig, GX6/609.

52. Circular of the DVP national headquarters, 4 Mar. 1931, BA: R 45 II/22/31–32.

53. Eduard Dingeldey, *Staatsautorität und Parlamentarismus im heutigen Deutschland. Vortrag, gehalten am 17. Februar 1931 vor der Vereinigung für Handel und Industrie bei der Deutschen Volkspartei Berlin im Hotel Esplanade zu Berlin* (Berlin, [1931]), pp. 4–6. See also the statement that Dingeldey read to the Reichstag on behalf of the DVP, Center, and other moderate bourgeois parties, 10 Feb. 1931, BA: NL Dingeldey, 36/105–6.

54. Eduard Dingeldey, *Kampf und Politik der Deutschen Volkspartei. Rede in der Sitzung des Zentralvorstandes der Deutschen Volkspartei am 19. April 1931* (Berlin, 1931), p. 5. See also pp. 15–17 and 32–35 in this work, as well as the report of Dingeldey's speech in Cologne, 28 Feb. 1931, in *KZ*, 2 Mar. 1931, no. 120.

55. Dingeldey, *Kampf und Politik*, pp. 41–52. For further information on the "Kampfziele," see the critical analysis by Lothar Döhn, *Politik und Interesse. Die Interessenstruktur der Deutschen Volkspartei* (Meisenheim an Glan, 1970), pp. 211–23. On the DVP's proposals for a reform of the Weimar Constitution, see also "Vorschläge der Deutschen Volkspartei zu einer Verfassungsreform," June 1931, BA: R 45 II/63/101–11.

56. For example, see Glatzel to Dingeldey, 23 Apr. 1931, BA: NL Dingeldey, 55/71–72.

57. Minutes of the DVP Reichstag delegation, 8 Mar. 1931, BA: R 45 II/67/319. See also Kalle to Dingeldey, 8 Mar. 1931, BA: NL Dingeldey, 75/6, and Gilsa to Kellermann, 23 Mar. 1931, HA/GHH: NL Reusch, 400101290/4, as well as Dingel-

dey's speech in Munich, 15 Mar. 1931, reported in *DAZ*, 17 Mar. 1931, nos. 119–20.

58. Minutes of the DVP Reichstag delegation, 16 May 1931, BA: R 45 II/67/322–24.

59. Dingeldey to Brüning, 18 May 1931, BA: NL Dingeldey, 36/90–96.

60. *KZ*, 6 June 1931, no. 300. See also the report of Dingeldey's speech in Trier, 8 June 1931, in *DAZ*, 9 June 1931, nos. 253–54.

61. Minutes of the DVP Reichstag delegation, 11 June 1931, BA: R 45 II/67/327–29.

62. Brüning, *Memoiren*, pp. 285–86. See also Brüning's opening statement at a meeting with representatives from the moderate bourgeois parties, 15 June 1931, BA: R 43 I/2370/125–26.

63. Dingeldey's memorandum of a conversation with Brüning, Kaas, and Vögler, 13 June 1931, BA: NL Dingeldey, 36/79–85.

64. Entry in Luther's diary, 12 June 1931, in Ilse Maurer and Udo Wengst, eds., *Politik und Wirtschaft in der Krise 1930–1932. Quellen zur Ära Brüning*, with an introduction by Gerhard Schulz, 2 vols. (Düsseldorf, 1980), 1:655–58.

65. Wirtschaftspolitischer Informationsdienst, 13 June 1931, HA/GHH: NL Reusch, 4001012024/8.

66. In this respect, see the correspondence between Kalle and Dingeldey, 12–14 June 1931, BA: NL Dingeldey, 75/8–13.

67. Minutes of the DVP Reichstag delegation, 15 June 1931, BA: R 45 II/67/329–30.

68. For example, see Hembeck and Schütz to Dingeldey, 15 June 1931, HSA Düsseldorf, NL Klingspor, 6.

69. Minutes of the DVP Reichstag delegation, 16 June 1931, BA: R 45 II/67/332–33. See also the resolution that the delegation released at the conclusion of its meeting in *Erneuerung*, 20 June 1931, no. 12.

70. For example, see Zapf to Dingeldey, 8 July 1931, BA: NL Zapf, 1.

71. Dingeldey, "Was wir wollten und weiter wollen. Die Haltung der Deutschen Volkspartei," *KZ*, 18 June 1931, no. 324.

CHAPTER THIRTY-ONE

1. Gilsa to Reusch, 17 Jan. 1931, HA/GHH: NL Reusch, 400101290/4b.

2. Volker R. Berghahn, *Der Stahlhelm. Bund der Frontsoldaten 1918–1935* (Düsseldorf, 1966), pp. 156–60.

3. Wagner to the state and provincial leaders of the Stahlhelm, 31 Oct. 1930, Bayerisches Kriegsarchiv, Munich, Stahlhelm, 77.

4. Kempkes's memorandum of a meeting between representatives from the Stahlhelm, DNVP, WP, CNBLP, and DVP, 12 Nov. 1930, BA: R 45 II/22/13–17. See also Brosius to Hugenberg, 12 Nov. 1930, BA: NL Hugenberg, 189.

5. For further information, see the undated memorandum from Dec. 1930, Bayerisches Kriegsarchiv, Munich, Stahlhelm, 77, as well as Gilsa to Reusch, 31 Jan. 1931, HA/GHH: NL Reusch, 400101290/4, and Hugenberg to Hitler, 5 Feb. 1931, BA: NL Schmidt-Hannover, 30.

6. Schmidt-Hannover to Wegener, 7 Feb. 1931, BA: NL Schmidt-Hannover, 75.
7. For example, see Brauweiler to Seldte, 11 Feb. 1931, StA Mönchen-Gladbach, NL Brauweiler, 111.
8. Gilsa to Mahnken, 12 Feb. 1931, BA: NL Jarres, 58.
9. Gilsa to Stendel, 20 Feb. 1931, BA: R 45 II/22/21–25. See also Gilsa to Dingeldey, 12 and 19 Feb. 1931, BA: NL Jarres, 58.
10. Circular from the DVP national headquarters, 4 Mar. 1931, BA: R 45 II/22/31–32. See also Hans Winter, *Der Kampf um Preußen* (Berlin, 1931).
11. On the DVP's difficulties, see Jochmus to Mahnken, 14 Mar. 1931, BA: R 45 II/22/50–53.
12. Ferdinand Friedensburg, *Lebenserinnerungen. Kaiserreich—Weimarer Republik—Hitlerzeit* (Frankfurt am Main and Bonn, 1969), pp. 200–202. For further details, see Larry Eugene Jones, "Sammlung oder Zersplitterung? Die Bestrebungen zur Bildung einer neuen Mittelpartei in der Endphase der Weimarer Republik 1930–1933," *VfZ* 25 (1977): 272–73.
13. Friedensburg to Luther, 24 Feb. 1931, BA: NL Friedensburg, 25/287. See also the memorandum of a meeting in Friedensburg's home, 23 Feb. 1931, ibid., 288–89.
14. An invitation dated 16 Mar. 1931, and signed by Friedensburg, Otte, and Pfeiffer can be found along with a list of those to whom invitations were sent in BA: NL Friedensburg, 33a/68, 94–95.
15. Friedensburg, *Lebenserinnerungen*, p. 205. See also Friedensburg to Fleischmann, 8 Aug. 1931, BA: NL Friedensburg, 25/264.
16. In this respect, see the correspondence between Dingeldey and Wagner, 11–15 July 1931, BA: NL Dingeldey, 40/20–24, as well as Dingeldey to Gilsa, 24 July 1931, ibid., 69/51–52.
17. For example, see Hembeck to Dingeldey, 24 June 1931, BA: NL Dingeldey, 46/45.
18. Köngeter to Gilsa, 22 June 1931, HA/GHH: NL Reusch, 400101293/4.
19. In this respect, see Hugo, "Die politische Verantwortung der Deutschen Volkspartei," *Erneuerung*, 11 July 1931, no. 15, as well as the minutes of the DVP Reichstag delegation, 16 July 1931, BA: R 45 II/67/332–33, and Gilsa to Reusch, 16 July 1931, HA/GHH: NL Reusch, 400101293/4.
20. For example, see the correspondence between Gilsa and Hugenberg, 12–17 Aug. 1931, HA/GHH: NL Reusch, 400101293/4.
21. Memorandum by Dingeldey on his conversation with Hitler, 28 July 1931, BA: NL Dingeldey, 37/1–4. See also Dingeldey's remarks before the DVP Reichstag delegation, 3 Aug. 1931, BA: R 45 II/67/331.
22. Hugenberg to Hitler, 1 Aug. 1931, BA: NL Wegener, 73/183.
23. Dohna, "Gegengründe," *KZ*, 4 Aug. 1931, no. 418.
24. *KZ*, 6 Aug. 1931, no. 422, and 7 Aug. 1931, no. 424.
25. For example, see Gilsa to Dingeldey, 6 Aug. 1931, BA: NL Dingeldey, 69/53–55, and Hugo to Dingeldey, 8 Aug. 1931, ibid., 73/80.
26. Zapf to Dingeldey, 7 Sept. 1931, BA: NL Zapf, 1. See also Kahl to Dingeldey, 28 Aug. 1931, BA: NL Dingeldey, 74/2–3.
27. Schnell to Dingeldey, 10 and 20 Aug. 1931, BA: NL Dingeldey, 101/48–60.
28. Dingeldey to Schnell, 31 Aug. 1931, BA: NL Dingeldey, 101/61.

598 *Notes to Pages 427–30*

29. For further details, see Julius Curtius, *Sechs Jahre Minister der deutschen Republik* (Heidelberg, 1948), pp. 188–212.

30. Dingeldey to Curtius, 4 Sept. 1931, BA: NL Dingeldey, 57/1–3. See also Dingeldey's report before the DVP Reichstag delegation, 8 Sept. 1931, BA: R 45 II 67/334–38.

31. In this respect, see Dietrich's remarks before the DStP executive committee, 15 Aug. 1931, BA: R 45 III/49/90–92, as well as Winschuh to Kluthe, 18 Aug. 1931, BA: NL Kluthe, 17/133.

32. Dietrich's announcement before the DStP executive committee, 15 Aug. 1931, BA: R 45 III/49/91.

33. Entry in Passarge's diary, 8 Sept. 1931, BA: NL Passarge, 6/3–7.

34. See Pünder's memorandum on his conversation with Hamm, 21 Sept. 1931, BA: NL Pünder, 140/151–53.

35. Entry in Passarge's diary, 13 Sept. 1931, BA: NL Passarge, 6/10–11.

36. Minutes of the meeting in the Deutsche Gesellschaft 1914, 15 Sept. 1931, BA: NL Passarge, 6/13–21. See also the entry in Passarge's diary, 18 Sept. 1931, ibid., 6/23–24, as well as Weber's remarks before the DStP executive committee, 26 Sept. 1931, BA: R 45 III/49/134–37, and his speech at the DStP's Berlin party congress, 26 Sept. 1931, ibid., 47/3–4. For further details, see Jones, "Sammlung oder Zersplitterung?," pp. 273–76.

37. Minutes of the meeting in the Deutsche Gesellschaft 1914, 21 Sept. 1931, BA: NL Passarge, 6/29–32. See also Passarge to Schlange-Schöningen, 23 Sept. 1931, ibid., 6/33–37.

38. Gustav Hülser, *Der Christlich-soziale Volksdienst und die Parteien*, Schriften des Christlich-sozialen Volksdienstes, no. 15 (Berlin, [1931]), pp. 3–4.

39. *BTB*, 25 Sept. 1931, no. 452.

40. Passarge to Schlange-Schöningen, 29 Sept. 1931, BA: NL Passarge, 6/39–45.

41. Confidential circular from Glatzel, 26 Sept. 1931, StA Braunschweig, GX6/613.

42. For example, see Zapf to Dingeldey, 7 Sept. 1931, BA: NL Zapf, 1, and Klingspor to Hembeck, 5 Sept. 1931, HSA Düsseldorf, NL Klingspor, 5.

43. Dingeldey to Bredt, 15 Sept. 1931, BA: NL Dingeldey, 36/31–32.

44. *DAZ*, 25 Sept. 1931, nos. 439–40.

45. Heinrich Brüning, *Memoiren 1918–1934* (Stuttgart, 1970), p. 420.

46. For example, see Gilsa to Reusch, 9 Oct. 1931, HA/GHH: NL Reusch, 400101293/4.

47. *DAZ*, 11 Oct. 1931, nos. 467–68. See also the minutes of the DVP Reichstag delegation, 10 Oct. 1931, BA: R 45 II/67/340–43, as well as the text of Dingeldey's speech in the DVP Reichsklub, 11 Oct. 1931, BA: NL Dingeldey, 7/137–65.

48. On the course of the Harzburg rally, see the reports from Blank to Reusch, 12 Oct. 1931, HA/GHH: NL Reusch, 4001012024/9, and Gilsa to Reusch, 13 Oct. 1931, ibid., 400101293/4, as well as the official report in *Unsere Partei* 9, no. 20 (17 Oct. 1931): 245–53. For further information on the origins and goals of the Harzburg Front, see Berghahn, *Stahlhelm*, pp. 179–86, and John A. Leopold, *Alfred Hugenberg: The Radical Nationalist Campaign against the Weimar Republic* (New Haven, 1977), pp. 84–106.

49. *KZ*, 12 Oct. 1931, no. 556.

50. *DAZ*, 13 Oct. 1931, nos. 469–70. On Seeckt's career as a DVP Reichstag deputy, see Hans Maier-Welcker, *Seeckt* (Frankfurt, 1967), pp. 596–625.

51. *KZ*, 12 Oct. 1931, no. 556. See also Eynern, "Notrecht und Parteien," *Berliner Börsen-Courier*, 24 Oct. 1931, no. 497.

52. Minutes of the DVP Reichstag delegation, 10 Oct. 1931, BA: R 45 II/67/341–43. For the position of the DVP's left wing, see Mittelmann, "Die Haltung der Deutschen Volkspartei," *Vossische Zeitung*, 13 Oct. 1931, no. 482, and Glatzel, "Berliner Briefe," 13 Oct. 1931, BA: NL Dingeldey, 53/101–7.

53. In this respect, see Hugo to Dingeldey, 12 Oct. 1931, BA: NL Dingeldey, 73/41–43, and Hembeck to Dingeldey, 13 Oct. 1931, ibid., 46/49–51.

54. *Erneuerung*, 17 Oct. 1931, no. 29. See also the minutes of the DVP Reichstag delegation, 16 Oct. 1931, BA: R 45 II/67/344–47.

55. For further details, see Schmalenbach (Büro Otto Thiel), Sozialpolitischer Eildienst, 17 Oct. 1931, StA Braunschweig, GX6/606.

56. *Hannoverscher Kurier*, 28 Apr. 1931, no. 195.

57. *Kölner Nachrichten*, 13 June 1931, no. 24, and 20 June 1931, no. 25.

58. *Kölnische Zeitung*, 3 Aug. 1931, no. 416. For further information, see Martin Schumacher, *Mittelstandsfront und Republik. Die Wirtschaftspartei—Reichspartei des deutschen Mittelstandes 1919–1933* (Düsseldorf, 1972), pp. 164–77.

59. *Kölner Nachrichten*, 22 Aug. 1931, no. 34.

60. Ibid., 12 Sept. 1931, no. 37.

61. On the WP's negotiations with Brüning and the leaders of the national opposition, see the circular from the WP party leadership, 21 Oct. 1931, NL Bredt. For further information, see Johann Victor Bredt, *Erinnerungen und Dokumente von Joh. Victor Bredt 1914 bis 1933*, ed. Martin Schumacher (Düsseldorf, 1970), pp. 272–74, and Brüning, *Memoiren*, pp. 427–29, as well as the report of Drewitz's speech before the WP's Thuringian and Saxon state organizations in the *KZ*, 21 Oct. 1931, no. 574.

62. In this respect, see *Hannoverscher Kurier*, 18 Oct. 1931, no. 489; *KZ*, 18 and 22 Oct. 1931, nos. 568 and 576; and *DAZ*, 20–21 Oct. 1931, nos. 481–84.

63. *Unsere Partei* 9, no. 21 (1 Nov. 1931): 266–67.

64. For example, see Gilsa to Dingeldey, 3 Nov. 1931, BA: NL Dingeldey, 69/67–68.

65. DStP, Reichsgeschäftsstelle, circular no. 11, 20 Oct. 1931, BA: R 45 III/60/125–31.

66. *Vossische Zeitung*, 25 Oct. 1931, no. 504. See also Leonhardt, "Offener Brief an die Wirtschaftspartei," *Deutscher Aufstieg*, 29 Nov. 1931, no. 13. For the DStP's strategy toward the WP, see the minutes of the DStP managing committee, 20 Oct. 1931, BA R 45 III/51/74–81.

67. For example, see Heuss to Hopf, 16 Oct. 1931, BA: NL Heuss, 57.

68. Werner Stephan, "Grenzen des nationalsozialistischen Vormarsches. Eine Analyse der Wahlziffern seit der Reichstagswahl 1930," *Zeitschrift für Politik* 21 (1931/32): 570–78.

69. In this respect, see Dingeldey to Hitler, 22 Oct. 1931, BA: NL Dingeldey, 37/6, and Dingeldey to Gilsa, 14 Nov. 1931, ibid., 69/71.

70. On the outcome of the elections in Hesse, see *Schulthess' europäischer Geschichtskalender* 72 (1931): 253.

1. Theodor Heuss, *Hitlers Weg. Eine historisch-politische Studie über den Nationalsozialismus* (Berlin, 1932), pp. 31–46, 74–96, 152–67.

2. Rudolf Breitscheid and August Weber, *Wider den Nationalsozialismus. Zwei mütige Reden*, Republikanische Bibliothek, no. 2 (Berlin, 1932), pp. 70–90.

3. Dingeldey to Gilsa, 16 Nov. 1931, BA: NL Dingeldey, 69/74–77.

4. Dingeldey to Hitler, 22 Oct. 1931, BA: NL Dingeldey, 37/6.

5. For example, see Mittelmann, "Deutsche Volkspartei und Nationalsozialisten," *Vossische Zeitung*, 27 Oct. 1931, no. 507.

6. For further information, see the minutes of the meetings of the Kunz-Dohna faction on 30 Oct. and 20 Nov. 1931, ZSA: DVP/22/3–8, 19–25, as well as Kunz to Morath, 15 Oct. 1931, ibid., 1–2, and Dohna to Kunz, 18 Nov. 1931, ibid., 14. For further details, see Werner Methfessel, "Die Deutsche Volkspartei am Ende der Weimarer Republik" (Ph.D. dissertation, Jena, 1966), pp. 247–71.

7. Glatzel's memorandum of the meeting between Dingeldey and representatives from the Kunz-Dohna faction, 6 Nov. 1931, ZSA: DVP/22/10–12.

8. In this respect, see the correspondence between the DHV's Bechly and Dingeldey, 12–17 Nov. 1931, BA: NL Dingeldey, 35/26–30, 80–82. For the background of this conflict, see Bernd Weisbrod, "Die Befreiung von den 'Tariffesseln.' Deflationspolitik als Krisenstrategie der Unternehmer in der Ära Brüning," *Geschichte und Gesellschaft* 11 (1985), 295–325.

9. Bechly to Dingeldey, 30 Nov. 1931, BA: NL Dingeldey, 35/83–85.

10. Minutes of the meeting of the Kunz-Dohna faction, 20 Nov. 1931, ZSA: DVP/22/19–25. See also Dohna to Dingeldey, 30 Nov. 1931, ibid., 41–42, and the circular signed by Dohna, Kunz, Schwarz, and Willemsen, 30 Nov. 1931, StA Braunschweig, GX6/610.

11. Dingeldey to Kunz, 28 Nov. 1931, ZSA: DVP/22/37.

12. In this respect, see Gilsa to Dingeldey, 3 and 14 Nov. 1931, BA: NL Dingeldey, 69/67–71, and Gilsa to Reusch, 22 Oct. and 3 Nov. 1931, HA/GHH: NL Reusch, 400101293/4.

13. "Der Kurs der Deutschen Volkspartei," Dec. 1931, BA: R 45 II/63/121–24. See also the reports of this meeting in *KZ*, 7 Dec. 1931, no. 667, and *DAZ*, 8 Dec. 1931, nos. 563–64, as well as the DVP's official account in *Erneuerung*, 12 Dec. 1931, no. 37.

14. For example, see Kalle to Dingeldey, 7 and 12 Dec. 1931, BA: NL Dingeldey, 75/36–47, 55–57.

15. Dohna to Kardorff, 8 Dec. 1931, BA: NL Kardorff, 9/30.

16. Dingeldey to the members of the DVP executive committee, 10 Nov. [*sic*; Dec.] 1931, BA: NL Jarres, 40.

17. Mittelmann to Friedensburg, 7 Dec. 1931, BA: NL Friedensburg, 25/274.

18. Dohna to Kunz, 11 Dec. 1931, ZSA: DVP/22/54–55.

19. For example, see Dingeldey to Kalle, 9 Dec. 1931, BA: NL Dingeldey, 74/48–53.

20. Correspondence between Morath and Weber, 27 Nov.–3 Dec. 1931, NL Westarp.

21. Westarp's memorandum of his conversation with Sachsenberg, 11 Jan. 1932,

NL Westarp. See also Bredt to Dingeldey, 4 and 8 Feb. 1932, BA: NL Dingeldey, 42/36–38. For further details, see Larry Eugene Jones, "Sammlung oder Zersplitterung? Die Bestrebungen zur Bildung einer neuen Mittelpartei in der Endphase der Weimarer Republik 1930–1933," *VfZ* 25 (1977): 278–79.

22. Dingeldey to Bredt, 8 Feb. 1932, BA: NL Dingeldey, 42/37.

23. In this respect, see Gilsa to Köngeter, 21 Dec. 1931, HA/GHH: NL Reusch, 400101293/4, as well as his article, "Was nun?," *DAZ*, 16 Dec. 1931, nos. 577–78, and the text of his eight-page memorandum, "Was fordert die innenpolitische Lage von uns?," 19 Dec. 1931, BA: NL Jarres, 42.

24. On the preparations and course of this meeting, see Heinrichsbauer to Kellermann, 2 Jan. 1932, as well as Gilsa's report from 5 Jan. 1932, both in HA/GHH: NL Kellermann, 400101308/9.

25. Mahnken to the West German district organizations of the DVP, 14 Jan. 1932, BA: NL Dingeldey, 40/43.

26. Kuhbier to Jarres, 2 Feb. 1932, BA: NL Jarres, 42. See also Kuhbier to Mahnken, 29 Jan. 1932, BA: NL Dingeldey, 40/45–46.

27. Gilsa to Reusch, 8 and 15 Feb. 1932, HA/GHH: NL Reusch, 400101293/4.

28. Mahnken to Kuhbier, 12 Feb. 1932, BA: NL Dingeldey, 40/50–51.

29. Documentation on the secession of the DVP's South Westphalian organization is quite extensive. Above all, see Hugo's memorandum of a telephone conversation with Eberlein, 27 Feb. 1932, BA: NL Dingeldey, 73/46–48, and the correspondence between Dingeldey and Klingspor, 27 Feb.–14 Mar. 1932, HSA Düsseldorf, NL Klingspor, 6. For Hueck's position, see his letter to Dingeldey, 27 Feb. 1932, BA: NL Dingeldey, 46/83. For further information, see Horst Romeyk, "Die Deutsche Volkspartei in Rheinland und Westfalen 1918–1933," *Rheinische Vierteljahrsblätter* 39 (1975): 230–32.

30. Henry Ashby Turner, Jr., *German Big Business and the Rise of Hitler* (Oxford, 1984), pp. 222–24. See also Moldenhauer to Warburg, 3 Mar. 1932, BA: NL Dingeldey, 78/7–10.

31. For example, see the report of Dingeldey's speech before the DVP's South Westphalian organization, 14 Mar. 1932, reported in *KZ*, 15 Mar. 1932, no. 148.

32. Minutes of the DVP Reichstag delegation, 22 and 24 Feb. 1932, BA: R 45 II/67/360–66.

33. Dingeldey to Thiel, 22 and 26 Feb. 1932, BA: NL Dingeldey, 92/60–63.

34. Minutes of the DVP Reichstag delegation, 25 Feb. 1932, BA: R 45 II/67/267–70.

35. Ibid., 26 Feb. 1932, BA: R 45 II/67/371. See also Dingeldey to Curtius, 27 Feb. 1932, BA: NL Dingeldey, 53/27, and to Kardorff, 27 Feb. 1932, ibid., 61/126.

36. Dingeldey to Schnell, 22 Feb. 1932, BA: NL Dingeldey, 101/80–81.

37. For example, see Weber to Brüning, 7 Dec. 1931, BA: R 43 I/2661/103.

38. For the DStP's attitude toward the Brüning government and the considerations that led it to support the chancellor, see the debate at the meeting of the DStP executive committee, 21 Feb. 1932, in Lothar Albertin, ed., *Linksliberalismus in der Weimarer Republik. Die Führungsgremien der Deutschen Demokratischen Partei und der Deutschen Staatspartei 1918–1933* (Düsseldorf, 1980), pp. 688–97.

39. Johann Victor Bredt, *Erinnerungen und Dokumente von Joh. Victor Bredt 1914*

602 *Notes to Pages 442–45*

bis 1933, ed. Martin Schumacher (Düsseldorf, 1970), p. 276. On the WP's negotiations with the Brüning government, see Drewitz to Bredt, 15 Feb. 1932, NL Bredt, and Pünder's memorandum from 27 Feb. 1932, BA: R 43 I/2685/53–54.

40. *Unsere Partei* 10, no. 4 (15 Feb. 1932): 31–32. See also Weber, "Warum der Mittelstand für Hugenberg," *Berliner Lokal-Anzeiger*, 22 Apr. 1932, no. 191.

41. Deposition by Dingeldey from 15 Dec. 1932 on his meeting with Hitler, Jan. 1932, BA: NL Dingeldey, 2/11–14. On the background of Hindenburg's nomination, see Andreas Dorpalen, *Hindenburg and the Weimar Republic* (Princeton, 1964), pp. 254–71, and Thilo Vogelsang, *Reichswehr, Staat und NSDAP. Beiträge zur deutschen Geschichte 1930–1932* (Stuttgart, 1962), pp. 147–55.

42. DStP, Reichsgeschäftsstelle, circular no. 10, 25 Feb. 1932, BA: NL Dietrich, 250/99–105. See also Bäumer, "Zur Kandidatur Hindenburgs," *Blätter der Staatspartei* 2, no. 2 (Mar. 1932): 51–53.

43. For example, see Dingeldey, "Die Politik der Deutschen Volkspartei," *Erneuerung*, 5 Mar. 1932, no. 10.

44. Martin to Dietrich, 5 Mar. 1932, BA: NL Dietrich, 226/137.

45. For example, see the circular from the National Committee of German Democratic Civil Servants, 5 Oct. 1931, and Vogt to Dietrich, 28 Oct. 1931, BA: R 45 III/60/109–14, 140–42.

46. Remarks by Weber before the DStP executive committee, 19 Jan. 1932, BA: R 45 III/52/20. On the activity of the DStP's left wing, see the remarks by Hauff, ibid., 20–21, as well as the reports in *BTB*, 14 and 19 Jan. 1932, nos. 23 and 30.

47. On the state of the DStP party organization in the spring of 1932, see the minutes of the DStP organizational committee, 19 Mar. 1932, BA: R 45 III/58/48–52. On the DStP's financial difficulties, see Lemmer to Dietrich, 5 Mar. 1932, BA: NL Dietrich, 251/555–56; Nacher to Fischer, 22 Mar. 1932, ibid., 246/147; and Elsas to Dietrich, 5 Apr. 1932, ibid., 254/85–89.

48. Klingspor to Hintzmann, 30 Mar. 1932, HSA Düsseldorf, NL Klingspor, 6.

49. Kalle to Dingeldey, 7 Mar. 1932, BA: NL Dingeldey, 75/67–73.

50. On the crisis within the RjV and the mutiny against Glatzel's leadership of the organization, see the protocol of the RjV delegate conference in Hanover, 20 Mar. 1932, StA Braunschweig, GX6/613.

51. See the memorandum by Witzleben on the meeting of the Curatorium, 28 Aug. 1930, as well as Witzleben to Borsig, 1 Sept. 1930, both in SAA: NL Siemens, 4/Lf 646.

52. In this respect, see Siemens to Merten (DStP), 16 Apr. 1932; Siemens to Reichert (KVP), 18 Apr. 1932; and Siemens to Moldenhauer (DVP), 21 Apr. 1932, all in SAA: NL Siemens, 4/Lf 670.

53. Wilmowsky to Reusch, 18 Mar. 1932, HA/GHH: NL Reusch, 400101290/39, and Wilmowsky to Siemens, 18 Mar. 1932, SAA: NL Siemens, 4/Lf 670.

54. On the collapse of these efforts, see Wilmowsky to Krupp, 24 Mar.–1 Apr. 1932, HA Krupp, FAH 23/506, and Wilmowsky to Reusch, 7 Apr. 1932, HA/GHH: NL Reusch, 400101290/39. For further details, see Turner, *Big Business*, pp. 222–23, and Reinhard Neebe, *Großindustrie, Staat und NSDAP 1930–1933. Paul Silverberg und der Reichsverband der Deutschen Industrie in der Krise der Weimarer Republik* (Göttingen, 1981), p. 127.

55. On the DVP's financial difficulties, see Dingeldey to Thiel, 20 Jan. 1932, BA:

NL Dingeldey, 92/53–56, and Dingeldey to Reusch, 26 Jan. 1932, HA/GHH: NL Reusch, 400101293/12, as well as the correspondence between Moldenhauer and Zapf, 23–26 Mar. 1932, BA: NL Zapf, 4.

56. Memorandum by Dingeldey, n.d., appended to the letter from Hermann (DVP) to Westarp, 23 Mar. 1932, NL Westarp.

57. Hugenberg, "Rumtopf? Nein, nationaler Wiedergeburt," *Der Tag*, 30 Mar. 1932, no. 77.

58. DVP, Reichsgeschäftsstelle, ed., *Der Kampf um Preußen* (Berlin, [1932]), pp. 5–7. See also Dingeldey to Hugenberg, open letter from 4 Apr. 1932, in *Erneuerung*, 9 Apr. 1932, no. 14.

59. *KZ*, 2 Apr. 1932, no. 180, and 13 Apr. 1932, no. 201.

60. Minutes of the DStP organizational committee, 10 Feb. 1932, BA: R 45 III/58/43–46.

61. *Deutscher Aufstieg*, 6 Mar. 1932, no. 10. For the DStP's campaign strategy, see the speech by Schreiber before the DStP executive committee, 5 Apr. 1932, in Albertin, *Linksliberalismus*, pp. 698–702.

62. DVP, Reichsgeschäftsstelle, *Kampf um Preußen*, pp. 7–14.

63. Dingeldey, "Kampf und Ziel in Preußen," *DAZ*, 23 Apr. 1932, nos. 187–88.

64. For the most useful analyses of the election results, see Werner Stephan, "Die Parteien nach den großen Frühjahrswahlkämpfen. Eine Analyse der Wahlziffern des Jahres 1932," *Zeitschrift für Politik* 22 (1932/33): 110–18, and Alfred Milatz, "Das Ende der Parteien im Spiegel der Wahlen 1930 bis 1933," in *Das Ende der Parteien 1933*, ed. Erich Matthias and Rudolf Morsey (Düsseldorf, 1960), pp. 766–70.

65. For example, see Carl Petersen, *Die Schicksalsstunde des hamburgischen Bürgertums* (Hamburg, 1932), pp. 8–19.

CHAPTER THIRTY-THREE

1. Minutes of the DStP managing committee, 28 Apr. 1932, BA: R 45 III/52/50–61. See also Heuss to Hopf, Maier, and Bruckmann, 29 Apr. 1932, BA: NL Heuss, 58.

2. For example, see Dingeldey's "Führerbrief" from 25 Apr. 1932, BA: R 45 II/76. See also Dingeldey to Löffler, 29 Apr. 1932, BA: NL Dingeldey, 42/45, and to Thiel, 29 Apr. 1932, ibid., 92/85.

3. Kalle, "Sammlung der bürgerlichen Mitte," 20 May 1932, appended to Kalle to Dingeldey, 21 May 1932, BA: NL Dingeldey, 42/77–82.

4. Fecht to Dingeldey, 9 May 1932, with an enclosure on the "politische Neugestaltung der Mitte," BA: NL Dingeldey, 42/51–70.

5. Friedensburg, "Zusammenschluß der Mittelgruppen?," *BTB*, 30 Apr. 1932, no. 204.

6. Ziebell to Friedensburg, 9 May 1932, BA: NL Friedensburg, 25/254–55. See also Gruber to Dietrich, 26 May 1932, BA: NL Dietrich, 135/94–96.

7. Hermann Fischer and Ernst Mosich, *Wirtschaftsfreiheit gegen Wirtschaftsnot. Kampf dem internationalen und nationalen Kommunismus. Ansprachen auf der Tagung der Wirtschaftspolitischen Gesamtausschusses des Hansa-Bundes, Berlin, 10. Januar 1931*, Flugschriften des Hansa-Bundes, no. 27 (Berlin, [1931]), pp. 17–31.

8. Mosich to Jarres, 27 May 1932, BA: NL Jarres, 44. See also the guidelines for

the Central Office for Bourgeois Politics, [May 1932], ibid. Although the exact date of its founding is not clear, the organization had been founded prior to the state elections of 24 April 1932. See Gudell and Mosich to Schleicher, 25 Apr. 1932, BA-MA: NL Schleicher, N42/91/80.

9. For further details, see Dingeldey to Schnell, 23 May 1932, BA: NL Dingeldey, 101/95–97, and Westarp to Keudell, 28 May 1932, NL Westarp.

10. For example, see Fischer to Dietrich, 25 June 1932, BA: NL Dietrich, 254/95–101.

11. DStP campaign leaflets, July 1932, BA: ZSg 1/27 (20).

12. DVP, Reichsgeschäftsstelle, ed., *Eine Materialsammlung als Unterlage für Vorträge. Reichstagswahlen 1932* (Berlin, n.d. [1932]), pp. 5–12.

13. For a more detailed discussion of these negotiations, see Larry Eugene Jones, "Sammlung oder Zersplitterung? Die Bestrebungen zur Bildung einer neuen Mittelpartei in der Endphase der Weimarer Republik 1930–1933," *VfZ* 25 (1977): 283–91.

14. DVP, confidential circular no. 8, 8 June 1932, ZSA: DVP/225/70.

15. Minutes of a joint session of the DStP managing committee and Reichstag delegation, 6 June 1932, BA: R 45 II/52/87–92. See also Heuss to Hopf, 8 June 1932, BA: NL Heuss, 57.

16. Entry for 9 June 1932 in a memorandum by Jänicke, 30 May–9 June 1932, BA: NL Jänicke, 59. For a particularly candid statement of Dietrich's reasons for opposing the founding of a new middle party, see his letter to Fischer, 16 June 1932, BA: NL Dietrich, 223/77–78.

17. Schmid to Dingeldey, 8 June 1932, BA: NL Dingeldey, 86/8.

18. DVP, confidential memorandum no. 9, 10 June 1932, ZSA: DVP/225/69. See also Moldenhauer to Kardorff, 6 June 1932, BA: NL Kardorff, 11/167.

19. Weber to Wildermuth, 11 June 1932, BA: NL Dietrich, 223/41–43. See also Weber's remarks before the DStP executive committee, 12 June 1932, BA: R 45 III/50/76, and Jänicke to Friedensburg, 13 June 1932, BA: NL Jänicke, 15, as well as the entry in Passarge's diary for 13 June 1932, BA: NL Passarge, 6/208.

20. Invitation signed by Eckener, Solf, Wildhagen, and Plate, [10 June 1932], BA: NL Solf, 90/2.

21. For example, see Ziebell to Friedensburg, 8 June 1932, BA: NL Friedensburg, 25/248.

22. Mosich to Dingeldey, 10 June 1932, BA: NL Dingeldey, 42/98–100.

23. Eckener to Solf, telegram, 13 June 1932, BA: NL Solf, 90/16.

24. Mosich to Dingeldey, 13 June 1932, BA: NL Dingeldey, 42/105–06.

25. Dingeldey to Wildhagen, 20 June 1932, BA: NL Dingeldey, 42/117–23.

26. Heuss to Hopf, 17 June 1932, BA: NL Heuss, 57. See also Petersen to Kardorff, 14 June 1932, BA: NL Kardorff, 14/40.

27. For the most revealing statement of the DVP's objectives in the negotiations to form a united middle party, see Dingeldey's speech before the DVP central executive committee, 19 June 1932, BA: NL Dingeldey, 7/166–99. See also Jarres to Mosich, 11 June 1932, and to Aschoff, 13 June 1932, BA: NL Jarres, 44.

28. Lindeiner-Wildau to Kohlhaas, 17 June 1932, NL Kohlhaas.

29. Dingeldey to Wildhagen, 20 June 1932, BA: NL Dingeldey, 42/117–23.

30. *NLC*, 20 June 1932, no. 115.

31. For the details of this arrangement, see Dingeldey's circular from 9 July 1932, BA: NL Jarres, 43.

32. Cremer to Hermann, 2 July 1932, BA: NL Dingeldey, 101/102.

33. *Der Deutsche*, 7 July 1932, no. 157. See also Thiel to Dingeldey, 4 July 1932, BA: NL Dingeldey, 92/103–4, and Glatzel to Dingeldey, 6 July 1932, ibid., 53/199–201.

34. For example, see Schreiber to Dietrich, 17 June 1932, BA: NL Dietrich, 224/9–12. For further information on these contacts, see Schreiber's remarks before the DStP managing committee, 16 June 1932, BA: R 45 III/52/102–3, and Heuss to Hopf, 17 June 1932, BA: NL Heuss, 57.

35. For further details, see the minutes of the DStP executive committee, 7 July 1932, BA: R 45 III/50/118–29, as well as Heuss to Mück, 8 July 1932, BA: NL Heuss, 269.

36. Mosich to Külz, 20 July 1932, BA: NL Külz, 17/79.

37. For example, see Witzleben to Croll, 16 June [*sic*; July] 1932, as well as the handwritten note on the letter from Dietrich to Siemens, 20 July 1932, both in SAA: NL Siemens, 4/Lf 670.

38. On industry's efforts to force Hugenberg's removal from the chairmanship of the DNVP, see John A. Leopold, *Alfred Hugenberg: The Radical Nationalist Campaign against the Weimar Republic* (New Haven, 1977), pp. 116–17, and Henry Ashby Turner, Jr., *German Big Business and the Rise of Hitler* (Oxford, 1984), pp. 230–31.

39. The exact amount of assistance which the DVP received from Schleicher cannot be established on the basis of existing documentation. For evidence of such support, see Dingeldey to Schleicher, 18 July 1932, BA-MA: NL Schleicher, N42/22/55.

40. For example, see DStP Hamburg, ed., *Der gefesselte Staat. Die Schicksalsfrage an das deutsche Volk* (Hamburg, [1932]), pp. 3–20.

41. "An die jüdischen Wähler in Baden!," July 1932, BA: NL Dietrich, 223/235.

42. "12 Pünkte für das Kabinett Brüning-Dietrich. Seine wichtigsten Maßnahmen zugunsten des Mittelstandes," [July 1932], BA: NL Dietrich, 223/231–32.

43. For example, see the correspondence between Dingeldey and Albrecht, 24–25 June 1932, StA Braunschweig, GX6/607.

44. *NLC*, 22 July 1932, no. 137.

45. Hoff to the DVP Ortsgruppe Schöneberg, 23 July 1932, BA: NL Zapf, 2.

46. Dingeldey to Kalle, 8 July 1932, BA: NL Dingeldey, 75/80–82. See also Dingeldey's circular from 9 July 1932, BA: NL Jarres, 43, as well as DVP, Reichsgeschäftsstelle, *Materialsammlung als Unterlage*, pp. 21–24.

47. Alfred Milatz, "Das Ende der Parteien im Spiegel der Wahlen 1930 bis 1933," in *Das Ende der Parteien 1933*, ed. Erich Matthias and Rudolf Morsey (Düsseldorf, 1960), pp. 771–81. See also Werner Stephan, "Die Reichstagswahlen vom 31. Juli 1932. Eine Analyse der Wahlziffern," *Zeitschrift für Politik* 22 (1932/33): 353–60. On the social bases of the Nazi electoral victory, see Thomas Childers, *The Nazi Voter: The Social Foundations of Fascism in Germany, 1919–1933* (Chapel Hill, 1983), pp. 192–261, and Richard F. Hamilton, *Who Voted for Hitler?* (Princeton, 1982), pp. 64–228.

48. Weber to Jänicke, 26 Aug. 1932, BA: NL Jänicke, 26.

49. Minutes of the DStP managing committee, 2 Sept. 1932, BA: R 45 III/52/115–21.

606 *Notes to Pages 456–59*

50. Reinhold Maier, *Nationale Demokratie gegen Diktatur. Vortrag, gehalten auf dem Süddeutschen Demokratentag in Bietigheim* (Berlin, [1932]), pp. 1–8. See also Maier to Dietrich, 6 Sept. 1932, BA: NL Dietrich, 224/141–42, as well as the official reports of the conference in *Der Beobachter*, 10 Sept. 1932, no. 37, and *Deutscher Aufstieg*, 11 Sept. 1932, no. 37.

51. Minutes of the DStP executive committee, 11 Sept. 1932, BA: R 45 III/50/135–55. See also circular no. 21 from the DStP Reichsgeschäftsstelle, 19 Sept. 1932, BA: NL Lüders, 100.

52. See the statutes and founding protocol of the DNV, 18 Sept. 1932, appended to the letter from Kunz to Wildermuth, 19 Sept. 1932, BA: NL Wildermuth, 47. For further details, see Jones, "Sammlung oder Zersplitterung?," pp. 291–93.

53. [Deutscher Nationalverein], *Was will der Deutsche Nationalverein?*, Schriften des Deutschen Nationalvereins, no. 1 (Berlin, [1932]). See also Glatzel, "Der Nationalverein von 1932," *Die Hilfe* 38, no. 40 (1 Oct. 1932): 937–41.

54. See the membership list of the members of the DNV executive committee in BA: NL Solf, 90/139. On Wildermuth's involvement in the efforts to consolidate the bourgeois middle, see Wilhelm Kohlhaas, *Eberhard Wildermuth. Ein Aufrechter Bürger. Ein Lebensbild* (Bonn, 1960), pp. 78–81.

55. Kohlhaas to Wildermuth, 21 Sept. 1932, NL Kohlhaas. On Wildermuth's overtures to Schlange-Schöningen, see the entry in Passarge's diary, 16 Sept. 1932, BA: NL Passarge, 6/303–4.

56. Moldenhauer to Wildermuth, 28 Sept. 1932, BA: NL Dingeldey, 42/152–55.

57. Wildermuth to Dingeldey, 23 Sept. 1932, BA: NL Dingeldey, 41/1–2, and to Dietrich, 23 Sept. 1932, BA: NL Dietrich, 224/288–89.

58. Morath to Schneider, 17 Sept. 1932, BA: NL Dingeldey, 42/148–49. See also Heuss to Dürr, 17 Sept. 1932, BA: NL Heuss, 55.

59. Dingeldey to Regh, 14 Sept. 1932, BA: NL Dingeldey, 116/85. See also Jarres's handwritten notes on the meeting of the DVP executive committee, [15 Sept. 1932], BA: NL Jarres, 43.

60. Dingeldey to Schleicher, 22 Sept. 1932, BA-MA: NL Schleicher, N42/22/151.

61. Wildermuth to Solf, 23 Sept. 1932, BA: NL Solf, 90/134–35.

62. Heuss to Hopf, 27 Sept. 1932, BA: NL Heuss, 57. See also Eynern to Friedensburg, 26 Sept. 1932, BA: NL Friedensburg, 25/225.

63. DStP, Reichsgeschäftsstelle, circular no. 23, 7 Oct. 1932, BA: NL Külz, 18/39–40.

64. Hermann Dietrich, Carl Petersen, and Reinhold Maier, *Der Weg der nationalen Demokratie. Reden auf der Kundgebung der Deutschen Staatspartei in Mannheim am 2. Oktober 1932*, with an introduction by Max Clauß (Mannheim, [1932]). See also Dietrich, "Wege der nationalen Demokratie," *Deutscher Aufstieg*, 2 Oct. 1932, no. 40.

65. Eduard Dingeldey, *Botschaft an das nationale Deutschland. Rede vor dem Zentralvorstand der Deutschen Volkspartei in Erfurt am 9. Oktober 1932* (Berlin, 1932), pp. 4–10, 18–23. See also DVP, Reichsgeschäftsstelle, ed., *Materialsammlung als Unterlage für Vorträge. Zweite Reichstagswahl 1932* (Berlin, [1932]), pp. 12–23, 40–45.

66. Hopf to Dietrich, 2 Dec. 1932, BA: NL Dietrich, 256/65.

67. For example, see Jarres's marginalia on a draft of a letter that he sent to five Ruhr businessmen, 6 Oct. 1932, BA: NL Jarres, 43, as well as Krüger's report on the DVP's campaign in West Düsseldorf, 6 Dec. 1932, BA: NL Dingeldey, 113/2–12.

68. Turner, *Big Business*, pp. 293–96. See also Blank's minutes of a meeting of Germany's industrial leadership, 19 Oct. 1932, HA/GHH: NL Reusch, 4001012024/10, as well as Siemens's circular letter of 24 Oct. 1932, SAA: NL Siemens, 4/Lf 670.

69. For example, see Dingeldey to Kalle, 13 Oct. 1932, BA: NL Dingeldey, 75/91.

70. Heino Kaack, *Geschichte und Struktur des deutschen Parteiensystems. Ein Handbuch* (Opladen, 1971), pp. 118–19. For further details, see Milatz, "Ende der Parteien," pp. 781–87. On the NSDAP's losses, see Thomas Childers, "The Limits of National Socialist Mobilisation: The Elections of 6 November 1932 and the Fragmentation of the Nazi Constituency," in *The Formation of the Nazi Constituency, 1918–1933*, ed. Thomas Childers (Totowa, 1986), pp. 232–59.

CHAPTER THIRTY-FOUR

1. On the demise of the Papen government, see the classic studies by Karl Dietrich Bracher, *Die Auflösung der Weimarer Republik. Eine Studie zum Problem des Machtverfalls in der Demokratie*, 3d ed. (Villingen/Schwarzwald, 1960), pp. 656–62, and Thilo Vogelsang, *Reichswehr, Staat und NSDAP. Beiträge zur deutschen Geschichte 1930–1932* (Stuttgart, 1962), pp. 311–18, as well as the more recent contribution by Volker Hentschel, *Weimars letzte Monate. Hitler und der Untergang der Republik* (Düsseldorf, 1979), pp. 59–74.

2. The record of these negotiations has been published as an appendix to Kurt Gossweiler, "Karl Dietrich Brachers 'Auflösung der Weimarer Republik,'" *Zeitschrift für Geschichtswissenschaft* 6 (1958): 543–57.

3. Vogelsang, *Reichswehr*, pp. 318–34. For a more recent assessment of Schleicher's strategy and objectives, see Peter Hayes, "A 'Question Mark with Epaulettes'? Kurt von Schleicher and Weimar Politics," *JMH* 52 (1980): 35–65.

4. For example, see Heuss to Hopf, 17 Dec. 1932, BA: NL Heuss, 57.

5. See the circular from Maier to the members of the DStP *Arbeitsausschuß*, 9 Nov. 1932, BA: NL Dietrich, 224/503–5, as well as his letter to Dietrich, 17 Nov. 1932, ibid., 255/351–52.

6. Jänicke, Lüders, Meyer, Reinhold, Richthofen, and Weber to Dietrich, 5 Nov. 1932, BA: NL Jänicke, 59. See also the correspondence between Weber and Jänicke, 22–29 Sept. 1932, ibid., as well as Lüders to Weber, 22 Oct. 1932, BA: NL Lüders, 100.

7. Report on the meeting of the DStP *Arbeitsausschuß*, 23 Nov. 1932, BA: NL Külz, 18/111–13. See also Meyer to Jänicke, 25 Nov. 1932, BA: NL Jänicke, 19, and Dietrich to Lemmer, 28 Nov. 1932, BA: NL Dietrich, 138/17.

8. Maier's remarks before the DStP executive committee, 8 Jan. 1933, BA: R 45 III/50/170–71. See also Landahl to Heuss, 7 Dec. 1932, BA: NL Heuss, 58, and Weber to Nuschke, 13 Dec. 1932, BA: NL Jänicke, 59.

9. Heuss to Hopf, 17 Dec. 1932, BA: NL Heuss, 57.

10. Dingeldey to Schleicher, 26 Nov. 1932, BA-MA: NL Schleicher, N42/31/75–76.

11. DVP, Reichsgeschäftsstelle, circular no. 17, 12 Dec. 1932, BA: NL Dingeldey, 34/11–12.

12. For example, see DNVP, circular no. 11, 6 Dec. 1932, NL Weilnböck.

13. [Deutscher Nationalverein], *Das Gebot der Stunde. Sammlung des Bürgertums*, Schriften des Deutschen Nationalvereins, no. 2 (Berlin, [1932–33]).

14. Wildermuth to Dingeldey, 19 Dec. 1932, BA: NL Dingeldey, 41/19–21.

15. Report of the meeting of the DStP *Arbeitsausschuß*, 23 Nov. 1932, BA: NL Külz, 18/111–13. See also Wildermuth to Petersen, 5 Nov. 1932, and Solf to Wildermuth, 8 Nov. 1932, BA: NL Solf, 90/188–90.

16. Wildermuth to the DStP national headquarters, 18 Nov. 1932, BA: NL Dietrich, 255/363.

17. Glatzel, "Die Reichsgemeinschaft," 31 Oct. 1932, BA: NL Dingeldey, 53/204–10.

18. For example, see Dingeldey to Wildermuth, 21 Nov. and 19 Dec. 1932, BA: NL Dingeldey, 41/14–18.

19. Dingeldey to Wildermuth, 30 Dec. 1932, BA: NL Dingeldey, 41/25–26.

20. Wildermuth to Solf, 7 Jan. 1933, BA: NL Solf, 90/208–10.

21. Wilamowitz-Möllendorf to Solf, 24 Jan. 1933, BA: NL Solf, 90/229. On Treviranus's election as "speaker of the leadership circle" of the VKV, see the mimeographed protocol of the meeting of the expanded leadership circle of the VKV, 27 Nov. 1932, NL Westarp.

22. DStP, Reichsgeschäftsstelle, circular no. 1, 10 Jan. 1933, BA: NL Heuss, 382.

23. Dingeldey to Wildermuth, 30 Dec. 1932, BA: NL Dingeldey, 41/25–26.

24. For example, see the remarks by Albrecht, Schiftan, Sauerborn, and others at a meeting of the DVP national committee, 15 Jan. 1933, ZSA: DVP/222/31–39.

25. Schütt to Baumgardt, 21 Jan. 1933, BA: NL Dietrich, 142/129.

26. Wildermuth to Dingeldey, 23 Jan. 1933, BA: NL Dingeldey, 41/29.

27. On the collapse of the Schleicher government, see Andreas Dorpalen, *Hindenburg and the Weimar Republic* (Princeton, 1964), pp. 397–446, and Vogelsang, *Reichswehr*, pp. 335–404, as well as Hentschel, *Weimars letzte Monate*, pp. 79–101. On the failure of Schleicher's negotiations with the free trade unions, see Richard Breitman, "On German Social Democracy and General Schleicher," *CEH* 9 (1976): 352–78. For the most informed discussion of the Strasser fiasco, see Peter D. Stachura, *Gregor Strasser and the Rise of Nazism* (London, 1983), pp. 103–20.

28. The secondary literature on the formation of the Hitler-Papen cabinet is far too extensive for citation here. Above all else, see Karl Dietrich Bracher, Wolfgang Sauer, and Gerhard Schulz, *Die nationalsozialistische Machtergreifung. Studien zur Errichtung des totalitären Herrschaftssystems in Deutschland 1933/34* (Cologne and Opladen, 1960), pp. 45–53.

29. Minutes of the DVP national committee, 5 Feb. 1933, StA Braunschweig, GX6/601.

30. *Deutscher Aufstieg*, 5 Feb. 1933, no. 6.

31. Wildermuth to Dingeldey, 1 Feb. 1933, BA: NL Dingeldey, 41/30. See also

DNV, "Aufruf zur Sammlung der volksbürgerlichen Mitte," 1 Feb. 1933, BA: NL Solf, 90/239.

32. Wildermuth to Planck, 24 Jan. 1933, BA: NL Solf, 90/234–36.

33. See Dingeldey's speech, "Es geht um die wahre und große nationale Front," before the DVP national committee, 5 Feb. 1933, BA: NL Dingeldey, 50/158–59.

34. Wolfhard to Vögele, 13 Feb. 1933, BA: NL Dietrich, 265/19–20.

35. Ibid. See also the appeal from the DStP party leadership, 11 Feb. 1933, BA: NL Külz, 19/28.

36. For the details of this agreement, see the circular from the DStP Reichsgeschäftsstelle, 11 Feb. 1933, BA: NL Külz, 19/28.

37. Dingeldey to Papen, 4 Feb. 1933, BA: NL Dingeldey, 81/11. See also the minutes of the meeting of the DVP national council, 5 Feb. 1933, StA Braunschweig, GX6/601, as well as "Um die bürgerlich-nationale Front!," Feb. 1933, BA: ZSg 1-42/8 (5).

38. *NLC*, 10 Feb. 1933, no. 26. For the terms of the agreement, see "Wahlabkommen zur Reichstagswahl am 5. März 1933," 7 Feb. 1933, BA: NL Dingeldey, 43/23–25. For further information, see Dingeldey's "Führerbrief" of 10 Feb. 1933, StA Braunschweig, GX6/641.

39. Eduard Dingeldey, *Klarer nationaler Kurs in stürmischer Zeit. Rede gehalten in Darmstadt am 19. Februar 1933* (Berlin, [1933]), pp. 7–11.

40. Ibid., pp. 12–15. See also DVP, Reichsgeschäftsstelle, ed., *Materialsammlung als Unterlage für Vorträge. Reichstagswahl 1933* (Berlin, [1933]), pp. 17–20, 24–31.

41. "Für den gewerblichen Mittelstand. Programmatische Forderungen des Reichsausschusses der Deutschen Volkspartei für den gewerblichen Mittelstand," [Feb. 1933], BA: ZSg 1-42/8 (5).

42. For example, see Dingeldey, "Unsre Stellung in der nationalen Front," *KZ*, 28 Feb. 1933, no. 116.

43. Dietrich to Külz, 15 Feb. 1933, BA: NL Külz, 19/40.

44. *Deutscher Aufstieg*, 12 Feb. 1933, no. 7.

45. "Zum 5. März. Was am Rundfunk nicht gesagt wird," [Mar. 1933], BA: ZSg 1-27/20 (6).

46. Bracher, Sauer, and Schulz, *Machtergreifung*, pp. 59–60. For Papen's goals, see his letter to Hugenberg, 12 Feb. 1933, BA: NL Hugenberg, 38/149–50, as well as his article, "Die Stunde des nationalen Bürgertums," *KZ*, 26 Feb. 1933, no. 112.

47. DNVP, circular no. 2, Feb. 16, 1933, BA: NL Dingeldey, 43/16–22.

48. Bracher, Sauer, and Schulz, *Machtergreifung*, pp. 70–71.

49. For further details of this meeting, see the memorandum by Blank, 21 Feb. 1933, HA/GHH: NL Reusch, 4001012924/11, and Springorum to Reusch, 21 Feb. 1933, ibid., 400106/105. The role German big business played in the installation and stabilization of the Nazi regime has been the subject of considerable disagreement among historians. For two widely differing views, see Dirk Stegmann, "Zum Verhältnis von Großindustrie und Nationalsozialismus 1930–1933. Ein Beitrag zur Geschichte der sog. Machtergreifung," *Archiv für Sozialgeschichte* 13 (1973): 399–482, and Henry Ashby Turner, Jr., *German Big Business and the Rise of Hitler* (Oxford, 1984), pp. 313–39. On the industrial financing of the NSDAP, see Thomas Trumpp,

"Zur Finanzierung der NSDAP durch die deutsche Großindustrie. Versuch einer Bilanz," *Geschichte in Wissenschaft und Unterricht* 32 (1981): 223–41.

50. In this respect, see Witzleben to Dingeldey, 2 Mar. 1933, SAA: NL Siemens, 4/Lf 670, as well as Gutehoffnungshütte, "Wahlen am 5. und 12. März 1933," n.d., HA/GHH: Allgemeine Verwaltung, 400106/104.

51. Siemens to Merten, 1 Mar. 1933, SAA: NL Siemens, 4/Lf 670.

52. For the most detailed analyses of the 1933 election results, see Alfred Milatz, "Das Ende der Parteien im Spiegel der Wahlen 1930 bis 1933," in *Das Ende der Parteien 1933*, ed. Erich Matthias and Rudolf Morsey (Düsseldorf, 1960), pp. 790–93, and Bracher, Sauer, and Schulz, *Machtergreifung*, pp. 88–136.

53. On the origins of this bill, see Bracher, Sauer, and Schulz, *Machtergreifung*, pp. 152–58.

54. For further information, see Hans Booms, "Die Deutsche Volkspartei," in *Das Ende der Parteien*, ed. Matthias and Morsey, p. 535.

55. On Brüning's efforts to amend the Enabling Act, see Rudolf Morsey, *Der Untergang des politisches Katholizismus. Die Zentrumspartei zwischen christlichem Selbstverständnis und "Nationaler Erhebung" 1932/33* (Zurich, 1977), pp. 142–47. On Dietrich's contacts with Brüning, see his testimony before the Württemberg Landtag, quoted by Erich Matthias and Rudolf Morsey, "Die Deutsche Staatspartei," in *Das Ende der Parteien*, ed. Matthias and Morsey, p. 69.

56. For further details, see Matthias and Morsey, "Staatspartei," pp. 68–70, and Modris Eksteins, *Theodor Heuss und die Weimarer Republik. Ein Beitrag zur Geschichte des deutschen Liberalismus* (Stuttgart, 1969), pp. 113–16.

57. DStP, Reichsgeschäftsstelle, circular no. 6, 24 Mar. 1933, BA: NL Külz, 19/108–10. See also the statement released by the five DStP deputies, 24 Mar. 1933, BA: NL Heuss, 382.

58. "Erklärung der DStP zum Ermächtigungsgesetz im Reichstag," [23 Mar. 1933], BA: NL Heuss, 382.

59. Cited in Matthias and Morsey, "Staatspartei," p. 69.

60. Minutes of the DStP executive committee, 14 May 1933, in Lothar Albertin, ed., *Linksliberalismus in der Weimarer Republik. Die Führungsgremien der Deutschen Demokratischen Partei und der Deutschen Staatspartei 1918–1933* (Düsseldorf, 1980), pp. 764–65.

61. DStP, Reichsgeschäftsstelle, circular no. 7, 19 May 1933, BA: NL Heuss, 382.

62. For example, see *Deutscher Aufstieg*, 4 and 11 June 1933, nos. 23–24.

63. *Deutscher Aufstieg*, 2 July 1933, no. 27.

64. Hugo to Dingeldey, 28 Mar. 1933, BA: NL Dingeldey, 73/75–77.

65. *Erneuerung*, 8 Apr. 1933, no. 14.

66. Hugo to Dingeldey, 6 Apr. 1933, BA: NL Dingeldey, 73/78–80. See also the circular from the DVP Reichsgeschäftsstelle, 13 Apr. 1933, BA: ZSg 1-42/10, as well as the report in *Erneuerung*, 22 Apr. 1933, no. 16.

67. *NLC*, 13 Apr. 1933, no. 64. See also Horst Romeyk, "Die Deutsche Volkspartei in Rheinland und Westfalen 1918–1933," *Rheinische Vierteljahrsblätter* 39 (1975): 233–35.

68. *Erneuerung*, 29 Apr. 1933, no. 17.

69. Circular from Wittig to the members of the DVP executive committee and officials of the DVP's national organization, 4 July 1933, BA: NL Jarres, 42.

Bibliography

UNPUBLISHED SOURCES

Archiv für Christlich-Demokratische Politik der Konrad Adenauer-Stiftung, Sankt
    Augustin bei Bonn
  Nachlaß Ernst Lemmer
  Nachlaß Adam Stegerwald
  Nachlaß Hugo Stinnes
Badisches Generallandesarchiv, Karlsruhe
  Nachlaß Willy Hugo Hellpach
Bayerisches Hauptstaatsarchiv, Munich
  Abteilung IV (Kriegsarchiv)
    Records of the Stalhelm, Landesverband Bayern
  Abteilung V (Nachlässe und Sammlungen)
    Flugblätter-Sammlung
    Rehse-Archiv
Bundesarchiv, Koblenz
  Records of the Reichskanzlei (Bestand R 43 I)
  Records of the Deutsche Volkspartei (Bestand R 45 II)
  Records of the Deutsche Demokratische Partei/Deutsche Staatspartei (Bestand R
    45 III)
  Records of the Jungdeutscher Order (Bestand R 161)
  Records of the Nationalsozialistische Deutsche Arbeiterpartei (Bestand NS 22)
  Records of the NSDAP Hauptarchiv (Bestand NS 26)
  Nachlaß Otto Becker
  Nachlaß Hermann Dietrich
  Nachlaß Eduard Dingeldey
  Nachlaß Anton Erkelenz
  Nachlaß Ferdinand Friedensburg
  Nachlaß Heinrich Gerland
  Nachlaß Otto Gessler
  Nachlaß Georg Gothein
  Nachlaß Wilhelm Heile
  Nachlaß Theodor Heuss
  Nachlaß Rudolf ten Hompel
  Nachlaß Alfred Hugenberg
  Nachlaß Wolfgang Jänicke
  Nachlaß Karl Jarres
  Nachlaß Jakob Kaiser

Nachlaß Siegfried von Kardorff
Nachlaß Hans Albert Kluthe
Nachlaß Erich Koch-Weser
Nachlaß Wilhelm Külz
Nachlaß Marie Elizabeth Lüders
Nachlaß Hans Luther
Nachlaß Paul Moldenhauer
Nachlaß Karl Passarge
Nachlaß Friedrich Payer
Nachlaß Hermann Pünder
Nachlaß Reinhold Quaatz
Nachlaß Hartmann von Richthofen
Nachlaß Eugen Schiffer
Nachlaß Otto Schmidt-Hannover
Nachlaß Walther Schücking
Nachlaß Paul Silverberg
Nachlaß Wilhelm Solf
Nachlaß Gustav Stolper
Nachlaß Leo Wegener
Nachlaß Eberhard Wildermuth
Nachlaß Alfred Zapf
Kleine Erwerbung 384: August Weber, "Rückblick und Ausblick (1871–1956)"
Kleine Erwerbung 484: "Akten des nordwestdeutschen Februar-Klubs, Köln, Februar 1928–März 1933" (cited as NL Sieling)
Kleine Erwerbung 549: Letters from Jakob Riesser to his son, 1920–30 (cited as NL Riesser)
Kleine Erwerbung 557: Correspondence between Gustav Stresemann and Theodor Boehm, 1919–27
Zeitgeschichtliche Sammlung 1/27 DDP/DStP
                                    1/42 DVP
                                    1/44 DNVP
                                    1/176 WP
                                    1/194 Liberale Vereinigung
                                    1/261 VRP
Zeitgeschichtliche Sammlung 109: Sammlung Lauterbach
Bundesarchiv-Militärarchiv, Freiburg im Breisgau
    Nachlaß Kurt von Schleicher
Hauptstaatsarchiv Düsseldorf
    Nachlaß Hermann Klingspor (Bestand RWN 216)
Hauptstaatsarchiv Stuttgart
    Nachlaß Conrad Haußmann
Historisches Archiv der Friedrich Krupp GmbH, Essen
    Correspondence between Gustav Krupp von Bohlen und Halbach and Tilo Freiherr von Wilmowsky (Bestand FAH 23)
Historisches Archiv der Gutehoffnungshütte, Oberhausen
    Akten der Allgemeinen Verwaltung

Nachlaß Hermann Kellermann
Nachlaß Paul Reusch
Landesarchiv Schleswig-Holstein, Schleswig
Nachlaß Anton Schifferer
Politisches Archiv des Auswärtigen Amts, Bonn
Nachlaß Gustav Stresemann
Siemens-Museum, Munich
Nachlaß Carl Friedrich von Siemens
Staatsarchiv Hamburg
Nachlaß Carl Petersen
Hans Robinsohn, "Erinnerungsbericht über die Umwandlung der Deutsch-
    Demokratischen Partei zur Deutschen Staatspartei in Hamburg im Sommer
    1930," 20 Apr. 1971, Handschriftensammlung 1233
Stadtarchiv Braunschweig
    Records of the Deutsche Volkspartei, Landesverband Braunschweig (Bestand GX6)
Stadtarchiv Mönchen-Gladbach
    Nachlaß Heinz Brauweiler (Bestand 15/13)
Stadtarchiv München
    Nachlaß Pius Dirr
Stadtarchiv Nürnberg
    Nürnberger Prozeß-Akten, Fall 6 (I.G. Farben)
Werksarchiv Bayer A.G., Leverkusen
    Autographen-Sammlung Carl Duisberg
    Records of I. G. Farben
    Records of the Reichsverband der Deutschen Industrie
Yale University Archives, New Haven
    Nachlaß Marie Baum (in the private papers of Hajo Holborn)
Zentrales Staatsarchiv der Deutschen Demokratischen Republik, Potsdam
    Records of the Deutsche Volkspartei (available on microfilm in the Bundesarchiv,
    Koblenz)
Private Possession
    "Büchner-Protokolle. Redaktionssitzungen der Kölnischen Zeitung 22. März 1929
    bis 2. Dezember 1935"
    Wilhelm Ferdinand Kalle, "Es war einmal. . . . Erinnerungen an die Zeit von 1870
    bis 1932"
    Nachlaß Johann Victor Bredt
    Nachlaß Eduard Hamm
    Nachlaß Wilhelm Kohlhaas
    Nachlaß Luitpold von Weilnböck
    Nachlaß Kuno Graf von Westarp

PUBLISHED DOCUMENTS

Akten der Reichskanzlei:
    Das Kabinett Fehrenbach. 25. Juni 1920 bis 4. Mai 1921. Edited by Peter Wulf.
    Boppard am Rhein, 1972.

Die Kabinette Wirth I u. II. 10. Mai 1921 bis 26. Oktober 1921. 26. Oktober 1921 bis 22. November 1922. Edited by Ingrid Schulze-Bidlingmaier. 2 vols. Boppard am Rhein, 1973.

Das Kabinett Cuno. 22. November 1922 bis 12. August 1923. Edited by Karl-Heinz Harbeck. Boppard am Rhein, 1968.

Die Kabinette Stresemann I u. II. 13. August 1923 bis 6. Oktober 1923. 6. Oktober 1923 bis 30. November 1923. Edited by Karl Dietrich Erdmann and Martin Vogt. 2 vols. Boppard am Rhein, 1978.

Die Kabinette Marx I und II. 30. November 1923 bis 3. Juni 1924. 3. Juni 1924 bis 15. Januar 1925. Edited by Günter Abramowski. 2 vols. Boppard am Rhein, 1973.

Die Kabinette Luther I und II. 15. Januar 1925 bis 20. Januar 1926. 20. Januar 1926 bis 17. Mai 1926. Edited by Karl-Heinz Minuth. 2 vols. Boppard am Rhein, 1977.

Das Kabinett Müller II. 28. Juni 1928 bis 27. März 1930. Edited by Martin Vogt. 2 vols. Boppard am Rhein, 1970.

Die Kabinette Brüning I u. II. 30 März 1930 bis 10. Oktober 1931. 10. Oktober 1931 bis 1. Juni 1932. Edited by Tilman Koops. 2 vols. Boppard am Rhein, 1982.

Albertin, Lothar, ed. *Linksliberalismus in der Weimarer Republik. Die Führungsgremien der Deutschen Demokratischen Partei und der Deutschen Staatspartei 1918–1933.* Düsseldorf, 1980.

Heilfron, Eduard, ed. *Die deutsche Nationalversammlung im Jahre 1919 in ihrer Arbeit für den Aufbau des neuen deutschen Volksstaates.* 9 vols. Berlin, 1919–20.

Maurer, Ilse, and Udo Wengst, eds. *Politik und Wirtschaft in der Krise 1930–1932. Quellen zur Ära Brüning.* With an introduction by Gerhard Schulz. 2 vols. Düsseldorf, 1980.

Morsey, Rudolf. "Neue Quellen zur Vorgeschichte der Reichskanzlerschaft Brünings." In *Staat, Wirtschaft und Politik in der Weimarer Republik. Festschrift für Heinrich Brüning*, edited by Ferdinand A. Hermens and Theodor Schieder, pp. 207–32. Berlin, 1967.

————, ed. *Die Protokolle der Reichstagsfraktion und des Fraktionsvorstandes der Deutschen Zentrumspartei 1926–1933.* Mainz, 1969.

Morsey, Rudolf, and Karsten Ruppert, eds. *Die Protokolle der Reichstagsfraktion der Deutschen Zentrumspartei 1920–1925.* Mainz, 1981.

Preußisches Statistisches Landesamt, ed. *Die Wahlen zum Preußischen Landtag am 20. Februar 1921 und 19. November 1922.* Berlin, 1924.

Statistisches Reichsamt, ed. *Wirtschaft und Statistik.* Berlin, 1921–33.

Stenographische Berichte über die Verhandlungen des Reichstags. Berlin, 1920–33.

HANDBOOKS, BIBLIOGRAPHIES, AND OTHER REFERENCE WORKS

Deutscher Geschichtskalender. Leipzig, 1919–33.

Egelhaafs historisch-politische Jahresübersicht. Stuttgart, 1924–33.

Fricke, Dieter, ed. *Die bürgerlichen Parteien in Deutschland. Handbuch der Ge-*

schichte der bürgerlichen Parteien und anderer bürgerlicher Interessenorganisationen vom Vormärz bis zum Jahre 1945. 2 vols. [East] Berlin, 1968 and 1970.

Gatzke, Hans W. "The Stresemann Papers." Journal of Modern History 26 (1954): 49–59.

Granier, Gerhard; Josef Henke; and Klaus Oldenhage. Das Bundesarchiv und seine Bestände. 3d ed. Boppard am Rhein, 1977.

Hess, Jürgen C., and E. van Steensel van der Aa. Bibliographie zum deutschen Liberalismus. Göttingen, 1981.

Mommsen, Wilhelm. Die Nachlässe in deutschen Archiven (mit Ergänzungen aus anderen Beständen). Boppard am Rhein, 1971.

Schulthess' europäischer Geschichtskalender. Munich, 1918–33.

Schumacher, Martin. Wahlen und Abstimmungen 1918–1933. Ein Bibliographie. Düsseldorf, 1976.

Schwarz, Max. MdR. Biographisches Handbuch der Reichstage. Hanover, 1965.

Trumpp, Thomas, and Renate Köhne, eds. Archivbestände zur Wirtschafts- und Sozialgeschichte der Weimarer Republik. Übersicht über Quellen in Archiven der Bundesrepublik Deutschland. Boppard am Rhein, 1979.

Walsdorff, Martin. Bibliographie Gustav Stresemann. Düsseldorf, 1972.

NEWSPAPERS

Berliner Börsen-Courier. Berlin, 1928–31.
Berliner Börsen-Zeitung. Berlin, 1925–29.
Berliner Lokal-Anzeiger. Berlin, 1932.
Berliner Tageblatt. Berlin, 1920–32.
Deutsche Allgemeine Zeitung. Berlin, 1924–32.
Frankfurter Nachrichten. Frankfurt, 1929–30.
Frankfurter Zeitung. Frankfurt, 1924–30.
Frankischer Kurier. Nuremberg, 1924.
Hamburger Fremdenblatt. Hamburg, 1922–28.
Hannoverscher Kurier. Hannover, 1924, 1928–31.
Kölnische Zeitung. Cologne, 1924–33.
Königsberger Allgemeine Zeitung. Königsberg, 1929–30.
Leipziger Neueste Nachrichten. Leipzig, 1930.
Neue Zürcher Zeitung. Zurich, 1929–30.
Stuttgarter Neues Tageblatt. Stuttgart, 1930.
Der Tag. Berlin, 1922–24, 1932.
Vossische Zeitung. Berlin, 1923–31.

CONTEMPORARY POLITICAL PERIODICALS

Die Aufwertung. Offizielles Organ des Hypotheken-Gläubiger- und Sparer-Schutzverbandes für das Deutsche Reich. Berlin, 1924–25.

Bayer. Bauern- und Mittelstandsbund. Beilage der "Neuen freien Volkszeitung" in München. Munich, 1928–32.

Das Bayernblatt. Wochenschrift der Deutschen Volkspartei/Nationalliberalen Partei in Bayern r.d.Rh. Munich, 1921–22.

Der Beobachter. Ein Volksblatt aus Schwaben. Stuttgart, 1929–33.

Berliner Stimmen. Zeitschrift für Politik. Berlin, 1924–31.

Blätter der Staatspartei. Organ der Deutschen Staatspartei. Berlin, 1930–32.

Briefe aus dem Nationalverein. Herausgegeben vom Deutschen Nationalverein. Neue Folge der Briefe aus der Mitte. Berlin, 1932–33.

Der Bündler. Organ für fortschrittliche Bauern- und Mittelstandspolitik. Munich, 1919–27.

Christlicher Volksdienst. Evangelisch-soziales Wochenblatt Süddeutschlands. Korntal-Stuttgart, 1929–32.

Der Demokrat. Mitteilungen aus der Deutschen Demokratischen Partei. Berlin, 1920–30.

Das demokratische Deutschland. Hamburg, 1919–24.

Demokratische Partei-Korrespondenz. Berlin, 1918–20.

Deutsche Bauernzeitung. Zentralorgan der Deutschen Bauernschaft. Berlin, 1927–32.

Deutsche Einheit. Hamburg and Berlin, 1925–28.

Deutsche Handels-Warte. Beiträge zur deutschen Wirtschaftspolitik. Nuremberg, 1922–32.

Das Deutsche Handwerksblatt. Mitteilungen des Deutschen Handwerks- und Gewerbekammertages. Hanover, 1921–28.

Deutsche Stimmen. Berlin, 1919–30.

Deutscher Aufstieg. Wochenschrift der Deutschen Staatspartei. Magdeburg, 1931–33.

Deutscher Bauernbund. Wirtschaftspolitische Zeitschrift des Deutschen Bauernbundes. Berlin, 1918–27.

Deutsches Volksrecht. Zentralorgan des Sparerbundes/Offizielles Nachrichtenblatt der Volksrechts-Partei. Berlin, 1928–33.

Das Echo der jungen Demokratie. Nuremberg, 1927–30.

Erneuerung. Wochenblatt der Deutschen Volkspartei. Berlin, 1931–33.

Die grüne Zukunft. Zeitschrift für deutsche Bauernpolitik. Breslau, 1928–30.

Der Herold der deutschen Jungdemokratie. Organ des Reichsbundes Deutscher Demokratischer Jugend. Berlin, 1929–30.

Die Hilfe. Wochenschrift für Politik, Literatur und Kunst. Berlin, 1919–32.

Der Jungdeutsche. Tageszeitung für Volkskraft und Standesfrieden. Berlin, 1929–30.

Kölner Nachrichten. Wochenschrift der Reichspartei des deutschen Mittelstandes (Wirtschaftspartei). Cologne, 1928–33.

Der Landbürger. Kommunalpolitisches Organ der Christlich-Nationalen Bauern- und Landvolkpartei. Berlin, 1929–32.

Der Meister. Jungdeutsche Monatsschrift für Führer und denkende Brüder. Berlin, 1928–30.

Der Mittelstand. Das Organ der Reichspartei des deutschen Mittelstandes (Wirtschaftspartei). Cologne, 1926–27.

Nassauische Bauern-Zeitung. Organ und Verlage der Bezirksbauernschaft für Nassau und den Kreis Wetzlar e.V. Limburg an der Lahn, 1928–32.

Nationalliberale Correspondenz. Pressedienst der Deutschen Volkspartei. Berlin, 1919–33.

Die Reichsgemeinschaft. Blätter der "Reichsgemeinschaft junger Volksparteiler." Berlin, 1930–32.

Der Reichs-Landbund. Agrarpolitische Wochenschrift. Berlin, 1928–32.

Das Staatsschiff. Halbmonatsschrift für Politik und Kultur. Berlin, 1929–30.

Süddeutsche demokratische Korrespondenz. Munich, 1919–22.

Das Tagebuch. Berlin, 1930.

Der Thüringer Landbund. Thüringer Bauernzeitung für die im Thüringer Landbund zusammengeschlossenen Bauernvereinigungen. Weimar, 1928–32.

Unsere Partei. Berlin, 1931–33.

Volkskonservative Stimmen. Zeitschrift der Volkskonservativen Vereinigung. Berlin, 1930–32.

Der Waffenschmied. Monatshefte des Liberalen Preßvereins. Mitteilungen der Deutschen Demokratischen Partei in Bayern. Munich, 1918–19.

Wille und Weg. Eine politische Halbmonatsschrift. Berlin, 1925–29.

CONTEMPORARY POLITICAL LITERATURE

Allgemeine Werbeflugschriften der Deutschen demokratischen Partei. Berlin-Zehlendorf, 1918.

Aufruf und Gründung. Volkskonservative Flugschriften, no. 1. Berlin, 1930.

Aufstieg oder Niedergang? Deutsche Wirtschafts- und Finanzreform 1929. Eine Denkschrift des Präsidiums des Reichsverbandes der Deutschen Industrie. Veröffentlichungen des Reichsverbandes der Deutschen Industrie, no. 49. Berlin, 1929.

Backhaus, Alexander. *Aufgaben der Landwirtschaft und ihre Vertretung durch die Deutsche Volkspartei.* Berlin, 1929.

Bahr, Max. *Das Reichsmietengesetz.* Berlin, [1922].

Barth, Theodor, and Friedrich Naumann. *Die Erneuerung des Liberalismus. Ein politischer Weckruf.* Berlin, 1906.

Bäumer, Gertrud. *Grundlagen demokratischer Politik.* Karlsruhe, 1928.

————. *Sinn und Form geistiger Führung.* Berlin, 1930.

————. *Soziale Erneuerung. Amtliches Stenogramm der Rede in der Nationalversammlung vom 21. Februar 1919.* Demokratische Reden, no. 3. Berlin, 1919.

Bauser, Adolf, ed. *Für Wahrheit und Recht. Der Endkampf um eine gerechte Aufwertung. Reden und Aufsätze.* Stuttgart, 1927.

Bayerischer Bauernbund, Hauptgeschäftsstelle, ed. *Der Bayerischer Bauernbund im Jahre 1919.* Flugschriften des Bayerischen Bauernbundes, no. 1. Munich, [1919].

Becker, Johann. *Die neuen Steuern. Vortrag gehalten in Hamburg am 5. Oktober 1919.* Hamburger Flugschriften, no. 1. Hamburg, [1919].

————. *Steuerkompromiß und Deutsche Volkspartei.* Flugschriften der Deutschen Volkspartei, no. 41. Berlin, 1922.

Bernhard, Henry. *Das Kabinett Stresemann.* Berlin, 1924.

Beythien, Heinrich. *Der gewerbliche Mittelstand und die Deutsche Volkspartei. Rede, gehalten im Reichstag am 1.12.1920.* Flugschriften der Deutschen Volkspartei, no. 21. Berlin, 1921.

———. *Die Lage des gewerblichen Mittelstandes.* Flugschriften der Deutschen Volkspartei, no. 39. Berlin, 1922.

Boelitz, Otto. *Der nationale und kulturelle Beruf Preußens. Rede auf dem ersten Preußentag der Deutschen Volkspartei in Potsdam am 9. Januar 1921.* Berlin, 1922.

Böhme, Karl. *Der Bauernstand in Knechtschaft und Freiheit.* Berlin, 1924.

———. *Der nationale Liberalismus und die Bauern.* Flugschriften der Deutschen Volkspartei, no. 69. Berlin, 1927.

———. *Zum Streit der landwirtschaftlichen Organisationen! Ein Wort zur Abwehr.* Leipzig, [1928].

Bredt, Johann Victor. *Hypotheken-Aufwertung.* Munich, [1924].

———. "Das politische Parlament und die berufsständischen Vertretungen." In *Volk und Reich der Deutschen,* edited by Bernhard Harms, 2:282–300. Berlin, 1929.

Breitscheid, Rudolf, and August Weber. *Wider den Nationalsozialismus. Zwei mütige Reden.* Republikanische Bibliothek, no. 2. Berlin, 1932.

Brodauf, Max. *Beamtenbesoldung und andere Beamtenfragen. Rede im Reichstage am 25. Juni 1924.* Berlin, [1924].

Brüning, Heinrich. *Das Programm der Reichsregierung. Rede im Reichstage am 16. Oktober 1930.* Berlin, 1930.

Brüning, Heinrich, and Julius Curtius. *Um Deutschlands Zukunft. Zwei Reden.* Berlin, 1931.

Christlicher Mittelstand, Generalsekretariat, ed. *Christlicher Mittelstand. Mittelstandstagung für das westliche Deutschland am 24. und 25. Februar 1920 im Vortragssaal der Bürgergesellschaft zu Köln.* Cologne, [1920].

David, Eduard, Johannes Giesberts, and Conrad Haußmann. *Warum brauchen wir eine Regierung der Mitte? Drei Beiträge.* Berlin, 1920.

Delius, Karl. *Deutsche Demokratische Partei und Beamtenbesoldung.* Berlin, [1920].

———. *Die Stellung der Beamtenschaft im neuen Staat.* Berlin, [1922].

Deutsche Demokratische Partei, Preußische Landtagsfraktion, ed. *Preußen-Tag der Deutschen Demokratischen Partei am 22. und 23. Oktober 1927 in Berlin (Stenographischer Bericht).* Berlin, 1927.

Deutsche Demokratische Partei, Reichs-Arbeitnehmerausschuß, ed. *Bericht über die Verhandlungen der 2. ordentlichen Tagung des Reichs-Arbeitnehmerausschusses der Deutschen Demokratischen Partei, abgehalten am 17. und 18. September 1921 in Berlin.* Berlin, [1921].

———. *Die Gründungstagung des Reichs-Arbeitnehmerausschusses der Deutschen Demokratischen Partei am 10. Dezember 1920 auf dem 2. ordentlichen Parteitag zu Nürnberg.* Berlin, [1921].

Deutsche Demokratische Partei, Reichsausschuß für Handel, Industrie und Gewerbe beim Hauptvorstand der Deutschen Demokratischen Partei, ed. *Protokoll der Gründungsversammlung des Reichsausschusses für Handel, Industrie und Gewerbe beim Hauptvorstand der DDP vom 16. Oktober 1920.* Berlin, [1920].

Deutsche Demokratische Partei, Reichsausschuß für Handel, Industrie und Gewerbe und Reichsmittelstandsausschuß, ed. *Heidelberger Tagung des Reichsausschusses für Handel, Industrie und Gewerbe und des Reichsmittelstandsausschusses der Deutschen Demokratischen Partei 3. Oktober 1929.* Berlin, [1929].

Deutsche Demokratische Partei, Reichsgeschäftsstelle, ed. *Bericht über die Verhandlungen des Preußenausschusses der Deutschen Demokratischen Partei am 28. November 1920 in Hannover.* Berlin, [1920].

_____. *Bericht über die Verhandlungen des 1. Parteitages der Deutschen Demokratischen Partei abgehalten in Berlin vom 19. bis 22. Juli 1919. Bericht über die Tagung der Demokratischen Frauen in Berlin, den 18. und 19. Juli 1919. Bericht über die Tagung des Reichsbundes demokratischer Jugendvereine am 18. und 19. Juli 1919.* Berlin, [1919].

_____. *Bericht über die Verhandlungen des 2. außerordentlichen Parteitages der Deutschen Demokratischen Partei, abgehalten in Leipzig vom 13.–15. Dezember 1919.* Berlin, [1920].

_____. *Bericht über die Verhandlungen des 2. ordentlichen Parteitages der Deutschen Demokratischen Partei, abgehalten in Nürnberg, 11.–14. Dezember 1920.* Berlin, [1921].

_____. *Bericht über die Verhandlungen des 3. (ordentlichen) Parteitages der Deutschen Demokratischen Partei, abgehalten in Bremen vom 12. bis 14. November 1921 in den Gesamträumen des Parkhauses (Bürgerpark).* Berlin, [1921].

_____. *Bericht über die Verhandlungen des 4. ordentlichen Parteitages der Deutschen Demokratischen Partei, abgehalten in Elberfeld am 9. und 10. Oktober 1922 in den Gesamträumen der Stadthalle.* Berlin, [1922].

_____. *Bericht über die Verhandlungen des 5. ordentlichen Parteitages der Deutschen Demokratischen Partei, abgehalten in Weimar am 5. und 6. April 1924.* Berlin, [1924].

_____. *D.D.P. und Landwirtschaft.* Materialien zur demokratischen Politik, no. 84. Berlin, 1924.

_____. *Die Demokratie und die Aufwertung.* Materialien zur demokratischen Politik, no. 112. Berlin, 1924.

_____. *Die Deutsche Demokratische Partei und der Beamtenstreik.* Berlin, [1922].

_____. *Die Deutsche Wirtschaftspartei.* Materialien zur demokratischen Politik, no. 132. Berlin, 1927.

_____. *Die Liberale Vereinigung.* Materialien zur demokratischen Politik, no. 120. Berlin, 1924.

_____. *Niederschrift über die Tagung der Parteisekretäre der Deutschen demokratischen Partei am 17. und 18. Mai 1919 im Anwaltshause in Berlin.* Berlin, [1919].

_____. *Organisationshandbuch der Deutschen Demokratischen Partei.* Berlin, 1926.

_____. *Ultimatum und Regierungsbildung. Die Haltung der Deutschen Demokratischen Partei.* Berlin, [1921].

Deutsche Staatspartei, ed. *Entwurf einer Wahlrede für bäuerliche Versammlungen.* Berlin, [1930].

_____. *Spiegel der Parteien.* Materialien zur demokratischen Politik, no. 151. Berlin, [1930].

Deutsche Staatspartei Hamburg. *Der gefesselte Staat. Die Schicksalsfrage an das deutsche Volk.* Hamburg, [1932].

Deutsche Volkspartei, Landesverband Baden, ed. *Badische Politik 1918–1921. Wahlhandbuch der Deutschen liberalen Partei (Landesverband Baden der Deutschen Volkspartei).* Heidelberg, [1921].

————. *Entstehung und Entwicklung der Deutschen Volkspartei (Deutschen liberalen Volkspartei) im ersten Revolutionsjahr. Aufklärungsschrift.* Heidelberg, [1919].

Deutsche Volkspartei, Reichsgeschäftsstelle, ed. *8. Reichsparteitag der Deutschen Volkspartei in Mannheim vom 21. bis 23. März 1930.* Berlin, [1930].

————. *Beamtenpolitik der Deutschen Volkspartei.* Flugschriften der Deutschen Volkspartei, no. 55. Berlin, 1924.

————. *Die Bemühungen der Deutschen Volkspartei um die Bildung einer nationalen Einheitsfront.* Berlin, [1921].

————. *Bericht über den ersten Parteitag der Deutschen Volkspartei am 13. April 1919 in den akademischen Rosensälen in Jena.* Berlin, 1919.

————. *Bericht über den zweiten Parteitag der Deutschen Volkspartei am 18., 19. und 20. Oktober 1919 im Kristallpalast in Leipzig.* Berlin, 1920.

————. *Das Betriebsrätegesetz, die Parteien und wirtschaftliche Berüfe.* Flugschriften der Deutschen Volkspartei, no. 21. Berlin, 1920.

[————.] *Die Demokratische Partei ist als Verräterin des Bürgertums und des Mittelstandes entlarvt.* Berlin, [1920].

————. *Deutsche Jugend—Deutsche Volkspartei.* Jugend-Schriften der Deutschen Volkspartei, no. 5. Berlin, 1924.

————. *Die Deutsche Volkspartei in der Preußischen Landesversammlung.* Berlin, 1921.

————. *Die Deutsche Volkspartei und die Beamten.* Flugschriften der Deutschen Volkspartei, no. 13. Berlin, 1919.

————. *Die Entstehung der Deutschen Volkspartei.* Berlin, 1919.

————. *Die finanziellen und sozialpolitischen Probleme bei der Reichstagswahl 1930. Reden der Reichstagsabgeordneten Dr. Cremer, Dr. Hoff, Keinath, Morath und Thiel, gehalten bei einer volksparteilichen Tagung am 25. Juli 1930 im Reichstage.* Berlin, [1930].

————. *Grundsätze der Deutschen Volkspartei. Beschlossen auf dem Parteitag in Leipzig am 19. Oktober 1919.* Berlin, 1931.

————. *Der Kampf um Preußen.* Berlin, [1932].

————. *Kapp-Putsch und Bolschewismus in der Nationalversammlung. Vier Reden der Führer der Deutschen Volkspartei.* Flugschriften der Deutschen Volkspartei, no. 16. Berlin, 1920.

————. *Eine Materialsammlung als Unterlage für Vorträge. Reichstagswahlen 1932.* Berlin, [1932].

————. *Materialsammlung als Unterlage für Vorträge. Reichstagswahl 1933.* Berlin, [1933].

————. *Materialsammlung als Unterlage für Vorträge. Zweite Reichstagswahl 1932.* Berlin, [1932].

————. *Mit Hindenburg für Deutschlands Rettung!* Printed as a manuscript. Berlin, [1930].

————. *Mittelstandspolitik der Deutschen Volkspartei.* Flugschriften der Deutschen Volkspartei, no. 55. Berlin, 1924.

_____. *Nachtrag zum Wahlhandbuch 1924.* Berlin, 1924.

_____. *Die Reichspolitik. Überblick über die wichtigsten Vorgänge der Reichspolitik vom Januar bis September 1925.* Berlin, [1925].

_____. *60 Jahr-Feier der Nationalliberalen Partei am 19. und 20. März 1927 in Hannover.* Berlin, [1927].

_____. *Stichworte für den Wahlkampf 1930.* Berlin, 1930.

_____. *Wahlhandbuch 1924.* Berlin, 1924.

_____. *Wahlhandbuch 1928.* Berlin, 1928.

_____. *Der Wolf ohne Schafspelz. Oder: Was das deutsche Volk sich alles anbieten läßt!* Cologne, [1930].

Deutscher Bauernbund, ed. *Politisches ABC. Taschenbuch für Bauernbündler.* Berlin, 1920.

_____. *Politisches ABC. Taschenbuch für Bauernbündler (Nachtrag).* Berlin, 1924.

Deutscher Nationalverein. *Das Gebot der Stunde. Sammlung des Bürgertums.* Schriften des Deutschen Nationalvereins, no. 2. Berlin, [1932–33].

_____. *Was will der Deutsche Nationalverein?* Schriften des Deutschen Nationalvereins, no. 1. Berlin, [1932].

Dietrich, Hermann. *Aufwertung und Deutsche Demokratische Partei. Der Wahlschwindel der Deutschnationalen. Rede gehalten im Deutschen Reichstag am 8. Mai 1925.* Berlin, [1925].

_____. *Gegen die Ausbeutung des Mittelstandes zugunsten des Großkapitals. Für eine gerechte Entschädigung aller Kriegs- und Inflationsgeschädigten. Rede im Reichstag am 20. Februar 1925.* Berlin, [1925].

_____. *Ein Jahr Agrarpolitik.* Berlin, 1929.

_____. *Was wird aus den Sparguthaben?* Karlsruhe, 1924.

_____. *Ziele und Aufgaben der Staatspartei. Rede, gehalten auf dem Gründungsparteitag der Deutschen Staatspartei, Hannover, den 9. November 1930.* Berlin, [1930].

Dietrich, Hermann, Carl Petersen, and Reinhold Maier. *Der Weg der nationalen Demokratie. Rede auf der Kundgebung der Deutschen Staatspartei in Mannheim am 2. Oktober 1932.* With an introduction by Max Clauß. Mannheim, [1932].

Dingeldey, Eduard. *Botschaft an das nationale Deutschland. Rede vor dem Zentralvorstand der Deutschen Volkspartei in Erfurt am 9. Oktober 1932.* Berlin, 1932.

_____. *Die Deutsche Volkspartei seit dem 14. September 1930. Rede in der Sitzung des Reichsausschusses der Deutschen Volkspartei am 2. November 1930.* Berlin, [1930].

_____. *Kampf und Politik der Deutschen Volkspartei. Rede in der Sitzung des Zentralvorstandes der Deutschen Volkspartei am 19. April 1931.* Berlin, 1931.

_____. *Klarer nationaler Kurs in stürmischer Zeit. Rede gehalten in Darmstadt am 19. Februar 1933.* Berlin, [1933].

_____. *Staatsautorität und Parlamentarismus im heutigen Deutschland. Vortrag, gehalten am 17. Februar 1931 vor der Vereinigung für Handel und Industrie bei der Deutschen Volkspartei Berlin im Hotel Esplanade zu Berlin.* Berlin, [1931].

Durch deutschen Sieg zum deutschen Frieden. Fünf Reden zur Lage gehalten 19. Januar 1917 in der Versammlung des "Unabhängigen Ausschusses für einen deutschen Frieden" im Sitzungssaale des Abgeordnetenhauses zu Berlin. Berlin, 1917.

Dusche, Wilhelm. *Die Deutsche Volkspartei und die Landwirtschaft.* Berlin, 1919.

Eggeling, Erich. *Partei oder Bewegung? Der jungdeutsche Kampf und die Staatspartei.* Berlin, 1930.

Ehlermann, Hans. *Der Wahlkampf 1928 (Einführung und Überblick).* Schriftenreihe für politische Werbung der DDP, no. 1. Berlin, 1928.

Erkelenz, Anton. *Die Aufgaben der Arbeitnehmer im demokratischen Staat. Rede auf der Tagung des Reichs-Arbeitnehmerausschusses der D.D.P. am 28. September 1921 zu Berlin.* Schriften des Reichs-Arbeitnehmerausschusses der Deutschen Demokratischen Partei, no. 1. Berlin, [1921].

————. *Demokratie und Parteiorganisation. Dem Andenken an Friedrich Naumann und Wilhelm Ohr.* Berlin, 1925.

————. *Unternehmer und Arbeitnehmer in der neuen Wirtschaft.* Berlin, 1922.

————, ed. *Zehn Jahre Deutsche Republik. Ein Handbuch für republikanische Politik.* Berlin-Zehlendorf, 1928.

Fischer, Hermann. *Gegen eine neue Inflation! Für Revision der Beamtenabbauverordnung! Für Hebung des Mittelstandes! Gegen die Münchener Hochverräter! Rede in der Reichstagssitzung vom 7. März 1924.* Berlin, [1924].

————. *Volk, Staat und Wirtschaft. Vortrag auf dem Parteitag der Deutschen Demokratischen Partei 5. April 1924.* Berlin, [1924].

Fischer, Hermann, and Oskar Meyer. *Die Politik des Hansa-Bundes. Programmreden gehalten auf der Haupt-Versammlung des Hansa-Bundes in Nürnberg vom 5. bis 7. Mai 1922.* N.p., [1922].

Fischer, Hermann, and Ernst Mosich. *Wirtschaftsfreiheit gegen Wirtschaftsnot! Kampf dem internationalen und nationalen Kommunismus. Ansprachen auf der Tagung der Wirtschaftspolitischen Gesamtausschusses des Hansa-Bundes, Berlin, 10. Januar 1931.* Flugschriften des Hansa-Bundes, no. 27. Berlin, [1931].

Friedberg, Robert, Conrad Haußmann, and Ludwig Quidde. *Der Entwurf des Friedenvertrages. Reden gehalten in der Nationalversammlung vom 12. Mai 1919 sowie in der Preußischen Landesversammlung vom 13. Mai 1919.* Berlin, 1919.

Geisler, Fritz. *Die nationale, wirtschaftsfriedliche Gewerkschaftsbewegung beim Wiederaufbau Deutschlands. Rede gehalten im National-Klub von 1919 in Hamburg am 31. August 1920.* Hamburg, [1920].

Gewerkschaftsbund der Angestellten, ed. *Epochen der Angestellten-Bewegung 1774– 1930.* Berlin, 1930.

Gildemeister, Alfred. *Was wir wollen! Rede auf der Tagung der Nationalliberalen Vereinigung der Deutschen Volkspartei am Mittwoch, den 26. Mai 1924.* [Berlin, 1924].

Graefe, Arthur. *3 Jahre Aufbaupolitik. Zu den Sachsenwahlen 1926.* Edited by Sächsischer Wahlkreisverbände der Deutschen Volkspartei. Dresden, 1926.

Haas, Ludwig. *Die deutsche Demokratie und das Kabinett Luther. Reichstags-Rede vom 22. Januar 1925.* Berlin, [1925].

Haas, Ludwig, and Robert Friedberg. *Die Deutsche Demokratische Partei und der Kapp-Putsch. Zwei Reden deutschdemokratischer Parteiführer.* Berlin, 1920.

Hanemann, Alfred. *Materialien für deutschnationale Wahlredner.* Freiburg im Breisgau, 1928.

Hansa-Bund für Gewerbe, Handel und Industrie, ed. *Der künftige Kurs der deutschen*

Sozialpolitik. Verhandlungen des Wirtschaftspolitischen Ausschusses des Hansa-Bundes für Gewerbe, Handel und Industrie, Berlin, 4. Dezember 1926. Flugschriften des Hansa-Bundes, no. 8. Berlin, 1927.

————. *Stenogramm der Verhandlungen des Wirtschaftspolitischen Gesamtausschusses des Hansa-Bundes für Gewerbe, Handel und Industrie, Berlin, am 17. und 18. Juni 1931.* Berlin, 1931.

Helfferich, Karl. *Die Lage der deutschen Finanzen. Rede auf dem 3. deutschnationalen Parteitag in München am 3. September 1921.* Deutschnationale Flugschrift, no. 121. Berlin, 1921.

————. *Die Politik der Erfüllung.* Munich, 1922.

Hepp, Karl. *Ernährung und Landwirtschaft.* Flugschriften der Deutschen Volkspartei, no. 40. Berlin, 1922.

————. *Lage und Aufgaben der deutschen Landwirtschaft. Nach einem Vortrag gehalten in Darmstadt am 1. April 1921 auf dem Parteitage der Deutschen Volkspartei in Hessen.* Aufklärungsschriften der Deutschen Volkspartei in Hessen, no. 13. Darmstadt, 1921.

Hergt, Oskar. *Auf zum Preußenkampf! Aus der Rede am Sonntag, den 9. Januar 1921, in der Philharmonie in Berlin.* Deutschnationale Flugschrift, no. 83. Berlin, 1921.

————. *Gegenwart und Zukunft der Deutschnationalen Volkspartei. Rede auf dem Parteitag der Deutschnationalen Volkspartei in Berlin am 12. und 13. Juli 1919.* Deutschnationale Flugschrift, no. 21. Berlin, 1919.

Heuss, Theodor. "Die Deutsche Demokratische Partei." In *Volk und Reich der Deutschen,* edited by Bernhard Harms, 2:104–21. Berlin, 1929.

————. *Hitlers Weg. Eine historisch-politische Studie über den Nationalsozialismus.* Berlin, 1932.

————. *Kapp-Lüttwitz. Das Verbrechen gegen die Nation.* Berlin, 1920.

Heym, Walther. *Die Vertretung des gewerblichen Mittelstandes durch den 3. Landtag von Thüringen.* Rudolstadt, 1926.

Hindenburgbund, Jugendgruppe der Deutschen Volkspartei, ed. *Staatsbürgerliche Jugendbildung. Unsere Reichsschulungswoche in Braunlage/Harz vom 22. bis 27. April 1930.* Berlin, [1930].

Hoff, Ferdinand. *Politische Zeit- und Streitfragen in demokratischer Beleuchtung. Ein Wort zur Aufklärung für die kommenden Wahlen.* Berlin, [1920].

Hömberg, Heinrich Albert. *Hitlerpartei oder Wirtschaftspartei—Phrase oder Vernunft? Eine Sammlung national-sozialistischer Pressestimmen und Aussprüchen von Führern der N.S.D.A.P.* Recklinghausen, [1930].

Horneffer, Ernst. *Die Krise der Wirtschaftspartei.* Leipzig, [1931].

Hugenberg, Alfred. *Klare Front zum Freiheitskampf! Rede gehalten auf dem 9. Reichsparteitag der Deutschnationalen Volkspartei in Kassel am 22. November 1929.* Deutschnationale Flugschrift, no. 339. Berlin, 1929.

Hugo, Otto. *Der Mittelstand und die Deutsche Volkspartei.* Berlin, 1919.

Hülser, Gustav. *Der Christlich-soziale Volksdienst und die Parteien.* Schriften des Christlich-sozialen Volksdienstes, no. 15. Berlin, [1931].

Ißberner, Rudolf, ed. *Demokratisches ABC-Buch.* Berlin, [1920].

Jansen, Robert. *Der Berliner Militärputsch und seine politischen Folgen.* Berlin, [1920].

————. *Die große Koalition in Preußen.* Berlin, [1921].

————. *Die Regierungsbildung in Preußen.* Berlin, [1921].

Jörissen, Franz. *Hausbesitz und Mittelstand. Nach einem Vortrage gehalten auf dem Verbandestage des Zentralverbandes deutscher Haus- und Grundbesitzer-Vereine Köln a. Rhein 1921.* Schriften des Zentralverbandes der Haus- und Grundbesitzer-Vereine Deutschlands, no. 22. Spandau, 1921.

Kahl, Wilhelm. *Die Deutsche Volkspartei und das Reich.* Flugschriften der Deutschen Volkspartei, no. 14. Berlin, 1919.

————. "Der Liberalismus der Deutschen Volkspartei." In *Volk und Reich der Deutschen,* edited by Bernhard Harms, 2:88–103. Berlin, 1929.

Der Kampf um die Aufwertung. Deutschnationale Flugschrift, no. 215. Berlin, 1925.

Kaufhold, Josef. *Die Sünden der Demokratischen Partei und des Deutschen Bauernbundes an der Landwirtschaft.* Deutschnationale Flugschrift, no. 134. Berlin, 1922.

Keinath, Otto, Gustav Schneider, and Hermann Fischer. *Der Kampf um die neuen Steuern. Referate, gehalten im Parteiausschuß der D.D.P. am 4.12.1921.* Edited by Reichsgeschäftsstelle der Deutschen Demokratischen Partei. Berlin, [1921].

Kempkes, Adolf, ed. *Deutscher Aufbau. Nationalliberale Arbeit der Deutschen Volkspartei.* Berlin, 1927.

Klett, Hans. *Der Untergang des Mittelstandes. Der Zerfall der Wirtschaftspartei.* Berlin, [1931].

Koch-Weser, Erich. *Die Deutsche Demokratische Partei in der Opposition. Rede bei der Beratung der Regierungserklärung am Freitag, 4. Februar 1927.* Berlin, [1927].

————. *Gerade aus—nicht rechts, nicht links! Rede auf dem demokratischen Parteitag am 2. November 1924 zu Berlin.* Berlin, [1924].

————. *Wider den Rechtsblock! Rede im Reichstag, am 21. Januar 1925.* Berlin, [1925].

Koch-Weser, Erich, and Hermann Luppe. *Der großdeutsche Einheitsstaat. Das Ziel und der Weg. Die Verhandlungen des Hamburger Parteitages der Deutschen Demokratischen Partei.* Edited by Reichsgeschäftsstelle der Deutschen Demokratischen Partei. Berlin, [1927].

Koester, Adolf. *Gegen den schwarz-rot-goldenen Block! Vortragsfolge für politische Ausbildungskurse der Deutschen Volkspartei. Ein Nachschlagebuch für den Wahlkampf.* Edited by Generalsekretariat der Deutschen Volkspartei in Dortmund. Dortmund, 1920.

Köhler, Julius. *Der Jungliberalismus. Eine historisch-politische Darstellung.* Cologne, 1912.

Kroschel, A. W. *Das deutschnationale Gewissen.* Berlin, 1920.

Kugelmann, Herbert. *Die deutsch-demokratische Jugendbewegung. Ihre Ziele und Bestrebungen.* Berlin-Zehlendorf-West, 1919.

Lantzsch, Rudolf. *Die Agrarpolitik der Deutschen Demokratischen Partei.* Schriftenreihe für politische Werbung der DDP, no. 8. Berlin, 1928.

Leidig, Eugen. *Liberalismus und Demokratie.* Berlin, 1919.

Lemmer, Ernst, ed. *1. Freiheitlich-nationaler Kongreß des Gewerkschaftsringes deutscher Arbeiter-, Angestellten- und Beamtenverbände 27. bis 29. November 1920 in Berlin.* [Berlin, 1930].

Liberale Vereinigung. *Liberale Politik im neuen Staate. Leitsätze, Vorträge und Ansprachen.* Munich, 1927.

————. *Die Liberale Vereinigung.* Berlin, [1926].

————. *Liberaler Tag im deutschen Reichstag, Berlin, den 1. Juli 1928.* Dresden, 1928.

————. *Mitglieder- und Vertreter-Versammlung zu Berlin im Gebäude des Reichswirtschaftsrats am 16. Mai 1925.* Berlin-Charlottenburg, [1925].

————. *Zum Reichsschulgesetz. Kundgebung zum Entwurf eines Reichsschulgesetzes am 23. Oktober 1927.* Berlin, 1927.

Lindeiner-Wildau, Hans-Erdmann von. *Erneuerung des politischen Lebens. Reichstagsrede gehalten am 13. Dezember 1929.* Schriften der Deutschnationalen Arbeitsgemeinschaft, no. 1. Berlin-Charlottenburg, 1929.

Luther, Hans. *Feste Mark—Solide Wirtschaft. Rückblick auf die Arbeit der Regierung während der Wintermonate 1923/24.* Berlin, 1924.

Mahraun, Artur. *Der Aufbruch. Sinn und Zweck der Volksnationalen Reichsvereinigung.* Berlin, 1930.

————. *Die Deutsche Staatspartei. Eine Selbsthilfeorganisation deutschen Staatsbürgertums.* Berlin, 1930.

————. *Gegen getarnte Gewalten. Weg und Kampf einer Volksbewegung.* Berlin, 1928.

————. *Das jungdeutsche Manifest. Volk gegen Kaste und Geld. Sicherung des Friedens durch Neubau der Staaten.* Berlin, 1927.

————. *Die neue Front. Hindenburgs Sendung.* Berlin, 1928.

————. *Parole 1929.* Berlin, 1929.

Maier, Reinhold. *Nationale Demokratie gegen Diktatur. Vortrag, gehalten auf dem Süddeutschen Demokratentag in Bietigheim.* Berlin, [1932].

Mann, Thomas. *Deutsche Ansprache. Ein Appell an die Vernunft. Rede, gehalten am 17. Oktober 1930 im Beethovensaal zu Berlin.* Berlin, 1930.

————. *Von deutscher Republik. Rede, gehalten am 15. Oktober 1922 im Beethovensaal zu Berlin.* Berlin, 1922.

Marwitz, Bruno. *Deutsche Demokratie und nationaler Liberalismus.* Deutschdemokratische Ziele, no. 6. Berlin, 1919.

Meyer, E. H. *Die Stellung des gewerblichen Mittelstandes nach den neuen Steuergesetzen. Vortrag gehalten auf Veranlassung der Handelskammer Berlin am 3. März 1921.* Zeit- und Streitfragen des deutschen Handwerks, no. 4. Hanover, 1921.

Morath, Albrecht. *Nachrevolutionäre Beamtenpolitik.* Flugschriften der Deutschen Volkspartei, no. 42. Berlin, 1922.

Mosich, Ernst. *Materialien zur Finanzreform.* Druckschriften des Hansa-Bundes für Gewerbe, Handel und Industrie, n.s., no. 2. Berlin, 1929.

Most, Otto; Gustav Stresemann; and Wilhelm Kahl. *Deutscher Liberalismus. Reden in der Sitzung des Zentralvorstandes der Deutschen Volkspartei am 23. Mai 1925 in Berlin.* Berlin, 1925.

Naumann, Friedrich. *Demokratie als Staatsgrundlage. Vortrag, gehalten am 4. März 1919 in der Stadtkirche in Jena.* Demokratische Reden, no. 5. Berlin, 1919.

————. *Die Demokratie in der Nationalversammlung. Rede gehalten in der deutschen Nationalversammlung am 13. Februar 1919.* Berlin, 1919.

————. *Der Kaiser im Volksstaat.* Berlin-Schöneberg, 1917.

————. *Der Weg zum Volksstaat.* Berlin, [1918].

Pautsch, Otto. *Demokratie und Landwirtschaft. Vortrag gehalten am 30. März 1919 auf dem Parteitage des Brandenburgischen Provinzialverbandes der Deutschen demokratischen Partei.* Berlin-Zehlendorf, [1919].

Payer, Friedrich von. *Anno 1848.* Frankfurt am Main, 1923.

―――. *Demokratie und Mehrheitsregierung. Etatsrede, Weimar, 11. April 1919.* Weimar, 1919.

Petersen, Carl. *Die Schicksalsstunde des hamburgischen Bürgertums.* Hamburg, 1932.

―――. *Zum Wahlkampf. Rede gehalten am 24. April 1920 in Görlitz.* Berlin, [1920].

Philipp, Albrecht. *Von Stresemann zu Marx. Sechs Monate deutschnationaler Politik (August 1923–Januar 1924).* Deutschnationale Flugschrift, no. 146. Berlin, 1924.

Posadowsky-Wehner, Adolf von. *Die Enteignung des Gläubiger-Vermögens. Eine Sammlung von Aufsätzen.* Berlin, [1928].

Radikaldemokratische Partei, Reichsgeschäftsstelle, ed. *Radikale Demokratie!* Berlin, [ca. 1930–31].

Raschig, Felix. *Zolltariffvorlage und Deutsche Demokratische Partei.* Berlin, 1925.

Rathje, Johannes. *Deutsche Volkspartei oder Deutsche Demokratische Partei.* Berlin-Zehlendorf, [1919].

Reichsgemeinschaft junger Volksparteiler. *Aufmarsch und Ziel.* Lobau, [1929].

Reichs-Landbund, e.V., ed. *Der 8. Reichs-Landbund-Tag. Die Reden der Präsidenten und des Ernährungsministers Schiele.* Berlin, [1928].

Reichspartei des deutschen Mittelstandes, ed. *Jahrbuch der Reichspartei des deutschen Mittelstandes.* [Berlin], 1929.

―――. *Die Satzungen und Görlitzer Richtlinien der Reichspartei des deutschen Mittelstandes e.V. (Wirtschaftspartei).* Berlin, [1929].

―――. *Unsere Arbeit und unsere Gegner. 1930 Wahlhandbuch der Reichspartei des deutschen Mittelstandes (Wirtschaftspartei).* Berlin, 1930.

―――. *Wahrheiten. 1928 Wahlhandbuch der Reichspartei des deutschen Mittelstandes (Wirtschaftspartei).* Berlin, 1928.

Reichsverband des deutschen Handwerks, ed. *Stenographischer Bericht über die Verhandlungen der 2. (24.) Vertreterversammlung des Deutschen Handwerks- und Gewerbekammertages und der 5. Vollversammlung des Reichsverbandes des deutschen Handwerks am 27. und 28. Mai in Berlin.* Hanover, 1924.

Reif, Hans. *Mittelstandspolitik.* Schriftenreihe für politische Werbung der DDP, no. 9. Berlin, 1928.

Reinhardt, Paul Gustav. *Die Deutsche Volkspartei und ihre Ziele. Vortrag gehalten am 27. Mai 1919 in der Aula des Nikolaigymnasiums in Leipzig.* Leipzig, [1919].

Rheinbaben, Rochus von. *Liberale Politik im neuen Reiche.* Karlsruhe, 1928.

Riedel, Oswald, ed. *Das ABC der DDP.* Berlin, 1927.

Riesser, Jakob. *Das Reichsnotopfer und die Deutsche Volkspartei. Rede in der Nationalversammlung vom 9.12.19.* Flugschriften der Deutschen Volkspartei, no. 18. Berlin, 1919.

Schacht, Hjalmar. *Zwölf Monate demokratischer Politik. Rede am 4. November in Dessau.* Berlin, [1924].

Schiffer, Eugen. *Deutschlands Finanzlage nach dem Kriege. Rede gehalten in der deutschen Nationalversammlung am 15. Februar 1919.* Berlin, 1919.

―――. *Von der Nationalversammlung zum Reichstag. Rede gehalten am 16. April 1920 in Magdeburg.* Berlin, [1920].

Schneider, Gustav. *Der Angestellte im demokratischen Volksstaat.* Flugschriften aus der Deutschen demokratischen Partei, no. 4. Leipzig, 1920.

———. *Die Kraft der Angestellten, der Rätegedanke, die Einheits-Gewerkschaft. Betrachtungen über die Zukunft der Angestellten-Bewegung.* Leipzig, [1919].

———. *Staat und Gewerkschaft.* Schriftenfolge des Gewerkschaftsbundes der Angestellten, no. 8. Berlin, [1921].

Schneider, Rudolf. *Warum brauchen wir die Zollvorlage? Rede gehalten im Reichstag am 24. Juni 1925.* Flugschriften der Deutschen Volkspartei, no. 65. Berlin, 1925.

Schroeder, Georg. "Der Sozialismus der nationalen Jugend." *Der Arbeitgeber. Zeitschrift der Vereinigung der Deutschen Arbeitgeberverbände* 20, no. 8 (14 April 1930): 218–20.

Schücking, Walther. *Annehmen oder Ablehnen? Rede in der Fraktion der Demokratischen Partei zu Weimar am 19. Juni 1919.* N.p., [1919].

Spahn, Martin. *Der Weg zur deutschen Rechten. Rede auf dem dritten Parteitag der Deutschnationalen Volkspartei in München am 2. September 1921.* Deutschnationale Flugschrift, no. 115. Berlin, 1921.

Stegerwald, Adam. *Deutsche Lebensfragen. Vortrag gehalten auf dem 10. Kongreß der christlichen Gewerkschaften Deutschlands am 21. November 1920 in Essen.* Cologne, 1920.

———. *Die Notverordnung vom 5. Juni 1931. Ihr Hintergrund, Wesen und Ziel.* Berlin, 1931.

———. *Zusammenbruch und Wiederaufbau.* Berlin, 1922.

Stephan, Werner. *Die Deutsche Demokratische Partei im Berichtsjahr 1926. Jahresbericht der Reichsparteileitung.* N.p., [1927].

———. "Grenzen des nationalsozialistischen Vormarsches. Eine Analyse der Wahlen seit der Reichstagswahl 1930." *Zeitschrift für Politik* 21 (1931/32): 570–78.

———. "Die Parteien nach den großen Frühjahrswahlkämpfen. Eine Analyse der Wahlziffern des Jahres 1932." *Zeitschrift für Politik* 22 (1932/33): 110–18.

———. *Parteiorganisation im Wahlkampf.* Berlin, [1928].

———. "Die Reichstagswahlen vom 31. Juli 1932. Eine Analyse der Wahlziffern." *Zeitschrift für Politik* 22 (1932/33): 353–60.

Steuer, Lothar. *Die deutsche Landwirtschaft und die politischen Parteien. Eine Wahlkampfbetrachtung.* Kassel, 1928.

———. *Die deutschnationale Wahlniederlage vom 20. Mai 1928. Ihre Ursachen, Zusammenhänge, Folgerungen.* Anklam, 1928.

Stinnes, Hugo. *Mark-Stabilisierung und Arbeitsleistung. Rede gehalten am 9. November 1922 im Reichswirtschaftsrat.* Berlin, 1922.

Stolper, Gustav. *Die wirtschaftlich-soziale Weltanschauung der Demokratie. Programmrede auf dem Mannheimer Parteitag der Deutschen Demokratischen Partei am 5. Oktober 1929.* Berlin, 1929.

Stresemann, Gustav. *Deutsche Gegenwart und Zukunft. Vortrag gehalten in Stuttgart am 18. November 1917.* Stuttgart, 1917.

———. *Die Deutsche Volkspartei und ihr politisches Programm. Rede auf dem Leipziger Parteitag der Deutschen Volkspartei am 18. Oktober 1919.* Flugschriften der Deutschen Volkspartei, no. 11. Berlin, 1919.

———. *Deutsche Volkspartei und Regierungspolitik. Rede gehalten auf dem 3. Partei-*

tag der Deutschen Volkspartei in Nürnberg am 3. Dezember 1920. Flugschriften der Deutschen Volkspartei, no. 26. Berlin, 1921.

————. *Die Märzereignisse und die Deutsche Volkspartei.* Berlin, 1920.

————. *Nationale Realpolitik. Rede auf dem 6. Parteitag der Deutschen Volkspartei in Dortmund am 14. November 1924.* Flugschriften der Deutschen Volkspartei, no. 56. Berlin, 1924.

————. *Neue Zeiten. Rede am 27. März 1917 im Reichstag.* Berlin, 1917.

————. *Rede zu Magdeburg am 3. November 1919.* Magdeburg, [1919].

————. *Schutz der Verfassung.* Flugschriften der Deutschen Volkspartei, no. 43. Berlin, 1922.

————. *Weimar und die Politik.* Berlin, 1919.

————. "Der Wiederaufbau Deutschlands und die Industrie." In *Bericht über die 16. Hauptversammlung des Verbandes Sächsischer Industrieller am 5. Mai 1920,* pp. 93–121. Veröffentlichungen des Verbandes Sächsischer Industrieller, no. 32. Dresden, 1920.

————. *Der Wille zur Verständigung. Rede vor dem "Deutschen Industrie- und Handelstag" am 24. August 1923.* Berlin, [1923].

Thiel, Otto. "Die Deutsche Volkspartei." In *Internationales Handwörterbuch des Gewerkschaftswesens,* edited by Ludwig Heyde, 1:347–49. 2 vols. Berlin, 1931–32.

————. *Die sozialen Aufgaben des Wiederaufbaues. Rede gehalten auf dem Nürnberger Parteitag am 4. Dezember 1920.* Flugschriften der Deutschen Volkspartei, no. 30. Berlin, 1921.

————. *Wie kommen wir zu einer großen Deutschen Volkspartei? Vortrag, geh. auf der Tagung der Reichsgemeinschaft junger Volksparteiler in Berlin am 26. Oktober 1930.* N.p., [1930].

Treviranus, G. R. *Auf neuen Wegen.* Volkskonservative Flugschriften, no. 2. Berlin, 1930.

Vögler, Albert. *Die Organisation der Wirtschaft. Wortlaut der Rede vom 14. Januar nach dem stenographischen Bericht der Nationalversammlung.* Flugschriften der Deutschen Volkspartei, no. 20. Berlin, 1920.

Vogt, Gerhard, ed. *Handbuch für die Mitglieder des Reichsausschusses der deutschen demokratischen Beamten, für Vorsitzende der Ortsbeamtenausschüsse und Vertrauenspersonen.* Berlin, 1925.

Volksnationale Reichsvereinigung. *Der erste Reichsvertretertag am 5. und 6. April 1930.* Berlin, 1930.

Wallraf, Max. *Die deutschen Parteien am Scheidewege. Rede auf dem deutschnationalen Reichsparteitage in Görlitz am 28. Oktober 1922.* Deutschnationale Flugschrift, no. 139. Görlitz, 1922.

Weinhausen, Friedrich. *Demokraten und Oberschlesische Krisis.* Berlin, [1921].

Westarp, Kuno von. *Bauernnot—Volksnot. Das Arbeitsprogramm des Reichstages und das landwirtschaftliche Programm der Deutschnationalen Volkspartei.* Deutschnationale Flugschrift, no. 317. Berlin, 1928.

Winschuh, Josef. "Bündische Bewegung und Sozialpolitik." *Soziales Praxis. Zentralblatt für Sozialpolitik und Wohlfahrtspflege* 39, no. 24 (12 June 1930): 561–65.

————. "Die Rolle der Sozialpolitik in den neuen politischen Strömungen," *Der*

Arbeitgeber. Zeitschrift der Vereinigung der Deutschen Arbeitgeberverbände 20, no. 8 (15 April 1930): 214–18.

Winter, Hans. *Der Kampf um Preußen.* Berlin, 1931.

Wirth, Joseph, ed. *Der Aufbruch. Republikanische Flugschriften.* Berlin and Frankfurt am Main, 1926.

Wirtschaftspartei des deutschen Mittelstandes, Generalsekretariat, ed. *Verhandlungen des 1. Parteitages der Wirtschaftspartei des deutschen Mittelstandes zu Breslau vom 23., 24. und 25. April 1921.* Berlin, [1921].

Wirtschaftspartei des deutschen Mittelstandes, Parteivorstand, ed. *Handbuch der Wirtschaftspartei des deutschen Mittelstandes für die Reichstags- und Gemeindewahlen 1924.* Berlin, [1924].

Wolff, Richard. *Ideenkrisis—Parteienwirrwarr. Eine historisch-politische Betrachtung.* Berlin, 1931.

Wüst, Reinhard. *Das Aufwertungsproblem und die 3. Steuernotverordnung. Eine gemeinverständliche Betrachtung.* Halle, 1924.

―――――. *Im Aufwertungskampf für Wahrheit und Recht gegen "Luthertum" und "Marxismus." Eine gemeinverständliche Auseinandersetzung mit den Trugschlüssen und Schlagworten der Aufwertungsgegnern.* Halle, 1924.

Zweck und Ziele des Deutsch-demokratischen Gewerkschaftsbundes. Schriften des Deutsch-demokratischen Gewerkschaftsbundes, no. 1. Berlin, 1919.

MEMOIRS, DIARIES, AND COLLECTED ESSAYS, SPEECHES, AND LETTERS

Bredt, Johann Victor. *Erinnerungen und Dokumente von Joh. Victor Bredt 1914 bis 1933.* Edited by Martin Schumacher. Düsseldorf, 1970.

Brüning, Heinrich. *Memoiren 1918–1934.* Stuttgart, 1970.

Curtius, Julius. *Sechs Jahre Minister der deutschen Republik.* Heidelberg, 1948.

Egelhaaf, Gottlob. *Lebens-Erinnerungen.* Edited by Adolf Rapp. Stuttgart, 1960.

Erkelenz, Anton. *Junge Demokratie. Reden und Schriften politischen Inhalts.* Berlin, 1925.

―――――. *Moderne Sozialpolitik.* Berlin, 1926.

Feder, Ernst. *Heute sprach ich mit. . . . Tagebuch eines Berliner Publizisten 1926–1932.* Edited by Cecile Löwenthal-Hensel and Arnold Paucker. Stuttgart, 1971.

Friedensburg, Ferdinand. *Lebenserinnerungen. Kaiserreich—Weimarer Republik—Hitlerzeit.* Frankfurt am Main and Bonn, 1969.

Gessler, Otto. *Reichswehrpolitik in der Weimarer Republik.* Edited by Kurt Sendtner. Stuttgart, 1958.

Haußmann, Conrad. *Aus Conrad Haußmanns politischer Arbeit.* Frankfurt am Main, 1923.

―――――. *Schlaglichter. Reichstagsbriefe und Aufzeichnungen.* Edited by Ulrich Zeller. Frankfurt am Main, 1924.

Hellpach, Willy. *Wirken in Wirren. Lebenserinnerungen. Eine Rechenschaft über Wert und Glück, Schuld und Sturz meiner Generation.* 2 vols. Hamburg, 1949.

Lemmer, Ernst. *Manches war doch anders. Erinnerungen eines deutschen Demokraten.* Frankfurt am Main, 1968.

Luther, Hans. *Politiker ohne Partei. Erinnerungen.* Stuttgart, 1960.

Müller-Meiningen, Ernst. *Aus Bayerns schwersten Tagen. Erinnerungen und Betrachtungen aus der Revolutionszeit.* Berlin and Leipzig, 1924.

Payer, Friedrich von. *Von Bethmann-Hollweg bis Ebert. Erinnerungen und Bilder.* Frankfurt am Main, 1923.

Rathenau, Walther. *Gesammelte Reden.* Berlin, 1924.

————. *Politische Briefe.* Berlin, 1929.

Schiffer, Eugen. *Ein Leben für Liberalismus.* Berlin, 1951.

Stephan, Werner. *Acht Jahrzehnte erlebtes Deutschland. Ein Liberaler in vier Epochen.* Düsseldorf, 1983.

Stresemann, Gustav. *Reden und Schriften. Politik—Geschichte—Literatur 1897–1926.* Edited by Rochus von Rheinbaben. 2 vols. Dresden, 1926.

————. *Vermächtnis. Der Nachlaß in drei Bänden.* Edited by Henry Bernhard. 3 vols. Berlin, 1932–33.

————. *Von der Revolution bis zum Frieden von Versailles. Reden und Aufsätze.* Berlin, 1919.

————. *Wirtschaftspolitische Zeitfragen.* Dresden, 1910.

Wirth, Joseph. *Reden während der Kanzlerschaft.* Berlin, 1925.

Wolff, Theodor. *Tagebücher 1914–1919. Der erste Weltkrieg und die Entstehung der Weimarer Republik in Tagebüchern, Leitartikeln und Briefen des Chefredakteur am "Berliner Tageblatt" und Mitbegründer der "Deutschen Demokratischen Partei."* Edited with an introduction by Bernd Sösemann. 2 vols. Boppard am Rhein, 1984.

SECONDARY LITERATURE

Abraham, David. *The Collapse of the Weimar Republic: Political Economy and Crisis.* Princeton, 1981.

————. "Constituting Hegemony: The Bourgeois Crisis of Weimar Germany." *Journal of Modern History* 51 (1979): 417–33.

————. "State and Classes in Weimar Germany." *Politics and Society* 7 (1977): 229–66.

Acker, Detlef. *Walther Schücking (1871–1935).* Münster, 1970.

Albertin, Lothar. "German Liberalism and the Foundation of the Weimar Republic: A Missed Opportunity?" In *German Democracy and the Triumph of Hitler*, edited by Anthony Nicholls and Erich Matthias, pp. 29–46. London, 1971.

————. "Liberalismus in der Weimarer Republik." *Neue Politische Literatur* 19 (1974): 220–34.

————. *Liberalismus und Demokratie am Anfang der Weimarer Republik. Eine vergleichende Analyse der Deutschen Demokratischen Partei und Deutschen Volkspartei.* Düsseldorf, 1972.

————. "Der unzeitige Parlamentarismus der Liberalen. Versäumnisse seiner parteiendemokratischen Fundierung." In *Politische Parteien auf dem Weg zur parlamen-*

tarischen Demokratie in Deutschland. Entwicklungslinien bis zur Gegenwart, edited by Lothar Albertin and Werner Link, pp. 31–62. Düsseldorf, 1981.

————. "Die Verantwortung der liberalen Parteien für das Scheitern der großen Koalition im Herbst 1921." *Historische Zeitschrift* 205 (1967): 566–627.

Arns, Günter. "Die Krise des Weimarer Parlamentarismus im Frühherbst 1923." *Der Staat* 8 (1969): 181–216.

Barth, Hans Martin. "Der demokratische Volksbund. Zu den Anfängen des politischen Engagements der Unternehmer der Berliner Elektroindustrie im November 1918." *Jahrbuch für die Geschichte Mittel- und Ostdeutschlands* 16/17 (1968/69): 254–66.

Becker, Josef. "Joseph Wirth und die Krise des Zentrums während des IV. Kabinetts Marx (1927–1928)." *Zeitschrift für die Geschichte des Oberrheins* 109 (1961): 361–482.

Beeck, Karl-Hermann. "Die Gründung der Deutschen Staatspartei im Jahre 1930 im Zusammenhang der Neuordnungsversuche des Liberalismus." Ph.D. dissertation, Cologne, 1957.

Berghahn, Volker R. *Der Stahlhelm. Bund der Frontsoldaten 1918–1935*. Düsseldorf, 1966.

Bertram, Jürgen. *Die Wahlen zum Deutschen Reichstag vom Jahre 1912. Parteien und Verbände in der Innenpolitik des Wilhelminischen Reiches*. Düsseldorf, 1964.

Bessel, Richard, and E. J. Feuchtwanger, eds. *Social Change and Political Development in the Weimar Republic*. London, 1981.

Beyer, Hans. *Die Agrarkrise und die Landvolkbewegung in den Jahren 1928–1932. Ein Beitrag zur Geschichte "revolutionärer" Bauernbewegung zwischen den beiden Weltkriegen*. Itzehoe, 1962.

Blackbourn, David. "The *Mittelstand* in German Society and Politics, 1871–1914." *Social History*, no. 4 (Jan. 1977): 409–33.

Blackbourn, David, and Geoff Eley. *The Peculiarities of German History: Bourgeois Society and Politics in Nineteenth-Century Germany*. Oxford, 1984.

Block, Hermann. *Die parlamentarische Krisis der Nationalliberalen Partei 1879–80*. Hamburg, 1930.

Bowers, Peter M. "The Failure of the German Democratic Party, 1918–1930." Ph.D. dissertation, University of Pittsburgh, 1973.

Bracher, Karl Dietrich. *Die Auflösung der Weimarer Republik. Eine Studie zum Problem des Machtverfalls in der Demokratie*. 4th ed. Villingen, 1960.

Brantz, Rennie William. "Anton Erkelenz, the Hirsch-Duncker Trade Unions, and the German Democratic Party." Ph.D. dissertation, Ohio State University, 1973.

Brose, Eric Dorn. *Christian Labor and the Politics of Frustration in Imperial Germany*. Washington, D.C., 1985.

Busch, Otto, and Gerald D. Feldman, eds. *Historische Prozesse der deutschen Inflation 1914 bis 1924. Ein Tagungsbericht*. Berlin, 1978.

Büttner, Ursula. *Hamburg in der Staats- und Wirtschaftskrise 1928–1931*. Hamburg, 1982.

————. "Vereinigte Liberale und Deutsche Demokraten in Hamburg 1906–1930." *Zeitschrift des Vereins für Hamburgische Geschichte* 63 (1977): 1–34.

Chanady, Attila A. "Anton Erkelenz and Erich Koch-Weser: A Portrait of Two German Democrats." *Historical Studies: Australia and New Zealand* 12 (1967): 491–505.

————. "The Disintegration of the German National People's Party, 1924–1930." *Journal of Modern History* 39 (1967): 65–91.

————. "The Dissolution of the German Democratic Party in 1930." *American Historical Review* 70 (1968): 1433–53.

————. "Erich Koch-Weser and the Weimar Republik." *Canadian Journal of History* 7 (1972): 51–63.

Childers, Thomas. "Inflation, Stabilization, and Political Realignment in Germany, 1924–1928." In *Die deutsche Inflation. Eine Zwischenbilanz/The German Inflation Reconsidered: A Preliminary Balance*, edited by Gerald D. Feldman, Carl-Ludwig Holtfrerich, Gerhard A. Ritter, and Peter-Christian Witt, pp. 409–31. Berlin and New York, 1982.

————. "Interest and Ideology: Anti-System Politics in the Era of Stabilization." In *Die Nachwirkungen der Inflation auf die deutsche Geschichte 1924–1933*, edited by Gerald D. Feldman, pp. 1–20. Munich, 1985.

————. "The Limits of National Socialist Mobilisation: The Elections of 6 November 1932 and the Fragmentation of the Nazi Constituency." In *The Formation of the Nazi Constituency, 1919–1933*, edited by Thomas Childers, pp. 232–59. Totowa, 1986.

————. *The Nazi Voter: The Social Foundations of Fascism in Germany, 1924–1933.* Chapel Hill, 1983.

Conze, Werner. "Friedrich Naumann. Grundlagen und Ansatz seiner Politik in der nationalsozialen Zeit (1895–1903)." In *Schicksalswege deutscher Vergangenheit. Beiträge zur geschichtlichen Deutung der letzten hundertfünfzig Jahren*, edited by Walther Hubatsch, pp. 355–86. Düsseldorf, 1950.

————. "Die Krise des Parteienstaates in Deutschland 1929/30." *Historische Zeitschrift* 178 (1954): 47–83.

Cornebise, Alfred E. "Gustav Stresemann and the Ruhr Occupation: The Making of a Statesman." *European Studies Review* 2 (1972): 43–67.

Dahrendorf, Ralf. *Society and Democracy in Germany.* Garden City, 1967.

Diehl, James M. *Paramilitary Politics in Weimar Germany.* Bloomington, 1977.

Dix, Arthur. *Die deutschen Reichstagswahlen 1871–1930 und die Wandlungen der Volksgliederung.* Tübingen, 1930.

Döhn, Lothar. *Politik und Interesse. Die Interessenstruktur der Deutschen Volkspartei.* Meisenheim an Glan, 1970.

————. "Wirtschafts- und Sozialpolitik der Deutschen Demokratischen Partei und der Deutschen Volkspartei." In *Sozialer Liberalismus*, edited by Karl Holl, Günter Trautmann, and Hans Vorländer, pp. 84–107. Göttingen, 1986.

Domansky, Elisabeth. "Politische Dimensionen von Jugendprotest und Generationenkonflikt in der Zwischenkriegszeit in Deutschland." In *Jugendprotest und Generationenkonflikt in Europa im 20. Jahrhundert. Deutschland, England, Frankreich und Italien im Vergleich*, edited by Dieter Dowe, pp. 113–37. Brunswick and Bonn, 1986.

Domurad, Frank. "The Politics of Corporatism: Hamburg Handicraft in the Late Weimar Republic, 1927–1933." In *Social Change and Political Development in Weimar Germany*, edited by Richard Bessel and E. J. Feuchtwanger, pp. 174–206. London and New York, 1981.

Eisfeld, Gerhard. *Die Entstehung der liberalen Parteien in Deutschland 1858–70. Studien zu den Organisationen und Programmen der Liberalen und Demokraten.* Hanover, 1969.

Eksteins, Modris. *The Limits of Reason: The German Democratic Press and the Collapse of Weimar Democracy.* Oxford, 1975.

Eley, Geoff. *Reshaping the German Right: Radical Nationalism and Political Change after Bismarck.* New Haven and London, 1980.

————. "What Produces Fascism: Preindustrial Traditions or a Crisis of a Capitalist State?" *Politics and Society* 12 (1983): 53–82.

Elm, Ludwig. *Zwischen Fortschritt und Reaktion. Geschichte der Parteien der liberalen Bourgeoisie in Deutschland 1893–1918.* [East] Berlin, 1968.

Epstein, Klaus. *Matthias Erzberger und das Dilemma der deutschen Demokratie.* Berlin and Frankfurt am Main, 1963.

Erger, Johannes. *Der Kapp-Lüttwitz Putsch. Ein Beitrag zur deutschen Innenpolitik 1919/20.* Düsseldorf, 1967.

Evans, Ellen. "The Center Wages *Kulturpolitik*: Conflict in the Marx-Keudell Government of 1927." *Central European History* 2 (1969): 139–58.

Farr, Ian. "Populism in the Countryside: The Peasant Leagues in Bavaria in the 1890's." In *Society and Politics in Wilhelmine Germany*, edited by Richard J. Evans, pp. 136–59. London and New York, 1978.

Feldman, Gerald D. "Bayern und Sachsen in der Hyperinflation 1922/23." *Historische Zeitschrift* 238 (1984): 569–609.

————. "Big Business and the Kapp Putsch." *Central European History* 4 (1971): 99–130.

————. *Iron and Steel in the German Inflation, 1916–1923.* Princeton, 1977.

————. "The Political Economy of Germany's Relative Stabilization during the 1920/21 World Depression." In *Die deutsche Inflation. Eine Zwischenbilanz/The German Inflation Reconsidered: A Preliminary Balance*, edited by Gerald D. Feldman, Carl-Ludwig Holtfrerich, Gerhard A. Ritter, and Peter-Christian Witt, pp. 180–206. Berlin and New York, 1982.

Felix, David. *Walther Rathenau and the Weimar Republic. The Politics of Reparations.* Baltimore, 1970.

Flemming, Jens. *Landwirtschaftliche Interessen und Demokratie. Ländliche Gesellschaft, Agrarverbände und Staat 1890–1925.* Bonn, 1978.

Friedenthal, Elizabeth. "Volksbegehren und Volksentscheid über den Young Plan und die deutschnationale Sezession." Ph.D. dissertation, Tübingen, 1957.

Fritz, Stephen G. " 'The Center Cannot Hold.' Educational Policies and the Collapse of the Democratic Middle in Germany: The School Bill Crisis in Baden, 1927–28." *History of Education Quarterly* 25 (1985): 413–37.

————. "The Search for *Volksgemeinschaft*: Gustav Stresemann and the Baden DVP, 1926–1930." *German Studies Review* 7 (1984): 249–80.

Frye, Bruce B. "The German Democratic Party and the 'Jewish Problem' in the Weimar Republic." *Year Book of the Leo Baeck Institute* 21 (1976): 143–72.

————. *Liberal Democrats in the Weimar Republic: The History of the German Democratic Party and the German State Party.* Carbondale, 1985.

Gall, Lother. "Liberalismus und 'bürgerliche Gesellschaft.' Zu Charakter und Entwicklung der liberalen Bewegung in Deutschland." *Historische Zeitschrift* 220 (1975):
324–56.

Gessner, Dieter. *Agrarverbände in der Weimarer Republik. Wirtschaftliche und soziale
Voraussetzungen agrarkonservativer Politik vor 1933*. Düsseldorf, 1976.

Grathwohl, Robert P. *Stresemann and the DNVP: Reconciliation or Revenge in German
Foreign Policy*. Lawrence, 1980.

Gutleben, Burkhard. "Radikaldemokratische Partei—aufrechte Liberale ohne Erfolg."
Liberal 28 (1986): 65–75.

Hamel, Iris. *Völkischer Verband und nationale Gewerkschaft. Der Deutschnationale
Handlungsgehilfen-Verband 1893–1933*. Hamburg, 1967.

Hartenstein, Wolfgang. *Die Anfänge der Deutschen Volkspartei 1918–1920*. Düsseldorf, 1962.

Haushofer, Heinz. "Der Bayerische Bauernbund (1893–1933)." In *Europäische Bauernparteien im 20. Jahrhundert*, edited by Heinz Gollwitzer, pp. 562–86. Stuttgart
and New York, 1977.

Hayes, Peter. *Industry and Ideology: I.G. Farben in the Nazi Era*. Cambridge, 1987.

———. " 'A Question Mark with Epaulettes'? Kurt von Schleicher and Weimar Politics." *Journal of Modern History* 52 (1980): 35–65.

Heckart, Beverly. *From Bassermann to Bebel: The Grand Bloc's Quest for Reform in
the Kaiserreich, 1900–1914*. New Haven, 1974.

Hertzman, Lewis. *DNVP: Right-Wing Opposition in the Weimar Republic, 1918–1924*.
Lincoln, 1963.

———. "Gustav Stresemann: The Problem of Political Leadership in the Weimar
Republic." *International Review of Social History* 5 (1960): 361–77.

Hess, Jürgen C. "Die Desintegration des Liberalismus in der Weimarer Republik." In
*Auf dem Weg zum modernen Parteienstaat. Zur Entstehung, Organisation und Struk-
tur politischer Parteien in Deutschland und den Niederlanden*, edited by Hermann
W. von der Dunk and Horst Lademacher, pp. 249–72. Kassel, 1986.

———. "Europagedanke und nationaler Revisionismus. Überlegungen zu ihrer Ver-
knüpfung in der Weimarer Republik am Beispiel Wilhelm Heiles." *Historische Zeitschrift* 225 (1977): 572–622.

———. *"Das ganze Deutschland soll es sein." Demokratischer Nationalismus in der
Weimarer Republik am Beispiel der Deutschen Demokratischen Partei*. Stuttgart,
1978.

———. "Wandlungen im Staatsverständnis des Linksliberalismus der Weimarer Re-
publik 1930 bis 1933." In *Wirtschaftskrise und liberale Demokratie. Das Ende der
Weimarer Republik und die gegenwärtige Situation*, edited by Karl Holl, pp. 46–88.
Göttingen, 1978.

Heuss, Theodor. *Friedrich Naumann. Der Mann, das Werk, die Zeit*. Stuttgart and
Berlin, 1937.

Holl, Karl. "Der Austritt Theodor Wolffs aus der Deutschen Demokratischen Partei."
Publizistik 3 (1971): 294–302.

———. "Pazifismus oder liberaler Neu-Imperialismus? Zur Rolle der Pazifisten in der
Deutschen Demokratischen Partei 1918–1930." In *Imperialismus im 20. Jahr-*

hundert. Gedenkschrift für George W. Hallgarten, edited by Joachim Radkau and Imanuel Geiss, pp. 171–95. Munich, 1976.

Hollenberg, Günter. "Bürgerliche Sammlung oder sozialliberale Koalition? Sozialstruktur, Interessenlage und politisches Verhalten der bürgerlichen Schichten 1918/19 am Beispiel der Stadt Frankfurt am Main." *Vierteljahrshefte für Zeitgeschichte* 29 (1979): 392–430.

Holtfrerich, Carl-Ludwig. *Die deutsche Inflation 1914–1923. Ursachen und Folgen in internationaler Perspektive.* Berlin and New York, 1980.

Holzbach, Heidrun. *Das "System Hugenberg." Die Organisation bürgerlicher Sammlungspolitik vor dem Aufstieg der NSDAP.* Munich, 1980.

Hornung, Klaus. *Der Jungdeutsche Orden.* Düsseldorf, 1958.

Hughes, Michael. "Economic Interest, Social Attitudes, and Creditor Ideology: Popular Responses to Inflation." In *Die deutsche Inflation. Eine Zwischenbilanz/The German Inflation Reconsidered: A Preliminary Balance*, edited by Gerald D. Feldman, Carl-Ludwig Holtfrerich, Gerhard A. Ritter, and Peter-Christian Witt, pp. 385–408. Berlin and New York, 1982.

Hunt, James C. "The Bourgeois Middle in German Politics, 1871–1933." *Central European History* 11 (1978): 83–106.

――――. "The 'Egalitarianism' of the Right: The Agrarian League in Southwest Germany, 1893–1914." *Journal of Contemporary History* 10 (1975): 513–30.

――――. *The People's Party in Württemberg and Southern Germany, 1890–1914.* Stuttgart, 1975.

James, Harold. *The German Slump: Politics and Economics, 1924–1936.* Oxford, 1986.

Jarausch, Konrad H. "The Crisis of German Professions 1918–1933." *Journal of Contemporary History* 20 (1985): 379–98.

――――. "Illiberalism and Beyond: German History in Search of a Paradigm." *Journal of Modern History* 55 (1983): 268–84.

Jasper, Gotthard. *Der Schutz der Republik. Studien zur staatlichen Sicherung der Demokratie in der Weimarer Republik 1922–1930.* Tübingen, 1963.

Jochmann, Werner. "Brünings Deflationspolitik und der Untergang der Weimarer Republik." In *Industrielle Gesellschaft und politisches System. Beiträge zur politischen Sozialgeschichte*, edited by Dirk Stegmann, Bernd-Jürgen Wendt, and Peter-Christian Witt, pp. 87–112. Bonn, 1978.

Jonas, Erasmus. *Die Volkskonservativen 1928–1933. Entwicklung, Struktur, Standort und staatspolitische Zielsetzung.* Düsseldorf, 1965.

Jones, Larry Eugene. "Adam Stegerwald und die Krise des deutschen Parteiensystems. Ein Beitrag zur Deutung des 'Essener Programms' vom November 1920." *Vierteljahrshefte für Zeitgeschichte* 27 (1979): 1–29.

――――. "Between the Fronts: The German National Union of Commercial Employees from 1928 to 1933." *Journal of Modern History* 48 (1976): 462–82.

――――. "Crisis and Realignment: Agrarian Splinter Parties in the Late Weimar Republic, 1928–33." In *Peasants and Lords in Modern Germany: Recent Studies in Agricultural History*, edited by Robert G. Moeller, pp. 198–232. London, 1986.

――――. "The Dissolution of the Bourgeois Party System in the Weimar Republic." In

Social Change and Political Development in Weimar Germany, edited by Richard Bessel and E. J. Feuchtwanger, pp. 268–88. London, 1981.

––––––. " 'The Dying Middle': Weimar Germany and the Failure of Bourgeois Unity, 1924–1930." Ph.D. dissertation, University of Wisconsin, 1970.

––––––. " 'The Dying Middle': Weimar Germany and the Fragmentation of Bourgeois Politics." *Central European History* 5 (1972): 23–54.

––––––. "Gustav Stresemann and the Crisis of German Liberalism." *European Studies Review* 4 (1974): 141–63.

––––––. "Inflation, Revaluation, and the Crisis of Middle-Class Politics, 1923–28: A Study in the Dissolution of the German Party System." *Central European History* 12 (1979): 143–68.

––––––. "In the Shadow of Stabilization: German Liberalism and the Legitimacy Crisis of the Weimar Party System, 1924–30." In *Die Nachwirkungen der Inflation auf die deutsche Geschichte 1924–1933*, edited by Gerald D. Feldman, pp. 21–41. Munich, 1985.

––––––. "Sammlung oder Zersplitterung? Die Bestrebungen zur Bildung einer neuen Mittelpartei in der Endphase der Weimarer Republik 1930–1933." *Vierteljahrshefte für Zeitgeschichte* 25 (1977): 265–304.

Kaack, Heino. *Geschichte und Struktur des deutschen Parteiensystems. Ein Handbuch.* Opladen, 1971.

Kessler, Alexander. *Der Jungdeutsche Orden auf dem Wege zur Deutschen Staatspartei.* Munich, 1980.

––––––. *Der Jungdeutsche Orden in den Jahren der Entscheidung (I) 1928–1930.* Munich, 1975.

Kessler, Harry. *Walther Rathenau: His Life and Work.* New York, 1930.

Kocka, Jürgen. *Klassengesellschaft im Krieg. Deutsche Sozialgeschichte 1914–1918.* Göttingen, 1973.

Krieger, Leonard. *The German Idea of Freedom: History of a Political Tradition.* Chicago, 1957.

Kunz, Andreas. *Civil Servants and the Politics of Inflation in Germany 1914–1924.* Berlin, 1986.

Laqueur, Walter Z. *Young Germany: A History of the German Youth Movement.* With an introduction by R. H. S. Crossman. New York, 1962.

Laubach, Ernst. *Die Politik der Kabinette Wirth 1921–1922.* Lübeck and Hamburg, 1968.

Leopold, John A. *Alfred Hugenberg: The Radical Nationalist Campaign against the Weimar Republic.* New Haven, 1977.

Lepsius, M. Rainer. "From Fragmented Party Democracy to Government by Emergency Decree and National Socialist Takeover: Germany." In *The Breakdown of Democratic Regimes: Europe*, edited by Juan J. Linz and Alfred Stephan, pp. 34–79. Baltimore, 1978.

Link, Werner. "Der Nationalverein für das liberale Deutschland (1907–1918)." *Politische Vierteljahresschrift* 5 (1964): 422–44.

Lüth, Erich, and Hans-Dieter Loose. *Bürgermeister Carl Petersen 1868–1933.* Hamburg, 1971.

Maier, Charles S. *Recasting Bourgeois Europe: Stabilization in France, Germany, and Italy in the Decade after World War I.* Princeton, 1975.

Maste, Ernst. *Die Republik der Nachbarn. Die Nachbarschaft und der Staatsgedanke Artur Mahrauns.* Giessen, 1957.

Matthias, Erich, and Rudolf Morsey. "Die Deutsche Staatspartei." In *Das Ende der Parteien 1933*, edited by Erich Matthias and Rudolf Morsey, pp. 31–97. Düsseldorf, 1960.

Maurer, Ilse. *Reichsfinanzen und große Koalition. Zur Geschichte der Reichskabinetts Müller (1928–1930).* Bonn and Frankfurt am Main, 1973.

Methfessel, Werner. "Die Deutsche Volkspartei am Ende der Weimarer Republik." Ph.D. dissertation, Jena, 1966.

―――. *Der Weg in den Abgrund. Zur Geschichte der Deutschen Volkspartei 1930–1933.* Edited by Sekretariat des Zentralvorstandes der Liberal-Demokratischen Partei Deutschlands. [East Berlin], 1978.

Mielke, Siegfried. *Der Hansa-Bund für Gewerbe, Handel und Industrie 1909–1914. Der gescheiterte Versuch einer antifeudalen Sammlungspolitik.* Göttingen, 1976.

Milatz, Alfred. "Das Ende der Parteien im Spiegel der Wahlen 1930 bis 1933." In *Das Ende der Parteien 1933*, edited by Erich Matthias and Rudolf Morsey, pp. 743–93. Düsseldorf, 1960.

―――. "Die linksliberalen Parteien und Gruppen in den Reichstagswahlen 1871–1912." *Archiv für Sozialgeschichte* 12 (1972): 273–92.

Moeller, Robert G. *German Peasants and Agrarian Politics, 1914–1924: The Rhineland and Westphalia.* Chapel Hill, 1986.

―――. "Winners as Losers in the German Inflation: Peasant Protest over the Controlled Economy, 1920–1923." In *Die deutsche Inflation. Eine Zwischenbilanz/The German Inflation Reconsidered: A Preliminary Balance*, edited by Gerald D. Feldman, Carl-Ludwig Holtfrerich, Gerhard A. Ritter, and Peter-Christian Witt, pp. 255–82. Berlin and New York, 1982.

Mommsen, Hans. "Die Auflösung des Bürgertums seit dem späten 19. Jahrhundert." In *Bürger und Bürgerlichkeit im 19. Jahrhundert*, edited by Jürgen Kocka, pp. 288–315. Göttingen, 1987.

―――. "Generationskonflikt und Jugendrevolte in der Weimarer Republik." In *"Mit uns zieht die neue Zeit." Der Mythos Jugend*, edited by Thomas Koebner, Rolf-Peter Janz, and Frank Trommler, pp. 50–67. Frankfurt am Main, 1985.

―――. "Heinrich Brünings Politik als Reichskanzler: Das Scheitern eines politischen Alleingangs." In *Wirtschaftskrise und liberale Demokratie. Das Ende der Weimarer Republik und die gegenwärtige Situation*, edited by Karl Holl, pp. 16–45. Göttingen, 1978.

―――. "Staat und Bürokratie in der Ära Brüning." In *Tradition und Reform in der deutschen Politik. Gedenkschrift für Waldemar Besson*, edited by Gotthard Jasper, pp. 81–137. Frankfurt am Main, 1976.

―――. "Die Stellung der Beamtenschaft in Reich, Ländern und Gemeinden in der Ära Brüning." *Vierteljahrshefte für Zeitgeschichte* 21 (1973): 151–65.

Mommsen, Hans, Dietmar Petzina, and Bernd Weisbrod, eds. *Industrielles System und politische Entwicklung in der Weimarer Republik. Verhandlungen des Internationalen Symposiums in Bochum vom 12.–17. Juni 1973.* Düsseldorf, 1974.

Mommsen, Wolfgang J. *Max Weber and German Politics, 1890–1920.* Translated by Michael S. Steinberg. Chicago, 1984.

―――. "Wandlungen der liberalen Idee im Zeitalter des Imperialismus." In *Liberalis-*

638   Bibliography

mus und imperialistischer Staat. Der Imperialismus als Problem liberaler Parteien in Deutschland 1890–1914, edited by Karl Holl and Günther List, pp. 109–47. Göttingen, 1975.

Morsey, Rudolf. Die Deutsche Zentrumspartei 1917–1923. Düsseldorf, 1966.

Mundle, G. F. "The German National Liberal Party, 1900–1914." Ph.D. dissertation, University of Illinois, 1975.

Neebe, Reinhard. Großindustrie, Staat und NSDAP 1930–1933. Paul Silverberg und der Reichsverband der Deutschen Industrie in der Krise der Weimarer Republik. Göttingen, 1981.

Netzband, Karl-Bernhard, and Hans Peter Widmaier. Währungs- und Finanzpolitik in der Ära Luther 1923–1925. Tübingen, 1964.

Neumann, Sigmund. Die deutschen Parteien. Wesen und Wandel nach dem Kriege. Berlin, 1932.

Nipperdey, Thomas. "Die Organisation der bürgerlichen Parteien in Deutschland vor 1918." Historische Zeitschrift 185 (1958): 550–602.

O'Donnell, Anthony J. "National Liberalism and the Mass Politics of the German Right, 1890–1907." Ph.D. dissertation, Princeton University, 1973.

Osmond, Jonathan. "Peasant Farming in South and West Germany during War and Inflation 1914 to 1924: Stability or Stagnation?" In Die deutsche Inflation. Eine Zwischenbilanz/The German Inflation Reconsidered: A Preliminary Balance, edited by Gerald D. Feldman, Carl-Ludwig Holtfrerich, Gerhard A. Ritter, and Peter-Christian Witt, pp. 255–307. Berlin and New York, 1982.

Panzer, Arno. "Parteipolitische Ansätze der deutschen Bauernbewegung bis 1933." In Europäische Bauernparteien im 20. Jahrhundert, edited by Heinz Gollwitzer, pp. 524–42. Stuttgart and New York, 1977.

Patch, William L., Jr. Christian Trade Unions in the Weimar Republic, 1918–1933: The Failure of "Corporate Pluralism." New Haven, 1985.

Portner, Ernst. "Der Ansatz zur demokratischen Massenpartei im deutschen Linksliberalismus." Vierteljahrshefte für Zeitgeschichte 13 (1965): 150–61.

———. Die Verfassungspolitik der Liberalen—1919. Ein Beitrag zur Deutung der Weimarer Reichsverfassung. Bonn, 1973.

Priamus, Heinz-Jürgen. Angestellte und Demokratie. Die nationalliberale Angestelltenbewegung in der Weimarer Republik. Stuttgart, 1979.

Pryce, Donald B. "The Reich Government versus Saxony, 1923: The Decision to Intervene." Central European History 10 (1977): 112–47.

Puhle, Hans-Jürgen. "Parlament, Parteien und Interessenverbände 1890–1914." In Das kaiserliche Deutschland. Politik und Gesellschaft 1870–1918, edited by Michael Stürmer, pp. 340–77. Düsseldorf, 1970.

———. Politische Agrarbewegungen in kapitalistischen Industriegesellschaften. Deutschland, USA und Frankreich im 20. Jahrhundert. Göttingen, 1975.

Raabe, Felix. Die bündische Jugend. Ein Beitrag zur Geschichte der Weimarer Republik. Stuttgart, 1961.

Rachfahl, Felix. "Eugen Richter und der Linksliberalismus im neuen Reiche." Zeitschrift für Politik 5 (1912): 261–374.

Riemann, Joachim. Ernst Müller-Meiningen senior und der Linksliberalismus in seiner

Zeit. Zur Biographie eines bayerischen und deutschen Politikers (1866–1944). Munich, 1968.

———. "Der politische Liberalismus in der Krise der Revolution." In *Bayern im Umbruch. Die Revolution von 1918, ihre Voraussetzungen, ihr Verlauf und ihre Folgen*, edited by Karl Bosl, pp. 165–99. Munich, 1969.

Ritter, Gerhard A. "Kontinuität und Umformung des deutschen Parteiensystems 1918–1920." In *Entstehung und Wandel der modernen Gesellschaft. Festschrift für Hans Rosenberg zum 65. Geburtstag*, edited by Gerhard A. Ritter, pp. 342–84. Berlin, 1970.

Robson, Stuart T. "German Left Liberals and the First World War." *Canadian Historical Association. Historical Papers Presented at the Annual Meeting Held at Ottawa, June 7–10, 1967*, pp. 216–34.

Romeyk, Horst. "Die Deutsche Volkspartei in Rheinland und Westfalen 1918–1933." *Rheinische Vierteljahrsblätter* 39 (1975): 189–236.

Rommel, Hans-Otto. "Die Weimarer Jungdemokraten." *Liberal* 13 (1971): 915–24.

Rupieper, Hermann J. *The Cuno Government and Reparations, 1922–1923: Politics and Economics*. The Hague, 1979.

Saldern, Adelheid von. *Hermann Dietrich. Ein Staatsmann der Weimarer Republik*. Boppard am Rhein, 1966.

Schelm-Spangenburg, Ursula. *Die Deutsche Volkspartei im Lande Braunschweig. Gründung, Entwicklung, soziologische Struktur, politische Arbeit*. Brunswick, 1964.

Schieder, Theodor. *Staat und Gesellschaft im Wandel unserer Zeit. Studien zur Geschichte des 19. und 20. Jahrhunderts*. Munich, 1958.

Schieder, Wolfgang, ed. *Liberalismus in der Gesellschaft des deutschen Vormärz*. Göttingen, 1983.

Schmidt, Gustav. "Die Nationalliberalen—eine regierungsfähige Partei? Zur Problematik der inneren Reichsgründung 1870–1878." In *Die deutschen Parteien vor 1918*, edited by Gerhard A. Ritter, pp. 208–23. Düsseldorf, 1973.

———. "Parlamentarisierung oder 'Präventive Konterrevolution'? Die deutsche Innenpolitik im Spannungsfeld zwischen konservativer Sammlungsbewegungen und latenter Reformbestrebungen 1907–1914." In *Gesellschaft, Parlament und Regierung. Zur Geschichte des Parlamentarismus in Deutschland*, edited by Gerhard A. Ritter, pp. 249–74. Düsseldorf, 1974.

Schneider, Werner. *Die Deutsche Demokratische Partei in der Weimarer Republik 1924–1930*. Munich, 1978.

Schulz, Gerhard. "Räte, Wirtschaftsstände und Verbandswesen am Anfang der Weimarer Republik." In *Gesellschaft, Parlament und Regierung. Zur Geschichte des Parlamentarismus in Deutschland*, edited by Gerhard A. Ritter, pp. 355–66. Düsseldorf, 1974.

———. "Über Entstehung und Formen von Interessengruppen in Deutschland seit dem Beginn der Industrialisierung." *Politische Vierteljahresschrift* 2 (1961): 124–54.

Schumacher, Martin. *Land und Politik. Eine Untersuchung über politische Parteien und agrarische Interessen 1914–1923*. Düsseldorf, 1978.

_____. *Mittelstandsfront und Republik. Die Wirtschaftspartei—Reichspartei des deutschen Mittelstandes 1919–1933*. Düsseldorf, 1972.

_____. "Stabilität und Instabilität. Wahlentwicklung und Parlament in Baden und Braunschweig 1918–1933." In *Gesellschaft, Parlament und Regierung. Zur Geschichte des Parlamentarismus in Deutschland*, edited by Gerhard A. Ritter, pp. 389–417. Düsseldorf, 1974.

Schustereit, Hartmut. *Linksliberalismus und Sozialdemokratie in der Weimarer Republik. Eine vergleichende Betrachtung der Politik von DDP und SPD 1919–1930*. Düsseldorf, 1975.

Schwarz, Gotthard. *Theodor Wolff und das "Berliner Tageblatt." Eine liberale Stimme in der deutschen Politik 1926–1933*. Tübingen, 1968.

Schwering, Leo. "Stegerwalds und Brünings Vorstellungen über Parteireform und Parteiensystem." In *Staat, Wirtschaft und Politik in der Weimarer Republik. Festschrift für Heinrich Brüning*, edited by Ferdinand Hermens and Theodor Schieder, pp. 23–40. Berlin, 1967.

Seeber, Gustav. *Zwischen Bebel und Bismarck. Zur Geschichte des Linksliberalismus in Deutschland 1871–1893*. [East] Berlin, 1965.

Sheehan, James J. *German Liberalism in the Nineteenth Century*. Chicago, 1978.

Simons, Klaus. *Die württembergischen Demokraten. Ihre Stellung und Arbeit im Parteien- und Verfassungssystem in Württemberg und im Deutschen Reich 1890–1920*. Stuttgart, 1969.

Stachura, Peter, ed. *Unemployment and the Great Depression in Weimar Germany*. New York, 1986.

Stegmann, Dirk. *Die Erben Bismarcks. Parteien und Verbände in der Spätphase des Wilhelminischen Deutschlands. Sammlungspolitik 1897–1918*. Cologne, 1970.

_____. "Zum Verhältnis von Großindustrie und Nationalsozialismus 1930–1933. Ein Beitrag zur Geschichte der sog. Machtergreifung." *Archiv für Sozialgeschichte* 13 (1979): 399–482.

Stephan, Werner. *Aufstieg und Verfall des Linksliberalismus. Geschichte der Deutschen Demokratischen Partei*. Göttingen, 1973.

Stern, Fritz. *The Failure of Illiberalism: Essays on the Political Culture of Modern Germany*. New York, 1972.

Struve, Walter. *Elites against Democracy: Leadership Ideals in Bourgeois Political Thought in Germany, 1890–1933*. Princeton, 1973.

Stürmer, Michael. *Koalition und Opposition in der Weimarer Republik 1924–1928*. Düsseldorf, 1967.

Thieme, Hartwig. *Nationaler Liberalismus in der Krise. Die nationalliberale Fraktion des Preußischen Abgeordnetenhauses 1914–1918*. Boppard am Rhein, 1963.

Thimme, Roland. *Stresemann und die Deutsche Volkspartei 1923–25*. Lübeck and Hamburg, 1961.

Timm, Helga. *Deutsche Sozialpolitik und der Bruch der großen Koalition im März 1930*. Düsseldorf, 1952.

Trumpp, Thomas. "Zur Finanzierung der NSDAP durch die deutsche Großindustrie. Versuch einer Bilanz." *Geschichte in Wissenschaft und Unterricht* 32 (1981): 223–41.

Turner, Henry Ashby, Jr. *German Big Business and the Rise of Hitler*. Oxford, 1984.

————. "The Ruhrlade: Secret Cabinet of Heavy Industry in the Weimar Republic." *Central European History* 3 (1970): 195–228.

————. *Stresemann and the Politics of the Weimar Republic.* Princeton, 1963.

Vallentin, Antonina. *Stresemann. Vom Werden einer Staatsidee.* Leipzig, 1930.

Vogelsang, Thilo. *Reichswehr, Staat und NSDAP. Beiträge zur deutschen Geschichte 1930–1932.* Stuttgart, 1962.

Walker, David P. "The German Nationalist People's Party: The Conservative Dilemma in the Weimar Republic." *Journal of Contemporary History* 14 (1979): 627–47.

Warren, Donald K. *The Red Kingdom of Saxony: Lobbying Grounds for Gustav Stresemann, 1901–1909.* The Hague, 1964.

Wegner, Konstanze. "Linksliberalismus im wilhelminischen Deutschland und in der Weimarer Republik." *Geschichte und Gesellschaft* 4 (1978): 120–38.

————. *Theodor Barth und die Freisinnige Vereinigung. Studien zur Geschichte des Linksliberalismus im wilhelminischen Deutschland (1893–1910).* Tübingen, 1968.

Weisbrod, Bernd. "Die Befreiung von 'Tariffesseln.' Deflationspolitik als Krisenstrategie der Unternehmer in der Ära Brüning." *Geschichte und Gesellschaft* 11 (1985): 295–325.

————. *Schwerindustrie in der Weimarer Republik. Interessenpolitik zwischen Stabilisierung und Krise.* Wuppertal, 1978.

White, Dan S. *The Splintered Party: National Liberalism in Hesse and the Reich, 1867–1918.* Cambridge, Mass., 1976.

Wiener, P. B. "Die Parteien der Mitte." In *Entscheidungsjahr 1932. Zur Judenfrage in der Endphase der Weimarer Republik,* edited by Werner E. Mosse, pp. 289–321. Tübingen, 1965.

Williamson, John G. *Karl Helfferich 1872–1924: Economist, Financier, Politician.* Princeton, 1971.

Winkler, Heinrich August. *Mittelstand, Demokratie und Nationalsozialismus. Die politische Entwicklung von Handwerk und Kleinhandel in der Weimarer Republik.* Cologne, 1972.

————. *Preußischer Liberalismus und deutscher Nationalstaat. Studien zur Geschichte der Deutschen Fortschrittspartei 1861–1866.* Tübingen, 1964.

————. *Der Schein der Normalität. Arbeiter und Arbeiterbewegung in der Weimarer Republik 1924 bis 1930.* Berlin and Bonn, 1985.

————. "Vom linken zum rechten Nationalismus. Der deutsche Liberalismus in der Krise von 1878/79." *Geschichte und Gesellschaft* 4 (1978): 5–28.

————. *Von der Revolution zur Stabilisierung. Arbeiter und Arbeiterbewegung in der Weimarer Republik 1918 bis 1924.* Berlin and Bonn, 1984.

Witt, Peter-Christian. "Finanzpolitik als Verfassungs- und Gesellschaftspolitik. Überlegungen zur Finanzpolitik des Deutschen Reiches in den Jahren 1930 bis 1932." *Geschichte und Gesellschaft* 8 (1982): 386–414.

————. "Inflation, Wohnungszwangswirtschaft und Hauszinssteuer. Zur Regelung von Wohnungsbau und Wohnungsmarkt in der Weimarer Republik." In *Wohnen im Wandel. Beiträge zur Geschichte des Alltages in der bürgerlichen Gesellschaft,* edited by Lutz Niethammer, pp. 385–407. Wuppertal, 1979.

Wulf, Peter. "Die Auseinandersetzungen um die Sozialisierung der Kohle in Deutschland 1920/21." *Vierteljahrshefte für Zeitgeschichte* 25 (1977): 46–98.

————. *Hugo Stinnes. Wirtschaft und Politik 1918–1924.* Stuttgart, 1979.

Zeender, John K. "German Catholics and the Concept of an Interconfessional Party, 1900–1922." *Journal of Central European Affairs* 23 (1964): 424–39.

Ziegler, Wilhelm. *Die Deutsche Nationalversammlung 1919/20 und ihr Verfassungs-werk.* Berlin, 1932.

Index

Abegg, Wilhelm, 428, 430
Adolf, Arthur, 370
Agrarian League (BdL), 7, 31, 180, 280
Agrarian splinter parties, 177, 279–90 passim. *See also* Bavarian Peasants' League; Christian-National Peasants and Farmers' Party; German Peasants' Party; Württemberg Peasants and Wine Growers' League
Agricultural interest organizations, 7, 10, 73–74, 113–14, 167–69, 180–81, 225–26, 231, 279–90 passim, 358–59. *See also* Agrarian League; Association of Christian Peasant Unions; Baden Rural League; Bavarian Peasants' League; Christian peasant unions; German Peasantry; German Peasants' League; Hessian Rural League; League of Agricultural Tenants and Small Peasants; National Federation of Small and Middle-Sized Agricultural Enterprises; National Rural League; Thuringian Rural League
Agriculture, 279–90, 298–99, 410–11; and DVP, 49, 79, 95, 167, 175–76, 180–81; and DDP, 73–74, 113, 167–69, 281–83, 288–90, 299. *See also* Peasantry
Albertin, Lothar, 3
Alliance against Profiteering and High Prices, 260
Alliance of Clerk Unions, 100
Alliance of the Constitutional Middle, 153–56, 158–59, 228; and Wirth, 184–87; and Cuno, 189, 193–94; and Stresemann, 197
Anti-Semitism, 61, 68–69, 71, 381, 435–36

Arendt, Otto, 70
Artisanry, 5, 252–53; and DDP, 24–25, 78, 99, 105, 113, 233–34; and DVP, 46, 95, 221, 388; and WP, 254–59, 264, 297–98; and DStP, 387, 415
Association of Christian Peasant Unions, 7, 280. *See also* Christian peasant unions
Austria, 47, 427, 429

Baden, 177, 360, 379
Baden Rural League, 171, 181
Baltrusch, Fritz, 26, 335, 354, 370, 389, 425
Barth, Theodor, 8
Bartschat, Franz, 99, 233
Bassermann, Ernst, 45
Bauer, Gustav, 40, 42, 56–57, 61, 63, 65
Bäumer, Gertrud, 32, 85, 122, 166, 228, 325, 369; and DStP, 383, 389–90
Bauser, Adolf, 262, 457–58
Bavaria, 203–4, 278–79, 285–86, 310, 314; and DDP, 156–59, 212, 221–22, 228, 233; and DVP, 199, 221–22
Bavarian Peasant and Middle-Class League, 237, 285, 299. *See also* Bavarian Peasants' League
Bavarian Peasants' League (BBB), 7, 156, 279–80, 284–88, 310; and WP, 256–58, 286; and DBP, 286–87, 410–11
Bavarian People's Party (BVP), 79, 84, 145, 148, 156, 166, 168, 205–6, 209, 221, 226–27, 241, 244, 249, 286, 294, 359, 387, 422, 455, 467–68
Bazille, Wilhelm, 360
Bechly, Hans, 26, 49, 270, 437, 453

Schnell, Walter, 403–5
Scholz, Ernst, 86, 200–201, 205, 215, 276, 292–93, 311, 318, 329, 333, 340, 348; and Stresemann, 315–16, 321; as DVP national chairman, 349, 355–57, 403–6; and bourgeois concentration, 355–76 passim, 428; and DStP, 373–75, 382, 397, 399
School bill, 295–97, 310
Schücking, Walter, 37, 122, 228, 242
Schuldt, Otto, 233, 242
Schultz, Ludwig, 440
Second Emergency Decree for the Protection of the Economy and Finance, 415–16, 418–21, 425, 427
Seeckt, Hans von, 200–201, 205, 430
Seldte, Franz, 467–68
Siehr, Ernst, 154
Siemens, Carl Friedrich von, 100, 444, 453, 470; and Curatorium for the Reconstruction of German Economic Life, 25, 51–52, 75; and DDP, 72, 98, 105, 220, 228; and LV, 232, 272, 278
Siemens, Wilhelm von, 51
Silesian Peasants' League, 286
Silverberg, Paul, 171, 277, 398, 444
Simons, Walter, 87, 242, 244
Small business, 409–10; and DDP, 24–25; and DVP, 175–76; and WP, 298
Social Democratic Party of Germany (SPD), 6, 16, 37, 39–40, 60, 79, 92, 101, 108, 176, 178, 211, 226, 238, 242, 245–46, 249, 260–62, 268, 297–98, 302, 304, 309, 328, 360, 366–67, 372, 395, 460, 472–73, 477; and liberal parties, 30–31, 185–87, 379; and DDP, 33–36, 56–58, 67–68, 127, 137, 141–43, 167, 267, 276–77, 283; and cabinet negotiations (1919), 33–34, (1920), 83–87, 91, (1922), 152, 196–97, 230, (1925), 247–48, (1926), 292; and DVP, 69–70, 126–27, 143, 200–202, 206, 282, 320, 356, 385, 396, 405, 416–18; in Prussia, 112, 114–17, 315, 319–20; and

Wirth, 123–25, 129; and Independent Socialists, 150, 151–53; and Brüning, 379, 411; and DStP, 453, 458, 468
Socialization, 90–93, 137, 254; and DDP, 35–36, 60, 99–100, 105, 166; and DVP, 90–93
Social Republican Circle, 350, 361, 372
Solf, Wilhelm, 451–52, 456
Sorge, Kurt, 52, 88, 203
South German Democrats, 463
Spa Conference, 86–88
Spahn, Martin, 134
Sparrer, Georg, 231, 272
Spengler, Oswald, 102
Springorum, Friedrich, 301, 367, 376, 444, 453
Stabilization, currency, 4, 146–47, 182, 185, 198, 208–11, 223, 266, 291, 304–5, 366, 479–80; and middle class, 210–11, 216–18, 251–52, 256, 259–61, 478–79; and agriculture, 281, 285
Stadtler, Eduard, 136
Stahlhelm, 263, 317–18, 321, 331, 338–39, 352, 381, 430, 439, 457, 467; and DVP, 318, 423–24, 440; and Prussian referendum, 422–25
Stegerwald, Adam, 24, 100–101, 103, 111, 118, 141, 153, 155, 208, 359; and Essen Program, 107–9
Stendel, Ernst, 320
Stephan, Werner, 190, 311
Stern, Fritz, 3
Stingl, Karl, 241
Stinnes, Hugo, 32, 51, 88–89, 90, 92–93, 99–100, 110–11, 130, 141, 174, 182, 186, 192, 203, 216; and DVP, 52, 75, 127, 135, 142, 191, 201, 214–15
Stolper, Gustav, 342–44, 373, 381–82, 388–89, 451, 455
Strasser, Gregor, 386, 462
Streiter, Georg, 26, 75
Stresemann, Gustav, 70, 110–12, 158, 243, 281–82, 288, 309, 347–48, 385,